Collins EUROPE
ESSENTIAL ROAD ATLAS

Published by Collins
An imprint of HarperCollins Publishers
Westerhill Road
Bishopbriggs
Glasgow G64 2QT
www.harpercollins.co.uk

First published 2004

New edition 2016

© HarperCollins Publishers Ltd 2016
Maps © Collins Bartholomew Ltd 2016

Collins® is a registered trademark of HarperCollins Publishers Ltd

The contents of this publication are believed correct at the time of printing. Nevertheless the publisher can accept no responsibility for errors or omissions, changes in the detail given or for any expense or loss thereby caused.

HarperCollins does not warrant that any website mentioned in this title will be provided uninterrupted, that any website will be error free, that defects will be corrected, or that the website or the server that makes it available are free of viruses or bugs. For full terms and conditions please refer to the site terms provided on the website.

A catalogue record for this book is available from the British Library

ISBN 978-0-00-820358-0

10 9 8 7 6 5 4 3 2 1

Printed by RR Donnelley APS Co Ltd, China

All mapping in this atlas is generated from Collins Bartholomew digital databases. Collins Bartholomew, the UK's leading independent geographical information supplier, can provide a digital, custom, and premium mapping service to a variety of markets.
For further information:
Tel: +44 (0)141 306 3752
e-mail: collinsbartholomew@harpercollins.co.uk
or visit our website at: www.collinsbartholomew.com

If you would like to c... above address or onl... e-mail: collinsmaps(...

facebook.com/c...

Contents

Map symbols

Road maps	Carte routière	Strassenkarten
E55 Euro route number	Route européenne	Europastrasse
A13 Motorway	Autoroute	Autobahn
Motorway – toll	Autoroute à péage	Gebührenpflichtige Autobahn
Motorway – toll (vignette)	Autoroute à péage (vignette)	Gebührenpflichtige Autobahn (Vignette)
37 Motorway junction – full access	Echangeur d'autoroute avec accès libre	Autobahnauffahrt mit vollem Zugang
12 Motorway junction – restricted access	Echangeur d'autoroute avec accès limité	Autobahnauffahrt mit beschränktem Zugang
Motorway services	Aire de service sur autoroute	Autobahnservicestelle
309 Main road – dual carriageway	Route principale à chaussées séparées	Hauptstrasse – Zweispurig
Main road – single carriageway	Route principale à une seule chaussée	Hauptstrasse – Einspurig
516 Secondary road – dual carriageway	Route secondaire à chaussées séparées	Zweispurige Nebenstrasse
Secondary road – single carriageway	Route secondaire à seule chaussée	Einspurige Nebenstrasse
Other road	Autre route	Andere Strasse
Motorway tunnel	Autoroute tunnel	Autobahntunnel
Main road tunnel	Route principale tunnel	Hauptstrassetunnel
Motorway/road under construction	Autoroute/route en construction	Autobahn/Strasse im Bau
Road toll	Route à péage	Gebührenpflichtige Strasse
Distance marker 16 Distances in kilometres 10 Distances in miles (UK only)	Marquage des distances Distances en kilomètres Distances en miles (GB)	Distanz-Markierung Distanzen in Kilometern Distanzen in Meilen (GB)
Steep hill	Colline abrupte	Steile Strasse
2587 Mountain pass (height in metres)	Col (Altitude en mètres)	Pass (Höhe in Metern)
Scenic route	Parcours pittoresque	Landschaftlich schöne Strecke
International airport	Aéroport international	Internationaler Flughafen
Car transport by rail	Transport des autos par voie ferrée	Autotransport per Bahn
Railway	Chemin de fer	Eisenbahn
Tunnel	Tunnel	Tunnel
Funicular railway	Funiculaire	Seilbahn
Rotterdam Car ferry	Bac pour autos	Autofähre
▲2587 Summit (height in metres)	Sommet (Altitude en mètres)	Berg (Höhe in Metern)
▲ Volcano	Volcan	Vulkan
Canal	Canal	Kanal
International boundary	Frontière d'Etat	Landesgrenze
Disputed International boundary	Frontière litigieuse	Umstrittene Staatsgrenze
GB Country abbreviation	Abréviation du pays	Regionsgrenze
Urban area	Zone urbaine	Stadtgebiet
28 Adjoining page indicator	Indication de la page contigüe	Randhinweis auf Folgekarte
National Park	Parc national	Nationalpark

1:1 000 000

1 centimetre to 10 kilometres

0	10	20	30	40	50	60	70	80 km
0		10		20		30		40	50 miles

1 inch to 16 miles

City maps and plans	Plans de ville	Stadtpläne
★ Place of interest	Site d'interêt	Sehenswerter Ort
▬ Railway station	Gare	Bahnhof
Parkland	Espace vert	Parkland
Woodland	Espace boisé	Waldland
General place of interest	Site d'interêt général	Sehenswerter Ort
Academic/Municipal building	Établissement scolaire/installations municipales	Akademisches/Öffentliches Gebäude
Place of worship	Lieu de culte	Andachtsstätte
Transport location	Infrastructure de transport	Verkehrsanbindung

Places of interest

English	French	German
Museum and Art Gallery	Musée / Gallerie d'art	Museum / Kunstgalerie
Castle	Château	Burg / Schloss
Historic building	Monument historique	historisches Gebäude
Historic site	Site historique	historische Stätte
Monument	Monument	Denkmal
Religious site	Site religieux	religiöse Stätte
Aquarium / Sea life centre	Aquarium / Parc Marin	Aquarium
Arboretum	Arboretum	Arboretum, Baumschule
Botanic garden (National)	Jardin botanique national	botanischer Garten
Natural place of interest (other site)	Réserve naturelle	landschaftlich interessanter Ort
Zoo / Safari park / Wildlife park	Parc Safari / Réserve sauvage / Zoo	Safaripark / Wildreservat / Zoo
Other site	Autres sites	Touristenattraktion
Theme park	Parc à thème	Freizeitpark
World Heritage site	Patrimoine Mondial	Weltkulturerbe
Athletics stadium (International)	Stade international d'athlétisme	internationales Leichtathletik Stadion
Football stadium (Major)	Stade de football	Fußballstadion
Golf course (International)	Parcours de golf international	internationaler Golfplatz
Grand Prix circuit (Formula 1) / Motor racing venue / MotoGP circuit	Circuit auto-moto	Autodrom
Rugby ground (International - Six Nations)	Stade de rugby	internationales Rugbystadion
International sports venue	Autre manifestation sportive	internationale Sportanlage
Tennis venue	Court de tennis	Tennis
Winter sports resort	Sports d'hiver	Wintersport

Country identifiers

A	Austria	Autriche	Österreich	I	Italy	Italie	Italien
AL	Albania	Albanie	Albanien	IRL	Ireland	Irlande	Irland
AND	Andorra	Andorre	Andorra	IS	Iceland	Islande	Island
B	Belgium	Belgique	Belgien	L	Luxembourg	Luxembourg	Luxemburg
BG	Bulgaria	Bulgarie	Bulgarien	LT	Lithuania	Lituanie	Litauen
BIH	Bosnia and Herzegovina	Bosnie-et-Herzégovine	Bosnien und Herzegowina	LV	Latvia	Lettonie	Lettland
BY	Belarus	Bélarus	Belarus	M	Malta	Malte	Malta
CH	Switzerland	Suisse	Schweiz	MA	Morocco	Maroc	Marokko
CY	Cyprus	Chypre	Zypern	MC	Monaco	Monaco	Monaco
CZ	Czechia (Czech Republic)	République tchèque	Tschechische Republik	MD	Moldova	Moldavie	Moldawien
D	Germany	Allemagne	Deutschland	MK	Macedonia (F.Y.R.O.M.)	Ancienne République yougoslave de Macédoine	Ehemalige jugoslawische Republik Mazedonien
DK	Denmark	Danemark	Dänemark	MNE	Montenegro	Monténégro	Montenegro
DZ	Algeria	Algérie	Algerien	N	Norway	Norvège	Norwegen
E	Spain	Espagne	Spanien	NL	Netherlands	Pays-Bas	Niederlande
EST	Estonia	Estonie	Estland	P	Portugal	Portugal	Portugal
F	France	France	Frankreich	PL	Poland	Pologne	Polen
FIN	Finland	Finlande	Finnland	RKS	Kosovo	Kosovo	Kosovo
FL	Liechtenstein	Liechtenstein	Liechtenstein	RO	Romania	Roumanie	Rumänien
FO	Faroe Islands	Iles Féroé	Färöer-Inseln	RSM	San Marino	Saint-Marin	San Marino
GB	United Kingdom GB & NI	Grande-Bretagne	Grossbritannien	RUS	Russia	Russie	Russland
GBA	Alderney	Alderney	Alderney	S	Sweden	Suède	Schweden
GBG	Guernsey	Guernsey	Guernsey	SK	Slovakia	République slovaque	Slowakei
GBJ	Jersey	Jersey	Jersey	SLO	Slovenia	Slovénie	Slowenien
GBM	Isle of Man	île de Man	Insel Man	SRB	Serbia	Sérbie	Serbien
GBZ	Gibraltar	Gibraltar	Gibraltar	TN	Tunisia	Tunisie	Tunisien
GR	Greece	Grèce	Griechenland	TR	Turkey	Turquie	Türkei
H	Hungary	Hongrie	Ungarn	UA	Ukraine	Ukraine	Ukraine
HR	Croatia	Croatie	Kroatien				

International road signs and travel web links

Informative signs

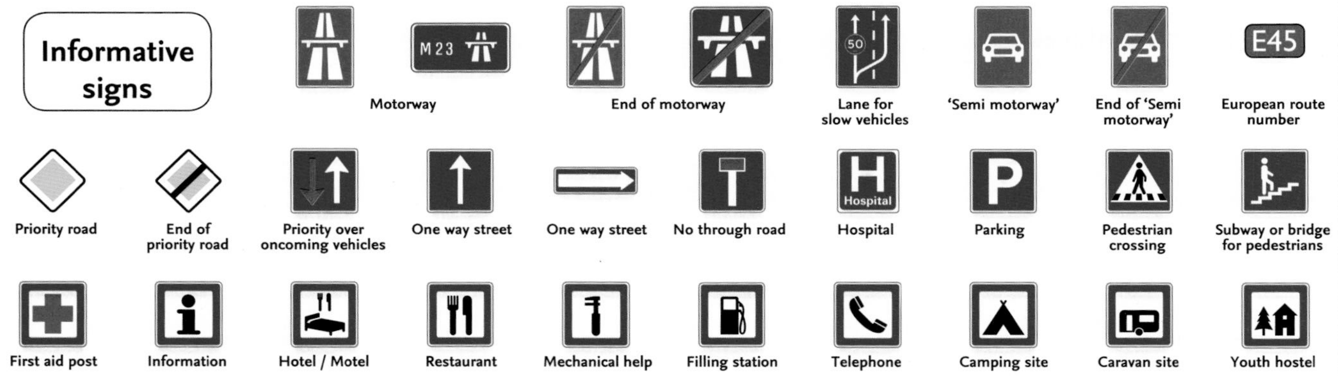
M23
E45
Motorway
End of motorway
Lane for slow vehicles
'Semi motorway'
End of 'Semi motorway'
European route number
Priority road
End of priority road
Priority over oncoming vehicles
One way street
One way street
No through road
Hospital
Parking
Pedestrian crossing
Subway or bridge for pedestrians
First aid post
Information
Hotel / Motel
Restaurant
Mechanical help
Filling station
Telephone
Camping site
Caravan site
Youth hostel

Warning signs

Right bend
Left bend
Double bend
Roundabout
Intersection with non-priority road
Traffic merges from left
Traffic merges from right
Road narrows
Road narrows at left
Road narrows at right
Give way
Slippery road
Uneven road
10%
Steep hill – descent
Tunnel
Opening bridge
Road works
Loose chippings
Level crossing with barrier
Level crossing without barrier
Tram
'Count down' posts
'Danger' level crossing
Low flying aircraft
Falling rocks
Cross wind
Quayside or river bank
Two-way traffic
Traffic signals ahead
Pedestrians
Children
Animals
Wild animals
Other dangers
3,5 m
Width of carriageway
Beginning of regulation
Repetition sign
End of regulation

Regulative signs

End of all restrictions
STOP
Halt sign
STOP KONTROL
Customs
No stopping ("clearway")
No parking/waiting
Priority to oncoming vehicles
Use of horns prohibited
Roundabout
Direction to be followed
Pass this side
50
Minimum speed limit
50
End of minimum speed limit
Cycle path
Footpath
Riders only
All vehicles prohibited
No entry for all vehicles
No right turn
No u-turns
No entry for motor cars
No entry for all motor vehicles
Lorries prohibited
Buses and coaches prohibited
No trailers
Motorcycles prohibited
Mopeds prohibited
Cycles prohibited
No entry for pedestrians
No overtaking
End of no overtaking
No overtaking for lorries
End of no overtaking for lorries
5 t
Laden weight limit
2 t
Axle weight limit
2 m
Width limit
3,5 m
Height limit
60
Maximum speed limit
60
End of speed limit

Travel & route planning

Driving information	www.drive-alive.co.uk
The AA	www.theaa.com
The RAC	www.rac.co.uk
ViaMichelin	www.viamichelin.com
Bing Maps	www.bing.com/mapspreview
Motorail information	www.seat61.com/Motorail
Ferry information	www.aferry.com
Eurotunnel information	www.eurotunnel.com/uk/home/

General information

UK Foreign & Commonwealth Office	www.gov.uk/government/organisations/foreign-commonwealth-office
Country profiles	www.cia.gov/library/publications/resources/the-world-factbook/index.html
World Heritage sites	whc.unesco.org/en/list
World time	wwp.greenwichmeantime.com
Weather information	www.metoffice.gov.uk

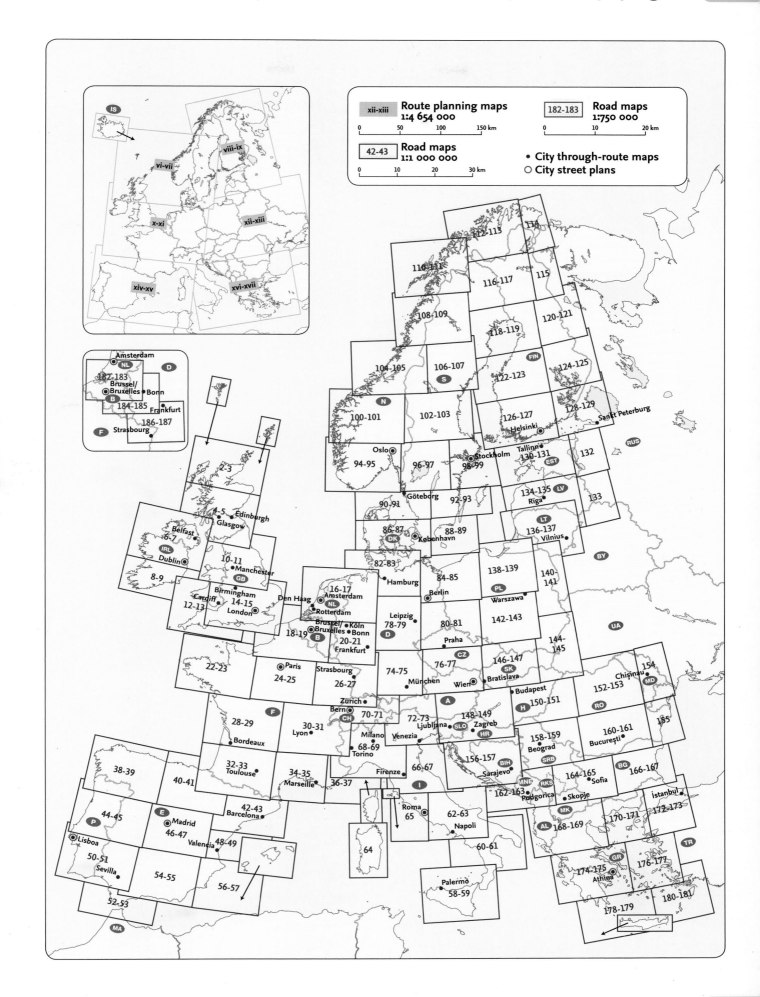

Route planning maps
1:4 654 000

xii-xiii

0   50   100   150 km

Road maps
1:750 000

182-183

0   10   20 km

Road maps
1:1 000 000

42-43

0   10   20   30 km

• City through-route maps
○ City street plans

IS

24° Straumnes Horn Grímsey Rifstangi Fontur Arctic Circle
Öxarfjörður
66° Ísafjörður Reiphólsfjöll Húnaflói Saudárkrókur Akureyri Borgarfjörður 66°
881 Egilsstaðir Seydisfjörður
Bjargtangar Breiðafjörður Ódáðahraun Snæfell Breiddalsvík
1763 1833
Hafursfjörður 1491 Bárðarbunga
Faxaflói 2009 Vesturhorn
Borgarnes IS
Grímsvötn 1719
Sviahnúkar
64° REYKJAVÍK 64°
Keflavík 1491 2119
Reykjanestá Hvannadalshnúkur
Skaftárós
Vestmannaeyjar Surtsey Vík Kötlutangi 18°
Vestmannaeyjar

FO
Eysturoy Slættaratindur
682 Klaksvík
FAROE Vágar Borðoy
ISLANDS Torshavn
(FOROYAR) Sandoy
(Denmark) Gluggarnín 610
DK Suðuroy

Unst
Yell
Shetland
60° Islands
Foula Lerwick

A T L A N T I C
Fair Isle

O C E A N
Kirkwall
Hoy Orkney
Islands
Cape Thurso
58° Wrath
Lewis A9
Stornoway
Western The Minch
St Kilda Clisham Ullapool
South 799 A835
Harris A9
North Uist Moray Firth
Benbecula Portree A96 Elgin
South Uist 993 Carn Eighe A82 Inverness Peterhead
Skye 1183 A9 Ben Macdui
56° Barra A87 1309 A96
Rum Ben Nevis A9 Aberdeen
Fort William 1345 Grampian Mountains
Coll A82 A90
Tiree Ben A9
Mull Lawers Dundee Arbroath
966 Oban 1214 Perth
Colonsay A85 A85 A84 A9 M90 N O
Stirling Kirkcaldy
Jura Loch M9
Lomond Firth of Forth
Islay Greenock Glasgow Edinburgh
Paisley M8 Berwick-upon-Tweed
Arran 873 Hamilton M74 Southern Uplands A1
Kilmarnock 840 Galashiels S
Campbeltown Ayr 816 Hawick
Malin Head Merrick Dumfries GB Morpeth
Tory Island 843 A74(M) South Shields
752 Coleraine A77 Carlisle A69 Newcastle
Errigal Ballymoney Stranraer Solway Firth A75 upon Tyne Sunderland
Letterkenny Londonderry A26 Ballymena Workington Durham
Donegal (Derry) A6 x Penrith Hartlepool
Donegal N15 Magherafelt Cross Fell A1(M)
Bay N15 Lower Omagh M1 Belfast Bangor Snaefell 893 Middlesbrough
Sligo Enniskillen Neagh Newtown Scafell A66 Darlington
Nephin Upper N17 N4 Armagh Lisburn Pike 977
806 Erne Monaghan 852

Achill
Island

1:4 654 000
0 100 200 km
0 50 100 miles

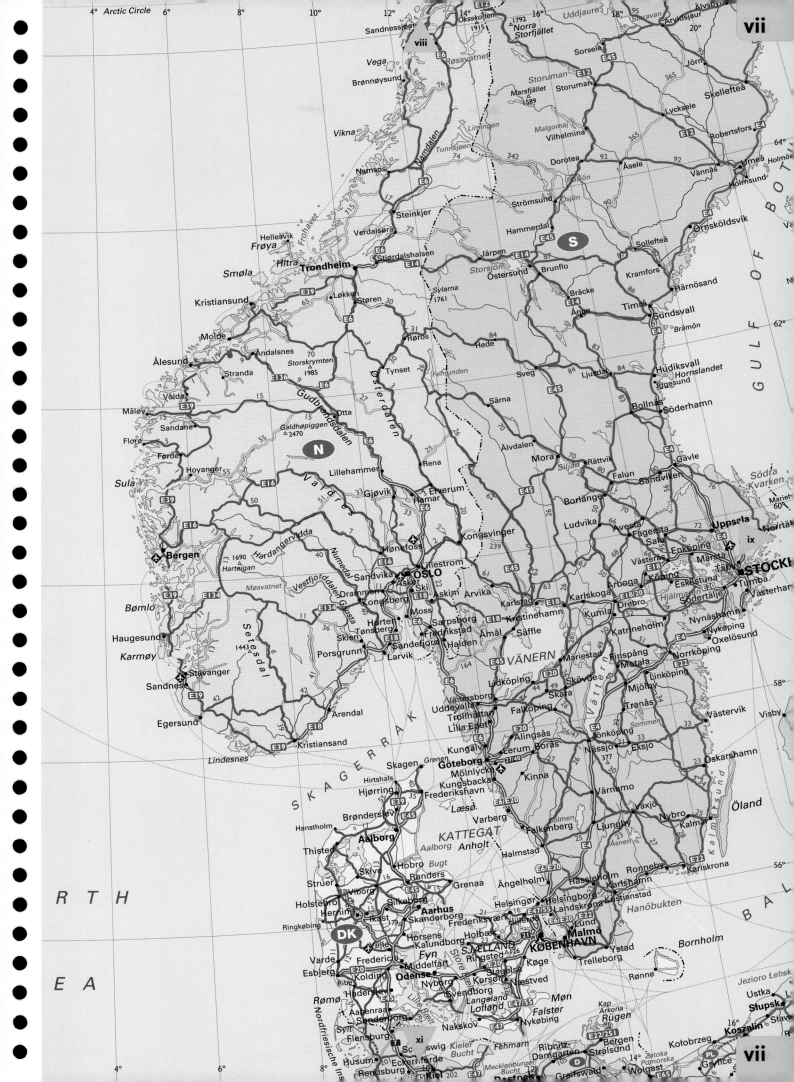

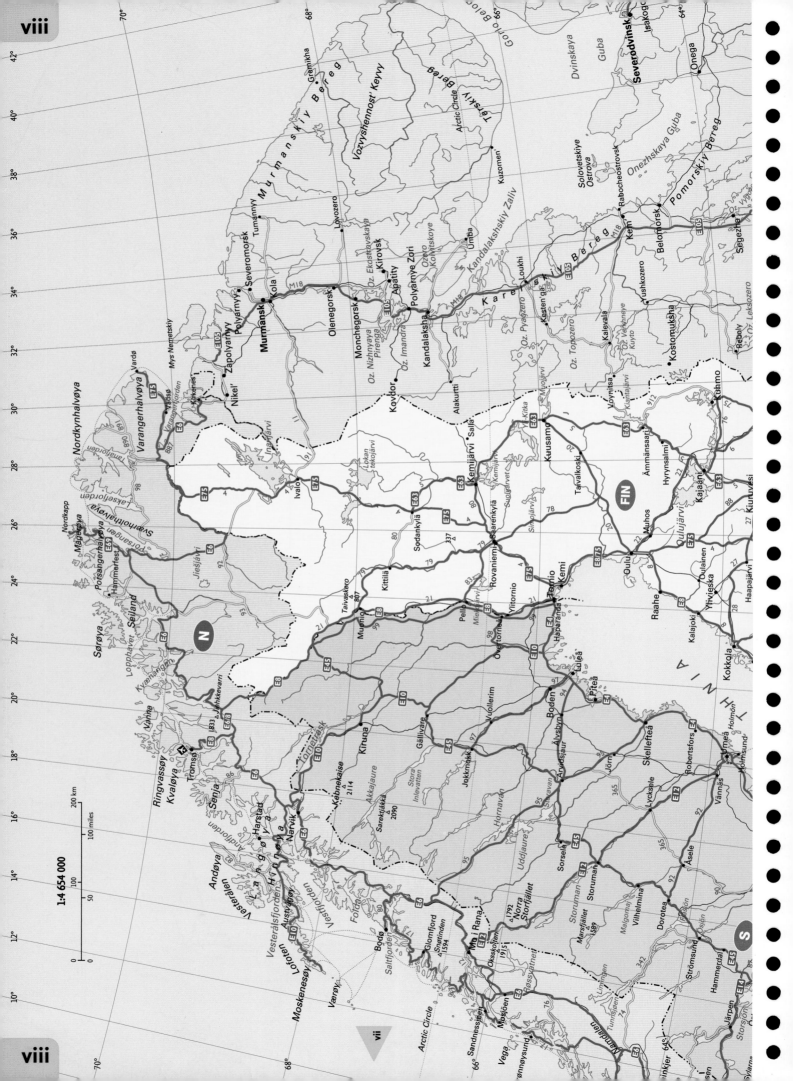

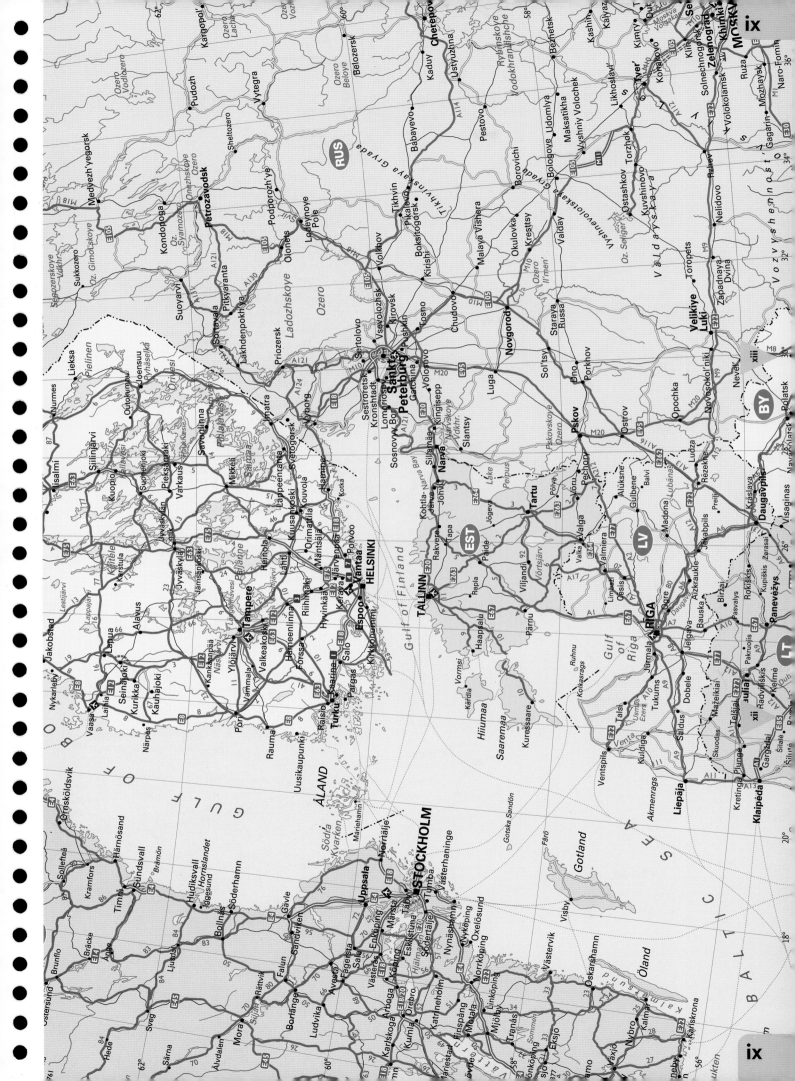

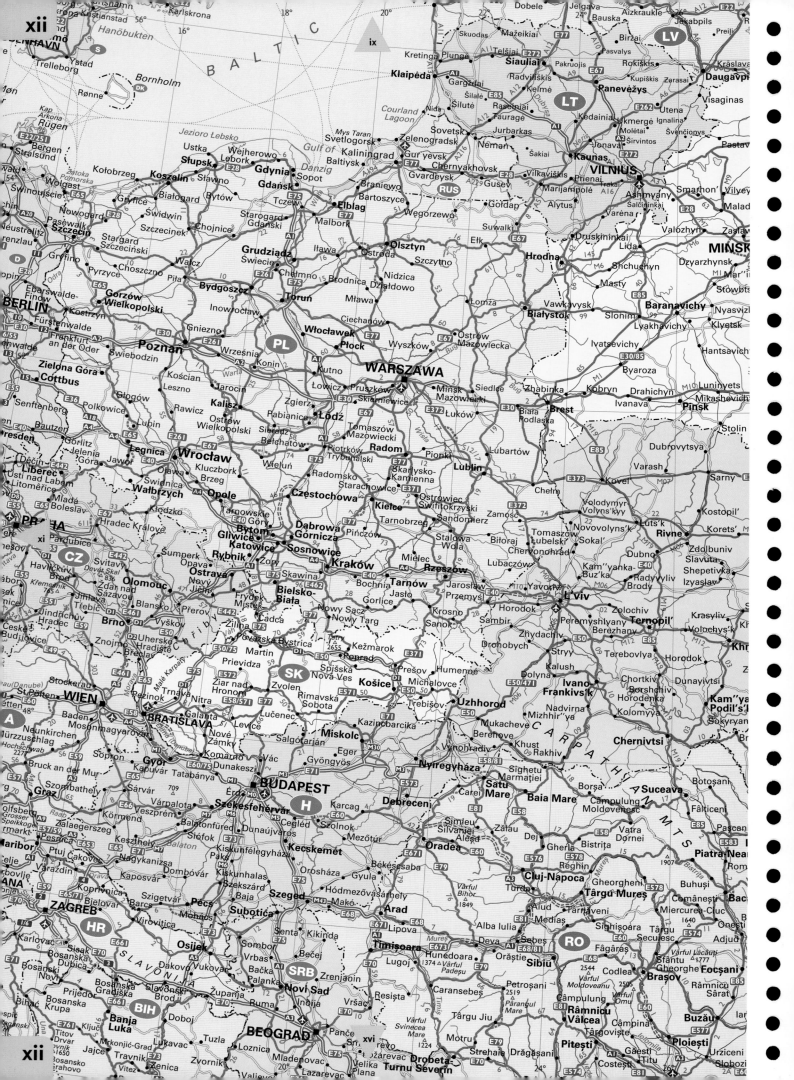

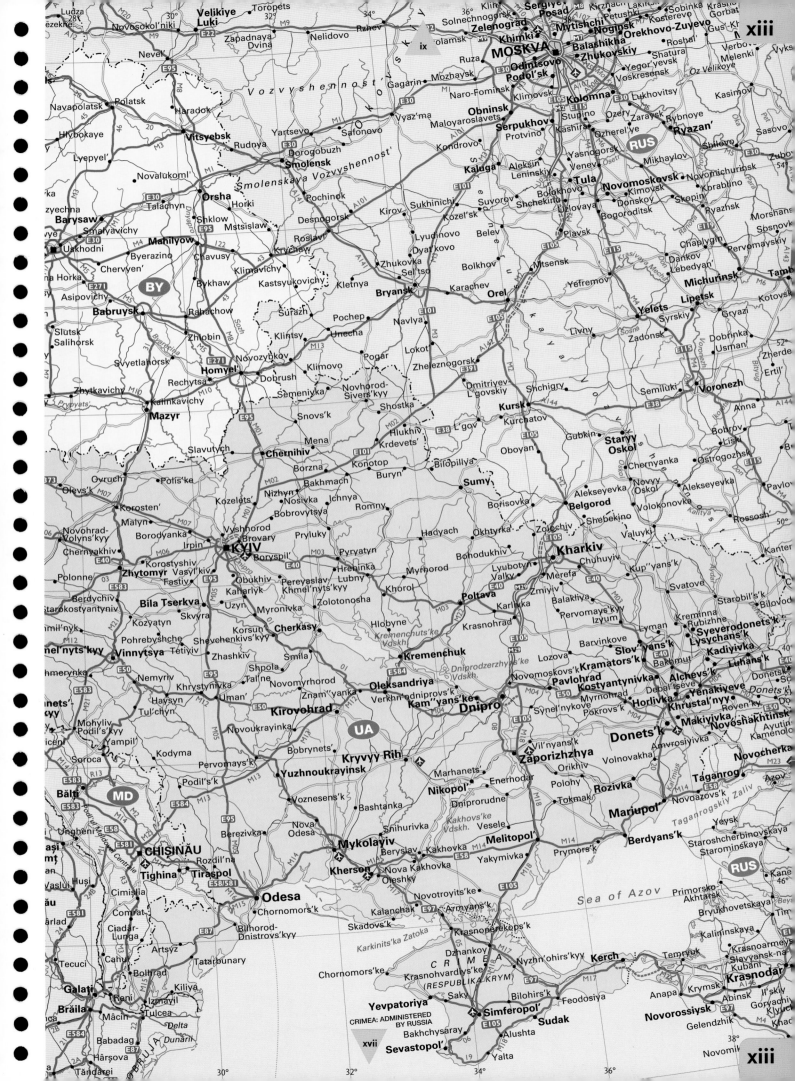

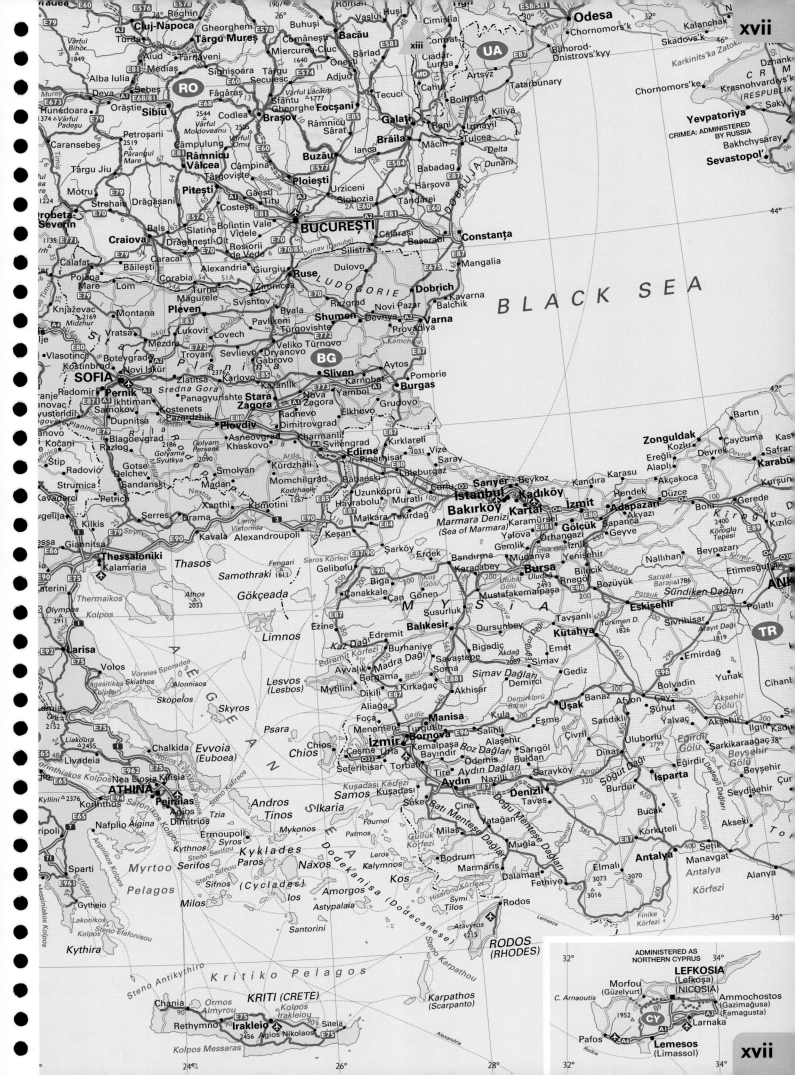

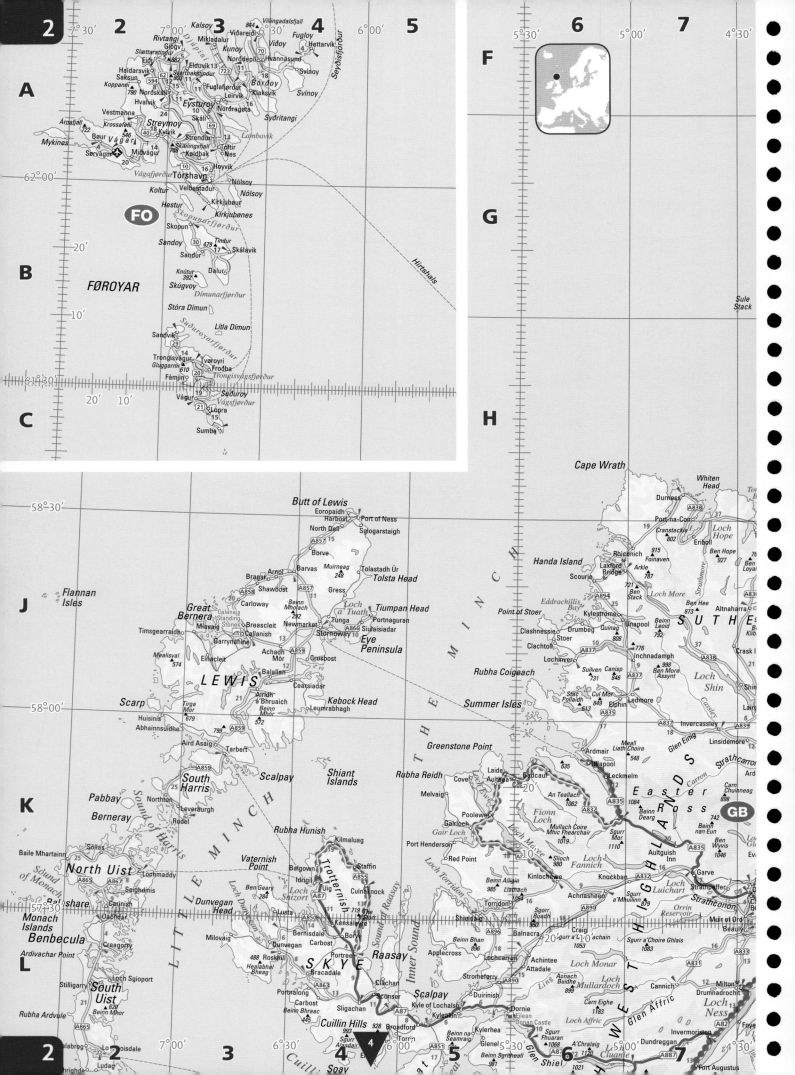

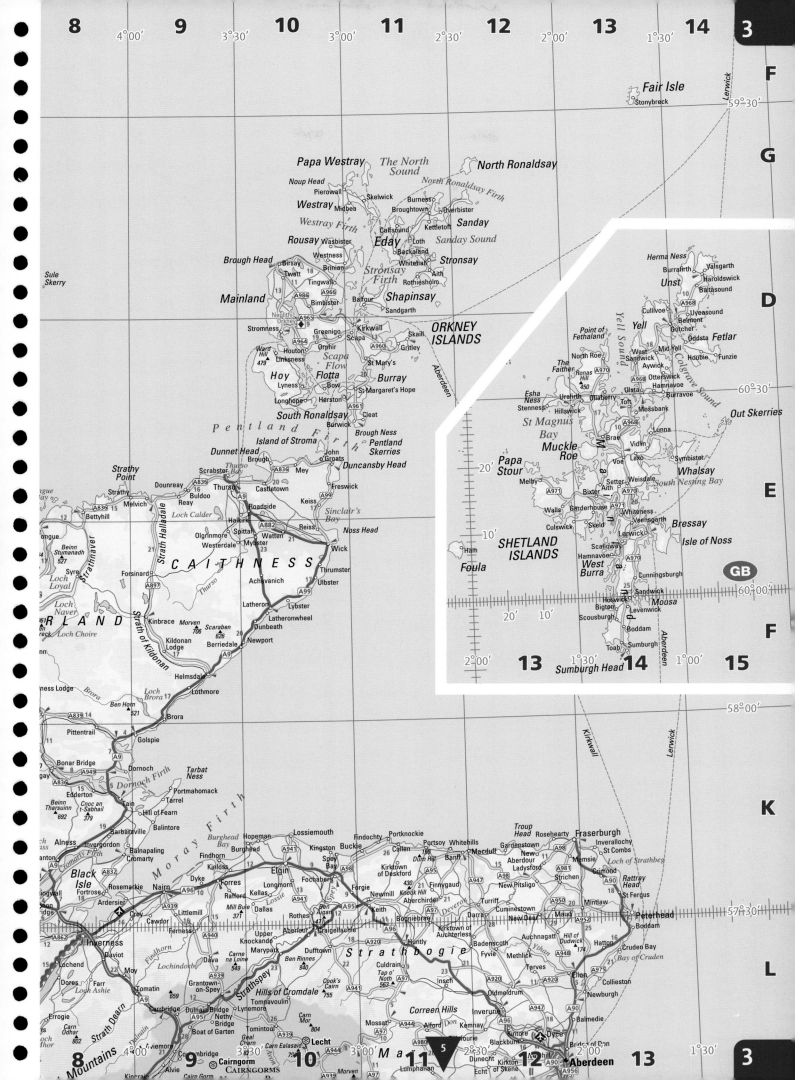

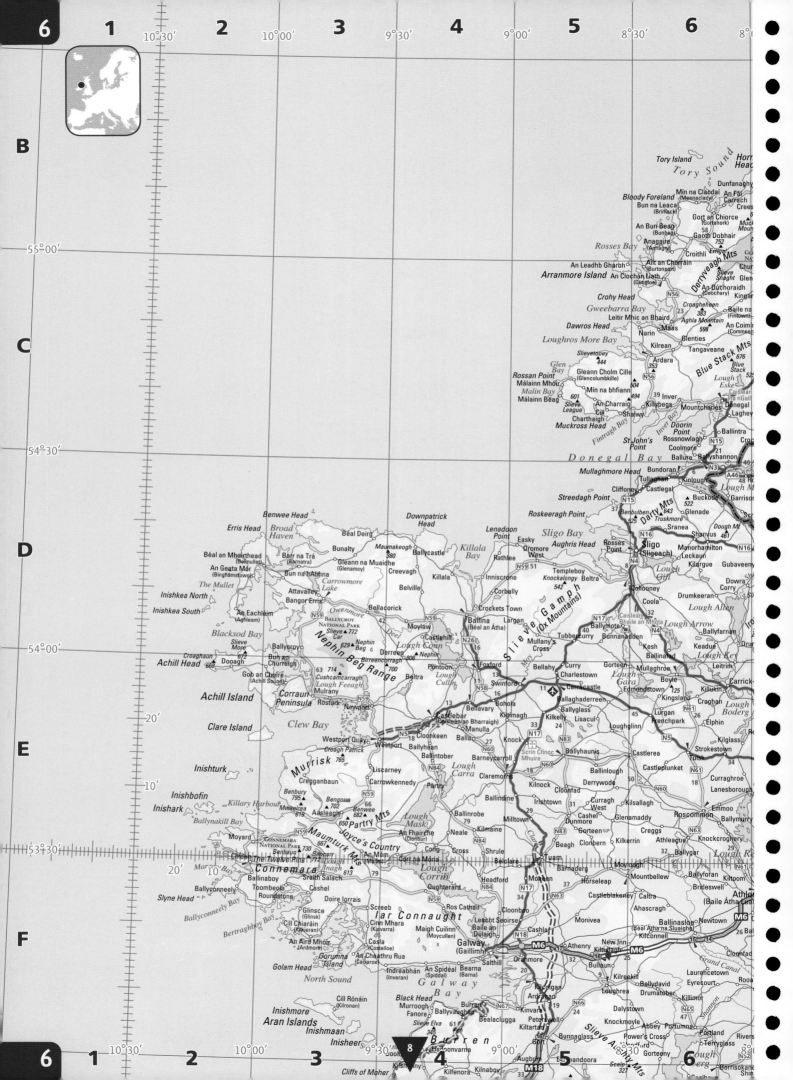

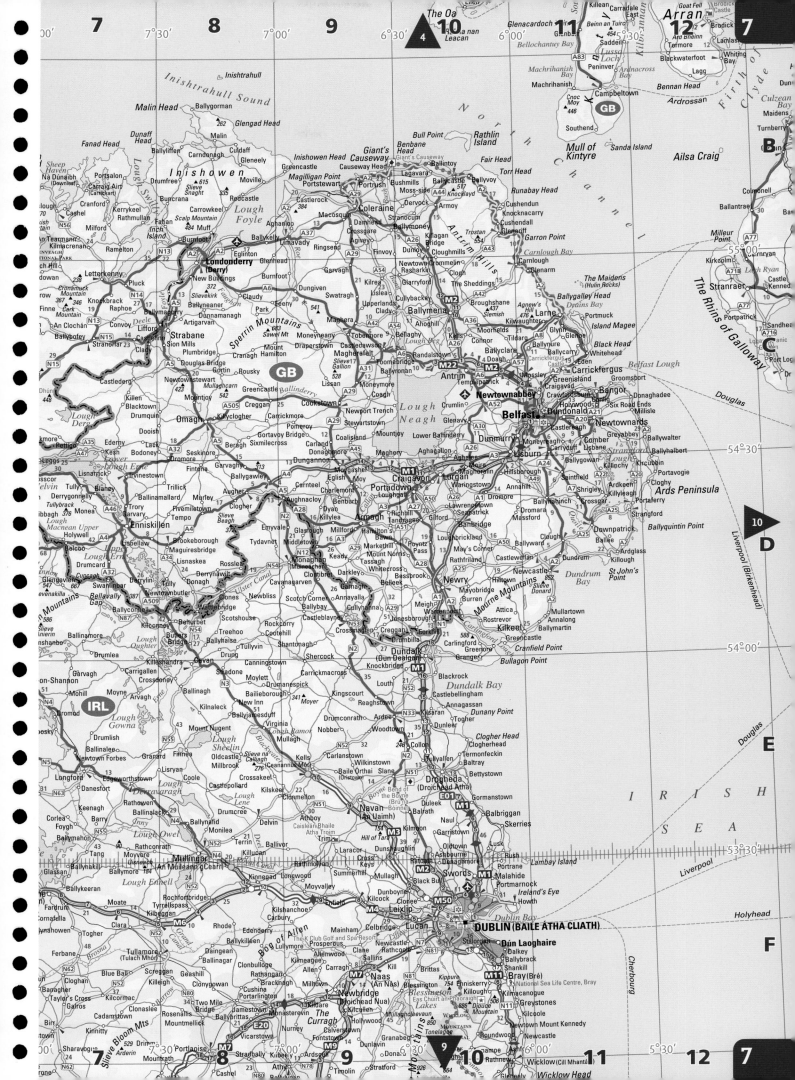

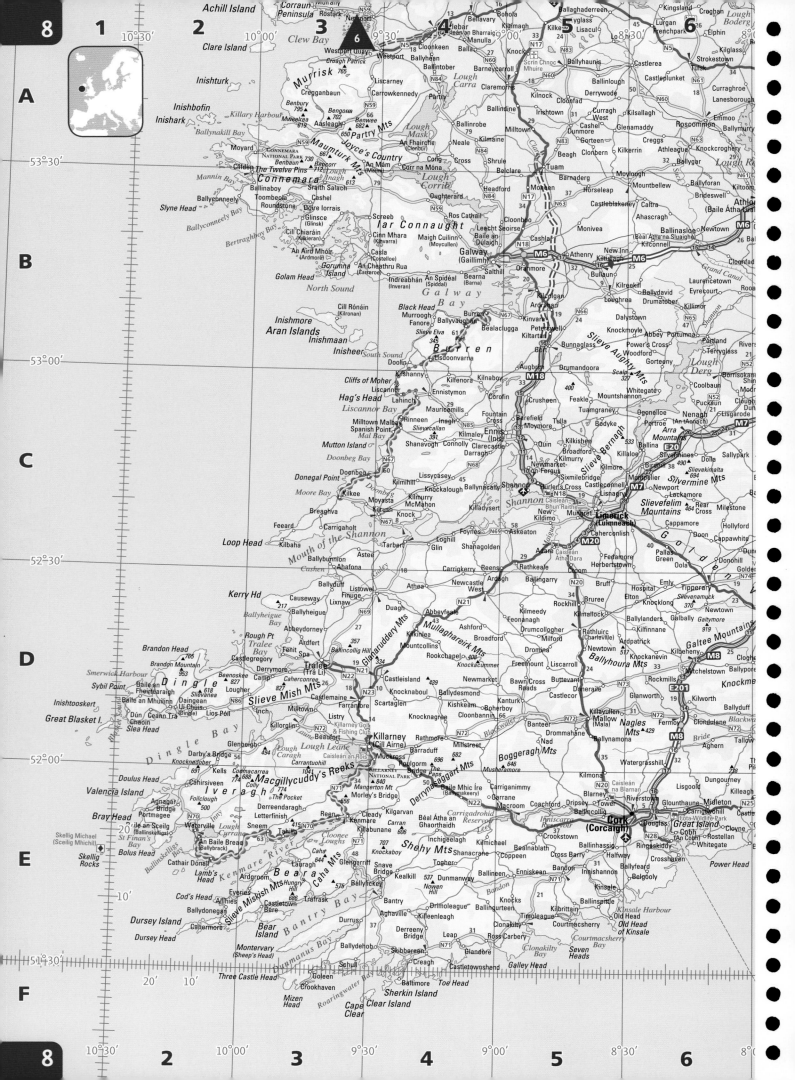

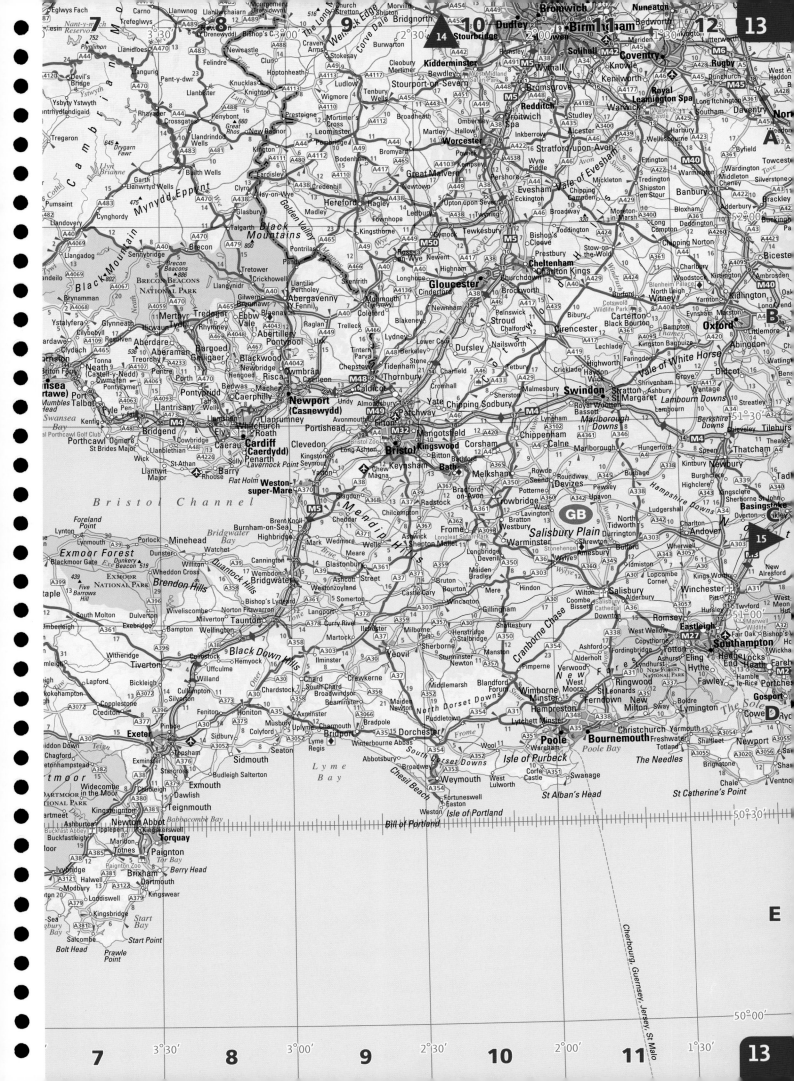

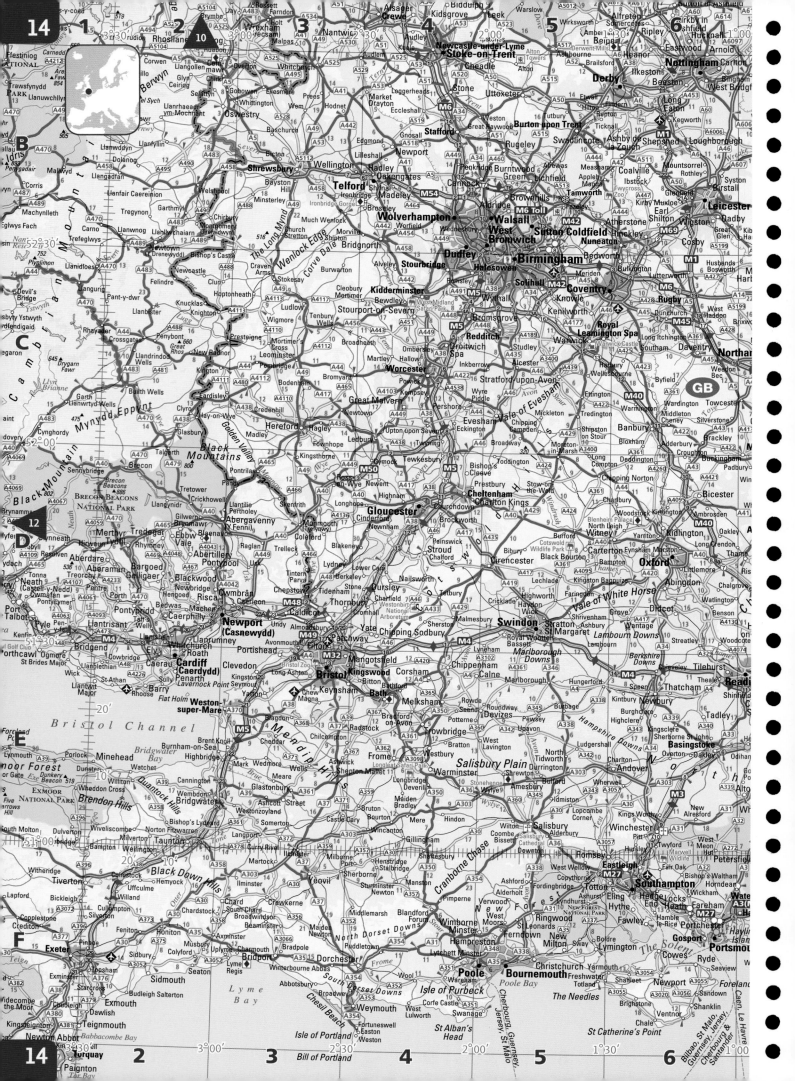

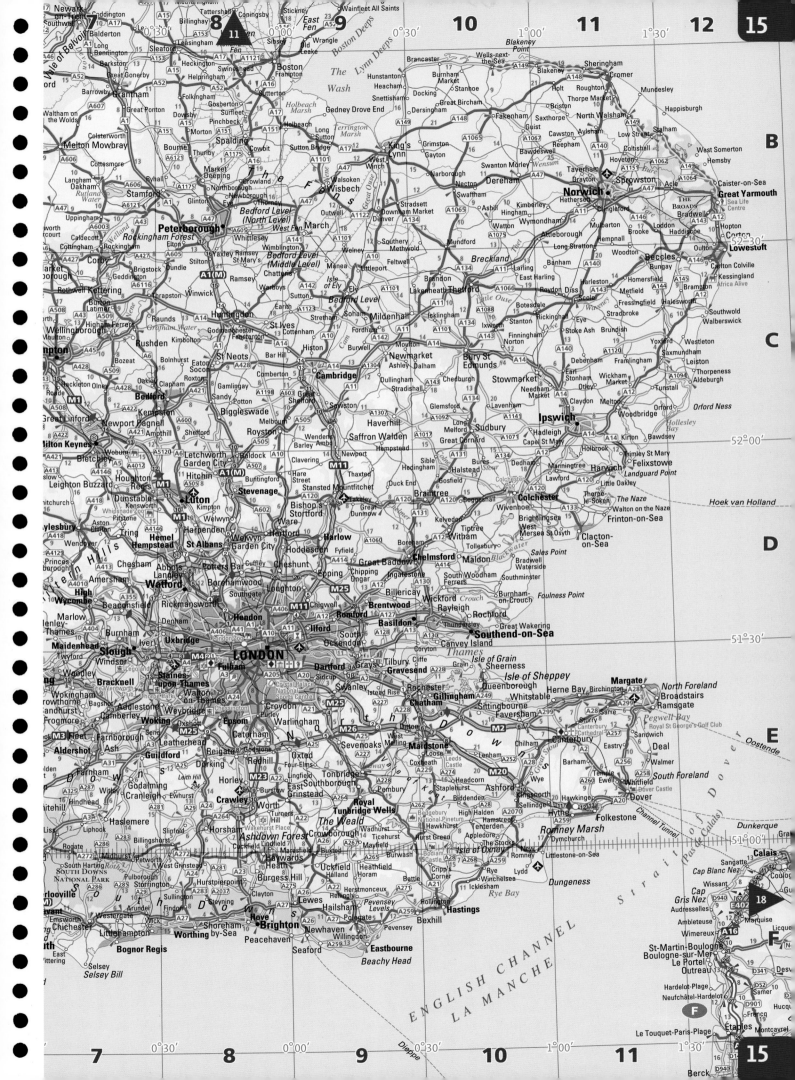

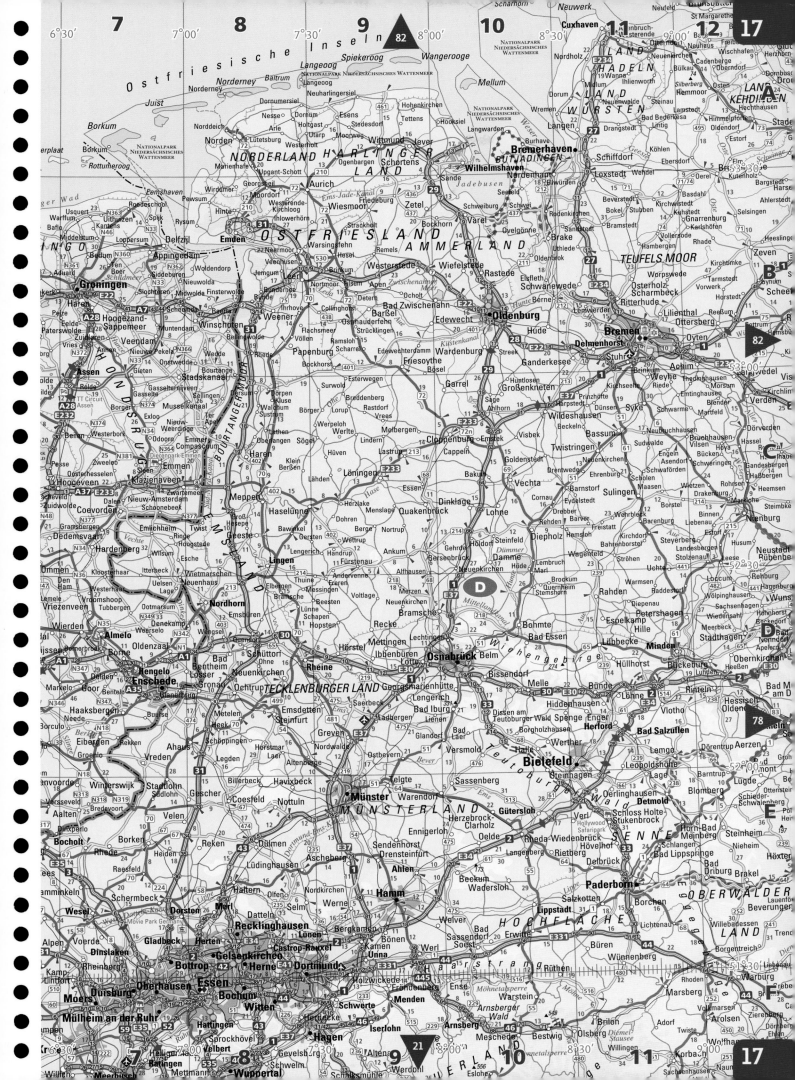

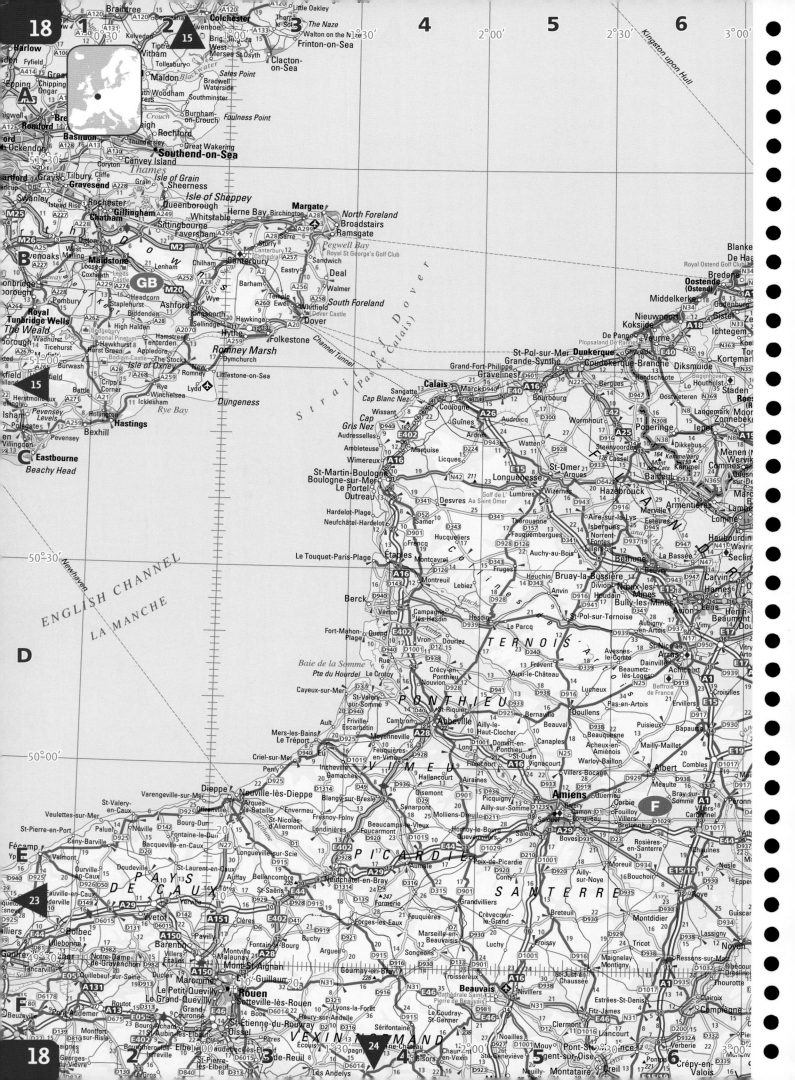

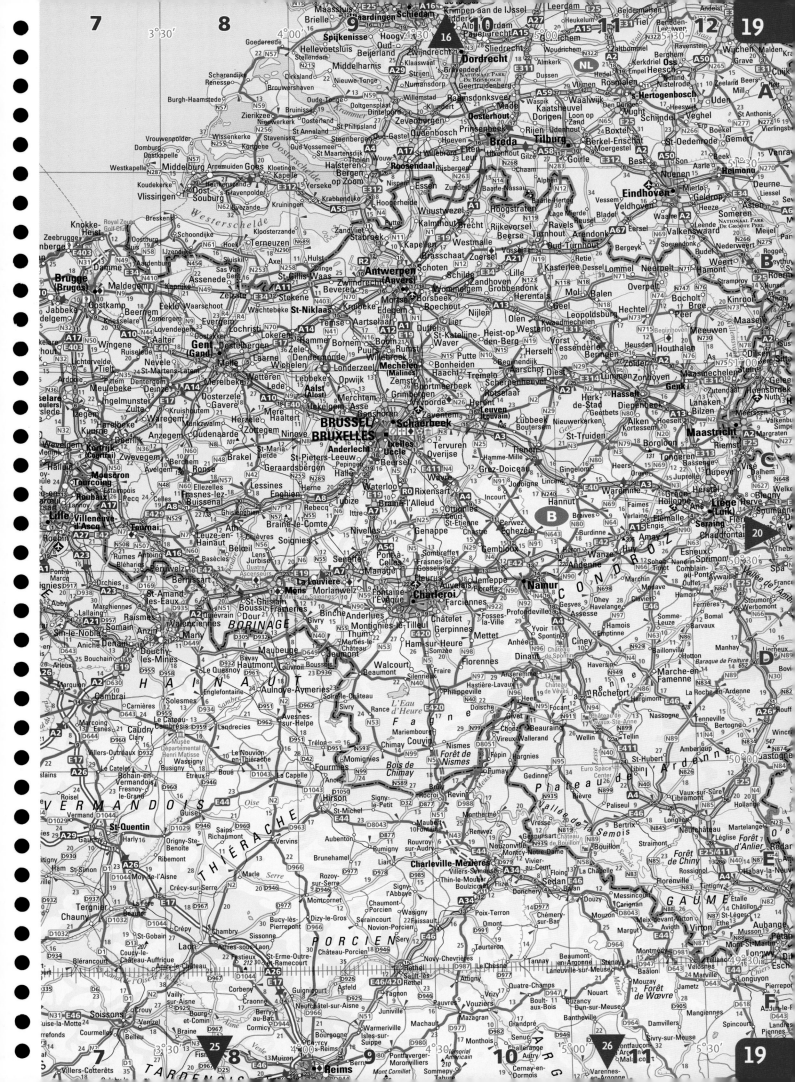

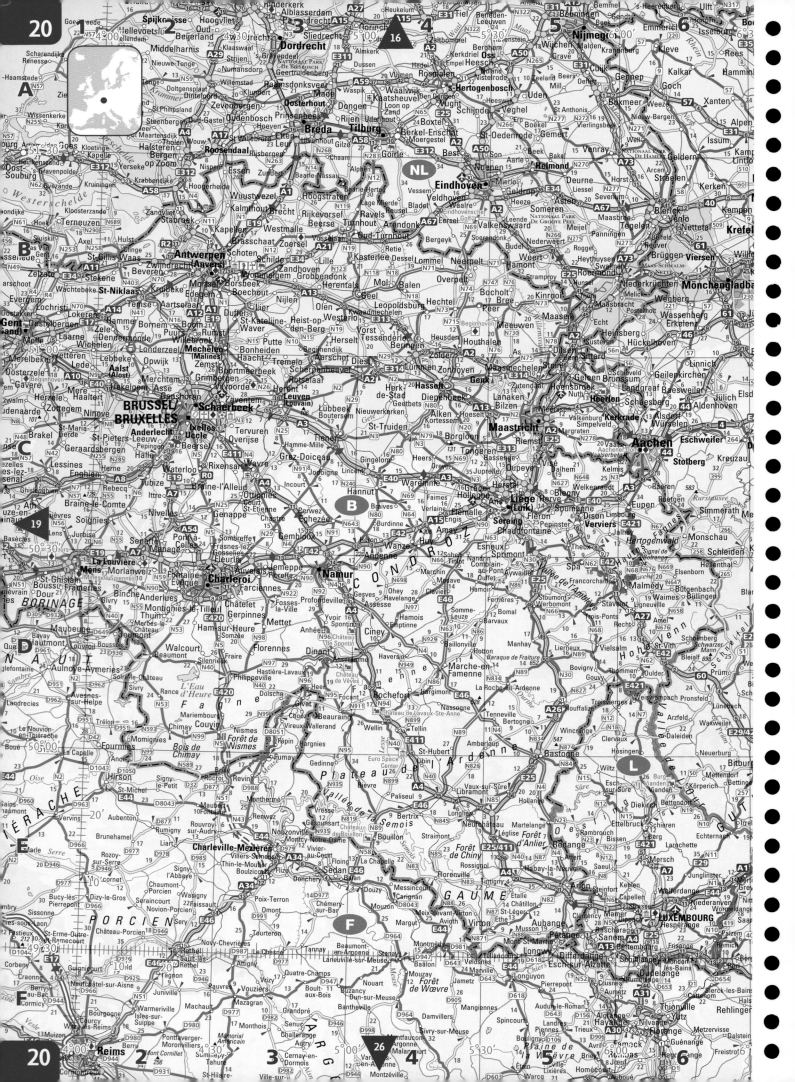

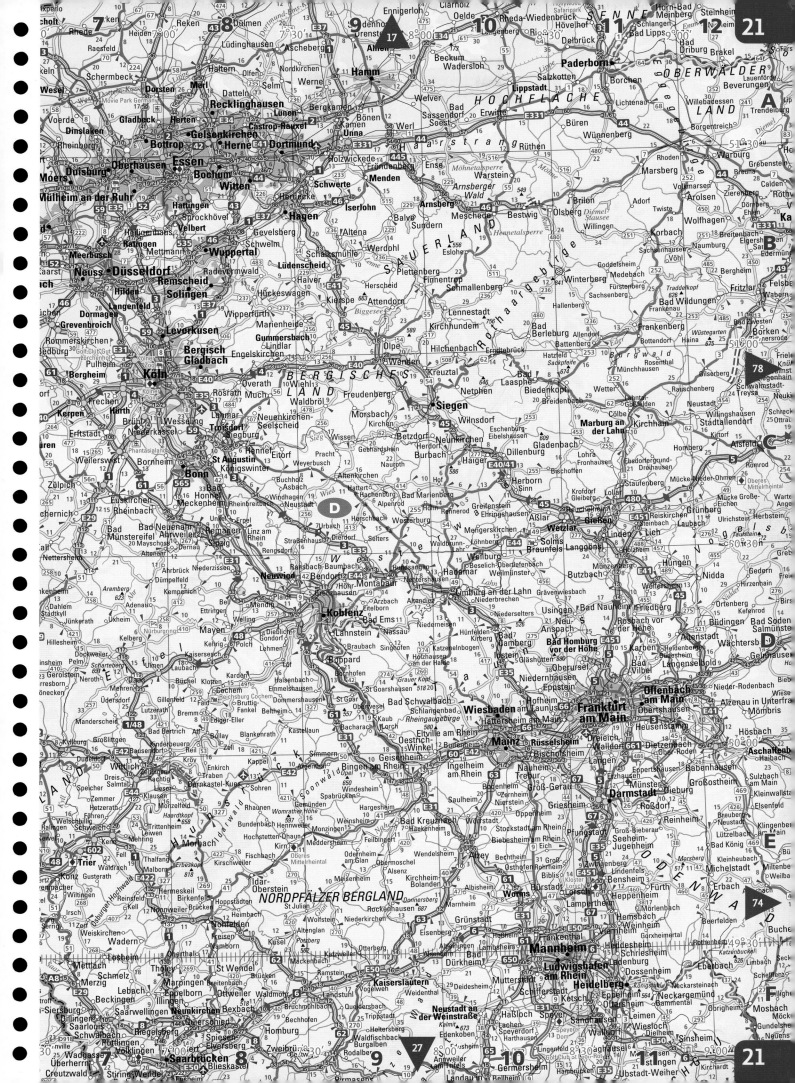

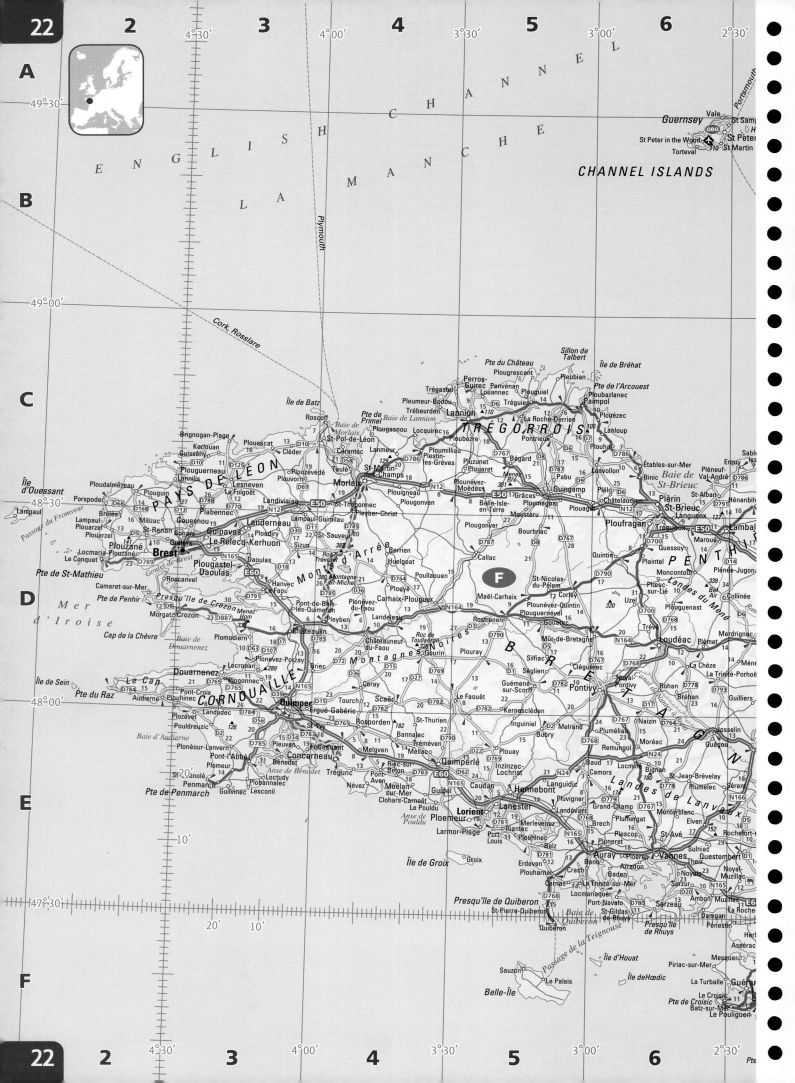

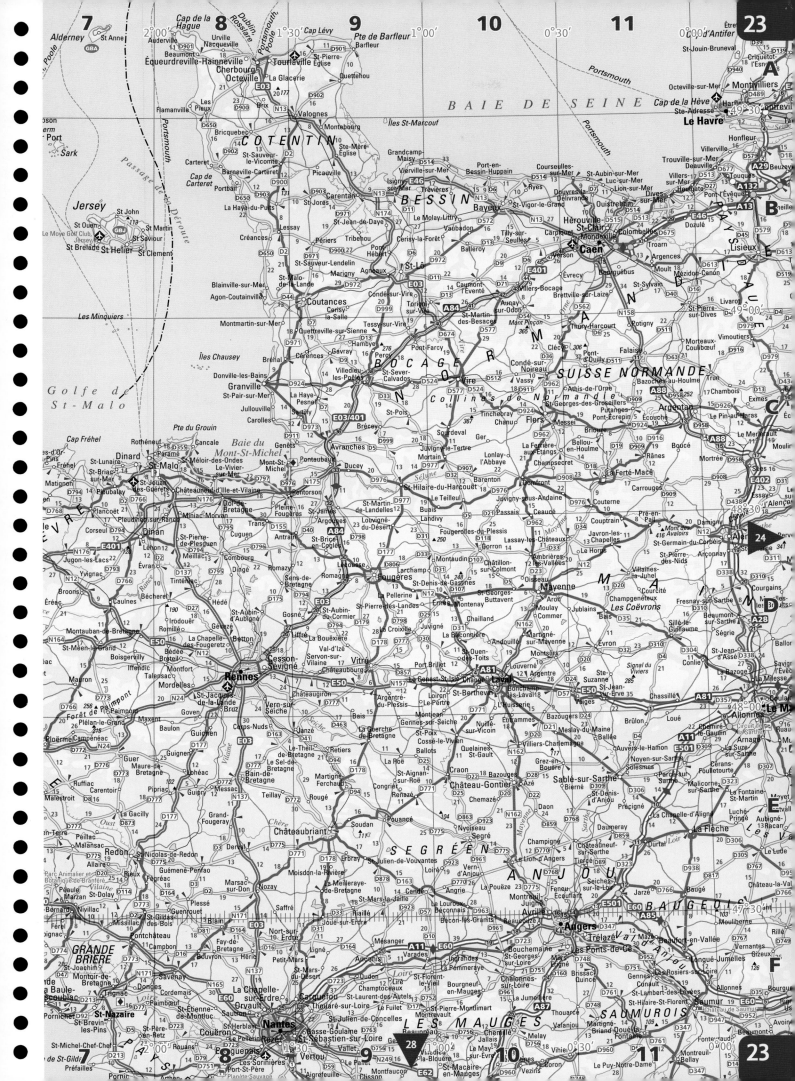

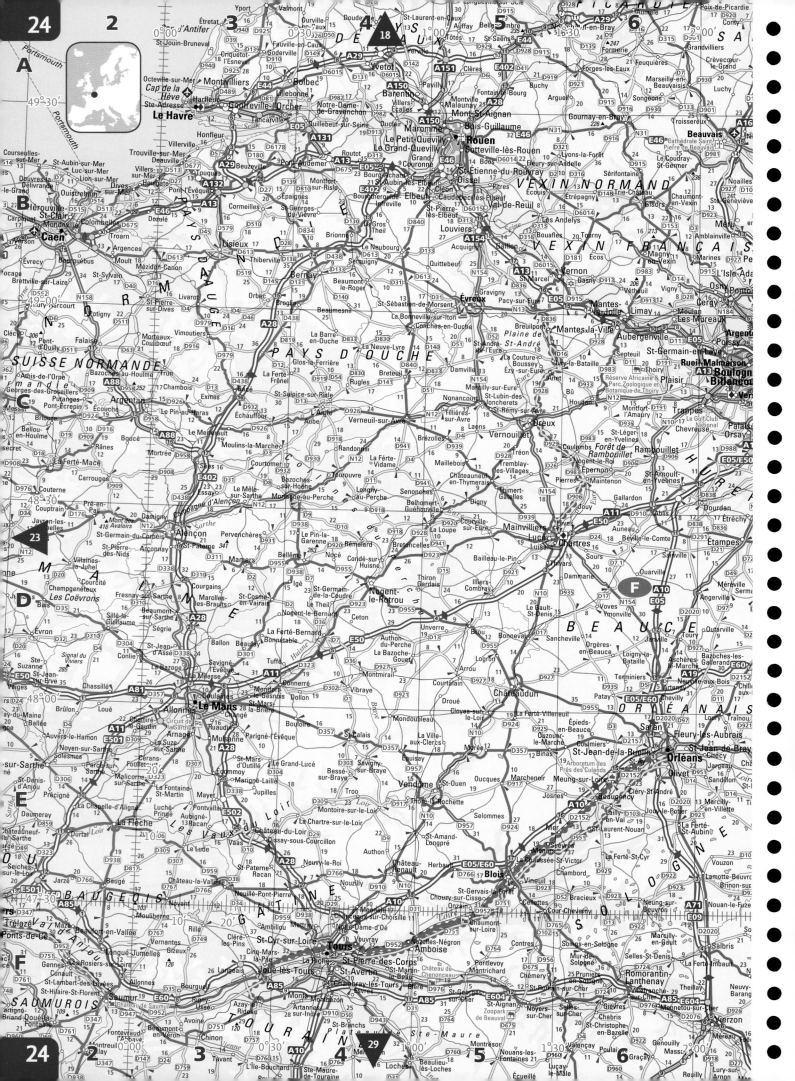

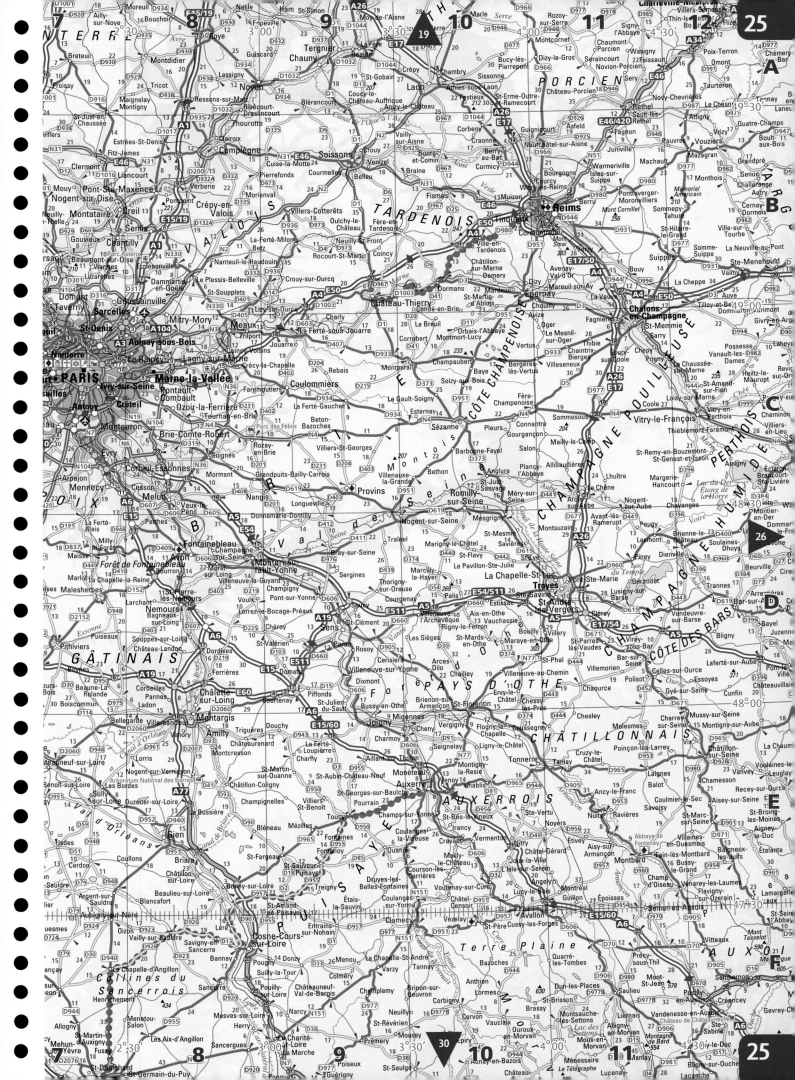

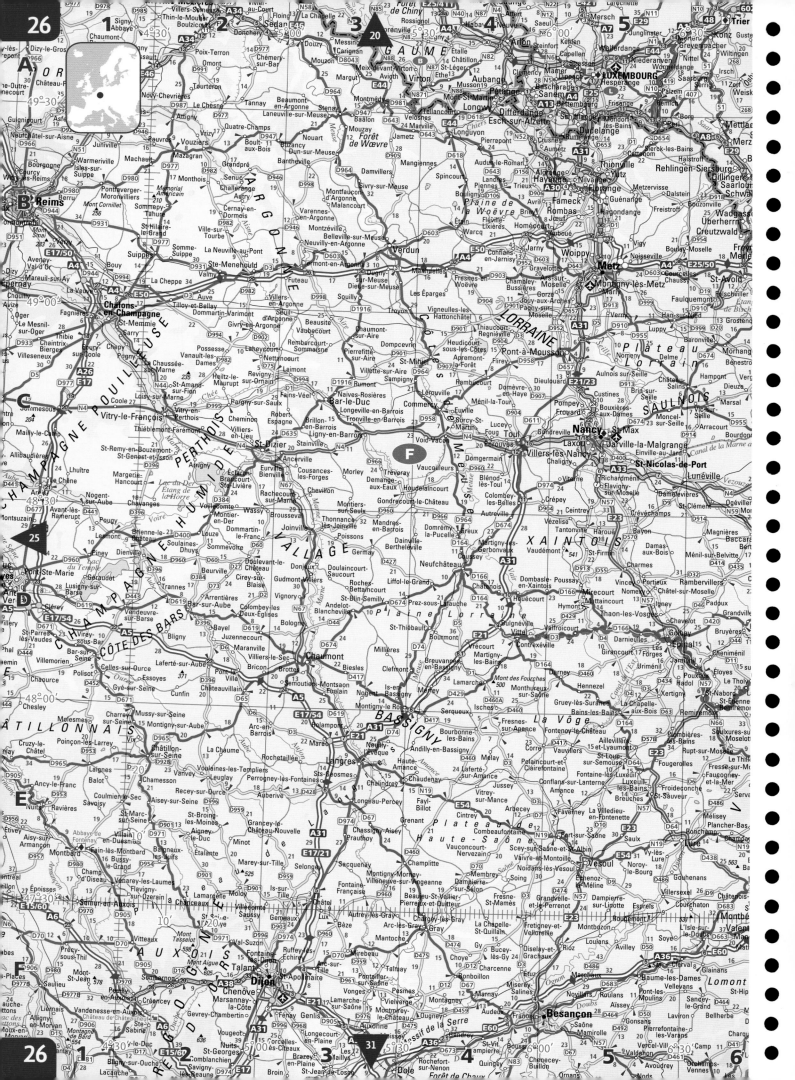

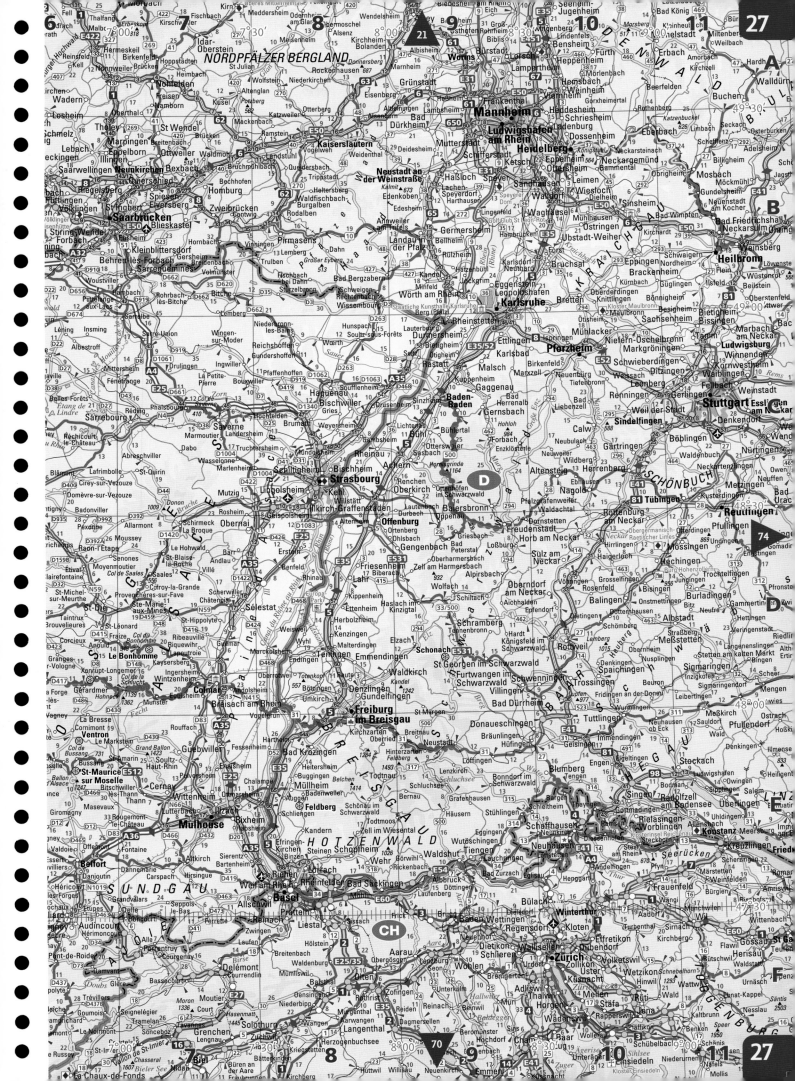

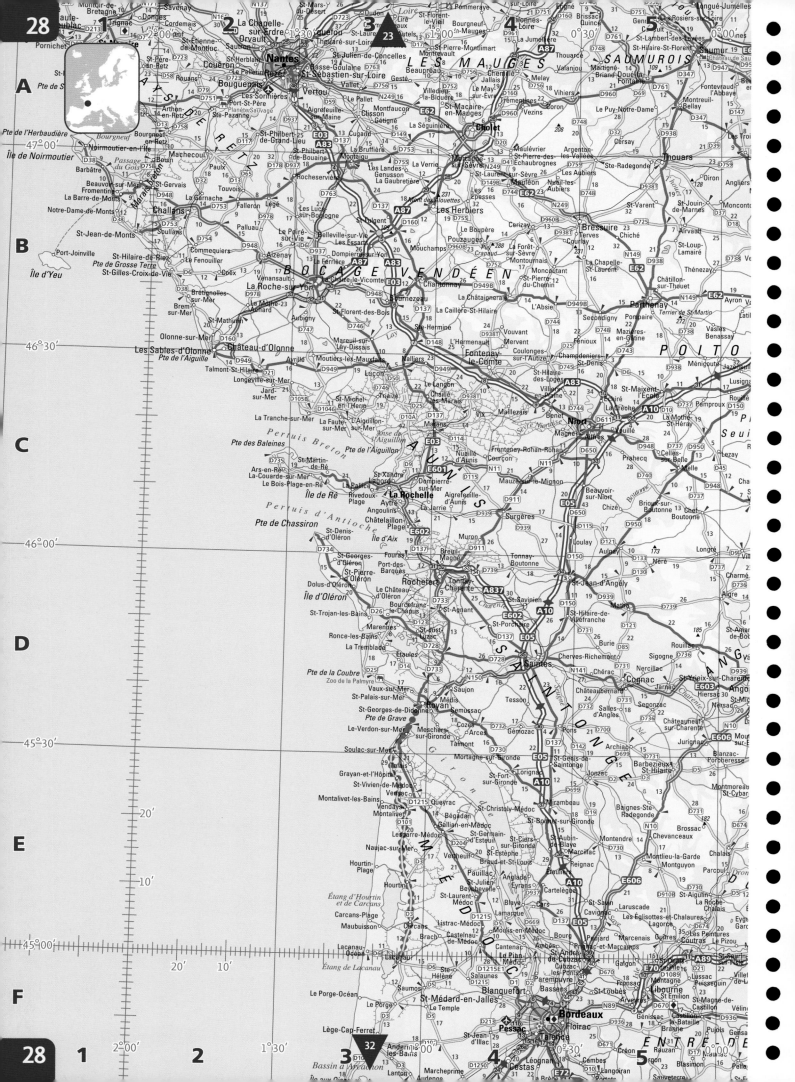

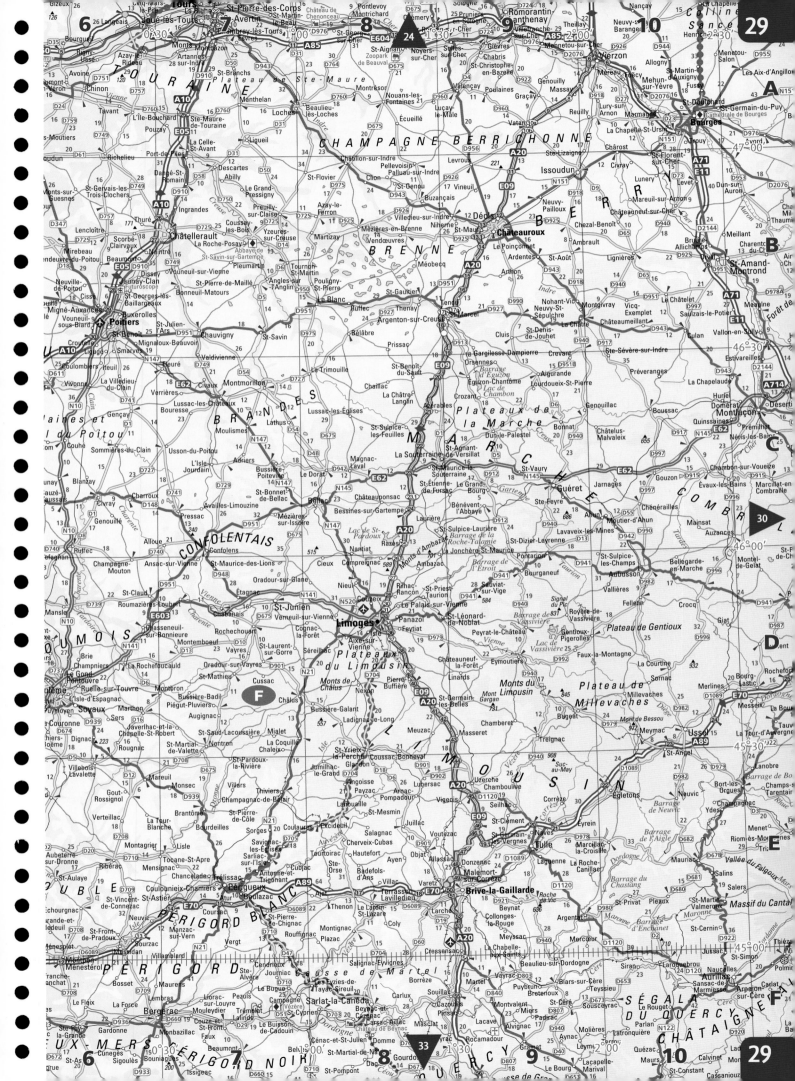

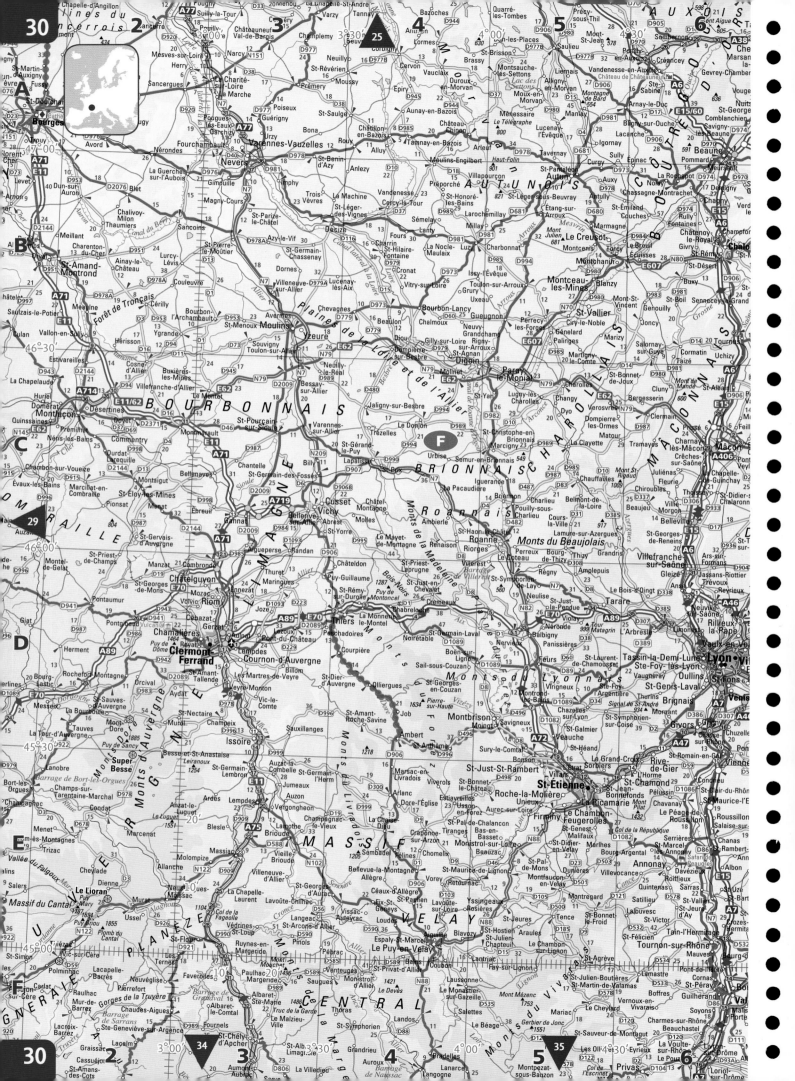

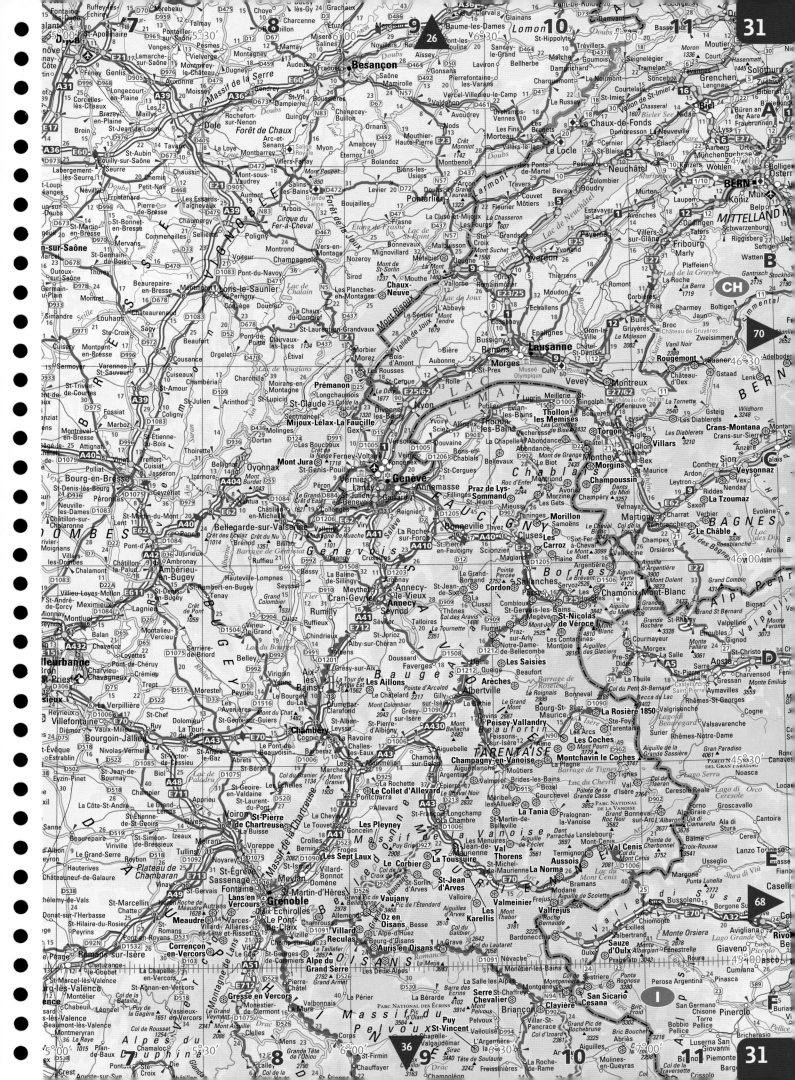

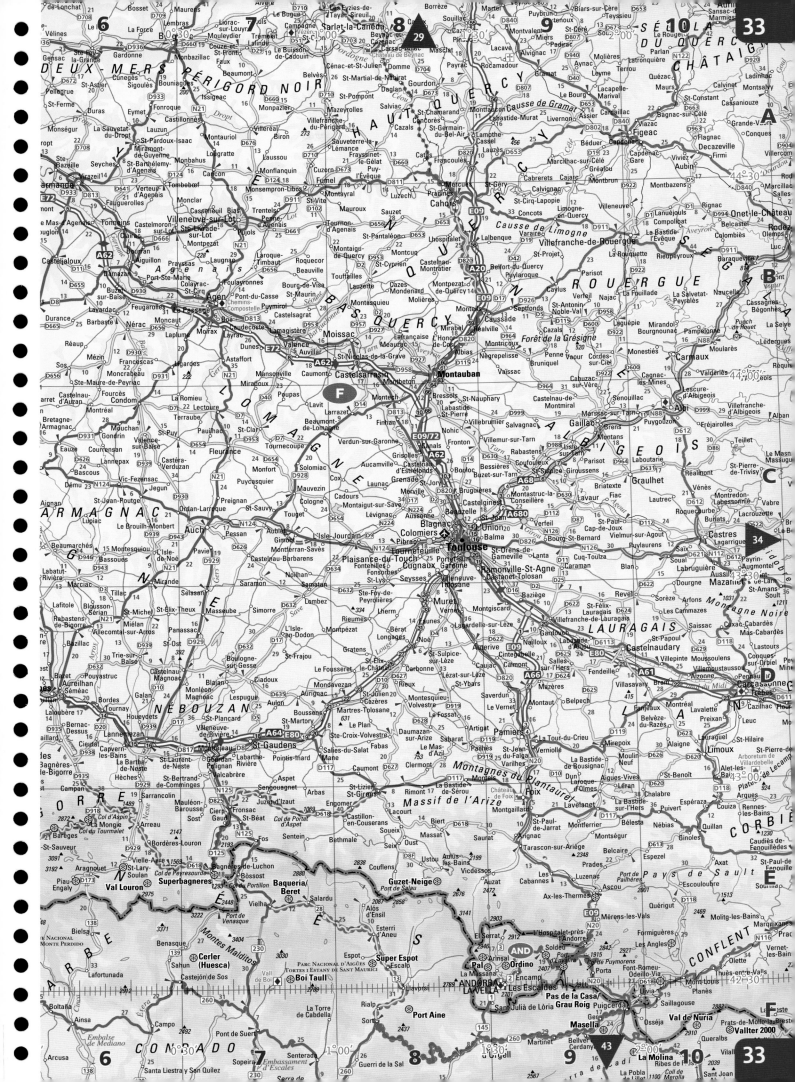

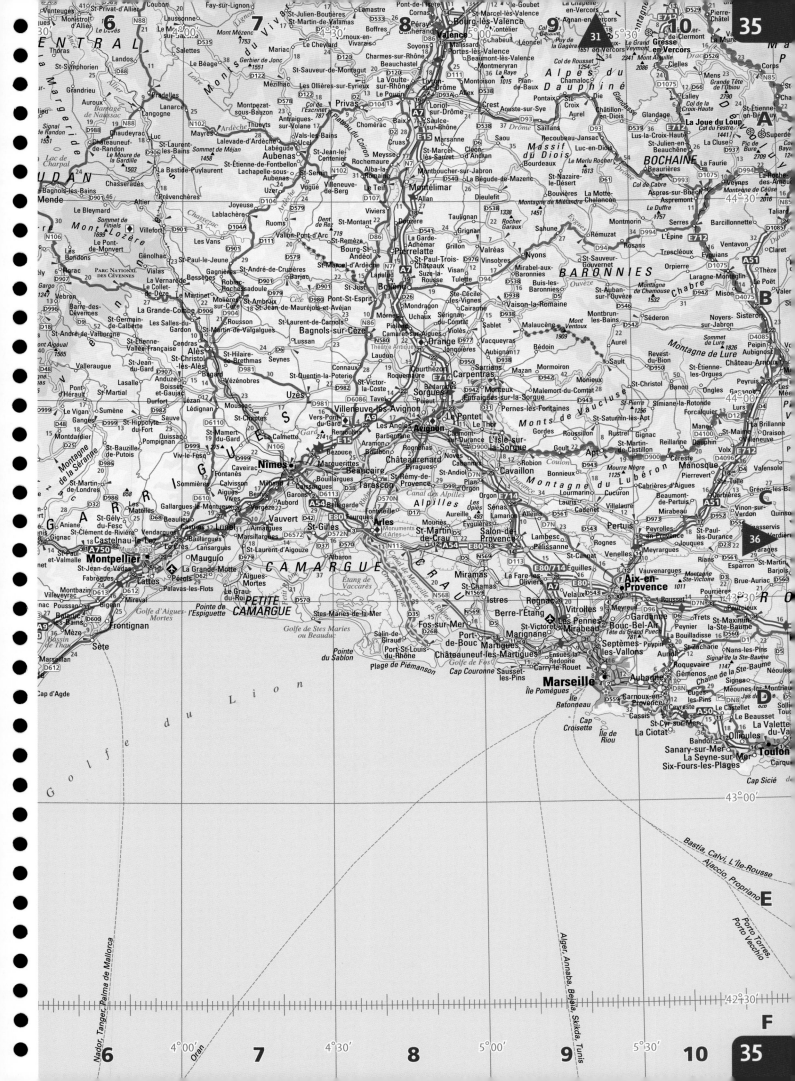

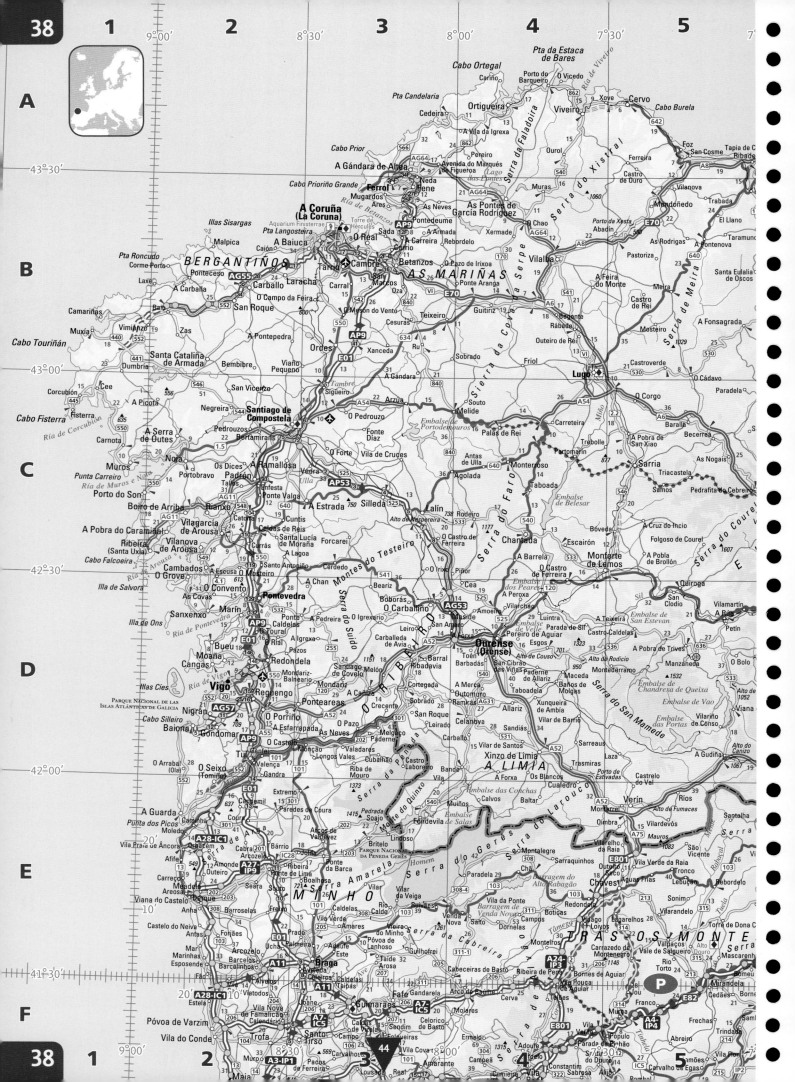

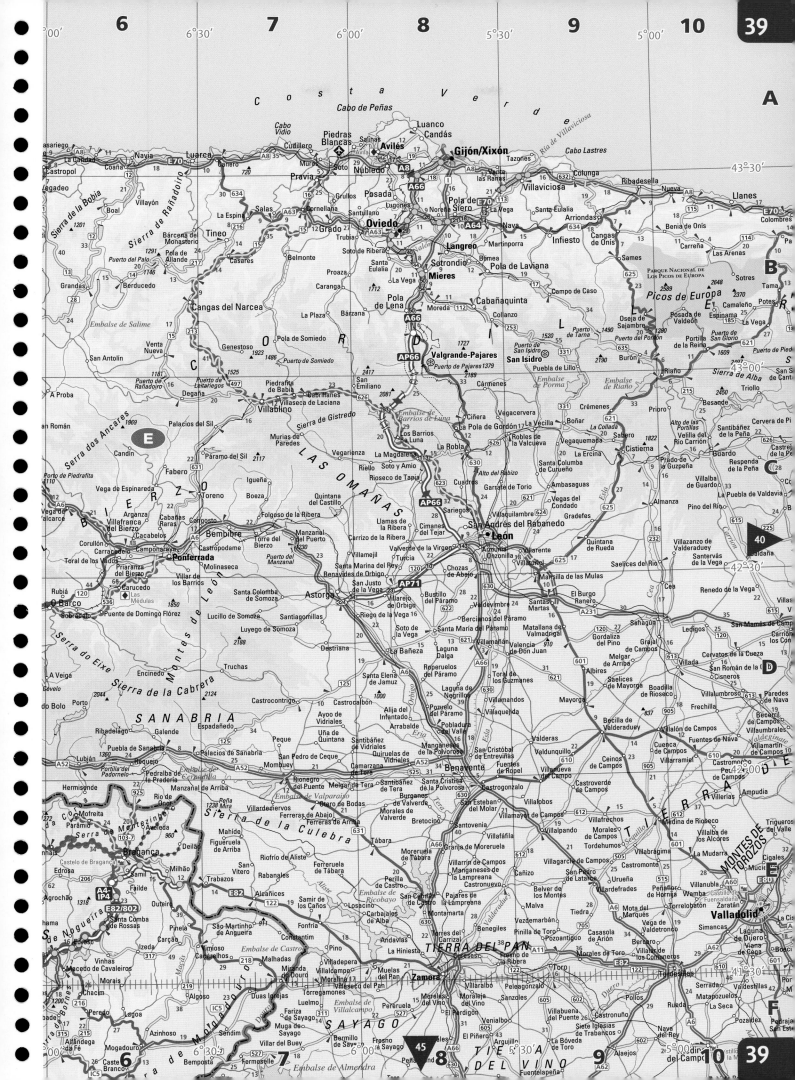

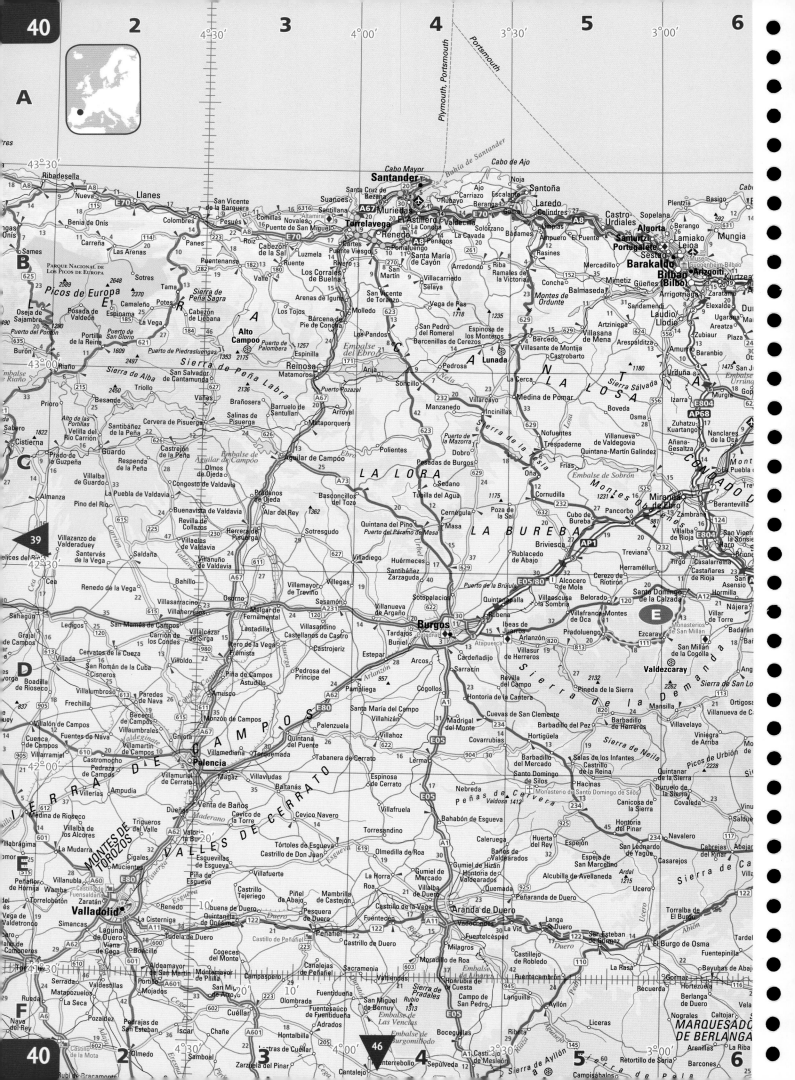

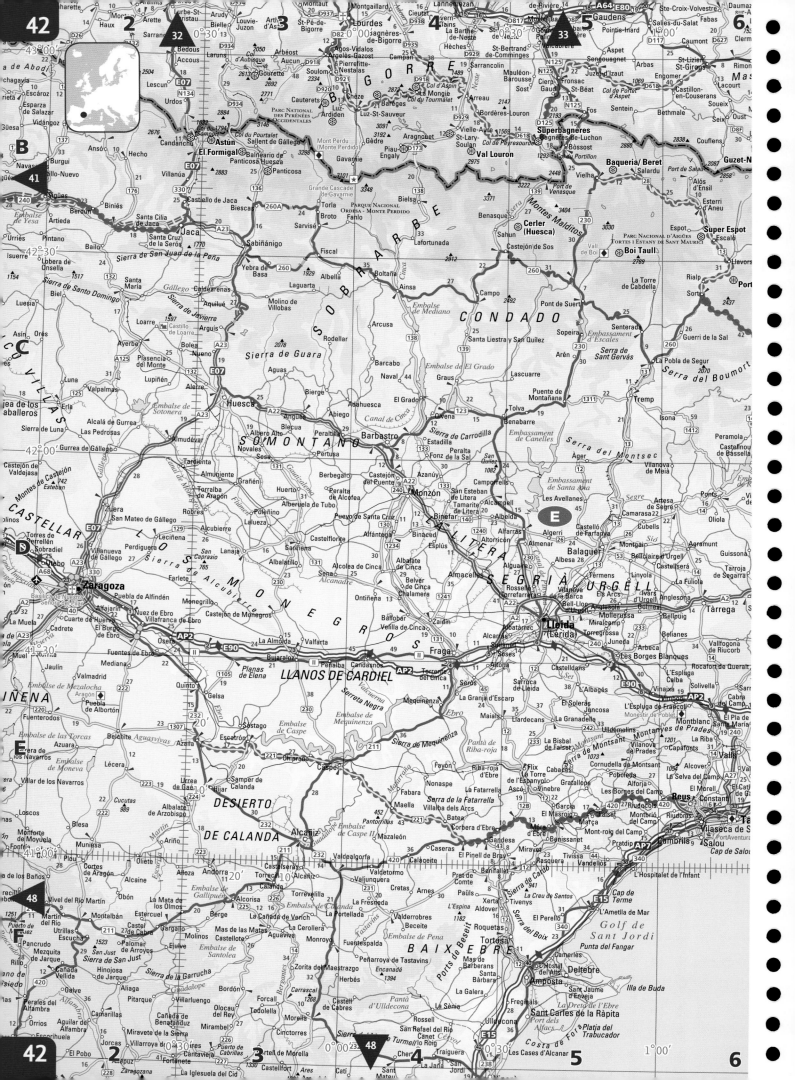

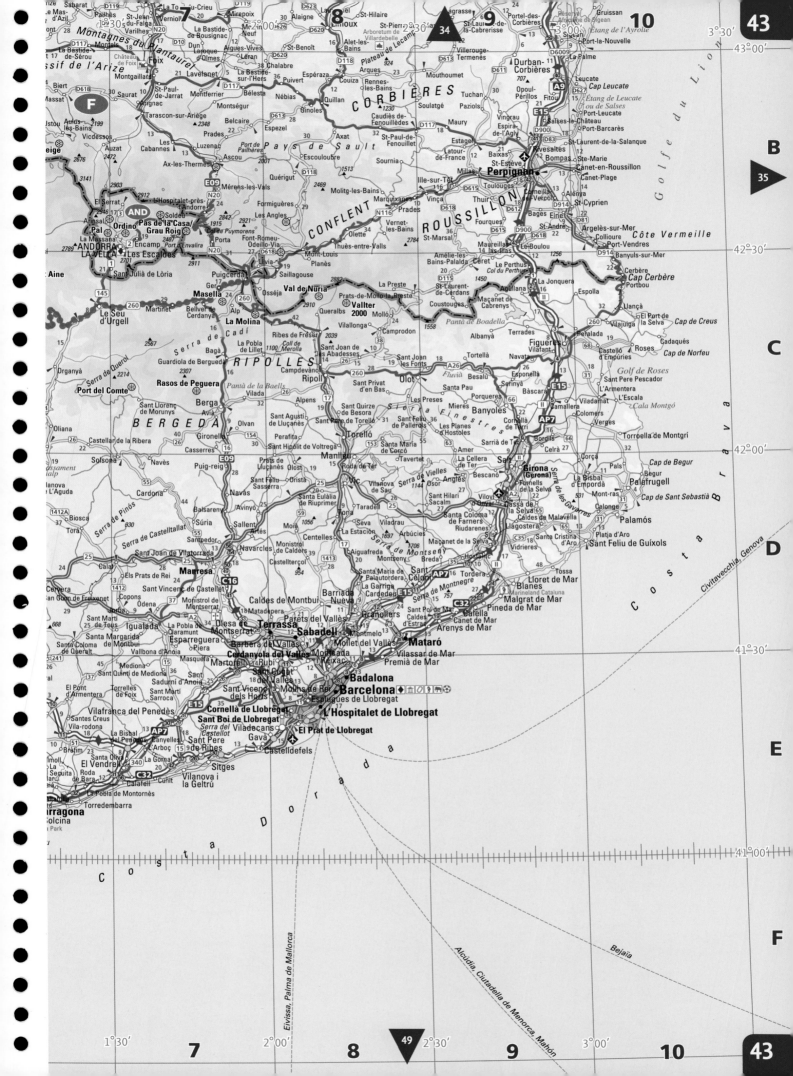

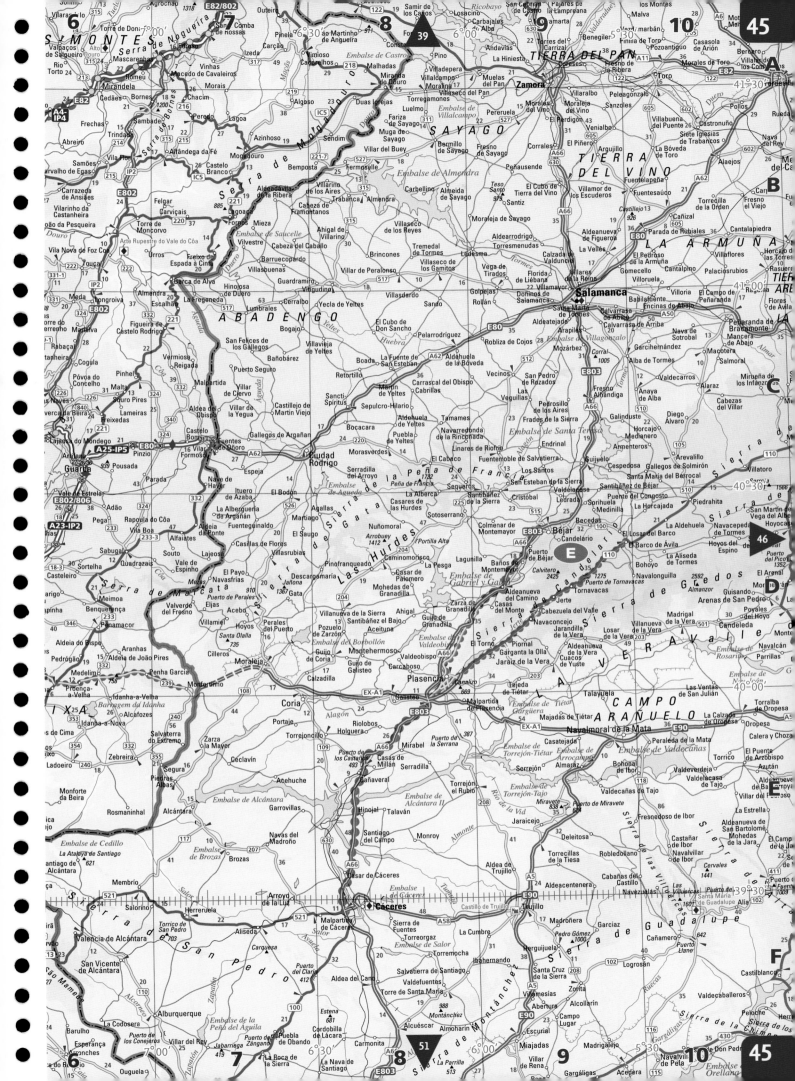

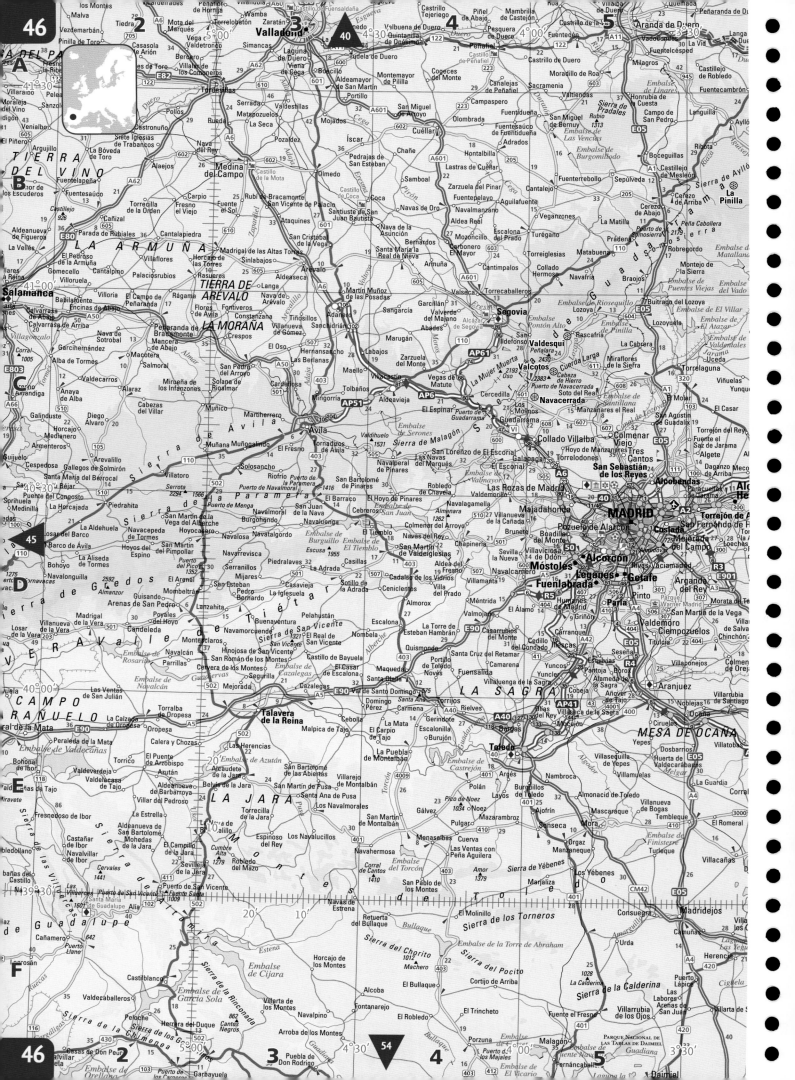

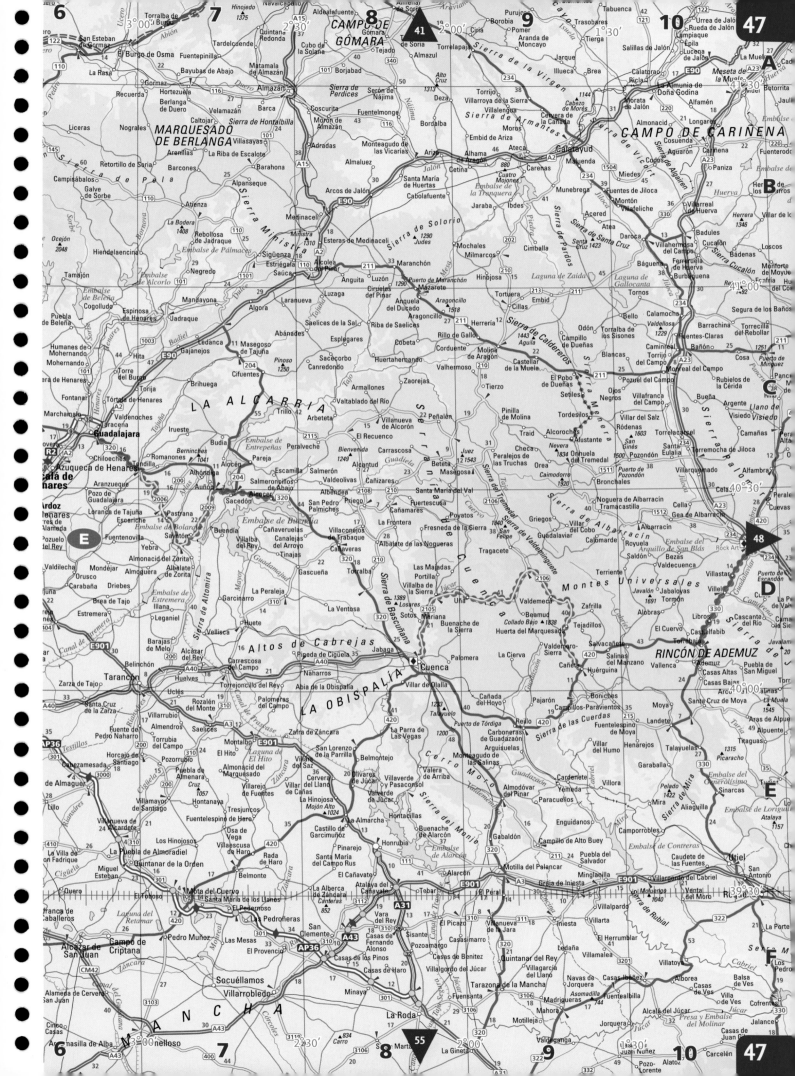

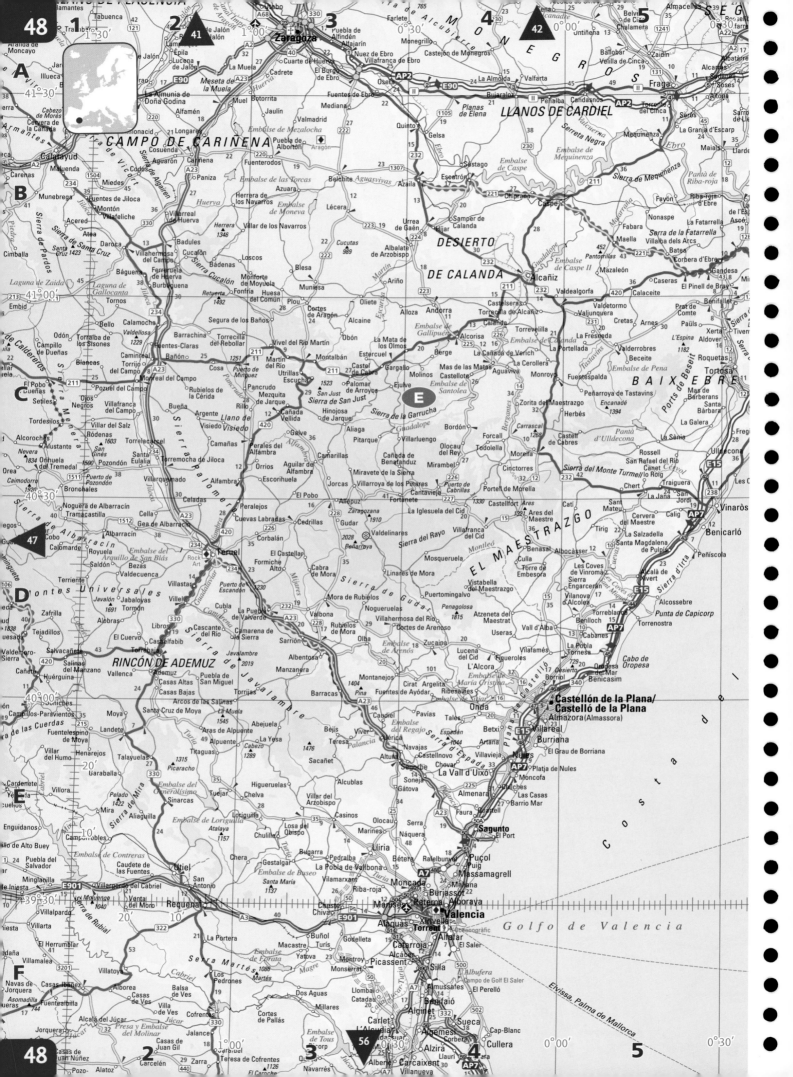

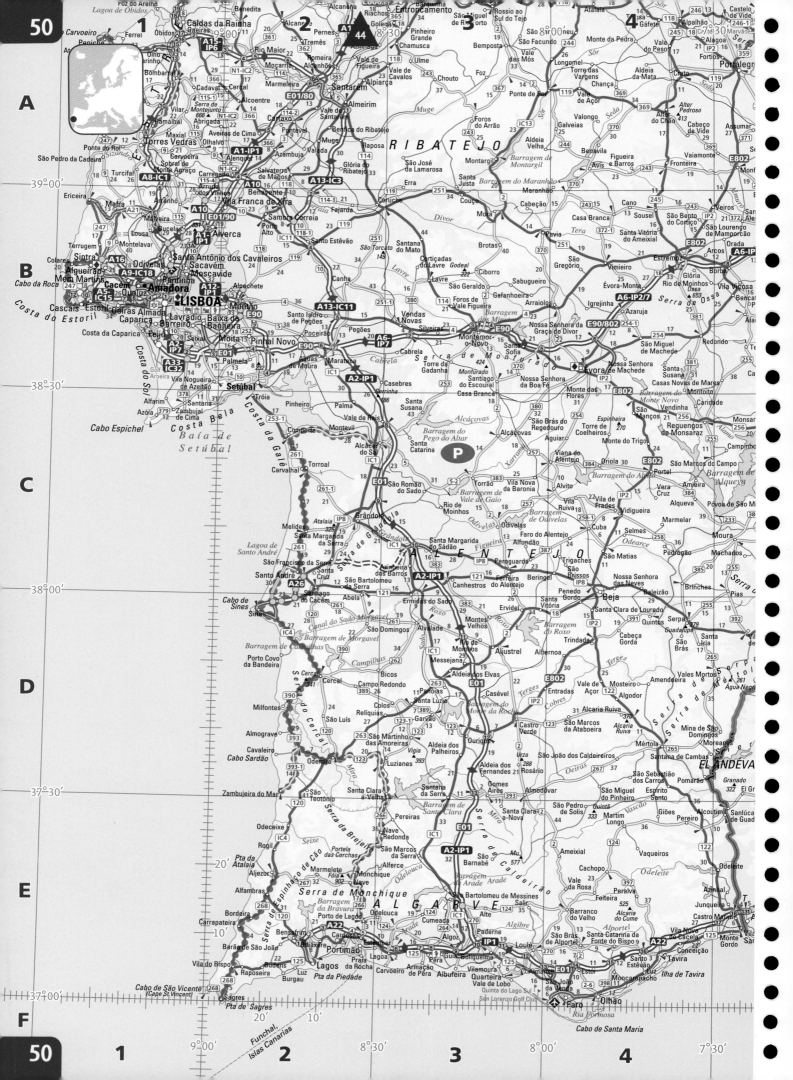

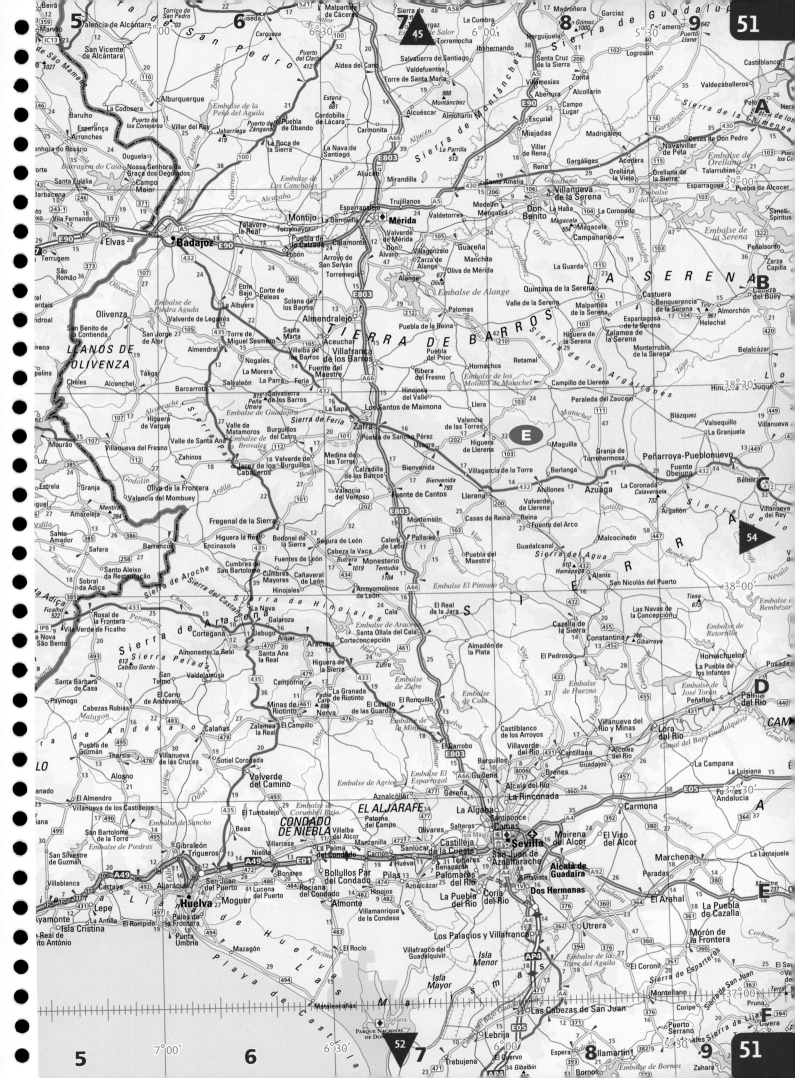

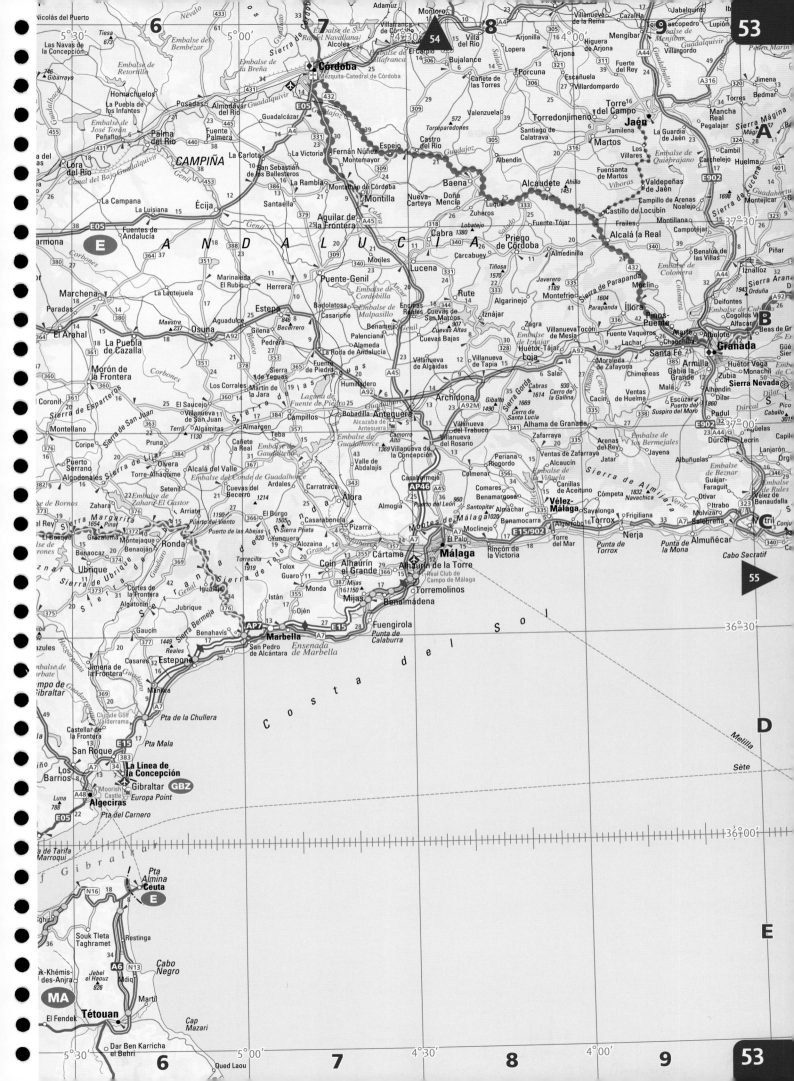

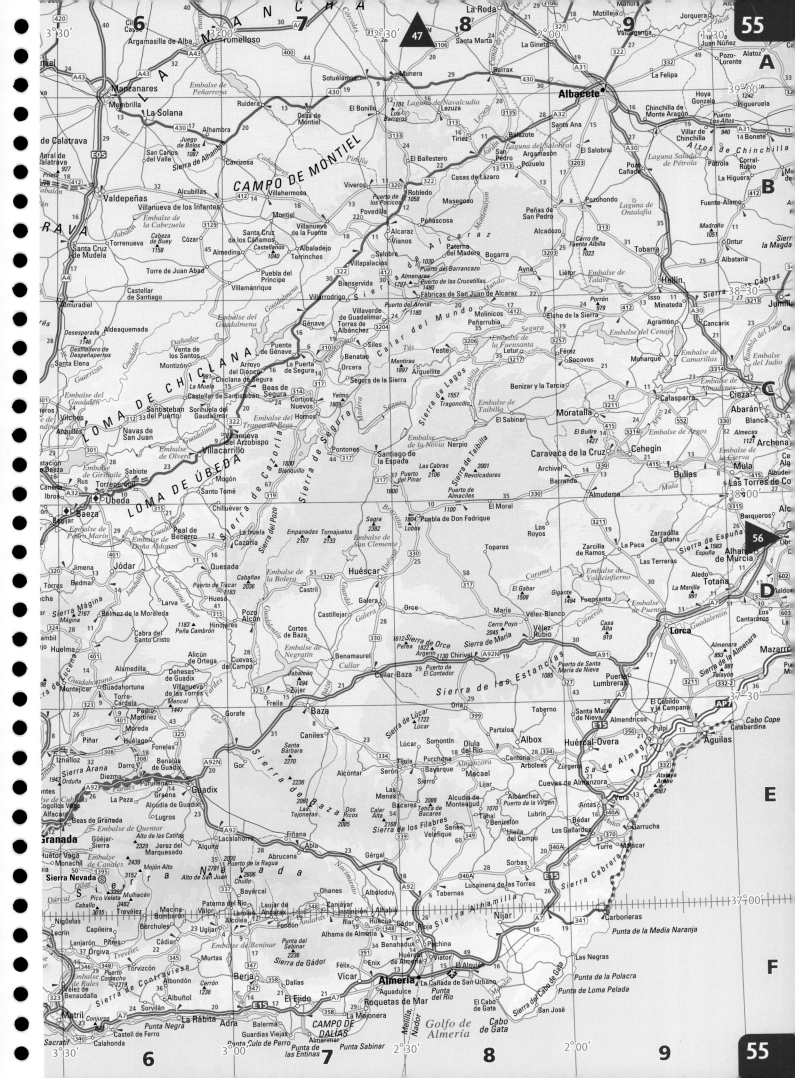

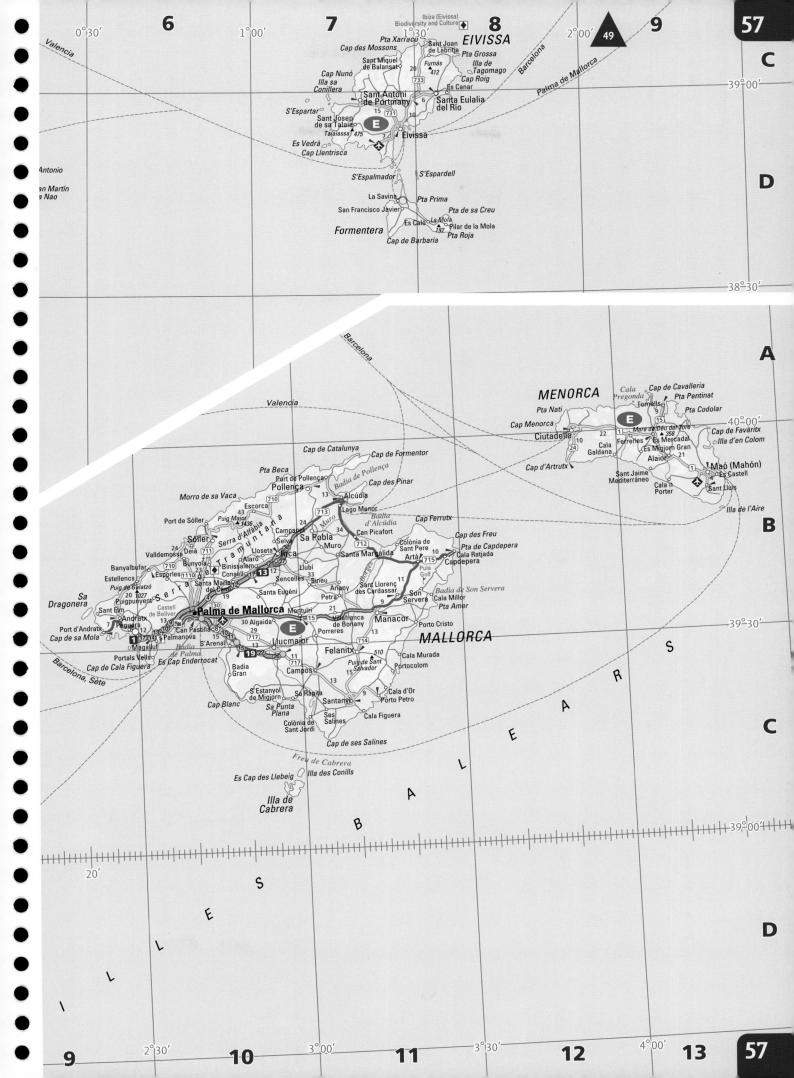

0°30'   1°00'   1°30'   2°00'   49

Valencia

Ibiza (Eivissa)
Biodiversity and Culture

EIVISSA

Pta Xarraco
Cap des Mossons
Sant Joan de Labritja
Pta Grossa
Illa de Tagomago

Sant Miquel de Balansat
Furnás 412
Cap Roig

Barcelona
Palma de Mallorca

39°00'

Cap Nunó
Illa sa Conillera
20
733
Es Canar

Sant Antoni de Portmany
6
Santa Eulalia del Río

S'Espartar
15 731
Sant Josep de sa Talaia
10

S'Espalmador
S'Espardell

Es Vedrà
Talaiassa 475
E
Cap Llentrisca
EIVISSA

San Antonio
en Martín e Nao

La Savina
Pta Prima

San Francisco Javier
Pta de sa Creu

Es Caló
La Mola 192
Pilar de la Mola
Pta Roja

Formentera
Cap de Barbaria

38°30'

Barcelona

A

Valencia
40°00'

MENORCA
Cala Pregonda
Cap de Cavalleria
Pta Pentinat

Pta Nati
Fornells
Pta Codolar

Cap de Catalunya
Pta Beca
Cap de Formentor

Cap Menorca
Mare de Déu del Toro
Cap de Favàritx

Morro de sa Vaca
Port de Pollença
Cap des Pinar
Ciutadella
10
22
1
358
Illa d'en Colom

Pollença
Badia de Pollença
24
Cala Galdana
Es Mercadal
Ferreries
Es Migjorn Gran
Alaior
21

Escorca
710
13
Alcúdia
Cap d'Artrutx
1
Maó (Mahón)

Port de Sóller
Puig Major 1436
713
Lago Menor
Sant Jaime Mediterráneo
Cala n Porter
Es Castell
Sant Lluís

Sóller
Serra d'Alfàbia
24
Muro
34
Badia d'Alcúdia
Cap Ferrutx
Illa de l'Aire

Deià
711
Campanet
712
Can Picafort

Valldemossa
Selva
Sa Pobla
Muro
Colònia de Sant Pere
Cap des Freu
B

Banyalbufar
Lloseta
30
Santa Margalida
Artà
Pta de Capdepera
Cala Ratjada

Estellencs
710
Alaró
Inca
715
10
Capdepera

Esporles
1110
Binissalem
13
12
Llubí
33
Pula Golf

Puig de Galatzó
23
Consell
Llombards
Son Llorenç des Cardassar
Son Servera
Badia de Son Servera

Sa Dragonera
1027
Santa Maria del Camí
Sencelles
Sineu
11
9
Cala Millor

Puigpunyent
19
Santa Eugènia
Petra
Anyany
Pta Amer

Sant Elm
Castell de Bellver
Montuïri
21
Villafranca de Bonany
Manacor
Porto Cristo

Andratx
Peguera
13
9
30 Algaida
29
15
Badia de Son Servera

Port d'Andratx
7
12
717
Porreres
13

Cap de sa Mola
1
17 14
Can Pastilla
8
Llucmajor
714
510
Cala Murada

Magaluf
Palmanova
10 11
S'Arenal
Felanitx
Puig de Sant Salvador
Portocolom

Palma de Mallorca
E

Portals Vells
15
19 22
717
11
Campos
15
Cala d'Or
Porto Petro

Barcelona, Sète
Cap de Cala Figuera
Badia de Palma
26
13
9

Es Cap Enderrocat
Badia Gran
Santanyí

S'Estanyol de Migjorn
Sa Ràpita
Santanyí
Ses Salines
Cala Figuera

Cap Blanc
Sa Punta Plana
Colònia de Sant Jordi

MALLORCA

Cap de ses Salines

39°30'

B A L E A R S

C

Freu de Cabrera
Es Cap des Llebeig
Illa des Conills

Illa de Cabrera
B

39°00'

20'

I L L E S

D

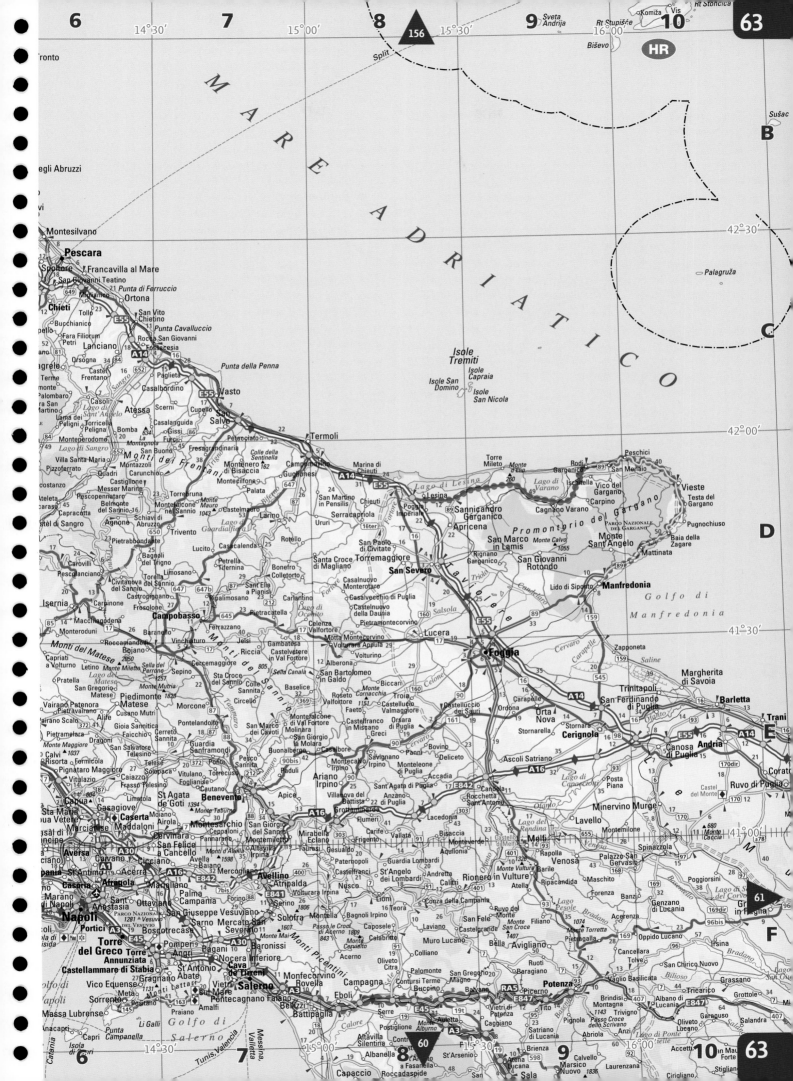

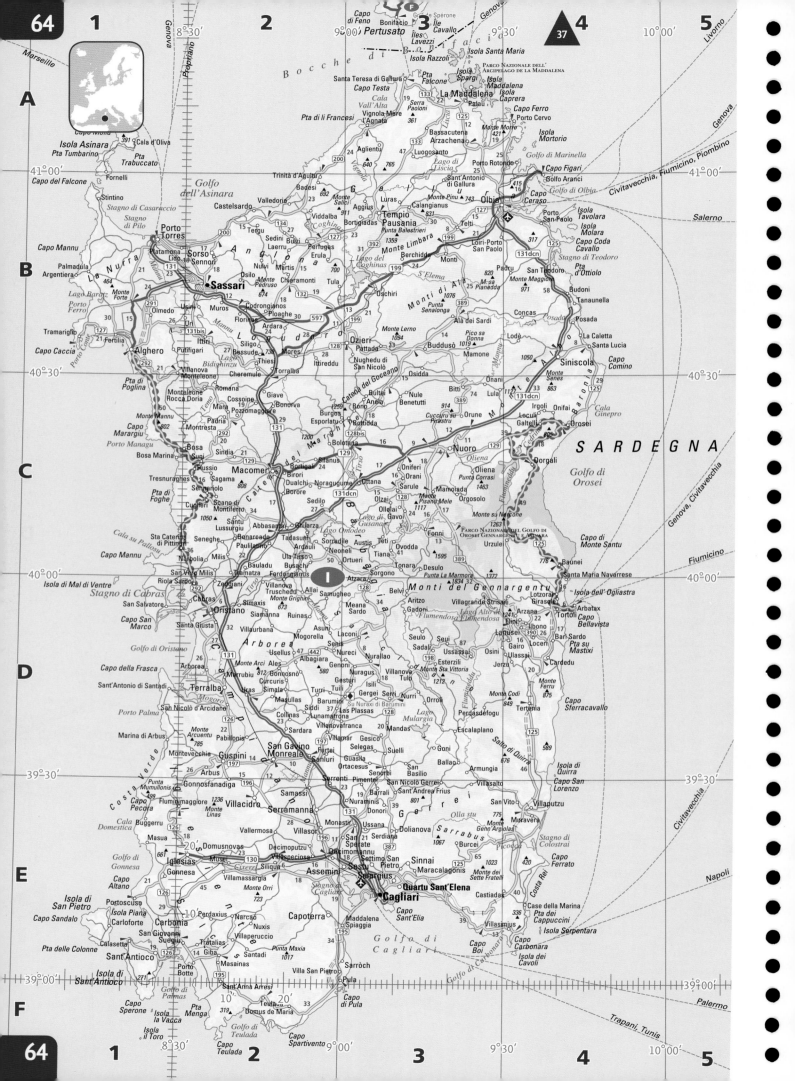

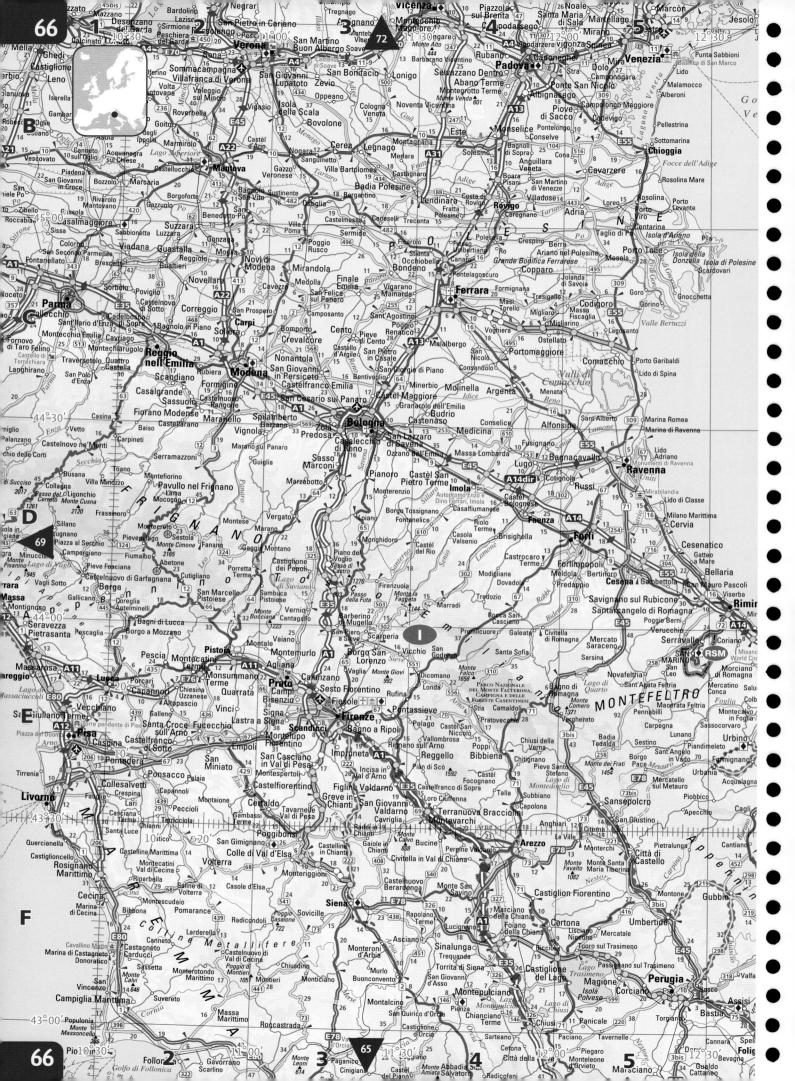

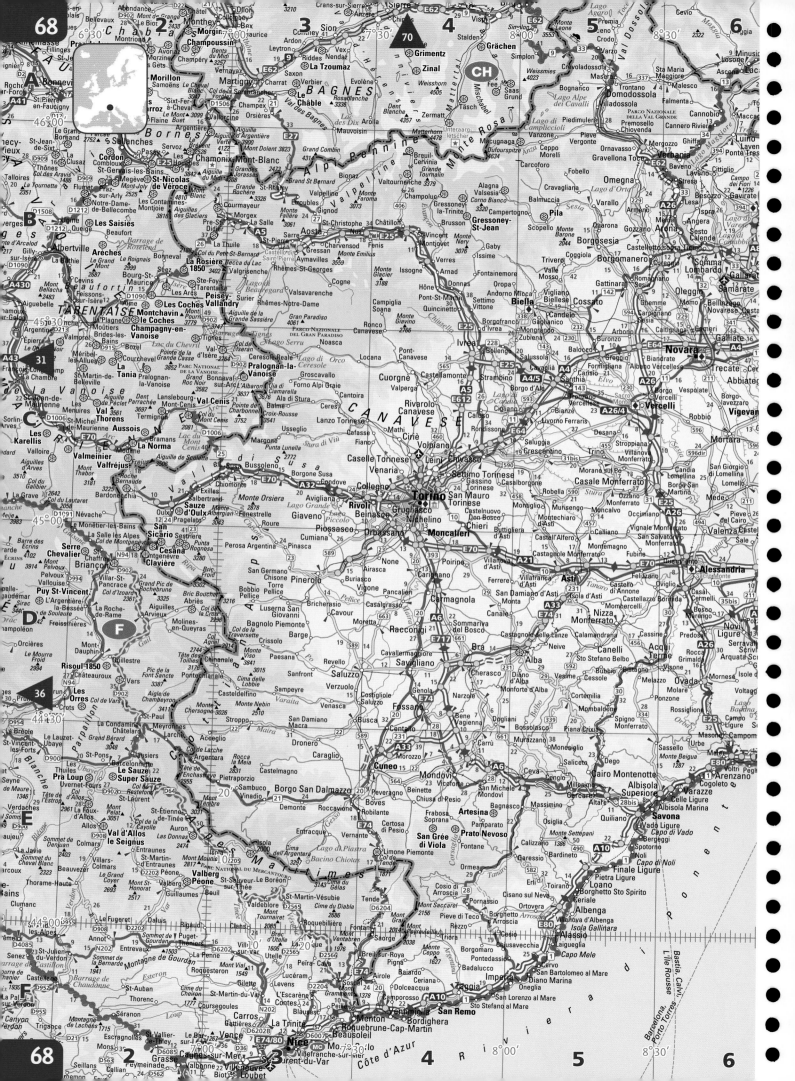

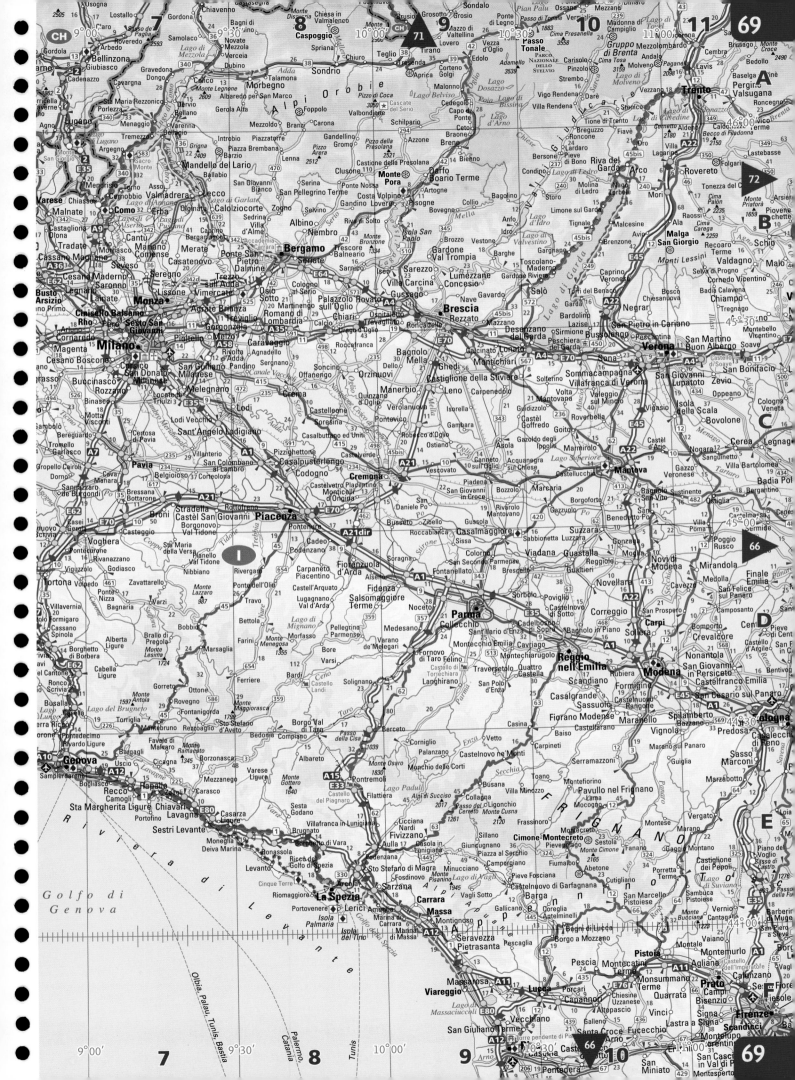

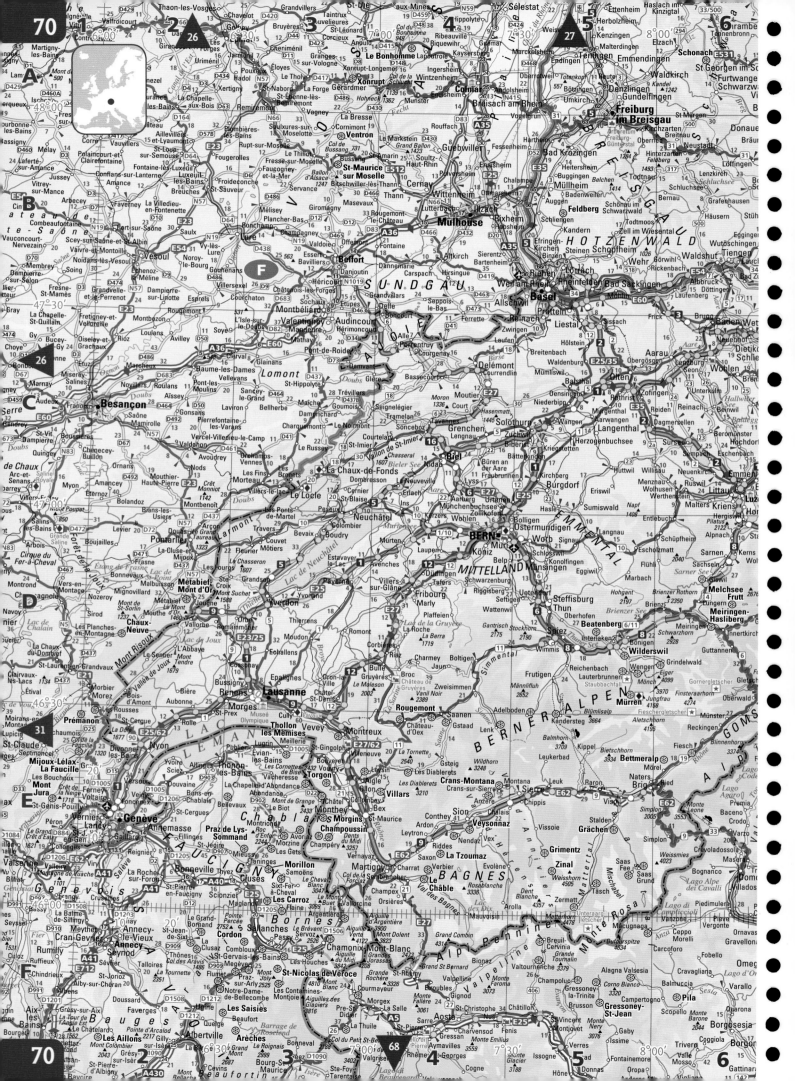

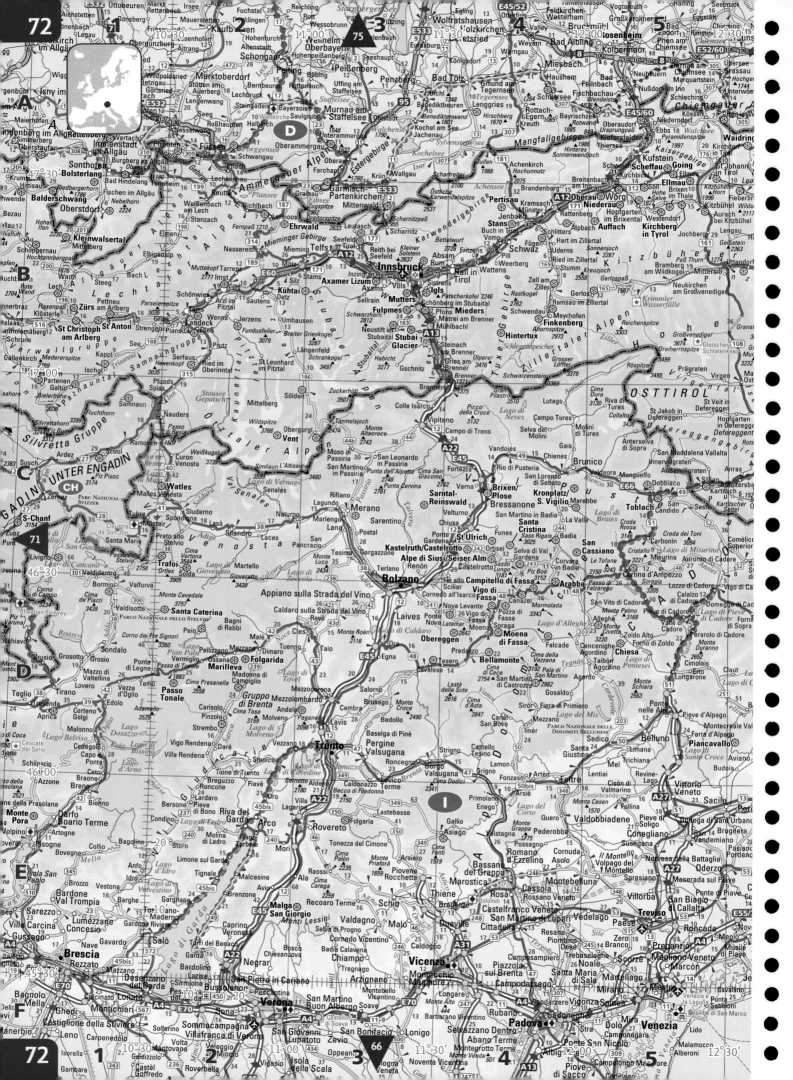

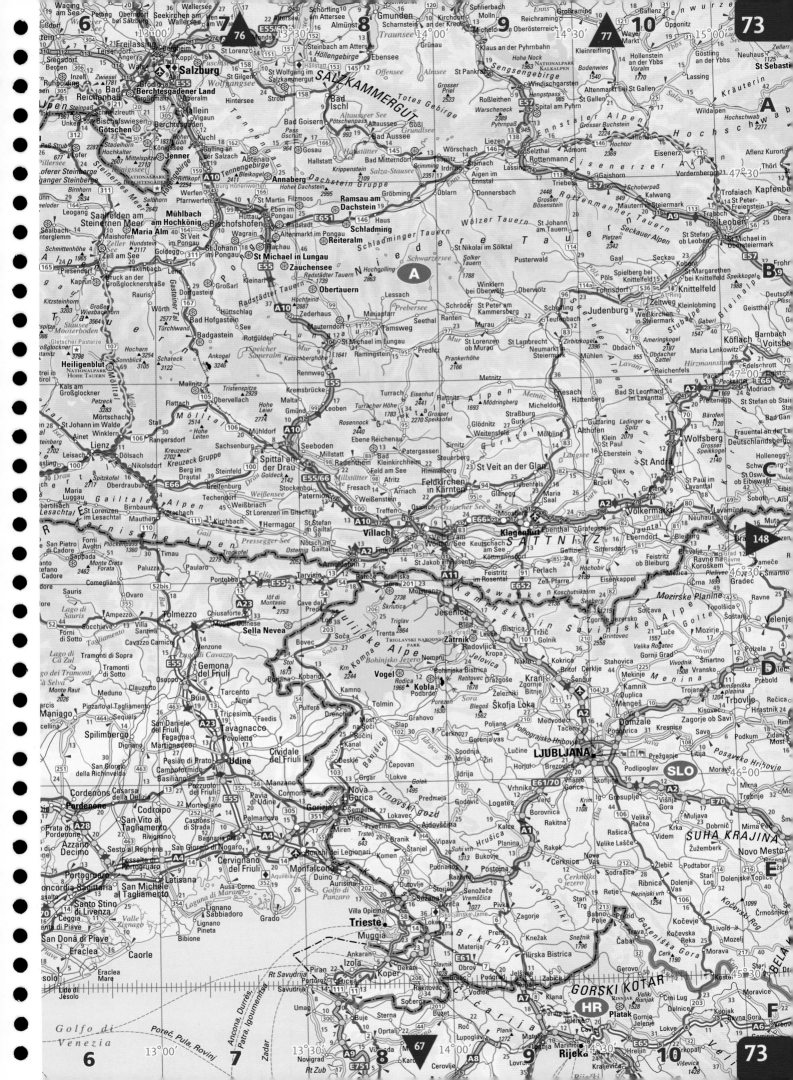

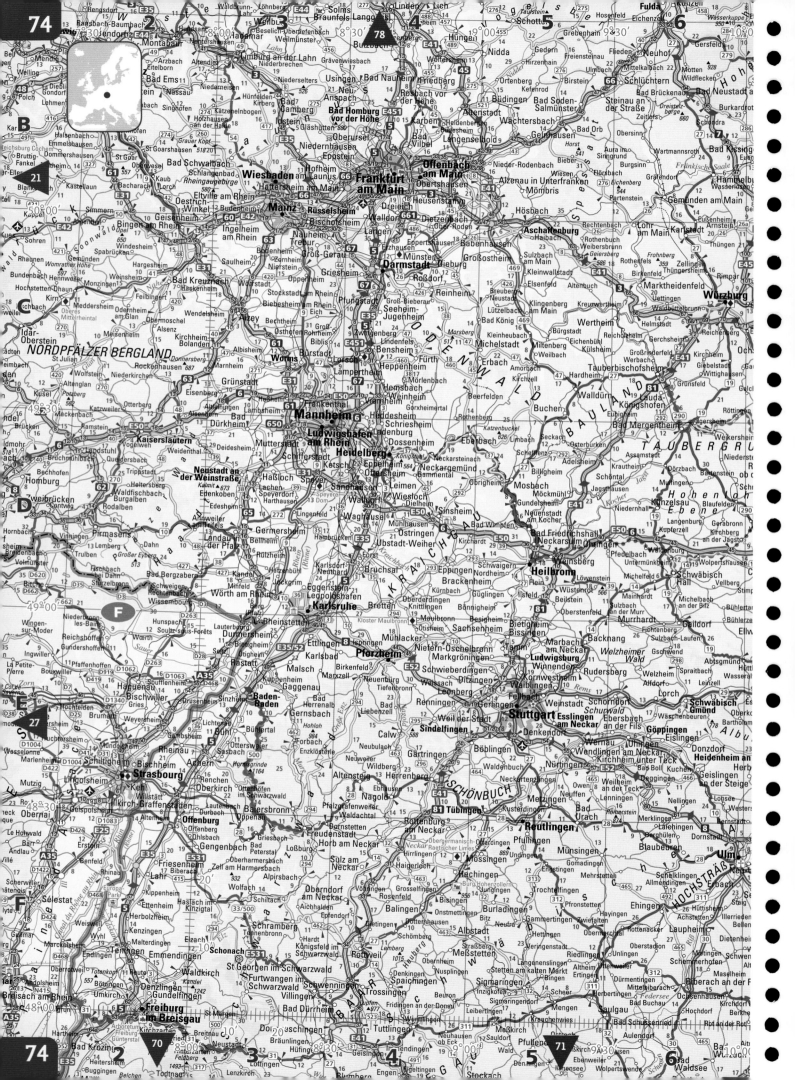

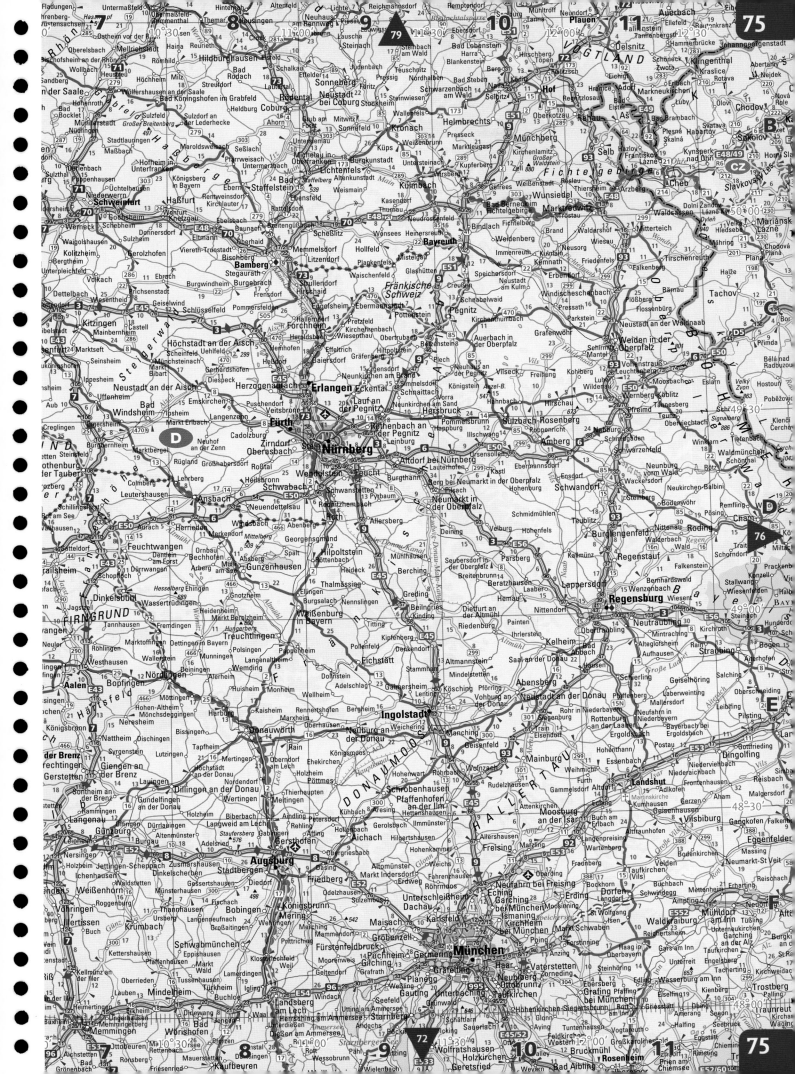

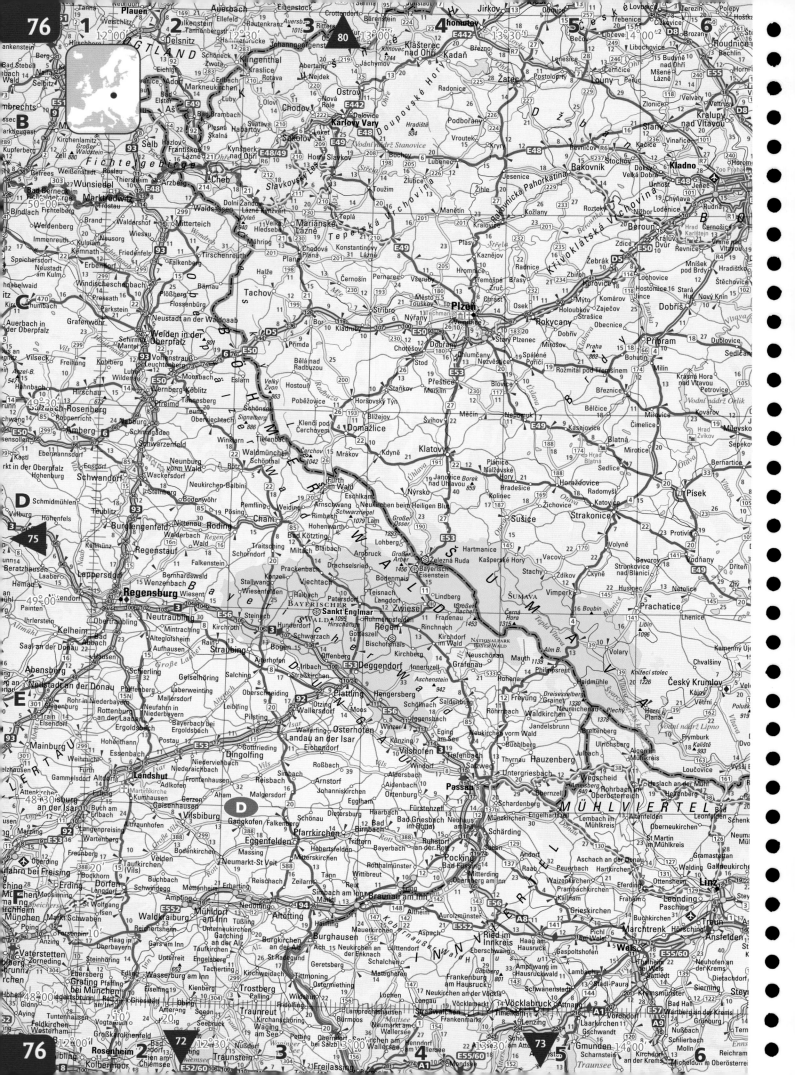

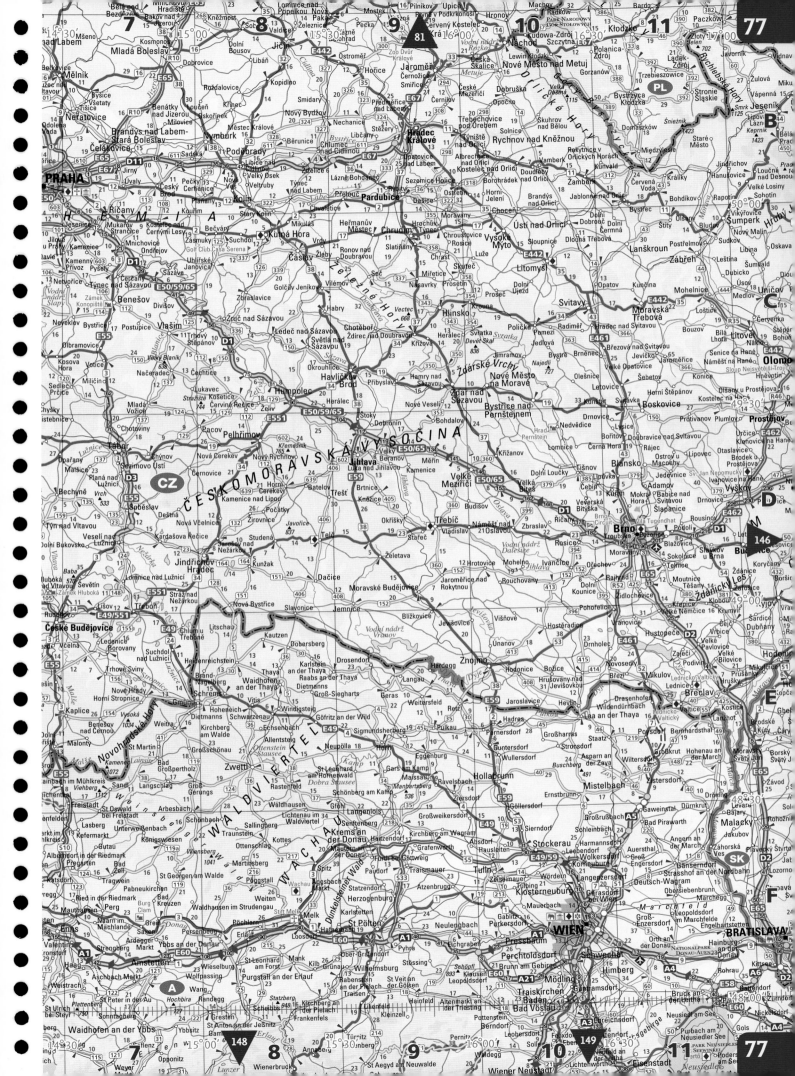

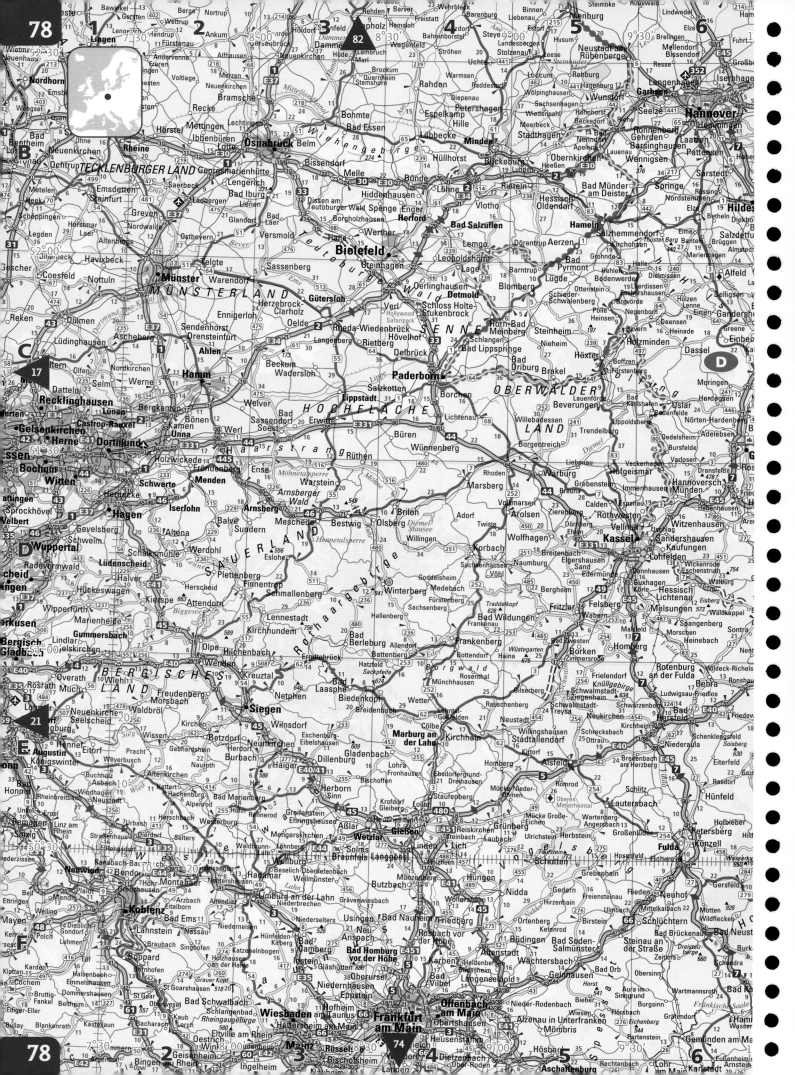

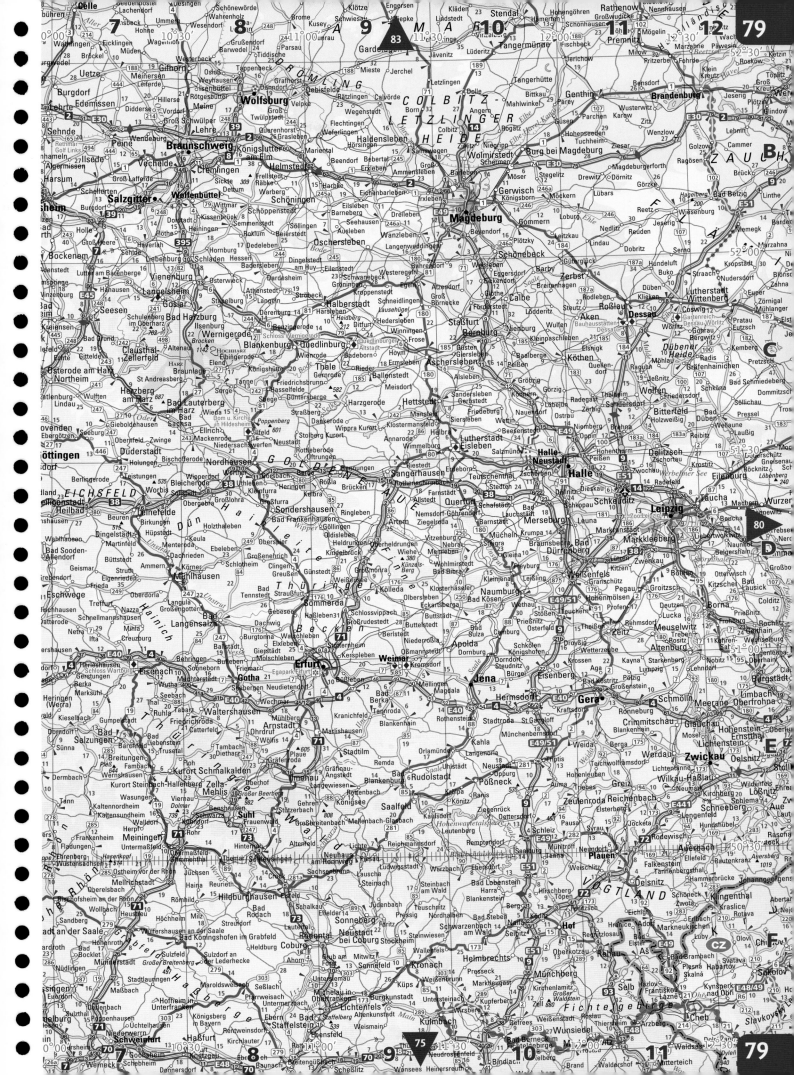

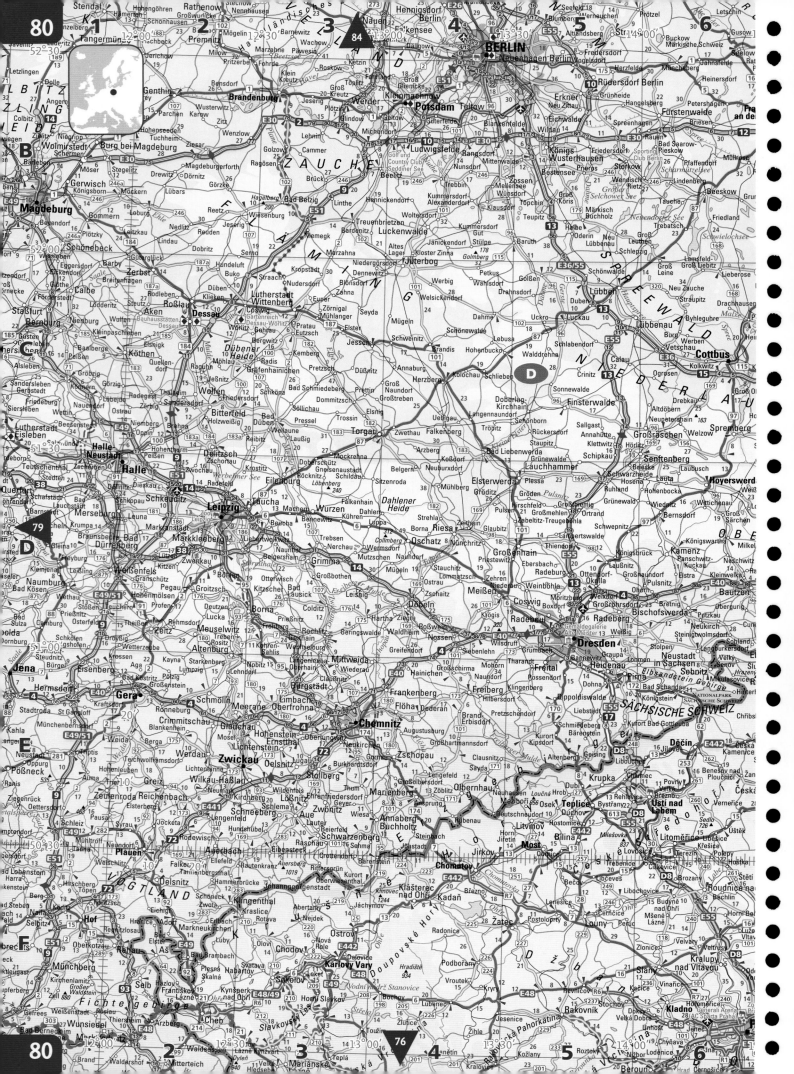

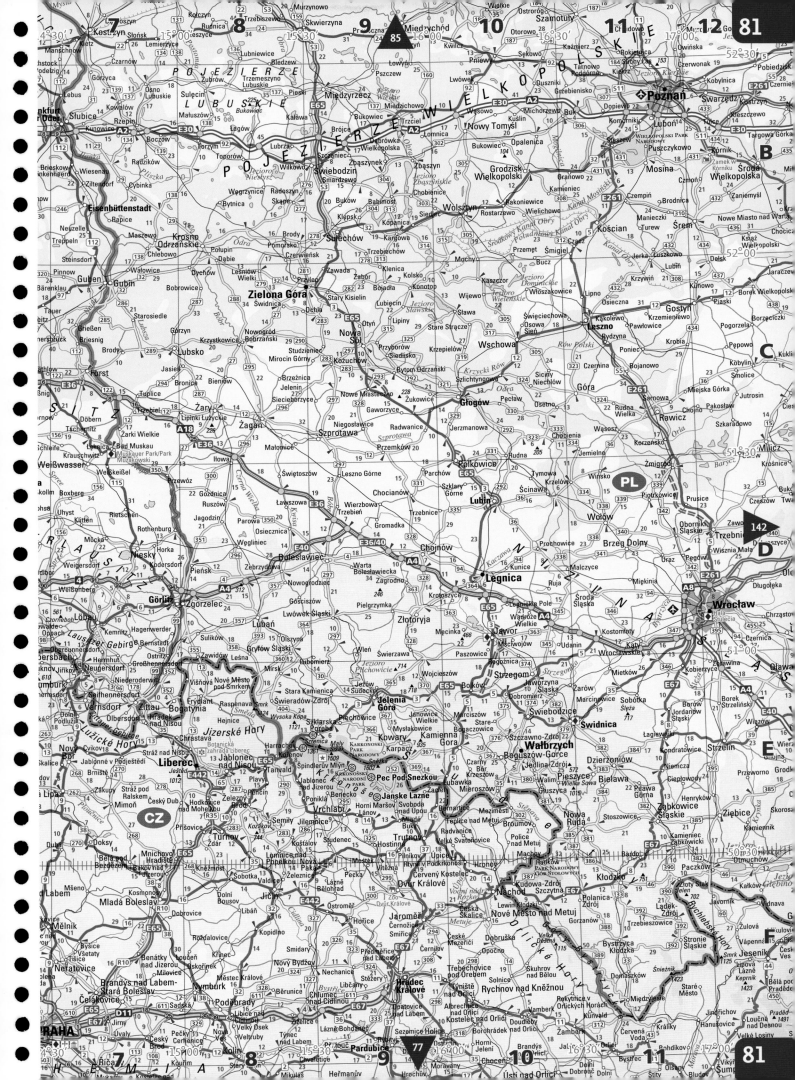

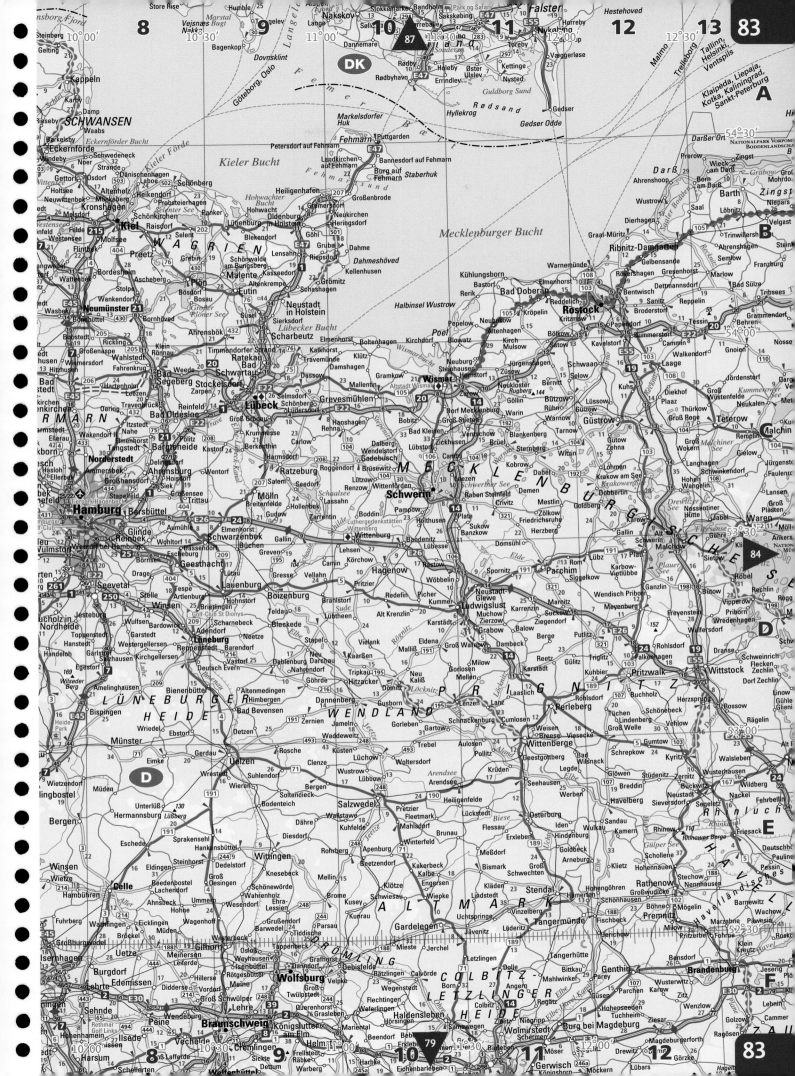

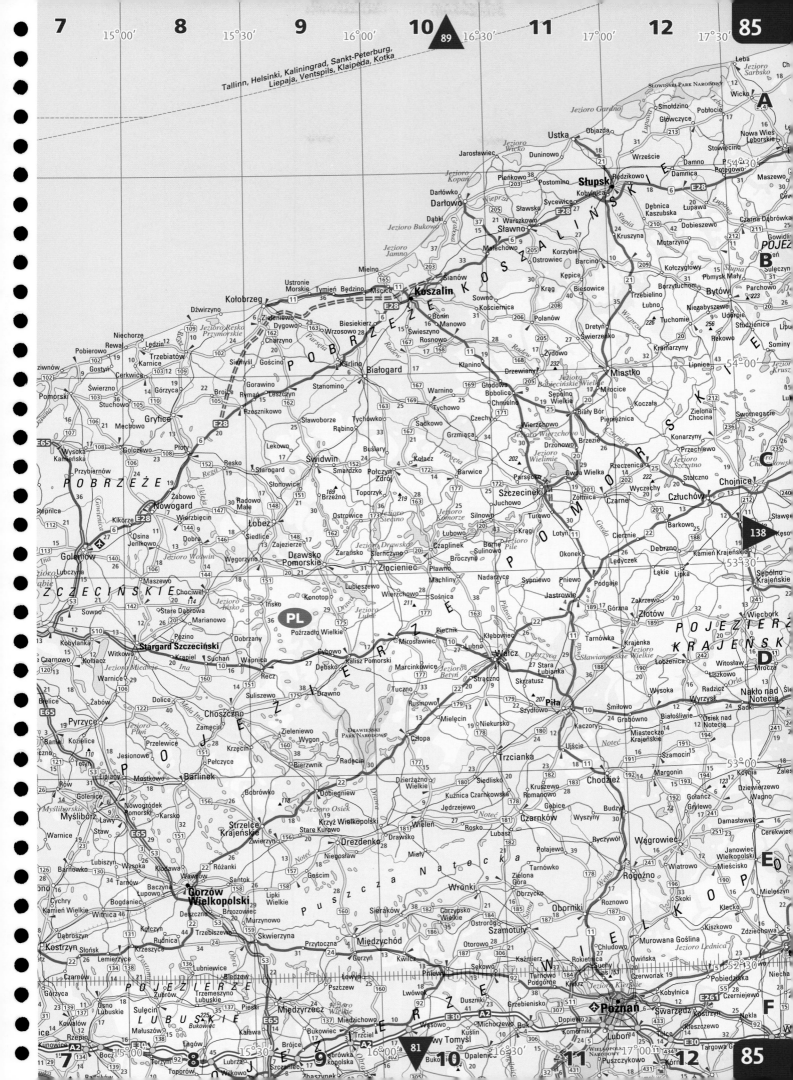

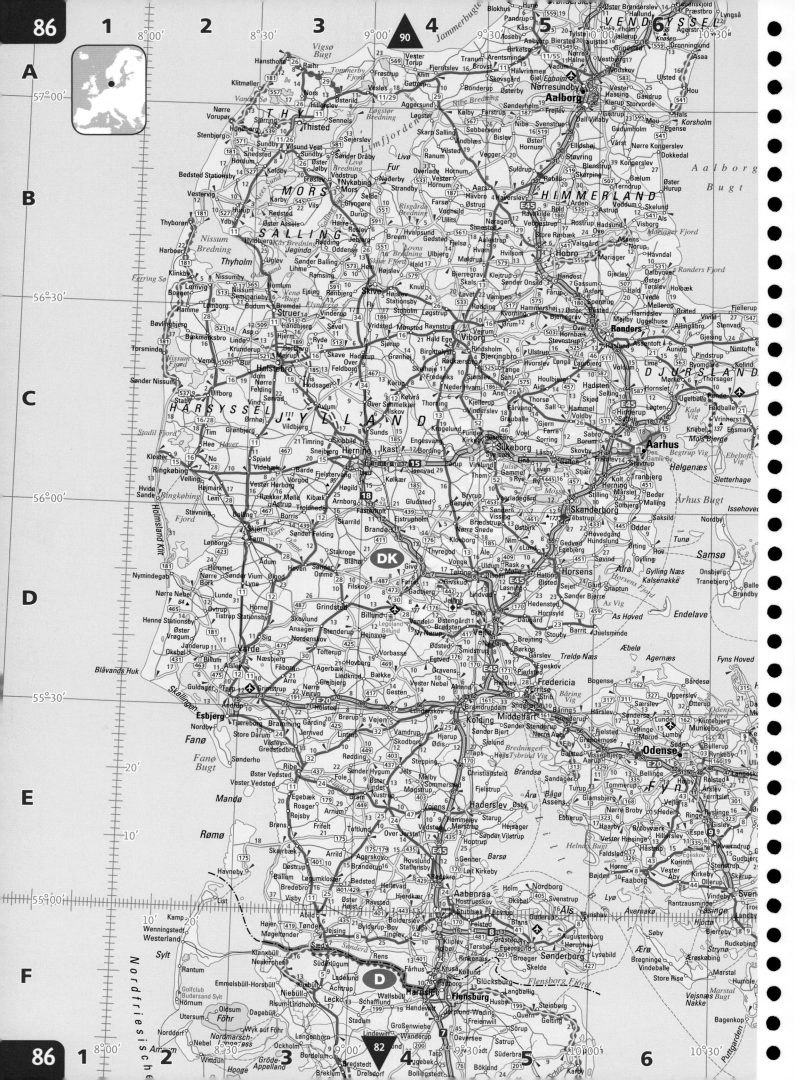

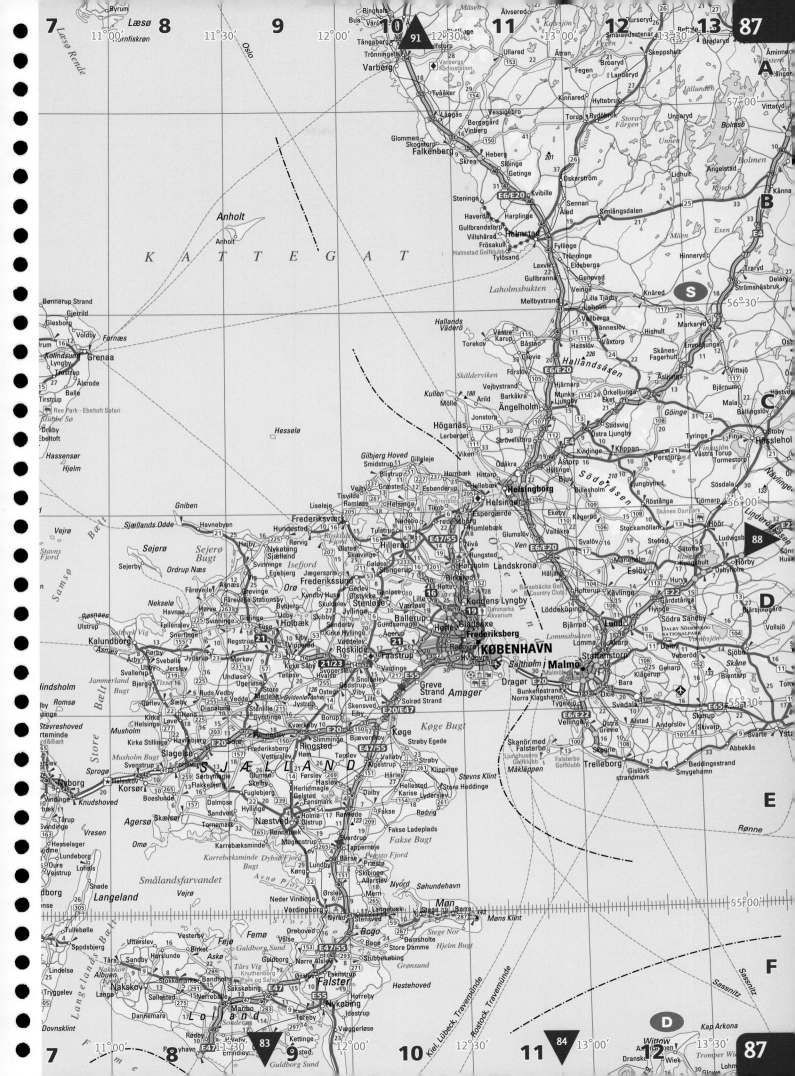

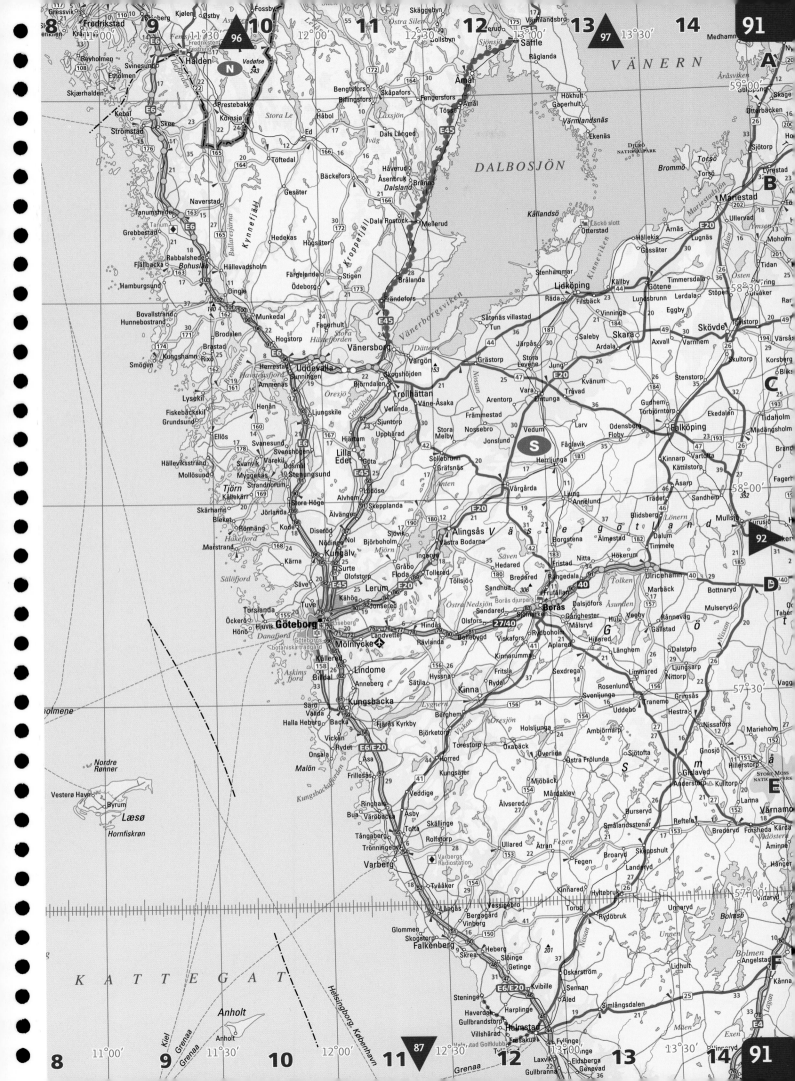

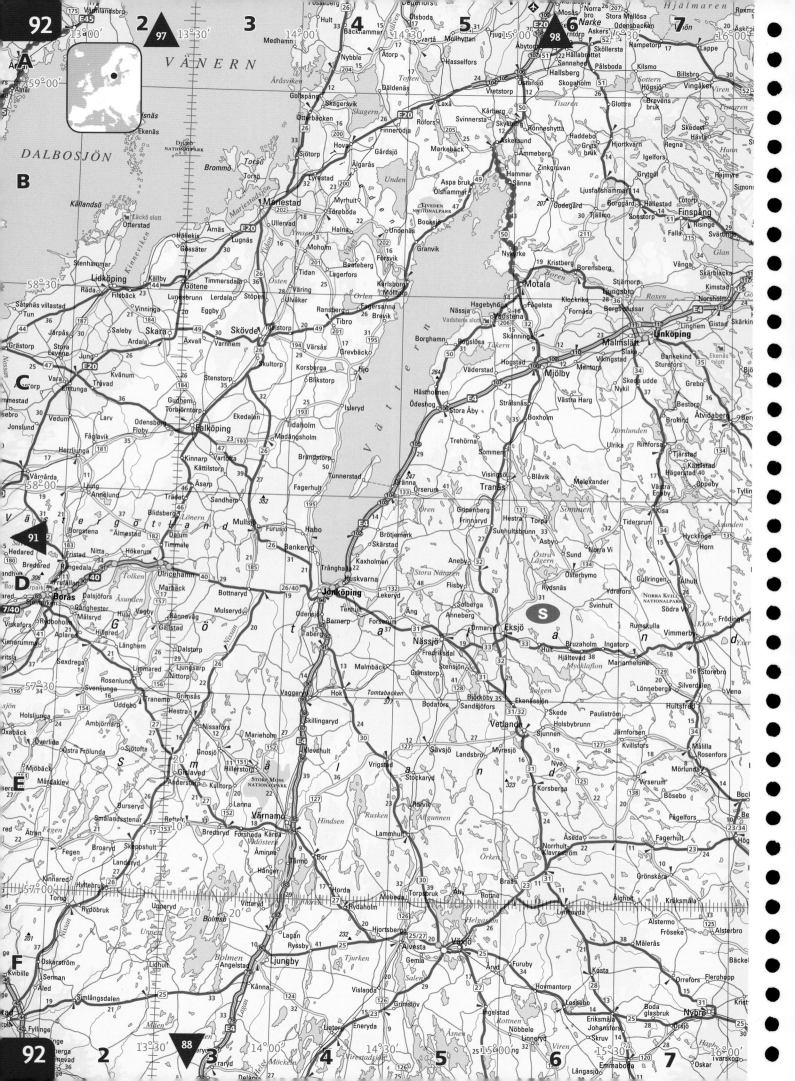

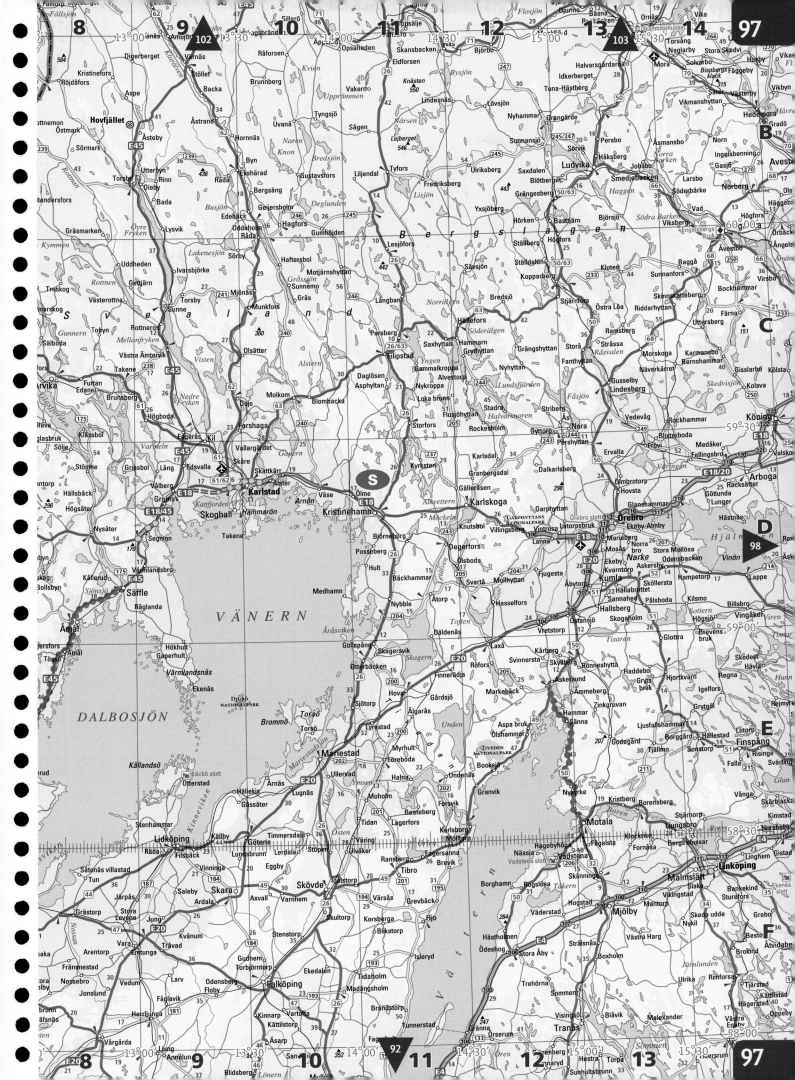

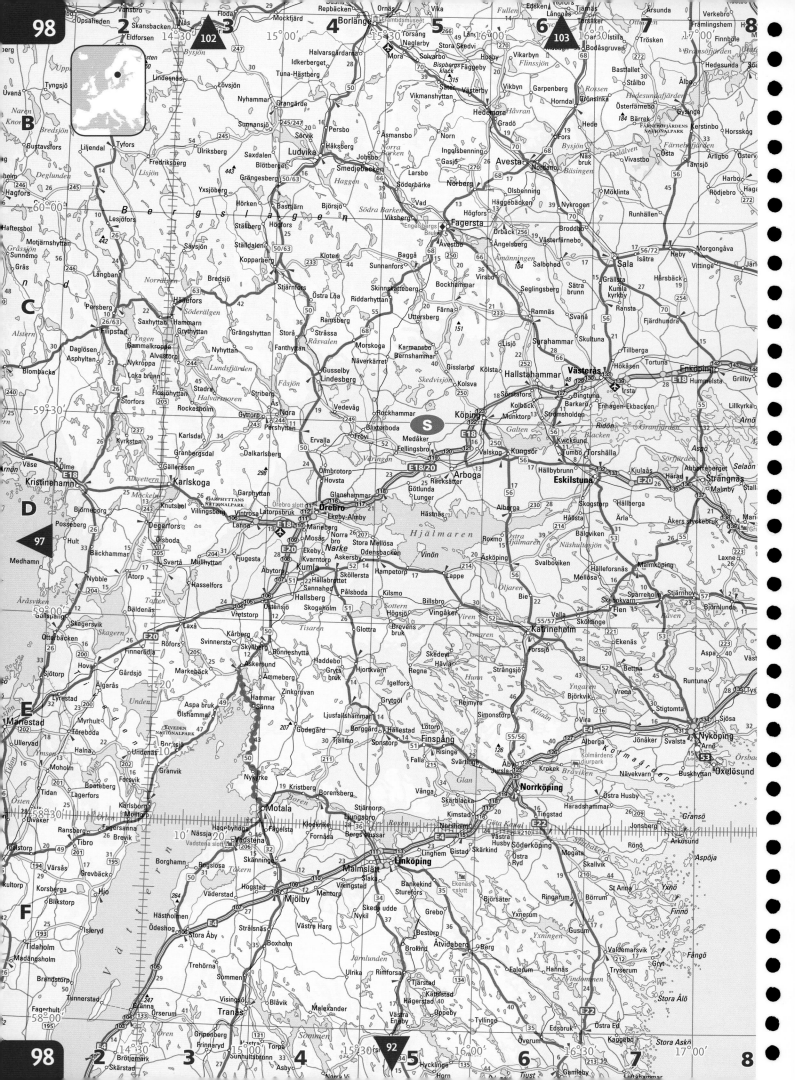

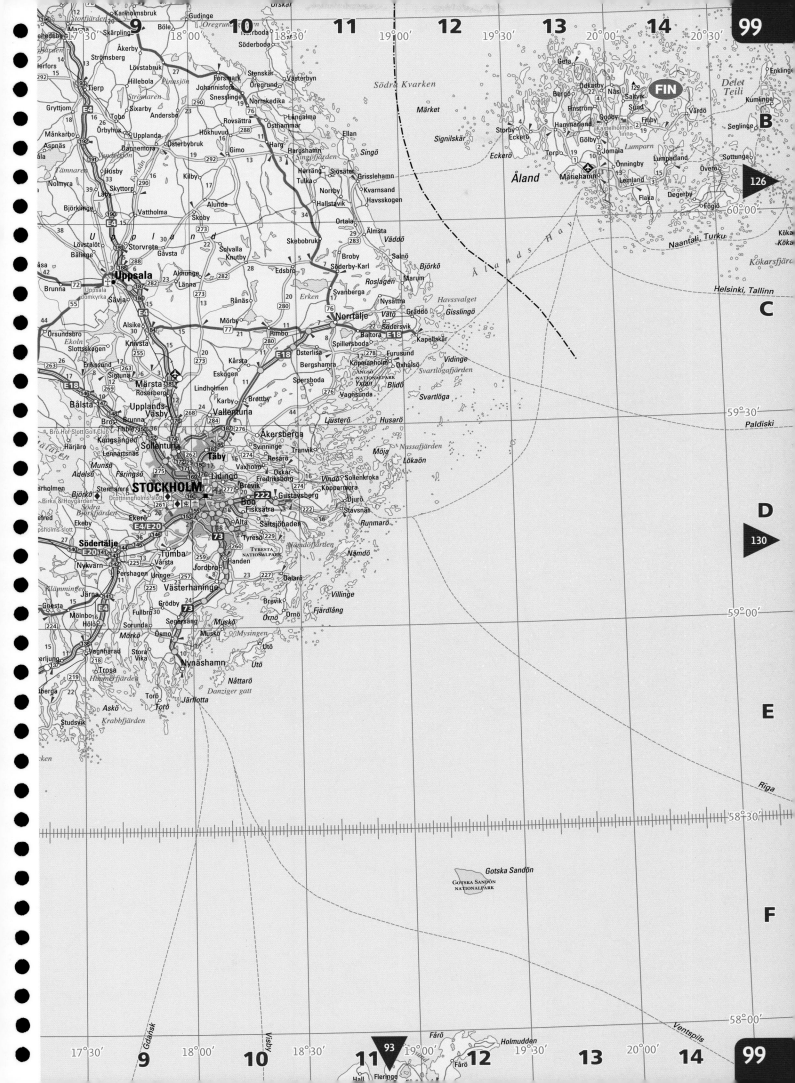

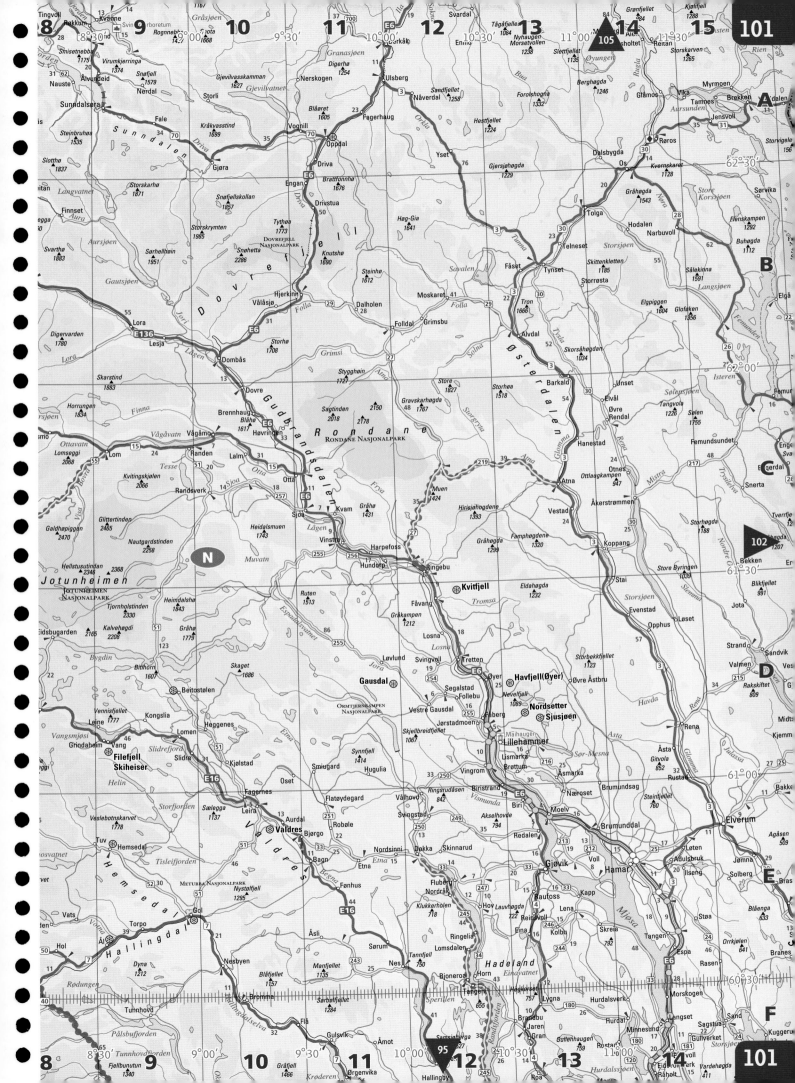

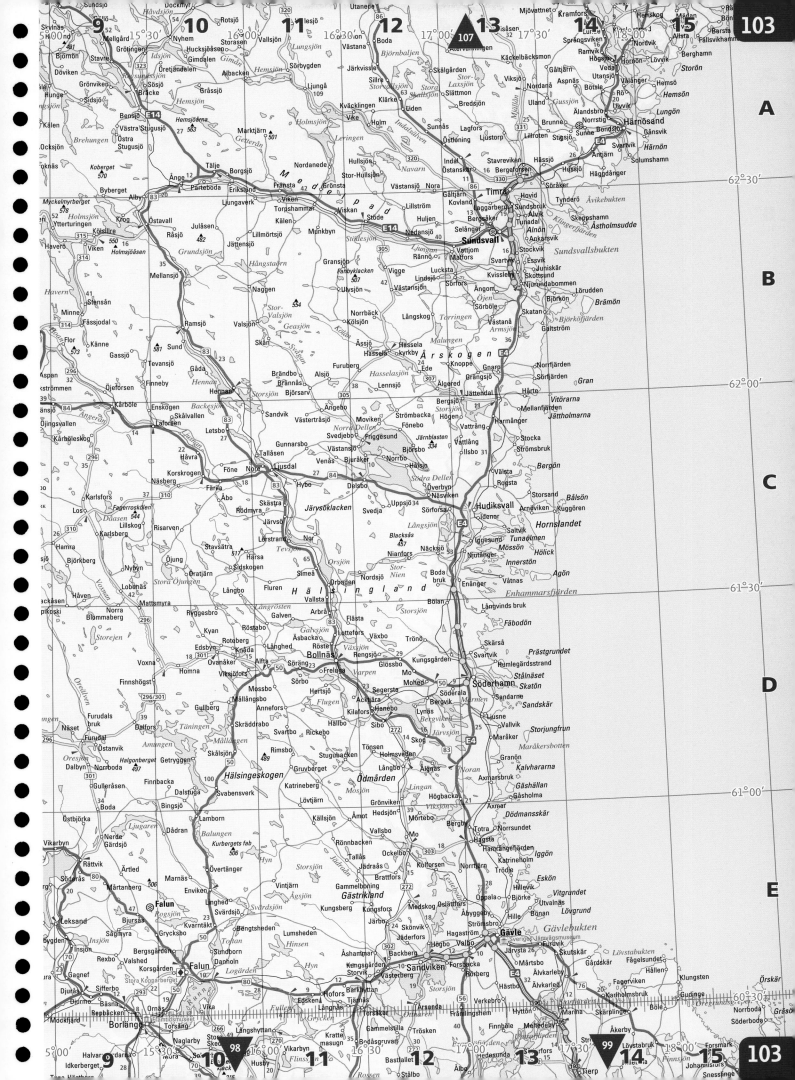

A

B

C

D

E

F

65°00'

64°30'

64°00'

63°30'

20'

10'

63°00'

1   7°00'   2   7°30'   3   8°00'   4   8°30'   5   9°00'   6   9°30'   7   10°00'   8   10°

Brandsfjorden

Sætter
Svefjo
Vingsand

Bessaker
Utro   Roan   Hoff
Kiran   Nordskjør
Harbak   Kjerringheia   540
Tørrvika   Harsvik   37
Ratvika   30   715   By
Tårnes   723   Afjord
Selnes   Eide   Mørrevatnet   Fle
Vallersund   Lysøysund
Oksvoll   721   Teksdal   22   715
Bjugn   26   13   Bjøljelia   710   3
Botngård   24
Uthaug   Opphaug   718   23
Brekstad   Austrått   42   61
Fevåg   14   Olsøy   L
715   Rissa   809
Grønningen   710   717   Storvatnet   30
Reinskloster   13   Hindrem   755   Vannvikan
Lensvik   656   13   8
Åstan   Selbekken   Stadsbygd
Sunde   9   Øyangen   Ringve
Flesvik   Kjøra   Flakkfjorden   Botaniske
Heim   34   Flakk   715
Krokstadøra   Nidarosdomen   566   ☩
Skorild   707   Byneset   Trondhe
Berdal   23   710   387
Gjølme   E39   13   Børsa
Omnsfjellet   714   15   709   Buvika
847   Orkanger   Heimda
Fannrem   15   704
Hoston   17   20   Vormstad   Melhus
65   Svorkmo   708   Ler
Svartkmo   708
Gråfjellet   19   Løkken   Korsveggen
1040   700   Gåsbakken   33
Storås   701   Meldal   Hovin   Anova
Rindal   31   65   23   Løkken   Støren
Harang   Sætra   Restfjellet   30
Suna   1162   A   19   Rog
Follsjøen   Soknedal   E6
Honnstadknyken   30
1071   Tindfjellet   Ilfjellet   Okdal
1167   1218
Grindal   37   700   Svardal
Gråsjøen   E6   19   Ila   Enmo
Rognnebba   Snota   Berkåk
1497   1668   Soknu   ☩
Gjevilvatnet   254   Ulsberg

Frohavet

Norddyrøy   Svellingen
Tuvnes   Helfesvik
16   716   714
Frøyhavet   Frøya   Sistranda
Flatvål   17   Hammarvika
13   716   Selvåg
Titran   Storhallaren   Knarrlagsund
Frøyfjorden   Kjerringvåg   16   714
Veidholmen   Hestnes   6   Fillan   19
Kvenvær   Straum   714   Hestvika
713   12   Sandstad   21   Kongsvoll
Havmyran   Hitra   10   Sunde
Dyrnes   Forsnes   17   Gjengstø
28   345   Helland   Heim
Smøla   Vikan   Fonna   9
669   Vihalsen   722   Storodden
Austsmøla   16   Årvågen   14
Straumen   Svinvika   Todalsfjellet   Rovatnet
Rossvoll   8   Ånes   821   13   Søya   29
Korsvoll   Aure   680   Søvassli
Solskjela   682   Vinjeøra   E39
Leira   Åmo   Vinjøra
680   Aukan   Ervik   Todal   14
Kristiansund   15   Stabblandet   E39
Sveggesundet   6   908   Arasvika   Gråfjellet
Hasløya   Tustna   Renndal   Drystølen   1040
Reinsvik   Litlbøen   Betna   929   Brattset
Karvåg   Kvalvåg   Hennset   65
Bruhagen   13   70   Hjelmen   Valsøybotn   Søvassli
Øydegarden   Førvikan   Kanestraum   Bøverfjord
Veiøy   Halsa   7   Åsskard   978
Hurtigruten   Heggem   31   Rindal
Hustadvika   Ørj.   20   Mork   Aksnes   Torvik   Kvanne   Alvund
Bud   Skalten   Høgset   666   Hoem   Årnes   670   Surnadalsøra
Hostadvatnet   664   Eide   Reinsfjellet   994   Tingvoll   1071
Elnesvågen   692   Torvikbukt   35   Ångvik   Rokkum
663   Bårnfjordsøra   665   Alvund   Svinvik Arboretum
Gossen   Urfjellet   Hjelset   Steinløysa   Kvanne   70   Gråsjøen
979   NORDMØRE   10   Kleive   62   Eidsøra   70   Rognnebba
Aureosen   Tornes   664   15   E39   62   Smisetnebba   Virumkjerringa
Aukra   662   Molde   Hjelset   Tjelle   660   Eidsvåg   1175   1374
Ørten   Gr.7°30'   Hesjestranda   17   Alvundeid   Nauste   Nerdal   579   Gjevilvatnet

Vevång   Averøya
Svinvika

Edøyfjorden

Tjusøya

Vinjefjorden

Kvernesfjorden

Trondheimsleia

Fillfjorden   Kråkvågfjorden

Tarvefjorden

Tarva

Ramsøyfjorden

Frostadheia

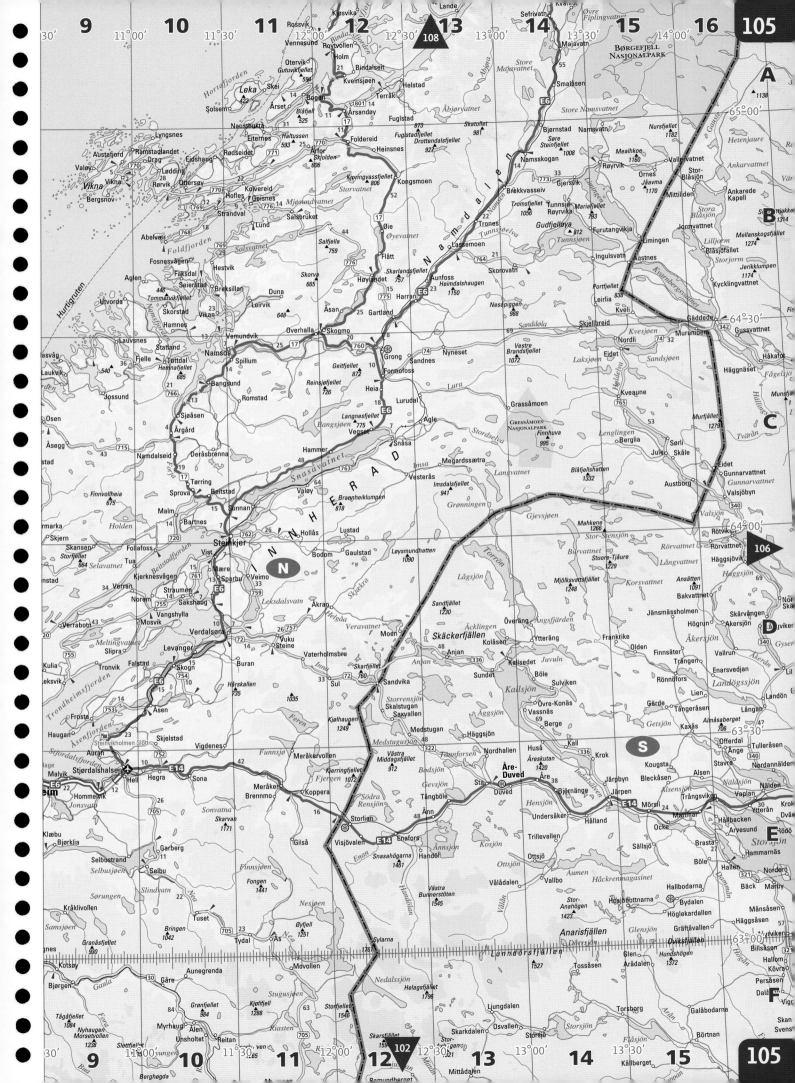

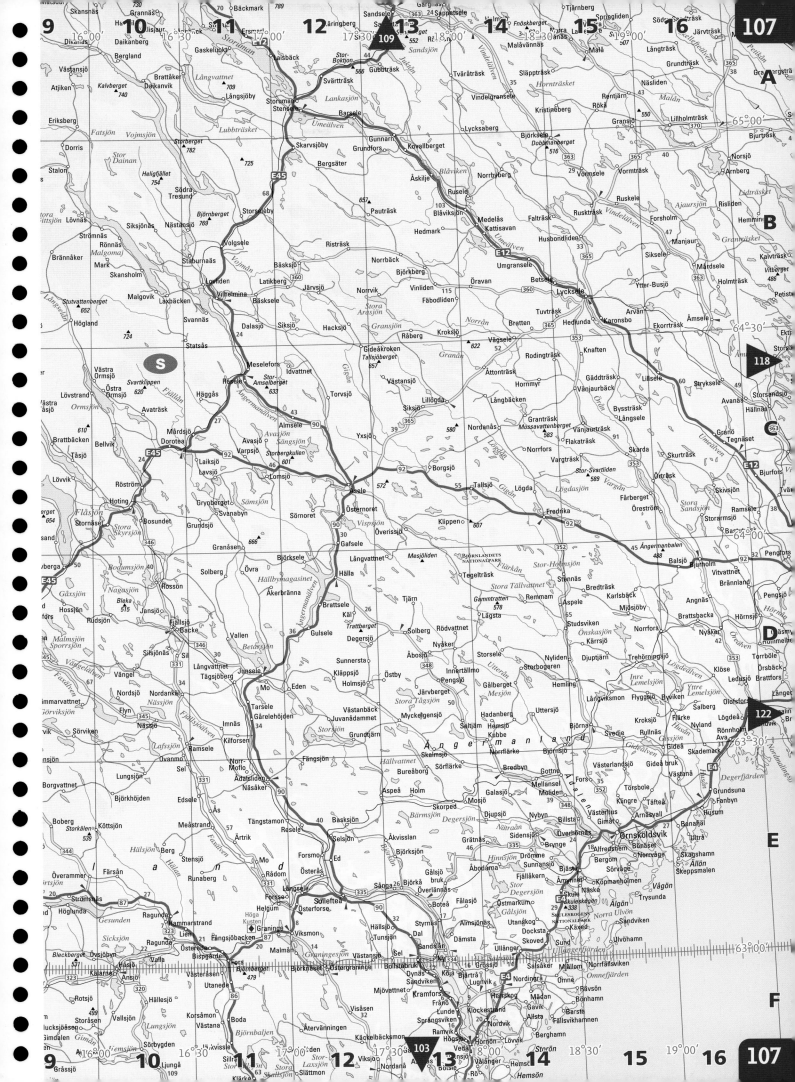

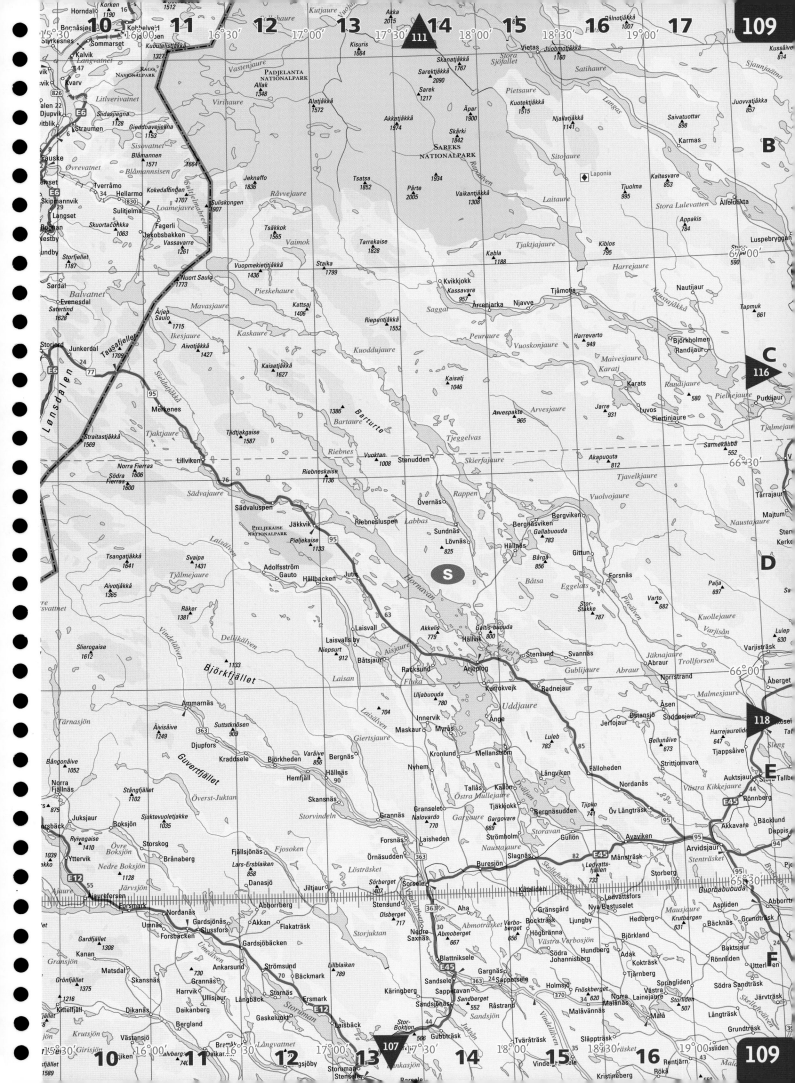

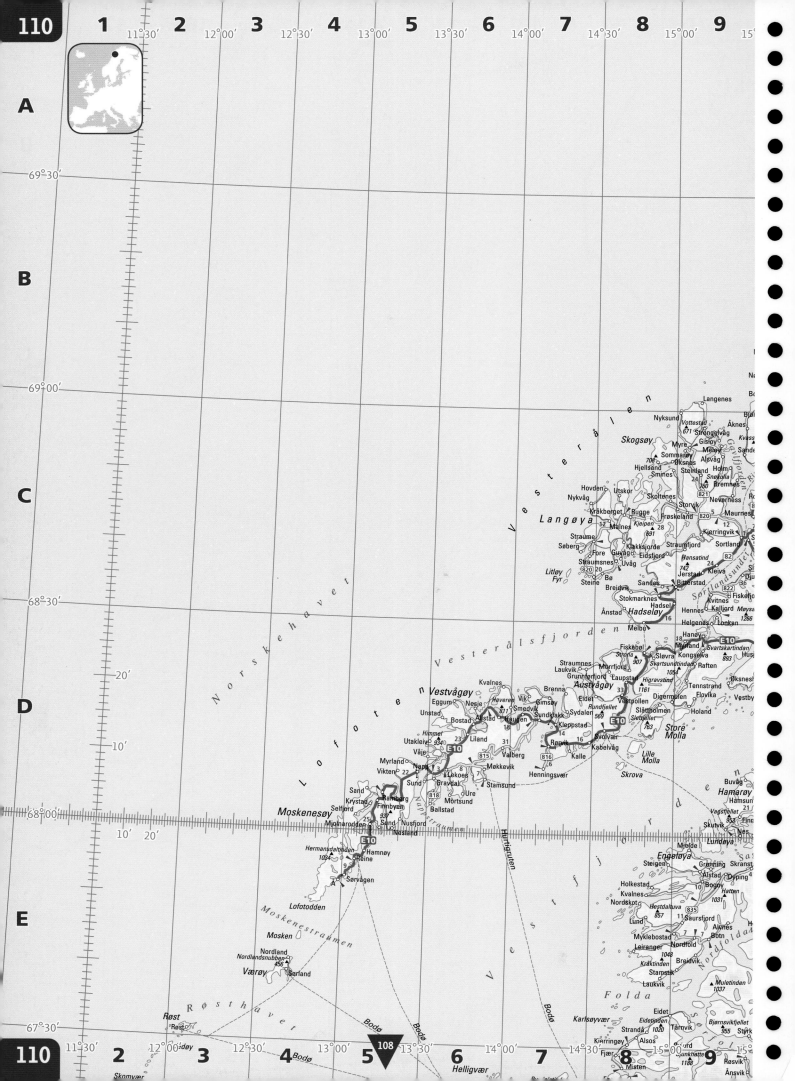

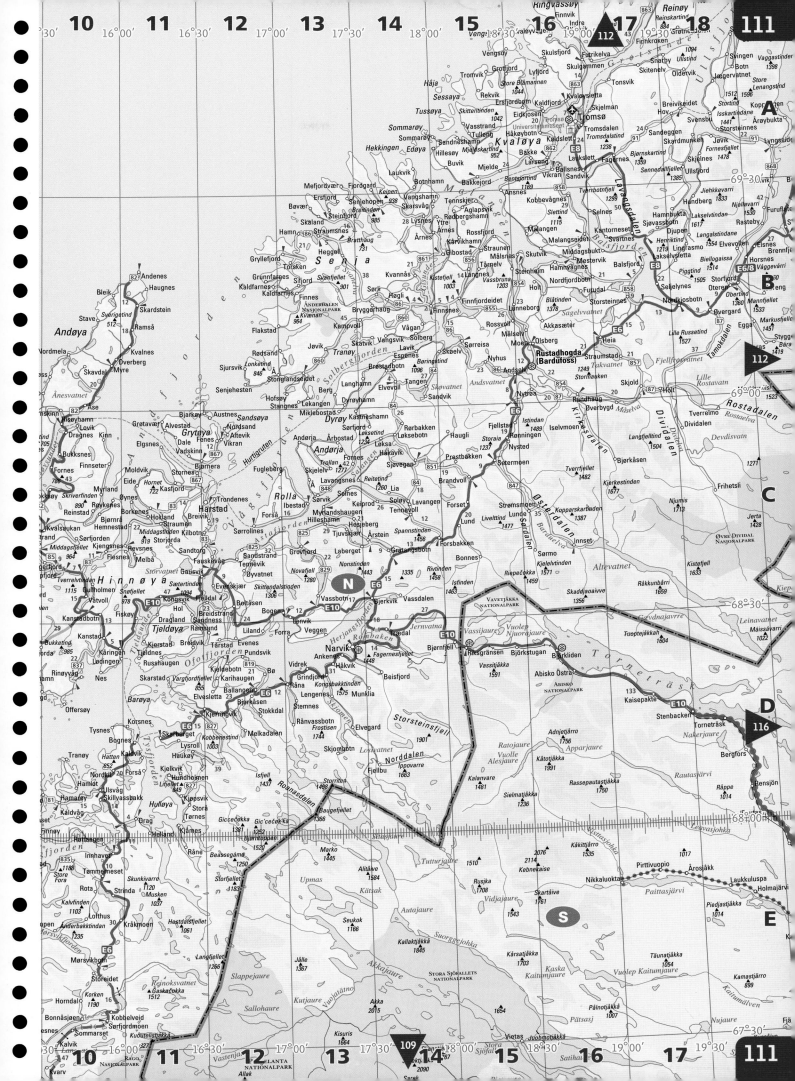

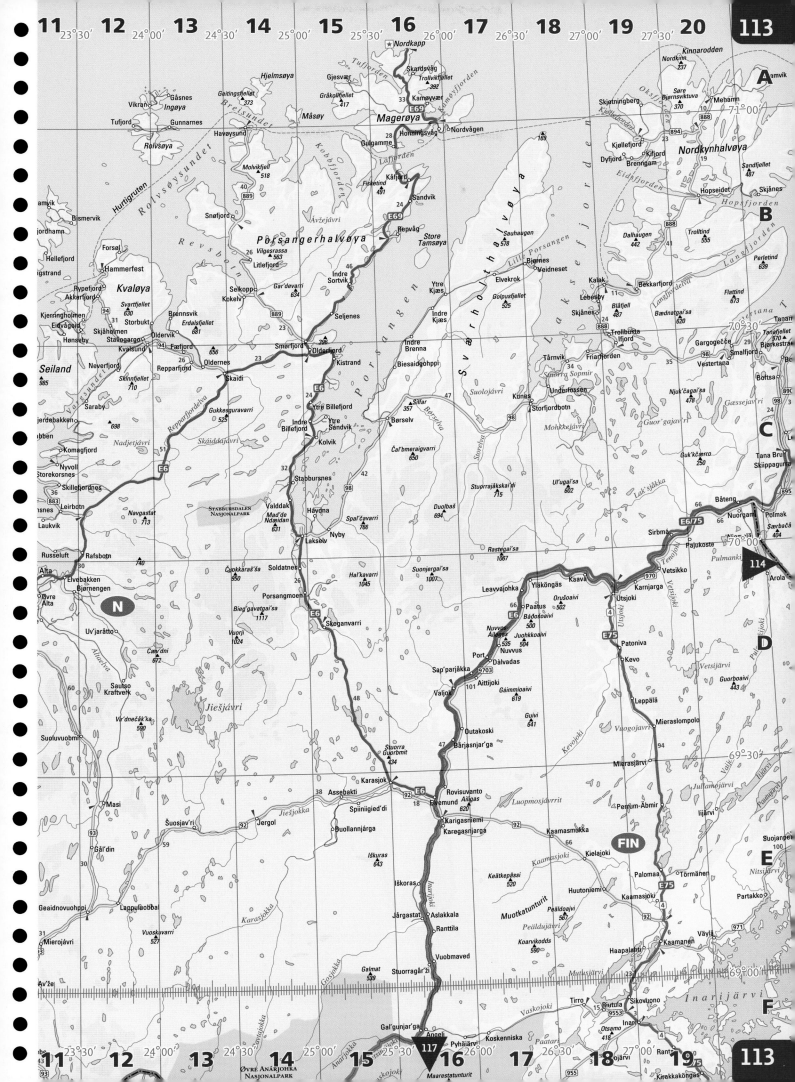

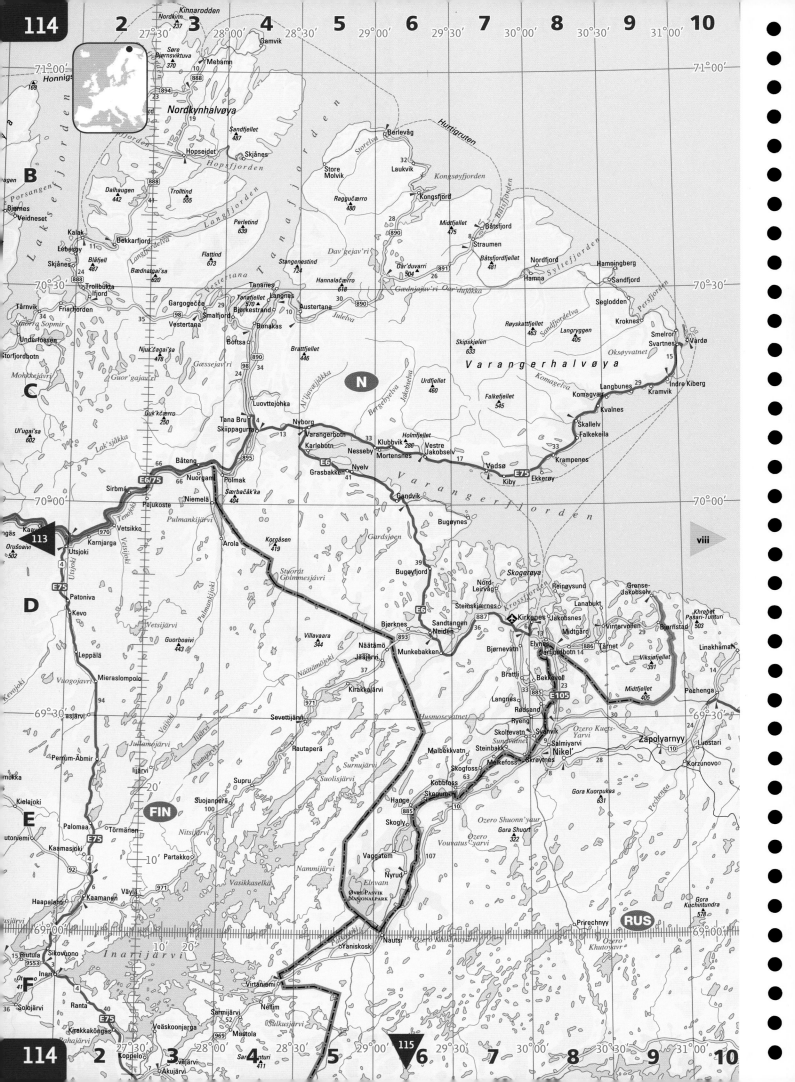

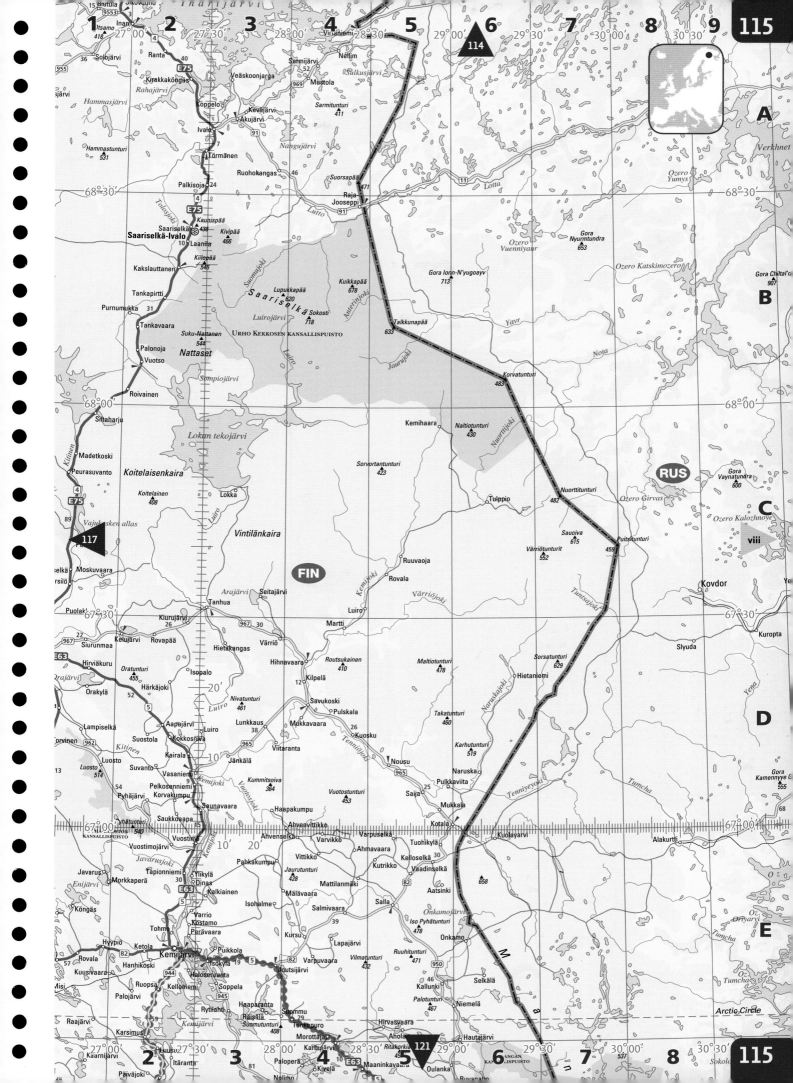

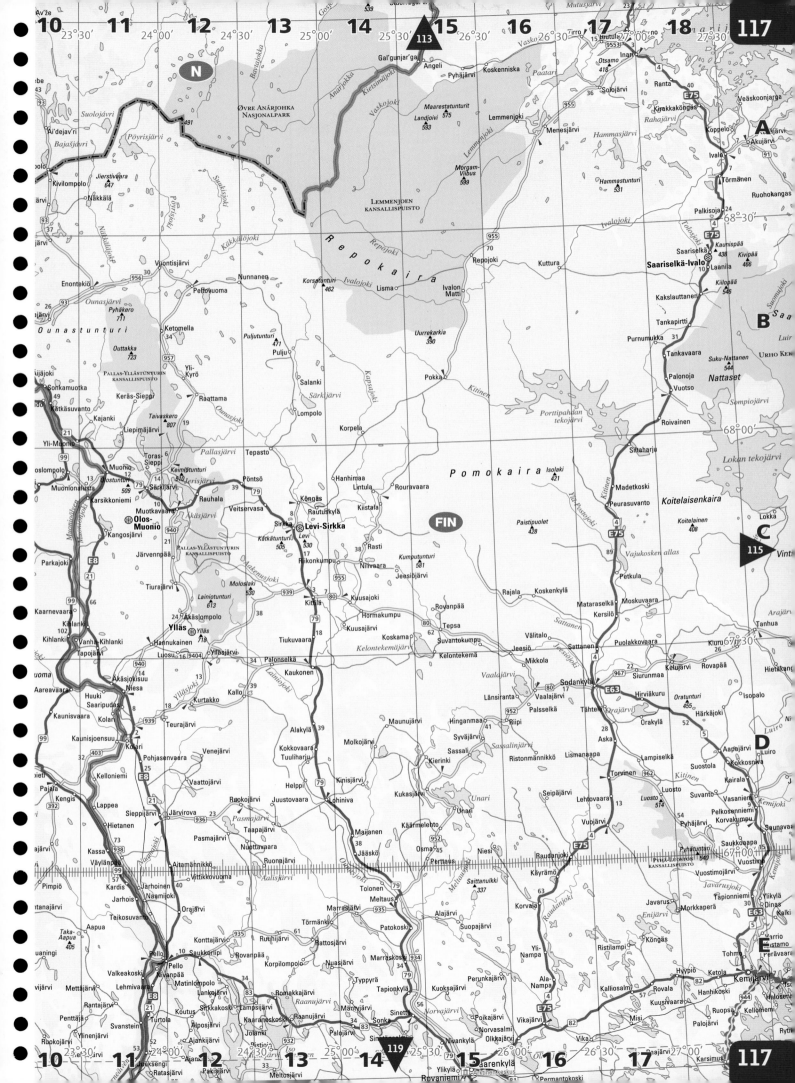

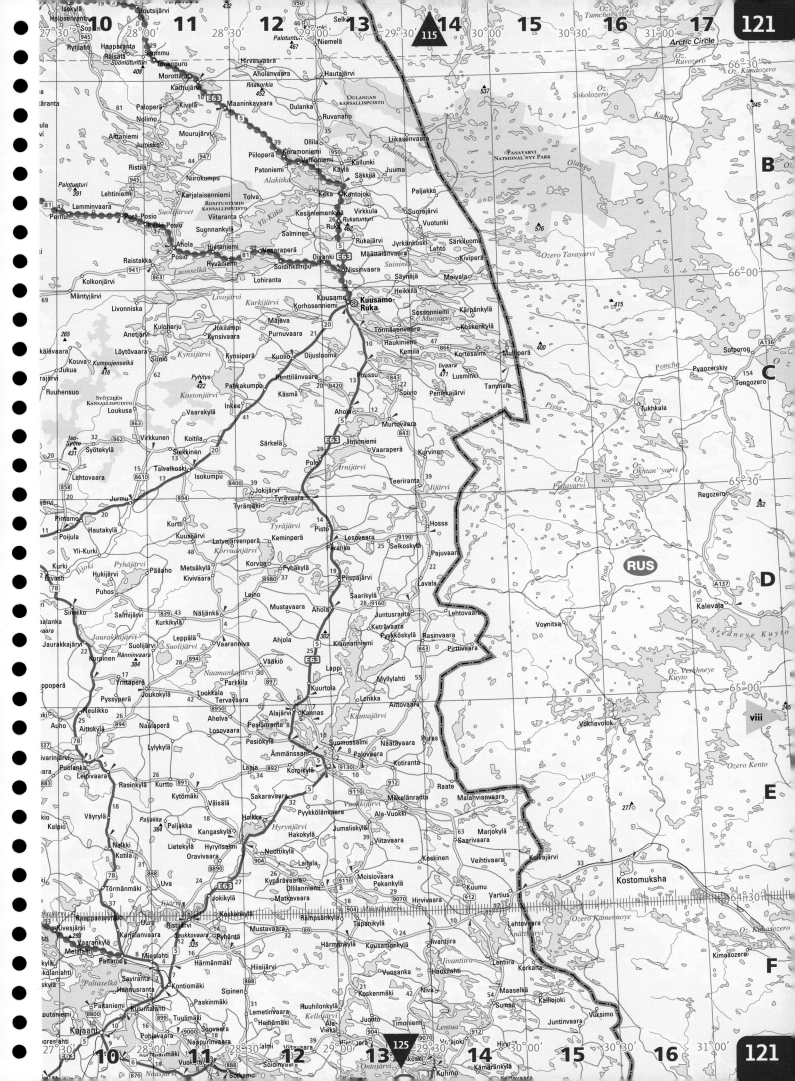

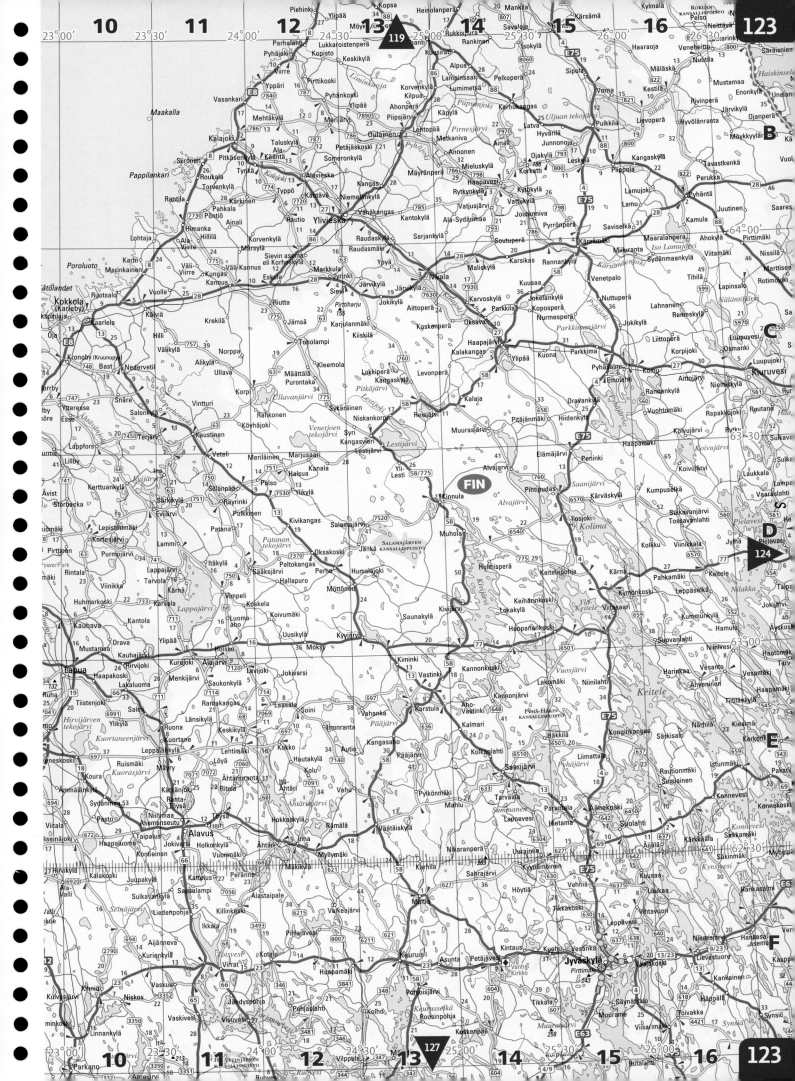

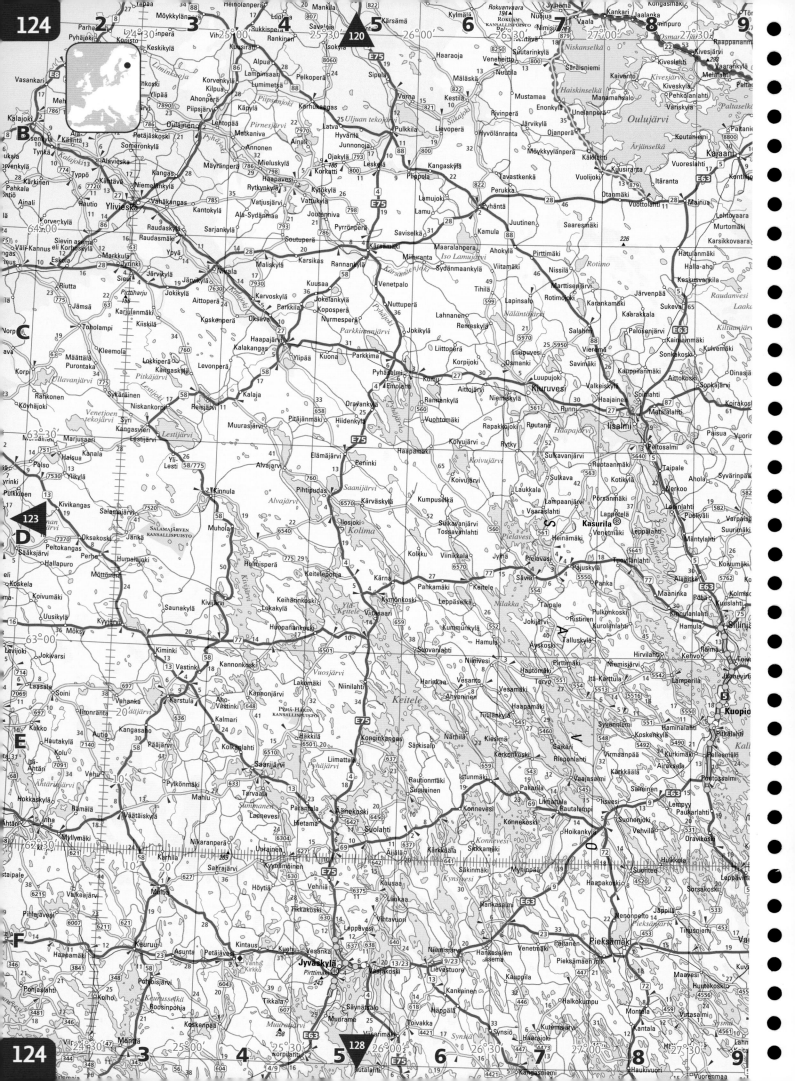

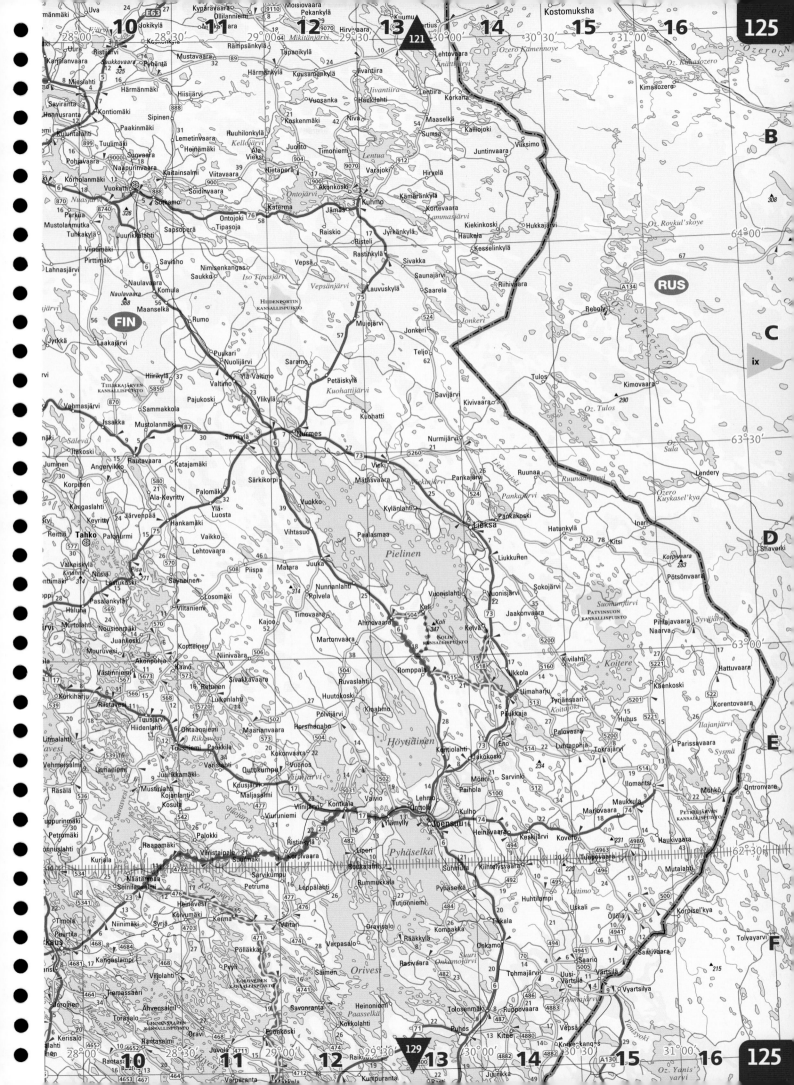

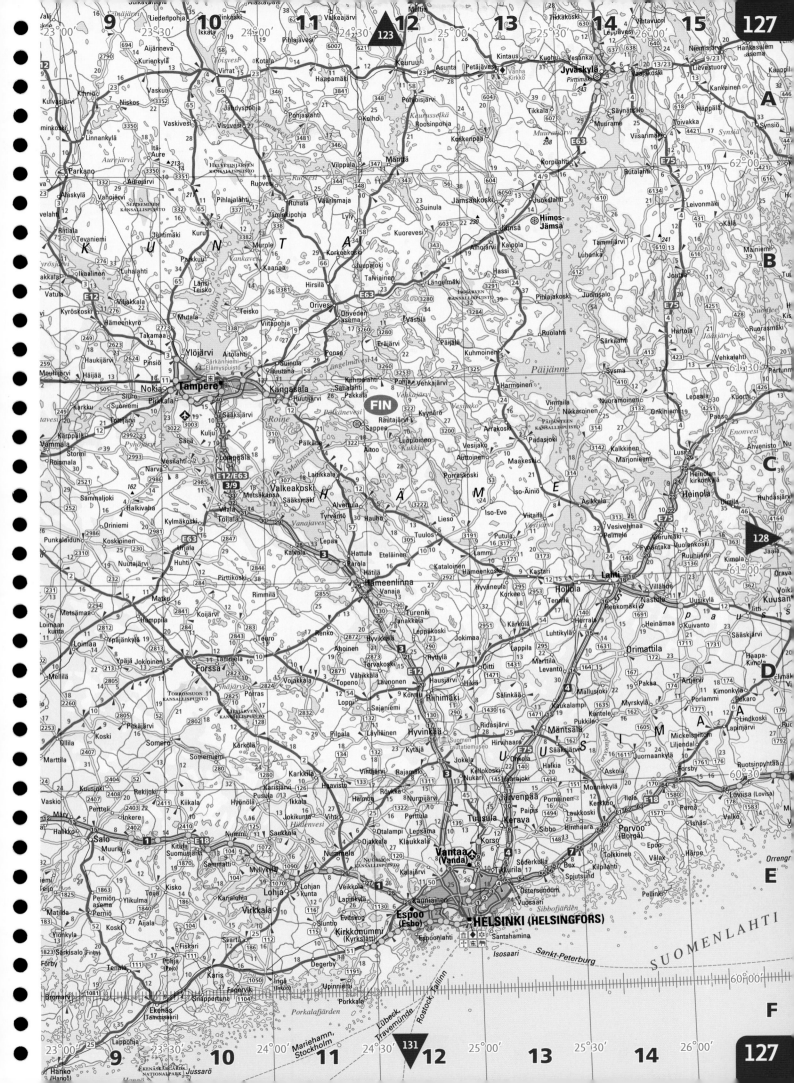

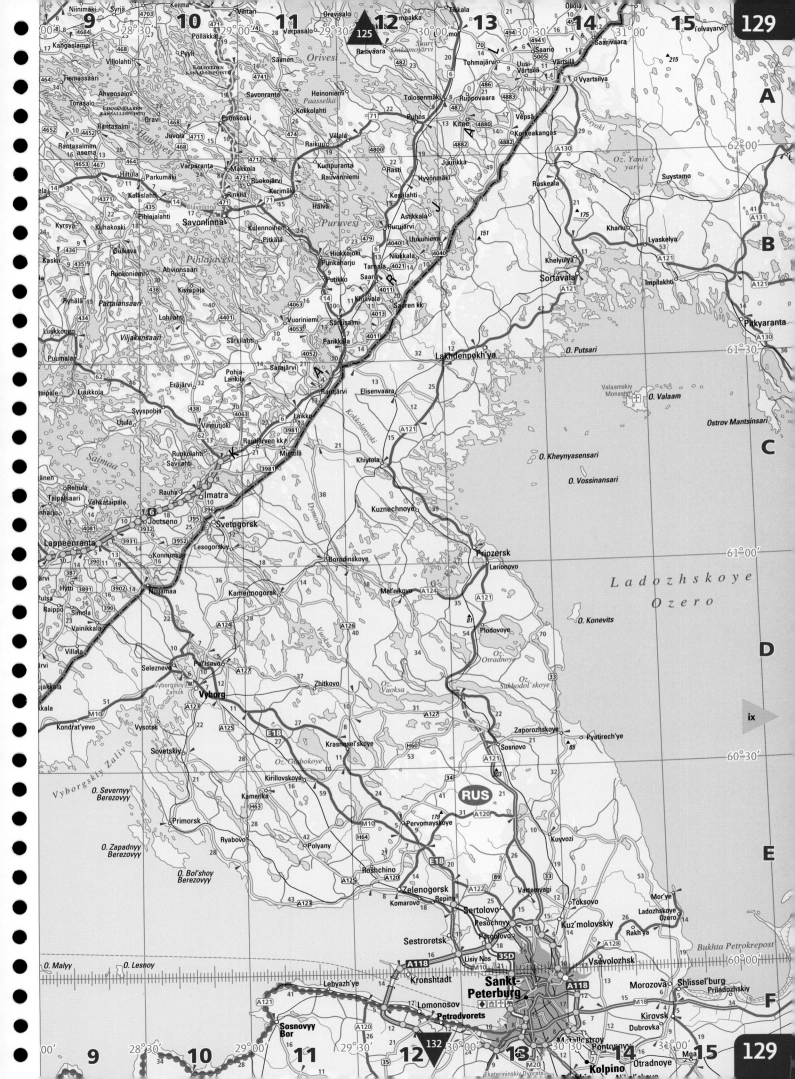

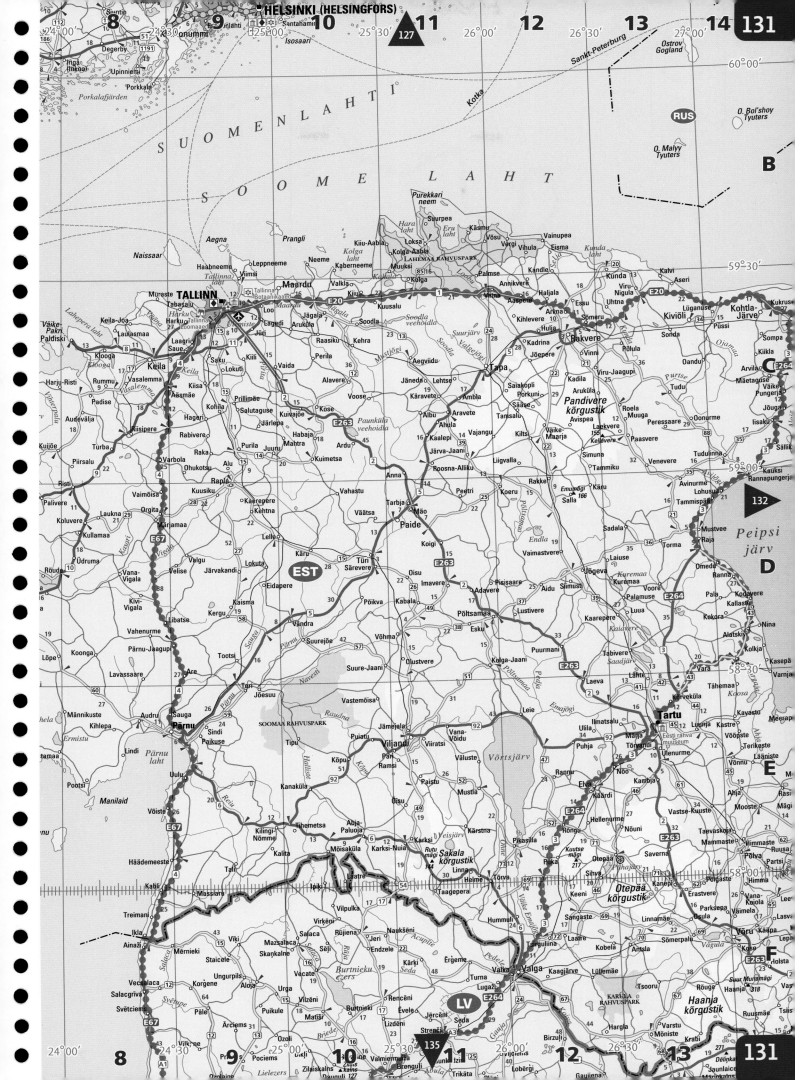

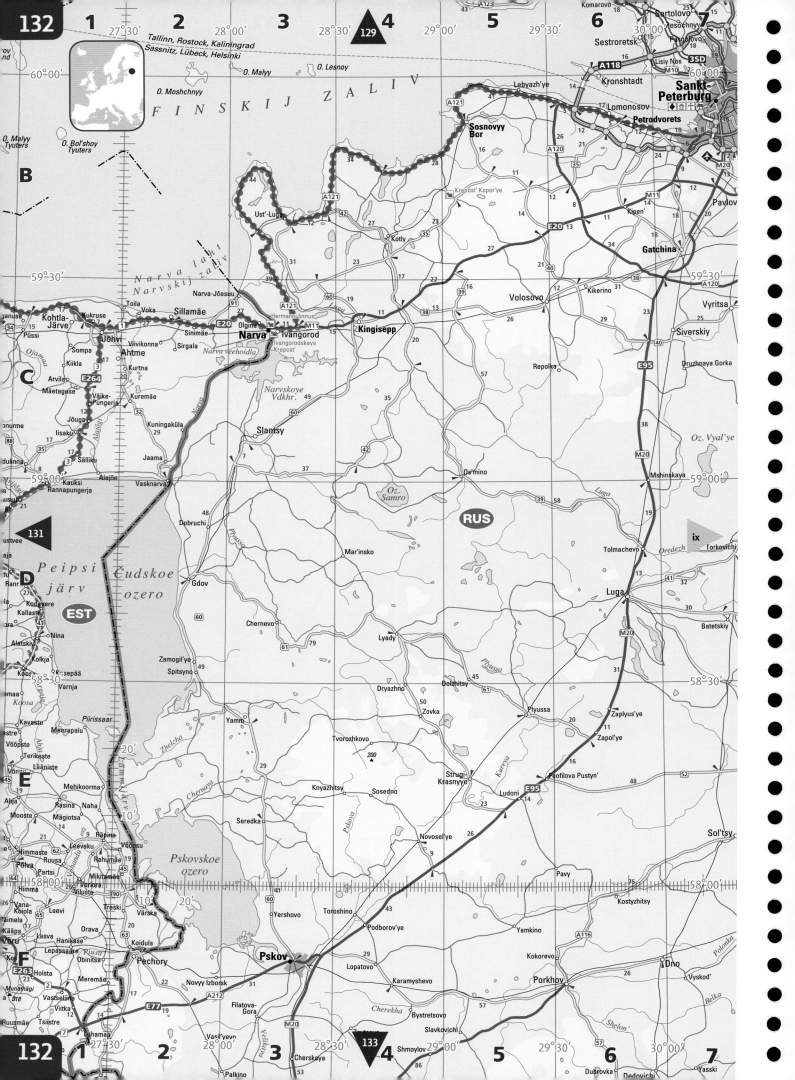

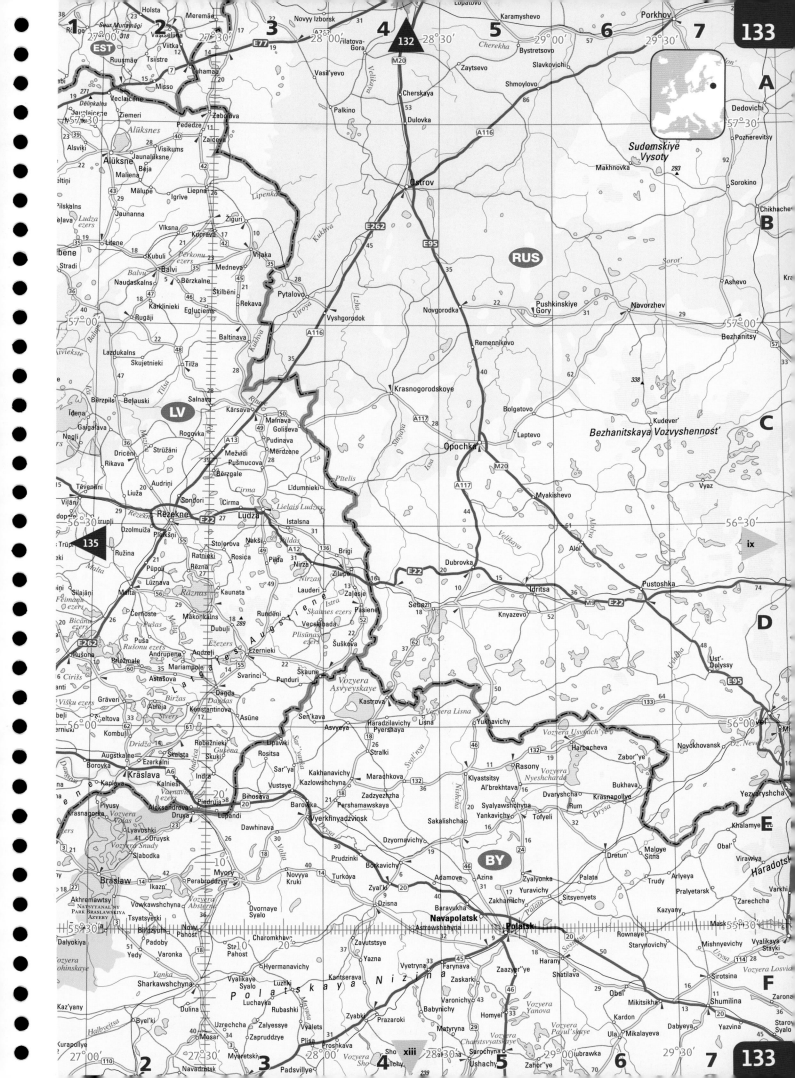

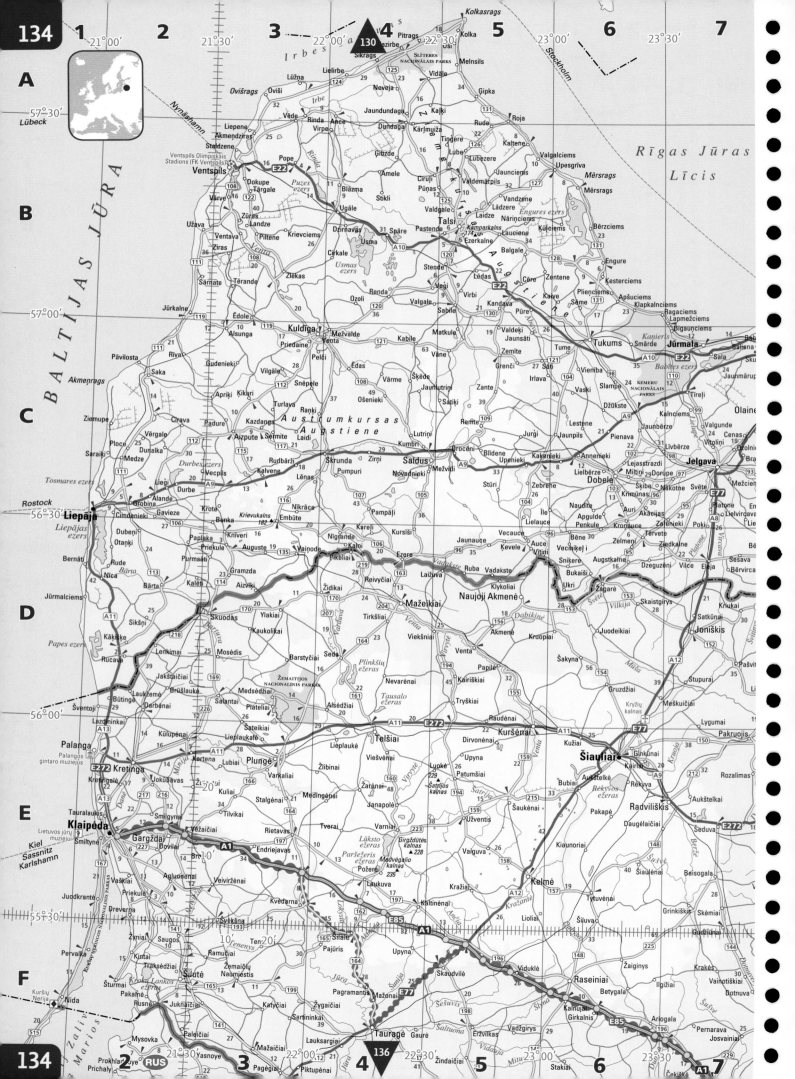

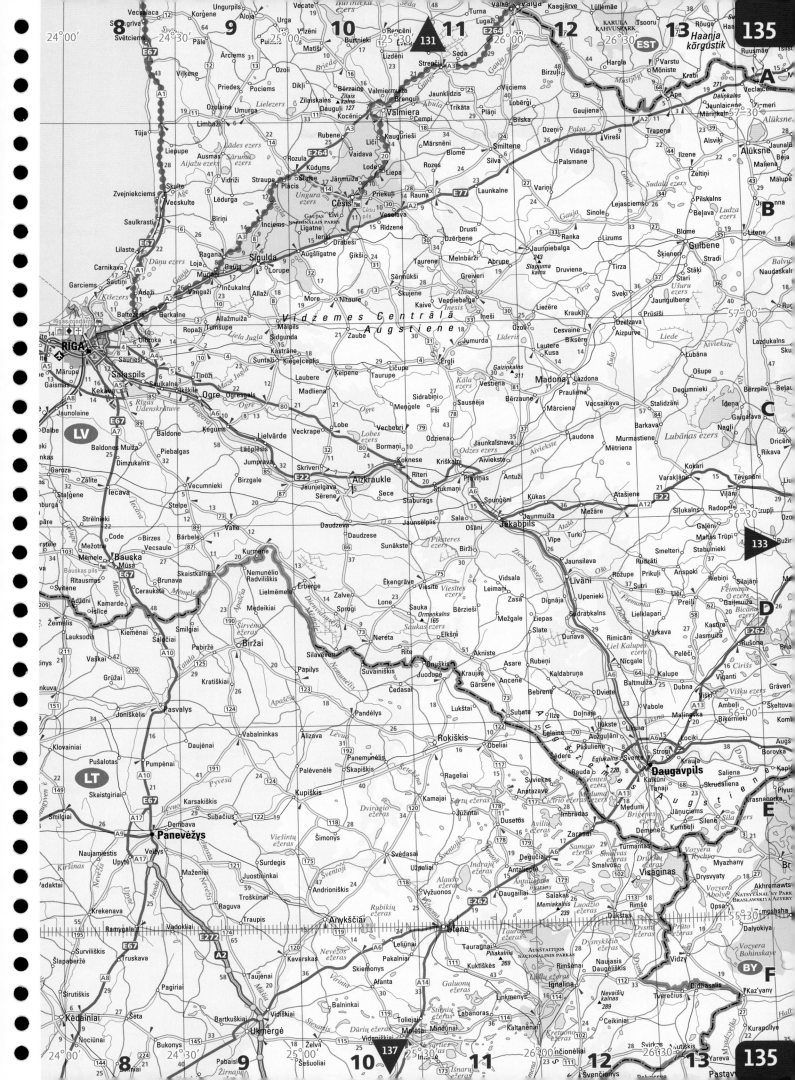

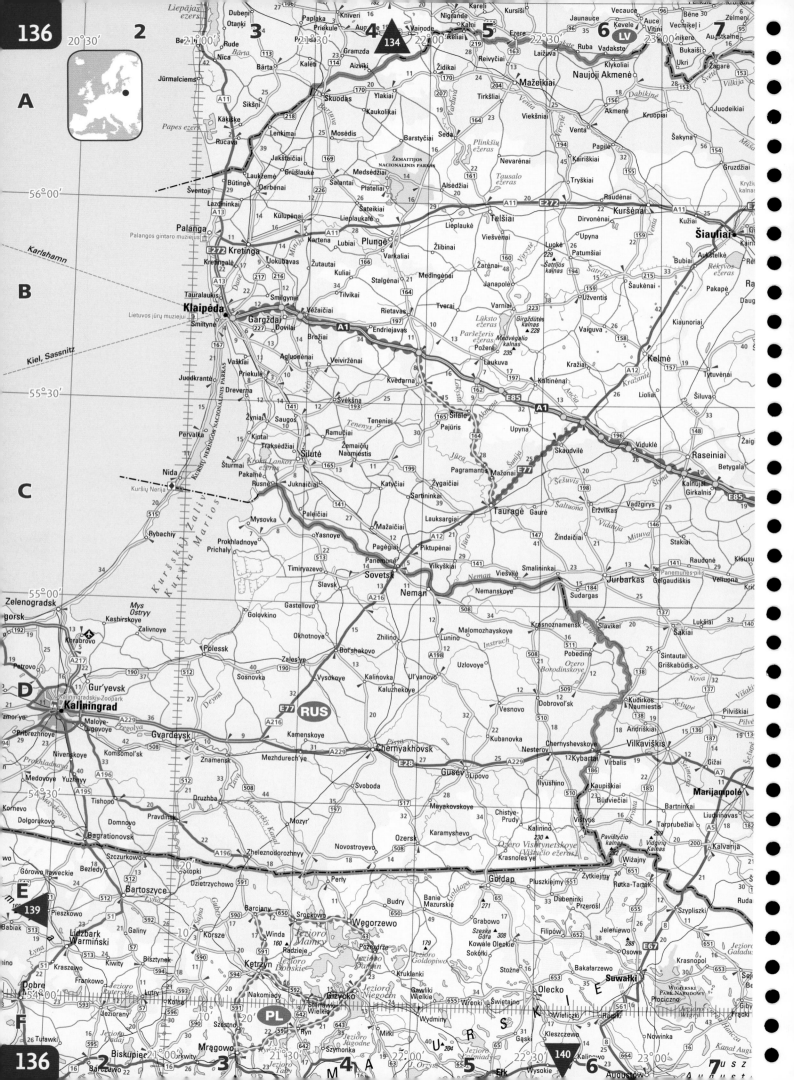

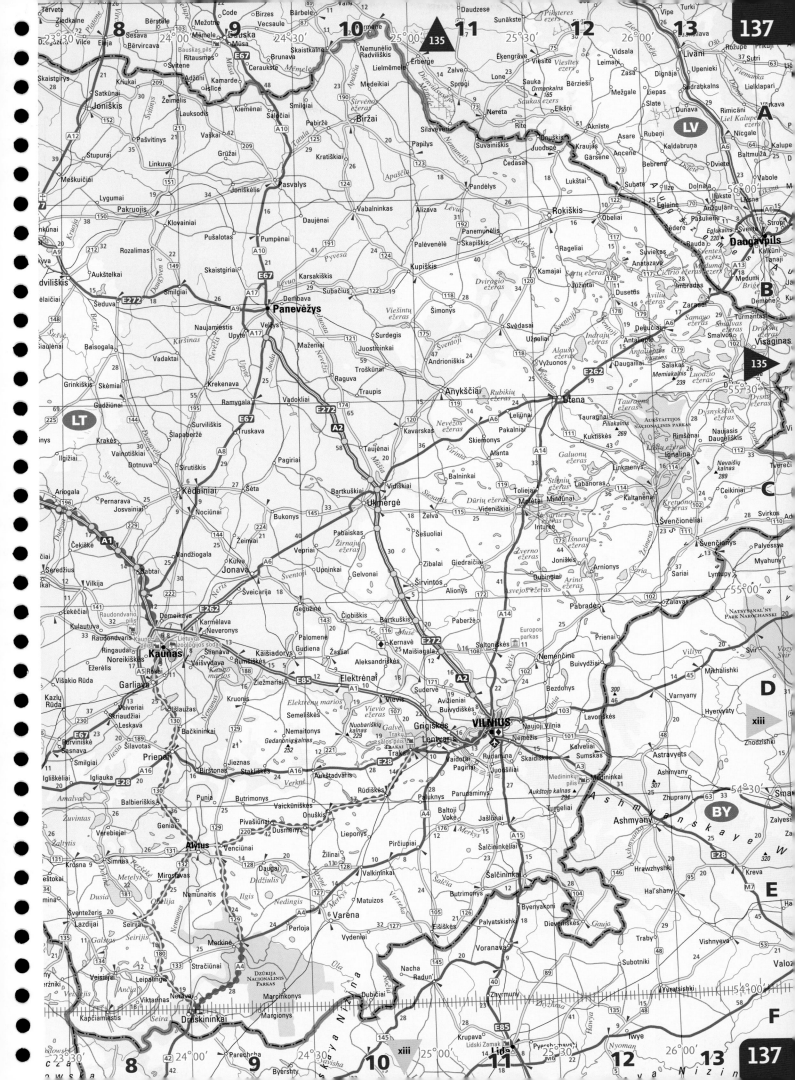

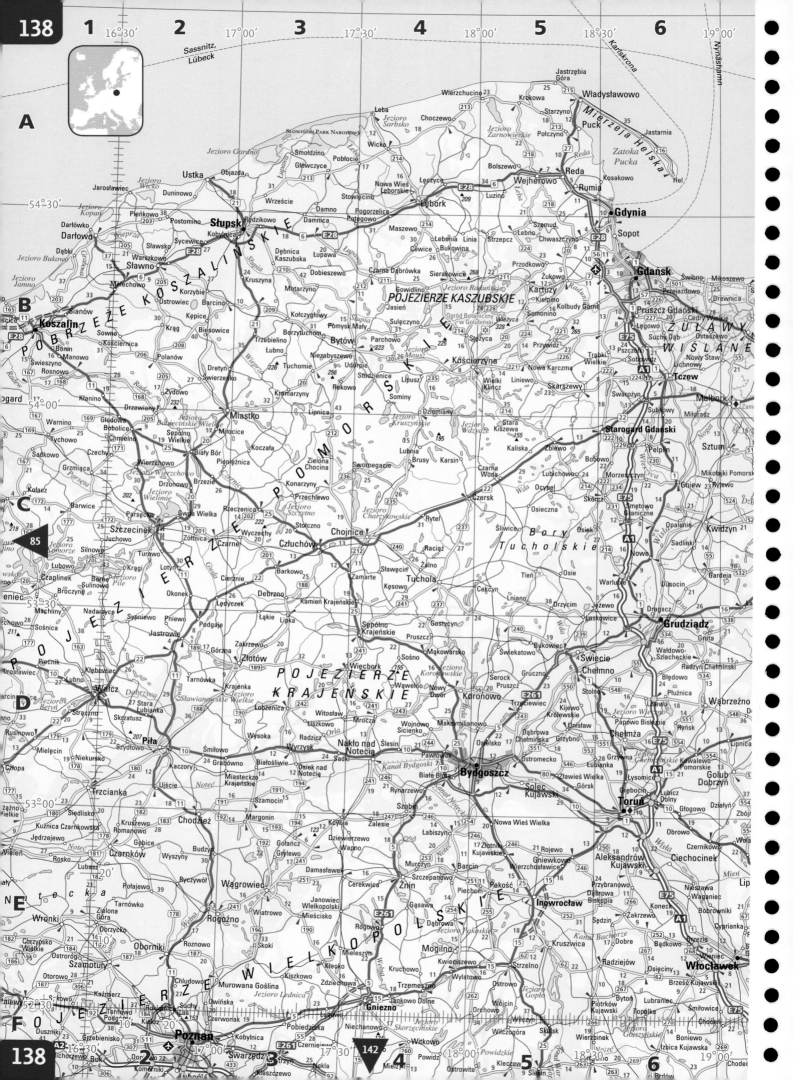

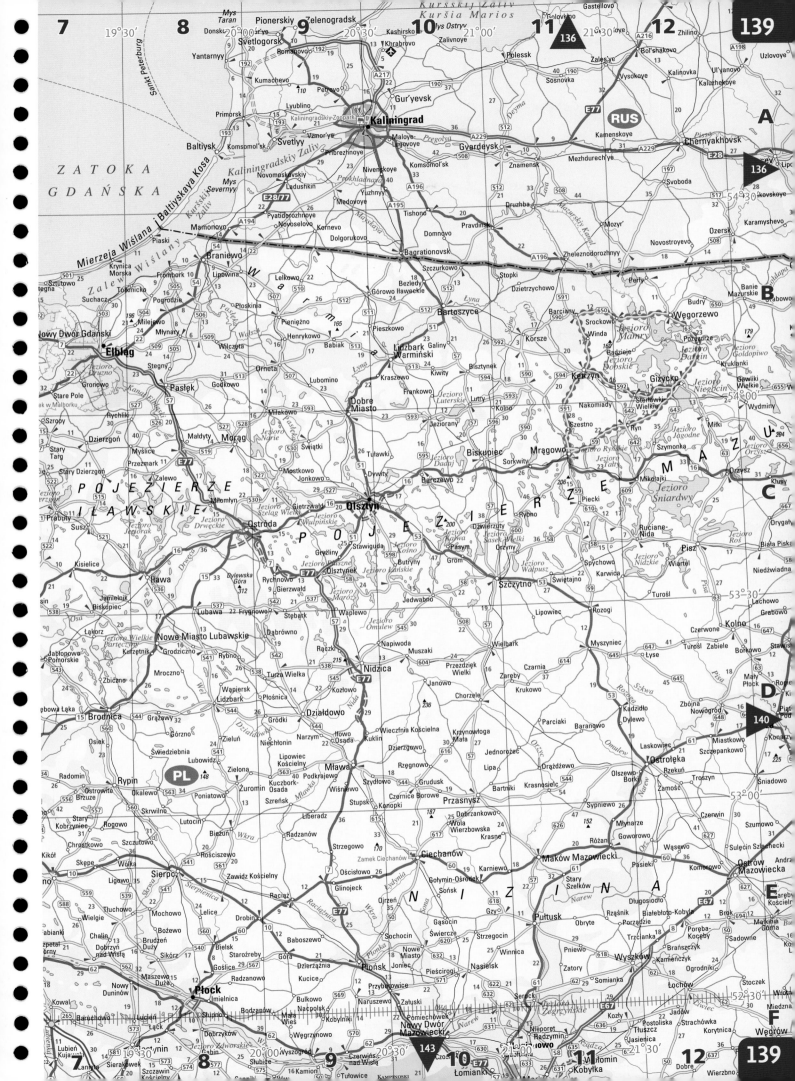

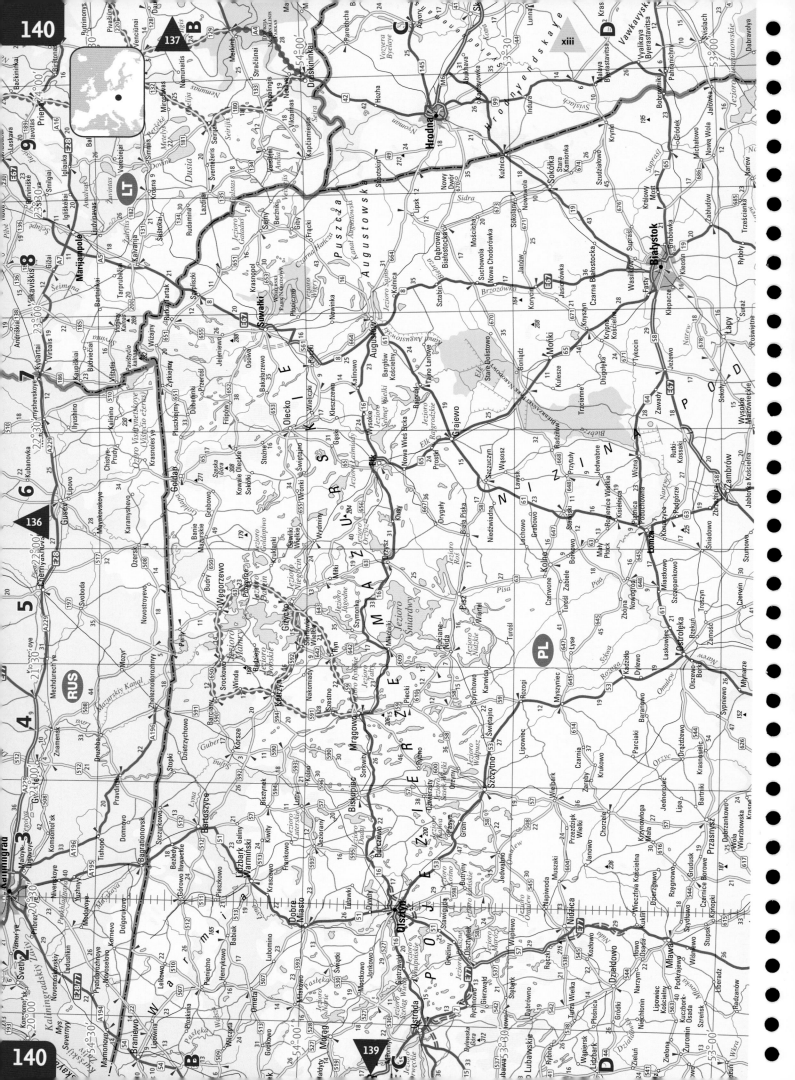

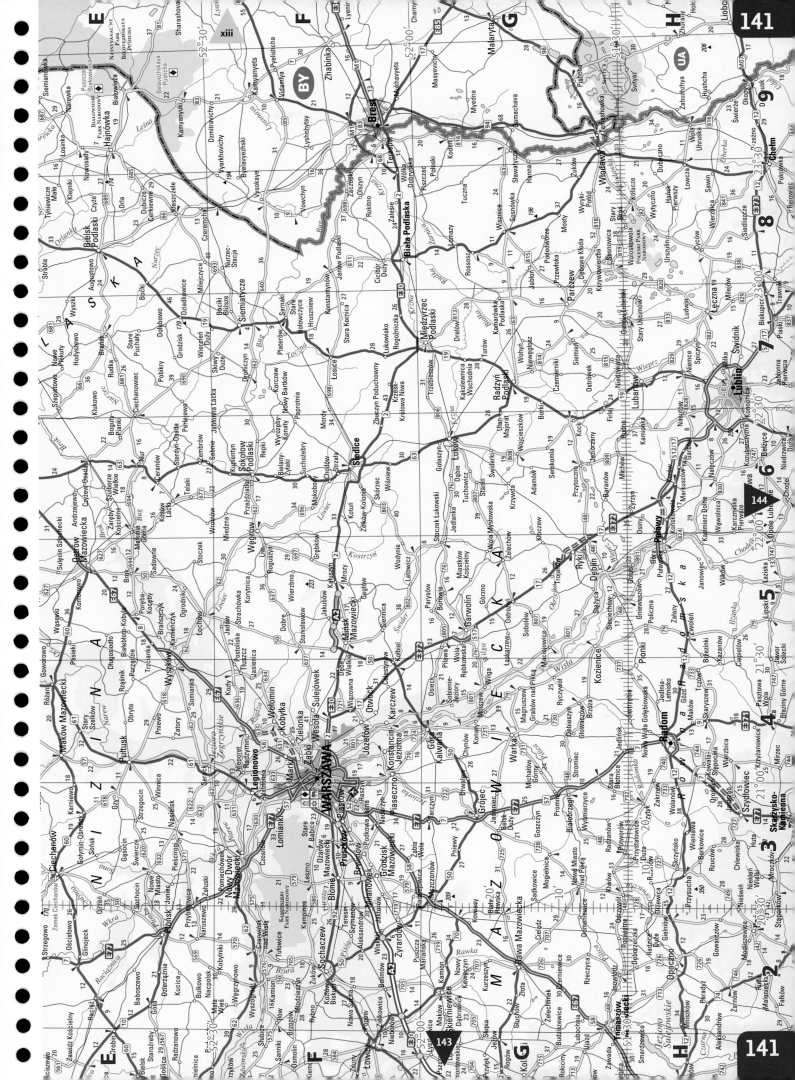

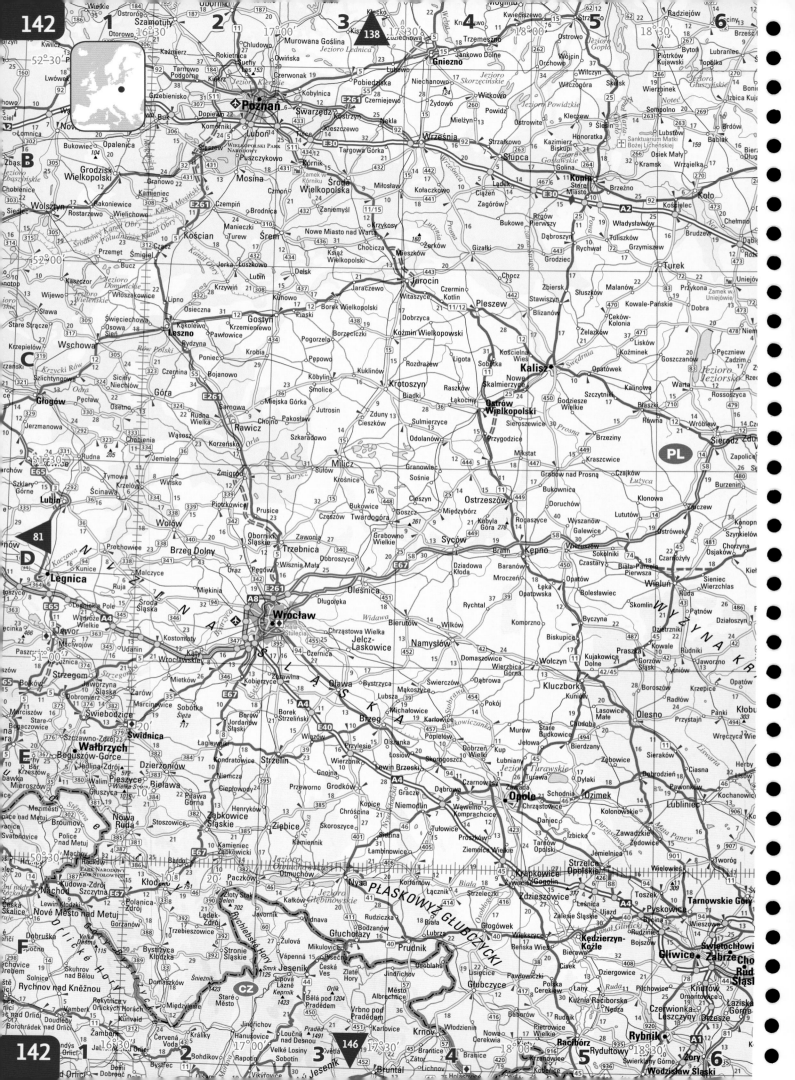

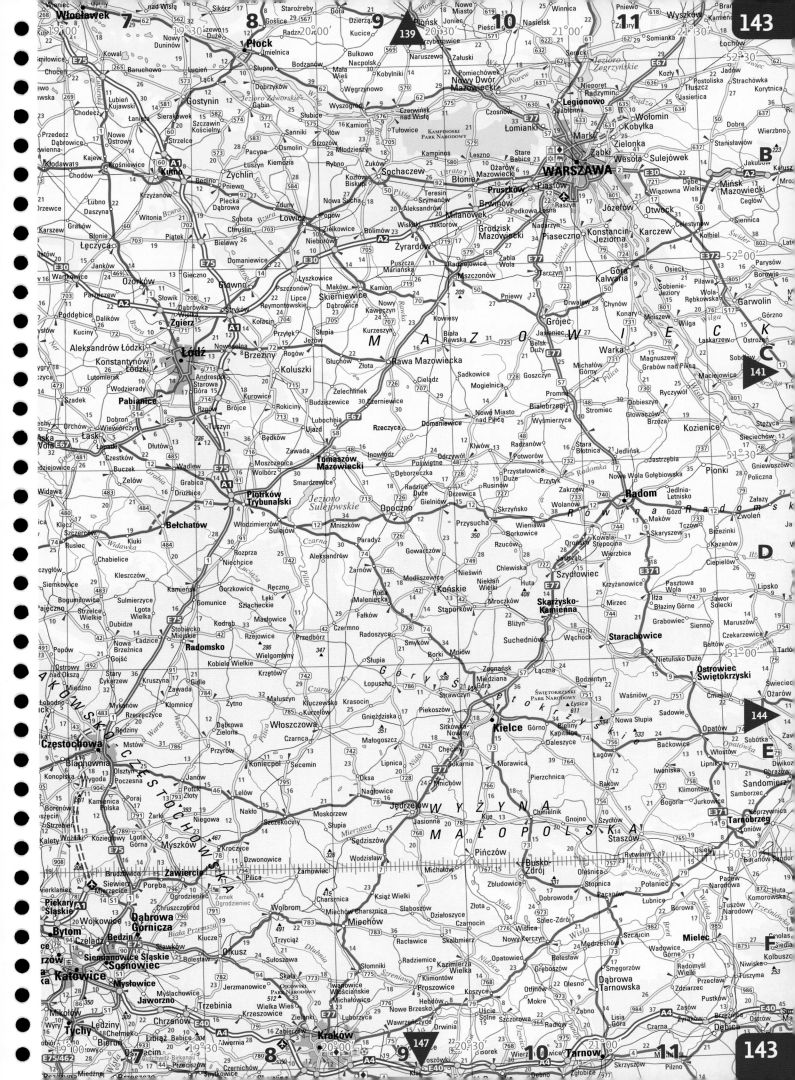

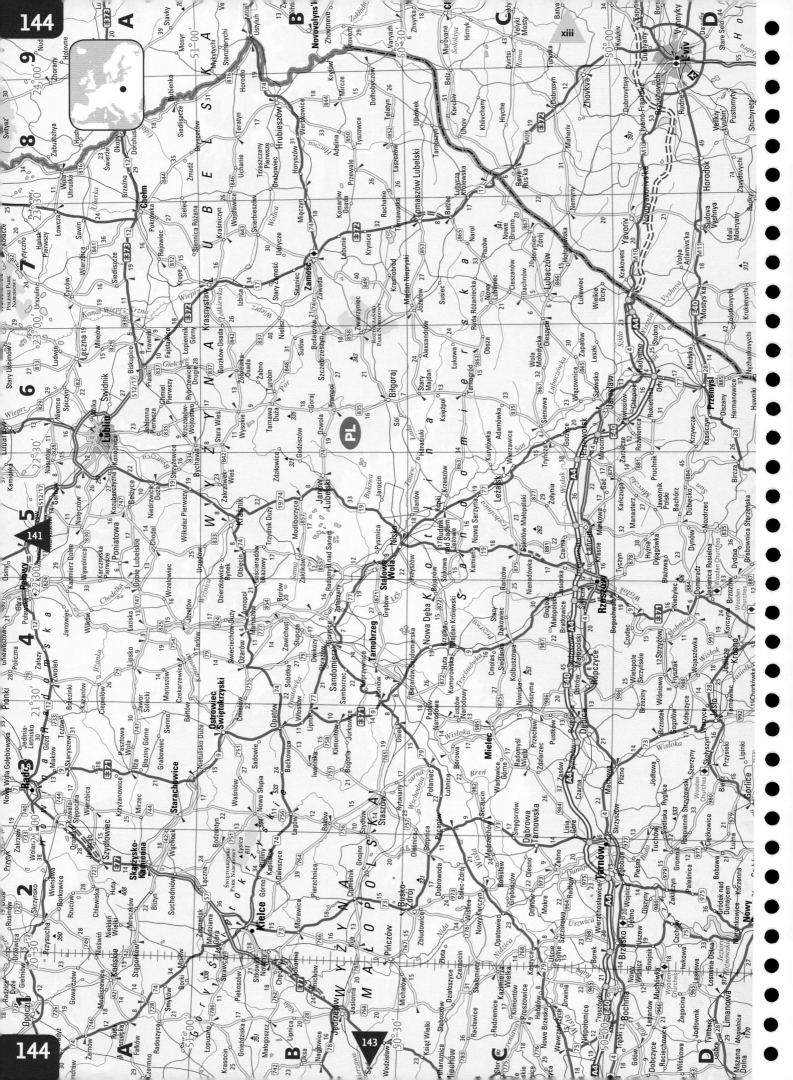

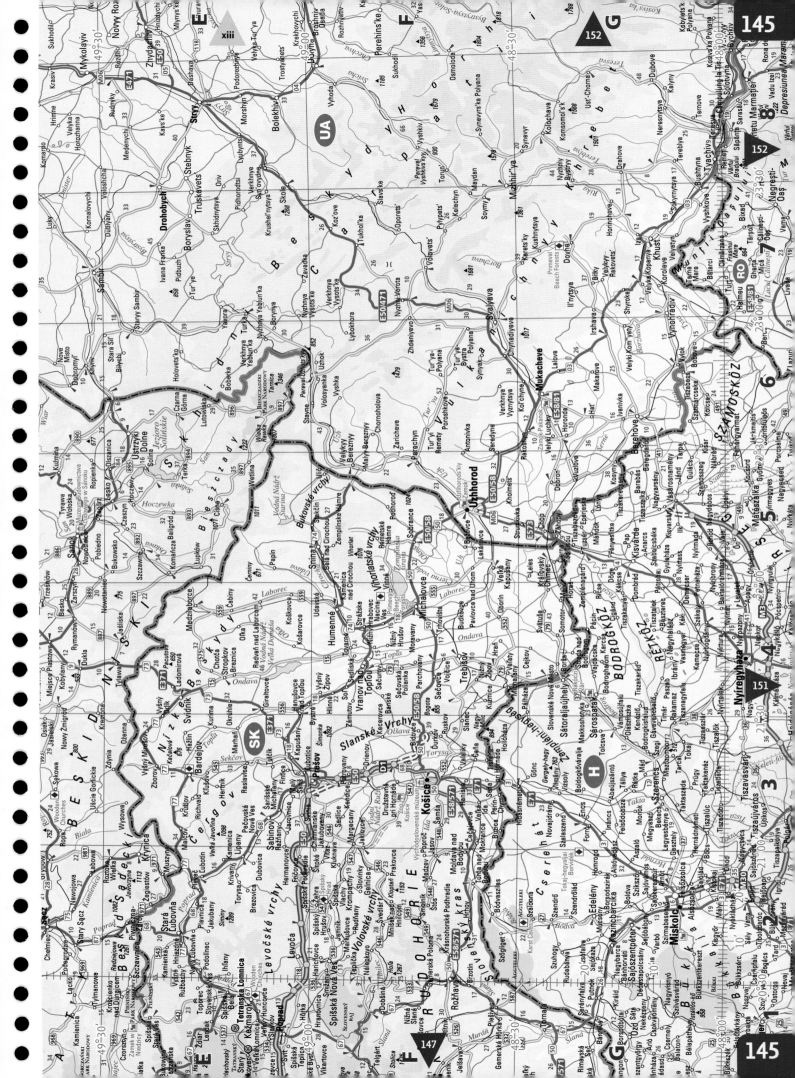

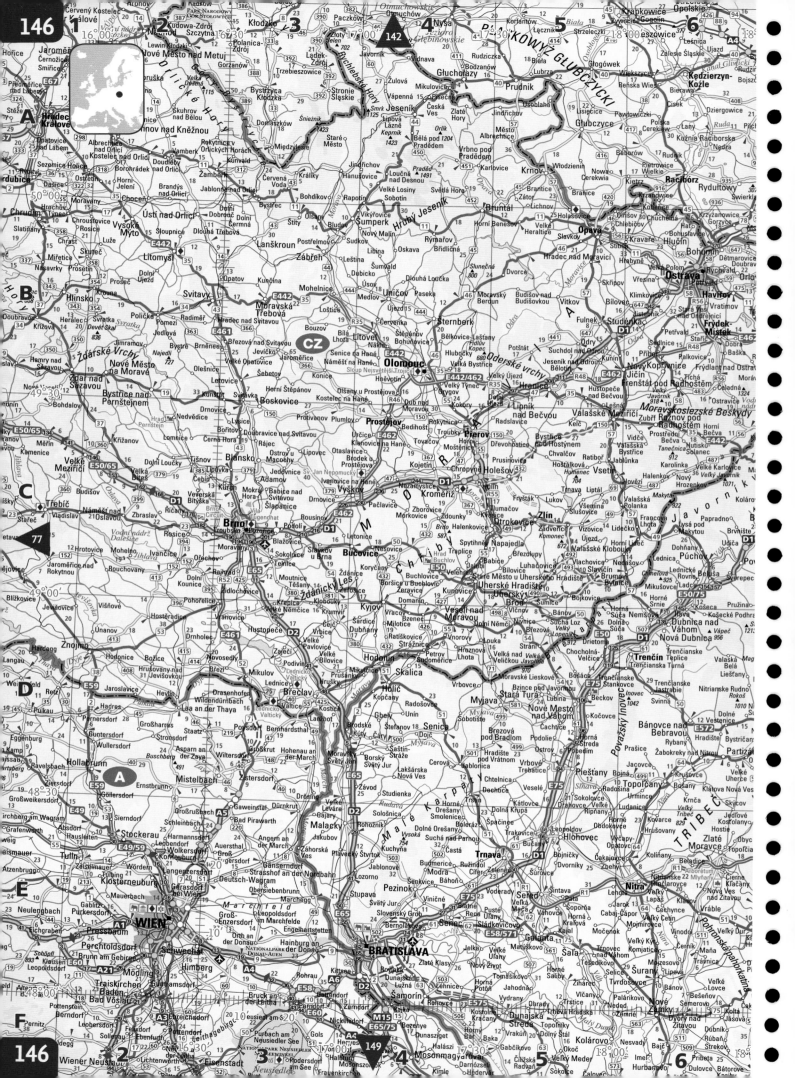

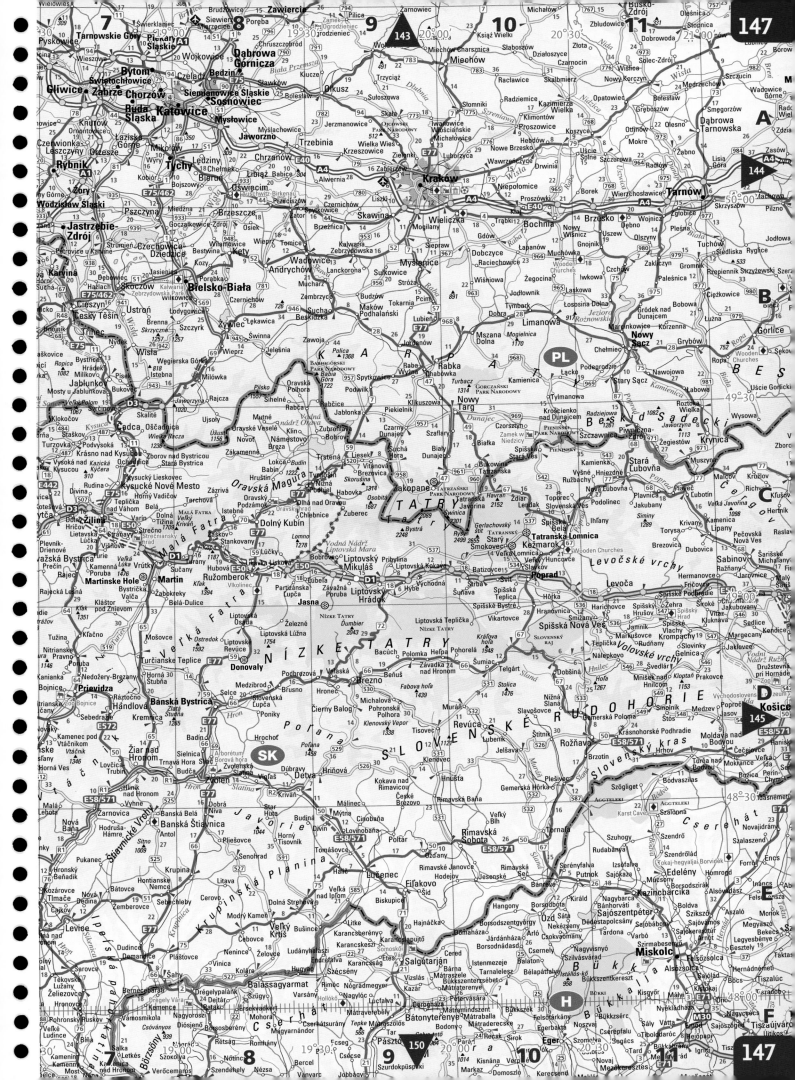

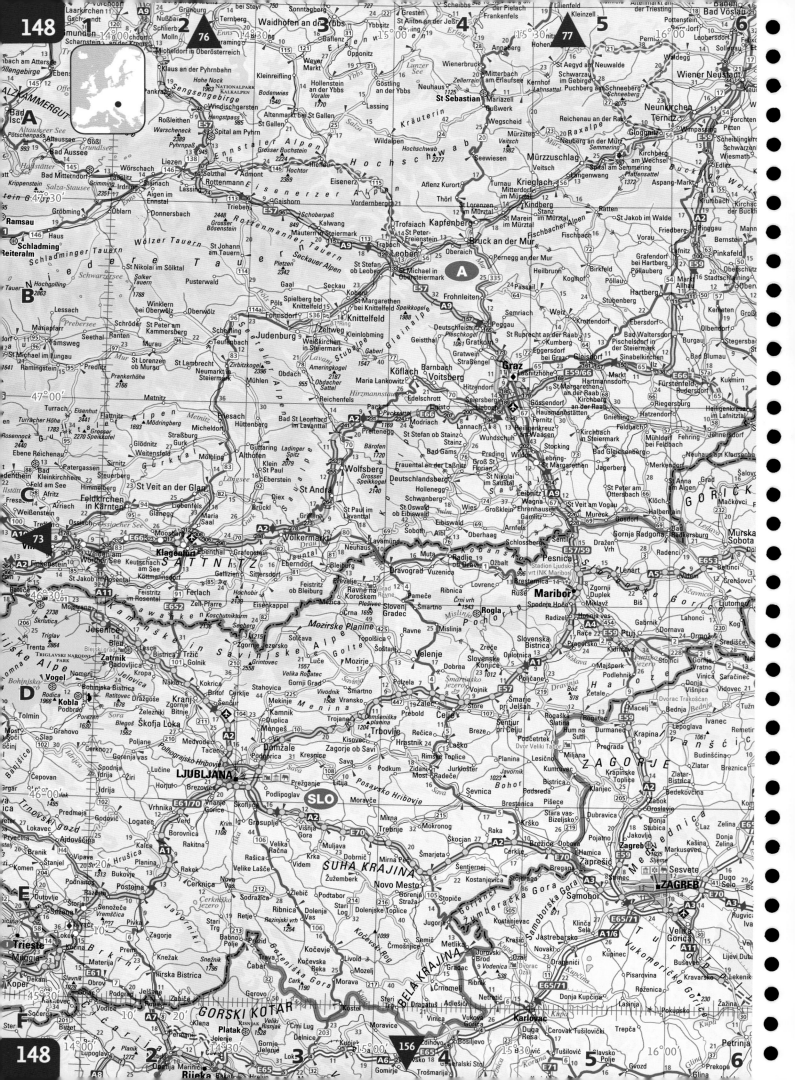

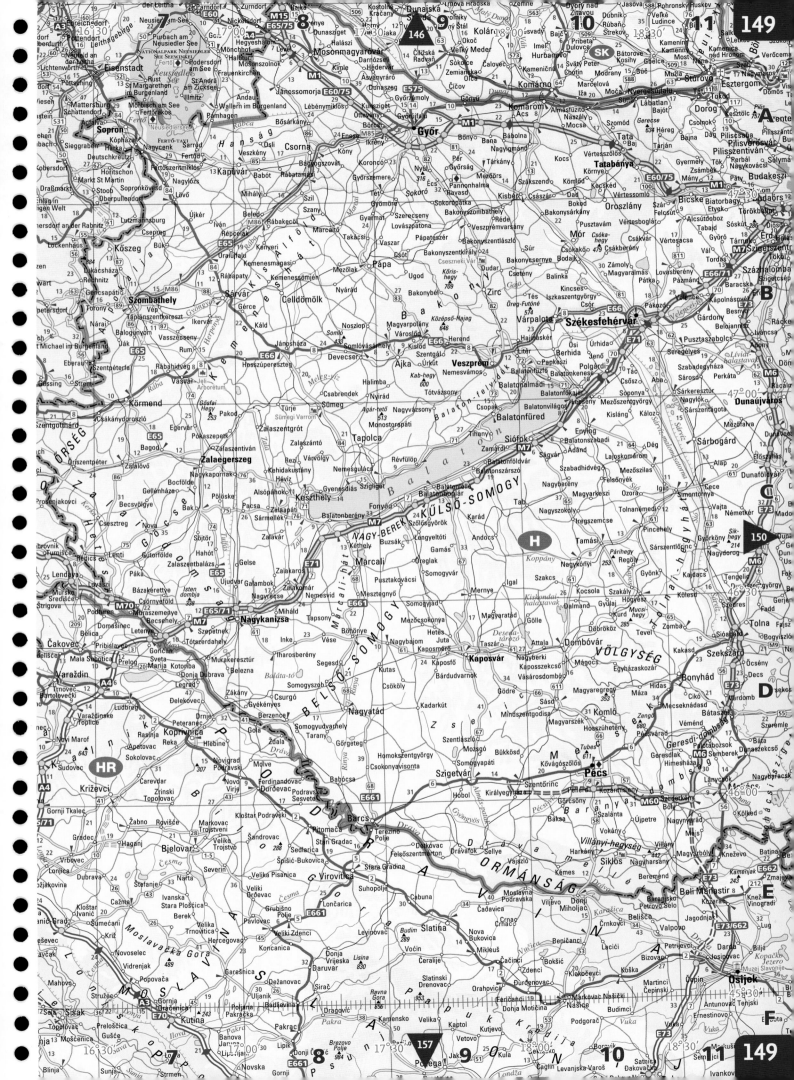

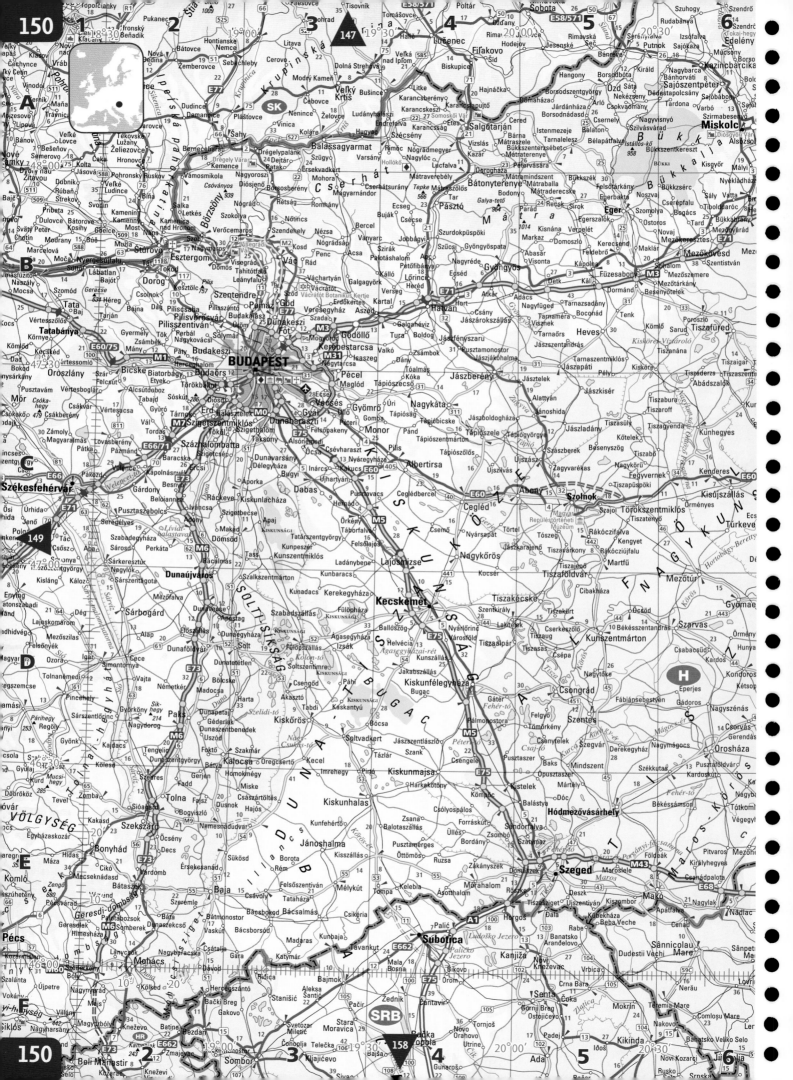

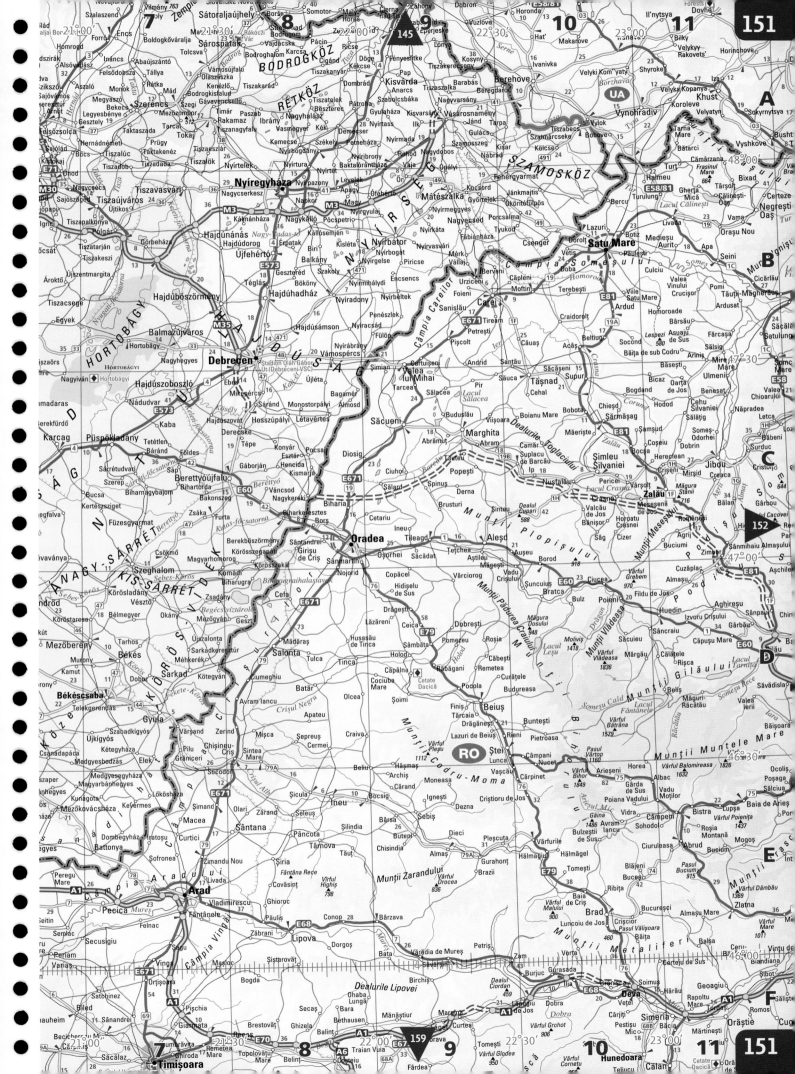

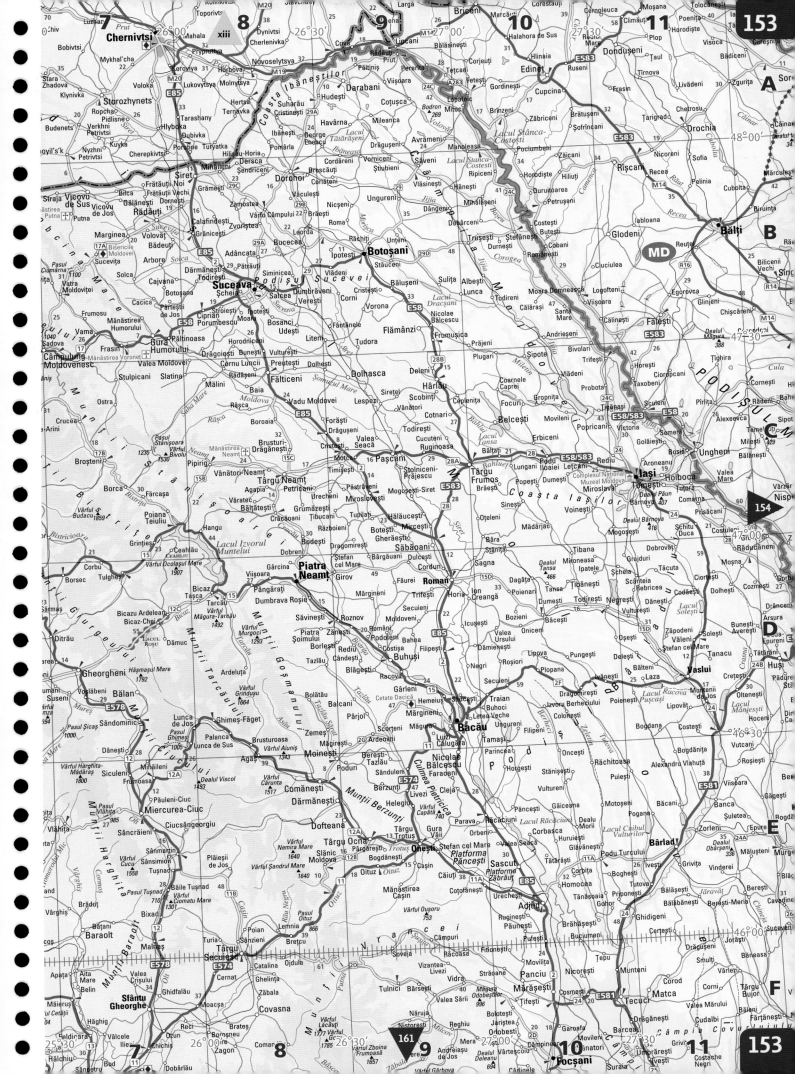

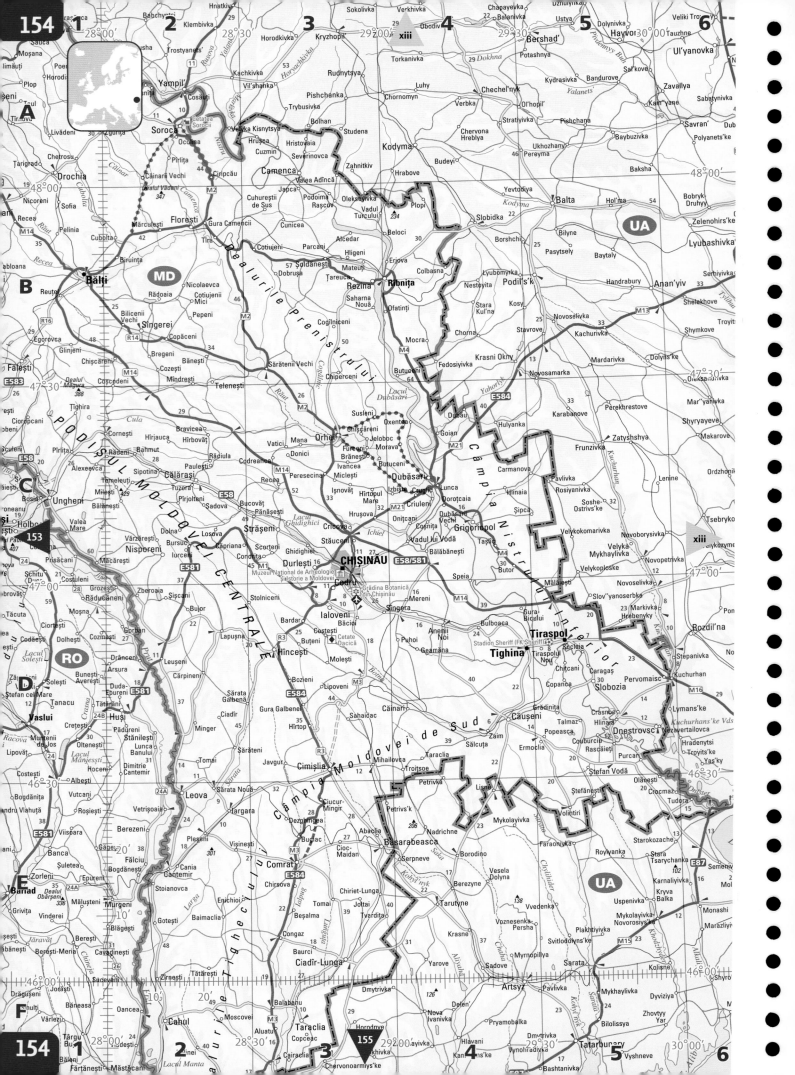

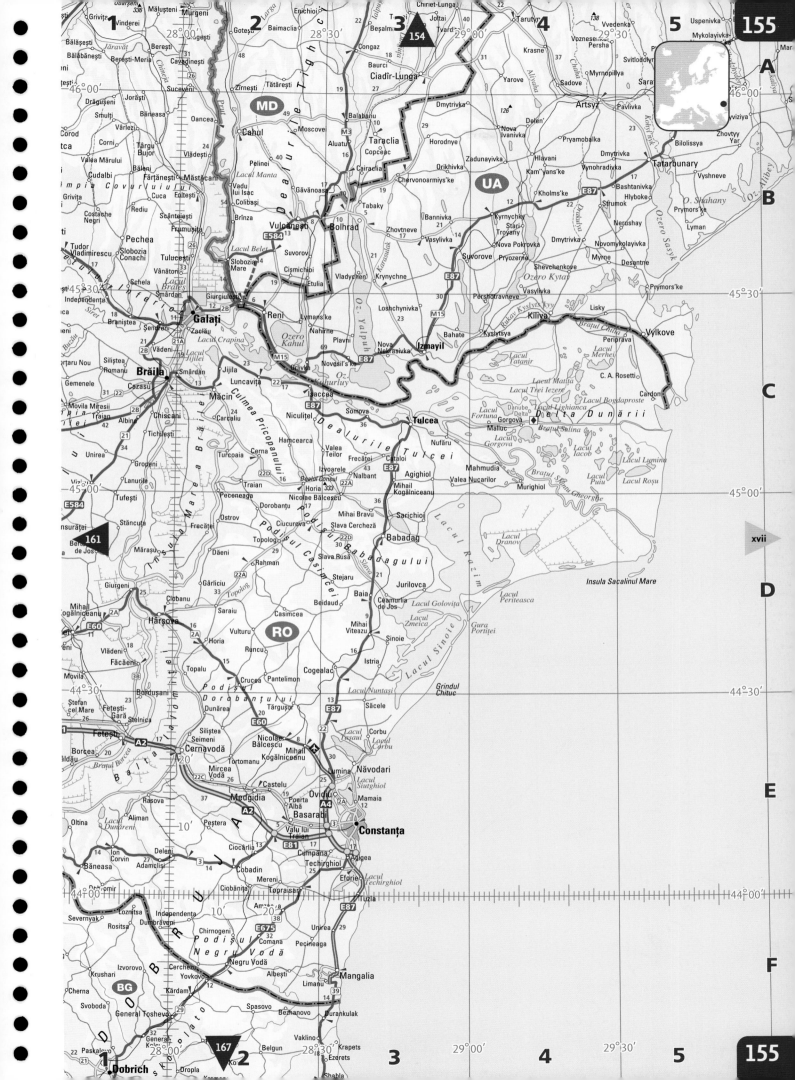

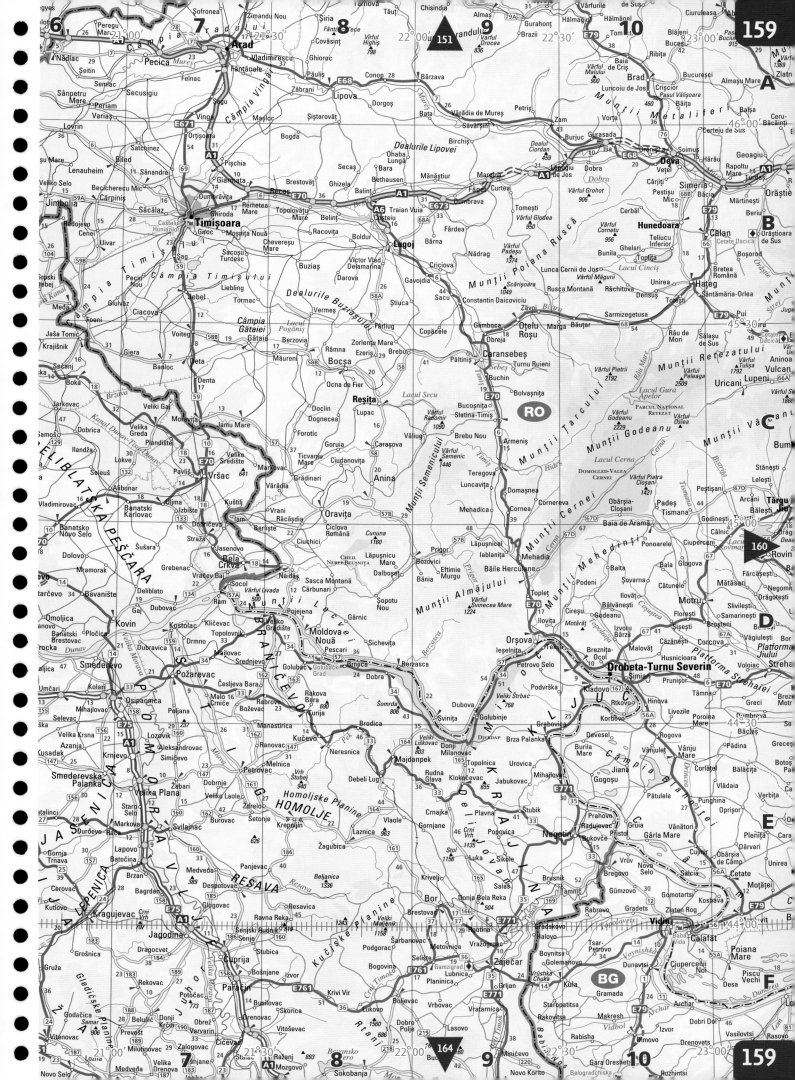

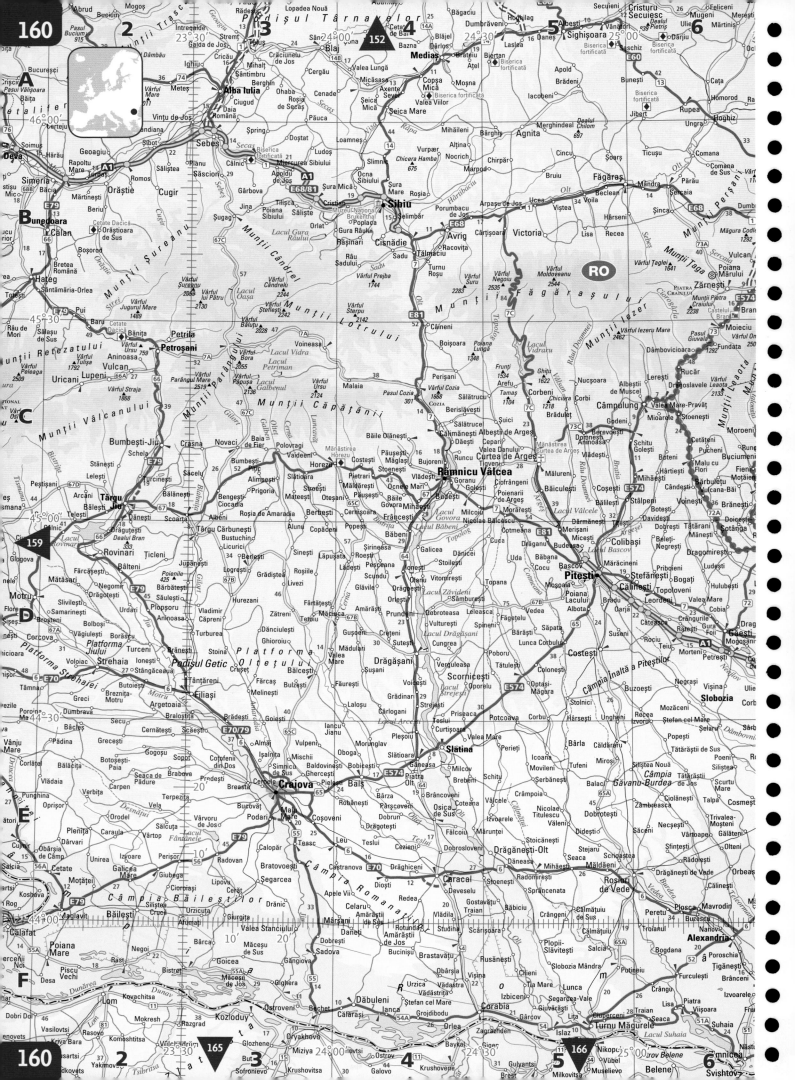

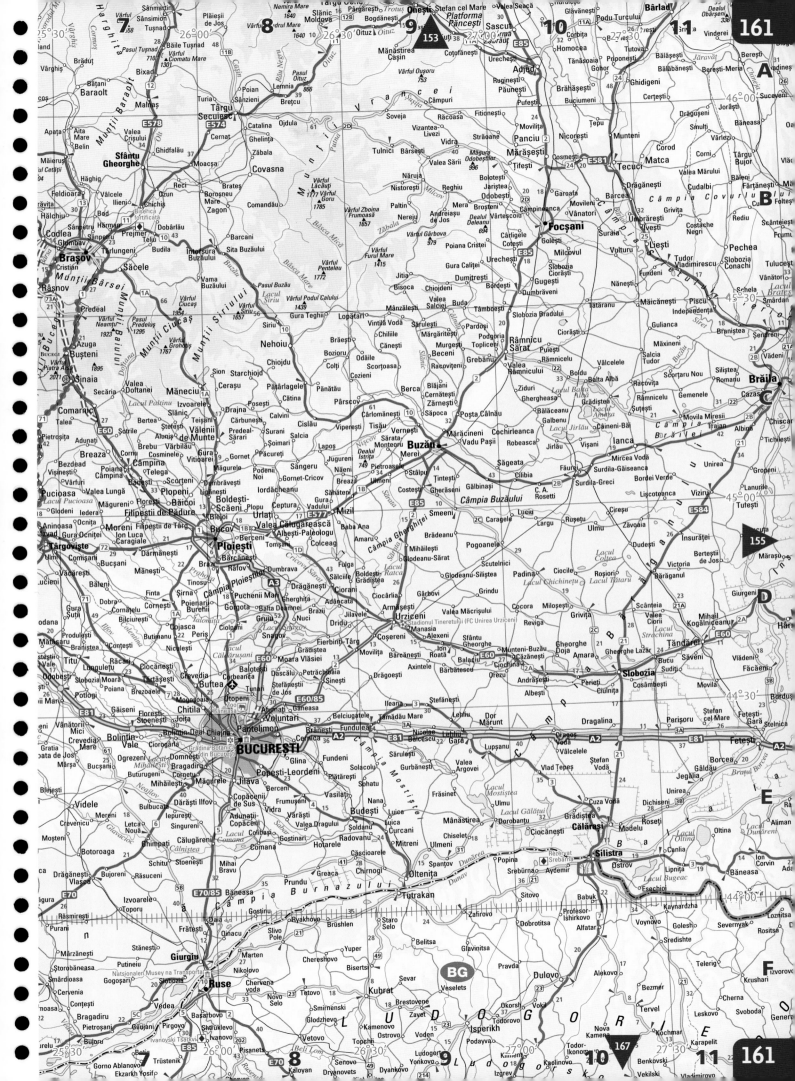

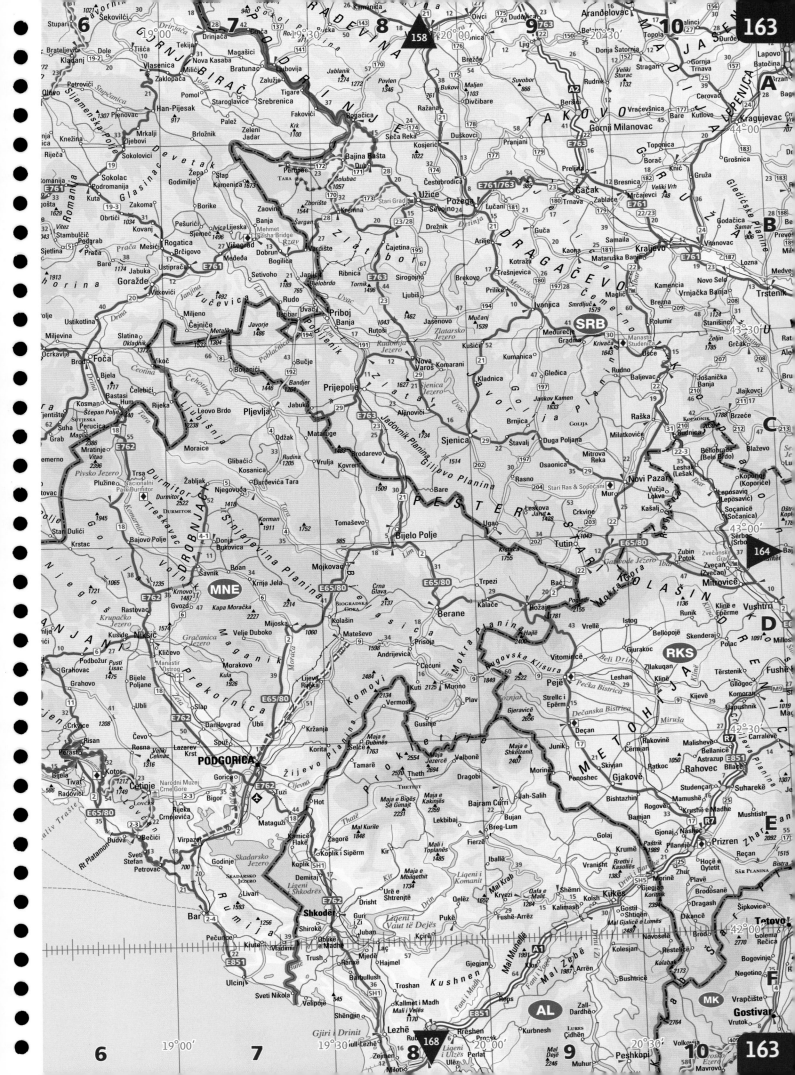

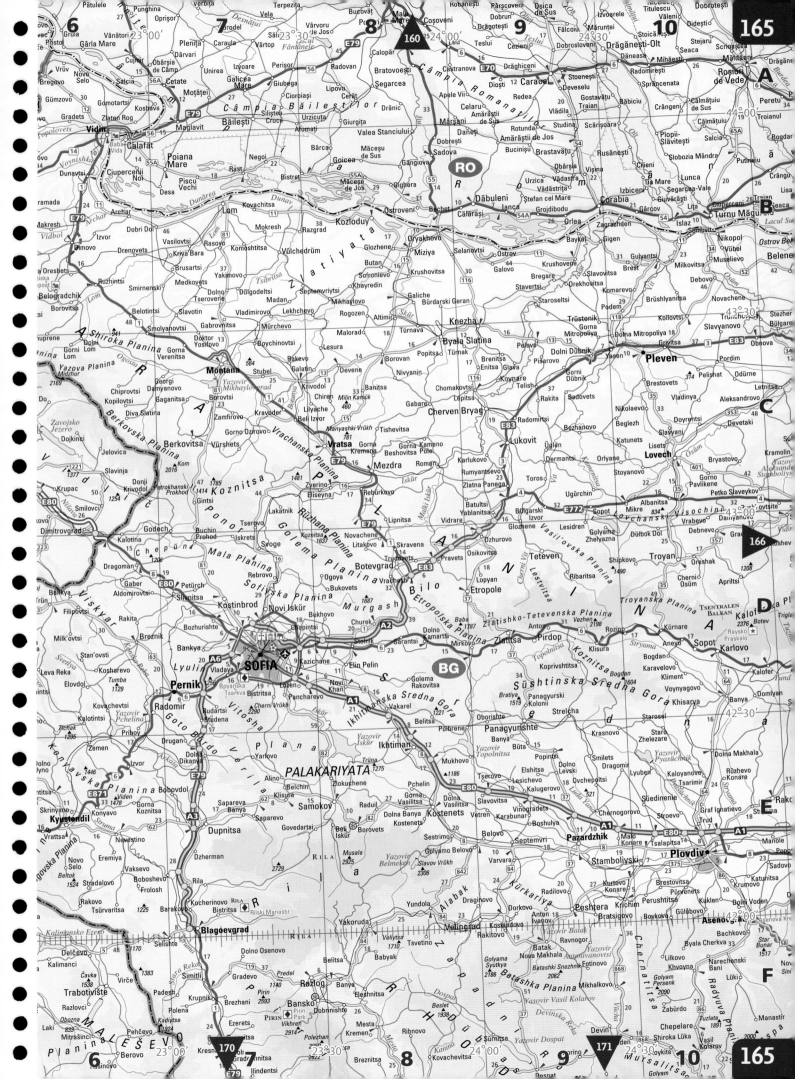

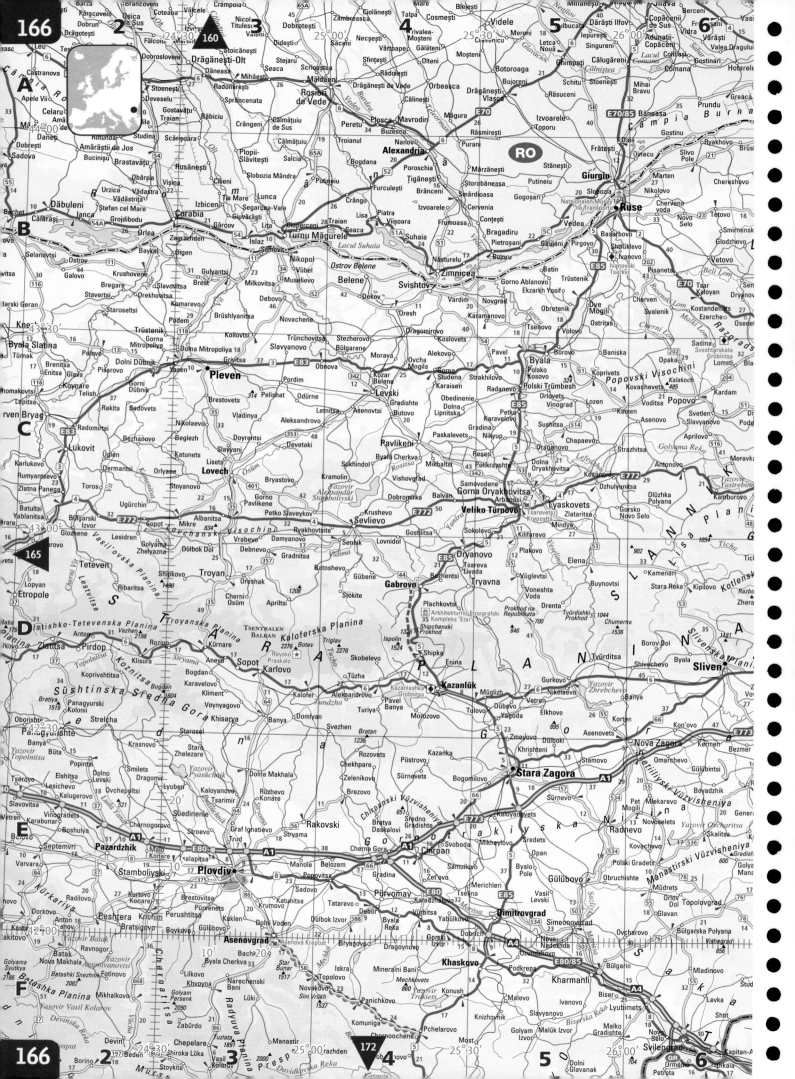

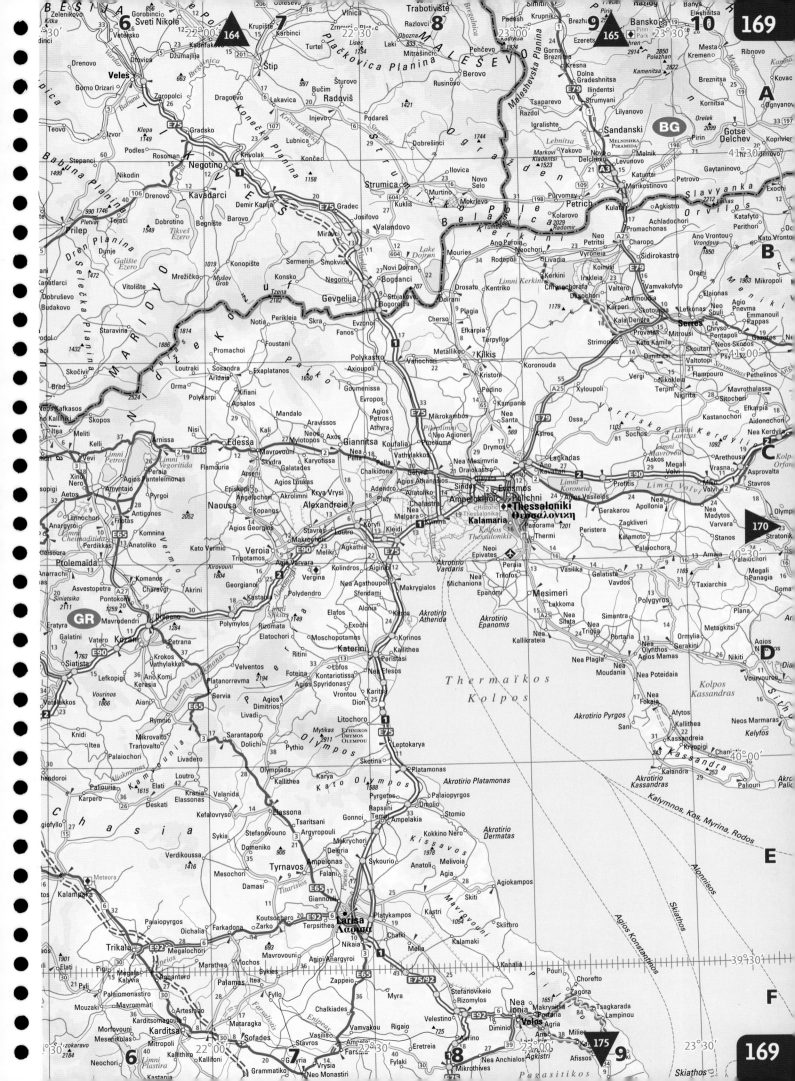

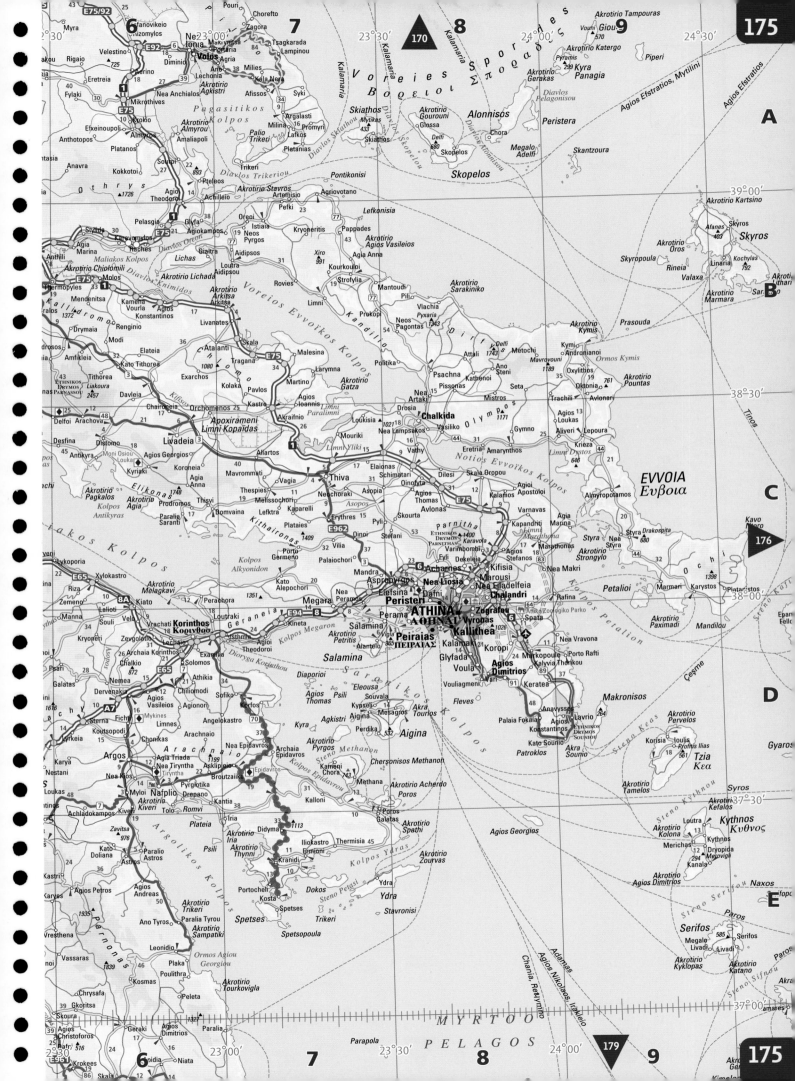

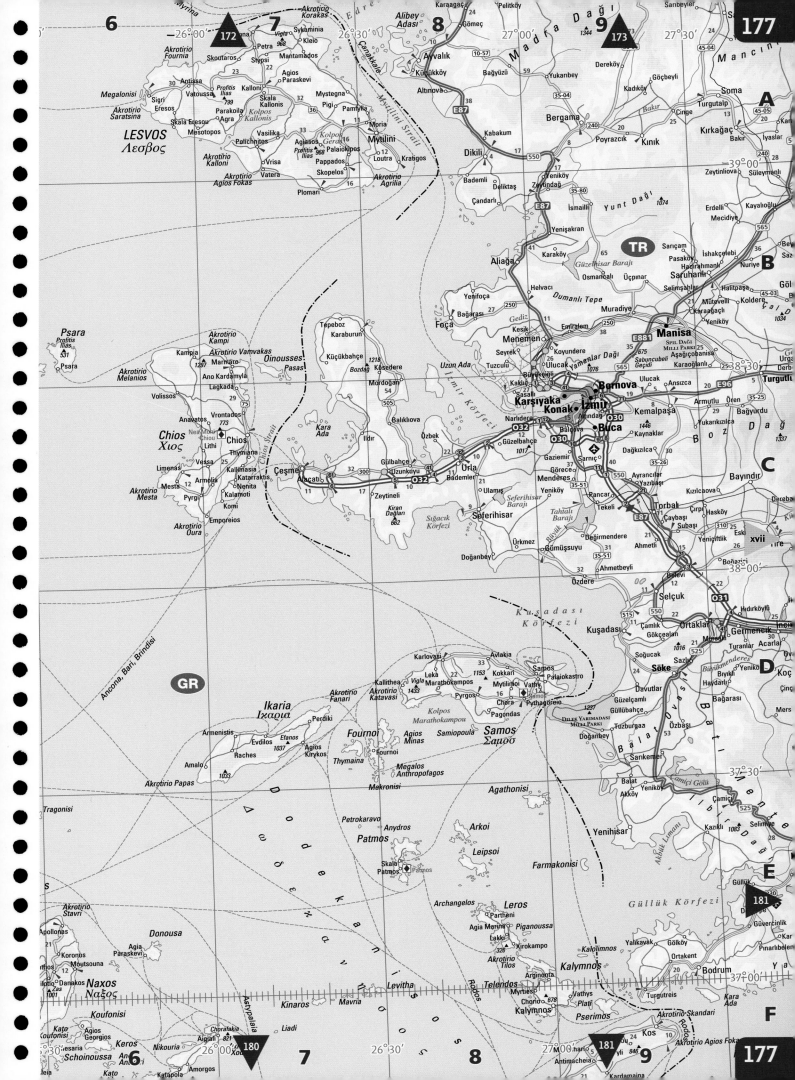

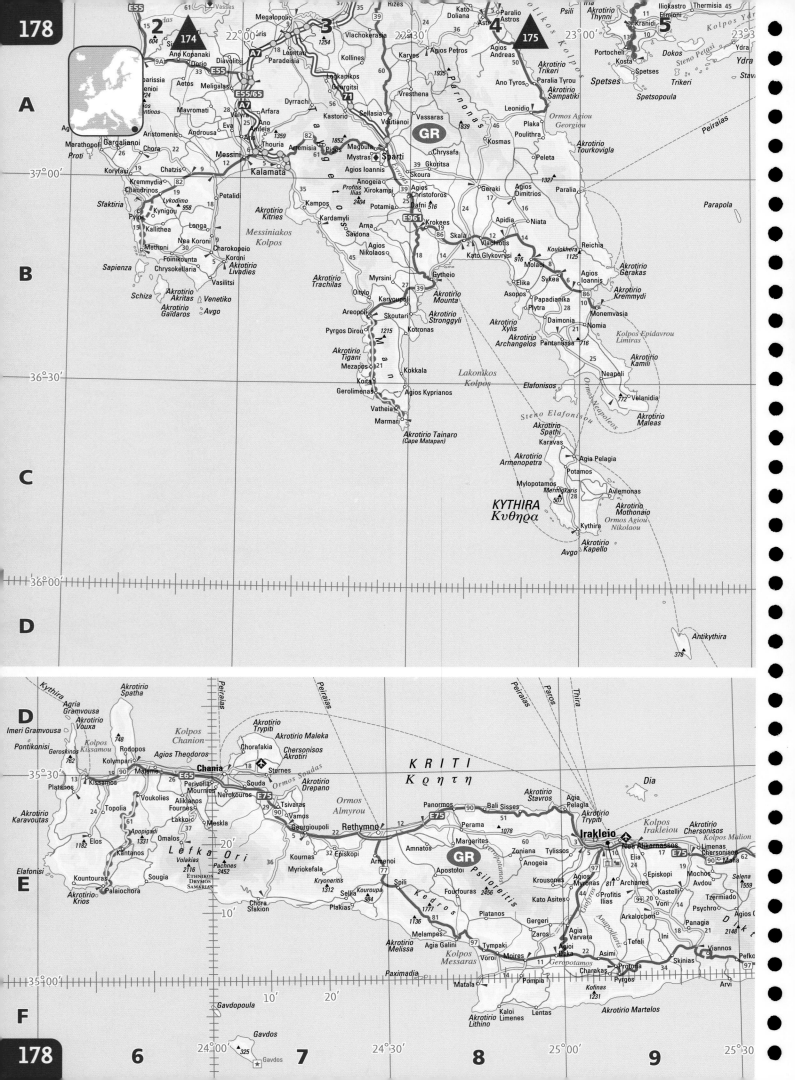

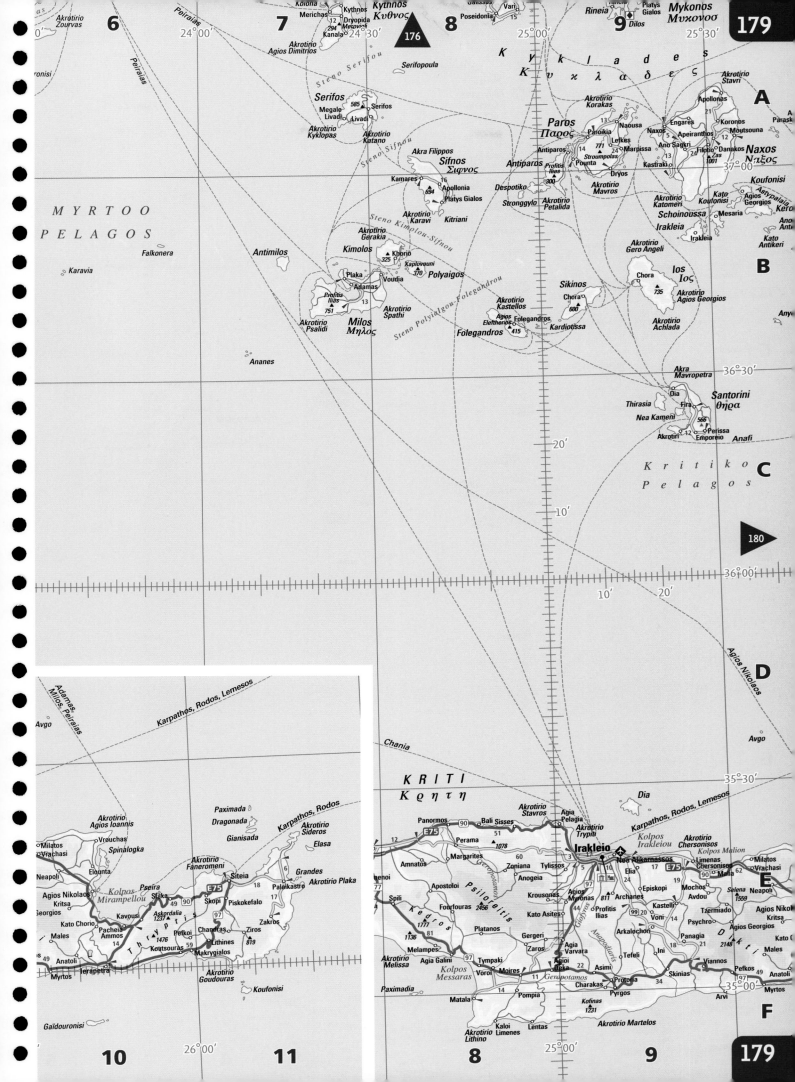

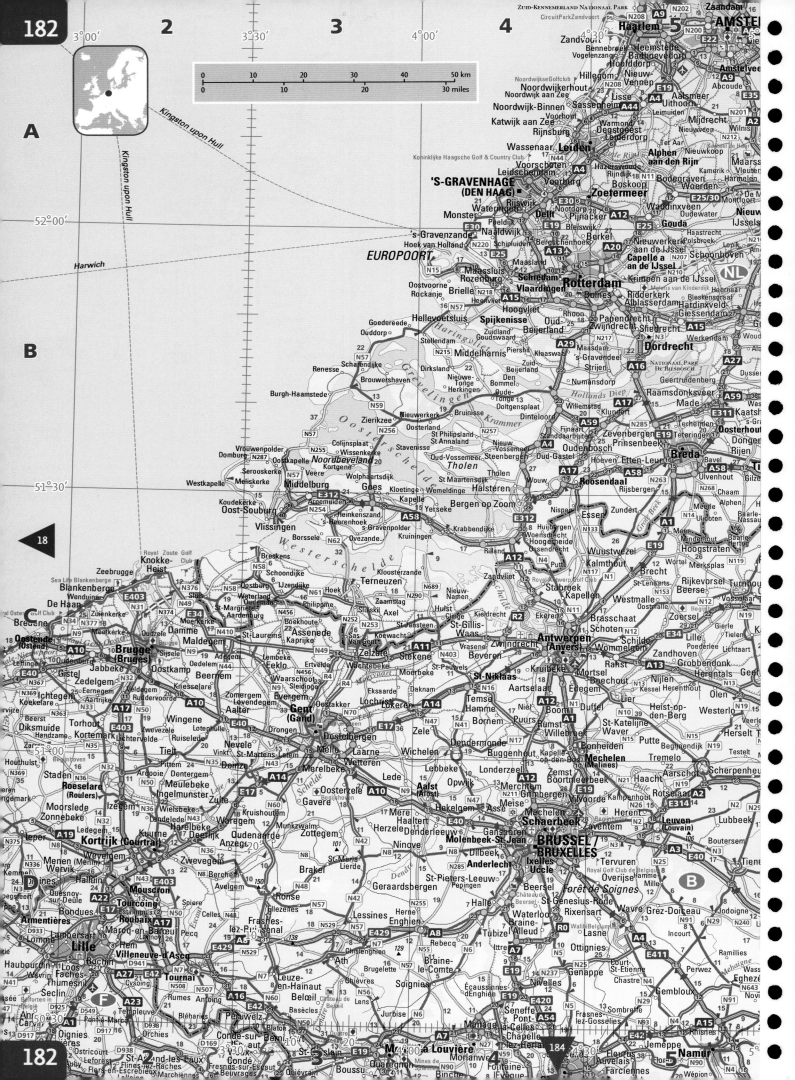

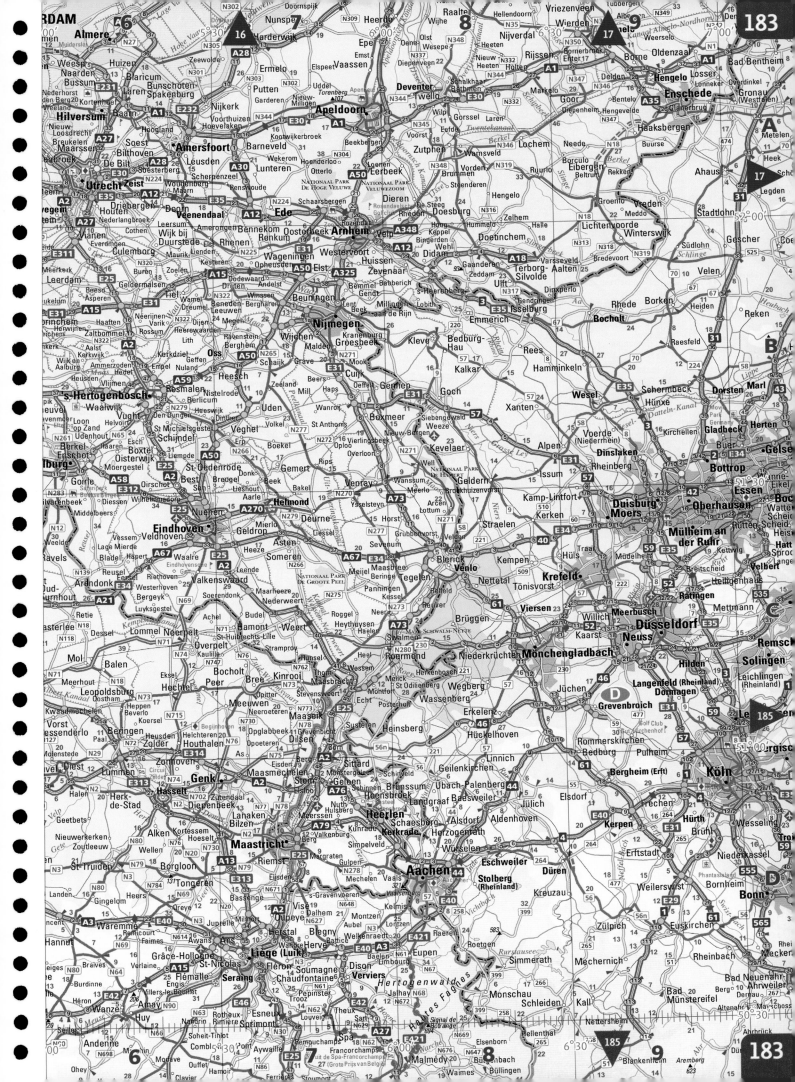

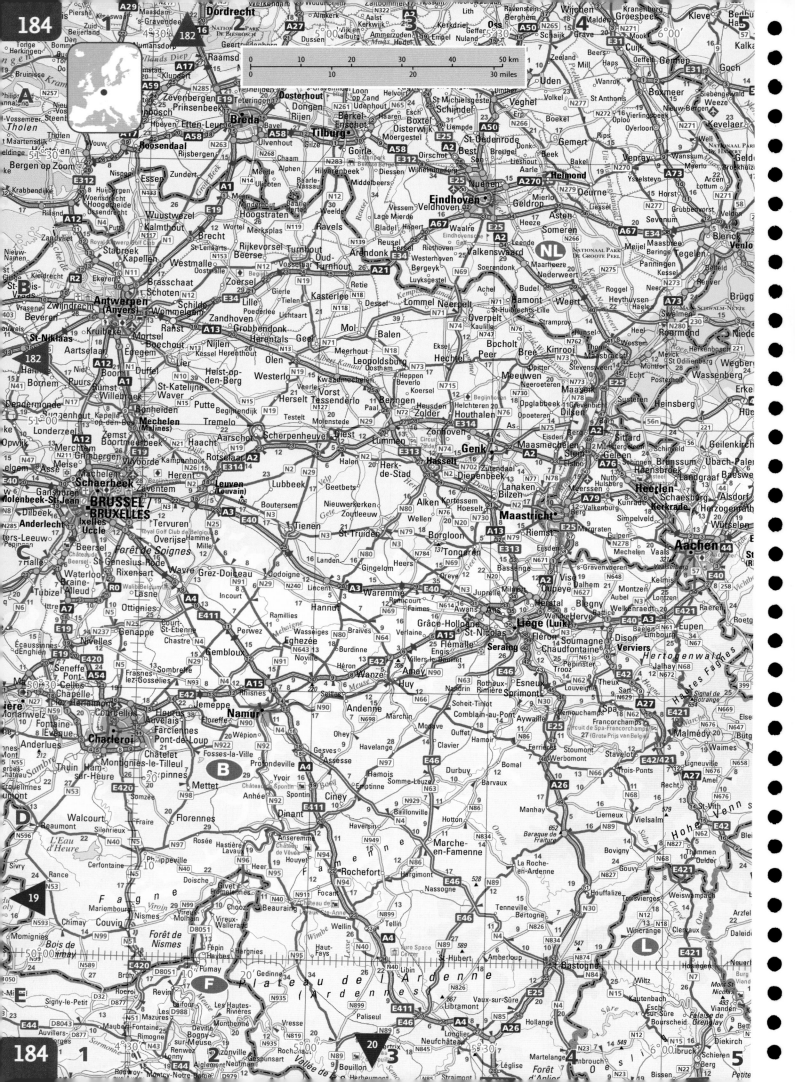

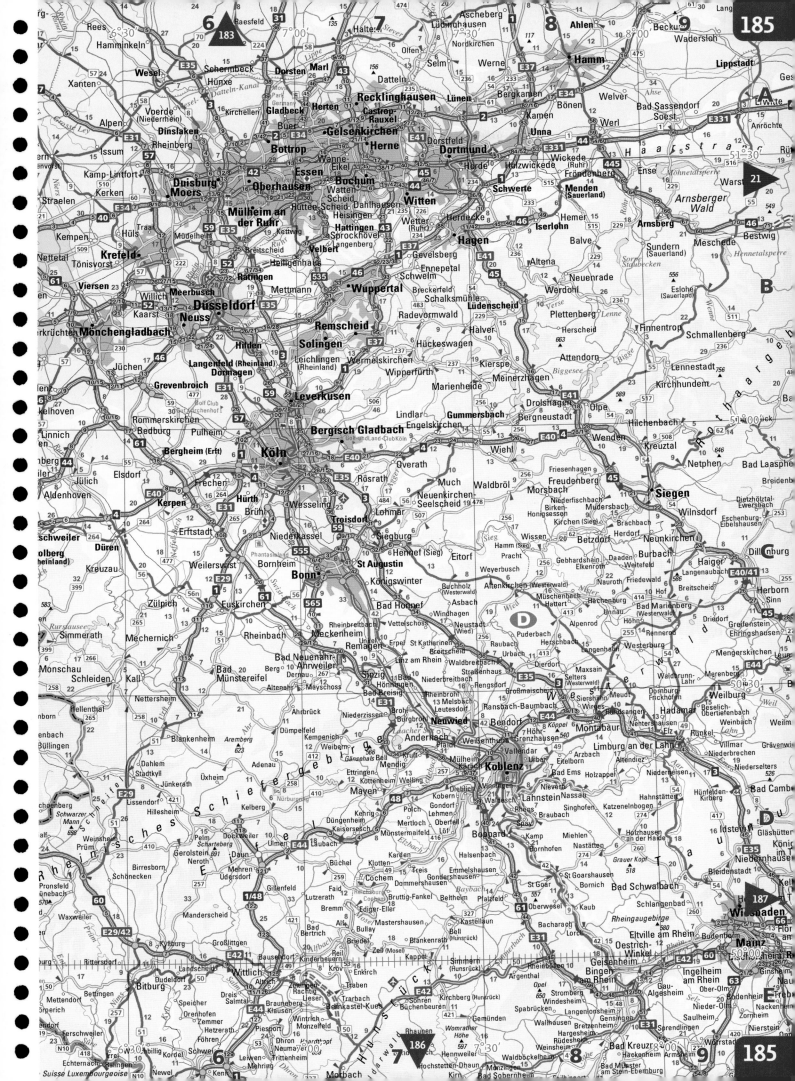

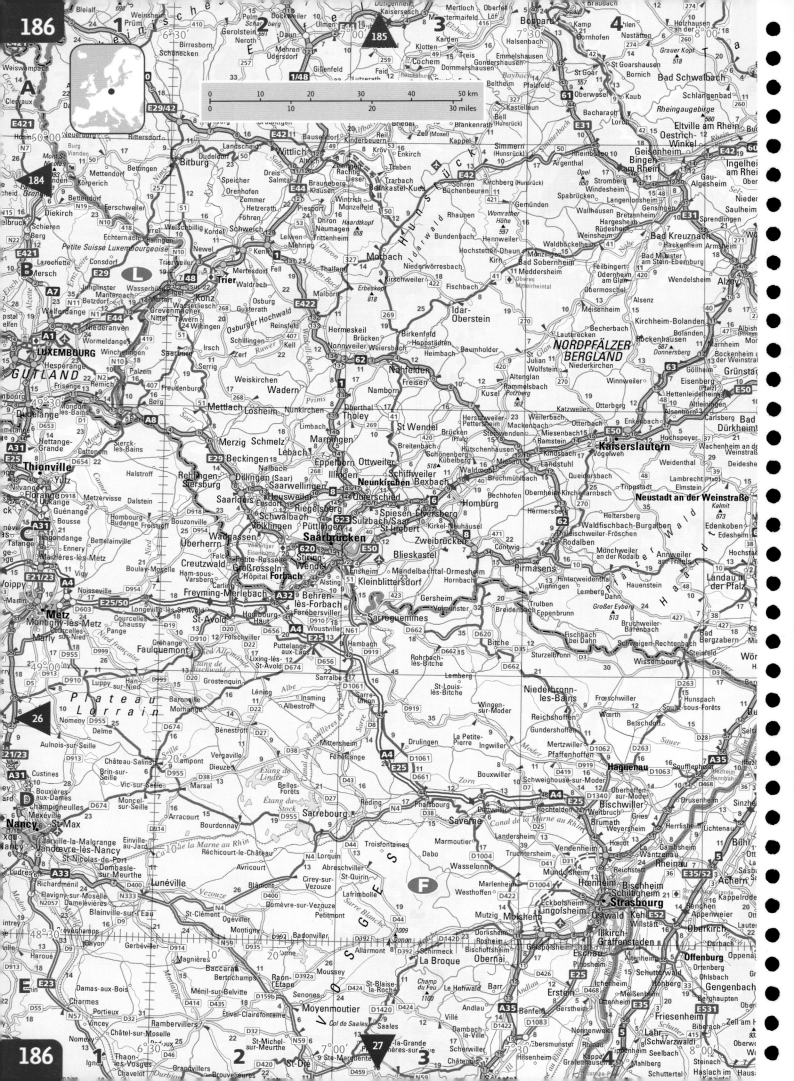

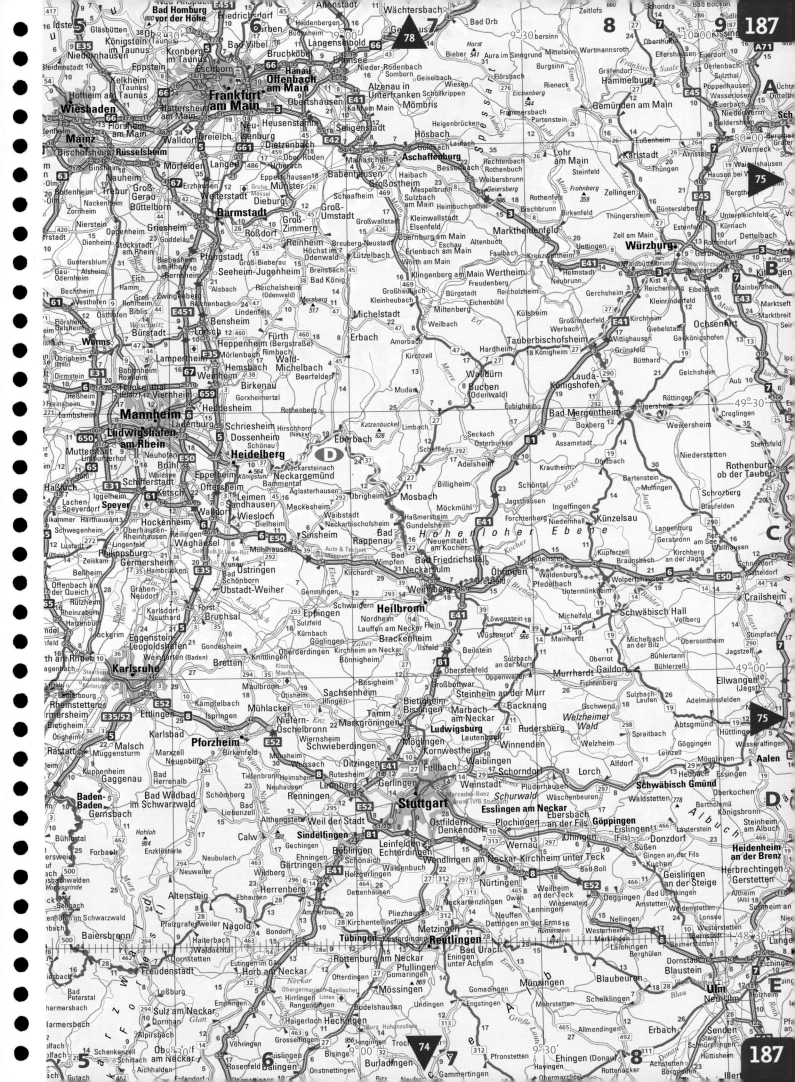

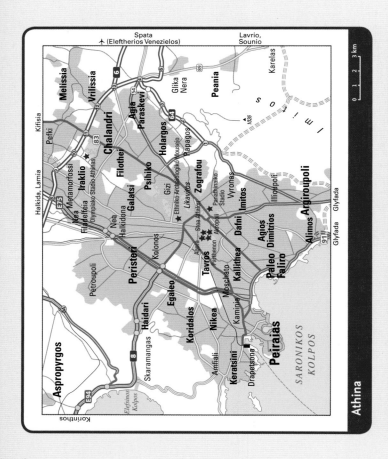

Athina

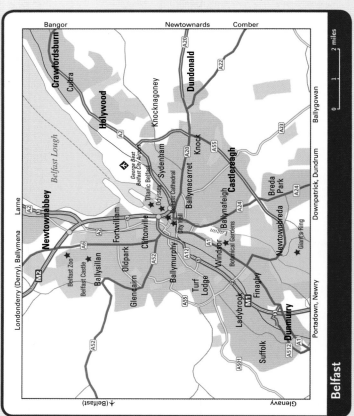

Belfast

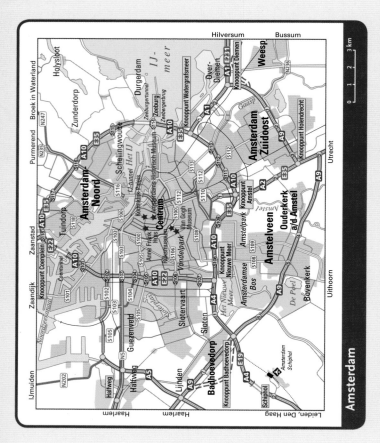

Amsterdam

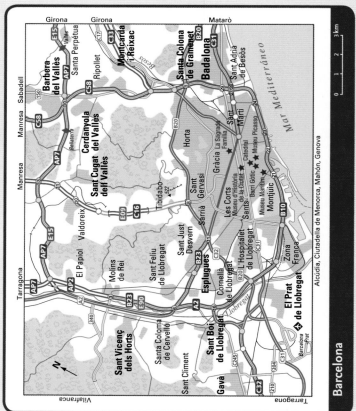

Barcelona

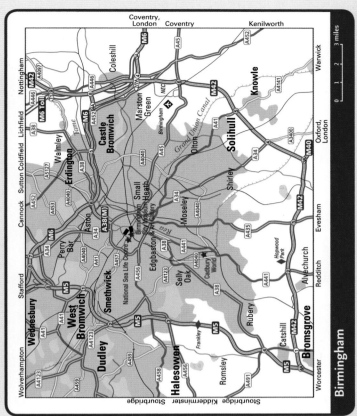

Berlin

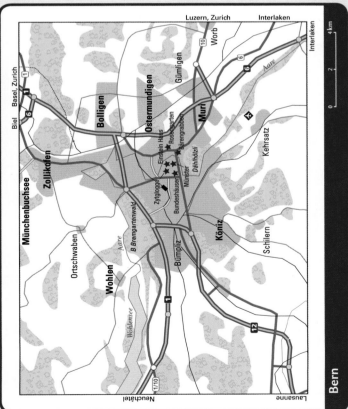

Birmingham

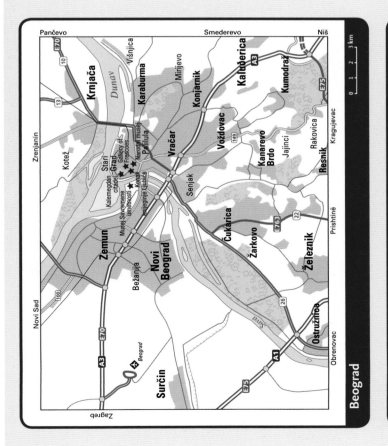

Beograd

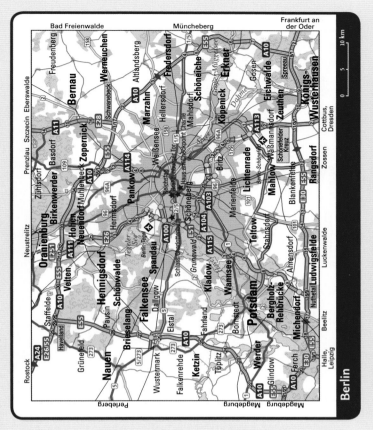

Bern

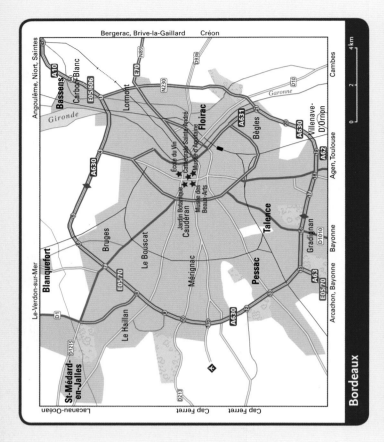

Bonn

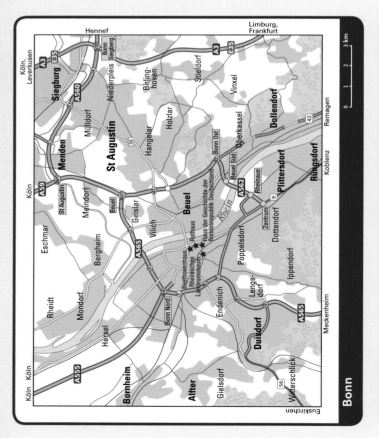

Bordeaux

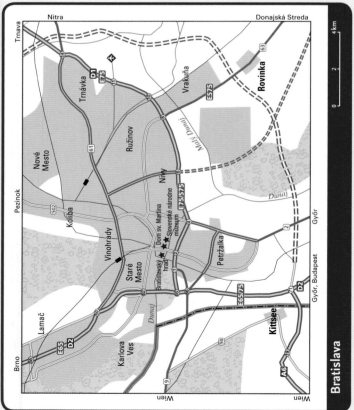

Brussel/Bruxelles

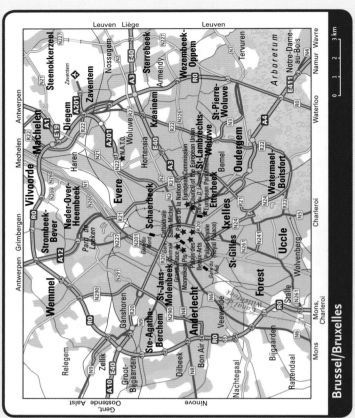

Bratislava

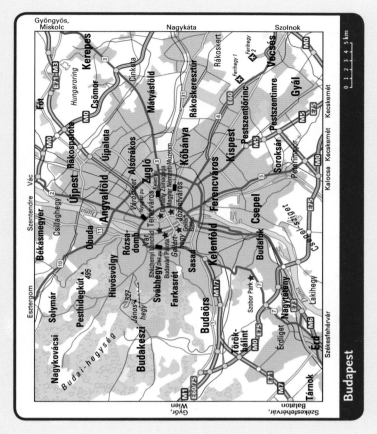

Budapest

Gyöngyös, Miskolc
Nagykáta
Szolnok

Kerepes
Csömör
Fót
Kerepes
Mátyásföld
Rákoskert
Vecsés
Rákospalota
Rákoskeresztúr
Gyál
Újpest
Újpalota
Kőbánya
Pestszentőrinc
Pestszentimre
Kispest
Soroksár
Angyalföld
Zugló
Ferencváros
Csepel
Békásmegyer
Óbuda
Rózsa-domb
Kelenföld
Budafok
Hűvösvölgy
Sasad
Nagytétény
Solymár
Svábhegy
Farkasrét
Budakeszi
Budaörs
Érd
Nagykovácsi
Török-bálint
Tárnok
Budai-hegység
Gyór, Wien
Balaton
Székesfehérvár

Szentendre
Vác
Esztergom
Kalocsa Kecskemét
Kecskemét

km
0 1 2 3 4 5km

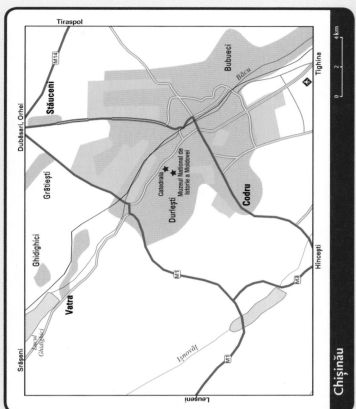

Chişinău

Tiraspol
Bubueci
Stăuceni
Băcu
Tighina
Dubăsari, Orhei
Grătieşti
Durleşti
Codru
Ghidighici
Catedrala
Muzeul Naţional de Istorie a Moldovei
Sărăseni
Iacul Ghidighici
Vatra
Isnovăţ
Leuşeni
Hinceşti

km
0 2 4km

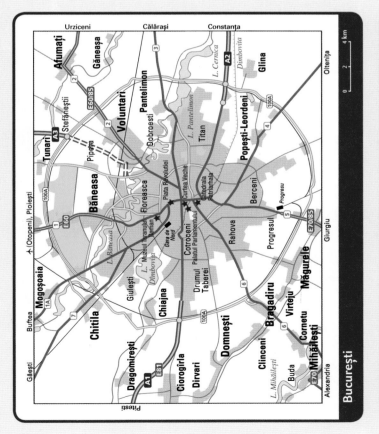

Bucureşti

Urziceni
Călăraşi
Constanţa
Afumaţi
Găneasa
Tunari
Voluntari
Pantelimon
Glina
Ştefăneşti
L. Cernica
Dâmboviţa
L. Pantelimon
Pipera
Dobroeşti
Oltenţa
Băneasa
Floreasca
Titan
Popeşti-Leordeni
(Otopeni), Ploieşti
Piaţa Revoluţiei
Curtea Veche
Berceni
Progresu
Muzeul Ţăranului Român
Catedrala Patriarhală
Magoşoaia
Cotroceni
Palatul Parlamentului
Rahova
Gara de Nord
Progresul
Giuleşti
Drumul Taberei
Chitila
Chiajna
Bragadiru
Virţeju
Măgurele
Domneşti
Dragomireşti
Cornetu
Mihăileşti
Clinceni
Buda
Ciorogârla
Dirvari
L. Mihăileşti
Buftea
Găeşti
Pieteşti
Alexandria
Giurgiu

km
0 2 4km

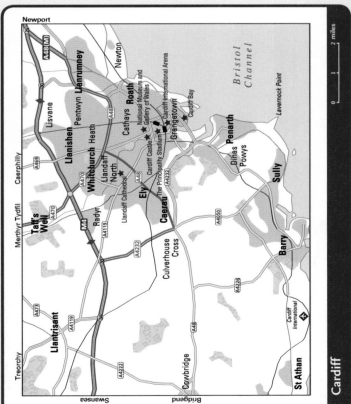

Cardiff

Newport
Bristol Channel
A48(M)
Newton
Lisvane
Llanrumney
Caerphilly
Pentwyn
Roath
Llanishen
Cathays
National Museum and Gallery of Wales
Cardiff International Arena
Whitchurch Heath
Cardiff Bay
Lavernock Point
Llandaff North
Cardiff Castle
Grangetown
Merthyr Tydfil
Radyr
Llandaff Cathedral
The Principality Stadium
Ely
Dinas Powys
Penarth
Caerau
Sully
Taff's Well
Culverhouse Cross
Barry
Llantrisant
Gwbridge
St Athan
Cardiff International
Treorchy
Bridgend
Swansea

miles
0 1 2 miles

195

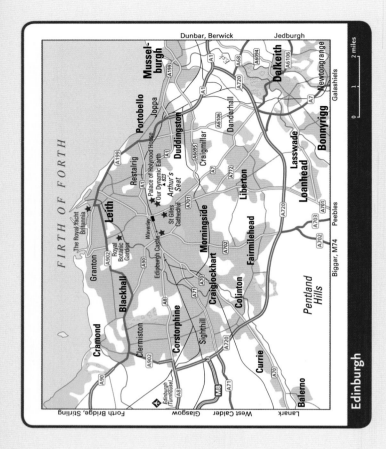

Edinburgh

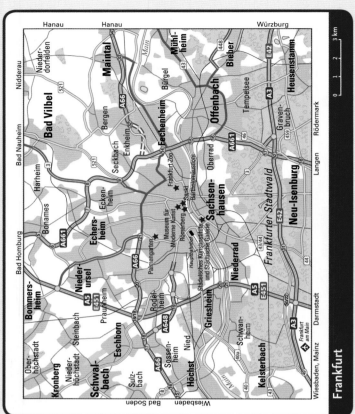

Frankfurt

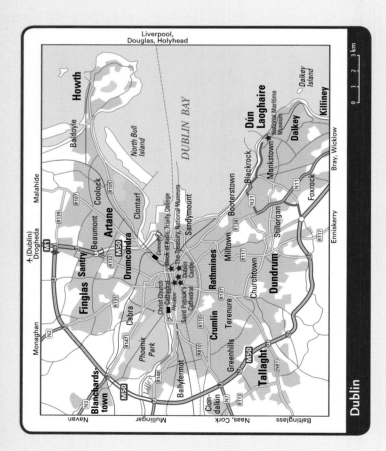

Dublin

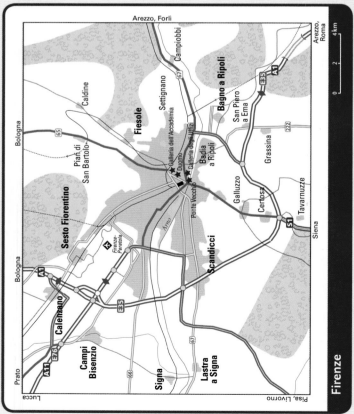

Firenze

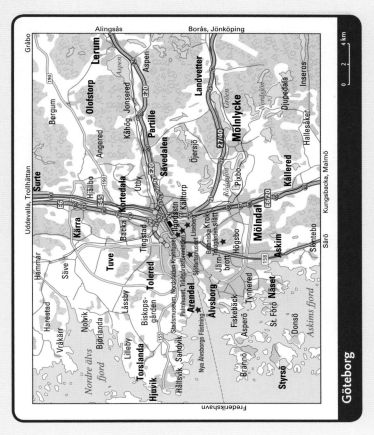

Göteborg

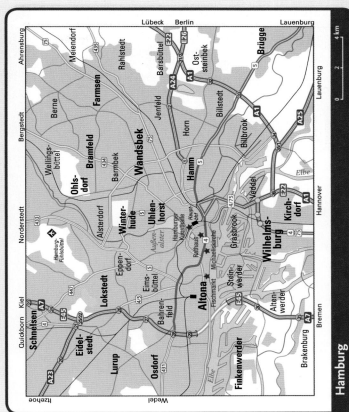

Hamburg

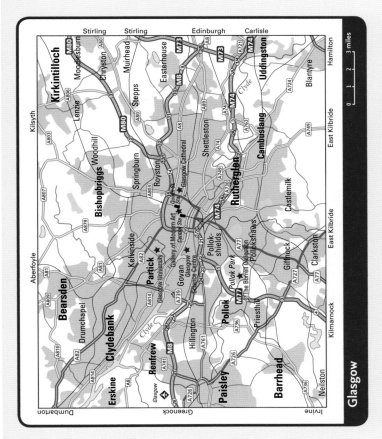

Glasgow

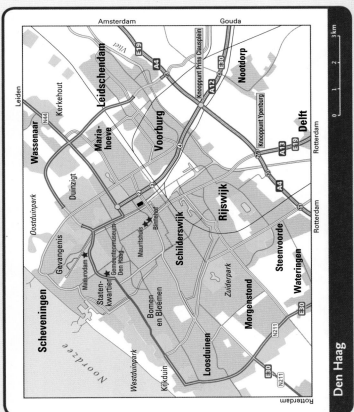

Den Haag

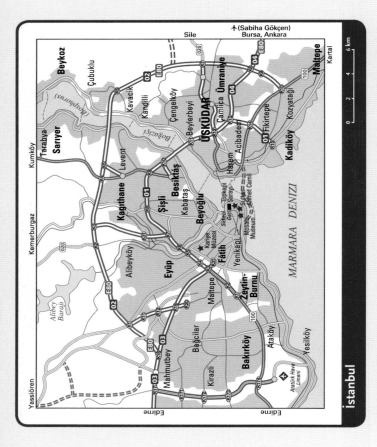

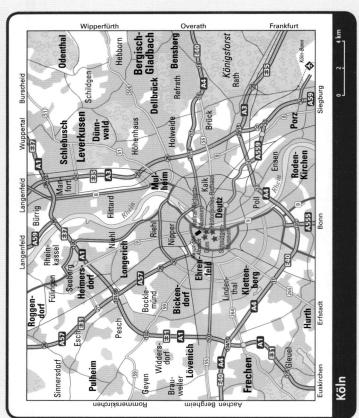

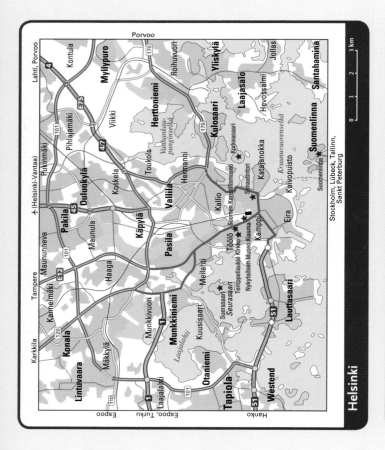

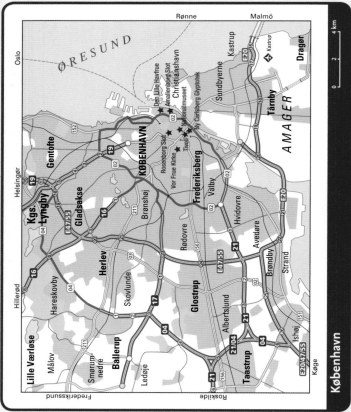

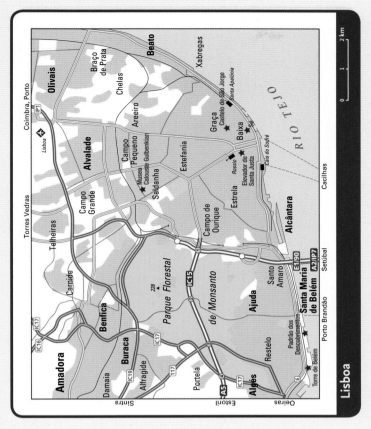

Lisboa

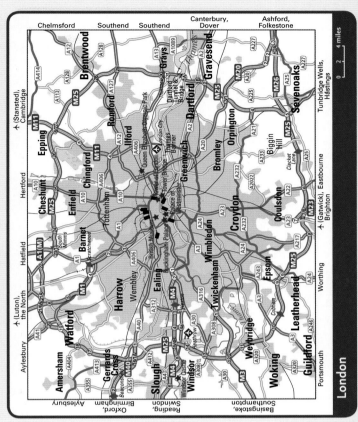

London

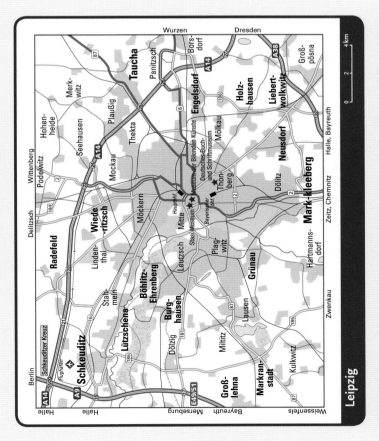

Leipzig

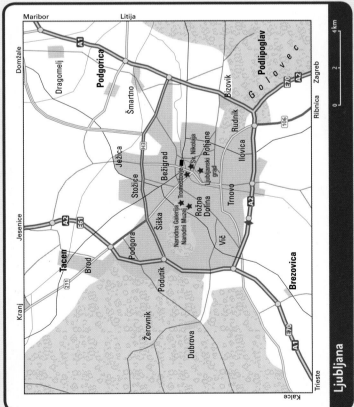

Ljubljana

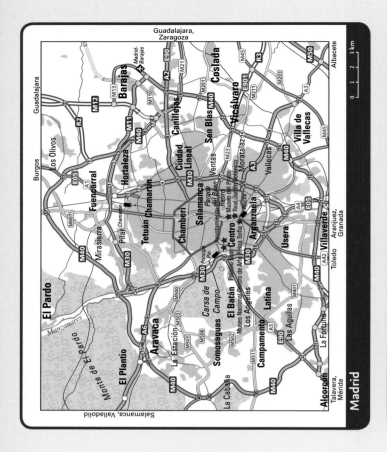

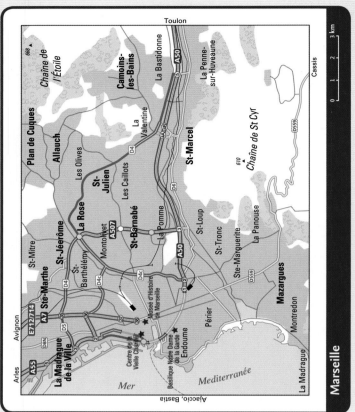

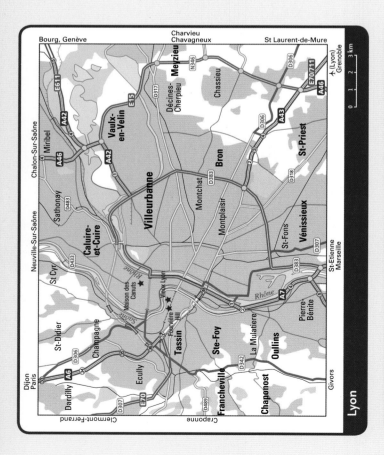

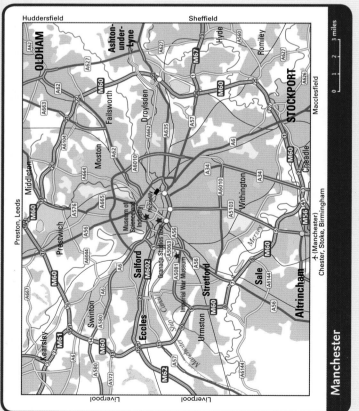

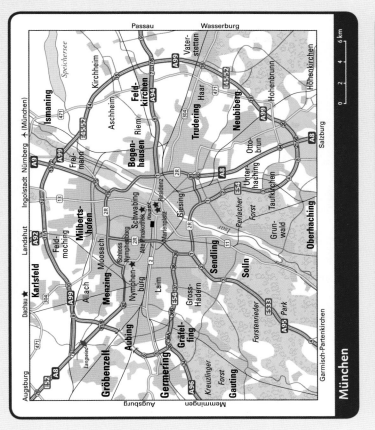

München

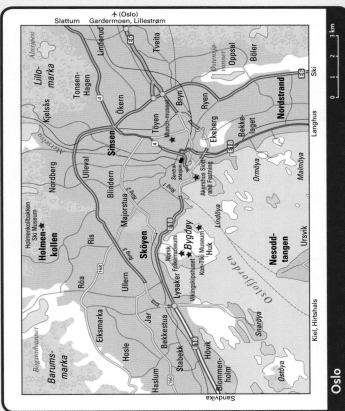

Oslo

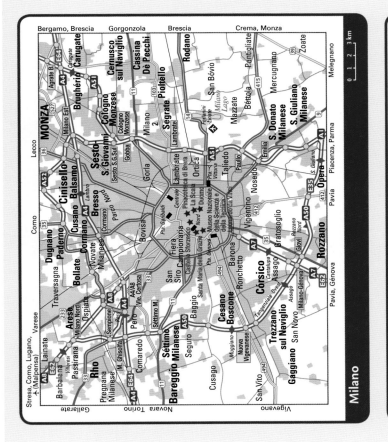

Milano

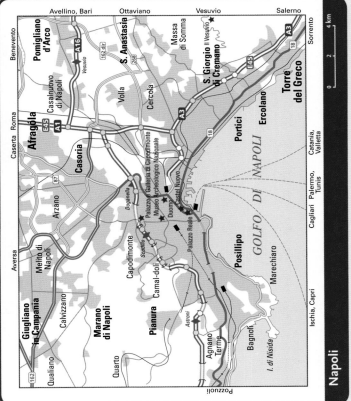

Napoli

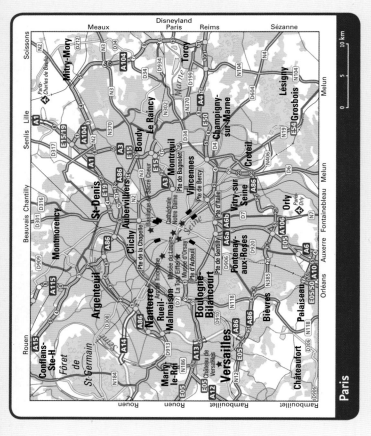

Paris

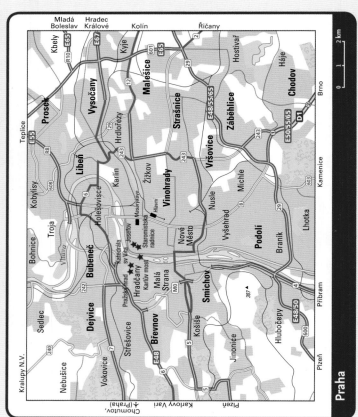

Praha

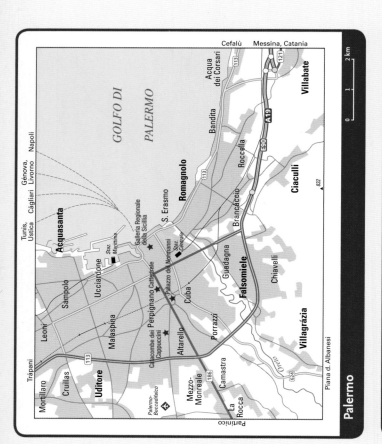

Palermo

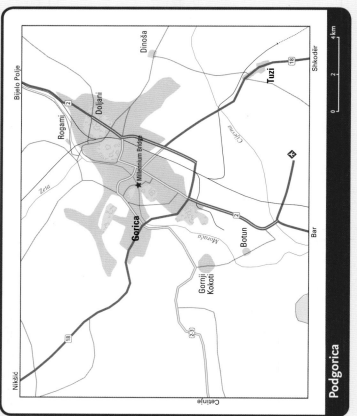

Podgorica

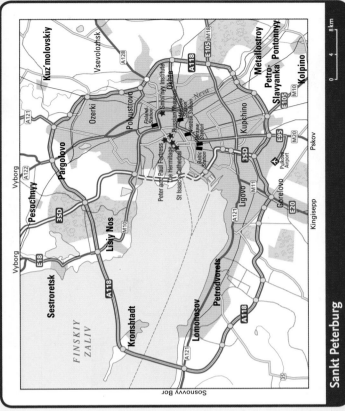

Roma

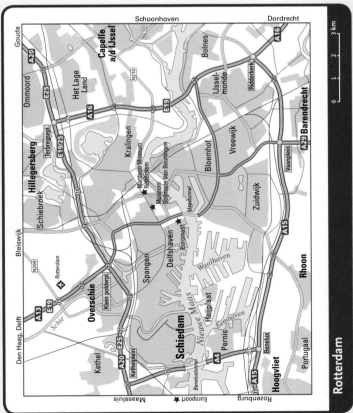

Sankt Peterburg

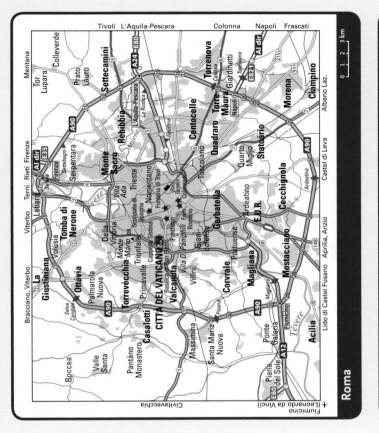

Rīga

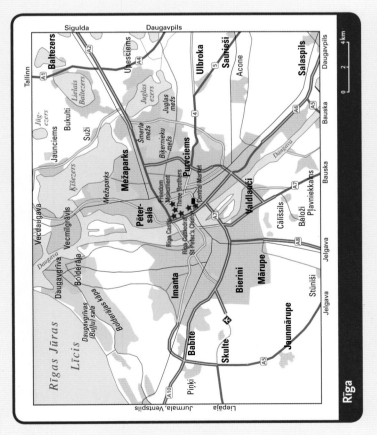

Rotterdam

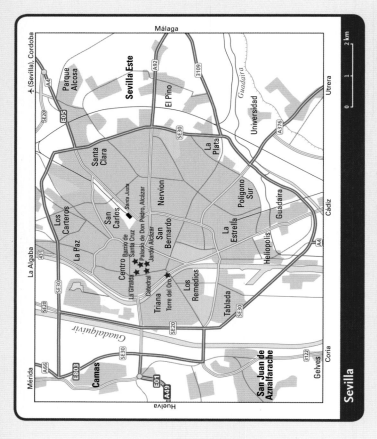

Sevilla

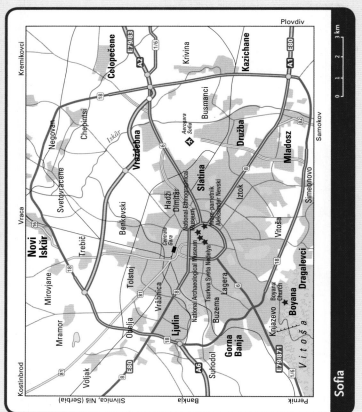

Sofia

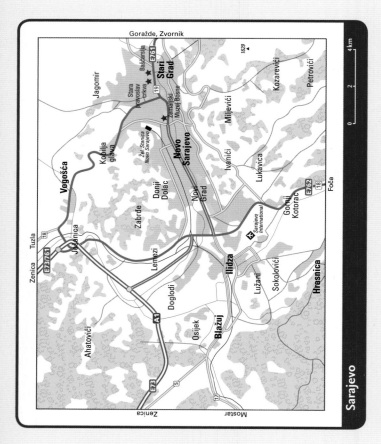

Sarajevo

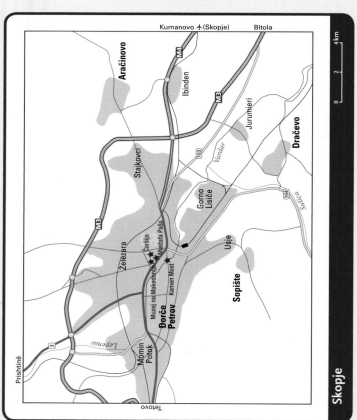

Skopje

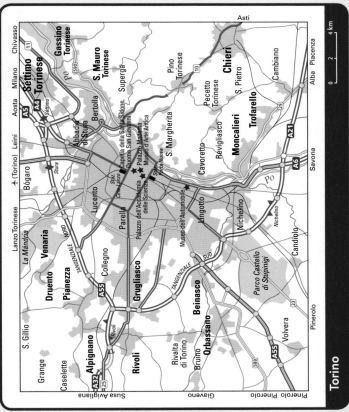

Strasbourg

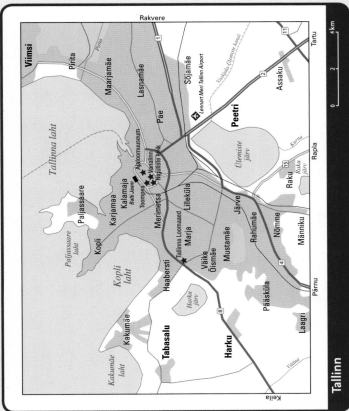

Torino

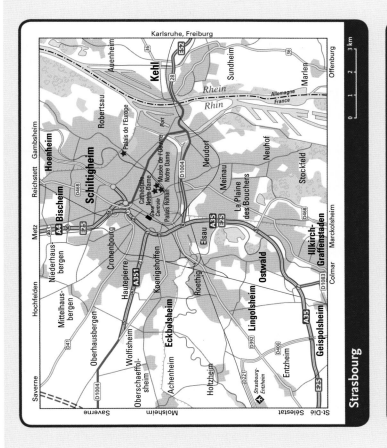

Stockholm

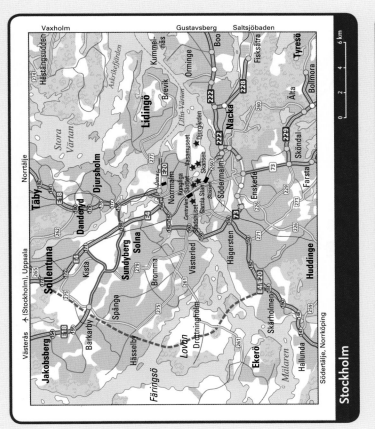

Tallinn

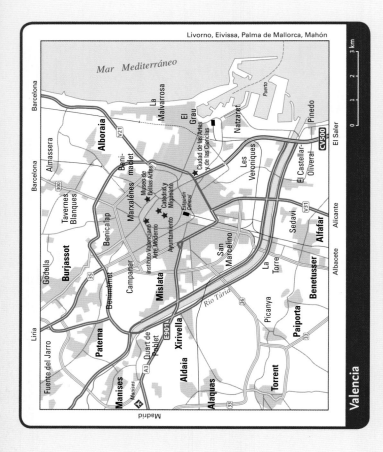

Valencia

Livorno, Eivissa, Palma de Mallorca, Mahón

Mar Mediterráneo

Barcelona · Barcelona · Almassera · Godella · Fuente del Jarro · Liria · Paterna · Manises · Madrid · Aldaia · Alaquas · Torrent · Xirivella · Quart de Poblet · Tavernes Blanques · Alboraia · Benimàmet · Campanar · Benicalap · Mislata · Burjassot · Marxalénes · Benimaclet · Beni-maclet · Ayuntamiento · Instituto Valenciano Arte Moderno · Museo de Bellas Artes · Catedral y Miguelete · Ciudad de las Artes y de las Ciencias · Estación Central · La Malvarrosa · El Grau · Natzaret · Puerto · Les Veroniques · El Castellar-Oliveral · San Marcelino · La Torre · Sedavi · Picanya · Paiporta · Benetusser · Alfafar · Pinedo · El Saler · Albacete · Alicante · CV500 · V21 · V31

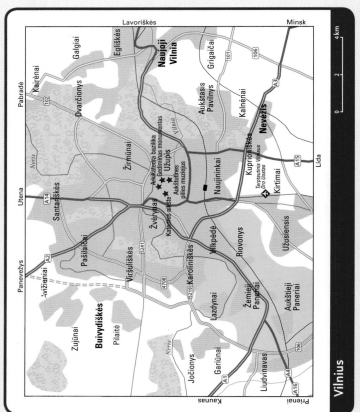

Vilnius

Lavoriškės · Minsk

Pabradè · Kairenai · Galgiai · Eglišķes · Dvarčionys · Naujoji Vilnia · Grigaičiai · Nevėžis · Lida · Aukštasis Pavilnys · Kalnėnai · Utena · Žirmūnai · Arkikatedra bazilika Gedimino monumentas · Užupis · Santariškés · Žvėrynas · Kaupros salelé · Aukštutinès pilies muziejus · Naujininkai · Kuprioniškés · Kirtimai · Tarptautinis Vilniaus Oro Uostas · Pašilaičiai · Viršuliškés · Karoliniškés · Vilkpedé · Riovonys · Užusiensis · Aukštieji Paneriai · Avižieniai · Panevežys · Lazdynai · Žemieji Paneriai · Zujūnai · Buivydiškès · Pilaité · Gariūnai · Aukštieji Paneriai · Jočionys · Liudvinavas · Kaunas · Prienai · Neris · Neris · Neris

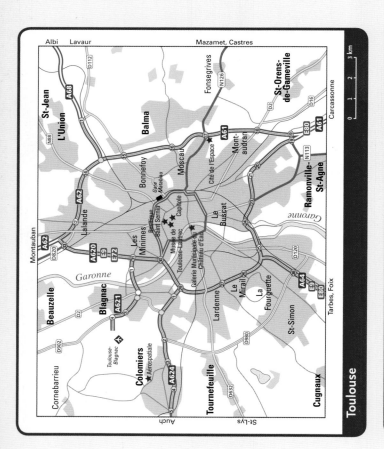

Toulouse

Albi · Lavaur · Mazamet, Castres · Fonsegrives · St-Orens-de-Gameville · Carcassonne · St-Jean · St-Union · Balma · Montaudran · Moscou · Bonnefoy · Cité de l'Espace · Ramonville-St-Agne · Gare Matabiau · Capitole · La Buscat · Lalande · Basilique Saint-Sernin · Galerie Municipale du Château d'Eau · Les Minimes · Musée des Toulouse-Lautrec · Le Mirail · Lardenne · La Fourguette · St-Simon · Beauzelle · Blagnac · Toulouse-Blagnac Aéro-spatiale · Colomiers · Cornebarrieu · Tournefeuille · Cugnaux · Montauban · Garonne · Garonne · Auch · St-Lys · Tarbes, Foix

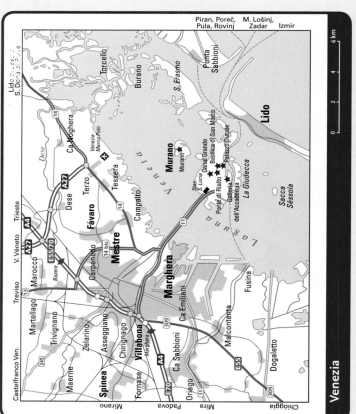

Venezia

Piran, Poreč, M. Lošinj, Pula, Rovinj · Zadar · Izmir

Lido, S. Dona di Piave · Torcello · Burano · Punta Sabbioni · S. Erasmo · Lido · Ca Noghera · Venezia-Marco-Polo · Murano · Murano · Canal Grande · Basilica di San Marco · Palazzo Ducale · Staz. S. Lucia · Ponte di Rialto · Galleria dell'Accademia · La Giudecca · Sacca Sessola · Deseo · Terzo · Tessera · Campalto · Laguna · Laguna Veneta · Fàvaro · Dese · Mestre · Trieste · V. Veneto · Marocco · Carpenedo · Marghera · Fusina · Treviso · Bazera · Ca Sabbioni · Ca Emiliani · Malcontenta · Martellago · Trivignano · Zelarino · Assegiano · Chirignago · Villabona · Marghera · Dogaletto · Castelfranco Ven. · Maerne · Fornase · Oriago · Spinea · Mirano · Mira · Padova · Chioggia

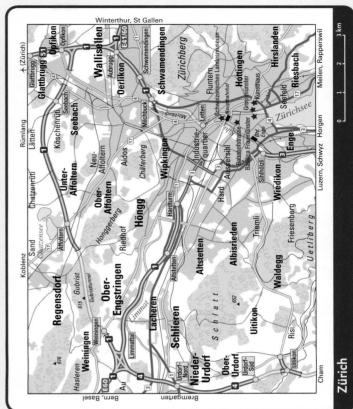

Wien

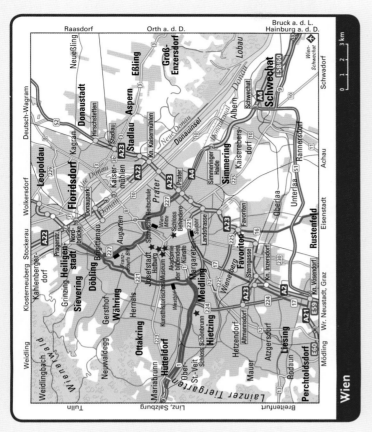

Zürich

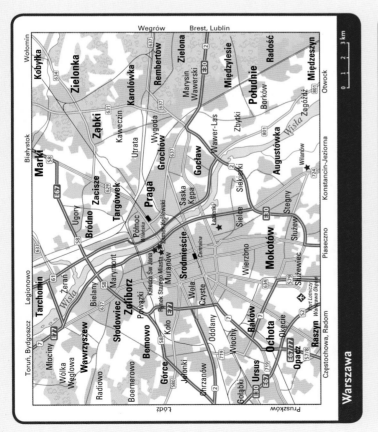

Warszawa

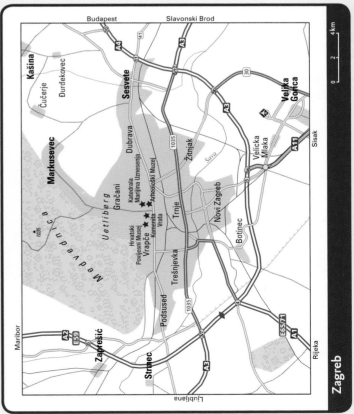

Zagreb

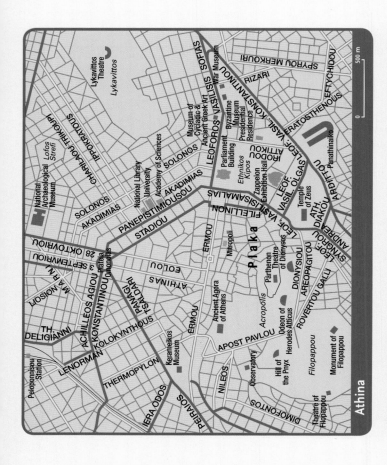

Athina

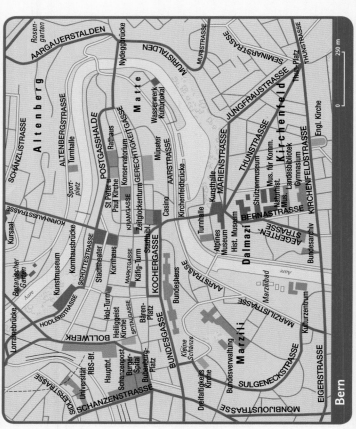

Bern

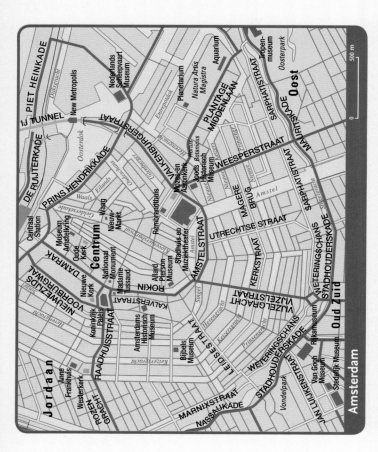

Amsterdam

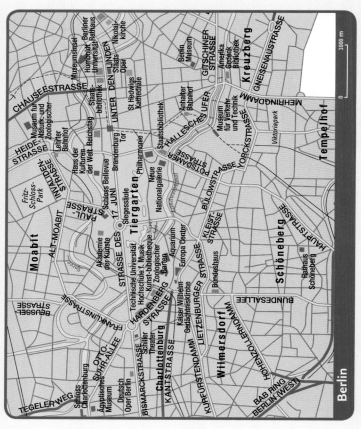

Berlin

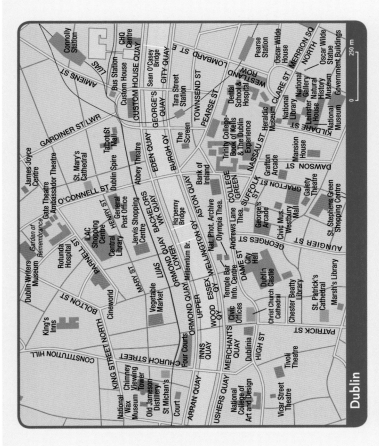

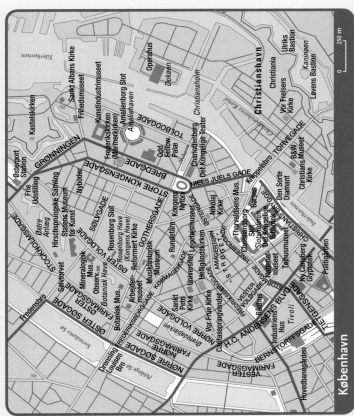

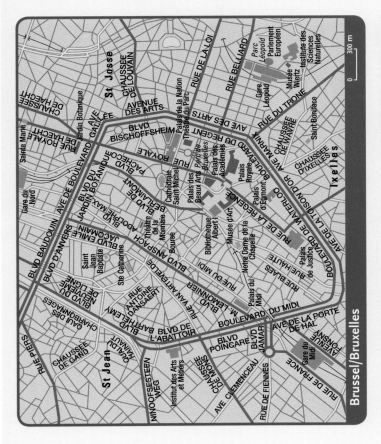

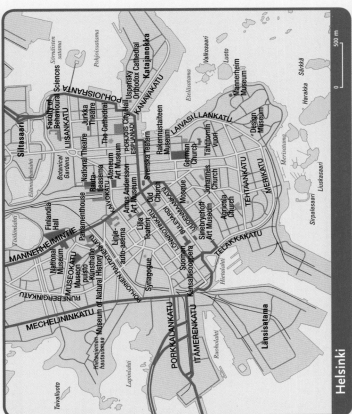

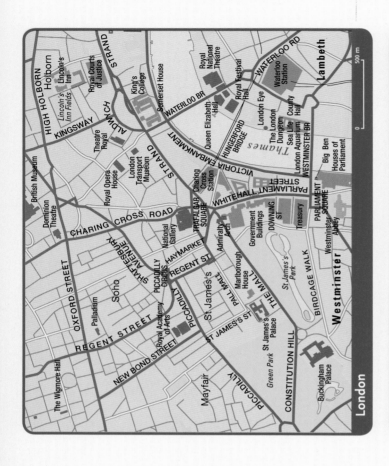

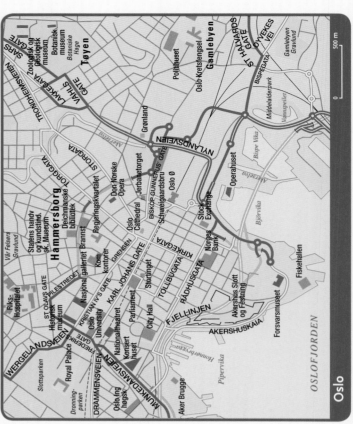

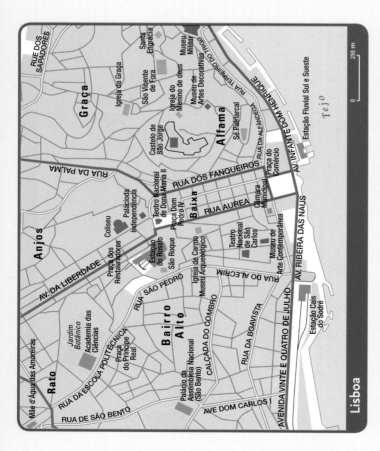

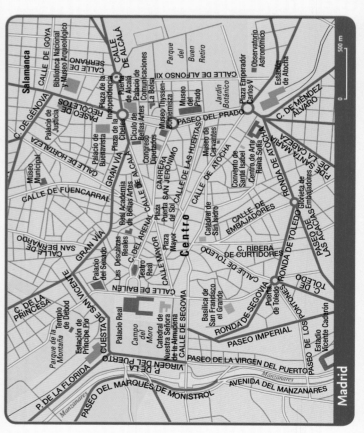

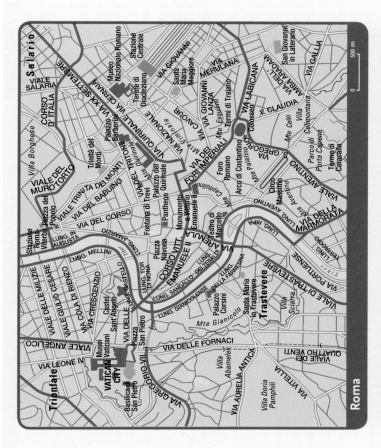

Roma

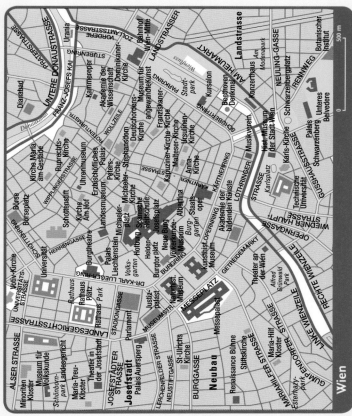

Wien

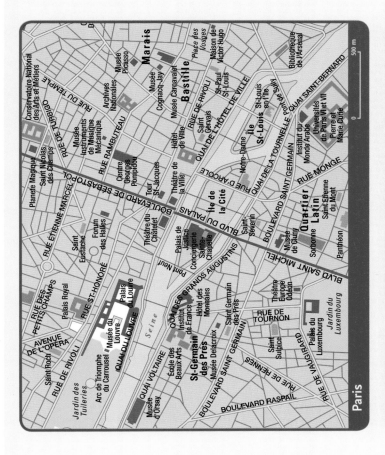

Paris

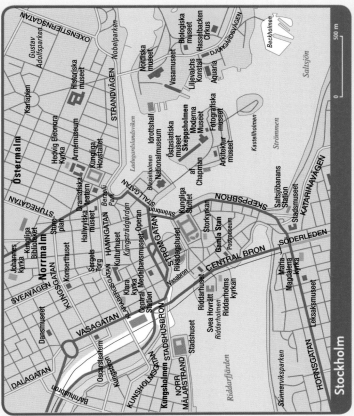

Stockholm

A

Å N 104 F7
Å N 110 E4
Å N 111 B12
Å N 111 C13
Aabenraa DK 86 E4
Aabybro DK 86 A5
Aachen D 20 C6
Aadorf CH 27 F10
Aakirkeby DK 89 E7
Aalborg DK 86 A5
Aalen D 75 E7
Aalestrup DK 86 B4
Aalsmeer NL 16 D3
Aalst B 19 C9
Aalst NL 183 B6
Aalten NL 17 E7
Aalter B 19 B7
Äänekoski FIN 123 E15
Aapajärvi FIN 115 D2
Aapajärvi FIN 119 B12
Aapajoki FIN 119 B12
Aapua S 117 E11
Aarau CH 27 F9
Aarberg CH 31 A11
Aardenburg NL 19 B7
Aareavaara S 117 D10
Aarhus DK 86 C6
Aarle NL 16 F5
A Armada E 38 B3
Aars DK 86 B5
Aarschot B 19 C10
Aartrijke B 182 C2
Aartselaar B 19 B9
Aarup DK 86 E6
Aarwangen CH 27 F8
Aasleagh IRL 6 E3
Ääsmäe EST 131 C9
Aaspere EST 131 C12
Aatsinki FIN 115 E5
Aavajärvi S 119 C11
Aavasaksa FIN 119 B11
Aba H 149 B11
Abaclia MD 154 E3
Abades E 46 C4
Abadín E 38 B5
Abadiño-Zelaieta E 41 B6
Abádszalók H 150 C6
A Baiuca E 38 B3
Abak TR 181 A7
Abalar TR 172 A6
Abánades E 47 C8
Abanilla E 56 E2
Abano Terme I 66 B4
Abarán E 55 C10
A Barrela E 38 C4
Abasár H 150 B5
Abaújszántó H 145 G3
Abbadia San Salvatore I 62 B1
Abbasanta I 64 C2
Abbekås S 87 E13
Abbeville F 18 D4
Abbey IRL 6 F6
Abbeydorney IRL 8 D3
Abbeyfeale IRL 8 D4
Abbeyleix IRL 9 C8
Abbey Town GB 5 F10
Abbiategrasso I 69 C6
Abborrberg S 109 F12
Abborreberget S 98 D8
Abborrträsk S 109 F17
Abbotsbury GB 13 D9
Abbots Langley GB 15 D8
Abcoude NL 16 D3
Abejar E 40 E6
Abejuela E 48 E3
Abela P 50 C2
Abelvær N 105 B10
Abenberg D 75 D8
Abenójar E 54 B4
Abensberg D 75 E10
Aberaeron GB 12 A6
Aberaman GB 13 B8
Aberchirder GB 3 K11
Aberdare GB 13 B8
Aberdaron GB 10 F2
Aberdeen GB 3 L12
Aberdovey GB 10 F3
Aberfeldy GB 5 B9
Aberffraw GB 10 E3
Aberford GB 11 D9
Aberfoyle GB 5 C8
Abergavenny GB 13 B8
Abergele GB 10 E4
Åberget S 109 E18
Abergwaun GB 12 B5
Abergynolwyn GB 10 F4
Aberlady GB 5 C11
Aberlour GB 3 L10
Abernethy GB 5 C10
Aberporth GB 12 A5
Abersoch GB 10 F2
Abertamy CZ 75 B12
Abertawe GB 13 B7
Abertillery GB 13 B8
Abertura E 45 F9
Aberuthven GB 5 C9
Aberystwyth GB 12 A6
Abetone I 66 D2
Abfaltersbach A 72 C6
Abhainnsuidhe GB 2 K2
Abia de la Obispalía E 47 D8
Abiego E 42 C3
Abild DK 86 F3
Abilly F 29 B7
Abingdon GB 13 B12
Abington GB 5 E9
Abisko Östra S 111 D16
Abja-Paluoja EST 131 E10
Abla E 55 E7
Ablis F 24 C6
Ablitas E 41 E8
Abmelaseter N 112 E6
Abo FIN 126 E7
Åbo S 103 C10
Åbodarna S 107 E14
Åbogen N 96 B7
Abondance F 31 C10
Abony H 150 C5
Åbosjö S 107 D13
Aboyne GB 5 A11
Abragão P 44 B4
Abram RO 151 C9
Abrămuț RO 151 C9
Abrantes P 44 F4
Abraur S 109 D16
Abreiro P 38 F5
Abreschviller F 27 C7
Abrest F 30 C3
Abriès F 31 F10
Abrigada P 44 F2
Abriola I 60 B5
Abrucena E 55 E7
Abrud RO 151 E11
Abrupe LV 135 B11
Absam A 72 B4
Absberg D 75 D8
Absdorf A 77 F9
Abtenau A 73 A7
Abtsgmünd D 74 E6
Abukhava BY 140 C10
Åby S 89 A7
Åby S 93 B8
Åbyen DK 90 D7
Åbyggeby S 103 E13
Åbyn S 118 D6
Åbytorp S 92 A6
Acaill IRL 6 E3
A Cañiza E 38 D3
A Carballa E 38 B2
Acarlar TR 177 D10
A Carreira E 38 B3
Acâș RO 151 B10
Acate I 58 E5
Accadia I 60 A4
Acceglio I 36 C5
Accettura I 60 C6
Acciano I 62 C5
Acciaroli I 60 C4
Accous F 32 E4
Accrington GB 11 D7
Accumoli I 62 B4
Acebo E 45 D7
Acedera E 45 F9
Acedo E 32 E1
Acehuche E 45 E7
Aceituna E 45 D8
Acered E 47 B9
Acerenza I 60 B5
Acerno I 60 B4
Acerra I 60 B2
Aceuchal E 51 B7
Ach A 76 F3
Achadh Mòr GB 2 J3
A Chan E 38 D3
Acharacle GB 4 B5
Acharnes GR 175 C8
Achavanich GB 3 J10
Achel B 183 C6
Achenkirch A 72 A4
Achern D 27 C9
Acheux-en-Amiénois F 18 D6
Achicourt F 18 D6
Achill IRL 6 E3
Achilleio GR 175 A6
Achim D 17 B12
Achintee GB 2 L6
Achladochori GR 169 B10
Achladokampos GR 175 D6
Achnacroish GB 4 B6
Achnasheen GB 2 K6
Achosnich GB 4 B4
Achstetten D 71 A9
Achtrup D 82 A6
Aci Castello I 59 D7
Aci Catena I 59 D7
Acireale I 59 D7
Aci Sant'Antonio I 59 D7
Aci Trezza I 59 D7
Acktjära S 103 D11
Acle GB 15 B12
A Coruña E 38 B3
Acquacalda I 59 B6
Acqualagna I 67 E6
Acquanegra sul Chiese I 66 B1
Acquapendente I 62 B1
Acquappesa I 60 E5
Acquaro I 59 B9
Acquarossa CH 71 E7
Acquasanta Terme I 62 B4
Acquasparta I 62 B3
Acquaviva Picena I 62 B5
Acquedolci I 59 C6
Acquigny F 24 B5
Acqui Terme I 37 B8
Acri I 61 E6
A Cruz do Incio E 38 C5
Ács H 149 A10
Acsa H 150 B3
Acuto I 62 D4
Ada SRB 150 F5
Adács H 150 B4
Adahuesca E 42 C3
Adak S 109 F16
Ådalsliden S 107 E11
Adamas GR 179 B7
Adamclisi RO 155 E1
Adamov CZ 77 D11
Adamova BY 133 E4
Adamów PL 141 G6
Adamówka PL 144 C6
Adamstown IRL 9 D9
Adămuș RO 152 E4
Adamuz E 53 A7
Adâncata RO 153 B8
Adâncata RO 161 D8
Ádánd H 149 C10
Adanero E 46 C3
Adão P 45 D6
Adare IRL 8 C5
Adatepe TR 173 D6
Adaúfe P 38 E3
Adavere EST 131 D11
Ādaži LV 135 B8
Adderbury GB 13 A12
Addlestone GB 15 E8
Adegem B 182 C2
Adelboden CH 31 C12
Adelebsen D 78 C6
Adelfia I 61 A7
Adelina PL 144 B8
Adelmannsfelden D 187 D8
Adelschlag D 75 E9
Adelsheim D 27 B11
Adelsried D 75 F8
Ademuz E 47 D10
Adenau D 21 D7
Adendorf D 83 D8
Adendro GR 169 C8
Adenstedt D 78 C6
Adjud RO 153 E10
Adlešiči SLO 148 E4
Adliswil CH 27 F10
Adlkofen D 75 E11
Admont A 73 A9
Adolfsström S 109 D12
Adony H 149 B11
Adorf D 75 B11
Adorf (Diemelsee) D 17 F11
Adoufe P 38 F4
Adra E 55 F6
Adradas E 41 F7
Adrados E 40 F3
Adrano I 59 D6
Adria I 66 B5
Adriani GR 171 B6
Adriers F 29 C7
Aduard NL 17 B6
Adulsbruk N 101 E14
Ådum DK 86 D3
Adunați RO 161 C7
Adunații-Copăceni RO 161 E8
Adutiškis LT 135 F13
Adzaneta de Albaida E 56 D4
Adžūni LV 135 D8
Aegviidu EST 131 C11
Aerino GR 169 F8
Ærøskøbing DK 86 F6
Aerzen D 17 D12
A Escusa E 38 C2
A Esfarrapada E 38 D2
A Estrada E 38 C3
Aetos GR 169 C6
Aetos GR 174 B3
Aetos GR 174 E4
Äetsä FIN 126 C8
Afantou GR 181 D8
Åfarnes N 100 A7
A Feira do Monte E 38 B4
Affing D 75 F8
Afife P 38 E2
Afissos GR 169 F9
Åfjord N 104 D8
Aflenz Kurort A 73 A11
A Fonsagrada E 38 B5
A Forxa E 38 D4
A Forxa E 38 D4
Åfoss N 90 A6
Afragola I 60 B2
Afritz A 73 C8
Afumați RO 160 E2
Afumați RO 161 D8
Afytos GR 169 D9
Aga D 79 E11
Ağaçli TR 173 B10
Ağaköy TR 173 D7
Agalas GR 174 D2
Agallas E 45 D8
A Gándara E 38 B3
A Gándara de Altea E 38 A3
Agapia RO 153 C8
Agăș RO 153 D8
Ágasegyháza H 150 D3
Agde F 34 D5
Agen F 33 B7
Ager E 42 C5
Agerbæk DK 86 D3
Agerskov DK 86 E4
Agersted DK 86 A6
Agerup DK 87 D10
Ágfalva H 149 A7
Aggersund DK 86 A4
Aggius I 64 B3
Aggsbach Markt A 77 F8
Aghaboe IRL 9 C7
Aghagallon GB 7 C10
Aghalee GB 7 C10
Aghanloo GB 4 E3
Aghaville IRL 8 E4
Aghern IRL 8 D6
Aghione F 37 G10
Aghireșu RO 151 D11
Aghleam IRL 6 D2
Aghnagar Bridge IRL 8 E2
Agia GR 169 E8
Agia Anna GR 175 B7
Agia Anna GR 175 C6
Agia Effimia GR 174 C2
Agia Efthymia GR 174 C5
Agia Galini GR 178 E8
Agia Kyriaki GR 174 E4
Agia Marina GR 175 B6
Agia Marina GR 175 C9
Agia Marina GR 177 E8
Agia Paraskevi GR 168 D4
Agia Paraskevi GR 174 A3
Agia Paraskevi GR 177 E6
Agia Pelagia GR 178 C4
Agia Pelagia GR 178 E9
Agiasma GR 171 C7
Agiasos GR 177 A7
Agia Triada GR 174 D4
Agia Triada GR 175 D6
Agia Varvara GR 169 D7
Agia Varvara GR 178 E9
Agigea RO 155 E3
Agighiol RO 155 C3
Agino Selo BIH 157 C7
Agiofyllo GR 169 E6
Agioi Anargyroi GR 169 E7
Agioi Apostoloi GR 175 C8
Agioi Deka GR 178 E8
Agioi Theodoroi GR 169 E5
Agioi Theodoroi GR 175 A6
Agioi Theodoroi GR 175 D7
Agiokampos GR 169 E8
Agiokampos GR 175 B7
Agionori GR 175 D6
Agios Andreas GR 175 E6
Agios Athanasios GR 169 C8
Agios Athanasios GR 171 B6
Agios Charalampos GR 171 B8
Agios Christoforos GR 175 F5
Agios Dimitrios GR 169 D7
Agios Dimitrios GR 175 D8
Agios Dimitrios GR 175 F6
Agios Efstratios GR 171 E7
Agios Georgios GR 169 C7
Agios Georgios GR 174 B4
Agios Georgios GR 175 C6
Agios Georgios GR 177 F6
Agios Georgios GR 178 E9
Agios Germanos GR 168 C5
Agios Ioannis GR 174 E5
Agios Ioannis GR 175 C7
Agios Ioannis GR 178 B4
Agios Kirykos GR 177 D7
Agios Konstantinos GR 174 B3
Agios Konstantinos GR 174 D5
Agios Konstantinos GR 175 B6
Agios Konstantinos GR 175 D9
Agios Kyprianos GR 178 C3
Agios Leon GR 174 D2
Agios Loukas GR 169 C7
Agios Loukas GR 175 C9
Agios Mamas GR 169 D9
Agios Matthaios GR 168 F2
Agios Myronas GR 178 E9
Agios Nikolaos GR 168 E3
Agios Nikolaos GR 168 E5
Agios Nikolaos GR 169 D10
Agios Nikolaos GR 174 B2
Agios Nikolaos GR 174 B4
Agios Nikolaos GR 174 B4
Agios Nikolaos GR 178 B3
Agios Nikolaos GR 179 E10
Agios Panteleimonas GR 169 C6
Agios Paraskevi GR 171 F10
Agios Petros GR 169 C8
Agios Petros GR 174 B2
Agios Petros GR 175 E6
Agios Spyridonas GR 169 D7
Agios Spyridonas GR 174 A2
Agios Stefanos GR 175 C8
Agios Stefanos GR 176 E5
Agios Thomas GR 175 C8
Agios Vasileios GR 169 C9
Agios Vasileios GR 175 D6
Agira I 59 D6
Agivey GB 4 E3
Agkathia GR 169 C7
Agkistro GR 169 B9
Aglapsvik N 111 B15
Aglasterhausen D 187 C6
Agle N 105 C13
Aglen N 105 B10
Agliana I 66 E3
Aglientu I 64 A3
Aglish IRL 9 D7
Agluonėnai LT 134 E2
Agnadello I 69 C8
Agnagar Bridge IRL 8 E2
Agnanta GR 168 F5
Agnantero GR 169 F6
Agneaux F 23 B9
Agnita RO 152 F5
Agno CH 69 A6
Agnone I 63 D6
Agolada E 38 C3
Agoncillo E 32 F1
Agon-Coutainville F 23 B8
Agordo I 72 D5
Agost E 56 E3
Agos-Vidalos F 32 D5
Ågotnes N 94 B2
Agra GR 177 A7
Agramón E 55 C9
Agramunt E 42 D6
Agrate Brianza I 69 B7
Agreda E 41 E8
Agrés E 56 D4
Agria GR 169 F9
Agridi GR 174 D4
Agrigento I 58 E4
Agrij RO 151 C11
Agrili GR 174 E4
Agrinio GR 174 B3
Agriovotano GR 175 A7
Agrochão P 39 E5
Agropoli I 60 C3
Ågskaret N 108 C5
Aguadulce E 53 B7
Aguadulce E 55 F7
A Guarda E 38 E2
Aguarón E 41 F9
Aguas E 42 C3
Águas Belas P 44 E4
Águas de Busot E 56 D4
Águas de Moura P 50 B2
Águas Frias P 38 E5
Aguaviva E 42 F3
A Gudiña E 38 D5
Agudo E 54 B3
Águeda P 44 C4
Aguessac F 34 B5
Agugliano I 67 E7
Aguiar P 50 C4
Aguiar da Beira P 44 C5
Aguilafuente E 46 B4
Aguilar de Alfambra E 42 F2
Aguilar de Campóo E 40 C3
Aguilar de la Frontera E 53 A7
Aguilar del Río Alhama E 41 E8
Águilas E 55 E9
Agullana E 34 F4
Agullent E 56 D3
Aha S 109 F14
Ahafona IRL 8 C3
Aham D 75 E11
Ahascragh IRL 6 F6
Ahaus D 17 D8
Åheim N 100 B3
Ahelva FIN 121 E11
Ahigal E 45 D8
Ahigal de Villarino E 45 B8
Ahillones E 51 C8
Ahja EST 131 E14
Ahjola FIN 121 D12
Ahlainen FIN 126 B6
Ahlatlı TR 167 E8
Ahlbeck D 84 C6
Ahlbeck D 84 C6
Ahlden (Aller) D 82 E7
Ahlen D 17 E9
Ahlerstedt D 17 B12
Ahlhorn D 17 C10
Ahmas FIN 119 E17
Ahmavaara FIN 115 E4
Ahmetbey TR 173 B8
Ahmetbeyli TR 177 C9
Ahmetçeeli TR 172 E6
Ahmetli TR 177 C9
Ahmovaara FIN 125 D13
Ahnsbeck D 79 A7
Ahoghill GB 4 F4
Ahoinen FIN 127 D11
Ahokylä FIN 123 C17
Ahola FIN 121 B11
Ahola FIN 121 C13
Ahola FIN 121 D13
Ahola FIN 124 D9
Aholanvaara FIN 115 E5
Ahonperä FIN 119 F13
Ahorn D 75 B8
Aho-Vastinki FIN 123 E14
Ahrbrück D 21 D7
Ahrensbök D 83 B9
Ahrensburg D 83 C8
Ahrenshagen D 83 B13
Ahrenshoop D 83 B12
Ähtäri FIN 123 E12
Ähtärinranta FIN 123 E12
Ahtme EST 132 C1
Ahula EST 131 C11
Ahun F 29 C10
Åhus S 88 D6
Ahveninen FIN 123 E16
Ahvenisto FIN 127 C16
Ahvensalmi FIN 125 F10
Ahvenselkä FIN 115 E4
Ahvenvittikko FIN 115 D4
Ahvionsaari FIN 129 B10
Aiani GR 169 D6
Aianteio GR 175 D7
Aibar E 32 E3
Aibl A 73 C11
Aichach D 75 F9
Aichhalden D 27 D9
Aichstetten D 71 B10
Ai'dejav'ri N 117 A10
Aidenbach D 76 E4
Aidipsos GR 175 B7
Aidone I 58 E5
Aidonochori GR 169 C10
Aidt DK 86 C5
Aidu EST 131 D12
Aiello Calabro I 59 A9
Aielo de Malferit E 56 D3
Aieta I 60 D5
Aiffres F 28 C5
Aigeira GR 174 C5
Aigen im Ennstal A 73 A9
Aigen im Mühlkreis A 76 E5
Aigiali GR 177 F6
Aigina GR 175 D7
Aiginio GR 169 D8
Aigio GR 174 C5
Aigle CH 31 C10
Aiglemont F 184 E2
Aignan F 33 C6
Aignay-le-Duc F 25 E12
Aigre F 28 D6
Aigrefeuille-d'Aunis F 28 C4
Aigrefeuille-sur-Maine F 28 A3
A Igrexa E 38 D3
Aiguafreda E 43 D8
Aiguebelle F 31 D9
Aigueblanche F 31 D10
Aigueperse F 30 C3
Aigues-Mortes F 35 C7
Aigues-Vives F 33 E9
Aigues-Vives F 34 D4
Aigues-Vives F 35 C7
Aiguilhe F 30 E4
Aiguilles F 31 F10
Aiguillon F 33 B6
Aigurande F 29 C9
Äijäjoki FIN 116 B10
Äijälä FIN 123 E16
Aijala FIN 127 E9
Aijänneva FIN 123 F11
Aillant-sur-Tholon F 25 E9
Aillas F 32 B5
Ailevillers-et-Lyaumont F 26 E5
Ailly-le-Haut-Clocher F 18 D4
Ailly-sur-Noye F 18 E5
Ailly-sur-Somme F 18 E5
Ailt an Chorráin IRL 6 C6
Aimargues F 35 C7
Aime F 31 D10
Ainali FIN 119 F14
Ainali FIN 123 B11
Ainay-le-Château F 29 B11
Ainaži LV 131 F8
Aindling D 75 E8
Ainet A 73 C6
Ainsa E 33 F6
Ainzón E 41 E9
Airaines F 18 E4
Airaksela FIN 124 E8
Airasca I 31 F11
Aird Asaig GB 2 K3
Airdrie GB 5 D9
Aire-sur-l'Adour F 32 C5
Aire-sur-la-Lys F 18 C5
Airidh a'Bhruaich GB 2 J3
Airola I 60 A3
Airole I 37 D7
Airolo CH 71 D7
Airvault F 28 B5
Aisey-sur-Seine F 25 E12
Aïssey F 26 F5
Aisymi GR 171 B9
Aisy-sur-Armançon F 25 E11
Aitamännikkö FIN 117 D12
Aita Mare RO 153 F7
Aiterhofen D 75 E12
Aith GB 3 E14
Aith GB 3 G11
Aitolahti FIN 127 B10
Aitoliko GR 174 C3
Aiton RO 152 D3
Aitona E 42 E4
Aitoo FIN 127 C11
Aitrach D 71 B10
Aitrang D 71 B11
Aittaniemi FIN 121 B10
Aittijoki FIN 113 D17
Aittojärvi FIN 119 D17
Aittojärvi FIN 123 C16
Aittokoski FIN 124 C8
Aittokylä FIN 121 E10
Aittoperä FIN 123 C13
Aittovaara FIN 121 D13
Aiud RO 152 E3
Aiviekste LV 135 C11
Aix-en-Othe F 25 D10
Aix-en-Provence F 35 C9
Aixe-sur-Vienne F 29 D8
Aix-les-Bains F 31 D8
Aizenay F 28 B2
Aizkraukle LV 135 C10
Aizpún E 32 E2
Aizpurve LV 135 C12
Aizpute LV 134 C3
Aizvīķi LV 134 D3
Ajaccio F 37 H9
Ajanki FIN 117 E12
Ajankijärvi FIN 117 E12
Ajat F 29 E8
Ajaureforsen S 109 E10
Ajdovščina SLO 73 E8
Ajka H 149 B9
Ajo E 40 B4
Ajofrín E 46 E5
Ajos FIN 119 C13
Akācijas LV 134 C6
Åkarp S 87 D12
Äkäsjokisuu FIN 117 D11
Äkäslompolo FIN 117 C12
Akasztó H 150 D3
Akçaova TR 181 B7
Akçasusurluk TR 173 D9
Akeld GB 5 D12
Aken D 79 C11
Åkerbränna S 107 D11
Åkerby S 99 B9
Åkerholmen S 118 C6
Åkersberga S 99 D10
Akersjön S 105 D16
Åkers styckebruk S 98 D8
Åkerstrømmen N 101 C14
Akheloy BG 167 D9
Akhremawtsy BY 133 E2
Akhtopol BG 167 E9
Akkan S 109 F12
Akkarfjord N 113 B12
Akkarvik N 112 C5
Akkasæter N 111 B16
Akkavare S 109 E17
Akkerhaugen N 95 D10
Akköy TR 171 E10
Akköy TR 177 E9
Akkrum NL 16 B5
Akmeņdziras LV 134 B3
Akmenė LT 134 D5
Åknes N 110 C9
Aknīste LV 135 D11
Akonkoski FIN 121 F13
Akonpohja FIN 125 D10
Akpinar TR 173 B10
Akraifnio GR 175 C7
Åkran N 105 D12
Akrata GR 174 C5
Åkrehamn N 94 D2
Akrini GR 169 D6
Akrolimni GR 169 C7
Akropotamos GR 170 C6
Akrotiri GR 179 C9
Aksakal TR 173 D9
Aksaz TR 173 D7
Aksdal N 94 D2
Aksnes N 104 F4
Akujärvi FIN 114 F3
Åkullsjön S 118 F5
Åkvisslan S 107 E13
Ål N 101 E9
Ala I 69 B11
Ala S 93 E13
Alacaat TR 173 E10
Alacant E 56 E4
Alacaoğlu TR 173 B7
Alaçati TR 177 C7
Alà dei Sardi I 64 B3
Ala di Stura I 31 E11
Alaejos E 39 F9
Alagna Valsesia I 68 B4
A Lagoa E 38 C2
Alagoa P 44 F5
Alagón E 41 E9
Alahärmä FIN 122 D9
Ala-Honkajoki FIN 126 B7
Alaigne F 33 D10
Alaior E 57 B13
Alájar E 51 D6
Alajärvi FIN 117 E15
Alajärvi FIN 121 E12
Alajärvi FIN 123 D11
Alajõe EST 132 C1
Ala-Jokikylä FIN 119 C14
Ala-Kääntä FIN 119 F12
Ala-Keyritty FIN 125 D10
Alakurtti RUS 115 E8
Alakylä FIN 117 D13
Alakylä FIN 119 D15
Alakylä FIN 126 B6
Ala-Livo FIN 119 D17
Alameda E 53 B7
Alameda de Cervera E 47 F6
Alameda de la Sagra E 46 D5
Alamedilla E 55 D6
Alamillo E 54 B3
Alan HR 67 B10
Ala-Nampa FIN 117 E16
Alanäs S 106 C9
Ålande LV 134 C2
Alandroal P 50 B5
Ålandsbro S 103 A14
Alange E 51 B7
Alaniemi FIN 119 C14
Alanís E 51 C8
Alanta LT 135 F10
Alap H 149 C11
Alapitkä FIN 124 D9
Alaquàs E 48 F4
Alaranta FIN 119 D14
Alaraz E 45 C10
Alarcón E 47 E8
Alar del Rey E 40 C3
Alaró E 49 E10
Alarup AL 168 C4
Ålåsen S 106 D7
Alaskylä FIN 127 B8
Alassio I 37 C8
Alastaipale FIN 123 F11
Alastaro FIN 126 D8
Ala-Sydänmaa FIN 123 B14
Alata F 37 H9
Ala-Temmes FIN 119 E15
Alatoz E 47 F10
Alatri I 62 D4
Alatskivi EST 131 D14
Alattyán H 150 C5
Ala-Valli FIN 123 F9
Alavattnet S 106 C9
Alavere EST 131 C10
Ala-Vieksi FIN 121 F12
Alavieska FIN 119 F12
Ala-Viirre FIN 123 B11
Ala-Vuokki FIN 121 E13
Ala-Vuotto FIN 119 D16
Alavus FIN 123 E11
Alba I 37 B8
Alba Adriatica I 62 B5
Albac RO 151 E10
Albacete E 55 A9
Albacken S 103 A11
Alba de Tormes E 45 C9
Ålbæk DK 90 D7
Albagiara I 64 D2
Albaida E 56 D4
Alba Iulia RO 152 E3
Albaladejo E 55 B7
Albala-la-Romaine F 35 A8
Albalate de Arzobispo E 42 E3
Albalate de Cinca E 42 D4
Albalate de las Nogueras E 47 D8
Albalate de Zorita E 47 D7
Albalatillo E 42 D3
Alban F 33 C10
Albánchez E 55 E8
Albanella I 60 C4
Albanitsa BG 165 C10
Albano di Lucania I 60 B6
Albano Laziale I 62 D3
Albano Vercellese I 68 C5
Albanyà E 43 C9
Albaredo per San Marco I 69 A8
Albaret-le-Comtal F 30 F3
Albareto I 69 E8
Albaret-Ste-Marie F 30 F3
Albaron F 35 C7
Albarracín E 47 D10
Albatana E 55 B9
Albatàrrec E 42 D5
Albatera E 56 E3
Albbruck D 27 E9
Albelda E 42 D4
Albelda de Iregua E 41 D7
Albella E 32 F5
Albendea E 47 C8
Albendín E 53 A8
Albenga I 37 C8
Albeni RO 160 C3
Albens F 31 D8
Albentosa E 48 D3
Ålberga S 93 B9
Alberga S 98 D6
Albergaria-a-Velha P 44 C4
Albergaria dos Doze P 44 E3
Albergen NL 183 A9
Alberic E 48 F4
Alberndorf in der Riedmark A 77 F6
Albernoa P 50 D4
Albero Alto E 41 D11
Alberobello I 61 B8
Alberona I 60 A4
Alberoni I 66 B5
Alberschwende A 71 C9
Albersdorf D 82 B6
Albert F 18 E6
Albertacce F 37 G9
Alberta Ligure I 37 B10
Albertirsa H 150 C4
Albertshofen D 187 B9
Albertville F 31 D9
Albertuela de Tubo E 42 D3
Albesa E 42 D5
Albești RO 152 E5
Albești RO 153 B10
Albești RO 153 D11
Albești RO 155 F2
Albești RO 161 D10
Albeștii de Argeș RO 160 C5
Albeștii de Muscel RO 160 C6
Albești-Paleologu RO 161 D8
Albestroff F 27 C6
Albi F 33 C10
Albias F 33 B8
Albidona I 61 D6
Albignasego I 66 B4
Albina RO 155 C1
Albino I 69 B8
Albires E 39 D9
Albisheim (Pfrimm) D 21 E10
Albisola Marina I 37 C9
Albisola Superiore I 37 C9
Alblasserdam NL 16 E3
Ålbo S 98 B7
Albocàsser E 48 D5
Alboloduy E 55 E7
Albolote E 53 B9
Albon F 30 E6
Albondón E 55 F6
Alboraya E 48 E4
Alborea E 47 F10
Albota RO 160 D5
Albox E 55 E8
Albrechtice nad Orlicí CZ 77 B10
Al'brekhtava BY 133 E5
Albstadt D 27 D11
Albu EST 131 C11
Albudeite E 55 C10
Albufeira P 50 E3
Albujón E 56 F2
Albuñol E 55 F6
Albuñuelas E 53 C9
Alburquerque E 45 F7
Alby S 89 C11
Alby S 103 A9
Alby-sur-Chéran F 31 D9
Alcácer E 48 F4
Alcácer do Sal P 50 C2
Alcáçovas P 50 C3
Alcadozo E 55 B9
Alcafozes P 45 E6
Alcaine E 42 F2
Alcains P 44 E6
Alcalá de Guadaira E 51 E8
Alcalá de Gurrea E 41 D10
Alcalá de Henares E 46 D6
Alcalá del Júcar E 47 F10
Alcalá de los Gazules E 52 D5
Alcalá del Río E 51 D8
Alcalá del Valle E 51 F9
Alcalà de Xivert E 48 D5
Alcalá la Real E 53 B9
Alcalalí E 56 D4
Alcamo I 58 D2
Alcampell E 42 D4
Alcanadre E 32 F1
Alcanede P 44 F3
Alcanena P 44 F3
Alcanhões P 44 F3
Alcañices E 39 E7
Alcañiz E 42 E3
Alcántara E 45 E7
Alcantarilla E 56 F2
Alcantud E 47 C8
Alcaracejos E 54 C3
Alcara li Fusi I 59 C6
Alcaraz E 55 B8
Alcaria Ruiva P 50 D4
Alcarràs E 42 D5
Alcaudete E 53 A8
Alcaucín E 53 C8
Alcaudete E 53 A8
Alcaudete de la Jara E 46 E3
Alçay-Alçabéhéty-Sunharette F 32 D4
Alcázar del Rey E 47 D7
Alcázar de San Juan E 47 F6
Alcedar MD 154 B3
Alcester GB 13 A11
Alçitepe TR 171 D10
Alcoba E 46 F4
Alcobaça P 44 E3
Alcobendas E 46 C5
Alcocer E 47 D7
Alcocero de Mola E 40 D5
Alcochete P 50 B2
Alcoentre P 44 F3
Alcoi E 56 D4
Alcolea E 53 A7
Alcolea E 55 F7
Alcolea de Calatrava E 54 B4
Alcolea de Cinca E 42 D4
Alcolea del Pinar E 47 B8
Alcolea del Río E 51 D8
Alcollarín E 45 F9
Alconchel E 51 B5
Alcóntar E 55 E7
Alcorcón E 46 D5
Alcorisa E 42 F3
Alcoroches E 47 C9
Alcossebre E 48 D5
Alcoutim P 50 E5
Alcover E 42 E6
Alcoy E 56 D4
Alcsútdoboz H 149 B11
Alcubierre E 41 E11
Alcubilla de Avellaneda E 40 E5
Alcubillas E 55 B6
Alcublas E 48 E3
Alcúdia E 57 B11
Alcudia de Guadix E 55 E6
Alcudia de Monteagud E 55 E8
Alcuéscar E 45 F8
Aldbrough GB 11 D11
Aldeacentenera E 45 E9

Aldeadávila de la Ribera E 45 B7
Aldea del Cano E 45 F8
Aldea del Fresno E 46 D4
Aldea del Obispo E 45 C7
Aldea del Rey E 54 B5
Aldea de Trujillo E 45 E9
Aldealafuente E 41 E7
Aldealpozo E 41 E7
Aldeamayor de San Martín E 39 E10
Aldeanueva de Barbarroya E 45 E10
Aldeanueva de Ebro E 41 D8
Aldeanueva de Figueroa E 45 B9
Aldeanueva de la Vera E 45 D9
Aldeanueva del Camino E 45 D9
Aldeanueva de San Bartolomé E 45 E10
Aldeaquemada E 55 C6
Aldea Real E 46 B4
Aldearrodrigo E 45 B9
Aldeaseca E 46 B3
Aldeatejada E 45 C9
Aldeavieja E 46 C4
Aldeburgh GB 15 C12
Aldehuela de la Bóveda E 45 C8
Aldehuela de Yeltes E 45 C8
Aldeia da Mata P 44 F5
Aldeia da Ponte P 45 D7
Aldeia de João Pires P 45 D6
Aldeia do Bispo P 45 D6
Aldeia dos Elvas P 50 D3
Aldeia dos Fernandes P 50 D3
Aldeia dos Palheiros P 50 D3
Aldeia Velha P 44 F4
Aldenhoven D 20 C6
Aldeno I 69 B11
Alderbury GB 13 C11
Alderholt GB 13 D11
Alderley Edge GB 11 E7
Aldersbach D 76 E4
Aldershot GB 15 E7
Aldinac SRB 164 B5
Aldinci MK 164 F3
Aldingham GB 10 C5
Aldomirovtsi BG 165 D6
Aldover E 42 F5
Aldridge GB 11 F8
Aldudes F 32 D3
Åle DK 86 D5
Åled S 87 B11
Aledo E 55 D9
Alekovo BG 161 F10
Alekovo BG 166 C4
Aleksandriškės LT 137 D10
Aleksandrova LV 133 E2
Aleksandrovac SRB 159 E7
Aleksandrovac SRB 163 C11
Aleksandrovo BG 165 C10
Aleksandrovo BG 166 D4
Aleksandrovo BG 167 E7
Aleksandrów PL 141 F2
Aleksandrów PL 141 H1
Aleksandrów Kujawski PL 138 E6
Aleksandrów Łódzki PL 143 C7
Aleksa Šantić SRB 150 F3
Aleksinac SRB 164 B4
Ålem S 89 B10
Ålen N 101 A14
Alençon F 23 D12
Alenquer P 44 F3
Alénya F 34 E4
Alerheim D 75 E8
Aléria F 37 G11
Alerre E 41 D11
Alès F 35 B7
Ales I 64 D2
Aleşd RO 151 C9
Alesón E 41 D6
Alessandria I 37 B9
Alessandria del Carretto I 61 D6
Alessandria della Rocca I 58 D3
Alessano I 61 D10
Ålesund N 100 B4
Alet-les-Bains F 33 D10
Alexandreia GR 169 C7
Alexandria GB 4 D7
Alexandria RO 160 F6
Alexandroupoli GR 171 C9
Alexandru Vlahuţă RO 153 E11
Alexeevca MD 153 C11
Alexeni RO 161 D9
Alexsandrów PL 144 C6
Alezio I 61 C10
Alf D 21 D8
Alfacar E 53 B9
Alfafar E 48 F4
Alfaiates P 45 D7
Alfajarín E 41 E10
Alfambra E 42 F1
Alfambras P 50 E2
Alfamén E 41 F9
Alfândega da Fé P 39 F6
Alfántega E 42 D4
Alfarim P 50 C1
Alfaro E 41 D8
Alfarràs E 42 D5
Alfatar BG 161 F10
Alfdorf D 74 E6
Alfedena I 62 D6
Alfeizerão P 44 E2
Alfeld (Leine) D 78 C6
Alfena P 44 B3
Alferce P 50 E3
Alfhausen D 17 C9
Alfonsine I 66 D5
Alford GB 3 L11
Alford GB 11 E12
Alforja E 42 E5
Alfredshem S 107 E15
Alfreton GB 11 E9
Alfta S 103 D11
Alfundão P 50 C3
Algaida E 57 B10
Algajola F 37 F9
Algámitas E 53 B6
Algar E 52 C5
Älgarås S 92 B4
Ålgård N 94 E3
Algarinejo E 53 B8
Algarrobo E 53 C8
Algatocín E 53 C6
Algeciras E 53 D6
Algemesí E 48 F4
Älgered S 103 B12
Algermissen D 79 B6
Algerri E 42 D5
Algestrup DK 87 E10
Algete E 46 C6
Alghero I 64 B1
Älghult S 89 A9
Alginet E 48 F4
Älgnäs S 103 D12
Algodonales E 51 F9
Algodor P 50 D4
Algora E 47 C7
Algorta E 40 B6
Algoso P 39 F6
Algoz P 50 E3
Algrange F 20 F6
Alguaire E 42 D5
Alguazas E 56 E2
Algueirão-Mem Martins P 50 B1
Algueña E 56 E3
Algutsrum S 89 B11
Alhabia E 55 F7
Alhama de Almería E 55 F7
Alhama de Aragón E 41 F8
Alhama de Granada E 53 B9
Alhama de Murcia E 55 D10
Alhambra E 55 B6
Alhamn S 118 D7
Alhaurín de la Torre E 53 C7
Alhaurín el Grande E 53 C7
Alhendín E 53 B9
Alhojärvi FIN 127 B13
Alhóndiga E 47 C7
Ålhult S 92 D7
Alía E 45 F10
Alia I 58 D4
Aliaga E 42 F2
Aliağa TR 177 B8
Aliaguilla E 47 E10
Aliano I 60 C6
Aliartos GR 175 C7
Alibunar SRB 159 C6
Alicante E 56 E4
Alicún de Ortega E 55 D6
Alife I 60 A2
Alija del Infantado E 39 D8
Alijó P 38 F5
Alikianos GR 178 E6
Alikylä FIN 123 C11
Aliman RO 155 E1
Alimena I 58 D5
Aliminusa I 58 D4
Alimpeşti RO 160 C3
Alingsås S 91 D12
Alino BG 165 E7
Alionys 1 LT 137 C11
Aliseda E 45 F7
Alistrati GR 170 B5
Alì Terme I 59 C7
Aliveri GR 175 C9
Alizava LT 135 E10
Aljaraque E 51 E5
Aljezur P 50 E2
Aljinovići SRB 163 C8
Aljubarrota P 44 E3
Aljucén E 51 A7
Aljustrel P 50 D3
Alken B 19 C11
Alkkia FIN 122 F9
Alkmaar NL 16 C3
Allai I 64 D2
Allaire F 23 E7
Allambres AL 168 C2
Allan F 35 A8
Allanche F 30 E2
Allariz E 38 D4
Allarmont F 27 D7
Allassac F 29 E8
Allaži LV 135 B9
Allažmuiža LV 135 B9
Alle CH 27 F7
Alleghe I 72 D5
Allègre F 30 E4
Alleins F 35 C9
Allemond F 31 E9
Allen IRL 7 F9
Allendale Town GB 5 F12
Allendorf (Eder) D 21 B11
Allenheads GB 5 F12
Allensbach D 27 E11
Allentsteig A 77 E8
Allenwood IRL 7 F9
Allepuz E 42 G2
Allerona I 62 B1
Allersberg D 75 D9
Allershausen D 75 F10
Allerslev DK 87 E10
Allevard F 31 E9
Allex F 30 F6
Allibaudières F 25 C11
Alligny-en-Morvan F 25 F11
Allihies IRL 8 E2
Allingåbro DK 86 C6
Allinges F 31 C9
Allinge-Sandvig DK 89 E7
Alliste I 61 D10
Allmendingen D 74 F6
Allo E 32 E1
Alloa GB 5 C9
Allogny F 25 F7
Ålloluokta S 109 B17
Allonby GB 5 F10
Allonnes F 23 E12
Allonnes F 23 F12
Allons F 32 B5
Allos F 36 C5
Alloue F 29 C7
Alloza E 42 F2
Allschwil CH 27 E8
Allsta S 103 A15
Allstad N 110 D6
Allstedt D 79 D9
Allumiere I 62 C1
Alluy F 30 A4
Almacelles E 42 D4
Almáchar E 53 C8
Almada P 50 B1
Almadén E 54 B3
Almadén de la Plata E 51 D7
Almadenejos E 54 B3
Almagro E 54 B5
Almăj RO 160 E3
Almajano E 41 E7
Almalaguês P 44 D4
Almaluez E 41 F7
Almansa E 56 D2
Almansil P 50 E3
Almanza E 39 C9
Almaraz E 45 E9
Almargen E 53 B6
Almarza E 41 E7
Almaş RO 151 E9
Almásfüzitő H 149 A10
Almaşu RO 151 D11
Almaşu Mare RO 151 E11
Almazán E 41 F6
Almazora E 48 E4
Almazul E 41 E7
Almedina E 55 B7
Almedinilla E 53 B8
Almeida de Sayago E 39 F7
Almeirim P 44 F3
Almelo NL 17 D7
Almenar E 42 D5
Almenara E 48 E4
Almenar de Soria E 41 E7
Almendra E 45 B8
Almendra P 45 B6
Almendral E 51 B6
Almendralejo E 51 B7
Almendricos E 55 E9
Almendros E 47 E7
Almere NL 16 D4
Almería E 55 F8
Almerimar E 55 F7
Älmestad S 91 D13
Älmhult S 88 B6
Almind DK 86 D4
Almkerk NL 16 E3
Ålmo N 104 E4
Almodôvar P 50 D3
Almodóvar del Campo E 54 B4
Almodóvar del Pinar E 47 E9
Almodóvar del Río E 53 A6
Almofala P 44 C5
Almogía E 53 C7
Almograve P 50 D2
Almoguera E 47 D7
Almoharín E 45 F8
Almonacid de la Sierra E 41 F9
Almonacid del Marquesado E 47 E7
Almonacid del Zorita E 47 D7
Almonacid de Toledo E 46 E5
Almonaster la Real E 51 D6
Almondsbury GB 13 B9
Almonte E 51 E6
Almoradí E 56 E3
Almorchón E 51 B9
Almorox E 46 D4
Álmosd H 151 C8
Almoster P 44 E4
Almsele S 107 C12
Almsjönäs S 107 E14
Älmsta S 99 C11
Almstedt D 79 B6
Almudema E 55 C9
Almudévar E 41 D10
Almuñécar E 53 C9
Almunge S 99 C10
Almuniente E 41 E11
Almünster A 73 A8
Álmuradiel E 55 B6
Almussafes E 48 F4
Almvik S 93 D9
Almyropotamos GR 175 C9
Almyros GR 175 A6
Alnes N 100 B4
Alness GB 3 K8
Alnwick GB 5 E13
Alobras E 47 D10
Alocén E 47 C7
Aloja LV 131 F9
Alol' RUS 133 D6
Alonia GR 169 D8
Álora E 53 C7
Alós d'Ensil E 33 E8
Alosno E 51 D5
Alost B 19 C9
Alost B 182 D4
Alovera E 47 C6
Alozaina E 53 C7
Alp E 33 F9
Alpalhão P 44 F5
Alpanseque E 41 F6
Alpbach A 72 B4
Alpedrinha P 44 D6
Alpedriz P 44 E3
Alpen D 17 E7
Alpenrod D 21 C9
Alpens E 43 C8
Alpera E 56 D2
Alphen NL 16 F3
Alphen aan den Rijn NL 16 D3
Alpiarça P 44 F3
Alpirsbach D 27 D9
Alpnach CH 70 D6
Alposjärvi FIN 117 E12
Alpua FIN 119 F14
Alpuente E 47 E11
Alpullu TR 173 B7
Alquería de la Condesa E 56 D4
Alquerías E 56 E2
Alqueva P 50 C4
Alquife E 55 E6
Alrance F 34 B4
Alrewas GB 11 F8
Als DK 86 B6
Alsager GB 11 E7
Alsån S 119 B9
Alsbach D 187 B6
Alsdorf D 20 C6
Alsėdžiai LT 134 D4
Alsen S 105 E15
Alsenborn D 21 F9
Alseno I 69 D8
Alsenz D 21 E9
Alsfeld D 21 C12
Alsheim D 185 E9
Alsike S 99 C9
Alsjö S 103 B11
Alsleben (Saale) D 79 C10
Alslev DK 86 D2
Alsmo N 100 D6
Alsónémedi H 150 C3
Alsópáhok H 149 C8
Alsos N 108 A8
Alsóvadász H 145 G2
Alsózsolca H 145 G2
Ålsrode DK 87 C7
Ålstad N 110 E9
Alstad S 87 E12
Alstahaug N 108 E3
Alstakan S 97 C8
Alster S 97 D10
Alsterbro S 89 B9
Alstermo S 89 B9
Alsting F 186 C2
Alston GB 5 F12
Alsunga LV 134 C3
Alsvåg N 110 C9
Alsvik N 108 B7
Alsviķi LV 133 B1
Alta N 113 D11
Älta S 99 D10
Altafulla E 43 E6
Altamura I 61 B7
Altare I 37 C8
Altatornio FIN 119 C12
Altaussee A 73 A8
Altavilla Irpina I 60 B3
Altavilla Silentina I 60 B4
Altdöbern D 80 C6
Altdorf CH 71 D7
Altdorf D 75 E11
Altdorf bei Nürnberg D 75 D9
Alt Duvenstedt D 82 B7
Alte P 50 E3
Altea E 56 D4
Altefähr D 84 B4
Alteglofsheim D 75 E11
Alteidet N 112 C9
Altena D 17 F9
Altenahr D 21 C7
Altenau D 79 C7
Altenberg D 80 E5
Altenberge D 17 D8
Altenbruch-Westerende D 17 A11
Altenbuch D 74 C5
Altenburg D 79 E11
Altendiez D 21 D9
Altenfeld D 75 A8
Altenfelden A 76 F5
Altenglan D 21 E8
Altenhagen D 83 B11
Altenheim D 27 D8
Altenhof D 84 E5
Altenholz D 83 B8
Altenkirchen D 84 A4
Altenkirchen (Westerwald) D 21 C9
Altenkrempe D 83 B9
Altenkunstadt D 75 B9
Altenmarkt an der Triesting A 77 F9
Altenmarkt bei Sankt Gallen A 73 A10
Altenmarkt im Pongau A 73 B7
Altenmedingen D 83 D9
Altenmünster D 75 F8
Altenstadt D 21 D11
Altenstadt D 71 A10
Altenstadt D 71 B11
Altensteig D 27 C10
Altentreptow D 84 C4
Alter do Chão P 44 F5
Altes Lager D 80 B4
Altevik N 111 C12
Altfraunhofen D 75 F11
Altheim A 76 F4
Altheim D 27 D11
Altheim (Alb) D 187 D9
Althengstett D 187 D6
Althofen A 73 C9
Altier F 35 B6
Altimir BG 165 B8
Alţina RO 152 F4
Altindag TR 177 C9
Altinoluk TR 172 E6
Altinova TR 177 A8
Altintaş TR 181 A8
Altkirch F 27 E7
Alt Krenzlin D 83 D10
Altlandsberg D 80 A5
Altleiningen D 21 E10
Altmannstein D 75 E10
Altnaharra GB 2 J8
Altofonte I 58 C3
Altomonte I 60 D6
Altomünster D 75 F9
Alton GB 11 F8
Alton GB 14 E7
Altopascio I 66 E2
Altorricón E 42 D4
Altötting D 75 F12
Altrich D 185 E6
Altrincham GB 11 E7
Alt Ruppin D 84 E3
Altsasu E 32 E1
Alt Schwerin D 83 C12
Altshausen D 71 B9
Altstätten CH 71 C9
Alttajärvi S 116 C5
Altura E 48 E4
Altusried D 71 B10
Alu EST 131 C9
Aluatu MD 154 F3
Alūksne LV 133 B2
Ålund S 118 D6
Alunda S 99 B10
Aluniş RO 152 C3
Aluniş RO 152 D5
Aluniş RO 161 C7
Alunu RO 160 C3
Alustante E 47 C9
Alva S 93 E12
Alvaiázere P 44 E4
Alvajarvi FIN 123 D14
Alvalade P 50 D3
Alvaneu CH 71 D9
Älvängen S 91 D11
Alvarenga P 44 C4
Álvares P 44 D4
Álvaro P 44 E5
Alvdal N 101 B13
Älvdalen S 102 D7
Alvega P 44 F4
Alveley GB 13 A10
Alvelos P 38 E2
Alverca P 50 B1
Alverca da Beira P 45 C6
Alvesta S 88 B7
Alvestad N 111 C11
Alvestorp S 97 C12
Alvettula FIN 127 C11
Alvhem S 91 C11
Älvho S 102 D8
Alviano I 62 B2
Alvie GB 3 L9
Alvignac F 29 F9
Ålvik N 94 B4
Alvik S 102 E8
Alvik S 103 B13
Alvik S 118 C7
Alvito I 62 D5
Alvito P 50 C4
Älvkarleby S 103 E13
Älvkarleö S 99 A8
Alvnes N 108 B9
Alvnes N 110 E9
Alvoco da Serra P 44 D5
Älvros S 102 B8
Älvsbyn S 118 C6
Älvsered S 87 A11
Ålvund N 101 A9
Ålvundeid N 101 A9
Alwernia PL 143 F8
Alyki GR 174 A3
Alyth GB 5 B10
Alytus LT 137 E9
Alzenau in Unterfranken D 21 D12
Alzey D 21 E10
Alzira E 48 F4
Alzon F 34 C5
Alzonne F 33 D10
Ämådalen S 102 D8
Amadora P 50 B1
Amaiur-Maia E 32 D3
Åmål S 91 A12
Åmål S 91 B12
Amalfi I 60 B3
Amaliada GR 174 D3
Amaliapoli GR 175 A6
Amalo GR 177 D6
Amance F 26 E5
Amancey F 31 A9
Amandola I 62 B4
Amantea I 60 E6
Amara RO 161 D10
Amarante P 38 F3
Amarantos GR 168 E5
Amărăşti RO 160 D4
Amărăştii de Jos RO 160 F4
Amărăştii de Sus RO 160 F4
Amareleja P 51 C5
Amares P 38 E3
Amaroni I 59 B9
Amaru RO 161 D9
Amarynthos GR 175 C8
Amaseno I 62 E4
Amatrice I 62 B4
Amaxades GR 171 B8
Amay B 19 C11
Ambasaguas E 39 C9
Ambazac F 29 D8
Ambel E 41 E8
Ambeļi LV 135 D13
Amberg D 75 D10
Ambergate GB 11 E9
Ambérieu-en-Bugey F 31 D7
Amberloup B 19 D12
Ambert F 30 D4
Ambès F 28 E4
Ambierle F 30 C4
Ambillou F 24 F3
Ambjörby S 97 B9
Ambjörnarp S 91 E13
Ambla EST 131 C11
Amblainville F 24 B7
Amble GB 5 E13
Ambleside GB 10 C6
Ambleteuse F 15 F12
Amboise F 24 F4
Ambon F 22 E6
Ambrault F 29 B9
Ambrières-les-Vallées F 23 D10
Ambronay F 31 C7
Ambrosden GB 13 B12
Åmdals Verk N 95 D8
Ameglia I 69 E8
Ameide NL 182 B5
Ameixial P 50 E4
Amel B 20 D6
Amele LV 134 B4
Amelia I 62 B2
Amélie-les-Bains-Palalda F 34 F4
Amelinghausen D 83 D8
Amêndoa P 44 E4
Amendoeira P 50 D4
Amendolara I 61 D7
Amer E 43 C9
Amerang D 75 G11
A Merca E 38 D4
Amerongen NL 183 B6
Amersfoort NL 16 D4
Amersham GB 15 D7
Amesbury GB 13 C11
Amezketa E 32 D1
Amfikleia GR 175 B6
Amfilochia GR 174 B3
Amfipoli GR 169 C10
Amfissa GR 174 B5
Amieira P 50 C4
Amiens F 18 E5
Amilly F 25 E8
Åminne FIN 122 E7
Åminne S 87 A14
Åmland N 94 F5
Åmli N 90 A3
Åmli N 90 B3
Amlwch GB 10 E3
Ämmälänkylä FIN 123 E9
Ammanford GB 12 B7
Ämmänsaari FIN 121 E12
Ammarnäs S 109 E11
Åmmeberg S 92 B6
Ammenäs S 91 C10
Ammerbuch D 187 D6
Ammern D 79 D7
Ammersbek D 83 C8
Ammerzoden NL 183 B6
Ammochori GR 169 C5
Ammotopos GR 168 F4
Ammoudia GR 169 B9
Amnatos GR 178 E8
Amnéville F 186 C1
Amoeiro E 38 D4
Amonde P 38 E2
Amorbach D 21 E12
Amorebieta E 40 B6
Amorgos GR 177 F6
Amori GR 171 B10
Åmot N 94 C7
Åmot N 95 B11
Åmot N 95 C8
Åmot N 95 C11
Åmot S 103 E11
Åmotfors S 96 C7
Amou F 32 C4
Åmøyhamn N 108 C5
Ampelakia GR 169 E8
Ampeleia GR 169 F7
Ampelokipoi GR 169 C8
Ampelonas GR 169 E7
Ampezzo I 73 D6
Ampfing D 75 F11
Ampflwang im Hausruckwald A 76 F5
Amplepuis F 30 D5
Amposta E 42 F5
Ampthill GB 15 C8
Ampudia E 39 E10
Ampuero E 40 B5
Ampus F 36 D4
Amriswil CH 27 E11
Åmsele S 107 B16
Åmsosen N 94 D3
Amstelveen NL 16 D3
Amsterdam NL 16 D3
Amstetten A 77 F7
Amstetten D 187 D8
Amulree GB 5 B9
Amurrio E 40 B6
Amusco E 40 D3
Amvrosia GR 171 B8
Amygdaleonas GR 171 C6
Amygdalia GR 174 C5
Åmynnet S 107 E15
Amyntaio GR 169 C6
Amzacea RO 155 F2
Anacapri I 60 B2
Anadia P 44 D4
Anafi GR 180 D3
Anafonitria GR 174 D2
Anagaire IRL 6 B6
Anagni I 62 D4
An Aird Mhóir IRL 6 F3
Añana-Gesaltza E 40 C6
Anan'yiv UA 154 B5
Anarcs H 145 G5
Anargyroi GR 169 C6
Anarrachi GR 169 D6
Ånäset S 118 F6
Åna-Sira N 94 F4
Anatazavė LT 135 E11
Anatoli GR 168 E4
Anatoli GR 169 E8
Anatoli GR 179 E10
Anatoliki Fragkista GR 174 B4
Anatoliko GR 169 C6
Anatoliko GR 169 C8
Anavatos GR 177 C7
Anavra GR 174 A5
Anavra GR 175 A6
Anavyssos GR 175 D8
Anaya de Alba E 45 C10
An Baile Breac IRL 8 E2
An Baile Nua IRL 8 D5
An Bhlarna IRL 8 E5
An Bun Beag IRL 6 B6
An Cabhán IRL 7 E8
An Caiseal IRL 6 F3
An Caisleánn Riabhach IRL 6 E6
An Caisléan Nua IRL 7 F10
An Caisléan Nua IRL 8 D4
An Cathair IRL 9 D7
Ance LV 134 A4
Ancelle F 36 B4
Ancene LV 135 D11
Ancenis F 23 F9
Ancerville F 26 C3
An Charraig IRL 6 C5
An Cheathru Rua IRL 6 F3
An Chill IRL 7 F9
Ancín E 32 E1
An Cionn Garbh IRL 6 C6
An Clochán IRL 7 C7
An Clochán Liath IRL 6 C6
An Cóbh IRL 8 E6
An Coimín IRL 7 C7
An Coireán IRL 8 E2
Ancona I 67 E8
Ancroft GB 5 D13
Ancrum GB 5 D11
Ancy-le-Franc F 25 E11
Anda N 100 C4
Andalo I 69 A11
Åndalsnes N 100 A7
Andau A 149 A8
Andavías E 39 E8
Anddalsvågen N 108 E3
Andebu N 95 D12
Andechs D 75 G9
Andeer CH 71 D8
Andelfingen CH 27 E10
Andelot-Blancheville F 26 D3
Andelst NL 16 E5
Andenes N 111 B11
Andenne B 19 D11
Anderlecht B 19 C9
Anderlues B 19 D9
Andermatt CH 71 D7
Andernach D 185 D7
Andernos-les-Bains F 28 F3
Andersbo S 99 B9
Anderslöv S 87 E12
Anderstorp S 88 A5
Andervenne D 17 C9
Andfiskå N 108 D7
Andijk NL 16 C4
Andilly-en-Bassigny F 26 E4
Andlau F 27 D7
Andoain E 32 D1
Andocs H 149 C9
Andolsheim F 27 D7
Andorf A 76 F5
Andørja N 111 C13
Andorno Micca I 68 B5
Andorra E 42 F3
Andorra la Vella AND 33 E9
Andosilla E 32 F2
Andouillé F 23 D10
Andover GB 13 C12
Andrano I 61 D10
Andrăşeşti RO 161 D10
Andratx E 49 E9
Andravida GR 174 D3
Andreas GBM 10 C3
Andreiaşu de Jos RO 153 F9
Andrespol PL 143 C8
Andrest F 33 D6
Andretta I 60 B4
Andria I 60 A6
Andrid RO 151 B9
Andrieşeni RO 153 B10
Andrijaševci HR 157 B10
Andrijevica MNE 163 D8
Andrioniškis LT 135 E10
Andriškiai LT 136 D6
Andritsaina GR 174 E4
Andronianoi GR 175 B9
Andros GR 176 D4
Androusa GR 174 E4
Andrup DK 86 D3
Andrupene LV 133 D2
Andrychów PL 147 B8
Andrzejewo PL 141 E6
Andselv N 111 B15
Andsnes N 112 C7
An Dúchoraidh IRL 6 C6
Andújar E 53 A8
Anduze F 35 B6
Andzeļi LV 133 D3
An Eachléim IRL 6 D2
Åneby N 95 B13
Aneby S 92 D5
Anela I 64 C3
Anenii Noi MD 154 D4
Ånes N 104 E4
Anet F 24 C5
Anetjärvi FIN 121 C10
Anevo BG 165 D10
Aneza GR 174 A2
An Fál Carrach IRL 6 B6
An Féar Bán IRL 7 F7
An Fhairche IRL 6 E4
Anfo I 69 B9
Äng S 92 D5
Anga S 93 E13
Ånge S 103 A10
Änge S 105 E16
Ånge S 109 E14
An Geata Mór IRL 6 D2
Ängebo S 103 C11
Angeja P 44 C3
Ängelholm S 87 C11
Angeli FIN 113 F16
Angelniemi FIN 127 E8
Angelochori GR 169 C7
Angelokastro GR 174 B3
Angelokastro GR 175 D7
Ångelsberg S 97 C15
Angelstad S 87 B13
Angely F 25 E11
Anger D 73 A6
Angera I 68 B6
Angermünde D 84 D6
Angern D 79 B10
Angern an der March A 77 F11
Angers F 23 F10
Ångersjö S 102 C8
Ängersjö S 122 C3
Angersnes N 108 D4
Angervikko FIN 125 D10
Angerville F 24 D7
Ängesån S 116 E8
Ängeslevä FIN 119 E15
Ängesträsk S 118 B8
Anghiari I 66 E5
Anglade F 28 E4
Angle GB 9 E12
Anglès E 43 D9
Anglès F 34 C4
Anglesola E 42 D5
Anglesona E 42 D6
Angles-sur-l'Anglin F 29 B7
Anglet F 32 D2
Angliers F 29 B6
Anglure F 25 C10
Angnäs S 107 D16
Angoisse F 29 E8
Ängom S 103 B13
An Gort IRL 6 F5
Angoulême F 29 D6
Angoulins F 28 C3
Angri I 60 B3
Angrie F 23 E10
Angüés E 42 C3
Anguiano E 40 D6
Anguillara Sabazia I 62 C2
Anguillara Veneta I 66 B4
Anguita E 47 B8
Angvik N 100 A8
Anha P 38 E2
Anhée B 19 D10
Anholt DK 87 B9
Aniane F 35 C6
Aniche F 19 D7
Anif A 73 A7
Anina RO 159 C8
Aninoasa RO 160 C2
Aninoasa RO 160 C5
Aninoasa RO 160 D2
Aninoasa RO 161 D6
Anizy-le-Château F 19 E7
Anjalankoski FIN 128 D6
Anjan S 105 D13
Anjum NL 16 B6
Ankaran SLO 73 E8
Ankarede Kapell S 105 B16
Ankarsrum S 93 D8
Ankarsund S 109 F12
Ankarsvik S 103 B13
Ankenes N 111 D13
Ankerlia N 112 E6
Ankershagen D 84 D3
Anklam D 84 C5
Ankum D 17 C9
Anlaby GB 11 D11
An Leadhb Gharbh IRL 6 C5
Anlezy F 30 B4
An Longfort IRL 7 E7
An Mám IRL 6 E3
An Mhala Raithní IRL 6 E3
An Móta IRL 7 F7
An Muileann gCearr IRL 7 E8
Ånn S 105 E13
Anna E 56 C3
Anna EST 131 C11
Annaberg A 77 G8
Annaberg-Buchholtz D 80 E4
Annaburg D 80 C4
Annagassan IRL 7 E10
Annagry IRL 6 B6
Annahilt GB 7 D10
Annahütte D 80 C5
Annalong GB 7 D11
Annamoe IRL 7 F10
Annan GB 5 F10
Anna Paulowna NL 16 C3
Annarode D 79 C9
An Nás IRL 7 F9
Annayalla IRL 7 D9
Annbank GB 4 E7
Anneberg S 91 D11
Anneberg S 92 D5
Annecy F 31 D9
Annecy-le-Vieux F 31 D9
Annefors S 103 D11
Annelund S 91 D13
Annemasse F 31 C9
Annen NL 17 B7
Annenieki LV 134 C6
Annestown IRL 9 D8
Anneyron F 30 E6
Annikvere EST 131 C12
Annœullin F 182 D1
Annonay F 30 E6
Annonen FIN 119 F14
Annopol PL 144 B4
Annot F 36 D5
Annweiler am Trifels D 21 F9
Ano Agios Vlasios GR 174 B4
Ano Amfeia GR 174 E5
Ano Chora GR 174 B4
Ano Diakofto GR 174 C5
Ano Drosini GR 171 B9
Anoeta E 32 D1
Anogeia GR 174 F5
Anogeia GR 178 E8
Ano Kalliniki GR 168 C5
Ano Kardamyla GR 177 B7
Ano Kavallari GR 169 C9
Ano Komi GR 169 D6
Ano Kopanaki GR 174 E4
Ano Lechonia GR 169 F9
Ano Lefkimmi GR 168 F3
Ano Mera GR 176 E5
Añón E 41 E8
Ano Poroia GR 169 B9
Anor F 19 E9
Añora E 54 C3
Ano Sagkri GR 176 E5
Ano Steni GR 175 B8

Ballyferriter IRL 8 D2
Ballyforan IRL 6 F6
Ballygar IRL 6 E6
Ballygarrett IRL 9 C10
Ballygawley GB 7 D8
Ballygeary IRL 9 D10
Ballyglass IRL 6 E5
Ballygorman IRL 4 E2
Ballygowan GB 7 C11
Ballyhaise IRL 7 D8
Ballyhalbert GB 7 D12
Ballyhale IRL 9 D8
Ballyhaunis IRL 6 E5
Ballyhean IRL 6 E4
Ballyheigue IRL 8 D3
Ballyjamesduff IRL 7 E8
Ballykeeran IRL 7 F7
Ballykelly GB 4 E2
Ballykilleen IRL 7 F8
Ballylanders IRL 8 D6
Ballylaneen IRL 9 D8
Ballylickey IRL 8 E4
Ballyliffen IRL 4 E2
Ballyliffin IRL 4 E2
Ballylynan IRL 9 C8
Ballymacarberry IRL 9 D7
Ballymacmague IRL 9 D7
Ballymadog IRL 9 E7
Ballymagorry GB 4 F2
Ballymahon IRL 7 E7
Ballymakeery IRL 8 E4
Ballymartin GB 7 D11
Ballymena GB 4 F4
Ballymoney GB 4 E3
Ballymore IRL 7 F7
Ballymote IRL 6 D5
Ballymurphy IRL 9 C9
Ballymurry IRL 6 E6
Ballynacally IRL 8 C4
Ballynafid IRL 7 E8
Ballynahinch GB 7 D11
Ballynahowen IRL 7 F7
Ballynakill IRL 7 F7
Ballynamona IRL 8 D5
Ballyneaner GB 4 F2
Ballynunty IRL 9 C7
Ballynure GB 4 F5
Ballyporeen IRL 8 D6
Ballyragget IRL 9 C8
Ballyroan IRL 9 C8
Ballyronan GB 4 F3
Ballyshannon IRL 6 C6
Ballyvaldon IRL 9 D10
Ballyvaughan IRL 6 F4
Ballyvoy GB 4 E4
Ballyvoyle IRL 9 D7
Ballywalter GB 7 C12
Ballyward GB 7 D10
Balma F 33 C9
Balmaha GB 4 C7
Balmaseda E 40 B5
Balmazújváros H 151 B7
Balme I 31 E11
Balmedie GB 3 L12
Balmuccia I 68 B5
Balnacra GB 2 L6
Balnapaling GB 3 K8
Balneario de Panticosa Huesca E 32 E5
Balninkai LT 135 F10
Balocco I 68 C5
Balogunyom H 149 B7
Balot F 25 E11
Balotaszállás H 150 E4
Balotești RO 161 D8
Balow D 83 D11
Balrath IRL 7 E10
Balș RO 160 E4
Balșa RO 151 E11
Balsa de Ves E 47 F10
Balsa Pintada E 56 F2
Balsareny E 43 D7
Balsfjord N 111 B17
Balsicas E 56 F3
Balsjö S 107 D16
Balsorano I 62 D5
Bålsta S 99 C9
Balsthal CH 27 F8
Balta RO 159 D10
Balta UA 154 B5
Balta Albă RO 161 C10
Balta Berilovac SRB 164 C5
Balta Doamnei RO 161 D8
Baltanás E 40 E3
Baltar E 38 E4
Baltasound GB 3 D15
Bălțătești RO 153 C8
Bălțați RO 153 C10
Bălteni RO 153 D11
Bâlteni RO 159 D11
Baltezers LV 135 B8
Bălți MD 153 B11
Baltimore IRL 8 F4
Baltinava LV 133 C3
Baltinglass IRL 9 C9
Baltiysk RUS 139 A8
Baltmuiža LV 135 D13
Baltoji Vokė LT 137 E11
Baltora S 99 C11
Bałtów PL 143 D12
Baltray IRL 7 E10
Băluşeni RO 153 B9
Balvan BG 166 C4
Bâlvănești RO 159 D10
Balvano I 60 B5
Balve D 17 F9
Balvi LV 133 B2
Balvicar GB 4 C5
Balya TR 173 E8
Balzers FL 71 C9
Bamberg D 75 C8
Bamburgh GB 5 D13
Bammental D 21 F11
Bampini GR 174 B3
Bampton GB 13 B11
Bampton GB 13 D8
Bana H 149 A9
Banafjäl S 107 E16
Banagher IRL 7 F7
Banarli TR 173 B7
Banassac F 34 B5
Banatski Brestovac SRB 159 D6
Banatski Dvor SRB 158 B6
Banatski Karlovac SRB 159 C7
Banatsko Aranđelovo SRB 150 E5
Banatsko Karađorđevo SRB 158 B6
Banatsko Novo Selo SRB 159 D6
Banatsko Veliko Selo SRB 150 F6
Banbridge GB 7 D10
Banbury GB 13 A12
Banca RO 153 E11
Banchory GB 5 A12
Band RO 152 D4
Bande E 38 D4
Bandenitz D 83 D10
Bandholm DK 83 A10
Bandirma TR 173 D8
Bandol F 35 D10
Bandon IRL 8 E5
Bandurove UA 154 A5
Băneasa RO 153 F11
Băneasa RO 155 E1
Băneasa RO 161 E8
Bănești MD 154 B2
Bănești RO 161 C7
Banevo BG 167 D8
Banff GB 3 K11
Bångnäs S 106 B9
Bangor GB 4 F5
Bangor GB 10 E3
Bangor IRL 6 D3
Bangor Erris IRL 6 D3
Bangsund N 105 C10
Banham GB 15 C11
Bánhorváti H 145 G2
Bănia RO 159 D9
Banie PL 85 D7
Banie Mazurskie PL 136 E5
Baniska BG 166 C5
Bănișor RO 151 C10
Bănița RO 159 C11
Banite BG 171 A8
Banitsa BG 165 C8
Banja BIH 158 F3
Banja SRB 163 B8
Banja Lučica BIH 157 D10
Banja Luka BIH 157 C7
Banjani SRB 158 D4
Banja Vrućia BIH 157 C8
Bankekind S 92 C7
Bankeryd S 92 D4
Bankfoot GB 5 B9
Bankya BG 165 D6
Bankya BG 165 D7
Banloc RO 159 C7
Bannalec F 22 E4
Bannay F 25 F8
Bannesdorf auf Fehmarn D 83 B10
Bannewitz D 80 E5
Bannivka UA 155 B3
Bannockburn GB 5 C9
Bañobárez E 45 C7
Bañón E 47 C10
Banon F 35 B10
Baños de la Encina E 54 C5
Baños de Molgas E 38 D4
Baños de Montemayor E 45 D9
Baños de Río Tobía E 40 D6
Baños de Valdearados E 40 E4
Bánov CZ 146 D5
Bánov SK 146 E6
Banova Jaruga HR 149 F7
Bánovce nad Bebravou SK 146 D6
Banoviči BIH 157 D10
Bánréve H 145 G1
Bansin D 84 C6
Banská Belá SK 147 E7
Banská Bystrica SK 147 D8
Banská Štiavnica SK 147 E7
Banské SK 145 F4
Bansko BG 165 F7
Bant NL 16 C5
Banteer IRL 8 D5
Banteln D 78 B6
Bantheville F 19 F11
Bantry IRL 8 E4
Banya BG 165 D10
Banya BG 165 E9
Banya BG 165 F8
Banya BG 166 D5
Banya BG 167 D9
Banyalbufar E 49 E10
Banyeres de Mariola E 56 D3
Banyliv UA 152 A6
Banyliv-Pidhirnyy UA 152 A7
Banyoles E 43 C9
Banyuls-sur-Mer F 34 F5
Banzi I 60 B6
Banzkow D 83 C11
Bapaume F 18 D6
Bar MNE 163 E7
Bara RO 151 F8
Bâra RO 153 C10
Bara S 87 D12
Barabás H 145 G5
Baracska H 149 B11
Bărăganul RO 161 D11
Baragiano I 60 B5
Barahona E 41 F6
Barajas de Melo E 47 D7
Barajevo SRB 158 D5
Barakaldo E 40 B6
Barakovo BG 165 E7
Baralla E 38 C5
Barañain E 32 E2
Baranbio E 40 B6
Báránd H 151 C7
Baranello I 63 D7
Baranjsko Petrovo Selo HR 149 E10
Barano d'Ischia I 62 F5
Baranów PL 141 G6
Baranów PL 142 D5
Baranowo PL 139 D11
Baranów Sandomierska PL 143 F12
Barão de São João P 50 E2
Baraolt RO 153 E7
Baraqueville F 33 B10
Barásoain E 32 E2
Barassie GB 4 D7
Bărăști RO 160 D5
Baravukha BY 133 E5
Barbacena P 51 B5
Barbadás E 38 D4
Barbadillo de Herreros E 40 D5
Barbadillo del Mercado E 40 D5
Barbadillo del Pez E 40 D5
Barban HR 67 B9
Barbarano Vicentino I 66 B4
Barbaraville GB 3 K8
Barbaros TR 173 C7
Barbaste F 33 B6
Barbastro E 42 C4
Barbat HR 67 C10
Barbate de Franco E 52 D5
Bărbătescu RO 161 D9
Bărbătești RO 160 D3
Barbatovac SRB 164 C3
Barbâtre F 28 B1
Bărbele LV 135 D9
Barbentane F 35 C8
Barberá del Vallès E 43 D8
Barberaz F 31 D8
Barberino di Mugello I 66 D3
Barbezieux-St-Hilaire F 28 E5
Barbonne-Fayel F 25 C10
Bărbulețu RO 160 C6
Barbullush AL 163 F8
Barby (Elbe) D 79 C10
Barç AL 168 C4
Barca E 41 F6
Bârca RO 160 F3
Barcabo E 42 C4
Barcada BIH 157 B8
Barca de Alva P 45 B7
Bărcănești RO 161 D8
Bărcănești RO 161 D9
Barcani RO 161 B8
Barcarrota E 51 B6
Barcea RO 153 F10
Barcelinhos P 38 E2
Barcellona Pozzo di Gotto I 59 C7
Barcelona E 43 E8
Barcelonne-du-Gers F 32 C5
Barcelonnette F 36 C5
Barcelos P 38 E2
Bárcena del Monasterio E 39 B6
Bárcena de Pie de Concha E 40 B3
Barcenillas de Cerezos E 40 B4
Barchfeld D 79 E7
Barciany PL 136 E3
Barcillonnette F 35 B10
Barcin PL 138 E4
Barcino PL 85 B11
Barcis I 72 D6
Barcones E 40 F6
Barcos P 44 B5
Barcs H 149 E8
Barcus F 32 D4
Barczewo PL 136 F2
Bardal N 108 D5
Bardar MD 154 D3
Barde DK 86 C3
Bardejov SK 145 E3
Bárdena E 41 D9
Bardenitz D 80 B3
Bårdesø DK 86 D6
Bardi I 69 D8
Bardineto I 37 C8
Bardney GB 11 E11
Bardo PL 77 B11
Bardolino I 66 A2
Bardonecchia I 31 E10
Bardos F 32 D3
Bardowick D 83 D8
Bardsea GB 10 C5
Bárdudvarnok H 149 D9
Bare BIH 157 E10
Bare SRB 158 E6
Bare SRB 163 C8
Barefield IRL 8 C5
Barèges F 33 E6
Barenburg D 17 C11
Barendorf D 83 D9
Bärenklau D 81 C7
Bärenstein D 76 B4
Bärenstein D 80 E5
Barentin F 18 E2
Barenton F 23 C10
Barevo BIH 157 D7
Barfleur F 23 A9
Barga I 66 D1
Bargagli I 37 C10
Bargas E 46 E4
Bârgăuani RO 153 D9
Barge I 31 F11
Bargemon F 36 D5
Bargen CH 27 E10
Bargenstedt D 82 B6
Barghe I 69 B9
Bârghiș RO 152 F5
Bargischow D 84 C5
Barglów Kościelny PL 140 C7
Bargoed GB 13 B8
Bargrennan GB 4 E7
Bargstedt D 17 B12
Bargteheide D 83 C8
Bargullas AL 168 C3
Barham GB 15 E11
Bar Hill GB 15 C9
Bari I 61 A7
Barić Draga HR 156 D3
Barile I 60 B5
Barilović HR 148 F5
Barinas E 56 E2
Båring DK 86 E5
Barì Sardo I 64 D4
Barisciano I 62 C5
Barjac F 35 B7
Bårjasnjar'ga N 113 D15
Barjols F 35 C11
Barkåkar N 95 D12
Barkåkra S 87 C11
Barkald N 101 C13
Barkarö S 98 C7
Barkava LV 135 C13
Barkelsby D 83 A7
Barkhyttan S 103 E11
Barkowo PL 85 C12
Barkston GB 11 F10
Bârla RO 160 E5
Bârlad RO 153 E11
Barleben D 79 B10
Bar-le-Duc F 26 C3
Barles F 36 C4
Barletta I 60 A6
Barley GB 15 C9
Barlinek PL 85 E8
Barlingbo S 93 D12
Barmouth GB 10 F3
Barmstedt D 82 C7
Bárna H 147 E9
Barna IRL 6 F4
Bârna RO 159 B9
Barnaderg IRL 6 F5
Barnard Castle GB 11 B8
Barnarp S 92 D4
Barnatra IRL 6 D3
Bärnau D 75 C11
Barnbach A 73 B11
Barneberg D 79 B9
Barneveld NL 16 D5
Barneville-Carteret F 23 B8
Barnewitz D 79 A12
Barneycarroll IRL 6 E5
Barnoldswick GB 11 D7
Bârnova RO 153 C11
Barnowko PL 85 E7
Barnsley GB 11 D9
Barnstädt D 79 D10
Barnstaple GB 12 C6
Barnstorf D 17 C11
Barntrup D 17 E12
Baronissi I 60 B3
Baronville F 26 C6
Baroševac SRB 158 E5
Barovo MK 169 B7
Barowka BY 133 E3
Barqueros E 55 D10
Barr F 27 D7
Barr GB 4 E7
Barracas E 48 D3
Barrachina E 47 C10
Barraduff IRL 8 D4
Barrafranca I 58 E5
Barral E 38 D3
Barrali I 64 E3
Barranco do Velho P 50 E4
Barrancos P 51 C6
Barranda E 55 C9
Barrapoll GB 4 C3
Barrax E 55 A8
Barre-des-Cévennes F 35 B6
Barreiro P 50 B1
Bärrek S 98 B7
Barrême F 36 D4
Barrhead GB 5 D8
Barrhill GB 4 E7
Barriada Nueva E 43 D8
Bárrio P 38 E2
Barrio del Peral E 56 F3
Barrio Mar E 48 E4
Barrit DK 86 D5
Barr na Trá IRL 6 D3
Barroca P 44 D5
Barroselas P 38 E2
Barrowby GB 11 F10
Barrow-in-Furness GB 10 C5
Barruecopardo E 45 B7
Barruelo de Santullan E 40 C3
Barry GB 13 C8
Barry IRL 7 E7
Bârsa RO 151 E9
Barsac F 32 A5
Bârsana RO 145 H9
Bârsău RO 151 B11
Barsbüttel D 83 C8
Bårse DK 87 E9
Barsele S 107 A12
Bârsești RO 153 F9
Barsinghausen D 78 B5
Barßel D 17 B9
Barsta S 103 A15
Barstyčiai LT 134 D3
Bar-sur-Aube F 25 D12
Bar-sur-Seine F 25 D11
Bārta LV 134 D2
Bartenheim F 27 E7
Bartenstein D 74 D6
Barth D 83 B13
Bartholomä D 74 E6
Bartholomäberg A 71 C9
Bartkuškiai LT 135 F9
Bartkuškis LT 137 D10
Bartnes N 105 C10
Bartniki PL 139 D10
Bartninkai LT 136 E7
Barton GB 10 D6
Barton-upon-Humber GB 11 D11
Bartoszyce PL 136 E2
Baru RO 159 C11
Baruchowo PL 139 F7
Barulho P 45 F6
Barumini I 64 D3
Baruth D 80 B5
Barvas GB 2 J3
Barvaux B 19 D11
Barver D 17 C11
Barwedel D 79 A8
Barwice PL 85 C10
Barxeta E 56 C4
Bârza RO 160 E4
Bárzana E 39 B8
Bârzava RO 151 E9
Barzio I 69 B7
Bašaid SRB 158 B5
Basarabeasca MD 154 E3
Basarabi RO 155 E2
Basarbovo BG 161 F7
Bàscara E 43 C9
Bascharage L 20 E5
Baschi I 62 B2
Baschurch GB 10 F6
Basciano I 62 B5
Basconcillos del Tozo E 40 C4
Bascons F 32 C5
Bascous F 33 C6
Bascov RO 160 D5
Basdahl D 17 B12
Basècles B 19 C8
Basel CH 27 E8
Baselga di Pinè I 69 A11
Baselice I 60 A3
Bas-en-Basset F 30 E5
Băsești RO 151 C11
Båsheim N 95 B10
Bashtanivka UA 154 F4
Basigo E 40 B6
Basildon GB 15 D9
Basiliano I 73 D7
Basingstoke GB 13 C12
Baška CZ 146 B6
Baška HR 67 C10
Baška Voda HR 157 F6
Baskemölla S 88 D6
Bäsksele S 107 B11
Bäsksjö S 107 B12
Basksjön S 107 E12
Baslow GB 11 E8
Bäsna S 97 A13
Bassacutena I 64 A3
Bassano del Grappa I 72 E4
Bassano Romano I 62 C2
Bassecourt CH 27 F7
Basse-Goulaine F 23 F9
Bassenge B 19 C12
Bassens F 28 F4
Bassiano I 62 D4
Bassoues F 33 C6
Bassum D 17 C11
Bassy F 31 D8
Bast FIN 123 C10
Båstad S 87 C11
Bastardo I 62 B3
Bastasi BIH 156 D5
Bastasi BIH 157 F10
Bastelica F 37 G10
Bastelicaccia F 37 H9
Bastennes F 32 C4
Bastfallet S 98 B7
Bastia F 37 F10
Bastia I 62 A3
Bastogne B 19 D12
Bastorf D 83 B11
Basttjärn S 97 B12
Bastumarks by S 118 E3
Bastuträsk S 107 C16
Bastuträsk S 118 E4
Báta H 149 D11
Bata RO 151 E9
Batajnica SRB 158 D5
Batak BG 165 F9
Batalha P 44 E3
Bățani RO 153 E7
Batăr RO 151 D8
Bătarci RO 145 G7
Båtas S 106 B8
Bátaszék H 149 D11
Batea E 42 E4
Batelov CZ 77 D8
Båteng N 113 C20
Baterno E 54 B3
Batetskiy RUS 132 D7
Bath GB 13 C10
Bathford GB 13 C10
Bathgate GB 5 D9
Bathmen NL 16 D6
Batin BG 161 F7
Batina HR 149 E11
Batizovce SK 145 E1
Batković BIH 158 D3
Batley GB 11 D8
Batllavë RKS 164 D3
Bátmonostor H 150 E2
Båtnfjordsøra N 100 A7
Batočina SRB 159 E7
Bátonyterenye H 147 F9
Bátorove Kosihy SK 146 F6
Batoș RO 152 D5
Batoshevo BG 166 D4
Bátovce SK 147 E7
Batovo BG 167 C9
Batrina HR 157 B8
Båtsfjord N 114 B7
Batsi GR 176 D4
Båtsjaur S 109 D13
Båtskärsnäs S 119 C10
Battenberg (Eder) D 21 B11
Bätterkinden CH 27 F8
Battice B 183 D7
Battipaglia I 60 B3
Battle GB 15 F9
Battonya H 151 E7
Batultsi BG 165 C9
Bátya H 150 E2
Batyatychi UA 144 C9
Batz-sur-Mer F 22 F7
Baucina I 58 D4
Baud F 22 E5
Bauduen F 36 D4
Bauen CH 71 D7
Baugé F 23 E11
Baugy F 25 F8
Bauladu I 64 C2
Baulon F 23 E8
Baume-les-Dames F 26 F5
Baumholder D 186 B3
Baunach D 75 C8
Baunei I 64 C4
Baurci MD 154 E3
Bausendorf D 21 D7
Bauska LV 135 D8
Băuțar RO 159 B10
Bautzen D 80 D6
Bavanište SRB 159 D6
Bavay F 19 D8
Bavel NL 182 B5
Baveno I 68 B6
Bavilliers F 27 E6
Bavorov CZ 76 D6
Bawdeswell GB 15 B11
Bawdsey GB 15 C11
Bawinkel D 17 C8
Bawn Cross Roads IRL 8 D5
Bayárcal E 55 E7
Bayarque E 55 E8
Baybuzivka UA 154 A5
Baye F 25 C10
Bayel F 25 D12
Bayerbach D 76 F4
Bayerbach bei Ergoldsbach D 75 E11
Bayerisch Eisenstein D 76 D4
Bayeux F 23 B10
Bayindir TR 177 C10
Bayir TR 181 B8
Bayirköy TR 172 D6
Baykal BG 160 F4
Bayon F 26 D5
Bayonne F 32 D3
Bayramiç TR 172 E6
Bayramiç TR 173 C6
Bayramli TR 173 B6
Bayreuth D 75 C10
Bayrischzell D 72 A5
Bayston Hill GB 10 F6
Baytaly UA 154 B5
Bayubas de Abajo E 40 E6
Baza E 55 D7
Bázakerettye H 149 C7
Bazas F 32 B5
Bazet F 33 D6
Baziège F 33 D9
Bazillac F 33 D6
Bazna RO 152 E4
Bazoches F 25 F10
Bazoches-au-Houlme F 23 C11
Bazoches-les-Gallerandes F 24 D7
Bazoches-sur-Hoëne F 24 C3
Bazougers F 23 D10
Bazouges F 23 E10
Bazzano I 66 D3
Beaconsfield GB 15 D7
Beadnell GB 5 D13
Beagh IRL 6 E5
Bealach A Doirín IRL 6 E5
Bealach Conglais IRL 9 C9
Bealach Feich IRL 7 C7
Bealaclugga IRL 6 F4
Béal an Átha IRL 6 D4
Béal an Mhuirthead IRL 6 D3
Béal Átha an Ghaorthaidh IRL 8 E4
Béal Átha Beithe IRL 7 D9
Béal Átha hAmhnais IRL 6 E5
Béal Átha Liag IRL 7 E7
Béal Átha na Muice IRL 6 E5
Béal Átha na Sluaighe IRL 6 F6
Béal Átha Seanaidh IRL 6 C6
Béal Deirg IRL 6 D3
Béal Easa IRL 6 E4
Bealnablath IRL 8 E5
Beaminster GB 13 D9
Beamud E 47 D9
Beannchar IRL 7 F7
Beantraí IRL 8 E4
Beariz E 38 D3
Bearna IRL 6 F4
Bearsden GB 5 D8
Beas E 51 E6
Beasain E 32 D1
Beas de Granada E 53 B10
Beas de Segura E 55 C7
Beateberg S 92 B4
Beattock GB 5 E10
Beaucaire F 35 C8
Beaucamps-le-Vieux F 18 E4
Beauchastel F 30 F6
Beaucouzé F 23 F10
Beaufay F 24 D3
Beaufort F 31 B7
Beaufort F 31 D10
Beaufort IRL 8 D3
Beaufort-en-Vallée F 23 F11
Beaugency F 24 E6
Beaujeu F 30 C6
Beaujeu F 36 C4
Beaujeu-St-Vallier-Pierrejux-et-Quitteur F 26 E4
Beaulieu F 35 C7
Beaulieu-lès-Loches F 24 F5
Beaulieu-sur-Dordogne F 29 F9
Beaulieu-sur-Loire F 25 E8
Beaulon F 30 B4
Beauly GB 2 L8
Beaumarchés F 33 C6
Beaumaris GB 10 E3
Beaumesnil F 24 B4
Beaumetz-lès-Loges F 18 D6
Beaumont B 19 D9
Beaumont F 23 A8
Beaumont F 29 B6
Beaumont F 29 F7
Beaumont-de-Lomagne F 33 C7
Beaumont-de-Pertuis F 35 C10
Beaumont-en-Argonne F 19 E11
Beaumont-en-Véron F 23 F12
Beaumont-le-Roger F 24 B4
Beaumont-lès-Valence F 30 F6
Beaumont-sur-Oise F 25 B7
Beaumont-sur-Sarthe F 23 D12
Beaune F 30 A6
Beaune-La Rolande F 25 D7
Beaupréau F 23 F10
Beauquesne F 18 D5
Beauraing B 19 D10
Beaurepaire F 31 E7
Beaurepaire-en-Bresse F 31 B7
Beaurières F 35 A10
Beausite F 26 C3
Beausoleil F 37 D6
Beautor F 19 E7
Beauvais F 18 F5
Beauval F 18 D5
Beauvezer F 36 C5
Beauville F 33 B7
Beauvoir-sur-Mer F 28 B1
Beauvoir-sur-Niort F 28 C5
Beauzac F 30 E5
Beauzelle F 33 C8
Beba Veche RO 150 E5
Bebertal D 79 B9
Bebington GB 10 E5
Bebra D 78 E6
Bebrene LV 135 D12
Bebrina HR 157 B8
Beccles GB 15 C12
Becedas E 45 D9
Beceite E 42 F4
Bečej SRB 158 B5
Beceni RO 161 C9
Becerreá E 38 C5
Becerril de Campos E 39 D10
Becherbach D 186 B4
Bécherel F 23 D8
Bechet RO 160 F3
Bechhofen D 21 F8
Bechhofen D 75 D8
Bechlín CZ 76 B6
Bechtheim D 21 E10
Bechyně CZ 77 D6
Becicherecu Mic RO 151 F7
Bečići MNE 163 E6
Becilla de Valderaduey E 39 D9
Beçin TR 181 B7
Beckdorf D 82 D7
Beckedorf D 17 D12
Beckeln D 17 C11
Beckingen D 21 F7
Beckingham GB 11 E10
Beckov SK 146 D5
Beckum D 17 E10
Beclean RO 152 C4
Beclean RO 152 F5
Bécon-les-Granits F 23 F10
Bečov CZ 76 B5
Becsehely H 149 D7
Becsvölgye H 149 C7
Bečváry CZ 77 C8
Bedale GB 11 C8
Bédar E 55 E9
Bédarieux F 34 C5
Bédarrides F 35 B8
Bedburg D 21 C7
Bedburg-Hau D 183 B8
Beddgelert GB 10 E3
Beddingestrand S 87 E12
Bédée F 23 D8
Bedekovčina HR 148 D5
Beden BG 165 F9
Beder DK 86 C6
Bedford GB 15 C8
Bedihošť CZ 77 D12
Bjdków PL 143 C8
Bedlington GB 5 E13
Bedlno PL 143 B8
Bedmar E 53 A10
Bednja HR 148 D5
Bédoin F 35 B9
Bedollo I 69 A11
Bedonia I 37 B11
Bedous F 32 D4
Bedsted DK 86 E4
Bedsted Stationsby DK 86 B2
Béduer F 33 A9
Bedum NL 17 B7
Bedwas GB 13 B8
Bedworth GB 13 A12
Bjdzin PL 143 F7
Bjdzino PL 85 B9
Beedenbostel D 79 A7
Beeford GB 11 D11
Beek NL 16 E5
Beek NL 16 E5
Beek NL 183 D7
Beekbergen NL 183 A7
Beelitz D 80 B3
Beendorf D 79 B9
Beenz D 84 D4
Beerfelden D 21 E11
Beernem B 19 B7
Beers NL 16 E5
Beerse B 16 F3
Beersel B 19 C9
Beerst B 182 C1
Beerta NL 17 B8
Beesd NL 183 B6
Beesenstedt D 79 C10
Beeskow D 80 B6
Beesten D 17 D9
Beeston GB 11 F9
Beetsterzwaag NL 16 B6
Beetzendorf D 83 E10
Bégaar F 32 C4
Bégadan F 28 E4
Begaljica SRB 158 D6
Bégard F 22 C5
Begejci SRB 158 B6
Beğendik TR 172 C6
Begíjar E 53 A9
Begijnendijk B 19 B10
Beglezh BG 165 C10
Begnište MK 169 B6
Begonte E 38 B4
Begur E 43 D10
Behramkale TR 171 F10
Behren-lès-Forbach F 27 B6
Behren-Lübchin D 83 B13
Behringen D 79 D8
Beica de Jos RO 152 D5
Beidaud RO 155 D3
Beierfeld D 79 E12
Beierstedt D 79 B8
Beilen NL 17 C7
Beilngries D 75 D9
Beilstein D 27 B11
Beimerstetten D 187 E8
Beinasco I 37 A7
Beinette I 37 C7
Beinwil CH 27 F9
Beirã P 44 F6
Beisfjord N 111 D14
Beisland N 90 C3
Beith GB 4 D7
Beitostølen N 101 D9
Beitstad N 105 C10
Beiuș RO 151 D9
Beja LV 133 B2
Beja P 50 C4
Bejar AL 168 D2
Béjar E 45 D9
Bejís E 48 E3
Bekecs H 145 G3
Békés H 151 D7
Békéscsaba H 151 D7
Békéssámson H 150 E6
Békésszentandrás H 150 D5
Bekkarfjord N 113 B19
Bekken N 101 C15
Bekkevoll N 114 D8
Belá SK 147 C7
Bélâbre F 29 B8
Bela Crkva SRB 159 D7
Beladice SK 146 E6
Belá-Dulice SK 147 C7
Belalcázar E 51 B9
Belá nad Cirochou SK 145 F5
Bělá nad Radbuzou CZ 75 C12
Belanovce MK 164 E4
Belanovica SRB 158 E5
Bela Palanka SRB 164 C5
Bélapátfalva H 145 G1
Bělá pod Bezdězem CZ 77 A7
Bělá pod Pradědem CZ 77 B12
Belascoáin E 32 E2
Belauski LV 133 C2
Belava LV 135 B13
Belazaima do Chão P 44 C4
Belcaire F 33 E9
Belcastel F 33 B10
Belcești RO 153 C10
Bełchatów PL 143 D7
Belchin BG 165 E7
Belchite E 41 F10
Bělčice CZ 76 C5
Belciugatele RO 161 E8
Belclare IRL 6 F5
Belcoo GB 7 D7
Belderg IRL 6 D3
Beldibi TR 181 C8
Beled H 149 B8
Belegiš SRB 158 C5
Belej HR 67 C9
Belene BG 160 F6
Bélesta F 33 E9
Beleți-Negrești RO 160 D6
Belevi TR 177 C9
Belezna H 149 D7
Belfast GB 7 C11
Belfeld NL 16 F6
Belford GB 5 D13
Belfort F 27 E6
Belfort-du-Quercy F 33 B9
Belforte del Chienti I 67 F7
Belgern D 80 D4
Belgershain D 79 D12
Belgioioso I 69 C7
Belgodère F 37 F10
Belgooly IRL 8 E6
Belgun BG 155 F2
Belhomert-Guéhouville F 24 C5
Beli HR 67 B9
Belianes E 42 D6
Belica HR 149 D7
Beli Iskŭr BG 165 E8
Beli Izvor BG 165 C7
Beli Manastir HR 149 E11
Belin RO 153 F7
Belin-Béliet F 32 B4
Belinchón E 47 D6
Belinț RO 151 F8
Beli Potok SRB 164 B5
Beliș RO 151 D11
Belišće HR 149 E10
Belitsa BG 161 F9
Belitsa BG 165 D8
Belitsa BG 165 F8
Beliu RO 151 E9
Bělkovice-Lašťany CZ 146 B4
Bell D 21 D8
Bell (Hunsrück) D 185 D7
Bella I 60 B5
Bellac F 29 C8
Bellacorick IRL 6 D3
Bellaghy GB 4 F3
Bellaghy IRL 6 E5
Bellagio I 69 B7
Bellahy IRL 6 E5
Bellanicë RKS 163 E10
Bellano I 69 A7

Bellante I 62 B5
Bellaria I 66 D5
Bellavary IRL 6 E4
Bellavista E 51 E8
Bellclaire d'Urgell E 42 D5
Belleek GB 7 D10
Bellegarde F 25 E7
Bellegarde F 35 C8
Bellegarde-en-Marche F 29 D10
Bellegarde-sur-Valserine F 31 C8
Belle-Isle-en-Terre F 22 C5
Bellême F 24 D4
Bellenaves F 30 C3
Bellenberg D 71 A10
Bellencombre F 18 E3
Bellerive-sur-Allier F 30 C3
Belles-Forêts F 27 C6
Belleu F 19 F7
Bellevaux F 31 C10
Belleville F 30 C6
Belleville-sur-Meuse F 26 B3
Belleville-sur-Vie F 28 B3
Bellevue-la-Montagne F 30 E4
Belley F 31 D8
Bellheim D 21 F10
Bellherbe F 26 F6
Bellignat F 31 C8
Bellinge DK 86 E6
Bellingham GB 5 E12
Bellingwolde NL 17 B8
Bellinzago Novarese I 68 B6
Bellinzona CH 69 A7
Bellizzi I 60 B3
Bell-Lloc d'Urgell E 42 D5
Bello E 47 C10
Bellobradë RKS 163 C10
Bellopojë RKS 163 D10
Bellou-en-Houlme F 23 C11
Bellpuig E 42 D6
Bellreguard E 56 D4
Bellshill GB 5 D8
Belluno I 72 D5
Bellver de Cerdanya E 33 F9
Bellvik S 107 C10
Belm D 17 D10
Bélmegyer H 151 D7
Bélmez E 51 C9
Bélmez de la Moraleda E 53 A10
Belmont GB 3 D15
Belmont-de-la-Loire F 30 C5
Belmonte E 39 B7
Belmonte E 47 E7
Belmonte P 45 D6
Belmonte Calabro I 60 E6
Belmonte del Sannio I 63 D6
Belmonte in Sabina I 62 C3
Belmontejo E 47 E8
Belmont-sur-Rance F 34 C4
Belmullet IRL 6 D3
Belo Brdo RKS 163 C10
Beloci MD 154 B4
Belœil B 19 C8
Belogradchik BG 159 F10
Beloiannisz H 149 B11
Belojin SRB 164 C3
Belorado E 40 D5
Beloslav BG 167 C9
Bělotín CZ 146 B5
Belotintsi BG 165 B6
Belovo BG 165 E9
Belozem BG 166 E4
Belp CH 31 B11
Belpasso I 59 D6
Belpech F 33 D9
Belper GB 11 E9
Belsay GB 5 E13
Belsh AL 168 C2
Belsk Duży PL 141 G3
Beltheim D 21 D8
Beltinci SLO 148 C6
Beltiug RO 151 B10
Beltra IRL 6 D5
Beltra IRL 6 E4
Beltrum NL 183 A9
Belturbet IRL 7 D8
Beluša SK 146 C6
Belušić SRB 159 F7
Belvédère-Campomoro F 37 H9
Belvedere Marittimo I 60 D5
Belvedere Ostrense I 67 E7
Belver de Cinca E 42 D4
Belver de los Montes E 39 E9
Belvès F 29 F8
Belvèze-du-Razès F 33 D10
Belvì I 64 D3
Belville IRL 6 D4
Belvís de la Jara E 46 E3
Belz F 22 E5
Belz UA 144 C9
Bełżec PL 144 C7
Bełżyce PL 141 H6
Bembibre E 38 B2
Bembibre E 39 C7
Bemmel NL 16 E5
Bemposta P 39 F7
Bemposta P 44 F4
Bempton GB 11 C11
Benabarre E 42 C4
Benacazón E 51 E7
Benahadux E 55 F8
Benahavís E 53 C6
Benalmádena E 53 C7
Benalúa de Guadix E 55 E6
Benalúa de las Villas E 53 B9
Benalup de Sidonia E 52 D5
Benamargosa E 53 C8
Benamaurel E 55 D7
Benamejí E 53 B7
Benamocarra E 53 C8
Benaocaz E 53 C6
Benaoján E 53 C6
Benasal E 48 D4
Benasau E 56 D4
Benasque E 33 E7
Benassay F 28 B6
Benatae E 55 C7
Benátky nad Jizerou CZ 77 B7
Benavente E 39 D8
Benavente P 50 B2
Benavides de Orbigo E 39 D8
Benavila P 44 F5
Benburb GB 7 D9
Bencatel P 50 B5
Bendorf D 21 D9
Bēne LV 134 D6
Benecko CZ 81 E9
Beneden-Leeuwen NL 16 E4
Benediktbeuren D 72 A3
Benedita P 44 F3
Benegiles E 39 E8
Bénéjacq F 32 D5
Benejama E 56 D3
Benejúzar E 56 E3
Benesat RO 151 C11
Benešov CZ 77 C7
Benešov nad Černou CZ 77 E7
Benešov nad Ploučnicí CZ 80 E6
Bénesse-Maremne F 32 C3
Benestare I 59 C9
Bénestroff F 27 C6
Benet F 28 C4
Benetutti I 64 C3
Bene Vagienna I 37 B7
Bénévent-l'Abbaye F 29 C9
Benevento I 60 A3
Benfeld F 27 D8
Benfica do Ribatejo P 44 F3
Bengești-Ciocadia RO 160 C3
Bengtsfors S 91 A11
Bengtsheden S 103 E10
Benia de Onís E 39 B10
Beniarbeig E 56 D5
Beniarrés E 56 D4
Beničanci HR 149 E10
Benicarló E 48 D5
Benicasim E 48 D5
Benidorm E 56 D4
Beniel E 56 E3
Benifaió E 48 F4
Benifallet E 42 F5
Benifallim E 56 D4
Benigánim E 56 D4
Benilloba E 56 D4
Benissa E 56 D5
Benissanet E 42 E5
Benitachell E 56 D5
Benitses GR 168 E2
Benizalón E 55 E8
Benizar y la Tercia E 55 C9
Benken CH 27 F11
Benkovac HR 156 D4
Benkovski BG 161 F10
Benkovski BG 171 B8
Benllech GB 10 E3
Benlloch E 48 D5
Bennebroek NL 182 A5
Bennekom NL 183 A7
Bennewitz D 79 D12
Bennungen D 79 D9
Bénodet F 22 E3
Benquerença P 45 D6
Benquerenças P 44 E5
Benquerencia de la Serena E 51 B9
Benquet F 32 C4
Bensafrim P 50 E2
Bensbyn S 118 C8
Bensdorf D 79 B11
Benshausen D 79 E8
Bensheim D 21 E11
Bensjö S 103 A9
Benson GB 13 B12
Bentelo NL 17 D7
Bentivoglio I 66 C3
Bentley GB 11 D9
Bentwisch D 83 B12
Bentzin D 84 C4
Beňuš SK 147 D9
Benzingerode D 79 C8
Beočin SRB 158 C4
Beograd SRB 158 D5
Bera de Bidasoa E 32 D2
Beragh GB 7 C8
Berane MNE 163 D8
Beranga E 40 B4
Berango E 40 B6
Berantevilla E 40 C6
Berat AL 168 C2
Bérat F 33 D8
Beratzhausen D 75 D10
Berbegal E 42 D3
Berbești RO 160 C3
Berca RO 161 C9
Bercedo E 40 B5
Bercel H 147 F8
Berceni RO 161 D8
Berceni RO 161 E8
Bercero E 39 E9
Berceto I 69 D8
Berchem B 19 C8
Berchidda I 64 B3
Berching D 75 D9
Berchtesgaden D 73 A7
Bérchules E 55 F6
Bercianos del Páramo E 39 D8
Berck F 15 G12
Bercu RO 145 H6
Berdal N 104 E6
Berdalen N 94 D6
Berducedo E 39 B6
Berdún E 32 E4
Bere Alston GB 12 E6
Beregdaróc H 145 G6
Bereguardo I 69 C7
Berehomet UA 152 A6
Berehove UA 145 G6
Berek HR 149 E7
Berekböszörmény H 151 C8
Berekfürdő H 150 C6
Beremend H 149 E10
Berești RO 153 E11
Berești-Meria RO 153 E11
Berești-Tazlău RO 153 E9
Berettyóújfalu H 151 C8
Berevoești RO 160 C5
Berezeni RO 154 E2
Berezyne UA 154 E4
Berg D 71 B9
Berg D 75 B10
Berg D 183 D9
Berg L 20 E6
Berg N 96 B7
Berg N 108 F3
Berg N 111 B13
Berg NL 19 C12
Berg NL 183 D7
Berg S 92 C8
Berg S 102 A7
Berg S 107 E10
Berg (Pfalz) D 27 C9
Berga D 79 D9
Berga D 79 E11
Berga E 43 C7
Berga S 89 A10
Bergagård S 87 B11
Bergaland N 94 D4
Bergama TR 177 A9
Bergamo I 69 B8
Bergantino I 66 B3
Bergara E 32 D1
Bergasa E 32 F1
Bergatreute D 71 B9
Berg bei Neumarkt in der Oberpfalz D 75 D9
Bergby S 103 E13
Berge D 17 C9
Berge D 83 D11
Berge E 42 F3
Berge S 102 A8
Berge S 105 D14
Bergeforsen S 103 A13
Bergeggi I 37 C8
Bergen D 73 A6
Bergen D 83 E7
Bergen D 84 B4
Bergen N 94 B2
Bergen NL 16 C3
Bergen (Dumme) D 83 E9
Bergen op Zoom NL 16 F2
Berger N 95 C12
Bergerac F 29 F6
Bergères-lès-Vertus F 25 C11
Bergesserin F 30 C6
Berget N 108 D6
Bergeyk NL 16 F4
Bergfors S 111 D18
Berghamn S 103 A15
Bergharen NL 183 B7
Berghaupten D 186 E4
Bergheim A 73 A7
Bergheim D 75 E9
Bergheim (Edertal) D 21 B12
Bergheim (Erft) D 21 C7
Berghem NL 16 E5
Berghem S 91 E12
Berghin RO 152 E3
Berghülen D 74 F6
Berg im Drautal A 73 C7
Bergisch Gladbach D 21 C8
Bergkamen D 17 E9
Bergkarlås S 102 D8
Bergkvara S 89 C10
Bergland S 107 A10
Berglia N 105 C15
Bergmo N 112 D7
Bergnäs S 109 E13
Bergnäset S 118 C8
Bergnäsudden S 109 E15
Bergnäsviken S 109 D15
Bergneustadt D 185 B8
Bergö FIN 99 B13
Bergö FIN 122 E6
Bergom S 107 E15
Bergsåker S 103 B13
Bergsäng S 97 B10
Bergsäter S 107 B12
Bergsbyn S 118 E6
Bergschenhoek NL 182 B5
Bergsgården S 103 E10
Bergshamra S 99 C11
Bergsjö S 103 C13
Bergsnov N 105 B9
Bergs slussar S 92 C7
Bergstod N 95 D9
Bergstrøm N 96 D6
Bergsviken S 118 D6
Bergtheim D 75 C7
Bergues F 18 C5
Bergün CH 71 D9
Bergvik S 103 D12
Bergviken S 109 D16
Bergwitz D 79 C12
Berhida H 149 B10
Beringe NL 183 C7
Beringel P 50 C4
Beringen B 19 B11
Berislăvești RO 160 C4
Beriu RO 151 F11
Berja E 55 F7
Berka D 79 E7
Berkåk N 101 A12
Berkel NL 16 E2
Berkel-Enschot NL 16 E4
Berkeley GB 13 B10
Berkenthin D 83 C9
Berkheim D 71 A10
Berkhout NL 16 C4
Berkovići BIH 157 F9
Berkovitsa BG 165 C7
Berlanga E 51 C8
Berlanga de Duero E 40 F6
Berlești RO 160 D3
Berlevåg N 114 B6
Berlicum NL 183 B6
Berlin D 80 A4
Berlingerode D 79 D7
Berlişte RO 159 D7
Berlstedt D 79 D9
Bermatingen D 27 E11
Bermeo E 40 B6
Bermillo de Sayago E 39 F7
Bern CH 31 B11
Bernac-Dessus F 33 D6
Bernalda I 61 C7
Bernardos E 46 B4
Bernartice CZ 76 D6
Bernartice CZ 81 E9
Bernăti LV 134 D1
Bernau D 27 E9
Bernau D 84 E5
Bernau am Chiemsee D 72 A5
Bernaville F 18 D5
Bernay F 24 B4
Bernbeuren D 71 B11
Bernburg (Saale) D 79 C10
Berndorf A 77 G10
Berne D 17 B10
Bernecebaráti H 147 E7
Bernedo E 41 C7
Bernhardsthal A 77 E11
Bernhardswald D 75 D11
Bernin F 31 E8
Bernis F 35 C7
Bernisdale GB 2 L4
Bernissart B 19 D8
Bernitt D 83 C11
Bernkastel-Kues D 21 E8
Bernolákovo SK 146 E4
Bernsdorf D 80 D6
Bernshammar S 97 C14
Bernstadt D 74 E7
Bernstadt D 81 D7
Bernstein A 148 B6
Beromünster CH 27 F9
Beronovo BG 167 D7
Beroun CZ 76 C6
Berovo MK 165 F6
Berra I 66 C4
Berre-l'Étang F 35 D9
Berriedale GB 3 J9
Berrien F 22 D4
Berriozar E 32 E2
Berru F 19 F9
Berry-au-Bac F 19 F8
Bersenbrück D 17 C9
Bershad' UA 154 A5
Beršići SRB 158 E5
Bersone I 69 B10
Bērstele LV 135 D7
Bertamirans E 38 C2
Bertea RO 161 C7
Berteştii de Jos RO 155 D1
Bertinoro I 66 D5
Bertnes N 108 B8
Bertogne B 19 D12
Bertrange L 186 B1
Bertrichamps F 27 D6
Bertrix B 19 E11
Běrunice CZ 77 B8
Berveni RO 151 B9
Bērvircava LV 134 D7
Berwick-upon-Tweed GB 5 D12
Bērzaine LV 131 F10
Berzasca RO 159 D8
Bērzaune LV 135 C12
Bērzciems LV 134 B6
Berzence H 149 D8
Bērzgale LV 133 C3
Bērzieši LV 135 D11
Bērzkalne LV 133 B2
Berźniki PL 137 E7
Berzovia RO 159 C8
Bērzpils LV 133 C2
Berzunți RO 153 E9
Beşalma MD 154 E3
Besalú E 43 C9
Besançon F 26 F5
Besande E 39 C10
Bescanó E 43 D9
Beselich-Obertiefenbach D 21 D10
Beșeňov SK 146 E6
Besenyőtelek H 150 B5
Besenyszög H 150 C5
Besigheim D 27 C11
Beşiktaş TR 173 B11
Beška SRB 158 C5
Besko PL 145 D4
Besni Fok SRB 158 D5
Besnyő H 149 B11
Besozzo I 68 B6
Bessacarr GB 11 D9
Bessaker N 104 C8
Bessan F 34 D5
Bessay-sur-Allier F 30 C3
Bessbrook GB 7 D10
Besse F 31 E9
Besse-et-St-Anastaise F 30 D2
Bessèges F 35 B7
Bessenbach D 187 B7
Bessé-sur-Braye F 24 E4
Besse-sur-Issole F 36 E4
Bessières F 33 C9
Bessines-sur-Gartempe F 29 C8
Bessude I 64 B2
Best NL 16 E4
Bestensee D 80 B5
Bestorp S 92 C7
Bestwig D 17 F10
Bestwina PL 147 B8
Beszterec H 145 G4
Betanzos E 38 B3
Betelu E 32 D2
Bétera E 48 E4
Beteta E 47 C8
Bethausen RO 151 F8
Betheln D 78 B6
Bethesda GB 10 E3
Bethmale F 33 E8
Bethon F 25 C10
Béthune F 18 C6
Betna N 104 E4
Beton-Bazoches F 25 C9
Betschdorf F 186 D4
Betsele S 107 B15
Bettelainville F 186 C1
Bettembourg L 20 E6
Bettendorf L 20 E6
Bettingen D 20 E6
Bettna S 93 B9
Bettola I 37 B11
Betton F 23 D8
Bettyhill GB 3 H8
Bettystown IRL 7 E10
Betws-y-coed GB 10 E4
Betxi E 48 E4
Betygala LT 134 F6
Betz F 25 B8
Betzdorf D 21 C9
Betzdorf L 186 B1
Betzenstein D 75 C9
Betzigau D 71 B10
Beucha D 79 D12
Beuil F 36 C5
Beuningen NL 16 E5
Beuren D 79 D7
Beuron D 27 D10
Beurville F 25 D12
Beuvrages F 182 E2
Beuvry F 18 C6
Beuzeville F 18 F1
Bevagna I 62 B3
Bevaix CH 31 B10
Beveren B 19 B9
Beverley GB 11 D11
Beverlo B 183 C6
Bevern D 78 C5
Beverstedt D 17 B11
Beverungen D 21 A12
Beverwijk NL 16 D3
Béville-le-Comte F 24 D6
Bewdley GB 13 A10
Bex CH 31 C11
Bexbach D 21 F8
Bexhill GB 15 F9
Beyağaç TR 181 B9
Beyazköy TR 173 B8
Beyçayiri TR 173 D6
Beyel TR 173 E10
Beyendorf D 79 B10
Beykoz TR 173 B11
Beynac-et-Cazenac F 29 F8
Beynat F 29 E9
Beynost F 31 D7
Beyoba TR 177 B10
Beyobasi TR 181 C9
Bezas E 47 D10
Bezau A 71 C9
Bezdan SRB 150 F2
Bezdead RO 161 C6
Bezdonys LT 137 D12
Bèze F 26 F3
Bezenye H 146 F4
Bezhanitsy RUS 133 C7
Bezhanovo BG 155 F2
Bezhanovo BG 165 C9
Béziers F 34 D5
Bezledy PL 136 E2
Bezmer BG 161 F10
Bezmer BG 166 E6
Bezouce F 35 C8
Bežovce SK 145 F5
Biadki PL 142 C4
Biała PL 142 F4
Biała-Parcela Pierwsza PL 142 D5
Biała Piska PL 139 C13
Biała Podlaska PL 141 F8
Biała Rawska PL 141 G2
Białe Błota PL 138 D4
Białebłoto-Kobyla PL 139 E12
Białka PL 145 E1
Białobrzegi PL 141 G3
Białogard PL 85 C9
Białośliwie PL 85 D12
Białowieża PL 141 E9
Biały Bór PL 85 C11
Biały Dunajec PL 147 C10
Białystok PL 140 D8
Biancavilla I 59 D6
Bianco I 59 C9
Biandrate I 68 C5
Bians-les-Usiers F 31 B9
Bianzè I 68 C5
Biar E 56 D3
Biarritz F 32 D2
Biarrotte F 32 C3
Biars-sur-Cère F 29 F9
Bias F 32 B3
Bias F 33 B7
Biasca CH 71 E7
Biatorbágy H 149 B11
Bibbiena I 66 E4
Bibbona I 66 F2
Biberach D 27 D9
Biberach an der Riß D 71 A9
Biberbach D 75 E8
Biberist CH 27 F8
Bibinje HR 156 D3
Bibione I 73 E7
Biblis D 21 E10
Bibury GB 13 B11
Bicaz RO 151 C11
Bicaz RO 153 D8
Bicaz-Chei RO 153 D7
Bicazu Ardelean RO 153 D7
Biccari I 60 A4
Bicester GB 13 B12
Bichiș RO 152 E4
Bichl D 72 A3
Bichlbach A 71 C11
Bickleigh GB 13 D7
Bicorp E 48 F3
Bicos P 50 D3
Bicske H 149 A11
Bicton GB 10 F6
Bidache F 32 D3
Bidart F 32 D2
Biddenden GB 15 E10
Biddinghuizen NL 16 D5
Biddulph GB 11 E7
Bideford GB 12 C6
Bidjovagge N 112 E10
Bidos F 32 D4
Bidovce SK 145 F3
Bie S 93 A8
Bieber D 21 D12
Biebesheim am Rhein D 21 E10
Biecz PL 144 D3
Biedenkopf D 21 C11
Biel CH 27 F7
Biel E 32 F4
Bielany-Żyłaki PL 141 F6
Bielawa PL 81 E11
Bielawy PL 143 B8
Bielefeld D 17 D11
Bielice PL 85 D7
Bieliny Kapitulne PL 143 E10
Biella I 68 B5
Bielle F 32 D5
Bielsa E 33 E6
Bielsk PL 139 E8
Bielsko-Biała PL 147 B8
Bielsk Podlaski PL 141 E8
Bienenbüttel D 83 D8
Bieniów PL 81 C8
Bienno I 69 B9
Bienservida E 55 B7
Bienvenida E 51 C7
Bierawa PL 142 F5
Bierdzany PL 142 E5
Bière CH 31 B9
Bierge E 42 C3
Bierné F 23 E10
Biersted DK 86 A5
Biert F 33 E8
Biertan RO 152 E5
Bieruń PL 143 F7
Bierutów PL 142 D4
Bierzwienna-Długa PL 142 B6
Bierzwnik PL 85 D9
Biesaidgohppi N 113 C16
Biescas E 32 E5
Biesenthal D 84 E5
Biesiekierz PL 85 B10
Biesles F 26 D3
Biesowice PL 85 B11
Biessenhofen D 71 B11
Bietigheim D 27 C9
Bietigheim-Bissingen D 27 C11
Bietikow D 84 D5
Bièvre B 19 E11
Bieżuń PL 139 E8
Biga TR 173 D7
Bigadiç TR 173 F9
Biganos F 32 A4
Bigastro E 56 E3
Bigauņciems LV 134 C7
Bigbury-on-Sea GB 13 E7
Biggar GB 5 D9
Biggleswade GB 15 C8
Bignan F 22 E6
Bignasco CH 71 E7
Bigor MNE 163 E7
Bigüézal E 32 E3
Biguglia F 37 F10
Bihać BIH 156 C4
Biharia RO 151 C8
Biharkeresztes H 151 C8
Biharnagybajom H 151 C7
Bihartorda H 151 C7
Biharugra H 151 D8
Bihosava BY 133 E3
Bijela MNE 163 E6
Bijele Poljane MNE 163 D6
Bijeljani BIH 157 F9
Bijeljina BIH 158 D3
Bijelo Brdo HR 149 E11
Bijelo Bučje BIH 157 D8
Bijelo Polje MNE 163 C8
Bikernieki LV 135 E13
Bikovo SRB 150 F4
Biksēre LV 135 C12
Bílá Lhota CZ 77 C11
Bilalovac BIH 157 D9
Bilbao E 40 B6
Bilbo E 40 B6
Bilbor RO 153 C7
Bilca RO 153 B7
Bilciurești RO 161 D7
Bil'dzyuhi BY 133 F2
Bileća BIH 162 D5
Biled RO 151 F6
Biłgoraj PL 144 B6
Bilicenii Vechi MD 153 B12
Bílina CZ 80 E5
Bilisht AL 168 C4
Biljača SRB 164 E4
Bilje HR 149 E11
Bilky UA 145 G7
Billdal S 91 D10
Billerbeck D 17 E8
Billère F 32 D5
Billericay GB 15 D9
Billesholm S 87 C11
Billiat F 31 C8
Billigheim D 21 F12
Billingham GB 11 B9
Billinghay GB 11 E11
Billingsfors S 91 B11
Billingshurst GB 15 E8
Billom F 30 D3
Billsåsen S 105 F16
Billsbro S 92 A7
Billsta S 107 E15
Billum DK 86 D2
Billund DK 86 D4
Billy F 30 C3
Bilolissya UA 154 F5
Bílovec CZ 146 B6
Bílovice CZ 146 C5
Bilska LV 135 B11
Bilston GB 5 D10
Bilthoven NL 16 D4
Bilto N 112 E7
Bilton GB 11 D11
Bilyayivka UA 154 E6
Bilychi UA 145 E6
Bilyn UA 152 A4
Bilyne UA 154 B5
Bilzen B 19 C12
Bimbister GB 3 G10
Bíňa SK 147 F7
Binaced E 42 D4
Binas F 24 E5
Binasco I 69 C7
Binbrook GB 11 E11
Binche B 19 D9
Bindalseit N 105 A12
Bindlach D 75 C10
Bindslev DK 90 D7
Binefar E 42 D4
Bingen D 27 D11
Bingen am Rhein D 21 E9
Bingerden NL 183 B8
Bingham GB 11 F10
Binghamstown IRL 6 D2
Bingley GB 11 D8
Bingsjö S 103 D10
Binic F 22 C6
Biniés E 32 E4
Binissalem E 49 E10
Binnen D 17 C12
Binz D 84 B5
Binzen D 27 E8
Biograd na Moru HR 156 E3
Biokovina BIH 157 D7
Biol F 31 E7
Bionaz I 31 D11
Biorra IRL 7 F7
Biosca E 43 D6
Biot F 36 D6
Biota E 41 D9
Birchington GB 15 E11
Birchiș RO 151 F9
Bircza PL 144 D5
Birdhill IRL 8 C6
Birgittelyst DK 86 C4
Biri H 151 B8
Biri N 101 E13
Bīriņi LV 135 B9
Biristrand N 101 D12
Birkeland N 90 C3
Birkelse DK 86 A5
Birkenau D 187 B6
Birkenfeld D 21 E8
Birkenfeld D 27 C10
Birkenfeld D 74 C6
Birkenhead GB 10 E5
Birken-Honigsessen D 185 C8
Birkenwerder Berlin D 84 E4
Birkerød DK 87 D10
Birket DK 87 F8
Birketveit N 90 C2
Birkfeld A 148 B5
Birkungen D 79 D7
Birmingham GB 13 A11
Birnbaum A 73 C6
Biron F 33 A7
Birori I 64 C2
Birr IRL 7 F7
Birresborn D 21 D7
Birsay GB 3 G10
Birstall GB 11 F9
Birstein D 21 D12
Birštonas LT 137 D9
Birtavarre N 112 E6
Birtley GB 5 F13
Biruința MD 153 B12
Biržai LT 135 D9
Birzes LV 135 D8
Birzgale LV 135 C9
Birži LV 135 D11
Birzuli LV 131 F12
Biš SLO 148 C5
Bisaccia I 60 A4
Bisacquino I 58 D3
Biscarrosse F 32 B3
Biscarrosse-Plage F 32 B3
Bisceglie I 61 A7
Bischberg D 75 C8
Bischbrunn D 187 B7
Bischhausen (Waldkappel) D 78 D6
Bischheim F 27 C8
Bischoffen D 21 C10
Bischofferode D 79 D7
Bischoffsheim F 186 E3
Bischofsheim D 21 E10
Bischofsheim an der Rhön D 74 B7
Bischofshofen A 73 B7
Bischofsmais D 76 E4
Bischofswerda D 80 D6
Bischofswiesen D 73 A6
Bischofszell CH 27 E11
Bischwiller F 27 C8
Bisenti I 62 B5
Biser BG 166 F5
Bisertsi BG 161 F9
Bishop Auckland GB 5 F13
Bishop's Castle GB 10 G6
Bishop's Cleeve GB 13 B10
Bishop's Lydeard GB 13 C8
Bishop's Stortford GB 15 D9
Bishop's Waltham GB 13 D12
Bishqem AL 168 B2
Bishtazhin RKS 163 E10
Bisignano I 60 D6
Bisingen D 27 D10
Biskupice PL 141 H7
Biskupice PL 142 D5
Biskupice SK 147 E9
Biskupiec PL 136 F2
Biskupiec PL 139 C7
Bislev DK 86 B5
Bismark (Altmark) D 83 E11
Bismervik N 113 B11
Bismo N 101 C8
Bisoca RO 161 B9
Bispgården S 107 E11
Bispingen D 83 D8
Bissen L 20 E6
Bissendorf D 17 D10
Bissendorf (Wedemark) D 78 A6
Bissingen D 75 E8
Bistagno I 37 B8
Bistarac BIH 157 C10
Bistra RO 151 E11
Bistra RO 152 B4
Bistreț RO 160 F3
Bistrets BG 167 E8
Bistrica BIH 157 B7
Bistrica BIH 157 C7
Bistrica BIH 157 E8
Bistrica BIH 157 E10
Bistrica SLO 73 D9
Bistrica SLO 148 D5
Bistričak BIH 157 D8
Bistrița RO 152 C5
Bistrița Bârgăului RO 152 C5
Bistritsa BG 165 D7
Bistritsa BG 165 E7
Bisztynek PL 136 E2
Bitburg D 21 E7
Bitche F 27 B7
Bitetto I 61 A7
Bitinckë AL 168 C4
Bitola MK 168 B5
Bitonto I 61 A7
Bitritto I 61 A7
Bitschwiller-lès-Thann F 27 E7
Bitterfeld D 79 C11
Bitterstad N 110 C9
Bitti I 64 C3
Bittkau D 79 B10
Bitton GB 13 C10
Bitz D 27 D11
Biurrun E 32 E2
Bivio CH 71 E9
Bivolari RO 153 B10
Bivona I 58 D3
Bixad RO 145 H7
Bixad RO 153 E7
Bixter GB 3 E14
Biyikali TR 173 B7
Biyikli TR 177 D10
Bizanet F 34 D4
Bizanos F 32 D5
Bizovac HR 149 E10
Bjåen N 94 C6
Bjærangen N 108 C6
Bjæverskov DK 87 E10
Bjännberg S 122 C3
Bjarkøy N 111 C12
Bjärnum S 87 C13
Bjärred S 87 D12
Bjärsjölagård S 87 D13
Bjärtrå S 107 F13
Bjästa S 107 E15
Bjela BIH 157 F10
Bjelajci BIH 157 B6
Bjelopolje HR 156 C4
Bjelovar HR 149 E7
Bjergby DK 90 D7
Bjerge DK 87 D8
Bjerka N 108 D6
Bjerkvik N 111 C14
Bjerreby DK 86 F7
Bjerregrav DK 86 B5
Bjerringbro DK 86 C5
Bjøllånes N 108 C8
Bjoneroa N 95 A12
Bjønnes N 108 D7
Björbo S 97 B12
Björboholm S 91 D11
Bjordal N 94 E4
Bjørgen N 105 F9
Bjørgo N 101 E10
Björkå S 107 E13
Bjørkåsen N 111 C17
Bjørkåsen N 111 D12
Björkberg S 103 C9
Björkberg S 107 B13
Björkberg S 118 C5
Björkboda FIN 126 E8
Björke S 93 D12
Björke S 103 E13
Bjørkeflåta N 95 B9
Bjørkelangen N 95 C15
Bjørkeset N 95 C10
Bjørkestrand N 114 C4
Björketorp S 91 E12
Björkfors S 119 C10
Björkheden S 109 E12
Björkhöjden S 107 E10
Björkholmen S 109 C17
Björkland S 109 F16
Bjørklia N 105 E9
Björkliden S 111 D16
Björklinge S 99 B9
Björknäset S 107 F12
Bjørknes N 96 B6
Bjørknes N 114 D6
Björkö FIN 122 E6
Björköby FIN 122 D6
Björköby S 92 D5
Björkön S 103 B14
Björksele S 107 B15
Björksele S 107 D12
Björksjön S 107 E13
Björkstugan S 111 D15
Björkvik S 93 B9
Bjorli N 100 B8
Bjørn N 108 D4
Björna S 107 D15
Björnänge S 105 E14
Björndalen S 97 C11
Björneborg S 97 D11
Bjørnengen N 113 D11

Bjørnera N 111 C12
Bjørnes N 113 B18
Bjørnevatn N 114 D7
Bjørnfjell N 111 D15
Björnhult S 89 A10
Björnliden S 102 B3
Björnlunda S 93 A10
Björnön S 103 A9
Bjørnrå N 111 C10
Björnrike S 102 B6
Björnsjö S 107 D14
Bjørnskinn N 111 B10
Bjørnstad N 105 B14
Bjørnstad N 114 D9
Björsarv S 103 B11
Björsäter S 92 C8
Björsbo S 103 C12
Björsjö S 97 B13
Bjugn N 104 D7
Bjurå S 118 B8
Bjuråker S 103 C12
Bjurberget S 97 A8
Bjurfors S 107 C17
Bjurfors S 118 E5
Bjurholm S 107 D16
Bjursås S 103 E9
Bjurselet S 118 E6
Bjurträsk S 107 B17
Bjuv S 87 C11
Blace MK 164 E3
Blace SRB 164 C3
Blachownia PL 143 E6
Black Bourton GB 13 B11
Black Bull IRL 7 F10
Blackburn GB 3 L12
Blackburn GB 5 D9
Blackburn GB 10 D7
Blackmoor Gate GB 13 C7
Blackpool GB 10 D5
Blackrock IRL 7 E10
Blackstad S 93 D8
Blacktown GB 7 C7
Blackwater IRL 9 D10
Blackwaterfoot GB 4 D6
Blackwood GB 13 B8
Bladel NL 16 F4
Blaenau Ffestiniog GB 10 F4
Blaenavon GB 13 B8
Blagaj BIH 157 F8
Blagaj Japra BIH 156 B5
Blagdon GB 13 C9
Blăgești RO 153 D9
Blăgești RO 153 E12
Blagnac F 33 C8
Blagoevgrad BG 165 E7
Blagoevo BG 166 C6
Blåhøj DK 86 D4
Blaibach D 75 D12
Blain F 23 F8
Blainville-sur-l'Eau F 186 D1
Blainville-sur-Mer F 23 B8
Blair Atholl GB 5 B9
Blairgowrie GB 5 B10
Blaj RO 152 E3
Blajan F 33 D7
Blăjani RO 161 C9
Blăjel RO 152 E4
Blăjeni RO 151 E10
Blakeney GB 13 B10
Blakeney GB 15 B11
Blakstad N 90 C4
Blâmont F 27 C6
Blan F 33 C10
Blanca E 55 C10
Blancafort F 25 E8
Blancas E 47 C10
Blandford Forum GB 13 D10
Blandiana RO 151 F11
Blanes E 43 D9
Blaney GB 7 D7
Blangy-sur-Bresle F 18 E4
Blankaholm S 93 D9
Blankenberg D 83 C11
Blankenberge B 19 B7
Blankenburg (Harz) D 79 C8
Blankenfelde D 80 B4
Blankenhain D 79 E9
Blankenhain D 79 E11
Blankenheim D 21 D7
Blankenrath D 21 D8
Blankensee D 84 D4
Blankenstein D 75 B10
Blanquefort F 28 F4
Blans DK 86 F5
Blansko CZ 77 D11
Blanzac-Porcheresse F 28 E6
Blanzay F 29 C6
Blanzy F 30 B5
Blaricum NL 183 A6
Blarney IRL 8 E5
Blasimon F 28 F5
Blåsjöfallet S 105 B16
Blåsmark S 118 D6
Błaszki PL 142 C5
Blatec MK 164 F6
Blatets BG 167 D7
Blatna BIH 156 C5
Blatná CZ 76 D5
Blatné SK 146 E4
Blatnica BIH 157 D8
Blato HR 162 D2
Blaton B 182 D3
Blattniksele S 109 F14
Blaubeuren D 74 F6
Blaufelden D 74 D6
Blausasc F 37 D6
Blaustein D 187 E8
Blåvik S 92 C6
Blåviksjön S 107 B14
Blavozy F 30 E4
Blaye F 28 E4
Blaževo SRB 163 C10
Błaziny Górne PL 141 H4
Blāzma LV 134 B4
Blažovice CZ 77 D11
Błażowa PL 144 D5
Blázquez E 51 C9
Blažuj BIH 157 E9
Bleckåsen S 105 E15
Bleckede D 83 D9
Blecua E 42 C3
Bled SLO 73 D9
Błędowo PL 138 D6
Bledzew PL 81 A8
Blegny B 19 C12
Bléharies B 19 C7
Bleialf D 20 D6
Bleiburg A 73 C10
Bleicherode D 79 D8
Bleidenstadt D 185 D9
Bleik N 111 B10
Bleikvassli N 108 E6
Bleiswijk NL 182 A5
Blejești RO 161 E6
Blejoi RO 161 D8
Blekendorf D 83 B9
Bleket S 91 D10
Blender D 17 C12
Bléneau F 25 E8
Blénod-lès-Toul F 26 C4
Blenstrup DK 86 B6
Blentarp S 87 D13
Blera I 62 C2
Blérancourt F 19 E7
Bléré F 24 F4
Blerick NL 16 F6
Blesa E 42 E2
Bleskensgraaf NL 182 B5
Blesle F 30 E3
Blessington IRL 7 F9
Blet F 29 B11
Bletchley GB 15 D7
Blīdene LV 134 C5
Blidsberg S 91 D14
Blieskastel D 21 F8
Bligny F 25 D12
Bligny-sur-Ouche F 25 F12
Blikstorp S 91 C15
Bliksund N 90 C3
Blimea E 39 B8
Blindow D 84 D5
Blinja HR 149 F6
Blistrup DK 87 C10
Blixterboda S 97 D13
Blizanów PL 142 C5
Bliżejov CZ 76 D3
Blížkovice CZ 77 E9
Bliznatsi BG 167 C9
Bliżyn PL 141 H3
Bllacë RKS 163 E10
Blois F 24 E5
Blokhus DK 86 A5
Blokzijl NL 16 C5
Blombacka S 97 C10
Blomberg D 17 E12
Blome LV 135 B11
Blome LV 135 B13
Blomsøy N 108 E3
Blomstermåla S 89 B10
Błonie PL 141 F3
Błonie PL 143 B7
Blönsdorf D 79 C12
Blötberget S 97 B13
Blousson-Sérian F 33 D6
Blovice CZ 76 C5
Blowatz D 83 C11
Bloxham GB 13 A12
Bludenz A 71 C9
Bludov CZ 77 C11
Blue Ball IRL 7 F7
Blumberg D 27 E10
Blumberg D 80 A5
Blumenhagen D 84 C5
Blumenholz D 84 D4
Blŭskovo BG 167 C8
Blyberg S 102 D7
Blyth GB 5 E13
Blyth GB 11 E9
Blyth Bridge GB 5 D10
Blyton GB 11 E10
Bø N 95 D10
Bø N 110 C8
Bo N 111 B10
Bø N 111 D12
Boada E 45 C8
Boadilla del Monte E 46 D5
Boadilla de Rioseco E 39 D10
Boal E 39 B6
Boalhosa P 38 E3
Boan MNE 163 D7
Boara Pisani I 66 B4
Boat of Garten GB 3 L9
Boa Vista P 44 E3
Boavista P 44 F2
Bobadilla E 53 B7
Bobâlna RO 152 C3
Bobbio I 37 B10
Bobbio Pellice I 31 F11
Bobenheim-Roxheim D 187 B5
Boberg S 107 E9
Boberka UA 145 E6
Bobicești RO 160 E4
Böbing D 71 B12
Bobingen D 71 A11
Böbitz D 83 C10
Bobivtsi UA 153 A7
Böblingen D 27 C11
Bobolice PL 85 C11
Boborás E 38 D3
Boboshevo BG 165 E7
Bobota HR 149 F11
Bobota RO 151 C10
Bobovdol BG 165 E7
Bobove UA 145 G6
Bobowa PL 144 D2
Bobowo PL 138 C6
Bobrov SK 147 C9
Bobrovec SK 147 C9
Bobrowice PL 81 C8
Bobrówko PL 85 E8
Bobrowniki PL 138 E6
Bobrowniki PL 140 D9
Bobryk-Druhyy UA 154 B6
Bocacara E 45 C8
Bocairent E 56 D3
Bočar SRB 150 F5
Bocchigliero I 61 E7
Boceguillas E 40 F4
Bocfölde H 149 C7
Bochnia PL 144 D1
Bocholt B 19 B12
Bocholt D 17 E7
Bochov CZ 76 B4
Bochum D 17 F8
Bockara S 89 A10
Bockenem D 79 B7
Bockenheim an der Weinstraße D 187 B5
Bockhammar S 97 C14
Bockhorn D 17 B10
Bockhorn D 75 F10
Bockhorst D 17 B9
Boćki PL 141 E8
Bocksjö S 92 B5
Bockträsk S 109 F15
Bocognano F 37 G10
Boconád H 150 B5
Bőcs H 145 G2
Bócsa H 150 D3
Bocșa RO 151 C10
Bocșa RO 159 C8
Bocsig RO 151 E8
Boczów PL 81 B7
Bod RO 153 F7
Böda S 89 A12
Boda S 103 A12
Boda S 103 D9
Boda bruk S 103 C12
Bodaczów PL 144 B7
Bodafors S 92 D5
Boda glasbruk S 89 B9
Bodajk H 149 B10
Bodåsgruvan S 98 B6
Bodbacka FIN 122 E6
Bodbyn S 122 B4
Boddam GB 3 F14
Boddam GB 3 L13
Boddin D 83 C10
Bodegraven NL 182 A5
Bodelshausen D 187 E6
Boden S 118 C7
Bodenfelde D 78 C6
Bodenham GB 13 A9
Bodenheim D 21 E10
Bodenkirchen D 75 F11
Bodenmais D 76 D4
Bodenteich D 83 E9
Bodenwerder D 78 C6
Bodenwöhr D 75 D11
Bodești RO 153 C8
Bodman D 27 E11
Bodmin GB 12 E5
Bodnegg D 71 B9
Bodø N 108 B7
Bodom N 105 D11
Bodonal de la Sierra E 51 C6
Bodoney GB 7 C8
Bodony H 147 F10
Bodroghalom H 145 G4
Bodrogkisfalud H 145 G3
Bodrum TR 177 E9
Bodsjö S 102 A8
Bodsjöbyn S 102 A8
Bodträskfors S 118 B5
Bődvaszilas H 145 F2
Bodyke IRL 8 C5
Bodzanów PL 139 E9
Bodzanów PL 142 F3
Bodzentyn PL 143 E10
Boé F 33 B7
Boechout B 19 B9
Boecillo E 39 E10
Boekel NL 16 E5
Boekhoute B 182 C3
Boën-sur-Lignon F 30 D5
Boeslunde DK 87 E8
Boeza E 39 C7
Boffres F 30 F6
Boffzen D 21 A12
Boftsa N 113 C21
Bogács H 145 H2
Bogajo E 45 C7
Bogarra E 55 B8
Bogați RO 160 D6
Bogatić SRB 158 D4
Bogatići BIH 157 E9
Bogatynia PL 81 E7
Boğaziçi TR 177 C10
Bogda RO 151 F8
Bogdan BG 165 D10
Bogdana RO 153 D11
Bogdana RO 160 F6
Bogdanci MK 169 B8
Bogdand RO 151 C10
Bogdănești RO 153 E9
Bogdănești RO 154 E2
Bogdaniec PL 85 E8
Bogdănița RO 153 E11
Bogdan Vodă RO 152 B4
Boge S 93 D13
Bogen D 75 E12
Bogen N 105 A11
Bogen N 111 C12
Bogense DK 86 D6
Boggsjö S 106 E8
Boghești RO 153 E10
Bogilice BIH 158 F3
Bogliasco I 37 C10
Bognanco I 68 A5
Bognelv N 112 C9
Bognes N 111 D11
Bogniebrae GB 3 L11
Bognor Regis GB 15 F7
Bogny-sur-Meuse F 184 E2
Bogø DK 87 F10
Bogodol BIH 157 F8
Bogojevo SRB 157 A11
Bogomilovo BG 166 E5
Bogoria PL 143 E11
Bogorojca MK 169 B8
Bogovina SRB 159 F8
Bogovinje MK 163 F10
Bogoy N 110 E9
Bograngen S 102 E4
Boguchwała PL 144 D4
Bogumiłowice PL 143 D7
Boguszów-Gorce PL 81 E10
Boguty-Pianki PL 141 E6
Bogyiszló H 149 D11
Bohain-en-Vermandois F 19 E7
Bohars F 22 D3
Bohdalov CZ 77 D9
Bohdan UA 152 A4
Bohdíkov CZ 77 B11
Boherboy IRL 8 D4
Boherbue IRL 8 D4
Bohinjska Bistrica SLO 73 D8
Böhl D 187 C5
Böhlen D 79 D11
Böhme D 82 E6
Bohmte D 17 D10
Böhne D 79 A11
Bohola IRL 6 E4
Bohonal de Ibor E 45 E10
Böhönye H 149 D8
Bohoyo E 45 D10
Bohumín CZ 146 B6
Bohuňovice CZ 146 B4
Bohuslavice CZ 146 B6
Bohutín CZ 76 C5
Boianu Mare RO 151 C10
Boiro de Arriba E 38 C2
Boiscommun F 25 D7
Bois-d'Amont F 31 B9
Boisgervilly F 23 D7
Bois-Guillaume F 18 F3
Boișoara RO 160 C4
Boisset-et-Gaujac F 35 B7
Boissezon F 33 C10
Boitzenburg D 84 D5
Boiu Mare RO 152 C3
Boizenburg D 83 D9
Bojadła PL 81 C9
Bojano I 63 E6
Bojanów PL 144 C4
Bojanowo PL 81 C11
Bøjden DK 86 E6
Bojkovice CZ 146 C5
Bojná SK 146 D6
Bojnice SK 147 D7
Bojničky SK 146 E5
Bojnik SRB 164 C4
Bojszów PL 142 F5
Bojszowy PL 143 F7
Boka SRB 159 C6
Bokel D 17 B11
Böklund D 82 A7
Bokod H 149 A10
Bököny H 151 B8
Bokšić HR 149 E10
Boksjön S 109 E10
Bol HR 156 F6
Bölan S 103 D12
Bolanden D 186 B5
Bolandoz F 31 A9
Bolaños de Calatrava E 54 B5
Bolătău RO 153 D8
Bolayir TR 173 C6
Bolbaite E 56 C3
Bolbec F 18 E1
Bolboși RO 159 D11
Bölcske H 150 D2
Boldekow D 84 C5
Bolderslev DK 86 F4
Boldești-Grădiștea RO 161 D9
Boldești-Scăeni RO 161 C8
Boldog H 150 B4
Boldogkőváralja H 145 G3
Boldre GB 13 D11
Boldu RO 161 C10
Boldur RO 159 B8
Boldva H 145 G2
Böle S 99 B9
Böle S 102 B7
Böle S 105 D14
Böle S 105 E15
Böle S 118 C8
Böle S 118 D6
Bolea E 41 D10
Bolekhiv UA 145 E8
Bolerác SK 146 E5
Bolesław PL 143 F7
Bolesław PL 143 F10
Bolesławiec PL 81 D9
Bolesławiec PL 142 D5
Boleszkowice PL 84 E7
Bolga N 108 C5
Bolgatovo RUS 133 C5
Bolhan UA 154 A3
Bolhrad UA 155 B3
Boliden S 118 E4
Bolimów PL 141 F2
Bolintin-Deal RO 161 E7
Bolintin-Vale RO 161 E7
Boliqueime P 50 E3
Boljanić BIH 157 C9
Boljanići MNE 163 C7
Boljevac SRB 159 F8
Boljevci SRB 158 D5
Bölkow D 83 B11
Bolków PL 81 E10
Bollebygd S 91 D12
Bollène F 35 B8
Bollengo I 68 C4
Bollermoen N 108 D6
Bolligen CH 31 B11
Bolling DK 86 D3
Bollingstedt D 82 A6
Bollnäs S 103 D11
Bollsbyn S 91 A12
Bollstabruk S 107 E13
Bollullos Par del Condado E 51 E6
Bolnes NL 182 B5
Bolnhurst GB 15 C8
Bologna I 66 D3
Bologne F 26 D3
Bolognetta I 58 D3
Bolognola I 62 B4
Bolotana I 64 C2
Boloteşti RO 153 F10
Bolsena I 62 B1
Bol'shakovo RUS 136 D4
Bolsover GB 11 E9
Bolsward NL 16 B5
Bolszewo PL 138 A5
Boltaña E 33 F6
Boltåsen N 111 C12
Boltenhagen D 83 C10
Boltigen CH 31 B11
Bolton GB 5 D11
Bolton GB 11 D7
Bolüntü TR 181 A7
Bolvașnița RO 159 C9
Bóly H 149 E11
Bolyarovo BG 167 E7
Bolzano I 72 D3
Bomal B 19 D12
Bomba I 63 C6
Bombarral P 44 F2
Bomlitz D 82 E7
Bompas F 34 E4
Bompensiere I 58 E4
Bompietro I 58 D5
Bomporto I 66 C3
Bomsund S 107 E9
Bona F 30 A3
Bonaduz CH 71 D8
Bonakas N 113 C21
Bonäs S 103 E13
Bonanza E 52 C4
Boñar E 39 C9
Bonar Bridge GB 3 K8
Bonarcado I 64 C2
Bonares E 51 E6
Bonäs S 102 D7
Bonäset S 106 D8
Bonäset S 107 E15
Bonassola I 37 C11
Bonawe GB 4 C6
Bonboillon F 26 F4
Bonchamp-lès-Laval F 23 D10
Bonchester Bridge GB 5 E11
Boncourt CH 27 F7
Bondeno I 66 C3
Bondersbyn S 119 C9
Bonderup DK 86 A4
Bondorf D 187 D6
Bondsjö S 103 A14
Bondues F 182 D2
Bönebüttel D 83 B8
Bonefro I 63 D7
Bönen D 17 E9
Bo'ness GB 5 C9
Bonete E 55 B10
Bönhamn S 103 A15
Bonheiden B 19 B10
Boniches E 47 E9
Boniewo PL 138 F6
Bonifacio F 37 J10
Bonifati I 60 D5
Bönigen CH 70 D5
Bonin PL 85 B10
Bonn D 21 C8
Bonnåsjøen N 109 A10
Bonnat F 29 C9
Bonndorf im Schwarzwald D 27 E9
Bønnerup Strand DK 87 B7
Bonnes N 111 C15
Bonnet DK 86 B2
Bonnétable F 24 D3
Bonneuil-Matours F 29 B7
Bonneval F 24 D5
Bonneval F 31 D10
Bonneval-sur-Arc F 31 E11
Bonnevaux F 31 B9
Bonneville F 31 C9
Bonnieux F 35 C9
Bönnigheim D 27 B11
Bonnyrigg GB 5 D10
Bonny-sur-Loire F 25 E8
Bono F 22 E6
Bono I 64 C3
Bonorva I 64 C2
Bons-en-Chablais F 31 C9
Bonson F 30 D5
Bonțida RO 152 D3
Bőny H 149 A9
Bonyhád H 149 D11
Boo S 99 D10
Boock D 84 D6
Boom B 19 B9
Boortmeerbeek B 19 C10
Boos F 18 F3
Boostedt D 83 B8
Bootle GB 10 E6
Bopfingen D 75 E7
Boppard D 21 D9
Bor CZ 75 C12
Bor S 88 A6
Bor SRB 159 E9
Borač SRB 158 F6
Borås S 91 D12
Borăscu RO 160 D2
Borba P 50 B5
Borbjerg DK 86 C3
Borca RO 153 C7
Borča SRB 158 D5
Borcea RO 155 E1
Borchen D 17 E11
Borci BIH 157 C7
Borci BIH 157 E9
Börcs H 149 A9
Borculo NL 17 D7
Bordalba E 41 F7
Bordány H 150 E4
Bordeaux F 28 F4
Bordeira P 50 E2
Bordei Verde RO 161 C11
Bordelum D 82 A5
Bordères-Louron F 33 E6
Bordères-sur-l'Échez F 33 D6
Bordes F 32 D5
Bordes F 33 D6
Bordesholm D 83 B8
Bordești RO 161 B10
Bordighera I 37 D7
Bordils E 43 C9
Bording DK 86 C4
Bordón E 42 F3
Bordușani RO 155 E1
Bore I 69 D8
Boreham GB 15 D10
Borehamwood GB 15 D8
Borek PL 143 F10
Borek Strzeliński PL 81 E12
Borek Wielkopolski PL 81 C12
Boreland GB 5 E10
Børelva N 108 B8
Borensberg S 92 B6
Borg D 20 E6
Borgå FIN 127 E14
Borgafjäll S 106 B8
Borgentreich D 17 E12
Börger D 17 C9
Borger NL 17 C7
Borggård S 92 B7
Borghamn S 92 C5
Borgheim N 90 A7
Borghetto d'Arroscia I 37 C7
Borghetto di Borbera I 37 B9
Borghetto di Vara I 69 E8
Borghetto Santo Spirito I 37 C8
Borgholm S 89 B11
Borgholzhausen D 17 D10
Borgia I 59 B10
Borgloon B 19 C11
Børglum DK 90 E6
Borgo F 37 F10
Borgo a Mozzano I 66 E2
Borgo d'Ale I 68 C5
Borgoforte I 66 B2
Borgofranco d'Ivrea I 68 B4
Borgo Grappa I 61 C10
Borgo-lavezzaro I 68 C6
Borgomanero I 68 B5
Borgomaro I 37 D7
Borgone Susa I 31 E11
Borgonovo Val Tidone I 69 C7
Borgo Pace I 66 E5
Borgorose I 62 C4
Borgo San Dalmazzo I 37 C6
Borgo San Lorenzo I 66 E3
Borgo San Martino I 68 C6
Borgosesia I 68 B5
Borgo Tossignano I 66 D4
Borgo Val di Taro I 69 E8
Borgo Valsugana I 72 D3
Borgo Velino I 62 C4
Borgo Vercelli I 68 C5
Borgsjö S 103 A10
Borgsjö S 107 C13
Borgstedt D 82 B7
Borgstena S 91 D13
Borgue GB 5 F8
Borgvattnet S 107 E9
Borhaug N 94 F5
Boriaeva BG 171 B7
Borike BIH 157 E11
Borino BG 165 F9
Bořitov CZ 77 D11
Borja E 41 E8
Borjabad E 41 E7
Borjana SLO 73 D7
Borjelslandet S 118 C8
Borkan S 106 A8
Borkavichy BY 133 E4
Borken D 17 E7
Borken (Hessen) D 21 B12
Borkenes N 111 C11
Borki PL 141 G7
Borki PL 143 D9
Børkop DK 86 D5
Borkowice PL 141 H3
Borkowo PL 139 D12
Borkum D 17 A7
Borlänge S 97 B13
Borlești RO 153 D9
Bormani LV 135 C10
Børmarka N 104 C8
Bormio I 71 E10
Born D 79 B9
Born NL 183 C7
Borna D 79 D12
Borna D 80 D4
Born am Darß D 83 B13
Borne NL 17 D7
Bornem B 19 B9
Bornerbroek NL 17 D7
Bornes P 39 F6
Bornes de Aguiar P 38 E4
Borne Sulinowo PL 85 C11
Bornheim D 21 C7
Bornhofen D 21 D9
Bornhöved D 83 B8
Bornich D 185 D8
Bornos E 51 F8
Bornova TR 177 C9
Börnsen D 83 D8
Boroaia RO 153 C8
Borobia E 41 E8
Borod RO 151 D10
Borodino UA 154 E4
Borodinskoye RUS 129 C11
Borohrádek CZ 77 B10
Borojevići BIH 157 F8
Boronów PL 143 E6
Borore I 64 C2
Boroșneu Mare RO 153 F8
Boroszów PL 142 E5
Borota H 150 E3
Boroughbridge GB 11 C9
Borovan BG 165 C8
Borovany CZ 77 E7
Borov Dol BG 166 D6
Borovets BG 165 E8
Borovik HR 149 F10
Borovitsa BG 165 B6
Borovka LV 133 E1
Borovnica BIH 157 D9
Borovnica SLO 73 E9
Borovo BG 166 C5
Borovo Selo HR 157 B10
Borovtsi BG 165 C7
Borów PL 81 E11
Borów PL 144 B4
Borowa PL 143 F11
Borowie PL 141 G5
Borox E 46 D5
Borrby S 88 E6
Borre DK 87 F10
Borre N 95 D12
Borrentin D 84 C3
Borrèze F 29 F8
Borriol E 48 D4
Borris DK 86 D3
Borris IRL 9 C9
Borris-in-Ossory IRL 9 C7
Borrisokane IRL 6 G6
Borrisoleigh IRL 9 C7
Borrowdale GB 10 B5
Børrud N 96 C7
Börrum S 93 C9
Borș RO 151 C8
Børsa N 104 E8
Borșa RO 152 B5
Borșa RO 152 D3
Borša SK 145 G4
Borsbeek B 19 B10
Borsec RO 153 D7
Børselv N 113 C16
Borsh AL 168 D2
Borshchi UA 154 B5
Borshchovychi UA 144 D9
Boršice u Buchlovic CZ 146 C4
Borsio GR 174 D3
Borský Svätý Jur SK 77 E12
Borsodbóta H 145 G1
Borsodnádasd H 145 G1
Borsodszentgyörgy H 145 G1
Borsodszirák H 145 G2
Borsosberény H 147 F8
Borssele NL 182 C3
Borstel D 17 C11
Borth GB 10 G3
Bortigali I 64 C2
Bortigiadas I 64 B3
Bort-les-Orgues F 29 E10
Börtnan S 102 A6
Bortnen N 100 C2
Borum DK 86 C6
Borup DK 87 E9
Borve GB 2 L4
Borynya UA 145 E6
Boryslav UA 145 D7
Borzęciczki PL 81 C12
Borzonasca I 37 C10
Borzytuchom PL 85 B12
Bosa I 64 C2
Bošáca SK 146 D5
Bosa Marina I 64 C1
Bosanci RO 153 B8
Bosanka Rača BIH 158 D3
Bosanska Dubica BIH 157 B6
Bosanska Gradiška BIH 157 B7
Bosanska Kostajnica BIH 156 B6
Bosanska Krupa BIH 156 C5
Bosanski Brod BIH 157 B9
Bosanski Kobas BIH 157 B8
Bosanski Novi BIH 156 B5
Bosanski Petrovac BIH 156 C5
Bosanski Šamac BIH 157 B9
Bosansko Grahovo BIH 156 D5
Bošany SK 146 D6
Bősárkány H 149 A8
Bosau D 83 B8
Boscastle GB 12 D5
Bosco I 66 F5
Bosco Chiesanuova I 69 B11
Bosco Marengo I 37 B9
Boscotrecase I 60 B2
Bösdorf D 83 B8
Bösebo S 89 A9
Bösel D 17 B9
Boshulya BG 165 E9
Bosia RO 153 C11
Bosilegrad SRB 164 E5
Bosiljevo HR 148 F4
Boskoop NL 16 D3
Boskovice CZ 77 D11
Bošnjace SRB 164 D4
Bošnjaci HR 157 B10
Bošnjane SRB 159 F7
Bošnjane SRB 159 F7
Boșorod RO 159 B11
Bössbod S 102 D7
Bosset F 29 F6
Bossolasco I 37 B8
Bössost E 33 E7
Bostad N 110 D6
Bostan BIH 157 F7
Bøstølen N 100 B6
Boston GB 11 F11
Boston Spa GB 11 D9
Bostrak N 90 A4
Bosundet S 107 C10
Botão P 44 D4
Boteå S 107 E13
Boteni RO 160 C6
Botesdale GB 15 C11
Botești RO 153 C9
Botești RO 160 C6
Botevgrad BG 165 D8
Botevo BG 167 C9
Bothel GB 5 F10
Boticas P 38 E4
Botiz RO 151 B10
Botiza RO 152 B4
Botn N 110 E9
Botn N 111 A18
Botn N 112 D4
Botngård N 104 D7
Botnhamn N 111 A14
Botoroaga RO 161 E7
Botorrita E 41 E9
Botoš SRB 158 C6
Botoșana RO 153 B7
Botoșani RO 153 B9
Botoșești-Paia RO 159 E11
Botricello I 61 F7
Bötsle S 103 A14
Botsmark S 118 F4
Bottendorf (Burgwald) D 21 B11
Bottesford GB 11 D10
Bottidda I 64 C3
Bottnaryd S 91 D14
Bottrop D 17 E7
Botun MK 168 B4
Bötzingen D 27 D8
Bouafles F 24 B5
Boucau F 32 C3
Bouc-Bel-Air F 35 D9
Boucé F 23 C11
Bouchain F 19 D7
Bouchemaine F 23 F10
Bouchoir F 18 E6
Boudry CH 31 B10
Boué F 19 D8
Bouglon F 33 B6
Bouguenais F 23 F8
Bouillargues F 35 C7
Bouillon B 19 E11
Bouilly F 25 D10
Bouin F 28 B1
Boujailles F 31 B9
Boujan-sur-Libron F 34 D5
Boulay-Moselle F 26 B5
Boulazac F 29 E7
Boulbon F 35 C8
Bouligny F 19 F12
Bouloc F 33 C8
Boulogne-Billancourt F 25 C7
Boulogne-sur-Gesse F 33 D7
Boulogne-sur-Mer F 15 F12
Bouloire F 24 E4
Boulouris F 36 E5
Boult-aux-Bois F 19 F10
Boulzicourt F 19 E10
Bouniagues F 29 F7
Bøur FO 2 A2
Bourbon-Lancy F 30 B4
Bourbon-l'Archambault F 30 B3
Bourbonne-les-Bains F 26 E4
Bourbourg F 18 C5
Bourbriac F 22 D5
Bourcefranc-le-Chapus F 28 D3
Bourdeaux F 35 A9
Bourdeilles F 29 E7
Bourdonnay F 27 C6
Bouresse F 29 C7
Bourg F 28 E4
Bourg-Achard F 18 F2
Bourganeuf F 29 D9
Bourg-Argental F 30 E6
Bourg-de-Péage F 31 E7
Bourg-de-Thizy F 30 C5
Bourg-de-Visa F 33 B7
Bourg-Dun F 18 E2
Bourg-en-Bresse F 31 C7
Bourges F 29 A10
Bourg-et-Comin F 19 F8
Bourg-Lastic F 29 D11
Bourg-lès-Valence F 30 F6
Bourgneuf-en-Mauges F 23 F10
Bourgneuf-en-Retz F 28 A2
Bourgogne F 19 F9
Bourgoin-Jallieu F 31 D7
Bourg-St-Andéol F 35 B8
Bourg-St-Bernard F 33 C9
Bourg-St-Maurice F 31 D10
Bourgtheroulde-Infreville F 18 F2
Bourguébus F 23 B11
Bourgueil F 23 F12
Bourmont F 26 D4
Bourne GB 11 F11
Bournemouth GB 13 D11
Bournezeau F 28 B3
Bourran F 33 B6
Bourriot-Bergonce F 32 B5
Bourron-Marlotte F 25 D8
Bourscheid L 184 E5
Bourtange NL 17 B8
Bourton GB 13 C10
Boussac F 29 C10
Bousse F 186 C1
Boussens F 33 D7
Boussières F 26 F4
Boussois F 19 D9
Boussu B 19 D8
Boutersem B 19 C10
Bouveret CH 31 C10
Bouvières F 35 A9
Bouvron F 23 F8
Bouxières-aux-Dames F 26 C5
Bouxwiller F 27 C7
Bouy F 25 B11
Bouzonville F 21 F7
Bouzov CZ 77 C11
Bova I 59 C8
Bøvær N 111 B13
Bovalino I 59 C9
Bovallstrand S 91 C9
Bova Marina I 59 D8
Bovan SRB 159 F8
Bovec SLO 73 D8
Bóveda E 38 C5

Boveda E 40 C5
Bovegno I 69 B9
Bovenden D 78 C6
Bøverfjord N 104 E5
Boves F 18 E5
Boves I 37 C7
Bovigny B 20 D5
Boviken S 118 E6
Boville Ernica I 62 D4
Bovino I 60 A4
Bøvlingbjerg DK 86 C2
Bovolone I 66 B3
Bovrup DK 86 F5
Bow GB 3 H10
Bowes GB 11 B7
Bowmore GB 4 D4
Box FIN 127 E13
Boxberg D 81 D7
Boxberg D 187 C8
Boxdorf D 80 D5
Boxholm S 92 C6
Boxmeer NL 16 E5
Boxtel NL 16 E4
Boyadzhik BG 166 E6
Boyanovo BG 167 E7
Boychinovtsi BG 165 C7
Boykovo BG 165 E10
Boyle IRL 6 E6
Bøylefoss N 90 B4
Boynes F 25 D7
Boynitsa BG 159 F10
Bøyum N 100 D5
Božava HR 67 D10
Bozburun TR 181 C8
Bozeat GB 15 C7
Bozel F 31 E10
Boževac SRB 159 D7
Bożewo PL 139 E8
Bozhentsi BG 166 D4
Bozhurishte BG 165 D7
Božica SRB 164 D5
Božice CZ 77 E10
Bozieni MD 154 D3
Bozieni RO 153 D10
Bozioru RO 161 C8
Božjakovina HR 148 E6
Bozlar TR 173 D7
Bozouls F 34 B4
Bozovici RO 159 D9
Bozveliysko BG 167 C8
Bozzolo I 66 B1
Bra I 37 B7
Braås S 89 A8
Bråbo S 89 A10
Brabova RO 160 E2
Bracadale GB 2 L4
Bracciano I 62 C2
Brach F 28 E4
Brachbach D 185 C8
Bracieux F 24 E6
Bräcke S 103 A9
Brackenheim D 27 B11
Brackley GB 13 A12
Bracknagh IRL 7 F8
Bracknell GB 15 E7
Braco GB 5 C9
Brad RO 151 E10
Bradashesh AL 168 B3
Brădeanu RO 161 D9
Brădeni RO 152 E5
Brădești RO 152 E6
Brădești RO 160 E3
Bradford GB 11 D8
Bradford-on-Avon GB 13 C10
Bradpole GB 13 D9
Bradu RO 160 D5
Brăduleț RO 160 C5
Brăduț RO 153 E7
Bradwell GB 15 B12
Bradwell Waterside GB 15 D10
Brae GB 3 E14
Brædstrup DK 86 D5
Braehead of Lunan GB 5 B11
Braemar GB 5 A10
Brăești RO 153 B8
Brăești RO 153 C10
Brăești RO 161 C9
Brăfim E 43 E6
Braga P 38 E3
Bragadiru RO 161 E7
Bragadiru RO 161 F7
Bragança P 39 E6
Bragar GB 2 J3
Brăhășești RO 153 E10
Brahlstorf D 83 D9
Brăila RO 155 C1
Brailsford GB 11 F8
Braine F 19 F8
Braine-l'Alleud B 19 C9
Braine-le-Comte B 19 C9
Braintree GB 15 D10
Braives B 19 C11
Brajkovići BIH 157 D8
Brake (Unterweser) D 17 B10
Brakel B 19 C8
Brakel D 17 E12
Bräkne-Hoby S 89 C8
Brålanda S 91 B11
Bralin PL 142 D4
Brallo di Pregola I 37 B10
Bralos GR 174 B5
Braloștița RO 160 D3
Bram F 33 D10
Bramans F 31 E10
Bramberg am Wildkogel
A 72 B5
Bramdrupdam DK 86 D4
Bramming DK 86 E3
Brampton GB 5 F11
Brampton GB 15 C12
Bramsche D 17 D8
Bramsche D 17 D10
Bramstedt D 17 B11
Bran RO 160 B6
Brånaberg S 109 E11
Branäs S 102 E4
Brancaleone I 59 D9
Brancaster GB 15 B10
Brânceni RO 160 F6
Brâncovenești RO 152 D5
Brâncoveni RO 160 E4
Brand A 71 C9
Brand D 75 C10
Brandal N 100 B4
Brändåsen S 102 B4
Brändbo S 103 B11
Brandbu N 95 B13
Brande DK 86 D4
Brande-Hörnerkirchen D 82 C7
Brandenberg A 72 B4
Brandenburg D 79 B12
Brand-Erbisdorf D 80 E4
Branderup DK 86 E4
Brandesburton GB 11 D11
Brandis D 80 C4
Brand-Nagelberg A 77 E8
Brando F 37 F10
Brändö FIN 126 E5
Brandon GB 15 C10
Brändön S 118 C8
Brändövik FIN 122 D6
Brandshagen D 84 B4
Brandstorp S 92 C4
Brandsvoll N 90 C2
Brandval N 96 B7
Brandvoll N 111 C15
Brandýs nad Labem-Stará
Boleslav CZ 77 B7
Brandýs nad Orlicí CZ 77 B10
Branes N 96 A6
Brănești MD 154 C3
Brănești RO 160 C6
Brănești RO 160 D2
Brănești RO 161 E8
Branice PL 142 F4
Braniewo PL 139 B8
Branik SLO 73 E8
Brănișca RO 151 F10
Braniștea RO 152 C4
Braniștea RO 155 C1
Braniștea RO 161 D7
Brankas LV 134 C7
Bränna S 91 B11
Brännåker S 107 B9
Brännäs S 103 B11
Brännberg S 118 C6
Branne F 28 F5
Brännland S 107 D16
Brännland S 122 C4
Brañosera E 40 C3
Brańsk PL 141 E7
Branston GB 11 E11
Brańszczyk PL 139 E12
Brantevik S 88 D6
Brantice CZ 142 F4
Brantôme F 29 E7
Branzi I 69 A8
Braojos E 46 B5
Braone I 69 B9
Braskereidfoss N 101 E15
Braslaw BY 133 E2
Brașov RO 161 B7
Brassac F 33 C10
Brasschaat B 16 F2
Brassy F 25 F10
Brasta S 105 E16
Brastad S 91 C10
Brastavățu RO 160 F4
Břasy CZ 76 C5
Brataj AL 168 D2
Bratca RO 151 D10
Bråte N 95 C14
Brateiu RO 152 E4
Brateljevici BIH 157 D10
Brateș RO 153 F8
Bratislava SK 77 F12
Bratkowice PL 144 C4
Bratovoești RO 160 E3
Bratsigovo BG 165 E9
Brattåker S 107 A11
Brattbäcken S 107 C9
Bratten S 107 B14
Brattfors S 103 E12
Brattfors S 107 D17
Brattli N 114 D7
Brattmon S 102 E4
Bratton GB 13 C10
Brattsbacka S 107 D16
Brattsele S 107 D12
Brattset N 104 E5
Brattvåg N 100 A4
Bratunac BIH 158 E3
Brătușeni MD 153 A10
Bratya Daskalovi BG 166 E4
Braubach D 21 D9
Braud-et-St-Louis F 28 E4
Braunau am Inn A 76 F4
Brauneberg D 185 E6
Braunfels D 21 C10
Braunlage D 79 C8
Bräunlingen D 27 E9
Braunsbach D 187 C8
Braunsbedra D 79 D10
Braunschweig D 79 B8
Braunton GB 12 C6
Bravicea MD 154 C2
Bravnica BIH 157 D7
Bray IRL 7 F10
Bray-sur-Seine F 25 D9
Bray-sur-Somme F 18 E6
Brazatortas E 54 B4
Brazey-en-Plaine F 26 F3
Brazi RO 161 D8
Brazii RO 151 E9
Brazii RO 161 D8
Brbinj HR 67 D11
Brčigovo BIH 157 E11
Brčko BIH 157 C10
Brdów PL 138 F6
Bré IRL 7 F10
Brea E 41 E8
Brea de Tajo E 47 D6
Breaghva IRL 8 C3
Breascleit GB 2 J3
Breasta RO 160 E3
Breaza RO 152 B6
Breaza RO 152 D5
Breaza RO 161 C7
Breaza RO 161 C9
Brebeni RO 160 E4
Brebu RO 159 C8
Brebu RO 161 C7
Brebu Nou RO 159 C9
Brécey F 23 C9
Brech F 22 E6
Brechfa GB 12 B6
Brechin GB 5 B11
Brecht B 16 F3
Breckerfeld D 185 B7
Břeclav CZ 77 E11
Brecon GB 13 B8
Breda E 43 D9
Breda NL 16 E3
Bredared S 91 D12
Bredaryd S 87 A13
Bredbyn S 107 E14
Breddenberg D 17 C9
Breddin D 83 E12
Bredebro DK 86 E3
Bredene B 18 B6
Bredereiche D 84 D4
Bredevoort NL 17 E7
Bredkälen S 106 D8
Bredsätra S 89 B11
Bredsel S 118 C4
Bredsjö S 97 C12
Bredsjön S 103 A13
Bredstedt D 82 A5
Bredsten DK 86 D4
Bredträsk S 107 D15
Bredvik S 107 D17
Bredviken S 108 D8
Bredviken S 119 C10
Bree B 19 B12
Breese D 83 D11
Bregana HR 148 E5
Breganze I 72 E4
Bregare BG 165 B9
Bregeni MD 153 B12
Bregenz A 71 B9
Breg-Lum AL 163 E9
Breg-Lum AL 168 B2
Bregninge DK 86 F6
Bregovo BG 159 E10
Breguzzo I 69 B10
Bréhal F 23 C8
Bréhan F 22 D6
Brehna D 79 C11
Breidenbach D 21 C10
Breidenbach F 27 B7
Breidstrand N 111 C12
Breidvik N 108 B9
Breidvik N 110 C8
Breidvik N 110 E9
Breidvik N 111 D11
Breiholz D 82 B7
Breil CH 71 D8
Breil-sur-Roya F 37 D7
Breisach am Rhein D 27 D8
Breistein N 94 B2
Breitenbach CH 27 F8
Breitenbach D 21 F8
Breitenbach (Schauenburg)
D 17 F12
Breitenbach am Herzberg
D 78 E6
Breitenbach am Inn A 72 B4
Breitenberg D 76 E5
Breitenbrunn D 75 D10
Breitenburg D 82 C7
Breitenfelde D 83 C9
Breitengüßbach D 75 C8
Breitenhagen D 79 C10
Breitnau D 27 E9
Breitscheid D 183 C9
Breitscheid D 185 C7
Breitscheid D 185 C9
Breitungen D 79 E7
Breivik N 111 C12
Breivik N 112 B9
Breivikbotn N 112 B9
Breivikeidet N 111 A18
Brejning DK 86 D5
Brekka N 108 B9
Brekken N 101 A15
Brekken N 108 E5
Brekkestø N 90 C3
Brekkhus N 100 E4
Brekkvasseiv N 105 B14
Breklum D 82 A5
Brekovo SRB 158 F5
Breksillan N 105 B10
Brekstad N 104 D7
Brélès F 22 D2
Brelingen (Wedemark) D 78 A6
Bremdal DK 86 B3
Bremen D 17 B11
Bremerhaven D 17 A11
Bremervörde D 17 B12
Bremgarten CH 27 F9
Bremm D 21 D8
Bremnes N 94 C2
Bremnes N 110 C9
Brem-sur-Mer F 28 B2
Brenderup DK 86 E5
Brenes E 51 D8
Brenguļi LV 131 F11
Brenitsa BG 165 C9
Brenna N 108 F5
Brenna N 110 D7
Brenna PL 147 B7
Brennero I 72 C4
Brennes N 112 D5
Brennfjell N 112 E5
Brenngam N 113 B19
Brennhaug N 101 C10
Brennmo N 105 E11
Brennsvik N 113 B13
Breno I 69 B9
Brénod F 31 C8
Brens F 33 C9
Brensbach D 187 B6
Brent Knoll GB 13 C9
Brentwood GB 15 D9
Brenzone I 69 B10
Bresalc RKS 164 E3
Brescello I 66 C2
Brescia I 66 A1
Breskens NL 16 F1
Bresnica SRB 158 F6
Bressana Bottarone I 69 C7
Bressanone I 72 C4
Bressols F 33 C8
Bressuire F 28 B5
Brest BG 160 F5
Brest BY 141 F9
Brest F 22 D3
Brestak BG 167 C9
Brestanica SLO 148 E4
Bresternica SLO 148 C5
Brestova HR 67 B9
Brestovac SRB 159 E9
Brestovac SRB 164 C4
Brestovac Požeški HR 149 F9
Brestovăț RO 151 F8
Brestovene BG 161 F9
Brestovets BG 165 C10
Brestovitsa BG 165 E10
Bretagne-d'Armagnac F 33 C6
Brețcu RO 153 E8
Bretea Română RO 159 B11
Breteil F 23 D8
Bretenoux F 29 F9
Breteuil F 18 E5
Breteuil F 24 C4
Brétignolles-sur-Mer F 28 B2
Bretnig D 80 D6
Bretocino E 39 E8
Bretoncelles F 24 D4
Bretten D 27 B10
Bretton GB 10 E6
Brettville-sur-Laize F 23 B11
Bretzenheim D 185 E8
Bretzfeld D 187 C7
Breuberg-Neustadt D 21 E12
Breuches F 26 E5
Breugel NL 183 B7
Breuil-Cervinia I 68 B4
Breuil-Magné F 28 D4
Breuilpont F 24 C5
Breukelen NL 16 D4
Breum DK 86 B4
Breuna D 17 F12
Breuvannes-en-Bassigny
F 26 D4
Brevens bruk S 92 A7
Brevik N 90 A6
Brevik S 92 C4
Brevik S 93 A12
Brevik S 99 D10
Breviken S 96 D7
Brevörde D 78 C5
Breza BIH 157 D9
Breza SK 147 C8
Brežđe SRB 158 E5
Breze SLO 148 D4
Brezhani BG 165 F7
Březí CZ 77 E11
Brezičani BIH 157 B6
Brežice SLO 148 E5
Brezna SRB 163 B10
Breznica HR 148 D6
Breznica SK 145 E4
Březnice CZ 76 C5
Breznik BG 165 D6
Breznița-Motru RO 159 D11
Breznița-Ocol RO 159 D10
Breznitsa BG 165 F8
Březno CZ 76 B4
Brezno SK 147 D9
Brezoaele RO 161 D7
Brézolles F 24 C5
Březolupy CZ 146 C5
Březová CZ 146 D5
Březová nad Svitavou CZ 77 C11
Brezová pod Bradlom SK 146 D5
Brezovica SK 145 E2
Brezovica SK 147 C9
Brezovica SLO 73 D9
Brezovo BG 166 E4
Brezovo Polje BIH 157 C10
Brezovo Polje HR 156 B5
Briançon F 31 F10
Briare F 25 E8
Briatexte F 33 C9
Briceni MD 153 A10
Bricherasio I 31 F11
Bricon F 26 D2
Bricquebec F 23 B8
Brides-les-Bains F 31 E10
Brideswell IRL 6 F6
Bridgeland IRL 9 C9
Bridgend GB 4 C6
Bridgend GB 4 D4
Bridgend GB 13 B7
Bridge of Cally GB 5 B10
Bridge of Don GB 3 L12
Bridge of Dye GB 5 B11
Bridge of Earn GB 5 C10
Bridge of Orchy GB 4 B7
Bridge of Weir GB 4 D7
Bridgetown IRL 9 D9
Bridgnorth GB 11 F7
Bridgwater GB 13 C8
Břidličná CZ 146 B4
Bridlington GB 11 C11
Bridport GB 13 D9
Brie F 29 D6
Briec F 22 D4
Brie-Comte-Robert F 25 C8
Briedel D 185 D7
Brielle NL 16 E2
Brienne-le-Château F 25 D12
Briennon F 30 C5
Brienon-sur-Armançon F 25 D10
Brienz CH 70 D6
Brienza I 60 C5
Briesen D 80 B6
Brieske D 80 D5
Brieskow-Finkenheerd D 81 B7
Briesnig D 81 C7
Brietlingen D 83 D8
Briey F 20 F5
Brig CH 68 A4
Brigg GB 11 D11
Brighstone GB 13 D12
Brightlingsea GB 15 D11
Brighton GB 15 F8
Brigi LV 133 D4
Brignais F 30 D6
Brignogan-Plage F 22 C3
Brignoles F 36 E4
Brigstock GB 15 C7
Brihuega E 47 C7
Brijesta HR 162 D4
Brillon-en-Barrois F 26 C3
Brilon D 17 F11
Brimington GB 11 E9
Brimnes N 94 B5
Brinches P 50 C4
Brincones E 45 B8
Brindisi I 61 B9
Brindisi Montagna I 60 B5
Bringsinghaug N 100 B2
Bringsli N 108 B9
Brinian GB 3 G11
Brinje HR 67 B11
Brinkum D 17 B9
Brinkum D 17 B11
Brinlack IRL 6 B6
Brinon-sur-Beuvron F 25 F9
Brinon-sur-Sauldre F 25 E7
Brin-sur-Seille F 26 C5
Brînza MD 155 B2
Brînzeni MD 153 A10
Brion F 30 F3
Briones E 40 C6
Brionne F 24 B4
Brioude F 30 E3
Brioux-sur-Boutonne F 28 C5
Briouze F 23 C11
Briscous F 32 D3
Brisighella I 66 D4
Brissac-Quincé F 23 F11
Bristol GB 13 C9
Briston GB 15 B11
Britelo P 38 E3
Britof SLO 73 D9
Briton Ferry GB 13 B7
Brittas IRL 7 F10
Brittas Bay IRL 9 C10
Britvica BIH 157 F8
Britz D 84 E5
Brive-la-Gaillarde F 29 E9
Briviesca E 40 C5
Brix F 23 A8
Brixen im Thale A 72 B5
Brixham GB 13 E7
Brixworth GB 15 C7
Brka BIH 157 C10
Brložnik BIH 157 D11
Brna HR 162 D2
Brnaze HR 157 E6
Brněnec CZ 77 C11
Brniště CZ 81 E7
Brnjica SRB 159 D8
Brnjica SRB 163 C9
Brno CZ 77 D11
Bro S 93 D12
Bro S 99 C9
Broadford GB 2 L5
Broadford IRL 8 C5
Broadford IRL 8 D5
Broad Haven GB 9 E12
Broadheath GB 13 A10
Broadstairs GB 15 E11
Broadway GB 13 A11
Broadwey GB 13 D10
Broadwindsor GB 13 D9
Broager DK 86 F5
Broaryd S 87 A12
Broby S 88 C6
Broby S 99 C11
Brobyværk DK 86 E6
Broc CH 31 B11
Broćanac BIH 157 F7
Brocas F 32 B4
Brocēni LV 134 C5
Bröckel D 79 A7
Brockum D 17 D10
Brockworth GB 13 B10
Broczyno PL 85 C10
Brod BIH 157 F10
Brod MK 168 A5
Brod MK 169 C6
Brod RKS 163 F10
Brod RKS 164 E3
Brodalen S 91 C10
Brodarevo SRB 163 C8
Broddbo S 98 C6
Brodek u Prostějova CZ 77 D12
Broderstorf D 83 B12
Brodica SRB 159 E8
Brodick GB 4 D6
Brodilovo BG 167 E9
Brodina RO 152 B6
Brodnica PL 81 B11
Brodnica PL 139 D7
Brodosanë RKS 163 E10
Brodské SK 77 E12
Brodski Stubnik HR 157 B8
Brody PL 81 B8
Brody PL 81 C7
Broekhuizenvorst NL 183 C8
Broglie F 24 B4
Brohl D 185 D7
Brohm D 84 C5
Broin F 26 F3
Brójce PL 81 B9
Brojce PL 85 C8
Brójce PL 143 C8
Brok PL 139 E12
Brokdorf D 17 A12
Brokind S 92 C7
Brokka N 90 C2
Brokstedt D 83 C7
Brolo I 59 C6
Bromarv FIN 127 F9
Brome D 79 A8
Bromma N 95 B10
Bromnes N 112 C2
Bromölla S 88 C6
Brömsebro S 89 C10
Bromsgrove GB 13 A10
Bromyard GB 13 A9
Bron F 30 D6
Bronchales E 47 C9
Brønderslev DK 86 A5
Broni I 69 C7
Bronice PL 81 C7
Brønnøysund N 108 F3
Bronnytsya UA 154 A1
Brøns DK 86 E3
Bronte I 59 D6
Bronzani Majdan BIH 157 C6
Brooke GB 15 B11
Brookeborough GB 7 D8
Broons F 23 D7
Broquiès F 34 B4
Brora GB 3 J9
Brørup DK 86 E4
Brösarp S 88 D6
Broscăuți RO 153 B8
Broseley GB 10 F7
Broshniv Osada UA 145 F9
Brossac F 28 E5
Brøstadbotn N 111 B14
Broșteni RO 153 C7
Broșteni RO 153 F10
Broșteni RO 159 D10
Brotas P 50 B3
Brötjemark S 92 D4
Broto E 32 E5
Brottby S 99 C10
Brottes F 26 D3
Brotton GB 11 B10
Brøttum N 101 D13
Brou F 24 D5
Brough GB 3 H10
Brough GB 11 B7
Broughshane GB 4 F4
Broughton GB 5 D10
Broughton GB 10 E6
Broughton in Furness GB 10 C5
Broughtown GB 3 G11
Broughty Ferry GB 5 C11
Broumov CZ 81 E10
Brousseval F 26 D2
Broutzaiika GR 175 D6
Brouvelieures F 26 D6
Brouwershaven NL 16 E1
Brovst DK 86 A5
Brownhills GB 11 F8
Broxburn GB 5 D10
Brozany CZ 76 B6
Brozas E 45 E7
Brožiai LT 134 E3
Brozzo I 69 B9
Brštanovo HR 156 E5
Brtnice CZ 77 D9
Bruay-la-Bussière F 18 D6
Bruchhausen-Vilsen D 17 C12
Bruchköbel D 187 A6
Bruchmühlbach D 21 F8
Bruchsal D 27 B10
Bruchweiler-Bärenbach
D 186 C4
Brück D 79 B12
Bruck an der
Großglocknerstraße A 73 B6
Bruck an der Leitha A 77 F11
Bruck an der Mur A 73 B11
Brücken D 21 E8
Brücken (Helme) D 79 D9
Brücken (Pfalz) D 21 F8
Brückl A 73 C10
Bruckmühl D 72 A4
Brudzeń Duży PL 139 E8
Brudzew PL 142 B6
Brudzowice PL 143 E7
Brue-Auriac F 35 C10
Brüel D 83 C11
Bruère-Allichamps F 29 B10
Bruff IRL 8 D5
Brugelette B 182 D3
Bruges B 19 B7
Bruges B 182 C2
Brugg CH 27 F9
Brugge B 19 B7
Brüggen D 16 F6
Brüggen D 78 B6
Brugnato I 69 E8
Brugnera I 72 E6
Bruguières F 33 C8
Bruhagen N 104 E3
Brühl D 21 C7
Brühl D 187 C6
Bruinisse NL 16 E2
Bruiu RO 152 F5
Bruksvallarna S 102 A3
Brûlon F 23 E11
Brûly B 19 E10
Brumath F 27 C8
Brummen NL 183 A8
Brumov-Bylnice CZ 146 C6
Brumunddal N 101 E13
Brumundsag N 101 E13
Brunau D 83 E10
Brunava LV 135 D8
Brundby DK 86 D7
Brundish GB 15 C11
Brunehamel F 19 E9
Brunete E 46 D5
Brunflo S 106 E7
Brunico I 72 C4
Bruniquel F 33 B9
Brunkeberg N 95 D8
Brunn D 84 C4
Brunna S 99 C8
Brunna S 99 C9
Brunn am Gebirge A 77 F10
Brunnberg S 97 B10
Brunne S 103 A14
Brunnen CH 71 C7
Brunnsberg S 102 D6
Brunsberg S 97 C8
Brunsbüttel D 17 A12
Brunssum NL 20 C5
Bruntál CZ 142 G3
Bruravik N 94 B5
Bruree IRL 8 D5
Brus SRB 163 C11
Brusago I 69 A11
Brusand N 94 E3
Brušane HR 156 C3
Brusartsi BG 159 F11
Brüsewitz D 83 C10
Brŭshlen BG 161 F8
Brŭshlyanitsa BG 165 B10
Brusio CH 69 A9
Brusnik SRB 159 E9
Brusnika Velika BIH 157 B9
Brusno SK 147 D8
Brusque F 34 C4
Brussel B 19 C9
Brusson I 68 B4
Brüssow D 84 D6
Brusturi RO 151 C9
Brusturi-Drăgănești RO 153 C8
Brusturiv UA 152 A5
Brusturoasa RO 153 D8
Brusy PL 138 C4
Bruton GB 13 C10
Bruttig-Fankel D 21 D8
Bruvno HR 156 D4
Bruxelles B 19 C9
Bruyères F 26 D6
Bruz F 23 D8
Bruzaholm S 92 D6
Brvnište SK 146 C6
Brwinów PL 141 F3
Bryagovo BG 166 F4
Bryastovo BG 165 C10
Bryggerhaug N 111 B14
Brymbo GB 10 E5
Brynamman GB 13 B7
Bryne N 94 E3
Brynford GB 10 E5
Brynge S 107 E14
Bryngelhögen S 102 B7
Brynje S 102 A8
Brynje S 106 E7
Brynmawr GB 13 B8
Bryrup DK 86 D5
Bryukhovychi UA 144 D8
Brzan SRB 159 E7
Brza Palanka SRB 159 E9
Brzeće SRB 163 C10
Brzeg PL 142 E3
Brzeg Dolny PL 81 D11
Brześć Kujawski PL 138 E6
Brzesko PL 143 G10
Brzeszcze PL 143 G7
Brzezie PL 85 C11
Brzezie PL 138 E6
Brzeziny PL 141 H5
Brzeziny PL 142 C5
Brzeziny PL 143 C8
Brzeziny PL 144 D4
Brzeźnica PL 81 C8
Brzeźnica PL 143 F11
Brzeźnica PL 147 B9
Brzeźno PL 85 C9
Brzeźno PL 141 H9
Brzeźno PL 142 B5
Brzostek PL 144 D3
Brzotín SK 145 F1
Brzóza PL 141 G4
Brzózów PL 141 F2
Brzozów PL 144 D5
Brzozowiec PL 81 A8
Brzuze PL 139 D7
Bû F 24 C6
Bua S 87 A10
Buais F 23 C10
Buarcos P 44 D3
Buavågen N 94 C2
Bubbio I 37 B8
Bubiai LT 134 E6
Bubry F 22 E5
Bubwith GB 11 D10
Búč SK 149 A10
Buca TR 177 C9
Bučany SK 146 E5
Buccheri I 59 E6
Bucchianico I 63 C6
Buccinasco I 69 C7
Buccino I 60 B4
Bucecea RO 153 B8
Bucelas P 50 B1
Buceș RO 151 E10
Bucey-lès-Gy F 26 F4
Buch D 71 A10
Buch am Erlbach D 75 F11
Buchbach D 75 F11
Buchboden A 71 C9
Büchel D 21 D8
Büchen D 83 D9
Buchen (Odenwald) D 27 A11
Büchenbeuren D 185 E7
Buchholz D 83 D12
Buchholz (Aller) D 82 E7
Buchholz (Westerwald) D 21 C8
Buchin RO 159 C9
Buchin Prohod BG 165 D7
Buch in Tirol A 72 B4
Buchkirchen A 76 F6
Büchlberg D 76 E5
Buchloe D 71 A11
Buchlovice CZ 146 C4
Bucholz in der Nordheide
D 83 D7
Buchs CH 71 C8
Buchy F 18 E3
Bučim MK 164 F5
Buçimas AL 168 C4
Bučin MK 168 B5
Bucine I 66 F4
Bucinișu RO 160 F4
Bučište MK 164 F5
Bucium RO 151 E11
Buciumeni RO 153 F10
Buciumeni RO 161 C6
Buciumi RO 151 C11
Bučje SRB 159 F9
Bučje SRB 163 C7
Buckden GB 11 C7
Bückeburg D 17 D12
Bücken D 17 C12
Buckfastleigh GB 13 E7
Buckhaven GB 5 C10
Buckie GB 3 K11
Buckingham GB 14 D7
Buckley GB 10 E5
Buckode IRL 6 D6
Buckow Märkische Schweiz
D 80 A6
Bückwitz D 83 E12
Bucoșnița RO 159 C9
Bucov RO 161 D8
Bucovăț MD 154 C2
Bucovăț RO 160 E3
Bucovica BIH 157 E7
Bučovice CZ 77 D12
Bucsa H 151 C7
Bucșani RO 161 D7
Bucșani RO 161 E7
Bucu RO 161 D11
București RO 151 E10
București RO 161 E8
Bucy-lès-Pierrepont F 19 E8
Bucz PL 81 B10
Buczek PL 143 D7
Bud N 100 A5
Buda RO 161 B9
Budacu de Jos RO 152 C5
Budakalász H 150 B3
Budakeszi H 149 A11
Budakovo MK 168 B5
Budaörs H 149 B11
Budapest H 150 C3
Budča SK 147 D8
Buddusò I 64 B3
Bude GB 12 D5
Budeasa RO 160 D5
Budel NL 16 F5
Büdelsdorf D 82 B7
Budenets' UA 153 A7
Budenheim D 21 D10
Budens P 50 E2
Büdesheim D 21 D11
Budești RO 152 B3
Budești RO 152 D4
Budești RO 160 C4
Budești RO 161 E8
Budeyi UA 154 A4
Budia E 47 C7
Budila RO 161 B7
Budimci HR 149 F10
Budimlič Japra BIH 156 C5
Budiná SK 147 E8
Büdingen D 21 D12
Budinščina HR 148 D6
Budišov CZ 77 D9
Budišov nad Budišovkou
CZ 146 B5
Budkovce SK 145 F4
Budleigh Salterton GB 13 D8
Budmerice SK 146 E4
Budoia I 72 D6
Budoni I 64 B4
Budrio I 66 C4
Budry PL 136 E4
Budureasa RO 151 D10
Buduslău RO 151 C9
Budva MNE 163 E6
Būdviečiai LT 136 D6
Budyně nad Ohří CZ 76 B6
Budziszewice PL 141 G1
Budzów PL 147 B9
Budzyń PL 85 E11
Bue N 94 E3
Bueña E 47 C10
Buenache de Alarcón E 47 E8
Buenache de la Sierra E 47 D8
Buenaventura E 46 D3
Buenavista de Valdavia E 39 C10
Buendía E 47 D7
Buer D 183 B10
Buer N 96 D6
Bueu E 38 D2
Bufleben D 79 D8
Buftea RO 161 D7
Bugac H 150 D4
Bugarra E 48 E3
Buğdayli TR 173 D8
Bugeat F 29 D9
Buggenhout B 182 C4
Buggerru I 64 E1
Buggingen D 27 E8
Bugiac MD 154 E3
Bugnara I 62 C5
Bugnein F 32 D4
Bugojno BIH 157 D7
Bugøyfjord N 114 D6
Bugøynes N 114 D7
Bugyi H 150 C3
Bühl D 27 C9
Bühlertal D 27 C9
Bühlertann D 74 D6
Bühlerzell D 74 D6

Caorle I 73 E6
Capaccio I 60 C4
Capaci I 58 C3
Capafonts E 42 E6
Capalbio I 65 C4
Căpâlna RO 151 D9
Căpâlnița RO 153 E6
Capannoli I 66 E2
Capannori I 66 E2
Caparde BIH 157 D10
Capari MK 168 B5
Caparica P 50 B1
Caparrosa P 44 C4
Caparroso E 32 F2
Cap-Blanc E 48 F4
Capbreton F 32 C3
Cap d'Agde F 34 D6
Capdenac F 33 A10
Capdenac-Gare F 33 A10
Capdepera E 57 B11
Capel Curig GB 10 E4
Capelins P 51 B5
Capelle aan de IJssel NL 16 E3
Capellen L 20 E6
Capel St Mary GB 15 C11
Capendu F 34 D4
Capestang F 34 D5
Capestrano I 62 C5
Cap Ferret F 32 A3
Capileira E 55 F6
Capilla E 54 B2
Capinha P 44 D6
Capistrello I 62 D4
Capizzi I 58 D5
Căpleni RO 151 B10
Čaplje BIH 157 C6
Čapljina BIH 157 F8
Capodimonte I 62 B1
Capo di Ponte I 69 A9
Capo d'Orlando I 59 C6
Capoliveri I 65 B2
Capolona I 66 E4
Caposele I 60 B4
Capoterra I 64 E2
Cappadocia I 62 C4
Cappagh White IRL 8 C6
Cappamore IRL 8 C6
Cappawhite IRL 8 C6
Cappeen IRL 8 E5
Cappelle sul Tavo I 62 C6
Cappeln (Oldenburg) D 17 C10
Cappercleuch GB 5 E10
Cappoquin IRL 9 D7
Capracotta I 63 D6
Capraia Isola I 65 A1
Capranica I 62 C2
Caprarola I 62 C2
Căpreni RO 160 D3
Capri I 60 B2
Căpriana MD 154 C2
Capriati a Volturno I 63 E6
Capri Leone I 59 C6
Caprino Bergamasco I 69 B7
Caprino Veronese I 69 B10
Captieux F 32 B5
Capua I 60 A2
Capurso I 61 A7
Căpușu Mare RO 151 D11
Capvern-les-Bains F 33 D6
Carabaña E 47 D6
Caracal RO 160 E4
Caracuel de Calatrava E 54 B4
Caragaș MD 154 D5
Caragele RO 161 D10
Caraglio I 37 C6
Caraman F 33 C9
Caramanico Terme I 62 C6
Caramulo P 44 C4
Cărand RO 151 E9
Caranga E 39 B7
Caranguejeira P 44 E3
Caransebeș RO 159 C9
Carantec F 22 C4
Carapelle I 60 A5
Carapinheira P 44 D3
Carasco I 37 C10
Carașova RO 159 C8
Caraula RO 159 E11
Caravaca de la Cruz E 55 C9
Caravaggio I 69 C8
Carbajales de Alba E 39 E8
Carballeda de Avia E 38 D3
Carballo E 38 B2
Carballo E 38 D4
Carbellino E 45 B8
Carbonera de Frentes E 41 E6
Carboneras E 55 F9
Carboneras de Guadazaón
E 47 E9
Carbonero El Mayor E 46 B4
Carboneros E 54 C5
Carbonia I 64 E2
Carbonìn I 72 C5
Carbonne F 33 D8
Carbost GB 2 L4
Carbost GB 2 L4
Cărbunari RO 159 D8
Cărbunești RO 161 C8
Carbury IRL 7 F9
Carcaboso E 45 D8
Carcabuey E 53 B8
Carcaixent E 48 F4
Carcaliu RO 155 C2
Carcans F 28 E3
Carcans-Plage F 28 E3
Carção P 39 E6
Cárcar E 32 F2
Carcare I 37 C8
Carcassonne F 33 D10
Carcastillo E 32 F3
Carcelén E 47 F10
Carcès F 36 E4
Carchelejo E 53 A9
Carcoforo I 68 B5
Cardaillac F 29 F9
Çardak TR 172 D6
Cardedeu E 43 D8
Cardedu I 64 D4
Cardeña E 54 C4
Cardeñadijo E 40 D4
Cardenden GB 5 C10
Cardenete E 47 E9
Cardeñosa E 46 C3
Cardeto I 59 C8
Cardiff GB 13 C8
Cardigan GB 12 A5
Cardigos P 44 E4
Cardinale I 59 B9
Cardito I 62 D5
Cardon RO 155 C5
Cardona E 43 D7
Cardosas P 50 E2
Carei RO 151 B9
Carenas E 41 F8
Carentan F 23 B9
Carentoir F 23 E7
Carevdar HR 149 D7
Carev Dvor MK 168 B5
Cargenbridge GB 5 E9
Cargèse F 37 G9
Carhaix-Plouguer F 22 D4
Caria P 44 D6
Cariati I 61 E7
Caridade P 50 C4
Carife I 60 A4
Carignan F 19 E11
Carignano I 37 B7
Cariñena E 41 F9
Carini I 58 C3
Carinish GB 2 K2
Cariño E 38 A4
Carinola I 60 A1
Carisio I 68 C5
Carisolo I 69 A10
Cârjiți RO 151 F10
Carland GB 7 C9
Carlanstown IRL 7 E9
Carlantino I 63 D7
Carlat F 29 F11
Carlentini I 59 E7
Carlet E 48 F3
Cârlibaba RO 152 B6
Cârligele RO 153 F10
Carling F 186 C2
Carlingford IRL 7 D10
Carlisle GB 5 F11
Carloforte I 64 E1
Cârlogani RO 160 D4
Carlomănești RO 161 C9
Carlopoli I 59 A9
Carlops GB 5 D10
Carlow D 83 C9
Carlow IRL 9 C9
Carloway GB 2 J3
Carlsberg D 186 C5
Carlton GB 11 F9
Carlton Colville GB 15 C12
Carluke GB 5 D9
Carlux F 29 F8
Carmagnola I 37 B7
Carmanova MD 154 C5
Carmarthen GB 12 B6
Carmaux F 33 B10
Carmena E 46 E4
Cármenes E 39 C8
Carmiano I 61 C10
Carmona E 51 E8
Carmonita E 45 F8
Carmyllie GB 5 B11
Carnac F 22 E5
Carnagh GB 7 D9
Carndonagh IRL 4 E2
Carnew IRL 9 C10
Carnforth GB 10 C6
Carnières F 19 D7
Carnikava LV 135 B8
Carnlough GB 4 F5
Carno GB 10 F4
Carnota E 38 C1
Carnoules F 36 E4
Carnoustie GB 5 B11
Carnoux-en-Provence F 35 D10
Carnteel GB 7 D9
Carnwath GB 5 D9
Carolei I 60 E6
Carolles F 23 C8
Carona I 69 A8
Caronia I 58 C5
C. A. Rosetti RO 155 C5
C. A. Rosetti RO 161 C10
Carosino I 61 C8
Carovigno I 61 B9
Carovilli I 63 D6
Carpaneto Piacentino I 69 D8
Carpegna I 66 E5
Carpen RO 159 E11
Carpenedolo I 66 B1
Carpentras F 35 B9
Carpi I 66 C2
Carpignano Salentino I 61 C10
Carpignano Sesia I 68 B5
Cărpineni MD 154 D2
Carpinet RO 151 E10
Carpineti I 66 D1
Carpineto Romano I 62 D4
Cărpiniș RO 151 F6
Carpino I 63 D9
Carpinone I 63 D6
Carpio E 40 F1
Carpiquet F 23 B11
Carquefou F 23 F9
Carqueiranne F 36 E4
Carracastle IRL 6 E5
Carracedelo E 39 C6
Carradale East GB 4 D6
Carragh IRL 7 F9
Carraig Airt IRL 7 B7
Carraig na Siuire IRL 9 D8
Carraig Thuathail IRL 8 E6
Carral E 38 B3
Carralevë RKS 163 E10
Carranque E 46 D5
Carrapateira P 50 E2
Carrapichana P 44 C6
Carrara I 69 E9
Carraroe IRL 6 F3
Carrascal del Obispo E 45 C9
Carrascosa E 47 C8
Carrascosa del Campo E 47 D7
Carratraca E 53 C7
Carrazeda de Ansiães P 45 B6
Carrazedo de Montenegro
P 38 E5
Carrbridge GB 3 L9
Carreço P 38 E2
Carregado P 50 A2
Carregal do Sal P 44 D5
Carregueiros P 44 E4
Carreira P 44 E3
Carreña E 39 B10
Carreteira E 38 C4
Carriazo E 40 B4
Carrick IRL 6 C5
Carrick IRL 9 D9
Carrickart IRL 7 B7
Carrickfergus GB 4 F5
Carrickmacross IRL 7 E9
Carrickmore GB 4 F2
Carrick-on-Shannon IRL 6 E6
Carrick-on-Suir IRL 9 D8
Carriço P 44 E3
Carrigaholt IRL 8 C3
Carrigallen IRL 7 E7
Carriganima IRL 8 E4
Carriganimmy IRL 8 E4
Carrigart IRL 7 B7
Carrigkerry IRL 8 D4
Carrig Mhachaire IRL 7 E9
Carrigtohill IRL 8 E6
Carrigtwohill IRL 8 E6
Carrio E 38 B3
Carrión de Calatrava E 54 A5
Carrión de los Céspedes
E 51 E7
Carrión de los Condes E 39 D10
Carrizo de la Ribera E 39 C8
Carrizosa E 55 B7
Carronbridge GB 5 E9
Carros F 37 D6
Carrouges F 23 C11
Carrowkeel IRL 4 E2
Carrowkeel IRL 7 B7
Carrowkennedy IRL 6 E3
Carrù I 37 C7
Carryduff GB 7 C11
Carry-le-Rouet F 35 D9
Cars F 28 E4
Carsac-Aillac F 29 F8
Carsluith GB 5 F8
Carsoli I 62 C4
Carspach F 27 E7
Carsphairn GB 5 E8
Carstairs GB 5 D9
Cartagena E 56 F3
Cártama E 53 C7
Cartaxo P 44 F3
Cartaya E 51 E5
Cartelègue F 28 E4
Carteret F 23 B8
Carterton GB 13 B11
Cartes E 40 B3
Cârțișoara RO 152 F5
Cartoceto I 67 E6
Carucedo E 39 D6
Carunchio I 63 D7
Carvalhal P 44 E4
Carvalhal P 50 C2
Carvalho de Egas P 38 F5
Carvalhosa P 38 F3
Carviçais P 45 B7
Carvin F 18 D6
Carvoeira P 44 F2
Carvoeiro P 50 E3
Čáry SK 77 E12
Casabermeja E 53 C8
Casabona I 61 E7
Casa Branca P 50 B3
Casa Branca P 50 B4
Casacalenda I 63 D7
Casagiove I 60 A2
Casaglione F 37 G9
Casa l'Abate I 61 C10
Casalanguida I 63 C6
Casalarreina E 40 C6
Casalbordino I 63 C7
Casalbore I 60 A4
Casalborgone I 68 C4
Casalbuono I 60 C5
Casalbuttano ed Uniti I 69 C8
Casàl Cermelli I 37 B9
Casàl di Principe I 60 A2
Casalecchio di Reno I 66 D3
Casale Monferrato I 68 C5
Casaletto Spartano I 60 C5
Casalfiumanese I 66 D4
Casalgrande I 66 C2
Casalgrasso I 37 B7
Casalmaggiore I 66 C1
Casalnuovo Monterotaro
I 63 D8
Casalpusterlengo I 69 C8
Casalvecchio di Puglia I 63 D8
Casàl Velino I 60 C4
Casamassima I 61 B7
Casamozza F 37 F10
Casarabonela E 53 C7
Casarano I 61 C10
Casar de Cáceres E 45 E8
Casar de Palomero E 45 D8
Casarejos E 40 E5
Casares E 39 B7
Casares E 53 D6
Casares de las Hurdes E 45 D8
Casariche E 53 B7
Casarrubios del Monte E 46 D4
Casarsa della Delizia I 73 E6
Casarza Ligure I 37 C10
Casas Altas E 47 D10
Casas Bajas E 47 D10
Casas de Benítez E 47 F8
Casas de Don Pedro E 45 F10
Casas de Fernando Alonso
E 47 F8
Casas de Haro E 47 F8
Casas de Juan Gil E 47 F10
Casas de Juan Núñez E 47 F9
Casas de Lázaro E 55 B8
Casas del Monte E 45 D9
Casas de los Pinos E 47 F8
Casas del Puerto E 56 E2
Casas de Millán E 45 E8
Casas de Reina E 51 C8
Casas de Ves E 47 F10
Casas-Ibáñez E 47 F10
Casasimarro E 47 F8
Casas Novas de Mares P 50 B5
Casasola de Arión E 39 E9
Casatejada E 45 E9
Casatenovo I 69 B7
Casavieja E 46 D3
Cascais P 50 B1
Cascante E 41 D8
Cascante del Río E 47 D10
Cascia I 62 B4
Casciana Terme I 66 E2
Cascina I 66 E2
Căscioarele RO 161 E8
Casebres P 50 B2
Cáseda E 32 E3
Case della Marina I 64 E4
Casei Gerola I 37 A9
Căşeiu RO 152 C3
Casekow D 84 D6
Casella I 37 B9
Caselle in Pittari I 60 C5
Caselle Torinese I 68 C4
Case Perrone I 61 B7
Caseras E 42 E4
Caserta I 60 A2
Casével P 50 D3
Cashel IRL 6 E5
Cashel IRL 6 F3
Cashel IRL 7 B7
Cashel IRL 7 G8
Cashel IRL 9 C7
Cashla IRL 6 F5
Casillas E 46 D3
Casillas de Flores E 45 D7
Casimcea RO 155 D2
Cașin RO 153 E9
Casina I 66 C1
Casinos E 48 E3
Casla IRL 6 F3
Čáslav CZ 77 C8
Casnewydd GB 13 B9
Casola in Lunigiana I 66 D1
Casola Valsenio I 66 D4
Casole d'Elsa I 66 F3
Casoli I 63 C6
Casoria I 60 B2
Caspe E 42 E3
Casperia I 62 C3
Cassà de la Selva E 43 D9
Cassagnes-Bégonhès F 33 B11
Cassaniouze F 29 F10
Cassano allo Ionio I 61 D6
Cassano delle Murge I 61 B7
Cassano Magnano I 69 B6
Cassano Spinola I 37 B9
Cassaro I 59 E6
Cassel F 18 C5
Casseneuil F 33 B7
Casserres E 43 C7
Cassibile I 59 F7
Cassine I 37 B9
Cassino I 62 E5
Cassis F 35 D10
Cassola I 72 E4
Cassuéjouls F 30 F2
Častá SK 146 E4
Castagliona Olona I 69 B6
Castagnaro I 66 B3
Castagneto Carducci I 66 F2
Castagnole delle Lanze I 37 B8
Castagnole Monferrato I 37 B8
Castalla E 56 D3
Castañar de Ibor E 45 E10
Castañares de Rioja E 40 C6
Castanet-Tolosan F 33 C9
Castanheira P 44 C6
Castanheira de Pêra P 44 D4
Castano Primo I 68 B6
Castasegna CH 69 A8
Casteggio I 37 A10
Castejón E 41 D8
Castejón del Puente E 42 D4
Castejón de Monegros E 42 D3
Castejón de Sos E 33 E6
Castejón de Valdejasa E 41 E10
Castelbellino I 67 F7
Castèl Bolognese I 66 D4
Castelbuono I 58 D5
Castelcivita I 60 C4
Castèl d'Ario I 66 B2
Castel de Cabra E 42 F2
Casteldelfino I 36 B6
Castèl del Monte I 62 C5
Castèl del Piano I 65 B5
Castèl del Rio I 66 D4
Castèl di Iudica I 59 E6
Castèl di Lama I 62 B5
Castèl di Lucio I 58 D5
Castèl di Sangro I 62 D6
Casteleiro P 45 D6
Castelfidardo I 67 F8
Castelfiorentino I 66 E2
Castelflorite E 42 D3
Castèl Focognano I 66 E4
Castelforte I 62 E5
Castelfranci I 60 B4
Castelfranco di Sopra I 66 E4
Castelfranco di Sotto I 66 E2
Castelfranco Emilia I 66 C3
Castelfranco in Miscano I 60 A4
Castelfranco Veneto I 72 E4
Castèl Frentano I 63 C6
Castèl Gandolfo I 62 D3
Castelginest F 33 C8
Castèl Giorgio I 62 B1
Castèl Goffredo I 66 B1
Castelgrande I 60 B4
Casteljaloux F 33 B6
Castell D 75 C7
Castellabate I 60 C3
Castell'Alfero I 37 B8
Castellalto I 62 B5
Castellammare del Golfo I 58 C2
Castellammare di Stabia I 60 B2
Castellamonte I 68 C4
Castellana Grotte I 61 B8
Castellane F 36 D5
Castellaneta I 61 B7
Castellanos de Castro E 40 D3
Castellarano I 66 C2
Castellar de la Frontera E 53 D6
Castellar de la Muela E 47 C9
Castellar de la Ribera E 43 C6
Castellar de Santiago E 55 B6
Castellar de Santisteban E 55 C6
Castell'Arquato I 69 D8
Castell'Azzara I 62 B1
Castellazzo Bormida I 37 B9
Castelldans E 42 E5
Castell de Cabres E 42 F4
Castell de Castells E 56 D4
Castelldefels E 43 E7
Castell de Ferro E 55 F6
Castelleone I 69 C8
Castelletto sopra Ticino I 68 B6
Castellfort E 42 F3
Castellina in Chianti I 66 F3
Castellina Marittima I 66 F2
Castelliri I 62 D5
Castellnou de Bassella E 43 C6
Castellnovo E 48 E4
Castello d'Argile I 66 C3
Castelló de Farfanya E 42 D5
Castelló de la Plana E 48 E4
Castelló d'Empúries E 43 C10
Castelló de Rugat E 56 D4
Castello di Annone I 37 B8
Castellón de la Plana E 48 E4
Castellote E 42 F3
Castello Tesino I 72 D4
Castellserá E 42 D5
Castellterçol E 43 D8
Castellucchio I 66 B2
Castelluccio dei Sauri I 60 A4
Castelluccio Inferiore I 60 C5
Castelluccio Valmaggiore I 60 A4
Castell'Umberto I 59 C6
Castelluzzo I 58 C2
Castell-y-Nedd GB 13 B7
Castèl Madama I 62 D3
Castèl Maggiore I 66 C3
Castelmagno I 37 C6
Castelmassa I 66 B3
Castelmauro I 63 D7
Castelmoron-sur-Lot F 33 B6
Castelnau-Barbarens F 33 C7
Castelnaudary F 33 D9
Castelnau-d'Auzan F 33 C6
Castelnau-de-Médoc F 28 E4
Castelnau-de-Montmiral
F 33 C9
Castelnau d'Estréfonds F 33 C8
Castelnau-le-Lez F 35 C6
Castelnau-Magnoac F 33 D7
Castelnau-Montratier F 33 B8
Castelnau-Rivière-Basse F 32 C5
Castelnovo di Sotto I 66 C2
Castelnovo ne'Monti I 66 D1
Castelnuovo Berardenga I 66 F4
Castelnuovo della Daunia
I 63 D8
Castelnuovo di Garfagnana
I 66 D1
Castelnuovo di Porto I 62 C3
Castelnuovo di Val di Cecina
I 66 F2
Castelnuovo Don Bosco I 68 C4
Castelnuovo Rangone I 66 C2
Castelnuovo Scrivia I 37 B9
Castelo Bom P 45 C7
Castelo Branco P 39 F6
Castelo Branco P 44 E6
Castelo de Paiva P 44 B4
Castelo de Vide P 44 F6
Castelo do Neiva P 38 E2
Castelões P 44 B4
Castelplanio I 67 F7
Castelraimondo I 67 F7
Castèl Ritaldi I 62 B3
Castelrotto I 72 C4
Castelsagrat F 33 B7
Castèl San Giovanni I 69 C7
Castèl San Lorenzo I 60 C4
Castèl San Niccolò I 66 E4
Castèl San Pietro Terme I 66 D4
Castèl Sant'Angelo I 62 C4
Castelsantangelo sul Nera
I 62 B4
Castelsaraceno I 60 C5
Castelsardo I 64 B2
Castelsarrasin F 33 B8
Castelseras E 42 F3
Casteltermini I 58 D4
Castelu RO 155 E2
Castelverde I 69 C8
Castelvetere in Val Fortore
I 60 A3
Castelvetrano I 58 D2
Castelvetro Placentino I 69 C8
Castèl Viscardo I 62 B2
Castèl Volturno I 60 A1
Castenaso I 66 C3
Castéra-Verduzan F 33 C6
Castetnau-Camblong F 32 D4
Castets F 32 C3
Castiadas I 64 E4
Castielfabib E 47 D10
Castiello de Jaca E 32 E4
Castiglioncello I 66 F1
Castiglione dei Pepoli I 66 D3
Castiglione del Lago I 66 F5
Castiglione della Pescaia I 65 B3
Castiglione delle Stiviere I 66 B1
Castiglione di Sicilia I 59 D7
Castiglione d'Orcia I 65 A5
Castiglione in Teverina I 62 B2
Castiglione Messer Marino
I 63 D6
Castiglion Fiorentino I 66 F4
Castignano I 62 B5
Castilblanco E 45 F10
Castilblanco de los Arroyos
E 51 D8
Castiliscar E 32 F3
Castilleja de la Cuesta E 51 E7
Castillejar E 55 D7
Castillejo de Martin Viejo E 45 C7
Castillejo de Mesleón E 40 F4
Castillejo de Robledo E 40 E5
Castillo de Bayuela E 46 D3
Castillo de Garcimuñoz E 47 E8
Castillo de Locubín E 53 A9
Castillon-en-Couserans F 33 E8
Castillon-la-Bataille F 28 F5
Castillonnès F 33 A7
Castillo-Nuevo E 32 E3
Castilruiz E 41 E7
Castione della Presolana I 69 B9
Castiòns di Strada I 73 E7
Castlebar IRL 6 E4
Castlebay GB 4 B2
Castlebellingham IRL 7 E10
Castleblakeney IRL 6 F6
Castleblayney IRL 7 D9
Castlebridge IRL 9 D10
Castle Carrock GB 5 F11
Castle Cary GB 13 C9
Castlecomer IRL 9 C8
Castleconnell IRL 8 C5
Castlecor IRL 8 D5
Castledawson GB 4 F3
Castlederg GB 4 F1
Castledermot IRL 9 C9
Castle Douglas GB 5 F9
Castleellis IRL 9 D10
Castlefinn IRL 4 F1
Castleford GB 11 D9
Castlegal IRL 6 D6
Castlegregory IRL 8 D2
Castlehill IRL 6 D4
Castleisland IRL 8 D4
Castle Kennedy GB 4 F7
Castlellis IRL 9 D10
Castlemaine IRL 8 D3
Castlemartin GB 12 B4
Castlemartyr IRL 8 E6
Castleplunket IRL 6 E6
Castlepollard IRL 7 E8
Castlerea IRL 6 E6
Castlereagh GB 7 C11
Castlerock GB 4 E3
Castletown GB 3 H10
Castletown GB 11 F7
Castletown GBM 10 C2
Castletown IRL 7 G8
Castletown Bere IRL 8 E3
Castletownshend IRL 8 E4
Castlewellan GB 7 D11
Castranova RO 160 E4
Castrejón de la Peña E 39 C10
Castrelo do Val E 38 E5
Castres F 33 C10
Castricum NL 16 C3
Castries F 35 C6
Castrignano del Capo I 61 D10
Castril E 55 D7
Castrillo de Don Juan E 40 E3
Castrillo de Duero E 40 E3
Castrillo de la Reina E 40 E5
Castrillo de la Vega E 40 E4
Castrillo Tejeriego E 40 E3
Castro I 61 C10
Castrobarto E 40 B5
Castrocalbón E 39 D8
Castro Caldelas E 38 D5
Castrocaro Terme I 66 D4
Castrocontrigo E 39 D7
Castro Daire P 44 C5
Castro dei Volsci I 62 D5
Castro del Río E 53 A8
Castro de Ouro E 38 A5
Castro de Rei E 38 B5
Castrofilippo I 58 E4
Castrogonzalo E 39 E8
Castrojeriz E 40 D3
Castro Laboreiro P 38 D3
Castro Marim P 50 E5
Castromocho E 39 D10
Castromonte E 39 E9
Castronuevo E 39 E8
Castronuño E 39 F9
Castronuovo di Sant'Andrea
I 60 C6
Castronuovo di Sicilia I 58 D4
Castropignano I 63 D7
Castropodame E 39 C7
Castropol E 39 A5
Castrop-Rauxel D 17 E8
Castroreale I 59 C7
Castro-Urdiales E 40 B5
Castroverde E 38 B5
Castro Verde P 50 D3
Castroverde de Campos E 39 E9
Castrovillari I 60 D6
Castuera E 51 B8
Cața RO 152 E6
Catadau E 48 F3
Çatalca TR 173 B9
Catalina RO 153 F8
Cataloi RO 155 C3
Catania I 59 E7
Catanzaro I 59 B10
Catanzaro Marina I 59 B10
Catarroja E 48 F4
Cătcău RO 152 C3
Căteasca RO 160 D6
Catenanuova I 59 D6
Caterham GB 15 E8
Cateri F 37 F9
Cathair Dónall IRL 8 E2
Cathair na Mart IRL 6 E3
Cathair Saidhbhín IRL 8 E2
Catherdaniel IRL 8 E2
Catí E 42 G4
Čatići BIH 157 D9
Catignano I 62 C5
Cătina RO 152 D4
Cătina RO 161 C8
Cativelos P 44 C5
Catoira E 38 C2
Caton GB 10 C6
Catral E 56 E3
Cattenom F 20 F6
Catterfeld D 79 E8
Catterick GB 11 C8
Catterline GB 5 B12
Cattolica I 67 E6
Cattolica Eraclea I 58 E3
Cătunele RO 159 D10
Catus F 33 A8
Căuaș RO 151 B10
Caudan F 22 E5
Caudebec-lès-Elbeuf F 18 F3
Caudecoste F 33 B7
Caudete E 56 D3
Caudete de las Fuentes E 47 E10
Caudiel E 48 E3
Caudiès-de-Fenouillèdes
F 33 E10
Caudry F 19 D7
Caulnes F 23 D7
Caulonia I 59 C9
Caumont F 33 B8
Caumont F 33 D8
Caumont-l'Éventé F 23 B10
Caumont-sur-Durance F 35 C8
Caunes-Minervois F 34 D4
Cauro F 37 H9
Căușeni MD 154 D4
Causeway IRL 8 D3
Causeway Head GB 4 E3
Caussade F 33 B9
Cautano I 60 A3
Cauterets F 32 E5
Cava de'Tirreni I 60 B3
Cavadinești RO 153 E12
Cavaglià I 68 C5
Cavaillon F 35 C9
Cavalaire-sur-Mer F 36 E5
Cavaleiro P 50 D2
Cavalese I 72 D3
Cavallermaggiore I 37 B7
Cavallino I 66 B6
Cava Manara I 69 C7
Cavan IRL 7 E8
Cavanagarven IRL 7 D9
Cavargna I 69 A7
Cavarzere I 66 B5
Cavazzo Carnico I 73 D7
Cave I 62 D3
Cave del Predil I 73 D8
Caveirac F 35 C7
Cavezzo I 66 C3
Cavignac F 28 E5
Čavle HR 67 B9
Cavnic RO 152 B3
Cavour I 68 D3
Cavriago I 66 C2
Cavriglia I 66 E3
Cavtat HR 162 D5
Çavuşköy TR 171 C10
Cawdor GB 3 K9
Cawood GB 11 D9
Cawston GB 15 B11
Caxarias P 44 E3
Çaybaşı TR 177 C9
Çayboyu TR 181 B8
Cayeux-sur-Mer F 18 D4
Çayirdere TR 173 B9
Caylus F 33 B9
Cazalegas E 46 D3
Cazalilla E 53 A9
Cazalla de la Sierra E 51 D8
Cazals F 33 A8
Cazals F 33 B9
Căzănești RO 159 D10
Căzănești RO 161 D10
Cazasu RO 155 C1
Cazaubon F 32 C5
Cazères F 33 D8
Cazes-Mondenard F 33 B8
Cazilhac F 33 D10
Cazin BIH 156 C4
Cazis CH 71 D8
Čazma HR 149 E7
Cazorla E 55 D7
Cazoulès F 29 F8
Cea E 38 D4
Cea E 39 D10
Ceahlău RO 153 C7
Ceamurlia de Jos RO 155 D3
Ceanannus Mór IRL 7 E9
Ceann Toirc IRL 8 D5
Ceann Trá IRL 8 D2
Ceanu Mare RO 152 D3
Cearsiadar GB 2 J3
Ceatharlach IRL 9 C9
Ceaucé F 23 D10
Ceaușu de Câmpie RO 152 D5
Céaux-d'Allègre F 30 E4
Cébazat F 30 D3
Čebín CZ 77 D10
Cebolla E 46 E3
Čebovce SK 147 E8
Cebreros E 46 D4
Ceccano I 62 D4
Cece H 149 C11
Čečejovce SK 145 F3
Čechtice CZ 77 C8
Čechynce SK 146 E6
Cecina I 66 F2
Ceclavín E 45 E7
Cecuni MNE 163 D8
Cedães P 38 F5
Čedasai LT 135 D10
Cedegolo I 69 A9
Cedeira E 38 A3
Cedillo E 44 E6
Cedillo del Condado E 46 D5
Cedrillas E 48 D3
Cedry Wielkie PL 138 B6
Cedynia PL 84 E6
Cee E 38 C1
Cefa RO 151 D8
Cefalù I 58 C5
Cefn-mawr GB 10 F5
Ceggia I 73 E6
Cegléd H 150 C4
Ceglédbercel H 150 C4
Ceglie Messapica I 61 B9
Cegłów PL 141 F5
Čegrane MK 163 F10
Cehal RO 151 C10
Cehegín E 55 C9
Cehu Silvaniei RO 151 C11
Ceica RO 151 D9
Ceikiniai LT 135 F12
Ceilhes-et-Rocozels F 34 C5
Ceinos de Campos E 39 D9
Ceintrey F 26 C5
Ceira P 44 D4
Čejč CZ 77 E11
Čejkov SK 145 G4
Cekcyn PL 138 C5
Çekirdekli TR 173 F9
Čekiškė LT 134 F7
Ceków-Kolonia PL 142 C5
Celadas E 47 D10
Čeladná CZ 146 B6
Čelákovice CZ 77 B7
Celaliye TR 173 A7
Celano I 62 C5
Celanova E 38 D4
Čelarevo SRB 158 C4
Celaru RO 160 E4
Celbridge IRL 7 F9
Čelebić BIH 157 E6
Čelebići BIH 157 F10
Celeiros P 38 E3
Celenza Valfortore I 63 D7
Celestynów PL 141 F4
Čelić BIH 157 C10
Celico I 61 E6
Čelinac Donji BIH 157 C7
Celje SLO 148 D4
Cella E 47 D10
Celldömölk H 149 B8
Celle D 79 A7
Celle Ligure I 37 C9
Cellere I 62 C1
Celles B 19 C7
Celles-sur-Belle F 28 C5
Celles-sur-Ource F 25 D11
Cellettes F 24 E5
Cellino Attanasio I 62 B5
Cellole I 62 E5
Čelopeci MK 168 B5
Čelopek MK 164 F3
Celorico da Beira P 44 C6
Celorico de Basto P 38 F4
Celrà E 43 C9
Çeltikçi TR 173 D9
Cembra I 69 A11
Čemerno BIH 157 F10
Cempi LV 135 A11
Cénac-et-St-Julien F 29 F8
Cenad RO 150 E6
Cenade RO 152 E4
Cenas LV 134 C7
Cencenighe Agordino I 72 D4
Cendras F 35 B7
Cendrieux F 29 F7
Cenei RO 159 B6
Ceneselli I 66 B3
Cengio I 37 C8
Cenicero E 41 D6
Cenicientos E 46 D4
Čenta SRB 158 C5
Centallo I 37 B7
Centelles E 43 D8
Cento I 66 C3
Centola I 60 C4
Centuri F 37 F10
Centuripe I 59 D6
Cepagatti I 62 C6
Cepari RO 160 C5
Čepin HR 149 E11
Ceplenița RO 153 C9
Čepovan SLO 73 D8
Ceppaloni I 60 A3
Ceppo Morelli I 68 B5
Ceprano I 62 D5
Ceptura RO 161 C8
Čeralije HR 149 E9
Cerami I 59 D6
Cerani BIH 157 C8
Cerano I 68 C6
Ceranów PL 141 E6
Cérans-Foulletourte F 23 E12
Cerasi I 59 C8
Ceraso I 60 C4
Cerașu RO 161 C8
Cerăt RO 160 E3
Ceraukste LV 135 D8
Čeravë AL 168 C4
Cerbăl RO 151 F10

Cerbère F 34 F5
Cercal P 44 F3
Cercal P 50 D2
Čerčany CZ 77 C7
Cercedilla E 46 C4
Cercemaggiore I 63 E7
Cerchezu RO 155 F2
Cerchiara di Calabria I 61 D6
Cerchio I 62 C5
Cercy-la-Tour F 30 B4
Cerda I 58 D4
Cerdanyola del Vallès E 43 E8
Cerdedo E 38 C3
Cerdeira P 44 D5
Cerdon F 25 E7
Cēre LV 134 B5
Cerea I 66 B3
Cered H 147 E9
Ceregnano I 66 B4
Cerekwica PL 85 E13
Cérences F 23 C9
Ceres GB 5 C11
Ceres I 31 E11
Ceresole Reale I 31 E11
Céreste F 35 C10
Céret F 34 F4
Čerević SRB 158 C4
Cerezo de Abajo E 46 B5
Cerezo de Arriba E 40 F4
Cerezo de Riotirón E 40 C5
Cerfontaine B 184 D1
Cergău RO 152 E3
Cergy F 24 B7
Cerhenice CZ 77 B8
Ceriale I 37 C8
Ceriana I 37 D7
Cerignola I 60 A5
Cérilly F 30 B2
Čerin BIH 157 F8
Cerisano I 60 E6
Cerisiers F 25 D9
Cerisy-la-Forêt F 23 B10
Cerisy-la-Salle F 23 B9
Cerizay F 28 B4
Çerkezköy TR 173 B9
Çerkezmüsellim TR 173 B7
Cerklje SLO 73 D9
Cerklje SLO 148 E5
Cerknica SLO 73 E9
Cerkno SLO 73 D8
Cerkwica PL 85 B8
Cermei RO 151 D8
Çermë-Proshkë AL 168 B2
Cermignano I 62 B5
Cërmjan RKS 163 E9
Cerna HR 157 B10
Cerna RO 155 C2
Cernache do Bonjardim P 44 E4
Černá Hora CZ 77 D11
Cernat RO 153 F8
Cernătești RO 160 E2
Cernătești RO 161 C9
Cernavodă RO 155 E2
Cernay F 27 E7
Cernay-en-Dormois F 19 F10
Černčice CZ 76 B5
Cernégula E 40 C4
Cernele RO 160 E3
Cernești RO 152 C3
Cernica RO 161 E8
Cernier CH 31 A10
Černik HR 157 B7
Černík SK 146 E6
Černilov CZ 77 B9
Cernișoara RO 160 C4
Cernobbio I 69 B7
Cernoleuca MD 153 A11
Černošice CZ 76 C6
Černošín CZ 76 C3
Černilov LV 133 D2
Černovice CZ 77 D7
Černožice CZ 77 B9
Cerová SK 146 D4
Cerovac SRB 159 E6
Cerovak Tušilovički HR 148 F5
Ceroviljani BIH 157 B7
Cerovlje HR 67 B9
Cerovo SK 147 E8
Cerralbo E 45 C7
Cerreto d'Esi I 67 F6
Cerreto di Spoleto I 62 B3
Cerreto Sannita I 60 A3
Cerrigydrudion GB 10 E4
Cërrik AL 168 B2
Cerro al Volturno I 62 D6
Cersay F 28 A5
Cersosimo I 61 C6
Certaldo I 66 E3
Certeju de Sus RO 151 F10
Certești RO 153 E11
Certeze RO 145 H7
Certosa di Pavia I 69 C7
Certosa di Pesio I 37 C7
Ceru-Băcăinți RO 151 F11
Cërujë AL 168 C3
Cerva P 38 F4
Cervaro I 62 E5
Cervatos de la Cueza E 39 D10
Červená Voda CZ 77 B11
Cervenia RO 161 F6
Červená Voda CZ 77 C12
Červený Kostelec CZ 77 B10
Cervera E 42 D6
Cervera de la Cañada E 41 F8
Cervera del Llano E 47 E8
Cervera del Maestre E 48 D5
Cervera de los Montes E 46 D3
Cervera del Río Alhama E 41 D8
Cervera de Pisuerga E 40 C3
Cerveteri I 62 D2
Cervia I 66 D5
Cervignano del Friuli I 73 E7
Cervinara I 60 A3
Červiná Řečice CZ 77 C8
Cervione F 37 G10
Cervo E 38 A5
Cervo I 37 D8
Cervon F 25 F10
Cerzeto I 60 E6
Cesano Boscone I 69 C7
Cesano Maderno I 69 B7
Cesarò I 59 D6
Cesena I 66 D5
Cesenatico I 66 D5
Cesio I 37 C7
Cēsis LV 135 B10
Česká Kamenice CZ 80 E6
Česká Lípa CZ 81 E7
Česká Skalice CZ 77 B10
Česká Ves CZ 77 B12
České Brezovo SK 147 E9
České Budějovice CZ 77 E6
České Meziříčí CZ 77 B10
Český Brod CZ 77 B7
Český Dub CZ 81 E7
Český Krumlov CZ 76 E6
Český Těšín CZ 147 B7
Češljeva Bara SRB 159 D7
Çeşme TR 177 C7
Cespedosa E 45 C9
Cessalto I 73 E6
Cessenon-sur-Orb F 34 D5
Cessole I 37 B8
Cesson F 25 C8
Cesson-Sévigné F 23 D8
Cestas F 28 F4
Čestobrodica SRB 158 F5
Cesuras E 38 B3
Cesvaine LV 135 C12
Cetariu RO 151 C9
Cetate RO 152 C5
Cetate RO 159 E11
Cetatea de Baltă RO 152 E4
Cetățeni RO 160 C6
Cetina E 41 F8
Cetingrad HR 156 B4
Cetinje MNE 163 E6
Ceto I 69 A9
Ceton F 24 D4
Cetona I 62 B1
Cetraro I 60 D5
Ceuta WHAT 53 E6
Ceutí E 56 E2
Ceva I 37 C8
Cevico de la Torre E 40 E3
Cevico Navero E 40 E3
Cevins F 31 D9
Cevio CH 68 A6
Cevizköy TR 173 A8
Čevo MNE 163 D6
Cewice PL 85 B13
Ceyreste F 35 D10
Ceyzériat F 31 C7
Cezieni RO 160 E4
Chã P 38 E4
Chaam NL 16 F3
Chabanais F 29 D7
Chabeuil F 31 F7
Chabielice PL 143 D7
Chablis F 25 E10
Chabówka PL 147 B9
Chabreloche F 30 D4
Chabris F 24 F6
Chacim P 39 F6
Chagford GB 13 D7
Chagny F 30 B6
Chaïkali GR 174 C4
Chaillac F 29 C8
Chailland F 23 D10
Chaillé-les-Marais F 28 C3
Chailley F 25 D10
Chaintrix-Bierges F 25 C11
Chaironeia GR 175 C6
Chalabre F 33 E10
Chalais CH 31 C12
Chalais F 28 E6
Chalamera E 42 D4
Chalamont F 31 C7
Chalampé F 27 E8
Chalandri GR 175 C8
Chalandritsa GR 174 C4
Chalastra GR 169 C8
Chale GB 13 D12
Chaleix F 29 D7
Châlette-sur-Loing F 25 D8
Chalford GB 13 B10
Chalgrove GB 13 B12
Chaligny F 26 C5
Chalin PL 139 E7
Chalindrey F 26 E3
Chalivoy-Milon F 29 B11
Chalki GR 169 E8
Chalki GR 181 D7
Chalkiades GR 169 F7
Chalkiades GR 174 A2
Chalkida GR 175 C8
Chalkidona GR 169 C8
Chalkio GR 175 D6
Challans F 28 B2
Challerange F 19 F10
Challes-les-Eaux F 31 D8
Chalmoux F 30 B4
Chalonnes-sur-Loire F 23 F10
Châlons-en-Champagne
F 25 C11
Chalon-sur-Saône F 30 B6
Châlus F 29 D7
Cham CH 27 F9
Cham D 75 D12
Chamalières F 30 D3
Chamaloc F 31 F7
Chamberet F 29 D9
Chambéria F 31 C8
Chambéry F 31 D8
Chambley-Bussières F 26 B4
Chambois F 23 C12
Chambon-sur-Voueize F 29 C10
Chambord F 24 E6
Chamboulive F 29 E9
Chambray-lès-Tours F 24 F4
Chambry F 19 E8
Chamesson F 25 E12
Chamonix-Mont-Blanc F 31 D10
Chamoux-sur-Gelon F 31 D9
Champagnac F 29 E10
Champagnac-de-Belair F 29 E7
Champagnac-le-Vieux F 30 E4
Champagne-Mouton F 29 D6
Champagne-sur-Seine F 25 D8
Champagney F 26 E6
Champagnole F 31 B8
Champaubert F 25 C10
Champdeniers-St-Denis F 28 C5
Champ-d'Oiseau F 25 E11
Champeix F 30 D3
Champéry CH 31 C10
Champex CH 31 C11
Champforgeuil F 30 B6
Champgenéteux F 23 D11
Champier F 31 E7
Champigné F 23 E10
Champignelles F 25 E9
Champigneulles F 186 D1
Champigny F 25 D9
Champlemy F 25 F9
Champlitte F 26 E4
Champniers F 29 D6
Champoléon F 31 F9
Champoluc I 68 B4
Champsecret F 23 C10
Champs-sur-Tarentaine-
Marchal F 29 E11
Champs-sur-Yonne F 25 E10
Champ-sur-Drac F 31 E8
Champtoceaux F 23 F9
Chamrousse F 31 E8
Chamusca P 44 F4
Chanac F 34 B5
Chanas F 30 E6
Chança P 44 F5
Chanceaux F 25 E12
Chanceaux-sur-Choisille F 24 F4
Chancelade F 29 E7
Chancelaria P 44 E3
Chandras GR 179 E11
Chandrinos GR 174 F4
Chañe E 40 F3
Changé F 23 D10
Changé F 23 E12
Changy F 30 C5
Chania GR 178 D7
Chaniotis GR 169 D10
Chantada E 38 C4
Chantelle F 30 C3
Chantilly F 25 B7
Chantonnay F 28 B3
Chanu F 23 C10
Chaource F 25 D11
Chapaevo BG 166 C4
Chapayevka UA 154 A5
Chapel-en-le-Frith GB 11 E8
Chapelle-lez-Herlaimont
B 182 E4
Chapeltown GB 11 E9
Chapinería E 46 D4
Charakas GR 178 E9
Charavgi GR 169 D6
Charbonnat F 30 B5
Charcenne F 26 F4
Charchilla F 31 C8
Chard GB 13 D9
Chardstock GB 13 D9
Charenton-du-Cher F 29 B11
Charfield GB 13 B10
Chargey-lès-Gray F 26 F4
Charlbury GB 13 B12
Charlemont GB 7 D9
Charleroi B 19 D9
Charlestown IRL 6 E5
Charleville IRL 8 D5
Charleville-Mézières F 19 E10
Charlieu F 30 C5
Charlottenberg S 96 C7
Charlton GB 13 C12
Charlton Kings GB 13 B10
Charly F 25 C9
Charmé F 29 D6
Charmes F 26 D5
Charmes-sur-Rhône F 30 F6
Charmey CH 31 B11
Charmouth GB 13 D9
Charmoy F 25 E9
Charnay-lès-Mâcon F 30 C6
Charny F 25 E9
Charokopeio GR 178 B2
Charolles F 30 C5
Charomkhava BY 133 F3
Charopo GR 169 B9
Chârost F 29 B10
Charquemont F 27 F6
Charrat CH 31 C11
Charrey-sur-Seine F 25 E12
Charrin F 30 B4
Charroux F 29 C6
Charsznica PL 143 F8
Chartres F 24 D5
Charvensod I 31 D11
Charvieu-Chavagneux F 31 D7
Charzyno PL 85 B9
Chassagne-Montrachet F 30 B6
Chasseneuil-sur-Bonnieure
F 29 D6
Chasseradès F 35 A6
Chasse-sur-Rhône F 30 D6
Chassigny-Aisey F 26 E3
Chassillé F 23 D11
Chastre B 19 C10
Château-Arnoux F 35 B10
Châteaubernard F 28 D5
Châteaubourg F 23 D9
Châteaubriant F 23 E9
Château-Chinon F 30 A4
Château-d'Oex CH 31 C11
Château-d'Olonne F 28 B2
Château-du-Loir F 24 E3
Châteaudun F 24 D5
Châteaugiron F 23 D8
Château-Gontier F 23 E10
Château-Landon F 25 D8
Château-la-Vallière F 24 E3
Châteaulin F 22 D3
Châteaumeillant F 29 B10
Châteauneuf-de-Galaure
F 31 E6
Châteauneuf-de-Randon
F 35 A6
Châteauneuf-d'Ille-et-Vilaine
F 23 C8
Châteauneuf-du-Faou F 22 D4
Châteauneuf-en-Thymerais
F 24 C5
Châteauneuf-la-Forêt F 29 D9
Châteauneuf-les-Martigues
F 35 D9
Châteauneuf-sur-Charente
F 28 D5
Châteauneuf-sur-Cher F 29 B10
Châteauneuf-sur-Loire F 25 E7
Châteauneuf-sur-Sarthe
F 23 E11
Châteauneuf-Val-de-Bargis
F 25 F9
Châteauponsac F 29 C8
Château-Porcien F 19 E9
Châteauredon F 36 C4
Châteaurenard F 25 E8
Châteaurenard F 35 C8
Châteaurenaud F 31 B7
Château-Renault F 24 E4
Châteauroux F 29 B9
Châteauroux F 36 B5
Château-Salins F 26 C6
Château-Thierry F 25 B9
Châteauvillain F 25 D12
Châtel F 31 C10
Châtelaillon-Plage F 28 C3
Châtelaudren F 22 C6
Châtel-Censoir F 25 E10
Châteldon F 30 D4
Châtelet B 19 D10
Châtel-Gérard F 25 E11
Châtelguyon F 30 D3
Châtellerault F 29 B7
Châtel-Montagne F 30 C4
Châtel-St-Denis CH 31 B10
Châtel-sur-Moselle F 26 D5
Châtelus-Malvaleix F 29 C10
Châtenois F 26 D4
Châtenois F 27 D7
Châtenois-les-Forges F 27 E6
Châtenoy-le-Royal F 30 B6
Chatham GB 15 E10
Châtillon B 19 E12
Châtillon I 68 B4
Châtillon-Coligny F 25 E8
Châtillon-en-Bazois F 30 A4
Châtillon-en-Diois F 35 A9
Châtillon-en-Michaille F 31 C8
Châtillon-la-Palud F 31 D7
Châtillon-sur-Chalaronne
F 31 C6
Châtillon-sur-Colmont F 23 D10
Châtillon-sur-Indre F 29 B8
Châtillon-sur-Loire F 25 E8
Châtillon-sur-Marne F 25 B10
Châtillon-sur-Seine F 25 E12
Châtillon-sur-Thouet F 28 B5
Chatte F 31 E7
Chatteris GB 15 C9
Chatton GB 5 D13
Chatuzange-le-Goubet F 31 F7
Chatzis GR 174 E4
Chauchina E 53 B9
Chaudenay F 26 E4
Chaudes-Aigues F 30 F3
Chaudeyrac F 35 A6
Chaudfontaine B 19 C12
Chauffailles F 30 C5
Chauffayer F 31 F9
Chaulnes F 18 E6
Chaumergy F 31 B7
Chaumont F 26 D3
Chaumont-en-Vexin F 18 F4
Chaumont-Porcien F 19 E9
Chaumont-sur-Aire F 26 C3
Chaumont-sur-Loire F 24 F5
Chaunay F 29 C6
Chauny F 19 E7
Chaussin F 31 B7
Chauvigny F 29 B7
Chavanay F 30 E6
Chavanges F 25 C12
Chavanoz F 31 D7
Chavari GR 174 D3
Chavelot F 26 D5
Chaves P 38 E5
Chazelles-sur-Lyon F 30 D5
Cheadle GB 11 F8
Cheb CZ 75 B11
Checa E 47 C9
Chechel'nyk UA 154 A4
Chęciny PL 143 E9
Chécy F 24 E7
Chedburgh GB 15 C10
Cheddar GB 13 C9
Chef-Boutonne F 28 C5
Chekhpare BG 166 E4
Cheles E 51 B5
Chella E 56 C3
Chełm PL 141 H8
Chełmek PL 143 F7
Chełmiec PL 145 D2
Chełmno PL 138 D5
Chełmno PL 142 B6
Chelmsford GB 15 D9
Chełmża PL 138 D6
Cheltenham GB 13 B10
Chelva E 47 E11
Chemazé F 23 E10
Chémery F 24 F5
Chémery-sur-Bar F 19 E10
Chemillé F 23 F10
Chemin F 31 B7
Cheminon F 25 C12
Chemiré-le-Gaudin F 23 E11
Chemnitz D 80 E3
Chenecey-Buillon F 26 F4
Chénérailles F 29 C10
Cheniménil F 26 D6
Chenôve F 26 F3
Cheny F 25 E10
Chepelare BG 165 F10
Chepintsi BG 165 D7
Chepstow GB 13 B9
Chepy F 25 C11
Chera E 48 E3
Chérac F 28 D5
Cherasco I 37 B7
Chéraute F 32 D4
Cherbourg-Octeville F 23 A8
Cheremule I 64 B2
Cherepkivtsi UA 153 A7
Chereshovo BG 161 F8
Cherlenivka UA 153 A8
Cherna BG 155 F1
Cherna Gora BG 166 E4
Chernevo BG 167 C9
Chernevo RUS 132 D3
Cherni Osŭm BG 165 D10
Cherni Vrŭkh BG 167 E8
Chernivtsi UA 153 A7
Chernogorovo BG 165 E9
Cherno More BG 167 D8
Chernoochene BG 166 F4
Chernyakhovsk RUS 136 D4
Chernyshevskoye RUS 136 D6
Chéroy F 25 D9
Cherskaya RUS 132 F3
Cherso GR 169 B8
Chert E 42 F4
Cherveix-Cubas F 29 E8
Cherven BG 161 F8
Chervena voda BG 161 F8
Cherven Bryag BG 165 C9
Cherventsi BG 167 B8
Cherves-Richemont F 28 D5
Chervona Hreblya UA 154 A4
Chervonoarmiys'ke UA 154 F3
Chervonohrad UA 144 C9
Chesham GB 15 D7
Cheshunt GB 15 D8
Chesley F 25 E11
Chessy-les-Prés F 25 D10
Cheste E 48 F3
Chester GB 10 E6
Chesterfield GB 11 E9
Chester-le-Street GB 5 F13
Chețani RO 152 E4
Chetrosu MD 153 A10
Chevagnes F 30 B4
Chevanceaux F 28 E5
Chevereșu Mare RO 159 B7
Chevillon F 26 C3
Chevilly F 24 D6
Chevreuse F 24 C7
Chew Magna GB 13 C9
Cheylade F 30 E2
Chezal-Benoît F 29 B10
Chèze F 32 E5
Chiajna RO 161 E8
Chiampo I 66 A3
Chianciano Terme I 62 A1
Chianni I 66 E2
Chiaramonte Gulfi I 59 E6
Chiaramonti I 64 B2
Chiaravalle I 67 E7
Chiaravalle Centrale I 59 B9
Chiari I 69 B8
Chiaromonte I 60 C6
Chiasso CH 69 B7
Chiavari I 37 C10
Chiavenno I 69 A7
Chiché F 28 B5
Chichester GB 15 F7
Chichiș RO 153 F7
Chiclana de la Frontera E 52 D4
Chiclana de Segura E 55 C6
Chieming D 72 A6
Chienes I 72 C4
Chieri I 37 A7
Chiesa in Valmalenco I 69 A8
Chieșd RO 151 C10
Chiesina Uzzanese I 66 E2
Chieti I 63 C6
Chieuti I 63 D8
Chieveley GB 13 C12
Chièvres B 19 C8
Chigwell GB 15 D9
Chiheru de Jos RO 152 D5
Chikhachevo RUS 133 B7
Chilches E 48 E4
Chilcompton GB 13 C9
Chilham GB 15 E10
Chiliile RO 161 C9
Chiliomodi GR 175 D6
Chilleurs-aux-Bois F 24 D7
Chillón E 54 B3
Chilluévar E 55 C6
Chiloeches E 47 C6
Chimay B 19 D9
Chimeneas E 53 B9
Chinanale I 68 B5
Chinchilla de Monte Aragón
E 55 B9
Chinchón E 46 D6
Chindrieux F 31 D8
Chinon F 23 F12
Chinteni RO 152 D3
Chiochiș RO 152 D4
Chioggia I 66 B5
Chiojdeni RO 161 B9
Chiojdu RO 161 C8
Chiomonte I 31 E10
Chiona GR 174 C4
Chionata GR 174 C2
Chios GR 177 C7
Chiperceni MD 154 B3
Chipiona E 52 C4
Chippenham GB 13 C10
Chipping Campden GB 13 A11
Chipping Norton GB 13 B11
Chipping Ongar GB 15 D9
Chipping Sodbury GB 13 B10
Chippis CH 31 C12
Chiprana E 42 E3
Chiprovtsi BG 165 C6
Chirbury GB 10 F5
Chiren BG 165 C8
Chiriet-Lunga MD 154 E3
Chirivel E 55 D8
Chirk GB 10 F5
Chirnogeni RO 155 F2
Chirnogi RO 161 E9
Chirnside GB 5 D12
Chiroubles F 30 C6
Chirpan BG 166 E4
Chirpăr RO 152 F5
Chirsova MD 154 E3
Chiscani RO 155 C1
Chișcăreni MD 153 B12
Chișcăreni MD 154 C3
Chiselet RO 161 E9
Chișinău MD 154 C3
Chisindia RO 151 E9
Chișineu-Criș RO 151 D8
Chistye-Prudy RUS 136 E5
Chițcani MD 154 D5
Chitignano I 66 E4
Chitila RO 161 D7
Chiuiești RO 152 C3
Chiuro I 69 A8
Chiusa I 72 C4
Chiusa di Pesio I 37 C7
Chiusaforte I 73 D7
Chiusa Sclafani I 58 D3
Chiusavecchia I 37 D7
Chiusdino I 66 F3
Chiusi I 62 A1
Chiusi della Verna I 66 E4
Chiuza RO 152 C4
Chiva E 48 F3
Chivasso I 68 C4
Chizé F 28 C5
Chlebičov CZ 146 B5
Chlebnice SK 147 C8
Chlebowo PL 81 B7
Chlewiska PL 141 H3
Chłopice PL 144 D6
Chludowo PL 81 A11
Chlumčany CZ 76 C4
Chlumec CZ 80 E5
Chlumec nad Cidlinou CZ 77 B8
Chlum u Třeboně CZ 77 E7
Chmielnik PL 143 E10
Chmielno PL 85 C10
Chmiel Pierwszy PL 144 A6
Chminianske Jakubovany
SK 145 F3
Chobienia PL 81 C10
Chobienice PL 81 B9
Choceň CZ 77 B10
Choceń PL 138 F7
Chocholná-Velčice SK 146 D5
Chocianów PL 81 D9
Chocicza PL 81 B12
Chociwel PL 85 D8
Chocz PL 142 C4
Choczewo PL 138 A4
Chodecz PL 138 F7
Chodel PL 141 H6
Chodov CZ 75 B12
Chodová Planá CZ 75 C12
Chodów PL 141 F6
Chodów PL 143 B7
Chodzież PL 85 E11
Chojna PL 84 E6
Chojnice PL 85 C13
Chojno PL 81 C12
Chojnów PL 81 D9
Cholet F 28 A4
Chomakovtsi BG 165 C9
Chomelix F 30 E4
Chomérac F 35 A8
Chomutov CZ 76 B4
Chonikas GR 175 D6
Chooz F 19 D10
Chop UA 145 G5
Chora GR 174 E4
Chora GR 175 A8
Chora GR 177 D8
Chora GR 179 B9
Chora GR 179 B9
Chorafakia GR 178 D7
Chora Sfakion GR 178 E7
Chorefto GR 169 F9
Chorges F 36 B4
Chorio GR 177 F8
Choristi GR 171 B6
Chorkówka PL 145 D4
Chorley GB 10 D6
Chorna UA 154 B4
Chorna Tysa UA 152 A4
Chornoholova UA 145 F6
Chornomyn UA 154 A4
Chorzele PL 139 D10
Chorzów PL 143 F6
Chorzyna PL 142 D6
Choszczno PL 85 D8
Chotča SK 145 E4
Chotěboř CZ 77 C9
Chotěšov CZ 76 C4
Chotín SK 149 A10
Chouilly F 25 B11
Chouni GR 174 B4
Chouto P 44 F4
Chouzy-sur-Cisse F 24 E5
Chovar E 48 E4
Choye F 26 F4
Chozas de Abajo E 39 C8
Chrást CZ 76 C4
Chrast CZ 77 C9
Chrastava CZ 81 E7
Chřibská CZ 81 E6
Christchurch GB 13 D11
Christiansfeld DK 86 E4
Christon Bank GB 5 E13
Chropyně CZ 146 C4
Chróścina PL 142 E3
Chrostkowo PL 139 E7
Chroustovice CZ 77 C9
Chrudim CZ 77 C9
Chruślin PL 143 B8
Chruszczobród PL 143 F7
Chrysa GR 171 B7
Chrysafa GR 175 E6
Chryso GR 169 B10
Chrysochorafa GR 169 B9
Chrysochori GR 171 C7
Chrysokellaria GR 178 B2
Chrysoupoli GR 171 C7
Chrzanów PL 143 F7
Chrząstowa Wielka PL 81 D12
Chrząstowice PL 142 E5
Chrzypsko Wielkie PL 81 A10
Chtelnica SK 146 D5
Chuchelná CZ 142 G5
Chudleigh GB 13 D7
Chudoba PL 142 E5
Chulilla E 48 E3
Chulmleigh GB 13 D7
Chuprene BG 165 B6
Chur CH 71 D9
Churchdown GB 13 B10
Church Hill IRL 7 C7
Church Stretton GB 10 F6
Churek BG 165 D8
Churwalden CH 71 D9
Chuzelles F 30 D6
Chvalčov CZ 146 C5
Chvaletice CZ 77 B8
Chvalšiny CZ 76 E6
Chwaszczyno PL 138 B5
Chynadiyeve UA 145 F6
Chyňava CZ 76 B6
Chýnov CZ 77 D7
Chynów PL 141 G4
Chyšky CZ 77 C6
Ciacova RO 159 B7
Ciadîr MD 154 D2
Ciadîr-Lunga MD 154 E3
Ciadoux F 33 D7
Ciampino I 62 D3
Cianciana I 58 D3
Ciasna PL 142 E6
Ciążeń PL 142 B4
Cibakháza H 150 D5
Ciborro P 50 B3
Ciboure F 32 D2
Cicagna I 37 C10
Cicărlău RO 151 B11
Cicciano I 60 B3
Cicerale I 60 C4
Ćićevac SRB 159 F7
Cicibór Duży PL 141 F8
Ciclova Română RO 159 C8
Cičov SK 149 A9
Çidhën AL 163 F9
Cidones E 41 E6
Ciechanów PL 139 E10
Ciechanowiec PL 141 E7
Ciechocinek PL 138 E6
Ciełądz PL 141 G2
Ciempozuelos E 46 D5
Ciepielów PL 141 H5
Ciepłowody PL 81 E11
Čierna nad Tisou SK 145 G5
Čierne Kľačany SK 146 E6
Čierny Balog SK 147 D9
Cierp-Gaud F 33 E7
Cierznie PL 85 C12
Cieszanów PL 144 C7
Cieszków PL 81 C12
Cieszyn PL 142 D4
Cieszyn PL 147 B7
Cieutat F 33 D6
Cieux F 29 D8
Cieza E 55 C10
Ciężkowice PL 144 D2
Cifer SK 146 E5
Çifliq AL 168 E3
Çiftlikköy TR 173 B7
Çiftlikköy TR 173 B9
Cifuentes E 47 C7
Cigales E 39 E10
Cigánd H 145 G4
Cigliano I 68 C5
Cikó H 149 D11
Cilibia RO 161 C10
Cilieni RO 160 F5
Čilipi HR 162 D5
Čiližská Radvaň SK 146 F5
Cill Airne IRL 8 D4
Cillas E 47 C9
Cill Chainnigh IRL 9 C8
Cill Chaoi IRL 8 C3
Cill Charthaigh IRL 6 C5
Cill Chiaráin IRL 6 F3
Cill Choca IRL 7 F9
Cill Chomhghaill IRL 7 F10
Cill Chormaic IRL 7 F7
Cill Chuillin IRL 7 F9
Cill Dalua IRL 8 C6
Cill Dara IRL 7 F9
Cill Dhéagláin IRL 7 E10
Cill Droichid IRL 7 F9
Cille Bhrighde GB 2 L2
Cilleros E 45 D7
Cill Mhantáin IRL 7 G10
Cill Mocheallóg IRL 8 D5
Cill na Mallach IRL 8 D5
Cill Orglan IRL 8 D3
Cill Rois IRL 8 C4
Cill Rónáin IRL 6 F3
Cilybebyll GB 13 B7
Cimanes del Tejar E 39 C8
Cimballa E 47 B9
Cimdenieki LV 134 C2
Čimelice CZ 76 D6
Ciminna I 58 D4
Cimișlia MD 154 D3
Cimolais I 72 D5
Çinarcik TR 173 C11
Cinco Casas E 47 F6
Cinctorres E 42 F3
Cincu RO 152 F5
Cinderford GB 13 B10
Çine TR 181 A8
Ciñera E 39 C8
Ciney B 19 D11
Cinfães P 44 B4
Cinge TR 177 A9
Cingoli I 67 F7
Cinigiano I 65 B4
Cinisello Balsamo I 69 B7
Cinn Mhara IRL 6 F3
Cinobaňa SK 147 E9
Cinq-Mars-la-Pile F 24 F3
Cinquefrondi I 59 C9
Cintegabelle F 33 D9
Cintrey F 26 E4
Cintruénigo E 41 D8
Ciobănița RO 155 E2
Ciobanu RO 155 D1
Čiobiškis LT 137 D10
Ciocănești RO 161 D7
Ciocănești RO 161 E10
Ciocârlia RO 155 E2
Ciocârlia RO 161 D9
Ciochina RO 161 D10
Ciocile RO 161 D10
Cioc-Maidan MD 154 E3
Ciofrângeni RO 160 C5
Cióirtheach IRL 7 F7
Ciolănești RO 160 E6
Ciolpani RO 161 D8
Cionn tSáile IRL 8 E5
Ciorani RO 161 D8
Ciorăști RO 161 C10
Ciorogârla RO 161 E7
Cioroiași RO 160 E2
Cioropcani MD 153 C11
Ciortești RO 153 D11
Ciprian Porumbescu RO 153 B8
Cirat E 48 D4
Cirauqui E 32 E2
Cīrava LV 134 C2
Circello I 60 A3
Cirencester GB 13 B11
Cireșu RO 159 D10
Cireșu RO 161 D10
Cirey-sur-Blaise F 26 D2
Cirey-sur-Vezouze F 27 C6
Ciria E 41 E8
Ciriè I 68 C4
Cirigliano I 60 C6
Ciripcău MD 154 A2
Cirkale LV 134 B4
Cirma LV 133 C3
Cirò I 61 E8
Cirò Marina I 61 E8
Çirpi TR 177 C10
Ciruelos E 46 E5
Ciruelos del Pinar E 47 B8
Cīruļi LV 134 B4
Ciry-le-Noble F 30 B5
Cisano sul Neva I 37 C8
Cisek PL 142 F5
Cislău RO 161 C8
Cișmichioi MD 155 B2
Cisna PL 145 E5
Cisnădie RO 160 B4
Cisneros E 39 D10
Cisòn di Valmarino I 72 E5
Cissé F 29 B6
Cista Provo HR 157 E6
Cisterna di Latina I 62 D3
Cisternino I 61 B8
Cistierna E 39 C9
Citerna I 66 F5
Čitluk BIH 157 B6
Čitluk BIH 157 F8
Cittadella I 72 E4
Città della Pieve I 62 B2
Città di Castello I 66 F5
Cittanova I 59 C9
Cittareale I 62 B4
Città Sant'Angelo I 62 B6
Cittiglio I 68 B6
Ciucea RO 151 D10
Ciuchici RO 159 D8
Ciuciulea MD 153 B10
Ciucsângeorgiu RO 153 E7
Ciucur-Mingir MD 154 E3
Ciucurova RO 155 D2
Ciudad Real E 54 B5
Ciudad Rodrigo E 45 C7
Ciudanovița RO 159 C8
Ciugud RO 152 E3
Ciuhoi RO 151 C9
Ciulnița RO 161 D10
Ciumani RO 153 D7
Ciumeghiu RO 151 D8
Ciuperceni RO 159 D11
Ciuperceni RO 160 F5
Ciupercenii Noi RO 159 F10
Ciurila RO 152 D3
Ciuruleasa RO 151 E11
Ciutadella E 57 A12
Civaux F 29 C7
Cividale del Friuli I 73 D7
Civita I 61 D6
Civita Castellana I 62 C2
Civita d'Antino I 62 D4
Civitanova del Sannio I 63 D6
Civitanova Marche I 67 F8
Civitaquana I 62 C5
Civitavecchia I 62 C1
Civitella Casanova I 62 C5
Civitella del Tronto I 62 B5
Civitella di Romagna I 66 D4
Civitella in Val di Chiana I 66 F4

Civitella Roveto I 62 D4
Civray F 29 B10
Civray F 29 C6
Cizer RO 151 C10
Čížkovice CZ 76 B6
Čkyně CZ 76 D5
Clabhach GB 4 B3
Clachan GB 2 L4
Clachan GB 4 C7
Clachan of Glendaruel GB 4 C6
Clachtoll GB 2 J6
Clackmannan GB 5 C9
Clacton-on-Sea GB 15 D11
Cladich GB 4 C6
Clady GB 4 F1
Clady GB 4 F3
Claggan GB 4 B5
Clairac F 33 B6
Clairoix F 18 F6
Clairvaux-les-Lacs F 31 B8
Claix F 31 E8
Clamecy F 25 F10
Clane IRL 7 F9
Clans F 36 C6
Claonadh IRL 7 F9
Claonaig GB 4 D6
Clapham GB 11 C7
Clapham GB 15 C8
Clara IRL 7 F7
Clár Chlainne Mhuiris IRL 6 E5
Clarecastle IRL 8 C5
Claremorris IRL 6 E5
Claret F 35 B10
Claro CH 69 A7
Clary F 19 D7
Clashmore IRL 9 D7
Clashnessie GB 2 J6
Claudy GB 4 F2
Clausnitz D 80 E4
Claußnitz D 80 E3
Clausthal-Zellerfeld D 79 C7
Claut I 72 D6
Clauzetto I 73 D6
Clavering GB 15 D9
Clavier B 19 D11
Clay Cross GB 11 E9
Claydon GB 15 C11
Clayton GB 15 F8
Cleady IRL 8 E3
Cleat GB 3 H11
Cleator Moor GB 10 B4
Clécy F 23 C11
Cléder F 22 C3
Cleethorpes GB 11 D11
Clefmont F 26 D4
Cléguérec F 22 D5
Cleja RO 153 E9
Clelles F 31 F8
Clémency L 20 E5
Clenze D 83 E9
Cleobury Mortimer GB 13 A10
Cléon F 18 F3
Cléon-d'Andran F 35 A8
Cléré-les-Pins F 24 F3
Clères F 18 E3
Clérey F 25 D11
Clermain F 30 C6
Clermont F 18 F5
Clermont F 33 D8
Clermont-en-Argonne F 26 B3
Clermont-Ferrand F 30 D3
Clermont-l'Hérault F 34 C5
Clerval F 26 F6
Clervaux L 20 D6
Cléry-St-André F 24 E6
Cles I 72 D3
Clevedon GB 13 C9
Cleveleys GB 10 D5
Clifden IRL 6 F2
Cliffe GB 15 E9
Cliffoney IRL 6 D6
Climăuți MD 153 A11
Clinge NL 16 F2
Clingen D 79 D8
Clion F 29 B8
Clisson F 28 A3
Clitheroe GB 11 D7
Cloch na Rón IRL 6 F3
Clogh GB 4 F4
Clogh IRL 9 C7
Clogh IRL 9 C8
Clogh IRL 9 C10
Cloghan IRL 7 C7
Cloghan IRL 7 F7
Clogheen IRL 8 D7
Clogher GB 7 D8
Clogherhead IRL 7 E10
Cloghy GB 7 D12
Clohars-Carnoët F 22 E4
Clohernagh IRL 9 D8
Cloich na Coillte IRL 8 E5
Clonakilty IRL 8 E5
Clonaslee IRL 7 F7
Clonbern IRL 6 E5
Clonbulloge IRL 7 F8
Clonbur IRL 6 E4
Clondrohid IRL 8 E4
Clondulane IRL 8 D6
Clonea IRL 9 D8
Clonee IRL 7 F10
Cloneen IRL 9 D7
Clones IRL 7 D8
Clonmel IRL 9 D7
Clonmellon IRL 7 E8
Clonoulty IRL 9 C7
Clonroche IRL 9 D9
Clontibret IRL 7 D9
Clonygowan IRL 7 F8
Cloonbannin IRL 8 D4
Cloonboo IRL 6 F4
Cloonfad IRL 6 E5
Cloonfad IRL 6 F6
Cloonkeen IRL 6 E4
Cloppenburg D 17 C10
Closeburn GB 5 E9
Clough GB 7 D11
Cloughjordan IRL 8 C6
Cloughmills GB 4 E4
Cloughton GB 11 C11
Clova GB 5 B10
Clovelly GB 12 D6
Clovullin GB 4 B6
Cloyes-sur-le-Loir F 24 E5
Cloyne IRL 8 E6
Cluain Bú IRL 6 F4
Cluain Eois IRL 7 D8
Cluainín IRL 6 D6
Cluain Meala IRL 9 D7
Cluis F 29 B9
Cluj-Napoca RO 152 D3
Clumanc F 36 C4
Clun GB 13 A8
Cluny F 30 C6
Cluses F 31 C10
Clusone I 69 B8
Clydach GB 13 B7
Clydebank GB 5 D8
Clynderwen GB 12 B5
Clyro GB 13 A8
Ćmielów PL 143 E12
Ćmolas PL 143 F12
Coachford IRL 8 E5
Coagh GB 4 F3
Coalburn GB 5 D9
Coalisland GB 7 C9
Coalville GB 11 F9
Coaña E 39 A6
Coarnele Caprei RO 153 C10
Coarraze F 32 D5
Coast GB 2 K5
Coatbridge GB 5 D8
Cobadin RO 155 E2
Cobani MD 153 B10
Cobeja E 46 D5
Cobeta E 47 C8
Cobh IRL 8 E6
Cobia RO 160 D6
Coburg D 75 B8
Coca E 46 B3
Cocentaina E 56 D4
Cochem D 21 D8
Cochirleanca RO 161 C10
Cociuba Mare RO 151 D9
Cockburnspath GB 5 D12
Cockenzie and Port Seton
GB 5 D11
Cockerham GB 10 D6
Cockermouth GB 5 F10
Cockett GB 12 B7
Cocora RO 161 D10
Cocu RO 160 D5
Cocumont F 32 B6
Codăești RO 153 D11
Coddington GB 11 E10
Code LV 135 D8
Codevigo I 66 B5
Codigoro I 66 C5
Codlea RO 161 B6
Codogno I 69 C8
Codos E 41 F9
Codreanca MD 154 C3
Codroipo I 73 E6
Codrongianos I 64 B2
Codru MD 154 D3
Coesfeld D 17 E8
Coevorden NL 17 C7
Coëx F 28 B2
Cofrentes E 47 F10
Cogealac RO 155 D3
Cogeces del Monte E 40 E3
Coggeshall GB 15 D10
Coggia F 37 G9
Coggiola I 68 B5
Cogîlniceni MD 154 B3
Çöğmen TR 181 C10
Cognac F 28 D5
Cognac-la-Forêt F 29 D8
Cogne I 31 D11
Cognin F 31 D8
Cogoleto I 37 C9
Cogolin F 36 E5
Cogollos E 40 D4
Cogollos Vega E 53 B9
Cogolludo E 47 C6
Cogula P 45 C6
Coillan Chollaigh IRL 7 E9
Coimbra P 44 D4
Coimbrão P 44 E3
Coín E 53 C7
Coincy F 25 B9
Coja P 44 D5
Cojasca RO 161 D7
Cojocna RO 152 D3
Čoka SRB 150 F5
Colares P 50 B1
Colayrac-St-Cirq F 33 B7
Colbasna MD 154 B4
Cölbe D 21 C11
Colbitz D 79 B10
Colbordola I 67 E6
Colceag RO 161 D8
Colchester GB 15 D10
Coldingham GB 5 D12
Colditz D 79 D12
Coldstream GB 5 D12
Coleford GB 13 B9
Coleraine GB 4 E3
Colibași MD 155 B2
Colibași RO 160 D5
Colibași RO 161 E8
Colibița RO 152 C5
Colico I 69 A7
Coligny F 31 C7
Colijnsplaat NL 182 B3
Colindres E 40 B5
Colintraive GB 4 D6
Collado Hermoso E 46 B5
Collado Villalba E 46 C5
Collagna I 66 D1
Collanzo E 39 B8
Collarmele I 62 C5
Collazzone I 62 B2
Collecchio I 66 C1
Collecorvino I 62 C5
Colledara I 62 B5
Colle di Val d'Elsa I 66 F3
Colleferro I 62 D4
Collegno I 68 C4
Colle Isarco I 72 C3
Collelongo I 62 D5
Collepardo I 62 D4
Collepasso I 61 C10
Collesalvetti I 66 E1
Colle Sannita I 60 A3
Collesano I 58 D4
Colletorto I 63 D7
Colliano I 60 B4
Colli a Volturno I 62 D6
Collieston GB 3 L13
Collinas I 64 D2
Collinée F 22 D6
Collinghorst (Rhauderfehn)
D 17 B9
Collio I 69 B9
Collioure F 34 E5
Collobrières F 36 E4
Collombey CH 31 C10
Collon IRL 7 E10
Collonges F 31 C8
Collonges-la-Rouge F 29 E9
Collooney IRL 6 D6
Colmar F 27 D7
Colmars F 36 C5
Colmberg D 75 D7
Colmeal P 44 D5
Colmenar E 53 C8
Colmenar del Arroyo E 46 D4
Colmenar de Montemayor
E 45 D9
Colmenar de Oreja E 46 D6
Colmenar Viejo E 46 C5
Colméry F 25 F9
Colmonell GB 4 E7
Colne GB 11 D7
Colobraro I 61 C6
Cologna Veneta I 66 B3
Cologne F 33 C7
Cologno al Serio I 69 B8
Colombelles F 23 B11
Colombey-les-Belles F 26 C4
Colombey-les Deux-Églises
F 25 D12
Colombier CH 31 B10
Colombiès F 33 B10
Colombres E 39 B10
Colomers E 43 C9
Colomiers F 33 C8
Colonești RO 153 D10
Colonești RO 160 D5
Colònia de Sant Jordi E 57 C11
Colònia de Sant Pere E 57 B11
Colonnella I 62 B5
Colorno I 66 C1
Colos P 50 D3
Cölpin D 84 C4
Colquhar GB 5 D10
Colroy-la-Grande F 27 D7
Colsterworth GB 11 F10
Colți RO 161 C8
Coltishall GB 15 B11
Colunga E 39 B9
Colwyn Bay GB 10 E4
Coly F 29 E8
Colyford GB 13 D8
Comacchio I 66 C5
Comana RO 152 F6
Comana RO 155 F2
Comana RO 161 E8
Comana de Sus RO 152 F6
Comandău RO 153 F8
Comănești RO 153 E8
Comares E 53 C8
Comarna RO 153 C11
Comarnic RO 161 C7
Combeaufontaine F 26 E4
Combe Martin GB 12 C6
Comber GB 7 C11
Comberton GB 15 C9
Comblain-au-Pont B 19 D12
Comblanchien F 26 F2
Combles F 18 D6
Combloux F 31 D10
Combourg F 23 D8
Combronde F 30 D3
Comeglians I 73 C6
Comelico Superiore I 72 C6
Comillas E 40 B3
Comines B 18 C6
Comișani RO 161 D7
Comiso I 59 F6
Comitini I 58 E4
Comloșu Mare RO 150 F6
Commeen IRL 7 C7
Commenailles F 31 B7
Commensacq F 32 B4
Commentry F 30 C2
Commequiers F 28 B2
Commer F 23 D10
Commercy F 26 C4
Como I 69 B7
Cómpeta E 53 C9
Compiano I 37 B11
Compiègne F 18 F6
Compolibat F 33 B10
Comporta P 50 C2
Compreignac F 29 D8
Comps-sur-Artuby F 36 D5
Comrat MD 154 E3
Comrie GB 5 C9
Comunanza I 62 B4
Cona I 66 B5
Conca F 37 H10
Concarneau F 22 E4
Concas I 64 B4
Conceição P 50 E4
Concesio I 69 B9
Concha E 40 B5
Conches-en-Ouche F 24 C4
Concordia Sagittaria I 73 E6
Concorès F 33 A8
Concots F 33 B9
Condat F 30 E2
Condé-en-Brie F 25 B10
Condeixa-a-Nova P 44 D4
Condé-sur-Huisne F 24 D4
Condé-sur-l'Escaut F 182 E3
Condé-sur-Noireau F 23 C10
Condé-sur-Vire F 23 B9
Condino I 69 B10
Condofuri I 59 C8
Condom F 33 C6
Condove I 31 E11
Condrieu F 30 E6
Condrița MD 154 C3
Conegliano I 72 E5
Conflans-en-Jarnisy F 26 B4
Conflans-sur-Lanterne F 26 E5
Conflenti I 59 A9
Confolens F 29 C7
Cong IRL 6 E4
Congaz MD 154 E3
Congdon's Shop GB 12 D6
Congleton GB 11 E7
Congosto E 39 C7
Congosto de Valdavia E 39 C10
Congrier F 23 E9
Conil de la Frontera E 52 D4
Coningsby GB 11 E11
Coniston GB 10 C5
Conlie F 23 D11
Conliège F 31 B8
Conlig GB 4 F5
Connah's Quay GB 10 E5
Connantre F 25 C10
Connaux F 35 B8
Connel GB 4 C6
Connerré F 24 D3
Connolly IRL 8 C4
Connor GB 4 F4
Conon Bridge GB 2 K8
Conop RO 151 E8
Čonoplja SRB 150 F3
Conow D 84 D4
Conques F 33 A10
Conques-sur-Orbiel F 33 D10
Conquista E 54 C3
Consandolo I 66 C4
Consdorf L 186 B1
Conselice I 66 C4
Consell E 49 E10
Conselve I 66 B4
Consett GB 5 F13
Constância P 44 F4
Constanța RO 155 E3
Constantí E 42 E6
Constantim P 38 F4
Constantim P 39 E7
Constantina E 51 D8
Constantin Daicoviciu RO
159 B9
Constanzana E 46 C3
Consuegra E 46 F5
Contarina I 66 B5
Contes F 37 D6
Contessa Entellina I 58 D3
Contești RO 161 D7
Contești RO 161 F6
Conthey CH 31 C11
Contigliano I 62 C3
Contis-Plage F 32 B3
Contres F 24 F5
Contrexéville F 26 D4
Controne I 60 B4
Contursi Terme I 60 B4
Contwig D 21 F8
Conty F 18 E5
Conversano I 61 B8
Convoy IRL 7 C7
Conwy GB 10 E4
Conza della Campania I 60 B4
Cookstown GB 4 F3
Coola IRL 6 D6
Coolbaun IRL 6 G6
Coole F 25 C11
Coole IRL 7 E8
Coolmore IRL 6 C6
Coombe Bissett GB 13 C11
Cootehill IRL 7 D8
Copăcel RO 151 D9
Copăcele RO 159 C9
Copăceni MD 154 B2
Copăceni RO 160 D3
Copăcenii de Sus RO 161 E8
Copalnic-Mănăștur RO 152 B3
Copanca MD 154 D5
Copanello I 59 B10
Copceac MD 154 F3
Copertino I 61 C10
Çöpköy TR 173 B6
Copley GB 5 F13
Copons E 43 D7
Copparo I 66 C4
Coppeen IRL 8 E5
Copplestone GB 13 D7
Coppull GB 10 D6
Copșa Mică RO 152 E4
Copythorne GB 13 D11
Corabia RO 160 F4
Cora Chaitlín IRL 8 C5
Cora Droma Rúisc IRL 6 E6
Čoralići BIH 156 C4
Corato I 61 A6
Coray F 22 D4
Corbalán E 47 D11
Corbally IRL 6 D4
Corbasca RO 153 E10
Corbeanca RO 161 D8
Corbeil-Essonnes F 25 C7
Corbeilles F 25 D8
Corbeni RO 160 C5
Corbeny F 19 F8
Corbera E 48 F4
Corbera d'Ebre E 42 E4
Corbi RO 160 C5
Corbie F 18 E6
Corbières CH 31 B11
Corbières F 35 C10
Corbigny F 25 F10
Corbii Mari RO 161 D6
Corbița RO 153 E10
Corbridge GB 5 F12
Corbu RO 153 D7
Corbu RO 155 E3
Corbu RO 160 D5
Corby GB 11 G10
Corçà E 43 D10
Corcaigh IRL 8 E6
Corcelles-lès-Cîteaux F 26 F3
Corchiano I 62 C2
Corciano I 66 F5
Corcieux F 27 D6
Corcova RO 159 D11
Corcubión E 38 C1
Cordăreni RO 153 B9
Cordemais F 23 F8
Cordenòns I 73 E6
Cordes-sur-Ciel F 33 B9
Córdoba E 53 A7
Cordobilla de Lácara E 45 F8
Corduente E 47 C9
Cordun RO 153 D9
Coreglia Antelminelli I 66 D2
Corella E 41 D8
Coreses E 39 E8
Corestăuți MD 153 A10
Corfe Castle GB 13 D10
Corfinio I 62 C5
Cori I 62 D3
Coria E 45 E7
Coria del Río E 51 E7
Coriano I 66 E6
Corigliano Calabro I 61 D7
Corinaldo I 67 E7
Coripe E 51 F9
Corjeuți MD 153 A10
Cork IRL 8 E6
Corlățel RO 159 E10
Corlăteni RO 153 B9
Corlay F 22 D5
Corlea IRL 7 E7
Corleone I 58 D3
Corleto Perticara I 60 C6
Çorlu TR 173 B8
Cormatin F 30 B6
Cormeilles F 18 F1
Corme Porto E 38 B2
Cormicy F 19 F8
Cormons I 73 E7
Cormontreuil F 20 F2
Cornafulla IRL 6 F7
Cornago E 41 D7
Cornamona IRL 6 E4
Cornaredo I 69 B7
Cornas F 30 F6
Cornățelu RO 161 D7
Cornau D 17 C10
Cornea RO 159 C9
Cornedo all'Isarco I 72 D3
Cornedo Vicentino I 69 B11
Corneilla-del-Vercol F 34 E4
Cornellà de Llobregat E 43 E8
Cornellà de Terri E 43 C9
Cornellana E 39 B7
Cornereva RO 159 C9
Cornești MD 153 C12
Cornești RO 152 C3
Cornești RO 161 D7
Cornetu RO 161 E7
Corni RO 153 B9
Corni RO 153 F11
Corniglio I 69 E9
Cornimont F 27 E6
Cornu RO 161 C7
Cornuda I 72 E5
Cornudella de Montsant E 42 E5
Cornudilla E 40 C5
Cornu Luncii RO 153 C8
Cornus F 34 C5
Corod RO 153 F11
Corofin IRL 8 C4
Coroieni RO 152 C3
Coroisânmărtin RO 152 E5
Coron F 23 F10
Çorovodë AL 168 C3
Corps F 31 F8
Corps-Nuds F 23 E8
Corral de Almaguer E 47 E6
Corral de Calatrava E 54 B4
Corrales E 39 F8
Corral-Rubio E 55 B10
Corre F 26 E5
Correggio I 66 C2
Corrèze F 29 E9
Corridonia I 67 F8
Corrie GB 4 D6
Corris GB 10 F4
Corr na Móna IRL 6 E4
Corrobert F 25 C10
Corry IRL 6 D6
Corsano I 61 D10
Corseul F 23 D7
Corsham GB 13 C10
Corsico I 69 C7
Corsock GB 5 E9
Cortale I 59 B9
Corte F 37 G10
Corteconcepción E 51 D7
Corte de Peleas E 51 B6
Cortegada E 38 D3
Cortegana E 51 D6
Cortemilia I 37 B8
Corteno Golgi I 69 A9
Corteolona I 69 C7
Cortes E 41 E9
Cortes de Aragón E 42 F2
Cortes de Arenoso E 48 D3
Cortes de Baza E 55 D7
Cortes de la Frontera E 53 C6
Cortes de Pallás E 48 F3
Cortiçadas do Lavre P 50 B3
Cortijo de Arriba E 46 F4
Cortijos Nuevos E 55 C7
Cortina d'Ampezzo I 72 C5
Corton GB 15 B12
Cortona I 66 F4
Coruche P 50 B2
Corullón E 39 C6
Corund RO 152 E6
Corvara in Badia I 72 C4
Corvera E 56 F2
Corwen GB 10 F5
Coryton GB 15 D10
Cosa E 47 C10
Cosâmbești RO 161 D10
Cosăuți MD 154 A2
Coșbuc RO 152 C4
Cosby GB 11 F9
Coșcodeni MD 153 B12
Coscurita E 41 F7
Coșeiu RO 151 C11
Cosenza I 60 E6
Coșereni RO 161 D9
Coșești RO 160 C5
Coshieville GB 5 B9
Ćosići BIH 157 D8
Cosio di Arroscia I 37 C7
Coslada E 46 D5
Cosmești RO 153 F10
Cosmești RO 160 E6
Cosminele RO 161 C7
Cosne-Cours-sur-Loire F 25 F8
Cosne-d'Allier F 30 C2
Coșnița MD 154 C4
Cosoleto I 59 C8
Coșoveni RO 160 E3
Cossato I 68 B5
Cossé-le-Vivien F 23 E10
Cossoine I 64 C2
Cossonay CH 31 B10
Costacciaro I 67 F6
Costache Negri RO 153 F11
Costa da Caparica P 50 B1
Costa di Rovigo I 66 B4
Costa Volpino I 69 B9
Costeiu RO 151 F8
Costelloe IRL 6 F3
Costești MD 153 B10
Costești MD 154 D3
Costești RO 153 D11
Costești RO 160 C4
Costești RO 160 D5
Costești RO 161 C9
Costeștii din Vale RO 161 D6
Costigliole Saluzzo I 37 B6
Costișa RO 153 D9
Costuleni RO 153 C11
Cosuenda E 41 F9
Coswig D 79 C11
Coswig D 80 D5
Coteana RO 160 E4
Cotești RO 161 B10
Cothen NL 16 D4
Coti-Chiavari F 37 H9
Cotignac F 36 D4
Cotignola I 66 D4
Cotiujeni MD 154 B3
Cotiujenii Mici MD 154 B2
Cotmeana RO 160 D5
Cotnari RO 153 C9
Coțofănești RO 153 E9
Coțofenii din Dos RO 160 E3
Cotronei I 61 E7
Cottanello I 62 C3
Cottbus D 80 C6
Cottenham GB 15 C9
Cottesmore GB 11 F10
Cottingham GB 11 F10
Coțușca RO 153 A9
Coubon F 30 E4
Couburciu MD 154 D5
Couches F 30 B6
Couço P 50 B3
Coucy-le-Château-Auffrique
F 19 E7
Coudekerque-Branche F 18 B5
Couëron F 23 F8
Couflens F 33 E8
Coufouleux F 33 C9
Couhé F 29 C6
Couiza F 33 E10
Coulaines F 23 D12
Coulanges-la-Vineuse F 25 E10
Coulanges-sur-Yonne F 25 E10
Coulaures F 29 E7
Couleuvre F 30 B2
Coullons F 25 E7
Coulmier-le-Sec F 25 E11
Coulmiers F 24 E6
Coulogne F 15 F12
Coulombiers F 29 C6
Coulombs F 24 C6
Coulommiers F 25 C9
Coulonges-sur-l'Autize F 28 C4
Coulounieix-Chamiers F 29 E7
Coulport GB 4 C7
Coupar Angus GB 5 B10
Couptrain F 23 D11
Coura P 38 E2
Courcelles B 182 E4
Courcelles-Chaussy F 26 B5
Courcelles-sur-Nied F 186 C1
Courchaton F 26 E6
Courchevel F 31 E10
Cour-Cheverny F 24 E5
Courcité F 23 D11
Courçon F 28 C4
Courcy F 19 F9
Courgains F 23 D12
Courgenay CH 27 F7
Courgenay F 25 D10
Courlay F 28 B4
Courmayeur I 31 D10
Courmelles F 19 F7
Cournon-d'Auvergne F 30 D3
Courpière F 30 D4
Courrendlin CH 27 F7
Courrensan F 33 C6
Courrières F 182 E1
Coursac F 29 E7
Coursan F 34 D5
Coursegoules F 36 D6
Courseulles-sur-Mer F 23 B11
Cours-la-Ville F 30 C5
Courson-les-Carrières F 25 E9
Court CH 27 F7
Courtalain F 24 D5
Courtelary CH 27 F7
Courtenay F 25 D9
Courthézon F 35 B8
Courtmacsherry IRL 8 E5
Courtomer F 24 C3
Courtown IRL 9 C10
Courtrai B 19 C7
Courtrai B 182 D2
Court-St-Etienne B 19 C10
Courville-sur-Eure F 24 D5
Cousance F 31 B7
Cousances-les-Forges F 26 C3
Coussac-Bonneval F 29 D8
Coussay-les-Bois F 29 B7
Coussegrey F 25 E11
Coussey F 26 D4
Coustouges F 34 F4
Coutances F 23 B9
Couterne F 23 C11
Couto de Cima P 44 C5
Coutras F 28 E5
Couvet CH 31 B10
Couvin B 19 D10
Couze-et-St-Front F 29 F7
Couzeix F 29 D8
Covaleda E 40 E6
Covarrubias E 40 D5
Covăsinț RO 151 E8
Covasna RO 153 F8
Cove GB 2 K5
Cove Bay GB 3 L12
Coventry GB 13 A11
Covilhã P 44 D6
Cowbit GB 11 F11
Cowbridge GB 13 C8
Cowdenbeath GB 5 C10
Cowes GB 13 D12
Cox E 56 E3
Cox F 33 C8
Coxheath GB 15 E9
Coxhoe GB 5 F13
Coylumbridge GB 3 L9
Cózar E 55 B6
Cozes F 28 D4
Cozești MD 154 B2
Cozieni RO 161 C9
Cozmești RO 153 D11
Cozzano F 37 H10
Craanford IRL 9 C10
Crăcăoani RO 153 C8
Crach F 22 E5
Crăciunelu de Jos RO 152 E3
Crăciunești RO 152 E5
Craco I 61 C6
Craidorolț RO 151 B10
Craig GB 2 L6
Craigavad GB 4 F5
Craigavon GB 7 D10
Craigellachie GB 3 L10
Craignure GB 4 C5
Crail GB 5 C11
Crailsheim D 75 D7
Craiova RO 160 E3
Craiva RO 151 D8
Cramlington GB 5 E13
Crămpoia RO 160 E5
Cranage GB 11 E7
Cranagh GB 4 F2
Cranford IRL 7 B7
Crângeni RO 160 E5
Cran-Gevrier F 31 D9
Crângu RO 160 F6
Crângurile RO 160 D6
Cranleigh GB 15 E8
Crans-sur-Sierre CH 31 C11
Craon F 23 E10
Craonne F 19 F8
Craponne-sur-Arzon F 30 E4
Crask Inn GB 2 J7
Crasna RO 151 C10
Crasna RO 160 C3
Crasnoe MD 154 D5
Crathie GB 5 A10
Crato P 44 F5
Cravagliana I 68 B5
Cravant F 25 E10
Craven Arms GB 13 A9
Crawfordjohn GB 5 E9
Crawfordsburn GB 4 F5
Crawley GB 15 E8
Creaca RO 151 C11
Creagh IRL 8 E4
Creagorry GB 2 L2
Creamhghort IRL 7 B7
Créances F 23 B8
Créancey F 25 F12
Crecente E 38 D3
Crêches-sur-Saône F 30 C6
Crécy-en-Ponthieu F 18 D4
Crécy-la-Chapelle F 25 C8
Crécy-sur-Serre F 19 E8
Credenhill GB 13 A9
Crediton GB 13 D7
Creeslough IRL 7 B7
Creevagh IRL 6 D4
Creggan GB 4 F2
Creggan GB 7 D9
Cregganbaun IRL 6 E3
Creggs IRL 6 E6
Creglingen D 75 D7
Cregneash GBM 10 C2
Créhange F 186 C2
Creil F 18 F5
Creil NL 16 C5
Creissels F 34 B5
Crema I 69 C8
Cremeaux F 30 D4
Crémenes E 39 C9
Crémieu F 31 D7
Cremlingen D 79 B8
Cremona I 69 C9
Črenšovci SLO 148 C6
Créon F 28 F5
Crepaja SRB 158 C6
Crépey F 26 C4
Crépy F 19 E8
Crépy-en-Valois F 18 F6
Cres HR 67 C9
Crescentino I 68 C5
Crespina I 66 E2
Crespino I 66 C4
Crespos E 46 C3
Cressensac F 29 E9
Crest F 31 F7
Creswell GB 11 E9
Cretas E 42 F4
Créteil F 25 C7
Crețeni RO 160 D4
Crețești RO 153 D11
Creußen D 75 C10
Creutzwald F 21 F7
Creuzburg D 79 D7
Crevalcore I 66 C3
Crevant F 29 C9
Crévéchamps F 26 C5
Crèvecœur-le-Grand F 18 E5
Crevedia RO 161 D7
Crevedia Mare RO 161 E7
Crevenicu RO 161 E7
Crevillente E 56 E3
Crevoladossola I 68 A5
Crewe GB 10 E7
Crewkerne GB 13 D9
Crianlarich GB 4 C7
Cricău RO 152 E3
Criccieth GB 10 F3
Criciova RO 159 B9
Crickhowell GB 13 B8
Cricklade GB 13 B11
Cricova MD 154 C3
Crieff GB 5 C9
Criel-sur-Mer F 18 D3
Crikvenica HR 67 B10
Crimmitschau D 79 E11
Crimond GB 3 K13
Crinan GB 4 C5
Cringleford GB 15 B11
Crinitz D 80 C5
Cripán E 41 C7
Cripp's Corner GB 15 F10
Criquetot-l'Esneval F 18 E1
Criscior RO 151 E10
Crișeni RO 151 C11
Crispiano I 61 B8
Crissolo I 31 F11
Cristești RO 152 D4
Cristești RO 153 B9
Cristești RO 153 C9
Cristian RO 152 F4
Cristian RO 161 B6
Cristinești RO 153 A8
Criștioru de Jos RO 151 E10
Cristóbal E 45 D9
Cristolț RO 151 C11
Cristuru Secuiesc RO 152 E6
Criuleni MD 154 C4
Criva MD 153 A9
Crivitz D 83 C11
Crkvice BIH 157 D8
Crkvice HR 162 D3
Crkvice MNE 163 D6
Crkvina BIH 157 B9
Crkvine SRB 163 C9
Crljivica BIH 156 D5
Črmošnjice SLO 73 E11
Črna SLO 73 D10
Crna Bara SRB 150 F5
Crna Bara SRB 158 D3
Crnac HR 149 E9
Crnajka SRB 159 E9
Crna Trava SRB 164 D5
Crnča SRB 158 E3
Crni Lug BIH 156 D6
Crni Lug HR 67 B10
Crnjelovo BIH 157 C11
Črnkovci HR 149 E10
Crnoklište SRB 164 C5
Črnomelj SLO 148 E4
Crock D 75 B8
Crocketford GB 5 E9
Crockets Town IRL 6 D4
Crockmore IRL 7 C7
Crocmaz MD 154 E5
Crocq F 29 D10
Crodo I 68 A5
Crofty GB 12 B6
Croghan IRL 6 E6
Crognaleto I 62 B4
Croisilles F 18 D6
Croithlí IRL 6 B6
Crolles F 31 E8
Crolly IRL 6 B6
Cromadh IRL 8 C5
Cromarty GB 3 K8
Cromer GB 15 B11
Cromhall GB 13 B10
Cronat F 30 B4
Crook GB 5 F13
Crookham GB 5 D12
Crookhaven IRL 8 F3
Crookstown IRL 8 E5
Croom IRL 8 C5
Cropalati I 61 D7
Cropani I 59 B10
Crosbost GB 2 J4

Digny F 24 C5
Digoin F 30 C4
Dihtiv UA 144 B9
Dijon F 26 F3
Dikaia GR 166 F6
Dikanäs S 107 A10
Dikancë RKS 163 E10
Dikili TR 177 A8
Dikkebus B 18 C6
Dikļi LV 131 F10
Diksmuide B 18 B6
Dilar E 53 B9
Dilbeek B 182 D4
Dilesi GR 175 C8
Dilinata GR 174 C2
Dillenburg D 21 C10
Dilling N 95 D13
Dillingen (Saar) D 21 F7
Dillingen an der Donau D 75 E7
Dilove UA 145 H9
Dilsen B 19 B12
Dimaro I 71 E11
Diminio GR 169 F8
Dimitrie Cantemir RO 153 D12
Dimitritsi GR 169 C9
Dimitrovgrad BG 166 E5
Dimitrovgrad SRB 165 C6
Dimitsana GR 174 D5
Dimovo BG 159 F10
Dimzukalns LV 135 C8
Dinami I 59 B9
Dinan F 23 D7
Dinant B 19 D10
Dinard F 23 C7
Dingé F 23 D8
Dingelstädt D 79 D7
Dingelstedt am Huy D 79 C8
Dingle IRL 8 D2
Dingle S 91 B10
Dingolfing D 75 E12
Dingtuna S 98 C6
Dingwall GB 2 K8
Dinjiška HR 67 D11
Dinkelsbühl D 75 D7
Dinkelscherben D 75 F8
Dinklage D 17 C10
Dinnet GB 5 A11
Dinslaken D 17 E7
Dinteloord NL 16 E2
Dinther NL 183 B6
Dinxperlo NL 17 E6
Diö S 88 B6
Dion GR 169 D7
Diósd H 149 B11
Diosig RO 151 C9
Diósjenő H 147 F8
Dioşti RO 160 E4
Diou F 30 B4
Dipignano I 60 E6
Dipotama GR 171 B7
Dipotamia GR 168 D4
Dippach L 20 E6
Dippoldiswalde D 80 E5
Dirdal N 94 E4
Dirhami EST 130 C7
Dirivaara S 116 E8
Dirkshorn NL 16 C3
Dirksland NL 16 E2
Dirlewang D 71 A11
Dirmstein D 187 B5
Dirvonėnai LT 134 E5
Dischingen D 75 E7
Disentis Muster CH 71 D7
Diseröd S 91 D11
Dison B 19 C12
Diss GB 15 C11
Dissay F 29 B6
Dissay-sous-Courcillon F 24 E3
Dissen am Teutoburger Wald D 17 D10
Distington GB 10 B4
Distomo GR 175 C6
Distrato GR 168 D5
Ditfurt D 79 C9
Ditrău RO 153 D7
Ditton GB 15 E9
Ditzingen D 27 C11
Divača SLO 73 E8
Divarata GR 174 C2
Diva Slatina BG 165 C6
Divci SRB 158 E5
Divčibare SRB 158 E5
Dives-sur-Mer F 23 B11
Dividalen N 111 C18
Divieto I 59 C7
Divín SK 147 E9
Divina SK 147 C7
Divion F 18 D6
Divišov CZ 77 C7
Divjakë AL 168 C2
Divonne-les-Bains F 31 C9
Divuša HR 156 B5
Dixmont F 25 D9
Dizy F 25 B10
Dizy-le-Gros F 19 E9
Djäkneboda S 122 B5
Djäkneböle S 122 C4
Djupen N 111 B18
Djupfjord N 110 C9
Djupfors S 109 E11
Djupsjö S 107 E14
Djuptjärn S 107 D15
Djupvik N 109 B10
Djupvik N 112 D5
Djupvik S 89 A11
Djura S 103 E8
Djurås S 97 A13
Djurmo S 97 A13
Djurö S 99 D11
Dlhá nad Oravou SK 147 C8
Dlouhá Loučka CZ 77 C12
Dlouhá Třebová CZ 77 C10
Długołęka PL 81 D12
Długołęka PL 140 D7
Długosiodło PL 139 E12
Dłutów PL 143 C7
Dlŭzhka Polyana BG 166 C6
Dmytrivka UA 154 F3
Dmytrivka UA 154 F4
Dmytrivka UA 155 B4
Dnestrovsc MD 154 D5
Dno RUS 132 F6
Doagh GB 4 F4
Doba RO 151 B10
Dobanovci SRB 158 D5
Dobârceni RO 153 B10
Dobârlău RO 153 F7
Dobbertin D 83 C12
Dobbiaco I 72 C5
Dobczyce PL 144 D1
Dobele LV 134 C6
Döbeln D 80 D4
Doberçan RKS 164 E4
Doberlug-Kirchhain D 80 C5
Döbern D 81 C7
Dobersberg A 77 E8
Doberschütz D 79 D12
Dobiegniew PL 85 E9
Dobieszewo PL 85 B12
Dobieszyn PL 141 G4
Doboj BIH 157 C9
Dobova SLO 148 E5
Doboz H 151 D7
Dobrá CZ 146 B6
Dobra PL 85 C8
Dobra PL 142 C6
Dobra PL 144 D1
Dobra RO 151 F10
Dobra RO 161 D7
Dobra SRB 159 D8
Dobrá Niva SK 147 E8
Dobřany CZ 76 C4
Dobre PL 138 E6
Dobre PL 139 F12
Dobre Miasto PL 136 F1
Dobreni RO 153 D8
Dobreşinci MK 169 A8
Dobreşti RO 151 D9
Dobreşti RO 160 D6
Dobreşti RO 160 F3
Dobrevo MK 164 E5
Dobrica SRB 159 C6
Dobričevo SRB 159 D7
Dobrich BG 155 F1
Dobrich BG 166 E5
Dobri Do SRB 164 D3
Dobri Dol BG 159 F11
Dobrin RO 151 C11
Dobrinishte BG 165 F8
Dobříš CZ 76 C6
Dobritz D 79 B11
Dobřív CZ 76 C5
Dobrljin BIH 156 B5
Dobrna SLO 73 D11
Dobrnič SLO 73 E10
Dobrnja BIH 157 C7
Dobrnja BIH 157 C10
Dobrnje SRB 159 E7
Dobro E 40 C4
Dobrodzień PL 142 E5
Döbrököz H 149 D10
Dobromierz PL 81 E10
Dobromir RO 155 E1
Dobromirka BG 166 C4
Dobromirtsi BG 171 B8
Dobromyl' UA 145 D6
Dobroń PL 143 C7
Dobron' UA 145 G5
Dobronín CZ 77 D9
Dobro Polje BIH 157 E10
Dobro Polje SRB 159 F9
Dobrošane MK 164 E4
Dobrosloveni RO 160 E4
Dobrosyn UA 144 C8
Dobroszyce PL 81 D12
Dobroteasa RO 160 D4
Dobroteşti RO 160 E5
Dobrotić SRB 164 C4
Dobrotich BG 167 C8
Dobrotino MK 169 B6
Dobrotitsa BG 161 F9
Dobrovăţ RO 153 D11
Dobrovci BIH 157 C9
Dobrovice CZ 77 B7
Dobrovnik SLO 149 C6
Dobrovol'sk RUS 136 D5
Dobrowoda PL 143 F10
Dobruchi RUS 132 D2
Dobrun BIH 158 F3
Dobrun RO 160 E4
Dobruşa MD 154 B3
Dobruševo MK 169 B5
Dobruška CZ 77 B10
Dobrzankowo PL 139 E10
Dobrzany PL 85 D8
Dobrzeń Wielki PL 142 E4
Dobrzyca PL 142 C4
Dobrzyków PL 139 F8
Dobrzyń nad Wisłą PL 139 E7
Dobšiná SK 145 F1
Dóc H 150 E5
Docking GB 15 B10
Dockmyr S 103 A10
Docksta S 107 E14
Dockweiler D 21 D7
Doclin RO 159 C8
Doddington GB 5 D12
Dodewaard NL 183 B7
Dodonoupoli GR 168 E4
Dödre S 102 A8
Doesburg NL 16 D6
Doetinchem NL 16 E6
Dofteana RO 153 E9
Doğanbey TR 177 C8
Doğanbey TR 177 D9
Doğanci TR 173 D10
Doğanköy TR 173 D10
Döge H 145 G5
Dogliani I 37 B7
Dognecea RO 159 C8
Döğüşbelen TR 181 C9
Dohna D 80 E5
Dohňany SK 146 C6
Dohren D 17 C9
Doiceşti RO 160 D6
Doïrani GR 169 B8
Doire Iorrais IRL 6 F3
Doische B 19 D10
Dojč SK 146 D4
Dojkinci SRB 165 C6
Dokka N 101 E12
Dokkas S 116 D6
Dokkedal DK 86 B6
Dokkum NL 16 B5
Doksy CZ 76 B6
Doksy CZ 81 E7
Doktor Yosifovo BG 165 C7
Dokupe LV 134 B3
Dolanog GB 10 F5
Dolbenmaen GB 10 F3
Dolceacqua I 37 D7
Dol-de-Bretagne F 23 C8
Dole BIH 157 D10
Dole F 26 F3
Dølemo N 90 B3
Dolenci MK 168 B5
Dolenja Vas SLO 73 E10
Dolenjske Toplice SLO 73 E11
Dolgarrog GB 10 E4
Dolgellau GB 10 F4
Dolgen D 84 D4
Dolgorukovo RUS 136 E2
Dolhan TR 167 F8
Dolhasca RO 153 C9
Dolheşti RO 153 C9
Dolheşti RO 153 D11
Dołhobyczów PL 144 B9
Dolianova I 64 E3
Dolice PL 85 D8
Dolichi GR 169 D7
Doljani BIH 157 E8
Doljani HR 156 D5
Doljevac SRB 164 C4
Dolla IRL 8 C6
Dolle D 79 B10
Dollern D 82 C7
Döllnitz D 79 D11
Dollnstein D 75 E9
Dollon F 24 D4
Dolna MD 154 C2
Dolna Banya BG 165 E8
Dolna Dikanya BG 165 E7
Dolna Gradeshnitsa BG 165 F7
Dolnaja LV 135 D12
Dolná Krupá SK 146 E5
Dolna Lipnitsa BG 166 C4
Dolna Makhala BG 165 E10
Dolna Melna BG 164 D6
Dolna Mitropoliya BG 165 C10
Dolna Oryakhovitsa BG 166 C5
Dolná Strehová SK 147 E8
Dolná Súča SK 146 D6
Dolná Tižina SK 147 C7
Dolna Vasilitsa BG 165 E8
Dolna Zelina HR 148 E6
Dolné Orešany SK 146 E4
Dolné Vestenice SK 146 D6
Dolní Bousov CZ 77 B8
Dolní Bukovsko CZ 77 D7
Dolní Čermná CZ 77 C11
Dolni Chiflik BG 167 D9
Dolní Dobrouč CZ 77 C11
Dolni Dŭbnik BG 165 C9
Dolní Dvořiště CZ 77 E6
Dolni Glavanak BG 166 F5
Dolní Kounice CZ 77 D10
Dolni Lom BG 165 C6
Dolní Loučky CZ 77 D10
Dolní Němčí CZ 146 D5
Dolní Podluží CZ 81 E7
Dolní Újezd CZ 77 C10
Dolní Újezd CZ 146 B5
Dolni Voden BG 165 E10
Dolní Žandov CZ 75 B12
Dolno Dupeni MK 168 C5
Dolno Ezerovo BG 167 D8
Dolno Kamartsi BG 165 D8
Dolno Konjare MK 164 F4
Dolno Levski BG 165 E9
Dolno Osenovo BG 165 F7
Dolno Selo BG 164 E5
Dolno Tserovene BG 159 F11
Dolno Uyno BG 164 E6
Dolný Hričov SK 147 C7
Dolný Kubín SK 147 C8
Dolný Pial SK 146 E6
Dolný Štál SK 146 F5
Dolo I 66 B5
Dolomieu F 31 D8
Dolores E 56 E3
Dolovo SRB 159 D6
Dölsach A 73 C6
Dolsk PL 81 C12
Dołubowo PL 141 E7
Dolus-d'Oléron F 28 D3
Dolyna UA 145 F8
Dolynivka UA 154 A5
Dolyns'ke UA 154 B5
Dolzhitsy RUS 132 D5
Domaháza H 147 E10
Domaniewice PL 141 G2
Domaniewice PL 143 B8
Domanín CZ 146 C4
Domaradz PL 144 D4
Domart-en-Ponthieu F 18 D5
Domaševo BIH 162 D5
Domašinec HR 149 D7
Domaşnea RO 159 C9
Domaszek H 150 E5
Domaszków PL 77 B11
Domaszowice PL 142 D4
Domat Ems CH 71 D8
Domats F 25 D9
Domažlice CZ 76 D3
Dombås N 101 B10
Dombasle-en-Xaintois F 26 D4
Dombasle-sur-Meurthe F 186 D1
Dombegyház H 151 E7
Dombóvár H 149 D10
Dombrád H 145 G4
Dombresson CH 31 A10
Domburg NL 16 E1
Domegge di Cadore I 72 D5
Domeikava LT 137 D8
Domène F 31 E8
Domeniko GR 169 E7
Domérat F 29 C11
Domèvre-en-Haye F 26 C4
Domèvre-sur-Vezouze F 27 C6
Domfront F 23 C10
Domgermain F 26 C4
Dominće HR 162 D3
Domingo Pérez E 46 E4
Dömitz D 83 D10
Domlyan BG 165 D10
Dommartin-le-Franc F 26 D2
Dommartin-Varimont F 25 C12
Domme F 29 F8
Dommershausen D 21 D8
Dommitzsch D 80 C3
Domneşti RO 160 C5
Domneşti RO 161 E7
Domnitsa GR 174 B4
Domnovo RUS 136 E2
Domodossola I 68 A5
Domokos GR 174 A5
Domont F 25 B7
Domoroc RKS 164 D4
Dömös H 149 A11
Domoszló H 147 F10
Dompcevrin F 26 C3
Dompierre-les-Ormes F 30 C5
Dompierre-sur-Besbre F 30 B4
Dompierre-sur-Mer F 28 C3
Dompierre-sur-Yon F 28 B3
Domrémy-la-Pucelle F 26 D4
Dömsöd H 150 C3
Domsühl D 83 D11
Domus de Maria I 64 F2
Domusnovas I 64 E2
Domvaina GR 175 C6
Domžale SLO 73 D10
Donagh GB 7 D8
Donaghadee GB 4 F5
Donaghmore GB 7 C9
Donaghmore IRL 7 F10
Don Álvaro E 51 B7
Doña Mencía E 53 A8
Donard IRL 7 F9
Donaueschingen D 27 E9
Donauwörth D 75 E8
Don Benito E 51 B8
Doncaster GB 11 D9
Donchery F 19 E10
Donduşeni MD 153 A11
Donegal IRL 6 C6
Doneraile IRL 8 D5
Doneztebe E 32 D2
Dønfoss N 100 C8
Dongen NL 16 E3
Donges F 23 F7
Dongo I 69 A7
Donici MD 154 C3
Doñinos de Salamanca E 45 C9
Donja Bela Reka SRB 159 E9
Donja Brela HR 157 F6
Donja Bukovica MNE 163 C7
Donja Dubrava HR 149 D7
Donja Kupčina HR 148 E5
Donja Lepenica BIH 157 B8
Donja Mahala BIH 157 B10
Donja Motičina HR 149 F10
Donja Šatornja SRB 158 E6
Donja Stubica HR 148 E5
Donja Višnjica HR 148 D6
Donja Vrijeska HR 149 E8
Donja Zelina HR 148 E6
Donje Pazarište HR 67 C11
Donjeux F 26 D3
Donji Andrijevci HR 157 B9
Donji Čaglić HR 149 F8
Donji Dubovnik BIH 156 C5
Donji Dušnik SRB 164 C5
Donji Kosinj HR 156 C3
Donji Krčin SRB 159 F7
Donji Krivodol SRB 165 C6
Donji Lapac HR 156 C4
Donji Miholjac HR 149 E10
Donji Milanovac SRB 159 E9
Donji Proložac HR 157 F7
Donji Rujani BIH 157 E6
Donji Seget HR 156 E5
Donji Srb HR 156 D5
Donji Striževac SRB 164 C5
Donji Svilaj BIH 157 B9
Donji Vakuf BIH 157 D7
Donji Vijačani BIH 157 C8
Donji Zemunik HR 156 D3
Donji Širovac HR 156 B5
Donk NL 183 B7
Donkerbroek NL 16 B6
Donnalucata I 59 F6
Donnas I 68 B4
Donnemarie-Dontilly F 25 D9
Donnersbach A 73 B9
Donnersdorf D 75 C7
Donohill IRL 8 C6
Donori I 64 E3
Donostia E 32 D2
Donskoye RUS 139 A8
Donville-les-Bains F 23 C8
Donzdorf D 74 E6
Donzenac F 29 E9
Donzère F 35 B8
Donzy F 25 F9
Dooagh IRL 6 E2
Doochary IRL 6 C6
Dooish GB 4 F2
Doolin IRL 6 F4
Doon IRL 8 C6
Doonbeg IRL 8 C3
Doorn NL 16 D4
Doornspijk NL 183 A7
Dopiewo PL 81 B11
Đorče Petrov MK 164 E3
Dorchester GB 13 D10
Dørdal N 90 B5
Dordives F 25 D8
Dordrecht NL 16 E3
Dore-l'Église F 30 E4
Dörentrup D 17 D12
Dores GB 3 L8
Dorfen D 75 F11
Dorfgastein A 73 B7
Dorfmark D 82 E7
Dorf Mecklenburg D 83 C10
Dorf Zechlin D 83 D13
Dorgali I 64 C4
Dorgoş RO 151 E8
Dorio GR 174 E4
Dorking GB 15 E8
Dorkovo BG 165 E9
Dorlisheim F 186 D3
Dormagen D 21 B7
Dormánd H 150 B5
Dormans F 25 B10
Dor Mărunt RO 161 E9
Dorna-Arini RO 152 C6
Dorna Candrenilor RO 152 C6
Dornava SLO 148 D5
Dörnberg (Habichtswald) D 17 F12
Dornbirn A 71 C9
Dornburg (Saale) D 79 D10
Dornburg-Frickhofen D 185 C9
Dornbusch D 17 A12
Dorndorf D 79 E7
Dorndorf-Steudnitz D 79 D10
Dornelas P 38 E4
Dornes F 30 B3
Dorneşti RO 153 B8
Dornhan D 187 E6
Dornie GB 2 L5
Dornişoara RO 152 C6
Dörnitz D 79 B11
Dorno I 69 C6
Dornoch GB 3 K8
Dornstadt D 74 F6
Dornstetten D 27 D9
Dornum D 17 A8
Dornumersiel D 17 A8
Dorobanţu RO 155 D2
Dorobanţu RO 161 E9
Dorog H 149 A11
Dorogháza H 147 F9
Dorohoi RO 153 B8
Dorohusk PL 141 H9
Dorolţ RO 151 B10
Dorotcaia MD 154 C4
Dorotea S 107 C10
Dörpen D 17 C8
Dorras N 112 D8
Dorris S 107 B9
Dorstadt D 79 B8
Dorsten D 17 E7
Dorstfeld D 185 A7
Dortan F 31 C8
Dortmund D 17 E8
Dörttepe TR 177 D10
Doruchów PL 142 D5
Dorum D 17 A11
Dorupe LV 134 C7
Dörverden D 17 C12
Dörzbach D 74 D6
Dos Aguas E 48 F3
Dosbarrios E 46 E6
Dos Hermanas E 51 E8
Dospat BG 165 F9
Dossenheim D 21 F11
Doştat RO 152 F3
Dos Torres E 54 C3
Døstrup DK 86 E3
Dotnuva LT 134 F7
Dotternhausen D 27 D10
Döttingen CH 27 E9
Douai F 19 D7
Douarnenez F 22 D3
Doubrava CZ 147 B7
Doubravice nad Svitavou CZ 77 D11
Doubs F 31 B9
Douchy F 25 E9
Douchy-les-Mines F 19 D7
Doucier F 31 B8
Doudeville F 18 E2
Doudleby nad Orlicí CZ 77 B10
Doué-la-Fontaine F 23 F11
Douglas GB 5 D9
Douglas GBM 10 C3
Douglas IRL 8 E6
Douglas Bridge GB 4 F2
Doulaincourt-Saucourt F 26 D3
Doulevant-le-Château F 25 D12
Doullens F 18 D5
Dounaiika GR 174 D3
Doune GB 5 C8
Dounreay GB 3 H9
Dour B 19 D8
Dourdan F 24 C7
Dourgne F 33 D10
Douriez F 18 D4
Doussard F 31 D9
Douvaine F 31 C9
Douvres-la-Délivrande F 23 B11
Douzy F 19 E11
Dovadola I 66 D4
Dover GB 15 E11
Dovhe UA 145 G7
Döviken S 103 A9
Dovilai LT 134 E2
Dovre N 101 C10
Dowally GB 5 B9
Downham Market GB 11 F12
Downpatrick GB 7 D11
Downton GB 13 D11
Dowra IRL 6 D6
Dowsby GB 11 F11
Doxato GR 171 B6
Doyet F 30 C2
Doyrentsi BG 165 C10
Dozulé F 23 B11
Drabeši LV 135 B10
Dråby DK 86 C7
Dračevo BIH 162 D5
Dračevo MK 164 F4
Drachhausen D 80 C6
Drachselsried D 76 D4
Drachten NL 16 B6
Drag N 105 B10
Drag N 111 D11
Dragacz PL 138 C6
Dragalijevac BIH 157 C11
Dragalina RO 161 E10
Dragalovci BIH 157 C8
Drăgăneşti RO 151 D9
Drăgăneşti RO 153 F10
Drăgăneşti RO 161 D8
Drăgăneşti de Vede RO 160 E6
Drăgăneşti-Olt RO 160 E5
Drăgăneşti-Vlaşca RO 161 E7
Draganići HR 148 E5
Draganovo BG 166 C5
Drăganu RO 160 D5
Drăgăşani RO 160 D4
Dragash RKS 163 E10
Dragatuš SLO 67 A11
Drage D 83 D8
Drage HR 156 E4
Drăgeşti RO 151 D9
Drăghiceni RO 160 E4
Draginac SRB 158 D3
Draginje SRB 158 D4
Draginovo BG 165 E8
Dragland N 111 C11
Dragnes N 111 C10
Dragnić BIH 157 D7
Dragobi AL 163 E8
Dragočaj BIH 157 C7
Dragocvet SRB 159 F7
Dragodana RO 160 D6
Drăgoeşti RO 160 D4
Drăgoeşti RO 161 D9
Dragoevo BG 167 C7
Dragoevo MK 164 F5
Drăgoieşti RO 153 B8
Dragoman BG 165 D6
Dragomance MK 164 E4
Dragomir BG 165 E9
Dragomireşti RO 152 B4
Dragomireşti RO 153 C9
Dragomireşti RO 153 D10
Dragomireşti RO 160 D6
Dragomirovo BG 166 B4
Dragoni I 60 A2
Dragør DK 87 D11
Dragoš MK 168 C5
Dragoslavele RO 160 C6
Dragoş Vodă RO 161 E10
Drăgoteşti RO 159 D11
Drăgoteşti RO 160 E4
Dragotina HR 156 B5
Dragović HR 149 F8
Dragovishtitsa BG 165 E6
Dragoychintsi BG 164 D5
Dragoynovo BG 166 F4
Dragsfjärd FIN 126 E7
Draguignan F 36 D4
Drăguşeni RO 153 A9
Drăguşeni RO 153 C8
Drăguşeni RO 153 F11
Drăguteşti RO 159 D11
Drahnsdorf D 80 C5
Drahovce SK 146 D5
Drahove UA 145 G8
Drahovica Donja BIH 157 C9
Drajna RO 161 C8
Draka BG 167 E8
Drakenburg D 17 C12
Draksenič BIH 157 B6
Dralfa BG 167 C6
Drama GR 170 B6
Drammen N 95 C12
Drânceni RO 153 D12
Drange N 94 F5
Drangedal N 90 A5
Drangstedt D 17 A11
Drănic RO 160 E3
Dranse D 83 D13
Dransfeld D 78 D6
Dranske D 84 A4
Draperstown GB 4 F3
Drasenhofen A 77 E11
Draßmarkt A 149 A6
Drávafok H 149 E9
Dravagen S 102 B6
Draviskos GR 170 C5
Dravograd SLO 73 C11
Drawno PL 85 D9
Drawsko PL 85 E10
Drawsko Pomorskie PL 85 C9
Drayton GB 15 B11
Drążdżewo PL 139 D11
Dražen Vrh SLO 148 C5
Draževac SRB 158 D5
Dražgoše SLO 73 D9
Drebber D 17 C10
Drebkau D 80 C6
Drégelypalánk H 147 E8
Dreieich D 21 D11
Dreileben D 79 B9
Dreis D 21 E7
Drelów PL 141 G7
Drelsdorf D 82 A6
Drem GB 5 C11
Drenchia I 73 D8
Drenovac SRB 159 F7
Drenovci HR 157 C10
Drenovë AL 168 C4
Drenovets BG 159 F10
Drenovicë AL 168 C2
Drenovo MK 164 F4
Drenovo MK 169 B6
Drense D 84 D5
Drensteinfurt D 17 E9
Drenta BG 166 D5
Drentwede D 17 C11
Drepano GR 169 D6
Drepano GR 175 D6
Dresden D 80 D5
Dretun' BY 133 E6
Dretyń PL 85 B11
Dreumel NL 183 B6
Dreux F 24 C5
Dreverna LT 134 E2
Drevja N 108 E5
Drevjesætra N 102 D4
Dřevohostice CZ 146 C5
Drevsjø N 102 C3
Drevvatn N 108 D5
Drewitz D 79 B11
Drewnica PL 138 B6
Drezdenko PL 85 E9
Drežnica BIH 157 E8
Drežnik SRB 158 F4
Driceni LV 133 C2
Dridu RO 161 D8
Driebergen NL 16 D4
Driebes E 47 D6
Driedorf D 185 C9
Drienov SK 145 F3
Drietoma SK 146 D5
Driffield GB 11 C11
Drimmo IRL 7 F7
Drimnin GB 4 B5
Drimoleague IRL 8 E4
Drinić BIH 156 C5
Drinjača BIH 157 D11
Drinovci BIH 157 F7
Dripsey IRL 8 E5
Drisht AL 163 E8
Dřiteň CZ 76 D6
Drithas AL 168 C4
Driva N 101 A11
Drivstua N 101 B11
Drmno SRB 159 D7
Drnholec CZ 77 E11
Drniš HR 156 E5
Drnje HR 149 D7
Drnovice CZ 77 D11
Drnovice CZ 77 D11
Dro I 69 B10
Drøbak N 95 C13
Drobeta-Turnu Severin RO 159 D10
Drobin PL 139 E8
Drochia MD 153 A11
Drochtersen D 17 A12
Drogheda IRL 7 E10
Drohiczyn PL 141 F7
Drohobych UA 145 E8
Droichead Abhann IRL 8 C5
Droichead Átha IRL 7 E10
Droichead na Bandan IRL 8 E5
Droichead Nua IRL 7 F9
Droitwich Spa GB 13 A10
Drolshagen D 185 B8
Drolsum N 95 B12
Dromara GB 7 D10
Dromina IRL 8 D5
Drommahane IRL 8 D5
Drömme S 107 E14
Dromod IRL 7 E7
Dromore GB 7 C8
Dromore GB 7 D10
Dromore West IRL 6 D5
Dronero I 37 C6
Dronfield GB 11 E9
Drongan GB 5 E8
Drongen B 182 C3
Dronninglund DK 86 A6
Dronrijp NL 16 B5
Dronten NL 16 C5
Dropla BG 155 F2
Drosato GR 169 B8
Drosbacken S 102 C3
Drosendorf A 77 E9
Drosia GR 175 C8
Drösing A 77 E11
Drosopigi GR 168 C5
Droué F 24 D5
Droyßig D 79 D11
Drugan BG 165 E7
Drugovo MK 168 B4
Druid GB 10 F5
Druimdrishaig GB 4 D5
Drulingen F 27 C7
Drumandoora IRL 6 G5
Drumanespick IRL 7 E8
Drumatober IRL 6 F6
Drumbeg GB 2 J6
Drumbilla IRL 7 D9
Drumcard GB 7 D7
Drumcollogher IRL 8 D5
Drumcondra IRL 7 E9
Drumconrath IRL 7 E9
Drumcree IRL 7 E8
Drumettaz-Clarafond F 31 D8
Drumevo BG 167 C8
Drumfree IRL 4 E2
Drumkeeran IRL 6 D6
Drumlea IRL 7 D7
Drumlish IRL 7 E7
Drumlithie GB 5 B12
Drummin IRL 9 D9
Drummore GB 4 F7
Drumnadrochit GB 2 L8
Drumquin GB 4 F2
Drumshanbo IRL 6 D6
Drung IRL 7 D8
Drusenheim F 27 C8
Druskininkai LT 137 F9
Drusti LV 135 B11
Druten NL 183 B7
Druviena LV 135 B12
Druya BY 133 E2
Druyes-les-Belles-Fontaines F 25 E9
Druysk BY 133 E2
Družbice PL 143 D7
Druzhba RUS 136 E3
Druzhnaya Gorka RUS 132 C7
Družstevná pri Hornáde SK 145 F3
Drvenik HR 157 F7
Drwalew PL 141 G4
Drwinia PL 143 F9
Dryanovets BG 161 F8
Dryanovo BG 166 D4
Dryazhno RUS 132 E4
Drygały PL 139 C13
Drymaia GR 175 B6
Drymen GB 5 C8
Drymos GR 169 C8
Dryna N 100 A5
Dryopida GR 175 E9
Dryos GR 176 E5
Drysvyaty BY 135 E13
Dryszczów PL 144 A8
Drzewce PL 142 B6
Drzewiany PL 85 C11
Drzewica PL 141 H2
Drzonowo PL 85 C11
Drzycim PL 138 C5
Duagh IRL 8 D4
Dualchi I 64 C2
Dually IRL 9 C7
Duas Igrejas P 39 F7
Dub SRB 158 F4
Dubá CZ 77 A7
Dubăsari MD 154 C4
Dubăsarii Vechi MD 154 C4
Duba Stonska HR 162 D4
Dubău MD 154 C4
Dubecno PL 141 H8
Düben D 79 C11
Duben D 80 C5
Dübendorf CH 27 F10
Dubeņi LV 134 D2
Dubeninki PL 136 E6
Dubí CZ 80 E5
Dubičiai LT 137 E10
Dubicko CZ 77 C11
Dubicze Cerkiewne PL 141 E8
Dubidze PL 143 D7
Dubiecko PL 144 D5
Dubienka PL 144 A8
Dubingiai LT 137 C11
Dubino I 69 A7
Dubivka UA 153 A8
Dublin IRL 7 F10
Dublje SRB 158 D4
Dublovice CZ 76 C6
Dublyany UA 144 D9
Dublyany UA 145 E7
Dubna LV 135 D13
Dub nad Moravou CZ 146 C4
Dubňany CZ 77 E12
Dubnica nad Váhom SK 146 D6
Dubník SK 146 F6
Duboštica BIH 157 D9
Dubova RO 159 D9
Dubovac SRB 159 D7
Dubove UA 145 G8
Dŭbovets BG 166 F5
Dubovica SK 145 E2
Dŭbovo BG 166 D5
Dubovo SRB 164 C4
Dubovsko BIH 156 C5
Dubrava BIH 157 C8
Dubrava HR 149 E7
Dubrave BIH 157 C10
Dubrave BIH 157 D6
Dubrave BIH 157 D10
Dubravica BIH 157 D8
Dubravica HR 148 E5
Dubravica SRB 159 D7
Dúbravy SK 147 D8
Dubrawka BY 133 F6
Dubrovka RUS 129 F14
Dubrovka RUS 132 F6
Dubrovka RUS 133 D5
Dubrovnik HR 162 D5
Dubrovytsya UA 144 D8
Dubuļi LV 133 D3
Dubynove UA 154 A6
Ducey F 23 C9
Ducherow D 84 C5
Duchov CZ 80 E5
Duck End GB 15 D9
Duclair F 18 F2
Duda-Epureni RO 153 D12
Dudar H 149 B9
Duddo GB 5 D12
Dudelange L 20 F6
Dudeldorf D 21 E7
Duderstadt D 79 C7
Dudeşti RO 161 D10
Dudeştii Vechi RO 150 E5
Dudince SK 147 E7
Düdingen CH 31 B11
Dudley GB 11 F7
Dudovica SRB 158 E5
Dueñas E 40 E2
Duesund N 100 E2
Dueville I 72 E4
Duffel B 19 B10
Dufftown GB 3 L10
Duga Poljana SRB 163 C9
Duga Resa HR 148 F5
Dugi Rat HR 156 F6
Dugny-sur-Meuse F 26 B3
Dugopolje HR 156 E6
Dugo Selo HR 148 E6
Düğüncübaşı TR 173 B7
Duhort-Bachen F 32 C5
Duino I 73 E8
Duirinish GB 2 L5
Duisburg D 17 F7
Dukas AL 168 C2
Dukat AL 168 D2
Dukat i Ri AL 168 D1

Dukla PL 145 D4
Dūkštas LT 135 E12
Dŭlbok Dol BG 165 D10
Dŭlboki BG 166 E5
Dŭlbok Izvor BG 166 E4
Dulcești RO 153 D9
Duleek IRL 7 E10
Dŭlgodeltsi BG 160 F2
Dŭlgopol BG 167 C8
Dulina BY 133 F2
Duljci BIH 157 D7
Dullingham GB 15 C9
Dülmen D 17 E8
Dulnain Bridge GB 3 L9
Dulovce SK 146 F6
Dulovka RUS 133 A4
Dulovo BG 161 F10
Dulverton GB 13 C7
Dumbarton GB 4 D7
Dumbrava RO 151 F9
Dumbrava RO 159 D11
Dumbrava RO 161 D8
Dumbrava Roșie RO 153 D8
Dumbrăveni RO 152 E5
Dumbrăveni RO 153 B8
Dumbrăveni RO 155 F1
Dumbrăveni RO 161 B10
Dumbrăvești RO 161 C7
Dumbrăvița RO 151 F7
Dumbrăvița RO 152 B3
Dumbrăvița RO 153 F6
Dumbría E 38 B1
Dumești RO 153 C10
Dumești RO 153 D10
Dumfries GB 5 E9
Dumitra RO 152 C4
Dumitrești RO 161 B9
Dummerstorf D 83 C12
Dumnicë e Poshtme RKS 164 D3
Dümpelfeld D 21 D7
Dun F 33 D9
Duna N 105 B11
Dunaegyháza H 149 C11
Dunaföldvár H 149 C11
Dunaharaszti H 150 C3
Dunajská Lužná SK 146 E4
Dunajská Streda SK 146 F5
Dunakeszi H 150 B3
Dunalka LV 134 C2
Dún an Rí IRL 7 E9
Dunapataj H 150 D3
Dunărea RO 155 E2
Dunaszeg H 149 A9
Dunaszekcső H 149 D11
Dunaszentbenedek H 149 C11
Dunaszentgyörgy H 149 C11
Dunasziget H 146 F4
Dunatetétlen H 150 D3
Dunaújváros H 149 C11
Dunava LV 135 D12
Dunavarsány H 150 C3
Dunavecse H 150 D2
Dunavtsi BG 159 F10
Dunbar GB 5 C11
Dunbeath GB 3 J10
Dunblane GB 5 C9
Dunboyne IRL 7 F10
Dún Búinne IRL 7 F10
Duncannon IRL 9 D9
Dún Chaoin IRL 8 D2
Dunchurch GB 13 A12
Duncormick IRL 9 D9
Dundaga LV 134 A4
Dundalk IRL 7 D10
Dún Dealgan IRL 7 D10
Dun Dealgan IRL 7 D10
Dundee GB 5 C11
Dunderland N 108 D8
Dundonald GB 7 C11
Dundreggan GB 2 L7
Dundrennan GB 5 F9
Dundrum GB 7 D11
Dundrum IRL 8 C6
Dunecht GB 3 L12
Dunes F 33 B7
Dunfanaghy IRL 7 B7
Dunfermline GB 5 C10
Dungannon GB 7 C9
Dún Garbhán IRL 9 D7
Dungarvan IRL 9 C8
Dungarvan IRL 9 D7
Düngenheim D 185 D7
Dungiven GB 4 F3
Dungloe IRL 6 C6
Dungourney IRL 8 E6
Dunholme GB 11 E11
Dunicë AL 168 C4
Dunières F 30 E5
Duninowo PL 85 A11
Dunje MK 169 B6
Dunkeld GB 5 B9
Dunkerque F 18 B5
Dunkerrin IRL 9 C7
Dunkitt IRL 9 D8
Dún Laoghaire IRL 7 F10
Dunlavin IRL 7 F9
Dunleer IRL 7 E10
Dún Léire IRL 7 E10
Dun-le-Palestel F 29 C9
Dun-les-Places F 25 F11
Dunlop GB 4 D7
Dunloy GB 4 E4
Dún Mánmhaí IRL 8 E4
Dunmanway IRL 8 E4
Dún Mór IRL 9 D9
Dunmore IRL 6 E5
Dunmore East IRL 9 D9
Dunmurry GB 7 C11
Dunnamanagh GB 4 F2
Dún na nGall IRL 6 C6
Dunning GB 5 C9
Dunoon GB 4 D7
Dunquin IRL 8 D2
Duns GB 5 D12
Dunscore GB 5 E9
Dünsen D 17 C11
Dunshaughlin IRL 7 E9
Dunstable GB 15 D7
Dunster GB 13 C8
Dun-sur-Auron F 29 B11
Dun-sur-Meuse F 19 F11
Dunure GB 4 E7
Dunvant GB 12 B6
Dunvegan GB 2 L3
Duplica SLO 73 D10
Dupnitsa BG 165 E7
Durach D 71 B10
Durak TR 173 E9
Durana E 41 C6
Durance F 33 B6
Durango E 41 B6
Durankulak BG 155 F3
Duras F 33 A6
Durbach D 27 C9
Durban-Corbières F 34 E4
Durbe LV 134 C2
Durbuy B 184 D3
Dúrcal E 53 C9
Durdat-Larequille F 29 C11
Đurđenovac HR 149 E10
Đurđevac HR 149 D8
Đurđevića Tara MNE 163 C7
Đurđevik BIH 157 D10
Đurđevo SRB 158 C5
Đurđevo SRB 159 E6
Düren D 20 C6
Durfort F 35 C6
Durham GB 5 F13
Ďurkov SK 145 F3
Durlas IRL 9 C7
Durlești MD 154 C3
Durmanec HR 148 D5
Dürmentingen D 71 A9
Durmersheim D 27 C9
Durness GB 2 H7
Durnești RO 153 B10
Dürnkrut A 77 F11
Durrës AL 168 B1
Durrington GB 13 C11
Dürrlauingen D 75 F7
Durrow IRL 9 C8
Durrus IRL 8 E3
Dürrwangen D 75 D7
Dursley GB 13 B10
Dursunbey TR 173 E10
Durtal F 23 E11
Duruelo de la Sierra E 40 E6
Duruitoarea MD 153 B10
Durup DK 86 B3
Durusu TR 173 B10
Dusetos LT 135 E11
Dushk i Madh AL 168 C2
Dusina BIH 157 E8
Dŭskotna BG 167 D8
Duškovci SRB 158 F5
Dusmenys LT 137 E9
Dusnok H 150 E2
Dusocin PL 138 C6
Düsseldorf D 21 B7
Dussen NL 16 E3
Dußlingen D 187 E7
Düßnitz D 79 C12
Duszniki PL 81 B10
Dutluca TR 173 E11
Dutovlje SLO 73 E8
Duvberg S 102 B7
Duved S 105 E13
Düvertepe TR 173 F9
Duži BIH 162 D5
Dvärsätt S 106 E6
Dvaryshcha BY 133 E6
Dve Mogili BG 161 F7
Dverberg N 111 B10
Dviete LV 135 D12
Dvirtsi UA 144 C9
Dvor HR 156 B5
Dvorce CZ 146 B5
Dvornaye Syalo BY 133 E3
Dvorníky SK 146 E5
Dvory nad Žitavou SK 146 F6
Dvůr Králové CZ 77 B9
Dwikozy PL 144 B4
Dwingeloo NL 16 C6
Dyan GB 7 D9
Dyankovo BG 161 F9
Dybvad DK 90 E7
Dyce GB 3 L12
Dychów PL 81 C8
Dydnia PL 144 D5
Dyfjord N 113 B19
Dygowo PL 85 B9
Dyke GB 3 K9
Dykehead GB 5 B11
Dykhtynets' UA 152 A6
Dylągówka PL 144 D5
Dylaki PL 142 E5
Dylewo PL 139 D11
Dymchurch GB 15 E10
Dymock GB 13 B10
Dynäs S 107 F13
Dynivtsi UA 153 A8
Dynów PL 144 D5
Dyo F 30 C5
Dyping N 110 E9
Dyrnes N 104 E3
Dyrøyhamn N 111 B13
Dyrrachi GR 174 E5
Dyulevo BG 167 E8
Dyulino BG 167 D9
Dyviziya UA 154 F5
Dywity PL 136 F1
Dzeguzēni LV 134 D6
Dzelzava LV 135 C12
Dzeņi LV 135 B12
Dzērbene LV 135 B11
Dzhebel BG 171 A8
Dzherman BG 165 E7
Dzhulynka UA 154 A5
Dzhulyunitsa BG 166 C5
Dzhuriv UA 152 A6
Dzhurovo BG 165 D9
Dziadkowice PL 141 E7
Dziadowa Kłoda PL 142 D4
Działdowo PL 139 D9
Działoszyce PL 143 F9
Działoszyn PL 142 D6
Działyń PL 138 D7
Dziemiany PL 138 B4
Dziergowice PL 142 F5
Dzierzążnia PL 139 E9
Dzierżążno Wielkie PL 85 E10
Dzierzgoń PL 139 C7
Dzierzgowo PL 139 D10
Dzierzkowice-Rynek PL 144 B5
Dzierżoniów PL 81 E11
Dzietrzniki PL 142 D6
Dzietrzychowo PL 136 E3
Dziewierzewo PL 85 E13
Džigolj SRB 164 C4
Dzirnavas LV 134 B4
Dzisna BY 133 E4
Dziwnów PL 85 B7
Dzmitravichy BY 141 F9
Džūkste LV 134 C6
Džumajlija MK 164 F4
Dźwierzuty PL 139 C10
Dźwirzyno PL 85 B8
Dzwola PL 144 B6
Dzwonowice PL 143 E8
Dzyornavichy BY 133 E4

E

Éadan Doire IRL 7 F8
Eaglesfield GB 5 E10
Eardisley GB 13 A8
Earith GB 15 C9
Earl Shilton GB 11 F9
Earlston GB 5 D11
Earl Stonham GB 15 C11
Earsairidh GB 4 B2
Easdale GB 4 C5
Easington GB 5 F14
Easington GB 11 D12
Easingwold GB 11 C9
Easky IRL 6 D5
Eastbourne GB 15 F9
Eastburn GB 11 D11
Eastfield GB 11 C11
Eastgate GB 5 F12
East Grinstead GB 15 E8
East Harling GB 15 C10
East Kilbride GB 5 D8
Eastleigh GB 13 D12
East Linton GB 5 D11
East Looe GB 12 E6
Eastoft GB 11 D10
Easton GB 13 D10
East Retford GB 11 E10
Eastriggs GB 5 F10
Eastry GB 15 E11
East Wemyss GB 5 C10
East Wittering GB 15 F7
Eastwood GB 11 E9
Eaton Socon GB 15 C8
Eaunes F 33 D8
Eauze F 33 C6
Ebberup DK 86 E5
Ebbs A 72 A5
Ebbw Vale GB 13 B8
Ebecik TR 181 A9
Ebeleben D 79 D8
Ebelsbach D 75 C8
Ebeltoft DK 86 C7
Ebene Reichenau A 73 C8
Ebenfurth A 77 G10
Eben im Pongau A 73 B7
Ebensee A 73 A8
Ebensfeld D 75 B8
Ebenthal A 73 C9
Ebenweiler D 71 B9
Eberau A 149 B6
Eberbach D 21 F11
Ebergötzen D 79 C7
Ebermannsdorf D 75 D10
Ebermannstadt D 75 C9
Ebern D 75 B8
Eberndorf A 73 C10
Ebersbach D 80 D5
Ebersbach D 81 D7
Ebersbach an der Fils D 74 E6
Ebersberg D 75 F10
Eberschwang A 76 F5
Ebersdorf A 148 B5
Ebersdorf D 17 A12
Ebersdorf D 75 B10
Ebersmunster F 186 E4
Eberstein A 73 C10
Eberswalde-Finow D 84 E5
Ebes H 151 C8
Ebhausen D 27 C10
Ebikon CH 27 F9
Ebnat-Kappel CH 27 F11
Eboli I 60 B4
Ebrach D 75 C7
Ebreichsdorf A 77 G10
Ébreuil F 30 C3
Ebsdorfergrund-Dreihausen D 21 C11
Ebstorf D 83 D8
Écaussinnes-d'Enghien B 182 D4
Ecclefechan GB 5 E10
Eccles GB 5 D12
Eccleshall GB 11 F7
Eceabat TR 171 D10
Echallens CH 31 B10
Echarri E 32 E2
Échauffour F 24 C3
Échenoz-la-Méline F 26 E5
Eching D 75 E11
Eching D 75 F10
Echinos GR 171 B7
Échiré F 28 C5
Échirolles F 31 E8
Échourgnac F 29 E6
Echsenbach A 77 E8
Echt GB 3 L12
Echt NL 19 B12
Echte D 79 C7
Echternach L 20 E6
Écija E 53 A6
Ečka SRB 158 C5
Eckartsberga D 79 D10
Eckbolsheim F 186 D4
Eckental D 75 C9
Eckernförde D 83 B7
Eckerö FIN 99 B13
Eckington GB 11 E9
Eckington GB 13 A10
Éclaron-Braucourt-Ste-Livière F 25 C12
Écommoy F 23 E12
Écos F 24 B6
Écouché F 23 C11
Écouflant F 23 E10
Écouis F 18 F3
Écrouves F 26 C4
Écs H 149 A9
Ecséd H 150 B4
Ecseg H 147 F9
Ecsegfalva H 151 C6
Ecser H 150 C3
Écueillé F 29 A8
Écuisses F 30 B6
Écury-sur-Coole F 25 C11
Ed S 91 B10
Ed S 107 E12
Eda glasbruk S 96 C7
Edam NL 16 C4
Edane S 97 C8
Ēdas LV 134 C4
Eddelak D 82 C6
Edderton GB 3 K8
Eddleston GB 5 D10
Ede NL 16 D5
Ede S 103 B12
Edebäck S 97 B10
Edefors S 118 B5
Edegem B 19 B9
Edelény H 145 G2
Edelschrott A 73 B11
Edemissen D 79 B7
Eden GB 4 F5
Eden S 107 D12
Edenderry IRL 7 F8
Edenkoben D 21 F10
Edermünde D 78 D5
Ederny GB 7 C7
Edesheim D 21 F10
Edessa GR 169 C7
Edewecht D 17 B9
Edewechterdamm D 17 B9
Edgeworthstown IRL 7 E7
Edgmond GB 11 F7
Ediger-Eller D 21 D8
Edinburgh GB 5 D10
Edincik TR 173 D8
Edineț MD 153 A10
Edirne TR 171 A11
Edland N 94 C7
Edling D 75 F11
Edlingham GB 5 E13
Edlitz A 148 A6
Edmondstown IRL 6 E5
Edmundbyers GB 5 F13
Ēdole LV 134 B3
Edolo I 69 A9
Edremit TR 173 E7
Edrosa P 39 E6
Edroso P 39 E6
Edsbro S 99 C10
Edsbruk S 93 C8
Edsbyn S 103 D10
Edsele S 107 E11
Edsken S 98 A6
Edsvalla S 97 D9
Edzell GB 5 B11
Eefde NL 183 A8
Eeklo B 19 B8
Eelde-Paterswolde NL 17 B7
Eerbeek NL 16 D6
Eernegem B 182 C2
Eersel NL 16 F4
Eferding A 76 F6
Effelder D 75 B9
Effeltrich D 75 C9
Effretikon CH 27 F10
Efkarpia GR 169 B8
Efkarpia GR 169 C10
Eforie RO 155 E3
Efpalio GR 174 C4
Efringen-Kirchen D 27 E8
Eftimie Murgu RO 159 D9
Efxeinoupoli GR 175 A6
Egby S 89 B11
Egebæk DK 86 E3
Egebjerg DK 86 D5
Egebjerg DK 87 D9
Egeln D 79 C9
Egense DK 86 B6
Eger H 145 H1
Egerbakta H 145 H1
Egernsund DK 86 F5
Egersund N 94 F4
Egerszalók H 145 H1
Egervár H 149 C7
Egeskov DK 86 D5
Egestorf D 83 D8
Egga N 111 B19
Eggby S 91 C14
Eggebek D 82 A6
Eggenburg A 77 E9
Eggenfelden D 75 F12
Eggenstein-Leopoldshafen D 27 B9
Eggersdorf D 79 C10
Eggersdorf bei Graz A 148 B5
Eggesbønes N 100 B3
Eggesin D 84 C6
Eggingen D 27 E9
Eggiwil CH 70 D5
Egglham D 76 E4
Eggolsheim D 75 C9
Eggstätt D 72 A5
Eggum N 110 D6
Eghezée B 19 C10
Eging am See D 76 E4
Églaine LV 135 E12
Égletons F 29 E10
Egling D 72 A4
Eglingham GB 5 E13
Eglinton GB 4 E2
Eglisau CH 27 E10
Eglish GB 7 D9
Egļuciems LV 133 B2
Eglwys Fach GB 10 F4
Eglwyswrw GB 12 A5
Egmond aan Zee NL 16 C3
Egna I 69 A11
Egorovca MD 153 B11
Egremont GB 10 C4
Egsmark DK 86 C7
Egtved DK 86 D4
Éguilles F 35 C9
Eguisheim F 27 D7
Éguzon-Chantôme F 29 C9
Egyek H 151 B6
Egyházaskozár H 149 D10
Ehekirchen D 75 E9
Ehingen D 75 D8
Ehingen (Donau) D 71 A9
Ehlen (Habichtswald) D 17 F12
Ehningen D 187 D6
Ehra-Lessien D 79 A8
Ehrenberg-Wüstensachsen D 74 B7
Ehrenburg D 17 C11
Ehrenfriedersdorf D 80 E3
Ehrenhausen A 148 C5
Ehringshausen D 21 C10
Eibar E 41 B7
Eibelstadt D 74 C7
Eibenstock D 75 B12
Eibergen NL 17 D7
Eibiswald A 148 C4
Eich D 21 E10
Eichenbarleben D 79 B9
Eichenbühl D 27 A11
Eichendorf D 76 E3
Eichenzell D 74 B6
Eichgraben A 77 F9
Eichigt D 75 B11
Eichstätt D 75 E9
Eichwalde D 80 B5
Eickendorf D 79 C10
Eicklingen D 79 A7
Eidapere EST 131 D9
Eide N 100 A6
Eide N 104 D8
Eide N 111 C11
Eidem N 108 E2
Eidet N 105 C15
Eidet N 105 C16
Eidet N 108 A9
Eidet N 110 D8
Eidfjord N 94 B6
Eiði FO 2 A2
Eidkjosen N 111 A16
Eidsbugarden N 101 D8
Eidsdal N 100 B6
Eidsfjord N 110 C8
Eidsfoss N 95 C12
Eidshaug N 105 B10
Eidsnes N 112 C10
Eidsøra N 100 A8
Eidstranda N 111 A19
Eidsund N 94 D3
Eidsvåg N 100 A8
Eidsvoll N 95 B14
Eidsvoll Verk N 95 B14
Eidvågeid N 113 B12
Eigeltingen D 27 E10
Eigenrieden D 79 D7
Eijsden NL 183 D7
Eik N 94 D3
Eikelandsosen N 94 B3
Eiken N 94 F6
Eikesdal N 100 B8
Eikjaberg N 100 D6
Eikjeskog N 94 E4
Eikjil N 90 B1
Eiksund N 100 B3
Eilenburg D 79 D12
Eilenstedt D 79 C9
Eilsleben D 79 B9
Eime D 78 B6
Eimen D 78 C6
Eimke D 83 E8
Eina N 101 E13
Einacleit GB 2 J3
Einbeck D 78 C6
Eindhoven NL 16 F4
Einsiedeln CH 27 F10
Einville-au-Jard F 26 C5
Eivollen N 108 F3
Eisden B 183 D7
Eiselfing D 75 F11
Eisenach D 79 E7
Eisenberg D 79 E10
Eisenberg (Pfalz) D 21 E10
Eisenerz A 73 A10
Eisenhüttenstadt D 81 B7
Eisenkappel A 73 D10
Eisenstadt A 77 G11
Eisfeld D 75 B8
Eišiškės LT 137 E10
Eislandet N 100 E3
Eisleben, Lutherstadt D 79 C10
Eislingen (Fils) D 74 E6
Eisma EST 131 B12
Eitelborn D 21 D9
Eiterfeld D 78 E6
Eiternes N 105 B11
Eiterstraum N 108 E5
Eitorf D 21 C8
Eivinvik N 100 E2
Eivissa E 57 D7
Eja P 44 B4
Ejby DK 86 E5
Ejby DK 87 D9
Ejby DK 87 E10
Ejea de los Caballeros E 41 D9
Ejsing DK 86 B3
Ejstrupholm DK 86 D4
Ejulve E 42 F2
Ekeby S 87 C11
Ekeby S 92 A6
Ekeby S 99 D9
Ekeby-Almby S 97 D13
Ekedalen S 91 C14
Ekenäs FIN 127 F9
Ekenäs S 91 B13
Ekenäs S 93 B9
Ekenässjön S 92 E6
Ēķengrāve LV 135 D11
Ekeren B 182 C4
Ekerö S 99 D9
Eket S 87 C12
Ekkerøy N 114 C8
Ekmekçi TR 173 D9
Ekola FIN 122 D9
Ekorrträsk S 107 B16
Eksaarde B 182 C3
Eksel B 183 C6
Ekshärad S 97 B9
Eksjö S 92 D5
Ekšta S 93 E12
Ekträsk S 118 F3
Ekzarkh-Antimovo BG 167 D7
Ekzarkh Yosif BG 161 F7
Elafos GR 169 D7
Elafotopos GR 168 E4
Elaiochori GR 171 C6
Elaionas GR 169 B10
Elaionas GR 174 B5
Elaionas GR 175 C7
El Álamo E 46 D5
El Algar E 56 F3
El Almendro E 51 D5
El Alquián E 55 F8
Elämäjärvi FIN 123 D15
El Arahal E 51 E8
El Arenal E 45 D10
Elassona GR 169 E7
El Astillero E 40 B4
Elateia GR 175 B6
Elati GR 169 E6
Elati GR 169 E6
Elatochori GR 169 D7
Elatou GR 174 B4
El Ballestero E 55 B8
El Barco de Ávila E 45 D9
El Barraco E 46 D3
Elbasan AL 168 B3
Elbergen D 17 D8
Elbeuf F 18 F3
Elbigenalp A 71 C10
Elbingerode (Harz) D 79 C8
Elbląg PL 139 B7
El Bodón E 45 D7
El Bonillo E 55 B7
El Bosque E 53 C6
El Bullaque E 46 F4
El Burgo E 53 C7
El Burgo de Ebro E 41 E10
El Burgo de Osma E 40 E5
El Burgo Ranero E 39 D9
El Buste E 41 E8
El Cabaco E 45 C8
El Cabildo y la Campana E 55 E9
El Cabo de Gata E 55 F8
El Campillo E 51 D6
El Campillo de la Jara E 45 E10
El Campo de Peñaranda E 45 C10
El Cañavate E 47 E8
El Carpio E 53 A8
El Carpio de Tajo E 46 E4
El Casar E 46 C6
El Casar de Escalona E 46 D3
El Castellar E 48 D3
El Castillo de las Guardas E 51 D7
El Catllar de Gaià E 43 E6
El Centenillo E 54 C5
El Cerro de Andévalo E 51 D6
Elche E 56 E3
Elche de la Sierra E 55 C8
Elchingen D 187 E9
Elciego E 41 C6
Elçili TR 172 B6
El Coronil E 51 E8
El Cubo de Don Sancho E 45 C8
El Cubo de Tierra del Vino E 39 F8
El Cuervo E 47 D10
El Cuervo E 51 F7
Elda E 56 E3
Eldalsosen N 100 D4
Eldena D 83 D10
Eldforsen S 97 B11
Eldingen D 83 E8
Eldsberga S 87 B12
Elduvík FO 2 A3
Elefsina GR 175 C8
Eleftheres GR 171 C6
Elefthero GR 168 D4
Eleftheroupoli GR 171 C6
Eleja LV 134 D7
El Ejido E 55 F7
Elek H 151 D7
Elektrėnai LT 137 D10
Elemir SRB 158 C5
Elena BG 166 D5
Elend D 79 C8
Eleousa GR 168 E4
El Escorial E 46 C4
Eleshnitsa BG 165 F8
El Espinar E 46 C4
El Estrecho E 56 F3
Elexalde E 40 B6
El Fendek MA 53 E5
Elfershausen D 187 A8
El Fresno E 46 C3
Elgå N 101 B15
El Garrobo E 51 D7
Elgershausen (Schauenburg) D 21 B12
Elgeta E 41 B7
Elgin GB 3 K10
Elgoibar E 32 D1
Elgol GB 2 L4
El Grado E 42 C4
El Granado E 50 D5
El Grau de Borriana E 48 E4
Elgsnes N 111 C11
El Herrumblar E 47 F9
El Hito E 47 E7
El Hoyo de Pinares E 46 C4
Elia GR 178 E9
Elice I 62 B5
Elie GB 5 C11
Elika GR 178 B4
Elimäki FIN 127 D15
Eling GB 13 D12
Elini I 64 D4
Elin Pelin BG 165 D8
Elisenvaara RUS 129 C12
Eliseyna BG 165 C8
Elizondo E 32 D2
Eljas E 45 D7
Ełk PL 136 F5
Elkenroth D 185 C8
Elkhovo BG 166 D5
Elkhovo BG 167 E7
Elkšņi LV 135 D11
Ellan S 99 B11
Elland GB 11 D8
Ellefeld D 75 B11
Ellenberg D 187 C9
Ellerau D 83 C7
Ellerbek D 83 C7
Ellesmere GB 10 F6
Ellesmere Port GB 10 E6
Ellezelles B 19 C8
Ellidshøj DK 86 B5
Elling DK 90 E7
Ellingen D 75 D8
Ellington GB 5 E13
El Llano E 38 B5
Ellmau A 72 A5
Ellon GB 3 L12
Ellös S 91 C9
El Losar del Barco E 45 D9
Elloughton GB 11 D10
Ellrich D 79 C8
Ellwangen (Jagst) D 75 E7
Ellwürden D 17 B10
Elm CH 71 D8
Elm D 17 A12
Elmacık TR 167 F8
El Masroig E 42 E5
Elmen A 71 C11
Elmenhorst D 83 B12
Elmenhorst D 83 C8
Elmenhorst D 83 C9
Elmenhorst D 83 C10
El Molar E 46 C5
El Molinillo E 46 F4
El Moral E 55 D8
El Morell E 42 E6
Elmshorn D 82 C7
Elne F 34 E4
Elnesvågen N 100 A6
Elorrio E 41 B6
Elorz E 32 E2
Elos GR 178 E6
El Oso E 46 C3
Előszállás H 149 C11
Elounta GR 179 E10
Elovdol BG 165 D6
Éloyes F 26 D6
El Palmar E 56 F2
El Palo E 53 C8
El Payo E 45 D7
El Pedernoso E 47 F7
El Pedroso E 51 D8
El Pedroso de la Armuña E 45 B10
El Peral E 47 E9
El Perdigón E 39 F8
El Perelló E 42 F5
El Perelló E 48 F4
Elpersbüttel D 82 B6
Elphin GB 2 J6
Elphin IRL 6 E6
El Picazo E 47 F8
El Pinell de Bray E 42 E5
El Piñero E 39 F8
El Pla de Santa María E 43 E6
El Pobo E 42 F2
El Pobo de Dueñas E 47 C9
El Pont d'Armentera E 43 E6
El Port E 48 E4
El Port de la Selva E 34 F5
El Prat de Llobregat E 43 E8
El Provencio E 47 F7
El Puente E 40 B5
El Puente de Arzobispo E 45 E10
El Puerto de Santa María E 52 C4
El Real de la Jara E 51 D7
El Real de San Vicente E 46 D3
El Recuenco E 47 C8
El Robledo E 46 F4
El Rocío E 51 E7
El Romeral E 46 E6
El Rompido E 51 E5
El Ronquillo E 51 D7
El Royo E 41 E6
El Rubio E 53 B7
El Sabinar E 41 D9
El Sabinar E 55 C8
El Saler E 48 F4
El Salobral E 55 B9
Els Arcs E 42 D5
El Saucejo E 53 B6
El Saugo E 45 D7
Elsdon GB 5 E12
Elsdorf D 21 C7
Elsenborn B 20 D6
Elsendorf D 75 E10
Elsenfeld D 21 E12
El Serrat AND 33 E9
Elsfjord N 108 D6
Elsfleth D 17 B10
Elshitsa BG 165 E9
Elsloo NL 183 D7
Elsnes N 111 B19
Elsnig D 80 C3
Elsnigk D 79 C11
El Soleràs E 42 E5
Elspeet NL 16 D5
Els Prats de Rei E 43 D7
Elst NL 16 E5
Elst NL 183 B6
Elster D 79 C12
Elsterberg D 79 E11
Elsterwerda D 80 D5
Elstra D 80 D6
El Tiemblo E 46 D4
Eltmann D 75 C8
El Toboso E 47 E7
Elton GB 11 F11
Elton IRL 8 D6
El Torno E 45 D9
El Trincheto E 46 F4
El Tumbalejo E 51 E6
Eltville am Rhein D 21 D10
Elva EST 131 E12
Elvål N 101 C14
Elvanfoot GB 5 E9
Elvas P 51 B5
Elvebakken N 113 D11
Elvegard N 111 D13
Elvekrok N 113 B17
Elvelund N 112 E6
Elvemund N 113 E16
Elven F 22 E6
El Vendrell E 43 E7
El Verger E 56 D5
Elverum N 101 E15
Elvesletta N 111 D12
Elvevoll N 111 B14
Elvevollen N 111 B18
El Villar de Arnedo E 32 F1
Elvington GB 11 D10
El Viso E 54 C3
El Viso del Alcor E 51 E8
Elvnes N 114 D8
Elx E 56 E3
Elxleben D 79 D8
Ely GB 13 C8
Ely GB 15 C9
Elz D 185 D9
Elzach D 27 D9
Elze D 78 B6
Elze (Wedemark) D 78 A6
Embid E 47 C9
Embid de Ariza E 41 F8
Embleton GB 5 E13
Embrun F 36 B4
Emburga LV 135 C7
Embūte LV 134 C3
Emden D 17 B8
Emecik TR 181 C7
Emiralem TR 177 B9
Emirali TR 173 B8
Emlichheim D 17 C7
Emly IRL 8 D6
Emmaboda S 89 B9
Emmaljunga S 87 C13
Emmanouil Pappas GR 169 B10
Emmaste EST 130 D5
Emmeloord NL 16 C5
Emmelsbüll-Horsbüll D 82 A5
Emmelshausen D 21 D9
Emmen CH 27 F9
Emmen NL 17 C7
Emmendingen D 27 D8
Emmer-Compascuum NL 17 C8
Emmerich D 16 E6
Emmoo IRL 6 E6
Emőd H 145 H2
Emolahti FIN 123 C15
Empel NL 16 E4
Empesos GR 174 A3
Empfingen D 187 E6
Empoli I 66 E2
Emponas GR 181 D7
Emporeio GR 179 C9
Emporeios GR 177 C7
Emptinne B 19 D11
Emsbüren D 17 D8
Emsdetten D 17 D9
Emsfors S 89 A10
Emskirchen D 75 C8
Emst NL 16 D5
Emstek D 17 C10
Emsworth GB 15 F7
Emtinghausen D 17 C11
Emtunga S 91 C12
Emyvale IRL 7 D9
Enafors S 105 E12
Enäjärvi FIN 128 D7
Enånger S 103 C13
Enarsvedjan S 105 D16
Encamp AND 33 E9
Encinas de Abajo E 45 C10
Encinasola E 51 C6
Encinas Reales E 53 B8
Encinedo E 39 D6
Enciso E 41 D7
Encs H 145 G3
Encsencs H 151 B9
Endingen D 27 D8
Endre S 93 D12
Endrefalva H 147 E9
Endriejavas LT 134 E3
Endrinal E 45 C9

Fuente el Sol E 46 B3
Fuenteguinaldo E 45 D7
Fuentelapeña E 39 F9
Fuentelcésped E 40 E4
Fuentelespino de Haro E 47 E7
Fuentelespino de Moya E 47 E10
Fuentelmonge E 41 F7
Fuentenovilla E 47 D6
Fuente Obejuna E 51 C9
Fuente Palmera E 53 A6
Fuentepelayo E 46 B4
Fuentepinilla E 40 E6
Fuenterodos E 41 F10
Fuenterrebollo E 40 F4
Fuenterroble de Salvatierra E 45 C9
Fuentesaúco E 45 B10
Fuentesaúco de Fuentidueña E 40 F3
Fuentes-Claras E 47 C10
Fuentes de Andalucía E 51 E9
Fuentes de Ebro E 41 E10
Fuentes de Jiloca E 41 F8
Fuentes de León E 51 C6
Fuentes de Nava E 39 D10
Fuentes de Oñoro E 45 C7
Fuentes de Ropel E 39 E8
Fuentespalda E 42 F4
Fuente-Tójar E 53 A8
Fuente Vaqueros E 53 B9
Fuentidueña E 40 F4
Fuerte del Rey E 53 A9
Fuertescusa E 47 D8
Fügen A 72 B4
Fuglafjørður FO 2 A3
Fugleberg N 111 C12
Fuglebjerg DK 87 E9
Fuglstad N 105 A13
Fuhrberg (Burgwedel) D 78 A6
Fulda D 74 A6
Fulford GB 11 D9
Fulga RO 161 D8
Fulham GB 15 E8
Fullbro S 93 A11
Fulnek CZ 146 B5
Fülöp H 151 B9
Fülöpháza H 150 D3
Fülöpszállás H 150 D3
Fulunäs S 102 D5
Fumay F 19 E10
Fumel F 33 B7
Fumone I 62 D4
Funäsdalen S 102 A4
Fundada P 44 E4
Fundão P 44 D6
Fundata RO 160 C6
Fundeni RO 161 B11
Fundeni RO 161 E8
Funder Kirkeby DK 86 C4
Fundulea RO 161 E9
Fundu Moldovei RO 152 B6
Funes E 32 F2
Funes I 72 C4
Funzie GB 3 D15
Furadouro P 44 C3
Furceni MD 154 C3
Furci I 63 C7
Furci Siculo I 59 D7
Furculeşti RO 160 F6
Furiani F 37 F10
Furnace GB 4 C6
Furnari I 59 C7
Furraleigh IRL 9 D8
Fürstenau D 17 C9
Fürstenberg D 21 A12
Fürstenberg D 84 D4
Fürstenberg (Lichtenfels) D 21 B11
Fürstenfeld A 148 B6
Fürstenfeldbruck D 75 F9
Fürstenwalde D 80 B6
Fürstenwerder D 84 D5
Fürstenzell D 76 E4
Furta H 151 C7
Furtan S 97 C8
Furtei I 64 D2
Fürth D 21 E11
Fürth D 75 D8
Furth D 75 E11
Furth bei Göttweig A 77 F9
Furth im Wald D 76 D3
Furtwangen im Schwarzwald D 27 D9
Furuberg S 103 B12
Furuby S 89 B8
Furudal N 111 B16
Furudal S 103 D9
Furudals bruk S 103 D9
Furuflaten N 111 B19
Furuögrund S 118 E6
Furusjö S 91 D14
Furusund S 99 C11
Furutangvikja N 105 B14
Furuvik S 103 E13
Fusa N 94 B3
Fuscaldo I 60 E6
Fushë-Arrëz AL 163 E9
Fushë-Bardhe AL 168 D3
Fushë Kosovë RKS 164 D3
Fushë-Krujë AL 168 B2
Fushë-Kuqe AL 168 A2
Fusignano I 66 D4
Fußach A 71 C9
Füssen D 71 B11
Fussy F 25 F7
Fustiñana E 41 D9
Futeau F 26 B3
Futog SRB 158 C4
Futrikelva N 111 A17
Füzesabony H 150 B5
Füzesgyarmat H 151 C7
Fužine HR 67 B10
Fyfield GB 15 D9
Fylaki GR 169 F8
Fyli GR 175 C8
Fyllinge S 87 B11
Fyllo GR 169 F7
Fynshav DK 86 F5
Fyrås S 106 D8
Fyrde N 100 B4
Fyresdal N 90 A3
Fyteies GR 174 B3
Fyvie GB 3 L12

G

Gaal A 73 B10
Gaanderen NL 183 B8
Gabaldón E 47 E9
Gabare BG 165 C8
Gabarret F 32 C6
Gabčíkovo SK 146 F5
Gabela BIH 157 F8
Gaber BG 165 D6
Gabia la Grande E 53 B9
Gabicce Mare I 67 E6
Gąbin PL 139 F8
Gablingen D 75 F8
Gablitz A 77 F10
Gáborján H 151 C8
Gabriac F 34 B4
Gabrnik SLO 148 D5
Gabrovnitsa BG 165 B7
Gabrovo BG 166 D4
Gaby I 68 B4
Gać PL 144 C5
Gacé F 23 C12
Gacko BIH 157 F10
Gåda S 103 B10
Gadbjerg DK 86 D4
Gäddede S 105 B16
Gäddträsk S 107 C15
Gadebusch D 83 C10
Gadmen CH 70 D6
Gadoni I 64 D3
Gádor E 55 F8
Gádoros H 150 D6
Gadstrup DK 87 D10
Gadžin Han SRB 164 C5
Gaeiras P 44 F2
Gærum DK 90 E7
Găeşti RO 160 D6
Gaeta I 62 E5
Gafanha da Boa Hora P 44 C3
Gafanha da Nazaré P 44 C3
Gafanha do Carmo P 44 C3
Gafanhoeira P 50 B3
Gåfete P 44 F5
Gaflenz A 73 A10
Gafsele S 107 C12
Gaganitsa BG 165 C7
Găgeşti RO 153 E11
Gaggenau D 27 C9
Gaggi I 59 D7
Gaggio Montano I 66 D2
Gagliano I 68 B5
Gagliano Castelferrato I 59 D6
Gagliano del Capo I 61 D10
Gagnef S 103 E9
Gagnières F 35 B7
Gagsmark S 118 D6
Găiceana RO 153 E10
Gaigalava LV 133 C2
Gaildorf D 74 E6
Gaillac F 33 C9
Gaillac-d'Aveyron F 34 B4
Gaillard F 31 C9
Gaillimh IRL 6 F4
Gaillon F 24 B5
Gaiļmui LV 135 D13
Gaimersheim D 75 E9
Gainsborough GB 11 E10
Gaiole in Chianti I 66 F3
Gaios GR 174 A1
Gairloch GB 2 K5
Gairo I 64 D4
Gais CH 71 C8
Gais I 72 C4
Găiseni RO 161 D7
Gaishorn A 73 A10
Gaismas LV 135 C8
Gaj SRB 159 D7
Gajanejos E 47 C7
Gajary SK 77 F11
Gakovo SRB 150 F3
Galåbodarna S 102 A6
Galambok H 149 C8
Galan F 33 D6
Gălăneşti RO 153 B7
Gálaniitu N 112 F10
Galanta SK 146 E5
Galapagar E 46 C5
Galaroza E 51 D6
Galåsen N 102 D4
Galashiels GB 5 D11
Galasjö S 107 E14
Galata BG 167 C9
Galatades GR 169 C7
Galatas GR 175 D6
Galatas GR 175 E7
Gălăteni RO 160 E6
Galaţi RO 155 C2
Galaţii Bistriţei RO 152 D4
Galati Mamertino I 59 C6
Galatin BG 165 C8
Galatina I 61 C10
Galatini GR 169 D6
Galatista GR 169 D9
Galatone I 61 C10
Gălăuţaş RO 152 D6
Galaxidi GR 174 C5
Galbally IRL 8 D6
Galbarra E 32 E1
Galbenu RO 161 C10
Gålberget S 107 D14
Gălbinaşi RO 161 C9
Galda de Jos RO 152 E3
Gâldău RO 161 E11
Gál'din N 113 E12
Galeata I 66 E4
Galende E 39 D6
Galēni LV 135 D13
Galera E 55 D7
Galéria F 37 G9
Găleşti RO 152 E5
Galewice PL 142 D5
Galgagyörk H 150 B3
Galgahéviz H 150 B4
Gâlgău RO 152 C3
Galgon F 28 F5
Gal'gunjar'ga N 113 F16
Galicea RO 160 D4
Galicea Mare RO 160 E2
Galiche BG 165 B8
Galinduste E 45 C9
Galiny PL 136 E2
Galissas GR 176 E4
Galisteo E 45 E8
Gallarate I 68 B6
Gallardon F 24 C6
Gallargues-le-Montueux F 35 C7
Galleberg N 95 C12
Gallegos de Argañan E 45 C7
Gallegos de Solmirón E 45 C10
Galleno I 66 E2
Gälleråsen S 97 D11
Gallese I 62 C2
Gallian-en-Médoc F 28 E4
Galliate I 68 C6
Gallicano I 66 D1
Gallicano nel Lazio I 62 D3
Gallin D 83 C9
Gallin D 83 C12
Gallio I 72 E4
Gallipoli I 61 C10
Gällivare S 116 D5
Gallizien A 73 C10
Gallneukirchen A 76 F6
Gällö S 103 A9
Gällstad S 91 D13
Galluccio I 60 A1
Gallur E 41 E9
Galovo BG 160 F4
Galros IRL 7 F7
Gålsjö bruk S 107 E13
Galston GB 5 D8
Galtelli I 64 C4
Galten DK 86 C5
Galterud N 96 B6
Gåltjärn S 103 A13
Gåltjärn S 103 A14
Galtström S 103 B13
Galtür A 71 D10
Galve E 42 F2
Galve de Sorbe E 47 B6
Galveias P 44 F5
Galven S 103 D11
Gálvez E 46 E4
Galway IRL 6 F4
Gama E 40 B5
Gamaches F 18 E4
Gamarde-les-Bains F 32 C4
Gamás H 149 C9
Gambara I 66 B1
Gambarie I 59 C8
Gambassi Terme I 66 E2
Gambatesa I 63 D7
Gambettola I 66 D5
Gambolò I 69 C6
Gambsheim F 27 C8
Gaming A 77 G8
Gamleby S 93 D8
Gamlingay GB 15 C8
Gamlitz A 148 C5
Gammalkroppa S 97 C11
Gammelboning S 103 E11
Gammelgården S 119 C10
Gammelgarn S 93 E13
Gammel Rye DK 86 C5
Gammelsdorf D 75 E10
Gammelstaden S 118 C8
Gammelstilla S 98 B7
Gammertingen D 27 D11
Gams CH 71 C8
Gamvik N 112 C9
Gamvik N 113 A21
Gamvik N 113 B11
Gan F 32 D5
Ganagobie F 35 B10
Gand B 19 B8
Gand B 182 C3
Gandarela P 38 F3
Gandellino I 69 B8
Ganderkesee D 17 B11
Gandesa E 42 E4
Gandesbergen D 17 C12
Gandía E 56 D4
Gandino I 69 B8
Gandra P 38 D2
Gandrup DK 86 A6
Gandvik N 114 C6
Găneasa RO 160 E4
Găneasa RO 161 D8
Găneşti RO 152 E4
Ganfei P 38 D2
Ganges F 35 C6
Gånghester S 91 D13
Gangi I 58 D5
Gângiova RO 160 F3
Gangkofen D 75 F12
Ganløse DK 87 D10
Gannat F 30 C3
Gänserndorf A 77 F11
Ganshoren B 19 C9
Gänsvik S 103 A15
Ganzlin D 83 D12
Gaoth Dobhair IRL 6 B6
Gap F 36 B4
Gaperhult S 91 B13
Gara H 150 E3
Garaballa E 47 E10
Garagarza E 32 D1
Garaguso I 60 B6
Gara Khitrino BG 167 C7
Gara Oreshets BG 159 F10
Gârbău RO 151 D11
Garbayuela E 46 F3
Garberg N 105 E10
Gârbou RO 151 C11
Gârbova RO 152 F3
Gârbovi RO 161 D9
Garbów PL 141 H6
Garbsen D 78 B6
Garching an der Alz D 75 F12
Garching bei München D 75 F10
Garchizy F 30 A3
Garcia E 42 E5
Garciaz E 45 F9
Garciems LV 135 B8
Garcihernández E 45 C10
Garcillán E 46 C4
Garčin HR 157 B9
Gârcina RO 153 D8
Garcinarro E 47 D7
Gârcov RO 160 F5
Garda I 69 B10
Gârda de Sus RO 151 E10
Gardanne F 35 D9
Gårdås S 102 E6
Gårdby S 89 B11
Garde S 93 E13
Gärde S 105 D15
Gardeja PL 138 C6
Gardelegen D 79 A9
Gardenstown GB 3 K12
Garderen NL 183 A7
Garderhouse GB 3 E14
Gardermoen N 95 B14
Gardiki GR 174 B4
Garding D 82 B5
Gärdnäs S 106 C8
Gardone Riviera I 69 B10
Gardone Val Trompia I 69 B9
Gardonne F 29 F6
Gárdony H 149 B11
Gardouch F 33 D9
Gårdsjö S 92 B4
Gardsjöbäcken S 109 F12
Gårdsjönås S 109 F11
Gårdskär S 103 E14
Gårds Köpinge S 88 D6
Gårdslösa S 89 B11
Gårdstånga S 87 D12
Gåre N 102 A1
Garein F 32 B4
Gärelehöjden S 107 D11
Garelochhead GB 4 C7
Garéoult F 36 E4
Garešnica HR 149 E7
Garessio I 37 C8
Garforth GB 11 D9
Gargalianoi GR 174 E4
Gargáligas E 45 F9
Gargallo E 42 F2
Garganta la Olla E 45 D9
Gargazzone I 72 C3
Gargilesse-Dampierre F 29 B9
Gargnano I 69 B10
Gargnäs S 107 A13
Gargogečče N 113 C20
Gargždai LT 134 E2
Garijp NL 16 B5
Garkalne LV 135 B8
Gârla Mare RO 159 E10
Garlasco I 69 C6
Gârleni RO 153 D9
Garliava LT 137 D8
Gârliciu RO 155 D2
Garlieston GB 5 F8
Garlin F 32 C5
Garlitos E 54 B2
Garlstorf D 83 D8
Garmisch-Partenkirchen D 72 B3
Garnes N 100 B3
Gârnic RO 159 D8
Garoafa RO 153 F10
Garons F 35 C7
Garoza LV 135 C7
Garpenberg S 98 B6
Garphyttan S 97 D12
Garrafe de Torio E 39 C8
Garralda E 32 E3
Garrane IRL 8 E4
Garray E 41 E7
Garrel D 17 C10
Garrison GB 6 D6
Garristown IRL 7 E10
Garrovillas E 45 E7
Garrucha E 55 E9
Garrynahine GB 2 J3
Garryvoe IRL 8 E6
Gars am Inn D 75 F11
Gars am Kamp A 77 E9
Garsås S 102 E8
Garsdale Head GB 11 C7
Gârsene LV 135 D11
Gårslev DK 86 D5
Gärsnäs S 88 D6
Garstang GB 10 D6
Garstedt D 83 D8
Garten N 104 D7
Garth GB 13 A7
Garthmyl GB 10 F5
Gartland N 105 B12
Gartow D 83 D10
Gärtringen D 27 C10
Gartz D 84 D6
Garvagh GB 4 F3
Garvagh IRL 7 E7
Garvaghy GB 7 D8
Garvald GB 5 D11
Garvamore GB 5 A8
Garvão P 50 D3
Garvard GB 4 C4
Garvary GB 7 D7
Garve GB 2 K7
Garwolin PL 141 G5
Garz D 84 B4
Gąsawa PL 138 E4
Gåsbakken N 104 E7
Gaschurn A 71 D10
Gascueña E 47 D7
Gåsholma S 103 D13
Gasjö S 97 B14
Gaskeluokt S 107 A11
Gąski PL 136 F5
Gåsnes N 112 D8
Gåsnes N 113 A13
Gasny F 24 B6
Gąsocin PL 139 E10
Gasperina I 59 B10
Gaspoltshofen A 76 F5
Gasselte NL 17 C7
Gasselternijveen NL 17 C7
Gassino Torinese I 68 C4
Gassjö S 103 B9
Gassum DK 86 B6
Gastellovo RUS 136 C4
Gastes F 32 B3
Gastouni GR 174 D3
Gastouri GR 168 E2
Gata E 45 D7
Gata de Gorgos E 56 D5
Gătaia RO 159 C7
Gatchina RUS 132 B7
Gatehouse of Fleet GB 5 F8
Gátér H 150 D4
Gateshead GB 5 F13
Gátova E 48 E3
Gattendorf A 77 F11
Gatteo a Mare I 66 D5
Gattières F 37 D6
Gattinara I 68 B5
Gau-Algesheim D 185 E9
Gauchy F 19 E7
Gaucín E 53 C6
Gauja LV 135 B9
Găujani RO 161 F7
Gaujiena LV 131 F12
Gaukönigshofen D 74 C6
Gaulstad N 105 D12
Gau-Odernheim D 185 E9
Gaupne N 100 D6
Gaurė LT 134 F4
Gausvik N 111 C11
Gautestad N 90 B2
Gauting D 75 F9
Gauto S 109 D12
Gavà E 43 E8
Gavalou GR 174 B4
Găvănoasa MD 155 B2
Gavardo I 69 B9
Gavarnie F 32 E5
Gávavencsellő H 145 G4
Gavere B 19 C8
Gavi I 37 B9
Gavião P 44 F5
Gavieze LV 134 C2
Gavik S 103 A15
Gavirate I 68 B6
Gävle S 103 E13
Gavoi I 64 C3
Gavojdia RO 159 B9
Gavorrano I 65 B3
Gavray F 23 C9
Gavrio GR 176 D4
Gavrolimni GR 174 C4
Gåvsta S 99 C9
Gaweinstal A 77 F11
Gawliki Wielkie PL 136 E5
Gaworzyce PL 81 C9
Gåxsjö S 106 D8
Gaytaninovo BG 169 B10
Gayton GB 11 F13
Gaziemir TR 177 C9
Gaziköy TR 173 C7
Gazioğlu TR 173 B8
Gaziosmanpaşa TR 173 B10
Gazolaz E 32 E2
Gazoldo degli Ippoliti I 66 B2
Gazoros GR 169 B10
Gazzo Veronese I 66 B3
Gazzuolo I 66 B2
Gbelce SK 147 F7
Gbely SK 77 E12
Gdańsk PL 138 B6
Gdinj HR 157 F6
Gdov RUS 132 D2
Gdów PL 144 D1
Gdynia PL 138 A6
Geaca RO 152 D4
Gea de Albarracín E 47 D10
Geaidnovuohppi N 113 E12
Geamăna MD 154 D4
Geashill IRL 7 F8
Geaune F 32 C5
Gebesee D 79 D8
Gebhardshain D 21 C9
Gįbice PL 85 E11
Gechingen D 187 D6
Geçkinli TR 167 F7
Geddington GB 15 C7
Géderlak H 149 C11
Gedern D 21 D12
Gedinne B 19 E10
Gedney Drove End GB 11 F12
Gèdre F 32 E6
Gedser DK 83 A11
Gedsted DK 86 B4
Gedved DK 86 D5
Geel B 19 B11
Geertruidenberg NL 16 E3
Geeste D 17 C8
Geesteren NL 183 A9
Geestgottberg D 83 E11
Geesthacht D 83 D8
Geetbets B 19 C11
Geffen NL 183 B6
Gefrees D 75 B10
Gefyra GR 169 C8
Gefyria GR 169 F7
Gegai AL 168 C2
Gegužinė LT 137 D9
Gehrde D 17 C10
Gehrden D 78 B6
Gehren D 79 E9
Geijersholm S 97 B10
Geilenkirchen D 20 C6
Geilo N 95 A8
Geiranger N 100 B6
Geisa D 78 E6
Geiselbach D 187 A7
Geiselhöring D 75 E11
Geiselwind D 75 C7
Geisenfeld D 75 E10
Geisenhausen D 75 F11
Geisenheim D 21 E9
Geising D 80 E5
Geisingen D 27 E10
Geislingen D 187 E6
Geislingen an der Steige D 74 E6
Geismar D 79 D7
Geisnes N 105 B11
Geispolsheim F 27 C8
Geistthal A 73 B11
Geithain D 79 D12
Geithus N 95 C11
Geitvågen N 108 B8
Gela I 58 E5
Gelbensande D 83 B12
Gelchsheim D 74 C7
Geldermalsen NL 16 E4
Geldern D 16 E6
Geldersheim D 75 B7
Geldrop NL 16 F5
Geleen NL 19 C12
Gelgaudiškis LT 136 C6
Gelibolu TR 172 D6
Gellénháza H 149 C7
Gelligaer GB 13 B8
Gelnhausen D 21 D12
Gelnica SK 145 F2
Gelos F 32 D5
Gelsa E 41 F11
Gelse H 149 C7
Gelsenkirchen D 17 E8
Gelsted DK 86 E5
Gelsted DK 87 E9
Geltendorf D 71 A12
Gelting D 83 A7
Geltow D 80 B3
Gelvonai LT 137 C10
Gembloux B 19 C10
Gemeaux F 26 F3
Gemenele RO 155 C1
Gémenos F 35 D10
Gemerská Hôrka SK 145 F1
Gemerská Poloma SK 145 F1
Gemert NL 16 E5
Gemla S 88 B7
Gemmingen D 187 C6
Gemona del Friuli I 73 D7
Gémozac F 28 D4
Gemünden D 21 E8
Gemünden am Main D 74 B6
Genappe B 19 C9
Genarp S 87 D12
Génave E 55 C7
Genazzano I 62 D3
Gençay F 29 C6
Gencsapáti H 149 B7
Gendrey F 26 F4
Gendringen NL 16 E6
Gendt NL 16 E5
Génelard F 30 B5
Genemuiden NL 16 C6
General-Inzovo BG 167 E6
General-Kolevo BG 155 F1
Generalski Stol HR 148 F4
General Toshevo BG 155 F2
Genestoso E 39 B7
Genêts F 23 C9
Genevad S 87 B12
Genève CH 31 C9
Genevilla E 32 E1
Genga I 67 F6
Gengenbach D 27 D9
Geniai LT 137 E8
Genisea GR 171 B7
Génissac F 28 F5
Genk B 19 C12
Genlis F 26 F3
Gennadi GR 181 D7
Gennep NL 16 E5
Genner DK 86 E4
Gennes F 23 F11
Gennes-sur-Seiche F 23 E9
Genola I 37 B7
Génolhac F 35 B6
Genoni I 64 D3
Genouillac F 29 C9
Genouillé F 29 C6
Genouilly F 24 F6
Genouilly F 30 B6
Genova I 37 C9
Genovés E 56 D4
Gensac F 28 F6
Gensingen D 185 E8
Gent B 19 B8
Genthin D 79 B11
Gentioux-Pigerolles F 29 D9
Genzano di Lucania I 60 B6
Genzano di Roma I 62 D3
Geoagiu RO 151 F11
George Enescu RO 153 A9
Georgensgmünd D 75 D9
Georgianoi GR 169 D7
Georgianoi GR 170 C6
Georgi Damyanovo BG 165 C7
Georgioupoli GR 178 E7
Georgitsi GR 174 E5
Georgsheil D 17 B8
Georgsmarienhütte D 17 D10
Ger E 33 F9
Ger F 23 C10
Ger F 32 D5
Gera D 79 E11
Geraardsbergen B 19 C8
Gerabronn D 74 D6
Gerace I 59 C9
Geraci Siculo I 58 D5
Gerakarou GR 169 C9
Geraki GR 175 F6
Gerakini GR 169 D9
Gérardmer F 27 D6
Geras A 77 E9
Gerasdorf bei Wien A 77 F10
Géraudot F 25 D11
Gerbéviller F 186 E2
Gerbrunn D 187 B8
Gerbstedt D 79 C10
Gérce H 149 B8
Gerchsheim D 74 C6
Gerdau D 83 E8
Gerena E 51 D7
Gerendás H 151 D6
Geresdlak H 149 D11
Geretsberg A 76 F3
Geretsried D 72 A3
Gérgal E 55 E7
Gergei I 64 D3
Gergeri GR 178 E8
Gerhardshofen D 75 C8
Gerindote E 46 E4
Geringswalde D 80 D3
Gerjen H 149 D11
Gerlev DK 87 D10
Gerlingen D 27 C11
Gerlos A 72 B5
Germas GR 168 D5
Germay F 26 D3
Germencik TR 177 D10
Germering D 75 F9
Germersheim D 21 F10
Gernika-Lumo E 41 B6
Gernrode D 79 C9
Gernsbach D 27 C9
Gernsheim D 187 B5
Gerola Alta I 69 A8
Gerolimenas GR 178 C3
Gerolsbach D 75 F9
Gerolstein D 21 D7
Gerolzhofen D 75 C7
Gerovo HR 67 A10
Gerpinnes B 19 D10
Gersau CH 71 D7
Gersfeld (Rhön) D 74 B6
Gersheim D 27 B7
Gersten D 17 C9
Gerstetten D 74 E7
Gerstheim F 186 E4
Gersthofen D 75 F8
Gerstungen D 79 E7
Gerswalde D 84 D5
Gerwisch D 79 B10
Gerzat F 30 D3
Gerzen D 75 E11
Gesäter S 91 B10
Gescher D 17 E8
Gesico I 64 D3
Gespunsart F 19 E10
Gessertshausen D 75 F8
Gestalgar E 48 E3
Gesté F 23 F9
Gesten DK 86 D4
Gesturi I 64 D3
Gesualdo I 60 A4
Gesunda S 102 E8
Gesves B 19 D11
Geszt H 151 D8
Gesztely H 145 G2
Geszteréd H 151 B8
Geta FIN 99 B13
Getafe E 46 D5
Getaria E 32 D1
Gétigné F 28 A3
Getinge S 87 B11
Getryggen S 103 D10
Getterum S 93 D8
Gettjärn S 97 C8
Gettorf D 83 B7
Gevelsberg D 17 F8
Gévezé F 23 D8
Gevgelija MK 169 B7
Gevrey-Chambertin F 26 F2
Gex F 31 C9
Geyer D 80 E3
Geyikli TR 171 E10
Gezavesh AL 168 B3
Gföhl A 77 E8
Ghedi I 66 B1
Ghelari RO 159 B10
Ghelinţa RO 153 F8
Ghemme I 68 B5
Gheorghe Doja RO 161 D10
Gheorghe Lazăr RO 161 D10
Gheorgheni RO 153 D7
Gherăeşti RO 153 C9
Gherăseni RO 161 C9
Gherceşti RO 160 E3
Gherghеasa RO 161 C10
Gherghiţa RO 161 D8
Gherla RO 152 C3
Gherţa Mică RO 145 H7
Ghidfalău RO 153 F7
Ghidigeni RO 153 E10
Ghidighiei MD 154 C3
Ghiffa I 68 B6
Ghilarza I 64 C2
Ghimbav RO 161 B7
Ghimeş-Făget RO 153 D8
Ghimpaţi RO 161 E7
Ghindari RO 152 E5
Ghioroc RO 151 E8
Ghioroiu RO 160 D3
Ghiroda RO 151 F7
Ghislenghien B 19 C8
Ghisonaccia F 37 G10
Ghisoni F 37 G10
Ghizela RO 151 F8
Ghyvelde F 18 B6
Gialtra GR 175 B6
Giannades GR 168 E2
Giannitsa GR 169 C7
Giannouli GR 169 E7
Giano dell'Umbria I 62 B3
Giardini-Naxos I 59 D7
Giarmata RO 151 F7
Giarratana I 59 E6
Giarre I 59 D7
Giat F 29 D10
Giave I 64 C2
Giaveno I 31 E11
Giba I 64 E2
Gibellina Nuova I 58 D2
Gibostad N 111 B15
Gibraleón E 51 E6
Gibraltar GBZ 53 D6
Giby PL 136 E7
Ģibzde LV 134 B4
Gideå S 107 E15
Gideå bruk S 107 E16
Gideåkroken S 107 C12
Gidle PL 143 E7
Giebelstadt D 74 C6
Gieboldehausen D 79 C7
Gieczno PL 143 C7
Giedraičiai LT 137 C11
Gielniów PL 141 H2
Gielow D 83 C13
Gien F 25 E8
Giengen an der Brenz D 75 E7
Giera RO 159 C6
Gierle B 182 C5
Giersleben D 79 C10
Gierstädt D 79 D8
Gierzwałd PL 139 C9
Gießen D 21 C11
Gieten NL 17 B7
Gietrzwałd PL 139 C9
Gièvres F 24 F6
Giffnock GB 5 D8
Gifford GB 5 D11
Gifhorn D 79 B8
Gigean F 35 C6
Gigen BG 160 F4
Gighera RO 160 F3
Giglio Castello I 65 C3
Gignac F 35 C6
Gignac F 35 C10
Gignod I 31 D11
Gijón E 39 A8
Ģikši LV 135 B10
Gilău RO 151 D11
Gilching D 75 F9
Gilena E 53 B7
Gilette F 37 D6
Gilford GB 7 D10
Gilleleje DK 87 C10
Gillenfeld D 21 D7
Gillhov S 102 A8
Gillingham GB 13 C10
Gillingham GB 15 E10
Gilling West GB 11 C8
Gilly-sur-Isère F 31 D9
Gilly-sur-Loire F 30 B4
Gilmerton GB 5 C9
Gilså N 105 E11
Gilserberg D 21 C12
Gilsland GB 5 F11
Gilten D 82 E7
Gilwern GB 13 B8
Gilze NL 16 E3
Gimåt S 107 E15
Gimdalen S 103 A10
Gimigliano I 59 B10
Gimo S 99 B10
Gimont F 33 C7
Gimouille F 30 B3
Gimsøy N 110 D7
Ginasservis F 35 C10
Ginestas F 34 D4
Gingelom B 19 C11
Gingen an der Fils D 187 D8
Gingst D 84 B4
Ginkūnai LT 134 E6
Ginoles F 33 E10
Ginosa I 61 B7
Ginostra I 59 B7
Ginsheim D 185 E9
Gintsi BG 165 C7
Giões P 50 E4
Gioi I 60 C4
Gioia dei Marsi I 62 D5
Gioia del Colle I 61 B7
Gioia Sannitica I 60 A2
Gioia Tauro I 59 C8
Gioiosa Ionica I 59 C9
Gioiosa Marea I 59 C6
Giornico CH 71 E7
Giovinazzo I 61 A7
Ģipka LV 130 F5
Giraltovce SK 145 E4
Girancourt F 26 D5
Girasole I 64 D4
Girifalco I 59 B9
Girişu de Criş RO 151 C8
Girkalnis LT 134 F6
Giroc RO 159 B7
Giromagny F 27 E6
Girona E 43 D9
Gironde-sur-Dropt F 32 A5
Gironella E 43 C7
Giroussens F 33 C9
Girov RO 153 D9
Girvan GB 4 E7
Gislaved S 88 A5
Gislev DK 86 E7
Gislinge DK 87 D9
Gislövs strandmark S 87 E12
Gisløy N 110 C9
Gisors F 18 F4
Gissi I 63 C7
Gisslarbo S 97 C14
Gistad S 92 C7
Gistel B 18 B6
Gistrup DK 86 B5
Giswil CH 70 D6

Gittelde D 79 C7
Gittun S 109 D16
Giubega RO 160 E2
Giubiasco CH 69 A7
Giugliano in Campania I 60 B2
Giulești RO 152 B3
Giuliano di Roma I 62 D4
Giulianova I 62 B5
Giulvăz RO 159 B6
Giuncugnano I 66 D1
Giurgeni RO 155 D1
Giurgița RO 160 E3
Giurgiu RO 161 F7
Giurgiulești MD 155 C2
Giuvărăști RO 160 F5
Give DK 86 D4
Givet F 19 D10
Givors F 30 D6
Givry B 19 D9
Givry F 30 B6
Givry-en-Argonne F 25 C12
Givskud DK 86 D4
Gižai LT 136 D7
Giżałki PL 142 B4
Gizeux F 23 F12
Giżycko PL 136 E4
Gizzeria I 59 B9
Gjakovë RKS 163 E9
Gjærnes N 90 B5
Gjegjan AL 163 E9
Gjegjan AL 163 F9
Gjengstø N 104 E6
Gjerde N 100 C6
Gjerdebakken N 113 C11
Gjerdrum N 95 B14
Gjerlev DK 86 B6
Gjermungshamn N 94 B3
Gjern DK 86 C5
Gjerrild DK 87 C7
Gjerstad N 90 B5
Gjersvik N 105 B14
Gjesing DK 86 C6
Gjesvær N 113 A15
Gjevaldshaugen N 101 D15
Gjilan RKS 164 E3
Gjirokastër AL 168 D3
Gjógv FO 2 A3
Gjøl DK 86 A5
Gjøljelia N 104 D7
Gjølme N 104 E7
Gjonaj RKS 163 E10
Gjonëm AL 168 A2
Gjøra N 101 A10
Gjorm AL 168 D2
Gjøvåg N 94 B2
Gjøvik N 101 E13
Gjurakoc RKS 163 D9
Gjuvberget N 102 E3
Gkoritsa GR 175 E6
Gladbeck D 17 E7
Gladenbach D 21 C11
Gladsaxe DK 87 D10
Gladstad N 108 E2
Glainans F 26 F6
Glamis GB 5 B11
Glamoč BIH 157 D6
Glåmos N 101 A14
Glamsbjerg DK 86 E6
Glandage F 35 A10
Glandon F 29 E8
Glandore IRL 8 E4
Glandorf D 17 D10
Glanegg A 73 C9
Glanerbrug NL 17 D7
Glanshammar S 97 D13
Glanworth IRL 8 D6
Glarryford GB 4 F4
Glarus CH 71 C8
Glasbury GB 13 A8
Glasgow GB 5 D8
Gläshütten D 21 D10
Glashütten D 75 C9
Glaslough IRL 7 D9
Glassan IRL 7 F7
Glastonbury GB 13 C9
Glaubitz D 80 D4
Glauchau D 79 E12
Glava BG 165 C9
Glava S 97 C8
Glava glasbruk S 96 C7
Glavan BG 166 E6
Glăvănești RO 153 E10
Glavanovtsi BG 164 D6
Glavatićevo BIH 157 F9
Glavice HR 157 E6
Glavičice BIH 157 C11
Glăvile RO 160 D4
Glavinitsa BG 161 F9
Glavki GR 171 B7
Gleann Cholm Cille IRL 6 C5
Gleann Doimhin IRL 7 C7
Gleann na Muaidhe IRL 6 D3
Gledića SRB 163 C9
Glein N 108 D4
Gleina D 79 D10
Gleisdorf A 148 B5
Gleizé F 30 D6
Glejbjerg DK 86 D3
Glemsford GB 15 C10
Glen S 102 A6
Glenade IRL 6 D6
Glenamaddy IRL 6 E5
Glenamoy IRL 6 D3
Glenariff GB 4 E4
Glenarm GB 4 F5
Glenavy GB 7 C10
Glenbarr GB 4 D5
Glenbeg GB 4 B5
Glenbeigh IRL 8 D3
Glencaple GB 5 E9
Glencar IRL 6 D6
Glencoe GB 4 B6
Glencolumbkille IRL 6 C5
Glendowan IRL 7 C7
Gleneagles GB 5 C9
Glenealy IRL 7 G10
Gleneely IRL 4 E2
Glenegedale GB 4 D4
Glenelg GB 2 L5
Glenfield GB 11 F9
Glenfinnan GB 4 B6
Glengarriff IRL 8 E3
Glengavlen IRL 7 D7
Glenhead GB 4 E2
Glenluce GB 4 F7
Glenmore IRL 9 D8
Glenoe GB 4 F5
Glenrothes GB 5 C10
Glenties IRL 6 C6
Glère F 27 F6
Glesborg DK 87 C7
Gletsch CH 71 D6
Glewitz D 84 B3
Glibaći MNE 163 C7
Glimåkra S 88 C6
Glimboca RO 159 C9
Glin IRL 8 C4
Glina HR 148 F6
Glina RO 161 E8
Glinde D 83 C8
Glindow D 79 B12
Glinjeni MD 153 B11
Glinojeck PL 139 E9
Glinsce IRL 6 F3
Glinsk IRL 6 F3
Glinton GB 11 F11
Glissjöberg S 102 B7
Gliwice PL 142 F6
Gllamnik RKS 164 D3
Glloboçicë RKS 164 E3
Gllogoc RKS 163 D10
Glodeanu-Sărat RO 161 D9
Glodeanu-Siliștea RO 161 D9
Glodeni MD 153 B11
Glodeni RO 152 D5
Glodeni RO 161 C6
Glödnitz A 73 C9
Glodowa PL 85 C11
Glodzhevo BG 161 F8
Gloggnitz A 148 A5
Glogova RO 159 D10
Glogovac SRB 159 E7
Głogów PL 81 C10
Głogówek PL 142 F4
Głogów Małopolski PL 144 C4
Glogowo PL 138 D6
Glomfjord N 108 C6
Glommen S 87 B10
Glommersträsk S 107 A17
Glonn D 75 G10
Glória P 50 B4
Glória do Ribatejo P 44 F3
Glos-la-Ferrière F 24 C4
Glossa GR 175 A8
Glössbo S 103 D12
Glossop GB 11 E8
Glöte S 102 B5
Glöthe D 79 C10
Glottra S 92 B6
Gloucester GB 13 B10
Glounthaune IRL 8 E6
Głowaczów PL 141 G4
Główczyce PL 85 A12
Glowe D 84 A4
Glöwen D 83 E12
Głowno PL 143 C8
Gložan SRB 158 C4
Glozhene BG 160 F3
Glozhene BG 165 C9
Głubczyce PL 142 F4
Głuchołazy PL 142 F3
Głuchów PL 141 G2
Glücksburg (Ostsee) D 82 A7
Glückstadt D 17 A12
Glud DK 86 D5
Gludsted DK 86 C4
Gluggvasshaugen N 108 E5
Glumslöv S 87 D11
Glumsø DK 87 E9
Glusburn GB 11 D8
Glušci SRB 158 D4
Głuszyca PL 81 E10
Glyfa GR 175 B7
Glyfada GR 175 D8
Glyki GR 168 F4
Glyn Ceiriog GB 10 F5
Glyngøre DK 86 B3
Glynn GB 4 F5
Glynn IRL 9 D9
Glynneath GB 13 B7
Gmünd A 73 C8
Gmünd A 77 E7
Gmund am Tegernsee D 72 A4
Gmunden A 73 A8
Gnarp S 103 B13
Gnarrenburg D 17 B12
Gneisenaustadt Schildau D 80 D3
Gnesta S 93 A10
Gniebing A 148 C5
Gniew PL 138 C6
Gniewkowo PL 138 E5
Gniewoszów PL 141 H5
Gnieździska PL 143 E9
Gniezno PL 85 E13
Gnisvärd S 93 D12
Gnocchetta I 66 C5
Gnoien D 83 C13
Gnojna PL 81 E12
Gnojnice BIH 157 F8
Gnojnik PL 144 D2
Gnojno PL 143 E10
Gnosall GB 11 F7
Gnosjö S 91 E14
Gnotzheim D 75 D8
Gnutz D 83 B7
Göbel TR 173 D9
Gobowen GB 10 F5
Göçbeyli TR 177 A9
Göcek TR 181 C9
Göçerler TR 173 B8
Goch D 16 E6
Gochsheim D 75 B7
Goczałkowice-Zdrój PL 147 B7
Göd H 150 B3
Godačica SRB 159 F6
Godal N 95 D11
Godalming GB 15 E7
Godby FIN 99 B13
Goddelau D 187 B6
Goddelsheim (Lichtenfels) D 21 B11
Godeanu RO 159 D10
Godech BG 165 C7
Godega di Sant'Urbano I 72 E5
Godegård S 92 B6
Godelleta E 48 F3
Godeni RO 160 C5
Goderville F 18 E1
Godiasco I 37 B10
Godimilje BIH 157 E11
Godinești RO 159 C10
Godinje MNE 163 E7
Godkowo PL 139 B8
Godmanchester GB 15 C8
Gödöllő H 150 B3
Godovič SLO 73 E9
Gödre H 149 D9
Godstone GB 15 E8
Goduš BIH 157 C10
Godziesze Wielkie PL 142 C5
Godziszów PL 144 B5
Goedereede NL 16 E1
Goes NL 16 E1
Göfritz an der Wild A 77 E8
Göggingen D 187 D8
Gogolin PL 142 F5
Gogołów PL 144 D4
Gogoșari RO 161 F7
Gogoșu RO 159 E10
Gogoșu RO 160 E2
Göhl D 83 B9
Gohor RO 153 E10
Gohrau D 79 C11
Göhrde D 83 D9
Göhren D 84 B5
Göhren-Lebbin D 83 D13
Goian MD 154 C4
Goicea RO 160 F3
Goiești RO 160 E3
Goirle NL 16 E4
Góis P 44 D4
Goito I 66 B2
Goizueta E 32 D2
Gojść PL 143 D7
Gökçealan TR 177 D9
Gökçebayir TR 171 E10
Gökçedağ TR 173 E10
Gökçeören TR 181 B9
Gökçeyazi TR 173 E8
Gokels D 82 B6
Gökova TR 181 B8
Göktepe TR 181 B9
Göktürk TR 173 B10
Gol N 101 E9
Gola HR 149 D8
Gołąb PL 141 H5
Golac SLO 67 A9
Golăiești RO 153 C11
Golaj AL 163 E9
Gołańcz PL 85 E12
Gołaszyn PL 141 G6
Golbey F 26 D5
Gölby FIN 99 B13
Gölcük TR 173 F8
Golčův Jeníkov CZ 77 C8
Golczewo PL 85 C7
Goldach CH 71 C8
Gołdap PL 136 E5
Goldbeck D 83 E11
Goldberg D 83 C12
Goldegg A 73 B7
Goldelund D 82 A6
Golden IRL 9 D7
Golden Pot GB 14 E7
Goldenstedt D 17 C10
Goleen IRL 8 F3
Golegã P 44 F4
Golemanovo BG 159 F9
Golema Rakovitsa BG 165 D8
Golema Rečica MK 163 F10
Golenice PL 85 E7
Goleniów PL 85 C7
Golesh BG 161 F11
Golești RO 153 F10
Golești RO 160 C4
Golfo Aranci I 64 B4
Golina PL 142 B5
Golinhac F 33 A11
Goliševa LV 133 C3
Gölköy TR 177 E9
Gölle H 149 D10
Göllersdorf A 77 F10
Göllheim D 186 B5
Göllin D 83 C11
Gollin D 84 D5
Golling an der Salzach A 73 A7
Göllingen D 79 D9
Gollmitz D 84 D5
Golmes E 42 D5
Golnik SLO 73 D9
Gøløse DK 87 D10
Golovkino RUS 136 D3
Golpejas E 45 B9
Gols A 77 G11
Golspie GB 3 K9
Golßen D 80 C5
Golubac SRB 159 D8
Golub-Dobrzyń PL 138 D7
Golubić HR 156 D5
Golubinje SRB 159 D9
Golyama Zhelyazna BG 165 D9
Golyam Izvor BG 166 F5
Golyam Manastir BG 166 E6
Golyamo Belovo BG 165 E8
Gölyazi TR 173 D9
Gołymin-Ośrodek PL 139 E10
Golzow D 79 B12
Gomadingen D 27 D11
Gómara E 41 E7
Gomaringen D 187 E7
Gomati GR 169 D10
Gomba H 150 C4
Gömeç TR 173 F6
Gomecello E 45 B9
Gomes Aires P 50 D3
Gomirje HR 67 B11
Gommern D 79 B10
Gomotartsi BG 159 E10
Gomunice PL 143 D7
Gönc H 145 G3
Gonçalo P 44 D6
Gencelin F 31 E8
Gondelsheim D 187 C6
Gondershausen D 185 D7
Gondomar E 38 D2
Gondomar P 44 B3
Gondorf D 21 D8
Gondrecourt-le-Château F 26 C4
Gondreville F 26 C4
Gondrin F 33 C6
Gönen TR 173 D8
Gonfaron F 36 E4
Gonfreville-l'Orcher F 18 E1
Goni I 64 D3
Goniądz PL 140 D7
Gonnesa I 64 E1
Gonnoi GR 169 E7
Gonnosfanadiga I 64 E2
Gonnosnò I 64 D2
Gonsans F 26 F5
Gönyű H 149 A9
Gonzaga I 66 C2
Goodwick GB 12 A5
Goole GB 11 D10
Goonhavern GB 12 E4
Goor NL 17 D7
Gopegi E 40 C6
Göppingen D 74 E6
Gor E 55 E7
Góra PL 81 C11
Góra PL 139 E9
Gorafe E 55 E6
Goraj PL 144 B6
Góra Kalwaria PL 141 G4
Goranu RO 160 C4
Góra Puławska PL 141 H5
Gorawino PL 85 C8
Goražde BIH 157 E10
Gorban RO 153 D12
Görbeháza H 151 B7
Görcsöny H 149 E10
Gördalen S 102 C3
Gordaliza del Pino E 39 D9
Gordes F 35 C9
Gordinești MD 153 A10
Gørding DK 86 E3
Gordola CH 69 A6
Gordon GB 5 D11
Gordona I 69 A7
Gorebridge GB 5 D10
Görece TR 177 C9
Gorenja Straža SLO 73 E11
Gorenja vas SLO 73 D9
Gorey IRL 9 C10
Görgeteg H 149 D8
Gorgoglione I 60 C6
Gorgonzola I 69 B7
Gorgota RO 161 D8
Gorgova RO 155 C4
Gorica BIH 157 D7
Gorica BIH 157 F7
Gorica BIH 162 D5
Gorica MNE 163 E7
Goričan HR 149 D7
Gorinchem NL 16 E3
Gorino I 66 C5
Gorishovë AL 168 C2
Görisried D 71 B11
Goritsa BG 167 D9
Goritsa BG 167 D9
Göritz D 84 D5
Gorizia I 73 E8
Gorleben D 83 D10
Gørlev DK 87 D8
Gorlice PL 144 D3
Görlitz D 81 D7
Gorlosen D 83 D10
Gormanston IRL 7 E10
Gormanstown IRL 7 E10
Gormaz E 40 E6
Görmin D 84 C4
Gorna Belica MK 164 F3
Gorna Beshovitsa BG 165 C8
Gorna Breznitsa BG 165 F7
Gorna Koznitsa BG 165 E6
Gorna Kremena BG 165 C8
Gorna Mitropoliya BG 165 C9
Gorna Oryakhovitsa BG 166 C5
Gorna Studena BG 166 C4
Gornau D 80 E4
Gorna Vasilitsa BG 165 E8
Gorna Verenitsa BG 165 C7
Gornești RO 152 D5
Gornet RO 161 C8
Gornet-Cricov RO 161 C8
Gorni Dŭbnik BG 165 C9
Gorni Lom BG 165 C6
Gornja Golubinja BIH 157 D8
Gornja Grabovica BIH 157 E8
Gornja Gračenica HR 149 E7
Gornja Ljubata SRB 164 D5
Gornja Ljuta BIH 157 E9
Gornjane SRB 159 E9
Gornja Ploča HR 156 D4
Gornja Radgona SLO 148 C5
Gornja Sanica BIH 157 C6
Gornja Slatina BIH 157 C9
Gornja Toponica SRB 164 C4
Gornja Trnava SRB 159 E6
Gornja Tuzla BIH 157 C10
Gornje Jelenje HR 67 B10
Gornje Peulje BIH 156 D6
Gornje Ratkovo BIH 157 C6
Gornje Vratno HR 148 D6
Gornji Agići BIH 156 C5
Gornji Babin Potok HR 156 C4
Gornji Breg SRB 150 F5
Gornji Dolac HR 157 E6
Gornji Grad SLO 73 D10
Gornji Humac HR 157 F6
Gornji Kosinj HR 156 C3
Gornji Lapac HR 156 C5
Gornji Lukavac BIH 157 F9
Gornji Majkovi HR 162 D4
Gornji Malovan BIH 157 E7
Gornji Matejevac SRB 164 C4
Gornji Milanovac SRB 158 E5
Gornji Očcauš BIH 157 C8
Gornji Podgradći BIH 157 B7
Gornji Rajić HR 157 B7
Gornji Ribnik BIH 157 D6
Gornji Tkalec HR 149 E6
Gornji Vakuf BIH 157 E8
Górno PL 143 E10
Gorno Ablanovo BG 161 F7
Gorno Aleksandrovo BG 167 D7
Gorno Orizari MK 164 F4
Gorno Ozirovo BG 165 C7
Gorno Pavlikene BG 165 C10
Goro I 66 C5
Gorobinci MK 164 F4
Górowo Iławeckie PL 136 E2
Gorredijk NL 16 B6
Gorreto I 37 B10
Gorron F 23 D10
Görsbach D 79 D8
Gorseinon GB 12 B6
Görsk PL 138 D5
Gorska Polyana BG 167 E7
Gorski Izvor BG 166 E4
Gorsko Novo Selo BG 166 C5
Gorssel NL 16 D6
Gort IRL 6 F5
Gortahork IRL 6 B6
Gort an Choirce IRL 6 B6
Gortavoy Bridge GB 7 C9
Gorteen IRL 6 E5
Gorteen IRL 6 E6
Gorteeny IRL 6 F6
Gortin GB 4 F2
Goruia RO 159 C8
Görükle TR 173 D10
Gorun BG 167 B10
Görvik S 106 D9
Görwihl D 27 E9
Gorxheimertal D 21 E11
Gorzanów PL 77 B11
Gorze F 26 B5
Görzig D 79 C10
Görzke D 79 B11
Gorzkowice PL 143 D8
Gorzków-Osada PL 144 B7
Górzna PL 85 D11
Górzno PL 139 D8
Górzno PL 141 G5
Gorzów Śląski PL 142 D5
Gorzów Wielkopolski PL 85 E8
Górzyca PL 81 B7
Górzyca PL 85 C8
Gorzyce PL 144 B4
Gorzyce PL 144 C6
Gorzyce PL 146 B6
Gorzyń PL 81 A9
Górzyn PL 81 C7
Gosaldo I 72 D4
Gosau A 73 A8
Gosberton GB 11 F11
Gościeradów Ukazowy PL 144 B4
Gościm PL 85 E9
Gościno PL 85 B9
Gósciszów PL 81 D8
Gosdorf A 148 C5
Gosë AL 168 B2
Gosfield GB 15 D10
Gosforth GB 5 E13
Gosforth GB 10 C5
Goslar D 79 C7
Goślice PL 139 E8
Gosné F 23 D9
Gospić HR 156 C3
Gospođinci SRB 158 C4
Gosport GB 13 D12
Gössäter S 91 B13
Gossau CH 27 F11
Gössendorf A 148 C5
Gößl A 73 A8
Gostavățu RO 160 E5
Gostil AL 163 E9
Gostilitsa BG 166 C4
Gostinari RO 161 E8
Gostinu RO 161 E8
Gostivar MK 163 F10
Göstling an der Ybbs A 73 A10
Gostoviči BIH 157 D9
Gostycyn PL 138 D4
Gostyń PL 81 C12
Gostyń PL 85 B7
Gostynin PL 139 F7
Goszcz PL 142 D3
Goszczanów PL 142 C6
Goszczyn PL 141 G3
Göta S 91 C11
Göteborg S 91 D10
Götene S 91 B13
Gotești MD 154 E2
Gotha D 79 E8
Gothem S 93 D13
Götlunda S 97 D14
Gotse Delchev BG 169 A10
Gottböle FIN 122 F6
Gotteszell D 76 E3
Gottfrieding D 75 E12
Göttingen D 78 C6
Gottmadingen D 27 E10
Gottne S 107 E14
Gøttrup DK 86 A4
Götzis A 71 C9
Gouarec F 22 D5
Gouda NL 16 D3
Goudswaard NL 182 B4
Gouesnou F 22 D3
Gouhenans F 26 E5
Goult F 35 C9
Goumenissa GR 169 C7
Goumois F 27 F6
Gourdan-Polignan F 33 D7
Gourdon F 29 F8
Gourdon GB 5 B12
Gourette F 32 E5
Gourgançon F 25 C11
Gouria GR 174 C3
Gourin F 22 D4
Gournay-en-Bray F 18 F4
Goussainville F 25 B7
Gout-Rossignol F 29 E6
Gouveia P 44 D5
Gouvia GR 168 E2
Gouvieux F 25 B7
Gouvy B 20 D5
Gouzon F 29 C10
Gove P 44 B4
Goveđari HR 162 D3
Govedartsi BG 165 E7
Goven F 23 D8
Gowarczów PL 141 H2
Gowidlino PL 138 B4
Goworowo PL 139 E12
Gowran IRL 9 C8
Goxhill GB 11 D11
Göynükbelen TR 173 E11
Gózd PL 141 H4
Gozdnica PL 81 D8
Gozdowice PL 84 E6
Gözsüz TR 173 C6
Gozzano I 68 B5
Graal-Müritz D 83 B12
Grab BIH 157 F10
Grab BIH 162 D5
Graben-Neudorf D 187 C5
Grabica PL 143 D8
Grabjan AL 168 C2
Grabo S 91 D11
Grabovac HR 157 F7
Grabovci SRB 158 D4
Grabovica SRB 159 E10
Grabow D 83 D11
Grabów PL 143 B7
Grabowiec PL 143 D11
Grabowiec PL 144 B8
Grabówka PL 140 D8
Grabów nad Pilicą PL 141 G4
Grabów nad Prosną PL 142 C5
Grabownica Starzeńska PL 144 D5
Grabówno PL 85 D12
Grabowno Wielkie PL 142 D3
Grabowo PL 136 E5
Grabowo PL 139 D13
Grabs CH 71 C8
Gračac HR 156 D4
Gračanica BIH 157 C9
Gračanica BIH 157 D10
Gračanica BIH 157 E8
Graçay F 24 F6
Grâce-Hollogne B 19 C11
Grâces F 22 C5
Gračianica BIH 157 E8
Gracze PL 142 E4
Grad SLO 148 C6
Gradac BIH 162 D5
Gradac HR 157 F7
Gradac SLO 148 E4
Gradačac BIH 157 C9
Gradara I 67 E6
Grăddö S 99 C12
Gradec HR 149 E6
Gradec MK 169 B8
Gradefes E 39 C9
Gradets BG 159 E10
Gradets BG 167 D7
Gradevo BG 165 F7
Gradina BG 166 C5
Gradina BG 166 E4
Gradina BIH 157 F9
Gradina SRB 163 C9
Grădinari RO 159 C8
Grădinari RO 160 D4
Grădinița MD 154 D5
Gradishte BG 166 C4
Gradište HR 157 B10
Gradište SRB 164 B5
Gradište SRB 164 C5
Grădiștea RO 160 D3
Grădiștea RO 161 C10
Grădiștea RO 161 D8
Grădiștea RO 161 E10
Gradište Bekteško HR 149 F9
Gradnitsa BG 165 D10
Grado E 39 B7
Grado I 73 E7
Gradö S 97 B15
Gradojević SRB 158 D4
Gradoli I 62 B1
Gradsko MK 169 A6
Gradskovo SRB 159 E9
Graena E 55 E6
Græsted DK 87 C10
Gräfelfing D 75 F9
Grafenau D 76 E4
Gräfenberg D 75 C9
Gräfendorf D 74 B6
Grafendorf bei Hartberg A 148 B5
Gräfenhainichen D 79 C11
Grafenhausen D 27 E9
Grafenrheinfeld D 187 B9
Gräfenroda D 79 E8
Grafenstein A 73 C9
Grafenwöhr D 75 C10
Grafenworth A 77 F9
Graffignano I 62 B2
Grafhorst D 79 B8
Graf Ignatievo BG 165 E10
Gräfinau-Angstedt D 79 E9
Grafing bei München D 75 F10
Grafrath D 75 F9
Gräfsnäs S 91 C11
Gräftåvallen S 105 E15
Gragnano I 60 B3
Grahovac MNE 163 D6
Grahovo MNE 163 D6
Grahovo SLO 73 D8
Gráig na Manach IRL 9 C9
Graigue IRL 9 C9
Graiguenamanagh IRL 9 C9
Grain GB 15 E10
Grainau D 71 C12
Grainet D 76 E5
Graissac F 30 F2
Graissessac F 34 C5
Graja de Iniesta E 47 E9
Grajal de Campos E 39 D9
Grajduri RO 153 D11
Grajewo PL 140 C6
Grällsta S 98 C7
Grålum N 95 D14
Gram DK 86 E4
Gramada BG 159 F10
Gramastetten A 76 F6
Gramat F 29 F9
Gramatikovo BG 167 E9
Grambow D 84 D6
Grămești RO 153 B8
Gramków D 83 C10
Grammatiko GR 169 F7
Grammendorf D 83 B13
Grammenitsa GR 174 A2
Grammeno GR 168 E4
Grammichele I 59 E6
Gramsbergen NL 17 C7
Gramsh AL 168 C3
Gramzda LV 134 D3
Gramzow D 84 D6
Gran N 95 B13
Granabeg IRL 7 F10
Granada E 53 B9
Granån S 119 C10
Granard IRL 7 E8
Granarolo dell'Emilia I 66 C3
Granåsen S 107 C11
Granátula de Calatrava E 54 B5
Granberg S 118 D3
Granberget N 102 D3
Granbergsdal S 97 D12
Granbergsträsk S 107 A17
Grančarevo BIH 162 D5
Grancey-le-Château-Nouvelle F 26 E3
Grandas E 39 B6
Grandcamp-Maisy F 23 B9
Grand-Champ F 22 E6
Grand-Couronne F 18 F3
Grande-Synthe F 18 B5
Grande-Vabre F 33 A10
Grand-Fort-Philippe F 18 B5
Grand-Fougeray F 23 E8
Grândola P 50 C2
Grandpré F 19 F10
Grandpuits-Bailly-Carrois F 25 C8
Grandrieu F 30 F4
Grandris F 30 C5
Grandson CH 31 B10
Grandtully GB 5 B9
Grandvelle-et-le-Perrenot F 26 E5
Grandvillars F 27 E6
Grandvillers F 26 D6
Grandvilliers F 18 E4
Grañén E 41 E11
Grangärde S 97 B12
Grange IRL 7 E10
Grange IRL 9 E7
Grangemouth GB 5 C9
Grange-over-Sands GB 10 C6
Grängesberg S 97 B13
Granges-sur-Vologne F 27 D6
Grängshyttan S 97 C12
Grängsjö S 103 B13
Granhult S 116 D7
Granica BIH 162 D5
Grăniceri RO 151 D7
Grănicești RO 153 B8
Graninge S 107 E11
Granitola-Torretta I 58 D2
Granitsa GR 174 A4
Granja P 51 C5
Granja de Moreruela E 39 E8
Granja de Torrehermosa E 51 C8
Granja do Ulmeiro P 44 D3
Gränna S 92 C4
Grannäs S 107 A10
Grannäs S 109 E13
Granneset N 108 E6
Granö S 107 C16
Granollers E 43 D8
Granön S 103 D13
Granowiec PL 142 D4
Granowo PL 81 B11
Granschütz D 79 D11
Gransee D 84 D4
Granselet S 109 E14
Gränsgård S 109 F15
Gransjö S 107 A15
Gransjön S 103 B11
Grånssjö S 108 F8
Grantham GB 11 F10
Grantown-on-Spey GB 3 L9
Granträsk S 107 C14
Granträskmark S 118 D6
Grantshouse GB 5 D12
Granum S 88 C7
Granvik S 92 B5
Granville F 23 C8
Granvin N 94 A5
Grapska BIH 157 C9
Gräs S 97 C10
Grasbakken N 114 C5
Gräsgård S 89 C11
Grasleben D 79 B9
Gräsmarken S 97 B8
Grasmere GB 10 C5
Gräsmyr S 107 D17
Grassåmoen N 105 C14
Grassano I 60 B6
Grassau D 72 A5
Grasse F 36 D5
Grassington GB 11 C8
Grässjö S 103 A10
Gråsten DK 86 F5
Grästorp S 91 C12
Gratallops E 42 E5
Gratangsbotn N 111 C14
Gratens F 33 D8
Gratia RO 161 E6
Gratini GR 171 B9
Gratkorn A 148 B4
Grātnäs S 107 E14
Gråträsk S 118 D3
Gratteri I 58 D4
Gratwein A 148 B4
Grauballe DK 86 C5
Graulhet F 33 C9
Graupa D 80 D5
Graus E 42 C4
Grávalos E 41 D8
Gravberget N 102 E3
Gravbränna S 106 D7
Gravdal N 110 D6
Grave NL 16 E5
Gravedona I 69 A7
Gravelines F 18 C5
Gravellona Toce I 68 B5
Gravelotte F 26 B5
Gravens DK 86 D4
Grävenwiesbach D 21 D10
Grāveri LV 133 D2
Gravesend GB 15 E9
Gravia GR 174 B5
Gravigny F 24 B5
Grävika N 100 E1
Gravina di Catania I 59 D7
Gravina in Puglia I 61 B6
Gravmark S 118 F4
Gray F 26 F4
Grayan-et-l'Hôpital F 28 E3
Grays GB 15 E9
Graz A 148 B4
Grazalema E 53 C6
Grążawy PL 139 D8
Grazzanise I 60 A2
Grčak SRB 163 C10
Grdelica SRB 164 D5
Greaca RO 161 E8
Greåker N 95 D14
Grèalou F 33 A9
Great Baddow GB 15 D10
Great Bircham GB 15 B10
Great Clifton GB 5 F10
Great Cornard GB 15 C10
Great Dunmow GB 15 D9
Great Glen GB 11 F9
Great Gonerby GB 11 F10
Greatham GB 11 B9
Great Harwood GB 11 D7
Great Haywood GB 11 F8
Great Linford GB 15 C7
Great Malvern GB 13 A10
Great Ponton GB 11 F10
Great Salkeld GB 5 F11
Great Shelford GB 15 C9
Great Torrington GB 12 D6
Great Wakering GB 15 D10
Great Yarmouth GB 15 B12
Grebănu RO 161 C9
Grebaštica HR 156 E4
Grebbestad S 91 B9
Grebci BIH 162 D5
Grebenac SRB 159 D7
Grebendorf (Meinhard) D 79 D7
Grebenhain D 21 D12
Grebenișu de Câmpie RO 152 D4
Grebenstein D 21 B12
Grebin D 83 B8
Grjbków PL 141 F5
Grebo S 92 C7
Grjbocin PL 138 D6
Grjboszów PL 143 F10
Grjbów PL 144 B4
Greccio I 62 C3
Grecești RO 160 E2
Greci I 60 A4
Greci RO 159 D11
Gredelj BIH 157 F10
Greding D 75 D9
Gredstedbro DK 86 E3
Greencastle GB 4 F2
Greencastle GB 7 D10
Greencastle IRL 4 E3
Greene D 78 C6
Greengairs GB 5 D9
Greenhead GB 5 F11
Greenigo GB 3 H10
Greenisland GB 4 F5
Greenlaw GB 5 D12
Greenloaning GB 5 C9
Greenock GB 4 D7
Greenodd GB 10 C5
Greenore IRL 7 D10
Greenway GB 12 B5
Greggio I 68 C5
Greifenburg A 73 C7
Greifendorf D 80 D4
Greifenstein D 21 C10
Greiffenberg D 84 D5
Greifswald D 84 B4
Grein A 77 F7

Greiveri LV 135 B11
Greiz D 79 E11
Grejs DK 86 D5
Gremersdorf D 83 B9
Grenaa DK 87 C7
Grenade F 33 C8
Grenade-sur-l'Adour F 32 C5
Grenant F 26 E4
Grenås S 106 D8
Grenchen CH 27 F7
Grenči LV 134 C5
Grenoble F 31 E8
Grense-Jakobselv N 114 D9
Gréoux-les-Bains F 35 C10
Gresenhorst D 83 B12
Gress GB 2 J4
Gressan I 31 D11
Gresse D 83 D9
Gressoney-la-Trinite I 68 B4
Gressvik N 91 A8
Gresten A 77 G8
Grésy-sur-Aix F 31 D8
Grésy-sur-Isère F 31 D9
Gretna GB 5 F10
Greußen D 79 D8
Greux F 26 D4
Grevbäck S 92 C4
Greve in Chianti I 66 E3
Greven D 17 D9
Greven D 83 D9
Grevena GR 168 D5
Grevenbicht NL 183 C7
Grevenbroich D 21 B7
Greveniti GR 168 E5
Grevenmacher L 20 E6
Grevesmühlen D 83 C10
Greve Strand DK 87 D10
Grevie S 87 C11
Grevinge DK 87 D9
Greyabbey GB 7 C11
Greystoke GB 5 F11
Greystones IRL 7 F10
Grez-Doiceau B 19 C10
Grez-en-Bouère F 23 E10
Grgar SLO 73 D8
Grgurevci SRB 158 C4
Griegos E 47 D9
Gries F 27 C8
Gries am Brenner A 72 B3
Griesbach D 27 D9
Griesheim D 21 E11
Grieskirchen A 76 F5
Grießen D 81 C7
Griesstätt D 75 G11
Griffen A 73 C10
Grigiškės LT 137 D11
Grignan F 35 B8
Grigno I 72 D4
Grignols F 32 B5
Grigny F 30 D6
Grigoriopol MD 154 C4
Grijota E 40 D2
Grijpskerk NL 16 B6
Grillby S 98 C8
Grillon F 35 B8
Grimaldi I 60 E6
Grimaud F 36 E5
Grimbergen B 19 C9
Grimma D 79 D12
Grimmen D 84 B4
Grimoldby GB 11 E12
Grimsås S 91 E14
Grimsbu N 101 B12
Grimsby GB 11 D11
Grimslöv S 88 B7
Grimstad N 90 C4
Grimston GB 11 F13
Grimstorp S 92 D5
Grimstrup DK 86 D3
Grindafjord N 94 D2
Grindaheim N 101 D9
Grindal N 101 A11
Grindelwald CH 70 D6
Grinder N 96 B7
Grindjord N 111 D13
Grindsted DK 86 A6
Grindsted DK 86 D3
Grindu RO 161 D9
Grinkiškis LT 134 E7
Griñón E 46 D5
Grins A 71 C11
Grinsbol S 97 D8
Grinţieş RO 153 C7
Gripenberg S 92 D5
Grisén E 41 E9
Griškabūdis LT 136 D7
Grisolia I 60 D5
Grisolles F 33 C8
Grisslehamn S 99 B11
Gritley GB 3 H11
Griviţa RO 153 E11
Griviţa RO 153 F11
Griviţa RO 161 D10
Grivitsa BG 165 C10
Grkinja SRB 164 C4
Grljan SRB 159 F9
Grnčari MK 168 B5
Grobbendonk B 19 B10
Gröbenzell D 75 F9
Grobiņa LV 134 C2
Gröbming A 73 B8
Gröbzig D 79 C10
Grocka SRB 158 D6
Grödby S 93 A11
Gródek PL 140 D9
Gródek nad Dunajcem PL 144 D2
Gröden D 80 D5
Grödig A 73 A7
Gröditz D 80 D4
Gródki PL 139 D9
Grodków PL 142 E3
Grodziczno PL 139 D8
Grodziec PL 142 B5
Grodzisk PL 141 E7
Grodzisk Mazowiecki PL 141 F3
Grodzisk Wielkopolski PL 81 B10
Groenlo NL 17 D7
Groesbeek NL 183 B7
Grohnde (Emmerthal) D 78 B5
Groitzsch D 79 D11
Groix F 22 E5
Grojdibodu RO 160 F4
Grójec PL 141 G3
Grom PL 139 C10
Gromadka PL 81 D9
Grömitz D 83 B9
Gromnik PL 144 D2
Gromo I 69 B8
Gronau (Westfalen) D 17 D8
Grønbjerg DK 86 C3
Grönbo S 118 D5
Gröndal S 108 E8
Grong N 105 C12
Grönhögen S 89 C10
Grønhøj DK 86 C4
Gröningen D 79 C9
Groningen NL 17 B7
Grønnemose DK 86 E6
Grønnes N 100 A6
Grønning N 110 E9
Grønningen N 104 D7
Gronowo PL 139 B7
Grönsinka S 98 B7
Grönskåra S 89 A9
Grönsta S 103 A11
Grønvik N 94 D4
Grönviken S 103 A9
Grönviken S 103 D12
Groomsport GB 4 F5
Grootegast NL 16 B6
Gropello Cairoli I 69 C6
Gropeni RO 155 C1
Gropniţa RO 153 C10
Grorud N 95 D11
Groscavallo I 31 E11
Groşi RO 152 B3
Grosio I 69 A9
Grošnica SRB 159 F6
Grosotto I 69 A9
Großaitingen D 71 A11
Groß Ammensleben D 79 B10
Großarl A 73 B7
Groß-Bieberau D 21 E11
Groß Börnecke D 79 C9
Großbothen D 79 D12
Großbottwar D 27 C11
Großbreitenbach D 79 E9
Großburgwedel (Burgwedel) D 78 B6
Groß Dölln D 84 E5
Grosselfingen D 27 D10
Großenaspe D 83 C7
Großenbrode D 83 B10
Großenehrich D 79 D8
Groß Engersdorf A 77 F11
Großengottern D 79 D8
Großenhain D 80 D5
Großenkneten D 17 C10
Großenlüder D 78 E6
Großensee D 83 C8
Großenstein D 79 E11
Großenwiehe D 82 A6
Groß-Enzersdorf A 77 F11
Grosseto I 65 B4
Grosseto-Prugna F 37 H9
Großfurra D 79 D8
Groß-Gerau D 21 E10
Groß-Gerungs A 77 E7
Groß Glienicke D 80 B4
Großgmain D 73 A6
Groß Grönau D 83 C9
Großhabersdorf D 75 D8
Großhansdorf D 83 C8
Großharras A 77 E10
Groß Fredenwalde D 84 D5
Großhartmannsdorf D 80 E4
Groß Heere (Heere) D 79 B7
Großhennersdorf D 81 E7
Groß-Hesepe D 17 C8
Großheubach D 187 B7
Grössjö S 107 F14
Großkarolinenfeld D 72 A5
Groß Kiesow D 84 B4
Großklein A 148 C4
Groß Köris D 80 B5
Groß Kreutz D 79 B12
Großkrut A 77 E11
Groß Lafferde (Lahstedt) D 79 B7
Großlangheim D 187 B9
Groß Leine D 80 B6
Groß Leuthen D 80 B6
Großlittgen D 21 D7
Großlohra D 79 D8
Großmaischeid D 185 C8
Großmehlen D 80 D5
Groß Miltzow D 84 C5
Groß Mohrdorf D 84 B3
Großmonra D 79 D9
Groß Naundorf D 80 C3
Großnaundorf D 80 D5
Groß Nemerow D 84 D4
Groß Oesingen D 79 A7
Großolbersdorf D 80 E4
Groß Oßnig D 80 C6
Großostheim D 21 E12
Großpetersdorf A 149 B6
Groß Plasten D 83 C13
Großraming A 73 A10
Großräschen D 80 C6
Großrinderfeld D 74 C6
Groß Roge D 83 C13
Groß-Rohrheim D 21 E10
Großröhrsdorf D 80 D6
Großrosseln D 186 C2
Großrudestedt D 79 D9
Großrußbach A 77 F10
Groß Sankt Florian A 148 C4
Groß Särchen D 80 D6
Großschirma D 80 E4
Großschönau A 77 E7
Groß Schönebeck D 84 E5
Groß Schwechten D 83 E11
Groß Schwülper (Schwülper) D 79 B7
Groß-Siegharts A 77 E8
Groß Stieten D 83 C10
Großthiemig D 80 D5
Großtreben D 80 C3
Groß Twülpstedt D 79 B8
Groß-Umstadt D 187 B6
Großwallstadt D 187 B7
Groß Warnow D 83 D11
Großweikersdorf A 77 F9
Groß Welle D 83 D12
Groß Wittensee D 82 B7
Groß Wokern D 83 C12
Großwudicke D 79 A11
Groß Wüstenfelde D 83 C13
Groß Ziethen D 84 E5
Groß-Zimmern D 187 B6
Grostenquin F 27 C6
Grosuplje SLO 73 E10
Grøtavær N 111 C11
Grotfjord N 111 A16
Grötholen S 102 C4
Grötingen S 103 A9
Grotli N 100 B7
Grötlingbo S 93 E12
Grøtnesdalen N 111 A18
Grottaferrata I 62 D3
Grottaglie I 61 B8
Grottaminarda I 60 A4
Grottammare I 62 B5
Grottazzolina I 62 A5
Grotte I 58 E4
Grotte di Castro I 62 B1
Grotteria I 59 C9
Grottole I 61 B6
Grou NL 16 B5
Grova N 90 A4
Grove GB 13 B12
Grövelsjön S 102 B3
Grovfjord N 111 C13
Grozd'ovo BG 167 C9
Grozeşti RO 153 D12
Grub am Forst D 75 B9
Grubbenvorst NL 183 C8
Grubbnäsudden S 119 B10
Grube D 83 B10
Grubišno Polje HR 149 E8
Gruczno PL 138 D5
Gruda HR 162 D5
Grude BIH 157 F7
Grudusk PL 139 D10
Grudziądz PL 138 D6
Gruey-lès-Surance F 26 D5
Gruġliasco I 68 C4
Gruia RO 159 E10
Gruissan F 34 D5
Gruiu RO 161 D8
Grullos E 39 B7
Grumăzeşti RO 153 C8
Grumbach D 80 D5
Grumo Appula I 61 A7
Grums S 97 D9
Grünau A 73 A8
Grünau A 77 F9
Grünberg D 21 C11
Grünburg A 76 G6
Grundagssätern S 102 B4
Grundfors S 106 A8
Grundfors S 107 B13
Grundforsen S 102 D4
Grundsanden S 118 B5
Grundsel S 118 C4
Grundsjö S 107 C11
Grundsuna S 107 E16
Grundsund S 91 C9
Grundtjärn S 107 D12
Grundträsk S 107 A16
Grundträsk S 109 F17
Grundträsk S 118 B7
Grundvattnet S 118 C4
Grünendeich D 82 C7
Grünewald D 80 D5
Grünewalde D 80 C5
Grungebru N 94 C7
Grünheide D 80 B5
Grünkraut D 71 B9
Grunnfarnes N 111 B12
Grunnfjord N 112 C4
Grunnførfjord N 110 D8
Grunow D 80 B6
Grünsfeld D 74 C6
Grünstadt D 21 E10
Grünwald D 75 F10
Grupčin MK 164 F3
Grury F 30 B4
Grūšlaukė LT 134 D2
Grußendorf (Sassenburg) D 79 A8
Gruta PL 138 D6
Gruvberget S 103 D11
Gruyères CH 31 B11
Gruža SRB 159 F6
Grūžai LT 135 D8
Gruzdžiai LT 134 D6
Grybów PL 145 D2
Grycksbo S 103 E9
Gryfice PL 85 C8
Gryfino PL 84 D6
Gryfów Śląski PL 81 D8
Grygov CZ 146 B4
Grylewo PL 85 E12
Gryllefjord N 111 B13
Grynberget S 107 C11
Gryt S 93 C9
Grytan S 106 E7
Grytgöl S 92 B7
Grythyttan S 97 C12
Gryts bruk S 92 B6
Grytsjö S 106 A9
Gryttjom S 99 B8
Gryźliny PL 139 C9
Grzebienisko PL 81 B11
Grzmiąca PL 85 C10
Grzybno PL 84 D7
Grzybno PL 138 D5
Grzymiszew PL 142 B5
Grzywna PL 138 D6
Gschnitz A 72 B3
Gschwandt A 73 A8
Gschwend D 74 E6
Gstaad CH 31 C11
Gsteig CH 31 C11
Guadahortuna E 53 A10
Guadajoz E 51 D8
Guadalajara E 47 C6
Guadalaviar E 47 D9
Guadalcanal E 51 C8
Guadalcázar E 53 A7
Guadalest E 56 D4
Guadalmez E 54 B3
Guadarrama E 46 C4
Guadassuar E 48 F4
Guadix E 55 E6
Guaire IRL 9 C10
Guájar-Faraguit E 53 C9
Gualöv S 88 C6
Gualdo Cattaneo I 62 B3
Gualdo Tadino I 67 F6
Gualtieri I 66 C2
Guarcino I 62 D4
Guarda P 45 C6
Guardamar del Segura E 56 E3
Guardavalle I 59 B9
Guardea I 62 B2
Guardiagrele I 63 C6
Guardia Lombardi I 60 B4
Guardia Perticara I 60 C6
Guardia Piemontese I 60 E6
Guardia Sanframondi I 60 A3
Guardias Viejas E 55 F7
Guardiola de Berguedà E 43 C7
Guardo E 39 C10
Guardramiro E 45 B8
Guareña E 51 B7
Guaro E 53 C7
Guarromán E 54 C5
Guasila I 64 D3
Guastalla I 66 C2
Gubaveeny IRL 7 D7
Gubbhögen S 106 C9
Gubbio I 66 F6
Gubbträsk S 107 A13
Guben D 81 C7
Gübene BG 166 D4
Gubin PL 81 C7
Guča SRB 158 F5
Guča Gora BIH 157 D8
Gudar E 48 D3
Gudavac BIH 156 C5
Gudbjerg DK 86 E7
Gudenieki LV 134 C3
Guderup DK 86 F5
Gudhem S 91 C14
Gudhjem DK 89 E7
Gudiena LT 137 D9
Gudinge S 99 A9
Gudme DK 87 E7
Gudmont-Villiers F 26 D3
Gudow D 83 C9
Gudum DK 86 B2
Gudumholm DK 86 B6
Gudvangen N 100 E5
Gudžiūnai LT 134 E7
Guebwiller F 27 E7
Guégon F 22 E6
Güéjar-Sierra E 53 B10
Guémar F 27 D7
Guémené-Penfao F 23 E8
Guémené-sur-Scorff F 22 D5
Guénange F 20 F6
Güeñes E 40 B5
Guenrouet F 23 E8
Guer F 23 E7
Guérande F 22 F7
Guéret F 29 C9
Guérigny F 25 F9
Guerri de la Sal E 33 F8
Güesa E 32 E3
Gueugnon F 30 B5
Gugeşti RO 161 B10
Güglingen D 27 B10
Guglionesi I 63 D7
Gugutka BG 171 B9
Gühlen-Glienicke D 83 D13
Guia P 44 E3
Guia P 50 E3
Guichen F 23 E8
Guidel F 22 E5
Guide Post GB 5 E13
Guidizzolo I 66 B2
Guidonia-Montecelio I 62 D3
Guiglia I 66 D2
Guignen F 23 E8
Guignes F 25 C8
Guignicourt F 19 F8
Guijo de Coria E 45 D8
Guijo de Galisteo E 45 D8
Guijo de Granadilla E 45 D8
Guijuelo E 45 C9
Guildford GB 15 E7
Guilers F 22 D2
Guilherand F 30 F6
Guilhofrei P 38 E3
Guilhovai P 44 C3
Guillaumes F 36 C5
Guillena E 51 D7
Guillestre F 36 B5
Guilliers F 22 D7
Guillon F 25 E11
Guillos F 32 A4
Guilvinec F 22 E3
Guimarães P 38 F3
Guînes F 15 F12
Guingamp F 22 C5
Guipavas F 22 D3
Guipry F 23 E8
Guisando E 45 D10
Guisborough GB 11 B9
Guiscard F 19 E7
Guise F 19 E8
Guisény F 22 C3
Guissona E 42 D6
Guist GB 15 B10
Guitiriz E 38 B4
Guîtres F 28 E5
Gujan-Mestras F 32 A3
Gulács H 145 G5
Gülbahçe TR 177 C8
Gulbene LV 135 B13
Guldager DK 86 D2
Guldborg DK 84 A1
Gulgamme N 113 B16
Gulianca RO 161 C11
Gülitz D 83 D11
Gullabo S 89 C9
Gullane GB 5 C11
Gullberg S 103 D10
Gullbrå N 100 E4
Gullbrandstorp S 87 B11
Gullbranna S 87 B11
Gulleråsen S 103 D9
Gullholmen N 111 C10
Gullön S 109 E15
Gullringen S 92 D7
Gullspång S 91 B15
Gullträsk S 118 B6
Güllübahçe TR 177 D9
Güllüce TR 173 D9
Güllük TR 177 E10
Gullverket N 95 B14
Gulpen NL 183 D7
Gülpinar TR 171 E10
Gulsele S 107 D12
Gulsvik N 95 B11
Gültz D 84 C4
Gülübintsi BG 166 E6
Gülübovo BG 165 E10
Gülübovo BG 166 E5
Gulyantsi BG 160 F5
Gülzow D 83 C12
Gumhöjden S 97 B10
Gumiel de Hizán E 40 E4
Gumiel de Mercado E 40 E4
Gummark S 118 E5
Gummersbach D 21 B9
Gumpelstadt D 79 E7
Gumtow D 83 E12
Gümüşçay TR 173 D7
Gümüşsuyu TR 177 C9
Gümüşyaka TR 173 B9
Gümzovo BG 159 E10
Gunaroš SRB 150 F4
Gundelfingen D 27 D8
Gundelfingen an der Donau D 75 E7
Gundelsheim D 21 F12
Gundershoffen F 27 C8
Gundinci HR 157 B9
Gündoğan TR 173 D8
Gündoğdu TR 173 D7
Gundsømagle DK 87 D10
Güneyli TR 172 D6
Güngörmez TR 173 B8
Gunja HR 157 C10
Gunnarn S 107 A13
Gunnarnes N 113 A13
Gunnarsbo S 103 C11
Gunnarsbyn S 118 B7
Gunnarskog S 97 C8
Gunnarvattnet S 105 C16
Gunnebo S 93 D9
Günstedt D 79 D9
Güntersberge D 79 C8
Guntersblum D 185 E9
Guntersdorf A 77 E10
Güntersleben D 187 B8
Guntramsdorf A 77 F10
Günzburg D 75 F7
Gunzenhausen D 75 D8
Gura-Bicului MD 154 D4
Gura Caliţei RO 161 B9
Gura Camencii MD 154 B2
Gura Foii RO 160 D6
Gura Galbenei MD 154 D3
Gurahonţ RO 151 E9
Gura Humorului RO 153 B7
Gura Ocniţei RO 161 D7
Gura Râului RO 152 F3
Gurasada RO 151 F10
Gura Ştiţii RO 161 D7
Gura Teghii RO 161 C8
Gura Vadului RO 161 C8
Gura Văii RO 153 E9
Gura Vitioarei RO 161 C8
Gurbăneşti RO 161 E9
Gurghiu RO 152 D5
Guri i Bardhë AL 168 B3
Guri i Zi AL 163 E8
Gurk A 73 C9
Gurkovo BG 166 D5
Gurkovo BG 167 C10
Gŭrlyano BG 164 E6
Gurrea de Gállego E 41 D10
Gurrë e Madhe AL 168 A3
Gurteen IRL 6 E6
Gur'yevsk RUS 136 D2
Gusborn D 83 D10
Gušće HR 149 F7
Güsen D 79 B10
Gusev RUS 136 D5
Gusinje MNE 163 D8
Guşoeni RO 160 D4
Gusow D 80 A6
Guspini I 64 D2
Gussago I 69 B9
Gusselby S 97 C13
Güssing A 149 B6
Gussola I 66 B1
Gussvattnet S 105 C16
Gußwerk A 148 A4
Gustavsberg S 99 D10
Gustavsfors S 97 B10
Güsten D 79 C10
Gusterath D 21 E7
Güstrow D 83 C12
Gusum S 93 C8
Gutach (Schwarzwaldbahn) D 187 E5
Gutau A 77 F7
Gutcher GB 3 D14
Güterfelde D 80 B4
Güterglück D 79 C10
Gütersloh D 17 E10
Guthrie GB 5 B11
Gutorfölde H 149 C7
Gutow D 83 C12
Guttannen CH 70 D6
Guttaring A 73 C10
Gützkow D 84 C4
Guvåg N 110 C8
Güvemalani TR 173 D7
Güvercinlik TR 177 E10
Guxhagen D 78 D5
Güzelbahçe TR 177 C8
Güzelçamli TR 177 D9
Gvardeysk RUS 136 D3
Gvarv N 95 D10
Gvozd HR 148 F5
Gvozd MNE 163 D7
Gvozdansko HR 156 B5
Gwda Wielka PL 85 C11
Gweedore IRL 6 B6
Gwithian GB 12 E4
Gy F 26 F4
Gyál H 150 C3
Gyarmat H 149 B8
Gyékényes H 149 D8
Gyenesdiás H 149 C8
Gyermely H 149 A11
Gyé-sur-Seine F 25 D11
Gyhum D 17 B12
Gyljen S 118 B9
Gylling DK 86 D6
Gymno GR 175 C8
Gyomaendrőd H 150 D6
Gyömöre H 149 A9
Gyömrő H 150 C3
Gyöngyös H 150 B4
Gyöngyöspata H 150 B4
Gyönk H 149 C10
Győr H 149 A9
Györköny H 149 C11
Győrság H 149 A9
Győrszemere H 149 A9
Győrtelek H 145 H5
Győrújbarát H 149 A9
Győrújfalu H 149 A9
Győrzámoly H 149 A9
Gyrstinge DK 87 E9
Gysinge S 98 B7
Gytheio GR 178 B4
Gyttorp S 97 C12
Gyueshevo BG 164 E5
Gyula H 151 D7
Gyulaháza H 145 G5
Gyulaj H 149 D10
Gyúró H 149 B11
Gzy PL 139 E10

H

Haabneeme EST 131 B9
Haacht B 19 C10
Hääd emeeste EST 131 E8
Haaften NL 183 B6
Haag A 77 F7
Haag am Hausruck A 76 F5
Haag in Oberbayern D 75 F11
Haajainen FIN 124 C7
Haaksbergen NL 17 D7
Haaltert B 19 C9
Haanja EST 131 F14
Haapajärvi FIN 123 C14
Haapa-Kimola FIN 127 D15
Haapakoski FIN 123 E10
Haapakoski FIN 124 F8
Haapakumpu FIN 115 D3
Haapalahti FIN 113 E19
Haapaluoma FIN 123 E10
Haapamäki FIN 123 C16
Haapamäki FIN 123 E17
Haapamäki FIN 123 F12
Haapamäki FIN 125 E10
Haaparanta FIN 115 E3
Haapavesi FIN 119 F14
Haapsalu EST 130 D7
Haar D 75 F10
Haarajoki FIN 123 F17
Haarajoki FIN 127 E13
Haaraoja FIN 119 F16
Haarasaajo FIN 119 B12
Haarbach D 76 E4
Haarby DK 86 E6
Haaren NL 183 B6
Haarlem NL 16 D3
Haastrecht NL 16 E3
Haavisto FIN 127 D11
Habaja EST 131 C10
Habartov CZ 75 B12
Habas F 32 C4
Habay-la-Neuve B 19 E12
Häbbersliden S 118 E4
Habiller TR 167 F7
Hablingbo S 93 E12
Habo S 91 D15
Håbol S 91 B11
Habovka SK 147 C9
Habry CZ 77 C8
Habsheim F 27 E7
Hachenburg D 21 C9
Haciaslanlar TR 173 E7
Hacidanişment TR 167 F7
Hacigelen TR 172 D6
Hacıköy TR 172 C6
Hacinas E 40 E5
Hacirahmanli TR 177 B10
Haciumur TR 167 F7
Hacivelioba TR 173 D8
Hackås S 102 A8
Hackenheim D 21 E9
Hacketstown IRL 9 C9
Hackleton GB 15 C7
Hacksjö S 107 B12
Hadamar D 21 D10
Hadanberg S 107 D14
Haddebo S 92 B6
Haddington GB 5 D11
Haddiscoe GB 15 B12
Haderslev DK 86 E4
Haderup DK 86 C3
Hadimköy TR 173 B10
Hadleigh GB 15 C10
Hadley GB 10 F7
Hadol F 26 D5
Hadres A 77 E10
Hadsel N 110 C8
Hadsten DK 86 C6
Hadsund DK 86 B6
Hadžići BIH 157 E9
Haelen NL 183 C7
Hafnerbach A 77 F8
Haftersbol S 97 C10
Haga S 98 B8
Haganj HR 149 E7
Hagaström S 103 E13
Hagby S 89 B10
Hagebyhöga S 92 C5
Hagen D 17 F8
Hagenbach D 187 C5
Hagenburg D 17 D12
Hagenow D 83 D10
Hagenwerder D 81 D7
Hageri EST 131 C9
Hägerstad S 92 C7
Hagetaubin F 32 C4
Hagetmau F 32 C4
Hagfors S 97 B10
Häggås S 107 C11
Häggdånger S 103 A14
Häggebäcken S 98 B6
Häggenås S 106 E7
Häggnäset S 105 C16
Häggsåsen S 105 E16
Häggsjön S 105 D13
Häggsjövik S 105 D16
Häghig RO 153 F7
Hagley GB 13 A9
Hagondange F 20 F6
Hagsta S 103 E13
Haguenau F 27 C8
Hahausen D 79 C7
Hahnbach D 75 C10
Hahnstätten D 185 D9
Hahót H 149 C7
Haibach D 21 E12
Haibach D 75 D12
Haidmühle D 76 E5
Haiger D 21 C10
Haigerloch D 27 D10
Häijää FIN 127 B9
Hailsham GB 15 F9
Hailuoto FIN 119 D13
Haiming D 76 F3
Haimoo FIN 127 E11
Haina D 75 B8
Haina (Kloster) D 21 B11
Hainburg an der Donau A 77 F11
Hainfeld A 77 F9
Hainichen D 80 E4
Haiterbach D 187 D6
Haitzendorf A 77 F9
Hajala FIN 127 E8
Hajdúböszörmény H 151 B8
Hajdúdorog H 151 B8
Hajdúhadház H 151 B8
Hajdúnánás H 145 H3
Hajdúsámson H 151 B8
Hajdúszoboszló H 151 C7
Hajdúszovát H 151 C7
Hajmáskér H 149 B10
Hajmel AL 163 F8
Hajnáčka SK 147 E9
Hajnoc RKS 164 D4
Hajnówka PL 141 E9
Hajós H 150 E3
Hakadal N 95 B13
Håkafot S 105 C16
Håkansvallen S 102 B7
Håkavik N 111 C14
Hakkas S 116 E7
Hakkenpää FIN 126 D6
Häkkilä FIN 123 E14
Hakokylä FIN 121 E12
Håkøybotn N 111 A16
Håksberg S 97 B13
Hakstabben N 112 C11
Håkvik N 111 D13
Halahora de Sus MD 153 A10
Håland N 94 C4
Halapić BIH 157 D6
Halászi H 146 F4
Halásztelek H 150 C2
Hălăuceşti RO 153 C9
Halbe D 80 B5
Halbenrain A 148 C5
Hålberg S 109 F18
Halberstadt D 79 C9
Halbjerg DK 90 E7
Halblech D 71 B11
Halbturn A 77 G11
Hălchiu RO 153 F7
Hald DK 86 B4
Hald DK 86 B6
Haldarsvik FO 2 A2
Hald Ege DK 86 C4
Halden N 91 A9
Haldensleben D 79 B9
Hale GB 11 E7
Halen B 183 D6
Halenkov CZ 146 C6
Halenkovice CZ 146 C4
Halesowen GB 13 A10
Halesworth GB 15 C12
Halfing D 72 A5
Halfway IRL 8 E5
Halfweg NL 16 D3
Halhjem N 94 B2
Halič SK 147 E9
Halifax GB 11 D8
Halikko FIN 127 E9
Halimba H 149 B9
Halitpaşa TR 177 B10
Haljala EST 131 C12
Häljarp S 87 D11
Halkia FIN 127 D13
Halkirk GB 3 H10
Halkivaha FIN 127 C9
Halkokumpu FIN 124 F7
Hall S 93 D13
Hälla S 107 D12
Halla-aho FIN 124 C9
Hallabro S 89 C8
Hällabrottet S 92 A6
Halla Heberg S 91 E10
Halland GB 15 F9
Hälland S 105 E14
Hallapuro FIN 123 D12
Hällaryd S 89 C7
Hällbacken S 105 E16
Hällbacken S 109 D12
Hällberga S 98 D7
Hällbo S 103 D11
Hallbodarna S 105 E15
Hällbybrunn S 98 D6
Halle B 19 C9
Halle D 78 C6
Halle NL 183 B8
Halle (Saale) D 79 D10
Halle (Westfalen) D 17 D10
Hällefors S 97 C12
Hälleforsnäs S 93 A9
Hallein A 73 A7
Hällekis S 91 B13
Hällen S 103 E14
Hallen S 105 E16
Hallenberg D 21 B11
Hallencourt F 18 E4
Halle-Neustadt D 79 D10
Hallerndorf D 75 C8
Hällesjö S 103 A11
Hällestad S 92 B7
Hällevadsholm S 91 B10
Hällevik S 88 C7
Hälleviksstrand S 91 C9
Hall-Häxåsen S 106 D8
Hallingby N 95 B12
Hallingeberg S 93 D8
Hällinmäki FIN 124 F9
Hall in Tirol A 72 B4
Hällnäs S 107 C17
Hällnäs S 109 D15
Hällnäs S 109 E13
Hallom S 102 A7
Hallow GB 13 A10
Hällsbäck S 97 D8
Hällsberg S 92 A6
Hällsjö S 107 E13
Hällsta S 98 D6
Hallstahammar S 98 C6
Hallstatt A 73 A8
Hallstavik S 99 B11
Halltorp S 89 C10
Halluin B 19 C7
Hallund DK 86 A6
Hällvik S 109 D14
Hällviken S 106 D8
Hallworthy GB 12 D5
Hälmägel RO 151 E10
Hălmagiu RO 151 E10
Halmeu RO 145 H7
Halmstad S 87 B11
Halna S 92 B4
Halosenniemi FIN 119 D14
Halosenranta FIN 115 E2
Halovo SRB 159 F9
Hals DK 86 B6
Halsa N 104 E4
Halsenbach D 21 D9
Hal'shany BY 137 E13
Hälsingby FIN 122 D7
Hälsjo S 103 C12
Halsøy N 108 E5
Halsskov DK 87 E8
Halstead GB 15 D10
Halstenbek D 83 C7
Halsteren NL 16 E2
Halstroff F 20 F6
Halsua FIN 123 D12
Haltern D 17 E8
Halttula FIN 119 C14
Haltwhistle GB 5 F12
Haluna FIN 125 D10
Hälvä FIN 129 B11
Halvarsgårdarna S 97 B13
Halver D 21 B8
Halvrimmen DK 86 A5
Halwell GB 13 E7
Halže CZ 75 C12
Ham F 19 E7
Ham GB 3 E12
Hamar N 101 E14
Hamari FIN 119 C14
Hamarøy N 108 D5
Hamarøy N 111 D10
Hambach F 27 B7
Hambergen D 17 B11
Hamble-le-Rice GB 13 D12
Hambrücken D 21 F11
Hambühren D 79 A6
Hamburg D 83 C7
Hamburgsund S 91 B9
Hambye F 23 C9
Hamcearca RO 155 C2
Hamdibey TR 173 E7
Hämeenkoski FIN 127 C13

Hämeenkyrö FIN 127 B9
Hämeenlinna FIN 127 D11
Hämelhausen D 17 C12
Hameln D 17 D12
Hämerten D 79 A10
Hamica HR 148 E5
Hamidiye TR 167 F9
Hamidiye TR 172 B6
Hamilton GB 5 D8
Hamilton's Bawn GB 7 D9
Hamina FIN 128 D7
Haminalahti FIN 124 E9
Hamit TR 181 C9
Hamitabat TR 173 A7
Hamlagrø N 94 A4
Hamlot N 111 D10
Hamm D 17 E9
Hamm (Sieg) D 185 C8
Hammar S 92 B5
Hammarland FIN 99 B13
Hammarn S 97 C12
Hammarnäs S 105 E16
Hammarsbyn S 102 E5
Hammarstrand S 107 E10
Hammarvika N 104 D5
Hamme B 19 B9
Hammel DK 86 C5
Hammelburg D 74 B6
Hammelev DK 86 E4
Hammelspring D 84 D4
Hamme-Mille B 19 C10
Hammenhög S 88 D6
Hammer N 105 C12
Hammerbrücke D 75 B11
Hammerdal S 106 D8
Hammerfest N 113 B12
Hammershøj DK 86 C5
Hammerum DK 86 C4
Hamminkeln D 17 E7
Hamn N 108 E3
Hamn N 111 B13
Hamna N 114 B8
Hamnavoe GB 3 D14
Hamnavoe GB 3 E14
Hamnbukt N 112 C8
Hamnbukta N 111 B18
Hamneidet N 112 D6
Hamnes N 105 B10
Hamnes N 108 E4
Hamnes N 112 D6
Hamningberg N 114 B9
Hamnøy N 110 E5
Hamnvågnes N 111 B16
Hamoir B 19 D12
Hamois B 19 D11
Hamont B 16 F5
Hampen DK 86 C4
Hampetorp S 92 A7
Håmpjåkk S 116 D4
Hampont F 26 C6
Hampreston GB 13 D11
Hamra S 93 F12
Hamra S 103 C9
Hamrångefjärden S 103 E13
Hamre N 112 C4
Hamry nad Sázavou CZ 77 C9
Ham-sous-Varsberg F 186 C2
Hamstreet GB 15 E10
Hamsund N 111 D10
Ham-sur-Heure B 19 D9
Hamula FIN 123 D16
Hamula FIN 124 D9
Hamzabeyli TR 167 F7
Hanaskog S 88 C6
Hanau D 187 A6
Handbjerg DK 86 C3
Handeloh D 83 D7
Handen S 93 A12
Handest DK 86 B5
Handewitt D 82 A6
Handlová SK 147 D7
Handog S 106 E7
Handöl S 105 E12
Handrabury UA 154 B5
Handrup D 17 C9
Handsjö S 102 B8
Handstein N 108 D4
Handzame B 182 C2
Hanebo S 103 D12
Hanerau-Hademarschen
D 82 B6
Hanestad N 101 C13
Hănești RO 153 B9
Hangastenmaa FIN 128 B7
Hangelsberg D 80 B5
Hånger S 87 A13
Hangö FIN 127 F8
Hangony H 145 G1
Hangu RO 153 C8
Hangvar S 93 D13
Hanhikoski FIN 115 E2
Hanhimaa FIN 117 C14
Han i Elezit RKS 164 E3
Hanikase EST 132 F1
Haniska SK 145 F3
Hankamäki FIN 125 D10
Hankasalem asema FIN 123 F16
Hankasalmi FIN 123 F16
Hankensbüttel D 83 E9
Han Knežica BIH 157 B6
Hanko FIN 127 F8
Hanna PL 141 G9
Hannäs S 93 C8
Hannover D 78 B6
Hannoversch Münden D 78 D6
Hannukainen FIN 117 C11
Hannusperä FIN 119 D15
Hannusranta FIN 121 F10
Hannut B 19 C11
Hanøy N 110 D9
Han-Pijesak BIH 157 D10
Hanshagen D 83 C10
Hańsk Pierwszy PL 141 H8
Hansnes N 112 D4
Hanstedt D 83 D8
Hanstholm DK 86 A3
Han-sur-Nied F 26 C5
Hanušovce nad Topľou SK
145 E4
Hanušovice CZ 77 B11
Hanvec F 22 D3
Haparanda S 119 C12
Hapert NL 183 C6
Häppälä FIN 123 F16
Happburg D 75 D9
Happisburgh GB 15 B12
Haps NL 183 B7
Hapträsk S 118 B4
Hara S 106 E6
Hårad S 98 D7
Haradok BY 133 F7
Harads S 118 B5
Häradsbäck S 88 B6
Häradsbygden S 103 E9
Haradshammar S 93 B9
Haradzilavichy Pyershaya
BY 133 D4
Haraldseng N 112 B9
Haram N 100 A4
Harang N 104 E6
Harany BY 133 F6
Harasiuki PL 144 C5
Hărău RO 151 F10
Haraudden S 116 E3
Harbacheva BY 133 E6
Harbak N 104 C8
Harbke D 79 B9
Harbo S 98 B8
Harboør DK 86 B2
Harbost GB 2 J4
Harburg (Schwaben) D 75 E8
Harbury GB 13 A12
Hard A 71 C9
Hardbakke N 100 D1
Hardegg A 77 E9
Hardegsen D 78 C6
Hardelot-Plage F 15 F12
Hardenberg NL 17 C7
Harderwijk NL 16 D5
Hardheim D 27 A11
Hardinxveld-Giessendam
NL 182 B5
Hardt D 27 D9
Hareid N 100 B4
Harelbeke B 19 C7
Haren NL 17 B7
Haren (Ems) D 17 C8
Hare Street GB 15 D9
Harestua N 95 B13
Harfleur F 23 A12
Harg S 99 B10
Hargesheim D 21 E9
Hargimont B 19 D11
Hargla EST 131 F12
Hargnies F 19 D10
Hargshamn S 99 B10
Harichovce SK 145 F2
Harinkaa FIN 123 E16
Harjakangas FIN 126 B6
Härjäro S 99 D8
Härjåsjön S 102 C7
Harjavalta FIN 126 C7
Harjula FIN 119 C15
Harjumaa FIN 128 B7
Harjunkylä FIN 122 E7
Harjunpää FIN 126 C6
Harju-Risti EST 131 C7
Harka H 149 A7
Härkäjoki FIN 115 D2
Harkakötöny H 150 E4
Harkány H 149 E10
Härkmeri FIN 122 F6
Härkönen FIN 119 C13
Harku EST 131 C9
Hârlău RO 153 C9
Harlech GB 10 F3
Harleston GB 15 C11
Hårlev DK 87 E10
Harlingen NL 16 B4
Harlow GB 15 D9
Harly F 19 E7
Hărman RO 153 F7
Harmånger S 103 C13
Härmänkylä FIN 121 F13
Harmanli TR 173 D9
Härmänmäki FIN 121 F11
Harmannsdorf A 77 F10
Harmelen NL 182 A5
Harmoinen FIN 127 C13
Harmsdorf D 83 C9
Harmston GB 11 E10
Harnes F 18 D6
Härnösand S 103 A14
Haro E 40 C6
Harodz'ki BY 137 E13
Haroldswick GB 3 D15
Haroué F 26 D5
Härpe FIN 127 E14
Harpefoss N 101 C11
Harpenden GB 15 D8
Harplinge S 87 B11
Harpstedt D 17 C11
Harra D 75 B10
Harrachov CZ 81 E8
Harran N 105 B13
Harre DK 86 B3
Harridslev DK 86 C6
Harrietfield GB 5 C9
Harrioja S 119 C11
Harrislee D 82 A6
Harrogate GB 11 D8
Harrsjö S 106 B9
Harrström FIN 122 E6
Harrvik S 107 A10
Harsa S 103 C10
Hårsbäck S 98 C7
Harsefeld D 82 D7
Hărseni RO 152 F6
Hărsești RO 160 D5
Harsleben D 79 C9
Hårslev DK 86 D6
Hârșova RO 155 D1
Harsprånget S 116 E3
Harstad N 111 C12
Harsum D 78 B6
Harsvik N 104 C8
Harta H 150 D3
Hartberg A 148 B5
Hårte S 103 C13
Hartenholm D 83 C8
Hartha D 80 D3
Harthausen D 21 F10
Hartheim D 27 E8
Hârtiești RO 160 C6
Hart im Zillertal A 72 B4
Hartkirchen A 76 F5
Hartland GB 12 D6
Hartlepool GB 11 B9
Hartmanice CZ 76 D4
Hartola FIN 127 B15
Harwich GB 15 D11
Harzgerode D 79 C9
Hasanağa TR 173 D10
Hasbuğa TR 173 A8
Haselünne D 17 C8
Hasirciarnavutköy TR 171 B10
Håsjö S 107 F10
Hasköy TR 173 A6
Hasköy TR 177 C9
Haslach an der Mühl A 76 E6
Haslach im Kinzigtal D 27 D9
Hasle CH 70 C5
Hasle DK 88 E7
Haslemere GB 15 E7
Haslev DK 87 E9
Hasloh D 83 C7
Hasløya N 104 E2
Haslund DK 86 C6
Hășmaș RO 151 D9
Hasparren F 32 D3
Haßbergen D 17 C12
Hassel (Weser) D 17 C12
Hassela S 103 B12
Hassela kyrkby S 103 B12
Hasselfelde D 79 C8
Hasselfors S 92 A5
Hasselt B 19 C11
Hasselt NL 16 C6
Haßfurt D 75 B8
Hassi FIN 127 B13
Hässjö S 103 A14
Haßleben D 79 D9
Haßleben D 84 D5
Hässleholm S 87 C13
Hasslö S 89 C8
Haßloch D 21 F10
Hasslöv S 87 C12
Haßmersheim D 187 C7
Hästbo S 103 E13
Hästholmen S 92 C5
Hastière-Lavaux B 19 D10
Hastings GB 15 F10
Hästnäs S 97 D14
Håstrup DK 86 E6
Hästveda S 87 C13
Hasvåg N 105 C9
Hasvik N 112 C9
Hať CZ 146 B6
Hat' UA 145 G6
Hațeg RO 159 B10
Hatfield GB 11 D10
Hatherleigh GB 12 D6
Hätilä FIN 127 C11
Hatipkışlasi TR 181 B7
Hatsola FIN 128 B8
Hattarvík FO 2 A4
Hattem NL 16 D6
Hattersheim am Main D 21 D10
Hattert D 21 C9
Hattfjelldal N 108 E6
Hatting DK 86 D5
Hattingen D 17 F8
Hatton GB 3 L13
Hattstedt D 82 A6
Hattula FIN 127 C11
Hattuvaara FIN 125 E16
Hatulanmäki FIN 124 C8
Hatunkylä FIN 125 D15
Hatvan H 150 B4
Hatzenbühl D 27 B9
Hatzendorf A 148 C6
Hatzfeld (Eder) D 21 C11
Haubourdin F 18 C6
Hauenstein D 186 C4
Haugan N 105 D9
Haugastøl N 94 A7
Hauge N 94 F4
Hauge N 114 E6
Haugen N 110 D7
Haugesund N 94 D2
Haugh of Urr GB 5 F9
Haugland N 108 D5
Haugli N 111 C15
Haugnes N 111 B11
Haugnes N 112 C6
Haugset N 112 D7
Hauho FIN 127 C12
Haukå N 100 C2
Haukela FIN 125 B14
Haukeligrend N 94 C7
Haukijärvi FIN 127 B9
Haukilahti FIN 121 F13
Haukiniemi FIN 121 C13
Haukipudas FIN 119 D14
Haukivaara FIN 125 E15
Haukivuori FIN 124 F8
Haukøy N 111 D11
Haulerwijk NL 16 B6
Haurukylä FIN 119 E15
Haus A 73 B8
Haus N 94 B2
Hausach D 187 E5
Hausen D 75 E11
Hausen bei Würzburg D 187 B9
Häusern D 27 E9
Hausham D 72 A4
Hausjärvi FIN 127 D12
Hauske N 94 D3
Hausleiten A 77 F10
Hausmannstätten A 148 C5
Hautajärvi FIN 115 E6
Hautakylä FIN 121 D10
Hautakylä FIN 123 E12
Haute-Amance F 26 E4
Hautefort F 29 E8
Hauterives F 31 E7
Hauteville-Lompnes F 31 D8
Haut-Fays B 184 D3
Hautmont F 19 D8
Hautomäki FIN 123 E17
Haux F 32 D4
Hauzenberg D 76 E5
Havant GB 14 F7
Havårna RO 153 A9
Havbro DK 86 B4
Havdhem S 93 E12
Hävdna N 113 C15
Havelange B 19 D11
Havelberg D 83 E12
Havelte NL 16 C6
Håven S 103 C9
Haverdal S 87 B11
Haverfordwest GB 12 B5
Haverhill GB 15 C9
Haverlah D 79 B7
Haverö S 103 B9
Haversin B 19 D11
Haverslev DK 86 B5
Håverud S 91 B11
Havířov CZ 146 B6
Havixbeck D 17 E8
Hävla S 92 B7
Havlíčkův Brod CZ 77 C9
Havndal DK 86 B6
Havneby DK 86 E3
Havnebyen DK 87 D8
Havnsø DK 87 D8
Havøysund N 113 A14
Håvra S 103 C10
Havran TR 173 E7
Havrebjerg DK 87 E8
Havsa TR 173 A6
Havsskogen S 99 B11
Havtun N 94 B2
Hawarden GB 10 E5
Hawes GB 11 C7
Hawick GB 5 E11
Hawkhurst GB 15 E10
Hawkinge GB 15 E11
Haxby GB 11 C9
Hayange F 20 F6
Haybes F 184 D2
Haydarli TR 177 D10
Haydere TR 181 A8
Haydon Bridge GB 5 F12
Haydon Wick GB 13 B11
Hayingen D 71 A8
Hayle GB 12 E4
Hay-on-Wye GB 13 A8
Hayrabolu TR 173 B7
Hayton GB 11 D10
Hayvoron UA 154 A5
Haywards Heath GB 15 F8
Hazebrouck F 18 C6
Hazerswoude-Rijndijk NL
182 A5
Hažlach PL 147 B7
Hažlín SK 145 E3
Hazlov CZ 75 B11
Heacham GB 11 F12
Headcorn GB 15 E10
Headford IRL 6 F4
Healeyfield GB 5 F13
Heanor GB 11 E9
Heathfield GB 15 F9
Hebdów PL 143 F9
Hebenhausen (Neu-Eichenberg)
D 78 D6
Heberg S 87 B11
Hebertsfelden D 76 F3
Hebnes N 94 D3
Heby S 98 C7
Hèches F 33 D6
Hechingen D 27 D10
Hecho E 32 E4
Hechtel B 19 B11
Hechthausen D 17 A12
Heckelberg D 84 E5
Heckington GB 11 F11
Hedared S 91 D12
Hedberg S 109 F16
Heddesheim D 21 F11
Hédé F 23 D8
Hede S 98 B6
Hede S 102 B6
Hedekas S 91 B10
Hedel NL 16 E4
Hedemora S 97 B14
Heden DK 86 E6
Heden S 102 C4
Heden S 118 C7
Hedenäset S 119 B11
Hedensbyn S 118 E6
Hedensted DK 86 D5
Hedersleben D 79 C9
Hédervár H 146 F4
Hedesunda S 98 B8
Hedeviken S 102 B6
Hedge End GB 13 D12
Hedlunda S 107 B15
Hedmark S 107 B13
Hedsjön S 103 E12
Hee DK 86 C2
Heeg NL 16 C5
Heek D 17 D8
Heel NL 183 C7
Heemsen D 17 C12
Heemskerk NL 16 C3
Heemstede NL 16 D3
Heenvliet NL 182 B4
Heer B 19 D10
Heerde NL 16 D6
Heerenveen NL 16 C5
Heerewaarden NL 183 B6
Heerhugowaard NL 16 C3
Heerlen NL 20 C5
Heers B 19 C11
Heesch NL 16 E5
Heeslingen D 17 B12
Heeßen D 17 D12
Heeswijk NL 16 E4
Heeten NL 183 A8
Heeze NL 16 F5
Heggeli N 111 B13
Heggem N 104 E4
Heggenes N 101 D10
Heggjabygda N 100 C4
Heggland N 90 A5
Heggmoen N 108 B8
Hegra N 105 E10
Hegyeshalom H 146 F4
Hehlen D 78 C5
Heia N 105 C12
Heia N 111 B17
Heide D 82 B6
Heideck D 75 D9
Heidelberg D 21 F11
Heiden D 17 E7
Heidenau D 80 E5
Heidenheim D 75 D8
Heidenheim an der Brenz
D 75 E7
Heidenreichstein A 77 E8
Heigenbrücken D 187 A7
Heikendorf D 83 B8
Heikkilä FIN 121 C14
Heikkilä FIN 122 F7
Heiland N 90 B4
Heilbronn D 27 B11
Heilbrunn A 148 B5
Heiligenberg D 27 E11
Heiligenfelde D 83 E10
Heiligenhafen D 83 B9
Heiligenhaus D 17 F7
Heiligenkreuz am Waasen
A 148 C5
Heiligenkreuz im Lafnitztal
A 148 C6
Heiligenstadt Heilbad D 79 D7
Heiligenstedten D 82 C6
Heiloo NL 16 C3
Heilsbronn D 75 D8
Heiltz-le-Maurupt F 25 C12
Heim N 104 E6
Heimbach D 21 E8
Heimbuchenthal D 187 B7
Heimdal N 100 E3
Heimdal N 104 E8
Heimertingen D 71 A10
Heimseta N 100 C3
Heimsheim D 187 D6
Heinade D 78 C6
Heinämaa FIN 127 D14
Heinämäki FIN 121 F12
Heinämäki FIN 123 D17
Heinävaara FIN 125 E14
Heinävesi FIN 125 F11
Heinebach (Alheim) D 78 D6
Heinersbrück D 81 C7
Heinersdorf D 80 B6
Heinersreuth D 75 C10
Heinijärvi FIN 119 E14
Heinijoki FIN 126 D7
Heiningen D 79 B8
Heinisuo FIN 119 C16
Heinkenszand NL 16 F1
Heinlahti FIN 128 E6
Heino NL 183 A8
Heinola FIN 127 C15
Heinolan kirkonkylä FIN 127 C15
Heinolanperä FIN 119 E14
Heinoniemi FIN 125 F13
Heinsberg D 20 B6
Heinsen D 78 C5
Heinsnes N 105 B12
Heisingen D 183 C10
Heistadmoen N 95 C11
Heist-op-den-Berg B 19 B10
Heitersheim D 27 E8
Heituinlahti FIN 128 C8
Hejls DK 86 E5
Hejnice CZ 81 E8
Hejnsvig DK 86 D4
Hejőpapi H 145 H2
Hejsager DK 86 E5
Hekelgem B 19 C9
Hel PL 138 A6
Helbra D 79 C9
Helchteren B 183 C6
Heldburg D 75 B8
Heldenbergen D 21 D11
Heldrungen D 79 D9
Helechal E 51 B9
Helegiu RO 153 E9
Helensburgh GB 4 C7
Helfenberg A 76 E6
Helgenes N 110 C9
Helgeroa N 90 B6
Helgum S 107 E11
Hell N 105 E9
Hella N 100 D5
Helland N 104 E5
Helland N 111 D11
Hellanmaa FIN 122 D9
Hellarmo N 109 B10
Helle N 90 B5
Hellebæk DK 87 C11
Hellefjord N 113 B11
Hellendoorn NL 183 A8
Hellenthal D 20 D6
Hellenurme EST 131 E12
Hellesøy N 100 E1
Hellested DK 87 E10
Hellesvik N 104 D5
Hellesylt N 100 B5
Hellevad DK 86 E4
Hellevoetsluis NL 16 E2
Helligskogen N 112 E6
Hellín E 55 B9
Hellingly GB 15 F9
Hellnes N 112 C6
Hellsö FIN 126 F4
Hellvi S 93 D13
Hellvik N 94 F3
Helmbrechts D 75 B10
Helme EST 131 E11
Helmond NL 16 F5
Helmsdale GB 3 J9
Helmsley GB 11 C9
Helmstadt D 74 C6
Helmstedt D 79 B9
Heľpa SK 147 D9
Helppi FIN 117 D13
Helpringham GB 11 F11
Helse D 82 C6
Helsingborg S 87 C11
Helsinge DK 87 C10
Helsingfors FIN 127 E12
Helsingør DK 87 C11
Helsinki FIN 127 E12
Helstad N 105 A12
Helston GB 12 E4
Heltermaa EST 130 D6
Heltersberg D 21 F9
Helvaci TR 177 B9
Helvécia H 150 D4
Helvoirt NL 183 B6
Hem DK 86 B3
Hem F 182 D2
Hemau D 75 D10
Hemavan S 108 E9
Hemeiuș RO 153 D9
Hemel Hempstead GB 15 D8
Hemer D 185 B8
Hemfjäll S 109 E12
Hemfjällstangen S 102 D5
Hemhofen D 75 C8
Hemling S 107 D15
Hemme D 82 B6
Hemmet DK 86 D2
Hemmingen D 78 B6
Hemmingen S 107 B17
Hemmingsmark S 118 D6
Hemmoor D 17 A12
Hemnesberget N 108 D6
Hemnestad N 111 C11
Hempnall GB 15 C11
Hempstead GB 15 C9
Hemsbach D 21 E11
Hemsbünde D 82 D6
Hemsby GB 15 B12
Hemse S 93 E12
Hemsedal N 101 E9
Hemsjö S 107 D14
Hemslingen D 82 D7
Hemsloh D 17 C11
Hemsö S 103 A15
Hemyock GB 13 D8
Henån S 91 C10
Hénanbihen F 23 C7
Henarejos E 47 E10
Hencida H 151 C8
Hendaye F 32 D2
Hendon GB 15 D8
Hengelo NL 16 D6
Hengelo NL 17 D7
Hengersberg D 76 E4
Hengevelde NL 183 A9
Henggart CH 27 E10
Hengoed GB 13 B8
Hénin-Beaumont F 18 D6
Henley-on-Thames GB 15 D7
Hennan S 103 B10
Henndorf am Wallersee A 73 A7
Hennebont F 22 E5
Hennef (Sieg) D 21 C8
Hennes N 110 C9
Henne Stationsby DK 86 D2
Hennezel F 26 D5
Hennickendorf D 80 B4
Hennigsdorf Berlin D 80 A4
Henningskälen S 106 D8
Henningsvær N 110 D7
Hennseid N 90 A5
Hennset N 104 E4
Hennstedt D 82 B6
Hennweiler D 21 E8
Henrichemont F 25 F8
Henryków PL 81 E12
Henrykowo PL 139 B9
Henstridge GB 13 D10
Hepola FIN 119 C13
Heppen B 183 C6
Heppenheim (Bergstraße)
D 21 E11
Herálec CZ 77 C8
Herálec CZ 77 C9
Herbault F 24 E5
Herbertingen D 27 D11
Herbertstown IRL 8 C6
Herbés E 42 F3
Herbeumont B 184 E3
Herbignac F 23 F7
Herbolzheim D 27 D8
Herborn D 21 C10
Herbrechtingen D 75 E7
Herbstein D 21 C12
Herby PL 142 E6
Herceghalom H 149 A11
Herceg-Novi MNE 162 E6
Hercegovac HR 149 E8
Hercegszántó H 150 F2
Herdecke D 17 F8
Herdorf D 21 C9
Hereclean RO 151 C11
Heréd H 150 B4
Hereford GB 13 A9
Héreg H 149 A11
Herencia E 46 F6
Herend H 149 B9
Herent B 19 C10
Herentals B 19 B10
Herenthout B 182 C5
Hérépian F 34 C5
Herford D 17 D11
Hergatz D 71 B9
Hergiswil CH 70 D6
Herguijuela E 45 F9
Héric F 23 F8
Héricourt F 27 E6
Hérimoncourt F 27 F6
Heringen (Helme) D 79 D8
Heringen (Werra) D 79 E7
Heringsdorf D 83 B10
Heringsdorf D 84 C6
Heriot GB 5 D11
Herisau CH 27 F11
Hérisson F 29 B11
Herk-de-Stad B 19 C11
Herkenbosch NL 183 C8
Herkingen NL 182 B4
Herleshausen D 79 D7
Herlev DK 87 D10
Herlufmagle DK 87 E9
Herm F 32 C3
Hermagor A 73 C7
Hermannsburg D 83 E8
Hermanovce SK 145 E3
Hermanowice PL 144 D6
Hermansverk N 100 D5
Heřmanův Městec CZ 77 C9
Herment F 29 D11
Hermersberg D 186 C4
Hermeskeil D 21 E7
Hermisende E 39 E6
Hermsdorf D 79 E10
Hernád H 150 C3
Hernádnémeti H 145 G2
Hernani E 32 D2
Hernansancho E 46 C3
Herne B 19 C9
Herne D 17 E8
Herne Bay GB 15 E11
Herning DK 86 C3
Heroldsbach D 75 C8
Héron B 19 C11
Hérouville-St-Clair F 23 B11
Herøy N 100 B3
Herpf D 79 E7
Herrala FIN 127 D13
Herramélluri E 40 C5
Herräng S 99 B11
Herré F 32 C5
Herre N 90 A6
Herrenberg D 27 C10
Herrera E 53 B7
Herrera del Duque E 45 F10
Herrera de los Navarros E 42 E1
Herrera de Pisuerga E 40 C3
Herreria E 47 C9
Herreruela E 45 F7
Herrestad S 91 C10
Herrieden D 75 D8
Herringbotn N 108 E6
Herrlisheim F 186 D4
Herrljunga S 91 C13
Herrnhut D 81 D7
Herrö S 102 B7
Herrsching am Ammersee
D 75 G9
Herrskog S 103 A15
Herrvik S 93 E13
Herry F 25 F8
Hersbruck D 75 C9
Herschbach D 21 C9
Herscheid D 21 B9
Herschweiler-Pettersheim
D 186 C3
Herselt B 19 B10
Herslev DK 86 D5
Herstal B 19 C12
Herstmonceux GB 15 F9
Herston GB 3 H11
Herten D 17 E8
Hertford GB 15 D8
Hertník SK 145 E3
Hertsa UA 153 A8
Hertsånger S 118 F6
Hertsjö S 103 D11
Herve B 19 C12
Hervik N 94 D3
Herwijnen NL 183 B6
Herzberg D 80 C4
Herzberg D 83 C11
Herzberg D 84 E3
Herzberg am Harz D 79 C7
Herzebrock-Clarholz D 17 E10
Herzele B 19 C8
Herzfelde D 80 B5
Herzhorn D 17 A12
Herzlake D 17 C9
Herzogenaurach D 75 C8
Herzogenbuchsee CH 27 F8
Herzogenburg A 77 F9
Herzogenrath D 183 D8
Herzsprung D 83 D12
Hesdin F 18 D5
Hesel D 17 B9
Hesjeberg N 111 C13
Hesjestranda N 100 A6
Heskestad N 94 F4
Hespérange L 20 E6
Heßdorf D 75 C8
Hesselager DK 87 E7
Hessen D 79 B8
Hessfjorden N 112 D3
Heßheim D 21 E10
Hessisch Lichtenau D 78 D6
Hessisch Oldendorf D 17 D12
Hest N 100 D3
Hestenesøyri N 100 C4
Hestnes N 104 D5
Hestøy N 108 E3
Hestra S 91 E14
Hestra S 92 D6
Hestvik N 105 B10
Hestvika N 104 D6
Heswall GB 10 E5
Hetekylä FIN 119 D17
Hetés H 149 D9
Hethersett GB 15 B11
Hetlingen D 82 C7
Hettange-Grande F 186 C1
Hettenleidelheim D 186 B5
Hettenshausen D 75 E10
Hettingen D 27 D11
Hetton GB 11 C7
Hettstedt D 79 C10
Hetzerath D 21 E7
Heubach D 187 D8
Heuchelheim D 21 C11
Heuchin F 18 D5
Heudicourt-sous-les-Côtes
F 26 C4
Heukelum NL 16 E4
Heusden B 19 B11
Heusden NL 183 B6
Heusenstamm D 21 D11
Heustreu D 75 B7
Heusweiler D 186 C2
Heves H 150 B5
Hévíz H 149 C8
Hevlín CZ 77 E10
Hexham GB 5 F12
Heyrieux F 31 D7
Heysham GB 10 C6
Heythuysen NL 19 B12
Heywood GB 11 D7
Hida RO 151 C11
Hidas H 149 D10
Hidasnémeti H 145 G3
Hiddenhausen D 17 D11
Hiddensee D 84 A4
Hidirköylü TR 177 D10
Hidișelu de Sus RO 151 D9
Hieflau A 73 A10
Hiendelaencina E 47 B7
Hiersac F 28 D5
Hietakangas FIN 115 D3
Hietama FIN 123 E15
Hietanen FIN 117 D11
Hietanen FIN 128 B7
Hietaniemi FIN 115 D6
Hietaniemi FIN 121 B11
Hietaperä FIN 121 F13
Higham Ferrers GB 15 C7
Highampton GB 12 D6
High Bentham GB 10 C6
Highbridge GB 13 C9
Highclere GB 13 C12
High Halden GB 15 E10
High Hawsker GB 11 C10
High Hesket GB 5 F11
High Lorton GB 5 F10
Highnam GB 13 B10
Highworth GB 13 B11
High Wycombe GB 15 D7
Higuera de Arjona E 53 A9
Higuera de la Serena E 51 B8
Higuera de la Sierra E 51 D7
Higuera de Llerena E 51 C8
Higuera de Vargas E 51 C6
Higuera la Real E 51 C6
Higueruela E 55 B10
Higueruelas E 48 E3
Hihnavaara FIN 115 D4
Hiidenkylä FIN 123 C15
Hiidenlahti FIN 125 E10
Hiilikumpu FIN 119 C15
Hiirikylä FIN 125 C10
Hiirola FIN 128 B7
Hiisijärvi FIN 121 F12
Híjar E 42 E3
Hikiä FIN 127 D12
Hilbersdorf D 80 E4
Hilchenbach D 21 C10
Hildburghausen D 75 B8
Hilden D 21 B7
Hilders D 79 E7
Hilderthorpe GB 11 C11
Hildesheim D 78 B6
Hilgertshausen D 75 F9
Hilișeu-Horia RO 153 A8
Hiliuți MD 153 B10
Hillared S 91 D13
Hille D 17 D11
Hille S 103 E13
Hillebola S 99 B9
Hillegom NL 16 D3
Hillerød DK 87 D10
Hillerse D 79 B7
Hillerslev DK 86 A3
Hillerslev DK 86 E6
Hillerstorp S 88 A5
Hillesham N 111 C13
Hillesheim D 21 D7
Hillesøy N 111 A15
Hillevik S 103 E13
Hilli FIN 123 C11
Hillilä FIN 123 B11
Hill of Fearn GB 3 K9
Hillosensalmi FIN 128 C6
Hillsand S 106 C8
Hillsborough GB 7 D10
Hillside GB 5 B12
Hillswick GB 3 E14
Hilltown GB 7 D10
Hilpoltstein D 75 D9
Hilsenheim F 186 E4
Hilton GB 11 F8
Hiltpoltstein D 75 C9
Hiltula FIN 129 B9
Hilvarenbeek NL 183 C6
Hilversum NL 16 D4
Himalansaari FIN 128 C8
Himanka FIN 123 B11
Himarë AL 168 D2
Himberg A 77 F10
Himbergen D 83 D9
Himesháza H 149 D11
Himma EST 131 F14

Himmaste EST 131 E14
Himmelberg A 73 C9
Himmelpforten D 17 A12
Hîncești MD 154 D3
Hinckley GB 11 F9
Hindås S 91 D11
Hindenburg D 83 E11
Hinderwell GB 11 B10
Hindhead GB 15 E7
Hindley GB 10 D6
Hindon GB 13 C10
Hindrem N 104 D8
Hinganmaa FIN 117 D15
Hingham GB 15 B10
Hinnerjöki FIN 126 C6
Hinnerup DK 86 C6
Hinneryd S 87 B13
Hinojal E 45 E8
Hinojales E 51 C6
Hinojares E 55 D7
Hinojasas de Calatrava E 54 B4
Hinojos E 51 E7
Hinojosa E 47 B9
Hinojosa de Duero E 45 C7
Hinojosa de Jarque E 42 F2
Hinojosa del Duque E 51 B9
Hinojosa del Valle E 51 C7
Hinojosa de San Vicente
E 46 D3
Hinova RO 159 D10
Hinte D 17 B8
Hinterhermsdorf D 80 E6
Hinternah D 75 A8
Hinterrhein CH 71 D8
Hintersee A 73 A7
Hintersee D 84 C6
Hinterweidenthal D 186 C4
Hinterzarten D 27 E9
Hinthaara FIN 127 E13
Hinwil CH 27 F10
Hinx F 32 C4
Hippolytushoef NL 16 C3
Hîrbovăț MD 154 C2
Hîrjauca MD 154 C2
Hirka TR 181 B9
Hirnyk UA 144 C9
Hirrlingen D 27 D10
Hirschaid D 75 C9
Hirschau D 75 C10
Hirschberg D 75 B10
Hirschfeld D 80 D5
Hirschhorn (Neckar) D 187 C6
Hirsilä FIN 127 B11
Hirsingue F 27 E7
Hirson F 19 E9
Hîrtop MD 154 D3
Hîrtopul Mare MD 154 C3
Hirtshals DK 90 D6
Hirvas FIN 119 B14
Hirvaskoski FIN 120 D9
Hirvasperä FIN 119 E13
Hirvasvaara FIN 115 E5
Hirvelä FIN 119 D16
Hirvelä FIN 121 F14
Hirvensalmi FIN 128 B6
Hirviäkuru FIN 115 D1
Hirvihaara FIN 127 D13
Hirvijoki FIN 123 E10
Hirvikylä FIN 123 F9
Hirvilahti FIN 124 D8
Hirvineva FIN 119 E14
Hirvivaara FIN 121 E13
Hirvlax FIN 122 D8
Hirwaun GB 13 B7
Hirzenhain D 21 D12
Hisarönü TR 181 C8
Hishult S 87 C12
Hissjön S 122 C4
Histon GB 15 C9
Hita E 47 C6
Hitchin GB 15 D8
Hitis FIN 126 F8
Hittarp S 87 C11
Hittisau A 71 C9
Hitzacker D 83 D10
Hitzendorf A 148 B4
Hitzhusen D 83 C7
Hiukkajoki FIN 129 B12
Hiyche UA 144 C8
Hjäggsjö S 122 C3
Hjallerup DK 86 A6
Hjältevad S 92 D6
Hjärnarp S 87 C11
Hjärsås S 88 C6
Hjärtum S 91 C11
Hjarup DK 86 E4
Hjelle N 100 C6
Hjellestad N 94 B2
Hjellsand N 110 C8
Hjelmeland N 94 D4
Hjelset N 100 A7
Hjerkinn N 101 B11
Hjerm DK 86 C3
Hjo S 92 C4
Hjordkær DK 86 E4
Hjørring DK 90 E7
Hjorted S 93 D8
Hjortkvarn S 92 B6
Hjortsberga S 88 B6
Hjørungavåg N 100 B4
Hjuvik S 91 D10
Hlavani UA 154 F4
Hlebine HR 149 D7
Hligeni MD 154 B3
Hlinaia MD 153 A10
Hlinaia MD 154 C4
Hlinaia MD 154 D5
Hliník nad Hronom SK 147 D7
Hlinné SK 145 F4
Hlinsko CZ 77 C9
Hlohovec SK 146 E5
Hlubočky CZ 146 B4
Hluboká nad Vltavou CZ 77 D6
Hlučín CZ 146 B6
Hlyboka UA 153 A7
Hlybokaye BY 133 F3
Hlyboke UA 155 B5
Hnatkiv UA 154 A2
Hněvotín CZ 77 C12
Hniezdné SK 145 E2
Hnizdychiv UA 145 E9
Hnojník CZ 147 B7
Hnúšťa SK 147 D9
Hobol H 149 D9
Hobøl N 95 C13
Hobro DK 86 B5
Hoburg S 93 F12
Hoçë e Qytetit RKS 163 E10
Hoceni RO 153 D12
Hochdonn D 82 B6
Hochdorf CH 27 F9
Hochdorf D 71 A9
Hochfelden F 27 C8
Höchheim D 75 B7
Hochspeyer D 186 C4
Hochstadt (Pfalz) D 187 C5
Höchstadt an der Aisch D 75 C8
Höchstädt an der Donau
D 75 E8
Hochstetten-Dhaun D 21 E8
Höchst im Odenwald D 187 B6
Hoçisht AL 168 C4
Hockenheim D 187 C6
Hoczew PL 145 E5
Hodac RO 152 D5
Hodalen N 101 B14
Hoddesdon GB 15 D8
Hodejov SK 147 E10
Hodenhagen D 82 E7
Hodkovice nad Mohelkou
CZ 81 E8
Hódmezővásárhely H 150 E5
Hodnet GB 10 F6
Hodod RO 151 C11
Hodonice CZ 77 E10
Hodonín CZ 77 E12
Hodoșa RO 152 D5
Hodruša-Hámre SK 147 E7
Hodsager DK 86 C3
Hodyszewo PL 141 E7
Hoek NL 16 F1
Hoek van Holland NL 16 E2
Hoem N 104 F4
Hoenderloo NL 183 A7
Hœnheim F 186 D4
Hoensbroek NL 19 C12
Hœrdt F 186 D4
Hoeselt B 19 C11
Hoevelaken NL 16 D4
Hoeven NL 16 E3
Hof D 21 C10
Hof D 75 B10
Hof N 95 C12
Hofbieber D 78 E6
Hoffstad N 104 C8
Hofgeismar D 21 B12
Hofheim am Taunus D 21 D10
Hofheim in Unterfranken
D 75 B8
Hofles N 105 B11
Hofors S 98 A6
Hofsøy N 111 B13
Hofterup S 87 D11
Höganäs S 87 C11
Högås S 108 E9
Högbacka S 103 D12
Högbo S 103 E12
Högboda S 97 C9
Högbränna S 109 F15
Högen S 103 C13
Högfors S 97 B15
Högfors S 97 C13
Höghilag RO 152 E5
Hoghiz RO 152 F6
Høgild DK 86 C3
Högland S 107 B9
Höglekardalen S 105 E15
Høgli N 111 B14
Höglunda S 107 E9
Hogosht RKS 164 D4
Högrun S 105 D16
Högsåra FIN 126 F7
Högsäter S 91 B11
Högsäter S 96 C6
Högsäter S 97 D8
Högsby S 89 A10
Høgset N 104 F3
Högsjö S 92 A7
Högsjö S 103 A14
Hogstad S 92 C6
Hogstorp S 91 C10
Högträsk S 116 E5
Högvålen S 102 B4
Hőgyész H 149 C10
Hohberg D 186 E4
Hohen-Altheim D 75 E8
Hohenaspe D 82 C7
Hohenau D 76 E5
Hohenau an der March A 77 E11
Hohenberg A 77 G9
Hohenbocka D 80 D6
Hohenbucko D 80 C4
Hohenburg D 75 D10
Hohendorf D 84 B5
Hoheneich A 77 E8
Hohenems A 71 C9
Hohenfels D 75 D10
Hohenfurch D 71 B11
Hohengöhren D 79 A11
Hohenhameln D 79 B7
Hohenkammer D 75 F10
Hohenkirchen D 17 A9
Höhenkirchen-Siegertsbrunn
D 75 F10
Hohenleuben D 79 E11
Hohenlockstedt D 82 C7
Hohenmocker D 84 C4
Hohenmölsen D 79 D11
Hohennauen D 83 E12
Hohenpeißenberg D 71 B12
Hohenroth D 75 B7
Hohensaaten D 84 E6
Hohenseeden D 79 B11
Hohenstein-Ernstthal D 79 E12
Hohenthann D 75 E11
Hohenthurm D 79 C11
Hohen Wangelin D 83 C12
Hohenwart D 75 E9
Hohenwarth D 76 D3
Hohenwestedt D 82 B7
Höhn D 21 C9
Hohn D 82 B7
Hohne D 79 A7
Hohnhorst D 17 D12
Hohnstorf (Elbe) D 83 D9
Höhr-Grenzhausen D 21 D9
Hohwacht (Ostsee) D 83 B9
Hoikankylä FIN 124 E7
Hoikka FIN 121 E12
Hoisdorf D 83 C8
Hoisko FIN 123 D11
Højby DK 86 E6
Højby DK 87 D9
Højer DK 86 F3
Højmark DK 86 C2
Højslev DK 86 B4
Højslev Stationsby DK 86 B4
Hok S 92 D4
Hökåsen S 98 C7
Hökerum S 91 D13
Hökhult S 91 A13
Hökhuvud S 99 B10
Hokka FIN 128 B6
Hokkaskylä FIN 123 E12
Hokksund N 95 C11
Hokland N 111 C11
Hökmark S 118 F6
Hökön S 88 C6
Hol N 101 E8
Hol N 111 C11
Holand N 110 D9
Holandsvika N 108 E5
Holasovice CZ 142 G4
Holbæk DK 86 B6
Holbæk DK 87 D9
Holbeach GB 11 F12
Holboca RO 153 C11
Holbøl DK 86 F4
Holbrook GB 15 D11
Holdorf D 17 C10
Holeby DK 83 A10
Hølen N 95 C13
Holešov CZ 146 C5
Holevik N 100 D1
Holguera E 45 E8
Holíč SK 77 E12
Holice CZ 77 B9
Höljes S 102 E4
Holkestad N 110 E8
Holkonkylä FIN 123 E11
Hollabrunn A 77 E10
Hollandscheveld NL 17 C7
Hollange B 19 E12
Hollås N 105 C11
Holle D 79 B7
Høllen N 90 C2
Hollenbach D 75 F9
Hollenbek D 83 C9
Hollenegg A 73 C11
Hollenstedt D 82 D7
Hollenstein an der Ybbs
A 73 A10
Hollern-Twielenfleth D 82 C7
Hollfeld D 75 C9
Hollingstedt D 82 B6
Hollington GB 15 F10
Hollingworth GB 11 E8
Hollóháza H 145 F3
Hollola FIN 127 D14
Hollum NL 16 B5
Hollybush GB 4 E7
Hollyford IRL 8 C6
Hollywood IRL 7 F9
Holm D 82 C7
Holm DK 86 E5
Holm N 105 A12
Holm N 110 C9
Holm S 103 A12
Holm S 107 E13
Hol'ma UA 154 B5
Holmajärvi S 111 E18
Holme-Olstrup DK 87 E9
Holme-on-Spalding-Moor
GB 11 D10
Holmestrand N 95 D12
Holmfirth GB 11 D8
Holmfors S 118 D4
Holmisperä FIN 123 D14
Holmsjö S 89 C9
Holmsjö S 107 A14
Holmsjö S 107 D12
Holmsund S 122 C4
Holmsvattensel S 118 B6
Holmsveden S 103 D12
Holmträsk S 107 B16
Hölö S 93 A11
Holod RO 151 D9
Hołodowska PL 144 C7
Holoșnița MD 153 A12
Holoubkov CZ 76 C5
Holovets'ko UA 145 E6
Holovne UA 141 H10
Holsbybrunn S 92 E6
Holsljunga S 91 E12
Holsta EST 131 F14
Holstebro DK 86 C3
Holsted DK 86 D3
Hölstein CH 27 F8
Holsworthy GB 12 D6
Holt GB 10 E6
Holt GB 15 B11
Holt N 111 B16
Holt N 111 B17
Holte DK 87 D10
Holten NL 17 D6
Holtet N 102 E3
Holtgast D 17 A9
Holthusen D 83 C10
Holtsee D 83 B7
Holungen D 79 D7
Holwerd NL 16 B5
Holycross IRL 9 C7
Holyhead GB 10 E2
Holywell GB 7 D7
Holywell GB 10 E5
Holywood GB 4 F5
Holzappel D 185 D8
Holzen D 78 C6
Holzgerlingen D 187 D7
Holzhausen an der Haide
D 21 D9
Holzheim D 21 D11
Holzheim D 75 E8
Holzheim D 75 E8
Holzheim D 75 F7
Holzkirchen D 72 A4
Holzminden D 21 A12
Holzthaleben D 79 D8
Holzweißig D 79 C11
Holzwickede D 17 E9
Høm DK 87 E9
Homberg (Efze) D 21 B12
Homberg (Ohm) D 21 C11
Hombourg-Budange F 186 C1
Hombourg-Haut F 186 C2
Homburg D 21 F8
Homécourt F 20 F5
Homersfield GB 15 C11
Homesh AL 168 A3
Hommelstø N 108 F4
Hommelvik N 105 E9
Hommersåk N 94 E3
Homna S 103 D10
Homocea RO 153 E10
Homokmégy H 150 E3
Homokszentgyörgy H 149 D9
Homoroade RO 151 B11
Homorod RO 152 E6
Homrogd H 145 G2
Homyel' BY 133 F5
Hondarribia E 32 D2
Hondón de las Nieves E 56 E3
Hondón de los Frailes E 56 E3
Hondschoote F 18 C6
Hône I 68 B4
Hønefoss N 95 B12
Honfleur F 23 B12
Høng DK 87 D8
Honiton GB 13 D8
Honkajoki FIN 122 G8
Honkakoski FIN 126 B7
Honkakylä FIN 122 E9
Honkilahti FIN 126 D7
Honley GB 11 D8
Honningsvåg N 100 B2
Honningsvåg N 113 B16
Hönö S 91 D10
Honoratka PL 142 B5
Honrubia E 47 E8
Honrubia de la Cuesta E 40 F4
Hønseby N 113 B11
Hontacillas E 47 E8
Hontalbilla E 40 F3
Hontanaya E 47 E7
Hontianske Nemce SK 147 E7
Hontoria de la Cantera E 40 D4
Hontoria del Pinar E 40 E5
Hontoria de Valdearados
E 40 E4
Hoofddorp NL 16 D3
Hoogerheide NL 16 F2
Hoogersmilde NL 16 C6
Hoogeveen NL 17 C6
Hoogezand-Sappemeer
NL 17 B7
Hoogkarspel NL 16 C4
Hoog-Keppel NL 183 B8
Hoogkerk NL 17 B6
Hoogland NL 183 A6
Hoogstede D 17 C7
Hoogstraten B 16 F3
Hoogvliet NL 16 E2
Hook GB 11 D10
Hook GB 14 E7
Hooksiel D 17 A10
Höör S 87 D13
Hoorn NL 16 C4
Hoornaar NL 182 B5
Hopârta RO 152 E3
Hope GB 10 E5
Hope N 100 E3
Hopeman GB 3 K10
Hopen N 111 E10
Hopfgarten im Brixental
A 72 B5
Hopfgarten in Defereggen
A 72 C6
Hopland N 100 C4
Hoppstädten D 21 E8
Hoppula FIN 115 F2
Hopseidet N 113 B20
Hopsten D 17 D9
Hopton GB 15 B12
Hoptonheath GB 13 A9
Hoptrup DK 86 E4
Horam GB 15 F9
Horažďovice CZ 76 D5
Horb am Neckar D 27 D10
Horbova UA 153 A8
Hörbranz A 71 B9
Hørby DK 90 E7
Hörby S 87 D13
Horcajo de las Torres E 45 B10
Horcajo de los Montes E 46 F3
Horcajo de Santiago E 47 E7
Horcajo Medianero E 45 C10
Horda N 94 C5
Horda S 88 A6
Hörde D 185 B7
Horden GB 11 B9
Hordum DK 86 B3
Horea RO 151 E10
Horeb GB 12 A6
Horești MD 153 C11
Horezu RO 160 C3
Horgen CH 27 F10
Horgenzell D 71 B9
Horgești RO 153 E10
Horgoš SRB 150 E4
Horia RO 153 D9
Horia RO 155 C2
Horia RO 155 D2
Hořice CZ 77 B9
Horinchove UA 145 G7
Horitschon A 149 A7
Horjul SLO 73 D9
Horka D 81 D7
Hôrka SK 145 E1
Hörken S 97 B12
Horley GB 15 E8
Hörlitz D 80 C5
Hormakumpu FIN 117 C14
Hormilla E 40 D6
Horn A 77 E9
Horn N 95 A12
Horn N 108 E3
Horn S 92 D7
Hornachos E 51 B7
Hornachuelos E 51 D9
Horná Kraľová SK 146 E5
Horná Potôň SK 146 E4
Horná Streda SK 146 D5
Horná Štubňa SK 147 D7
Horná Súča SK 146 D5
Horná Ves SK 146 D6
Hornbach D 21 F8
Horn-Bad Meinberg D 17 E11
Hornbæk DK 87 C10
Hornburg D 79 B8
Hornby GB 10 C6
Horncastle GB 11 E11
Horndal N 109 A10
Horndal S 98 B6
Horndean GB 14 F6
Horne DK 86 D3
Horne DK 86 E6
Horne DK 90 D6
Horneburg D 82 C7
Hörnefors S 122 C3
Horné Obdokovce SK 146 E6
Horné Orešany SK 146 E4
Horné Saliby SK 146 E5
Horné Srnie SK 146 C6
Horní Bečva CZ 146 C6
Horní Benešov CZ 146 B5
Horní Beřkovice CZ 76 B6
Horní Cerekev CZ 77 D8
Horní Jelení CZ 77 B10
Horní Jiřetín CZ 80 E5
Horní Lideč CZ 146 C6
Horní Maršov CZ 81 E9
Horní Moštěnice CZ 146 C4
Hornindal N 100 C5
Hørning DK 86 C6
Horní Planá CZ 76 E6
Horní Slavkov CZ 75 B12
Horní Štěpánov CZ 77 C11
Horní Stropnice CZ 77 E7
Horní Suchá CZ 146 B6
Hornmyr S 107 C14
Hornnäs S 97 B9
Hornnes N 90 B2
Hornön S 103 A14
Hornos E 55 C7
Hornow D 81 C7
Hornoy-le-Bourg F 18 E4
Hornsea GB 11 D11
Hörnsjö S 107 D17
Hornslet DK 86 C6
Hornstorf D 83 C11
Hornsyld DK 86 D5
Hörnum D 82 A4
Hornum DK 86 B4
Horný Bar SK 146 F4
Horný Tisovník SK 147 E8
Horný Vadičov SK 147 C7
Horoatu Crasnei RO 151 C10
Horodiște MD 153 A11
Horodiște MD 153 B10
Horodkivka UA 154 A3
Horodło PL 144 B9
Horodniceni RO 153 B8
Horodnye UA 154 F3
Horodok UA 144 D8
Horoměřice CZ 76 B6
Horonda UA 145 G6
Horonkylä FIN 122 E7
Hořovice CZ 76 C5
Horrabridge GB 12 D6
Horreby DK 83 A11
Horred S 91 E11
Hörsching A 76 F6
Horsdal N 108 B7
Horseleap IRL 6 F5
Horsens DK 86 D5
Horsforth GB 11 D8
Horsham GB 15 E8
Hørsholm DK 87 D10
Hörsingen D 79 B9
Horslunde DK 87 F8
Horsmanaho FIN 125 E12
Horsnes N 111 B18
Horšovský Týn CZ 76 C3
Horsskog S 98 B8
Horst NL 16 F6
Horst (Holstein) D 82 C7
Horstedt D 17 B12
Hörstel D 17 D9
Horstmar D 17 D8
Hort H 150 B4
Horten N 95 D12
Hortezuela E 40 F6
Hortigüela E 40 D5
Hortlax S 118 D6
Hortobágy H 151 B7
Horton in Ribblesdale GB 11 C7
Høruphav DK 86 F5
Hørve DK 87 D8
Hörvik S 89 C7
Horw CH 70 C6
Horwich GB 10 D6
Horyniec-Zdrój PL 144 C7
Horyszów PL 144 B8
Hösbach D 21 D12
Hosena D 80 D6
Hosenfeld D 74 A5
Hoset N 108 B8
Hosingen L 20 D6
Hosio FIN 119 C15
Hosjö S 106 E8
Hosjöbottnarna S 105 E15
Hoşköy TR 173 C7
Hospital IRL 8 D6
Hossa FIN 121 D14
Hössjö S 122 C3
Hossjön S 107 D9
Hoßkirch D 27 E11
Hosszúhetény H 149 D10
Hosszúpályi H 151 C8
Hosszúpereszteg H 149 B8
Hošťálková CZ 146 C5
Hostalric E 43 D9
Hostens F 32 B4
Hostěradice CZ 77 E10
Hostie SK 146 E6
Hostinné CZ 81 E9
Hošťka CZ 76 B6
Hostomice CZ 76 C6
Hostomice CZ 80 E5
Hoston N 104 E7
Höstoppen S 106 C8
Hostouň CZ 75 C12
Hostrupskov DK 86 E4
Höstsätern S 102 C4
Hot AL 163 E7
Hotarele RO 161 E8
Hoting S 107 C10
Hotinja vas SLO 148 D5
Hotonj BIH 162 D4
Hotton B 19 D11
Hou DK 86 A6
Houbie GB 3 D15
Houdain F 18 D6
Houdan F 24 C6
Houdelaincourt F 26 C3
Houécourt F 26 D4
Houeillès F 32 B6
Houeydets F 33 D6
Houffalize B 19 D12
Houghton le Spring GB 5 F14
Houghton Regis GB 15 D7
Houlbjerg DK 86 C5
Houlgate F 23 B11
Hourtin F 28 E3
Hourtin-Plage F 28 E3
Houten NL 16 D4
Houthalen B 19 B11
Houthulst B 18 C6
Houton GB 3 H10
Houtsala FIN 126 E6
Houtskär FIN 126 E5
Houyet B 184 D3
Hov DK 86 D6
Hov N 101 E12
Hov N 108 D4
Hov N 111 A18
Hova S 92 B4
Hovborg DK 86 D3
Hovda N 94 D4
Hovde N 90 B4
Hovden N 110 C8
Hovdevik N 100 B2
Hove GB 15 F8
Hovedgård DK 86 D5
Hövelhof D 17 E11
Hoven DK 86 D3
Hoveton GB 15 B11
Hovězí CZ 146 C6
Hovid S 103 B13
Hovin N 104 E8
Hovingham GB 11 C10
Hovmantorp S 89 B8
Høvringen N 101 C10
Hovslund Stationsby DK 86 E4
Hovsta S 97 D13
Howden GB 11 D10
Howth IRL 7 F10
Höxter D 17 E12
Hoya D 17 C12
Hoya Gonzalo E 55 B9
Høyanger N 100 D4
Høydal N 90 A5
Hoyerswerda D 80 D6
Hoylake GB 10 E5
Høylandet N 105 B12
Hoym D 79 C9
Hoyocasero E 46 D3
Hoyo de Manzanares E 46 C5
Hoyos E 45 D7
Hoyos del Espino E 45 D10
Höytiä FIN 123 F14
Hoyvík FO 2 A3
Hozha BY 137 F8
Hrabove UA 154 A4
Hrabyně CZ 146 B6
Hradec Králové CZ 77 B9
Hradec nad Moravicí CZ 146 B5
Hradec nad Svitavou CZ 77 C10
Hrádek CZ 147 B7
Hrádek nad Nisou CZ 81 E7
Hradenytsi UA 154 D6
Hradešice CZ 76 D5
Hradište SK 146 D6
Hradište pod Vrátnom SK
146 D5
Hradištko CZ 76 C6
Hraň SK 145 F4
Hranice CZ 75 B11
Hranice CZ 146 B5
Hranovnica SK 145 F1
Hrasnica BIH 157 E9
Hrastnik SLO 73 D11
Hrawzhyshki BY 137 E12
Hrebenyky UA 154 D5
Hreljin HR 67 B10
Hrhov SK 145 F2
Hrimne UA 145 D8
Hriňová SK 147 D9
Hristovaia MD 154 A3
Hrnjadi BIH 156 D5
Hrob CZ 80 E5
Hrochot SK 147 D8
Hrochův Týnec CZ 77 C9
Hrodna BY 140 C9
Hromnice CZ 76 C4
Hronec SK 147 D9
Hronov CZ 77 B10
Hronovce SK 147 E7
Hronský Beň Beňx SK 147 E7
Hrotovice CZ 77 D10
Hroznová Lhota CZ 146 D4
Hrtkovci SRB 158 D4
Hrubieszów PL 144 B8
Hrușca MD 154 A3
Hrušky CZ 77 E11
Hrușova MD 154 C3
Hrušovany SK 146 E6
Hrušovany nad Jevišovkou
CZ 77 E10
Hruštín SK 147 C8
Hruszniew PL 141 F7
Hrvaćani BIH 157 C7
Hrvace HR 156 E6
Hrvatska Dubica HR 157 B6
Hrvatska Kostajnica HR 156 B6
Hrynyava UA 152 B5
Huaröd S 88 D5
Huarte E 32 E2
Hubová SK 147 C8
Hückelhoven D 20 B6
Hückeswagen D 21 B8
Hucknall GB 11 E9
Hucksjöåsen S 103 A10
Hucqueliers F 15 F12
Huddersfield GB 11 D8
Hüde D 17 C10
Hude (Oldenburg) D 17 B10
Hudești RO 153 A9
Hudiksvall S 103 C13
Huécija E 55 F7
Huedin RO 151 D11
Huélago E 55 E6
Huelgoat F 22 D4
Huelma E 53 A10
Huelva E 51 E6
Huelves E 47 D7
Huércal de Almería E 55 F8
Huércal-Overa E 55 E9
Huérguina E 47 D9
Huérmeces E 40 C4
Huerta del Marquesada E 47 D9
Huerta del Rey E 40 E5
Huerta de Valdecarábanos
E 46 E5
Huertahernando E 47 C8
Huerto E 42 D3
Huesa E 55 D6
Huesa del Común E 42 E2
Huesca E 41 D11
Huéscar E 55 D7
Huete E 47 D7
Huétor-Tájar E 53 B8
Huétor-Vega E 53 B9
Huévar E 51 E7
Hüfingen D 27 E9
Hufthamar N 94 B2
Hugh Town GB 12 F2
Hugulia N 101 D11
Hugyag H 147 E8
Huhdasjärvi FIN 127 C16
Huhmarkoski FIN 123 D10
Huhtamo FIN 127 C8
Huhti FIN 127 C10
Huhtilampi FIN 125 F14
Huhus FIN 125 E15
Huijbergen NL 182 C4
Huikola FIN 119 E16
Huisheim D 75 E8
Huisinis GB 2 K2
Huissen NL 16 E5
Huissinkylä FIN 122 E8
Huittinen FIN 126 C8
Huizen NL 16 D4
Hujakkala FIN 128 D8
Hukijärvi FIN 121 D10
Hukkajärvi FIN 125 B14
Hulín CZ 146 C4
Hulja EST 131 C12
Huljen S 103 B12
Hulkkola FIN 124 E8
Hull GB 11 D11
Hüllhorst D 17 D11
Hullo EST 130 D6
Hullsjön S 103 A12
Hüls D 183 C8
Hulsberg NL 183 D7
Hulst NL 16 F2
Hult S 91 A15
Hult S 92 D6
Hulterstad S 89 C11
Hultsfred S 92 D7
Hulu S 91 D13
Hulubești RO 160 D6
Hulyanka UA 154 C4
Hum BIH 157 F10
Hum BIH 162 D5
Humalajoki FIN 123 D13
Humanes de Madrid E 46 D5
Humanes de Mohernando
E 47 C6
Humberston GB 11 D11
Humbie GB 5 D11
Humble DK 83 A9
Humenné SK 145 F4
Humilladero E 53 B7
Humlebæk DK 87 D11
Humlegärdsstrand S 103 D13
Humlum DK 86 B3
Hummelholm S 107 D17
Hummelo NL 183 A8
Hummelsta S 98 C7
Hummuli EST 131 F12
Hum na Sutli HR 148 D5
Humpolec CZ 77 C8
Humppila FIN 127 D9
Humshaugh GB 5 E12
Huncovce SK 145 E1
Hundåla N 108 E4
Hundberg N 111 B18
Hundberg S 109 F16
Hundborg DK 86 B3
Hundeluft D 79 C11
Hunderdorf D 75 E12
Hundested DK 87 D9
Hundholmen N 111 D11
Hundorp N 101 C11
Hundsangen D 21 D9
Hundshübel D 79 E12
Hundsjön S 118 C7
Hundslund DK 86 D6
Hundvin N 100 E2
Hune DK 86 A5
Hunedoara RO 151 F10
Hünfeld D 78 E6
Hünfelden-Kirberg D 21 D10
Hunge S 103 A9
Hungen D 21 D11
Hungerford GB 13 C11
Hunnebostrand S 91 C9
Hunsel NL 19 B12
Hunspach F 27 C8
Hunstanton GB 11 F12
Huntingdon GB 15 C8
Huntlosen D 17 C10
Huntly GB 3 L11
Hünxe D 183 B9
Hunya H 151 D6
Huopanankoski FIN 123 D15
Hüpstedt D 79 D7
Hurbanovo SK 146 F6
Hurdal N 95 B14
Hurdalsverk N 95 B14
Hurezani RO 160 D3
Huriel F 29 C10
Hurissalo FIN 128 C8
Hurler's Cross IRL 8 C5
Hursley GB 13 C12
Hurst Green GB 15 E9
Hurstpierpoint GB 15 F8
Hurteles E 41 D7
Hürth D 21 C7
Huruiești RO 153 E10
Huruksela FIN 128 D6
Hurup DK 86 B2
Hurva S 87 D12
Huså S 105 E14
Husås S 106 E7
Husasău de Tinca RO 151 D8
Husbands Bosworth GB 13 A12
Husberget S 102 B6
Husbondliden S 107 B15
Husby D 82 A7
Husby S 97 B15
Husby S 99 B9
Hushcha UA 141 H9
Huși RO 153 D12
Husinec CZ 76 D5
Husjorda N 111 D9
Huskvarna S 92 D4
Husnes N 94 C3
Husnicioara RO 159 D10
Husøy N 108 D3
Hussjö S 103 A14
Hustopeče CZ 77 E11
Hustopeče nad Bečvou CZ
146 B5
Husum D 17 C12
Husum D 82 B6
Husum S 107 E16
Husvik N 108 E4
Huta PL 141 H3
Huta Komorowska PL 143 F12
Hutisko-Solanec CZ 146 C6
Hutovo BIH 162 D4
Hütschenhausen D 186 C3
Hüttau A 73 B7
Hüttenberg A 73 C10
Hüttisheim D 74 F6
Hüttlingen D 75 E7
Huttoft GB 11 E12
Hüttschlag A 73 B7
Huttukylä FIN 119 D15
Huttwil CH 27 F8
Huuhilonkylä FIN 121 F13
Huuki S 117 D11
Huutijärvi FIN 127 C11
Huutokoski FIN 124 F9
Huutokoski FIN 125 E12
Huutoniemi FIN 113 E18
Huvåsen S 118 D4
Hüven D 17 C9
Huwniki PL 145 D6
Huy B 19 C11
Hvalpsund DK 86 B4
Hvalsø DK 87 D9
Hvalvík FO 2 A2
Hvam DK 86 B5
Hvannasund FO 2 A3
Hvar HR 156 F5
Hvidbjerg DK 86 B3
Hvide Sande DK 86 C2
Hvidovre DK 87 D10
Hvilsom DK 86 B5
Hvittingfoss N 95 D11
Hvorslev DK 86 C5
Hwlffordd GB 12 B5
Hybe SK 147 C9
Hybo S 103 C11
Hycklinge S 92 D7
Hyères F 36 E4
Hyermanavichy BY 133 F3

Jävenitz D 79 A10
Javerlhac-et-la-Chapelle-St-Robert F 29 D7
Javgur MD 154 D3
Javier E 32 E3
Javorani BIH 157 C7
Javorník CZ 77 B12
Jävre S 118 D6
Javron-les-Chapelles F 23 D11
Jawor PL 81 D10
Jawornik Polski PL 144 D5
Jawor Solecki PL 141 H4
Jaworzno PL 142 D6
Jaworzno PL 143 F7
Jaworzyna Śląska PL 81 E10
Jayena E 53 C9
Jazeneuil F 28 C6
Jebel RO 159 B7
Jebjerg DK 86 B4
Jedburgh GB 5 E11
Jedlanka PL 141 G6
Jedlicze PL 144 D4
Jedlina-Zdrój PL 81 E10
Jedlińsk PL 141 G4
Jedlnia-Letnisko PL 141 H4
Jedlová CZ 77 C10
Jedľové Kostolany SK 146 E6
Jednorożec PL 139 D11
Jedovnice CZ 77 D11
Jjdrzejewo PL 85 E10
Jjdrzejów PL 143 E9
Jédula E 52 C5
Jedwabne PL 140 D6
Jedwabno PL 139 C10
Jeesiö FIN 117 D16
Jeesiöjärvi FIN 117 C14
Jegălia RO 161 E11
Jegun F 33 C6
Jegunovce MK 164 E3
Jejsing DK 86 F3
Jēkabpils LV 135 C11
Jektvik N 108 C5
Jelah BIH 157 C8
Jelašca BIH 157 F9
Jelcz-Laskowice PL 81 D12
Jelenia Góra PL 81 E9
Jeleniewo PL 136 E6
Jelenin PL 81 C8
Jelenje HR 67 B9
Jeleśnia PL 147 B8
Jelgava LV 134 C7
Jelka SK 146 E5
Jelling DK 86 D4
Jeloboc MD 154 C3
Jelovica SRB 165 C6
Jełowa PL 142 E5
Jels DK 86 E4
Jelsa HR 157 F6
Jelšane SLO 67 A9
Jelšava SK 145 F1
Jelsi I 63 D7
Jemeppe B 19 D10
Jemgum D 17 B8
Jemielnica PL 142 E5
Jemielno PL 81 C11
Jemnice CZ 77 D9
Jena D 79 E10
Jenbach A 72 B4
Jeneč CZ 76 B6
Jengen D 71 B11
Jenikowo PL 85 C8
Jennersdorf A 148 C6
Jenny S 93 D9
Jenő H 149 B10
Jensvoll N 101 A15
Jeppo FIN 122 D9
Jērcēni LV 131 F11
Jerchel D 79 B9
Jerez de la Frontera E 52 C4
Jerez del Marquesado E 55 E6
Jerez de los Caballeros E 51 C6
Jerfojaur S 109 E16
Jergol N 113 E14
Jergucat AL 168 E3
Jeri LV 131 F10
Jérica E 48 E3
Jerichow D 79 A11
Jerka PL 81 C11
Jernved DK 86 E3
Jerslev DK 87 D8
Jerslev DK 90 E7
Jerstad N 110 C9
Jerte E 45 D9
Jerup DK 90 D7
Jerzens A 71 C11
Jerzmanowa PL 81 C10
Jerzmanowice PL 143 F8
Jerzu I 64 D4
Jesenice CZ 76 B4
Jesenice CZ 77 C7
Jesenice HR 156 D4
Jesenice HR 156 F6
Jesenice SLO 73 D9
Jeseník CZ 77 B12
Jeseník nad Odrou CZ 146 B5
Jesenské SK 147 E10
Jeserig D 79 B11
Jeserig D 79 B12
Jesi I 67 E7
Jesionowo PL 85 D8
Jesolo I 66 A6
Jessen D 80 C3
Jessheim N 95 B14
Jeßnitz D 79 C11
Jesteburg D 83 D7
Jettingen-Scheppach D 75 F7
Jeumont F 19 D9
Jevenstedt D 82 B7
Jever D 17 A9
Jevíčko CZ 77 C11
Jevišovice CZ 77 E10
Jevnaker N 95 B12
Jezera BIH 157 D8
Jezerane HR 67 B11
Jezerc RKS 164 E3
Jezero BIH 157 D7
Jezero HR 156 B3
Jeżewo PL 138 C5
Jeżewo PL 140 D7
Jeziorany PL 136 F2
Jeziorzany PL 141 G6
Jeżów PL 141 G1
Jeżowe PL 144 C5
Jeżów Sudecki PL 81 E9
Jiana RO 159 E10
Jibert RO 152 E6
Jibou RO 151 C11
Jichișu de Jos RO 152 C3
Jičín CZ 77 B8
Jidvei RO 152 E4
Jieznas LT 137 D9
Jihlava CZ 77 D9
Jijila RO 155 C2
Jijona-Xixona E 56 D4
Jilava RO 161 E8
Jilavele RO 161 D9
Jilemnice CZ 81 E9
Jílové CZ 80 E6
Jílové u Prahy CZ 77 C7
Jiltjaur S 109 E12
Jimbolia RO 150 F6
Jimena E 53 A10
Jimena de la Frontera E 53 D6
Jimramov CZ 77 C10
Jina RO 152 F3
Jince CZ 76 C5
Jindřichov CZ 77 B12
Jindřichov CZ 142 F4
Jindřichův Hradec CZ 77 D8
Jiříkov CZ 81 E7
Jirkov CZ 76 A4
Jirlău RO 161 C10
Jirnsum NL 16 B5
Jirny CZ 77 B7
Jistebnice CZ 77 D7
Jistebník CZ 146 B6
Jitia RO 161 B9
Jlajkovci SRB 163 C10
Joachimsthal D 84 E5
Jobbágyi H 147 F9
Jobsbo S 97 B13
Jochberg A 72 B5
Jocketa D 79 E11
Jockfall S 116 E9
Jockgrim D 27 B9
Jódar E 55 D6
Jodłowa PL 144 D3
Jodłownik PL 144 D1
Jodoigne B 19 C10
Joensuu FIN 125 E13
Jõepere EST 131 C12
Joesjö S 108 E8
Joeström S 108 E8
Jõesuu EST 131 E9
Jœuf F 20 F6
Jõgeva EST 131 D12
Jõgua EST 131 C14
Johanngeorgenstadt D 75 B12
Johannisfors S 99 B10
Johannishus S 89 C8
Johanniskirchen D 76 E3
Johansfors S 89 B9
John o'Groats GB 3 H10
Johnston GB 12 B5
Johnstone GB 4 D7
Johnstown IRL 9 C7
Johnstown IRL 9 C10
Johovac BIH 158 D3
Jöhstadt D 76 A4
Jõhvi EST 131 C14
Joigny F 25 E9
Joinville F 26 D3
Joița RO 161 E7
Jokela FIN 119 B16
Jokela FIN 119 E16
Jokela FIN 127 D12
Jokelankylä FIN 123 C14
Jøkelfjordeidet N 112 C9
Jokijärvi FIN 121 C12
Jokijärvi FIN 123 D17
Joki-Kokko FIN 119 D16
Jokikunta FIN 127 E11
Jokikylä FIN 121 E11
Jokikylä FIN 122 E8
Jokikylä FIN 123 C13
Jokikylä FIN 123 C15
Jokilampi FIN 121 C12
Jokimaa FIN 127 D12
Jokioinen FIN 127 D9
Jokiperä FIN 122 E8
Jokipii FIN 122 E9
Jokivarsi FIN 123 E11
Jokivarsi FIN 123 E12
Jokkmokk S 116 E3
Jokūbavas LT 134 E2
Jolanda di Savoia I 66 C4
Jolanki FIN 117 E13
Jolda P 38 E3
Joloskylä FIN 119 D16
Joltai MD 154 E3
Jomala FIN 99 B13
Jømna N 101 E15
Jona CH 27 F10
Jönåker S 93 B9
Jonava LT 137 C9
Joncy F 30 B6
Jondal N 94 B4
Jonesborough GB 7 D10
Joniec PL 139 E10
Joniškėlis LT 135 D8
Joniškis LT 134 D7
Joniškis LT 137 C12
Jonkeri FIN 125 C13
Jönköping S 92 D4
Jonkowo PL 139 C9
Jonku FIN 120 D9
Jonquières F 35 B8
Jonsberg S 93 B9
Jonsered S 91 D11
Jonslund S 91 C12
Jonstorp S 87 C11
Jonzac F 28 E5
Jõõdre EST 130 D7
Joppolo I 59 B8
Jorăști RO 153 F11
Jorba E 43 D7
Jorcas E 42 F2
Jordanów PL 147 B9
Jordanów Śląski PL 81 E11
Jordbro S 99 D10
Jordbru N 108 B9
Jordbrua N 108 D8
Jördenstorf D 83 C13
Jordet N 102 D3
Jork D 82 C7
Jörlanda S 91 D10
Jormvattnet S 105 B16
Jörn S 118 D4
Joroinen FIN 125 F9
Jørpeland N 94 D4
Jorquera E 47 F9
Jørstadmoen N 101 D12
Jošanica BIH 157 E9
Jošanička Banja SRB 163 C10
Jošavka BIH 157 C7
Joseni RO 153 D6
Josenii Bârgăului RO 152 C5
Josifovo MK 169 B7
Josipdol HR 156 B3
Josipovac HR 149 E11
Josnes F 24 E6
Jössefors S 96 C8
Josselin F 22 E6
Jossund N 105 C9
Josvainiai LT 134 F7
Jota N 101 D15
Jou P 38 F5
Jouarre F 25 C9
Joué-lès-Tours F 24 F4
Joué-sur-Erdre F 23 E9
Jougne F 31 B9
Joukokylä FIN 121 D10
Jouques F 35 C10
Joure NL 16 C5
Journiac F 29 F7
Joutenniva FIN 123 B15
Joutsa FIN 127 B15
Joutseno FIN 129 C10
Joutsijärvi FIN 115 E3
Joux-la-Ville F 25 E10
Jouy F 24 C6
Jouy-aux-Arches F 26 B5
Jouy-le-Potier F 24 E6
Jøvik N 111 A18
Jøvik N 111 B13
Joyeuse F 35 B7
Joze F 30 D3
Józefów PL 141 F4
Józefów PL 144 A4
Józefów PL 144 C7
Juankoski FIN 125 D10
Juan-les-Pins F 36 D6
Juban AL 163 E8
Jubë AL 168 B1
Jübek D 82 A6
Jublains F 23 D11
Jubrique E 53 C6
Jüchen D 20 B6
Juchowo PL 85 C10
Jüchsen D 75 B8
Jucu RO 152 D3
Judaberg N 94 D3
Judenbach D 75 B9
Judenburg A 73 B10
Judinsalo FIN 127 B14
Juelsminde DK 86 D6
Jugon-les-Lacs F 23 D7
Jugorje SLO 148 E4
Jugureni RO 161 C8
Juhonpieti S 116 D10
Juhtimäki FIN 127 B9
Juillac F 29 E8
Juillan F 32 D6
Jujurieux F 31 C7
Jukkasjärvi S 116 C5
Juknaičiai LT 134 F3
Juksjaur S 109 E10
Jukua FIN 121 C9
Julåsen S 103 B10
Julbach A 76 E5
Jule N 105 C15
Jülich D 20 C6
Juliénas F 30 C6
Jullouville F 23 C8
Jumaliskylä FIN 121 E13
Jumeaux F 30 E3
Jumilhac-le-Grand F 29 E8
Jumilla E 55 C10
Juminen FIN 125 D9
Jumisko FIN 121 B11
Jumprava LV 135 C9
Jumurda LV 135 C11
Juncal P 44 E3
Juncosa E 42 E5
Juneda E 42 D5
Jung S 91 C13
Jungingen D 27 D11
Junglinster L 20 E6
Jungsund FIN 122 D7
Junik RKS 163 E9
Juniskär S 103 B13
Juniville F 19 F9
Jünkerath D 21 D7
Junkerdal N 109 C10
Junnonoja FIN 119 F15
Junosuando S 116 D9
Junqueira P 50 E5
Junsele S 107 D11
Juntinvaara FIN 121 F15
Juntusranta FIN 121 D13
Juodeikiai LT 134 D6
Juodkrantė LT 134 E2
Juodšiliai LT 137 D11
Juodupė LT 135 D11
Juoksengi S 117 E11
Juoksenki FIN 117 E11
Juokslahti FIN 127 B13
Juokuanvaara FIN 119 C13
Juonto FIN 121 F13
Juorkuna FIN 120 E8
Juornaankylä FIN 127 D14
Juostininkai LT 135 E9
Juotasniemi FIN 119 B17
Jupânești RO 160 D3
Jupilles F 24 E3
Juprelle B 19 C12
Jurançon F 32 D5
Jurbarkas LT 136 C6
Jurbise B 19 C8
Jürgenshagen D 83 C11
Jürgenstorf D 84 C3
Jurgi LV 134 C5
Jüri EST 131 C9
Jurignac F 28 D5
Jurilovca RO 155 D3
Jurjevo HR 67 C10
Jürkalne LV 134 B2
Jurklošter SLO 148 D4
Jurkowice PL 143 E11
Jūrmala LV 134 C7
Jūrmalciems LV 134 D2
Jurmo FIN 126 D5
Jurmo FIN 126 F6
Jurmu FIN 121 D10
Jurovski Brod HR 148 E4
Jursla S 93 B8
Jurva FIN 122 E7
Jussac F 29 F10
Jussey F 26 E4
Juta H 149 D9
Jüterbog D 80 C4
Jutis S 109 D13
Jutrosin PL 81 C12
Jutsajaure S 116 D3
Juujärvi FIN 120 B9
Juuka FIN 125 D12
Juuma FIN 121 B13
Juupajoki FIN 127 B11
Juupakylä FIN 123 F10
Juurikka FIN 125 G14
Juurikkalahti FIN 125 B10
Juurikkamäki FIN 125 E10
Juurikorpi FIN 128 D6
Juuru EST 131 C9
Juustovaara FIN 117 D13
Juutinen FIN 123 B17
Juva FIN 128 B8
Juvanådammet S 107 D12
Juvigné F 23 D9
Juvigny-le-Tertre F 23 C9
Juvigny-sous-Andaine F 23 C10
Juvola FIN 125 F11
Juzennecourt F 26 D2
Juzet-d'Izaut F 33 E7
Jūžintai LT 135 E11
Jyderup DK 87 D8
Jylhä FIN 123 D17
Jylhämä FIN 119 E17
Jyllinge DK 87 D10
Jyllinkoski FIN 122 F8
Jyllintaival FIN 122 E8
Jyrinki FIN 123 C12
Jyrkänkoski FIN 121 B14
Jyrkänkylä FIN 125 B13
Jyrkkä FIN 125 C9
Jystrup DK 87 D9
Jyväskylä FIN 123 F15

K

Kaagjärve EST 131 F12
Kaakamo FIN 119 C12
Kaalepi EST 131 C11
Kaamanen FIN 113 E19
Kaamasjoki FIN 113 E19
Kaamasmukka FIN 113 E18
Kaanaa FIN 127 B11
Kääntöjärvi S 116 D7
Kääpa EST 131 F14
Kääpälä FIN 128 C6
Kaarakkala FIN 124 C8
Kaaraneskoski FIN 117 E12
Käärdi EST 131 E12
Kaarepere EST 131 D13
Kaaresuvanto FIN 116 B9
Kaarina FIN 126 E7
Kaarlela FIN 123 C10
Käärmelehto FIN 117 D15
Kaarnevaara S 117 C10
Kaarnijärvi FIN 115 F1
Kaarßen D 83 D10
Kaarst D 21 B7
Kaasmarkku FIN 126 C7
Kaatsheuvel NL 16 E4
Kaava FIN 113 D18
Kaavi FIN 125 E10
Kaba H 151 C7
Kabakça TR 173 B9
Kabaklar TR 173 E11
Kabakum TR 177 A8
Kabala EST 131 D11
Kåbdalis S 118 B4
Kabelvåg N 110 D7
Kaberneeme EST 131 B10
Kabile LV 134 C4
Kableshkovo BG 167 D9
Kabli EST 131 E8
Kać SRB 158 C4
Kaçanik RKS 164 E3
Kačarevo SRB 158 D6
Kachkivka UA 154 A2
Kachurivka UA 154 B5
Kačice CZ 76 B5
Käckelbäcksmon S 103 A13
Kaczory PL 85 D11
Kadaň CZ 76 B4
Kadarkút H 149 D9
Kadiköy TR 173 B9
Kadıköy TR 173 C6
Kadıköy TR 173 C11
Kadıköy TR 177 A9
Kadila EST 131 C12
Kadrifakovo MK 164 F5
Kadrina EST 131 C12
Kadzidło PL 139 D11
Käenkoski FIN 125 E15
Kaerepere EST 131 D9
Kåfjord N 112 D11
Kåfjord N 113 B16
Kåfjorddalen N 112 E6
Kåge S 118 E5
Kägeröd S 87 D12
Kaggebo S 93 D9
Kağıthane TR 173 B10
Kagkadi GR 174 C3
Kahla D 79 E10
Kahl am Main D 187 A7
Kahög S 91 D11
Kahraman TR 181 A8
Kähtävä FIN 119 F12
Kaiafa GR 174 D4
Käina EST 130 D5
Kainasto FIN 122 F8
Kainourgio GR 174 B3
Kainulasjärvi S 116 D9
Kainuunkylä FIN 119 B11
Kainuunmäki FIN 124 C8
Kaipiainen FIN 128 D7
Kaipola FIN 127 B13
Kairala FIN 115 D2
Kairiai LT 134 E6
Kairiškiai LT 134 D5
Kaisajoki FIN 119 B12
Kaisepakte S 111 D17
Kaisersesch D 21 D8
Kaiserslautern D 21 F9
Kaisheim D 75 E8
Kaišiadorys LT 137 D9
Kaisma EST 131 D9
Kaitainen FIN 124 F9
Kaitainsalmi FIN 121 F11
Kaitajärvi FIN 119 B13
Kaitum S 116 C4
Kaivanto FIN 120 F9
Kaive LV 134 B6
Kaive LV 135 B11
Kajaani FIN 121 F10
Kajal SK 146 E5
Kajanki FIN 117 B11
Kajdacs H 149 C11
Kajew PL 143 B7
Kajoo FIN 125 D12
Kájov CZ 76 E6
Kakanj BIH 157 D9
Kakasd H 149 D11
Kakavi AL 168 E3
Kakenieki LV 134 C6
Kakenstorf D 82 D7
Kakerbeck D 83 E10
Kakhanavichy BY 133 E4
Käkilahti FIN 120 F8
Kākišķe LV 134 D2
Kaklıç TR 177 C8
Kąkolewnica Wschodnia PL 141 G7
Kąkolewo PL 81 C11
Kakovatos GR 174 E4
Kakrukë AL 168 C3
Kakskerta FIN 126 E7
Kakslauttanen FIN 115 B2
Kakucs H 150 C3
Kál H 150 B5
Käl S 107 D12
Kälä FIN 127 B15
Kalabakbaşi TR 173 E7
Kålaboda S 118 F5
Kalače MNE 163 D9
Kala Dendra GR 169 B9
Kalaja FIN 123 C14
Kalajärvi FIN 127 E12
Kalajoki FIN 119 F11
Kalak N 113 B19
Kalakangas FIN 123 C14
Kalakoski FIN 123 F10
Kalamaki GR 169 E8
Kalamaki GR 174 D2
Kalamaki GR 175 D8
Kalamaria GR 169 C8
Kalamata GR 174 E5
Kalamos GR 175 C8
Kalamoti GR 177 C7
Kalamoto GR 169 C9
Kalampaka GR 169 E6
Kalampaki GR 171 B6
Kalana EST 130 D4
Kalandra GR 169 E9
Kala Nera GR 169 F9
Kalanistra GR 174 C4
Kalanti FIN 126 D6
Kälarne S 107 F10
Kalathos GR 181 D8
Kalavarda GR 181 D7
Kalavryta GR 174 C5
Kaława PL 81 B9
Kalbe (Milde) D 83 E10
Kalce SLO 73 E9
Kalchevo BG 167 E7
Káld H 149 B8
Kaldabruņa LV 135 D12
Kaldbak FO 2 A3
Kaldfarnes N 111 B12
Kaldfarnes N 111 B13
Kaldfjord N 111 A16
Kaldslett N 111 A16
Kaldvåg N 111 D10
Kaldvik N 111 D11
Kale TR 181 B9
Kalefeld D 79 C7
Kaleköy TR 171 D9
Kålen S 103 A8
Kålen S 103 B11
Kålen S 118 D6
Kalentzi GR 168 F4
Kalesija BIH 157 D10
Kalesmeno GR 174 B4
Kalēti LV 134 D2
Kalety PL 143 E6
Kalevala RUS 121 D17
Kali GR 169 C7
Kali HR 156 D3
Kalianoi GR 175 D5
Kalimanci MK 165 F6
Kalimash AL 163 E9
Kaliningrad RUS 136 D2
Kalinino RUS 136 E6
Kalinovik BIH 157 F9
Kalinovka RUS 136 D4
Kalinowa PL 142 C5
Kalinowo PL 136 F6
Kaliska PL 138 C5
Kalisz PL 142 C5
Kalisz Pomorski PL 85 D9
Kalita EST 131 E9
Kali Vrysi GR 170 B5
Kalix S 119 C10
Kalixforsen S 116 C4
Kalkar D 16 E6
Kalkhorst D 83 C10
Kalki LV 130 F4
Kalkiainen FIN 115 E3
Kalkim TR 173 E7
Kalkkimaa FIN 119 C12
Kalkkinen FIN 127 C14
Kałków PL 77 B12
Kalkūni LV 135 E12
Kall D 21 C7
Kall S 105 E14
Källa S 89 A11
Kallaste EST 131 D14
Kallax S 118 C8
Källberget S 102 A6
Källbomark S 118 D6
Källby FIN 122 C9
Källby S 91 B13
Kalle N 110 D7
Källeboda S 96 D7
Källekärr S 91 C10
Källered S 91 D11
Källerud S 91 A12
Kallham A 76 F5
Kallifoni GR 169 F6
Kallifytos GR 171 B6
Kallimasia GR 177 C7
Kallinge S 89 C8
Kalliojoki FIN 121 F15
Kalliopi GR 171 E8
Kalliosalmi FIN 117 E17
Kallirachi GR 171 C7
Kallislahti FIN 129 B10
Kallithea GR 169 D8
Kallithea GR 169 D9
Kallithea GR 169 E7
Kallithea GR 174 D4
Kallithea GR 174 F4
Kallithea GR 175 D8
Kallithea GR 177 D8
Kallithiro GR 169 F6
Kalljord N 110 C9
Kallmet i Madh AL 163 F8
Kallmünz D 75 D10
Kallo FIN 117 D12
Kálló H 150 B3
Kallön S 109 E15
Kalloni GR 171 F10
Kalloni GR 175 D7
Kalloni GR 176 D5
Kallósemjén H 145 H4
Kallsedet S 105 D13
Källsjön S 103 E11
Kallträsk FIN 122 F7
Kallunki FIN 115 E5
Kallunki FIN 121 B13
Kálmánháza H 145 H4
Kalmar S 89 B10
Kalmari FIN 123 E14
Kalmthout B 16 F2
Kalna SRB 164 C5
Kalna SRB 164 D5
Kalná nad Hronom SK 147 E7
Kalnciems LV 134 C7
Kalni LV 134 D4
Kalnieši LV 133 E2
Kalnujai LT 134 F6
Kalocsa H 150 D2
Kalofer BG 165 D10
Kaloi Limenes GR 178 F8
Kaloneri GR 169 D5
Kalo Nero GR 174 E4
Kalos Agros GR 170 B6
Kalotina BG 165 C6
Kalotintsi BG 165 D6
Kaloyanovets BG 166 E5
Kaloyanovo BG 165 E10
Káloz H 149 C10
Kalpaki GR 168 E4
Kalpio FIN 121 E10
Kals am Großglockner A 73 B6
Kaltanėnai LT 135 F11
Kaltbrunn CH 27 F11
Kaltene LV 134 B5
Kaltenkirchen D 83 C7
Kaltennordheim D 79 E7
Kaltensundheim D 79 E7
Kaltinėnai LT 134 E4
Kaluđerica SRB 158 D6
Kalugerovo BG 165 E9
Kalundborg DK 87 D8
Kalupe LV 135 D13
Kałuszyn PL 141 F5
Kaluzhekoye RUS 136 D4
Kalvåg N 100 C1
Kalvarija LT 136 E7
Kalvatn N 100 B4
Kalveliai LT 137 D12
Kalvene LV 134 C3
Kalvi EST 131 C13
Kälviä FIN 123 C10
Kalvik N 109 A10
Kalvitsa FIN 128 B7
Kalvola FIN 127 C11
Kalvträsk S 107 B17
Kalwang A 73 B10
Kalwaria Zebrzydowska PL 147 B9
Kalymnos GR 177 F8
Kalyny UA 145 G8
Kalythies GR 181 D8
Kalyves GR 171 C7
Kalyvia GR 174 B3
Kalyvia GR 174 B3
Kalyvia GR 174 D5
Kalyvia Thorikou GR 175 D8
Kamajai LT 135 E11
Kämäränkylä FIN 121 F14
Kamarde LV 135 D8
Kamares GR 174 C4
Kamares GR 175 F10
Kamariotissa GR 171 D8
Kambja EST 131 E13
Kamburovo BG 166 C6
Kamen BG 166 C5
Kamen D 17 E9
Kamenari BG 166 D6
Kamena Vourla GR 175 B6
Kamen Bryag BG 167 C11
Kamencia SRB 158 F6
Kamenec pod Vtáčnikom SK 147 D7
Kamengrad BIH 156 C6
Kamenica BIH 156 D5
Kamenica BIH 157 D9
Kamenica BIH 158 F3
Kamenica MK 164 E6
Kamenica SK 145 E2
Kamenica SRB 158 E4
Kamenica SRB 164 C5
Kamenica nad Cirochou SK 145 F4
Kamenica nad Hronom SK 147 F7
Kamenicë AL 168 C4
Kamenice CZ 77 C7
Kamenice CZ 77 D9
Kamenicë RKS 164 D4
Kamenice nad Lipou CZ 77 D8
Kameničná SK 146 F6
Kamenín SK 147 F7
Kamenka RUS 129 E11
Kamenná Poruba SK 147 C7
Kamennogorsk RUS 129 D11
Kamenný Most SK 147 F7
Kamenný Přívoz CZ 77 C7
Kamenný Újezd CZ 77 E6
Kameno BG 167 D8
Kameno Pole BG 165 C8
Kamenovo BG 161 F8
Kamensko BIH 157 D9
Kamensko HR 149 F8
Kamensko HR 157 E6
Kamenskoye RUS 136 D4
Kamenz D 80 D6
Kamerik NL 182 A5
Kamern D 83 E12
Kames GB 4 D6
Kamëz AL 168 B2
Kamičak BIH 157 C6
Kamicë-Flakë AL 163 E7
Kamień PL 144 C5
Kamieńczyk PL 139 E12
Kamienica PL 145 D1
Kamienica Polska PL 143 E7
Kamieniec PL 81 B10
Kamieniec Ząbkowicki PL 77 A11
Kamienka SK 145 E2
Kamień Krajeński PL 85 C13
Kamienna Gora PL 81 E10
Kamiennik PL 81 E12
Kamień Pomorski PL 85 C7
Kamieńsk PL 143 D8
Kamień Wielkie PL 81 A7
Kamilski Dol BG 171 A10
Kamion PL 139 F9
Kamion PL 141 G2
Kamionka PL 141 H6
Kamiros GR 181 D7
Kamlunge S 119 C9
Kammela FIN 126 D5
Kammen N 112 C4
Kamnik SLO 73 D10
Kamno SLO 73 D8
Kamøyvær N 113 A16
Kamp D 185 D8
Kampanis GR 169 C8
Kampen D 86 F2
Kampen NL 16 C5
Kampenhout B 182 D5
Kämpfelbach D 187 D6
Kampi GR 174 A2
Kampia GR 177 B6
Kampinkylä FIN 122 E8
Kampinos PL 141 F2
Kamp-Lintfort D 17 F7
Kampos GR 174 C5
Kampos GR 174 F5
Kampvoll N 111 B14
Kamsjö S 118 F3
Kamula FIN 123 B16
Kamut H 151 D6
Kam"yane UA 154 A5
Kam"yans'ke UA 154 F4
Kamyanyets BY 141 F9
Kamyanyuki BY 141 E9
Kanaküla EST 131 E10
Kanal SLO 73 D8
Kanala FIN 123 D12
Kanala GR 175 E9
Kanali GR 168 F4
Kanali GR 174 A2
Kanalia GR 169 F8
Kanallaki GR 168 F4
Kanan S 109 F10
Kanatlarci MK 169 B6
Kańczuga PL 144 D5
Kandava LV 134 B5
Kandel D 27 B9
Kandelin D 84 B4
Kandern D 27 E8
Kandersteg CH 70 E5
Kandila GR 174 B2
Kandila GR 174 D5
Kandle EST 131 B12
Kanepi EST 131 F13
Kanestraum N 104 E4
Kanfanar HR 67 B8
Kangas FIN 119 F13
Kangas FIN 122 D9
Kangasaho FIN 123 E13
Kangasala FIN 127 C11
Kangaskylä FIN 119 F16
Kangaskylä FIN 121 E11
Kangaskylä FIN 123 C13
Kangaslahti FIN 125 D10
Kangaslampi FIN 125 F10
Kangasniemi FIN 123 G17
Kangasvieri FIN 123 C13
Kangos S 116 D9
Kangosjärvi FIN 117 C11
Kanianka SK 147 D7
Kaninë AL 168 D2
Kanjiža SRB 150 E5
Kankaanpää FIN 126 B7
Kankaanpää FIN 126 C7
Kankainen FIN 123 F16
Kankari FIN 120 E8
Kånna S 87 B13
Kannas FIN 121 E12
Känne S 103 B9
Kannonjärvi FIN 123 E14
Kannonkoski FIN 123 E14
Kannus FIN 123 C11
Kannusjärvi FIN 128 D7
Kannuskoski FIN 128 D7
Kanpantxua E 41 B6
Kanstad N 111 D10
Kanstadbotn N 111 C10
Kantala FIN 124 F8
Kantanos GR 178 E6
Kantele FIN 127 D14
Kantens NL 17 B7
Kantia GR 175 D6
Kantojärvi FIN 119 C12
Kantojoki FIN 121 E13
Kantokylä FIN 123 B13
Kantola FIN 123 D10
Kantomaanpää FIN 119 B12
Kantorneset N 111 B17
Kantserava BY 133 F4
Kantti FIN 122 F9
Kanturk IRL 8 D5
Kaolinovo BG 161 F10
Kaona SRB 158 F5
Kaonik BIH 157 D8
Kaonik SRB 164 B3
Kapakli TR 173 B8
Kapakli TR 173 D10
Kapanbeleni TR 173 D7
Kapandriti GR 175 C8
Kaparelli GR 175 C7
Kapčiamiestis LT 137 F8
Kapelle NL 16 F2
Kapellen B 16 F2
Kapelle-op-den-Bos B 182 C4
Kapellskär S 99 C12
Kapfenberg A 148 B4
Kapikargin TR 181 C9
Kapitan-Andreevo BG 166 F6
Kapiz TR 181 B9
Kaplava LV 133 E2
Kaplice CZ 77 E7
Kapljuh BIH 156 C5
Kápolna H 150 B5
Kápolnásnyék H 149 B11
Kaposfő H 149 D9
Kaposmérő H 149 D9
Kaposszekcső H 149 D10
Kaposvár H 149 D9
Kapp N 101 E13
Kappel D 21 E8
Kappel-Grafenhausen D 186 E4
Kappeln D 83 A7
Kappelrodeck D 186 D5
Kappl A 71 C10
Kåpponis S 118 B4
Kaprijke B 16 F1
Kaprun A 73 B6
Kapsia GR 174 D5
Kaptol HR 149 F9
Kaptsyowka BY 140 C9
Kapušany SK 145 E3
Kapusta FIN 119 B12
Kapuvár H 149 A8
Käpylä FIN 119 F14
Karaağaç TR 173 A7
Karaağaç TR 173 F6
Karaağaçli TR 177 B9
Karabanove UA 154 C5
Karabiga TR 173 D7
Karaboğürtlen TR 181 B9
Karabunar BG 165 E9
Karaburun TR 173 B10
Karaburun TR 177 B7
Karaca TR 181 C8
Karacabey TR 173 D9
Karacadağ TR 167 F9
Karacakılavuz TR 173 B7
Karacaköy TR 173 B9
Karád H 149 C9
Karadzhalovo BG 166 E4
Karahalil TR 173 A7
Karaincirli TR 171 C10
Karainebeyli TR 171 D10
Karaisen BG 166 C4
Karakaja BIH 157 D11
Karakasim TR 172 A6
Karakaya TR 173 F9
Karakoca TR 173 D10
Karaköy TR 173 E6
Karaköy TR 177 B9

Karaköy TR 181 B9
Karakurt TR 177 A10
Karala EST 130 E3
Karaman TR 173 E9
Karamanovo BG 166 B5
Karamehmet TR 173 B8
Karamyshevo RUS 132 F4
Karamyshevo RUS 136 E5
Karancsberény H 147 E9
Karancskeszi H 147 E9
Karancslapujtő H 147 E9
Karancsság H 147 E9
Karankamäki FIN 124 C8
Karaoğlanli TR 177 B10
Karaorman TR 173 E9
Karaova TR 177 E10
Karapchiv UA 152 A6
Karapelit BG 161 F11
Karasjok N 113 E15
Karatoulas GR 174 D4
Karats S 109 C16
Karavas GR 178 C4
Karavelovo BG 165 D10
Karavelovo BG 167 E7
Käravete EST 131 C11
Karavomylos GR 175 B6
Karavukovo SRB 157 B11
Karben D 21 D11
Kårberg S 92 B5
Karbinci MK 164 F5
Kårböle S 103 C9
Kårböleskog S 103 C9
Karbow-Vietlübbe D 83 D12
Karbunarë e Vogël AL 168 C2
Karby D 83 A7
Karby DK 86 B3
Karby S 99 C10
Karcag H 151 C6
Karcsa H 145 G4
Karczew PL 141 F4
Karczmiska Pierwsze PL 141 H6
Kärda S 87 A13
Kardakata GR 174 C1
Kardam BG 155 F2
Kardam BG 166 C6
Kardamaina GR 177 F9
Kardamyli GR 174 F5
Kardašova Řečice CZ 77 D7
Karden D 21 D8
Kardiani GR 176 D5
Kardis S 117 E11
Karditsa GR 169 F6
Karditsomagoula GR 169 F6
Kärdla EST 130 D5
Kardon BY 133 F6
Kardos H 150 D6
Kardoskút H 150 E6
Karegasnjarga FIN 113 E16
Kareļi LV 134 D4
Karesuando S 116 B8
Kargowa PL 81 B9
Karhi FIN 123 C10
Karhila FIN 123 F13
Karhujärvi FIN 115 F4
Karhukangas FIN 119 F14
Karhula FIN 128 D6
Kariani GR 170 C5
Karigasniemi FIN 113 E16
Karihaugen N 111 D12
Karijoki FIN 122 F7
Karinainen FIN 126 D8
Käringberg S 107 A12
Käringen N 111 D10
Käringsjön S 102 B3
Käringsjövallen S 102 B4
Karinkanta FIN 119 E13
Karis FIN 127 E10
Karise DK 87 E10
Karisjärvi FIN 127 D11
Karitaina GR 174 E5
Karitsa GR 169 D7
Karjalaisenniemi FIN 121 B11
Karjalan kirkonkylä FIN 126 D7
Karjalankylä FIN 119 D15
Karjalankylä FIN 126 D7
Karjalanvaara FIN 120 B9
Karjalanvaara FIN 121 F10
Karjalohja FIN 127 E10
Kärjenkoski FIN 122 F7
Karjulanmäki FIN 123 C13
Karkalou GR 174 D5
Kärķi LV 131 F11
Kärkinen FIN 119 F12
Kärkkäälä FIN 123 E16
Kärkkäälä FIN 124 E8
Karkkila FIN 127 D11
Karkku FIN 127 C9
Kärklinieki LV 133 B2
Kärkölä FIN 127 D10
Kärkölä FIN 127 D13
Karksi EST 131 E11
Karksi-Nuia EST 131 E11
Kårkul S 118 B5
Kärla EST 130 E4
Karlå FIN 122 F7
Karlby FIN 126 F4
Karlebotn N 114 C5
Karleby FIN 123 C10
Karlholmsbruk S 99 A9
Karlino PL 85 B9
Kārļmuiža LV 134 B4
Karlobag HR 67 C11
Karlovac HR 148 F5
Karlovasi GR 177 D8
Karlovice CZ 142 F3
Karlovo BG 165 D10
Karlovy Vary CZ 76 B3
Karłowice PL 142 E4
Karlsbäck S 107 D15
Karlsbad D 27 C10
Karlsberg S 103 C9
Karlsborg S 92 B5
Karlsburg D 84 C5
Karlsdal S 97 D12
Karlsdorf-Neuthard D 27 B10
Karlsfeld D 75 F9
Karlsfors S 103 C9
Karlshagen D 84 B5
Karlshamn S 89 C7
Karlshöfen D 17 B12
Karlskoga S 97 D12
Karlskrona S 89 C9
Karlsøy N 112 C4
Karlsruhe D 27 B9
Karlstad S 97 D10
Karlstadt D 74 C6
Karlstein an der Thaya A 77 E8
Karlstetten A 77 F9
Karlukovo BG 165 C9
Karmansbo S 97 C14
Karmas S 109 B17
Karmēlava LT 137 D9
Kärnä FIN 123 D11
Kärnä FIN 123 D15
Kärna S 91 D10
Karnaliyivka UA 154 E6
Karnice PL 85 B8
Karniewo PL 139 E10
Karnjarga FIN 113 D19
Karnobat BG 167 D7
Karojba HR 67 B8
Karolinka CZ 146 C6
Karonsbo S 107 B15
Karoti GR 171 B10
Karousades GR 168 E2
Karow D 79 B11
Karow D 83 C12
Karpacz PL 81 E9
Kärpänkylä FIN 121 C14
Karpathos GR 181 E6
Karpenisi GR 174 B4
Karperi GR 169 B9
Karpero GR 169 E6
Kärppälä FIN 127 C9
Karpuzlu TR 171 C10
Karpuzlu TR 181 A7
Kärrbackstrand S 102 E4
Karrebæksminde DK 87 E9
Karrenzin D 83 D11
Kärrsjö S 107 D15
Karsakiškis LT 135 E9
Kärsämä FIN 119 E15
Kärsämäki FIN 123 C15
Kārsava LV 133 C3
Karsikas FIN 123 C14
Karsikkoniemi FIN 117 C11
Karsikkovaara FIN 124 B9
Karsimus FIN 115 E2
Karsin PL 138 C4
Karşiyaka TR 173 D9
Karşiyaka TR 177 C9
Karsko PL 85 E8
Kårsta S 99 C10
Karstädt D 83 D10
Karstädt D 83 D11
Kärstna EST 131 E11
Karstula FIN 123 E13
Karszew PL 142 B6
Kartal H 150 B4
Kartavoll N 94 E3
Kartena LT 134 E2
Kartitsch A 72 C6
Kartuzy PL 138 B5
Käru EST 131 D10
Käru EST 131 D12
Karuna FIN 126 E8
Karungi S 119 B11
Karunki FIN 119 B12
Karup DK 86 C4
Kårvåg N 104 E3
Karvala FIN 123 D11
Kärväskylä FIN 123 D15
Karvia FIN 122 F9
Kårvikhamn N 111 B15
Karviná CZ 147 B7
Karvoskylä FIN 123 C14
Karvounari GR 168 F3
Karwica PL 139 C11
Karya GR 169 E7
Karya GR 174 B2
Karya GR 175 D6
Karyes GR 171 D6
Karyes GR 175 E5
Karyotissa GR 169 C7
Karyoupoli GR 178 B3
Karystos GR 175 C9
Kås DK 86 A5
Kašalj SRB 163 C10
Kasejovice CZ 76 D5
Kasendorf D 75 B9
Kasepää EST 131 D14
Kåsfjord N 111 C11
Kashirskoye RUS 136 D2
Kaşikçi TR 173 B7
Kašina HR 148 E6
Kaskantyú H 150 D3
Kåskats S 116 F4
Kaskii FIN 129 B9
Kaskinen FIN 122 F6
Kaskö FIN 122 F6
Käsmä FIN 121 C12
Kåsmo N 108 B9
Kåsmolia N 108 B9
Käsmu EST 131 B11
Kaspakas GR 171 E8
Kašperské Hory CZ 76 D5
Kaspichan BG 167 C8
Kassa S 117 D11
Kassandreia GR 169 D9
Kasseedorf D 83 B9
Kassel D 78 D6
Kassiopi GR 168 E2
Kastania GR 168 D4
Kastania GR 168 E5
Kastania GR 169 D7
Kastania GR 169 F6
Kastanies GR 171 A10
Kastanochori GR 169 C10
Kastari FIN 127 C13
Kastellaun D 21 D8
Kastelli GR 178 E9
Kastellia GR 174 B5
Kaštel Stari HR 156 E5
Kaštel Sućurac HR 156 E5
Kaštel Šegarski HR 156 D4
Kasterlee B 16 F3
Kastīre LV 135 D13
Kastl D 75 D10
Kastlösa S 89 C10
Kastneshamn N 111 C13
Kastorf D 83 C9
Kastoria GR 168 C5
Kastorio GR 174 E5
Kastraki GR 174 B3
Kastraki GR 176 E5
Kastrāne LV 135 C10
Kastre EST 131 E14
Kastri GR 169 E8
Kastri GR 175 E6
Kastro GR 175 C7
Kastrosykia GR 174 A2
Kastrova BY 133 D4
Kaszaper H 150 E6
Kaszczor PL 81 C10
Katafyto GR 169 B10
Katajamäki FIN 125 D10
Katakolo GR 174 D3
Kåtaliden S 109 F15
Kataloinen FIN 127 C12
Katapola GR 177 F6
Katarraktis GR 177 C7
Kåtaselet S 118 D3
Katastari GR 174 D2
Katerini GR 169 D8
Katerma FIN 125 B12
Kathenoi GR 175 B8
Kathlow D 81 C6
Kätkänjoki FIN 123 E11
Kätkäsuvanto FIN 117 B10
Kätkävaara FIN 119 B13
Kätkesuando S 117 B10
Katlenburg-Lindau D 79 C7
Kátlovce SK 146 D5
Kato Achaïa GR 174 C4
Kato Alepochori GR 175 C7
Kato Asites GR 178 E9
Katochi GR 174 C3
Kato Chorio GR 179 E10
Kato Doliana GR 175 E6
Kato Glykovrysi GR 178 B4
Kato Kamila GR 169 B9
Kato Makrinou GR 174 C4
Kato Nevrokopi GR 169 B10
Kato Sounio GR 175 D9
Kato Tithorea GR 175 B6
Katouna GR 174 B3
Kato Vermio GR 169 C7
Katovice CZ 76 D5
Kato Vlasia GR 174 C4
Kato Vrontou GR 169 B10
Katowice PL 143 F7
Katranca TR 173 B7
Katrineberg S 103 D11
Katrineholm S 93 B8
Katrineholm S 103 E13
Katsdorf A 77 F6
Katsikas GR 168 E4
Kattavia GR 181 E7
Kattbo S 102 E7
Kattelus FIN 123 F11
Kattilasaari S 119 C11
Kättilstad S 92 C7
Kättilstorp S 91 C14
Kattisavan S 107 B14
Kattisträsk S 118 E3
Katundishtë AL 168 D3
Katunets BG 165 C10
Katunitsa BG 165 E10
Katuntsi BG 169 B9
Katwijk aan Zee NL 16 D2
Katyčiai LT 134 F3
Katymár H 150 E3
Kąty Wrocławskie PL 81 D11
Katzenelnbogen D 21 D9
Katzweiler D 21 E9
Kaub D 21 D9
Kaufbeuren D 71 B11
Kaufungen D 78 D6
Kaugurieši LV 135 B11
Kauhajärvi FIN 122 F8
Kauhajärvi FIN 123 D10
Kauhajoki FIN 122 F8
Kauhava FIN 123 D10
Kaukalampi FIN 127 D13
Kaukolikai LT 134 D3
Kaukonen FIN 117 D13
Kauksi EST 131 C14
Kaulille B 183 C7
Kaulinranta FIN 119 B11
Kaulsdorf D 79 E9
Kaunas LT 137 D8
Kaunata LV 133 D3
Kauniainen FIN 127 E12
Kaunisjoensuu S 117 D11
Kaunisvaara S 117 D10
Kaupanger N 100 D6
Kaupiškiai LT 136 D6
Kauppila FIN 123 F17
Kauppilanmäki FIN 124 C8
Kaurajärvi FIN 122 D9
Kaurissalo FIN 126 D5
Kaustinen FIN 123 C11
Kautenbach L 184 E5
Kautokeino N 112 E11
Kautzen A 77 E8
Kauvatsa FIN 126 C8
Kauvosaarenpää FIN 119 B11
Kavacik TR 172 B6
Kavacik TR 173 E9
Kavadarci MK 169 B7
Kavajë AL 168 B2
Kavak TR 173 C6
Kavakdere TR 173 A7
Kavakli TR 173 A7
Kavaklidere TR 181 B8
Kavala GR 171 C6
Kavarna BG 167 C10
Kavarskas LT 135 F9
Kavasilas GR 174 D3
Kavastu EST 131 E14
Kavelstorf D 83 C12
Kävlinge S 87 D12
Kavos GR 168 F3
Kavousi GR 179 E10
Kavs'ke UA 145 E8
Kavyli GR 171 A11
Kaxås S 105 D15
Kåxed S 107 E14
Kaxholmen S 92 D4
Kayabaşi TR 181 B9
Kayalar TR 173 E8
Kayali TR 167 F8
Kayalioğlu TR 177 B10
Kayapa TR 173 F7
Kayatepe TR 173 E7
Käylä FIN 121 B13
Käymäjärvi S 116 D9
Kayna D 79 E11
Kaynaklar TR 177 C9
Kaynarca TR 173 A7
Kaynardzha BG 161 F10
Käyrämö FIN 117 E16
Kaysersberg F 27 D7
Kazanka BG 166 E4
Kazanlŭk BG 166 D4
Kazanów PL 141 H4
Kazár H 147 E9
Kazdanga LV 134 C3
Kazichane BG 165 D7
Kazikli TR 177 E9
Kazimierza Wielka PL 143 F9
Kazimierz Biskupi PL 142 B5
Kazimierz Dolne PL 141 H5
Kazincbarcika H 145 G2
Kazlowshchyna BY 133 E4
Kazlų Rūda LT 137 D7
Kaźmierz PL 81 A11
Kaznějov CZ 76 C4
Kazyany BY 133 E7
Kaz'yany BY 135 F13
Kçirë AL 163 E8
Kcynia PL 85 E12
Kdyně CZ 76 D4
Keadue IRL 6 D6
Keady GB 7 D9
Kealkill IRL 8 E4
Kebal S 91 B9
Kecel H 150 D3
Kecerovce SK 145 F3
Kechrokampos GR 171 B7
Kechros GR 171 B9
Kecskéd H 149 A10
Kecskemét H 150 D4
Kėdainiai LT 135 F7
Kędzierzyn-Koźle PL 142 F5
Keele GB 11 E7
Keenagh IRL 7 E7
Keeni EST 131 F12
Kefalos GR 181 C5
Kefalovryso GR 169 E7
Kefenrod D 21 D12
Kefermarkt A 77 F7
Ķegums LV 135 C9
Kegworth GB 11 F9
Kehidakustány H 149 C8
Kehl D 27 C8
Kehlen L 20 E6
Kehra EST 131 C10
Kehrig D 21 D8
Kehtna EST 131 D9
Kehvo FIN 124 D9
Keighley GB 11 D8
Keihärinkoski FIN 123 D15
Keikyä FIN 126 C8
Keila EST 131 C8
Keila-Joa EST 131 C8
Keillmore GB 4 D5
Keinäsperä FIN 119 D17
Ķeipene LV 135 C10
Ķeiprod N 111 C14
Keiss GB 3 H10
Keitele FIN 123 D16
Keitelepohja FIN 123 D15
Keith GB 3 K11
Kék H 145 G4
Ķekava LV 135 C8
Kékcse H 145 G5
Kelankylä FIN 119 C18
Kelberg D 21 D7
Kelbra (Kyffhäuser) D 79 D9
Kelč CZ 146 C5
Këlcyrë AL 168 D3
Kelebia H 150 E4
Kelechyn UA 145 F7
Kelheim D 75 E10
Kelkheim (Taunus) D 187 A5
Kell D 21 E7
Kellas GB 3 K10
Kellas GB 5 B11
Kellenhusen D 83 B10
Kelli GR 169 C6
Kellinghusen D 82 C7
Kellmünz an der Iller D 71 A10
Kello FIN 119 D14
Kellokoski FIN 127 D13
Kelloniemi FIN 115 E3
Kelloniemi FIN 117 D11
Kelloselkä FIN 115 E5
Kells GB 4 F4
Kells IRL 7 E9
Kells IRL 8 E2
Kells IRL 9 C8
Kelmė LT 134 E5
Kelmis B 20 C6
Kelontekemä FIN 117 C15
Kelottijärvi FIN 116 A8
Kelso GB 5 D12
Kelujärvi FIN 115 D2
Kelvä FIN 125 D14
Kelvedon GB 15 D10
Kemalpaşa TR 177 C9
Kemberg D 79 C12
Kemecse H 145 G4
Kemence H 147 E7
Kemenesmagasi H 149 B8
Kemenessömjén H 149 B8
Kemerburgaz TR 173 B10
Kémes H 149 E10
Kemeten A 148 B6
Kemi FIN 119 C13
Kemihaara FIN 115 C5
Kemijärvi FIN 115 E2
Kemilä FIN 121 C14
Keminmaa FIN 119 C13
Keminperä FIN 121 D12
Kemishtaj AL 168 C2
Kemmel B 18 C6
Kemnath D 75 C10
Kemnay GB 3 L12
Kemnitz D 81 D7
Kemnitz D 84 B5
Kempele FIN 119 E15
Kempen D 16 F6
Kempenich D 21 D8
Kempsey GB 13 A10
Kempston GB 15 C8
Kempten (Allgäu) D 71 B10
Kendal GB 10 C6
Kenderes H 150 C6
Kendice SK 145 F3
Kenézlő H 145 G4
Kenfig GB 13 B7
Kengis S 117 D10
Kengyet H 150 C5
Kenilworth GB 13 A11
Kenmare IRL 8 E3
Kenmore GB 5 B9
Kenn D 21 E7
Kennacraig GB 4 D6
Kensaleyre GB 2 L4
Kensworth GB 15 D7
Kentavros GR 171 B7
Kentriko GR 169 B8
Kentro GR 174 D3
Kenyeri H 149 B8
Kenzingen D 27 D8
Kepez TR 171 D10
Kępice PL 85 B11
Kępno PL 142 D4
Kepsut TR 173 E9
Keqekollë RKS 164 D3
Keramitsa GR 168 E3
Keramoti GR 171 C7
Keräntöjärvi S 116 C9
Kerasia GR 169 D6
Kerasona GR 168 F4
Keräs-Sieppi FIN 117 B11
Keratea GR 175 D8
Kerava FIN 127 E13
Kerecsend H 147 F10
Kerekegyháza H 150 D3
Kerepestarcsa H 150 B3
Kerets'ky UA 145 G7
Kergu EST 131 D9
Keri GR 174 D2
Kerimäki FIN 129 B11
Kerisalo FIN 125 F9
Kerkdriel NL 16 E4
Kerkejaure S 118 B3
Kerken D 16 F6
Kerkini GR 169 B9
Kerkkoo FIN 127 E14
Kerkonkoski FIN 123 E17
Kerkrade NL 20 C6
Kerkwijk NL 183 B6
Kerkyra GR 168 E2
Kerlouan F 22 C3
Kerma FIN 125 F11
Kermen BG 166 D6
Kernascléden F 22 D5
Kernavė LT 137 D10
Kernhof A 148 A5
Kerns CH 70 D6
Kerpen D 21 C7
Kerrykeel IRL 7 B7
Kershopefoot GB 5 E11
Kersilö FIN 117 C17
Kerspleben D 79 D9
Kerstinbo S 98 B7
Kerteminde DK 86 E7
Kertészsziget H 151 C7
Kertezi GR 174 D4
Kerttuankylä FIN 123 D10
Kerzers CH 31 B11
Kesälahti FIN 129 B12
Keşan TR 172 C6
Kesäniemenkylä FIN 121 B12
Kesarevo BG 166 C5
Kesasjärv S 118 B8
Kesh GB 7 C7
Kesh IRL 6 D6
Kesik TR 177 B8
Keskijärvi FIN 125 E14
Keskikylä FIN 119 E13
Keskikylä FIN 119 E15
Keskikylä FIN 119 F13
Keskikylä FIN 122 F9
Keskikylä FIN 123 E11
Keskinen FIN 121 E13
Keskipiiri FIN 119 E14
Keski-Posio FIN 121 B11
Keskusvankila FIN 124 C8
Kjsowo PL 138 C4
Kessel B 182 C5
Kessel NL 183 C8
Kesselinkylä FIN 125 C14
Kessingland GB 15 C12
Ķesterciems LV 134 B6
Kesteren NL 183 B7
Kestilä FIN 119 D14
Kestilä FIN 119 F16
Kestrini GR 168 E3
Keswick GB 10 B5
Keszthely H 149 C8
Kesztölc H 149 A11
Kétegyháza H 151 D7
Kéthely H 149 C8
Ketola FIN 115 E2
Ketomella FIN 117 B12
Keträvaara FIN 121 D13
Kętrzyn PL 136 E3
Ketsch D 21 F11
Kétsoprony H 151 D6
Kettering GB 15 C7
Kettershausen D 71 A10
Kettinge DK 83 A11
Kettletoft GB 3 G11
Kettlewell GB 11 C7
Kettwig D 183 C9
Kęty PL 147 B8
Ketzin D 79 B12
Keula D 79 D8
Keuruu FIN 123 F13
Keutschach am See A 73 C9
Keväjärvi FIN 114 F3
Kevelaer D 16 E6
Ķevele LV 134 D5
Kevermes H 151 E7
Kevo FIN 113 D19
Keynsham GB 13 C9
Keyritty FIN 125 D10
Kežmarok SK 145 E1
Khadzhidimovo BG 169 A10
Khalamyer"ye BY 133 E7
Kharlu RUS 129 B14
Kharmanli BG 166 F5
Khaskovo BG 166 F5
Khayredin BG 160 F3
Khelyulya RUS 129 B14
Khisarya BG 165 D10
Khiytola RUS 129 C12
Khlivchany UA 144 C8
Kholmets' UA 145 F5
Kholms'ke UA 155 B4
Khorio GR 179 B8
Khrabrovo RUS 136 D2
Khrishteni BG 166 E5
Khust UA 145 G7
Khvoyna BG 165 F10
Khyriv UA 145 D6
Kiannanniemi FIN 121 D13
Kiato GR 175 C6
Kiaunoriai LT 134 E6
Kibæk DK 86 C3
Kibworth Harcourt GB 11 F10
Kiby N 114 C7
Kičevo MK 168 A4
Kichenitsa BG 161 F8
Kichevo BG 167 C9
Kidderminster GB 13 A10
Kidlington GB 13 B12
Kidričevo SLO 148 D5
Kidsgrove GB 11 E7
Kidwelly GB 12 B6
Kiefersfelden D 72 A5
Ķieģeļceplis LV 135 C10
Kiekinkoski FIN 125 B14
Kiekrz PL 81 B11
Kiel D 83 B8
Kielajoki FIN 113 E18
Kielce PL 143 E10
Kiełczygłów PL 143 D6
Kielder GB 5 E11
Kieldrecht B 182 C4
Kiełpino PL 138 B5
Kiemėnai LT 135 D8
Kiemozia PL 141 F1
Kienberg D 75 F11
Kierinki FIN 117 D15
Kierspe D 21 B9
Kieselbach D 79 E7
Kiesilä FIN 128 C7
Kiesimä FIN 123 E17
Kietrz PL 142 F5
Kietz D 81 A7
Kifisia GR 175 C8
Kifjord N 113 B19
Kihelkonna EST 130 E4
Kihlanki FIN 117 C11
Kihlanki S 117 C10
Kihlepa EST 131 E8
Kihlevere EST 131 C12
Kihniö FIN 123 F10
Kiihtelysvaara FIN 125 F14
Kiikala FIN 127 E10
Kiikka FIN 126 C8
Kiikla EST 131 C14
Kiikoinen FIN 126 C8
Kiili EST 131 C9
Kiiminki FIN 119 D15
Kiisa EST 131 C9
Kiiskilä FIN 123 C13
Kiistala FIN 117 C14
Kiiu EST 131 C10
Kiiu-Aabla EST 131 B11
Kije PL 143 E10
Kijevë RKS 163 D10
Kijevo HR 156 E5
Kijewo Królewskie PL 138 D5
Kikerino RUS 132 C6
Kikinda SRB 150 F5
Kików PL 138 E7
Kikorze PL 85 C8
Ķikuri LV 134 C3
Kil N 90 B5
Kil S 97 C9
Kilafors S 103 D12
Kilargue IRL 6 D6
Kilb A 77 F8
Kilbaha IRL 8 C3
Kilbeggan IRL 7 F8
Kilbeheny IRL 8 D6
Kilberry GB 4 D5
Kilberry IRL 7 F8
Kilbirnie GB 4 D7
Kilboghamn N 108 D5
Kilbotn N 111 C12
Kilbrittain IRL 8 E5
Kilby S 99 B10
Kilcar IRL 6 C5
Kilchoan GB 4 B4
Kilchrenan GB 4 C6
Kilcock IRL 7 F9
Kilcolgan IRL 6 F5
Kilcommon IRL 9 D7
Kilconnell IRL 6 F6
Kilconney IRL 7 D8
Kilcoole IRL 7 F10
Kilcormac IRL 7 F7
Kilcreggan GB 4 D7
Kilcullen IRL 7 F9
Kildare IRL 7 F9
Kildavin IRL 9 C9
Kilden DK 90 E7
Kildimo New IRL 8 C5
Kildonan Lodge GB 3 J9
Kile N 90 A2
Kilen N 95 D9
Kilfenora IRL 6 G4
Kilfinan GB 4 D6
Kilfinnane IRL 8 D6
Kilforsen S 107 D11
Kilgarvan IRL 8 E4
Kilgetty GB 12 B5
Kilglass IRL 6 E6
Kilglass IRL 6 F6
Kilham GB 5 D12
Kilidülbahir TR 171 D10
Kilifarevo BG 166 C5
Kilingi-Nõmme EST 131 E9
Kiliya UA 155 C4
Kilkea IRL 6 F6
Kilkee IRL 8 C3
Kilkeel GB 7 D11
Kilkelly IRL 6 E5
Kilkenny IRL 9 C8
Kilkerrin IRL 6 E5
Kilkhampton GB 12 D6
Kilkieran IRL 6 F3
Kilkinlea IRL 8 D4
Kilkis GR 169 C8
Kilkishen IRL 8 C5
Kill IRL 7 F9
Kill IRL 9 D8
Killabunane IRL 8 E3
Killadysert IRL 8 C4
Killagan Bridge GB 4 E4
Killala IRL 6 D4
Killaloe IRL 8 C6
Killamery IRL 9 D8
Killann IRL 9 C9
Killarga IRL 6 D6
Killarney IRL 8 D4
Killavullen IRL 8 D5
Killeagh IRL 8 E7
Killean GB 4 D5
Killearn GB 5 C8
Killeberg S 88 C6
Killeenleagh IRL 8 E4
Killeigh IRL 7 F8
Killen GB 7 C7
Killenaule IRL 9 C7
Killerrig IRL 9 C9
Killeshandra IRL 7 D7
Killichonan GB 5 B8
Killiecrankie GB 5 B9
Killimor IRL 6 F6
Killin GB 5 C8
Killinaboy IRL 6 G4
Killinchy GB 7 D11
Killinge S 116 C4
Killingworth GB 5 E13
Killinick IRL 9 D10
Killinkoski FIN 123 F11
Killorglin IRL 8 D3
Killough GB 7 D11
Killough IRL 7 F10
Killucan IRL 7 E8
Killukin IRL 6 E6
Killundine GB 4 B5
Killurin IRL 9 D9
Killybegs IRL 6 C6
Killyclogher GB 4 F2
Killylea GB 7 D9
Kilmacanogue IRL 7 F10
Kilmacrenan IRL 7 B7
Kilmacthomas IRL 9 D8
Kilmaganny IRL 9 D8
Kilmaine IRL 6 E4
Kilmaley IRL 8 C4
Kilmallock IRL 8 D5
Kilmaluag GB 2 K4
Kilmarnock GB 4 D8
Kilmartin GB 4 C6
Kilmeague IRL 7 F9
Kilmeedy IRL 8 D5
Kilmelford GB 4 C6
Kilmichael IRL 8 E4
Kilmihill IRL 8 C4
Kilmona IRL 8 E5
Kilmoon IRL 7 E10
Kilmore IRL 8 C5
Kilmore IRL 9 D9
Kilmore Quay IRL 9 D9
Kilmuckridge IRL 9 C10
Kilmurry IRL 8 C5
Kilmurry McMahon IRL 8 C4
Kilnaboy IRL 6 G4
Kilnaleck IRL 7 E8
Kilnamanagh IRL 9 C10
Kilninian GB 4 B4
Kilninver GB 4 C5
Kilnock IRL 6 E5
Kiloran GB 4 C4
Kilpelä FIN 115 D4
Kilpilahti FIN 127 E14
Kilpisjärvi FIN 112 E6
Kilpua FIN 119 F13
Kilquiggin IRL 9 C9
Kilrane IRL 9 D10
Kilrea GB 4 F3
Kilrean IRL 6 C6
Kilreekill IRL 6 F6
Kilrenny GB 5 C11
Kilronan IRL 6 F3
Kilrush IRL 8 C4
Kilsallagh IRL 6 E5
Kilsaran IRL 7 E10
Kilshanchoe IRL 7 F9
Kilshanny IRL 6 G4
Kilskeer IRL 7 E9
Kilsmo S 92 A7
Kilsund N 90 B4
Kilsyth GB 5 D8
Kiltartan IRL 6 F5
Kiltealy IRL 9 C9
Kiltegan IRL 9 C9
Kiltimagh IRL 6 E5
Kiltogan IRL 9 C9
Kiltoom IRL 6 F6
Kiltsi EST 131 C12
Kiltullagh IRL 6 F5
Kilvakkala FIN 127 B9
Kilvenaapa FIN 119 B16
Kilvo S 116 E6
Kilwaughter GB 4 F5
Kilwinning GB 4 D7
Kilworth IRL 8 D6
Kimasozero RUS 121 F17
Kimberley GB 15 B11
Kimbolton GB 15 C8
Kiminki FIN 123 E13
Kimito FIN 126 E8
Kimle H 146 F4
Kimmeria GR 171 B7
Kimo FIN 122 D8
Kimola FIN 127 C15
Kimonkylä FIN 127 D15
Kimovaara RUS 125 C16
Kimpton GB 15 D8
Kimstad S 92 B7
Kinahmo FIN 125 E13
Kinbrace GB 3 J9
Kincardine GB 5 C9
Kincraig GB 3 L9
Kincses H 149 B10
Kindberg A 148 A4
Kindelbrück D 79 D9
Kinderbeuern D 21 D8
Kinding D 75 E9
Kindsbach D 186 C4
Kindsjön S 102 E4
Kineta GR 175 D7
Kingarrow IRL 6 C6
Kingarth GB 4 D6
Kingisepp RUS 132 C4
Kingsbridge GB 13 E7
Kingsclere GB 13 C12
Kingscourt IRL 7 E9
Kingskerswell GB 13 E7
Kingsland IRL 6 E6
King's Lynn GB 11 F12
Kingsnorth GB 15 E10
Kingsteignton GB 13 D7
Kingsthorne GB 13 B9
Kingston GB 3 K10
Kingston Bagpuize GB 13 B12
Kingston Seymour GB 13 C9
Kingston upon Hull GB 11 D11
Kingswear GB 13 E7
Kingswood GB 13 C9
Kings Worthy GB 13 C12
Kington GB 13 A8
Kingussie GB 5 A8
Kingwilliamstown IRL 8 D4
Kinik TR 173 E10
Kinik TR 177 A9
Kinisjärvi FIN 117 D14
Kinloch GB 4 A4
Kinlochard GB 4 C8
Kinlochewe GB 2 K6
Kinlochleven GB 4 B7
Kinloch Rannoch GB 5 B8
Kinloss GB 3 K9
Kinlough IRL 6 D6
Kinn N 111 C10
Kinna S 91 D12
Kinnared S 87 A12
Kinnarp S 91 C14
Kinnarumma S 91 D12
Kinnegad IRL 7 F8
Kinnitty IRL 7 F7
Kinnula FIN 123 D13
Kinnulanlahti FIN 124 D8
Kinrooi B 19 B12
Kinross GB 5 C10
Kinsale IRL 8 E5
Kinsalebeg IRL 9 E7
Kinsarvik N 94 B5
Kintai LT 134 F2
Kintaus FIN 123 F14
Kintbury GB 13 C12
Kintore GB 3 L12
Kinvara IRL 6 F5
Kinvarra IRL 6 F3
Kioni GR 174 C2
Kipen' RUS 132 B6
Kipfenberg D 75 E9
Kipilovo BG 166 D6
Kipinä FIN 119 D17
Kipoi GR 168 E4
Kipoureio GR 168 E5
Kippel CH 70 E5
Kippen GB 5 C8
Kippenheim D 27 D8
Kir AL 163 E8
Kirakkajärvi FIN 114 D5
Kirakkaköngäs FIN 113 F19
Királd H 145 G1
Királyegyháza H 149 D9
Királyhegyes H 150 E6
Kiran N 104 C8
Kiran TR 181 B8
Kirazli TR 172 D6
Kirbla EST 131 D7
Kirby Muxloe GB 11 F9
Kircasalih TR 173 B6
Kirchanschöring D 73 A6
Kirchardt D 21 F11

Kirchbach A 73 C7
Kirchbach in Steiermark A 148 C5
Kirchberg CH 27 F11
Kirchberg CH 31 A12
Kirchberg D 76 E4
Kirchberg D 79 E12
Kirchberg (Hunsrück) D 185 E7
Kirchberg am Wagram A 77 F9
Kirchberg am Walde A 77 E8
Kirchberg am Wechsel A 148 A5
Kirchberg an der Jagst D 74 D6
Kirchberg an der Pielach A 77 F8
Kirchberg an der Raab A 148 C5
Kirchbichl A 72 A5
Kirchdorf D 17 C11
Kirchdorf D 83 C10
Kirchdorf an der Iller D 71 A10
Kirchdorf an der Krems A 73 A9
Kirchdorf im Wald D 76 E4
Kirchdorf in Tirol A 72 A5
Kirchehrenbach D 75 C9
Kirchellen D 183 B9
Kirchen (Sieg) D 21 C9
Kirchenlamitz D 75 B10
Kirchenthumbach D 75 C10
Kirchgellersen D 83 D8
Kirchhain D 21 C11
Kirchheim D 74 C6
Kirchheim D 78 E6
Kirchheim am Neckar D 187 C7
Kirchheim bei München D 75 F10
Kirchheim-Bolanden D 21 E10
Kirchheim unter Teck D 27 C11
Kirchhundem D 21 B10
Kirchlauter D 75 B8
Kirchlinteln D 17 C12
Kirch Mulsow D 83 C11
Kirchohsen (Emmerthal) D 78 B5
Kirchroth D 75 E12
Kirchschlag in der Buckligen Welt A 148 A6
Kirchseelte D 17 C11
Kirchtimke D 17 B12
Kirchwalsede D 17 B12
Kirchweidach D 75 F12
Kirchwistedt D 17 B11
Kirchzarten D 27 E8
Kirchzell D 21 E12
Kircubbin GB 7 D11
Kireç TR 173 E9
Kiremitçisalih TR 172 B6
Kirillovskoye RUS 129 E11
Kirjais FIN 126 E6
Kirjavala FIN 129 B12
Kirkağaç TR 177 A10
Kirkbean GB 5 F9
Kirkbride GB 5 F10
Kirkby GB 10 E6
Kirkby in Ashfield GB 11 E9
Kirkby Lonsdale GB 10 C6
Kirkbymoorside GB 11 C10
Kirkby Stephen GB 11 C7
Kirkby Thore GB 5 F11
Kirkcaldy GB 5 C10
Kirkcolm GB 4 F6
Kirkconnel GB 5 E8
Kirkcudbright GB 5 F8
Kirkeby DK 86 E7
Kirkehamn N 94 F5
Kirke Helsinge DK 87 D8
Kirke Hyllinge DK 87 D9
Kirkel-Neuhäusel D 186 C3
Kirkenær N 96 B7
Kirkenes N 114 D8
Kirke Såby DK 87 D9
Kirke Stillinge DK 87 E8
Kirkham GB 10 D6
Kirkinner GB 5 F8
Kirkintilloch GB 5 D8
Kirkjubøur FO 2 B3
Kirkkavak TR 173 B6
Kirkkepenekli TR 173 B8
Kirkkonummi FIN 127 E11
Kirklareli TR 167 F8
Kirkmichael GB 4 E7
Kirkmichael GB 5 B9
Kirk Michael GBM 10 C2
Kirknewton GB 5 D12
Kirkoswald GB 5 F11
Kirkpatrick-Fleming GB 5 E10
Kirkton GB 4 C5
Kirkton of Durris GB 5 A12
Kirkton of Glenisla GB 5 B10
Kirkton of Skene GB 3 L12
Kirktown of Auchterless GB 3 L12
Kirktown of Deskford GB 3 K11
Kirkwall GB 3 H11
Kirn D 21 E8
Kirnujärvi S 116 D10
Kirovsk RUS 129 F14
Kirriemuir GB 5 B10
Kirschweiler D 21 E8
Kirtik S 118 B5
Kirtlington GB 13 B12
Kirton GB 15 C11
Kirton in Lindsey GB 11 E10
Kirtorf D 21 C12
Kiruna S 116 C4
Kisa S 92 D7
Kisač SRB 158 C4
Kisar H 145 G6
Kisbér H 149 A10
Kiseljak BIH 157 C10
Kiseljak BIH 157 C11
Kiseljak BIH 157 E9
Kisgyőr H 145 G2
Kishkeam IRL 8 D4
Kisielice PL 139 C7
Kisielnica PL 139 D13
Kisko FIN 127 E9
Kisköre H 150 B5
Kiskőrös H 150 D3
Kiskunfélegyháza H 150 D4
Kiskunhalas H 150 E3
Kiskunlacháza H 150 C3
Kiskunmajsa H 150 E4
Kişlacik TR 167 F9
Kisláng H 149 C10
Kisléta H 151 B8
Kislőd H 149 B9
Kismarja H 151 C8
Kisnána H 147 F10
Kisovec SLO 73 D10
Kissakoski FIN 128 B6
Kissamos GR 178 E6
Kissenbrück D 79 B8
Kißlegg D 71 B9
Kisszállás H 150 E3
Kist D 187 B8
Kistanje HR 156 E4
Kistelek H 150 E4
Kistokaj H 145 G2
Kistrand N 113 C15
Kisújszállás H 150 C6
Kisvárda H 145 G5
Kisvarsány H 145 G5
Kiszkowo PL 81 A12
Kiszombor H 150 E5
Kitee FIN 125 F14
Kiten BG 167 E9
Kitinoja FIN 122 E9
Kitka FIN 121 B12
Kitkiöjärvi S 116 C10
Kitros GR 169 D8
Kitsi FIN 125 D15
Kittajaur S 118 B3
Kittelfjäll S 106 A8
Kittilä FIN 117 C13
Kittsee A 77 F12
Kitula FIN 127 E10
Kitzbühel A 72 B5
Kitzen D 79 D11
Kitzingen D 75 C7
Kitzscher D 79 D12
Kiucze PL 143 F8
Kiukainen FIN 126 C7
Kiuruvesi FIN 123 C17
Kiurujärvi FIN 115 D2
Kivarinjärvi FIN 121 E10
Kivelä FIN 115 F4
Kiveri GR 175 D6
Kivesjärvi FIN 121 F9
Kiveskylä FIN 121 F9
Kiveslahti FIN 120 F9
Kiviapaja FIN 129 B10
Kivijärvi FIN 123 D14
Kivijärvi S 116 E10
Kivik S 88 D6
Kivikangas FIN 123 D12
Kivilahti FIN 125 E14
Kivilompolo FIN 117 A10
Kivilompolo FIN 119 B12
Kivilompolo N 117 A10
Kivioja FIN 119 B14
Kiviõli EST 131 C13
Kiviperä FIN 121 B14
Kivivaara FIN 121 D11
Kivivaara FIN 125 C14
Kivi-Vigala EST 131 D8
Kivotos GR 168 D5
Kiwity PL 136 E2
Kıyıköy TR 173 A9
Kizilcaova TR 177 C10
Kizilcikdere TR 167 F8
Kizilpinar TR 173 B8
Kizilyaka TR 181 B8
Kjækan N 112 D9
Kjåmes N 111 D11
Kjeldebotn N 111 D12
Kjelkenes N 100 C2
Kjelkvik N 111 D11
Kjellerup DK 86 C4
Kjelling N 108 B7
Kjemmoen N 102 D2
Kjengsnes N 111 C11
Kjerknesvågen N 105 D10
Kjerret N 96 B7
Kjerringdal N 112 C9
Kjerringholmen N 113 B12
Kjerringøy N 108 A8
Kjerringvåg N 104 D5
Kjerringvik N 110 C9
Kjerringvik N 111 D12
Kjerstad N 111 D11
Kjølebrønn N 90 B5
Kjølen N 91 A9
Kjøllefjord N 113 B19
Kjølstad N 101 D10
Kjøpsvik N 111 D11
Kjura N 104 E7
Kjøsvika N 105 A12
Kjulaås S 98 D7
Klaaswaal NL 16 E2
Kľačno SK 147 D7
Kladanj BIH 157 D10
Kläden D 79 A10
Kladnica SRB 163 C9
Kladnice HR 156 E5
Kladno CZ 76 B6
Kladovo SRB 159 D10
Kladruby CZ 76 C3
Klæbu N 104 E8
Klagenfurt A 73 C9
Klågerup S 87 D12
Klaipėda LT 134 E2
Kłaj PL 143 G9
Klakksjorda N 110 C8
Klaksvík FO 2 A3
Klamila FIN 128 D7
Klana HR 67 B9
Klanac HR 156 C3
Klanino PL 85 B10
Klanjec HR 148 D5
Klanxbüll D 82 A5
Klapkalnciems LV 134 B6
Kläppsjö S 107 D12
Klärke S 103 A12
Klarup DK 86 A6
Klašnice BIH 157 C7
Klasov SK 146 E6
Klässbol S 97 C8
Klášterec nad Ohří CZ 76 B4
Kláštor pod Znievom SK 147 D7
Klátova Nová Ves SK 146 D6
Klatovy CZ 76 D4
Klaukkala FIN 127 E12
Klaus an der Pyhrnbahn A 73 A9
Klausdorf D 80 B4
Klausdorf D 84 B4
Klausen D 21 E7
Klausen Leopoldsdorf A 77 F10
Klausučiai LT 136 C7
Klauvnes N 112 D6
Klazienaveen NL 17 C7
Kłębowiec PL 85 D10
Klecko PL 81 A12
Klącz PL 143 D7
Kleczew PL 138 F5
Kleemola FIN 123 C12
Kleidi GR 169 C8
Kleinarl A 73 B7
Klein Berßen D 17 C8
Kleinblittersdorf D 27 B7
Klein Bünzow D 84 C5
Kleinfurra D 79 D8
Kleinheubach D 21 E12
Kleinjena D 79 D10
Klein Kreutz D 79 B12
Kleinlobming A 73 B10
Kleinmachnow D 80 B4
Kleinpaschleben D 79 C10
Kleinreifling A 73 A10
Kleinrinderfeld D 187 B8
Klein Rönnau D 83 C8
Klein Sankt Paul A 73 C10
Kleinwallstadt D 21 E12
Kleinwelka D 80 D6
Kleinzell A 77 G9
Kleio GR 171 F10
Kleisoura GR 168 C5
Kleitoria GR 174 D5
Kleiva N 110 C9
Kleive N 100 A7
Klejniki PL 141 E8
Klejtrup DK 86 B5
Klek SRB 158 C5
Klembivka UA 154 A2
Klemensker DK 89 E7
Klenčí pod Čerchovem CZ 75 D12
Klenica PL 81 C9
Klenike SRB 164 E4
Klenje SRB 158 D3
Klenovec SK 147 D9
Klenovice na Hané CZ 77 D12
Kleosin PL 140 D8
Klepacze PL 140 D8
Kleppe N 94 E3
Kleppestø N 94 B2
Kleppstad N 110 D7
Klipsk PL 81 B9
Kleszczele PL 141 E8
Kleszczewo PL 81 B12
Kleszczewo PL 136 F6
Kleszczów PL 143 D7
Klettwitz D 80 C5
Kleve D 16 E6
Klevshult S 92 E4
Kličevac SRB 159 D7
Kličevo MNE 163 D6
Klieken D 79 C11
Klietz D 83 E12
Klikuszowa PL 147 B9
Klim DK 86 A4
Kliment BG 161 F10
Kliment BG 165 D10
Klimentovo BG 167 C9
Klimkovice CZ 146 B6
Klimontów PL 143 E11
Klimontów PL 143 F9
Klimpfjäll S 106 A7
Klin SK 147 C8
Klinča Sela HR 148 E5
Klinë RKS 163 D10
Klinë e Epërme RKS 163 D10
Klingenberg D 80 E5
Klingenberg am Main D 21 E12
Klingenthal D 75 B11
Klingersel S 118 B7
Klingre S 107 E15
Klink D 83 D13
Klinkby DK 86 B2
Klinte S 93 E12
Klintebjerg DK 86 E6
Klintehamn S 93 E12
Kliplev DK 86 F4
Klippan S 87 C12
Klippen S 107 C13
Klippen S 108 E9
Klippinge DK 87 E10
Klis HR 156 E6
Klisura BG 165 D9
Klisura BG 165 E7
Klisura SRB 164 D5
Klitmøller DK 86 A3
Klitten D 81 D7
Klitten S 102 D7
Klixbüll D 82 A5
Kljajićevo SRB 150 F3
Ključ BIH 157 C6
Kllokot RKS 164 E3
Klobouky CZ 77 E11
Kłobuck PL 143 E6
Klobuk BIH 157 F7
Klöch A 148 C5
Klockestrand S 103 A14
Klockrike S 92 C6
Kłoczew PL 141 G5
Kłodawa PL 85 E8
Kłodawa PL 143 B6
Kłodzko PL 77 B11
Kloetinge NL 16 F1
Kløfta N 95 B14
Klokkarstua N 95 C12
Klokkerholm DK 86 A6
Klokočevac SRB 159 E9
Klokočevci HR 149 E10
Klokočov SK 147 C7
Kłomnice PL 143 E7
Klonowa PL 142 D5
Klooga EST 131 C8
Kloosterhaar NL 17 D7
Kloosterzande NL 16 F2
Klos AL 163 F9
Klos AL 168 B3
Klöse S 107 D16
Kloštar Ivanić HR 149 E6
Kloštar Podravski HR 149 E8
Kloster DK 86 C2
Klosterfelde D 84 E4
Klosterhäseler D 79 D10
Klösterle A 71 C10
Klosterlechfeld D 71 A11
Klostermansfeld D 79 C9
Klosterneuburg A 77 F10
Klosters CH 71 D9
Kloster Zinna D 80 B4
Kloten CH 27 F10
Kloten S 97 C13
Klotten D 21 D8
Klötze (Altmark) D 79 A9
Klovainiai LT 135 E7
Klovborg DK 86 D4
Klövertäsk S 118 C6
Kløvmoen N 108 E6
Klövsjö S 102 A7
Klubbfors S 118 D5
Klubbvik N 114 C6
Kluczbork PL 142 E5
Kluczewsko PL 143 E8
Kluki PL 143 D7
Kluknava SK 145 F2
Klukowo PL 141 E7
Klumpen S 106 D7
Klundert NL 16 E3
Klungsten S 99 A10
Klupe BIH 157 C8
Kluse D 17 C8
Kľušov SK 145 E3
Klusy PL 139 C13
Klutsjön S 102 B4
Klütz D 83 C10
Klwów PL 141 G3
Klyastsitsy BY 133 E5
Klykoliai LT 134 D5
Klynivka UA 153 A7
Knaben N 94 E6
Knåda S 103 D10
Knaften S 107 C15
Knäred S 87 B12
Knaresborough GB 11 C9
Knarrevik N 94 B2
Knarrlagsund N 104 D6
Knätten S 102 B7
Knebel DK 86 C6
Knesebeck D 83 E9
Knesselare B 19 B7
Knetzgau D 75 C8
Knežak SLO 73 E9
Kneževi Vinogradi HR 149 E11
Kneževo HR 149 E11
Knezha BG 165 C9
Kněžice CZ 77 D9
Knežina BIH 157 D10
Kněžmost CZ 77 B8
Knić SRB 158 F6
Knidi GR 169 D6
Knighton GB 13 A8
Knin HR 156 D5
Knislinge S 88 C6
Knittelfeld A 73 B10
Knittlingen D 27 B10
Knīveri LV 134 D3
Knivsta S 99 C9
Knizhovnik BG 166 F5
Knjaževac SRB 164 B5
Knock GB 4 C5
Knock IRL 6 E5
Knock IRL 8 C4
Knockalough IRL 8 C4
Knockanevin IRL 8 D6
Knockban GB 2 K7
Knockbrack IRL 7 C7
Knockbridge IRL 7 E10
Knockcroghery IRL 6 E6
Knocklong IRL 8 D6
Knockmoyle IRL 6 F6
Knocknaboul IRL 8 D4
Knocknacarry GB 4 E4
Knocknacree IRL 9 C9
Knocknagree IRL 8 D4
Knocks IRL 8 E5
Knocktopher IRL 9 D8
Knokke-Heist B 19 B7
Knoppe S 103 B12
Knorrendorf D 84 C4
Knottingley GB 11 D9
Knowle GB 13 A11
Knucklas GB 13 A8
Knud DK 86 B4
Knurów PL 142 F6
Knutbränna S 106 D7
Knutby S 99 C10
Knutsbol S 97 D12
Knutsford GB 11 E7
Knyazevo RUS 133 D5
Knyazhe UA 152 A6
Knyazhevo BG 167 E6
Knyazhitsy RUS 132 E4
Knyszyn PL 140 D7
Kobaky UA 152 A6
Kobarid SLO 73 D8
Kobatovci BIH 157 C7
Kobbelveid N 109 A10
Kobbevågnes N 111 B16
Kobbfoss N 114 E7
Kobela EST 131 F12
København DK 87 D11
Kobenz A 73 B10
Kobeřice CZ 142 G5
Kobern D 185 D7
Kobersdorf A 149 A6
Kobiele Wielkie PL 143 D8
Kobierzyce PL 81 E11
Kobilyane BG 171 A8
Kobiór PL 143 F6
Koblenz D 21 D9
Kobrow D 83 C11
Kobyla Góra PL 142 D4
Kobylanka PL 85 D7
Kobylany PL 145 D4
Kobylets'ka Polyana UA 145 G9
Kobylin PL 81 C12
Kobyłka PL 139 F11
Kobylnica PL 81 B12
Kobylnica PL 85 B12
Kobylniki PL 139 F9
Kocaavşar TR 173 E8
Kocahidir TR 171 C10
Kočani MK 164 F5
Kocapinar TR 173 E8
Koçarli TR 177 D10
Kocayazi TR 167 E8
Kocayazi TR 167 F8
Koceljevo SRB 158 E4
Kočeni LV 135 A10
Kočerin BIH 157 F8
Kočevje SLO 73 E10
Kočevska Reka SLO 73 E10
Kochanowice PL 142 E6
Kochel am See D 72 A3
Kocherinovo BG 165 E7
Kochmar BG 161 F10
Kochovo BG 167 C7
Kock PL 141 G6
Kočovce SK 146 D5
Kocs H 149 A10
Kocsér H 150 C4
Kocsola H 149 C10
Kocsord H 145 H5
Koczała PL 85 C12
Kodavere EST 131 D14
Kode S 91 D10
Kodeń PL 141 G9
Kodersdorf D 81 D7
Kodesjärvi FIN 122 F8
Kodiksami FIN 126 C6
Kodisjoki FIN 126 C6
Köditz D 75 B10
Kodrąb PL 143 D8
Kodyma UA 154 A4
Koekelare B 18 B6
Koersel B 183 C6
Koeru EST 131 D12
Koewacht NL 182 C3
Kofçaz TR 167 F8
Köflach A 73 B11
Kog SLO 148 D6
Køge DK 87 E10
Koglhof A 148 B5
Kohila EST 131 C9
Kohlberg D 75 C11
Köhlen D 17 A11
Kohren-Sahlis D 79 D12
Kohtla-Järve EST 131 C14
Koidula EST 132 F2
Koigi EST 131 D11
Koijärvi FIN 127 D10
Koikkala FIN 128 B8
Koiliomeno GR 174 D2
Koilovtsi BG 165 C10
Koimisi GR 169 B9
Koirakoski FIN 124 C9
Koita GR 178 B3
Koitila FIN 121 C11
Koivu FIN 119 B14
Koivujärvi FIN 123 C16
Koivujärvi FIN 123 D16
Koivumäki FIN 123 D12
Koivumäki FIN 124 D9
Koivumäki FIN 125 F11
Koivuniemi FIN 119 C15
Köja S 107 F13
Kojanlanti FIN 125 E11
Kojetín CZ 146 C4
Kóka H 150 C4
Kökar FIN 126 F4
Kokari LV 135 C13
Kokava nad Rimavicou SK 147 D9
Kokelv N 113 B14
Kokemäki FIN 126 C7
Kokkala GR 178 B3
Kokkari GR 177 D8
Kokkinochoma GR 171 C6
Kokkino Nero GR 169 E8
Kokkokylä FIN 119 C17
Kokkola FIN 123 C10
Kokkolahti FIN 125 F12
Kokkosniva FIN 115 D2
Kokkotoi GR 175 A6
Kokkovaara FIN 117 D13
Köklot FIN 122 D7
Koknese LV 135 C10
Kokonvaara FIN 125 E12
Kokora EST 131 D14
Kokorevo RUS 132 F6
Kokory CZ 146 C4
Kokrica SLO 73 D9
Koksijde B 18 B6
Kokträsk S 109 F16
Kola BIH 157 C7
Kołacin PL 141 G1
Kołacz PL 85 C10
Kołacze PL 141 H8
Kołaczkowo PL 142 B4
Kołaczyce PL 144 D3
Kolaka GR 175 B7
Koláre SK 147 E8
Kolari FIN 117 D11
Kolari S 117 D11
Kolari SRB 159 D6
Kolárovice SK 147 C7
Kolarovo BG 169 B9
Kolárovo SK 146 F5
Kolåsen S 105 D13
Kolašin MNE 163 D8
Kolbäck S 98 C6
Kołbacz PL 85 D7
Kołbaskowo PL 84 D6
Kolbermoor D 72 A5
Kołbiel PL 141 F4
Kolbotn N 95 C13
Kolbu N 101 E13
Kolbudy Górne PL 138 B5
Kolbuszowa PL 144 C4
Kølby DK 86 B4
Kol'chyne UA 145 G6
Kölcse H 145 G6
Kołczygłowy PL 85 B12
Kołczyn PL 81 A8
Koldby DK 86 B3
Koldere TR 177 B10
Kolding DK 86 E4
Koler S 118 D5
Kölesd H 149 C11
Kolesjan AL 163 F9
Koleska BIH 157 F9
Kolforsen S 103 E12
Kolga EST 131 C11
Kolga-Aabla EST 131 B11
Kolga-Jaani EST 131 D11
Kolho FIN 123 F13
Koli FIN 125 D13
Kolín CZ 77 B8
Kolíňany SK 146 E6
Kolind DK 86 C7
Kolindros GR 169 D7
Kolinec CZ 76 D4
Kolinkivtsi UA 153 A8
Koliri GR 174 D3
Kolisne UA 154 E5
Kolitzheim D 75 C7
Köljala EST 130 E5
Koljane HR 156 E5
Kolka LV 130 F5
Kølkær DK 86 C4
Kolkanlahti FIN 123 E14
Kölked H 149 E11
Kolkja EST 131 D14
Kolkku FIN 123 D16
Kolkonjärvi FIN 121 B10
Kolkwitz D 80 C6
Kollaja FIN 119 D17
Kölleda D 79 D9
Kollines GR 174 E5
Kölln-Reisiek D 82 C7
Kolltveit N 94 B2
Kollund DK 82 A6
Kolmisoppi FIN 124 D9
Köln D 21 C7
Kolnica PL 140 C8
Kolno PL 136 F2
Kolno PL 139 D12
Kolo BIH 157 E7
Koło PL 142 B6
Kołobrzeg PL 85 B9
Kolochau D 80 C4
Kolochava UA 145 G8
Kolonjë AL 168 C2
Kolonowskie PL 142 E5
Kölosen S 102 B4
Kolpino RUS 129 F14
Kolsätter S 102 B8
Kolsh AL 163 E9
Kölsillre S 103 B9
Kölsjön S 103 B11
Kolsko PL 81 C9
Kölsta S 97 C15
Kolsva S 97 C14
Kölsvallen S 102 C6
Kölsvallen S 102 C7
Kolt DK 86 C6
Kolta SK 146 E6
Kolu FIN 123 E12
Kolunič BIH 156 C5
Koluszki PL 141 G1
Koluvere EST 131 D8
Kölvallen S 102 B5
Kolvereid N 105 B11
Kolvik N 113 C15
Kølvrå DK 86 C4
Kolympari GR 178 D6
Kolympia GR 181 D8
Komádi H 151 C7
Komagfjord N 113 C11
Komagvær N 114 C9
Komańcza PL 145 E5
Komanos GR 169 D6
Komar BIH 157 D7
Komara GR 171 A10
Komarani SRB 163 C8
Komarevo BG 165 B10
Komarica BIH 157 C8
Komárno SK 149 A10
Komarno UA 145 D8
Komárom H 149 A10
Komárov CZ 76 C5
Komarovo RUS 129 E12
Komarówka Podlaska PL 141 G7
Komarów Osada PL 144 B7
Kombuļi LV 133 E2
Komen SLO 73 E8
Komėsi AL 168 A2
Komi GR 176 D5
Komi GR 177 C7
Komin HR 148 D6
Komin HR 157 F8
Komiža HR 63 A10
Komjatice SK 146 E6
Komletinci HR 157 B10
Komló H 149 D10
Kömlő H 150 B5
Kömlőd H 149 A10
Kommeno GR 174 A3
Komnina GR 169 C6
Komoran RKS 163 D10
Komorniki PL 81 B11
Komorowo PL 139 E12
Komorzno PL 142 D5
Komoshtitsa BG 160 F2
Komossa FIN 122 D9
Komotini GR 171 B8
Kompakka FIN 125 F13
Kompelusvaara S 116 D8
Kömpöc H 150 E4
Kompoti GR 174 A3
Komprachcice PL 142 E4
Komsi EST 130 D7
Komsomol's'k RUS 136 D2
Komsomol'sk RUS 139 A9
Komsomol's'k UA 145 G8
Komu FIN 123 C16
Komula FIN 125 C10
Komunari BG 167 C8
Komuniga BG 166 F4
Komylio GR 174 B2
Konak TR 177 C9
Konakpinar TR 173 F8
Konare BG 155 F2
Konary PL 141 G4
Konarzyce PL 139 D13
Konarzyny PL 85 C12
Koncanica HR 149 E8
Konče MK 169 A7
Kondolovo BG 167 E9
Kondoros H 150 D6
Kondratowice PL 81 E11
Kondrat'yevo RUS 129 D9
Kondrić HR 157 B9
Koneck PL 138 E6
Køng DK 87 E9
Konga S 89 B8
Köngäs FIN 115 E1
Köngäs FIN 117 C13
Kongasmäki FIN 121 E9
Kongens Lyngby DK 87 D11
Kongerslev DK 86 B6
Konginkangas FIN 123 E15
Kongsberg N 95 C11
Kongselva N 110 D9
Kongsfjord N 114 B6
Kongslia N 101 D9
Kongsmoen N 105 B12
Kongsvik N 111 C11
Kongsvinger N 96 B7
Kongsvoll N 104 D6
Konice CZ 77 C11
Koniecpol PL 143 E8
Königheim D 187 B8
Königsberg in Bayern D 75 B8
Königsborn D 79 B10
Königsbronn D 75 E7
Königsbrück D 80 D5
Königsbrunn D 75 F8
Königsdorf D 72 A3
Königsee D 79 E9
Königsfeld im Schwarzwald D 27 D9
Königshofen D 79 D10
Königshütte D 79 C8
Königslutter am Elm D 79 B8
Königsmoos D 75 E9
Königssee D 73 A6
Königstein D 75 C10
Königstein D 80 E6
Königstein im Taunus D 187 A5
Königswartha D 80 D6
Königswiesen A 77 F7
Königswinter D 21 C8
Königs Wusterhausen D 80 B5
Konin PL 142 B5
Konispol AL 168 E3
Konitsa GR 168 D4
Könitz D 79 E10
Köniz CH 31 B11
Konjevrate HR 156 E5
Konjic BIH 157 E8
Konjsko BIH 157 E7
Konjsko BIH 162 D5
Konnekoski FIN 123 E17
Könnern D 79 C10
Konnevesi FIN 123 E16
Könni FIN 122 E9
Konnunsuo FIN 129 C10
Konnuslahti FIN 125 E9
Könölä FIN 119 C12
Konolfingen CH 70 D5
Konopiska PL 143 E7
Konopište MK 169 B7
Konopki PL 139 D9
Konopnica PL 141 H6
Konopnica PL 142 D6
Konotop PL 81 C9
Konotop PL 85 D9
Kon'ovo BG 166 D6
Końskie PL 141 H2
Konsko MK 169 B7
Końskowola PL 141 H6
Konsmo N 90 C1
Konstancin-Jeziorna PL 141 F4
Konstantinova LV 133 D2
Konstantinovy Lázně CZ 76 C3
Konstantynów PL 141 F8
Konstantynów Łódzki PL 143 C7
Konstanz D 27 E11
Kontariotissa GR 169 D7
Kontiainen FIN 123 E10
Kontias GR 171 E8
Kontinjoki FIN 121 F10
Kontiokoski FIN 119 D15
Kontiolahti FIN 125 E13
Kontiomäki FIN 121 F11
Kontkala FIN 125 E12
Kontopouli GR 171 E8
Kontovazaina GR 174 D4
Konttajärvi FIN 117 E12
Konttila FIN 119 C17
Konttimäki FIN 125 D9
Konush BG 166 F4
Kóny H 149 A8
Konyár H 151 C8
Konyavo BG 165 E6
Konz D 21 E7
Konzell D 75 D12
Koog aan de Zaan NL 16 D3
Koonga EST 131 D8
Kööriilä FIN 126 B6
Koosa EST 131 D14
Kootstertille NL 16 B6
Kootwijkerbroek NL 183 A7
Kopani GR 168 F4
Kopanica PL 81 B9
Kopanos GR 169 C7
Kopardal N 108 D4
Koparnes N 100 B3
Kopčany SK 77 E12
Koper SLO 67 A8
Kopervik N 94 D2
Kópháza H 149 A7
Kopice PL 142 E3
Kopidlno CZ 77 B8
Kopilovtsi BG 165 C6
Köping S 97 C15
Köpingebro S 88 E5
Köpingsvik S 89 B11
Kopisto FIN 119 F12
Kopki PL 144 C5
Koplik AL 163 E7
Koplik i Sipërm AL 163 E7
Köpmanholm S 99 C11
Köpmanholmen S 107 E15
Koporiće RKS 163 C10
Koporiqë RKS 163 C10
Koposperä FIN 123 C14
Koppang N 101 C14
Koppangen N 111 A19
Kopparberg S 97 C13
Kopparmora S 99 D11
Kopparnäs S 118 D6
Koppelo FIN 114 F3
Koppera N 105 E11
Koppl A 73 A7
Koppom S 96 C7
Koprivets BG 166 C5
Koprivlen BG 169 A10
Koprivnica HR 149 D7
Kopřivnice CZ 146 B6
Koprivshtitsa BG 165 D9
Koprzywnica PL 143 E12
Kopsa FIN 119 E13
Kopstal L 186 B1
Kõpu EST 130 D4
Kõpu EST 131 E10
Koraj BIH 157 C10
Koramoniemi FIN 121 B12
Korbach D 17 F11
Korbevac SRB 164 D5
Korbovo SRB 159 D10
Korčanica BIH 156 C5
Korçë AL 168 C4
Korchiv UA 144 C8
Körchow D 83 D10
Korčula HR 162 D3
Korczew PL 141 F7
Korczyna PL 144 D4
Kordel D 185 E6
Korenita SRB 158 E3
Kořenov CZ 81 E8
Korentokylä FIN 120 D9
Korentovaara FIN 125 E16
Koretin RKS 164 D4
Korfantów PL 142 F4
Korfos GR 175 D7
Korgen N 108 D6
Korğene LV 131 F9
Kõrgessaare EST 130 D4
Korholanmäki FIN 121 F10
Korhoseniemi FIN 121 C12
Koria FIN 128 D6
Korinos GR 169 D8
Korinth DK 86 E6
Korinthos GR 175 D6
Korisia GR 175 D9
Korisos GR 168 D5
Korita BIH 156 D5
Korita BIH 157 F9
Korita HR 162 D4
Korita MNE 163 E8
Korithi GR 174 D2
Korkana FIN 121 F15
Korkatti FIN 119 F15
Korkeakangas FIN 125 F14
Korkeakoski FIN 127 B11
Korkee FIN 127 D13
Kõrkvere EST 130 E6
Körle D 78 D6
Körmend H 149 B7
Kormista GR 170 C6
Kormu FIN 127 D12
Korňa SK 147 C7
Kornalovychi UA 145 D7
Körner D 79 D8
Korneuburg A 77 F10
Kornevo RUS 136 E1
Kórnik PL 81 B12
Kornitsa BG 165 F8
Kornofolia GR 171 B10
Kornos GR 171 E8
Kornsjø N 91 B10
Kornwestheim D 27 C11
Környe H 149 A10
Koroleve UA 145 G7
Koromačno HR 67 C9
Koroncó H 149 A9
Koroneia GR 175 C6
Koroni GR 178 B2
Koronisia GR 174 A2
Koronos GR 177 E6
Koronouda GR 169 C9
Koronowo PL 138 D4
Koropi GR 175 D8
Körösladány H 151 D7
Körösszakál H 151 C8
Körösszegapáti H 151 C8
Köröstarcsa H 151 D7
Koroviya UA 153 A7

Korpela FIN 117 B14
Körperich D 20 E6
Korpi FIN 123 C12
Korpijärvi FIN 119 B13
Korpijoki FIN 123 C16
Korpikå S 119 C10
Korpikylä FIN 119 B11
Korpikylä FIN 121 E12
Korpikylä S 119 B11
Korpilahti FIN 123 F15
Korpilombolo S 116 E10
Korpilompolo FIN 117 E13
Korpinen FIN 121 D10
Korpinen FIN 125 D10
Korpisel'kya RUS 125 F16
Korpivaara FIN 125 E12
Korpo FIN 126 E6
Korpoström FIN 126 E6
Korsåmon S 103 A12
Korsbäck FIN 122 E6
Korsberga S 89 A8
Korsberga S 91 C15
Korsgården S 103 E10
Korsholm FIN 122 D7
Korskrogen S 103 C10
Korsmyrbränna S 106 E8
Korsnäs FIN 122 E6
Korsnes N 111 D11
Korso FIN 127 E13
Korsør DK 87 E8
Korssjön S 118 F5
Korssund N 100 D1
Korsträsk S 118 C5
Korsveggen N 104 E8
Korsvoll N 104 E4
Korsze PL 136 E3
Kortemark B 19 B7
Korten BG 166 D5
Kortenhoef NL 16 D4
Kortesalmi FIN 121 C14
Kortesjärvi FIN 123 D10
Kortessem B 19 C11
Kortevaara FIN 125 B13
Kortgene NL 16 E1
Korthi GR 176 D4
Kortrijk B 19 C7
Kortteenperä FIN 119 B17
Kortteinen FIN 125 D11
Korubaşi TR 171 E10
Korucu TR 173 F7
Koruköy TR 173 C6
Koruköy TR 177 E10
Korva S 119 B11
Korvakumpu FIN 115 D2
Korvala FIN 117 E16
Korvaluoma FIN 126 B8
Kõrveküla EST 131 E13
Korvenkylä FIN 119 D15
Korvenkylä FIN 119 F14
Korvenkylä FIN 123 B12
Korvua FIN 121 D12
Koryčany CZ 77 D12
Korycin PL 140 D8
Koryfasi GR 174 E4
Koryfi GR 169 C8
Korytnica PL 139 F12
Korzenna PL 144 D2
Korzeńsko PL 81 C11
Korzunovo RUS 114 E9
Korzybie PL 85 B11
Kos GR 177 F9
Kosakowo PL 138 A6
Kosanica MNE 163 C7
Košarovce SK 145 E4
Kösching D 75 E10
Kościan PL 81 B11
Kościelec PL 142 B6
Kościelna Wieś PL 142 C5
Kościernica PL 85 B10
Kościerzyna PL 138 B4
Kosd H 150 B3
Kose EST 131 C10
Kose EST 131 F14
Košeca SK 146 C6
Košecké Podhradie SK 146 D6
Kösedere TR 171 E10
Kösedere TR 177 B8
Köseilyas TR 173 B8
Kosel D 82 A7
Koselji BIH 157 E9
Koserow D 84 B6
Košetice CZ 77 C8
Kosharevo BG 165 D6
Koshava BG 159 E11
Košice SK 145 F3
Kosiv UA 152 A6
Kosivs'ka Polyana UA 145 G9
Kosjerić SRB 158 F4
Koška HR 149 E10
Koskama FIN 117 C14
Koskeby FIN 122 D8
Koskela FIN 119 E15
Koskela FIN 123 D11
Koskenkorva FIN 122 E8
Koskenkylä FIN 117 C16
Koskenkylä FIN 121 C14
Koskenkylä FIN 121 F11
Koskenkylä FIN 124 E8
Koskenkylä FIN 126 D7
Koskenmäki FIN 121 F13
Koskenniska FIN 113 F17
Koskenpää FIN 123 F14
Koskenperä FIN 123 C14
Koski FIN 127 D9
Koski FIN 127 E9
Koskimäki FIN 122 E7
Koskinou GR 181 D8
Koskioinen FIN 127 C9
Koškovce SK 145 E4
Koskue FIN 122 F9
Koskullskulle S 116 D5
Koslovets BG 166 C4
Kosmach UA 152 A5
Kosman BIH 157 F10
Kosmas GR 175 E6
Kosmio GR 171 B8
Kosmonosy CZ 77 B7
Kosola FIN 122 D9
Kosova Hora CZ 77 C6
Kosovo HR 156 E5
Kosovska Kamenicë RKS 164 D4
Kosów Lacki PL 141 E6
Koßdorf D 80 D4
Kössen A 72 A5
Kosta GR 175 E7
Kosta S 89 B8
Kostakioi GR 174 A2
Košťálov CZ 81 E8
Kostamo FIN 115 E2
Kostandenets BG 166 B6
Kostandovo BG 165 E9
Kostanjevac HR 148 E4
Kostanjevica SLO 148 E4
Kostel SLO 67 A10
Kostelec nad Černými Lesy CZ 77 C7
Kostelec nad Orlicí CZ 77 B10
Kostelec na Hané CZ 77 C12
Kostenets BG 165 E8
Kostenets BG 165 E8
Kostice CZ 77 E11
Kostinbrod BG 165 D7
Kostolac SRB 159 D7
Kostolné Kračany SK 146 F5
Kostomłoty PL 81 D11
Kostomuksha RUS 121 E16
Kostrzyn PL 81 A7
Kostrzyn PL 81 B12
Kostyzhitsy RUS 132 F6
Kosula FIN 125 E11
Košute HR 157 E6
Kosy UA 154 B5
Kosyny UA 145 G5
Koszalin PL 85 B10
Koszęcin PL 142 E6
Kőszeg H 149 B7
Koszyce PL 143 F10
Kotajärvi FIN 119 D15
Kotala FIN 115 D5
Kotala FIN 123 F12
Kotalanperä FIN 119 D15
Kotas GR 168 C5
Kotë AL 168 D2
Kötegyán H 151 D7
Kotel BG 167 D6
Kőtelek H 150 C5
Kotelow D 84 C5
Kotešová SK 147 C7
Köthen (Anhalt) D 79 C10
Kotikylä FIN 124 D8
Kotila FIN 121 E10
Kotiranta FIN 121 E13
Kotka FIN 128 E6
Kotlin PL 142 C4
Kotly RUS 132 B4
Kotor MNE 163 E6
Kotoriba HR 149 D7
Kotorsko BIH 157 C9
Kotor Varoš BIH 157 C7
Kotraža SRB 158 F5
Kotronas GR 178 B3
Kötschach A 73 C7
Kotsøy N 105 F9
Kottenheim D 185 D7
Kottes A 77 F8
Köttmannsdorf A 73 C9
Köttsjön S 107 E10
Kotuń PL 141 F6
Koudekerke NL 16 F1
Koudum NL 16 C4
Koufalia GR 169 C8
Koufovouno GR 171 B10
Kougsta S 105 E15
Kouklioi GR 168 E4
Koumanis GR 174 D4
Koura FIN 123 E10
Kouřim CZ 77 C7
Kourkouloi GR 175 B7
Kournas GR 178 E7
Koutaniemi FIN 121 F10
Koutojärvi S 119 B10
Koutsochero GR 169 E7
Koutsopodi GR 175 D6
Koutsouras GR 179 E10
Koutus FIN 117 E12
Kouva FIN 121 C10
Kouvola FIN 128 D6
Kovachevets BG 166 C6
Kovachevitsa BG 165 F8
Kovachevo BG 166 E6
Kovachevtsi BG 165 D6
Kovachitsa BG 160 F2
Kovači BIH 157 E7
Kovačica SRB 158 C6
Kővágószőlős H 149 D10
Kovallberget S 107 B13
Kovanj BIH 157 E10
Kovarce SK 146 E6
Kovářov CZ 76 C6
Kovdor RUS 115 C8
Kovelahti FIN 126 B8
Kovero FIN 125 E15
Kovilj SRB 158 C5
Kovin SRB 159 D6
Kovjoki FIN 122 C9
Kovland S 103 B13
Kõvra S 102 A7
Kovren MNE 163 C8
Kowal PL 139 F7
Kowala-Stjpocina PL 141 H4
Kowale PL 142 D5
Kowale Oleckie PL 136 E5
Kowale-Pańskie PL 142 C6
Kowalewo Pomorskie PL 138 D6
Kowalów PL 81 B7
Kowary PL 81 E9
Kowiesy PL 141 G2
Köyceğiz TR 181 C9
Köyhäjoki FIN 123 C11
Köyliö FIN 126 C7
Koynare BG 165 C9
Koyundere TR 177 B9
Koyunyeri TR 171 C10
Kozani GR 169 D6
Kozarac BIH 157 C6
Kozarac HR 149 E11
Kozar Belene BG 166 C4
Kozármisleny H 149 D10
Kozárovce SK 147 E7
Kozçeşme TR 173 D6
Kozica HR 157 F7
Koziegłowy PL 143 E7
Kozielice PL 85 D7
Kozienice PL 141 G5
Kozina SLO 73 E8
Kožlany CZ 76 C5
Kozloduy BG 160 F3
Kozłów Biskupi PL 141 F2
Kozłowo PL 139 D9
Kozluk BIH 157 C11
Kozły PL 139 F11
Koźminek PL 142 C5
Koźmin Wielkopowski PL 142 C3
Koz'ove UA 145 F7
Kozubszczyzna PL 141 H6
Kożuchów PL 81 C9
Kožuhe BIH 157 C9
Kozy PL 147 B8
Kozyörük TR 173 B6
Krabbendijke NL 16 F2
Krabi EST 131 F13
Kräckelbäcken S 102 C7
Krackow D 84 D6
Kraddsele S 109 E12
Kraftsdorf D 79 E10
Krąg PL 85 B11
Kragelund DK 86 C4
Kragerø N 90 B5
Krągi PL 85 C11
Kragujevac SRB 159 E6
Kraj HR 156 E6
Kraj HR 157 F7
Krajenka PL 85 D12
Krajišnik SRB 159 C6
Krajník Dolny PL 84 D6
Krakača BIH 156 B4
Kråkberget N 110 C8
Kråken S 122 C3
Kråkenes N 100 B2
Kråkerøy N 91 A8
Krakės LT 134 F7
Krakhella N 100 D2
Kråklingbo S 93 E13
Kråklivollen N 105 E9
Kråkmoen N 111 E10
Krakovets' UA 144 D7
Kraków PL 143 F8
Krakow am See D 83 C12
Kråksmåla S 89 A9
Kråkstad N 95 C13
Kralevo BG 167 C7
Králíky CZ 77 B11
Kraljeva BIH 157 D9
Kraljevica HR 67 B10
Kraljevo SRB 158 F6
Kralovice CZ 76 C4
Kráľovský Chlmec SK 145 G4
Kralupy nad Vltavou CZ 76 B6
Králův Dvůr CZ 76 C6
Kramarzyny PL 85 B12
Kramfors S 103 A14
Kramolin BG 166 C4
Krampenes N 114 C8
Kramsach A 72 B4
Kramsk PL 142 B5
Kramvik N 114 C9
Kranenburg D 16 E6
Kranevo BG 167 C10
Krångfors S 118 E4
Krania GR 168 E5
Krania Elassonas GR 169 E6
Kranichfeld D 79 E9
Kranidi GR 175 E7
Kranj SLO 73 D9
Kranjska Gora SLO 73 D8
Krapanj HR 156 E4
Krapets BG 155 F3
Krąpiel PL 85 D8
Krapina HR 148 D5
Krapinske Toplice HR 148 D5
Krapkowice PL 142 F4
Krašić HR 148 E5
Krasiczyn PL 144 D6
Krasiv UA 145 D8
Krāslava LV 133 E2
Kraslice CZ 75 B12
Krasnagorka BY 133 E2
Krásná Hora nad Vltavou CZ 76 C6
Krasnapollye BY 133 E6
Krasne PL 139 E10
Krasne PL 144 C5
Krasne UA 154 E4
Kraśniczyn PL 144 B7
Kraśnik PL 144 B5
Krasni Okny UA 154 B4
Krasnobród PL 144 B7
Krasnogorodskoye RUS 133 C4
Krásnohorské Podhradie SK 145 F2
Krasnoles'ye RUS 136 E5
Krásno nad Kysucou SK 147 C7
Krasnopol PL 136 E7
Krasno Polje HR 67 C11
Krasnosel'skoye RUS 129 D11
Krasnosielc PL 139 D11
Krasnovo BG 165 E9
Krasnoyil's'k UA 153 A7
Krasnoznamensk RUS 136 D5
Krasnystaw PL 144 B7
Krasocin PL 143 E9
Krastë AL 168 B3
Kraszewice PL 142 C5
Kraszewo PL 136 E2
Kratigos GR 177 A8
Kratiškiai LT 135 D9
Kratovo MK 164 E5
Kratte masugn S 98 B6
Krauchenwies D 27 D11
Krauja LV 135 E13
Kraujas LV 135 D11
Kraukļi LV 135 B12
Krauschwitz D 81 C7
Krautheim D 74 D6
Kravaře CZ 146 B6
Kravarsko HR 148 E6
Kravoder BG 165 C7
Kraymorie BG 167 E8
Kražiai LT 134 E5
Krčina BIH 157 C11
Krefeld D 17 F7
Kreiensen D 78 C6
Krekenava LT 135 E8
Krekhovychi UA 145 E9
Krekilä FIN 123 C11
Kremasti GR 181 D8
Kremen BG 165 F8
Kremena BG 155 F2
Kremintsi UA 152 A5
Kremmydia GR 174 F4
Kremna SRB 158 F4
Kremnica SK 147 D7
Krempe D 82 C7
Kremperheide D 17 A12
Krempna PL 145 D4
Krems an der Donau A 77 F9
Kremsbrücke A 73 C8
Kremsmünster A 76 F6
Křepice CZ 77 E11
Krepoljin SRB 159 E8
Krešev BIH 157 E9
Kreshpan AL 168 C2
Křešice CZ 76 A6
Kresna BG 165 F7
Kresnice SLO 73 D10
Kressbronn am Bodensee D 71 B9
Krestena GR 174 D4
Kretinga LT 134 E2
Kretingalė LT 134 E2
Kreuth D 72 A4
Kreuzau D 20 C6
Kreuzlingen CH 27 E11
Kreuztal D 21 C9
Kreuzwertheim D 74 C6
Kreva BY 137 E13
Krezluk BIH 157 D7
Krichim BG 165 E9
Krieglach A 148 A5
Kriegstetten CH 27 F8
Krien D 84 C4
Kriens CH 70 C6
Krievciems LV 134 B3
Krieza GR 175 C9
Krikello GR 174 B4
Krikellos GR 174 B3
Krimpen aan de IJssel NL 16 E3
Krimūnas LV 134 C6
Křinec CZ 77 B8
Krinida GR 170 C5
Krinides GR 171 B6
Kriškalni LV 135 C11
Kriškovci BIH 157 C7
Kristberg S 92 B6
Kristdala S 93 E8
Kristiansand N 90 C2
Kristianstad S 88 C6
Kristiansund N 104 E3
Kristiinankaupunki FIN 122 F6
Kristineberg S 107 A15
Kristinefors S 97 B8
Kristinehamn S 97 D11
Kristinestad FIN 122 F6
Kristoni GR 169 C8
Kristvallabrunn S 89 B10
Kritinia GR 181 D7
Kritsa GR 179 E10
Kritzmow D 83 B12
Kriukai LT 134 D7
Kriūkai LT 137 C7
Kriva Bara BG 159 F11
Krivača BIH 157 G9
Kriva Feja SRB 164 D5
Krivaja BIH 157 D9
Kriváň SK 147 D8
Krivany SK 145 E2
Kriva Palanka MK 164 E5
Krivelj SRB 159 E9
Krivi Put HR 67 B10
Krivi Vir SRB 159 F8
Krivodol BG 165 C7
Krivogaštani MK 168 B5
Krivolak MK 169 A7
Križ HR 149 E7
Křižanov CZ 77 D10
Križevci HR 149 D7
Křížová CZ 77 C9
Križpolje HR 67 B11
Krk HR 67 B10
Krka SLO 73 E10
Krmčina HR 156 D3
Krnča SK 146 D6
Krnica HR 67 C9
Krnjača SRB 158 D6
Krnja Jela MNE 163 D7
Krnjak HR 148 F5
Krnjeuša BIH 156 C5
Krnjevo SRB 159 E7
Krnov CZ 142 F4
Krobia PL 81 C11
Kroczyce PL 143 E8
Krøderen N 95 B11
Krofdorf Gleiberg D 21 C11
Krog S 103 B9
Krögis D 80 D4
Krok S 105 E14
Krokees GR 175 F6
Krokeide N 94 B2
Krokek S 93 B8
Kroken N 100 D6
Kroken N 108 F7
Krokfors S 108 E9
Krokfors S 118 B5
Krokio GR 175 A6
Kroknäs S 102 A8
Kroknes N 114 C9
Krokom S 106 E6
Krokos GR 169 D6
Krokowa PL 138 A5
Kroksjö S 107 B13
Kroksjö S 107 D15
Kroksjö S 118 F4
Krokstadelva N 95 C12
Krokstadøra N 104 E7
Krokstranda N 108 D9
Krokströmmen S 102 B8
Kroktjärn S 118 B4
Kroktråsk S 118 C6
Królowy Most PL 140 D8
Krölpa D 79 E10
Kroměříž CZ 146 C4
Krommenie NL 16 C3
Krompachy SK 145 F2
Kromsdorf D 79 E9
Kronach D 75 B9
Kronau D 187 C6
Kronauce LV 134 C6
Kronberg im Taunus D 187 A5
Kronlund S 109 E14
Kronoby FIN 123 C10
Kronprinzenkoog D 82 C5
Kronshagen D 83 B8
Kronshtadt RUS 129 F12
Kronstorf A 77 F6
Kropa SLO 73 D9
Kröpelin D 83 B11
Kropp D 82 B7
Kroppenstedt D 79 C9
Kropstädt D 79 C12
Krościenko nad Dunajcem PL 145 E1
Kröslin D 84 B5
Krosna LT 137 E8
Krośnice PL 81 D12
Krośniewice PL 143 B7
Krosno PL 144 D4
Krosno Odrzańskie PL 81 B8
Krossen D 79 E10
Krossen N 90 C2
Krossen N 95 C8
Krossmoen N 94 E4
Krostitz D 79 D11
Krote LV 134 C3
Krotoszyce PL 81 D10
Krotoszyn PL 142 C3
Krottendorf A 148 B5
Krouna CZ 77 C10
Krousonas GR 178 E8
Kröv D 21 E8
Krovik S 111 E19
Krovyli GR 171 C9
Krrabë AL 168 B2
Krš HR 156 C3
Kršan HR 67 B9
Krško SLO 148 E4
Krstac MNE 157 F10
Krstinja HR 156 B4
Krtova BIH 157 C9
Kruchowo PL 138 E4
Krüden D 83 E11
Kruft D 185 D7
Kruibeke B 19 B9
Kruiningen NL 16 F2
Kruishoutem B 19 C8
Krujë AL 168 A2
Krukenychi UA 144 D7
Kruklanki PL 136 E4
Krukowo PL 139 D11
Krumbach A 71 C9
Krumbach A 148 A6
Krumbach (Schwaben) D 71 A10
Krumë AL 163 E9
Krummesse D 83 C9
Krumovgrad BG 171 B9
Krumovo BG 165 E10
Krumovo BG 166 E6
Krumpa (Geiseltal) D 79 D10
Krumvíř CZ 77 E11
Krün D 72 A3
Krunderup DK 86 C3
Krūonis LT 137 D9
Kruopiai LT 134 D6
Krupac BIH 157 E9
Krupac SRB 165 C6
Krupa na Vrbasu BIH 157 C7
Krupanj SRB 158 E3
Krupava BY 137 F11
Krupe PL 144 A7
Krupina SK 147 E8
Krupište MK 164 F5
Krupka CZ 80 E5
Krupnik BG 165 F7
Kruså DK 82 A6
Kruševac SRB 164 B3
Kruševica SRB 158 E5
Kruševo MK 168 B5
Kruševo Grdo BIH 157 D8
Krushari BG 155 F1
Krushë e Madhe RKS 164 E2
Krushel'nytsya UA 145 E8
Krushevets BG 167 E8
Krushevo BG 166 C4
Krushovene BG 160 F4
Krushovitsa BG 160 F3
Krušovce SK 146 D6
Kruszewo PL 85 E11
Kruszwica PL 138 E5
Kruszyna PL 85 B12
Kruszyna PL 143 E7
Krutådal N 108 E7
Krute MNE 163 E7
Kruunupyy FIN 123 C10
Kružlov SK 145 E3
Krya Vrysi GR 169 C7
Kryekuq AL 168 C2
Kryezi AL 163 E9
Kryłów PL 144 B9
Krynica PL 145 E2
Krynica Morska PL 139 B7
Krynice PL 144 B7
Krynki PL 140 D9
Krynychne UA 155 B3
Kryoneri GR 175 D6
Kryoneritis GR 175 B7
Kryopigi GR 169 D9
Krypno Kościelne PL 140 D7
Kryry CZ 76 B4
Krystad N 110 D5
Krystallopigi GR 168 C5
Kryva Balka UA 154 E5
Kryve Ozero UA 154 B6
Kryvorivnya UA 152 A5
Kryzhopil' UA 154 A3
Kržanja MNE 163 D7
Krzanowice PL 142 F5
Krzątka PL 144 C4
Krzczonów-Wójtostwo PL 144 A6
Krzcin PL 85 D9
Krzelów PL 81 D11
Krzemieniewo PL 81 C11
Krzepice PL 142 E6
Krzepielów PL 81 C10
Krzesk-Królowa Niwa PL 141 F7
Krzeszów PL 81 E10
Krzeszów PL 144 C5
Krzeszowice PL 143 F8
Krzeszyce PL 81 A8
Krzytów PL 143 E8
Krzykosy PL 81 B12
Krzynowłoga Mała PL 139 D10
Krzystkowice PL 81 C8
Krzywcza PL 144 D6
Krzywda PL 141 G6
Krzywiń PL 81 C11
Krzywin PL 84 D6
Krzywowierzba PL 141 G8
Krzyżanów PL 143 B7
Krzyżanowice PL 141 H4
Krzyżanowice PL 146 B6
Krzyż Krzyż PL 85 E10
Ksar Sghir MA 53 E5
Książ Wielki PL 143 F9
Książ Wielkopolski PL 81 B12
Ksiżpol PL 144 C6
Kubanovka RUS 136 D5
Kubbe S 107 D14
Kübekháza H 150 E5
Kublichy BY 133 F4
Küblis CH 71 D9
Kubrat BG 161 F8
Kubuli LV 133 B2
Kuç AL 168 D2
Kučevo SRB 159 E8
Kuchen D 74 E6
Kuchl A 73 A7
Kuchurhan UA 154 D5
Kuchyňa SK 77 F12
Kučice PL 139 E9
Kuciny PL 143 C7
Kučište HR 162 D3
Kuçovë AL 168 C2
Küçükanafarta TR 171 D10
Küçükbahçe TR 177 B7
Küçükçekmece TR 173 B10
Küçükkariştiran TR 173 B7
Küçükkemerdere TR 177 C10
Küçükköy TR 172 F6
Küçükkumla TR 173 D11
Küçükkuyu TR 172 E6
Küçükyoncali TR 173 B8
Kucura SRB 158 B4
Kuczbork-Osada PL 139 D9
Kudever' RUS 133 C6
Kudirkos Naumiestis LT 136 D6
Kudowa-Zdrój PL 77 B10
Kūdums LV 135 B10
Kufstein A 72 A5
Kuggerud N 96 B6
Kuggören S 103 C14
Kuha FIN 119 C17
Kuhakoski FIN 129 B9
Kühbach D 75 F9
Kuhbier D 83 D12
Kuhfelde D 83 E10
Kühlungsborn D 83 B11
Kuhmalahti FIN 127 B12
Kuhmo FIN 121 F14
Kuhmoinen FIN 127 B13
Kühndorf D 79 E7
Kühren D 79 D12
Kuhs D 83 C12
Kuhstedt D 17 B11
Kuijõe EST 131 C7
Kuimetsa EST 131 C10
Kuinre NL 16 C5
Kuivajärvi FIN 121 E15
Kuivajõe EST 131 C10
Kuivakangas S 119 B11
Kuivalahti FIN 126 C6
Kuivaniemi FIN 119 C14
Kuivanto FIN 127 D15
Kuivasjärvi FIN 123 F9
Kuivastu EST 130 D6
Kujakowice Dolne PL 142 D5
Kūkas LV 135 C12
Kukasjärvi FIN 117 D15
Kukasjärvi S 119 B10
Kukës AL 163 E9
Kukko FIN 123 E12
Kukkola FIN 119 C12
Kukkola S 119 C12
Kuklen BG 165 E10
Kuklin PL 139 D9
Kuklinów PL 81 C12
Kukliš MK 169 B8
Kukljić HR 156 D4
Kukljica HR 156 D3
Kukljin SRB 164 B3
Kukmirn A 148 B6
Kukruse EST 131 C14
Kuktiškės LT 135 F11
Kukulje BIH 157 C7
Kukur AL 168 C3
Kukurečani MK 168 B5
Kula BG 159 F9
Kula HR 149 F9
Kula SRB 158 B4
Kulaši BIH 157 C8
Kulata BG 169 B9
Kulautuva LT 137 D8
Kūlciems LV 134 B6
Kuldīga LV 134 C3
Külefli TR 173 D8
Kuleli TR 173 B6
Kulennoinen FIN 129 B11
Kulen Vakuf BIH 156 C5
Kulesze PL 140 D7
Kulho FIN 125 E13
Kulia N 105 D9
Kuliai LT 134 E3
Kulju FIN 127 C10
Kullaa FIN 126 C7
Kullamaa EST 131 D8
Kulleseid N 94 C2
Kulltorp S 88 A5
Kulmain D 75 C10
Kulmbach D 75 B9
Kuloharju FIN 121 C11
Külsheim D 27 A12
Kultima FIN 116 B9
Kuluntalahti FIN 121 F10
Kūlupėnai LT 134 E2
Kulva LT 137 C9
Kulvemäki FIN 124 C9
Kulykiv UA 144 D9
Kumachevo RUS 139 A9
Kumane SRB 158 B5
Kumanica SRB 163 C9
Kumanovo MK 164 E4
Kumbağ TR 173 C7
Kumberg A 148 B5
Kumbri LV 134 C4
Kumbuļi LV 135 E13
Kumburun TR 171 E10
Kumhausen D 75 E11
Kumkadi TR 173 D9
Kumkale TR 171 E10
Kumköy TR 173 B11
Kumla S 92 A6
Kumla kyrkby S 98 C7
Kumlinge FIN 99 B15
Kummer D 83 D10
Kummerow D 83 C13
Kummersdorf-Alexanderdorf D 80 B4
Kummersdorf Gut D 80 B4
Kummunkylä FIN 123 D16
Kumpuranta FIN 125 G12
Kumpuselkä FIN 123 D16
Kumpuvaara FIN 119 C18
Kumrovec HR 148 D5
Kunadacs H 150 D3
Kunágota H 151 E7
Kunbaja H 150 E3
Kunbaracs H 150 D3
Kunčina CZ 77 C11
Kunda EST 131 B13
Kunes N 113 C18
Kunfehértó H 150 E3
Kungälv S 91 D10
Kungas FIN 123 C11
Kungsängen S 99 D9
Kungsäter S 88 A3
Kungsbacka S 91 E11
Kungsberg S 103 E11
Kungsfors S 103 E12
Kungsgården S 103 D12
Kungsgården S 103 E12
Kungshamn S 91 C9
Kungshult S 87 D12
Kungsör S 98 D6
Kunhegyes H 150 C6
Kunice PL 81 D10
Kunín CZ 146 B5
Kuningaküla EST 132 C2
Kuniów PL 142 E5
Kunmadaras H 150 C6
Kunovice CZ 146 C4
Kunowice PL 81 B7
Kunowo PL 81 C12
Kunpeszér H 150 C3
Kunrade NL 183 D7
Kunrau D 79 A9
Kunštát CZ 77 C11
Kunszállás H 150 D4
Kunszentmárton H 150 D5
Kunszentmiklós H 150 C3
Kunsziget H 149 A9
Kunvald CZ 77 B11
Kunžak CZ 77 D8
Künzell D 74 A6
Künzelsau D 74 D6
Künzing D 76 E4
Kuohatti FIN 125 C12
Kuohu FIN 123 F14
Kuoksajärvi FIN 117 E15
Kuoksu S 116 C7
Kuolayarvi RUS 115 E6
Kuolio FIN 121 C12
Kuomiokoski FIN 128 C7
Kuona FIN 123 C15
Kuopio FIN 124 E9
Kuoppala FIN 122 D9
Kuorevesi FIN 127 B12
Kuortane FIN 123 E11
Kuortti FIN 127 C15
Kuosku FIN 115 D4
Kuossakåbba S 116 D4
Kuouka S 116 E5
Kup PL 142 E4
Kupari HR 162 D5
Küpeler TR 173 E8
Kupferberg D 75 B10
Kupferzell D 74 D6
Kupientyn PL 141 F6
Kupinec HR 148 E5
Kupinovo SRB 158 D5
Kupiškis LT 135 E9
Kupjak HR 67 B10
Küplü TR 171 B10
Kuppenheim D 27 C9
Kuprava LV 133 B3
Kupres BIH 157 D7
Kuprešani BIH 157 D7
Küps D 75 B9
Kurapollye BY 135 F13
Kuratën AL 168 B2
Kurbnesh AL 163 F9
Kurd H 149 D10
Kürdzhali BG 171 A8
Kurejoki FIN 123 D11
Kuremaa EST 131 D13
Kuremäe EST 132 C2
Kuressaare EST 130 E4
Kurevere EST 130 E3
Kurienkylä FIN 123 F10
Kurikka FIN 122 E8
Kuřim CZ 77 D11
Kurima SK 145 E3
Kurjala FIN 125 E10
Kurjan AL 168 C2
Kurki FIN 121 D10
Kurkiharju FIN 125 E9
Kurkikylä FIN 121 D11
Kurkimäki FIN 124 E9
Kurmene LV 135 D9
Kürnach D 187 B9
Kürnare BG 165 D10
Kürnbach D 27 B10
Kurolanlahti FIN 124 D8
Kuropta RUS 115 D9
Kurort Bad Gottleuba D 80 E5
Kurort Kipsdorf D 80 E5
Kurort Oberwiesenthal D 76 B3
Kurort Schmalkalden D 79 E7
Kurort Steinbach-Hallenberg D 79 E8
Kurów PL 141 H6
Kurowice PL 143 C8
Kurravaara S 116 C4
Kurrokvejk S 109 E14
Kuršėnai LT 134 D5
Kursīši LV 134 D4
Kursu FIN 115 E4
Kuršumlija SRB 164 C3
Kuršumlijska Banja SRB 164 C3
Kurtakko FIN 117 D12
Kurtbey TR 172 B6
Kurtna EST 132 C2
Kurtovo Konare BG 165 E9
Kurtti FIN 121 D11
Kurtto FIN 121 E11
Kurtzea E 40 B6
Kuru FIN 127 B10
Kurvinen FIN 121 C14
Kuryłówka PL 144 C5
Kurzelów PL 143 E8
Kurzeszyn PL 141 G2
Kurzętnik PL 139 D8
Kusa LV 135 C12
Kusadak SRB 159 E6
Kuşadasi TR 177 D9
Kuşçayir TR 172 E6
Kusel D 21 E8
Kusey D 79 A9
Kusfors S 118 E4
Kushnytsya UA 145 G7
Kušići SRB 163 C9
Kuside MNE 163 D6
Kuślin PL 81 B10
Kusmark S 118 E5
Küsnacht CH 27 F10
Küssnacht CH 27 F9
Kustavi FIN 126 D5
Küsten D 83 E10
Kusterdingen D 27 C11
Kuštilj SRB 159 C7
Kuta BIH 157 E10
Kutalli AL 168 C2
Kutas H 149 D8
Kutemajärvi FIN 124 F7
Kutenholz D 17 B12
Kuti MNE 163 D8
Kutina HR 149 F7
Kutjevo HR 149 F9
Kutlovo SRB 159 E6
Kutná Hora CZ 77 C8
Kutno PL 143 B7
Kutrikko FIN 115 E5
Kuttainen S 116 B9
Kuttanen FIN 116 B9
Kuttura FIN 117 B16
Kúty SK 77 E12
Kuty UA 152 A6
Kuukasjärvi FIN 119 C17
Kuumu FIN 121 E14
Kuurne B 19 C7
Kuurtola FIN 121 D12
Kuusaa FIN 123 C15
Kuusaa FIN 123 F15
Kuusajärvi FIN 117 C14
Kuusajoki FIN 117 C14
Kuusalu EST 131 C10
Kuusamo FIN 121 C13
Kuusamonkylä FIN 121 F13
Kuusankoski FIN 128 D6
Kuusijärvi FIN 121 D11
Kuusijoki FIN 126 B8
Kuusiku EST 131 D9
Kuusiranta FIN 120 F9
Kuusirati FIN 119 F14
Kuusivaara FIN 115 E2
Kuusjärvi FIN 125 E11
Kuusjoki FIN 127 D9
Kuuslahti FIN 124 D9
Kuvansi FIN 125 F9
Kuvaskangas FIN 126 B6
Kuyka UA 153 A7
Kuyvozi RUS 129 E13
Kužiai LT 134 E6
Kuzmice SK 145 F4

Le Pouzin F 30 F6
Leppäjärvi FIN 117 B10
Leppäkoski FIN 127 D12
Leppälä FIN 113 D19
Leppälä FIN 121 D11
Leppälänkylä FIN 123 E11
Leppälahti FIN 124 D8
Leppälahti FIN 125 F12
Leppäselkä FIN 123 D16
Leppävesi FIN 123 F15
Leppävirta FIN 124 F9
Leppiaho FIN 119 C15
Leppikoski FIN 119 D17
Leppiniemi FIN 119 E16
Leppneeme EST 131 B9
Lepsala FIN 127 C15
Lepsäma FIN 127 E12
Lepsény H 149 B10
Leptokarya GR 169 D8
Le Puy-en-Velay F 30 E4
Le Puy-Notre-Dame F 23 F11
Le Quesnoy F 19 D8
Lequile I 61 C10
Ler N 104 E8
Le Raincy F 25 C8
Léran F 33 E9
Lerberget S 87 C11
Lercara Friddi I 58 D4
Lerdala S 91 C14
Léré F 25 F8
Le Relecq-Kerhuon F 22 D3
Lereşti RO 160 C6
Lerici I 69 E8
Lérida E 42 D5
Lerín E 32 F2
Lerkaka S 89 B11
Lerma E 40 D4
Lerm-et Musset F 32 B5
Lermoos A 71 C11
Lerot S 96 C7
Le Rouget F 29 F10
Lérouville F 26 C4
Le Rozier F 34 B5
Lerum S 91 D11
Le Russey F 26 F6
Lervik N 95 D13
Lerwick GB 3 E14
Lesa I 68 B6
Les Abrets F 31 D8
Les Aix-d'Angillon F 25 F8
Lešak RKS 163 C10
Lesaka E 32 D2
Les Andelys F 18 F3
Les Angles F 33 E10
Les Angles F 35 C8
Lešani MK 168 B4
Les Arcs F 31 D10
Les Arcs F 36 E4
Les Aubiers F 28 B4
Les Avellanes E 42 D5
Les Avenières F 31 D8
Les Bondons F 35 B6
Les Bordes F 25 E7
Les Borges Blanques E 42 D5
Les Borges del Camp E 42 E6
Les Bouchoux F 31 C8
Les Brenets CH 31 A10
Lesbury GB 5 E13
Les Cabannes F 33 E9
L'Escala E 43 C10
L'Escale F 35 B11
Les Cammazes F 33 D10
Lescar F 32 D5
L'Escarène F 37 D6
Les Cases d'Alcanar E 42 F5
Lesce SLO 73 D9
Lesconil F 22 E3
Les Contamines-Montjoie F 31 D10
Les Coves de Vinromà E 48 D5
Lescun F 32 E4
Lescure-d'Albigeois F 33 C10
Les Deux-Alpes F 31 E9
Les Diablerets CH 31 C11
Les Échelles F 31 E8
Les Églisottes-et-Chalaures F 28 E5
Le Sel-de-Bretagne F 23 E8
Le Sen F 32 B4
Le Sentier CH 31 B9
Les Éparges F 26 B4
Les Epesses F 28 B4
Les Escaldes AND 33 E9
Les Essards-Taignevaux F 31 B7
Les Essarts F 28 B3
Le Seu d'Urgell E 33 F8
Les Eyzies-de-Tayac-Sireuil F 29 F8
Les Fins F 31 A10
Les Forges F 26 D5
Les Fourgs F 31 B9
Les Gets F 31 C10
Leshak RKS 163 C10
Leshan RKS 163 D9
Les Hautes-Rivières F 184 E2
Les Herbiers F 28 B3
Les Houches F 31 D10
Lesichevo BG 165 E9
Lesično SLO 148 D5
Lesidren BG 165 D9
Lesina I 63 D8
Les Issambres F 36 E5
Lesja N 101 B9
Lesjöfors S 97 C11
Leskava LT 137 D8
Leskelä FIN 119 F15
Lesko PL 145 E5
Leskoec MK 168 B4
Leskova SRB 163 C9
Leskovac SRB 164 D4
Leskovik AL 168 D4
Leskovo BG 161 F11
Les Landes-Genusson F 28 B3
Leslie GB 5 C10
Les Lucs-sur-Boulogne F 28 B3
Lesmahagow GB 5 D9
Les Maillys F 26 F3
Les Marches F 31 E9
Les Martres-de-Veyre F 30 D3
Les Matelles F 35 C6
Les Mazures F 184 E2
Les Mées F 35 B10
Les Menuires F 31 E10
Lesmont F 25 D11
Les Mureaux F 24 C6
Lešná CZ 146 B5
Leśna PL 81 D8
Lesneven F 22 C3
Leśnica PL 142 F5
Lešnica SRB 158 D3
Leśniów Wielki PL 81 C8
Lesogorskiy RUS 129 C10
Les Ollières-sur-Eyrieux F 30 F6
Lesovaara FIN 121 D13
Lesovo BG 167 F7
Lesparre-Médoc F 28 E4
Les Peintures F 28 E5
Les Pennes-Mirabeau F 35 D9
Lesperon F 32 C3
Lespezi RO 153 C9
Les Pieux F 23 A8
Lespignan F 34 D5
Lespinassière F 34 D4
Les Planches-en-Montagne F 31 B9
Les Planes d'Hostoles E 43 C9
L'Espluga Calba E 42 E6
L'Espluga de Francolí E 42 E6
Les Ponts-de-Cé F 23 F10
Les Ponts-de-Martel CH 31 A10
Les Preses E 43 C8
Lespugue F 33 D7
Les Rosiers-sur-Loire F 23 F11
Les Rousses F 31 C9
Les Sables-d'Olonne F 28 C2
Lessach A 73 B8
Les Salles-du-Gardon F 35 B7
Lessay F 23 B8
Lessebo S 89 B8
Les Sièges F 25 D10
Lessines B 19 C8
Les Sorinières F 23 F8
Lestene LV 134 C6
Les Ternes F 30 E3
Les Thuiles F 36 C5
Lestijärvi FIN 123 C13
Leština CZ 77 C11
Lestrade F 34 B4
Les Trois-Moutiers F 24 F3
Leşu RO 152 C5
Lesura BG 165 C8
Les Vans F 35 B7
Les Vignes F 34 B5
Leszczyn PL 85 C9
Leszno PL 81 C11
Leszno PL 141 F3
Leszno Górne PL 81 D9
Létavértes H 151 C8
Letca RO 151 C11
Leţcani RO 153 C10
Letca Nouă RO 161 E7
Letchworth Garden City GB 15 D8
Letea Veche RO 153 D9
Le Teich F 32 A3
Le Teil F 35 A8
Le Teilleul F 23 C10
Le Temple F 28 F4
Letenye H 149 D7
Le Theil F 24 D4
Le-Theil-de-Bretagne F 23 E9
Le Thillot F 27 E6
Le Tholy F 27 D6
Le Thor F 35 C8
Letino I 63 E6
Letkés H 147 F7
Letnitsa BG 165 C11
Letoianni I 59 D7
Letonice CZ 77 D11
Le Touquet-Paris-Plage F 15 F12
Le Touvet F 31 E8
Letovice CZ 77 C11
L'Étrat F 30 E5
Le Trayas F 36 E5
Le Tréport F 18 D3
Letsbo S 103 C10
Letschin D 80 A6
Letterfinish IRL 8 E3
Letterkenny IRL 7 C7
Lettermacaward IRL 6 C6
Letterston GB 12 B5
Letur E 55 C8
Le Tuzan F 32 B4
Letzlingen D 79 B9
Leu RO 160 E4
Leuc F 33 D10
Leucate F 34 E5
Leuchars GB 5 C11
Leuchtenberg D 75 C11
Leud RO 152 B4
Leuenberg D 84 E5
Leuglay F 25 E12
Leuk CH 68 A4
Leukerbad CH 70 E5
Leumrabhagh GB 2 J4
Leun D 185 C9
Leuna D 79 D11
Leusden NL 16 D4
Leuşeni MD 154 D2
Leutasch A 72 B3
Leutenberg D 79 E9
Leutershausen D 75 D7
Leutesdorf D 185 D7
Leutkirch im Allgäu D 71 B10
Leuvanjoki FIN 119 D15
Leuven B 19 C10
Leuze-en-Hainaut B 19 C8
Levan AL 168 C1
Levänen FIN 128 C8
Levang N 108 D5
Levanger N 105 D10
Levanjska Varoš HR 149 F10
Levanto FIN 127 D13
Levanto I 37 C11
Leva Reka BG 165 D6
Leväsjoki FIN 126 B6
Levél H 146 F4
Levelek H 145 H4
Leven GB 5 C11
Leven GB 11 D11
Levens F 37 D6
Levens GB 10 C6
Levenwick GB 3 F14
Leverano I 61 C10
Leverburgh GB 2 K2
Le-Verdon-sur-Mer F 28 D3
Leverkusen D 21 B7
Le Vernet F 33 D9
Lèves F 24 D5
Levet F 29 B10
Levice SK 147 E7
Levico Terme I 69 A11
Levidi GR 174 D5
Levie F 37 H10
Levier F 31 B9
Le Vigan F 35 C6
Lévignac F 33 C8
Lévignacq F 32 B3
Levijoki FIN 123 E11
Le Ville I 66 F5
Levinovac HR 149 E8
Le-Vivier-sur-Mer F 23 C8
Levka BG 166 F6
Levkogeia GR 170 B5
Levoča SK 145 E2
Levonperä FIN 123 C14
Levo-oja FIN 119 D16
Levroux F 29 B9
Levski BG 166 C4
Levunovo BG 169 B9
Lewes GB 15 F9
Lewin Brzeski PL 142 E4
Lewin Kłodzki PL 77 B10
Leyburn GB 11 C8
Leyland GB 10 D6
Leyme F 29 F9
Leysin CH 31 C11
Leytron CH 31 C11
Leżajsk PL 144 C5
Lézan F 35 B7
Lézat-sur-Lèze F 33 D8
Lezay F 28 C5
Lezhë AL 163 F8
Lézignan-Corbières F 34 D4
Lezoux F 30 D3
Lezuza E 55 B8
Lgota Górna PL 143 E7
Lgota Wielka PL 143 D7
Lhenice CZ 76 D6
Lherm F 33 D8
L'Hermenault F 28 B4
L'Honor-de-Cos F 33 B8
L'Hôpital F 186 C2
L'Horme F 30 E6
Lhospitalet F 33 B8
L'Hospitalet de l'Infant E 42 F5
L'Hospitalet de Llobregat E 43 E8
L'Hospitalet-du-Larzac F 34 C5
L'Hospitalet-près-l'Andorre F 33 E9
L'Hostal del Alls E 42 F5
L'Huisserie F 23 D10
Lhuître F 25 C11
Lia N 111 C14
Liabøen N 104 E4
Liancourt F 18 F5
Liapades GR 168 E2
Liart F 19 E9
Liarvåg N 94 D3
Liatorp S 88 B6
Liatroim IRL 6 D6
Libáň CZ 77 B8
Libatse EST 131 D8
Libberton GB 5 D9
Libčany CZ 77 B9
Libčeves CZ 76 B5
Liberadz PL 139 D9
Liberec CZ 81 E8
Liběšice CZ 80 E6
Libiąż PL 143 F7
Libice nad Cidlinou CZ 77 B8
Libin B 19 E11
Libina CZ 77 C12
Libochovice CZ 76 B6
Libofshë AL 168 C2
Libohovë AL 168 D3
Libouchec CZ 80 E6
Libourne F 28 F5
Libramont B 19 E11
Librazhd AL 168 B3
Librilla E 55 D10
Libros E 47 D10
Licata I 58 E4
Licciana Nardi I 69 E9
Licenza I 62 C3
Liceras E 40 F5
Lich D 21 C11
Lichfield GB 11 F8
Lichnov CZ 142 F4
Lichnowy PL 138 B6
Lichtaart B 182 C5
Lichte D 75 A9
Lichtenau D 17 E11
Lichtenau D 27 C9
Lichtenau im Waldviertel A 77 E8
Lichtenfels D 75 B9
Lichtenstein D 79 E12
Lichtentanne D 79 E11
Lichtenvoorde NL 17 E7
Lichtenwörth A 77 G10
Lichterfelde D 84 E5
Lichtervelde B 19 B7
Līči LV 135 B10
Līči LV 135 D13
Lička Jesenica HR 156 C3
Lički Osik HR 156 C3
Licko Lešće HR 156 C3
Licodia Eubea I 59 E6
Licques F 15 F12
Līčupe LV 135 C10
Licurici RO 160 D3
Lida BY 137 F11
Lidečko CZ 146 C6
Liden S 103 A12
Lidhult S 87 B12
Lidingö S 99 D10
Lidköping S 91 B13
Lido I 66 B5
Lido Adriano I 66 D5
Lido di Classe I 66 D5
Lido di Foce Verde I 62 E3
Lido di Jesolo I 66 A6
Lido di Metaponto I 61 C7
Lido di Ostia I 62 D2
Lido di Siponto I 63 D9
Lido di Spina I 66 C5
Lidoriki GR 174 B5
Lidsälen S 102 E5
Lidsjöberg S 106 C8
Līdumnieki LV 133 C3
Lidzbark PL 139 D8
Lidzbark Warmiński PL 136 E2
Liebenau D 17 C12
Liebenau D 17 F12
Liebenburg D 79 B7
Liebenfels A 73 C9
Liebenwalde D 84 E4
Lieberose D 80 C6
Liebertwolkwitz D 79 D11
Liebling RO 159 B7
Lieboch A 148 C4
Liebstadt D 80 E5
Liedakkala FIN 119 C13
Liédena E 32 E3
Liedenpohja FIN 123 F11
Liège B 19 C12
Liegi LV 134 C2
Liehittäjä S 119 B10
Liekokylä FIN 119 C16
Lieksa FIN 125 D14
Lielauce LV 134 C5
Lielbērze LV 134 C6
Lielirbe LV 130 F4
Lielklapari LV 135 D13
Lielmēmele LV 135 D10
Lielvārde LV 135 C9
Lielvircava LV 134 C7
Liempde NL 183 B6
Lien S 105 D15
Lien S 107 E10
Lienden NL 183 B7
Lienen D 17 D9
Lienz A 73 C6
Liepa LV 135 B10
Liepāja LV 134 C2
Liepāre LV 134 C7
Liepas LV 135 D12
Liepe D 84 E5
Liepen D 84 C4
Liepene LV 134 B3
Liepgarten D 84 C6
Liepimäjärvi FIN 117 B11
Lieplaukalė LT 134 E3
Lieplaukė LT 134 E4
Liepna LV 133 B2
Lieponys LT 137 E10
Liepupe LV 135 B8
Lier B 19 B10
Lier N 96 B7
Lierbyen N 95 C12
Liernais F 25 F11
Lierneux B 19 D12
Liesek SK 147 C9
Lieser D 21 E8
Lieshout NL 183 B7
Lieso FIN 127 C12
Liessel NL 16 F5
Liestal CH 27 F8
Lieštany SK 146 D6
Lieşti RO 161 B11
Lietavská Lúčka SK 147 C7
Lietekylä FIN 121 E11
Lieto FIN 126 D7
Liétor E 55 B9
Lievestuore FIN 123 F16
Lievoperä FIN 119 F16
Liezen A 73 A9
Liezēre LV 135 B12
Liffol-le-Grand F 26 D4
Lifford IRL 4 F2
Liffré F 23 D8
Lifton GB 12 D6
Ligardes F 33 B6
Līgatne LV 135 B10
Ligist A 73 C11
Lignano Pineta I 73 E7
Lignano Sabbiadoro I 73 E7
Lignan-sur-Orb F 34 D5
Ligné F 23 F9
Ligneuville B 20 D6
Lignières F 29 B10
Ligny-en-Barrois F 26 C3
Ligny-le-Châtel F 25 E10
Ligonchio I 66 D1
Ligota PL 142 C4
Ligowo PL 139 E7
Ligueil F 29 A7
Ligugé F 29 B6
Lihme DK 86 B3
Lihula EST 130 D7
Liigvalla EST 131 C12
Liikasenvaara FIN 121 B14
Liikavaara S 116 D6
Liimattala FIN 123 E15
Liimattala FIN 123 E17
Liipantönkkä FIN 122 E9
Liittoperä FIN 123 C16
Liiva EST 130 D6
Lijar E 55 E8
Liješće BIH 157 B9
Lijeska BIH 158 F3
Lijeva Rijeka MNE 163 D7
Lijevi Dubravčak HR 149 E6
Likavka SK 147 C8
Likenäs S 102 E5
Likna LV 135 E12
Lilaia GR 175 B5
Liland N 110 D6
Liland N 111 D12
Lilaste LV 135 B8
L'Île-Bouchard F 24 F3
L'Île-Rousse F 37 F9
Lilienfeld A 77 F9
Lilienthal D 17 B11
Liljendal FIN 127 D15
Liljendal S 97 B11
Lilkovo BG 165 F10
Lillå S 118 B5
Lilla Edet S 91 C11
Lillåfors S 118 B6
Lilla Tjärby S 87 B12
Lillby FIN 123 D10
Lille B 16 F3
Lille F 19 C7
Lillebo N 102 C3
Lillebonne F 18 E2
Lillehammer N 101 D12
Lillers F 18 C5
Lillesand N 90 C3
Lilleshall GB 11 F7
Lille Skensved DK 87 D10
Lillestrøm N 95 C14
Lille Værløse DK 87 D10
Lillfjäten S 102 C4
Lillhamra S 102 C8
Lillhärdal S 102 C7
Lillholmsjö S 105 D16
Lillholmträsk S 107 B16
Lilliesleaf GB 5 D11
Lillkågeträsk S 118 E5
Lillkyrka S 98 C8
Lillmörtsjö S 103 B11
Lillo E 47 E6
Lillögda S 107 C13
Lillpite S 118 D6
Lillroten S 103 A14
Lillsaivis S 118 B7
Lillsele S 107 C16
Lillselet S 116 E9
Lillsjöhögen S 106 E8
Lillskog S 103 C9
Lillström S 103 B12
Lillsved S 102 A7
Lillviken S 109 C11
Lilyache BG 165 C8
Lilyak BG 167 C6
Lilyanovo BG 169 A9
Lima S 102 E5
Limana I 72 D5
Limanköy TR 167 F10
Limanowa PL 144 D1
Limanu RO 155 F3
Limatola I 60 A2
Limavady GB 4 E3
Limay F 24 B6
Limbach D 21 F12
Limbach D 186 C2
Limbach-Oberfrohna D 79 E12
Limbadi I 59 B8
Limbaži LV 135 A9
Limbourg B 20 C5
Limburg an der Lahn D 21 D10
Limburgerhof D 187 C5
Lime DK 86 C6
Limedsforsen S 102 E5
Limenaria GR 171 C7
Limenas GR 177 C6
Limenas Chersonisou GR 178 E9
Limerick IRL 8 C5
Limingen N 105 B15
Limingoån S 116 E9
Liminka FIN 119 E14
Liminpuro FIN 120 E9
Limmared S 91 D13
Limmen NL 16 C3
Limnes GR 175 D6
Limni GR 175 B7
Limnochori GR 169 C6
Limoges F 29 D8
Limogne-en-Quercy F 33 B9
Limone Piemonte I 37 C7
Limonest F 30 D6
Limone sul Garda I 69 B10
Limosano I 63 D7
Limoux F 33 D10
Limpias E 40 B5
Lin AL 168 B4
Linå DK 86 C5
Lina älv S 116 D4
Linakhamari RUS 114 D10
Linards F 29 D9
Linares E 54 C5
Linares de Mora E 48 D3
Linares de Riofrío E 45 C9
Linaria GR 175 B10
Lincent B 19 C11
Lincoln GB 11 E10
Lind DK 86 C3
Lindås N 100 E2
Lindau D 79 B11
Lindau D 82 A7
Lindau (Bodensee) D 71 B9
Lindberg D 76 D4
Linde DK 86 C2
Lindelse DK 87 F7
Linden D 21 C11
Linden D 82 B6
Lindenberg D 80 B6
Lindenberg D 83 D12
Lindenberg im Allgäu D 71 B9
Lindenfels D 21 E11
Lindern (Oldenburg) D 17 C9
Lindesberg S 97 C13
Lindesnäs S 97 B12
Lindewitt D 82 A6
Lindfield GB 15 E8
Lindholmen S 99 C10
Lindi EST 131 E8
Lindknud DK 86 D4
Lindkoski FIN 127 D15
Lindlar D 21 B8
Lindome S 91 D11
Lindores GB 5 C10
Lindos GR 181 D8
Lindoso P 38 E3
Lindow D 84 E3
Lindsdal S 89 B10
Lindsjö S 103 B12
Lindstedt D 79 A10
Lindved DK 86 D5
Lindwedel D 78 A6
Linge N 100 B6
Lingen (Ems) D 17 C8
Lingenfeld D 21 F10
Lingfield GB 15 E8
Linghed S 103 E10
Linghem S 92 C7
Lingolsheim F 27 C8
Lingrasmo N 111 B18
Linguaglossa I 59 D7
Linguizzetta F 37 G10
Linhares P 44 C6
Linia PL 138 B4
Liniewo PL 138 B5
Linkmenys LT 135 F11
Linköping S 92 C7
Linksness GB 3 H10
Linkuva LT 135 D7
Linlithgow GB 5 D9
Linna EST 131 E11
Linnamäe EST 130 D7
Linnamäe EST 131 F13
Linnankylä FIN 123 F10
Linneryd S 89 B8
Linnich D 20 C6
Linow D 83 D13
Linsell S 102 B6
Linsidemore GB 2 K8
Linthal CH 71 D8
Linthe D 79 B12
Lintig D 17 A11
Lintrup DK 86 E3
Lintula FIN 117 C14
Lintzoain E 32 E3
Linum D 84 E3
Linxe F 32 C3
Linyola E 42 D5
Linz A 76 F6
Linz am Rhein D 21 C8
Lioboml' UA 141 H10
Lioliai LT 134 E5
Lioni I 60 B4
Lion-sur-Mer F 23 B11
Liorac-sur-Louyre F 29 F7
Lios Mór IRL 9 D7
Lios Póil IRL 8 D2
Lios Tuathail IRL 8 D4
Lipa BIH 157 E7
Lipa PL 139 D10
Lipăneşti RO 161 C8
Lipany SK 145 E2
Lipar SRB 158 B4
Lipari I 59 C6
Lipawki BY 133 E3
Lipcani MD 153 A9
Lipce Reymontowskie PL 141 G1
Liperi FIN 125 E12
Liphook GB 15 E7
Lipiany PL 85 D7
Lipik HR 149 F8
Lipinki PL 144 D3
Lipinki Łużyckie PL 81 C8
Lipiny PL 81 C9
Lipjan RKS 164 D3
Lipka PL 85 D12
Lipki Wielkie PL 85 E9
Lipkovo MK 164 E4
Lipnica BIH 157 D9
Lipnica PL 85 C12
Lipnica PL 138 D7
Lipnica PL 143 E9
Lipnik PL 143 E11
Lipník nad Bečvou CZ 146 B5
Lipniţa RO 161 E11
Lipnitsa BG 165 C8
Lipno PL 81 C11
Lipno PL 139 E7
Lipolist SRB 158 D4
Liposthey F 32 B4
Lipova RO 151 E8
Lipova RO 153 D10
Lipová SK 146 E6
Lipovac HR 157 B11
Lipovac SRB 164 B4
Lipová-Lázně CZ 77 B12
Lipovăţ RO 153 D11
Lipovec CZ 77 D11
Lipoveni MD 154 D3
Lipovljani HR 149 F7
Lipovo RUS 136 D5
Lipovu RO 160 E3
Lipowiec PL 139 D11
Lipowiec Kościelny PL 139 D9
Lipowina PL 139 B8
Lippoldsberg (Wahlsburg) D 78 C6
Lippstadt D 17 E10
Lipsk PL 140 C8
Lipsko PL 141 H5
Liptál CZ 146 C5
Liptovská Kokava SK 147 C9
Liptovská Lúžna SK 147 D8
Liptovská Osada SK 147 D8
Liptovská Teplička SK 147 D10
Liptovské Revúce SK 147 D8
Liptovský Hrádok SK 147 C9
Liptovský Mikuláš SK 147 C9
Lipusz PL 138 B4
Lipůvka CZ 77 D11
Liqenas AL 168 C4
Liré F 23 F9
Lis AL 168 A3
Lisa RO 152 F5
Lisa RO 160 F6
Lisac BIH 157 D8
Lisac HR 162 D4
Iisaku EST 131 C14
Lisacul IRL 6 E5
Lisbane GB 7 C11
Lisbellaw GB 7 D7
Lisboa P 50 B1
Lisburn GB 7 C10
Liscannor IRL 8 C4
Liscarney IRL 6 E3
Liscarroll IRL 8 D5
Lisciano Niccone I 66 F5
Lişcoteanca RO 161 C11
Lisdoonvarna IRL 6 F4
Liseleje DK 87 C9
Lisets BG 165 C10
Lisewo PL 138 D6
Lisgarode IRL 8 C6
Lisgoold IRL 8 E6
Lisia Góra PL 143 F11
Lisiijcice PL 142 F4
Lisieux F 23 B12
Lisiy Nos RUS 129 E13
Lisjö S 97 C15
Liskeard GB 12 E6
Lisková SK 147 C8
Lisków PL 142 C5
Lisky UA 155 C4
Lisle F 29 E7
Lislea GB 4 F3
L'Isle-Adam F 25 B7
L'Isle-de-Noé F 33 C6
L'Isle-d'Espagnac F 29 D6
L'Isle-en-Dodon F 33 D7
L'Isle-Jourdain F 29 C7
L'Isle-Jourdain F 33 C8
L'Isle-sur-la-Sorgue F 35 C9
L'Isle-sur-le-Doubs F 26 F6
L'Isle-sur-Serein F 25 E11
Lisle-sur-Tarn F 33 C9
Lisma FIN 117 B14
Lismakin IRL 9 C7
Lismanaapa FIN 117 D17
Lismarka N 101 D13
Lismore IRL 9 D7
Lisna BY 133 D4
Lisnagry IRL 8 C5
Lisnakill IRL 9 D8
Lisnarrick GB 7 D7
Lisnaskea GB 7 D8
Lisne UA 154 E4
Lišov CZ 77 D7
Lisów PL 142 E6
Lispole IRL 8 D2
Lisronagh IRL 9 D7
Lisryan IRL 7 E8
Liss GB 15 E7
Lissan GB 4 F3
Lisse NL 16 D3
Lissendorf D 185 D6
Lisskogsbrändan S 97 A10
Lissone I 69 B7
Lissycasey IRL 8 C4
List D 86 E2
Listed DK 89 E8
Listerby S 89 C8
Listerlin IRL 9 D8
Listowel IRL 8 D4
Listrac-Médoc F 28 E4
Listry IRL 8 D3
Liszki PL 143 F8
Liszkowo PL 85 D12
Lit S 106 E7
Liţa RO 160 F5
Litakovo BG 165 D8
Litava SK 147 E8
Litene LV 133 B2
Liteni RO 153 B9
Litér H 149 B9
Lit-et-Mixe F 32 B3
Lith NL 183 B6
Lithakia GR 174 D2
Lithi GR 177 C7
Lithines GR 179 E11
Litija SLO 73 D10
Litke H 147 E9
Litlefjord N 113 B14
Litmalahti FIN 125 E9
Litmaniemi FIN 125 E10
Litochoro GR 169 D8
Litoměřice CZ 76 A6
Litomyšl CZ 77 C10
Litovel CZ 77 C12
Litschau A 77 E8
Littau CH 70 C6
Littleborough GB 11 D7
Littlehampton GB 15 F7
Littlemill GB 3 K9
Littlemore GB 13 B12
Little Oakley GB 15 D11
Littleport GB 15 C9
Littlestone-on-Sea GB 15 F10
Littleton IRL 9 C7
Littoinen FIN 126 E7
Litva BIH 157 D10
Litvínov CZ 80 E5
Litzendorf D 75 C9
Liudvinavas LT 136 E7
Liukkunen FIN 125 D14
Liuža LV 133 C2
Livada RO 145 H7
Livadaki GR 174 D4
Livadeia GR 175 C6
Livădeni MD 153 A11
Livadero GR 169 D6
Livadero GR 171 B6
Livadi GR 169 D7
Livadi GR 175 E10
Livadia GR 169 B9
Livanates GR 175 B7
Līvāni LV 135 D12
Livari MNE 163 E7
Livarot F 23 B12
Līvbērze LV 134 C6
Livernon F 33 A9
Liverpool GB 10 E6
Livezeni RO 152 D5
Livezi RO 153 E9
Livezi RO 160 D3
Livezile RO 152 C5
Livezile RO 152 E3
Livezile RO 159 D10
Līvi LV 135 B10
Livigno I 71 D10
Livingston GB 5 D9
Livno BIH 157 E7
Livo FIN 119 C17
Livold SLO 73 E10
Livonniska FIN 121 C10
Livorno I 66 E1
Livorno Ferraris I 68 C5
Livron-sur-Drôme F 30 F6
Liw PL 139 F12
Lixing-lès-St-Avold F 186 C2
Lixnaw IRL 8 D3
Lixouri GR 174 C1
Lizard GB 12 F4
Lizarraga E 32 E1
Lizdēni LV 131 F10
Lizums LV 135 B12
Lizy-sur-Ourcq F 25 B9
Lizzanello I 61 C10
Lizzano I 61 C8
Ljaljenča BIH 157 C11
Ljeskode Vode BIH 157 C8
Ljig SRB 158 E5
Ljønes N 108 B8
Ljørdal N 102 D4
Ljosland N 90 B1
Ljøsne N 100 D7
Ljuberađa SRB 164 C5
Ljubija BIH 156 C6
Ljubinje BIH 162 D5
Ljubiš SRB 158 F4
Ljubljana SLO 73 D10
Ljubogošta BIH 157 E10
Ljubovija SRB 158 E3
Ljubuški BIH 157 F8
Ljugarn S 93 E13
Ljung S 91 D13
Ljungå S 103 A11
Ljungaverk S 103 B11
Ljungby S 87 B13
Ljungby S 109 F15
Ljungbyhed S 87 C12
Ljungbyholm S 89 B10
Ljungdalen S 102 A4
Ljungsarp S 91 D14
Ljungsbro S 92 B7
Ljungskile S 91 C10
Ljupina HR 157 B7
Ljuša BIH 157 D7
Ljuså S 118 C7
Ljušći Palanka BIH 156 C5
Ljusdal S 103 C11
Ljusfallshammar S 92 B7
Ljusne S 103 D13
Ljusnedal S 102 A4
Ljustorp S 103 A13
Ljusträsk S 118 C3
Ljusvattnet S 118 E6
Ljuti Dolac BIH 157 F8
Ljutomer SLO 148 C6
Llabjan RKS 164 D3
Llagostera E 43 D9
Llamas de la Ribera E 39 C8
Llanaelhaearn GB 10 F3
Llanarth GB 12 A6
Llanarthney GB 12 B6
Llanbadarn Fawr GB 12 A6
Llanbadrig GB 10 E3
Llanbedr GB 10 F3
Llanbedrog GB 10 F3
Llanberis GB 10 E3
Llanbister GB 13 A8
Llanblethian GB 13 C8
Llançà E 34 F5
Llandanwg GB 10 F3
Llandderfel GB 10 F4
Llandeilo GB 12 B7
Llandissilio GB 12 B5
Llandovery GB 13 B7
Llandrillo GB 10 F5
Llandrindod Wells GB 13 A8
Llandudno GB 10 E4
Llandwrog GB 10 E3
Llandysul GB 12 A6
Llanegwad GB 12 B6
Llaneilian GB 10 E3
Llanelli GB 12 B6
Llanelltyd GB 10 F4
Llanelwy GB 10 E5
Llanes E 39 B10
Llanfaelog GB 10 E3
Llanfair Caereinion GB 10 F5
Llanfairfechan GB 10 E4
Llanfairpwllgwyngyll GB 10 E3
Llanfair Talhaiarn GB 10 E4
Llanfihangel-ar-arth GB 12 A6
Llanfyllin GB 10 F5
Llangadfan GB 10 F5
Llangadog GB 13 B7
Llangefni GB 10 E3
Llangeler GB 12 A6
Llangelynin GB 10 F3
Llangoed GB 10 E3
Llangollen GB 10 F5
Llangurig GB 13 A7
Llangynidr GB 13 B8
Llanidloes GB 13 A7
Llanilar GB 12 A6
Llanishen GB 13 B8

Llanllwchaiarn GB 10 F5
Llanllyfni GB 10 E3
Llannerch-y-medd GB 10 E3
Llan-non GB 12 A6
Llannon GB 12 B6
Llanrhaeadr-ym-Mochnant GB 10 F5
Llanrhidian GB 12 B6
Llanrhystud GB 12 A6
Llanrug GB 10 E3
Llanrumney GB 13 B8
Llanrwst GB 10 E4
Llansanffraid Glan Conwy GB 10 E4
Llansannan GB 10 E4
Llansawel GB 12 A6
Llantilio Pertholey GB 13 B8
Llantrisant GB 13 B8
Llantwit Major GB 13 C8
Llanuwchllyn GB 10 F4
Llanwddyn GB 10 F5
Llanwenog GB 12 A6
Llanwnda GB 10 E3
Llanwnog GB 10 F5
Llanwrtyd Wells GB 13 A7
Llanybydder GB 12 A6
Llapushnik RKS 163 D10
Llardecans E 42 E5
Llaurí E 48 F4
Llavorsí E 33 B8
Llay GB 10 E5
Lledrod GB 12 A7
Lleida E 42 D5
Llera E 51 C7
Llerena E 51 C7
Lliria E 48 E3
Llívia E 33 F9
Llodio E 40 B6
Llombai E 48 F3
Lloret de Mar E 43 D9
Lloseta E 49 E10
Llubí E 57 C10
Llucmajor E 57 C10
Lniano PL 138 C5
Lo B 18 C6
Loamneș RO 152 F4
Loano I 37 C8
Loarre E 32 F4
Löbau D 81 D7
Lobbæk DK 89 E7
Lobe LV 135 C10
Löbejün D 79 C10
Lobera de Onsella E 32 F3
Lobērģi LV 131 F12
Łobez PL 85 C9
Lobith NL 183 B8
Löbnitz D 83 B13
Łobodno PL 143 E6
Lobón E 51 B6
Lobonäs S 103 C9
Loburg D 79 B11
Łobżenica PL 85 D12
Locana I 31 E11
Locarno CH 68 A6
Locate di Triulzi I 69 C7
Loccum (Rehburg-Loccum) D 17 D12
Loceri I 64 D4
Lochaline GB 4 B5
Lochau A 71 B9
Lochawe GB 4 C6
Lochboisdale GB 2 L2
Lochcarron GB 2 L5
Lochdon GB 4 C5
Lochearnhead GB 5 C8
Lochem NL 16 D6
Lochen A 76 F4
Lochend GB 3 L8
Loches F 24 F4
Loch Garman IRL 9 D10
Lochgelly GB 5 C10
Lochgilphead GB 4 C6
Lochgoilhead GB 4 C7
Lochinver GB 2 J6
Lochmaben GB 5 E10
Lochmaddy GB 2 K2
Lochovice CZ 76 C5
Łochów PL 139 E12
Lochranza GB 4 D6
Lochristi B 19 B8
Loch Sgioport GB 2 L2
Lociki LV 133 E13
Lockenhaus A 149 B6
Lockerbie GB 5 E10
Lockne S 106 E7
Löcknitz D 84 D6
Locks Heath GB 13 D12
Lockton GB 11 C10
Locmaria-Plouzané F 22 D2
Locmariaquer F 22 E6
Locminé F 22 E6
Locorotondo I 61 B8
Locquirec F 22 C4
Locri I 59 C9
Locronan F 22 D3
Loctudy F 22 E3
Loculi I 64 C4
Löddeköpinge S 87 D12
Lödderitz D 79 C10
Loddin D 84 B6
Lødding N 105 B10
Loddiswell GB 13 E7
Loddon GB 15 B11
Lodè I 64 B4
Lode LV 135 B10
Loděnice CZ 76 B6
Löderup S 88 E6
Loděve F 34 C5
Lodi I 69 C8
Løding N 108 B8
Lødingen N 111 D10
Lodi Vecchio I 69 C7
Lodosa E 32 F1
Lödöse S 91 C11
Łodygowice PL 147 B8
Łódź PL 143 C7
Loeches E 46 D6
Loenen NL 183 A8
Löf D 21 D8
Løfallstrand N 94 B4
Lofer A 73 A6
Löffingen D 27 E9
Lofos GR 169 D7
Lofsdalen S 102 B5
Loftahammar S 93 D9
Lofthus N 94 B5
Lofthus N 111 E10
Loftus GB 11 B10
Log SLO 73 D8
Loga N 94 E5
Logan GB 5 E8
Logatec SLO 73 E9
Lögda S 107 D16

Lögdeå S 107 D16
Loggerheads GB 11 F7
Loghill IRL 8 C4
Logkanikos GR 174 E5
Logofteni MD 153 B11
Logrești RO 160 D3
Logroño E 41 D7
Logrosán E 45 F10
Løgstør DK 86 B4
Løgstrup DK 86 B4
Løgten DK 86 C6
Løgumkloster DK 86 E3
Lohals DK 87 E7
Lohberg D 76 D4
Lohéac F 23 E8
Lohe-Rickelshof D 82 B6
Lohfelden D 78 D6
Lohijärvi FIN 119 B12
Lohilahti FIN 129 B9
Lohiluoma FIN 122 E8
Lohiniva FIN 117 D13
Lohiranta FIN 121 B12
Lohja FIN 127 E11
Lohjan kunta FIN 127 E11
Lohmar D 21 C8
Lohmen D 84 A5
Lohmen D 80 E6
Lohmen D 83 C12
Löhnberg D 21 C10
Löhne D 17 D11
Lohne (Oldenburg) D 17 C10
Lohra D 21 C11
Lohr am Main D 74 C6
Lohsa D 81 D7
Lohtaja FIN 123 B11
Lohusuu EST 131 D14
Loiano I 66 D3
Loigny-la-Bataille F 24 D6
Loimaa FIN 126 D8
Loimaan kunta FIN 127 D8
Loiré F 23 E10
Loiri-Porto San Paolo I 64 B3
Loiron F 23 D10
Loisy-sur-Marne F 25 C12
Loitz D 84 C4
Loivos P 38 E5
Loivos do Monte P 44 B5
Loja E 53 B8
Loja LV 135 B9
Løjt Kirkeby DK 86 E4
Loka brunn S 97 C11
Lokakylä FIN 123 D14
Lokalahti FIN 126 D6
Lokavec SLO 73 E8
Lokca SK 147 C8
Loke S 106 E7
Løken N 95 C14
Lokeren B 19 B9
Loket CZ 75 B12
Lokev SLO 73 E8
Lokka FIN 115 C3
Løkken DK 90 E6
Løkken N 104 E7
Lokkiperä FIN 123 C13
Lőkösháza H 151 E7
Lokrume S 93 D13
Loksa EST 131 B11
Løksa N 111 C14
Løksebotn N 111 C14
Lokuta EST 131 D9
Lokuti EST 131 C9
Lokve HR 67 B10
Lokve SLO 73 D8
Lokve SRB 159 C7
Løkvoll N 112 D6
Lolishniy Shepit UA 152 A6
Lollar D 21 C11
L'Ollería E 56 D3
Lom BG 159 F11
Lom N 101 C9
Łomazy PL 141 G8
Lombez F 33 D7
Lombheden S 119 B9
Lomborg DK 86 B2
Lomello I 68 C6
Lomen N 101 D9
Łomianki PL 139 F10
Lomma S 87 D12
Lommatzsch D 80 D4
Lomme F 18 C6
Lommel B 19 B11
Łomnica PL 81 B9
Lomnice CZ 77 D10
Lomnice nad Lužnicí CZ 77 D7
Lomnice nad Popelkou CZ 77 A8
Lomonosov RUS 129 F12
Lompolo FIN 117 B13
Lomsdalen N 101 E12
Lomsjö S 107 C12
Lomsti BG 166 C6
Lomträsk S 109 E18
Lomträsk S 119 B9
Łomża PL 139 D13
Lonato I 66 B1
Lønborg DK 86 D2
Lončari BIH 157 C10
Lončarica HR 149 E8
Londa I 66 E4
Londerzeel B 19 C9
Londinières F 18 E3
London GB 15 D8
Londonderry GB 4 F2
Lone LV 135 D10
Long F 18 D4
Longa GR 174 F4
Longages F 33 D8
Longare I 66 B4
Longares E 41 F9
Longarone I 72 D5
Long Ashton GB 13 C9
Long Bennington GB 11 F10
Longbridge Deverill GB 13 C10
Longchaumois F 31 C8
Long Compton GB 13 B11
Long Crendon GB 14 D6
Long Eaton GB 11 F9
Longeau-Percey F 26 E3
Longecourt-en-Plaine F 26 F3
Longerak N 90 B2
Longeville-en-Barrois F 26 C3
Longeville-lès-St-Avold F 186 C2
Longeville-sur-Mer F 28 C2
Longford IRL 7 E7
Longframlington GB 5 E13
Longhope GB 3 H10
Longhope GB 13 B10
Longhorsley GB 5 E13
Longhoughton GB 5 E13
Long Itchington GB 13 A12
Longlier B 19 E11

Long Melford GB 15 C10
Longmorn GB 3 K10
Longny-au-Perche F 24 C4
Longobardi I 60 E6
Longobucco I 61 E7
Longomel P 44 F5
Longos GR 168 F3
Long Preston GB 11 C7
Longré F 28 C5
Longridge GB 10 D6
Longroiva P 45 C6
Long Stratton GB 15 C11
Long Sutton GB 11 F12
Longton GB 10 D6
Longtown GB 5 E11
Longueau F 18 E5
Longué-Jumelles F 23 F11
Longuenesse F 18 C5
Longueville F 25 D9
Longueville-sur-Scie F 18 E3
Longuyon F 19 E12
Longwood IRL 7 F9
Longwy F 19 E12
Lonigo I 66 B3
Lonin N 95 C10
Łoniów PL 143 E12
Lonja HR 149 F7
Lonjica HR 149 E6
Lonkan N 110 C9
Lonkka FIN 121 D13
Lonlay-l'Abbaye F 23 C10
Lonnig D 21 D7
Lons F 184 E2
Lons F 32 D4
Lönsboda S 88 C6
Lonsee D 74 E6
Lons-le-Saunier F 31 B8
Lønstrup DK 90 E6
Lontzen B 183 D8
Lónya H 145 G5
Loo EST 131 C9
Loon op Zand NL 16 E4
Loos F 182 D2
Loosdorf A 77 F8
Loose GB 15 E10
Lopadea Nouă RO 152 E3
Lopar HR 67 C10
Lopare BIH 157 C10
Łopatki PL 143 C7
Lopatnic MD 153 A10
Lopcombe Corner GB 13 C11
Lõpe EST 131 D7
Lopera E 53 A8
Łopiennik Górny PL 144 A7
Lopigna F 37 G9
Lopik NL 182 B5
Loppa N 112 C7
Loppersum NL 17 B7
Loppi FIN 127 D11
Lopra FO 2 C3
Lopushna UA 152 A6
Łopuszno PL 143 E9
Lopyan BG 165 D9
Lora N 101 B9
Lora del Río E 51 D8
Loranca de Tajuña E 47 D6
Loràs S 106 E8
Lörby S 88 C7
Lorca E 55 D9
Lorch D 21 D9
Lorch D 74 E6
Lorcha E 56 D3
Lordelo P 38 F4
Lordosa P 44 C5
Lørenskog N 95 C13
Loreo I 66 B5
Loreto I 67 F8
Loreto Aprutino I 62 C5
Lorgues F 36 D4
Lorient F 22 E5
Lorignac F 28 E4
Loriguilla E 48 E3
Lõrinci H 150 B4
Loriol-sur-Drôme F 30 F6
Lormes F 25 F10
Loro Ciuffenna I 66 E4
Loro Piceno I 67 F7
Lorquin F 186 D2
Lörrach D 27 E8
Lorrez-le-Bocage-Préaux F 25 D8
Lorris F 25 E8
Lorsch D 21 E11
Lørslev DK 90 E7
Lörstrand S 103 C11
Lörudden S 103 B14
Lorup D 17 C9
Lorupe LV 135 B9
Los S 103 C9
Losacino E 39 E7
Losa del Obispo E 48 E3
Los Alcázares E 56 F3
Los Algezares E 56 F2
Los Arcos E 32 E1
Losar de la Vera E 45 D9
Los Arenales del Sol E 56 E4
Los Barrios E 52 D6
Los Barrios de Luna E 39 C8
Los Belones E 56 F3
Los Cantareros E 55 D10
Los Corrales E 53 B9
Los Corrales de Buelna E 40 B3
Loscos E 42 E1
Los Dolores E 56 F2
Los Gallardos E 55 E9
Loshchynivka UA 155 C3
Losheim D 21 E7
Los Hinojosos E 47 E7
Łosice PL 141 F7
Łosinka PL 141 E9
Łosiów PL 142 E4
Los Maldonados E 56 F2
Los Molinos E 46 C4
Losna N 101 D12
Los Navalmorales E 46 E3
Los Navalucillos E 46 E3
Løsning DK 86 D5
Losomäki FIN 125 D11
Losone CH 68 A4
Łososina Dolna PL 144 D2
Losova MD 154 C2
Losovaara FIN 121 E11
Los Palacios y Villafranca E 51 E8
Los Pandos E 40 B4

Los Pedrones E 47 F10
Los Pozuelos de Calatrava E 54 B5
Los Rábanos E 41 E7
Los Royos E 55 D9
Los Santos E 45 C9
Los Santos de Maimona E 51 C7
Loßburg D 27 D9
Losse F 32 B5
Losser NL 17 D7
Lossiemouth GB 3 K10
Loßnitz D 79 E12
Lostallo CH 69 A7
Loštice CZ 77 C11
Los Tojos E 40 B3
Lostwithiel GB 12 E5
Los Villares E 53 A9
Los Yébenes E 46 E5
Löt S 89 B11
Lote N 100 C4
Loten N 94 D2
Lotenhulle B 182 C2
Loth GB 3 G11
Lothmore GB 3 J9
Lotorp S 92 B7
Lotte D 17 D9
Lottefors S 103 D11
Löttorp S 89 A11
Lottstetten D 27 E9
Lottum NL 183 C8
Lotyń PL 85 C11
Lotzorai I 64 D4
Louargel F 22 C5
Loučeň CZ 77 B8
Loučná nad Desnou CZ 77 B12
Loučovice CZ 76 E6
Loudéac F 22 D6
Loudes F 30 E4
Loudun F 28 A6
Loué F 23 E11
Loue FIN 119 B13
Louejärvi FIN 119 B14
Louejoki FIN 119 B14
Loughborough GB 11 F9
Loughbrickland GB 7 D10
Lougher IRL 8 D3
Loughgall GB 7 D9
Loughglinn IRL 6 E5
Loughrea IRL 6 F5
Loughton GB 15 D9
Louhans F 31 B7
Louka CZ 146 D4
Loukas GR 174 D5
Loukisia GR 175 C7
Loukkojärvi FIN 119 D15
Loukusa FIN 121 C10
Loulans F 26 F5
Loulay F 28 C4
Loulé P 50 E3
Louny CZ 76 B5
Loupiac F 32 A5
Lourdes F 32 D5
Lourdoueix-St-Pierre F 29 C9
Louriçal P 44 D3
Lourinhã P 44 F2
Lourmarin F 35 C9
Louros GR 174 A2
Loury F 24 E7
Lousã P 44 D4
Lousada P 38 F3
Louth GB 11 E11
Louth IRL 7 E9
Loutra GR 175 E9
Loutra GR 177 A8
Loutra Aidipsou GR 175 B7
Loutra Eleftheron GR 170 C6
Loutraki GR 169 C6
Loutraki GR 175 E9
Loutraki GR 175 D6
Loutra Kyllinis GR 174 D3
Loutra Smokovou GR 174 A5
Loutra Ypatis GR 174 B5
Loutro GR 169 C7
Loutro GR 169 E6
Loutro GR 174 B3
Loutros GR 171 C10
Louvain B 19 C10
Louveigné B 183 D7
Louverné F 23 D10
Louvie-Juzon F 32 D5
Louviers F 18 F3
Louvigné-du-Désert F 23 D9
Louvroil F 19 D8
Louze F 25 D12
Lov DK 87 E9
Lövånger S 118 F6
Lovasberény H 149 B11
Lovászi H 149 C7
Lovászpatona H 149 B9
Lovberg S 106 A7
Lövberga S 107 D9
Lovćenac SRB 158 B4
Løve DK 87 E8
Lovech BG 165 C10
Løvel DK 86 B4
Lovendegem B 19 B8
Lovere I 69 B9
Lovero I 69 A9
Lövestad S 88 D5
Loviisa FIN 127 E15
Lovik N 111 C10
Lovikka S 116 C9
Lovinac HR 156 D4
Lovinobaňa SK 147 E9
Loviste HR 157 F7
Lovliden S 107 B11
Løvlund N 101 D11
Lövnäs S 102 D5
Lövnäs S 109 D14
Lövnäsvallen S 102 C6
Lovnidol BG 166 D4
Lövö H 149 A7
Lovosice CZ 76 A6
Lovran HR 67 B9
Lovreč HR 67 B8
Lovreć HR 157 F7
Lovrenc SLO 73 D10
Lövsele S 118 F6
Lövsjö S 106 B8
Lövsjön S 97 B12
Lövstabruk S 99 B9
Lövstalöt S 99 C9

Lövtjärn S 103 D11
Lovund N 108 D3
Lövvik S 103 A15
Lövvik S 107 C9
Łowcza PL 141 H8
Löwenberg D 84 E4
Löwenstein D 27 B11
Lower Ballinderry GB 7 C10
Lower Cam GB 13 B10
Lower Kilchattan GB 4 C4
Lowestoft GB 15 C12
Lowick GB 5 D13
Łowicz PL 143 F8
Low Street GB 15 B11
Łowyń PL 81 B9
Loxstedt D 17 B11
Löya FIN 123 E11
Löytö FIN 128 B7
Löytökylä FIN 119 D16
Löytövaara FIN 121 C11
Lozarevo BG 167 D8
Lozen BG 165 F7
Lozen BG 166 C5
Lozenets BG 167 E9
Lozna RO 151 C11
Lozna SRB 159 F6
Loznica SRB 158 D3
Loznitsa BG 155 F1
Loznitsa BG 167 C7
Lozorno SK 77 F12
Lozovik SRB 159 E7
Lozoya E 46 C5
Lozoyuela E 46 C5
Lozuvata UA 154 A6
Lozzo di Cadore I 72 D5
Lú IRL 7 E9
Luanco E 39 A8
Luarca E 39 A6
Lubaczów PL 144 C7
Lubań PL 81 D8
Lubāna LV 135 C13
Lubanowo PL 84 D7
Lübars D 79 B11
Lubartów PL 141 H7
Lubasz PL 85 E11
Lubawa PL 139 C8
Lubawka PL 81 E10
Lübbecke D 17 D11
Lübbeek B 19 C10
Lübben D 80 C5
Lübbenau D 80 C5
Lübbow D 83 E10
Lubczyna PL 85 C7
Lube LV 134 B5
Lübeck D 83 C9
Lubeňa SK 147 C8
Lubenec CZ 76 B4
Lubeník SK 145 F1
Lübesse D 83 D10
Lubiaž LV 133 F11
Lügde D 17 E12
Lublon E 32 B2
Lugagnano Val d'Arda I 69 D8
Lubiany PL 142 E5
Lubichowo PL 138 C5
Lubicz Dolny PL 138 D6
Lubijcin PL 81 C9
Lubień PL 147 B9
Lubień Kujawski PL 139 F7
Lubienie PL 143 F11
Lubiewo PL 85 D9
Lubin PL 81 D10
Lubina SK 146 D5
Lubiszyn PL 85 E7
Lublin PL 141 H7
Lubliniec PL 142 E6
Lubmin D 84 B5
Lubnia PL 138 C4
Lubniany PL 142 E5
Lubnica MK 169 B7
Lubnica SRB 159 F9
Łubnice PL 143 F11
Lubniewice PL 81 A8
Łubno PL 85 B12
Łubno PL 85 D10
Łubno PL 143 B7
Lubochnia PL 141 G2
Lubomierz PL 81 D9
Lubomino PL 139 B9
Luboń PL 81 B11
Luborzyca PL 143 F9
Ľubotín SK 145 E2
Lubowidz PL 139 D8
Łubowo PL 85 C10
Lubraniec PL 138 E6
Lubrín E 55 E8
Lubrza PL 81 B8
Lubrza PL 142 F4
Lubsko PL 81 C7
Lübstorf D 83 C10
Lubstów PL 138 F5
Lubsza PL 142 E4
Lübtheen D 83 D10
Luby CZ 75 B11
Lubycza Królewska PL 144 C8
Lucainena de las Torres E 55 E8
Lucan IRL 7 F10
Lučani SRB 158 F5
Lúcar E 55 E8
Luçay-le-Mâle F 24 F5
Lucca I 66 E2
Lucca Sicula I 58 D3
Lucé F 24 D5
Luče SLO 73 D10
Lucena del Jalón E 41 E9
Lucena del Cid E 48 D4
Lucena del Puerto E 51 E6
Lucenay-lès-Aix F 30 B3
Lucenay-l'Évêque F 25 F11
Luc-en-Diois F 35 A9
Lučenec SK 147 E9
Luceni E 41 E9
Lucera I 63 D8
Lucéram F 37 D6
Lucey F 26 C4
Lucfalva H 147 E9
Luchachka BY 133 F3
Luché-Pringé F 23 E12
Lucheux F 18 D5
Lüchow D 83 E10
Luchy F 18 E5
Luciana I 54 B4
Lucień PL 139 F7
Lucieni RO 161 D6

Lucignano I 66 F4
Lucija SLO 67 A8
Lucillo de Somoza E 39 D7
Lucito I 63 D7
Lučka D 79 D11
Luckau D 80 C5
Luckenwalde D 80 B4
Lückstedt D 83 E11
Ľúčky SK 147 C8
Luco dei Marsi I 62 D4
Luçon F 28 C3
Lucq-de-Béarn F 32 D4
Luc-sur-Mer F 23 B11
Lucy-le-Bois F 25 E10
Ludag GB 2 L2
Ludanice SK 146 E6
Ludányhalászi H 147 E9
Ludbreg HR 149 D7
Lüdenscheid D 21 B9
Lüderitz D 79 A10
Lüdersdorf D 83 C9
Ludești RO 160 D6
Ludgershall GB 13 C11
Ludlow GB 13 A9
Lüdinghausen D 17 E8
Ludogortsi BG 161 F9
Ludoni RUS 132 E5
Ludoș RO 152 F3
Ludres F 186 D1
Luduș RO 152 E4
Ludvigsborg S 87 D13
Ludvika S 97 B13
Ludwigsau-Friedlos D 78 E6
Ludwigsburg D 27 C11
Ludwigsfelde D 80 B4
Ludwigshafen D 27 E11
Ludwigshafen am Rhein D 21 F10
Ludwigslust D 83 D10
Ludwigsstadt D 75 B9
Ludwin PL 141 H7
Ludza LV 133 C3
Lüe F 32 B4
Lüerdissen D 78 C6
Luesia E 32 F3
Lueta RO 153 E6
Lug BIH 162 D5
Lug HR 149 E11
Lugagnano Val d'Arda I 69 D8
Lugano CH 69 A6
Lüganuse EST 131 C14
Lugau D 79 E12
Lugaži LV 131 F11
Lügde D 17 E12
Luglon F 32 B4
Lugnano in Teverina I 62 B2
Lugnås S 91 B14
Lugnvik S 103 A14
Lugnvik S 106 E7
Lugo I 60 D4
Lugo-di-Nazza F 37 G10
Lugoj RO 159 B8
Lugones E 39 B8
Lugos F 32 B4
Lugrin F 31 C10
Lugros E 55 E6
Luhačovice CZ 146 C5
Luhalahti FIN 127 B9
Luhamaa EST 132 F1
Luhanka FIN 127 B14
Luhden D 17 D12
Luhe-Wildenau D 75 C11
Lühmannsdorf D 84 B5
Luhtapohja FIN 125 E15
Luhtikylä FIN 127 D13
Luhy UA 154 A4
Luica RO 161 E9
Luik B 183 D7
Luikonlahti FIN 125 E13
Luimneach IRL 8 C5
Luino I 68 B6
Luintra E 38 D4
Luiro FIN 115 C4
Luiro FIN 115 D3
Luizi Călugăra RO 153 D9
Luka SRB 159 E9
Lukácsháza H 149 B7
Luka nad Jihlavou CZ 77 D9
Lukavac BIH 157 C10
Lukavec CZ 77 C7
Lukavica BIH 157 C9
Łukawiec PL 144 C7
Luke MK 164 E5
Lukeswell IRL 9 D8
Lŭki BG 165 F10
Lukivtsi UA 152 A6
Luková CZ 146 C5
Lukovë AL 168 E2
Lukovit BG 165 C9
Lukovo HR 67 C10
Lukovo SRB 159 F8
Lukovo SRB 163 C11
Lukovo Šugare HR 67 D11
Lukovytsya UA 153 A8
Łuków PL 141 G6
Łukowa PL 144 C6
Łukowisko PL 141 F7
Łukowo PL 85 E11
Luksnėnai LT 136 D7
Lukštai LT 135 D11
Luky UA 145 F7
Lula I 64 C3
Luleå S 118 C8
Lüleburgaz TR 173 B7
Lüllemäe EST 131 F12
Lullymore IRL 7 F9
Lümanda EST 130 E4
Lumbarda HR 162 D3
Lumbier E 32 E2
Lumbrales E 45 C7
Lumbreras E 41 D6
Lumbres F 18 C5
Lumby DK 86 E6
Lumezzane I 69 B9
Lumijoki FIN 119 E14
Lumimetsä FIN 119 F14
Lumina RO 155 E3
Lumio F 37 F9
Lummen B 19 C11
Lumparland FIN 99 B14

Lumphanan GB 3 L11
Lumpiaque E 41 E9
Lumpzig D 79 E11
Lumsheden S 103 E11
Luna E 41 D10
Luna RO 152 D3
Lunamatrona I 64 D2
Lunano I 66 E5
Lunas F 34 C5
Lunca MD 154 C4
Lunca RO 151 B9
Lunca RO 152 D5
Lunca RO 153 B9
Lunca RO 160 F5
Lunca Banului RO 154 D2
Lunca Bradului RO 152 D6
Lunca Cernii de Jos RO 159 B10
Lunca Corbului RO 160 D5
Lunca de Jos RO 153 D7
Lunca de Sus RO 153 D7
Lunca Ilvei RO 152 C5
Lunca Mureșului RO 152 E3
Luncavița RO 155 C2
Luncavița RO 159 C9
Luncoiu de Jos RO 151 E10
Lund N 105 B11
Lund N 111 C15
Lund S 87 D12
Lundamo N 104 E8
Lundbjörken S 102 E8
Lundby DK 86 B4
Lundby DK 87 E9
Lunde DK 86 D2
Lunde DK 86 E6
Lunde N 95 D10
Lunde N 111 C11
Lunde S 103 A14
Lundeborg DK 87 E7
Lundebyvollen N 102 E3
Lundegård N 94 F6
Lunden D 82 B6
Lunderskov DK 86 E4
Lundsbrunn S 91 C13
Lundsjön S 106 D7
Lünebach D 20 D6
Lüneburg D 83 D8
Lunel F 35 C7
Lünen D 17 E8
Lunery F 29 B10
Lunéville F 26 C5
Lunger S 97 D14
Lungern CH 70 D6
Lungro I 60 D6
Lungsjön S 107 D11
Lungulețu RO 161 D7
Lunkkaus FIN 115 D5
Lunna BY 140 D10
Lunne D 17 D8
Lunnäset S 102 C6
Lünne D 17 D8
Lunneborg N 111 B16
Lunow D 84 E6
Luogosanto I 64 A3
Luohua FIN 119 E14
Luokė LT 134 E5
Luokkala FIN 121 D11
Luola-aapa FIN 119 C13
Luopa FIN 122 E9
Luopajärvi FIN 122 E9
Luopioinen FIN 127 C12
Luostari RUS 114 E10
Luosto FIN 115 C1
Luosu FIN 117 C12
Luotolahti FIN 128 C8
Luovankylä FIN 122 F7
Luovttejohka N 113 C21
Lupac RO 159 C8
Lupandi LV 133 E3
Łupawa PL 85 B12
Lupeni RO 152 D6
Lupeni RO 159 C11
Lupiac F 33 C6
Lupiñén E 41 D10
Lupión E 53 A9
Łupków PL 145 E5
Lupoglav HR 67 B9
Łupowo PL 85 E9
Luppa D 80 D3
Luppoperä FIN 121 D9
Luppy F 26 C5
Lupșa RO 151 E11
Lupșanu RO 161 E9
Luque E 53 A8
Luras I 64 B3
Lurbe-St-Christau F 32 D4
Lurcy-Lévis F 30 B2
Lure F 26 E5
Lurgan GB 7 D10
Lurgan IRL 6 E6
Luri F 37 F10
Lurøy N 108 D4
Lurs F 35 C10
Lurudal N 105 C13
Lury-sur-Arnon F 24 F7
Lusca IRL 7 E10
Lusciano I 60 B2
Luserna San Giovanni I 31 F11
Lushnjë AL 168 C2
Lusi FIN 127 C15
Lusignan F 29 C6
Lusigny-sur-Barse F 25 D11
Lusk IRL 7 E10
Lus-la-Croix-Haute F 35 A10
Lusminki FIN 121 C14
Lusnić BIH 157 E7
Luso P 44 D4
Luspa FIN 116 B8
Luspebryggan S 109 B18
Lussac F 28 E5
Lussac-les-Châteaux F 29 C7
Lussac-les-Églises F 29 C8
Lussan F 35 B7
Lüssow D 83 C12
Lusta GB 2 K3
Lustad N 105 C12
Lustadt D 187 C5
Lustenau A 71 C9
Luster N 100 D6
Lustivere EST 131 D12
Łuszkowo PL 81 B11
Luszyn PL 143 B8
Lutago I 72 C4
Lütau D 83 D7
Lütetsburg D 17 A8
Lutherstadt Wittenberg D 79 C12

Mesongi GR 168 F2
Mesopotamia GR 168 C5
Mesopotamos GR 168 F4
Mesoraca I 59 A10
Mesotopos GR 177 A7
Mespelbrunn D 187 B7
Mesquer F 22 F7
Messac F 23 E8
Messanges F 32 C3
Meßdorf D 83 E11
Messei F 23 C10
Messeix F 29 D11
Messejana P 50 D3
Messina I 59 C8
Messincourt F 19 E11
Messingen D 17 D8
Messini GR 174 E5
Meßkirch D 27 E11
Messlingen S 102 A4
Meßstetten D 27 D10
Mesta BG 165 F8
Mesta GR 177 C6
Mestanza E 54 B4
Městec Králové CZ 77 B8
Mestervik N 111 B16
Mesti GR 171 C9
Mestlin D 83 C11
Město Albrechtice CZ 142 F4
Město Touškov CZ 76 C4
Mestre I 66 B5
Mesves-sur-Loire F 25 F8
Mesztegnyő H 149 C8
Meta I 60 B2
Métabief F 31 B9
Metagkitsi GR 169 D10
Metajna HR 67 C11
Metalliko GR 169 B8
Metallostroy RUS 129 F14
Metaxades GR 171 B10
Metelen D 17 D8
Meteş RO 151 E11
Metfield GB 15 C11
Methana GR 175 D7
Metheringham GB 11 E11
Methlick GB 3 L12
Methoni GR 178 B2
Methven GB 5 C9
Methwold GB 11 F13
Metković HR 157 F8
Metlika SLO 148 E4
Metnitz A 73 C9
Metochi GR 174 C3
Metochi GR 175 B8
Metovnica SRB 159 F9
Mētriena LV 135 C12
Metsäkansa FIN 127 C10
Metsäkylä FIN 121 D11
Metsäkylä FIN 128 D7
Metsälä FIN 120 C9
Metsämaa FIN 127 D9
Metschow D 84 C3
Metsküla EST 130 D5
Metslawier NL 16 B6
Metsovo GR 168 E5
Mettäjärvi S 117 E11
Mettendorf D 20 E6
Mettenheim D 75 F11
Mettet B 19 D10
Mettevoll N 112 D7
Mettingen D 17 D9
Mettlach D 21 F7
Mettmann D 17 F7
Mettray F 24 F4
Metz F 26 B5
Metzervisse F 20 F6
Metzingen D 27 C11
Meudt D 185 D8
Meulan F 24 B6
Meulebeke B 19 C7
Meung-sur-Loire F 24 E6
Meursault F 30 B6
Meuselwitz D 79 D11
Meuzac F 29 D8
Mevagissey GB 12 E5
Mexborough GB 11 E9
Meximieux F 31 D7
Mey GB 3 H10
Meyenburg D 83 D12
Meylan F 31 E8
Meymac F 29 D10
Meyrargues F 35 C10
Meyreuil F 35 D10
Meyronnes F 36 C5
Meyrueis F 34 B5
Meyssac F 29 E9
Meysse F 35 A8
Meythet F 31 D9
Mezapos GR 178 B3
Mežāre LV 135 C12
Mežciems LV 134 C7
Mezdra BG 165 C8
Mèze F 35 D6
Mézel F 36 D4
Mežgale LV 135 D11
Mezhdurech'ye RUS 136 D4
Meziboří CZ 80 E5
Mežica SLO 73 C10
Mézidon-Canon F 23 B11
Mézières-en-Brenne F 29 B8
Mézières-sur-Issoire F 29 C7
Mézilhac F 30 F5
Mézilles F 25 E9
Meziměstí CZ 81 E10
Mézin F 33 B6
Mezio P 44 C5
Mezőberény H 151 D7
Mezőcsát H 147 F11
Mezőcsokonya H 149 D9
Mezőfalva H 149 C11
Mezőgyán H 151 D8
Mezőhegyes H 150 E6
Mezőkeresztes H 145 H2
Mezőkovácsháza H 151 E6
Mezőkövesd H 147 F11
Mezőlak H 149 B8
Mezőnyárád H 145 H2
Mezőörs H 149 A9
Mézos F 32 B3
Mezőszemere H 150 B6
Mezőszentgyörgy H 149 B10
Mezőszilas H 149 C10
Mezőtárkány H 150 B5
Mežotne LV 135 D8
Mezőtúr H 150 D6
Mezözombor H 145 G3
Mezquita de Jarque E 42 F2
Mežvalde LV 134 C4
Mežvidi LV 133 C3
Mežvidi LV 134 C4
Mezzana I 69 A10
Mezzanego I 37 C10
Mezzano I 72 D4
Mezzocorona I 69 A11
Mezzojuso I 58 D3
Mezzoldo I 69 A8
Mezzolombardo I 69 A11
Mga RUS 129 F15
Miączyn PL 144 B8
Miajadas E 45 F9
Mialet F 29 D7
Miały PL 85 E10
Miasteczko Krajeńskie PL 85 D12
Miastko PL 85 B11
Miastków Kościelny PL 141 G5
Miastkowo PL 139 D12
Miavaig GB 2 J3
Mica RO 152 C3
Mica RO 152 E4
Micăsasa RO 152 E4
Miceşti RO 160 D5
Miceştii de Câmpie RO 152 D4
Michaľany SK 145 F4
Michalová SK 147 D9
Michalovce SK 145 F4
Michałów PL 143 F9
Michałów Górny PL 141 G4
Michałowice PL 142 E3
Michałowice PL 143 F8
Michałowo PL 140 D9
Michelau in Oberfranken
D 75 B9
Michelbach an der Bilz D 74 D6
Micheldorf A 73 C9
Micheldorf in Oberösterreich
A 73 A9
Michelfeld D 74 D6
Michelstadt D 21 E12
Michendorf D 80 B4
Michorzewo PL 81 B10
Michów PL 141 G6
Mickelspiltom FIN 127 D15
Mickelsträsk S 118 F4
Mickleton GB 5 F12
Mickleton GB 13 A11
Micleşti MD 154 C3
Midbea GB 3 G11
Middagsbukt N 111 B17
Middelbeers NL 183 C6
Middelburg NL 16 E1
Middelfart DK 86 D5
Middelharnis NL 16 E2
Middelkerke B 18 B6
Middelstum NL 17 B7
Middenbeemster NL 16 C3
Middenmeer NL 16 C4
Middleham GB 11 C8
Middlemarsh GB 13 D10
Middlesbrough GB 11 B9
Middleton GB 11 D7
Middleton Cheney GB 13 A12
Middleton in Teesdale GB 5 F12
Middletown GB 7 D9
Middlewich GB 10 E7
Midhurst GB 15 F7
Midleton IRL 8 E6
Midlum D 17 A11
Midsund N 100 A5
Midtgård N 114 D8
Midtskogberget N 102 D3
Miðvágur FO 2 A2
Midwolda NL 17 B8
Mid Yell GB 3 D14
Miechów PL 143 F9
Miechów Charsznica PL 143 F8
Miedes E 41 F9
Miedziana Góra PL 143 E10
Miedzichowo PL 81 B9
Miedzna PL 139 F13
Miedźna PL 143 G7
Miedźno PL 143 E6
Międzybórz PL 142 D4
Międzychód PL 81 A9
Międzylesie PL 77 B11
Międzyrzec Podlaski PL 141 G7
Międzyrzecz PL 81 B9
Międzyzdroje PL 84 C6
Miehikkälä FIN 128 D8
Miehlen D 185 D8
Miejsce Piastowe PL 145 D4
Miejska Górka PL 81 C11
Miękinia PL 81 D11
Miekojärvi S 119 B10
Miélan F 33 D6
Mielec PL 143 F11
Mielęcin PL 85 D10
Mieleszyn PL 85 E12
Mielno PL 85 B10
Mieluskylä FIN 119 F14
Mielżyn PL 138 F4
Mieming A 71 C12
Mierasjärvi FIN 113 D19
Mieraslompolo FIN 113 D19
Miercurea-Ciuc RO 153 E7
Miercurea Nirajului RO 152 D5
Miercurea Sibiului RO 152 F3
Mieres E 39 B8
Mieres E 43 C9
Mierlo NL 16 F5
Mierojávri N 113 E11
Mieroszów PL 81 E10
Miers F 29 F9
Mierzęcice PL 143 F7
Mierzyn PL 84 D6
Miesau D 186 C3
Miesbach D 72 A4
Mieścisko PL 85 E12
Miesenbach D 186 C4
Mieslahti FIN 121 F10
Miessaure S 116 E4
Mieste D 79 B9
Mieszków PL 142 B3
Mieszkowice PL 84 E6
Mietingen D 71 A9
Mietków PL 81 E11
Mietoinen FIN 126 D6
Miettilä FIN 129 C11
Mieussy F 31 C10
Mieza E 45 B7
Migennes F 25 E10
Miglianico I 63 C6
Migliarino I 66 C4
Migliaro I 66 C4
Miglionica I 61 B6
Mignaloux-Beauvoir F 29 B6
Mignano Monte Lungo I 60 A1
Migné-Auxances F 29 B6
Mignovillard F 31 B9
Miguel Esteban E 47 E6
Miguelturra E 54 B5
Migushino RUS 133 E7
Mihăeşti RO 160 C4
Mihăeşti RO 160 C6
Mihăeşti RO 160 E5
Mihai Bravu RO 155 D3
Mihai Bravu RO 161 E8
Mihăileni RO 152 F4
Mihăileni RO 153 B8
Mihăileni RO 153 E7
Mihăileşti RO 161 D9
Mihăileşti RO 161 E7
Mihail Kogălniceanu RO 155 C3
Mihail Kogălniceanu RO 155 D1
Mihail Kogălniceanu RO 155 E2
Mihailovca MD 154 D3
Mihai Viteazu RO 152 D3
Mihai Viteazu RO 155 D3
Mihajlovac SRB 159 D6
Mihajlovac SRB 159 E9
Mihajlovo SRB 158 C5
Mihălăşeni RO 153 B10
Mihálď H 149 D8
Mihalţ RO 152 E3
Mihályi H 149 A8
Miheşu de Câmpie RO 152 D4
Mihla D 79 D7
Miiluranta FIN 123 C16
Mijares E 46 D3
Mijas E 53 C7
Mijdrecht NL 16 D3
Mijoska MNE 163 D7
Mikalayeva BY 133 F6
Mikepércs H 151 C8
Mikhalishki BY 137 D13
Mikhalkovo BG 165 F9
Mikhaltsi BG 166 C4
Mikhaylovo BG 165 B8
Mikhaylovo BG 166 E5
Mikitamäe EST 132 E2
Mikitsikha BY 133 F6
Mikkeli FIN 128 B7
Mikkelin mlk FIN 128 B7
Mikkelvik N 112 C3
Mikkola FIN 117 D16
Mikladalur FO 2 A3
Miklavž SLO 148 C5
Miklebostad N 111 C13
Mikleuš HR 149 E9
Mikołajki PL 136 F4
Mikołajki Pomorskie PL 139 C7
Mikołów PL 143 F6
Mikoszewo PL 138 B6
Mikre BG 165 C10
Mikri Volvi GR 169 C10
Mikro Dereio GR 171 B10
Mikrokambos GR 169 C8
Mikromilia GR 170 B6
Mikropoli GR 169 B10
Mikrothives GR 169 F8
Mikrovalto GR 169 D6
Mikstat PL 142 C4
Mikuláš CZ 77 C8
Mikulášovice CZ 80 E6
Mikulčice CZ 77 E12
Mikulov CZ 77 E11
Mikulovice CZ 142 F3
Mikušovce SK 146 C6
Miladinovci MK 164 F4
Milagro E 41 D8
Milagros E 40 E4
Miłakowo PL 139 B9
Milano I 69 C7
Milano Marittima I 66 D5
Milanówek PL 141 F3
Milaş RO 152 D4
Milas TR 181 B7
Milatkoviće SRB 163 C10
Milatos GR 179 E10
Milazzo I 59 C7
Milborne Port GB 13 D10
Milcoiu RO 160 C4
Milcov RO 160 E4
Milcovul RO 161 B10
Mildenhall GB 15 C10
Mildstedt D 82 B6
Mileanca RO 153 A9
Milejczyce PL 141 E8
Milejewo PL 139 B8
Milejów PL 141 H7
Milena I 58 E4
Mileşti MD 153 C12
Milestone IRL 8 C6
Mileto I 59 B9
Milevsko CZ 76 D6
Milfield GB 5 D12
Milfontes P 50 D2
Milford IRL 7 B7
Milford IRL 8 D5
Milford Haven GB 12 B4
Milhão P 39 E6
Milhaud F 35 C7
Milići BIH 157 D11
Milicz PL 81 C12
Milies GR 169 F9
Milíkov CZ 147 B7
Milín CZ 76 C6
Milina GR 175 A7
Milis I 64 C2
Militello in Val di Catania
I 59 E6
Miliyeve UA 152 A6
Milizac F 22 D2
Miljana HR 148 D5
Miljeno BIH 157 E11
Miljevina BIH 157 E10
Milkel D 81 D6
Miłki PL 136 F4
Milkovitsa BG 160 F5
Milk'ovtsi BG 165 D6
Mill NL 16 E5
Millares E 48 F3
Millas F 34 E4
Millau F 34 B5
Millay F 30 B5
Millbrook GB 12 E6
Millbrook IRL 7 E8
Millesimo I 37 C8
Millevaches F 29 D10
Millford GB 7 D9
Millhouse GB 4 D6
Millières F 26 D3
Millingen aan de Rijn NL 183 B8
Millisle GB 7 C11
Millom GB 10 C5
Milloshevë RKS 164 D3
Millport GB 4 D7
Millstatt A 73 C8
Millstreet IRL 8 D4
Millstreet IRL 9 D7
Milltown IRL 6 E5
Milltown IRL 7 F9
Milltown IRL 8 D2
Milltown IRL 8 D3
Milltown Malbay IRL 8 C4
Milly-la-Forêt F 25 D7
Milmarcos E 47 B9
Milmersdorf D 84 D5
Milmort B 183 D7
Milna HR 156 F5
Milnathort GB 5 C10
Milngavie GB 5 D8
Milnthorpe GB 10 C6
Milo I 59 D7
Miłocice PL 85 C11
Milohnić HR 67 B9
Miłomłyn PL 139 C8
Miłoradz PL 138 B6
Miloşeşti RO 161 D10
Miłosław PL 142 B3
Milot AL 163 F8
Milotice CZ 77 E12
Milovaig GB 2 L3
Milovice CZ 77 B7
Milow D 79 A11
Milow D 83 D11
Milówka PL 147 B8
Miltach D 75 D12
Miltenberg D 21 E12
Miltiņi LV 134 C6
Milton GB 2 L8
Milton GB 5 B9
Milton Keynes GB 15 C7
Miltzow D 84 B4
Milutinovac SRB 159 F7
Milverton GB 13 C8
Milz D 75 B8
Mimetiz E 40 B5
Mimizan F 32 B3
Mimizan-Plage F 32 B3
Mimoň CZ 81 E7
Mina de São Domingos P 50 D5
Mín an Chladaigh IRL 6 B6
Minas de Riotinto E 51 D6
Minateda E 55 C9
Minaya E 47 F8
Minde P 44 E3
Mindelheim D 71 A10
Mindelstetten D 75 E10
Minden D 17 D11
Minderhout B 182 C5
Mindnes N 108 E3
Mîndreşti MD 154 B2
Mindszent H 150 D5
Mindszentgodisa H 149 D10
Mindtangen N 108 E3
Mindūnai LT 135 F11
Mindya BG 166 C5
Minehead GB 13 C8
Mineo I 59 E6
Mineralni Bani BG 166 F4
Minerbio I 66 C3
Minervino Murge I 60 A6
Minfeld D 27 B9
Minger MD 154 D2
Minglanilla E 47 E9
Mingorría E 46 C3
Miniac-Morvan F 23 C8
Miničevo SRB 159 F9
Mín na bhFiann IRL 6 C5
Minne S 103 B9
Minnertsga NL 16 B5
Minnesund N 95 B14
Minnigaff GB 4 F8
Minot F 25 E12
Mińsk Mazowiecki PL 141 F5
Minsterley GB 10 F6
Mintiloglio GR 174 C4
Mintiu Gherlii RO 152 C3
Mintlaw GB 3 K13
Mintraching D 75 E11
Minturno I 62 E5
Minucciano I 66 D1
Minusio CH 68 A6
Mioarele RO 160 C6
Mionica SRB 158 E5
Mionnay F 30 D6
Mios F 32 A4
Mira E 47 E10
Mira I 66 B5
Mira P 44 D3
Mirabeau F 35 C10
Mirabel E 45 E8
Mirabel F 33 B8
Mirabel-aux-Baronnies F 35 B9
Mirabella Eclano I 60 A4
Mirabella Imbaccari I 58 E5
Miradoux F 33 C7
Miraflores de la Sierra E 46 C5
Miralcamp E 42 D5
Miramare I 66 D6
Miramas F 35 C9
Mirambeau F 28 E4
Mirambel E 42 F3
Miramont-de-Guyenne F 33 A6
Miranda de Arga E 32 F2
Miranda de Ebro E 40 C6
Miranda do Corvo P 44 D4
Miranda do Douro P 39 E7
Mirande F 33 C6
Mirandela P 38 F5
Mirandilla E 51 A7
Mirandola I 66 C3
Mirandol-Bourgnounac
F 33 B10
Miranje HR 156 E4
Mirano I 66 B5
Miras AL 168 C4
Mirash RKS 164 E3
Mirăslău RO 152 E3
Miratovac SRB 164 E4
Miravci MK 169 B7
Miravet E 42 E5
Miravete de la Sierra E 42 F2
Mircea Vodă RO 155 E2
Mircea Vodă RO 161 C10
Mirceşti RO 153 C9
Mircze PL 144 B8
Mirebeau F 26 F3
Mirebeau F 29 B6
Mirecourt F 26 D5
Miren SLO 73 E8
Mirepoix F 33 D9
Mireşu Mare RO 151 C11
Miřetice CZ 77 C9
Mireval F 35 C6
Miričina BIH 157 C9
Mirkovci HR 157 B10
Mirkovo BG 165 D9
Mirlović Zagora HR 156 E5
Mirna SLO 73 E11
Mirna Peč SLO 73 E11
Mirocin PL 144 C6
Mirocin Górny PL 81 C9
Mironeasa RO 153 D10
Miroševce SRB 164 D4
Miroşi RO 160 E5
Miroslava RO 153 C10
Miroslavas LT 137 E8
Mirosławiec PL 85 D10
Miroslovești RO 153 C9
Mirošov CZ 76 C5
Mirotice CZ 76 D6
Mirovice CZ 76 C6
Mirovtsi BG 167 C8
Mirow D 83 D13
Mirşid RO 151 C11
Mirsk PL 81 E8
Mirto Crosia I 61 D7
Mirueña de los Infanzones
E 45 C10
Mirzec PL 141 H4
Misano Adriatico I 67 E6
Mişca RO 151 D8
Mischii RO 160 E3
Miserey-Salines F 26 F4
Mishnyevichy BY 133 F7
Misi FIN 117 E17
Misilmeri I 58 C3
Mišinci BIH 157 C8
Miske H 150 E3
Miskolc H 145 G2
Mislina HR 162 D4
Mislinja SLO 73 D11
Mišnjak HR 67 C10
Mison F 35 B10
Missanello I 60 C6
Missenträsk S 107 A17
Missillac F 23 F7
Misso EST 131 F14
Mistelbach A 77 E11
Mistelgau D 75 C9
Misten N 108 B8
Misterbianco I 59 D7
Misterhult S 93 E9
Misterton GB 11 E10
Mistretta I 58 D5
Mistros GR 175 B8
Misurina I 72 C5
Misvær N 108 B9
Mitandersfors S 96 B7
Mitchelstown IRL 8 D6
Mithymna GR 171 F10
Mitoc RO 153 A10
Mitrašinci MK 165 F6
Mitreni RO 161 E9
Mitropoli GR 169 F6
Mitrousi GR 169 B9
Mitrova Reka SRB 163 C9
Mitrovicë RKS 163 D10
Mitry-Mory F 25 C8
Mittådalen S 102 A4
Mittelberg A 71 C10
Mittelberg A 71 D11
Mittelbiberach D 71 A9
Mittelkalbach D 74 B6
Mittelsinn D 187 A8
Mittenwald D 72 B3
Mittenwalde D 80 B5
Mittenwalde D 84 D5
Mitterbach am Erlaufsee
A 148 A4
Mitterding A 76 F4
Mitterdorf im Mürztal A 148 A5
Mittersheim F 27 C6
Mittersill A 72 B5
Mitterskirchen D 75 F12
Mitterteich D 75 C11
Mittet N 100 A7
Mittiliden S 105 B16
Mittweida D 80 E3
Mitwitz D 75 B9
Mizhhir"ya UA 145 F8
Mizil RO 161 C8
Miziya BG 160 F3
Mjällby S 88 C7
Mjällom S 107 F14
Mjedë AL 163 F8
Mjelde N 110 E9
Mjelde N 111 A15
Mjöbäck S 88 A3
Mjölby S 92 C6
Mjølfell N 100 E5
Mjolnarodden N 110 D5
Mjönäs S 97 C10
Mjøndalen N 95 C12
Mjønes N 108 B8
Mjösjöby S 107 D15
Mjösund FIN 126 E7
Mjöträsk S 119 B9
Mjövattnet S 103 A14
Mjövattnet S 118 E5
Mladá Boleslav CZ 77 B7
Mladá Vožice CZ 77 C7
Mladé Buky CZ 81 E9
Mladenovac SRB 158 E6
Mladenovo SRB 158 C3
Mladikovine BIH 157 D8
Mladinovo BG 166 F6
Mlado Nagoričane MK 164 E4
Mława PL 139 D9
Mlekarevo BG 166 E6
Mlinice BIH 157 D7
Mlinište BIH 157 D6
Młodzieszyn PL 141 F2
Młynary PL 139 B8
Młynarze PL 139 E11
Mlynys'ka UA 145 E9
Mnichovice CZ 77 C7
Mnichovo Hradiště CZ 77 A7
Mnichów PL 143 E9
Mniów PL 143 D9
Mníšek nad Hnilcom SK 145 F2
Mníšek pod Brdy CZ 76 C6
Mniszew PL 141 G4
Mniszków PL 141 H2
Mo N 100 E3
Mo S 103 D12
Mo S 103 E12
Mo S 107 D11
Mo S 107 E11
Moacşa RO 153 F7
Moaña E 38 D2
Moara RO 153 B8
Moara Domnească MD 153 B10
Moara Vlăsiei RO 161 D8
Moate IRL 7 F7
Mobberley GB 11 E7
Moča SK 149 A10
Moçarria P 44 F3
Mocejón E 46 E5
Močenok SK 146 E5
Mochales E 47 B9
Mochos GR 178 E9
Mochowo PL 139 E8
Mochy PL 81 B10
Mociu RO 152 D4
Möckern D 79 B10
Mockfjärd S 97 A12
Möckmühl D 27 B11
Mockrehna D 79 C12
Mockträsk S 118 C7
Moclín E 53 B9
Moclinejo E 53 C8
Mocra MD 154 B4
Mocsa H 149 A10
Modane F 31 E10
Modave B 19 D11
Modbury GB 13 E7
Modelu RO 161 E10
Modena I 66 C2
Modi GR 175 B6
Modica I 59 F6
Modigliana I 66 D4
Modliborzyce PL 144 B5
Mödling A 77 F10
Modliszewice PL 141 H2
Modra SK 146 E4
Modran BIH 157 C8
Modrany SK 146 F6
Modreeny IRL 8 C6
Modriach A 73 C11
Modriča BIH 157 C9
Modrište MK 168 A5
Modruš HR 156 B3
Modrý Kameň SK 147 E8
Modugno I 61 A7
Moëlan-sur-Mer F 22 E4
Moelfre GB 10 E3
Moelv N 101 E13
Moen N 105 D12
Moen N 111 B16
Moena I 72 D4
Moerbeke B 182 C3
Moergestel NL 16 E4
Moerkerke B 182 C2
Moers D 17 F7
Moffat GB 5 E10
Mofreita P 39 E6
Moftin RO 151 B10
Mogadouro P 39 F6
Mogata S 93 C8
Mögelin D 79 A11
Møgeltønder DK 86 F3
Mogenstrup DK 87 E9
Moggio Udinese I 73 D7
Mögglingen D 187 D8
Mogielnica PL 141 G3
Mogila MK 168 B5
Mogilany PL 147 B9
Mogilishte BG 167 C10
Mogilno PL 138 E4
Moglia I 66 C2
Mogliano I 67 F7
Mogliano Veneto I 66 A5
Möglingen D 187 D7
Mogón E 55 C6
Mogorella I 64 D2
Mogoş RO 151 E11
Mogoşani RO 160 D6
Mogoşeşti RO 153 C10
Mogoşeşti-Siret RO 153 C9
Mogoşoaia RO 161 D7
Moguer E 51 E6
Mogyoród H 150 B3
Mohács H 149 E11
Moharque E 55 C9
Mohed S 103 D12
Moheda S 88 A7
Mohedas de Granadilla E 45 D8
Mohedas de la Jara E 45 E10
Mohelnice CZ 77 C11
Mohelno CZ 77 D10
Mohernando E 47 C6
Mohil IRL 9 C8
Mohill IRL 7 E7
Möhkö FIN 125 E16
Möhlau D 79 C11
Möhlin CH 27 E8
Moholm S 91 B15
Mohora H 147 F8
Mohorn D 80 E4
Mohyliv Podil's'kyy UA 154 A1
Moi N 94 F5
Moi N 94 F6
Moià E 43 D8
Moiano I 60 A3
Moieciu RO 160 C6
Moimenta da Beira P 44 C5
Moineşti RO 153 E8
Moingt F 30 D5
Móinteach Milie IRL 7 F8
Moira GB 7 D10
Mo i Rana N 108 D7
Moirans F 31 E8
Moirans-en-Montagne F 31 C8
Moirax F 33 B7
Moires GR 178 E8
Mõisaküla EST 131 E10
Moisburg D 82 D7
Moisdon-la-Rivière F 23 E9
Moisei RO 152 B5
Moisiovaara FIN 121 E13
Moislains F 18 E6
Moissac F 33 B8
Moissac-Bellevue F 36 D4
Moissey F 26 F4
Moïta F 37 G10
Moita P 44 D4
Moita P 44 E3
Moita P 50 B2
Moixent-Mogente E 56 D3
Mojácar E 55 E9
Mojados E 39 F10
Mojkovac MNE 163 D8
Mojmírovce SK 146 E6
Mojstrana SLO 73 D8
Mojzesovo SK 146 E6
Møkkevik N 110 D6
Möklinta S 98 B7
Mokobody PL 141 F6
Mokrá Hora CZ 77 D11
Mokrance SK 145 F3
Mokre PL 143 F10
Mokren BG 167 D7
Mokresh BG 160 F2
Mokrievo MK 169 B8
Mokrin SRB 150 F5
Mokro BIH 157 E10
Mokronog SLO 73 E11
Mokronoge BIH 156 D5
Mokronoge BIH 157 E7
Möksy FIN 123 D12
Mol B 19 B11
Mol SRB 150 F5
Mola di Bari I 61 A8
Molaoi GR 178 B4
Molare I 37 B9
Molares P 38 F4
Molbergen D 17 C9
Mölbling A 73 C9
Mølby DK 86 E4
Mold GB 10 E5
Moldava nad Bodvou SK 145 F2
Molde N 100 A6
Moldjord N 108 B8
Moldova Nouă RO 159 D8
Moldova-Sulița RO 152 B6
Moldoveni RO 153 D9
Moldovița RO 153 B7
Møldrup DK 86 B5
Moldvik N 111 C11
Moledo P 38 E2
Moledo P 44 C5
Molelos P 44 C4
Molenbeek-St-Jean B 182 D4
Molenstede B 183 C6
Molescroft GB 11 D11
Molesmes F 25 E11
Moleşti MD 154 D3
Molėtai LT 135 F10
Molfetta I 61 A7
Molfsee D 83 B8
Moliden S 107 E14
Molières F 29 F9
Molières F 33 B8
Molières-sur-Cèze F 35 B7
Moliets-et-Maa F 32 C3
Molina Aterno I 62 C5
Molina de Aragón E 47 C9
Molina de Segura E 56 E2
Molina di Ledro I 69 B10
Molinara I 60 A3
Molinaseca E 39 C7
Molinella I 66 C4
Molines-en-Queyras F 31 F10
Molinet F 30 C4
Molinges F 31 C8
Molinicos E 55 C8
Molini di Tures I 72 C4
Molino de Villobas E 32 F5
Molinos E 42 F3
Molins de Rei E 43 E8
Moliterno I 60 C5
Molitg-les-Bains F 33 E10
Molkojärvi FIN 117 D14
Molkom S 97 C10
Mollas AL 168 C3
Mölle S 87 C11
Molledo E 40 B3
Möllenbeck D 84 D4
Möllenhagen D 84 C3
Mollerussa E 42 D5
Molles F 30 C4
Mollet del Vallès E 43 D8
Molliens-Dreuil F 18 E5
Mollis CH 27 F11
Molln A 73 A9
Mölln D 83 C9
Mölln D 84 C4
Molló E 33 F10
Mollösund S 91 C9
Mölltorp S 92 C4
Mölnbo S 93 A10
Mölnlycke S 91 D11
Molnytsya UA 153 A8
Moloha UA 154 E6
Molompize F 30 E3
Molos GR 175 B6
Moloy F 26 E2
Molpe FIN 122 E6
Molschleben D 79 D8
Molsheim F 186 D3
Molunat HR 162 E5
Molve HR 149 D8
Molveno I 69 A10
Molvízar E 53 C9
Mombaldone I 37 B8
Mombeltrán E 45 D10
Mombercelli I 37 B8
Mömbris D 21 D12
Mombuey E 39 D7
Momchilgrad BG 171 A8
Momignies B 19 D9
Momo I 68 B6
Monå FIN 122 D8
Monachil E 53 B9
Monacia-d'Aullène F 37 H10
Monaghan IRL 7 D9
Monamolin IRL 9 C10
Monäs FIN 122 D8
Monashi UA 154 E6
Monasterace I 59 C10
Monasterevin IRL 7 F8
Monastir I 64 E3
Monastiraki GR 174 B2
Monbahus F 33 A7
Monbazillac F 29 F6
Moncada E 48 E4
Moncalieri I 37 A7
Moncalvo I 68 C5
Monção P 38 D3
Moncarapacho P 50 E4
Moncaut F 33 B6
Moncel-sur-Seille F 26 C5
Mönchengladbach D 20 B6
Mönchhof A 77 G11
Monchio delle Corti I 66 D1
Monchique P 50 E2
Mönchsdeggingen D 75 E8
Monclar F 33 B7
Moncofa E 48 E4
Moncontour F 22 D6
Moncontour F 28 B5
Moncoutant F 28 B4
Moncrabeau F 33 B6
Monda E 53 C7
Mondariz E 38 D3
Mondariz-Balneario E 38 D3
Mondavezan F 33 D8
Mondavio I 67 E6
Mondéjar E 47 D6
Mondello I 58 C3
Mondeville F 23 B11
Mondolfo I 67 E7
Mondoñedo E 38 B5
Mondorf-les-Bains L 20 E6
Mondoubleau F 24 E4
Mondovì I 37 C7
Mondragon F 35 B8
Mondragone I 62 E5
Mondsee A 73 A7
Monea GB 7 D7
Moneasa RO 151 E9
Moneen IRL 6 F5
Moneglia I 37 C10
Monegrillo E 41 E11
Monein F 32 D4
Monemvasia GR 178 B5
Monesiglio I 37 C8
Monesterio E 51 C7
Monestier-de-Clermont F 31 F8
Monestiés F 33 B10
Monéteau F 25 E10
Moneygall IRL 9 C7
Moneymore GB 4 F3
Moneyneany GB 4 F3
Moneyreagh GB 7 C11
Monfalcone I 73 E8
Monfecorvino Rovella I 60 B3
Monflanquin F 33 A7
Monfort F 33 C7
Monforte P 44 F6

Monforte da Beira P 45 E6
Monforte d'Alba I 37 B7
Monforte del Cid E 56 E3
Monforte de Lemos E 38 C4
Monforte de Moyuela E 42 E2
Monfortinho P 45 D7
Monghidoro I 66 D3
Mongrando I 68 B5
Mongstad N 100 E2
Monguelfo I 72 C5
Monheim D 75 E8
Moniaive GB 5 E9
Monieux F 35 B9
Monifieth GB 5 C11
Monilea IRL 7 E8
Mõniste EST 131 F13
Monistrol-d'Allier F 30 F4
Monistrol de Calders E 43 D8
Monistrol de Montserrat E 43 D7
Monistrol-sur-Loire F 30 E5
Monivea IRL 6 F5
Mönkeberg D 83 B8
Mońki PL 140 D7
Monkokehampton GB 12 D6
Monléon-Magnoac F 33 D7
Monmouth GB 13 B9
Monnaie F 24 E4
Mönni FIN 125 E14
Monninkylä FIN 127 E14
Monok H 145 G3
Monolithos GR 181 D7
Monopoli I 61 B8
Monor H 150 C3
Monor RO 152 D5
Monostorapáti H 149 C9
Monostorpályi H 151 C8
Monóvar E 56 E3
Monpazier F 33 A7
Monreal E 32 E3
Monreal del Campo E 47 C10
Monreale I 58 C3
Monreith GB 4 F7
Monroy E 45 E8
Monroyo E 42 F3
Mons B 19 D8
Mons F 34 C4
Mons F 36 D5
Monsampolo del Tronto I 62 B5
Monsaraz P 51 C5
Monschau D 20 C6
Monsec F 29 E7
Monségur F 33 A6
Monselice I 66 B4
Monsempron-Libos F 33 B7
Monserrat E 48 F3
Monsheim D 187 B5
Mönsheim D 187 D6
Mønsted DK 86 C4
Monster NL 16 D2
Mönsterås S 89 A10
Monsummano Terme I 66 E2
Monta I 37 B7
Montabaur D 21 D9
Montaberner E 56 D4
Montady F 34 D5
Montagnac F 34 D5
Montagnana I 66 B3
Montagne F 28 F5
Montagney F 26 F4
Montagnol F 34 C5
Montagrier F 29 E6
Montaigu F 28 B3
Montaigu-de-Quercy F 33 B8
Montaigut F 30 C2
Montaigut-sur-Save F 33 C8
Montaione I 66 E2
Montalbán E 42 F2
Montalbán de Córdoba E 53 A7
Montalbano Elicona I 59 C7
Montalbano Jonico I 61 C7
Montalbo E 47 E7
Montalcino I 65 A4
Montale I 66 E3
Montalegre P 38 E4
Montalieu-Vercieu F 31 D7
Montalivet-les-Bains F 28 E3
Montallegro I 58 E3
Montalto delle Marche I 62 B5
Montalto di Castro I 65 C5
Montalto Marina I 65 C5
Montalto Uffugo I 60 E6
Montalvão P 44 E5
Montamarta E 39 E8
Montana BG 165 C7
Montana CH 31 C11
Montanejos E 48 D3
Montaner F 32 D5
Montano Antilia I 60 C4
Montans F 33 C9
Montaquila I 62 D6
Montargil P 44 F4
Montargis F 25 E8
Montastruc-la-Conseillère F 33 C9
Montataire F 18 F5
Montauban F 33 B8
Montauban-de-Bretagne F 23 D7
Montaudin F 23 D10
Montauriol F 33 A7
Montauroux F 36 D5
Montaut F 32 C4
Montaut F 32 D5
Montaut F 33 D9
Montayral F 33 B7
Montazzoli I 63 D6
Montbard F 25 E11
Montbarrey F 31 A8
Montbazens F 33 B10
Montbazin F 35 C6
Montbazon F 24 F4
Montbéliard F 27 E6
Montbenoît F 31 B9
Montbeton F 33 B8
Montblanc E 42 E6
Montboucher-sur-Jabron F 35 A8
Montbozon F 26 F5
Montbrió del Camp E 42 E6
Montbrison F 30 D5
Montbron F 29 D7
Montbrun F 33 A9
Montbrun-les-Bains F 35 B9
Montcada i Reixac E 43 E8
Montcavrel F 15 F12
Montceau-les-Mines F 30 B5
Montcenis F 30 B5
Montchanin F 30 B5
Montcornet F 19 E9
Montcresson F 25 E8
Montcuq F 33 B8
Montcy-Notre-Dame F 19 E10
Montdardier F 35 C6
Mont-Dauphin F 36 B5
Mont-de-Marsan F 32 C5
Montdidier F 18 E6
Mont-Dore F 30 D2
Monteagudo E 41 E8
Monteagudo de las Salinas E 47 E9
Monteagudo de las Vicarías E 41 F7
Montealegre del Castillo E 55 B10
Montebello Ionico I 59 D8
Montebello Vicentino I 66 B3
Montebelluna I 72 E5
Montebourg F 23 B9
Montebruno I 37 B10
Montecalvo in Foglia I 66 E6
Montecalvo Irpino I 60 A4
Monte-Carlo MC 37 D6
Montecarotto I 67 E7
Montecassiano I 67 F7
Monte Castello di Vibio I 62 B2
Montecastrilli I 62 B2
Montecatini Terme I 66 E2
Montecatini Val di Cecina I 66 F2
Montecchio I 67 E6
Montecchio Emilia I 66 C1
Montecchio Maggiore I 66 A3
Montech F 33 C8
Montechiaro d'Asti I 37 A8
Montechiarugolo I 66 C1
Montecilfone I 63 D7
Montecorice I 60 C3
Montecosaro I 67 F8
Montecreale Valcellina I 73 D6
Montecreto I 66 D2
Monte da Pedra P 44 F5
Monte das Flores P 50 B4
Montederramo E 38 D5
Monte di Procida I 60 B2
Monte do Trigo P 50 C4
Montefalco I 62 B3
Montefalcone di Val Fortore I 60 A4
Montefalcone nel Sannio I 63 D7
Montefano I 67 F7
Montefelcino I 67 E6
Montefiascone I 62 B2
Monteflore dell'Aso I 62 A5
Montefiorino I 66 D2
Montefortino I 62 B4
Montefranco I 62 B3
Montefrío E 53 B8
Montegiordano I 61 C7
Montegiorgio I 67 F8
Monte Gordo P 50 E5
Montegranaro I 67 F8
Montegrotto Terme I 66 B4
Montehermoso E 45 D8
Monteiasi I 61 C8
Monteils F 33 B9
Monteiros P 44 A5
Montejaque E 53 C6
Montejícar E 53 A10
Montejo de la Sierra E 46 B5
Montelabbate I 67 E6
Montelanico I 62 D4
Montelavar P 50 B1
Montel-de-Gelat F 29 D11
Monteleone di Puglia I 60 A4
Monteleone di Spoleto I 62 B3
Monteleone d'Orvieto I 62 B2
Monteleone Rocca Doria I 64 C2
Montelepre I 58 C3
Montelibretti I 62 C3
Montélier F 31 F7
Montélimar F 35 A8
Montella I 60 B4
Montellano E 51 E8
Montels F 33 D8
Montelupo Fiorentino I 66 E3
Montelupone I 67 F8
Montemaggiore Belsito I 58 D4
Montemagno I 37 B8
Montemarciano I 67 E7
Montemayor E 53 A7
Montemayor de Pililla E 40 E3
Montemboeuf F 29 D7
Montemesola I 61 B8
Montemiletto I 60 A3
Montemilone I 60 A5
Montemolín E 51 C7
Montemonaco I 62 B4
Montemor-o-Novo P 50 B3
Montemurlo I 66 E3
Montemurro I 60 C5
Montenay F 23 D10
Montendre F 28 E5
Montenegro de Cameros E 40 D6
Montenero di Bisaccia I 63 D7
Montenerodomo I 63 C6
Monte Porzio I 67 E7
Monteprandone I 62 B5
Montepulciano I 62 A1
Monterblanc F 22 E6
Monterchi I 66 F5
Monte Real P 44 E3
Montereale I 62 B4
Montereau-fault-Yonne F 25 D8
Monte Redondo P 44 E3
Monterenzio I 66 D3
Monteriggioni I 66 F3
Monteroduni I 63 D6
Monte Romano I 62 C1
Monteroni d'Arbia I 66 F3
Monteroni di Lecce I 61 C10
Monterosso Almo I 59 E6
Monterosso Calabro I 59 B9
Monterotondo I 62 C3
Monterotondo Marittimo I 66 F2
Monterrei E 38 E5
Monterroso E 38 C4
Monterrubio de la Serena E 51 B9
Monterubbiano I 62 A5
Montesa E 56 D3
Monte San Biagio I 62 E4
Monte San Giovanni Campano I 62 D5
Montesano Salentino I 61 D10
Montesano sulla Marcellana I 60 C5
Monte San Savino I 66 F4
Monte Santa Maria Tiberina I 66 F5
Monte Sant'Angelo I 63 D9
Monte San Vito I 67 E7
Montesarchio I 60 A3
Montescaglioso I 61 B7
Montesclaros E 46 D3
Montescudaio I 66 F2
Montese I 66 D2
Montesilvano I 63 B6
Montespertoli I 66 E3
Montesquieu F 33 B8
Montesquieu-Volvestre F 33 D8
Montesquiou F 33 C6
Montes Velhos P 50 D3
Monteux F 35 B8
Montevago I 58 D2
Montevarchi I 66 E4
Montevecchia I 64 D2
Monteverde I 60 A5
Montevil P 50 C2
Montfaucon F 23 F9
Montfaucon F 29 F9
Montfaucon-d'Argonne F 19 F11
Montfaucon-en-Velay F 30 E5
Montferran-Savès F 33 C7
Montferrat F 36 D4
Montferrier F 33 E9
Montfoort NL 182 A5
Montfort F 23 D8
Montfort F 32 D4
Montfort NL 183 C7
Montfort-en-Chalosse F 32 C4
Montfort-l'Amaury F 24 C6
Montfort-le-Gesnois F 24 D3
Montfort-sur-Risle F 18 F2
Montgai E 42 D5
Montgaillard F 33 D6
Montgaillard F 33 E9
Montgenèvre F 31 F10
Montgeron F 25 C7
Montgiscard F 33 D9
Montgivray F 29 B9
Montgomery GB 10 F5
Montguyon F 28 E5
Monthermé F 19 E10
Monthey CH 31 C10
Monthois F 19 F10
Monthureux-sur-Saône F 26 D4
Monti I 64 B3
Monticelli d'Ongina I 69 C8
Monticello F 37 F9
Montichiari I 66 B1
Monticiano I 65 A4
Montiel E 55 B7
Montier-en-Der F 25 D12
Montieri I 65 A4
Montiers-sur-Saulx F 26 C3
Montiglio I 68 C5
Montignac F 29 E8
Montignies-le-Tilleul B 19 D9
Montignoso I 66 D1
Montigny F 27 C6
Montigny-la-Resie F 25 E10
Montigny-le-Roi F 26 D3
Montigny-lès-Metz F 26 B5
Montigny-Mornay-Villeneuve-sur-Vingeanne F 26 E3
Montigny-sur-Aube F 25 E12
Montijo E 51 B6
Montijo P 50 B2
Montilla E 53 A7
Montillana E 53 A9
Montivilliers F 23 A12
Montizón E 55 C6
Montjaux F 34 B4
Montjean F 23 D10
Montjovet I 68 B4
Montlaur F 34 D4
Montlieu-la-Garde F 28 E5
Mont-Louis F 33 E10
Montluçon F 29 C11
Montluel F 31 D7
Montmarault F 30 C2
Montmartin-sur-Mer F 23 C8
Montmédy F 19 E11
Montmélian F 31 D9
Montmelo E 43 D8
Montmeyran F 31 F6
Montmeyan F 36 D4
Montmirail F 24 D4
Montmirail F 25 C10
Montmirey-le-Château F 26 F4
Montmoreau-St-Cybard F 29 E6
Montmorillon F 29 C7
Montmorin F 35 B10
Montmorot F 31 B8
Montmort-Lucy F 25 C10
Montoir-de-Bretagne F 23 F7
Montoire-sur-le-Loir F 24 E4
Montoison F 30 F6
Montoito P 50 B4
Montola FIN 124 F8
Montón E 47 B10
Montone I 66 F5
Montopoli di Sabina I 62 C3
Montorio al Vomano I 62 B5
Montoro E 53 A8
Montory F 32 D4
Montournais F 28 B4
Montpelier IRL 8 C6
Montpellier F 35 C6
Montpeyroux F 34 A4
Montpezat F 33 B7
Montpézat F 33 D7
Montpezat-de-Quercy F 33 B8
Montpezat-sous-Bauzon F 30 F5
Montpon-Ménestérol F 29 E6
Montpont-en-Bresse F 31 B7
Mont-ras E 43 D10
Montréal F 25 E11
Montréal F 33 C6
Montréal F 33 D10
Montredon-Labessonnié F 33 C10
Montregard F 30 E5
Montréjeau F 33 D7
Montrésor F 24 F5
Montresta I 64 C2
Montret F 31 B7
Montreuil F 15 G12
Montreuil-Bellay F 23 F11
Montreuil-Juigné F 23 E10
Montreux CH 31 C10
Montrevault F 23 F9
Montrevel-en-Bresse F 31 C7
Montrichard F 24 F5
Montricoux F 33 B9
Montriond F 31 C10
Mont-roig del Camp E 42 E5
Montrond F 31 B8
Montrond-les-Bains F 30 D5
Montrose GB 5 B12
Montroy E 48 F3
Monts F 24 F4
Montsalvy F 29 F10
Montsauche-les-Settons F 25 F11
Montségur F 33 E9
Montseny E 43 D8
Montsoué F 32 C4
Mont-sous-Vaudrey F 31 B8
Monts-sur-Guesnes F 29 B6
Mont-St-Aignan F 18 F3
Mont-St-Jean F 25 F11
Mont-St-Martin F 19 E12
Mont-St-Vincent F 30 B5
Montsûrs F 23 D10
Montsuzain F 25 D11
Mõntu EST 130 F4
Montuïri E 57 B10
Montvalent F 29 F9
Montville F 18 E3
Montzen B 183 D7
Montzéville F 20 F4
Monza I 69 B7
Monzelfeld D 21 E8
Monzingen D 21 E9
Monzón E 42 D4
Monzón de Campos E 40 D3
Mook NL 183 B7
Moone IRL 7 G9
Moordorf (Südbrookmerland) D 17 B8
Moorends GB 11 D10
Moorenweis D 75 F9
Moorfields GB 4 F4
Moorrege D 82 C7
Moorslede B 19 C7
Moorweg D 17 A9
Moos D 76 E3
Moosbach D 75 C11
Moosburg A 73 C9
Moosburg an der Isar D 75 F10
Moosinning D 75 F10
Mooste EST 131 E14
Mór H 149 B10
Mora E 46 E5
Mora P 50 B3
Mora S 97 B14
Mora S 102 D8
Móra d'Ebre E 42 E5
Mora de Rubielos E 48 D3
Moradillo de Roa E 40 E4
Morag PL 139 C8
Mórahalom H 150 E4
Moraice MNE 163 C7
Moraira E 56 D5
Morais P 39 E6
Moraïtika GR 168 E2
Morakovo MNE 163 D7
Moral de Calatrava E 54 B5
Moraleda de Zafayona E 53 B9
Moraleja E 45 D7
Moraleja del Vino E 39 F8
Moraleja de Sayago E 45 B9
Morales de Campos E 39 E9
Morales del Vino E 39 F8
Morales de Toro E 39 E9
Morales de Valverde E 39 E8
Moralina E 39 F7
Morång S 118 D3
Morano Calabro I 60 D6
Morano sul Po I 68 C5
Morar GB 4 B5
Morărești RO 160 C5
Morasverdes E 45 C8
Morata de Jalón E 41 F9
Morata de Tajuña E 46 D6
Moratalla E 55 C9
Moravia BG 166 C4
Morava MD 154 C4
Morava SLO 73 E10
Moravany CZ 77 B9
Moravany CZ 77 D11
Moravany SK 145 F4
Moravče SLO 73 E10
Moravice HR 67 B11
Moravița RO 159 C7
Moravka BG 166 C6
Morávka CZ 147 B7
Moravská Třebová CZ 77 C11
Moravské Budějovice CZ 77 D9
Moravské Lieskové SK 146 D5
MoravskýMoravskýx CZ 146 B4
Moravský Svätý Ján SK 77 E12
Morawica PL 143 E10
Morbach D 21 E8
Morbegno I 69 A8
Morbier F 31 B9
Mörbisch am See A 149 A7
Mörby S 99 C10
Mörbylånga S 89 B10
Morcenx F 32 B4
Morciano di Leuca I 61 D10
Morciano di Romagna I 66 E6
Morcone I 60 A3
Mordelles F 23 D8
Mordoğan TR 177 B8
Mordy PL 141 F7
More LV 135 B10
Moréac F 22 E6
Moreanes P 50 D4
Morebattle GB 5 D12
Morecambe GB 10 C6
Moreda E 39 B8
Moreda E 55 E6
Morée F 24 E5
Mörel CH 70 E6
Morella E 42 F3
Moreni RO 161 D7
Moresnish GB 5 C8
Morentín E 32 E1
Moreruela de Tábara E 39 E8
Mores I 64 B2
Morestel F 31 D7
Moretonhampstead GB 13 D7
Moreton-in-Marsh GB 13 B11
Moret-sur-Loing F 25 D8
Moretta I 37 B7
Moreuil F 18 E5
Morez F 31 B9
Morfa Nefyn GB 10 F2
Morfasso I 69 D8
Mörfelden D 187 B6
Morfi GR 168 D5
Morfi GR 168 F3
Morfovouni GR 169 F6
Morgat F 22 D2
Morgedal N 95 D8
Morges CH 31 B10
Morgex I 31 D11
Morgongåva S 98 C7
Morhange F 26 C6
Mori I 69 B10
Moria GR 177 A8
Moricone I 62 C3
Morienval F 18 F6
Moriles E 53 B7
Morinë AL 163 E10
Morinë RKS 163 E9
Moringen D 78 C6
Morino I 62 D4
Moritzburg D 80 D5
Morjärv S 118 B9
Mork N 104 F3
Mørke DK 86 C6
Morkkaperä FIN 115 E1
Mørkøv DK 87 D9
Morkovice CZ 77 D12
Mörkret S 102 C4
Morlaàs F 32 D5
Morlaix F 22 C4
Morlanne F 32 C4
Morlanwelz B 19 D9
Mörlenbach D 21 E11
Morley F 26 C3
Morley GB 11 D8
Morley's Bridge IRL 8 E4
Mörlunda S 89 A9
Mormanno I 60 D6
Mormant F 25 C8
Mormoiron F 35 B9
Mornant F 30 D6
Mornas F 35 B8
Mornese I 37 B9
Moroeni RO 161 C6
Morolo I 62 D4
Morón de Almazán E 41 F7
Morón de la Frontera E 51 E9
Moros E 41 F8
Morosaglia F 37 G10
Morottaja FIN 115 E4
Morović SRB 158 C3
Morozova RUS 129 F14
Morozovo BG 166 D4
Morozzo I 37 C7
Morpeth GB 5 E13
Mørrevatnet N 104 D8
Morrfjord N 110 D8
Morriston GB 13 B7
Morrovalle I 67 F8
Mörrum S 89 C7
Morsbach D 21 C9
Mörschen D 78 D6
Morshyn UA 145 E8
Mörsil S 105 E15
Morskoga S 97 C13
Morskogen N 95 B14
Morsum D 17 C12
Mørsvikbotn N 111 E10
Mortagne-au-Perche F 24 C4
Mortagne-sur-Gironde F 28 E4
Mortagne-sur-Sèvre F 28 A4
Mortágua P 44 D4
Mortain F 23 C10
Mortara I 68 C6
Morteau F 31 A10
Morteaux-Coulibœuf F 23 C11
Mortebo S 103 E12
Mortegliano I 73 E7
Mortelle I 59 C8
Morteni RO 160 D6
Mortensnes N 112 C11
Mortensnes N 114 C6
Mortimer's Cross GB 13 A9
Morton GB 11 F11
Mortrée F 23 C12
Mörtschach A 73 C6
Mortsel B 19 B9
Mörtsjön S 106 D7
Mortsund N 110 D6
Morud DK 86 E6
Morunglav RO 160 E4
Morville GB 10 F7
Mor'ye RUS 129 E15
Moryń PL 84 E6
Morzeszczyn PL 138 C6
Morzine F 31 C10
Moșana MD 153 A11
Mosar BY 133 F2
Mosås S 92 A6
Mosätt S 102 B7
Mosbach D 21 F12
Mosbjerg DK 90 D7
Mosborough GB 11 E9
Mosby N 90 C2
Moscavide P 50 B1
Moščenica HR 149 F6
Mošćenička Draga HR 67 B9
Moschopotamos GR 169 D7
Mosciano Sant'Angelo I 62 B5
Mościcka PL 141 C8
Moscovei MD 154 F2
Moscow GB 5 D8
Moseby DK 86 A5
Mosėdis LT 134 D3
Mosel D 79 E11
Mosel D 79 B10
Mosina PL 81 B11
Mosjö S 107 E13
Mosjøen N 108 E5
Moskaret N 101 B12
Mosko BIH 162 D5
Moskorzew PL 143 E8
Moskosel S 109 E17
Moskuvaara FIN 115 C1
Moslavna Podravska HR 149 E9
Moșna RO 152 E4
Moșna RO 153 D11
Moșnița Nouă RO 159 B7
Mosoaia RO 160 D5
Moso in Passiria I 72 C3
Mosonmagyaróvár H 146 F4
Mosonszolnok H 146 F4
Mošovce SK 147 D7
Mosqueruela E 48 D4
Moss N 95 D13
Mossala FIN 126 E5
Mossat GB 3 L11
Mossbo S 103 D11
Mössingen D 27 D11
Mossley GB 4 F5
Mossley GB 11 D7
Moss-side GB 4 E4
Mosstakan S 96 C7
Most BG 166 F5
Most CZ 76 A5
Mostar BIH 157 F8
Mosteiro E 38 B5
Mosteiro P 44 E5
Mosteiro P 50 D4
Mostek CZ 77 B9
Moșteni RO 161 E7
Mosterhamn N 94 C2
Mostkowo PL 85 E8
Mostkowo PL 139 C9
Most na Soči SLO 73 D8
Móstoles E 46 D5
Mosty PL 141 G8
Mostys'ka UA 144 D7
Mosty u Jablunkova CZ 147 B7
Mosvik N 105 D10
Mosyr UA 144 A9
Moszczenica PL 143 C8
Mota del Cuervo E 47 F7
Mota del Marqués E 39 E9
Moțăieni RO 160 C6
Motala S 92 B6
Motarzyno PL 85 B12
Moțăței RO 159 E11
Moțca RO 153 C9
Motherwell GB 5 D9
Môtiers CH 31 B10
Motike BIH 156 D6
Motike BIH 157 C7
Motilla del Palancar E 47 E9
Motilleja E 47 F9
Motjärnshyttan S 97 C10
Motoșeni RO 153 E10
Motovun HR 67 B8
Motril E 53 C9
Motru RO 159 D10
Motta Montecorvino I 63 D8
Motta San Giovanni I 59 C8
Motta Visconti I 69 C6
Motten D 74 B6
Möttingen D 75 E8
Mottola I 61 B8
Möttönen FIN 123 D13
Mötz A 71 C11
Mou DK 86 B6
Moucha GR 174 A4
Mouchamps F 28 B3
Mouchan F 33 C6
Moudon CH 31 B10
Moudros GR 171 E8
Mougins F 36 D6
Mouhijärvi FIN 127 B9
Moularès F 33 B10
Moulay F 23 D10
Mouleydier F 29 F7
Moulherne F 23 F12
Moulin-Neuf F 33 D9
Moulins F 30 B3
Moulins-Engilbert F 30 B4
Moulins-la-Marche F 24 C3
Moulis-en-Médoc F 28 E4
Moulismes F 29 C7
Moult F 23 B11
Moulton GB 15 C7
Moulton GB 15 C9
Mountbellew IRL 6 F6
Mount Bellew IRL 6 F6
Mountbenger GB 5 D10
Mountcharles IRL 6 C6
Mountcollins IRL 8 D4
Mount Hamilton GB 4 F2
Mountjoy GB 4 F2
Mountjoy GB 7 C9
Mountmellick IRL 7 F8
Mount Norris GB 7 D10
Mount Nugent IRL 7 E8
Mountrath IRL 7 F8
Mountshannon IRL 8 C6
Mountsorrel GB 11 F9
Moura P 50 C5
Mourão P 51 C5
Mourenx F 32 D4
Mouriès F 35 C8
Mouries GR 169 B8
Mouriki GR 175 C7
Mourisca do Vouga P 44 C4
Mouriscas P 44 E4
Mournies GR 178 E7
Mourujärvi FIN 121 B11
Mouscron B 19 C7
Moussac F 35 C7
Moussey F 27 D7
Moussoulens F 33 D10
Moussy F 25 F9
Moustéru F 22 C5
Moustey F 32 B4
Moustheni GR 170 C6
Moustiers-Ste-Marie F 36 D4
Mouthe F 31 B9
Mouthier-Haute-Pierre F 31 A9
Mouthiers-sur-Boëme F 29 D6
Mouthoumet F 34 E4
Moutier CH 27 F7
Moutier-d'Ahun F 29 C10
Moûtiers F 31 E10
Moutiers-les-Mauxfaits F 28 C3
Moutnice CZ 77 D11
Moutsouna GR 177 E6
Moux F 34 D4
Moux-en-Morvan F 25 F11
Mouy F 18 F5
Mouzaki GR 169 F6
Mouzaki GR 174 D4
Mouzay F 19 F11
Mouzon F 19 E11
Moviken S 103 C12
Movila RO 155 D1
Movila Miresii RO 155 C1
Movileni RO 153 C10
Movileni RO 153 F10
Movileni RO 160 E5
Movilița RO 153 F10
Movilița RO 161 D8
Moville IRL 4 E2
Movollen N 105 F11
Mowtie GB 5 B12
Moy GB 3 L8
Moy GB 7 D9
Moya E 47 E10
Moyard IRL 6 E2
Moyasta IRL 8 C3
Moycullen IRL 6 F4
Moy-de-l'Aisne F 19 E7
Moyenmoutier F 27 D6
Moyenneville F 18 D4
Moygashel GB 7 D9
Moyivka UA 154 A2
Möykkylänperä FIN 121 C15
Möykkylänperä FIN 119 F17
Moylaw IRL 6 D4
Moylett IRL 7 E8
Moylough IRL 6 F5
Moymore IRL 8 C5
Moyne IRL 7 E7
Moyvalley IRL 7 F9
Moyvore IRL 7 E7
Mozac F 30 D3
Mozăceni RO 160 D6
Mozárbez E 45 C9
Mozelj SLO 73 E10
Mozelos P 44 C5
Mozgovo SRB 159 F8
Mozirje SLO 73 D10
Mozoncillo E 46 B4
Mozsgó H 149 D9
Mozyr' RUS 136 E3
Mračaj BIH 157 E7
Mrągowo PL 136 F3
Mrákov CZ 76 D3
Mrakovica BIH 157 B6
Mramor BIH 157 F8
Mramorak SRB 159 D6
Mratinje MNE 157 F10
Mrčajevci SRB 158 F6
Mrežičko MK 169 B6
Mrkalji BIH 157 D10
Mrkonjić-Grad BIH 157 D7
Mrkopalj HR 67 B10
Mrmoš SRB 164 B3
Mrocza PL 85 D13
Mroczeń PL 142 D4
Mroczków PL 141 H3
Mroczno PL 139 D8
Mrozy PL 141 F5
Mścice PL 85 B10
Mściwojów PL 81 D10
Mšené Lázně CZ 76 B6
Mšeno CZ 77 B7
Mshinskaya RUS 132 C6
Mstów PL 143 E7
Mszana PL 147 B7
Mszana Dolna PL 144 D1
Mszczonów PL 141 G3
Muccia I 62 A4
Much D 21 C8
Muchalls GB 5 A12
Mucharz PL 147 B9
Mücheln (Geiseltal) D 79 D10
Muchow D 83 D11
Muchówka PL 144 D1
Much Wenlock GB 10 F6
Mucientes E 39 E10
Mücka D 81 D7
Mücke Große-Eichen D 21 C12
Mücke-Nieder-Ohmen D 21 C12
Muckross IRL 8 D4
Múcsony H 145 G2
Mudanya TR 173 D10
Mudau D 187 B7
Müdelheim D 183 C9
Müden (Aller) D 79 A7
Müden (Örtze) D 83 E8
Mudersbach D 185 C8
Müdrets BG 166 E6
Muel E 41 F9
Muelas del Pan E 39 E8
Muff IRL 4 E2
Muga de Sayago E 39 F7
Mugardos E 38 B3
Muge P 44 F3
Mügeln D 80 C4
Mügeln D 80 D4
Mugeni RO 152 E6
Muggensturm D 187 D5
Muggia I 73 E8
Muğla TR 181 B8
Müglen BG 167 D8
Müglizh BG 166 D5
Mugron F 32 C4
Mühlacker D 27 C10
Mühlanger D 79 C12
Mühlbachl A 72 B3
Mühlberg D 79 E8
Mühlberg D 80 D4
Mühldorf A 73 C7
Mühldorf am Inn D 75 F12
Mühldorf bei Feldbach A 148 C5
Mühlen A 73 B10
Mühlenbeck D 84 E4
Mühlhausen D 21 F11
Mühlhausen D 75 D9
Mühlhausen (Thüringen) D 79 D7
Mühltroff D 75 A10
Muhola FIN 123 D14
Muhos FIN 119 E15
Muhr am See D 75 D8
Muhur AL 163 F9
Muineachán IRL 7 D9
Muine Bheag IRL 9 C9
Muiños E 38 E4
Muirdrum GB 5 B11
Muirhead GB 5 C10
Muirkirk GB 5 D8
Muir of Ord GB 2 K8
Muizon F 19 F8
Mujdić BIH 157 D7
Mujejärvi FIN 125 C12
Mukacheve UA 145 G6
Mukařov CZ 77 C7
Mukhavyets BY 141 F9
Mukhovo BG 165 E8
Mukkala FIN 115 D5
Mukkavaara FIN 115 D4
Mula E 55 C10
Mulbarton GB 15 B11
Muleby DK 88 E7
Mulešići BIH 157 C9
Mulfingen D 74 D6
Mülheim an der Ruhr D 17 F7
Mülheim-Kärlich D 185 D7
Mulhouse F 27 E7
Muljava SLO 73 E10
Mullach Íde IRL 7 F10
Mullagh IRL 7 E9
Mullagh IRL 7 F9
Mullaghroe IRL 6 E6
Mullany's Cross IRL 6 D5
Mullartown GB 7 D11
Müllheim D 27 E8
Mullhyttan S 92 A5
Mullingar IRL 7 E8
Mullion GB 12 E4
Müllrose D 80 B6
Mullsjö S 91 D14
Mulrany IRL 6 E3
Mulsanne F 23 E12
Mulseryd S 91 D14
Multia FIN 123 F13
Multiperä FIN 121 C15
Mümliswil CH 27 F8
Munakka FIN 122 E9
Muñana E 45 C10
Munapirtti FIN 128 E6
Müncheberg D 75 B10
Müncheberg D 80 A6
München D 75 F10
Münchenbernsdorf D 79 E10
Münchenbuchsee CH 31 A11
Münchhausen D 21 C11
Münchsteinach D 75 C8
Münchweiler an der Rodalb D 186 C4
Münchwilen CH 27 F11
Mundaka E 41 B6
Munderkingen D 187 E8
Mundesley GB 15 B11
Mundford GB 15 B10
Mundheim N 94 B3
Mundolsheim F 27 C8
Munebrega E 41 F8
Munera E 55 A8

Mungia E 40 B6
Mungret IRL 8 C5
Muñico E 45 C10
Muniesa E 42 E2
Munilla E 41 D7
Munka-Ljungby S 87 C11
Munkbyn S 103 B11
Munkebakken N 114 D6
Munkebo DK 86 E7
Munkedal S 91 C10
Munken N 104 D6
Munkflohögen S 106 D7
Munkfors S 97 C10
Munklia N 111 D14
Munksund S 118 D7
Munktorp S 98 C6
Munkzwalm B 19 C8
Munne FIN 128 C7
Münnerstadt D 75 B7
Munningen D 75 E8
Muñogalindo E 46 C3
Munsala FIN 122 D8
Münsingen CH 31 B12
Münsingen D 74 F5
Münster A 72 B4
Münster CH 70 E6
Münster D 17 E9
Münster D 21 E11
Münster D 83 E8
Munster F 27 D7
Münsterdorf D 82 C7
Munstergeleen NL 183 D7
Münsterhausen D 75 F7
Münstermaifeld D 185 D7
Muntendam NL 17 B7
Munteni RO 153 F10
Munteni-Buzău RO 161 D9
Muntenii de Jos RO 153 D11
Münzenberg D 21 D11
Münzkirchen A 76 F5
Muodoslompolo S 117 C10
Muonio FIN 117 C11
Muonionalusta S 117 C11
Muotathal CH 71 D7
Muotkajärvi FIN 117 B10
Muotkavaara FIN 117 C12
Mur SRB 163 C9
Muradiye TR 173 D9
Muradiye TR 177 B9
Murakeresztúr H 149 D7
Muráň SK 147 D10
Muras E 38 B4
Murasson F 34 C4
Muraste EST 131 C8
Muraszemenye H 149 D7
Murat F 30 E2
Muratlar TR 181 B9
Muratli TR 173 B7
Murato F 37 F10
Murat-sur-Vèbre F 34 C4
Murau A 73 B9
Muravera I 64 E4
Murazzano I 37 C8
Murça P 38 F5
Murchante E 41 D8
Mŭrchevo BG 165 B7
Murchin D 84 C5
Murcia E 56 F2
Murczyn PL 138 E4
Mur-de-Barrez F 29 F11
Mûr-de-Bretagne F 22 D6
Mur-de-Sologne F 24 F6
Mureck A 148 C5
Mürefte TR 173 C7
Muret F 33 D8
Murgeni RO 153 E12
Murgenthal CH 27 F8
Murgești RO 161 C9
Murgia E 40 C6
Muri CH 27 F9
Muri CH 31 B11
Murias de Paredes E 39 C7
Muriedas E 40 B4
Murighiol RO 155 C4
Murillo de Río Leza E 32 F1
Murillo el Fruto E 32 F3
Murino MNE 163 D8
Murisengo I 68 C5
Murjāņi LV 135 B9
Murjek S 116 F5
Murley GB 7 D8
Murlo I 66 F3
Murmastiene LV 135 C13
Murnau am Staffelsee D 72 A3
Muro E 57 B11
Muro F 37 F9
Muro P 38 F2
Muro de Alcoy E 56 D4
Murol F 30 D2
Murole FIN 127 B10
Muro Lucano I 60 B4
Muron F 28 C4
Murony H 151 D7
Muros E 38 C1
Muros E 39 A7
Muros I 64 B2
Murovane UA 144 C9
Murów PL 142 E4
Murowana Goślina PL 81 A12
Murrë AL 168 A3
Murrhardt D 74 E6
Murronkylä FIN 119 E16
Murroogh IRL 6 F4
Mursalli TR 177 D10
Mûrs-Erigné F 23 F10
Murska Sobota SLO 148 C6
Mursko Središće HR 149 C6
Murtas E 55 F6
Murtede P 44 D4
Murten CH 31 B11
Murter HR 156 E4
Murtino MK 169 B8
Murto FIN 119 E15
Murtolahti FIN 125 D9
Murtomäki FIN 124 B9
Murtovaara FIN 121 C13
Murumoen N 105 C16
Murvica HR 156 D3
Murviel-lès-Béziers F 34 D5
Mürzsteg A 148 A5
Murzynowo PL 81 A8
Mürzzuschlag A 148 A5
Mūsa LV 135 D8
Musbury GB 13 D8
Müschenbach D 185 C8
Musei I 64 E2
Muselievo BG 160 F5
Mushtisht RKS 163 E10
Musile di Piave I 72 E6
Muskö S 93 B12
Mussalo FIN 128 E6
Musselburgh GB 5 D10
Musselkanaal NL 17 C8
Mussidan F 29 E6
Mussomeli I 58 D4
Musson B 19 E12
Mussy-sur-Seine F 25 E12
Mustafakemalpaşa TR 173 D9
Müstair CH 71 D10
Mustamaa FIN 119 F17
Mustamaa FIN 123 D10
Mustasaari FIN 122 D7
Mustavaara FIN 121 D12
Mustavaara FIN 121 F12
Mustinlahti FIN 125 E10
Mustjala EST 130 E4
Mustla EST 131 E11
Mustola FIN 114 F4
Mustolanmäki FIN 125 C10
Mustolanmutka FIN 125 B10
Mustvee EST 131 D13
Muszaki PL 139 D10
Muszyna PL 145 E2
Muta SLO 73 C11
Mutala FIN 127 B10
Mutalahti FIN 125 F16
Mütevelli TR 177 B10
Muthill GB 5 C9
Mutilva Baja E 32 E2
Mutné SK 147 C8
Mutriku E 32 D1
Mutterstadt D 21 F10
Mutxamel E 56 E4
Mutzig F 27 C7
Mutzschen D 80 D3
Muuga EST 131 C13
Muukajärvi S 116 E10
Muuksi EST 131 B11
Muurame FIN 123 F15
Muurasjärvi FIN 123 C14
Muurikkala FIN 128 D8
Muurla FIN 127 E9
Muurola FIN 119 B14
Muurola FIN 128 D8
Muuruvesi FIN 125 D10
Muxía E 38 B1
Muzillac F 22 E7
Mužla SK 149 A11
Myahuny BY 137 C14
Myakishevo RUS 133 C5
Myaretskiya BY 133 F3
Myazhany BY 135 E13
Mybster GB 3 J10
Myckelgensjö S 107 D13
Myckle S 118 E5
Myedna BY 141 G9
Myggenäs S 91 C10
Myggsjö S 102 C8
Myhinpää FIN 124 F7
Myjava SK 146 D5
Mykanów PL 143 E7
Mykhal'cha UA 153 A7
Mykhaylivka UA 154 F5
Myki GR 171 B7
Myklebostad N 110 E9
Mykolayiv UA 145 D8
Mykolayivka UA 154 E4
Mykolayivka-Novorosiys'ka UA 154 E5
Mykonos GR 176 E5
Mykulychyn UA 152 A5
Mykytychi UA 144 B9
Myllykoski FIN 128 D6
Myllykylä FIN 122 E8
Myllykylä FIN 127 E10
Myllykylä FIN 128 D7
Myllylahti FIN 121 D13
Myllymäki FIN 123 E12
Myloi GR 175 D6
Mylopotamos GR 178 C4
Mynämäki FIN 126 D7
Mynttilä FIN 128 C6
Myon F 31 A8
Myory BY 133 E3
Myra GR 169 F8
Myrås S 109 E14
Myre N 110 C9
Myre N 111 B10
Myresjö S 92 E5
Myrhaug N 101 A14
Myrheden S 118 D4
Myrhult S 92 B4
Myrina GR 171 E8
Myriokefala GR 178 E7
Myrkky FIN 122 F7
Myrland N 110 D5
Myrland N 110 D9
Myrland N 111 C10
Myrlandshaugen N 111 C13
Myrmoen N 101 A15
Myrne UA 155 B4
Myrnes N 112 C9
Myrnopillya UA 154 E4
Myrsini GR 174 D3
Myrsini GR 178 B3
Myrskylä FIN 127 D14
Myrties GR 177 F8
Myrtos GR 179 E10
Myrviken S 105 E16
Mysen N 95 C14
Myshall IRL 9 C9
Myślachowice PL 143 F7
Mysłakowice PL 81 E9
Myślenice PL 147 B9
Myślibórz PL 85 E7
Myślice PL 139 C8
Mysłowice PL 143 F7
Mysovka RUS 134 F2
Myssjö S 102 A7
Mystegna GR 177 A7
Mystras GR 174 E5
Myszków PL 143 E7
Myszyniec PL 139 D11
Mytikas GR 174 B2
Mytilini GR 177 A8
Mytilinioi GR 177 D8
Mýtna SK 147 E9
Mýto CZ 76 C5

N

Nå N 94 B5
Naaldwijk NL 16 E2
Naamankylä FIN 119 E17
Naamijoki FIN 117 E11
Naantali FIN 126 E7
Naapurinvaara FIN 121 F11
Naarden NL 183 A6
Näärinki FIN 128 B8
Naarn im Machlande A 77 F7
Naartijärvi S 119 C11
Naarva FIN 125 D16
Naas IRL 7 F9
Näätämö FIN 114 D6
Näätänmaa FIN 125 F10
Näätävaara FIN 121 E13
Nabburg D 75 D11
Nábrád H 145 G5
Na Cealla Beaga IRL 6 C6
Načeradec CZ 77 C7
Nacha BY 137 E10
Náchod CZ 77 B10
Nacina Ves SK 145 F4
Näckådalen S 102 D7
Nackel D 83 E13
Nackenheim D 185 E9
Näcksjö S 103 C12
Na Clocha Liathe IRL 7 F10
Nacpolsk PL 139 E9
Nad IRL 8 D5
Nadalj SRB 158 C4
Nadarzyce PL 85 D11
Nadarzyn PL 141 F3
Naddvik N 100 D7
Nadeș RO 152 E5
Nădlac RO 150 E6
Nădrag RO 159 B9
Nadrichne UA 154 E4
Nadudvar H 151 C7
Năeni RO 161 C8
Nærbø N 94 E3
Næroset N 101 E13
Nærsnes N 95 C13
Næsbjerg DK 86 D3
Næstved DK 87 E9
Näfels CH 27 F11
Nafferton GB 11 C11
Nafpaktos GR 174 C4
Nafplio GR 175 D6
Nagele NL 16 C5
Naggen S 103 B11
Naglarby S 97 B14
Na Gleannta IRL 6 C6
Nagli LV 133 C1
Nagłowice PL 143 E9
Nagold D 27 C10
Nagore E 32 E3
Nago-Torbole I 69 B10
Nagu FIN 126 E6
Nagyatád H 149 D8
Nagybajom H 149 D9
Nagybánhegyes H 151 E6
Nagybaracska H 149 D11
Nagybarca H 145 G2
Nagyberény H 149 C10
Nagyberki H 149 D10
Nagycenk H 149 A7
Nagycsécs H 145 H2
Nagycserkesz H 145 H4
Nagydobos H 145 G5
Nagydorog H 149 C11
Nagyecsed H 145 H5
Nagyfüged H 150 B5
Nagyhalász H 145 G4
Nagyharsány H 149 E10
Nagyhegyes H 151 B7
Nagyigmánd H 149 A10
Nagyiván H 151 C6
Nagykálló H 145 H4
Nagykanizsa H 149 D7
Nagykapornak H 149 C7
Nagykáta H 150 C4
Nagykereki H 151 C8
Nagykónyi H 149 C10
Nagykőrös H 150 C4
Nagykörű H 150 C5
Nagykovácsi H 149 A11
Nagylak H 150 E6
Nagylóc H 147 E9
Nagylók H 149 C11
Nagylózs H 149 A7
Nagymágocs H 150 D5
Nagymaros H 149 A11
Nagynyárád H 149 E11
Nagyoroszi H 147 F8
Nagyrécse H 149 C8
Nagyréde H 150 B4
Nagyszénás H 150 D6
Nagyszokoly H 149 C10
Nagytarcsa H 150 B3
Nagytőke H 150 D5
Nagyvarsány H 145 G5
Nagyvázsony H 149 C9
Nagyvisnyó H 145 G1
Naha EST 132 E1
Naharros E 47 D8
Nahe D 83 C8
Nahirne UA 155 C2
Nahrendorf D 83 D9
Naidăș RO 159 D8
Naila D 75 B10
Nailloux F 33 D9
Nailsworth GB 13 B10
Naimakka S 116 A7
Naintré F 29 B6
Naipköy TR 173 C7
Nairn GB 3 K9
Naives-Rosières F 26 C3
Naizin F 22 E6
Najac F 33 B9
Nájera E 40 D6
Näkkälä FIN 117 A11
Nakkerud N 95 B12
Nakkila FIN 126 C7
Náklo CZ 77 C12
Nakło PL 143 E8
Naklo SLO 73 D9
Nakło nad Notecią PL 85 D13
Nakomiady PL 136 E3
Näkotne LV 134 C6
Nakovo SRB 150 F6
Nakskov DK 83 A10
Nalbach D 186 C2
Nalbant RO 155 C3
Nalda E 41 D7
Nälden S 105 E16
Nałęczów PL 141 H6
Nálepkovo SK 145 F2
Näljänkä FIN 121 D11
Nalkki FIN 121 E10
Nalliers F 28 C3
Nalžovské Hory CZ 76 D5
Namborn D 21 E8
Nambroca E 46 E5
Namdalseid N 105 C10
Náměšť nad Oslavou CZ 77 D10
Náměšť na Hané CZ 77 C12
Námestovo SK 147 C8
Nämpnäs FIN 122 E6
Namsos N 105 C11
Namsskogan N 105 B14
Namsvatn N 105 B15
Namur B 19 D10
Namysłów PL 142 D4
Nana RO 161 E9
Nána SK 147 F7
Nançay F 24 F7
Nanclares de la Oca E 40 C6
Nancy F 26 C5
Nandrin B 183 D6
Nănești RO 161 B10
Nangis F 25 C9
Nannestad N 95 B13
Nanov RO 160 F6
Nans-les-Pins F 35 D10
Nant F 34 B5
Nanterre F 25 C7
Nantes F 23 F8
Nanteuil-le-Haudouin F 25 B8
Nantiat F 29 C8
Nantua F 31 C8
Nantwich GB 10 E6
Naousa GR 169 C7
Naousa GR 176 E5
Napajedla CZ 146 C5
Napiwoda PL 139 D9
Napkor H 145 H4
Napola I 58 D2
Napoli I 60 B2
Napp N 110 D5
Năpradea RO 151 C11
Náquera E 48 E4
När S 93 E13
Nåra N 100 D1
Nárai H 149 B7
Narberth GB 12 B5
Narbolia I 64 C2
Narbonne F 34 D5
Narbonne-Plage F 34 D5
Narborough GB 15 B10
Narbuvoll N 101 B14
Narcao I 64 E2
Narcy F 25 F9
Nardò I 61 C10
Narechenski Bani BG 165 F10
Narew PL 140 E9
Narewka PL 141 E9
Närhilä FIN 123 E16
Narin IRL 6 C6
Nāriņciems LV 134 B5
Narkaus FIN 119 B16
Narken S 116 E9
Narlidere TR 177 C9
Narni I 62 B3
Naro I 58 E4
Narol PL 144 C7
Närpes FIN 122 F6
Narrosse F 32 C3
Narta HR 149 E7
Nartë AL 168 D1
Naruja RO 153 F9
Naruska FIN 115 D6
Naruszewo PL 139 E9
Narva EST 132 C3
Narva FIN 127 C10
Narva-Jõesuu EST 132 C3
Närvijoki FIN 122 E7
Narvik N 111 D13
Narzole I 37 B7
Narzym PL 139 D9
Näs FIN 99 B14
Näs N 90 A5
Näs S 93 E12
Näs S 97 B12
Näs S 102 A8
Näsåker S 107 E11
Năsăud RO 152 C4
Nasavrky CZ 77 C9
Näsberg S 103 C10
Nasbinals F 34 A5
Näs bruk S 98 B6
Näsby S 89 C10
Na Sceirí IRL 7 E10
Näset S 103 D9
Nashec RKS 163 E10
Našice HR 149 F10
Nasielsk PL 139 E10
Näske S 107 E15
Näsliden S 107 A16
Naso I 59 C6
Nassau D 21 D9
Nassereith A 71 C11
Nässja S 92 C5
Nässjö S 92 D5
Nässjö S 107 D10
Nassogne B 19 D11
Nästansjö S 107 B11
Nastätten D 185 D8
Nästeln S 102 A7
Nastola FIN 127 D14
Năsturelu RO 161 F6
Näsum S 88 C7
Nasutów PL 141 H6
Näsviken S 103 C12
Näsviken S 106 D9
Naszály H 149 A10
Natalinci SRB 159 E6
Nateby GB 11 C7
Naters CH 68 A4
Nattavaara S 116 E5
Nattavaara by S 116 E6
Nattheim D 75 E7
Nättraby S 89 C9
Naturno I 71 D11
Naucelle F 33 B10
Naucelles F 29 F10
Naudaskalns LV 133 B2
Nauders A 71 D11
Naudīte LV 134 C6
Nauen D 79 A12
Nauendorf D 79 C10
Nauheim D 21 E10
Naujac-sur-Mer F 28 E3
Naujamiestis LT 135 E8
Naujasis Daugėliškis LT 135 F12
Naujoji Akmenė LT 134 D5
Naujoji Vilnia LT 137 D11
Naukšēni LV 131 F10
Naul IRL 7 E10
Naulaperä FIN 121 E10
Naulavaara FIN 125 C10
Naumburg (Hessen) D 17 F12
Naumburg (Saale) D 79 D10
Naundorf D 80 D4
Naundorf D 80 E4
Naunhof D 79 D12
Nauroth D 21 C9
Naurstad N 108 B8
Naustbukta N 105 B11
Naustdal N 100 C3
Nauste N 101 A8
Nautijaur S 109 C17
Nautsi RUS 114 E6
Nautsund N 100 D2
Nava E 39 B9
Navacepeda de Tormes E 45 D10
Navaconcejo E 45 D9
Nava de Arévalo E 46 C3
Nava de la Asunción E 46 B4
Nava del Rey E 39 F9
Nava de Sotrobal E 45 C10
Navadrutsk BY 133 F2
Navafría E 46 B5
Navahermosa E 46 E4
Navajas E 48 E4
Naval E 42 C4
Navalagamella E 46 D4
Navalcaballo E 41 E6
Navalcán E 45 D10
Navalcarnero E 46 D4
Navalero E 40 E6
Navalmanzano E 46 B4
Navalmoral E 46 D3
Navalmoral de la Mata E 45 E9
Navalonguilla E 45 D10
Navalosa E 46 D3
Navalperal de Pinares E 46 C4
Navalpino E 46 F3
Navaluenga E 46 D3
Navalvillar de Ibor E 45 E10
Navalvillar de Pela E 45 F10
Navamorcuende E 46 D3
Navan IRL 7 E9
Navapolatsk BY 133 E5
Navarcles E 43 D7
Navardún E 32 E3
Navarredonda de la Rinconada E 45 C8
Navarrenx F 32 D4
Navarrés E 48 F3
Navarrete E 41 D6
Navarrevisca E 46 D3
Navàs E 43 D7
Navascués E 32 E3
Navas de Estrena E 46 E3
Navas de Jorquera E 47 F9
Navas del Madroño E 45 E7
Navas del Rey E 46 D4
Navas de Oro E 46 B4
Navas de San Juan E 55 C6
Navasfrías E 45 D7
Navata E 43 C9
Navatalgordo E 46 D3
Nave I 69 B9
Nave P 50 E2
Nave de Haver P 45 C7
Nävekvarn S 93 B9
Navelli I 62 C5
Näverdal N 101 A12
Näverede S 106 E8
Nave Redonda P 50 E3
Näverkärret S 97 C14
Näverrys FIN 119 C15
Naverstad S 91 B10
Navès E 43 D7
Naves F 29 E9
Navezuelas E 45 E10
Navia E 39 A6
Navilly F 31 B7
Navit N 112 D8
Năvodari RO 155 E3
Nävragöl S 89 C9
Nawojowa PL 145 D2
Naxos GR 176 E5
Nay-Bourdettes F 32 D5
Nazaré P 44 E2
Nazelles-Négron F 24 F4
Nazza D 79 D7
Ndroq AL 168 B2
Nea Agathoupoli GR 169 D8
Nea Alikarnassos GR 178 E9
Nea Anchialos GR 169 F8
Nea Apollonia GR 169 C9
Nea Artaki GR 175 B8
Nea Efesos GR 169 D7
Nea Epidavros GR 175 D7
Nea Figaleia GR 174 E4
Nea Filadelfeia GR 175 C8
Nea Fokaia GR 169 D9
Nea Ionia GR 169 F8
Nea Iraklitsa GR 171 C6
Nea Kallikrateia GR 169 D9
Nea Karvali GR 171 C6
Nea Karya GR 171 C7
Nea Kerdylia GR 169 C10
Nea Kios GR 175 D6
Nea Koroni GR 174 F4
Nea Lampsakos GR 175 C8
Neale IRL 6 E4
Nea Liosia GR 175 C8
Nea Madytos GR 169 C10
Nea Makri GR 175 C8
Nea Malgara GR 169 C8
Nea Mesimvria GR 169 C8
Nea Michaniona GR 169 D8
Nea Moudania GR 169 D9
Nea Olynthos GR 169 D9
Nea Pella GR 169 C8
Nea Peramos GR 171 C6
Nea Peramos GR 175 C7
Nea Plagia GR 169 D9
Neapoli GR 168 D5
Neapoli GR 178 B5
Neapoli GR 179 E10
Nea Poteidaia GR 169 D9
Nea Roda GR 170 D5
Nea Santa GR 169 C8
Nea Santa GR 171 B9
Nea Silata GR 169 D9
Nea Styra GR 175 C9
Neath GB 13 B7
Nea Tiryntha GR 175 D6
Nea Triglia GR 169 D9
Neaua RO 152 E5
Nea Vravrona GR 175 D9
Nea Vyssa GR 171 A11
Nea Zichni GR 169 B10
Nebel D 82 A4
Nébias F 33 E10
Nebljusi HR 156 C4
Nebra (Unstrut) D 79 D10
Nebreda E 40 E4
Nechanice CZ 77 B9
Neckarbischofsheim D 187 C6
Neckargemünd D 21 F11
Neckarsteinach D 21 F11
Neckarsulm D 21 F12
Neckartenzlingen D 27 C11
Necșești RO 160 E6
Necton GB 15 B10
Nečujam HR 156 F5
Neda E 38 B3
Nedansjö S 103 B12
Nedašov CZ 146 C6
Neddemin D 84 C4
Neded SK 146 E5
Nedelino BG 171 B8
Nedelišće HR 149 D6
Nederby DK 86 B4
Nederhögen S 102 B7
Nederhorst den Berg NL 183 A6
Neder Hvam DK 86 C4
Nederlangbroek NL 183 A6
Nedervetil FIN 123 C10
Neder Vindinge DK 87 E9
Nederweert NL 16 F5
Nedlitz D 79 B11
Nedožery-Brezany SK 147 D7
Nedrebø N 94 E4
Nedre Saxnäs S 109 F14
Nedre Soppero S 116 B7
Nedstrand N 94 D3
Nedvědice CZ 77 D10
Nedyalsko BG 167 E7
Njdza PL 142 F5
Neede NL 17 D7
Needham Market GB 15 C11
Neer NL 183 C8
Neerijnen NL 183 B6
Neermoor D 17 B8
Neeroeteren B 183 C7
Neerpelt B 19 B11
Neetze D 83 D9
Nefyn GB 10 F2
Negenborn D 78 C6
Negoi RO 160 F2
Negomir RO 159 D11
Negorci MK 169 B7
Negoslavci HR 157 B11
Negotin SRB 159 E10
Negotino MK 163 F10
Negotino MK 169 B7
Negrar I 66 A2
Negrași RO 160 D6
Negredo E 47 B7
Negreira E 38 C2
Nègrepelisse F 33 B9
Negrești RO 153 D10
Negrești-Oaș RO 145 H7
Negri RO 153 D9
Negru Vodă RO 155 F2
Nehoiu RO 161 C8
Neiden N 114 D6
Neidin IRL 8 E3
Neitaskaite S 116 E8
Neitsuanto S 116 D5
Neittävä FIN 119 E17
Neive I 37 B8
Nejdek CZ 75 B12
Nekézseny H 145 G1
Nekla PL 81 B12
Neksø DK 89 E8
Nelas P 44 C5
Nellim FIN 114 F4
Nellingen D 74 E6
Nelson GB 11 D7
Nemaitonys LT 137 D9
Neman RUS 136 C5
Nemanjica MK 164 F4
Nemanskoye RUS 136 C5
Nembro I 69 B8
Nemea GR 175 D6
Nemenčinė LT 137 D11
Nemesgulács H 149 C8
Nemesnádudvar H 150 E3
Nemesvámos H 149 B9
Nemesvid H 149 C8
Némétkér H 149 C11
Nemėžis LT 137 D11
Nemours F 25 D8
Nemsdorf-Göhrendorf D 79 D10
Nemšová SK 146 D6
Nemunaitis LT 137 E9
Nemunėlio Radviliškis LT 135 D9
Nemyriv UA 144 C7
Nenagh IRL 8 C6
Nendaz CH 31 C12
Nenince SK 147 E8
Nenita GR 177 C7
Nennhausen D 79 A12
Nennslingen D 75 D9
Nenonpelto FIN 124 F8
Nentershausen D 21 D9
Nentershausen D 78 D6
Nenthead GB 5 F12
Nenzing A 71 C9
Neo Agioneri GR 169 C8
Neochoraki GR 175 C7
Neochori GR 169 B9
Neochori GR 169 F6
Neochori GR 171 B10
Neochori GR 174 A3
Neochori GR 174 C3
Neo Erasmio GR 171 C7
Neoi Epivates GR 169 C8
Neo Monastiri GR 169 F7
Neoneli I 64 C2
Neo Petritsi GR 169 B9
Neorić HR 156 E6
Neos Kafkasos GR 168 C5
Neos Marmaras GR 169 D10
Neos Mylotopos GR 169 C7
Neo Souli GR 169 B10
Neos Pagontas GR 175 B8
Neos Pyrgos GR 175 B7
Neos Skopos GR 169 B10
Néoules F 36 E4
Nepi I 62 C2
Nepomuk CZ 76 D5
Nérac F 33 B6
Neratovice CZ 77 B7
Nerău RO 150 F6
Neravai LT 137 E9
Nerchau D 79 D12
Nercillac F 28 D5
Nerdal N 101 A9
Nerde Gärdsjö S 103 E9
Néré F 28 D5
Nereju RO 153 F9
Neresheim D 75 E7
Neresnica SRB 159 E8
Neresnytsya UA 145 G8
Nereta LV 135 D10
Nereto I 62 B5
Nerezine HR 67 C9
Nerežišće HR 156 F6
Néris-les-Bains F 29 C11
Nerja E 53 C9
Nerkoo FIN 124 D8
Nerlia N 108 E7
Nerokouros GR 178 E7
Néronde F 30 D5
Nérondes F 30 B2
Neroth D 21 D7
Nerpio E 55 C8
Nersac F 28 D6
Nersingen D 75 F7
Nerskogen N 101 A11
Nerushay UA 155 B5
Nerva E 51 D6
Nervesa della Battaglia I 72 E5
Nervieux F 30 D5
Nes FIN 2 A3
Nes N 95 D9
Nes N 96 A2
Nes N 110 D9
Nes N 111 D10
Nes NL 16 B5
Nesbyen N 101 E10
Neschwitz D 80 D6
Nesebŭr BG 167 D9
Neset N 112 C7
Nes Flaten N 94 C5
Nesgrenda N 90 B4
Nesheim N 94 D3
Nesje N 110 D6
Nesjegjerde N 100 A6
Nesland N 110 D5
Neslandsvatn N 90 B5
Nesle F 18 E6
Nesna N 108 D5
Nesovice CZ 77 D12
Nessa F 37 F9
Nesse D 17 A8
Nesseby N 114 C6
Nesselwang D 71 B11
Nesslau CH 27 F11
Nessodtangen N 95 C13
Nestani GR 175 D5
Nestby N 108 B9
Nesterov RUS 136 D6
Neston GB 10 E5
Nestorio GR 168 D5
Nestoyita UA 154 B4
Nesttun N 94 B2
Nesvady SK 146 F6
Nesvatnstemmen N 90 B3
Nesvik N 94 D4
Nethy Bridge GB 3 L9
Netolice CZ 76 D6
Netphen D 21 C10
Netra (Ringgau) D 79 D7
Netretić HR 148 E4
Netstal CH 71 C8
Nettancourt F 25 C12
Nettersheim D 21 D7
Nettetal D 16 F6
Nettuno I 62 E3
Netvořice CZ 77 C7
Neu-Anspach D 21 D11
Neuberend D 82 A7
Neuberg an der Mürz A 148 A5
Neubeuern D 72 A5
Neubiberg D 75 F10
Neubrandenburg D 84 C4
Neubruchhausen D 17 C11
Neubrunn D 187 B8
Neubukow D 83 B11
Neubulach D 27 C10
Neuburg am Rhein D 187 D5
Neuburg an der Donau D 75 E9
Neuburg-Steinhausen D 83 C11
Neuburxdorf D 80 D4
Neuchâtel CH 31 B10
Neu Darchau D 83 D9
Neudietendorf D 79 E8
Neudorf A 146 F2
Neudrossenfeld D 75 B10
Neuenbürg D 27 C10
Neuendettelsau D 75 D8
Neuenhagen Berlin D 80 A5
Neuenhaus D 17 D7
Neuenhof CH 27 F9
Neuenkirch CH 27 F9
Neuenkirchen D 17 A11
Neuenkirchen D 17 C11
Neuenkirchen D 17 D8
Neuenkirchen D 17 D9
Neuenkirchen D 82 B6
Neuenkirchen D 82 D7
Neuenkirchen D 84 A4
Neuenkirchen D 84 B4
Neuenkirchen (Oldenburg) D 17 C10
Neuenkirchen-Seelscheid D 21 C8
Neuenrade D 185 B8
Neuenstadt am Kocher D 27 B11
Neuenstein D 187 C8
Neuenwalde D 17 A11
Neuerburg D 20 D6
Neufahrn bei Freising D 75 F10
Neufahrn in Niederbayern D 75 E11
Neufchâteau B 19 E11
Neufchâteau F 26 D4
Neufchâtel-en-Bray F 18 E3
Neufchâtel-Hardelot F 15 F12
Neufchâtel-sur-Aisne F 19 F9
Neufeld D 17 A12
Neufeld an der Leitha A 77 G10
Neuffen D 27 C11
Neufmanil F 184 E2
Neufra D 27 D11
Neugersdorf D 81 E7
Neuharlingersiel D 17 A9
Neuhaus A 73 A11
Neuhaus A 73 C10
Neuhaus (Oste) D 17 A12
Neuhaus am Inn D 76 F4
Neuhaus am Klausenbach A 148 C6
Neuhaus am Rennweg D 75 A9
Neuhaus an der Pegnitz D 75 C10
Neuhausen CH 27 E10
Neuhausen D 80 E4
Neuhausen D 187 D6
Neuhausen ob Eck D 27 E10
Neuhof D 74 B6
Neuhof an der Zenn D 75 D8
Neuhofen D 187 C5
Neuhofen an der Krems A 76 F6
Neuillé-Pont-Pierre F 24 E4
Neuilly F 25 F10
Neuilly-en-Thelle F 18 F5
Neuilly-le-Réal F 30 C3
Neuilly-l'Évêque F 26 E3
Neuilly-St-Front F 25 B9
Neu-Isenburg D 187 A6
Neukalen D 83 C13
Neu Kaliß D 83 D10
Neukirch D 80 D6
Neukirchen D 21 C12
Neukirchen D 80 E3
Neukirchen D 83 B10
Neukirchen D 86 F3
Neukirchen am Großvenediger A 72 B5
Neukirchen an der Enknach A 76 F4
Neukirchen an der Vöckla A 76 F5
Neukirchen-Balbini D 75 D11
Neukirchen beim Heiligen Blut D 76 D3
Neukirchen vorm Wald D 76 E4
Neukloster D 83 C11

Neulengbach A 77 F9
Neuler D 75 E7
Neulewin D 84 E6
Neulikko FIN 121 E10
Neulise F 30 D5
Neu Lübbenau D 80 B5
Neum BIH 162 D4
Neumagen D 185 E6
Neumark D 79 E11
Neumarkt am Wallersee A 73 A7
Neumarkt im Mühlkreis A 77 F6
Neumarkt in der Oberpfalz D 75 D9
Neumarkt in Steiermark A 73 B9
Neumarkt-Sankt Veit D 75 F12
Neu Mukran D 84 B5
Neumünster D 83 B7
Neunburg vorm Wald D 75 D11
Neundorf D 75 A11
Neung-sur-Beuvron F 24 E6
Neunkirch CH 27 E10
Neunkirchen A 148 A6
Neunkirchen D 21 C10
Neunkirchen D 21 F8
Neunkirchen am Brand D 75 C9
Neunkirchen am Sand D 75 C9
Neuötting D 75 F12
Neupetershain D 80 C6
Neupölla A 77 E8
Neureichenau D 76 E5
Neuruppin D 83 E13
Neuschönau D 76 E4
Neusiedl am See A 77 G11
Neusorg D 75 C10
Neuss D 21 B7
Neussargues-Moissac F 30 E2
Neustadt D 27 E9
Neustadt D 79 E10
Neustadt D 83 E12
Neustadt (Harz) D 79 C8
Neustadt (Hessen) D 21 C12
Neustadt (Wied) D 21 C8
Neustadt am Kulm D 75 C10
Neustadt am Rübenberge D 78 A5
Neustadt an der Aisch D 75 C8
Neustadt an der Donau D 75 E10
Neustadt an der Waldnaab D 75 C11
Neustadt an der Weinstraße D 21 F10
Neustadt bei Coburg D 75 B9
Neustadt-Glewe D 83 D11
Neustadt in Holstein D 83 B9
Neustadt in Sachsen D 80 D6
Neustift im Stubaital A 72 B3
Neustrelitz D 84 D4
Neutraubling D 75 E11
Neutrebbin D 80 A6
Neu-Ulm D 74 F7
Neuvéglise F 30 F2
Neuves-Maisons F 186 D1
Neuvic F 29 E6
Neuvic F 29 E10
Neuville-aux-Bois F 24 D7
Neuville-de-Poitou F 29 B6
Neuville-les-Dames F 31 C7
Neuville-lès-Dieppe F 18 E3
Neuville-sur-Saône F 30 D6
Neuvilly-en-Argonne F 26 B3
Neuvy-Grandchamp F 30 B4
Neuvy-le-Roi F 24 E4
Neuvy-Pailloux F 29 B9
Neuvy-St-Sépulchre F 29 B9
Neuvy-sur-Barangeon F 25 F7
Neuweiler D 27 C10
Neuwied D 21 D8
Neuwittenbek D 83 B8
Neu Wulmstorf D 83 D7
Neu Zauche D 80 C6
Neuzelle D 81 B7
Neu Zittau D 80 B5
Névache F 31 E10
Nevarėnai LT 134 D4
Neveja LV 130 F4
Neveklov CZ 77 C7
Nevel' RUS 133 D7
Nevele B 19 B8
Neverfjord N 113 C12
Nevernes N 108 F4
Neverness N 110 C9
Neveronys LT 137 D9
Nevers F 30 A3
Nevesinje BIH 157 F9
Nevestino BG 165 E6
Névez F 22 E4
Neviano I 61 C10
Néville F 18 E2
Nevlunghavn N 90 B6
Nevsha BG 167 C8
New Abbey GB 5 F9
New Aberdour GB 3 K12
New Alresford GB 13 C12
Newark-on-Trent GB 11 E10
Newbawn IRL 9 D9
Newbiggin-by-the-Sea GB 5 E13
Newbliss IRL 7 D8
Newborough GB 11 F11
Newbridge GB 13 B8
Newbridge IRL 7 F9
New Buildings GB 4 F2
Newburgh GB 3 L12
Newburgh GB 5 C10
Newbury GB 13 C12
Newby Bridge GB 10 C6
Newcastle GB 7 D11
Newcastle GB 13 A8
Newcastle IRL 7 F10
Newcastle IRL 7 F10
Newcastle Emlyn GB 12 A6
Newcastleton GB 5 E11
Newcastle-under-Lyme GB 11 E7
Newcastle upon Tyne GB 5 F13
Newcastle West IRL 8 D4
New Cumnock GB 5 E8
New Deer GB 3 K12
Newel D 21 E7
Newent GB 13 B10
New Galloway GB 5 E8
New Inn IRL 6 F6
New Inn IRL 7 E8
Newinn IRL 9 D7
New Kildimo IRL 8 C5
Newmarket GB 2 J4
Newmarket GB 15 C9
Newmarket IRL 8 D4
Newmarket IRL 9 D8
Newmarket-on-Fergus IRL 8 C5
Newmill GB 3 K11
New Milton GB 13 D11
Newnham GB 13 B10
New Pitsligo GB 3 K12
Newport GB 3 J10
Newport GB 11 F7
Newport GB 12 A5
Newport GB 13 B9
Newport GB 13 D12
Newport GB 15 D9
Newport IRL 6 E3
Newport IRL 8 C6
Newport-on-Tay GB 5 C11
Newport Pagnell GB 15 C7
Newport Trench GB 4 F3
New Quay GB 12 A6
Newquay GB 12 E4
New Radnor GB 13 A8
New Romney GB 15 F10
New Ross IRL 9 D9
Newry GB 7 D10
Newton GB 4 C6
Newton GB 10 D7
Newton Abbot GB 13 D7
Newton Aycliffe GB 5 F13
Newton Ferrers GB 12 E6
Newtonhill GB 5 A12
Newton-le-Willows GB 10 E6
Newton Mearns GB 5 D8
Newtonmore GB 5 A8
Newton Stewart GB 4 F8
Newtown GB 10 F5
Newtown GB 13 A9
Newtown IRL 6 F6
Newtown IRL 8 D5
Newtown IRL 8 D6
Newtown IRL 9 C8
Newtownabbey GB 4 F5
Newtownards GB 7 C11
Newtownbarry IRL 9 C9
Newtownbutler GB 7 D8
Newtown Crommelin GB 4 F4
Newtown Forbes IRL 7 E7
Newtown Mount Kennedy IRL 7 F10
Newtown St Boswells GB 5 D11
Newtownstewart GB 4 F2
Nexon F 29 D8
Neyland GB 12 B5
Nezamyslice CZ 77 D12
Nezavertailovca MD 154 D5
Nézsa H 147 F8
Nezvěstice CZ 76 C5
Nianfors S 103 C12
Niata GR 175 F6
Nibbiano I 37 B10
Nibe DK 86 B5
Nīca LV 134 D2
Nicastro I 59 B9
Nice F 37 D6
Nīcgale LV 135 D12
Nichelino I 37 A7
Nickelsdorf A 77 G12
Nicolae Bălcescu RO 153 B9
Nicolae Bălcescu RO 153 E9
Nicolae Bălcescu RO 155 D3
Nicolae Bălcescu RO 155 E2
Nicolae Bălcescu RO 160 D4
Nicolae Bălcescu RO 161 E9
Nicolae Titulescu RO 160 E5
Nicolaevca MD 154 B2
Nicolosi I 59 D7
Nicoreni MD 153 B11
Nicorești RO 153 F10
Nicosia I 58 D5
Nicotera I 59 B8
Nicșeni RO 153 B9
Niculești RO 161 D7
Niculițel RO 155 C2
Nida LT 134 F1
Nidau CH 27 F7
Nidda D 21 D12
Nidzica PL 139 D9
Niebla E 51 E6
Nieborów PL 141 F2
Niebüll D 82 A5
Niebylec PL 144 D4
Niechanowo PL 138 F4
Niechcice PL 143 D8
Niechłonin PL 139 D9
Niechlów PL 81 C10
Niechorze PL 85 B8
Niederaichbach D 75 E11
Niederanven L 20 E6
Niederau D 80 D5
Niederaula D 78 E6
Niederbipp CH 27 F8
Niederbrechen D 21 D10
Niederbreitbach D 185 C7
Niederbronn-les-Bains F 27 C8
Niederfinow D 84 E5
Niederfischbach D 185 C8
Niedergörsdorf D 80 C3
Niederkassel D 21 C8
Niederkirchen D 21 E9
Niederkrüchten D 20 B6
Niederndorf A 72 A5
Niederneisen D 21 D10
Niedernhall D 74 D6
Niedernhausen D 21 D10
Niederoderwitz D 81 E7
Nieder-Olm D 185 E9
Nieder-Rodenbach D 21 D12
Niederroßla D 79 D9
Niedersachswerfen D 79 C8
Niederselters D 21 D10
Niederstetten D 74 D6
Niederurnen CH 27 F11
Niederviehbach D 75 E11
Niederwerrn D 75 B7
Niederwörresbach D 186 B3
Niederzissen D 21 D8
Niedrzwica Duża PL 141 H6
Niedźwiada PL 141 G7
Niedźwiadna PL 139 C13
Niefern-Öschelbronn D 27 C10
Niegosław PL 85 E9
Niegosławice PL 81 C9
Niegowa PL 143 E7
Niegripp D 79 B10
Nieheim D 17 E12
Niekerk NL 16 B6
Niekłań Wielki PL 141 H3
Niekursko PL 85 D10
Niel B 182 C4
Nielisz PL 144 B7
Niemberg D 79 C11
Niemce PL 141 H7
Niemcza PL 81 E11
Niemegk D 79 B12
Niemelä FIN 113 C20
Niemelä FIN 115 E5
Niemelänkylä FIN 119 F12
Niemenkylä FIN 122 E7
Niemenkylä FIN 126 C6
Niemenpää FIN 119 B11
Niemis S 119 B11
Niemisel S 118 B7
Niemisjärvi FIN 123 F16
Niemisjärvi FIN 124 E8
Niemiskylä FIN 123 C17
Niemodlin PL 142 E4
Niemysłów PL 142 C6
Nienadówka PL 144 C5
Nienburg (Saale) D 79 C10
Nienburg (Weser) D 17 C12
Niepars D 84 B3
Niepołomice PL 143 F9
Nieporjt PL 139 F11
Nierstein D 21 E10
Niesa FIN 117 D11
Niesi FIN 117 D15
Niesky D 81 D7
Nieświń PL 141 H2
Nieszawa PL 138 E6
Nietsak S 116 D4
Nietulisko Duże PL 143 E11
Nieul F 29 D8
Nieuw-Amsterdam NL 17 C7
Nieuw-Bergen NL 16 E6
Nieuwegein NL 16 D4
Nieuwe-Niedorp NL 16 C3
Nieuwe Pekela NL 17 B7
Nieuwerkerk NL 16 E2
Nieuwerkerk aan de IJssel NL 16 E3
Nieuwerkerken B 19 C11
Nieuwe-Tonge NL 16 E2
Nieuw-Heeten NL 16 D6
Nieuwkoop NL 16 D3
Nieuw-Loosdrecht NL 183 A6
Nieuw-Milligen NL 183 A7
Nieuw-Namen NL 182 C4
Nieuwolda NL 17 B7
Nieuwpoort B 18 B6
Nieuwveen NL 182 A5
Nieuw-Vennep NL 16 D3
Nieuw-Vossemeer NL 182 B4
Nieuw-Weerdinge NL 17 C7
Nievern D 185 D8
Niewjgłosz PL 141 G7
Niezabyszewo PL 85 B12
Nigrán E 38 D2
Nīgrande LV 134 D4
Nigrita GR 169 C10
Nigüelas E 53 C9
Niherne F 29 B9
Niinilahti FIN 123 E15
Niinimaa FIN 123 E10
Niinimäki FIN 125 F10
Niinisalo FIN 126 B8
Niinivaara FIN 125 D11
Niinivesi FIN 123 E16
Niirokumpu FIN 121 B11
Níjar E 55 F8
Nijemci HR 157 B11
Nijkerk NL 16 D4
Nijlen B 19 B10
Nijmegen NL 16 E5
Nijverdal NL 17 D6
Nikaia GR 169 E7
Nikaranperä FIN 123 E14
Nikel' RUS 114 E8
Niki GR 168 C5
Nikisiani GR 170 C6
Nikiti GR 169 D10
Nikkala S 119 C11
Nikkaluokta S 111 E17
Nikkaroinen FIN 127 C14
Nikkeby N 112 C6
Nikodin MK 169 B6
Nikokleia GR 169 C9
Nikolaevo BG 165 C10
Nikolaevo BG 166 D5
Nikola-Kozlevo BG 161 F10
Nikolovo BG 161 F8
Nikolsdorf A 73 C6
Nikopol BG 160 F5
Nikopoli GR 174 A2
Nīkrāce LV 134 C3
Nikšić MNE 163 D6
Nikyup BG 166 C5
Nilivaara FIN 117 C14
Nilivaara S 116 D7
Nilsiä FIN 125 D10
Nilvange F 20 F6
Nim DK 86 D5
Nîmes F 35 C7
Nimigea RO 152 C4
Nimis I 73 D7
Nimisenkangas FIN 125 C11
Nimisjärvi FIN 119 E17
Nimtofte DK 86 C7
Nin HR 67 D11
Nina EST 131 D14
Nindorf D 82 B6
Ninemile Bar GB 5 E9
Ninemilehouse IRL 9 D8
Ninove B 19 C9
Niort F 28 C5
Nirza LV 133 D3
Niš SRB 164 C4
Nisa P 44 E5
Nisbet GB 5 D11
Niscemi I 58 E5
Niška Banja SRB 164 C5
Niskankorpi FIN 123 C13
Niskanpera FIN 119 B15
Nisko PL 144 B5
Niskos FIN 123 F10
Nismes B 19 D10
Nispen NL 16 F2
Nisporeni MD 154 C2
Nissafors S 91 E14
Nissan-lez-Enserune F 34 D5
Nissilä FIN 123 C17
Nissinvaara FIN 121 B13
Nissoria I 58 D5
Nissumby DK 86 B2
Nissum Seminarieby DK 86 B2
Nistelrode NL 16 E5
Nistorești RO 153 F9
Nītaure LV 135 B10
Nitra SK 146 E6
Nitrianske Hrnčiarovce SK 146 E6
Nitrianske Pravno SK 147 D7
Nitrianske Rudno SK 146 D6
Nitrianske Sučany SK 146 D6
Nitry F 25 E10
Nitta S 91 D13
Nittedal N 95 B13
Nittel D 20 E6
Nittenau D 75 D11
Nittendorf D 75 D10
Nittorp S 91 D14
Niukkala FIN 129 B12
Nivå DK 87 D11
Niva FIN 121 F14
Nivala FIN 123 C13
Nivankylä FIN 117 E15
Nivanpää FIN 117 E11
Nivelles B 19 C9
Nivenskoye RUS 136 D2
Nivillac F 23 E7
Nivillers F 18 F5
Nivnice CZ 146 D5
Nivolas-Vermelle F 31 D7
Nivyanin BG 165 C8
Niwiska PL 143 F12
Nižbor CZ 76 C6
Nižná SK 147 C9
Nižná Slaná SK 145 F1
Nižný Hrabovec SK 145 F4
Nižný Hrušov SK 145 F4
Nižný Šipov SK 145 F4
Nizza di Sicilia I 59 D7
Nizza Monferrato I 37 B8
Njavve S 109 C15
Njegovuđa MNE 163 C7
Një Maj AL 168 C3
Njetjavare S 116 E4
Njivice HR 67 B10
Njurundabommen S 103 B13
Njutånger S 103 C13
No DK 86 C2
Noaillan F 32 B5
Noailles F 18 F5
Noain E 32 E2
Noale I 66 A5
Noalejo E 53 A9
Noasca I 31 E11
Nöbbele S 89 B8
Nobber IRL 7 E9
Nobitz D 79 E11
Noblejas E 46 E6
Noćaj SRB 158 D4
Nocé F 24 D4
Nocera Inferiore I 60 B3
Nocera Terinese I 59 A9
Nocera Umbra I 62 A3
Noceto I 66 C1
Noci I 61 B8
Nociglia I 61 C10
Nociūnai LT 135 F8
Nocrich RO 152 F4
Nødebo DK 87 D10
Nodeland N 90 C2
Nödinge S 91 D11
Nodland N 94 F4
Nods F 26 F5
Noé F 33 D8
Noepoli I 61 C6
Noer D 83 B8
Nœux-les-Mines F 18 D6
Noez E 46 E4
Nofuentes E 40 C5
Nogales E 51 B6
Nogara I 66 B3
Nogaro F 32 C5
Nogent F 26 D3
Nogent-le-Bernard F 24 D3
Nogent-le-Roi F 24 C6
Nogent-le-Rotrou F 24 D4
Nogent-sur-Aube F 25 D11
Nogent-sur-Oise F 18 F5
Nogent-sur-Seine F 25 D10
Nogent-sur-Vernisson F 25 E8
Nogersund S 89 C7
Nógrád H 147 F8
Nógrádmegyer H 147 E9
Nógrádsáp H 147 F8
Nograles E 40 F6
Noguera de Albarracín E 47 D9
Noguères F 32 D4
Nogueruelas E 48 D3
Nohant-Vic F 29 B9
Nohfelden D 21 E8
Nohic F 33 C8
Noia E 38 C2
Noicattaro I 61 A7
Noidans-lès-Vesoul F 26 E5
Noilhan F 33 C7
Noirétable F 30 D4
Noirmoutier-en-l'Île F 28 A1
Noisseville F 26 B5
Noja E 40 B4
Nojorid RO 151 C8
Nokia FIN 127 C10
Nol S 91 D11
Nolay F 30 B6
Noli I 37 C8
Nolimo FIN 121 B11
Nolmyra S 99 B8
Nólsoy FO 2 A3
Nombela E 46 D4
Nomeland N 90 A2
Nomenj SLO 73 D9
Nomeny F 26 C5
Nomexy F 26 D5
Nomia GR 178 B5
Nonancourt F 24 C5
Nonantola I 66 C3
Nonaspe E 42 E4
None I 37 B7
Nonnenweier D 186 E4
Nonnweiler D 21 E7
Nontron F 29 D7
Nonza F 37 F10
Nõo EST 131 E13
Noordwijk aan Zee NL 182 A4
Noordwijk-Binnen NL 16 D2
Noordwijkerhout NL 16 D3
Noordwolde NL 16 C6
Noormarkku FIN 126 B6
Nootdorp NL 182 A4
Nopankylä FIN 122 E8
Noppikoski S 102 D8
Nor S 103 C11
Nora S 97 C13
Nora S 103 A12
Nørager DK 86 B5
Noragugume I 64 C2
Norberg S 97 B14
Norcia I 62 B4
Nordagutu N 95 D10
Nordanå S 103 A13
Nordanås S 107 C14
Nordanås S 109 E16
Nordanås S 109 F11
Nordanede S 103 A11
Nordankäl S 107 D10
Nordannälden S 105 E16
Nordano S 98 B6
Nordborg DK 86 E5
Nordbotn N 112 D9
Nordby DK 86 D7
Nordby DK 86 E2
Norddeich D 17 A8
NorŠdepil FO 2 A3
Norddorf D 82 A4
Norddyrøy N 104 D5
Nordeide N 100 D3
Nordeidet N 112 D4
Norden D 17 A8
Nordendorf D 75 E8
Nordenham D 17 B10
Nordenskov DK 86 D3
Norderåsen S 106 E7
Norderney D 17 A8
Norderö S 105 E16
Norderstedt D 83 C8
Nordfjord N 114 B8
Nordfjordbotn N 111 B17
Nordfjordeid N 100 C3
Nordfold N 110 E9
Nordhalben D 75 B10
Nordhallen S 105 E13
Nordhastedt D 82 B6
Nordhausen D 79 D8
Nordheim D 27 B11
Nordholz D 17 A11
Nordhorn D 17 D8
Nordhuglo N 94 C3
Nordingrå S 103 A15
Nordkil N 111 D10
Nordkirchen D 17 E9
Nordkisa N 95 B14
Nordkjosbotn N 111 B18
Nordland N 110 E4
Nord-Leirvåg N 114 D7
Nordlenangen N 111 A19
Nordli N 105 C15
Nördlingen D 75 E7
Nordmaling S 107 D17
Nordmannvik N 112 D5
Nordmela N 111 B10
Nordnesøy N 108 C4
Nordøyvågen N 108 D4
NorŠragøta FO 2 A3
Nordråk N 101 E12
Nordsand N 111 C12
Nordsinni N 101 E11
Nordsjö S 103 C12
Nordsjö S 107 D10
Nordsjona N 108 D5
NorŠskáli FO 2 A2
Nordskjør N 104 C8
Nordskot N 110 E8
Nordstemmen D 78 B6
Nord-Værnes N 108 C5
Nordvågen N 113 B17
Nordvik N 108 B9
Nordvik S 103 A14
Nordvika N 104 E4
Nordwalde D 17 D8
Nore S 103 C11
Noreikiškės LT 137 D8
Norem N 105 D10
Noreña E 39 B8
Noresund N 95 B11
Norg NL 17 B6
Norheimsund N 94 B4
Norinkylä FIN 122 E8
Norje S 88 C7
Norma I 62 D3
Norn S 97 B14
Nornäs S 102 D5
Noroy-le-Bourg F 26 E5
Norppa FIN 123 C11
Norra Åsum S 88 D6
Norra Blommaberg S 103 C9
Norra Bredåker S 118 C6
Norra bro S 92 A6
Norra Fjällnäs S 109 E10
Norra Holmnäs S 118 C3
Norråker S 106 C9
Norra Klagshamn S 87 D11
Norra Malånäs S 107 A15
Norra Prästholm S 118 C8
Norra Rödupp S 118 B9
Norra Skärvången S 105 D16
Norra Vallgrund FIN 122 D6
Norra Vi S 92 D6
Norrbäck S 103 B12
Norrbäck S 107 B13
Norrbo S 103 C12
Norrboda S 99 B10
Norrboda S 103 D9
Norrby FIN 122 C9
Norrby S 99 B11
Norrbyberg S 107 B14
Norrbyn S 122 C3
Norrbyskär S 122 C3
Nørre Aaby DK 86 E5
Nørre Alslev DK 84 A1
Nørreballe DK 83 A10
Nørre Bork DK 86 D2
Nørre Broby DK 86 E6
Nørre Felding DK 86 C3
Nørre Halne DK 86 A5
Nørre Kongerslev DK 86 B6
Nørre Nebel DK 86 D2
Norrent-Fontes F 18 C5
Nørre Snede DK 86 D4
Nørresundby DK 86 A5
Nørre Vejrup DK 86 D3
Nørre Vorupør DK 86 B2
Norrfällsviken S 107 F15
Norrfjärden S 103 B13
Norrfjärden S 118 D7
Norrfjärden S 122 C5
Norrflärke S 107 D14
Norrfors S 107 C14
Norrfors S 107 D15
Norrgårdssälen S 102 E6
Norr-Greningen S 106 E8
Norrhult-Klavreström S 89 A8
Norrköping S 93 B8
Norrlångträsk S 118 D5
Norr-Moflo S 107 E11
Norrnäs FIN 122 E6
Norrsjön S 106 B8
Norrskedika S 99 B10
Norrstig S 103 A14
Norrstrand S 109 E16
Norrsundet S 103 E13
Norrtälje S 99 C11
Norrtjärn S 103 E12
Norrvåge S 107 E15
Norrvik S 107 B13
Nors DK 86 A3
Norsholm S 92 B7
Norsjö S 107 B17
Nörten-Hardenberg D 78 C6
Northallerton GB 11 C9
Northam GB 12 C6
Northampton GB 15 C7
North Berwick GB 5 C11
Northborough GB 11 F11
North Cave GB 11 D10
North Dell GB 2 J4
North Duffield GB 11 D10
Northeim D 79 C6
North Ferriby GB 11 D10
North Grimston GB 11 C10
North Hykeham GB 11 E10
North Leigh GB 13 B12
North Shields GB 5 E14
North Somercotes GB 11 E12
North Sunderland GB 5 D13
North Tidworth GB 13 C11
Northton GB 2 K2
North Walsham GB 15 B11
Northwich GB 10 E6
Nortmoor D 17 B9
Norton GB 11 C10
Norton GB 15 C10
Norton Fitzwarren GB 13 C8
Nortorf D 83 B7
Nortrup D 17 C9
Nort-sur-Erdre F 23 F8
Norup DK 86 B6
Norvasalmi FIN 117 E15
Norwich GB 15 B11
Norwick GB 3 D15
Noșlac RO 152 E3
Nøss N 111 B10
Nossa Senhora da Boa Fé P 50 B3
Nossa Senhora da Graça de Póvoa e Meadas P 44 E5
Nossa Senhora da Graça do Divor P 50 B4
Nossa Senhora da Graça dos Degolados P 45 F6
Nossa Senhora das Neves P 50 C4
Nossa Senhora de Machede P 50 B4
Nossebro S 91 C12
Nossen D 80 D4
Nossendorf D 84 C3
Nossentiner Hütte D 83 C12
Noszlop H 149 B8
Noszvaj H 145 H1
Notaresco I 62 B5
Notia GR 169 B7
Nőtincs H 147 F8
Nötö FIN 126 F6
Noto I 59 F7
Notodden N 95 C10
Notre-Dame-de-Bellecombe F 31 D10
Notre-Dame-de-Gravenchon F 18 F2
Notre-Dame-de-Monts F 28 B1
Notre-Dame-d'Oé F 24 F4
Nötsch im Gailtal A 73 C8
Nottensdorf D 82 D7
Nottingham GB 11 F9
Nottuln D 17 E8
Notviken S 118 C8
Nouan-le-Fuzelier F 24 E7
Nouans-les-Fontaines F 24 F5
Nouart F 19 F11
Nõuni EST 131 E13
Nousiainen FIN 126 D7
Nousionmäki FIN 125 D10
Nousu FIN 115 D5
Nouvion F 18 D4
Nouzilly F 24 E4
Nouzonville F 19 E10
Nõva EST 130 C7
Nova H 149 C7
Nová Baňa SK 147 E7
Nova Breznica MK 164 F3
Nova Bukovica HR 149 E9
Nová Bystřice CZ 77 D8
Nová Cerekev CZ 77 D8
Novachene BG 165 B10
Novachene BG 165 D8
Novaci MK 168 B5
Novaci RO 160 C3
Nova Crnja SRB 158 B6
Nová Dedina SK 147 E7
Novadnieki LV 134 C4
Nová Dubnica SK 146 D6
Novafeltria I 66 E5
Nova Gorica SLO 73 E8
Nova Gradiška HR 157 B7
Nova Ivanivka UA 154 F4
Novaj H 145 H1
Novajidrány H 145 G3
Nova Kamena BG 161 F10
Nova Kasaba BIH 157 D11
Novaki HR 148 E5
Novakovo BG 166 F4
Nováky SK 147 D7
Novales E 40 B3
Novales E 41 D11
Nova Levante I 72 D4
Novalja HR 67 C10
Novallas E 41 E8
Nová Ľubovňa SK 145 E2
Nova Makhala BG 165 F9
Nova Nadezhda BG 166 E5
Nova Nekrasivka UA 155 C3
Nová Paka CZ 77 B9
Nova Pazova SRB 158 D5
Nova Pokrovka UA 155 B4
Novara I 68 C6
Novara di Sicilia I 59 C7
Nová Role CZ 75 B12
Nova Sela HR 157 F8
Nova Siri I 61 C7
Nova Siri Scalo I 61 C7
Novate Mezzola I 69 A7
Nova Topola BIH 157 B7
Nova Varoš SRB 163 C8
Nova Vas SLO 73 E9
Nová Včelnice CZ 77 D8
Nová Ves CZ 77 B8
Nová Ves nad Šitavou SK 146 E6
Nova Zagora BG 166 E6
Nové Hrady CZ 77 E7
Novelda E 56 E3
Novellara I 66 C2
Nové Město nad Metuj CZ 77 B10
Nové Mesto nad Váhom SK 146 D5
Nové Město na Moravé CZ 77 C10
Nové Město pod Smrkem CZ 81 E8
Nove Misto UA 145 D6
Noventa di Piave I 72 E6
Noventa Vicentina I 66 B4
Novés E 46 D4
Noves F 35 C8
Nové Veselí CZ 77 C9
Nové Zámky SK 146 F6
Novgorodka RUS 133 B5
Novgrad BG 161 F7
Novi Banovci SRB 158 D5
Novi Bečej SRB 158 B5
Novi di Modena I 66 C2
Novi Dojran MK 169 B8
Noviergas E 41 E7
Novi Grad BIH 157 B9
Novigrad HR 67 B8
Novigrad HR 156 D4
Novigrad Podravski HR 149 D7
Novi Iskŭr BG 165 D7
Novi Karlovci SRB 158 C5
Novi Khan BG 165 D8
Novi Kneževac SRB 150 E5
Novi Kozarci SRB 150 F6
Novi Ligure I 37 B9
Novillars F 26 F5
Noville B 182 D5
Novi Marof HR 149 D6
Novion-Porcien F 19 E9
Novi Pazar BG 167 C8
Novi Pazar SRB 163 C10
Novi Sad SRB 158 C4
Novi Šeher BIH 157 C9
Novi Slankamen SRB 158 C5
Novi Travnik BIH 157 D8
Novi Vinodolski HR 67 B10
Novo Beograd SRB 158 D5
Novoborysivka UA 154 C5
Novočići BIH 157 F9
Novo Delchevo BG 169 B9
Novokhovansk RUS 133 E7
Novo Korito SRB 159 F9
Novo Mesto SLO 73 E11
Novo Miloševo SRB 158 B5
Novomoskovskiy RUS 139 A9
Novomykolayivka UA 155 B5
Novo Orahovo SRB 150 F4
Novo Oryakhovo BG 167 D9
Novopetrivka UA 154 C5
Novorzhev RUS 133 B6
Novosamarka UA 154 B5
Novosedly CZ 77 E11
Novoselë AL 163 F10
Novoselë AL 168 C1
Novoselec HR 149 E7
Novoselets BG 166 E6
Novoselija BIH 157 C7
Novoselivka UA 154 B5
Novoselivka UA 154 D5
Novo Selo BG 159 E10
Novo Selo BG 161 F8
Novo Selo BG 165 E6
Novo Selo BG 166 F6
Novo Selo BIH 157 B8
Novo Selo BIH 157 B9
Novo Selo MK 169 B8
Novo Selo SRB 159 F6
Novoselovo RUS 139 B9
Novoseltsi BG 167 E8
Novosel'ye RUS 132 E4
Novoselytsya UA 153 A8
Novoselytsya UA 154 A6
Novosil's'ke UA 155 C3
Novostroyevo RUS 136 E4
Novot SK 147 C8
Novo Virje HR 149 D8
Novovolyns'k UA 144 B9
Novoyavorivs'ke UA 144 D8
Novska HR 149 F7
Nový Bor CZ 81 E7
Nový Bydžov CZ 77 B8
Novy-Chevrières F 19 E9
Novy Dvor BY 137 F10
Nový Hrozenkov CZ 146 C6
Nový Jičín CZ 146 B5
Nový Knín CZ 76 C6
Nový Malín CZ 77 C12
Novy Pahost BY 133 F2
Nový Rychnov CZ 77 D8
Novyya Kruki BY 133 E3
Novyy Izborsk RUS 132 F2
Novyy Rozdil UA 145 E9
Nový Život SK 146 E4
Nowa Brzeźnica PL 143 D7
Nowa Cerekwia PL 142 F4
Nowa Chodorówka PL 140 C8
Nowa Djba PL 143 F12
Nowa Karczma PL 138 B5
Nowa Ruda PL 81 E11
Nowa Sarzyna PL 144 C5
Nowa Słupia PL 143 E11
Nowa Sól PL 81 C9
Nowa Sucha PL 141 F2
Nowa Wieś Ełcka PL 140 C6
Nowa Wieś Ljborskie PL 85 A13
Nowa Wieś Wielka PL 138 E5
Nowa Wola PL 140 D9
Nowa Wola Gołjbiowska PL 141 H4
Nowe PL 138 C6
Nowe Brusno PL 144 C7
Nowe Brzesko PL 143 F9
Nowe Czarnowo PL 84 D6
Nowe Miasteczko PL 81 C9
Nowe Miasto PL 139 E10
Nowe Miasto Lubawskie PL 139 D8
Nowe Miasto nad Pilicą PL 141 G3
Nowe Miasto nad Wartą PL 81 B12
Nowe Ostrowy PL 143 B7
Nowe Piekuty PL 141 E7
Nowe Skalmierzyce PL 142 C4
Nowe Warpno PL 84 C6
Nowinka PL 136 F6
Nowogard PL 85 C8
Nowogród PL 139 D12
Nowogród Bobrzański PL 81 C8
Nowogródek Pomorski PL 85 E8
Nowogrodziec PL 81 D8
Nowosady PL 141 E9
Nowosielce PL 145 D5
Nowosolna PL 143 C8
Nowotaniec PL 145 D5
Nowowola PL 140 D8
Nowy Bartków PL 141 F7
Nowy Duninów PL 139 E7
Nowy Dwór PL 138 D4
Nowy Dwór PL 140 C9
Nowy Dwór Gdański PL 138 B7
Nowy Dwór Mazowiecki PL 139 F10
Nowy Kawjczyn PL 141 G2
Nowy Korczyn PL 143 F10
Nowy Lubliniec PL 144 C7
Nowy Sącz PL 145 D2
Nowy Staw PL 138 B7
Nowy Targ PL 147 C10
Nowy Tomyśl PL 81 B10
Nowy Wiśnicz PL 144 D1
Nowy Żmigród PL 145 D4
Noyal-Muzillac F 22 E7
Noyalo F 22 E6
Noyal-Pontivy F 22 D6
Noyant F 23 E12

Noyarey F 31 E8
Noyen-sur-Sarthe F 23 E11
Noyers F 25 E10
Noyers-sur-Cher F 24 F5
Noyers-sur-Jabron F 35 B10
Noyon F 18 E6
Nozay F 23 E8
Nozdrzec PL 144 D5
Nozeroy F 31 B9
Nuaillé-d'Aunis F 28 C4
Nuasjärvi FIN 117 E13
Nubledo E 39 A8
Nucet RO 151 E10
Nuci RO 161 D8
Nucşoara RO 160 C5
Nudersdorf D 79 C12
Nüdlingen D 75 B7
Nudyzhe UA 141 H10
Nueil-les-Aubiers F 28 B4
Nuenen NL 16 F5
Nueno E 41 D11
Nueva E 39 B10
Nueva-Carteya E 53 A8
Nueva Jarilla E 52 C4
Nuez de Ebro E 41 E10
Nufăru RO 155 C3
Nughedu di San Nicolò I 64 B3
Nuijamaa FIN 129 D10
Nuillé-sur-Vicoin F 23 E10
Nuits F 25 E11
Nuits-St-Georges F 26 F2
Nukari FIN 127 D12
Nukši LV 133 D3
Nuland NL 16 E4
Nule I 64 C3
Nules E 48 E4
Nulvi I 64 B2
Numana I 67 E8
Numansdorp NL 16 E2
Nummela FIN 127 E11
Nummi FIN 127 E10
Nummijärvi FIN 122 F8
Nummikoski FIN 122 F9
Nünchritz D 80 D4
Nuneaton GB 11 F9
Nunkirchen D 186 C2
Nunnanen FIN 117 B12
Nunnanlahti FIN 125 D12
Nuñomoral E 45 D8
Nunsdorf D 80 B4
Nunspeet NL 16 D5
Nuojua FIN 119 E17
Nuoksujärvi S 116 E9
Nuolijärvi FIN 125 C11
Nuoramoinen FIN 127 C14
Nuorgam FIN 113 C20
Nuoritta FIN 119 D16
Nuoro I 64 C3
Nuorunka FIN 120 C9
Nuottavaara FIN 117 D12
Nuottikylä FIN 121 E12
Nur PL 141 E6
Nuragus I 64 D3
Nurallao I 64 D3
Nuraminis I 64 E3
Nureci I 64 D2
Nuriye TR 177 B10
Nurmaa FIN 128 C6
Nurmes FIN 125 C12
Nurmesperä FIN 123 C15
Nurmijärvi FIN 125 C13
Nurmijärvi FIN 127 E12
Nurmo FIN 123 E9
Nürnberg D 75 D9
Nurney IRL 7 F9
Nurri I 64 D3
Nurste EST 130 D4
Nürtingen D 27 C11
Nurzec-Stacja PL 141 F8
Nus I 31 D11
Nusco I 60 B4
Nuşeni RO 152 C4
Nuşfalău RO 151 C10
Nusfjord N 110 D5
Nusnäs S 102 E8
Nusplingen D 27 D10
Nußbach A 76 G6
Nußdorf D 73 A6
Nußdorf am Inn D 72 A5
Nuštar HR 149 F11
Nustrup DK 86 E4
Nuth NL 19 C12
Nutheim N 95 C9
Nuttuperä FIN 123 C15
Nuuksujärvi S 116 C8
Nuupas FIN 119 B16
Nuutajärvi FIN 127 C9
Nuutila FIN 119 F16
Nuutilanmaki FIN 128 B8
Nuvsvåg N 112 C9
Nuvvus FIN 113 D17
Nuxis I 64 E2
Nüziders A 71 C9
Nya Bastuselet S 109 F16
Nyåker S 107 D13
Nyåker S 107 D16
Nyárád H 149 B8
Nyáregyháza H 150 C4
Nyárlőrinc H 150 D4
Nyársapát H 150 C4
Nybble S 91 A15
Nybergsund N 102 D3
Nyborg DK 87 E7
Nyborg N 114 C5
Nyborg S 119 C10
Nybro S 89 B9
Nybrostrand S 88 E5
Nyby FIN 122 E6
Nyby N 113 C15
Nyby S 106 E8
Nybyn S 103 C9
Nybyn S 107 E14
Nybyn S 118 D6
Nýdek CZ 147 B7
Nydri GR 174 B2
Nye S 89 A8
Nyékládháza H 145 H2
Nyelv N 114 C5
Nyergesújfalu H 149 A11
Nyhammar S 97 B12
Nyhem S 103 A10
Nyhem S 109 E14
Ny Højen DK 86 D5
Nyhus N 111 B15
Nyhyttan S 97 C12
Nyírábrány H 151 B9
Nyíracsád H 151 B8
Nyírád H 149 B8
Nyíradony H 151 B8
Nyírbátor H 151 B9
Nyírbéltek H 151 B9
Nyírbogát H 151 B9
Nyírbogdány H 145 G4
Nyíregyháza H 145 H4
Nyírgelse H 151 B8
Nyírgyulaj H 145 H5
Nyíribrony H 145 G4
Nyírkáta H 145 H5
Nyírmada H 145 G5
Nyírmeggyes H 145 H5
Nyírmihálydi H 151 B8
Nyírpazony H 145 H4
Nyírtass H 145 G5
Nyírtelek H 145 G4
Nyírtét H 145 G4
Nyírtura H 145 G4
Nyírvasvári H 151 B9
Nykarleby FIN 122 C9
Nyker DK 89 E7
Nykil S 92 C6
Nykøbing DK 83 A11
Nykøbing Mors DK 86 B3
Nykøbing Sjælland DK 87 D9
Nyköping S 93 B10
Nykrogen S 98 B6
Nykroppa S 97 C11
Nyksund N 110 C9
Nykvåg N 110 C7
Nykvarn S 93 A10
Nykyrke S 92 B5
Nyland S 107 D16
Nyland S 107 E13
Nyland S 122 C3
Nylars DK 89 E7
Nyliden S 107 D15
Nymburk CZ 77 B8
Nymfes GR 168 E2
Nymindegab DK 86 D2
Nymoen N 112 C6
Nynäshamn S 93 B11
Nyneset N 105 C13
Ny Nørup DK 86 D4
Nyoiseau F 23 E10
Nyon CH 31 C9
Nyons F 35 B9
Nyråd DK 87 E9
Nýřany CZ 76 C4
Nýrsko CZ 76 D4
Nyrud N 114 E6
Nysa PL 142 F3
Nysäter S 97 D8
Nysätern S 102 A5
Nysättra S 99 C11
Nysted DK 83 A11
Nysted N 111 C15
Nystrand S 118 C5
Nyträsk S 118 E4
Nytrøa N 111 B16
Nyúl H 149 A9
Nyvoll N 113 C11
Nyzhankovychi UA 144 D6
Nyzhni Petrivtsi UA 153 A7
Nyzhni Vorota UA 145 F7
Nyzhniy Bystryy UA 145 G8
Nyzhnya Vysots'ke UA 145 E7
Nyzhnya Yablun'ka
UA 145 E6

O

Oadby GB 11 F9
Oakengates GB 10 F7
Oakham GB 11 F10
Oakley GB 13 B12
Oakley GB 13 C12
Oakley GB 15 C7
Oancea RO 154 F2
Oandu EST 131 C13
Oarja RO 160 D5
O Arrabal E 38 D2
Oarța de Jos RO 151 C11
Obal' BY 133 E7
Obal' BY 133 F6
Obalj BIH 157 F9
Oban GB 4 C6
O Barco E 39 D6
Obârșia RO 160 F4
Obârșia-Cloșani RO 159 C10
Obârșia de Câmp RO 159 E11
Obbola S 122 C4
Obdach A 73 B10
Obecnice CZ 76 C5
Obedinenie BG 166 C5
Obejo E 54 C3
Obeliai LT 135 E11
Oberaich A 73 B11
Oberalm A 73 A7
Oberammergau D 71 B12
Oberasbach D 75 D8
Oberau D 72 A3
Oberaudorf D 72 A5
Obercunnersdorf D 81 D7
Oberderdingen D 27 B10
Oberding D 75 F10
Oberdorla D 79 D7
Oberdrauburg A 73 C6
Oberegg CH 71 C9
Oberelsbach D 75 B7
Oberfell D 185 D7
Obergebra D 79 D8
Obergösgen CH 27 F8
Ober-Grafendorf A 77 F9
Obergriesbach D 75 F9
Obergünzburg D 71 B10
Obergurgl A 72 C3
Obergurig D 80 D6
Oberhaag A 148 C4
Oberhaid D 75 C8
Oberharmersbach D 27 D9
Oberhausen D 17 F7
Oberhausen D 75 E9
Oberhausen-Rheinhausen
D 187 C5
Oberheldrungen D 79 D9
Oberhof D 79 E8
Oberhofen CH 70 D5
Oberhoffen-sur-Moder F 186 D4
Oberkirch D 27 C9
Oberkochen D 75 E7
Oberkotzau D 75 B10
Oberlangen D 17 C8
Oberlungwitz D 79 E12
Obermarchtal D 71 A9
Obermaßfeld-Grimmenthal
D 75 A7
Obermoschel D 21 E9
Obernai F 27 D7
Obernberg am Inn A 76 F4
Obernburg am Main D 187 B7
Oberndorf D 17 A12
Oberndorf am Lech D 75 E8
Oberndorf am Neckar D 27 D10
Oberndorf bei Salzburg A 73 A6
Oberneukirchen A 76 F6
Obernfeld D 79 C7
Obernheim D 27 D10
Obernheim-Kirchenarnbach
D 186 C4
Obernkirchen D 17 D12
Obernzell D 76 E5
Ober-Olm D 185 E9
Oberpullendorf A 149 A7
Oberried D 27 E8
Oberrieden D 71 A10
Oberriet CH 71 C9
Ober-Roden D 21 E11
Oberrot D 187 C8
Oberrotweil D 27 D8
Oberschneiding D 75 E12
Oberschützen A 148 B6
Obersiebenbrunn A 77 F11
Obersinn D 74 B6
Obersontheim D 187 C8
Oberspier D 79 D8
Oberstadion D 71 A9
Oberstaufen D 71 B10
Oberstdorf D 71 C10
Oberstenfeld D 27 B11
Oberthal D 21 E8
Oberthulba D 187 A8
Obertilliach A 73 C6
Obertraubling D 75 E11
Obertrubach D 75 C9
Obertshausen D 21 D11
Oberursel (Taunus) D 21 D11
Obervellach A 73 C7
Oberviechtach D 75 D11
Oberwald CH 70 D6
Oberwart A 148 B6
Oberwesel D 21 D9
Oberwolfach D 187 E5
Oberwölz A 73 B9
Óbidos P 44 F2
Obiliq RKS 164 D3
Obing D 75 F11
Obinitsa EST 132 F1
Obitel BG 167 C7
Objat F 29 E8
Objazda PL 85 A12
Öblarn A 73 B8
Oblešovo MK 164 F5
Oblikë e Madhe AL 163 E7
Obnova BG 165 C10
Obodivka UA 154 A4
Oboga RO 160 E4
O Bolo E 38 D5
Obón E 42 F2
Oborci BIH 157 D7
Oborín SK 145 F4
Oborishte BG 165 D9
Oborniki PL 81 A11
Oborniki Śląskie PL 81 D11
Obrazów PL 143 E12
Obreja RO 159 C9
Obrenovac SRB 158 D5
Obretenik BG 166 B5
Obrež SRB 158 D4
Obrež SRB 159 F7
Obrigheim D 21 F12
Obrigheim (Pfalz) D 187 B5
Obrnice CZ 76 A5
Obrochishte BG 167 C10
Obrov SLO 67 A9
Obrovac HR 156 D4
Obrovac SRB 158 C3
Obrowo PL 138 E6
Obrtići BIH 157 E10
Obruchishte BG 166 E5
Obryte PL 139 E11
Obrzycko PL 85 E11
Obsza PL 144 C6
Obudovac BIH 157 C10
Obyce SK 146 E6
Obzor BG 167 D9
O Cádavo E 38 B5
Ocaklar TR 173 D8
O Campo da Feira E 38 B3
Ocaña E 46 E6
Ocana F 37 H9
O Carballiño E 38 D3
O Castelo E 38 D3
O Castro E 38 C3
O Castro de Ferreira E 38 C4
Occhiobello I 66 C4
Occimiano I 68 C6
Očevlja BIH 157 D9
Ochagavía E 32 E3
O Chao E 38 B4
Ochiltree GB 5 E8
Ochla PL 81 C8
Ochodnica SK 147 C7
Ocholt D 17 B9
Ochsenfurt D 75 C7
Ochsenhausen D 71 A9
Ochtrup D 17 D8
Ocke S 105 E15
Ockelbo S 103 E12
Öckerö S 91 D10
Ockholm D 82 A5
Ocksjön S 102 A8
Ocland RO 152 E6
Ocna de Fier RO 159 C8
Ocna Mureş RO 152 E3
Ocna Sibiului RO 152 F4
Ocna Şugatag RO 152 B3
Ocnele Mari RO 160 C4
Ocniţa RO 161 D7
Ocolina MD 154 A2
Ocoliş RO 151 E11
O Convento E 38 D2
O Corgo E 38 C5
Ocrkavlje BIH 157 E10
Öcsa H 150 C3
Öcsény H 149 D11
Öcsöd H 150 D5
Octeville-sur-Mer F 23 A12
Ocypel PL 138 C5
Odăile RO 161 C9
Ödåkra S 87 C11
Odda N 94 B5
Odden N 112 D5
Oddense DK 86 B3
Odder DK 86 D6
Oddsta GB 3 D15
Ödeborg S 91 B10
Odeceixe P 50 E2
Odeleite P 50 E5
Odelouca P 50 E3
Odelzhausen D 75 F9
Odemira P 50 D2
Ödena E 43 D7
Odensbacken S 92 A7
Odensberg S 91 C13
Odense DK 86 E6
Odensjö S 92 D4
Odensvi S 93 D8
Oderberg D 84 E6
Oderin D 80 B5
Odernheim am Glan D 21 E9
Oderzo I 72 E5
Ödeshog S 92 C5
Odiáxere P 50 E2
Odiham GB 15 E7
Ødis DK 86 E4
Odivelas P 50 B1
Odivelas P 50 C3
Ödkarby FIN 99 B13
Odobeşti RO 153 F10
Odobeşti RO 161 D7
Odolanów PL 142 C4
Odolena Voda CZ 76 B6
Odón E 47 C9
Odoorn NL 17 C7
Odorheiu Secuiesc RO 152 E6
Odry CZ 146 B5
Odrzywół PL 141 G3
Ödsmål S 91 C10
Ødsted DK 86 D4
Odŭrne BG 165 C10
Odžaci BIH 157 E9
Odžaci SRB 158 B3
Odžak BIH 157 B9
Odžak BIH 157 E6
Odžak BIH 157 F9
Odžak MNE 163 C7
Odziena LV 135 C11
Oebisfelde D 79 B8
Oedelem B 182 C2
Oedelsheim (Oberweser) D 78 C6
Oederan D 80 E4
Oeffelt NL 16 E5
Oegstgeest NL 16 D3
Oeiras P 50 B1
Oelde D 17 E10
Oelixdorf D 82 C7
Oelsnitz D 75 B11
Oelsnitz D 79 E12
Oene NL 183 A8
Oenkerk NL 16 B5
Oensingen CH 27 F8
Oerel D 17 B12
Oering D 83 C8
Oerlenbach D 75 B7
Oerlinghausen D 17 E11
Oestrich-Winkel D 21 D9
Oettersdorf D 79 E10
Oettingen in Bayern D 75 E8
Oetz A 71 C11
Oetzen D 83 D9
Oeversee D 82 A6
Œyreluy F 32 C3
Ofatinţi MD 154 B4
Ófehértó H 145 H5
Ofena I 62 C5
Offanengo I 69 C8
Offemont F 27 E6
Offenbach am Main D 21 D11
Offenbach an der Queich
D 187 C5
Offenberg D 76 E3
Offenburg D 27 D8
Offerdal S 105 E16
Offersøy N 111 D10
Offida I 62 B5
Offingen D 75 F7
Offranville F 18 E3
O Forte E 38 C3
Ofte N 95 D8
Ofterdingen D 27 D11
Oftersheim D 21 F11
Ogenbargen D 17 A9
Oger F 25 C11
Ogeu-les-Bains F 32 D4
Ogéviller F 26 C6
Oggevatn N 90 C3
Ogliastro F 37 F10
Ogliastro Cilento I 60 C4
Ogmore GB 13 C7
Ognyanovo BG 169 A10
Ogonelloe IRL 8 C6
Ogoya BG 165 D8
Ogra RO 152 E4
Ogre LV 135 C9
Ogren AL 168 D3
Ogresgals LV 135 C9
Ogrezeni RO 161 E7
Ogrodniki PL 139 E12
Ogrodzieniec PL 143 F8
Ogrosen D 80 C6
O Grove E 38 D2
Ogulin HR 67 B11
Oğulpaşa TR 172 A6
Ohaba RO 152 E3
Ohaba Lungă RO 151 F8
Ohanes E 55 E7
Ohey B 19 D11
Ohkola FIN 127 D13
Ohlsbach D 27 D8
Ohlstadt D 72 A3
Ohne D 17 D8
Ohorn D 80 D6
Ohrady SK 146 E5
Ohrdruf D 79 E8
Ohrid MK 168 B4
Öhringen D 27 B11
Ohtaanniemi FIN 125 E11
Ohtanajärvi S 116 E10
Ohukotsu EST 131 C9
Oia GR 179 C9
Oiã P 44 C3
Oiartzun E 32 D2
Oichalia GR 169 E6
Øie N 105 B12
Oignies F 18 D6
O Igrexario E 38 D3
Oijärvi FIN 119 C15
Oijen NL 183 B6
Oijusluoma FIN 121 C13
Oikarainen FIN 119 B16
Oileán Ciarraí IRL 8 D4
Oilgate IRL 9 D9
Oímbra E 38 E5
Oinacu RO 161 F8
Oinas FIN 115 E2
Oinasjärvi FIN 124 C9
Oinofyta GR 175 C8
Oinoi GR 175 C7
Oion E 41 C7
O Irixo E 38 C3
Oiron F 28 B5
Oirschot NL 183 B6
Oiselay-et-Grachaux F 26 F4
Oisemont F 18 E4
Oisseau F 23 D10
Oissel F 18 F3
Oisterwijk NL 183 B6
Oisu EST 131 D11
Öisu EST 131 E11
Oitti FIN 127 D13
Oituz RO 153 E9
Oitylo GR 178 B3
Oivanki FIN 121 B13
Oizon F 25 F8
Öja FIN 123 C9
Öja S 93 E12
Ojakkala FIN 127 E11
Ojakylä FIN 119 D13
Ojakylä FIN 119 D14
Ojakylä FIN 119 F15
Ojanperä FIN 120 F8
Öjarn S 106 D8
Ojdula RO 153 F8
Öje S 102 E6
Öjebyn S 118 D6
Öjeforsen S 103 B9
Ojén E 53 C7
Öjingsvallen S 103 C8
Ojos Negros E 47 C10
Ojrzeń PL 139 E10
Öjung S 103 C10
Okalewo PL 139 D8
Okány H 151 D7
Okçular TR 181 C9
Økdal N 101 A12
Okehampton GB 12 D6
Okhotnoye RUS 136 D4
Oklaj HR 156 E5
Oknö S 89 A11
Okoč SK 146 F5
Okonek PL 85 C11
Okopy PL 141 H9
Ököritófülpös H 145 H6
Okorsh BG 161 F10
Okříšky CZ 77 D9
Okrouhlice CZ 77 C8
Okrúhle SK 145 E4
Oksa PL 143 E9
Öksajärvi S 116 C8
Oksakoski FIN 123 D12
Oksava FIN 123 C14
Oksbøl DK 86 D2
Oksbøl DK 86 E5
Øksfjord N 112 C9
Øksnes N 110 C8
Øksneshamn N 110 D9
Oksvoll N 104 D7
Oktonia GR 175 B9
Okučani HR 157 B7
Ola E 38 D2
Olague E 32 E2
Olaine LV 135 C7
Olalhas P 44 E4
Oland N 90 B3
Olăneşti MD 154 E5
Olanu RO 160 D4
Olargues F 34 C4
Olari RO 151 E8
Olaszliszka H 145 G3
Olave E 32 E2
Oława PL 81 E12
Olazti E 32 E1
Olba E 48 D3
Olbendorf A 148 B6
Olbernhau D 80 E4
Olbersdorf D 81 E7
Olbersleben D 79 D9
Olbia I 64 B3
Olbiĉjin PL 144 B5
Olbramovice CZ 77 C7
Olcea RO 151 D8
Oldcastle IRL 7 E8
Old Dailly GB 4 E7
Oldebroek NL 16 D5
Oldedalen N 100 C5
Oldehove NL 16 B6
Oldeide N 100 C2
Oldemarkt NL 16 C5
Olden N 100 C5
Olden S 105 D15
Oldenbrok D 17 B10
Oldenburg D 17 B10
Oldenburg in Holstein D 83 B9
Oldendorf D 17 A12
Oldenswort D 82 B5
Oldenzaal NL 17 D7
Olderdalen N 112 D6
Oldereid N 108 B8
Olderfjord N 113 C15
Oldernes N 113 C13
Oldervik N 108 C5
Oldervik N 111 A18
Oldervik N 113 B13
Oldham GB 11 D7
Old Head IRL 8 E5
Oldisleben D 79 D9
Old Leake GB 11 E12
Oldmeldrum GB 3 L12
Oldsum D 82 A4
Oldtown IRL 7 E10
Oleby S 97 B9
Olecko PL 136 E6
Oleggio I 68 B6
Oleiros P 44 E5
Oleksandrivka UA 154 C6
Olekseyivka UA 154 B3
Olemps F 33 B11
Olen B 19 B10
Ølen N 94 C3
Olesa de Montserrat E 43 D7
Oleśnica PL 142 D3
Oleśnica PL 143 F11
Olešnice CZ 77 C10
Olesno PL 142 E5
Olesno PL 143 F10
Oleszyce PL 144 C7
Olette F 33 E10
Olevano Romano I 62 D4
Olfen D 17 E8
Olgina EST 132 C3
Olginate I 69 B7
Ølgod DK 86 D3
Olgrinmore GB 3 J9
Olhalvo P 44 F2
Olhão P 50 E4
Olhava FIN 119 D14
Ølholm DK 86 D5
Olho Marinho P 44 F2
Ol'hopil' UA 154 A5
Oliana E 43 C6
Olías del Rey E 46 E5
Oliena I 64 C3
Oliete E 42 E2
Oligastro Marina I 60 C3
Olingdal S 102 C7
Olingsjövallen S 102 C7
Oliola E 42 D6
Olite E 32 F2
Oliva E 56 D4
Oliva de la Frontera E 51 C6
Oliva de Mérida E 51 B7
Olival P 44 E3
Olivares E 51 E7
Olivares de Júcar E 47 E8
Oliveira de Azeméis P 44 C4
Oliveira de Frades P 44 C4
Oliveira do Arda P 44 B4
Oliveira do Bairro P 44 C4
Oliveira do Conde P 44 D5
Oliveira do Douro P 44 B3
Oliveira do Hospital P 44 D5
Olivenza E 51 B5
Oliveri I 59 C7
Olivet F 24 E6
Oliveto Citra I 60 B4
Oliveto Lucano I 60 B6
Olivone CH 71 D7
Oľka SK 145 E4
Olkijoki FIN 119 E13
Olkiluoto FIN 126 C5
Olkkajärvi FIN 117 E16
Olkusz PL 143 F8
Ollaberry GB 3 D14
Ollerton GB 11 E9
Ollerup DK 86 E7
Olliergues F 30 D4
Ollila FIN 121 B13
Ollila FIN 127 D8
Ollilanniemi FIN 121 E12
Ollioules F 35 D10
Ollo E 32 E2
Öllölä FIN 125 F15
Ollolai I 64 C3
Ollon CH 31 C10
Ollsta S 106 E8
Ölmbrotorp S 97 D13
Ölme S 97 D11
Olmedilla de Roa E 40 E4
Olmedo E 46 B3
Olmedo I 64 B1
Olmeta-di-Tuda F 37 F10
Olmeto F 37 H9
Olmos de Ojeda E 40 C3
Olney GB 15 C7
Olocau E 48 E3
Olocau del Rey E 42 F3
Olofsfors S 107 D16
Olofstorp S 91 D11
Olofström S 88 C7
Olombrada E 40 F3
Olomouc CZ 146 B4
Olonne-sur-Mer F 28 B2
Olonzac F 34 D4
Oloron-Ste-Marie F 32 D4
Olost E 43 D8
Olot E 43 C8
Oloví CZ 75 B12
Olovo BIH 157 D10
Olpe D 21 B9
Olřišov CZ 142 G4
Olšany CZ 77 C11
Olšany u Prostějova CZ 77 C12
Olsätter S 97 C10
Olsbenning S 97 B15
Olsberg D 17 F10
Olsberg N 111 B16
Ölsboda S 92 A4
Olsfors S 91 D12
Olshammar S 92 B5
Olsøy N 104 D8
Olst NL 16 D6
Ølsted DK 86 D5
Ølsted DK 87 D10
Ølstykke DK 87 D10
Olszanica PL 145 E5
Olszanka PL 142 E3
Olszany PL 144 D6
Olszewo-Borki PL 139 D12
Olsztyn PL 136 F1
Olsztyn PL 143 E7
Olsztynek PL 139 C9
Olszyn PL 141 F8
Olszyna PL 81 D8
Olszyny PL 144 D2
Oltedal N 94 E4
Olten CH 27 F8
Olteneşti RO 153 D11
Olteni RO 160 E6
Olteniţa RO 161 E9
Oltina RO 155 E1
Olula del Río E 55 E8
Olustvere EST 131 D11
Olvan E 43 C7
Olvasjärvi FIN 120 D9
Ólvega E 41 E8
Olvena E 42 C4
Olvera E 51 F9
Olympiada GR 169 C10
Olympiada GR 169 E7
Olympos GR 181 E6
Olzai I 64 C3
Oma N 94 B3
Omagh GB 4 F2
Omalos GR 178 E6
Omarchevo BG 166 E6
Omarska BIH 157 C6
Ombersley GB 13 A10
Omedu EST 131 D14
Omegna I 68 B5
Ömerköy TR 173 E9
Ömerli TR 173 D9
O Mesón do Vento E 38 B3
Omessa F 37 G10
Omiš HR 157 F6
Omišalj HR 67 B10
Ommen NL 16 C6
Omne S 107 F14
Omolio GR 169 E8
Omoljica SRB 159 D6
Omont F 19 E10
Ömossa FIN 122 F7
O Mosteiro E 38 C2
Omurtag BG 167 C6
Omvriaki GR 174 A5
Oña E 40 C5
Ona N 100 A5
Onani I 64 C3
Onano I 62 B1
Oñati E 32 D1
Oncala E 41 E7
Onceşti RO 153 E10
Onchan GBM 10 C3
Onda E 48 E4
Ondara E 56 D5
Ondarroa E 32 D1
Ondřejov CZ 77 C7
Ondres F 32 C3
Oneglia I 37 D8
Onesse-et-Laharie F 32 B3
Oneşti RO 153 E9
Onet-le-Château F 33 B11
Ongles F 35 B10
Oniceni RO 153 D10
Onich GB 4 B6
Onifai I 64 C4
Oniferi I 64 C3
Oniţcani MD 154 C4
Onkamaa FIN 128 D7
Onkamo FIN 115 E6
Onkamo FIN 119 D15
Onkamo FIN 125 F14
Onkiniemi FIN 127 C15
Önnestad S 88 C6
Önningby FIN 99 B14
Ónod H 145 G2
Onøya N 108 D4
Onsala S 91 E11
Onsbjerg DK 86 D7
Ønslev DK 83 A11
Onslunda S 88 D6
Onstmettingen D 27 D10
Onstwedde NL 17 B8
Ontiñena E 42 D4
Ontinyent E 56 D3
Ontojoki FIN 125 B11
Ontronvara RUS 125 E16
Onttola FIN 125 E13
Ontur E 55 B10
Onuškis LT 135 D11
Onuškis LT 137 E10
Onzain F 24 E5
Onzonilla E 39 C8
Oola IRL 8 C6
Ooltgensplaat NL 16 E2
Oonurme EST 131 C13
Oostakker B 19 B8
Oostburg NL 19 B7
Oostende B 18 B6
Oostendorp NL 16 D5
Oosterbeek NL 183 B7
Oosterend NL 16 B3
Oosterhesselen NL 17 C7
Oosterhout NL 16 E3
Oosterland NL 16 E2
Oosterwolde NL 16 C6
Oosterzele B 19 C8
Oostham B 183 C6
Oosthuizen NL 16 C3
Oostkamp B 19 B7
Oostkapelle NL 16 E1
Oostmalle B 182 C5
Oost-Souburg NL 16 F1
Oostvleteren B 18 C6
Oost-Vlieland NL 16 B4
Oostvoorne NL 182 B4
Ootmarsum NL 17 D7
Opaka BG 166 C6
Opalenica PL 81 B10
Opalenie PL 138 C6
Ópályi H 145 H5
Opan BG 166 E5
Opařany CZ 77 D6
Opatija HR 67 B9
Opatov CZ 77 C10
Opatovice nad Labem CZ 77 B9
Opatów PL 142 D5
Opatów PL 142 E6
Opatów PL 143 E11
Opatówek PL 142 C5
Opatowiec PL 143 F10
Opava CZ 146 B5
O Pazo E 38 D3
O Pazo de Irixoa E 38 B3
Ope S 106 E7
O Pedrouzo E 38 C3
Opeinde NL 16 B6
Opfenbach D 71 B9
Opglabbeek B 183 C7
Opheusden NL 183 B7
Opi I 62 D5
Opitter B 183 C7
Oploo NL 183 B7
Oplotnica SLO 148 D4
Opmeer NL 16 C3
Opochka RUS 133 C5
Opočno CZ 77 B10
Opoczno PL 141 H2
Opoeteren B 183 C7
Opole PL 142 E4
Opole Lubelskie PL 141 H5
Oporelu RO 160 D4
Oporets' UA 145 F7
O Porriño E 38 D2
Opoul-Périllos F 34 E4
Opovo SRB 158 C5
Oppach D 81 D7
Oppala S 103 E13
Oppdal N 101 A11
Oppeano I 66 B3
Oppeby S 92 C7
Oppedal N 100 D3
Oppegard N 95 C13
Oppenau D 27 D9
Oppenheim D 21 E10
Oppenweiler D 187 D7
Opphaug N 104 D7
Opphus N 101 D14
Oppido Lucano I 60 B5
Oppido Mamertina I 59 C8
Oppin D 79 C11
Opponitz A 73 A10
Oppurg D 79 E10
Oprisavci HR 157 B9
Oprişor RO 159 E11
Oprtalj HR 67 B8
Opsa BY 135 E13
Opsaheden S 97 B10
Optaşi-Măgura RO 160 D5
Ópusztaszer H 150 E5
Opuzen HR 157 F8
Opwijk B 19 C9
Ór H 145 H5
Ora I 72 D3
Øra N 112 C8
Orada P 50 B5
Oradea RO 151 C8
Oradour-sur-Glane F 29 D8
Oradour-sur-Vayres F 29 D7
Orah BIH 157 F7
Orah BIH 162 D5
Orahovičko Polje BIH 157 D8
Orahova BIH 157 B7
Orahov Do BIH 162 D4
Orahovica HR 149 E9
Oraio GR 171 B7
Oraiokastro GR 169 C8
Oraison F 35 C10
Orajärvi FIN 117 E12
Orakylä FIN 115 D1
Orange F 35 B8
Orani I 64 C3
Oranienburg D 84 E4
Órán Mór IRL 6 F5
Oranmore IRL 6 F5
Orašac BIH 156 C5
Orašac HR 162 D5
Orašac SRB 164 C5
Orašje BIH 157 B10
Orăştie RO 151 F11
Orăştioara de Sus RO 151 F11
Orašu Nou RO 145 H7
Öratjärn S 103 C10

Orava EST 132 F1
Orava FIN 123 D10
Oravainen FIN 122 D8
Oravais FIN 122 D8
Oravala FIN 128 D6
Öravan S 107 B14
Oravankylä FIN 123 C15
Öravattnet S 106 E9
Oravi FIN 125 F11
Oravikoski FIN 124 E9
Oravisalo FIN 125 F13
Oravița RO 159 C8
Oravivaara FIN 121 E11
Oravská Polhora SK 147 B8
Oravské Veselé SK 147 C8
Oravský Podzámok SK 147 C8
Orba E 56 D4
Orbacém P 38 E2
Örbäck S 97 C15
Orbaden S 103 C11
Ørbæk DK 86 E7
Orbais-l'Abbaye F 25 C10
Orbara E 32 E3
Orbassano I 37 A7
Orbe CH 31 B10
Orbeasca RO 160 E6
Orbec F 24 B3
Orbeni RO 153 E10
Orbetello I 65 C4
Örbyhus S 99 B9
Orca P 44 D6
Orce E 55 D8
Orcera E 55 C7
Orchamps-Vennes F 26 F6
Orchies F 19 D7
Orchomenos GR 175 C6
Orchów PL 143 C7
Orchowo PL 138 E5
Orciano di Pesaro I 67 E6
Orcières F 36 B4
Orcival F 30 D2
Ordan-Larroque F 33 C6
Ordes E 38 B3
Ordizia E 32 D1
Ordona I 60 A5
Ordzhonikidze UA 154 C6
Orea E 47 C9
O Real E 38 B3
Örebäcken S 102 C4
Orebić HR 157 G7
Örebro S 97 D13
Ořechov CZ 77 D11
Öregcsertő H 150 D3
Öreglak H 149 C9
Öregrund S 99 B10
Orehoved DK 87 F9
Oreini GR 169 B10
Orekhovitsa BG 165 B9
Orellana de la Sierra E 51 A9
Orellana la Vieja E 51 A8
Ören TR 177 C10
Ören TR 181 B7
Orenhofen D 185 E6
Oreoi GR 175 B7
Orés E 32 F3
Oresh BG 166 B4
Oreshak BG 165 D10
Orestiada GR 171 B11
Öreström S 107 C16
Öretjändalen S 103 A10
Oreye B 19 C11
Orezu RO 161 D9
Orford GB 15 C12
Organi GR 171 B9
Organyà E 43 C6
Orgaz E 46 E5
Orgelet F 31 B8
Ørgenvika N 95 B11
Orgères-en-Beauce F 24 D6
Orgita EST 131 D8
Orgiva E 53 C10
Orgon F 35 C9
Orgosolo I 64 C3
Orhaneli TR 173 E10
Orhaniye TR 171 C10
Orhaniye TR 181 C8
Orhanlar TR 173 E8
Orhei MD 154 C3
Oria E 55 E8
Oria I 61 C9
O Rial E 38 D2
Origny-Ste-Benoîte F 19 E7
Orihuela E 56 E3
Orihuela del Tremedal E 47 C9
Orikhivka UA 154 F3
Orikum AL 168 D1
Orimattila FIN 127 D14
Oriniemi FIN 127 C9
Orio E 32 D1
Oriola P 50 C4
Oriolo I 61 C6
Oriolo Romano I 62 C2
Oripää FIN 126 D8
Orismala FIN 122 E8
Orissaare EST 130 D6
Oristà E 43 D8
Oristano I 64 D2
Oristown IRL 7 E9
Őriszentpéter H 149 C6
Oriv UA 145 E8
Oriveden asema FIN 127 B11
Orivesi FIN 127 B11
Orizare BG 167 D9
Orizari MK 164 F5
Ørjavik N 104 F2
Ørje N 96 D6
Orkanger N 104 E7
Örkelljunga S 87 C12
Örkény H 150 C3
Orla PL 141 E8
Orlamünde D 79 E10
Orlat RO 152 F3
Orlea RO 160 F4
Orléans F 24 E6
Orlești RO 160 D4
Orlivka UA 155 C2
Orllan RKS 164 D3
Orlová CZ 146 B6
Orlov Dol BG 166 E6
Orlovets BG 166 C5
Orły PL 144 D6
Orlyak BG 161 F10
Orlyane BG 165 C10
Orma GR 169 C6
Ormanli TR 173 B9
Ormaryd S 92 D5
Ormea I 37 C7
Örményes H 150 C6
Örménykút H 150 D6
Ormos GR 176 D4
Ormos Panormou GR 176 D5
Ormos Prinou GR 171 C7
Ormož SLO 148 D6
Ormskirk GB 10 D6
Ormylia GR 169 D10
Ornaisons F 34 D4
Ornans F 26 F5
Ornäs S 97 A14
Örnäsudden S 109 E13
Ornavasso I 68 B5
Ornbau D 75 D8
Ornes N 105 B15
Ørnes N 108 C6
Orneta PL 139 B9
Ørnhøj DK 86 C3
Ornö S 93 A12
Ornontowice PL 142 F6
Örnsköldsvik S 107 E15
Orodel RO 159 E11
Orolik HR 157 B11
Orom SRB 150 F4
Oron-la-Ville CH 31 B10
Oronoz E 32 D2
Orońsko PL 141 H3
Oropa I 68 B4
Oropesa E 45 E10
Oropesa del Mar E 48 D5
Ororbia E 32 E2
Orosei I 64 C4
Orosháza H 150 D6
Oroslavje HR 148 E5
Oroszlány H 149 B10
Orpierre F 35 B10
Orreaga E 32 D3
Orrefors S 89 B9
Orrios E 42 F2
Orrmo S 102 C7
Orroli I 64 D3
Orrviken S 106 E6
Orsa S 102 D8
Orsara di Puglia I 60 A4
Orsay F 24 C7
Örsbäck S 107 D17
Orsennes F 29 C9
Örserum S 92 C5
Orsières CH 31 C11
Örsjö S 89 B9
Ørslev DK 87 E9
Ørsnes N 100 A5
Orsogna I 63 C6
Orsomarso I 60 D5
Orșova RO 159 D9
Ørsta N 100 B4
Ørsted DK 86 C6
Örsundsbro S 99 C8
Ortaca TR 181 C9
Ortacesus I 64 D3
Ortakent TR 177 E9
Ortaklar TR 177 D9
Ortaköy TR 173 B9
Ortala S 99 C11
Orta Nova I 60 A5
Orte I 62 C2
Orten N 100 A5
Ortenberg D 21 D12
Ortenberg D 27 D8
Ortenburg D 76 E4
Orth an der Donau A 77 F11
Orthez F 32 D4
Ortholmen S 102 B6
Orthovouni GR 168 E5
Ortigosa E 41 D6
Ortigueira E 38 A4
Ørting DK 86 D6
Ortisei I 72 C4
Orțișoara RO 151 F7
Ortnevik N 100 D4
Orton GB 10 C6
Ortona I 63 C6
Ortovera I 37 C8
Ortrand D 80 D5
Orträsk S 107 C15
Ortueri I 64 C2
Örtülüce TR 173 D7
Ørum DK 86 C5
Ørum DK 86 C7
Orune I 64 C3
Orusco E 47 D6
Orval F 29 B10
Orvalho P 44 D5
Orvault F 23 F8
Orvieto I 62 B2
Örviken S 118 E6
Orvinio I 62 C3
Oryakhovo BG 160 F3
Orzesze PL 142 F6
Orzinuovi I 69 C8
Orzyny PL 139 C11
Orzysz PL 136 F4
Os N 101 B14
Osa N 100 E6
Osa de Vega E 47 E7
Ošāni LV 135 D11
Osaonica SRB 163 C9
Osbaldwick GB 11 D9
Os Blancos E 38 D4
Osburg D 186 B2
Øsby DK 86 E5
Osby S 88 C5
Osbyholm S 87 D13
Oščadnica SK 147 C7
Oschatz D 80 D4
Oschersleben (Bode) D 79 B9
Oschiri I 64 B3
Ościsłowo PL 139 E9
Os Dices E 38 C2
Osdorf D 83 B8
Osečina SRB 158 E4
O Seixo E 38 E2
Oseja de Sajambre E 39 B9
Osek CZ 76 C5
Osek CZ 80 E5
Osen N 105 C9
Osen N 108 D6
Osenets BG 166 B6
Ošenieki LV 134 C4
Osera E 41 E10
Oșești RO 153 D10
Øset N 101 D10
Osetno PL 81 C10
Ősi H 149 B10
Osica de Sus RO 160 E4
Osidda I 64 B3
Osie PL 138 C5
Osięciny PL 138 E6
Osieck PL 141 G4
Osieczna PL 81 C11
Osieczna PL 138 C5
Osiecznica PL 81 D8
Osiek PL 138 C5
Osiek PL 139 D7
Osiek PL 143 E11
Osiek PL 147 B8
Osiek Jasielski PL 145 D3
Osiek Mały PL 142 B6
Osiek nad Notecią PL 85 D12
Osielsko PL 138 D5
Osiglia I 37 C8
Osijek HR 149 E11
Osikovitsa BG 165 D9
Osilo I 64 B2
Osimo I 67 F7
Osina PL 85 C8
Osini I 64 D3
Osiny PL 141 H6
Osio Sotto I 69 B8
Osipaonica SRB 159 D7
Osjaków PL 142 D6
Oskar S 89 B9
Oskar-Fredriksborg S 99 D10
Oskarshamn S 93 E8
Oskarström S 87 B11
Oskava CZ 77 C12
Oskořínek CZ 77 B8
Osľany SK 146 D6
Oslättfors S 103 E12
Osli H 149 A8
Oslo N 95 C13
Osloß D 79 B8
Osma E 40 C5
Osma FIN 117 D15
Osmancali TR 177 B9
Osmancik TR 173 A7
Osmangazi TR 173 D11
Osmaniye TR 173 E10
Osmaniye TR 173 F10
Osmanki FIN 123 C16
Osmanli TR 173 A6
Os'mino RUS 132 C5
Ösmo S 93 B11
Osmolin PL 141 F1
Osmoloda UA 145 F9
Osnabrück D 17 D10
Osno Lubuskie PL 81 B7
Osny F 24 B7
Osoblaha CZ 142 F4
Osogna CH 69 A6
Osojnik HR 162 D5
Osoppo I 73 D7
Osor E 43 D9
Osor HR 67 C9
Oșorhei RO 151 C9
Osorno E 40 D3
Osowa PL 136 E6
Osowa Sień PL 81 C10
Osøyri N 94 B2
Ospitaletto I 69 B9
Oss NL 16 E5
Ossa GR 169 C9
Ossa de Montiel E 55 B7
Ossana I 69 A10
Osséja F 33 F9
Ossendrecht NL 182 C4
Ossès F 32 D3
Ossiach A 73 C8
Oßmannstedt D 79 D9
Ossun F 32 D5
Östa S 98 B7
Ostanå S 88 C6
Östanfjärden S 119 C10
Östansjö S 92 A5
Östansjö S 109 E16
Östanskär S 103 A13
Östanvik S 103 D9
Oštarije HR 156 B3
Ostaszewo PL 138 B6
Östavall S 103 B9
Ostbevern D 17 D9
Østbirk DK 86 D5
Östbjörka S 103 E9
Østby N 91 A9
Østby N 102 D4
Östby S 107 D13
Østed DK 87 D9
Ostellato I 66 C4
Osten D 17 A12
Ostend B 18 B6
Ostend B 182 C1
Ostenfeld (Husum) D 82 B6
Østengård DK 86 D4
Österås S 107 E12
Øster Assels DK 86 B3
Øster Bjerregrav DK 86 C5
Øster Brønderslev DK 86 A5
Osterburg (Altmark) D 83 E11
Osterburken D 27 B11
Osterby D 82 B7
Østerby DK 86 A5
Österbybruk S 99 B9
Österbymo S 92 D6
Österede S 107 E11
Österfärnebo S 98 B7
Osterfeld D 79 D10
Osterforse S 107 E12
Östergarn S 93 E13
Östergraninge S 107 F12
Österhankmo FIN 122 D7
Osterhever D 82 B5
Osterhofen D 76 E4
Øster Højst DK 86 E4
Osterholz-Scharmbeck D 17 B11
Øster Hornum DK 86 B5
Øster Hurup DK 86 B6
Østerild DK 86 A3
Øster Jølby DK 86 B3
Österjörn S 118 D4
Østerlars DK 89 E7
Øster Lindet DK 86 E4
Österlisa S 99 C11
Østermarie DK 89 E8
Östermark FIN 126 E8
Ostermiething A 76 F3
Ostermundigen CH 31 B11
Österneret S 107 C12
Östero FIN 122 D8
Osterode am Harz D 79 C7
Osterrönfeld D 82 B7
Österskucku S 102 A8
Östersund S 106 E7
Östersundom FIN 127 E13
Øster Tørslev DK 86 B6
Øster Ulslev DK 83 A11
Östervåla S 98 B8
Øster Vedsted DK 86 E3
Østervrå DK 90 E7
Øster Vrøgum DK 86 D2
Osterwieck D 79 C8
Østese N 94 B4
Ostfildern D 187 D7
Östhammar S 99 B10
Ostheim vor der Rhön D 75 B7
Osthofen D 21 E10
Ostia I 62 D2
Ostiano I 66 B1
Ostiglia I 66 B3
Ostiz E 32 E2
Östloning S 103 A13
Östmark S 97 B8
Östmarkum S 107 E14
Östnor S 102 D7
Ostojićevo SRB 150 F5
Ostoros H 145 H1
Ostra I 67 E7
Ostra RO 153 C7
Östra Åliden S 118 D4
Ostrach D 27 E11
Östra Ed S 93 C9
Östra Frölunda S 91 E13
Östra Granberg S 118 C4
Östra Grevie S 87 E12
Östra Husby S 93 B9
Östra Ljungby S 87 C12
Östra Lōa S 97 C13
Östra Lovsjön S 106 D7
Östra Ormsjö S 107 C10
Östra Ryd S 93 C8
Östra Skråmträsk S 118 E5
Östra Sönnarslöv S 88 D6
Östra Stugusjö S 103 A9
Ostrau D 79 C11
Ostrau D 80 D4
Ostrava CZ 146 B6
Östra Vemmerlöv S 88 D6
Ostravice CZ 146 B6
Östra Yttermark FIN 122 E6
Oštrelj BIH 156 D6
Ostren AL 168 B3
Ostřetín CZ 77 B10
Osthauderfehn D 17 B9
Ostricourt F 182 E2
Östringen D 21 F11
Ostritsa BG 166 B5
Ostritz D 81 D7
Ostróda PL 139 C8
Ostrołęka PL 140 D5
Ostromecko PL 138 D5
Ostroměř CZ 77 B9
Ostroróg PL 81 A10
Ostrov BG 160 F4
Ostrov CZ 76 B3
Ostrov RO 155 D2
Ostrov RO 161 E10
Ostrov RUS 133 B4
Ostrov SK 146 D5
Ostroveni RO 160 F3
Ostrovo BG 161 F9
Ostrov u Macochy CZ 77 D11
Ostrów PL 143 F12
Ostrówek PL 141 G7
Ostrówek PL 142 D6
Ostrowice PL 85 C9
Ostrowiec PL 85 B11
Ostrowiec Świętokrzyski PL 143 E11
Ostrowite PL 138 F5
Ostrowite PL 139 D7
Ostrów Lubelski PL 141 H7
Ostrów Mazowiecka PL 139 E12
Ostrowo PL 138 E5
Ostrów Wielkopolski PL 142 C4
Ostrowy nad Okszą PL 143 E7
Ostrožac BIH 156 C4
Ostrožac BIH 157 E8
Ostrzeń PL 141 G5
Østrup DK 86 B4
Ostrzeszów PL 142 D4
Ostuni I 61 B9
Ostvik S 118 E6
Ostwald F 186 D4
Osula EST 131 F13
Osuna E 53 B6
Ošupe LV 135 C13
Osvallen S 102 A4
Osvica BIH 157 C8
Oswaldkirk GB 11 C9
Oswestry GB 10 F5
Oświęcim PL 143 F7
Ota F 37 G9
Otaci MD 154 A1
Otalampi FIN 127 E12
Otaņķi LV 134 D2
Otanmäki FIN 120 F9
Otaslavice CZ 77 D12
Otava FIN 128 B7
Otavice HR 156 E5
Oteiza E 32 E2
Oțeleni RO 153 C10
Oțelu Roșu RO 159 B9
Otepää EST 131 E12
Oteren N 111 B18
Oterma FIN 120 E9
Otero de Bodas E 39 E7
Otervik N 105 A11
Oțeșani RO 160 C4
Oteševo MK 168 C4
Otfinów PL 143 F10
Othem S 93 D13
Ötigheim D 27 C9
Otisheim D 27 C10
Otišić HR 156 E5
Otívar E 53 C9
Otley GB 11 D8
Otley GB 15 C11
Otmuchów PL 77 B12
Otnes N 101 C14
Otočac HR 156 C3
Otok HR 157 B10
Otok HR 157 E6
Otoka BIH 156 C5
Otopeni RO 161 D8
Otorowo PL 81 A10
O Toural E 38 D2
Otovica MK 164 F4
Otradnoye RUS 129 F14
Otranto I 61 C10
Otricoli I 62 C2
Otrokovice CZ 146 C5
Otta N 101 C11
Ottana I 64 C3
Ottaviano I 60 B2
Ottenby S 89 C10
Ottendorf-Okrilla D 80 D5
Ottenheim D 186 E4
Ottenhöfen im Schwarzwald D 27 C9
Ottenschlag A 77 F8
Ottensheim A 76 F6
Ottenstein D 78 C5
Otterbach D 186 C4
Otterbäcken S 91 B15
Otterberg D 21 E9
Otterburn GB 5 E12
Otter Ferry GB 4 C6
Otterfing D 72 A4
Otterlo NL 16 D5
Otterndorf D 17 A11
Ottersberg D 17 B12
Ottersøy N 105 B10
Otterstad S 91 B13
Ottersweier D 27 C9
Otterswick GB 3 D14
Otterup DK 86 D6
Otterwisch D 79 D12
Öttevény H 149 A9
Ottignies B 19 C10
Ottmarsheim F 27 E8
Ottobeuren D 71 B10
Ottobrunn D 75 F10
Öttömös H 150 E4
Ottone I 37 B10
Ottrau D 21 C12
Ottsjö S 105 E14
Ottsjön S 106 D7
Ottweiler D 21 F8
Otwock PL 141 F4
Otxandio E 41 B6
Otyń PL 81 C9
Otzing D 76 E3
Ouanne F 25 E9
Ouarville F 24 D6
Ouca P 44 C3
Oucques F 24 E5
Oud-Beijerland NL 16 E2
Ouddorp NL 182 B3
Oudehaske NL 16 C5
Oudemirdum NL 16 C5
Oudenaarde B 19 C8
Oudenbosch NL 16 E3
Oudenburg B 18 B7
Oudeschild NL 16 B3
Oude-Tonge NL 16 E2
Oudewater NL 182 A5
Oud-Gastel NL 16 E2
Oudon F 23 F9
Oud-Turnhout B 16 F3
Oud-Vossemeer NL 16 E2
Oudzele B 182 C2
Oued Laou MA 53 F6
Ouffet B 19 D11
Oughterard IRL 6 F4
Ougney F 26 F4
Ouguela P 45 F6
Ouistreham F 23 B11
Oulainen FIN 119 F13
Oulanka FIN 115 F5
Oulchy-le-Château F 25 B9
Oulder B 20 D6
Oullins F 30 D6
Oulton GB 15 C12
Oulu FIN 119 D14
Oulunsalo FIN 119 E14
Oulx I 31 E10
Oundle GB 15 C8
Oupeye B 19 C12
Ouranoupoli GR 170 D5
Oure DK 87 E7
Ourém P 44 E3
Ourense E 38 D4
Ourique P 50 D3
Ourol E 38 A4
Ouroux-en-Morvan F 25 F10
Ouroux-sur-Saône F 31 B6
Ourville-en-Caux F 18 E2
Oust F 33 E8
Outakoski FIN 113 D16
Outarville F 24 D7
Outeiro P 38 E2
Outeiro P 39 E6
Outeiro de Rei E 38 B4
Outeiro Seco P 38 E5
Outokumpu FIN 125 E12
Outomuro E 38 D4
Outreau F 15 F12
Outwell GB 11 F12
Ouveillan F 34 D4
Ouzouer-le-Marché F 24 E6
Ouzouer-sur-Loire F 25 E7
Ovada I 37 B9
Ovanåker S 103 D10
Ovanmo S 107 D10
Ovar P 44 C3
Ovaro I 73 D6
Ovča SRB 158 D6
Ovcha Mogila BG 166 C4
Ovcharovo BG 166 E6
Ovchepoltsi BG 165 E9
Ove DK 86 B5
Ovelgönne D 17 B10
Överammer S 107 E9
Överäng S 105 D14
Overås N 100 A8
Overath D 21 C8
Överberg S 102 B7
Overbister GB 3 G11
Øverbygd N 111 C17
Överbyn S 103 C12
Overdinkel NL 183 A10
Over Feldborg DK 86 C3
Øvergard N 111 B18
Overhalla N 105 B11
Överhogdal S 102 B8
Överhörnäs S 107 E15
Over Hornbæk DK 86 C5
Overijse B 19 C10
Överissjö S 107 C13
Over Jerstal DK 86 E4
Överkalix S 119 B9
Overlade DK 86 B4
Överlännäs S 107 E13
Överlida S 91 E12
Overloon NL 183 B7
Övermalax FIN 122 E7
Övermark FIN 122 E6
Övermorjärv S 118 B9
Övernäs S 109 D14
Överö FIN 99 B15
Overøye N 100 B6
Overpelt B 19 B11
Over Simmelkær DK 86 C3
Överstbyn S 118 B7
Överträngér S 103 E10
Overton GB 10 F6
Overton GB 13 C12
Övertorneå S 119 B11
Överturingen S 102 B8
Överum S 93 D8
Ovezande NL 16 F1
O Vicedo E 38 A4
Ovidiu RO 155 E3
Oviedo E 39 B8
Oviglio I 37 B8
Oviken S 105 E16
Ovindoli I 62 C5
Oviši LV 130 F3
Öv Långträsk S 109 E16
Ovodda I 64 C3
Övra S 107 D11
Øvre Alta N 113 D11
Øvre Årdal N 100 D7
Øvre Åstbru N 101 D13
Övre Bredåker S 118 C6
Övre Flåsjön S 118 B7
Övre Kildal N 112 D7
Övre-Konäs S 105 D14
Øvrella N 95 C10
Øvre Rendal N 101 C14
Övre Soppero S 116 B7
Övre Tväråsel S 118 C5
Ovria GR 174 C4
Övsjöbyn S 107 E9
Ovtrup DK 86 D2
Owen D 27 C11
Owingen D 27 E11
Owińska PL 81 A11
Owschlag D 82 B7
Öxabäck S 91 E12
Oxberg S 102 D7
Oxelösund S 93 B10
Oxenhope GB 11 D8
Oxentea MD 154 C4
Oxford GB 13 B12
Oxhalsö S 99 C11
Oxie S 87 D12
Oxkangar FIN 122 D8
Oxshott GB 15 E8
Oxted GB 15 E9
Oxton GB 5 D11
Oxylithos GR 175 B9
Øyangen N 104 E7
Øydegarden N 104 E4
Øyenkilen N 91 A8
Øyer N 101 D12
Øyeren N 96 B7
Øyjord N 108 B9
Oy-Mittelberg D 71 B10
Øynes N 108 B9
Øynes N 111 C11
Oyonnax F 31 C8
Øyslebø N 90 C2
Oyten D 17 B12
Øyvatnet N 111 C12
Oza E 38 B3
Ozaeta E 41 C7
Ozalj HR 148 E4
Ożarów PL 143 E12
Ożarów Mazowiecki PL 141 F3
Ožbalt SLO 148 C4
Özbaşı TR 177 D9
Özbek TR 177 C8
Ózd H 145 G1
Ožďany SK 147 E9
Özdere TR 177 D9
Ožence PL 145 E3
Ozersk RUS 136 E5
Ozieri I 64 B3
Ozimek PL 142 E5
Ozimica BIH 157 D9
Özlüce TR 181 B9
Ozoir-la-Ferrière F 25 C8
Ozolaine LV 131 F9
Ozoli LV 131 F9
Ozoli LV 134 B4
Ozoli LV 135 C12
Ozolmuiža LV 133 D2
Ozolnieki LV 134 C7
Ozora H 149 C10
Ozorków PL 143 C7
Ozun RO 153 F7
Ozzano dell'Emilia I 66 D3
Ozzano Monferrato I 68 C5

P

Pääaho FIN 121 D10
Pääjärvi FIN 123 E13
Paakinmäki FIN 121 F11
Paakkila FIN 125 E11
Paakkola FIN 119 C13
Paal B 183 C6
Paalasmaa FIN 125 D12
Paaso FIN 127 C15
Paasvere EST 131 C13
Paatela FIN 129 B9
Paattinen FIN 126 D7
Paatus FIN 113 D17
Paavola FIN 119 E14
Pabaiskas LT 135 F9
Paberžė LT 137 D11
Pabianice PL 143 C7
Pabillonis I 64 D2
Pabiržė LT 135 D9
Pabneukirchen A 77 F7
Pabradė LT 137 D12
Pabu F 22 C5
Pacanów PL 143 F11
Paceco I 58 D2
Pacheia Ammos GR 179 E10
Pachino I 59 F7
Pachni GR 171 B7
Paciano I 62 A2
Pácin H 145 G4
Pačir SRB 150 F3
Pack A 73 C10
Pačlavice CZ 77 D12
Pacos de Ferreira P 38 F3
Pacov CZ 77 D8
Pacsa H 149 C8
Păcureți RO 161 C8
Pacyna PL 143 B8
Pacy-sur-Eure F 24 B5
Paczków PL 77 B12
Padasjoki FIN 127 C13
Padborg DK 82 A6
Padbury GB 14 D7
Padej SRB 150 F5
Pađene HR 156 D5
Paderborn D 17 E11
Paderne P 38 D3
Paderne P 50 E3
Paderne de Allariz E 38 D4
Padeș RO 159 C10
Padesh BG 165 F7
Padew Narodowa PL 143 F12
Padežine BIH 157 F8
Padiham GB 11 D7
Pădina RO 159 E11
Padina RO 161 D10
Padina SRB 159 C6
Padinska Skela SRB 158 D5
Padiract F 29 F9
Padise EST 131 C8
Padoby BY 133 F2
Padoux F 26 D6
Padova I 66 B4
Padria I 64 C2
Padrón E 38 C2
Padru I 64 B4
Padstow GB 12 D5
Padsvillye BY 133 F3
Padul E 53 B9
Padula I 60 C5
Paduli I 60 A3
Padure LV 134 C3
Pădureni RO 153 D12
Paesana I 37 B6
Paese I 72 E5
Pag HR 67 D11
Pagani I 60 B3
Paganica I 62 C4
Paganico I 65 B4
Pagėgiai LT 134 F3
Pagiriai LT 135 F8
Pagiriai LT 137 D11
Paglieta I 63 C6
Pagny-sur-Moselle F 26 C5
Pagondas GR 177 D8
Pagouria GR 171 B8
Pagramantis LT 134 F4
Paharova S 116 E8
Páhi H 150 D3
Pahkakoski FIN 119 D16
Pahkakumpu FIN 115 E3
Pahkakumpu FIN 121 C12
Pahkala FIN 119 F11
Pahkamäki FIN 123 D16
Pähl D 72 A3
Pahlen D 82 B6
Pahranichny BY 140 D9
Pahtaoja FIN 119 C14
Paião P 44 D3
Paide EST 131 D11
Paignton GB 13 E7
Paihola FIN 125 E13
Päijälä FIN 127 B12
Paikuse EST 131 E9
Pailhès F 33 D8
Paillet F 32 A5
Paimbœuf F 23 F7
Paimela FIN 127 C14
Paimio FIN 126 E8
Paimpol F 22 C5
Paimpont F 23 D7
Painswick GB 13 B10
Painten D 75 E10
Paipis FIN 127 E13
Paisley GB 5 D8
Paistu EST 131 E11
Paisua FIN 124 C9
Päiväjoki FIN 115 F2
Pajala S 117 D10
Pajares de la Lampreana E 39 E8
Pajarón E 47 E9
Pajęczno PL 143 D6
Pajukoski FIN 125 C11
Pajukoste FIN 113 C20
Pajūris LT 134 F4
Pajuskylä FIN 124 D7
Pajuvaara FIN 121 D14
Páka H 149 C7
Pakaa FIN 127 D14
Pakalnė LT 134 F2
Pakalniai LT 135 F10
Pakapė LT 134 E6
Pakarila FIN 123 E17
Pakisjärvi FIN 117 E12
Pakkala FIN 127 C11
Pakod H 149 C8
Pakość PL 138 E5
Pakosław PL 81 C12
Pakoštane HR 156 E4
Pákozd H 149 B11
Pakrac HR 149 F8
Pakruojis LT 134 E7
Paks H 149 C11
Paksuniemi S 116 C5
Pala EST 131 D14
Palacios del Sil E 39 C7
Palacios de Sanabria E 39 D6
Palaciosrubios E 45 B10
Palade EST 130 D5
Palafrugell E 43 D10
Palagianello I 61 B7
Palagiano I 61 B8
Palagonia I 59 E6
Palaia I 66 E2
Palaia Fokaia GR 175 D8
Palaikastro GR 179 E11
Palaiochora GR 169 C9
Palaiochora GR 178 E6
Palaiochori GR 169 C9
Palaiochori GR 169 D10
Palaiochori GR 175 C7
Palaiokastritsa GR 168 E2
Palaiokastro GR 177 D9
Palaiokipos GR 177 A7
Palaiokomi GR 170 C5
Palaiomonastiro GR 169 F6
Palaiopoli GR 176 D4
Palaiopyrgos GR 169 E6
Palaiopyrgos GR 169 E8
Palaiopyrgos GR 174 C4
Palaiovracha GR 174 B5
Palairos GR 174 B2
Palaiseau F 25 C7
Palamas GR 169 F7
Palamós E 43 D10
Palamuse EST 131 D13
Palanca RO 153 D8
Palanga LT 134 E2
Pålänge S 119 C9
Palanzano I 66 D1
Palárikovo SK 146 E6
Palas de Rei E 38 C4
Palata BY 133 E6
Palata I 63 D7
Pălatca RO 152 D4
Palau I 64 A3
Palavas-les-Flots F 35 C6
Palazzo Adriano I 58 D3
Palazzolo Acreide I 59 E6
Palazzolo sull'Oglio I 69 B8
Palazzo San Gervasio I 60 B6
Paldiski EST 131 C8
Pale BIH 157 E10
Päle LV 131 F9
Paleičiai LT 134 F2
Palena I 63 D6
Palencia E 40 D2
Palenciana E 53 B7
Palenzuela E 40 D3
Palermo AL 168 D2
Palermo I 58 C3
Paleśnica PL 144 D2
Palestrina I 62 D3
Palėvenėlė LT 135 E10
Palež BIH 158 E3
Palhaça P 44 C3
Pálháza H 145 G4
Palia Kavala GR 171 C6
Paliano I 62 D4
Palić SRB 150 E4
Palinges F 30 B5
Palinuro I 60 C4
Paliouri GR 169 E10
Paliouria GR 169 E6
Palis F 25 D10
Paliseul B 19 E11
Palivere EST 131 D7
Palizzi I 59 D9
Paljakka FIN 121 B14
Paljakka FIN 121 E11

Pälkäne FIN 127 C11
Pålkem S 118 B7
Palkino RUS 132 F3
Palkisoja FIN 115 A2
Palkovice CZ 146 B6
Palladio GR 171 B8
Pallagorio I 61 E7
Pallarés E 51 C7
Pallas Grean New IRL 8 C6
Pallas Green IRL 8 C6
Pälli FIN 119 E16
Palling D 75 F12
Palluau F 28 B2
Palluau-sur-Indre F 29 B8
Palma P 50 C2
Palma Campania I 60 B3
Palma del Río E 51 D9
Palma de Mallorca E 49 E10
Palma di Montechiaro I 58 E4
Palmadula I 64 B1
Palmanova E 49 E10
Palmanova I 73 E7
Palmaz P 44 C4
Palmeira P 38 E3
Palmela P 50 B2
Palmi I 59 C8
Pálmonostora H 150 D4
Palmse EST 131 B11
Palnackie GB 5 F9
Palneca F 37 H10
Palo del Colle I 61 A7
Palohuornas S 116 E6
Palojärvi FIN 115 E2
Palojärvi FIN 117 A10
Palojärvi FIN 117 E14
Palojoensuu FIN 116 B10
Palokki FIN 125 E11
Palomaa FIN 113 E19
Palomäki FIN 125 D11
Palomar de Arroyos E 42 F2
Palomares del Río E 51 E7
Palomas E 51 B7
Palombara Sabina I 62 C3
Palombaro I 63 C6
Palomenė LT 137 D9
Palomera E 47 D8
Palomeras del Campo E 47 E7
Palomonte I 60 B4
Palonoja FIN 115 B2
Palonselkä FIN 117 D13
Palonurmi FIN 125 D10
Paloperä FIN 115 F4
Palos de la Frontera E 51 E6
Palosenjärvi FIN 124 C8
Palotabozsok H 149 D11
Palotáshalom H 150 B4
Palovaara FIN 119 B12
Palovaara FIN 119 B16
Palovaara FIN 121 E13
Palovaara FIN 125 E14
Pals E 43 D10
Pålsboda S 92 A6
Palsmane LV 135 B12
Palsselkä FIN 117 D16
Pålsträsk S 118 C6
Paltamo FIN 121 F10
Paltanen FIN 124 F7
Paltaniemi FIN 121 F10
Paltin RO 153 F9
Păltiniș RO 153 A9
Păltiniș RO 159 C9
Păltinoasa RO 153 B7
Pal'tsevo RUS 129 D10
Paludi I 61 D7
Paluel F 18 E2
Paluknys LT 137 E10
Paluzza I 73 C7
Palyatskishki BY 137 E11
Palyessye BY 135 F12
Palzem D 20 E6
Pambukovica SRB 158 E4
Pameče SLO 73 C11
Pamfylla GR 177 A8
Pamhagen A 149 A7
Pamiers F 33 D9
Pampāļi LV 134 C4
Pamparato I 37 C7
Pampelonne F 33 B10
Pampilhosa P 44 D4
Pampilhosa da Serra P 44 D5
Pampliega E 40 D4
Pamplona E 32 E2
Pampow D 83 C10
Pamproux F 28 C5
Pamukçu TR 173 E8
Panaci RO 152 C6
Panagia GR 171 C7
Panagia GR 171 E8
Panagia GR 178 E9
Panagyurishte BG 165 D9
Panagyurski Kolonii BG 165 D9
Panahor AL 168 C2
Panaitolio GR 174 B3
Panaja AL 168 C1
Pănășești MD 154 C3
Panassac F 33 D7
Pănătău RO 161 C8
Panazol F 29 D8
Pancalieri I 37 B7
Pancar TR 177 C9
Pancarköy TR 173 B7
Păncești RO 153 E10
Pančevo SRB 158 D6
Pancharevo BG 165 D7
Panciu RO 153 F10
Pancorbo E 40 C5
Pâncota RO 151 E8
Pancrudo E 42 F1
Pánd H 150 C4
Pandėlys LT 135 D10
Pandino I 69 C8
Pandrup DK 86 A5
Pandy GB 13 B9
Panelia FIN 126 C6
Panemunė LT 136 C4
Panemunėlis LT 135 E10
Panes E 39 B10
Pănet RO 152 D4
Panevėžys LT 135 E8
Panga EST 130 D4
Pângărați RO 153 D8
Pange F 186 C1
Panicale I 62 A2
Panichkovo BG 166 F4
Panissières F 30 D5
Paniza E 41 F9
Panjas F 32 C5
Panjevac SRB 159 E8
Panjik BIH 157 C9
Panka FIN 124 D7
Pankajärvi FIN 125 D14
Pankakoski FIN 125 D14
Panker D 83 B9
Panki PL 142 E6
Pannarano I 60 A3
Pannes F 25 D8
Panni I 60 A4
Panningen NL 16 F5
Pannonhalma H 149 A9
Panóias P 50 D3
Panorama GR 169 C9
Panormos GR 178 E8
Panschwitz-Kuckau D 80 D6
Pantanassa GR 178 B4
Päntäne FIN 122 F8
Pantelimon RO 155 D2
Pantelimon RO 161 E8
Panticeu RO 152 C3
Panticosa E 32 E5
Pantoja E 46 D5
Panttikylä FIN 122 F8
Panttila FIN 122 E8
Pant-y-dwr GB 13 A8
Paola I 60 E6
Pap H 145 G5
Pápa H 149 B8
Papadianika GR 178 B4
Papasidero I 60 D5
Pápateszér H 149 B9
Papenburg D 17 B8
Papendorf D 83 B12
Papendrecht NL 16 E3
Papilė LT 134 D5
Papilys LT 135 D10
Papín SK 145 E5
Papkeszi H 149 B10
Paplaka LV 134 D2
Papowo Biskupie PL 138 D6
Pappades GR 175 B7
Pappados GR 177 A7
Pappenheim D 75 E8
Papradno SK 146 C6
Paprotnia PL 141 F6
Par GB 12 E5
Parabita I 61 C10
Paraćin SRB 159 F7
Paracuellos E 47 E9
Paracuellos de Jarama E 46 C5
Parád H 147 F10
Parada P 45 C6
Parada de Ester P 44 C4
Parada de Pinhão P 38 F4
Parada de Rubiales E 45 B10
Parada de Sil E 38 D4
Paradas E 51 E9
Paradeisi GR 181 D8
Paradeisia GR 174 E5
Paradeisos GR 171 B7
Paradela E 38 C5
Paradela P 38 E4
Paradela P 44 B5
Paradyż PL 141 H2
Parainen FIN 126 E7
Parakalamos GR 168 E4
Parakka S 116 D7
Parakoila GR 177 A7
Paralepa EST 130 D7
Paralia GR 174 C4
Paralia GR 175 F6
Paralia Avdiron GR 171 C7
Paralia Saranti GR 175 C6
Paralia Tyrou GR 175 E6
Paralio Astros GR 175 E6
Paramé F 23 C8
Parâmio P 39 E6
Páramo del Sil E 39 C7
Paramythia GR 168 F4
Paranesti GR 171 B6
Paranhos P 44 D5
Parantala FIN 123 E15
Parapotamos GR 168 E3
Paras N 111 B19
Părău RO 152 F6
Parava RO 153 E9
Paravola GR 174 B4
Paray-le-Monial F 30 C5
Parcani MD 154 B3
Parcent E 56 D4
Parcé-sur-Sarthe F 23 E11
Parchen D 79 B11
Parchim D 83 D11
Parchovany SK 145 F4
Parchów PL 81 D9
Parchowo PL 85 B13
Parciaki PL 139 D11
Parcoul F 28 E6
Parczew PL 141 G7
Pardais P 50 B5
Pardies F 32 D4
Pardilhó P 44 C3
Pardoși RO 161 C9
Pardubice CZ 77 B9
Parechcha BY 137 F9
Paredes de Coura P 38 E2
Paredes de Nava E 39 D10
Pareja E 47 C7
Parempuyre F 28 F4
Parenti I 61 E6
Parentis-en-Born F 32 B3
Parets del Vallès E 43 D8
Parey D 79 B10
Parga GR 168 F3
Pârgărești RO 153 E9
Pargas FIN 126 E7
Parghelia I 59 B8
Pargny-sur-Saulx F 25 C12
Pargolovo RUS 129 E13
Parhalahti FIN 119 F12
Päri EST 131 E11
Parigné-l'Évêque F 24 E3
Parikkala FIN 129 B12
Parincea RO 153 E10
Paris F 25 C7
Parisot F 33 B9
Parisot F 33 C9
Parissavaara FIN 125 E16
Pärjänsuo FIN 120 C9
Pârjol RO 153 D9
Park GB 4 F2
Parkajoki S 117 C10
Parkalompolo S 116 C9
Parkano FIN 123 F10
Parkkila FIN 121 D11
Parkkila FIN 123 C14
Parkkila FIN 128 B7
Parkkima FIN 123 C15
Parkkuu FIN 127 B10
Parksepa EST 131 F13
Parkstein D 75 C11
Parkua FIN 125 B9
Parkumäki FIN 129 B10
Parla E 46 D5
Parlan F 29 F10
Parma I 66 C1
Parndorf A 77 G11
Pärnu EST 131 E8
Pärnu-Jaagupi EST 131 D9
Paroikia GR 176 E5
Parola FIN 127 C11
Paron F 25 D9
Parowa PL 81 D8
Parrillas E 45 D10
Pärsama EST 130 D5
Parsau D 79 A8
Parsberg D 75 D10
Pârscov RO 161 C9
Pârșcoveni RO 160 E4
Parsęcko PL 85 C11
Parsteinsee D 84 E6
Partakko FIN 113 E20
Partaloa E 55 E8
Partanna I 58 D2
Parteboda S 103 A10
Partenen A 71 D10
Partenstein D 74 B6
Pârteștii de Jos RO 153 B7
Parthenay F 28 B5
Partheni GR 177 E8
Partinello F 37 G9
Partinico I 58 C3
Partizani BG 167 C8
Partizani SRB 158 E5
Partizánska Ľupča SK 147 C8
Partizánske SK 146 D6
Partney GB 11 E12
Parton GB 10 B4
Partry IRL 6 E4
Partsi EST 131 E14
Parudaminys LT 137 D11
Pårup DK 86 C4
Parva RO 152 C5
Parviainen S 119 C11
Påryd S 89 B9
Parysów PL 141 G5
Parzęczew PL 143 C7
Pasai Donibane E 32 D2
Paşaköy TR 171 C10
Paşaköy TR 171 E10
Paşaköy TR 173 E8
Pasaköy TR 177 B10
Pasalankylä FIN 125 D10
Paşayiğit TR 172 C6
Pașcani RO 153 C9
Pasching A 76 F6
Paseka CZ 77 C12
Pas-en-Artois F 18 D5
Pasewalk D 84 C6
Pasi FIN 128 D7
Pasiàn di Prato I 73 D7
Pasiano di Pordenone I 73 E6
Pasieki PL 139 E12
Pasiene LV 133 D4
Pasikovci HR 149 F9
Paskalevets BG 166 C4
Paskalevo BG 155 F1
Påskallavik S 89 A10
Pasłęk PL 139 B8
Pasmajärvi FIN 117 D12
Pašman HR 156 E3
Passage East IRL 9 D9
Passail A 148 B5
Passais F 23 C10
Passau D 76 E4
Passignano sul Trasimeno I 66 F5
Passow D 84 D6
Passy F 31 D10
Pastavy BY 135 F13
Pastende LV 134 B5
Pasto FIN 123 E10
Pastoriza E 38 B5
Pastrana E 47 D7
Păstrăveni RO 153 C9
Pašuliene LV 135 E12
Pasvalys LT 135 D8
Pašvitinys LT 134 D7
Pasym PL 139 C10
Pasytsely UA 154 B5
Paszab H 145 G4
Paszowice PL 81 D10
Pásztó H 147 F9
Pasztowa Wola PL 141 H4
Pata SK 146 E5
Pataias P 44 E3
Patak H 147 E8
Patana FIN 123 D11
Pătârlagele RO 161 C8
Patay F 24 D6
Patchway GB 13 B9
Pateley Bridge GB 11 C8
Pateniemi FIN 119 D14
Patergassen A 73 C8
Paterna E 48 E4
Paterna del Campo E 51 E7
Paterna del Madera E 55 B8
Paterna del Río E 55 E7
Paterna de Rivera E 52 C5
Paternion A 73 C8
Paternò I 59 D6
Paterno I 60 C5
Paternopoli I 60 B4
Patersdorf D 76 D3
Påterud S 96 C7
Patiška Reka MK 164 F3
Pátka H 149 B11
Patmos GR 177 E8
Patna GB 4 E7
Pątnów PL 142 D6
Patokoski FIN 117 E14
Patoniemi FIN 121 B12
Patoniva FIN 113 D19
Patos AL 168 C2
Patra GR 174 C4
Pătrăuți RO 153 B8
Patrica I 62 D4
Patrick GBM 10 C2
Patrimonio F 37 F10
Patrington GB 11 D11
Pátroha H 145 G4
Pattada I 64 B3
Pattensen D 78 B6
Patterdale GB 10 B6
Patti I 59 C6
Pattijoki FIN 119 E13
Pättikkä FIN 116 A7
Pătulele RO 159 E10
Patumšiai LT 134 E5
Pâturages B 182 E3
Páty H 149 A11
Pau F 32 D5
Păuca RO 152 E3
Paudorf A 77 F9
Pauilhac F 33 C7
Pauillac F 28 E4
Paukarlahti FIN 124 E9
Paukkaja FIN 125 E14
Paukkeri FIN 120 D9
Paul P 44 D5
Paularo I 73 C7
Păuleni-Ciuc RO 153 E7
Paulești MD 154 C2
Păulești RO 151 B10
Paulhac-en-Margeride F 30 F3
Paulhan F 34 C5
Paulilatino I 64 C2
Paulinenaue D 83 E13
Păuliș RO 151 E8
Paulistrôm S 92 E7
Paüls E 42 F4
Paulx F 28 B2
Păunești RO 153 E10
Pausa D 79 E11
Păușești RO 160 C4
Păușești-Măglași RO 160 C4
Pauträsk S 107 B13
Pauvres F 19 F10
Pavel BG 166 C5
Pavel Banya BG 166 D4
Pavia I 69 C7
Pavia P 50 B3
Pavia di Udine I 73 E7
Pavías E 48 E4
Pavie F 33 C7
Pavilly F 18 E2
Pāvilosta LV 134 C2
Pavlešenci MK 164 F4
Pavliani GR 174 B5
Pavlikeni BG 166 C4
Pavliš SRB 159 C7
Pavlivka UA 154 C5
Pavlivka UA 154 F4
Pavlos GR 175 B7
Pavlovac HR 149 E8
Pavlovce nad Uhom SK 145 F5
Pavullo nel Frignano I 66 D2
Pavy RUS 132 E6
Päwesin D 79 A12
Pawłosiów PL 144 D6
Pawłówek PL 138 D4
Pawłowice PL 81 C11
Pawłowiczki PL 142 F5
Pawonków PL 142 E6
Paxton GB 5 D12
Payerne CH 31 B10
Paymogo E 51 D5
Payrac F 29 F8
Payrin-Augmontel F 33 C10
Payzac F 29 E8
Pazardzhik BG 165 E9
Pazarič BIH 157 E9
Pazarköy TR 173 E7
Pazin HR 67 B8
Paziols F 34 E4
Pázmánd H 149 B11
Pazos E 38 D2
Pchelarovo BG 166 F4
Pchelin BG 165 E8
Pcim PL 147 B9
Pčinja MK 164 E4
Peacehaven GB 15 F8
Peal de Becerro E 55 D6
Péaule F 23 E7
Pébrac F 30 E4
Peccia CH 71 E7
Peccioli I 66 E2
Pécel H 150 C3
Peceneaga RO 155 C2
Pečenjevce SRB 164 C4
Pechea RO 155 B1
Pechenga RUS 114 D10
Pechina E 55 F8
Pechory RUS 132 F2
Peći BIH 156 D5
Pecica RO 151 E7
Pećigrad BIH 156 B4
Pećinci SRB 158 D4
Pecineaga RO 155 F2
Peciu Nou RO 159 B7
Pecka CZ 77 B9
Pecka SRB 158 E4
Pečky CZ 77 B8
Pęcław PL 81 C10
Pečovská Nová Ves SK 145 E3
Pecq B 19 C7
Pécs H 149 D10
Pécsvárad H 149 D10
Pečurice MNE 163 E7
Pęczniew PL 142 C6
Pedaso I 62 A5
Pededze LV 133 B2
Pederobba I 72 E4
Pedersker DK 89 E7
Pedersöre FIN 122 C9
Pedino GR 169 C8
Pedrafita do Cebreiro E 38 C5
Pedrajas de San Esteban E 40 F2
Pedralba E 48 E3
Pedralba de la Pradería E 39 D6
Pedraza de Campos E 39 E10
Pedrera E 53 B7
Pedro Abad E 53 A8
Pedro Bernardo E 46 D3
Pedroche E 54 C3
Pedrógão P 44 E3
Pedrógão P 45 D6
Pedrógão P 50 C4
Pedrógão Grande P 44 E4
Pedrógão Pequeno P 44 E4
Pedro-Martínez E 55 D6
Pedro Muñoz E 47 F7
Pedrosa E 40 B4
Pedrosa del Príncipe E 40 D3
Pedrosillo de los Aires E 45 C9
Pedroso E 41 D6
Pedroso P 44 B3
Pedrouzos E 38 C2
Peebles GB 5 D10
Peel GBM 10 C2
Peenemünde D 84 B5
Peer B 19 B11
Peera FIN 112 F7
Peetri EST 131 D11
Pefki GR 175 A7
Pefkofyto GR 168 D4
Pefkoi GR 179 E10
Pefkos GR 178 E9
Pega P 45 D6
Pegalajar E 53 A9
Pegau D 79 D11
Peggau A 148 B4
Pegli I 37 C9
Pegnitz D 75 C10
Pego E 56 D4
Pego P 44 F4
Pegões P 50 B2
Pęgów PL 81 D11
Peguera E 49 E9
Pehčevo MK 165 F6
Pehkolanlahti FIN 120 F9
Pehlivanköy TR 173 B6
Peillac F 23 E7
Peille F 37 D6
Peine D 79 B7
Peio I 71 E11
Peipin F 35 B10
Peipohja FIN 126 C7
Peïra-Cava F 37 D6
Peiraias GR 175 D8
Peißen D 79 C10
Peißen D 79 C11
Peißenberg D 72 A3
Peiting D 71 B11
Peitz D 80 C6
Peize NL 17 B7
Pejë RKS 163 D9
Pekankylä FIN 121 E13
Pekanpäa FIN 119 B11
Pekkala FIN 119 B17
Pelagićeyo BIH 157 C10
Pelago I 66 E4
Pelahustán E 46 D3
Pelarrodríguez E 45 C8
Pelasgia GR 175 B6
Pelči LV 134 C3
Pełczyce PL 85 D8
Peleagonzalo E 39 F9
Pelēči LV 135 D13
Pelekas GR 168 E2
Peleta GR 175 E6
Pelhřimov CZ 77 D8
Pelinei MD 154 F2
Pelinia MD 153 B11
Pelishat BG 165 C10
Pélissanne F 35 C9
Pelitköy TR 173 F6
Pelkoperä FIN 119 F15
Pelkosenniemi FIN 115 D2
Pella GR 169 C8
Pellaro I 59 C8
Pellegrino Parmense I 69 D8
Pellegrue F 28 F6
Pellérd H 149 D10
Pellesmäki FIN 124 E9
Pellestrina I 66 B5
Pellevoisin F 29 B8
Pellinki FIN 127 E14
Pellizzano I 69 A10
Pello FIN 117 E11
Pello S 117 E11
Pellosniemi FIN 128 C7
Pelm D 21 D7
Peloche E 45 F10
Pelovo BG 165 C9
Pelplin PL 138 C6
Pelsin D 84 C5
Pelso FIN 119 E16
Peltokangas FIN 123 D12
Peltosalmi FIN 124 C8
Peltovuoma FIN 117 B12
Pélussin F 30 E6
Pelvoux F 31 F9
Pély H 150 C5
Pelynt GB 12 E5
Pembrey GB 12 B6
Pembridge GB 13 A9
Pembroke GB 12 B5
Pembroke Dock GB 12 B5
Pembury GB 15 E9
Pemfling D 75 D12
Pempelijärvi S 116 E8
Peñacerrada E 41 C6
Penacova P 44 D4
Peñafiel E 40 E3
Penafiel P 44 B4
Peñaflor E 51 D9
Peñaflor de Hornija E 39 E10
Penagos E 40 B4
Peñalba E 42 E3
Peñalén E 47 C8
Peñalsordo E 51 B9
Penalva do Castelo P 44 C5
Penamacor P 45 D6
Peñaranda de Bracamonte E 45 C10
Peñaranda de Duero E 40 E5
Peñarroya de Tastavins E 42 F4
Peñarroya-Pueblonuevo E 51 C9
Peñarrubia E 55 C8
Penarth GB 13 C8
Peñascosa E 55 B8
Peñas de San Pedro E 55 B9
Peñausende E 39 F8
Penc H 150 B3
Pencader GB 12 A6
Pěnčín CZ 81 E8
Pendeen GB 12 E3
Pendilhe P 44 C5
Pendine GB 12 B5
Pendlebury GB 11 D7
Penedo Gordo P 50 D4
Penedono P 44 C6
Penela P 44 D4
Pénestin F 22 F7
Penészlek H 151 B9
Pengfors S 107 D17
Pengsjö S 107 D13
Pengsjö S 107 D17
Penha Garcia P 45 D6
Peniche P 44 F2
Penicuik GB 5 D10
Penikkajärvi FIN 121 C14
Peninki FIN 123 D15
Peninver GB 4 E5
Peñíscola E 48 D5
Penistone GB 11 D8
Penkridge GB 11 F7
Penkule LV 134 D6
Penkun D 84 D6
Penly F 18 E3
Penmarch F 22 E3
Pennabilli I 66 E5
Penna in Teverina I 62 C2
Pennapiedimonte I 63 C6
Pennautier F 33 D10
Penne F 33 B9
Penne I 62 C5
Penne-d'Agenais F 33 B7
Pennyghael GB 4 C4
Penrhiw-pâl GB 12 A6
Penrhyn Bay GB 10 E4
Penrith GB 5 F11
Penryn GB 12 E4
Pensala FIN 122 D9
Pentalofo GR 174 C3
Pentalofos GR 168 D5
Pentalofos GR 171 A10
Pentapoli GR 169 B10
Penteoria GR 174 C5
Pentinniemi FIN 119 C16
Pentir GB 10 E3
Pentone I 59 B10
Pentraeth GB 10 E3
Pentre GB 13 B8
Pentrefoelas GB 10 E4
Penttäjä S 117 E11
Penttilänvaara FIN 121 C12
Penvénan F 22 C5
Penybont GB 13 A8
Penybontfawr GB 10 F5
Pen-y-fai GB 13 B7
Penzance GB 12 E3
Penzberg D 72 A3
Penzlin D 84 D4
Péone F 36 C5
Pepelow D 83 B11
Pepeni MD 154 B2
Pepingen B 19 C9
Pepinster B 19 C12
Peplos GR 171 C10
Pępowo PL 81 C12
Pëqin AL 168 B2
Peque E 39 D7
Pér H 149 A9
Pêra P 50 E3
Perabroddzye BY 133 E2
Perachora GR 175 C6
Perafita E 43 C8
Perä-Hyyppä FIN 122 F8
Peraia GR 169 C6
Peraia GR 169 C8
Perais P 44 E5
Perälä FIN 122 F7
Peralada E 43 C10
Peraleda de la Mata E 45 E10
Peraleda del Zaucejo E 51 C8
Peralejos E 42 G1
Peralejos de las Truchas E 47 C9
Perales del Alfambra E 42 F2
Perales del Puerto E 45 D7
Peralta E 32 F2
Peralta de Alcofea E 42 D3
Peralta de la Sal E 42 D4
Peraltilla E 42 C3
Peralva P 50 E4
Peralveche E 47 C8
Perama GR 168 E4
Perama GR 175 D8
Perama GR 178 E8
Perämäki FIN 122 D9
Peramola E 42 C6
Peranka FIN 121 D13
Peränne FIN 123 F11
Perä-Posio FIN 121 B10
Perarolo di Cadore I 72 D5
Peräseinäjoki FIN 123 E10
Perast MNE 163 E6
Perävaara FIN 115 E2
Perbál H 149 A11
Perchtoldsdorf A 77 F10
Percy F 23 C9
Perdasdefogu I 64 D3
Perdaxius I 64 E2
Perdifumo I 60 C4
Perdiguera E 41 E10
Perdika GR 168 F3
Perdika GR 175 D7
Perdiki GR 177 D7
Perdikkas GR 169 C6
Perduhovo Selo BIH 157 D6
Perechyn UA 145 F5
Peredo P 39 F6
Peregu Mare RO 151 E6
Perehins'ke UA 145 F9
Pereiras P 50 E3
Pereiro E 38 A4
Pereiro P 50 E4
Pereiro de Aguiar E 38 D4
Perekhrestove UA 154 C5
Pererîta MD 153 A9
Pereruela E 39 F8
Peresecina MD 154 C3
Peressaare EST 131 C13
Peretu RO 160 E6
Pereyma UA 154 A5
Perfugas I 64 B2
Perg A 77 F7
Pergine Valdarno I 66 F4
Pergine Valsugana I 69 A11
Pergola I 67 E6
Perho FIN 123 D12
Periam RO 151 E6
Periana E 53 C8
Pericei RO 151 C10
Périers F 23 B9
Perieți RO 160 E5
Perieți RO 161 D10
Périgueux F 29 E7
Perikleia GR 169 B7
Perila EST 131 C10
Perilla de Castro E 39 E8
Perín-Chym SK 145 F3
Periprava RO 155 C5
Periș RO 161 D7
Perișani RO 160 C4
Perișor RO 160 E2
Perișoru RO 161 E11
Perissa GR 179 C9
Peristasi GR 169 D8
Peristera GR 169 C9
Peristeri GR 175 C8
Perithori GR 169 B10
Perivoli GR 168 E5
Perivoli GR 168 F3
Perivoli GR 174 A5
Perivoli GR 174 B5
Perivolia GR 178 E7
Perjasica HR 156 B3
Perkáta H 149 B11
Perkiömäki FIN 123 D9
Perl D 20 F6
Perlat AL 163 F8
Perleberg D 83 D11
Perlejewo PL 141 E7
Perlez SRB 158 C5
Perloja LT 137 E9
Perły PL 136 E4
Permani HR 67 B9
Permantokoski FIN 117 F16
Përmet AL 168 D3
Pernå FIN 127 E15
Pernarava LT 134 F7
Pernarec CZ 76 C4
Pernegg an der Mur A 148 B4
Pernersdorf A 77 E10
Pernes P 44 F3
Pernes-les-Fontaines F 35 C9
Perni GR 171 B7
Pernik BG 165 D7
Perniö FIN 127 E9
Perniön asema FIN 127 E9
Pernitz A 77 G9
Pernu FIN 121 B10
Pero I 69 B7
Peroguarda P 50 C3
Pérols F 35 C6
Péron F 31 C8
Perondi AL 168 C2
Péronnas F 31 C7
Péronne F 18 E6
Perosa Argentina I 31 F11
Pero Viseu P 44 D6
Perpignan F 34 E4
Perranporth GB 12 E4
Perrecy-les-Forges F 30 B5
Perreux F 30 C5
Perrigny F 31 B8
Perrogney-les-Fontaines F 26 E3
Perros-Guirec F 22 C5
Perrum-Äbmir FIN 113 E19
Persan F 25 B7
Persåsen S 102 A7
Persberg S 97 C11
Persbo S 97 B13
Persenbeug A 77 F8
Pershagen S 93 A11
Pershamawskaya BY 133 E4
Pershore GB 13 A10
Pershotravneve UA 155 C4
Pershyttan S 97 D13
Persnäs S 89 A11
Persön S 118 C8
Perstorp S 87 C12
Perth GB 5 C10
Perthes F 25 D8
Pertouli GR 168 E5
Perttaus FIN 117 D15
Pertteli FIN 127 E9
Perttula FIN 127 E12
Pertuis F 35 C10
Pertunmaa FIN 127 C15
Pertusa E 42 C3
Peruc CZ 76 B5
Perućac SRB 158 F3
Perucica BIH 157 F10
Perugia I 66 F5
Perukka FIN 119 F17
Perunkajärvi FIN 117 E15
Perushtitsa BG 165 E10
Perušić HR 156 C3
Péruwelz B 19 C8
Pervalka LT 134 F2
Pervenchères F 24 D3
Pervomaisc MD 154 D5
Pervomayskoye RUS 129 E12
Perwez B 19 C10
Pesadas de Burgos E 40 C4
Pesaro I 67 E6
Pescaglia I 66 E1
Pescantina I 66 B2
Pescara I 63 C6
Pescari RO 159 D8
Pescasseroli I 62 D5
Pesceana RO 160 D4
Peschadoires F 30 D3
Peschici I 63 D10
Peschiera del Garda I 66 B2
Pescia I 66 E2
Pescina I 62 C5
Pescocostanzo I 62 D6
Pescolanciano I 63 D6
Pescopennataro I 63 D6
Pescorocchiano I 62 C4
Pesco Sannita I 60 A3
Peseux CH 31 B10
Peshkopi AL 163 F9
Peshtera BG 165 E9
Pesiökylä FIN 121 E12
Pesiönranta FIN 121 E12
Pesmes F 26 F4
Pesnica SLO 148 C5
Pesochnyy RUS 129 E13
Peso da Régua P 44 B5
Pesquera de Duero E 40 E3
Pessac F 28 F4
Pessalompolo FIN 117 F12
Pessan F 33 C7
Pesse NL 17 C6
Pessin D 80 A3
Peštani MK 168 B4
Peștera RO 155 E2
Peștișani RO 159 C11
Pestișu Mic RO 151 F10
Pesués E 40 B3
Pešurići BIH 157 E11
Petacciato I 63 C7
Petäikkö FIN 119 E16
Petäiskylä FIN 125 C12
Petäjäjärvi FIN 119 C17
Petäjäkangas FIN 119 D17
Petäjäskoski FIN 119 B14
Petäjäskoski FIN 119 F13
Petäjävesi FIN 123 F14
Petalax FIN 122 E6
Petalidi GR 174 F4
Pétange L 20 E5
Petas GR 174 A3
Petelea RO 152 D5
Peteranec HR 149 D7
Peterborough GB 11 F11
Peterculter GB 3 L12
Peterhead GB 3 K13
Péteri H 150 C3
Peterlee GB 5 F14
Petersberg D 74 A6
Petersdorf D 75 E9
Petersdorf auf Fehmarn D 83 B10
Petersfield GB 15 E7
Petershagen D 17 D11
Petershagen D 80 B6
Peterswell IRL 6 F5
Pétervására H 147 E10
Pethelinos GR 169 C10
Petilia Policastro I 59 A10
Petín E 38 D5
Petisträsk S 107 B17
Petite-Rosselle F 186 C2
Petit-Mars F 23 F9
Petitmont F 186 D2
Petit-Noir F 31 B7
Petko Karavelovo BG 166 C5
Petko Slaveykov BG 165 C10
Petkula FIN 115 C1
Petkus D 80 C4
Petlovača SRB 158 D3
Pet Mogili BG 166 E6
Petneháza H 145 G5
Petőfibánya H 150 B4
Petra E 57 B11
Petra GR 171 F10
Petrăchioaia RO 161 D8
Petrades GR 172 B6
Petralia-Soprana I 58 D5
Petran AL 168 D3
Petrana GR 169 D6
Petrella Salto I 62 C4
Petrella Tifernina I 63 D7
Petrer E 56 E3
Petrești RO 151 B9
Petrești RO 160 D6
Petreștii de Jos RO 152 D3

Ravelsbach A 77 E9
Rävemåla S 89 B8
Ravenglass GB 10 C5
Ravenna I 66 D5
Ravensburg D 71 B9
Ravenstein NL 16 E5
Ravières F 25 E11
Ravijoki FIN 128 D8
Ravik N 108 B7
Rävlanda S 91 D12
Ravna Dubrava SRB 164 C5
Ravna Gora HR 67 B10
Ravna Reka SRB 159 E8
Ravne SLO 73 D11
Ravne na Koroškem SLO 73 C10
Ravnets BG 167 D8
Ravni BIH 157 F8
Ravnište SRB 164 C3
Ravnje SRB 158 D3
Ravnkilde DK 86 B5
Ravno BIH 157 E7
Ravno BIH 162 D4
Ravnogor BG 165 F9
Ravno Selo SRB 158 C4
Ravnshøj DK 90 E7
Ravnstrup DK 86 C4
Rävsön S 103 A15
Ravsted DK 86 E4
Rawa Mazowiecka PL 141 G2
Rawicz PL 81 C11
Rawmarsh GB 11 E9
Rawtenstall GB 11 D7
Raykovo BG 171 A7
Rayleigh GB 15 D10
Rayol-Canadel-sur-Mer F 36 E4
Räyrinki FIN 123 D11
Ražana SRB 158 E4
Ražanac HR 156 D3
Ražanj SRB 159 F8
Războieni RO 153 C9
Razboj BIH 157 B7
Razbojna SRB 164 C3
Razdelna BG 167 C9
Razdol BG 169 A9
Razdrto SLO 73 E9
Razès F 29 C8
Razgrad BG 160 F2
Razgrad BG 167 B7
Ražljevo BIH 157 C10
Razlog BG 165 F7
Razlovci MK 165 F6
Ražňany SK 145 E3
Ráztočno SK 147 D7
Răzvad RO 161 D6
Reading GB 14 E7
Reaghstown IRL 7 E9
Real P 38 F3
Réalmont F 33 C10
Realmonte I 58 E3
Réalville F 33 B8
Rear Cross IRL 8 C6
Réaup F 33 B6
Reay GB 3 H9
Rebais F 25 C9
Rebbenesbotn N 112 C2
Rebecq B 19 C9
Rébénacq F 32 D5
Rebild DK 86 B5
Rebollosa de Jadraque E 47 B7
Reboly RUS 125 C15
Rebordelo E 38 B3
Rebordelo P 38 E5
Rebra RO 152 C4
Rebricea RO 153 D11
Rebrişoara RO 152 C4
Rebrovo BG 165 D7
Rebŭrkovo BG 165 C8
Reca SK 146 E4
Reçan RKS 163 E10
Recanati I 67 F8
Recaş RO 151 F8
Recco I 37 C10
Recea MD 153 B11
Recea MD 154 C3
Recea RO 151 B12
Recea RO 152 F5
Recea RO 160 D6
Recea-Cristur RO 152 C3
Recess IRL 6 F3
Recey-sur-Ource F 25 E12
Réchicourt-le-Château F 27 C6
Rechlin D 83 D13
Rechnitz A 149 B6
Recht B 20 D6
Rechtenbach D 74 C6
Reci RO 153 F7
Rečica SLO 73 D11
Rečice BIH 157 F8
Recke D 17 D9
Reckingen CH 70 E6
Recklinghausen D 17 E8
Recoaro Terme I 69 B11
Recoubeau-Jansac F 35 A9
Recsk H 147 F10
Recuerda E 40 F6
Recz PL 85 D9
Rjczno PL 141 H1
Reda PL 138 A5
Redalen N 101 E13
Redange L 20 E5
Redcar GB 11 B9
Redcastle IRL 4 E2
Redcross IRL 9 C10
Reddelich D 83 B11
Redditch GB 13 A11
Réde H 149 B9
Redea RO 160 E4
Redefin D 83 D10
Redhill GB 15 E8
Rédics H 149 C6
Réding F 27 C7
Redinha P 44 D3
Rediu RO 153 C11
Rediu RO 153 D9
Rediu RO 153 F11
Rediul Mare MD 153 A11
Rednitzhembach D 75 D9
Redon F 23 E7
Redondela E 38 D2
Redondelo P 38 E4
Redondo P 50 B4
Redován E 56 E3
Red Point GB 2 K5
Redruth GB 12 E4
Redsted DK 86 B3
Reduzum NL 16 B5
Rjdzikowo PL 85 B12
Rjdziny PL 143 E7
Reen IRL 8 E3
Reens IRL 8 C5
Reepham GB 15 B11
Rees D 16 E6
Reeßum D 17 B12
Reetz D 79 B11
Reetz D 83 D11
Reftele S 87 A13
Regalbuto I 59 D6
Regen D 76 E4
Regensburg D 75 D11
Regensdorf CH 27 F9
Regenstauf D 75 D11
Reggello I 66 E4
Reggio di Calabria I 59 C8
Reggiolo I 66 C2
Reggio nell'Emilia I 66 C2
Reghin RO 152 D5
Reghiu RO 153 F9
Regna S 92 B7
Regnitzlosau D 75 B11
Régny F 30 D5
Regőly H 149 C10
Regozero RUS 121 D17
Regstrup DK 87 D9
Reguengo E 38 D2
Reguengos de Monsaraz P 50 C4
Rehau D 75 B11
Rehburg (Rehburg-Loccum) D 17 D12
Rehden D 17 C10
Rehling D 75 F8
Rehlingen-Siersburg D 21 F7
Řehlovice CZ 80 E5
Rehmsdorf D 79 D11
Rehna D 83 C10
Rehula FIN 129 C9
Reibitz D 79 C11
Reichelsheim (Odenwald) D 187 B6
Reichenau an der Rax A 148 A5
Reichenbach CH 70 D5
Reichenbach D 79 E11
Reichenbach D 187 B6
Reichenberg D 74 C6
Reichenfels A 73 B10
Reichenthal A 76 E6
Reichertsheim D 75 F11
Reichia GR 178 B5
Reichling D 71 B11
Reichmannsdorf D 75 A9
Reicholzheim D 74 C6
Reichraming A 73 A9
Reichshoffen F 27 C8
Reichstett F 186 D4
Reiden CH 27 F8
Reigada P 45 C7
Reigate GB 15 E8
Reignac F 28 E4
Reignier F 31 C9
Reil D 21 D8
Reilingen D 187 C6
Reillanne F 35 C10
Reillo E 47 E9
Reims F 19 F9
Reina E 51 C8
Reinach CH 27 F8
Reinach CH 27 F9
Reinbek D 83 C8
Reinberg D 84 B4
Reine N 110 E5
Reinfeld (Holstein) D 83 C8
Reinheim D 21 E11
Reinosa E 40 C3
Reinøysund N 114 D8
Reinsfeld D 21 E7
Reinskard N 112 D4
Reinskloster N 104 D7
Reinstad N 111 C10
Reinsvik N 104 E3
Reinsvoll N 101 E13
Reipa N 108 C6
Reisbach D 75 E12
Reischach D 75 F12
Reisjärvi FIN 123 C13
Reiskirchen D 21 C11
Reiss GB 3 J10
Reitan N 100 B8
Reitan N 101 A14
Reitano I 58 D5
Reith bei Seefeld A 72 B3
Reit im Winkl D 72 A5
Reittiö FIN 125 D9
Reivyčiai LT 134 D4
Rejmyre S 92 B7
Rejowiec PL 141 H8
Rejsby DK 86 E3
Reka HR 149 D7
Rekava LV 133 B3
Rekavice BIH 157 C7
Reken D 17 E8
Rekijoki FIN 127 E9
Rekken NL 17 D7
Reklynets' UA 144 C9
Rekovac SRB 159 F7
Rekowo PL 85 B12
Rekvik N 111 A15
Rėkyva LT 134 E6
Relíquias P 50 D3
Relletti FIN 119 E13
Relleu E 56 D4
Rellingen D 83 C7
Rém H 150 E3
Remagen D 21 C8
Rémalard F 24 D4
Rembercourt-Sommaisne F 26 C3
Remda D 79 E9
Remels (Uplengen) D 17 B9
Remennikovo RUS 133 C5
Remeskylä FIN 123 C16
Remetea RO 151 D9
Remetea RO 152 D6
Remetea Chioarului RO 152 B3
Remetea Mare RO 151 F7
Remeţi RO 145 H8
Remetinec HR 149 D6
Remetské Hámre SK 145 F5
Remich L 20 E6
Remicourt B 183 D6
Remiremont F 26 D6
Remmam S 107 D14
Remmen S 102 B8
Remmet S 102 B7
Remnes N 108 E4
Remolinos E 41 E9
Remouchamps B 183 E7
Remoulins F 35 C8
Remplin D 83 C13
Remptendorf D 75 A10
Remscheid D 21 B8
Remte LV 134 C5
Remungol F 22 E6
Rémuzat F 35 B9
Rena E 45 F9
Rena N 101 D14
Renaison F 30 C4
Renålandet S 106 D8
Renazé F 23 E9
Renceni LV 131 F10
Renchen D 27 C9
Renda LV 134 B4
Rende I 60 E6
Rendsburg D 82 B7
Renedo E 39 E10
Renedo E 40 B4
Renedo de la Vega E 39 D10
Renens CH 31 B10
Renesse NL 16 E1
Renfrew GB 5 D8
Renginio GR 175 B6
Rengsdorf D 21 C8
Rengsjö S 103 D12
Renholmen S 118 D6
Reni UA 155 C2
Renko FIN 127 D11
Renkomäki FIN 127 D14
Renkum NL 183 B7
Renndal N 104 E5
Rennerod D 21 C10
Rennertshofen D 75 E9
Rennes F 23 D8
Rennes-les-Bains F 33 E10
Renningen D 27 C10
Rennweg A 73 B8
Renòn I 72 C3
Rens DK 86 F4
Rensjön S 111 D18
Reńska Wieś PL 142 F5
Renström S 118 E4
Renswoude NL 183 A7
Rentina GR 174 A4
Rentjärn S 107 A15
Rentweinsdorf D 75 B8
Renwez F 19 E10
Renzow D 83 C10
Repbäcken S 97 A13
Répcelak H 149 B8
Repedea RO 152 B4
Repino RUS 129 E12
Repki PL 141 F6
Replot FIN 122 D6
Repojoki FIN 117 B15
Repolka RUS 132 C6
Reposaari FIN 126 B5
Repparfjord N 113 C13
Reppelin D 83 B12
Reppen N 108 C6
Reppenstedt D 83 D8
Reps AL 163 F9
Repton GB 11 F8
Repvåg N 113 B16
Requejo E 39 D6
Requena E 47 F10
Réquista F 33 B11
Rerik D 83 B11
Resana I 72 E4
Resarö S 99 D10
Resavica SRB 159 E8
Resele S 107 E12
Resen BG 166 C5
Resen MK 168 B5
Resenbro DK 86 C5
Resende P 44 B5
Rešetari HR 157 B7
Reşiţa RO 159 C8
Resko PL 85 C8
Resna MNE 163 E6
Resolven GB 13 B7
Respenda de la Peña E 39 C10
Resse (Wedemark) D 78 A6
Ressons-sur-Matz F 18 E6
Resteliçë RKS 163 F10
Restinga MA 53 E6
Reston GB 5 D12
Resuttano I 58 D5
Retamal E 51 B8
Retford GB 11 E10
Rethel F 19 E9
Rethem (Aller) D 17 C12
Rethymno GR 178 E7
Retie B 16 F4
Retiers F 23 E9
Retje SLO 73 E10
Retortillo E 45 C8
Retortillo de Soria E 40 F6
Retournac F 30 E5
Rétság H 147 F8
Retuerta del Bullaque E 46 F4
Retunen FIN 125 E11
Retz A 77 E9
Reuden D 79 B11
Reuilly F 24 F7
Reurieth D 75 B8
Reus E 42 E6
Reusel NL 16 F4
Reut D 76 F3
Reute D 27 D8
Reuţel MD 153 B11
Reuterstadt Stavenhagen D 84 C3
Reutlingen D 27 D11
Reutte A 71 C11
Reutuaapa FIN 119 B15
Reuver NL 16 F6
Revel F 33 D10
Revello I 37 B6
Revest-du-Bion F 35 B10
Révfülöp H 149 C9
Revholmen N 91 A8
Reviga RO 161 D10
Revigny-sur-Ornain F 26 C2
Revilla de Collazos E 40 C3
Revilla del Campo E 40 D4
Revin F 19 E10
Revine-Lago I 72 E5
Řevnice CZ 76 C6
Řevničov CZ 76 B5
Revò I 72 D3
Revonlahti FIN 119 E13
Revsnes N 100 D6
Revsnes N 111 C11
Revsund S 103 A9
Revúca SK 147 D10
Rewal PL 85 B8
Rexbo S 103 E9
Reyrieux F 30 D6
Rezé F 23 F8
Rēzekne LV 133 C2
Rezi H 149 C8
Rezina MD 154 B3
Rēzna LV 133 D2
Rezovo BG 167 F10
Rezzato I 66 A1
Rezzo I 37 C7
Rezzoaglio I 37 B10
Rgotina SRB 159 E9
Rhade D 17 B12
Rhaunen D 21 E8
Rhayader GB 13 A7
Rheda-Wiedenbrück D 17 E10
Rhede D 17 E7
Rhede (Ems) D 17 B8
Rheden NL 183 A8
Rheinau D 27 C8
Rheinbach D 21 C7
Rheinberg D 17 E7
Rheinböllen D 185 E8
Rheinbreitbach D 21 C8
Rheinbrohl D 185 D7
Rheine D 17 D8
Rheinfelden (Baden) D 27 E8
Rheinsberg D 84 D3
Rheinstetten D 27 C9
Rheinzabern D 187 C5
Rhêmes-Notre-Dame I 31 D11
Rhêmes-St-Georges I 31 D11
Rhenen NL 16 E5
Rhens D 185 D8
Rhiconich GB 2 J7
Rhinau F 27 D8
Rhinow D 83 E12
Rhisnes B 182 D5
Rho I 69 B7
Rhode IRL 7 F8
Rhoden (Diemelstadt) D 17 F12
Rhoon NL 182 B4
Rhoose GB 13 C8
Rhosllanerchrugog GB 10 E5
Rhôs-on-Sea GB 10 E4
Rhossili GB 12 B6
Rhuddlan GB 10 E5
Rhydaman GB 12 B7
Rhyl GB 10 E5
Rhymney GB 13 B8
Riace I 59 C9
Riachos P 44 F3
Riaillé F 23 E9
Rialp E 33 F8
Riaño E 39 C10
Riano I 62 C3
Rians F 35 C10
Riantec F 22 E5
Rianxo E 38 C2
Riaz CH 31 B11
Riba E 40 B4
Ribadavia E 38 D3
Ribadelago E 39 D6
Riba de Mouro P 38 D3
Ribadeo E 38 A5
Riba de Saelices E 47 C8
Ribadesella E 39 B9
Ribaforada E 41 D8
Ribafrecha E 32 F1
Ribarci SRB 164 E6
Ribare SRB 164 C4
Ribari SRB 158 D3
Ribaritsa BG 165 D9
Riba-roja d'Ebre E 42 E4
Riba-roja de Turia E 48 E3
Ribbåsen S 102 D7
Ribchester GB 10 D6
Ribe DK 86 E3
Ribeauvillé F 27 D7
Ribécourt-Dreslincourt F 18 E6
Ribeira E 38 C2
Ribeira P 38 E3
Ribeira de Pena P 38 E4
Ribemont F 19 E7
Ribera I 58 E3
Ribérac F 29 E6
Ribera del Fresno E 51 B7
Ribesalbes E 48 D4
Ribes de Freser E 33 F10
Ribiţa RO 151 E10
Ribnica BIH 157 D9
Ribnica SLO 73 E10
Ribnica SLO 148 C4
Ribnica SRB 158 F4
Ribnik HR 148 E4
Rîbniţa MD 154 B4
Ribnitz-Damgarten D 83 B12
Ribnovo BG 165 F8
Ribota E 40 F5
Ricadi I 59 B8
Říčany CZ 77 C7
Říčany CZ 77 D10
Riccia I 63 E7
Riccio I 66 F5
Riccione I 66 D6
Riccò del Golfo di Spezia I 69 E8
Richardménil F 26 C5
Richelieu F 29 A6
Richhill GB 7 D9
Richka UA 152 A5
Richmond GB 11 C8
Richvald SK 145 E3
Rickebo S 103 D11
Rickenbach D 27 E8
Rickinghall GB 15 C10
Rickling D 83 B8
Rickmansworth GB 15 D8
Ricla E 41 E9
Ricse H 145 G4
Ridasjärvi FIN 127 D13
Riddarhyttan S 97 C14
Ridderkerk NL 16 E3
Riddes CH 31 C11
Riđica SRB 150 F3
Rīdzene LV 135 B10
Riebiņi LV 135 D13
Riebnesluspen S 109 D13
Riec-sur-Belon F 22 E4
Ried CH 68 A5
Riede D 17 C11
Riedenburg D 75 E10
Rieder D 79 C9
Ried im Innkreis A 76 F4
Ried im Oberinntal A 71 C11
Ried im Zillertal A 72 B4
Ried in der Riedmark A 77 F7
Riedlingen D 71 A8
Riegelsberg D 21 F7
Riegersburg A 148 B5
Riego de la Vega E 39 D8
Riehe (Suthfeld) D 78 B5
Riehen CH 27 E8
Rielasingen-Worblingen D 27 E10
Riello E 39 C8
Rielves E 46 E4
Riemst B 19 C12
Rieneck D 187 A8
Rieni RO 151 D9
Rieponlahti FIN 124 E7
Riepsdorf D 83 B9
Riesa D 80 D4
Rieseby D 83 A7
Riesi I 58 E5
Riestedt D 79 D9
Rietavas LT 134 E3
Rietberg D 17 E10
Rieth D 84 C6
Riethoven NL 183 C6
Rieti I 62 C3
Rietschen D 81 D7
Rieumes F 33 D8
Rieupeyroux F 33 B10
Rieutort-de-Randon F 34 A5
Rieux F 23 E7
Rieux F 33 D8
Riez F 36 D4
Rifiano I 72 C3
Rīga LV 135 C8
Rigaio GR 169 F8
Rigaud F 36 D5
Riggisberg CH 31 B11
Rignac F 33 B10
Rignano Flaminio I 62 C2
Rignano Garganico I 63 D9
Rignano sull'Arno I 66 E3
Rigny-le-Ferron F 25 D10
Rigny-sur-Arroux F 30 B5
Rigny-Ussé F 24 F3
Rigside GB 5 D9
Rihtniemi FIN 126 C5
Riihimäki FIN 127 D12
Riihivaara FIN 125 C14
Riikonkumpu FIN 117 C14
Riipi FIN 117 D16
Riippi FIN 122 F7
Riisipere EST 131 C8
Riistavesi FIN 125 E10
Riitiala FIN 127 B8
Riječa BIH 157 E10
Rijeka BIH 157 D9
Rijeka BIH 157 F11
Rijeka HR 67 B9
Rijeka Crnojevića MNE 163 E7
Rijen NL 16 E3
Rijkevorsel B 16 F3
Rijnsburg NL 16 D2
Rijsbergen NL 16 E3
Rijsel F 19 C7
Rijssen NL 17 D7
Rijswijk NL 16 D2
Rikava LV 133 C2
Riksgränsen S 111 D15
Rila BG 165 E7
Rilhac-Rancon F 29 D8
Rilland NL 182 C4
Rillé F 23 F12
Rillieux-la-Pape F 30 D6
Rillo E 42 F2
Rillo de Gallo E 47 C9
Rimavská Baňa SK 147 D9
Rimavská Seč SK 145 G1
Rimavská Sobota SK 147 E10
Rimavské Janovce SK 147 E10
Rimbach D 76 D3
Rimbach D 187 B6
Rimbo S 99 C10
Rimetea RO 152 E3
Rimforsa S 92 C7
Rimicāni LV 135 D12
Rimini I 66 D6
Rimjokk S 118 B5
Rimmilä FIN 127 D11
Rimóc H 147 E9
Rimogne F 184 E2
Rimont F 33 E8
Rimpar D 74 C6
Rimsbo S 103 D11
Rimšė LT 135 E12
Rimšėnai LT 135 F12
Rimske Toplice SLO 73 D11
Rimsting D 72 A5
Rinchnach D 76 E4
Rincón de la Victoria E 53 C8
Rincón de Soto E 41 D8
Rinda LV 134 A3
Rindal N 104 E6
Rindsholm DK 86 C4
Rineia GR 176 E5
Rinella I 59 B6
Ringarum S 93 C8
Ringaudai LT 137 D8
Ringe D 17 C7
Ringe DK 86 E6
Ringebu N 101 C12
Ringelia N 101 E12
Ringen N 95 B12
Ringford GB 5 F8
Ringhals S 87 A10
Ringkøbing DK 86 C2
Ringleben D 79 D9
Ringsend GB 4 E3
Ringsta S 106 E7
Ringsted DK 87 E9
Ringvattnet S 106 C8
Ringville IRL 9 D7
Ringwood GB 13 D11
Rinkaby S 88 D6
Rinkabyholm S 89 B10
Rinkenæs DK 86 F5
Rinkilä FIN 129 B10
Rinloan GB 5 A10
Rinn S 97 B9
Rinneen IRL 8 C4
Rinøyvåg N 111 D10
Rintala FIN 123 D10
Rinteln D 17 D12
Rio GR 174 C4
Rio Caldo P 38 E3
Rio de Mel P 44 C6
Rio de Moinhos P 50 B4
Rio de Moinhos P 50 C3
Rio de Moinhos P 50 D3
Rio de Onor P 39 E6
Rio di Pusteria I 72 C4
Riofrío E 46 C3
Riofrío de Aliste E 39 E7
Rióqordo E 53 C8
Rioja E 55 F8
Riola Sardo I 64 D2
Riolobos E 45 E8
Riolo Terme I 66 D4
Riols F 34 C4
Riom F 30 D3
Riomaggiore I 69 E8
Rio Maior P 44 F3
Rio Marina I 65 B2
Riom-ès-Montagnes F 29 E11
Rion-des-Landes F 32 C4
Rionegro del Puente E 39 D7
Rio nell'Elba I 65 B2
Rionero in Vulture I 60 B5
Rionero Sannitico I 63 D6
Rions F 32 A5
Riorges F 30 C5
Ríos E 38 E5
Rioseco de Tapia E 39 C8
Rio Tinto P 44 B3
Rio Torto P 38 E5
Rioz F 26 F5
Ripač BIH 156 C4
Ripacandida I 60 B5
Ripalimosano I 63 D7
Ripanj SRB 158 D6
Riparbella I 66 F2
Ripatransone I 62 B5
Ripe I 67 E7
Ripi I 62 D4
Ripiceni RO 153 B10
Ripley GB 11 C8
Ripley GB 11 E9
Ripoll E 43 C8
Ripon GB 11 C8
Riposto I 59 D7
Rips NL 183 B7
Riquewihr F 27 D7
Risan MNE 163 D6
Risarven S 103 C10
Risbäck S 106 B9
Risberg S 102 D6
Risca GB 13 B8
Rişca RO 151 D11
Rîşcani MD 153 B11
Riscle F 32 C5
Risdal N 90 B3
Risede S 106 C8
Rish BG 167 D7
Risinge S 92 B7
Risliden S 107 B16
Risnabben S 118 D3
Risnes N 94 E5
Risør N 90 B5
Risøyhamn N 111 C10
Rissa N 104 D7
Rissna S 106 E8
Rissnaben S 118 D4
Riste FIN 126 C7
Risteli FIN 125 B12
Risti EST 131 D8
Ristiina FIN 128 B7
Ristijärvi FIN 121 F11
Ristilä FIN 121 B11
Ristilampi FIN 117 E17
Ristinen FIN 124 D7
Ristinkylä FIN 125 E12
Ristioja FIN 117 E13
Ristonmännikkö FIN 117 D16
Risträsk S 107 B12
Risudden S 119 B11
Risum-Lindholm D 82 A5
Rītausmas LV 135 D8
Rite LV 135 D10
Rīteri LV 135 C11
Ritini GR 169 D7
Ritola FIN 123 E11
Ritterhude D 17 B11
Rittersdorf D 185 D5
Rittersgrün D 75 B12
Riudarenes E 43 D9
Riudecols E 42 E5
Riudoms E 42 E6
Riutta FIN 123 C12
Riutula FIN 113 F18
Rīva LV 134 C2
Riva del Garda I 69 B10
Riva di Solto I 69 B9
Riva di Tures I 72 C5
Rivanazzano I 37 B10
Rivardo Ligure I 37 C9
Rivarolo Canavese I 68 C4
Rivarolo Mantovano I 66 B1
Rivas-Vaciamadrid E 46 D6
Rive-de-Gier F 30 D6
Rivedoux-Plage F 28 C3
Rivello I 60 C5
Riverchapel IRL 9 C10
Rivergaro I 37 B11
Rivero E 40 B3
Riverstown IRL 7 F7
Riverstown IRL 8 E6
Rivery F 18 E5
Rives F 31 E8
Rivesaltes F 34 E4
Rivière-sur-Tarn F 34 B5
Rivignano I 73 E7
Rivinperä FIN 119 F16
Rivodutri I 62 B3
Rivoli I 68 C4
Rivolta d'Adda I 69 C8
Rixensart B 19 C10
Rixheim F 27 E7
Rixö S 91 C9
Riza GR 175 C6
Rizes GR 174 E5
Rizia GR 171 A10
Rizomata GR 169 D7
Rizomylos GR 169 F8
Rizziconi I 59 C8
Rjånes N 100 B3
Rjukan N 95 C9
Rø DK 89 E7
Ro I 66 C4
Rö S 103 A14
Roa E 40 E4
Roa N 95 B13
Roade GB 15 C7
Roadside GB 3 H10
Roadside of Kinneff GB 5 B12
Roager DK 86 E3
Roaillan F 32 B5
Roald N 100 A4
Roan N 104 C8
Roanne F 30 C5
Roata de Jos RO 161 E7
Roath GB 13 C8
Röbäck S 122 C4
Robăneşti RO 160 E4
Robbio I 68 C6
Robeasca RO 161 C10
Robecco d'Oglio I 69 C9
Röbel D 83 D13
Robella I 68 C5
Robert-Espagne F 26 C3
Roberton GB 5 D9
Roberton GB 5 E11
Robertsfors S 118 F5
Robežnieki LV 133 E3
Robiac-Rochessadoule F 35 B7
Robilante I 37 C6
Robin Hood's Bay GB 11 C10
Robion F 35 C9
Robledo E 55 B8
Robledo de Chavela E 46 C4
Robledo del Mazo E 46 E3
Robledollano E 45 E9
Robles de la Valcueva E 39 C9
Robliza de Cojos E 45 C9
Robøle N 101 E11
Robregordo E 46 B5
Robres E 41 E11
Robres del Castillo E 32 F1
Roč HR 67 B9
Rocafort de Queralt E 43 E6
Rocamadour F 29 F9
Roca Vecchia I 61 C10
Roccabianca I 66 B1
Roccadaspide I 60 C4
Rocca d'Evandro I 60 A1
Rocca di Cambio I 62 C4
Rocca di Mezzo I 62 C5
Rocca di Neto I 61 E7
Rocca di Papa I 62 D3
Roccafranca I 69 C8
Roccagloriosa I 60 C4
Roccagorga I 62 D4
Rocca Grimalda I 37 B9
Rocca Imperiale I 61 C7
Roccalbegna I 65 B5
Roccalumera I 59 D7
Roccamandolfi I 63 D6
Rocca Massima I 62 D3
Roccamena I 58 D3
Roccamonfina I 60 A1
Roccamontepiano I 62 C6
Roccanova I 60 C6
Roccapalumba I 58 D4
Rocca Pia I 62 D5
Roccaraso I 62 D6
Rocca San Casciano I 66 D4
Rocca San Giovanni I 63 C6
Roccasecca I 62 D5
Roccasecca dei Volsci I 62 E4
Rocca Sinibalda I 62 C3
Roccastrada I 65 A4
Roccavione I 37 C6
Roccella Ionica I 59 C9
Rocchetta Sant'Antonio I 60 A4
Rochdale GB 11 D7
Roche GB 12 E5
Rochechouart F 29 D7
Rochefort B 19 D11
Rochefort F 28 D4
Rochefort-en-Terre F 23 E7
Rochefort-Montagne F 30 D2
Rochefort-sur-Nenon F 26 F4
Rochehaut B 184 E3
Roche-la-Molière F 30 E5
Rochemaure F 35 A8
Roches-Bettaincourt F 26 D3
Rocheservière F 28 B2
Rochester GB 5 E12
Rochester GB 15 E10
Rochetaillée F 26 E3
Rochford GB 15 D10
Rochfortbridge IRL 7 F8
Rochin F 19 C7
Rochlitz D 79 D12
Rociana del Condado E 51 E6
Ročinj SLO 73 D8
Rociu RO 160 D6
Rockanje NL 182 B4
Rockchapel IRL 8 D4
Rockcliffe GB 5 F9
Rockcorry IRL 7 D8
Rockenhausen D 21 E9
Rockesholm S 97 C12
Rockhammar S 97 C13
Rockhill IRL 8 D5
Rockingham GB 11 F10
Rockmills IRL 8 D6
Rockneby S 89 B10
Röcknitz D 79 D12
Rocourt-St-Martin F 25 B9
Rocroi F 19 E10
Roda de Bara E 43 E6
Roda de Ter E 43 D8
Rodalben D 21 F9
Rodaljice HR 156 D4
Rödåsel S 118 F3
Rodberg N 95 B9
Rødbergshamn N 111 B15
Rødby DK 83 A10
Rødbyhavn DK 83 A10
Rødding DK 86 B3
Rødding DK 86 C5
Rødding DK 86 E4
Rödeby S 89 C9
Rodeiro E 38 C4
Rødekro DK 86 E4
Rodel GB 2 K3
Rodellar E 32 F5
Rodelle F 34 A4
Roden NL 17 B6
Ródenas E 47 C10
Rodenkirchen (Stadland) D 17 B10
Rödental D 75 B9
Rodewald D 82 E6
Rodewisch D 75 A11
Rodez F 33 B11
Rodi Garganico I 63 D9
Roding D 75 D12
Rodingträsk S 107 C14
Rödjebro S 98 B8
Rødkærsbro DK 86 C4
Rodleben D 79 C11
Rødlia N 108 E7
Rödmyra S 103 C11
Rodna RO 152 C5
Rododafni GR 174 C5
Rodolivos GR 170 C5
Rödön S 105 E16
Rodopoli GR 169 B9
Rodopos GR 178 D6
Rodos GR 181 D8
Rødovre DK 87 D10
Rødsand N 111 B13
Rødsand N 114 D8
Rødseidet N 105 B11
Rödvattnet S 107 D13
Rødvig DK 87 E10
Roela EST 131 C13
Roermond NL 20 B5
Roeselare B 19 C7
Roeşti RO 160 D4
Roetgen D 20 C6
Röfors S 92 B5
Rofrano I 60 C4
Rogač HR 156 F5
Rogačica SRB 158 E4
Rogaška Slatina SLO 148 D5
Rogaszyce PL 142 D4
Rogate GB 15 E7
Rogatec SLO 148 D5
Rogatica BIH 157 E11
Rogätz D 79 B10
Roggel NL 16 F5
Roggenburg D 75 F7
Roggendorf D 83 C10
Roggentin D 84 D3
Roggiano Gravina I 60 D6
Roghudi I 59 C8
Rogienice Wielkie PL 139 D13
Rogil P 50 E2
Rogliano F 37 F10
Rogliano I 61 E6
Rognac F 35 D9

Sachsenberg (Lichtenfels) D 21 B11
Sachsenbrunn D 75 B8
Sachsenburg A 73 C7
Sachsenhagen D 17 D12
Sachsenhausen (Waldeck) D 17 F12
Sachsenheim D 27 C11
Sacile I 72 E5
Sacoșu Turcesc RO 159 B7
Sacović BIH 156 E6
Sacquenay F 26 E3
Sacramenia E 40 E4
Sacu RO 159 B9
Săcueni RO 151 C9
Săcuieu RO 151 D10
Sačurov SK 145 F4
Sada E 38 B3
Sádaba E 32 F3
Sadala EST 131 D13
Sadali I 64 D3
Saddell GB 4 D5
Sadina BG 166 C6
Sadki PL 85 D12
Sadkowice PL 141 G3
Sadkowo PL 85 C10
Sadlinki PL 138 C6
Sadova MD 154 C2
Sadova RO 152 B6
Sadova RO 160 F3
Sadove UA 154 E4
Sadovets BG 165 C9
Sadovo BG 165 E10
Sadowie PL 143 E11
Sadowne PL 139 E12
Sadská CZ 77 B7
Sadu RO 160 B4
Sädvaluspen S 109 D12
Sæbo N 94 B6
Sæbø N 100 B4
Sæbøvik N 94 C3
Sæby DK 87 D8
Sæby DK 90 E8
Sæd DK 86 F3
Saelices E 47 E7
Saelices de la Sal E 47 C8
Saelices del Rio E 39 C9
Saelices de Mayorga E 39 D9
Saerbeck D 17 D9
Særslev DK 86 D6
Sæter N 104 C8
Sætra N 104 E6
Sætre N 95 C13
Saeul L 20 E5
Sævareid N 94 B3
Safaalan TR 173 B9
Safara P 51 C5
Säffle S 91 A12
Saffré F 23 E8
Saffron Walden GB 15 C9
Săg RO 151 C10
Săg RO 159 B7
Sagama I 64 C2
Sagard D 84 A5
Sage D 17 C10
Săgeata RO 161 C9
Sågen S 97 B11
Sagiada GR 168 E3
Sağirlar TR 173 F9
Sağlamtaş TR 173 C7
Sågmyra S 103 E9
Sagna RO 153 D10
Sagone F 37 G9
Sagres P 50 E2
Sagstua N 95 B15
Săgu RO 151 E7
Sagunto E 48 E4
Sagvåg N 94 C2
Ságvár H 149 C10
Sagy F 31 B7
Sahagún E 39 D9
Sahaidac MD 154 D3
Sahalahti FIN 127 C11
Sahankylä FIN 122 F8
Saharna Nouă MD 154 B3
Săhăteni RO 161 C8
Şahin TR 173 B6
Şahinli TR 172 D6
Sahl DK 86 C5
Sahrajärvi FIN 123 F14
Sahun E 33 E6
Sahune F 35 B9
Šahy SK 147 E7
Saiakopli EST 131 C12
Saighdinis GB 2 K2
Saija FIN 115 D5
Säijä FIN 127 C10
Saikari FIN 124 E7
Saillagouse F 33 F10
Saillans F 35 A9
Sail-sous-Couzan F 30 D4
Saimaanharju FIN 129 C9
Säimen FIN 125 F12
Sains-Richaumont F 19 E8
St Abbs GB 5 D12
St-Affrique F 34 C4
St-Agnan F 30 B4
St-Agnan-en-Vercors F 31 F7
St-Agnant F 28 D4
St-Agnant-de-Versillat F 29 C9
St Agnes GB 12 E4
St-Agrève F 30 E5
St-Aignan F 24 F5
St-Aignan-sur-Roë F 23 E9
St-Aigulin F 28 E5
St-Albain F 30 C6
St-Alban F 22 C6
St-Alban-Leysse F 31 D8
St Albans GB 15 D8
St-Alban-sur-Limagnole F 30 F3
St-Amand-en-Puisaye F 25 E9
St-Amand-les-Eaux F 19 D7
St-Amand-Longpré F 24 E5
St-Amand-Montrond F 29 B11
St-Amand-sur-Fion F 25 C12
St-Amans F 34 A5
St-Amans-des-Cots F 30 F2
St-Amans-Soult F 33 D10
St-Amant-de-Boixe F 29 D6
St-Amant-Roche-Savine F 30 D4
St-Amant-Tallende F 30 D3
St-Amarin F 27 E7
St-Ambroix F 35 B7
St-Amour F 31 C7
St-Andiol F 35 C8
St-André F 34 E4
St-André-de-Corcy F 31 D6
St-André-de-Cruzières F 35 B7
St-André-de-Cubzac F 28 F5
St-André-de-l'Eure F 24 C5
St-André-de-Sangonis F 34 C6
St-André-de-Valborgne F 35 B6
St-André-le-Gaz F 31 D8
St-André-les-Alpes F 36 D5
St-André-les-Vergers F 25 D11
St Andrews GB 5 C11
St-Angel F 29 D10
St Anne GBG 23 A7
St-Anthème F 30 D4
St-Antonin-Noble-Val F 33 B9
St-Août F 29 B9
St-Apollinaire F 26 F3
St-Arcons-d'Allier F 30 E4
St-Arnoult-en-Yvelines F 24 C6
St Asaph GB 10 E5
St-Astier F 29 E7
St-Astier F 29 F6
St Athan GB 13 C8
St-Auban F 36 D5
St-Auban-sur-l'Ouvèze F 35 B9
St-Aubin F 31 A7
St-Aubin-Château-Neuf F 25 E9
St-Aubin-d'Aubigné F 23 D8
St-Aubin-de-Blaye F 28 E4
St-Aubin-du-Cormier F 23 D9
St-Aubin-lès-Elbeuf F 18 F3
St-Aubin-sur-Mer F 23 B11
St-Aulaye F 29 E6
St Austell GB 12 E5
St-Avé F 22 E6
St-Avertin F 24 F4
St-Avold F 26 B6
St-Ay F 24 E6
St-Aygulf F 36 E5
St-Barthélemy-d'Agenais F 33 A6
St-Barthélemy-de-Vals F 30 E6
St-Bauzille-de-Putois F 35 C6
St-Béat F 33 E7
St-Beauzély F 34 B4
St Bees GB 10 C4
St-Benin-d'Azy F 30 A3
St-Benoît F 29 B6
St-Benoît F 33 D10
St-Benoît-du-Sault F 29 C8
St-Benoît-sur-Loire F 25 E7
St-Béron F 31 D8
St-Berthevin F 23 D10
St-Bertrand-de-Comminges F 33 D7
St-Blaise CH 31 A10
St-Blaise-la-Roche F 27 D7
St-Blin-Semilly F 26 D3
St-Boil F 30 B6
St-Bonnet-de-Bellac F 29 C7
St-Bonnet-de-Joux F 30 C5
St-Bonnet-en-Bresse F 31 B7
St-Bonnet-en-Champsaur F 36 B4
St-Bonnet-le-Château F 30 E5
St-Bonnet-le-Froid F 30 E5
St-Bonnet-sur-Gironde F 28 E4
St-Branchs F 24 F4
St Brelade GBJ 23 B7
St-Brevin-les-Pins F 23 F7
St-Briac-sur-Mer F 23 C7
St-Brice-en-Coglès F 23 D9
St Brides Major GB 13 C7
St-Brieuc F 22 C6
St-Bris-le-Vineux F 25 E10
St-Brisson F 25 F11
St-Broing-les-Moines F 25 E12
St Buryan GB 12 E3
St-Calais F 24 E4
St-Cannat F 35 C9
St-Céré F 29 F9
St-Cergue CH 31 C9
St-Cergues F 31 C9
St-Cernin F 29 E10
St-Chaffrey F 31 F10
St-Chamarand F 33 A8
St-Chamas F 35 C9
St-Chamond F 30 E6
St-Chaptes F 35 C7
St-Chef F 31 D7
St-Chély-d'Apcher F 30 F3
St-Chély-d'Aubrac F 34 A4
St-Chinian F 34 D4
St-Christol F 35 B9
St-Christol-lès-Alès F 35 B7
St-Christoly-Médoc F 28 E4
St-Christophe I 31 D11
St-Christophe-en-Bazelle F 24 F6
St-Christophe-en-Brionnais F 30 C5
St-Ciers-sur-Gironde F 28 E4
St-Cirq-Lapopie F 33 B9
St-Clair-du-Rhône F 30 E6
St-Clar F 33 C7
St-Claud F 29 D6
St-Claude F 31 C8
St Clears GB 12 B6
St-Clément F 25 D9
St-Clément F 26 C6
St-Clément F 29 E9
St Clement GBJ 23 B7
St-Clément-de-Rivière F 35 C6
St Columb Major GB 12 E5
St Combs GB 3 K13
St-Constant F 29 F10
St-Cosme-en-Vairais F 24 D3
St-Cricq-Chalosse F 32 C4
St-Cyprien F 29 F8
St-Cyprien F 33 B8
St-Cyprien F 34 E5
St-Cyr-sur-Loire F 24 F4
St-Cyr-sur-Mer F 35 D10
St Cyrus GB 5 B12
St David's GB 9 E12
St Day GB 12 E4
St-Denis F 25 C7
St-Denis-d'Anjou F 23 E11
St-Denis-de-Gastines F 23 D10
St-Denis-de-Jouhet F 29 B9
St-Denis-de-Pile F 28 F5
St-Denis-d'Oléron F 28 C3
St-Denis-en-Bugey F 31 D7
St-Denis-lès-Bourg F 31 C7
St Dennis GB 12 E5
St-Désert F 30 B6
St-Didier-en-Velay F 30 E5
St-Didier-sur-Chalaronne F 30 C6
St-Dié F 27 D6
St-Dier-d'Auvergne F 30 D3
St-Dizier F 25 C12
St-Dizier-Leyrenne F 29 C9
St-Dolay F 23 E7
St-Donat-sur-l'Herbasse F 31 E6
St-Doulchard F 25 F7
Ste-Adresse F 23 A12
Ste-Alvère F 29 F7
Ste-Bazeille F 33 A6
Ste-Cécile-les-Vignes F 35 B8
Ste-Croix CH 31 B10
Ste-Croix F 31 B7
Ste-Croix F 31 F7
Ste-Croix-Volvestre F 33 D8
Ste-Engrâce F 32 D4
Ste-Énimie F 34 B5
Ste-Eulalie-d'Olt F 34 B4
Ste-Eulalie-en-Born F 32 B3
Ste-Feyre F 29 C9
Ste-Foy-de-Peyrolières F 33 D8
Ste-Foy-la-Grande F 29 F6
Ste-Foy-l'Argentière F 30 D5
Ste-Foy-lès-Lyon F 30 D6
Ste-Foy-Tarentaise F 31 D10
Ste-Geneviève F 18 F5
Ste-Geneviève-sur-Argence F 30 F2
St-Égrève F 31 E8
Ste-Hélène F 28 F4
Ste-Hermine F 28 B3
Ste-Livrade-sur-Lot F 33 B7
St-Élix-le-Château F 33 D8
St-Élix-Theux F 33 D6
Ste-Lizaigne F 29 A10
St-Éloy-les-Mines F 30 C2
Ste-Lucie-de-Tallano F 37 H10
Ste-Marguerite F 186 E2
Ste-Marie F 34 E5
Ste-Marie-aux-Mines F 27 D7
Ste-Maure-de-Peyriac F 33 B6
Ste-Maure-de-Touraine F 24 F4
Ste-Maxime F 36 E5
Ste-Menehould F 25 B12
Ste-Mère-Église F 23 B9
St-Émiland F 30 B5
St Endellion GB 12 D5
St Enoder GB 12 E5
Ste-Orse F 29 E8
Ste-Pazanne F 23 F8
Ste-Radegonde F 28 B5
St-Erme-Outre-et-Ramecourt F 19 E8
St Erth GB 12 E4
Saintes F 28 D4
Ste-Sabine F 25 F12
Ste-Savine F 25 D11
Ste-Sévère-sur-Indre F 29 C10
St-Esteben F 32 D3
St-Estèphe F 28 E4
St-Estève F 34 E4
Ste-Suzanne F 23 D11
St-Étienne F 30 E5
St-Étienne-de-Baïgorry F 32 D3
St-Étienne-de-Fontbellon F 35 A7
St-Étienne-de-Fursac F 29 C9
St-Étienne-de-Montluc F 23 F8
St-Étienne-de-St-Geoirs F 31 E7
St-Étienne-de-Tinée F 36 C5
St-Étienne-du-Bois F 31 C7
St-Étienne-du-Rouvray F 18 F3
St-Étienne-en-Dévoluy F 35 A10
St-Étienne-les-Orgues F 35 B10
St-Étienne-lès-Remiremont F 26 D6
St-Étienne-Vallée-Française F 35 B6
Ste-Tulle F 35 C10
Ste-Vertu F 25 E10
St-Fargeau F 25 E9
St-Félicien F 30 E6
St-Félix-Lauragais F 33 D9
St Fergus GB 3 K13
St-Ferme F 28 F6
Saintfield GB 7 D11
St Fillans GB 5 C8
St-Firmin F 26 D5
St-Firmin F 31 F9
St-Flavy F 25 D10
St-Florent F 37 F10
St-Florent-des-Bois F 28 B3
St-Florentin F 25 D10
St-Florent-le-Vieil F 23 F9
St-Florent-sur-Cher F 29 B10
St-Flour F 30 E3
St-Flovier F 29 B8
St-Fons F 30 D6
St-Fort-sur-Gironde F 28 E4
St-Frajou F 33 D7
St-François-Longchamp F 31 E9
St-Front-de-Pradoux F 29 E6
St-Fulgent F 28 B3
St-Galmier F 30 D5
St-Gaudens F 33 D7
St-Gaultier F 29 B8
St-Gein F 32 C5
St-Gély-du-Fesc F 35 C6
St-Genest-Malifaux F 30 E5
St-Geniez F 36 C4
St-Geniez-d'Olt F 34 B4
St-Genis-de-Saintonge F 28 E4
St-Genis-Laval F 30 D6
St-Genis-Pouilly F 31 C9
St-Genix-sur-Guiers F 31 D8
St-Genou F 29 B8
St-Geoire-en-Valdaine F 31 E8
St-Georges-Buttavent F 23 D10
St-Georges-d'Aurac F 30 E4
St-Georges-de-Commiers F 31 E8
St-Georges-de-Didonne F 28 D4
St-Georges-de-Luzençon F 34 B4
St-Georges-de-Mons F 30 D2
St-Georges-de-Reneins F 30 C6
St-Georges-des-Groseillers F 23 C10
St-Georges-d'Oléron F 28 D3
St-Georges-du-Vièvre F 18 F2
St-Georges-en-Couzan F 30 D4
St-Georges-lès-Baillargeaux F 29 B6
St-Georges-sur-Baulche F 25 E10
St-Georges-sur-Cher F 24 F5
St-Georges-sur-Loire F 23 F10
St-Geours-de-Maremne F 32 C3
St-Gérand-le-Puy F 30 C4
St-Germain-Chassenay F 30 B3
St-Germain-de-Calberte F 35 B6
St-Germain-de-la-Coudre F 24 D4
St-Germain-des-Fossés F 30 C3
St-Germain-d'Esteuil F 28 E4
St-Germain-du-Bel-Air F 33 A8
St-Germain-du-Bois F 31 B7
St-Germain-du-Corbéis F 23 D12
St-Germain-du-Plain F 31 B6
St-Germain-du-Puy F 25 F7
St-Germain-du-Teil F 34 B5
St-Germain-en-Laye F 24 C7
St-Germain-Laval F 30 D5
St-Germain-Lembron F 30 E3
St-Germain-les-Belles F 29 D8
St-Germain-les-Vergnes F 29 E9
St-Germain-l'Herm F 30 E4
St Germans GB 12 E6
St-Germé F 32 C5
St-Gervais F 28 B1
St-Gervais F 31 E7
St-Gervais-d'Auvergne F 30 C2
St-Gervais-la-Forêt F 24 E5
St-Gervais-les-Bains F 31 D10
St-Gervais-les-Trois-Clochers F 29 B6
St-Gervais-sur-Mare F 34 C5
St-Géry F 33 B9
St-Ghislain B 19 D8
St-Gildas-de-Rhuys F 22 E6
St-Gildas-des-Bois F 23 E7
St-Gilles F 35 C7
St-Gilles-Croix-de-Vie F 28 B2
St-Gingolph F 31 C10
St-Girons F 33 E8
St-Girons-Plage F 32 C3
St-Gobain F 19 E7
St-Guénolé F 22 E3
St-Guilhem-le-Désert F 35 C6
St-Haon-le-Châtel F 30 C4
St-Héand F 30 D5
St Helens GB 10 E6
St Helier GBJ 23 B7
St-Herblain F 23 F8
St-Hilaire F 33 D10
St-Hilaire-de-Brethmas F 35 B7
St-Hilaire-de-Riez F 28 B2
St-Hilaire-des-Loges F 28 C4
St-Hilaire-de-Villefranche F 28 D4
St-Hilaire-du-Harcouët F 23 C9
St-Hilaire-du-Rosier F 31 E7
St-Hilaire-Fontaine F 30 B4
St-Hilaire-le-Grand F 25 B11
St-Hilaire-St-Florent F 23 F11
St-Hippolyte F 27 D7
St-Hippolyte F 27 F6
St-Hippolyte-du-Fort F 35 C6
St-Honoré-les-Bains F 30 B4
St-Hostien F 30 E5
St-Hubert B 19 D11
St-Imier CH 27 F6
St-Ismier F 31 E8
St Ive GB 12 E6
St Ives GB 12 E4
St Ives GB 15 C8
St-Izaire F 34 C4
St-Jacques-de-la-Lande F 23 D8
St-James F 23 C9
St-Jean F 33 C8
St-Jean-Bonnefonds F 30 E5
St-Jean-Brévelay F 22 E6
St-Jean-d'Angély F 28 D4
St-Jean-d'Assé F 23 D12
St-Jean-de-Bournay F 31 D7
St-Jean-de-Braye F 24 E6
St-Jean-de-Daye F 23 B9
St-Jean-de-la-Ruelle F 24 E6
St-Jean-de-Losne F 26 F3
St-Jean-de-Luz F 32 D2
St-Jean-de-Marsacq F 32 C3
St-Jean-de-Mauréjols-et-Avéjan F 35 B7
St-Jean-de-Maurienne F 31 E9
St-Jean-de-Monts F 28 B1
St-Jean-de-Sixt F 31 D9
St-Jean-de-Védas F 35 C6
St-Jean-d'Illac F 28 F4
St-Jean-du-Bruel F 34 B5
St-Jean-du-Falga F 33 D9
St-Jean-du-Gard F 35 B6
St-Jean-le-Centenier F 35 A8
St-Jean-Pied-de-Port F 32 D3
St-Jean-Poutge F 33 C6
St-Jean-sur-Erve F 23 D11
St-Jeoire F 31 C9
St-Jeure-d'Ay F 30 E6
St-Jeures F 30 E5
St-Joachim F 23 F7
St John GBJ 23 B7
St John's Chapel GB 5 F12
St John's Town of Dalry GB 5 E8
St-Jores F 23 B9
St-Jorioz F 31 D9
St-Jory F 33 C8
St-Jouan-des-Guérets F 23 C8
St-Jouin-Bruneval F 23 A12
St-Jouin-de-Marnes F 28 B5
St-Julien F 31 C7
St-Julien F 33 D8
St-Julien-Beychevelle F 28 E4
St-Julien-Boutières F 30 F5
St-Julien-Chapteuil F 30 E5
St-Julien-de-Concelles F 23 F9
St-Julien-de-Vouvantes F 23 E9
St-Julien-du-Sault F 25 D9
St-Julien-du-Verdon F 36 D5
St-Julien-en-Beauchêne F 35 A10
St-Julien-en-Born F 32 B3
St-Julien-en-Genevois F 31 C9
St-Julien-l'Ars F 29 B7
St-Junien F 29 D7
St-Just F 35 B8
St Just GB 12 E3
St-Just-en-Chaussée F 18 E5
St-Just-en-Chevalet F 30 D4
St-Just-Ibarre F 32 D3
St-Justin F 32 C5
St Just in Roseland GB 12 E4
St-Just-la-Pendue F 30 D5
St-Just-Luzac F 28 D3
St-Just-Sauvage F 25 C10
St-Just-St-Rambert F 30 E5
St Keverne GB 12 E4
St-Lambert-des-Levées F 23 F11
St-Lary-Soulan F 33 E6
St-Laurent F 36 C5
St-Laurent-Bretagne F 32 D5
St-Laurent-d'Aigouze F 35 C7
St-Laurent-de-Carnols F 35 B8
St-Laurent-de-Cerdans F 34 F4
St-Laurent-de-Chamousset F 30 D5
St-Laurent-de-la-Cabrerisse F 34 D4
St-Laurent-de-la-Salanque F 34 E4
St-Laurent-de-Neste F 33 D6
St-Laurent-des-Autels F 23 F9
St-Laurent-du-Pont F 31 E8
St-Laurent-du-Var F 37 D6
St-Laurent-en-Caux F 18 E2
St-Laurent-en-Grandvaux F 31 B8
St-Laurent-les-Bains F 35 A6
St-Laurent-Médoc F 28 E4
St-Laurent-Nouan F 24 E6
St-Laurent-sur-Gorre F 29 D7
St-Laurent-sur-Sèvre F 28 B4
St-Léger B 19 E12
St-Léger-des-Vignes F 30 B3
St-Léger-en-Yvelines F 24 C6
St-Léger-sous-Beuvray F 30 B5
St-Léonard F 27 D6
St-Léonard-de-Noblat F 29 D8
St Leonards GB 13 D11
St-Lizier F 33 D8
St-Lô F 23 B9
St-Lon-les-Mines F 32 C3
St-Loubès F 28 F5
St-Louis-lès-Bitche F 186 D3
St-Loup-Géanges F 30 B6
St-Loup-Lamairé F 28 B5
St-Loup-sur-Semouse F 26 E5
St-Lubin-des-Joncherets F 24 C5
St-Lunaire F 23 C7
St-Lupicin F 31 C8
St-Lyé F 25 D11
St-Lys F 33 C8
St-Macaire F 32 A5
St-Macaire-en-Mauges F 23 F10
St-Magne F 32 A4
St-Magne-de-Castillon F 28 F5
St-Maime F 35 C10
St-Maixent-l'École F 28 C5
St-Malo F 23 C7
St-Malo-de-la-Lande F 23 B8
St-Mamert-du-Gard F 35 C7
St-Marcel F 24 B5
St-Marcel F 29 B9
St-Marcel F 30 B6
St-Marcel-d'Ardèche F 35 B8
St-Marcel-lès-Annonay F 30 E6
St-Marcel-lès-Sauzet F 35 A8
St-Marcel-lès-Valence F 31 F6
St-Marcellin F 31 E7
St-Marc-sur-Seine F 25 E12
St-Mards-en-Othe F 25 D10
St Margaret's Hope GB 3 H11
St-Marsal F 34 E4
St-Mars-d'Outillé F 24 E3
St-Mars-du-Désert F 23 F9
St-Mars-la-Brière F 24 D3
St-Mars-la-Jaille F 23 E9
St-Martial F 35 B6
St-Martial-de-Nabirat F 29 F8
St-Martial-de-Valette F 29 D7
St-Martin F 35 C10
St Martin GBG 22 B6
St Martin GBJ 23 B7
St-Martin-Boulogne F 15 F12
St-Martin-d'Ablois F 25 B10
St-Martin-d'Arrossa F 32 D3
St-Martin-d'Auxigny F 25 F7
St-Martin-de-Belleville F 31 E10
St-Martin-de-Castillon F 35 C10
St-Martin-de-Crau F 35 C8
St-Martin-de-Landelles F 23 C9
St-Martin-de-Londres F 35 C6
St-Martin-d'Entraunes F 36 C5
St-Martin-de-Ré F 28 C3
St-Martin-des-Besaces F 23 B10
St-Martin-des-Champs F 22 C4
St-Martin-de-Seignanx F 32 C3
St-Martin-de-Valamas F 30 F5
St-Martin-de-Valgalgues F 35 B7
St-Martin-d'Hères F 31 E8
St-Martin-d'Oney F 32 C4
St-Martin-du-Mont F 31 C7
St-Martin-du-Var F 37 D6
St-Martin-en-Bresse F 31 B7
St-Martin-le-Beau F 24 F4
St-Martin-sur-Ouanne F 25 E9
St-Martin-Valmeroux F 29 E10
St-Martin-Vésubie F 37 C6
St-Martory F 33 D7
St Mary's GB 3 H11
St-Mathieu F 29 D7
St-Mathurin F 28 B2
St-Maur F 29 B9
St-Maurice CH 31 C10
St-Maurice-de-Lignon F 30 E5
St-Maurice-des-Lions F 29 D7
St-Maurice-la-Souterraine F 29 C8
St-Maurice-l'Exil F 30 E6
St-Maurice-Navacelles F 35 C6
St-Maurin F 33 B7
St Mawes GB 12 E4
St-Max F 26 C5
St-Maximin-la-Ste-Baume F 35 D10
St-Médard-en-Jalles F 28 F4
St-Méen-le-Grand F 23 D7
St-Méloir-des-Ondes F 23 C8
St-Memmie F 25 C11
St-Menoux F 30 B3
St Merryn GB 12 D5
St-Mesmin F 25 D10
St-Mesmin F 29 E8
St-Michel F 19 E9
St-Michel F 28 D6
St-Michel F 33 D6
St-Michel-Chef-Chef F 23 F7
St-Michel-de-Castelnau F 32 B5
St-Michel-de-Maurienne F 31 E9
St-Michel-en-l'Herm F 28 C3
St-Michel-sur-Meurthe F 27 D6
St-Mihiel F 26 C4
St Monans GB 5 C11
St-Montant F 35 B8
St-Nabord F 26 D6
St-Nauphary F 33 C8
St-Nazaire F 23 F7
St-Nazaire-le-Désert F 35 A9
St-Nectaire F 30 D2
St Neots GB 15 C8
St-Nicolas B 183 D7
St-Nicolas F 18 D6
St-Nicolas-d'Aliermont F 18 E3
St-Nicolas-de-la-Grave F 33 B8
St-Nicolas-de-Port F 26 C5
St-Nicolas-de-Redon F 23 E7
St-Nicolas-du-Pélem F 22 D5
St-Oedenrode NL 16 E4
St-Omer F 18 C5
St-Orens-de-Gameville F 33 C9
St-Ost F 33 D6
St Osyth GB 15 D11
St-Ouen F 18 D5
St-Ouen F 24 E5
St Ouen GBJ 23 B7
St-Ouen-des-Toits F 23 D10
St-Pair-sur-Mer F 23 C8
St-Palais F 32 D3
St-Palais-sur-Mer F 28 D3
St-Pal-de-Chalancon F 30 E4
St-Pal-de-Mons F 30 E5
St-Pantaléon F 30 B5
St-Pantaléon F 33 B8
St-Papoul F 33 D10
St-Pardoux-Isaac F 33 A6
St-Pardoux-la-Rivière F 29 E7
St-Parize-le-Châtel F 30 B3
St-Parres-lès-Vaudes F 25 D11
St-Paterne F 23 D12
St-Paterne-Racan F 24 E3
St-Paul F 36 B5
St-Paul-Cap-de-Joux F 33 C9
St-Paul-de-Fenouillet F 33 E11
St-Paul-de-Jarrat F 33 E9
St-Paul-en-Born F 32 B3
St-Paul-en-Forêt F 36 D5
St-Paul-et-Valmalle F 35 C6
St-Paulien F 30 E4
St-Paul-le-Jeune F 35 B7
St-Paul-lès-Dax F 32 C3
St-Paul-lès-Durance F 35 C10
St-Paul-Trois-Châteaux F 35 B8
St-Pé-de-Bigorre F 32 D5
St-Pée-sur-Nivelle F 32 D2
St-Péray F 30 F6
St-Père F 25 F10
St-Père-en-Retz F 23 F7
St Peter in the Wood GBG 22 B6
St Peter Port GBG 22 B6
St-Phal F 25 D10
St-Philbert-de-Bouaine F 28 B2
St-Philbert-de-Grand-Lieu F 28 A2
St-Pierre I 31 D11
St-Pierre-d'Albigny F 31 D9
St-Pierre-de-Chignac F 29 E7
St-Pierre-de-Côle F 29 E7
St-Pierre-de-la-Fage F 34 C5
St-Pierre-de-Maillé F 29 B7
St-Pierre-de-Plesguen F 23 D8
St-Pierre-des-Champs F 34 D4
St-Pierre-des-Corps F 24 F4
St-Pierre-des-Échaubrognes F 28 A4
St-Pierre-des-Landes F 23 D9
St-Pierre-des-Nids F 23 D11
St-Pierre-de-Trivisy F 33 C10
St-Pierre-d'Irube F 32 D3
St-Pierre-d'Oléron F 28 D3
St-Pierre-du-Chemin F 28 B4
St-Pierre-du-Mont F 32 C4
St-Pierre-Église F 23 A9
St-Pierre-en-Faucigny F 31 C9
St-Pierre-en-Port F 18 E1
St-Pierre-le-Moûtier F 30 B3
St-Pierre-lès-Elbeuf F 18 F3
St-Pierre-lès-Nemours F 25 D8
St-Pierre-Montlimart F 23 F9
St-Pierre-Quiberon F 22 F5
St-Pierre-sur-Dives F 23 B11
St-Plancard F 33 D7
St-Pois F 23 C9
St-Poix F 23 E9
St-Pol-de-Léon F 22 C4
St-Pol-sur-Mer F 18 B5
St-Pol-sur-Ternoise F 18 D5
St-Pompont F 29 F8
St-Pons F 36 C5
St-Pons-de-Thomières F 34 D4
St-Porchaire F 28 D4
St-Pourçain-sur-Sioule F 30 C3
St-Prex CH 31 C9
St-Priest F 30 D6
St-Priest-de-Champs F 30 D2
St-Priest-Laprugne F 30 D4
St-Priest-Taurion F 29 D8
St-Privat F 29 E10
St-Privat-d'Allier F 30 F4
St-Prix F 30 C4
St-Projet F 33 B9
St-Puy F 33 C6
St-Quentin F 19 E7
St-Quentin-la-Poterie F 35 B7
St-Quirin F 27 C7
St-Rambert-d'Albon F 30 E6
St-Rambert-en-Bugey F 31 D7
St-Raphaël F 36 E5
St-Remèze F 35 B7
St-Rémy F 30 B6
St-Rémy-de-Provence F 35 C8
St-Remy-en-Bouzemont-St-Genest-et-Isson F 25 C12
St-Rémy-sur-Avre F 24 C5
St-Rémy-sur-Durolle F 30 D4
St-Renan F 22 D2
St-Révérien F 25 F10
St-Rhemy I 31 D11
St-Riquier F 18 D4
St-Romain-en-Gal F 30 D6
St-Romain-sur-Cher F 24 F5
St-Romans F 31 E7
St-Rome-de-Cernon F 34 B4
St-Rome-de-Tarn F 34 B4
St-Saëns F 18 E3
St Sampson GBG 22 B6
St-Saturnin-lès-Apt F 35 C9
St-Saud-Lacoussière F 29 D7
St-Saulge F 25 F10
St-Sauves-d'Auvergne F 29 D11
St-Sauveur F 22 D3
St-Sauveur F 26 E5
St-Sauveur-de-Montagut F 30 F6
St-Sauveur-en-Puisaye F 25 E9
St-Sauveur-Gouvernet F 35 B9
St-Sauveur-Lendelin F 23 B9
St-Sauveur-le-Vicomte F 23 B8
St-Sauveur-sur-Tinée F 36 C6
St-Sauvy F 33 C7
St-Savin F 28 E5
St-Savin F 29 B7
St-Savinien F 28 D4
St Saviour GBJ 23 B7
St-Sébastien-de-Morsent F 24 B5
St-Sébastien-sur-Loire F 23 F8
St-Seine-l'Abbaye F 25 F12
St-Sernin F 35 A7
St-Sernin-sur-Rance F 34 C4
St-Seurin-sur-l'Isle F 28 E5
St-Sever F 32 C4
St-Sever-Calvados F 23 C9
St-Siméon-de-Bressieux F 31 E7
St-Simon F 19 E7
St-Simon F 29 F11
St-Sorlin-d'Arves F 31 E9
St-Soupplets F 25 B8
St-Sulpice F 33 C9
St-Sulpice-Laurière F 29 C8
St-Sulpice-les-Champs F 29 D10
St-Sulpice-les-Feuilles F 29 C8
St-Sulpice-sur-Lèze F 33 D8
St-Sulpice-sur-Risle F 24 C4
St-Sylvain F 23 B11
St-Symphorien F 30 F4
St-Symphorien F 32 B5
St-Symphorien-de-Lay F 30 D5
St-Symphorien-sur-Coise F 30 D5
St Teath GB 12 D5
St-Thégonnec F 22 C4
St-Thibéry F 34 D5
St-Thiébault F 26 D4
St-Thurien F 22 E4
St-Trivier-de-Courtes F 31 C7
St-Trivier-sur-Moignans F 30 C6
St-Trojan-les-Bains F 28 D3
St-Tropez F 36 E5
St-Uze F 30 E6
St-Valérien F 25 D9
St-Valery-en-Caux F 18 E2
St-Valery-sur-Somme F 18 D4
St-Vallier F 30 B5
St-Vallier F 30 E6
St-Vallier-de-Thiey F 36 D5
St-Varent F 28 B5
St-Vaury F 29 C9
St-Victor F 30 E6
St-Victor-de-Cessieu F 31 D7
St-Victoret F 35 D9
St-Victor-la-Coste F 35 B8
St Vigeans GB 5 B11
St-Vigor-le-Grand F 23 B10
St-Vincent I 68 B4
St-Vincent-de-Connezac F 29 E6
St-Vincent-de-Paul F 32 C4
St-Vincent-les-Forts F 36 C4
St-Vit F 26 F4
St-Vite F 33 B7
St-Vith B 20 D6
St-Vivien-de-Médoc F 28 E3
St-Xandre F 28 C3
St-Yan F 30 C5
St-Ybars F 33 D8
St-Yorre F 30 C3
St-Yrieix-la-Perche F 29 D8
St-Yrieix-sur-Charente F 29 D6
St-Yvy F 22 E4
St-Zacharie F 35 D10
Sainville F 24 D6
Saissac F 33 D10
Saittarova S 116 D8
Saivomuotka S 116 B10
Saïx F 33 C10
Sajaniemi FIN 127 D11
Šahyajince SRB 164 E5
Sajkaš SRB 158 C5
Sajóbábony H 145 G2
Sajókaza H 145 G2
Sajókeresztúr H 145 G2
Sajólád H 145 G2
Sajószentpéter H 145 G2
Sajószöged H 145 H3
Sajóvámos H 145 G2
Säjvis S 119 C11
Saka LV 134 C2
Sakajärvi S 116 D5
Sakalishcha BY 133 E5
Sakaravaara FIN 121 E12
Sakiai LT 136 D7
Säkinmäki FIN 123 F16
Sakizköy TR 173 B7
Säkkilä FIN 121 B13
Sakshaug N 105 D10
Saksild DK 86 D6
Sakskøbing DK 83 A11
Saksun FO 2 A2
Saku EST 131 C9
Sakule SRB 158 C6
Säkylä FIN 126 C7
Šakyna LT 134 D6
Sala LV 134 C7
Sala LV 135 C11
Sala S 98 C7
Šaľa SK 146 E5
Salaca LV 131 F10
Sălacea RO 151 C9
Salacgrīva LV 131 F8
Sala Consilina I 60 C5
Salagnac F 29 E8
Salahmi FIN 124 C7
Salaise-sur-Sanne F 30 E6
Salakas LT 135 E12
Salakos GR 181 D7
Salakovac BIH 157 F8
Salamajärvi FIN 123 D13
Salamanca E 45 C9
Salamina GR 175 D7
Salandra I 61 B6
Salanki FIN 117 B13
Salantai LT 134 D3
Salar E 53 B8
Sălard RO 151 C9
Salardu E 33 E7
Salarli TR 172 B6
Salas E 39 B7
Salaš SRB 159 E9
Salas de los Infantes E 40 D5
Salash BG 164 B6
Salaspils LV 135 C8
Sălașu de Sus RO 159 C10
Sălățig RO 151 C11
Sălătrucel RO 160 C4
Sălătrucu RO 160 C5
Salaunes F 28 F4
Salberg S 107 D16
Salbertrand I 31 E10
Salboda S 97 C8
Salbohed S 98 C6
Salbris F 24 F7
Salbu N 100 D2
Salcea RO 153 B8
Salching D 75 E12
Salcia RO 159 E10
Salcia RO 160 F5
Salcia RO 161 C8
Salcia Tudor RO 161 C10
Sălciile RO 161 D8
Šalčininkai LT 137 E11
Šalčininkėliai LT 137 E11
Sălciua RO 151 E11
Salcombe GB 13 E7
Sălcuța MD 154 D4
Sălcuța RO 160 E2
Saldaña E 39 C10
Saldenburg D 76 E4
Saldón E 47 D10
Salduero E 40 E6
Saldus LV 134 C4
Sale GB 11 E7
Sale I 37 B9
Saleby S 91 C13
Salem D 27 E11
Salem D 83 C9
Salemi I 58 D2

Santiponce E 51 E7
Santisteban del Puerto E 55 C6
Santiuste de San Juan Bautista E 46 B3
Santiz E 45 B9
Sant Jaime Mediterráneo E 57 B13
Sant Jaume d'Enveja E 42 F5
Sant Joan de Labritja E 49 F8
Sant Joan de les Abadesses E 43 C8
Sant Joan de Vilatorrada E 43 D7
Sant Joan les Fonts E 43 C9
Sant Josep de sa Talaia E 57 D7
Sant Julià de Lòria AND 33 F9
Sant Llorenç de Morunys E 43 C7
Sant Llorenç des Cardassar E 57 B11
Sant Lluís E 57 B13
Sant Martí de Tous E 43 D7
Sant Martí Sarroca E 43 E7
Sant Mateu E 42 G4
Sant Miquel de Balansat E 57 C7
Santo Aleixo P 50 B5
Santo Aleixo da Restauração P 51 C5
Santo Amador P 51 C5
Santo André P 50 C2
Santo Antoniño E 38 C2
Santo António dos Cavaleiros P 50 B1
Santo Domingo de la Calzada E 40 D6
Santo Domingo de Silos E 40 E5
Santo Estêvão P 50 B2
Santo Estêvão P 50 E4
Santo Isidro de Pegões P 50 B2
Santok PL 85 E8
Santomera E 56 E2
Santo Omero I 62 B5
Santoña E 40 B5
Santo Pietro I 58 E6
Santo-Pietro-di-Tenda F 37 F10
Santo-Pietro-di-Venaco F 37 G10
Santo Stefano al Mare I 37 D7
Santo Stefano Belbo I 37 B8
Santo Stefano d'Aveto I 37 B10
Santo Stefano di Cadore I 72 C6
Santo Stefano di Camastra I 58 C5
Santo Stefano di Magra I 69 E8
Santo Stefano Quisquina I 58 D3
Santo Stino di Livenza I 73 E6
Santo Tirso P 38 F3
Santo Tomé E 55 C6
Santovenia E 39 E8
Santpedor E 43 D7
Sant Pere de Ribes E 43 E7
Sant Pere de Torelló E 43 C8
Sant Pere Pescador E 43 C10
Sant Pol de Mar E 43 D9
Santpoort NL 182 A5
Sant Privat d'en Bas E 43 C8
Sant Quintí de Mediona E 43 E7
Sant Quirze de Besora E 43 C8
Sant Sadurní d'Anoia E 43 E7
Santullano E 39 B8
Santu Lussurgiu I 64 C2
Santurtzi E 40 B5
Sant Vicenç dels Horts E 43 E8
Sant Vicenç de Castellet E 43 D7
San Venanzo I 62 B2
San Vendemiano I 72 E5
San Vero Milis I 64 C2
San Vicente de Alcántara E 45 F6
San Vicente de Arana E 32 E1
San Vicente de la Barquera E 40 B3
San Vicente de la Sonsierra E 40 C6
San Vicente del Raspeig E 56 E3
San Vicente de Palacio E 46 B3
San Vicente de Toranzo E 40 B4
San Vicenzo E 38 C2
San Vincenzo I 59 B7
San Vincenzo I 65 A3
San Vincenzo Valle Roveto I 62 D5
San Vitero E 39 E7
San Vito I 64 E4
San Vito al Tagliamento I 73 E6
San Vito Chietino I 63 C6
San Vito dei Normanni I 61 B9
San Vito di Cadore I 72 D5
San Vito lo Capo I 58 C2
San Vito Romano I 62 D3
San Vito sullo Ionio I 59 B9
San Vittoria in Matenano I 62 A4
Sanxenxo E 38 D2
Sanxhax AL 168 A2
Sanza I 60 C5
Sânzieni RO 153 E8
Sanzoles E 39 F8
São Barnabé P 50 E3
São Bartolomeu P 44 F5
São Bartolomeu da Serra P 50 C2
São Bartolomeu de Messines P 50 E3
São Bento do Cortiço P 50 B4
São Brás P 50 D4
São Brás de Alportel P 50 E4
São Brás do Regedouro P 50 C3
São Brissos P 50 C4
São Cosmado P 44 B5
São Domingos P 50 D2
São Facundo P 44 F4
São Francisco da Serra P 50 C2
São Geraldo P 50 B3
São Gregório P 50 B4
São Jacinto P 44 C3
São João da Madeira P 44 C4
São João da Pesqueira P 44 B6
São João da Venda P 50 E4
São João do Campo P 44 D4
São João dos Caldeireiros P 50 D4
São José da Lamarosa P 44 F4
São Lourenço de Mamporcão P 50 B4
São Luís P 50 D2
São Manços P 50 C4
São Marcos da Ataboeira P 50 D4
São Marcos da Serra P 50 E3
São Marcos do Campo P 50 C4
São Martinho da Cortiça P 44 D4
São Martinho das Amoreiras P 50 D3
São Martinho de Angueira P 39 E7
São Martinho do Porto P 44 E2
São Matias P 50 C4
São Miguel de Acha P 45 D6
São Miguel de Machede P 50 B4
São Miguel de Rio Torto P 44 F4
São Miguel do Outeiro P 44 C4
São Miguel do Pinheiro P 50 D4
Saône F 26 F5
São Pedro da Cadeira P 44 F2
São Pedro de Muel P 44 E2
São Pedro de Solis P 50 E4
São Pedro do Sul P 44 C4
Saorge F 37 D7
São Romão P 51 B5
São Romão do Sado P 50 C3
São Sebastião dos Carros P 50 D4
São Teotónio P 50 D2
Saou F 35 A9
São Vicente P 38 E5
São Vicente da Beira P 44 D5
Sáp H 151 C7
Sapanca TR 171 E10
Săpânța RO 145 H8
Sapareva Banya BG 165 E7
Saparevo BG 165 E7
Sapata RO 160 D5
Sapes GR 171 B9
Sapna BIH 157 C11
Sa Pobla E 57 B11
Săpoca RO 161 C9
Sapotskin BY 137 F8
Sappada I 73 C6
Sap'parjåkka N 113 D17
Sappee FIN 127 C11
Sappen N 112 D7
Sappetavan S 107 A13
Sappetsele S 107 A13
Sappisaasi S 116 C7
Sapri I 60 C5
Sapsalampi FIN 123 F11
Sapsoperä FIN 125 B11
Sara FIN 122 F9
Saraby N 113 C12
Saracena I 60 D6
Saračinec HR 148 D6
Sarafovo BG 167 D9
Saraikļ LV 134 C2
Säräisniemi FIN 119 F17
Saraiu RO 155 D2
Sarajärvi FIN 120 C9
Sarajärvi FIN 129 B11
Sarajevo BIH 157 E9
Saramo FIN 125 C12
Saramon F 33 C7
Saran F 24 E6
Saránd H 151 C8
Sarandë AL 168 E3
Sarantaporo GR 169 D7
Sarantsi BG 165 D8
Sa Ràpita E 57 C10
Sarasău RO 145 H8
Sarata UA 154 E5
Sărata Galbenă MD 154 D2
Sărata-Monteoru RO 161 C9
Sărata Nouă MD 154 E2
Sărăteni MD 154 D2
Sărătenii Vechi MD 154 B3
Saray TR 173 B8
Sarayakpinar TR 167 F7
Saraylar TR 173 C8
Šarbanovac SRB 159 F9
Sârbeni RO 161 E6
Sárbogárd H 149 C11
Sarcelles F 25 C7
Sarconi I 60 C5
Sardara I 64 D2
Šardice CZ 77 E12
Sardinia GR 174 B3
Sardoal P 44 E4
Sare F 32 D2
S'Arenal E 49 E10
Šarengrad HR 158 C3
Sarentino I 72 C3
Särevere EST 131 D10
Sarezzo I 69 B9
Sargans CH 71 C8
Sariai LT 137 C13
Saribeyler TR 173 F8
Saricaali TR 171 C10
Sariçam TR 177 B9
Sarichioi RO 155 D3
Saridanişment TR 167 F7
Sariegos E 39 C8
Sarikemer TR 177 D9
Sariköy TR 173 D8
Sariñena E 42 D3
Šarišské Michaľany SK 145 E3
Sariyer TR 173 B11
Sarjankylä FIN 123 B14
Sarkad H 151 D7
Sarkadkeresztúr H 151 D7
Särkelä FIN 121 C12
Sárkeresztúr H 149 B11
Särkijärvi FIN 117 C11
Särkijärvi FIN 119 C15
Särkijärvi FIN 120 E9
Särkikorpi FIN 125 D12
Särkikylä FIN 123 D11
Särkilahti FIN 127 B14
Särkilahti FIN 129 B11
Särkiluoma FIN 121 B14
Särkimo FIN 122 D8
Särkisalmi FIN 129 B11
Särkisalo FIN 123 E16
Särkisalo FIN 127 E8
Şarköy TR 173 C7
Sarlat-la-Canéda F 29 F8
Sarliac-sur-l'Isle F 29 E7
Sărmaş RO 152 D6
Sărmăşag RO 151 C10
Sărmaşu RO 152 D4
Sármellék H 149 C8
Sarmijärvi FIN 114 F4
Sărmizegetusa RO 159 B10
Särna S 102 C5
Sarnadas do Ródão P 44 E5
Sarnaki PL 141 F7
Sarnano I 62 A4
Sārnate LV 134 B2
Sarnen CH 70 D6
Sarnıç TR 177 C9
Sarnico I 69 B8
Sarno I 60 B3
Sarnowa PL 81 C11
Särnstugan S 102 C5
Särö S 91 D10
Sarochyna BY 133 F5
Saronno I 69 B7
Sárosd H 149 B11
Sárospatak H 145 G4
Šarovce SK 147 E7
Sarow D 84 C4
Sarpsborg N 95 D14
Sarracín E 40 D4
Sarral E 42 E6
Sarralbe F 27 C7
Sarrance F 32 D4
Sarrancolin F 33 E6
Sarraquinhos P 38 E4
Sarras F 30 E6
Sarre GB 15 E11
Sarre I 31 D11
Sarreaus E 38 D4
Sarrebourg F 27 C7
Sarreguemines F 27 B7
Sárrétudvari H 151 C7
Sarre-Union F 27 C7
Sarria E 38 C5
Sarrià de Ter E 43 C9
Sarrians F 35 B8
Sarrión E 48 D3
Sarroca de Lleida E 42 E5
Sarròch I 64 E3
Sarród H 149 A7
Sarrola-Carcopino F 37 G9
Sarron F 32 C5
Sarry F 25 C11
Sarsina I 66 E5
Sarstedt D 78 B6
Sárszentágota H 149 C11
Sárszentlőrinc H 149 C11
Sart B 183 D7
Sartaguda E 32 F1
Sarteano I 62 B1
Sartène F 37 H9
Sarti GR 170 D5
Sartilly F 23 C9
Sartininkai LT 134 F3
Sarud H 150 B6
Şaru Dornei RO 152 C6
Saruhanli TR 177 B10
Sarule I 64 C3
Săruleşti RO 161 C9
Săruleşti RO 161 E9
Sárvár H 149 B7
Sarvela FIN 122 F9
Sarvijoki FIN 122 E7
Sarvikumpu FIN 125 F12
Sarviluoma FIN 122 F8
Sarvinki FIN 125 E14
Sarvisé E 32 E5
Sarvisvaara S 116 E6
Särvsjön S 102 A5
Sar"ya BY 133 E3
Sarzana I 69 E8
Sarzeau F 22 E6
Sarzedas P 44 E5
Sarzedo P 44 B5
Sasa MK 164 E6
Sasalli TR 177 C8
Sasamón E 40 D3
Sasbach D 27 C9
Sasbachwalden D 186 D5
Sasca Montană RO 159 D8
Saschiz RO 152 E5
Sásciori RO 152 F3
Sascut RO 153 E10
Sásd H 149 D10
Sasina BIH 157 C6
Sasnava LT 137 D7
Sassali FIN 117 D15
Sassano I 60 C5
Sassari I 64 B2
Sassello I 37 C8
Sassen D 84 B4
Sassenage F 31 E8
Sassenberg D 17 E10
Sassenheim NL 16 D3
Sassetta I 65 A3
Sassnitz D 84 A5
Sassocorvaro I 66 E5
Sassoferrato I 67 F6
Sasso Marconi I 66 D3
Sassuolo I 66 C2
Sástago E 41 F11
Šaštín-Stráže SK 77 E12
Sas Van Gent NL 16 F1
Sáta H 145 G1
Satão P 44 C5
Satchinez RO 151 F7
Šateikiai LT 134 E3
Såtenäs villastad S 91 C12
Säter S 97 B14
Sätervallen S 102 A5
Sāti LV 134 C5
Satiķi LV 134 C5
Såtila S 91 D11
Satillieu F 30 E6
Satkūnai LT 134 D7
Satnica Đakovačka HR 149 F10
Såtofta S 87 D13
Sátoraljaújhely H 145 G4
Satovcha BG 170 A5
Satow D 83 C11
Sätra brunn S 98 C6
Satriano di Lucania I 60 B5
Satrup D 82 A7
Sattajärvi FIN 119 B12
Sattajärvi S 117 D10
Sattanen FIN 117 D17
Satteins A 71 C9
Satteldorf D 75 D7
Satter S 116 E7
Sattledt A 76 F6
Satulung RO 151 B11
Satu Mare RO 151 B10
Saubusse F 32 C3
Saúca E 47 B7
Sauca MD 154 A1
Săuca RO 151 C9
Saucats F 32 A4
Săuceşti RO 153 D9
Sauclières F 34 C5
Sauda N 94 C4
Saue EST 131 C9
Sauerlach D 75 G10
Sauga EST 131 E8
Saugnacq-et-Muret F 32 B4
Saugos LT 134 F2
Saugues F 30 F4
Saujon F 28 D4
Sauk AL 168 B2
Sauka LV 135 D10
Saukėnai LT 134 E5
Saukko FIN 125 C11
Saukkoaapa FIN 115 D2
Saukkojärvi FIN 119 B16
Saukkola FIN 127 E10
Saukkoriipi FIN 117 E12
Saukonkylä FIN 123 E11
Sauland N 95 C9
Saulce-sur-Rhône F 35 A8
Sauldorf D 27 E11
Saulepi EST 130 E7
Săuleşti RO 160 D2
Saulgau D 71 A9
Saulgrub D 71 B12
Saulheim D 21 E10
Şăulia RO 152 D4
Saulieu F 25 F11
Saulkalne LV 135 C8
Saulkrasti LV 135 B8
Sault F 35 B9
Sault-de-Navailles F 32 C4
Sault-lès-Rethel F 19 F9
Saulx F 26 E5
Saulxures-sur-Moselotte F 27 E6
Saulzais-le-Potier F 29 B11
Saumos F 28 F3
Saumur F 23 F11
Saunajärvi FIN 125 C13
Saunakylä FIN 123 D13
Saunavaara FIN 115 D3
Saundersfoot GB 12 B5
Saurat F 33 E9
Sauriešī LV 135 C8
Sauròch I 64 E3
Sauris I 73 D6
Saursfjord N 110 E9
Sausnēja LV 135 C11
Sausset-les-Pins F 35 D9
Saussy F 26 F2
Sautens A 71 C11
Sautiņl LV 135 B8
Sautron F 23 F8
Sautso Kraftverk N 113 D12
Sauvagnon F 32 D5
Sauve F 35 C6
Sauveterre-de-Béarn F 32 D4
Sauveterre-de-Guyenne F 28 F5
Sauveterre-la-Lémance F 33 A8
Sauviat-sur-Vige F 29 D9
Sauvo FIN 126 E8
Sauxillanges F 30 D3
Sauzet F 33 B8
Sauzé-Vaussais F 29 C6
Sauzon F 22 F5
Sava I 61 C9
Sava SLO 73 D10
Săvădisla RO 151 D11
Savalia GR 174 D3
Savaloja FIN 119 E15
Sävar S 122 C5
Săvârşin RO 151 E9
Sävast S 118 C7
Savaştepe TR 173 F8
Säve S 91 D10
Savelli I 61 E7
Savenay F 23 F8
Săveni RO 153 B9
Săveni RO 161 D11
Saverdun F 33 D9
Saverna EST 131 E13
Saverne F 27 C7
Sävi FIN 126 B8
Säviä FIN 123 D17
Saviaho FIN 125 C10
Savières F 25 D10
Savigliano I 37 B7
Savignac-les-Églises F 29 E7
Savignano Irpino I 60 A4
Savignano sul Rubicone I 66 D5
Savigné-l'Évêque F 23 D12
Savigneux F 30 D5
Savigny-en-Sancerre F 25 F8
Savigny-lès-Beaune F 25 F12
Savigny-sur-Braye F 24 E4
Savijärvi FIN 125 C13
Savikylä FIN 125 C11
Savilahti FIN 129 C10
Savimäki FIN 124 C7
Savines-le-Lac F 36 B4
Săvineşti RO 153 D8
Savino Selo SRB 158 B4
Savitaipale FIN 128 C8
Saviranta FIN 121 F10
Saviselkä FIN 123 B16
Sävja S 99 C9
Šavnik MNE 157 G11
Savognin CH 71 D9
Savoisy F 25 E11
Savona I 37 C8
Savonlinna FIN 129 B10
Savonranta FIN 125 F12
Savran' UA 154 A6
Sävsjö S 92 E5
Sävsjön S 97 C12
Savudrija HR 67 B7
Savukoski FIN 115 D4
Sawin PL 141 H8
Sawston GB 15 C9
Sax E 56 D3
Saxdalen S 97 B12
Saxen A 77 F7
Saxhyttan S 97 C11
Saxilby GB 11 E10
Saxmundham GB 15 C11
Saxnäs S 106 B8
Saxon CH 31 C11
Saxthorpe GB 15 B11
Saxvallen S 105 D12
Sayalonga E 53 C8
Sayatón E 47 D7
Sayda D 80 E4
Säynäjä FIN 121 B13
Säynätsalo FIN 123 F15
Säyneinen FIN 125 D10
Sázava CZ 77 C7
Sazli TR 171 E10
Sazli TR 177 D9
Sazoba TR 173 D7
Sazoba TR 177 B10
Scaër F 22 D4
Scăeşti RO 160 E3
Scafa I 62 C6
Scalasaig GB 4 C4
Scalby GB 11 C11
Scalea I 60 D5
Scaletta Zanclea I 59 C7
Scalloway GB 3 E14
Scandale I 61 E7
Scandiano I 66 C2
Scandicci I 66 E3
Scandriglia I 62 C3
Scanno I 62 D5
Scano di Montiferro I 64 C2
Scansano I 65 B4
Scânteia RO 153 D11
Scânteia RO 161 D10
Scânteieşti RO 153 F12
Scanzano Jonico I 61 C7
Scapa GB 3 H11
Scarborough GB 11 C11
Scardovari I 66 C5
Scarinish GB 4 B3
Scario I 60 C4
Scărişoara RO 160 F5
Scarlino I 65 B3
Scarperia I 66 E3
Scartaglen IRL 8 D4
Scartaglin IRL 8 D4
Šćenica-Bobani BIH 162 D5
Scerni I 63 C7
Scey-sur-Saône-et-St-Albin F 26 E4
Schaafheim D 187 B7
Schaan FL 71 C9
Schaarsbergen NL 183 A7
Schaerbeek B 19 C9
Schaesberg NL 20 C6
Schaffhausen CH 27 E10
Schafflund D 82 A6
Schafstädt D 79 D10
Schafstedt D 82 B6
Schäftlarn D 75 G9
Schagen NL 16 C3
Schaijk NL 183 B7
Schalchen A 76 F4
Schalkau D 75 B9
Schalkhaar NL 183 A8
Schalksmühle D 17 F9
Schänis CH 27 F11
Schapen D 17 D9
Scharbeutz D 83 B9
Schardenberg A 76 E4
Schärding A 76 F4
Scharendijke NL 16 E1
Scharnebeck D 83 D9
Scharnitz A 72 B3
Scharnstein A 73 A8
Scharrel (Oldenburg) D 17 B9
Scharwoude NL 16 C4
Schashagen D 83 B9
Schattendorf A 149 A7
Schebheim D 75 C7
Scheemda NL 17 B7
Scheer D 27 D11
Scheeßel D 82 D6
Schefflenz D 21 F12
Scheggia e Pascelupo I 67 F6
Scheggino I 62 B3
Şcheia RO 153 B8
Şcheia RO 153 D11
Scheibbs A 77 F8
Scheiblingkirchen A 148 A6
Scheidegg D 71 B9
Scheifling A 73 B9
Scheinfeld D 75 C7
Schela RO 155 B1
Schela RO 160 C2
Schelklingen D 74 F6
Schellerten D 79 B7
Schemmerhofen D 71 A9
Schenefeld D 82 B6
Schenefeld D 83 C7
Schenkenfelden A 76 E6
Schenkenzell D 187 E5
Schenklengsfeld D 78 E6
Schermbeck D 17 E7
Schermen D 79 B10
Schermerhorn NL 16 C3
Scherpenheuvel B 19 C10
Scherpenzeel NL 16 D4
Scherwiller F 27 D7
Scherzingen CH 27 E11
Scheßlitz D 75 C9
Schiavi di Abruzzo I 63 D6
Schiedam NL 16 E2
Schieder-Schwalenberg D 17 E12
Schieren L 20 E6
Schierling D 75 E11
Schiermonnikoog NL 16 B6
Schiers CH 71 D9
Schiffdorf D 17 A11
Schifferstadt D 21 F10
Schifflange L 20 E6
Schiffweiler D 186 C3
Schijndel NL 16 E4
Schilde B 16 F3
Schillingen D 186 B2
Schillingsfürst D 75 D7
Schilpario I 69 A9
Schiltach D 27 D9
Schiltigheim F 27 C8
Schimatari GR 175 C8
Schinnen NL 183 D7
Schinos GR 174 B3
Schinveld NL 20 C5
Schio I 69 B11
Schipkau D 80 C5
Schipluiden NL 182 B4
Schirmeck F 27 D7
Schirmitz D 75 C11
Schitu RO 160 E5
Schitu RO 161 E7
Schitu Duca RO 153 C11
Schitu Goleşti RO 160 C6
Schkeuditz D 79 D11
Schkölen D 79 D10
Schköna D 79 C12
Schkopau D 79 D10
Schlabendorf D 80 C5
Schladen D 79 B8
Schladming A 73 B8
Schlangen D 17 E11
Schlangenbad D 21 D10
Schleching D 72 A5
Schleiden D 20 C6
Schleife D 81 C7
Schleinbach A 77 F10
Schleitheim CH 27 E9
Schleiz D 79 E10
Schlema D 79 E12
Schlepzig D 80 B5
Schleswig D 82 A7
Schleusingen D 75 A8
Schlieben D 80 C4
Schliengen D 27 E8
Schlier D 71 B9
Schlierbach A 73 A9
Schlieren CH 27 F9
Schliersee D 72 A4
Schlitters A 72 B4
Schlitz D 78 E6
Schlossberg A 148 C4
Schloss Holte-Stukenbrock D 17 E11
Schlossvippach D 79 D9
Schlosswil CH 70 D5
Schlotheim D 79 D8
Schluchsee D 27 E9
Schlüchtern D 74 B6
Schlüsselfeld D 75 C8
Schmallenberg D 21 B10
Schmelz D 21 F7
Schmidgaden D 75 D11
Schmidmühlen D 75 D10
Schmiedeberg D 80 E5
Schmölln D 79 E11
Schmölln D 84 D6
Schnabelwaid D 75 C10
Schnackenburg D 83 D11
Schnaittach D 75 C9
Schneeberg D 79 E12
Schneidlingen D 79 C9
Schneizlreuth D 73 A6
Schnelldorf D 187 C9
Schnellmannshausen D 79 D7
Schneverdingen D 82 D7
Schnürpflingen D 187 E8
Schobüll D 82 A6
Schodnia PL 142 E5
Schoenberg B 20 D6
Scholen D 17 C11
Schollene D 83 E12
Schöllkrippen D 187 A7
Schöllnach D 76 E4
Schömberg D 27 D10
Schömberg D 187 D6
Schönaich D 187 D7
Schönau D 76 F3
Schönau im Schwarzwald D 27 E8
Schönbach A 77 F8
Schönberg D 83 C9
Schönberg D 84 E3
Schönberg (Holstein) D 83 B8
Schönberg am Kamp A 77 E9
Schönberg im Stubaital A 72 B3
Schönborn D 80 C5
Schondra D 74 B6
Schönebeck D 83 D12
Schönebeck (Elbe) D 79 B10
Schöneck D 75 B11
Schönecken D 20 D6
Schönenberg-Kübelberg D 186 C3
Schönermark D 84 D5
Schönewalde D 80 C4
Schönewörde D 79 A8
Schongau D 71 B11
Schönhausen D 79 A11
Schöningen D 79 B8
Schönkirchen D 83 B8
Schönow D 84 E5
Schönsee D 75 C12
Schöntal D 74 D6
Schönthal D 75 D12
Schönwalde D 80 C5
Schönwalde am Bungsberg D 83 B9
Schönwies A 71 C11
Schoondijke NL 16 F1
Schoonebeek NL 17 C7
Schoonhoven NL 16 E3
Schoorl NL 16 C3
Schopfheim D 27 E8
Schopfloch D 75 D7
Schöppenstedt D 79 B8
Schoppernau A 71 C10
Schöppingen D 17 D8
Schörfling am Attersee A 73 A8
Schorndorf D 74 E6
Schorndorf D 75 D12
Schortens D 17 A9
Schoten B 16 F2
Schotten D 21 D12
Schramberg D 27 D9
Schrecksbach D 21 C12
Schrems A 77 E8
Schrepkow D 83 E12
Schriesheim D 21 F11
Schrobenhausen D 75 E9
Schröder A 73 B9
Schrozberg D 74 D6
Schruns A 71 C9
Schübelbach CH 27 F10
Schuby D 82 A6
Schulenberg im Oberharz D 79 C7
Schull IRL 8 E3
Schulzendorf D 84 E6
Schüpfheim CH 70 D6
Schuttertal D 186 E4
Schutterwald D 186 E4
Schüttorf D 17 D8
Schwaan D 83 C12
Schwabach D 75 D9
Schwäbisch Gmünd D 74 E6
Schwäbisch Hall D 74 D6
Schwabmünchen D 71 A11
Schwabstedt D 82 B6
Schwaförden D 17 C11
Schwaigern D 27 B11
Schwalbach D 21 F7
Schwalmstadt-Treysa D 21 C12
Schwalmstadt-Ziegenhain D 21 C12
Schwanberg A 73 C11
Schwanden CH 71 C8
Schwandorf D 75 D11
Schwanebeck D 79 C9
Schwanenstadt A 76 F5
Schwanewede D 17 B11
Schwangau D 71 B11
Schwanstetten D 75 D9
Schwarme D 17 C12
Schwarmstedt D 82 E7
Schwarz D 83 D13
Schwarza D 79 E8
Schwarzach D 76 E3
Schwarzau im Gebirge A 148 A5
Schwarzenau A 77 E8
Schwarzenbach A 149 A6
Schwarzenbach am Wald D 75 B10
Schwarzenbek D 83 C8
Schwarzenberg D 79 E12
Schwarzenborn D 78 E5
Schwarzenburg CH 31 B11
Schwarzenfeld D 75 D11
Schwarzheide D 80 D5
Schwaz A 72 B4
Schwechat A 77 F10
Schwedeneck D 83 B8
Schwedt an der Oder D 84 D6
Schwegenheim D 187 C5
Schwei (Stadland) D 17 B10
Schweiburg D 17 B10
Schweich D 21 E7
Schweigen-Rechtenbach D 27 B8
Schweighouse-sur-Moder F 186 D4
Schweinfurt D 75 B7
Schweinitz D 80 C4
Schweinrich D 83 D13
Schwelm D 17 F8
Schwendau A 72 B4
Schwendi D 71 A9
Schwenningen D 27 D10
Schwepnitz D 80 D5
Schwerin D 83 C10
Schweringen D 17 C12
Schwerte D 17 F9
Schwichtenberg D 84 C5
Schwieberdingen D 27 C11
Schwiesau D 79 A9
Schwindegg D 75 F11
Schwinkendorf D 83 C13
Schwoich A 72 A5
Schwyz CH 71 C7
Sciacca I 58 D3
Sciara I 58 D4
Scicli I 59 F6
Sciez F 31 C9
Scigliano I 61 E6
Scilla I 59 C8
Šcinawa PL 81 D10
Scionzier F 31 C10
Scoarta RO 160 C2
Scobinţi RO 153 C9
Scoglitti I 58 F5
Scolaticci I 59 C6
Scole GB 15 C11
Scone GB 5 C10
Sconser GB 2 L4
Scopello I 68 B5
Scoppito I 62 C4
Scorbé-Clairvaux F 29 B6
Scordia I 59 E6
Scorniceşti RO 160 D5
Scorrano I 61 C10
Scorţaru Nou RO 161 C11
Scorţeni MD 154 C3
Scorţeni RO 153 D9
Scorţeni RO 161 C7
Scorţoasa RO 161 C9
Scorton GB 11 C8
Scorzè I 66 A5
Scotch Corner GB 11 C8
Scotch Corner IRL 7 D9
Scotshouse IRL 7 D8
Scourie GB 2 J6
Scousburgh GB 3 F14
Scrabster GB 3 H9
Screeb IRL 6 F3
Screggan IRL 7 F7
Scremerston GB 5 D13
Scribbagh GB 6 D6
Scrioaştea RO 160 E5
Scriob IRL 6 F3
Sculeni MD 153 C11
Scundu RO 160 D4
Scunthorpe GB 11 D10
Scuol CH 71 D10
Scurcola Marsicana I 62 C4
Scurtu Mare RO 160 E6
Scutelnici RO 161 D9
Seaca RO 160 E5
Seaca RO 160 F6
Seaca de Pădure RO 160 E2
Seaford GB 15 F9
Seaham GB 5 F14
Seahouses GB 5 D13
Seamer GB 11 C11
Seapatrick GB 7 D10
Seara P 38 E2
Seascale GB 10 C5
Seaton GB 5 F9
Seaton GB 13 D8
Seaton Delaval GB 5 E13
Seaton Sluice GB 5 E14
Seaview GB 13 D12
Sebal P 44 D3
Sébazac-Concourès F 34 B4
Sebbersund DK 86 B5
Sebechleby SK 147 E7
Sebedražie SK 147 D7
Sebeş RO 152 F3
Šebetov CZ 77 C11
Sebezh RUS 133 D4
Sebiş RO 151 E9
Sebnitz D 80 E6
Seč CZ 77 C9
Sečanj SRB 159 C6
Seča Reka SRB 158 E4
Secăria RO 161 C7
Secaş RO 151 F8
Sece LV 135 C10
Secemin PL 143 E8
Seckach D 27 B11
Seckau A 73 B10
Seclin F 19 C7
Secondigny F 28 B5
Sečovce SK 145 F4
Sečovská Polianka SK 145 F4
Secu RO 160 E2
Secuieni RO 152 E5
Secuieni RO 153 D9
Secuieni RO 153 D10
Secusigiu RO 151 E6
Seda LT 134 D4
Seda LV 131 F11
Sedan F 19 E10
Sedano E 40 C4
Sedbergh GB 10 C6
Seddülbahir TR 171 D10
Seden DK 86 E6
Sēdere LV 135 E12
Séderon F 35 B10
Sedgefield GB 5 F14
Sedico I 72 D5
Sedilo I 64 C2
Sedini I 64 B2
Sedlarica HR 149 E8
Sedlčany CZ 77 C6
Sedlec Prčice CZ 77 C7
Sedlice CZ 76 D5
Sedlice SK 145 F3
Sedliská SK 145 F4
Sedlnice CZ 146 B6
Sedrina I 69 B8
Šeduva LT 134 E7
Sjdziejowice PL 143 C7
Sjdzin PL 138 E6
Sjdziszów PL 143 E9
Sjdziszów Małopolski PL 143 F12
See A 71 C10
See A 73 B7
Seebach D 79 E7
Seebach D 187 D5
Seebergen D 79 E8
Seeboden A 73 C8
Seebruck D 72 A5
Seeburg D 79 C7
Seedorf D 83 C9
Seefeld D 75 F9
Seefeld D 80 A5
Seefeld (Stadland) D 17 B10

Sissach CH 27 F8
Sisses GR 178 E8
Sissonne F 19 E8
Șiștarovăț RO 151 E8
Sisteron F 35 B10
Sistranda N 104 D5
Sistrans A 72 B3
Sita Buzăului RO 161 B8
Sitaniec PL 144 B7
Siteia GR 179 E11
Sitges E 43 E7
Sitkówka-Nowiny PL 143 E10
Sitnica BIH 157 C7
Sitochori GR 169 C10
Sitovo BG 161 E10
Sitsyenyets BY 133 E6
Sittard NL 19 C12
Sittensen D 82 D7
Sittersdorf A 73 C10
Sittingbourne GB 15 E10
Sitzendorf an der Schmida A 77 E9
Sitzenroda D 80 D3
Siulaisiadar GB 2 J4
Siuntio FIN 127 E11
Siuro FIN 127 C9
Siurua FIN 119 D16
Siurunmaa FIN 115 D1
Sivac SRB 158 B3
Sivakka FIN 125 C13
Sivakkajoki FIN 119 B13
Sivakkavaara FIN 125 E11
Siverić HR 156 E5
Siverskiy RUS 132 C7
Sivertgården N 108 E7
Sivry B 19 D9
Sivry-sur-Meuse F 19 F11
Sixarby S 99 B9
Six-Fours-les-Plages F 35 D10
Sixmilebridge IRL 8 C5
Sixmilecross GB 7 C8
Six Road Ends GB 4 F5
Sixt-Fer-à-Cheval F 31 C10
Sizun F 22 D3
Sjemeć BIH 158 F3
Sjenica SRB 163 C9
Sjetlina BIH 157 E10
Sjoa N 101 C11
Sjøåsen N 105 C10
Sjöbo S 87 D13
Sjöbotten S 118 E6
Sjöbrånet S 107 C17
Sjøholt N 100 B5
Sjølund DK 86 E5
Sjömarken S 91 D12
Sjonbotn N 108 D6
Sjørring DK 86 B3
Sjørslev DK 86 C4
Sjørup DK 86 C4
Sjösa S 93 B10
Sjösäter S 99 B11
Sjötofta S 91 E13
Sjötorp S 91 B14
Sjoutnäset S 106 B7
Sjøvassbotn N 111 B17
Sjøvegan N 111 C14
Sjövik S 91 D11
Sjulsåsen S 106 C7
Sjulsmark S 118 C7
Sjunnen S 92 E6
Sjuntorp S 91 C11
Sjursvik N 111 B12
Skademark S 107 E16
Skælsør DK 87 E8
Skærbæk DK 86 E3
Skævinge DK 87 D10
Skaftung FIN 122 F6
Skagen DK 90 D8
Skagersvik S 91 B15
Skäggebyn S 91 A12
Skagshamn S 107 E16
Skaidi N 113 C13
Skaidiškės LT 137 D11
Skaill GB 3 H11
Skaista LV 133 E2
Skaistgiriai LT 135 E8
Skaistgirys LT 134 D6
Skaistkalne LV 135 D9
Skala GR 174 C2
Skala GR 175 B7
Skala GR 175 F6
Skala GR 177 E8
Skała PL 143 F8
Skala Eresou GR 177 A6
Skala Kallonis GR 177 A7
Skala Marion GR 171 C7
Skålan S 102 A7
Skaland N 111 B13
Skala Oropou GR 175 C8
Skálavik FO 2 B3
Skalbmierz PL 143 F9
Skåle N 105 C15
Skålevik N 90 C3
Skälgården S 103 A12
Skáli FO 2 A3
Skalica SK 146 D4
Skalice CZ 81 E7
Skalité SK 147 C7
Skalitsa BG 166 E6
Skallelv N 114 C8
Skällinge S 87 A10
Skallvik S 93 C9
Skalmodal S 108 F8
Skalmsjö S 107 D13
Skalná CZ 75 B11
Skålö S 97 A11
Skaloti GR 171 B6
Skals DK 86 B4
Skålsjön S 103 D10
Skalstugan S 105 D12
Skålsvik N 108 B7
Skålvallen S 103 C10
Skån S 103 B11
Skanderåsen S 102 A7
Skanderborg DK 86 C5
Skånes-Fagerhult S 87 C12
Skåne-Tranås S 88 D5
Skånevik N 94 C3
Skåningen N 112 C4
Skaņkalne LV 131 F10
Skänninge S 92 C6
Skanör med Falsterbo S 87 E11
Skansbacken S 97 B11
Skansen N 105 D9
Skansholm S 107 B10
Skansnäs S 107 A10
Skansnäs S 109 E13
Skansnäset S 106 C9
Skåpafors S 91 A11
Skąpe PL 81 B8
Skapiškis LT 135 E10
Skår N 94 D4
Skara S 91 C13
Skäran S 118 F6
Skarberget N 111 D11
Skärblacka S 92 B7
Skarda S 107 C15
Skardmodalen N 108 F7
Skardmunken N 111 A18
Skardstein N 111 B11
Skardsvåg N 113 A16
Skare N 94 C5
Skåre S 97 D9
Skärhamn S 91 D10
Skarkdalen S 102 A4
Skärkind S 92 C7
Skarnes N 96 B6
Skärplinge S 99 B9
Skarp Salling DK 86 B4
Skarrild DK 86 D3
Skärså S 103 D13
Skarsfjord N 112 D2
Skärsjövålen S 102 B5
Skarstad N 111 D11
Skärstad S 92 D4
Skarsvåg N 111 B15
Skarszewy PL 138 B5
Skårup DK 86 E7
Skarv N 112 C11
Skärvången S 105 D16
Skarvfjordhamn N 112 B11
Skarvsjöby S 107 B12
Skaryszew PL 141 H4
Skarżysko-Kamienna PL 141 H3
Skasenden N 96 B7
Skästra S 103 C11
Skatamark S 118 C7
Skatan S 103 B13
Skattkärr S 97 D10
Skattungbyn S 102 D8
Skatvik N 111 B14
Skaudvilė LT 134 F5
Skaugvoll N 108 C7
Skaulo S 116 D6
Šķaune LV 133 D3
Skavdal N 111 B10
Skave DK 86 C3
Skavnakk N 112 C7
Skawina PL 143 G8
Skebobruk S 99 C11
Skebokvarn S 93 A9
Skeda udde S 92 C7
Šķēde LV 134 C4
Skede S 92 E6
Skedevi S 92 B7
Skedsmokorset N 95 B14
Skee S 91 B9
Skegness GB 11 E12
Skegrie S 87 E12
Skei N 100 C4
Skei N 105 A11
Skela SRB 158 D5
Skelby DK 87 E9
Skelde DK 82 A7
Skelhøje DK 86 C4
Skellefteå S 118 E5
Skelleftehamn S 118 E6
Skelmersdale GB 10 D6
Skelton GB 11 B10
Šķeltova LV 133 D2
Skelund DK 86 B6
Skelwick GB 3 G11
Skėmiai LT 134 E7
Skenderaj RKS 163 D10
Skender Vakuf BIH 157 D7
Skenfrith GB 13 B9
Skepasto GR 174 C5
Skępe PL 139 E7
Skepplanda S 91 D11
Skeppshamn S 103 B14
Skeppshult S 87 A12
Skeppsmalen S 107 E16
Skerries IRL 7 E10
Skhidnytsya UA 145 E7
Ski N 95 C13
Skiathos GR 175 A7
Skibbereen IRL 8 E4
Skibbild DK 86 C3
Skibby DK 87 D9
Šķibe LV 134 C6
Skibinge DK 87 E10
Skibotn N 111 B19
Skidal' BY 140 C10
Skiemonys LT 135 F10
Skien N 90 A6
Šķieneri LV 135 B13
Skierbieszów PL 144 B7
Skierniewice PL 141 G2
Skiippagurra N 114 C4
Šķilbēni LV 133 B3
Skillebotn N 108 F3
Skillefjordnes N 113 C11
Skillingaryd S 92 E4
Skillinge S 88 E6
Skillvassbakk N 111 D10
Skinias GR 178 E9
Skinnarud N 101 E12
Skinnskatteberg S 97 C14
Skipmannvik N 109 B9
Skipness GB 4 D6
Skipsea GB 11 D11
Skipton GB 11 D7
Skiptvet N 95 D14
Skirlaugh GB 11 D11
Skitenelv N 111 A17
Skiti GR 169 E8
Skivarp S 87 E13
Skive DK 86 B4
Skivjan RKS 163 E9
Skivsjön S 107 C16
Skiwy Duże PL 141 F7
Skjærhalden N 91 A9
Skjåholmen N 113 B12
Skjånes N 113 B18
Skjånes N 113 B21
Skjåvika N 108 E6
Skjeberg N 91 A9
Skjeggedal N 90 B3
Skjelelv N 111 C13
Skjellbreid N 105 C14
Skjelman N 111 A17
Skjelnes N 111 A18
Skjelstad N 105 D10
Skjelvik N 108 B7
Skjern DK 86 D3
Skjern N 105 C9
Skjerstad N 108 B9
Skjervøy N 112 C6
Skjød DK 86 C5
Skjold N 111 B17
Skjoldastraumen N 94 D3
Skjolden N 100 D7
Skjombotn N 111 D13
Skjøtningberg N 113 A19
Sklithro GR 169 E8
Skobelevo BG 166 D4
Skoby S 99 B10
Skočivir MK 169 C6
Škocjan SLO 148 E4
Skoczów PL 147 B7
Skodborg DK 86 E4
Skodje N 100 A5
Skøelv N 111 B15
Škofja Loka SLO 73 D9
Škofljica SLO 73 E10
Skog S 103 D12
Skogaholm S 92 A6
Skoganvarri N 113 D15
Skoger N 95 C12
Skogfoss N 114 E7
Skoghall S 97 D9
Skogly N 114 E6
Skogmo N 105 B12
Skogn N 105 D10
Skogså S 118 C7
Skogsby S 89 B11
Skogsfjord N 112 C3
Skogshöjden S 91 C11
Skogstorp S 87 B10
Skogstorp S 98 D6
Skogstue N 112 D11
Skogum N 114 E6
Skoki PL 85 E12
Sköldinge S 93 A8
Skole UA 145 E8
Skollenborg N 95 C11
Sköllersta S 92 A6
Skoltenes N 110 C8
Skoltevatn N 114 E7
Skołyszyn PL 144 D3
Skomlin PL 142 D5
Skonseng N 108 D7
Skönvik S 103 E12
Skopelos GR 175 A8
Skopelos GR 177 A7
Skopi GR 179 E11
Skopje MK 164 F3
Skopos GR 169 C6
Skopos GR 171 B7
Skopun FO 2 B3
Skórcz PL 138 C6
Skorica SRB 159 F8
Skorild N 104 E6
Skorogoszcz PL 142 E4
Skoroszyce PL 142 E3
Skorovatn N 105 B14
Skorped S 107 E13
Skorpetorp S 89 A10
Skørping DK 86 B5
Skorstad N 105 B10
Skórzec PL 141 F6
Skoteini GR 174 D5
Skotfoss N 90 A6
Skotina GR 169 D8
Skotoussa GR 169 B9
Skotselv N 95 C11
Skotterud N 96 C7
Skottsund S 103 B13
Skoura GR 175 E5
Skourta GR 175 C8
Skoutari GR 169 B10
Skoutari GR 178 B4
Skoutaros GR 171 F10
Skovby DK 86 C5
Skövde S 91 C14
Skoved S 107 E14
Skovlund DK 86 D3
Skovsgård DK 86 A4
Skra GR 169 B7
Skräddrabo S 103 D10
Skradin HR 156 E4
Skråmestø N 100 E1
Skranstad N 110 E9
Skravena BG 165 D8
Skrea S 87 B11
Skreia N 101 E13
Skriaudžiai LT 137 D8
Skrinyano BG 165 E6
Skřipov CZ 146 B5
Skrīveri LV 135 C10
Skröven S 116 E7
Skrøytnes N 114 E7
Skrudaliena LV 135 E13
Skrunda LV 134 C4
Skruv S 89 B8
Skrwilno PL 139 D8
Skrzatusz PL 85 D11
Skrzyńsko PL 141 H3
Skrzyszów PL 143 G11
Skucani BIH 157 E6
Skudeneshavn N 94 D2
Skuhrov nad Bělou CZ 77 B10
Skujene LV 135 B10
Skujetnieki LV 133 C2
Skuķi LV 133 E3
Skuldelev DK 87 D10
Skule S 107 E14
Skulerud N 95 C15
Skulgammen N 111 A17
Skulsfjord N 111 A16
Skulsk PL 138 F5
Skulte LV 135 B8
Skulte LV 135 C7
Skultorp S 91 C14
Skultuna S 98 C6
Skuodas LT 134 D3
Skurträsk S 107 C16
Skurup S 87 E13
Skuteč CZ 77 C9
Skutskär S 103 E13
Skutvik N 110 D9
Skutvik N 111 B16
Skwierzyna PL 81 A9
Skýcov SK 146 D6
Skydra GR 169 C7
Skyllberg S 92 B6
Skylnäs S 103 A9
Skyros GR 175 B10
Skyttmon S 106 E9
Skyttorp S 99 B9
Slabodka BY 133 E2
Słaboszów PL 143 F9
Sládkovičovo SK 146 E5
Slagavallen S 102 B5
Slagelse DK 87 E8
Slagnäs S 109 E15
Slaidburn GB 10 D7
Slaka S 92 C7
Slampe LV 134 C6
Slane IRL 7 E9
Slanec SK 145 F3
Slangerup DK 87 D10
Slănic RO 161 C7
Slănic Moldova RO 153 E8
Slano HR 162 D4
Slantsy RUS 132 C3
Slaný CZ 76 B6
Slap BIH 158 F3
Slap MNE 163 D7
Slap SLO 73 D8
Šlapaberžė LT 135 F7
Šlapanice CZ 77 D11
Släppträsk S 107 A15
Slate LV 135 D12
Slatina BIH 157 C7
Slatina BIH 157 C8
Slatina BIH 157 E8
Slatina BIH 157 E10
Slatina HR 149 E9
Slatina RO 153 C8
Slatina RO 160 E4
Slatina SRB 158 E4
Slatiňany CZ 77 C9
Slatina-Timiș RO 159 C9
Slatino MK 168 B4
Slatinski Drenovac HR 149 E9
Slătioara RO 160 C3
Slătioara RO 160 E4
Slato BIH 157 F9
Slättberg S 102 D8
Slåttholmen N 110 D8
Slättmon S 103 A13
Slattum N 95 C13
Slava Cercheză RO 155 D3
Slava Rusă RO 155 D3
Slaveino BG 165 F10
Slavičín CZ 146 C5
Slavinja SRB 165 C6
Slavkov CZ 146 B5
Slavkovichi RUS 132 F5
Slavkov u Brna CZ 77 D11
Slavonice CZ 77 E8
Slavonski Brod HR 157 B9
Slavošovce SK 145 F1
Slavotin BG 165 B7
Slavovitsa BG 160 F4
Slavovitsa BG 165 E9
Slavsk RUS 136 C4
Slavs'ke UA 145 F7
Slavsko Polje HR 148 F5
Slavyani BG 165 C10
Slavyanovo BG 165 C10
Slavyanovo BG 166 C6
Slavyanovo BG 166 F5
Sława PL 81 C10
Sławatycze PL 141 G9
Sławięcin PL 85 C13
Sławków PL 143 F7
Sławno PL 85 B11
Sławoborze PL 85 C9
Sławsko PL 85 B11
Sleaford GB 11 F11
Sledmere GB 11 C10
Sleen NL 17 C7
Sleidinge B 182 C3
Sleights GB 11 C10
Slemmestad N 95 C12
Ślesin PL 138 D4
Ślesin PL 138 F5
Sletta N 112 C9
Slevik N 91 A8
Sliač SK 147 D8
Slidre N 101 D9
Sliedrecht NL 16 E3
Šlienava LT 137 D9
Sligachan GB 2 L4
Sligeach IRL 6 D6
Sligo IRL 6 D6
Slimminge DK 87 E9
Slimnic RO 152 F4
Slinfold GB 15 E8
Slipra N 105 D9
Slišane SRB 164 D4
Slite S 93 D13
Sliven BG 166 D6
Slivilești RO 159 D11
Slivnitsa BG 165 D7
Slivo Pole BG 161 F8
Śliwice PL 138 C5
Sllatinë e Madhe RKS 164 D3
Slobidka UA 154 B4
Slobozia MD 154 D5
Slobozia RO 160 D6
Slobozia RO 161 D10
Slobozia RO 161 F7
Slobozia Bradului RO 161 C10
Slobozia Ciorăști RO 161 B10
Slobozia Conachi RO 155 B1
Slobozia Mândra RO 160 F5
Slobozia Mare MD 155 B2
Slobozia Moară RO 161 D7
Slochteren NL 17 B7
Slöinge S 87 B11
Słomniki PL 143 F9
Słonowice PL 85 C9
Słońsk PL 81 A7
Slootdorp NL 16 C3
Slottsskogen S 99 C9
Slough GB 15 D7
Sloupnice CZ 77 C10
Sløvåg N 100 E2
Slovenj Gradec SLO 73 C11
Slovenska Bistrica SLO 148 D5
Slovenská Ľupča SK 147 D8
Slovenská Ves SK 145 E1
Slovenske Konjice SLO 148 D4
Slovenské Nové Mesto SK 145 G4
Slovenský Grob SK 146 E4
Slovinci HR 157 B6
Slovinky SK 145 F2
Sløvra N 110 D8
Slov"yanoserbka UA 154 D5
Słowik PL 143 C7
Słubice PL 81 B7
Słubice PL 139 F8
Sluderno I 71 D11
Sluis NL 19 B7
Sluiskil NL 16 F1
Šluknov CZ 81 D6
Slunj HR 156 B4
Słupca PL 142 B4
Słupcza PL 144 B4
Słupia PL 141 G1
Słupia PL 143 D9
Słupia PL 143 E8
Słupno PL 139 E8
Słupsk PL 85 B12
Slušovice CZ 146 C5
Slussfors S 109 F11
Słuszków PL 142 C5
Slyuda RUS 115 D8
Smailholm GB 5 D11
Smålandsstenar S 87 A12
Smalåsen N 105 A14
Smalfjord N 113 C21
Smalininkai LT 136 C6
Smalvos LT 135 E12
Smârdan RO 155 C1
Smârdan RO 155 C2
Smārde LV 134 C6
Smârdioasa RO 161 F6
Smardzewice PL 141 H2
Smardzewo PL 81 B9
Smardzko PL 85 C9
Smarhon' BY 137 E13
Šmarje pri Jelšah SLO 148 D5
Šmarjeta SLO 148 E4
Šmartno SLO 73 D10
Šmartno SLO 73 D11
Smarves F 29 B6
Smedby S 89 B10
Smederevo SRB 159 D6
Smederevska Palanka SRB 159 E6
Smedjebacken S 97 B13
Smedsbyn S 118 C8
Smedvik N 110 D6
Smeeni RO 161 C9
Smęgorzów PL 143 F11
Smelror N 114 C10
Smelteri LV 135 D13
Smętowo Graniczne PL 138 C6
Smidary CZ 77 B8
Smidstrup DK 86 D5
Smidstrup DK 87 C10
Śmigiel PL 81 B11
Smilčić HR 156 D4
Smilde NL 17 C6
Smilets BG 165 E9
Smilevo MK 168 B5
Smilgiai LT 135 D9
Smilgiai LT 135 E8
Smilgiai LT 137 D8
Smilgynai LT 134 E2
Smilovci SRB 165 C6
Śmiłowice PL 138 E7
Śmiłowo PL 85 D11
Smiltene LV 135 B11
Smiltynė LT 134 E2
Smilyan BG 171 A7
Smines N 110 C8
Smiřice CZ 77 B9
Smirnenski BG 159 F11
Smirnenski BG 161 F8
Smiugard N 101 D11
Smižany SK 145 F2
Smögen S 91 C9
Smokvica HR 162 D2
Smokvica MK 169 B7
Smołdzino PL 85 A12
Smolenice SK 146 D4
Smolice PL 81 C12
Smolmark S 96 C7
Smolnica PL 84 E7
Smolník SK 145 F2
Smolyan BG 171 A7
Smolyanovtsi BG 165 C6
Smørfjord N 113 B15
Smulți RO 153 F11
Smyadovo BG 167 C8
Smygehamn S 87 E12
Smyków PL 143 D9
Snagov RO 161 D8
Snainton GB 11 C10
Snaith GB 11 D9
Snålroa N 102 E2
Snappertuna FIN 127 E10
Snaptun DK 86 D6
Snarby N 111 A18
Snåre FIN 123 C10
Snartemo N 94 F6
Snåsa N 105 C12
Snave Bridge IRL 8 E4
Snedsted DK 86 B3
Sneek NL 16 B5
Sneem IRL 8 E3
Snejbjerg DK 86 C3
Snēpele LV 134 C3
Snerta N 101 C15
Snertinge DK 87 D8
Snesslinge S 99 B10
Snesudden S 118 B4
Snettisham GB 11 F13
Śniadowo PL 139 D12
Sniķere LV 134 D6
Snina SK 145 F5
Šnjegotina Velika BIH 157 C8
Snøde DK 87 E7
Snøfjord N 113 B14
Snogebæk DK 89 E8
Snoghøj DK 86 D5
Snoldelev DK 87 D10
Soajo P 38 E3
Șoarș RO 152 F5
Soave I 66 B3
Søberg N 110 C7
Soběslav CZ 77 D7
Sobienie-Jeziory PL 141 G4
Sobolew PL 141 G5
Sobota PL 143 B8
Soboth A 73 C11
Sobotín CZ 77 B12
Sobotište SK 146 D4
Sobotka CZ 77 B8
Sobótka PL 81 E11
Sobótka PL 142 C4
Sobótka PL 143 E12
Sobowidz PL 138 B6
Sobra HR 162 D4
Sobradelo E 39 D6
Sobradiel E 41 E9
Sobrado E 38 B3
Sobrado E 38 D3
Sobral da Adiça P 51 C5
Sobral de Monte Agraço P 50 A1
Sobrance SK 145 F5
Sobreira Formosa P 44 E5
Søby DK 86 F6
Soča SLO 73 D8
Sočanica RKS 163 C10
Soçanicë RKS 163 C10
Socchieve I 73 D6
Sočerga SLO 67 B8
Sochaczew PL 141 F2
Sochaux F 27 E6
Sochocin PL 139 E9
Sochos GR 169 C9
Socodor RO 151 D7
Socol RO 159 D7
Socond RO 151 B10
Socovos E 55 C9
Socuéllamos E 47 F7
Sodankylä FIN 117 D17
Söderåkra S 89 C10
Söderala S 103 D12
Söderås S 103 E9
Söderbärke S 97 B14
Söderboda S 99 B10
Söderby-Karl S 99 C11
Söderfors S 98 B8
Söderhamn S 103 D13
Söderköping S 93 C8
Söderkulla FIN 127 E13
Södersvik S 99 C11
Södertälje S 93 A11
Södra Åbyn S 118 E5
Södra Brännträsk S 118 C4
Södra Drängsmark S 118 E5
Södra Harads S 118 B5
Södra Johannisberg S 109 F15
Södra Löten S 102 E4
Södra Sandby S 87 D12
Södra Sandträsk S 107 A16
Södra Sunderbyn S 118 C7
Södra Tresund S 107 B11
Södra Vallgrund FIN 122 D6
Södra Vi S 92 D7
Sodražica SLO 73 E10
Soerendonk NL 16 F5
Soest D 17 E10
Soest NL 16 D4
Soesterberg NL 183 A6
Sofades GR 169 F7
Sofia BG 165 D7
Sofia MD 153 B11
Sofiko GR 171 B11
Sofiko GR 175 D7
Sofporog RUS 121 C17
Șofrîncani MD 153 A10
Șofronea RO 151 E7
Šofronievo BG 160 F3
Søften DK 86 C6
Søftestad N 90 A4
Sofular TR 181 A9
Sögel D 17 C9
Sogndalsfjøra N 100 D6
Søgne N 90 C2
Soğucak TR 173 A8
Soğucak TR 173 F8
Soğucak TR 177 D9
Soğukoluk TR 181 A7
Söğüt TR 181 C8
Söğütalan TR 173 D10
Soham GB 15 C9
Sohatu RO 161 E9
Soheit-Tinlot B 19 D11
Sohland D 80 D6
Sohodol RO 151 E11
Sohren D 21 E8
Soidinkumpu FIN 121 B12
Soidinvaara FIN 121 F12
Soignies B 19 C9
Soikko FIN 119 C14
Șoimari RO 161 C8
Șoimi RO 151 D9
Șoimuș RO 151 F10
Soing F 26 E4
Soings-en-Sologne F 24 F6
Soini FIN 123 E12
Soinilansalmi FIN 125 F10
Soinlahti FIN 124 C8
Soissons F 19 F7
Soivio FIN 121 C13
Soizy-aux-Bois F 25 C10
Sójkowa PL 144 C5
Söjtör H 149 C7
Sokal' UA 144 C9
Söke TR 177 D9
Soklot FIN 122 C9
Sokna N 95 B11
Soknedal N 104 F8
Sokobanja SRB 159 F8
Sokojärvi FIN 125 D14
Sokolac BIH 157 E10
Sokolany PL 140 D8
Sokolce SK 146 F5
Sokolivka UA 154 A3
Sokółka PL 140 D9
Sokółki PL 136 E5
Sokolnice CZ 77 D11
Sokolniki PL 142 D5
Sokolov CZ 75 B12
Sokolovac HR 149 D7
Sokolovce SK 146 D5
Sokolovici BIH 157 E10
Sokolovo BG 166 C5
Sokolovo BG 167 C10
Sokolovo BIH 157 C6
Sokołów Małopolski PL 144 C5
Sokołow Podlaski PL 141 F6
Sokoły PL 140 E7
Sokorópátka H 149 B9
Sokyrnytsya UA 145 G7
Sól PL 144 B6
Soľ SK 145 F4
Sola N 94 E3
Solacolu RO 161 E9
Solana de los Barros E 51 B6
Solana del Pino E 54 C4
Solana de Rioalmar E 45 C11
Søland N 95 B10
Solarino I 59 E7
Solaro F 37 H10
Solberg N 101 E15
Solberg N 111 B14
Solberg S 107 D11
Solberg S 107 D13
Solberga S 92 D5
Solbjerg DK 86 C6
Solca RO 153 B7
Solčava SLO 73 D10
Solda I 71 D11
Șoldănești MD 154 B3
Șoldanu RO 161 E9
Soldatnes N 113 D14
Sölden A 71 D12
Soldeu AND 33 E9
Solec Kujawski PL 138 D5
Solec-Zdrój PL 143 F10
Solenzara F 37 H10
Solesino I 66 B4
Solesmes F 19 D7
Solesmes F 23 E11
Solești RO 153 D11
Soleto I 61 C10
Solf FIN 122 D7
Solférino F 32 B4
Solferino I 66 B2
Solfjellsjøen N 108 D4
Soliera I 66 C2
Solignano I 69 D8
Solihull GB 13 A11
Solin HR 156 E5
Solina PL 145 E5
Solingen D 21 B8
Solivella E 42 E6
Soljani HR 157 C10
Sölje S 97 D8
Solkei FIN 128 C8
Söll A 72 A5
Sollacaro F 37 H9
Sollas GB 2 K2
Sollebrunn S 91 C12
Sollefteå S 107 E12
Sollenau A 77 G10
Sollenkroka S 99 D11
Sollentuna S 99 D9
Sóller E 49 E10
Sollerön S 102 E8
Søllested DK 83 A10
Söllichau D 79 C12
Solliès-Pont F 36 E4
Solliès-Toucas F 36 E4
Sollihøgda N 95 C12
Söllingen D 79 B8
Sollstedt D 79 D8
Solmaz TR 181 B9
Solms D 21 C10
Solnice CZ 77 B10
Solnik BG 167 D9
Solofra I 60 B3
Solojärvi FIN 113 F18
Solomiac F 33 C7
Solomos GR 175 D6
Solopaca I 60 A3
Solórzano E 40 B4
Solosancho E 46 C3
Sološnica SK 146 E4
Solothurn CH 27 F8
Solotvyna UA 145 H8
Soløy N 111 C14
Solre-le-Château F 19 D9
Solrød Strand DK 87 D10
Solsem N 105 A11
Solskjela N 104 E4
Sølsnes N 100 A6
Solsona E 43 D7
Solsvik N 94 B1
Solt H 150 D3
Soltau D 83 E7
Soltendieck D 83 E9
Sol'tsy RUS 132 E7
Soltszentimre H 150 D3
Soltvadkert H 150 D3
Solumshamn S 103 A14
Solva GB 9 E12
Solvalla S 99 C10
Solvarbo S 97 B14
Sölvesborg S 88 C7
Solvorn N 100 D6
Solymár H 149 A11
Soma TR 177 A10
Somain F 19 D7
Somberek H 149 D11
Sombernon F 25 F12
Sombor SRB 150 F3
Sombreffe B 19 C10
Șomcuța Mare RO 151 B11
Somercotes GB 11 E9
Someren NL 16 F5
Somerniemi FIN 127 D10
Somero FIN 127 D10
Someronkylä FIN 119 F12
Somerovaara FIN 119 D16
Sõmerpalu EST 131 F13
Somerton GB 13 C9
Sõmeru EST 131 C12
Someș-Odorhei RO 151 C11
Somianka PL 139 E11
Sominy PL 85 B13
Somlóvásárhely H 149 B8
Sommacampagna I 66 B2
Somma Lombardo I 68 B6
Sommariva del Bosco I 37 B7
Sommarøy N 110 C9
Sommarøy N 111 A15
Sommarset N 109 A10
Sommatino I 58 E4
Somme-Leuze B 19 D11
Sommen S 92 C5
Sommepy-Tahure F 19 F10
Sömmerda D 79 D9
Sommerfeld D 84 E4
Sommersted DK 86 E4
Sommesous F 25 C11
Somme-Suippe F 25 B12
Sommevoire F 25 D12
Sommières F 35 C7
Sommières-du-Clain F 29 C6
Somogyapáti H 149 D9
Somogyjád H 149 D9
Somogyszob H 149 D8
Somogyudvarhely H 149 D8
Somogyvár H 149 C9
Somonino PL 138 B5
Somontín E 55 E8
Somotor SK 145 G4
Somova RO 155 C3
Somovit BG 160 F5
Sompa EST 131 C14
Sompolno PL 138 F6
Sompujärvi FIN 119 C14
Somzée B 19 D9
Son N 95 C13
Son NL 16 E4
Sona I 66 B2
Sona N 105 E10
Șona RO 152 E4
Sonceboz CH 27 F7
Soncillo E 40 C4
Soncino I 69 C8
Sonda EST 131 C13
Sondalo I 69 A9
Søndeled N 90 B5
Sønder Balling DK 86 B3
Sønder Bjerre DK 86 D5
Sønder Bjert DK 86 E5
Sønderborg DK 86 F5
Sønderby DK 87 D10
Sønder Dråby DK 86 B3
Sønder Felding DK 86 D3
Sønderho DK 86 E2
Sønderholm DK 86 A5
Sønder Hygum DK 86 E3
Sønder Nissum DK 86 C2
Sønder Omme DK 86 D3
Sønder Onsild DK 86 B5
Sønder Rubjerg DK 90 E6
Sondershausen D 79 D8
Søndersø DK 86 E6
Sønder Stenderup DK 86 E5
Sønder Vilstrup DK 86 E5
Sønder Vissing DK 86 C5
Sønder Vium DK 86 D2
Sondori LV 133 C2
Sondrio I 69 A8
Soneja E 48 E4
Songe N 90 B5
Songeons F 18 E4
Sonim P 38 E5
Sonka FIN 117 E14
Sonkajärvi FIN 124 C9
Sonkakoski FIN 124 C9
Sonkamuotka FIN 117 B10
Sonneberg D 75 B9
Sonneborn D 79 E8
Sonnefeld D 75 B9
Sonnewalde D 80 C5
Sonnino I 62 E4
Sonntag A 71 C9

Stolac BIH 157 F8
Stolberg (Harz) Kurort D 79 C8
Stolberg (Rheinland) D 20 C6
Stołczno PL 85 C12
Stolerova LV 133 D3
Stollberg D 79 E12
Stöllet S 97 B9
Stolmen N 94 B2
Stolniceni MD 154 D3
Stolniceni-Prăjescu RO 153 C9
Stolnici RO 160 D5
Stolnik BG 165 D8
Stolno PL 138 D6
Stolpe D 83 B8
Stolpe D 84 E6
Stolpen D 80 D6
Stolzenau D 17 C12
Stomio GR 169 E8
Stömne S 97 D8
Ston HR 162 D4
Stone GB 11 F7
Stone GB 13 B10
Stonehaven GB 5 B12
Stonehouse GB 5 D9
Stong N 94 D3
Stongfjorden N 100 D2
Stonglandseidet N 111 B13
Stonybreck GB 3 F13
Stoob A 149 A7
Stöpen S 91 C14
Stopiče SLO 148 E4
Stopki PL 136 E3
Stopnica PL 143 F10
Storå N 111 D11
Storå S 97 C13
Stora Åby S 92 C5
Storåbränna S 106 D7
Stora Höga S 91 C10
Stora Levene S 91 C12
Stora Melby S 91 C12
Stora Mellösa S 92 A6
Storarmsjö S 107 C16
Storås N 104 E7
Storåsen S 103 A10
Storåsen S 106 D7
Stora Skedvi S 97 B14
Stora Tallberg S 109 E17
Stora Vika S 93 B11
Storbäck S 106 B9
Storbacka FIN 123 D10
Storbäcken S 102 C4
Storberg S 109 E16
Stor-Blåsjön S 105 B16
Storbo S 102 C3
Storbogaren S 107 D14
Storbränna S 106 D7
Storbrännan S 118 E4
Storbukt N 113 B12
Storby FIN 99 B13
Stordal N 100 B6
Štore SLO 148 D4
Storebø N 94 B2
Storebro S 92 D7
Storebru N 100 C3
Store Damme DK 84 A2
Store Darum DK 86 E3
Store Heddinge DK 87 E10
Storeidet N 111 E10
Storekorsnes N 112 C11
Storelv N 112 B10
Store Merløse DK 87 D9
Store Molvik N 114 B5
Støren N 104 E8
Storenga N 112 D7
Store Rise DK 83 A8
Store Rørbæk DK 86 B5
Storfjäten S 102 C5
Storfjord N 111 B18
Storfjordbotn N 113 C18
Storfors S 97 C11
Storforshei N 108 D8
Storhågna S 102 A7
Storhallaren N 104 D5
Stor-Hallen S 102 A7
Storhogen S 106 E8
Stor-Hullsjön S 103 A12
Štorje SLO 73 E8
Storjola S 106 B7
Storjord N 109 C9
Storjorda N 108 C6
Storjorda N 111 C11
Storkow D 80 B5
Storli N 101 A10
Storlien S 105 E12
Stormi FIN 127 C9
Stornara I 60 A5
Stornarella I 60 A5
Stornäs S 106 A8
Stornäs S 107 A11
Stornäset S 107 C10
Stornes N 111 C11
Storneshamn N 112 D7
Stornoway GB 2 J4
Storo I 69 B10
Štorobăneasa RO 161 F6
Štorodden N 104 E6
Storöhamn S 119 C10
Storozhynets' UA 153 A7
Storrington GB 15 F8
Storrøsta N 101 B13
Storsand S 103 C13
Storsand S 118 B5
Storsandsjö S 107 C17
Storsätern S 102 B3
Storsävarträsk S 118 F3
Storsele S 107 D14
Storseleby S 107 B11
Storseløy N 108 C4
Storsjö S 102 A5
Storskog S 109 E10
Storslett N 112 D7
Storsletta N 112 D6
Storsteinnes N 111 A18
Storsteinnes N 111 B17
Storsund S 118 C5
Storuman S 107 A12
Storvik N 108 C6
Storvik N 110 C9
Storvik N 112 C9
Storvik N 112 D7
Storvik S 103 E12
Storvorde DK 86 A6
Storvreta S 99 C9
Štós SK 145 F2
Stößen D 79 D10
Stössing A 77 F9
Stoszowice PL 81 E11
Støtt N 108 C5
Stötten am Auerberg D 71 B11
Stotternheim D 79 D9
Stouby DK 86 D5
Stoumont B 19 D12
Stourbridge GB 13 A10
Stourport-on-Severn GB 13 A10
Støvran N 108 B8
Støvring DK 86 B5
Støvset N 108 B8
Stow GB 5 D11
Stowijcino PL 85 A12
Stowmarket GB 15 C10
Stow-on-the-Wold GB 13 B11
Stoyan Mikhaylovski BG 167 C8
Stoyanovo BG 165 C10
Stoykite BG 165 F10
Stozher BG 167 C9
Stožne PL 136 E5
Stra I 66 B5
Straach D 79 C12
Strabane GB 4 F2
Strabla PL 141 E8
Strachan GB 5 A11
Strachówka PL 139 F12
Strachur GB 4 C6
Stracin MK 164 E5
Stračiūnai LT 137 E9
Strackholt (Großefehn) D 17 B9
Strączno PL 85 D10
Stradalovo BG 165 E6
Stradbally IRL 7 F8
Stradbroke GB 15 C11
Stradella I 69 C7
Stradi LV 135 B13
Stradishall GB 15 C10
Stradone IRL 7 E8
Stradsett GB 11 F12
Straelen D 16 F6
Stragari SRB 158 E6
Straia N 90 C2
Straimont B 19 E11
Straja RO 153 B7
Strakhilovo BG 166 C5
Strakonice CZ 76 D5
Straldzha BG 167 D7
Stralki BY 133 E4
Straloch GB 5 B9
Strålsnäs S 92 C6
Stralsund D 84 B4
Strambino I 68 C4
Stramproy NL 19 B12
Strâmtura RO 152 B4
Strářňavy SK 147 C7
Strančice CZ 77 C7
Strand N 101 D15
Strand N 110 C9
Strand S 106 D9
Stranda N 100 B5
Strandå N 108 A8
Strandby DK 86 B4
Strandby DK 90 E8
Strande D 83 B8
Strandnorum S 91 C10
Strandval N 105 B10
Strangford GB 7 D11
Stranghele N 100 E3
Strängnäs S 98 D8
Strangolagalli I 62 D4
Strångsjö S 93 B8
Strání CZ 146 D5
Stranocum GB 4 E4
Stranorlar IRL 7 C7
Stranraer GB 4 F6
Străoane RO 153 F10
Strasatti I 58 D2
Strasbourg F 27 C8
Strasburg D 84 D5
Strășeni MD 154 C3
Strašice CZ 76 C5
Stråssa S 97 C13
Straßberg D 27 D11
Straßberg D 79 C9
Straßburg A 73 C9
Strassen L 20 E6
Straßengel A 148 B4
Straßenhaus D 21 C9
Strasshof an der Nordbahn A 77 F11
Straßkirchen D 75 E12
Straßwalchen A 76 G4
Stratford IRL 7 G9
Stratford-upon-Avon GB 13 A11
Strathaven GB 5 D8
Strathblane GB 5 D8
Strathpeffer GB 2 K7
Strathy GB 3 H9
Strathyre GB 5 C8
Stratinska BIH 157 C6
Stratiyivka UA 154 A4
Stratoni GR 169 C10
Stratoniki GR 169 C10
Stratos GR 174 B3
Stratton GB 12 D5
Stratton St Margaret GB 13 B11
Straubing D 75 E12
Straum N 104 D5
Straum N 108 E5
Straume N 90 A2
Straume N 110 C7
Straumen N 104 E4
Straumen N 105 D10
Straumen N 108 B8
Straumen N 109 B10
Straumen N 111 A19
Straumen N 111 C11
Straumen N 114 B7
Straumfjord N 110 C9
Straumgjerde N 100 B5
Straumnes N 110 D7
Straumsnes N 108 B9
Straumsnes N 110 C8
Straumsnes N 111 B13
Straumstad N 111 B17
Straunen N 111 B15
Straupe LV 135 B9
Straupitz D 80 C6
Strausberg D 80 A5
Straußfurt D 79 D8
Stravaj AL 168 C3
Strawczyn PL 143 E9
Straža SRB 159 D7
Strazhitsa BG 166 C5
Stráž nad Nežárkou CZ 77 D7
Stráž nad Nisou CZ 81 E8
Strážnice CZ 146 D4
Stráž pod Ralskem CZ 81 E7
Strážske SK 145 F4
Štrba SK 147 C10
Streatley GB 13 B12
Strečno SK 147 C7
Streda nad Bodrogom SK 145 G4
Streek D 17 B10
Street GB 13 C9
Strehaia RO 159 D11
Strehla D 80 D4
Strejești RO 160 D4
Strekov SK 146 F6
Strelac SRB 164 D5
Strelcë AL 168 C4
Strelcha BG 165 D9
Strellc i Epërm RKS 163 D9
Strēlnieki LV 135 C8
Strem A 149 B6
Strembo I 69 A10
Stremț RO 152 E3
Strenči LV 131 F11
Strendur FO 2 A3
Strengberg A 77 F7
Strengelvåg N 110 C9
Strengen A 71 C10
Strengen N 95 D9
Stresa I 68 B6
Stretford GB 11 E7
Stretham GB 15 C9
Streufdorf D 75 B8
Strezimirovtsi BG 164 D5
Strib DK 86 D5
Striberg S 97 C12
Stříbro CZ 76 C3
Strichen GB 3 K12
Strigno I 72 D4
Štrigova HR 148 C6
Strijen NL 16 E3
Strimasund S 108 D8
Strimoniko GR 169 B9
Strinda N 111 E10
Strittjomvare S 109 E16
Strizivojna HR 157 B9
Strmec HR 148 E5
Strmen HR 149 F7
Strmica BIH 156 D5
Strmica HR 156 D5
Ströbeck D 79 C8
Strobl A 73 A7
Strøby DK 87 E10
Strøby Egede DK 87 E10
Stroeşti RO 160 C3
Stroevo BG 165 E10
Strofylia GR 175 B7
Ströhen D 17 C11
Stroiești RO 153 B8
Strokestown IRL 6 E6
Ström S 108 E8
Strömbäck S 122 C4
Strömbacka S 103 C12
Stromberg D 185 E8
Stromeferry GB 2 L5
Strömfors S 118 E4
Strömholm S 109 E15
Stromiec PL 141 G4
Strommen N 95 C13
Strömmer S 96 C6
Strömnäs S 107 B10
Strömnäs S 118 D5
Stromness GB 3 H10
Strömsberg S 99 B9
Strömsbro S 103 E13
Strömsbruk S 103 C13
Strömsholden S 98 C6
Strømsmoen N 111 C16
Strömsnäs S 107 E9
Strömsnäsbruk S 87 B13
Strömstad S 91 B9
Strömsund S 106 D9
Strömsund S 107 A11
Stronachlachar GB 4 C7
Stroncone I 62 C3
Strongoli I 61 E8
Stronie Śląskie PL 77 B11
Stronsdorf A 77 E10
Strontian GB 4 B5
Stropi LV 135 E13
Stropkov SK 145 E4
Stroppiana I 68 C5
Stroppo I 36 B6
Stroud GB 13 B10
Strövelstorp S 87 C11
Strovija MK 168 A5
Stróża PL 147 B9
Štrpce RKS 164 E3
Strücklingen (Saterland) D 17 B9
Struer DK 86 C3
Struga MK 168 B4
Strugi-Krasnyye RUS 132 E5
Strullendorf D 75 C8
Strumë AL 168 C2
Strumica MK 169 B8
Strumień PL 147 B7
Strumkivka UA 145 G5
Strumok UA 155 B4
Strumyani BG 169 A9
Strunkovice nad Blanicí CZ 76 D6
Strupļi LV 133 C1
Struth D 79 D7
Strūžāni LV 133 C2
Stružec HR 149 E7
Stryama BG 165 E10
Stryków PL 143 C8
Stryksele S 107 C16
Stryn N 100 C5
Stryy UA 145 E8
Strzała PL 141 F6
Strzałkowo PL 142 B4
Strzebień PL 143 E6
Strzegocin PL 139 E10
Strzegom PL 81 E10
Strzegowo PL 139 E9
Strzelce PL 143 B7
Strzelce Krajeńskie PL 85 E9
Strzelce Opolskie PL 142 E5
Strzelce Wielkie PL 143 D7
Strzeleczki PL 142 F4
Strzelin PL 81 E12
Strzelno PL 138 E5
Strzepcz PL 138 B5
Strzyżewice PL 144 A5
Strzyżów PL 144 D4
Sts-Geosmes F 26 E3
Stubbæk DK 86 F4
Stubbekøbing DK 84 A2
Stubben D 17 B11
Stubel BG 165 C7
Stubenberg A 148 B5
Stubica SRB 159 F7
Štubik SRB 159 E9
Stubline SRB 158 D5
Stubno PL 144 D6
Stuchowo PL 85 C8
Studena BG 165 D7
Studena BG 166 F6
Studená CZ 77 D8
Studena UA 154 A3
Studençan RKS 163 E10
Studenci HR 157 E7
Studenec CZ 81 E9
Studénka CZ 146 B6
Studienka SK 77 E12
Studina RO 160 F4
Studley GB 13 A11
Studsvik S 93 B10
Studsviken S 107 D14
Studzienice PL 85 B13
Studzieniec PL 81 C9
Stugubacken S 103 D11
Stuguflåten N 100 B8
Stugun S 106 E9
Stühlingen D 27 E9
Stuhr D 17 B11
Stukmaņi LV 135 C11
Stülpe D 80 B4
Stulpicani RO 153 C7
Stumm A 72 B4
Stumsnäs S 102 E8
Stuorajavrre N 112 E10
Stuorragårži N 113 E16
Stupari BIH 157 D10
Stupava SK 77 F12
Stupsk PL 139 D9
Stupurai LT 134 D7
Sturefors S 92 C7
Stūri LV 134 C5
Sturkö S 89 C9
Šturlić BIH 156 B4
Sturmai LT 134 F2
Sturminster Newton GB 13 D10
Štúrovo MK 164 F5
Štúrovo SK 149 A11
Sturry GB 15 E11
Sturzelbronn F 27 B8
Stuttgart D 27 C11
Stützerbach D 79 E8
Styggedalen N 111 B19
Stylida GR 175 B6
Stypsi GR 171 F10
Styra GR 175 C9
Styrkesnes N 109 A9
Styrnäs S 107 E13
Styrrmanstø N 111 A18
Suances E 40 B3
Suaningi S 117 E10
Suatu RO 152 D3
Subačius LT 135 E9
Subaşi TR 171 B10
Subaşı TR 173 B9
Subaşi TR 177 C9
Subate LV 135 D11
Subbiano I 66 E4
Suben A 76 F4
Subiaco I 62 D4
Subkowy PL 138 B6
Subotica SRB 150 E4
Subotište SRB 158 D4
Subotniki BY 137 E12
Sučany SK 147 C7
Suceava RO 153 B8
Suceveni RO 153 E12
Sučevići HR 156 D5
Sucevița RO 153 B7
Sucha Beskidzka PL 147 B9
Suchacz PL 139 B7
Suchá Hora SK 147 C9
Suchá Loz CZ 146 D5
Suchań PL 85 D8
Suchá nad Parnou SK 146 E4
Suchdol CZ 77 C8
Suchdol nad Lužnicí CZ 77 E7
Suchdol nad Odrou CZ 146 B5
Suchedniów PL 143 D10
Suchowola PL 140 C8
Suchożebry PL 141 F6
Suchy Dąb PL 138 B6
Suchy Las PL 81 B11
Sucina E 56 F3
Suciu de Sus RO 152 C4
Suckow D 83 D11
Suceleia MD 154 D5
Sučuraj HR 157 F7
Sudanell E 42 D5
Sudargas LT 136 C6
Sudbury GB 15 C10
Suddendorf D 183 A10
Suddesjaur S 109 E17
Süden D 82 B5
Süderbrarup D 82 A7
Süderhastedt D 82 B6
Süderlügum D 86 F3
Süderstapel D 82 B6
Suderve LT 137 D11
Sudiți RO 161 D11
Sudkov CZ 77 C11
Südlohn D 17 E7
Sudok S 118 B4
Sudoměřice CZ 146 D4
Sudova Vyshnya UA 144 D7
Sudovec HR 149 D6
Sudrabkalns LV 135 D12
Suďurad HR 162 D4
Sudwalde D 17 C11
Sueca E 48 F4
Suedinenie BG 165 E10
Suelli I 64 D3
Suèvres F 24 E5
Sugag RO 152 F3
Suha BIH 157 D9
Suha BIH 157 F10
Suhaia RO 160 F6
Suharău RO 153 A8
Suharekë RKS 163 E10
Suhl D 79 E8
Suhlendorf D 83 E9
Suhmura FIN 125 F13
Suho Polje BIH 157 C11
Suhopolje HR 149 E8
Suica BIH 157 E7
Suici RO 160 C5
Suijavaara S 116 B9
Suilly-la-Tour F 25 F9
Suinula FIN 127 B11
Suinula FIN 127 B12
Suippes F 25 B12
Sukeva FIN 124 C8
Sukhindol BG 166 C4
Sukhodil UA 145 D9
Sukhodil UA 145 F9
Sukošan HR 156 D3
Sükösd H 150 E2
Sukovo SRB 165 C6
Sukow D 83 C11
Sul N 105 D12
Suldrup DK 86 B5
Sulechów PL 81 B9
Sulęcin PL 81 B8
Suljcin Szlachecki PL 139 E12
Sulejczyno PL 138 B4
Sulejów PL 141 H1
Sulejówek PL 141 F4
Suleskar N 94 D5
Sulesund N 100 B4
Șuletea RO 153 E11
Süleymaniye TR 173 B6
Süleymaniye TR 173 C6
Süleymanli TR 177 B10
Sulików PL 81 D8
Sulingen D 17 C11
Suliszewo PL 85 D9
Sulița RO 153 B9
Sulitjelma N 109 B11
Sulkava FIN 123 D17
Sulkava FIN 129 B9
Sulkavanjärvi FIN 123 D16
Sulkavanjärvi FIN 123 D17
Sulkavankylä FIN 123 F11
Sułkowice PL 147 B9
Sullington GB 15 F8
Sully F 30 A5
Sully GB 13 C8
Sully-sur-Loire F 25 E7
Sulmierzyce PL 142 C4
Sulmierzyce PL 143 D7
Sulmona I 62 C5
Sulniac F 22 E6
Süloğlu TR 167 F7
Sułoszowa PL 143 F8
Sułów PL 81 D12
Sułów PL 144 B6
Sulsted DK 86 A5
Sultaniça TR 171 C10
Sultaniye TR 173 D9
Sultanköy TR 171 C10
Sultanköy TR 173 B8
Suluca TR 171 C10
Suluca TR 172 D6
Sulvik S 96 C7
Sulviken S 105 D14
Sulz A 71 C9
Sulz am Neckar D 27 D10
Sulzbach am Main D 21 E12
Sulzbach an der Murr D 27 B11
Sulzbach-Laufen D 74 E6
Sulzbach-Rosenberg D 75 C10
Sulzbach/Saar D 186 C3
Sulzdorf an der Lederhecke D 75 B8
Sulzemoos D 75 F9
Sulzfeld D 75 B7
Sulzfeld D 187 C6
Sulzheim D 75 C7
Sulzthal D 75 B7
Sumartin HR 157 F6
Sumba FO 2 C3
Sumburgh GB 3 F14
Šumećani HR 149 E6
Sümeg H 149 C8
Sumène F 35 C6
Šumiac SK 145 F1
Sumiainen FIN 123 E16
Šumice CZ 146 C5
Sumiswald CH 70 C5
Summer Bridge GB 11 C8
Summerhill IRL 7 F9
Šumperk CZ 77 C11
Sumsa FIN 121 F14
Šumvald CZ 77 C12
Sumvitg CH 71 D7
Sunākste LV 135 D11
Suňava SK 147 C10
Sunbilla E 32 D2
Șuncuiuș RO 151 D10
Sund FIN 99 B14
Sund N 108 B7
Sund N 110 D5
Sund N 110 D5
Sund S 92 D6
Sund S 103 B10
Sund S 107 E14
Sundborn S 103 E10
Sundby DK 86 B3
Sundby DK 86 B3
Sundby FIN 122 C9
Sundby N 108 B9
Sunde N 94 C3
Sunde N 104 E6
Sunderland GB 5 F14
Sundern (Sauerland) D 17 F10
Sundet S 105 D13
Sundklakk N 110 D7
Sundnäs S 109 D14
Sundom FIN 122 D7
Sundom S 118 C8
Sundre S 93 F12
Sunds DK 86 C4
Sundsbruk S 103 B13
Sundsjö S 103 A9
Sundsli N 90 A3
Sundsvall S 103 B13
Sundvollen N 95 B12
Sungurlare BG 167 D8
Sunhultsbrunn S 92 D5
Suni I 64 C2
Sunja HR 149 F7
Sünna D 79 E7
Sunnan N 105 C11
Sunnanfors S 97 C14
Sunnansjö S 97 B12
Sunnansjö S 107 E14
Sunnås S 103 A12
Sunndal N 94 B4
Sunndalsøra N 101 A9
Sunne S 97 C9
Sunne S 103 A14
Sunne S 106 E6
Sunnemo S 97 C10
Sunnersta S 107 D12
Sunningen S 91 C10
Suntaži LV 135 C9
Suodenniemi FIN 126 B8
Suojanperä FIN 114 E4
Suojoki FIN 122 F7
Suolahti FIN 123 E15
Suolijärvi FIN 121 D11
Suolijoki FIN 119 B14
Suoluvuobmi N 113 D12
Suomela FIN 119 C15
Suomenniemi FIN 128 C7
Suomijärvi FIN 122 F9
Suommu FIN 115 E4
Suomusjärvi FIN 127 E10
Suomussalmi FIN 121 E12
Suonenjoki FIN 124 E8
Suoniemi FIN 127 C9
Suonnankylä FIN 121 B11
Suontee FIN 124 F8
Suopajärvi FIN 117 E15
Suorajärvi FIN 121 B13
Suorsa FIN 120 B9
Šuosjav'ri N 113 E13
Suostola FIN 115 D2
Suovaara FIN 121 F11
Suovanlahti FIN 123 D16
Superdévoluy F 35 A10
Supersano I 61 C10
Supertarska Draga HR 67 C10
Supetar HR 156 F6
Supino I 62 D4
Suplac RO 152 E5
Suplacu de Barcău RO 151 C10
Suplai RO 152 C4
Supraśl PL 140 D8
Supru FIN 114 E4
Supur RO 151 C10
Súr H 149 B10
Surahammar S 98 C6
Suraia RO 153 F10
Şura Mare RO 152 F4
Şura Mică RO 152 F4
Šurani RO 161 C8
Šurany SK 146 E6
Suraż PL 140 E7
Surbo I 61 C10
Surčin SRB 158 D5
Surdegis LT 135 E9
Surdila-Găiseanca RO 161 C10
Surdila-Greci RO 161 C10
Surduc RO 151 C11
Surdulica SRB 164 D5
Surfleet GB 11 F11
Surgères F 28 C4
Surhuisterveen NL 16 B6
Súria E 43 D7
Surier I 31 D11
Surnadalsøra N 104 F5
Sŭrnevets BG 166 E4
Sŭrnevo BG 166 E5
Sŭrnitsa BG 165 F9
Šúrovce SK 146 E5
Sursee CH 27 F9
Surte S 91 D11
Surviliškis LT 135 F8
Surwold D 17 C9
Sury-le-Comtal F 30 D5
Surzur F 22 E6
Susa I 31 E11
Șușani RO 160 D4
Šušara SRB 159 D7
Susch CH 71 D10
Susegana I 72 E5
Susek SRB 158 C4
Süsel D 83 B9
Suseni RO 152 D5
Suseni RO 153 D7
Suseni RO 160 D5
Sushitsa BG 166 C5
Sušice CZ 76 D5
Susiec PL 144 C7
Suškova LV 133 D4
Susleni MD 154 C3
Susort N 94 D2
Susteren NL 19 B12
Sustinente I 66 B3
Sustrum D 17 C8
Susurluk TR 173 E9
Susuzmüsellim TR 173 B7
Susz PL 139 C7
Sutera I 58 D4
Sutești RO 160 D4
Șutești RO 161 C10
Šutina BIH 157 E7
Sutivan HR 156 F5
Sutjeska SRB 158 C6
Sütlüce TR 173 A8
Sutri I 62 C2
Sutri LV 135 D12
Sutterton GB 11 F11
Süttő H 149 A10
Sutton GB 15 C9
Sutton Bridge GB 11 F12
Sutton Coldfield GB 11 F8
Sutton in Ashfield GB 11 E9
Sutton-on-the-Forest GB 11 C9
Suure-Jaani EST 131 D10
Suurejõe EST 131 D10
Suuremõisa EST 130 D5
Suurimäki FIN 124 D9
Suurmaki FIN 125 E11
Suur-Miehikkälä FIN 128 D8
Suurpea EST 131 B11
Suutarinkylä FIN 119 E15
Suutarinkylä FIN 119 F17
Suvainiškis LT 135 D10
Suvanto FIN 115 D2
Suvantokumpu FIN 117 C15
Suvereto I 65 A3
Suviekas LT 135 E12
Suvodol MK 168 A5
Suvodol MK 169 B6
Suvorov MD 155 B2
Suvorove UA 155 B3
Suvorovo BG 167 C9
Suwałki PL 136 E6
Suystamo RUS 129 B15
Suze-la-Rousse F 35 B8
Suzzara I 66 C2
Svabensverk S 103 D10
Svalboviken S 93 A8
Svalenik BG 166 B6
Svallerup DK 87 D8
Svalöv S 87 D12
Svalsta S 93 B9
Svalyava UA 145 F6
Svanå S 98 C6
Svanabyn S 107 C11
Svanberga S 99 C11
Svaneke DK 89 E8
Svanesund S 91 C10
Svängsta S 89 C7
Svaningen S 106 C8
Svannäs S 107 B11
Svannäs S 109 D15
Svansele S 106 B8
Svansele S 107 B17
Svanskog S 91 A12
Svanstein S 117 E11
Svanström S 118 E5
Svantjärnåsen S 102 B7
Svanträsk S 118 D3
Svanvik N 114 E8
Svanvik S 91 C10
Svappavaara S 116 C6
Svardal N 101 A12
Svärdsjö S 103 E10
Svarinci LV 133 D3
Svarstad N 95 D11
Svartå FIN 127 E10
Svartå S 92 A5
Svartbo S 103 D11
Svartbyn S 119 B9
Svarte S 87 E13
Svartemyr N 100 D3
Svärtinge S 92 B8
Svartisdalhytta N 108 D7
Svartlå S 118 B6
Svartnes N 108 B8
Svartnes N 111 B17
Svartnes N 114 C10
Svartöstaden S 118 C8
Svärtträsk S 107 A12
Svartvik S 103 A14
Svartvik S 103 B13
Svartvik S 103 D13
Svatava CZ 75 B12
Svätuše SK 145 G4
Svätý Jur SK 146 E4
Svätý Peter SK 146 F6
Svebølle DK 87 D8
Svedala S 87 D12
Svėdasai LT 135 E10
Svedja S 103 C12
Svedje S 106 C9
Svedje S 107 D15
Svedjebo S 103 C12
Švedlár SK 145 F2
Sveg S 102 B7
Sveggesundet N 104 E3
Šveicarija LT 137 C9
Sveindal N 90 C1
Sveio N 94 C2
Svejbæk DK 86 C5
Svekl LV 135 B13
Švėkšna LT 134 E3
Svelgen N 100 C2
Svellingen N 104 D5
Svelvik N 95 C12
Švenčionėliai LT 135 F11
Švenčionys LT 135 F12
Svendborg DK 86 E7
Svene N 95 C11
Svenes N 90 B3
Svenljunga S 91 E13
Svenningdal N 108 F5
Svensbu N 111 A18
Svensbyn S 118 D6
Svenshögen S 91 C10
Svenstavik S 102 A7
Svenstrup DK 86 B5
Svenstrup DK 86 E5
Svenstrup DK 87 E8
Svente LV 135 E12
Šventežeris LT 137 E8
Šventoji LT 134 D2
Sverepec SK 146 C6
Sveta Marija HR 149 D7
Svētciems LV 131 F8
Svēte LV 134 C7
Sveti Nikola BG 167 C10
Sveti Nikola MNE 163 F7
Sveti Nikole MK 164 F4
Sveti Rok HR 156 D4
Sveti Stefan MNE 163 E6
Světlá Hora CZ 142 F3
Světlá nad Sázavou CZ 77 C8
Svetlen BG 166 C6
Svetlogorsk RUS 139 A9
Svetlyy RUS 139 A9
Svetogorsk RUS 129 C10
Svetozar Miletić SRB 150 F3
Svetvinčenat HR 67 B8
Svezhen BG 165 D11
Švica HR 67 C11
Švidník SK 145 E4
Šihov CZ 76 D4
Sviibi EST 130 D6
Svilajnac SRB 159 E7
Svilengrad BG 166 F6
Svindinge DK 86 E7
Svinesund S 91 A9
Svingen N 111 A18
Svingstad N 101 E12
Svingvoll N 101 D12
Svinhult S 92 D6
Svinia SK 145 E3
Svinița RO 159 D9
Svinná SK 146 D6
Svinnersta S 92 B5
Svinninge DK 87 D8
Svinninge DK 87 D9
Svinninge S 99 D10
Svínoy FO 2 A4
Svinvika N 104 E4
Svir BY 137 D13
Svirkos LT 135 F12
Svishtov BG 160 F6
Svislach BY 140 D10
Svit SK 145 E1
Svitávka CZ 77 C11
Svitavy CZ 77 C10
Svitene LV 135 D7
Svitlodolyns'ke UA 154 E5
Svityaz' UA 141 H9
Svoboda BG 155 F1
Svoboda BG 166 E4
Svoboda RUS 136 D4
Svoboda nad Úpou CZ 81 E9
Svobodinovo BG 166 F4
Svođe SRB 164 D5
Svodín SK 146 F6
Svodna BIH 156 B6
Svoge BG 165 D7
Svogerslev DK 87 D10
Svolvær N 110 D8
Svorkmo N 104 E7
Svratka CZ 77 C10
Svrčinovec SK 147 C7
Svrljig SRB 164 C5
Svullrya N 96 B7
Swadlincote GB 11 F8
Swaffham GB 15 B10
Swalmen NL 20 B6
Swan IRL 9 C9
Swanage GB 13 D11
Swanley GB 15 E9
Swanlinbar IRL 7 D7
Swansea GB 13 B7
Swanton Morley GB 15 B10
Swarożyn PL 138 B6
Swarzjdz PL 81 B12
Swatragh GB 4 F3
Sway GB 13 D11
Świątki PL 139 C9
Świbno PL 138 B6
Świderki PL 141 G6
Świdnica PL 81 C8
Świdnica PL 81 E10
Świdnik PL 141 H7
Świdwin PL 85 C9
Świebodzice PL 81 E10
Świebodzin PL 81 B9
Świecie PL 138 D5
Świjciechowa PL 81 C11
Świeciechów-Duży PL 144 B4
Świedziebnia PL 139 D8
Świekatowo PL 138 D5
Świeradów-Zdrój PL 81 E8
Świercze PL 139 E10
Świerczów PL 142 E4
Świerklaniec PL 143 F6
Świerklany Górne PL 142 F6
Świerzawa PL 81 D9
Świerże PL 141 H9
Świerzno PL 85 B11
Świerzno PL 85 C7

Świeszyno PL 85 B10
Świjtajno PL 136 E5
Świjtajno PL 139 C11
Świjtochłowice PL 143 F6
Świjtoszów PL 81 D8
Swifterbant NL 16 C5
Świlcza PL 144 C4
Swindon GB 13 B11
Swineshead GB 11 F11
Swinford IRL 6 E5
Świnna PL 147 B8
Świnoujście PL 84 C6
Swinton GB 5 D12
Swinton GB 11 D7
Swobnica PL 84 D7
Swords IRL 7 F10
Swornegacie PL 85 C13
Syalyawshchyna BY 133 E5
Sycewice PL 85 B11
Syców PL 142 D4
Sydalen N 110 D7
Sydänmaa FIN 123 E10
Sydänmaankylä FIN 123 C16
Sydnes N 94 C3
Syelishcha BY 133 F4
Syfteland N 94 B2
Sykaminia GR 171 F10
Sykäräinen FIN 123 C12
Syke D 17 C11
Sykea GR 178 B4
Syki GR 169 F9
Sykia GR 169 E7
Sykia GR 170 D5
Sykies GR 169 F7
Sykkylven N 100 B5
Sykorrachi GR 171 C9
Sykourio GR 169 E8
Sylling N 95 C12
Sylte N 100 B6
Symbister GB 3 E14
Symi GR 181 C7
Synej AL 168 B2
Synevyr UA 145 G8
Synevyrs'ka Polyana UA 145 F8
Synod Inn GB 12 A6
Synsiö FIN 123 F17
Synyak UA 145 F6
Syötekylä FIN 121 C10
Sypniewo PL 85 D11
Sypniewo PL 139 D11
Syrau D 75 A11
Syre GB 3 J8
Syrgenstein D 75 E7
Syri FIN 123 C13
Syrjä FIN 125 F10
Sysmä FIN 127 B14
Sysslebäck S 102 E4
Syston GB 11 F9
Syväjärvi FIN 117 D15
Syvänniemi FIN 124 E8
Syvärinpää FIN 125 D9
Syvde N 100 B3
Syvdsnes N 100 B3
Syvota GR 168 F3
Syvros GR 174 B2
Syvsten DK 90 E7
Syyspohja FIN 129 C10
Szabadegyháza H 149 B11
Szabadhidvég H 149 C10
Szabadkígyós H 151 D7
Szabadszállás H 150 D3
Szabolcsbáka H 145 G5
Szada H 150 B3
Szadek PL 143 C6
Szaflary PL 147 C10
Szajol H 150 C5
Szakály H 149 C10
Szakcs H 149 C10
Szakmár H 150 D3
Szakoly H 151 B8
Szákszend H 149 A10
Szalánta H 149 E10
Szalaszend H 145 G3
Szalkszentmárton H 150 D3
Szalonna H 145 G2
Szamocin PL 85 D12
Szamosszeg H 145 G5
Szamotuły PL 81 A11
Szank H 150 D4
Szany H 149 B8
Szár H 149 B11
Szarvas H 150 D6
Szászberek H 150 C5
Szatmárcseke H 145 G6
Szatymaz H 150 E5
Százhalombatta H 149 B11
Szczaniec PL 81 B9
Szczawin Kościelny PL 139 F8
Szczawne PL 145 E5
Szczawnica PL 145 E2
Szczawno-Zdrój PL 81 E10
Szczebrzeszyn PL 144 B6
Szczecin PL 84 D7
Szczecinek PL 85 C11
Szczekociny PL 143 E8
Szczepankowo PL 139 D12
Szczepanowo PL 138 E4
Szczerców PL 143 D7
Szczucin PL 143 F11
Szczuczyn PL 140 C6
Szczurkowo PL 136 E2
Szczurowa PL 143 F10
Szczutowo PL 139 E8
Szczyrk PL 147 B8
Szczytna PL 77 B10
Szczytniki PL 142 C5
Szczytno PL 139 C10
Szécsény H 147 E9
Szederkény H 149 D10
Szedres H 149 D11
Szeged H 150 E5
Szeghalom H 151 C7
Szegi H 145 G3
Szegvár H 150 D5
Székely H 145 G4
Székesfehérvár H 149 B10
Székkutas H 150 D6
Szekszárd H 149 D11
Szemud PL 138 B5
Szendehely H 147 F8
Szendrő H 145 G2
Szendrőlád H 145 G2
Szentendre H 150 B3
Szentes H 150 D5
Szentgál H 149 B9
Szentgotthárd H 148 C6
Szentistván H 150 B6
Szentkirály H 150 D4
Szentlászló H 149 D9
Szentőrinc H 149 D9
Szentpéterfa H 149 B6
Szepetnek H 149 D7
Szepietowo PL 141 E7
Szerecseny H 149 B9
Szeremle H 149 D11
Szerencs H 145 G3
Szerep H 151 C7
Szerzyny PL 144 D3
Szestno PL 136 F3
Szigetbecse H 149 B11
Szigetcsép H 149 B11
Szigethalom H 150 C2
Szigetszentmiklós H 150 C3
Szigetvár H 149 D9
Szigliget H 149 C8
Szihalom H 150 B5
Szikszó H 145 G2
Szil H 149 A8
Szilvásvárad H 145 G1
Szirák H 147 F9
Szirmabesenyő H 145 G2
Szkaradowo PL 81 C12
Szklarska Poręba PL 81 E9
Szklary Górne PL 81 D10
Szlichtyngowa PL 81 C10
Szob H 147 F7
Sződ H 150 B3
Szőgliget H 145 F2
Szokolya H 147 F8
Szolnok H 150 C5
Szőlősgyörök H 149 C9
Szombathely H 149 B7
Szomód H 149 A10
Szomolya H 145 H1
Szówsko PL 144 C6
Szpetal Górny PL 138 E7
Szprotawa PL 81 C9
Szreńsk PL 139 D9
Szropy PL 139 C7
Sztabin PL 140 C8
Sztum PL 138 C7
Sztutowo PL 139 B7
Szubin PL 138 D4
Szőcsi H 150 B4
Szudziałowo PL 140 D9
Szügy H 147 E8
Szuhogy H 145 G2
Szulborze Wielkie PL 141 E6
Szumowo PL 139 E13
Szurdokpüspöki H 147 F9
Szydłów PL 143 E11
Szydłowiec PL 141 H3
Szydłowo PL 85 D11
Szydłowo PL 139 D9
Szymanów PL 141 F2
Szymonka PL 136 F4
Szynkielów PL 142 D6
Szypliszki PL 136 E7

T

Taagepera EST 131 F11
Taalintehdas FIN 126 E8
Taapajärvi FIN 117 D13
Taastrup DK 87 D10
Tab H 149 C10
Tabajd H 149 B11
Tabaky UA 155 B3
Tabanera de Cerrato E 40 D3
Tábara E 39 E8
Tabarz D 79 E8
Tabasalu EST 131 C9
Tabdi H 150 D3
Taberg S 91 D15
Tabernas E 55 E8
Taberno E 55 E8
Tabivere EST 131 D13
Taboada E 38 C4
Taboadela E 38 D4
Tábor CZ 77 D7
Táborfalva H 150 C3
Tábua P 44 D4
Tabuaço P 44 B5
Tabuenca E 41 E8
Täby S 99 D10
Tác H 149 B10
Tacen SLO 73 D9
Tacherting D 75 F12
Tachov CZ 75 C12
Tackåsen S 103 C9
Tăcuta RO 153 D11
Tadasuni I 64 C2
Tadcaster GB 11 D9
Tadley GB 13 C12
Taebla EST 130 D7
Tælavåg N 94 B1
Taevaskoja EST 131 E14
Tafalla E 32 E2
Tafers CH 31 B11
Taff's Well GB 13 B8
Tafjord N 100 B6
Täfteå S 107 E15
Täfteå S 122 C4
Taga RO 152 D4
Tagaranna EST 130 D4
Taggia I 37 D7
Taghmon IRL 9 D9
Tagliacozzo I 62 C4
Taglio di Po I 66 B5
Taglio-Isolaccio F 37 G10
Tagnon F 19 F9
Tågsjöberg S 107 D11
Tahal E 55 E8
Tähemaa EST 131 E14
Tahilla IRL 8 E3
Tahitótfalu H 150 B3
Tähtelä FIN 117 D17
Taibòn Agordino I 72 D5
Taíde P 38 E3
Tain GB 3 K8
Tainiemi FIN 119 C15
Tainijoki FIN 119 C15
Tain-l'Hermitage F 30 E6
Taintrux F 27 D6
Taio I 72 D3
Taipale FIN 119 B15
Taipale FIN 119 C14
Taipale FIN 123 D17
Taipale FIN 124 D8
Taipale FIN 126 B8
Taipaleenharju FIN 119 D17
Taipalsaari FIN 129 C9
Taipalus FIN 123 E10
Taivalkoski FIN 121 C11
Taivassalo FIN 126 D6
Taizé F 30 B6
Tajmište MK 168 A4
Tajno Łanowe PL 140 C7
Takácsi H 149 B8
Takamaa FIN 127 B10
Takeley GB 15 D9
Takene S 97 C9
Takene S 97 D10
Taklax FIN 122 E6
Taksony H 150 C3
Taktakenéz H 145 G3
Taktaszada H 145 G3
Talais F 28 E3
Talamantes E 41 E8
Talamona I 69 A8
Talamone I 65 B4
Talange F 186 C1
Talant F 26 F3
Talarrubias E 51 A9
Talaván E 45 E8
Talavera de la Reina E 46 E3
Talavera la Real E 51 B6
Talayuela E 45 E9
Talayuelas E 47 E10
Talea RO 161 C7
Talence F 28 F4
Talensac F 23 D8
Tales E 48 E4
Taleža BIH 162 D5
Talgarreg GB 12 A6
Talgarth GB 13 B8
Talhadas P 44 C4
Tali EST 131 E9
Taliard F 36 C4
Taliesin GB 10 F4
Táliga E 51 B5
Tälje S 103 A10
Talla I 66 E4
Tallås S 103 E11
Tallås S 109 E14
Tallåsen S 103 C11
Tällberg S 103 E8
Tällberg S 118 B8
Taller F 32 C3
Tallinn EST 131 C9
Talljärv S 118 B8
Talloires F 31 D9
Tallone F 37 G11
Tallós E 38 C2
Tallow IRL 8 D6
Tallsjö S 107 C14
Talluskylä FIN 124 D7
Tallvik S 119 B9
Tállya H 145 G3
Tălmaciu RO 160 B4
Talmay F 26 F3
Talmaz MD 154 D5
Talmont F 28 D4
Talmont-St-Hilaire F 28 C2
Talpa RO 160 E6
Talsano I 61 C8
Talsi LV 134 B5
Taluskylä FIN 119 F12
Talviainen FIN 127 B12
Talvik N 112 C10
Tama E 39 B10
Tămădău Mare RO 161 E9
Tamajón E 47 B6
Tamames E 45 C8
Tamarë AL 163 E8
Tamarino BG 167 E7
Tamarite de Litera E 42 D4
Tamashowka BY 141 G9
Tamási H 149 C10
Tamaşi RO 153 D10
Tambach-Dietharz D 79 E8
Tâmboeşti RO 161 B10
Tâme S 118 E6
Tamins CH 71 D8
Tamiş TR 171 E10
Tamm D 27 C11
Tammela FIN 121 C15
Tammela FIN 127 D10
Tammensiel D 82 A5
Tammijärvi FIN 127 B14
Tammiku EST 131 C12
Tammisaari FIN 127 F9
Tammispää EST 131 D14
Tămna RO 159 D11
Tamnay-en-Bazois F 30 A4
Tamnes N 101 A15
Tamnič SRB 159 E9
Tampere FIN 127 C10
Tamsalu EST 131 C12
Tamsweg A 73 B8
Tamurejo E 54 B3
Tamworth GB 11 F8
Tana Bru N 113 C21
Tanacu RO 153 D11
Tanaji LV 135 E13
Tananes N 114 B4
Tananger N 94 E3
Tănăsoaia RO 153 E10
Tanaunella I 64 B4
Tancarville F 18 F1
Tandådalen S 102 D4
Tăndărei RO 161 D11
Tändö S 102 E5
Tandragee GB 7 D10
Tandsbyn S 106 E7
Tandsjöborg S 102 C8
Tang IRL 7 E7
Tångaberg S 87 A10
Tangaveane IRL 6 C6
Tångböle S 105 E13
Tange DK 86 C5
Tangen N 95 A12
Tangen N 101 E14
Tangen N 111 B14
Tanger MA 52 E5
Tångeråsen S 105 D15
Tangerhütte D 79 B10
Tangermünde D 79 A10
Tångstamon S 107 E11
Tangstedt D 83 C8
Tångvattnet S 108 E8
Tanhua FIN 115 C3
Taninges F 31 C10
Tankapirtti FIN 115 B2
Tankavaara FIN 115 B2
Tanlay F 25 E11
Tann D 76 F3
Tann (Rhon) D 79 E7
Tanna D 75 B10
Tannadice GB 5 B11
Tännäs S 102 B4
Tannay F 19 E10
Tannay F 25 F10
Tänndalen S 102 A3
Tanne D 79 C8
Tannenbergsthal D 75 B11
Tännesberg D 75 C11
Tannhausen D 75 E7
Tannheim A 71 C11
Tannila FIN 119 D15
Tännö S 88 A6
Tannroda D 79 E9
Tannsjön S 106 D9
Tanowo PL 84 C6
Tansa RO 153 D10
Țânțăreni RO 160 D2
Tantonville F 26 D5
Tanumshede S 91 B9
Tanvald CZ 81 E8
Taormina I 59 D7
Tapa EST 131 C11
Tapanikylä FIN 121 F13
Tapfheim D 75 E8
Tapia de Casariego E 39 A6
Tápióbicske H 150 C4
Tápiógyörgye H 150 C4
Tapionkylä FIN 117 E14
Tapionniemi FIN 115 E2
Tápióság H 150 C4
Tápiószecső H 150 C3
Tápiószele H 150 C4
Tápiószentmárton H 150 C4
Tápiószőlős H 150 C4
Táplánszentkereszt H 149 B7
Tapojärvi FIN 117 C11
Tapolca H 149 C8
Tappeluft N 112 C9
Tappenbeck D 79 B8
Tappernøje DK 87 E9
Taps DK 86 E4
Tapsony H 149 D8
Tar H 147 F9
Taracena E 47 C6
Taraclia MD 154 D4
Taraclia MD 154 F3
Taradeau F 36 E4
Taradell E 43 D8
Taramundi E 38 B5
Tarancón E 47 D6
Tarano I 62 C3
Taranto I 61 C8
Tarany H 149 D8
Tarare F 30 D5
Tarascon F 35 C8
Tarascon-sur-Ariège F 33 E9
Tarashany UA 153 A8
Tarazona E 41 E8
Tarazona de la Mancha E 47 F9
Tárbena E 56 D4
Tarbert GB 2 K3
Tarbert GB 4 D5
Tarbert GB 4 D6
Tarbert IRL 8 C4
Tarbes F 33 D6
Tarbja EST 131 D11
Tarbolton GB 4 D8
Tărcaia RO 151 D9
Tarcal H 145 G3
Tarcău RO 153 D8
Tarcea RO 151 C9
Tarcento I 73 D7
Tarčin BIH 157 E9
Tarczyn PL 141 G3
Tard H 145 H2
Tardajos E 40 D4
Tardelcuende E 41 E6
Tardets-Sorholus F 32 D4
Tardienta E 41 E10
Tardona H 145 G2
Tärendö S 116 D9
Tareuca MD 154 B3
Tärgale LV 134 B3
Targon F 28 F5
Târgovişte RO 161 D6
Targowa Górka PL 85 F12
Târgu Bujor RO 153 F11
Târgu Cărbuneşti RO 160 D3
Târgu Frumos RO 153 C9
Târgu Jiu RO 159 C11
Târgu Lăpuş RO 152 C3
Târgu Mureş RO 152 E5
Târgu Neamț RO 153 C8
Târgu Ocna RO 153 E9
Târgu Secuiesc RO 153 E8
Târguşor RO 155 E2
Târgu Trotuş RO 153 E9
Tarhos H 151 D7
Tarifa E 53 D5
Tarigrad MD 153 A11
Tarján H 149 A11
Tárkány H 149 A9
Tarleton GB 10 D6
Târlişua RO 152 C4
Tarłów PL 143 D12
Tărlungeni RO 161 B7
Tarm DK 86 D3
Tarmstedt D 17 B12
Tärnaby S 108 E9
Tärnafors S 108 E9
Tarnala FIN 129 B12
Tarnalelesz H 145 G1
Tarna Mare RO 145 G7
Tarnaméra H 150 B5
Tärnamo S 108 E9
Tarnaörs H 150 B5
Tarnaszentmiklós H 150 B5
Târnăveni RO 152 E4
Tarnawa Duża PL 144 B6
Tarnawatka PL 144 B7
Tarnazsadány H 150 B5
Tårnelv N 111 B15
Tärnes N 104 D7
Tärnet N 114 D8
Tarnobrzeg PL 143 E12
Tarnogród PL 144 C6
Tárnok H 149 B11
Tarnos F 32 C3
Tarnoszyn PL 144 C8
Târnova RO 151 E8
Tarnow D 83 C12
Tarnów PL 85 E7
Tarnów PL 143 F10
Tarnowiec PL 144 D4
Tarnówka PL 85 D11
Tarnówko PL 85 E11
Tarnowo Podgórne PL 81 B11
Tarnów Opolski PL 142 E5
Tarnowskie Góry PL 142 F6
Tärnsjö S 98 B7
Tårnvik N 108 A9
Tårnvik N 113 C18
Taron-Sadirac-Viellenave F 32 C5
Tarouca P 44 B5
Tarp D 82 A6
Tarp DK 86 D2
Tarpa H 145 G6
Tarprubežiai LT 136 E7
Tarquinia I 62 C1
Tarquinia Lido I 62 C1
Tarragona E 42 E6
Tärrajaur S 109 D18
Tàrrega E 42 D6
Tarrel GB 3 K9
Tarrenz A 71 C11
Tarrio E 38 B3
Tarroja de Segarra E 42 D6
Tårs DK 87 F8
Tårs DK 90 E7
Tarsele S 107 D11
Tarsia I 60 D6
Târşolț RO 145 H7
Târstad N 111 D12
Tartas F 32 C4
Tărtăşeşti RO 161 D7
Tartu EST 131 E13
Tårup DK 87 E7
Tarutyne UA 154 E4
Tarvaala FIN 123 E14
Tarvasjoki FIN 126 D8
Tarves GB 3 L12
Tarvisio I 73 C8
Tarvola FIN 123 D11
Taşağil TR 173 A7
Taşca RO 153 D8
Täsjö S 107 C9
Taşlîc MD 154 C4
Tăşnad RO 151 C10
Tass H 150 C3
Tassagh GB 7 D9
Tassin-la-Demi-Lune F 30 D6
Taszár H 149 D9
Tát H 149 A11
Tata H 149 A10
Tatabánya H 149 A10
Tataháza H 150 E3
Tătărăni RO 153 D11
Tătărani RO 160 D6
Tătăranu RO 161 B10
Tătărăşti RO 153 E10
Tătărăştii de Jos RO 160 E6
Tătărăştii de Sus RO 160 E6
Tătăruca MD 153 A12
Tatarbunary UA 154 F5
Tătăreşti MD 154 E2
Tatarevo BG 166 E4
Tatarköy TR 173 B7
Tatarlar TR 167 F7
Tatárszentgyörgy H 150 C3
Tating D 82 B5
Tatlisu TR 173 D8
Tatranská Javorina SK 145 E1
Tattershall GB 11 E11
Tătuleşti RO 160 D5
Tau N 94 D3
Tauberbischofsheim D 74 C6
Taucha D 79 D11
Tauche D 80 B6
Tauer D 81 C6
Taufkirchen D 75 F10
Taufkirchen D 75 F11
Taufkirchen (Vils) D 75 F11
Taujėnai LT 135 F9
Ţaul MD 153 A11
Taulé F 22 C4
Taulignan F 35 B8
Taunton GB 13 C8
Tauplitz A 73 A9
Tauragė LT 134 F4
Tauragnai LT 135 F11
Tauralaukis LT 134 E2
Taurasi I 60 B3
Taurene LV 135 B11
Taurianova I 59 C9
Taurisano I 61 D10
Taurupe LV 135 C10
Tauste E 41 E9
Ţăuţ RO 151 E8
Tăuteu RO 151 C9
Tăuţii-Măgherăuş RO 151 B12
Tauves F 29 D11
Tauvo FIN 119 E13
Tauzhne UA 154 A6
Tavaco F 37 G9
Tavagnacco I 73 D7
Tavaklı TR 171 E10
Tavankut SRB 150 E4
Tavannes CH 27 F7
Tavant F 24 F3
Tavarnelle Val di Pesa I 66 E3
Tavastila FIN 128 D6
Tavastkenkä FIN 119 F16
Tavaux F 31 A7
Taveiro P 44 D4
Tavel F 35 B8
Tavelsjö S 122 B4
Tavera F 37 G9
Taverham GB 15 B11
Taverna I 59 A10
Tavernay F 30 A5
Tavernelle I 62 A2
Tavernes F 36 D4
Tavernes de la Valldigna E 56 C4
Tavernspite GB 12 B5
Taverny F 25 B7
Tavertet E 43 D8
Taviano I 61 D10
Tavira P 50 E4
Tavistock GB 12 D6
Tavullia I 67 E6
Tawern D 186 B2
Taxenbach A 73 B6
Taxiarchis GR 169 D10
Taxobeni MD 153 C11
Tayfur TR 171 D10
Tayinloan GB 4 D5
Taylor's Cross IRL 7 F7
Taynuilt GB 4 C6
Tayport GB 5 C11
Tayvallich GB 4 C5
Tázlár H 150 D4
Tazlău RO 153 D8
Tazones E 39 A9
Tczew PL 138 B6
Tczów PL 141 H4
Teaca RO 152 D5
Teano I 60 A2
Tearce MK 164 E3
Teasc RO 160 E3
Teba E 53 C7
Tebar E 47 E8
Tebay GB 10 C6
Tebstrup DK 86 D5
Techendorf A 73 C7
Techirghiol RO 155 E3
Tecuci RO 153 F10
Tedavnet IRL 7 D8
Teeriranta FIN 121 C14
Teerivaara FIN 120 B9
Tefeli GR 178 E9
Tegelen NL 16 F6
Tegelträsk S 107 D13
Teggiano I 60 C5
Téglás H 151 B8
Teglio I 69 A9
Tegnäset S 107 C16
Teichwolframsdorf D 79 E11
Teignmouth GB 13 D8
Teijo FIN 127 E8
Teikosuvanto FIN 117 E11
Teillay F 23 E8
Teillet F 33 C10
Teişani RO 161 C8
Teisendorf D 73 A6
Teisko FIN 127 B10
Teisnach D 76 D4
Teistungen D 79 D7
Teiu RO 160 D6
Teiuş RO 152 E3
Teixeiro E 38 B3
Teixoso P 44 D6
Tejadillos E 47 D9
Tejado E 41 E7
Tejeda de Tiétar E 45 D9
Tejn DK 89 E7
Tekeler TR 181 A7
Tekeli TR 177 C9
Tekeriš SRB 158 D4
Tekija BIH 157 D11
Tekija SRB 159 D9
Tekirdağ TR 173 C7
Tekovské Lužany SK 147 E7
Teksdal N 104 D7
Telaki PL 141 E6
Telatyn PL 144 B8
Telč CZ 77 D8
Telciu RO 152 C4
Teldau D 83 D9
Telečka SRB 150 F3
Telega RO 161 C7
Telekgerendás H 151 D6
Teleneşti MD 154 B2
Telerig BG 161 F11
Telese I 60 A3
Teleşti RO 159 C11
Telford GB 10 F7
Telfs A 72 B3
Telgárt SK 145 F1
Telgte D 17 E9
Telhado P 44 D5
Telish BG 165 C9
Teliu RO 153 F7
Teliucu Inferior RO 159 B10
Teljo FIN 125 C13
Telkkälä FIN 119 C17
Tellancourt F 19 E12
Tellejåkk S 118 B3
Tellin B 19 D11
Tellingstedt D 82 B6
Telneset N 101 B13
Telnice CZ 77 D11
Teloes P 38 F4
Telšiai LT 134 E4
Telti I 64 B3
Teltow D 80 B4
Tembleque E 46 E6
Temeleuți MD 153 C12
Temeni GR 174 C5
Temerin SRB 158 C4
Temmes FIN 119 E15
Tempi GR 169 E8
Tempio Pausania I 64 B3
Temple Bar GB 12 A6
Templeboy IRL 6 D5
Temple Ewell GB 15 E11
Templemore IRL 9 C7
Templepatrick GB 4 F4
Temple Sowerby GB 5 F11
Templeton GB 12 B5
Templetuohy IRL 9 C7
Templeuve F 182 D2
Templin D 84 D5
Tempo GB 7 D8
Temse B 19 B9
Temska SRB 164 C6
Temû I 69 A9
Tenala FIN 127 E9
Tenay F 31 D8
Ten Boer NL 17 B7
Tenbury Wells GB 13 A9
Tenby GB 12 B5
Tence F 30 E5
Tende F 37 C7
Tendilla E 47 C7
Tendu F 29 B9
Teneniai LT 134 F3
Tenevo BG 167 E7
Tengelic H 149 C11
Tengen D 27 E10
Tengesdal N 94 C4
Tenhult S 92 D4
Teningen D 27 D8
Tenja HR 149 F11
Tenk H 150 B5
Tennänget S 102 D6
Tennenbronn D 27 D9
Tennevik N 111 C12
Tenneville B 19 D12
Tennevoll N 111 C14
Tennilä FIN 119 B16
Tennilä FIN 127 D13
Tennskjer N 111 B15
Tennstrand N 110 D9
Tenterden GB 15 E10
Tentúgal P 44 D3
Teora I 60 B4
Teovo MK 169 A6
Tepasto FIN 117 C13
Tépe H 151 C8
Tepeboz TR 177 B7
Tepecik TR 173 B10
Tepecik TR 173 E10
Tepelenë AL 168 D3
Teplá CZ 76 C3
Teplice CZ 80 E5
Teplice nad Metuj CZ 81 E10
Teplička SK 145 F2
Teplička nad Váhom SK 147 C7
Tepsa FIN 117 C15
Tepu RO 153 F10
Ter Aar NL 182 A5
Teramo I 62 B5
Terande LV 134 B3
Ter Apel NL 17 C8
Teratyn PL 144 B8
Terbaç AL 168 D2
Terborg-Silvolde NL 16 E6
Terchová SK 147 C8
Terebeşti RO 151 B10
Tereblya UA 145 G8
Teregova RO 159 C9
Teremia Mare RO 150 F6
Terena P 50 B5
Teresa E 48 E3
Teresa de Cofrentes E 47 F10
Teresin PL 141 F2
Terespol PL 141 F9
Teresva UA 145 G8
Terezín CZ 76 A6
Terezino Polje HR 149 E8
Tergnier F 19 E7
Tergu I 64 B2
Terheijden NL 182 B5
Terikeste EST 131 E14
Terjärv FIN 123 C11
Terka PL 145 E5
Terlano I 72 C3
Těrlicko CZ 146 B6
Terlizzi I 61 A7
Terme Luigiane I 60 E5
Térmens E 42 D5
Termignon F 31 E10
Terminiers F 24 D6
Termini Imerese I 58 D4
Termoli I 63 D7
Termon IRL 7 B7
Termonfeckin IRL 7 E10
Ternaard NL 16 B5
Ternavka UA 153 A8
Ternberg A 76 G6
Terndrup DK 86 B6
Terneuzen NL 16 F1
Terni I 62 B3
Ternitz A 148 A6
Ternove UA 145 G8
Terovo GR 168 F4
Terpezița RO 160 E3
Terpni GR 169 C9
Terpsithea GR 169 E7
Terpyllos GR 169 B8
Terracina I 62 E4
Terrades E 43 C9
Terråk N 105 A12
Terralba I 64 D2
Terranova da Sibari I 61 D6
Terranova di Pollino I 60 D6
Terranuova Bracciolini I 66 E4
Terrasini I 58 C3
Terrassa E 43 D8
Terrasson-Lavilledieu F 29 E8
Terraube F 33 C7
Terravecchia I 61 E7
Terricciola I 66 E2
Terriente E 47 D10
Terrin IRL 7 E8
Terrinches E 55 B7
Terrou F 29 F9
Terrugem P 50 B1
Terrugem P 51 B5
Terryglass IRL 6 F6
Terslev DK 87 E9
Tërstenik RKS 164 D2
Tertenia I 64 D4
Teruel E 47 D10
Tervajoki FIN 122 D8
Tervakoski FIN 127 D12
Tervavaara FIN 121 D11
Tervel BG 161 F10
Terves F 28 B4
Tērvete LV 134 D6
Tervo FIN 123 E17
Tervola FIN 119 B13
Tervolan asema FIN 119 B13
Tervuren B 19 C10
Tés H 149 B10
Tešanj BIH 157 C8
Těšany CZ 77 D11
Tešedíkovo SK 146 E5
Tesero I 72 D4
Tešica SRB 164 C4
Tesimo I 72 C3
Tesjoki FIN 127 E15
Teslić BIH 157 C8
Teslui RO 160 D4
Teslui RO 160 E4
Tespe D 83 D8
Tessenderlo B 19 B11
Tessin D 83 B12
Tesson F 28 D4
Tessy-sur-Vire F 23 C9
Testa del Gargano I 63 D10
Testa dell'Acqua I 59 F6
Testelt B 182 C5
Teşvikiye TR 173 C11
Tét H 149 A9
Tetbury GB 13 B10
Tețcani MD 153 A9
Tețchea RO 151 C9
Teteringen NL 182 B5
Teterow D 83 C13
Tetétlen H 151 C7
Teteven BG 165 D9
Teti I 64 C3
Tetney GB 11 E11
Tetoiu RO 160 D3
Tétouan MA 53 E6
Tetovo BG 161 F8
Tetovo MK 163 E10
Tettens D 17 A9
Tettnang D 71 B9
Tetyń PL 85 D7
Teublitz D 75 D11
Teuchern D 79 D11
Teufen CH 27 F11
Teufenbach A 73 B9
Teulada E 56 D5
Teulada I 64 F2
Teunz D 75 D11
Teupitz D 80 B5
Teurajärvi FIN 117 D11
Teurajärvi S 116 E9
Teuro FIN 127 D10
Teuschnitz D 75 B9
Teutschenthal D 79 D10
Teuva FIN 122 F7
Tevaniemi FIN 127 B9
Tevansjö S 103 B9
Tevel H 149 D10
Tēvenāni LV 133 C1
Tevfikiye TR 171 E10
Teviothead GB 5 E11
Tewkesbury GB 13 B10
Teyssieu F 29 F9
Thal D 79 E7
Thale (Harz) D 79 C9
Thaleischweiler-Fröschen D 186 C4
Thalfang D 21 E7
Thalheim D 79 C11
Thalheim bei Wels A 76 F6
Thaljina BIH 157 F7
Thalmässing D 75 D9
Thalwil CH 27 F10
Thame GB 14 D7
Thann F 27 E7
Thannhausen D 75 F7
Thaon-les-Vosges F 26 D5
Tharandt D 80 E5
't Harde NL 16 D5
Tharsis E 51 D5
Thasos GR 171 C7
Thatcham GB 13 C12
Thaumiers F 29 B11
Thaxted GB 15 D9
Thaya A 77 E8
Thayngen CH 27 E10
Theale GB 13 C12
Thedinghausen D 17 C12
Theillay F 24 F7
Theißen D 79 D11

Theix F 22 E6
Them DK 86 C5
Themar D 75 A8
The Mumbles GB 12 B6
Thenay F 29 B8
Thénezay F 28 B5
Thenon F 29 E8
Theologos GR 171 C7
Théoule-sur-Mer F 36 D5
The Pike IRL 9 D7
Therma GR 171 D9
Thermi GR 169 C9
Thermisia GR 175 E7
Thermo GR 174 B4
Thermopyles GR 175 B6
Thérouanne F 18 C5
The Sheddings GB 4 F4
Thespies GR 175 C7
Thesprotiko GR 168 F4
Thessaloniki GR 169 C8
The Stocks GB 15 E10
Thetford GB 15 C10
Theth AL 163 E8
Theux B 19 C12
Thèze F 32 D5
Thèze F 35 B10
Thiaucourt-Regniéville F 26 C4
Thiberville F 24 B3
Thibie F 25 C11
Thiéblemont-Farémont F 25 C12
Thiendorf D 80 D5
Thiene I 72 E3
Thierhaupten D 75 E8
Thierrens CH 31 B10
Thiers F 30 D4
Thiersee A 72 A5
Thiersheim D 75 B11
Thiesi I 64 B2
Thießow D 84 B5
Thiézac F 29 E11
Thimert-Gâtelles F 24 C5
Thin-le-Moutier F 19 E10
Thionville F 20 F6
Thiron Gardais F 24 D4
Thirsk GB 11 C9
Thisted DK 86 B3
Thisvi GR 175 C6
Thiva GR 175 C7
Thivars F 24 D5
Thiviers F 29 E7
Thizy F 30 C5
Thoirette F 31 C8
Thoiry F 24 C6
Thoissey F 30 C6
Tholen NL 16 E2
Tholey D 21 F8
Thomastown IRL 9 C8
Thommen B 20 D6
Thônes F 31 D9
Thonnance-lès-Joinville F 26 D3
Thonon-les-Bains F 31 C9
Thorame-Haute F 36 C5
Thoras F 30 F4
Thoré-la-Rochette F 24 E4
Thorenc F 36 D5
Thorigny-sur-Oreuse F 25 D9
Thörl A 73 A11
Thorn NL 19 B12
Thornaby-on-Tees GB 11 B9
Thornbury GB 13 B9
Thorne GB 11 D10
Thorney GB 11 F11
Thornhill GB 5 E9
Thorning DK 86 C4
Thornton GB 10 D5
Thorpe-le-Soken GB 15 D11
Thorpe Market GB 15 B11
Thorpeness GB 15 C12
Thorsager DK 86 C6
Thorshøj DK 90 E7
Thorsø DK 86 C5
Thouarcé F 23 F11
Thouaré-sur-Loire F 23 F9
Thouars F 28 B5
Thouria GR 174 E5
Thourotte F 18 F6
Thrapston GB 15 C7
Threshfield GB 11 C7
Thropton GB 5 E13
Thrumster GB 3 J10
Thuès-entre-Valls F 33 E10
Thueyts F 35 A7
Thuin B 19 D9
Thuine D 17 D9
Thuir F 34 E4
Thum D 80 E3
Thun CH 70 D5
Thundersley GB 15 D10
Thüngen D 74 C6
Thüngersheim D 74 C6
Thuré F 29 B6
Thuret F 30 D3
Thurey F 31 B7
Thüringen A 71 C9
Thurins F 30 D6
Thürkow D 83 C13
Thurlby GB 11 F11
Thurles IRL 9 C7
Thurnau D 75 B9
Thursby GB 5 F10
Thurso GB 3 H9
Thury-Harcourt F 23 C11
Thusis CH 71 D8
Thwaite GB 11 C7
Thyborøn DK 86 B2
Thyez F 31 C10
Thymiana GR 177 C7
Thyregod DK 86 D4
Thyrnau D 76 E5
Tia Mare RO 160 F5
Tiana I 64 C3
Ţibana RO 153 D10
Ţibăneşti RO 153 D10
Tibble S 99 D9
Tiberget S 102 D6
Tibi E 56 D3
Tibolddaróc H 145 H2
Tibro S 92 C4
Ţibucani RO 153 C9
Tice BIH 156 D6
Ticehurst GB 15 E9
Ticha BG 167 D6
Tichá CZ 146 B6
Tichileşti RO 155 C1
Tičići BIH 157 D9
Ticknall GB 11 F9
Ţicleni RO 160 D2
Ţicuşu RO 152 F6
Ticvaniu Mare RO 159 C8
Tidaholm S 91 C14
Tidan S 91 B15
Tiddische D 79 A8
Tidenham GB 13 B9
Tidersrum S 92 D7
Tiebas E 32 E2
Tiedra E 39 E9
Tiefenbach D 75 D12
Tiefenbach D 76 E4
Tiefenbronn D 27 C10
Tiefencastel CH 71 D9
Tiefensee D 84 E5
Tiel NL 16 E4
Tielen B 182 C5
Tielt B 19 C7
Tiemassaari FIN 125 F10
Tienen B 19 C10
Tiengen D 27 E9
Tiercé F 23 E11
Tierga E 41 E8
Tierp S 99 B9
Tierzo E 47 C9
Ţifeşti RO 153 F10
Ţigănaşi RO 153 C10
Ţigăneşti RO 160 F6
Tigare BIH 158 E3
Tighina MD 154 D4
Ţighira MD 153 C11
Tighnabruaich GB 4 D6
Tignale I 69 B10
Tignes F 31 E10
Tigveni RO 160 C5
Tigy F 25 E7
Tiha Bârgăului RO 152 C5
Tihany H 149 C9
Tihemetsa EST 131 E10
Tihilä FIN 123 C16
Tihusniemi FIN 124 F9
Tiistenjoki FIN 123 E10
Tiitilänkylä FIN 123 E17
Tijesno HR 156 E4
Tijnje NL 16 B5
Tíjola E 55 E8
Tikkakoski FIN 123 F15
Tikkala FIN 123 F14
Tikkala FIN 125 F14
Tikkurila FIN 127 E13
Tikob DK 87 C10
Tilburg NL 16 E4
Tilbury GB 15 E9
Til-Châtel F 26 E3
Tildarg GB 4 F4
Tileagd RO 151 C9
Tilehurst GB 13 C12
Tilh F 32 C4
Tilişca RO 152 F3
Tillac F 33 D6
Tillberga S 98 C7
Tillicoultry GB 5 C9
Tillières-sur-Avre F 24 C5
Tilloy-et-Bellay F 25 B12
Tillyfourie GB 3 L11
Tilly-sur-Seulles F 23 B10
Tilvikai LT 134 E3
Tilža LV 133 C2
Tim DK 86 C2
Timahoe IRL 7 G8
Timár H 145 G3
Timau I 73 C7
Timelkam A 76 F5
Timiryazevo RUS 136 C4
Timişeşti RO 153 C9
Timişoara RO 151 F7
Timmele S 91 D13
Timmendorfer Strand D 83 C9
Timmernabben S 89 B10
Timmersdala S 91 B14
Timola FIN 125 F9
Timoleague IRL 8 E5
Timolin IRL 7 G9
Timoniemi FIN 121 F13
Timovaara FIN 125 D12
Timrå S 103 A13
Timring DK 86 C3
Timsgearraidh GB 2 J2
Tinahely IRL 9 C10
Tinajas E 47 D7
Tinalhas P 44 E5
Tinca RO 151 D8
Tinchebray F 23 C10
Tineo E 39 B7
Tiņģere LV 134 B5
Tinglev DK 86 F4
Tingsryd S 89 B7
Tingstad S 93 B8
Tingstäde S 93 D13
Tingvatn N 94 F6
Tingvoll N 100 A8
Tingwall GB 3 G10
Tinja BIH 157 C10
Tinjan HR 67 B8
Tinn N 95 C9
Tinnoset N 95 C10
Tinos GR 176 D5
Tiñosillos E 46 C3
Tinosu RO 161 D8
Tinqueux F 19 F8
Tintagel GB 12 D5
Tinténiac F 23 D8
Tintern Parva GB 13 B9
Ţinteşti RO 161 C9
Tintigny B 19 E12
Tinūži LV 135 C9
Tiobraid Árann IRL 8 D6
Tione di Trento I 69 A10
Tipasoja FIN 125 B11
Tipperary IRL 8 D6
Tiptree GB 15 D10
Tipu EST 131 E10
Tîra MD 154 B2
Tiranë AL 168 B2
Tiranges F 30 E4
Tirano I 69 A9
Tiraspol MD 154 D5
Tiraspolul Nou MD 154 D5
Tire TR 177 C10
Tiream RO 151 B9
Tireļi LV 134 C7
Tirgo E 40 C6
Tiriez E 55 B8
Tírig E 48 D5
Tiriolo I 59 B10
Tirkšliai LT 134 D4
Tîrnova MD 153 A11
Tirrenia I 66 E1
Tirro FIN 113 F18
Tirschenreuth D 75 C11
Tirstrup DK 86 C7
Tirteafuera E 54 B4
Tirza LV 135 B12
Tisău RO 161 C9
Tišća BIH 157 D10
Tishevitsa BG 165 C8
Tishono RUS 136 E2
Tišice CZ 77 B7
Tismana RO 159 C10
Tišnov CZ 77 D10
Tisovec SK 147 D9
Tistrup Stationsby DK 86 D3
Tisvilde DK 87 C10
Tiszaalpár H 150 D4
Tiszabecs H 145 G6
Tiszabezdéd H 145 G5
Tiszabő H 150 C5
Tiszabura H 150 C5
Tiszacsege H 151 B7
Tiszadada H 145 G3
Tiszaderzs H 150 B6
Tiszadob H 145 G3
Tiszaeszlár H 145 G3
Tiszaföldvár H 150 D5
Tiszafüred H 150 B6
Tiszagyenda H 150 C6
Tiszaigar H 150 B6
Tiszajenő H 150 C5
Tiszakanyár H 145 G4
Tiszakarád H 145 G4
Tiszakécske H 150 D5
Tiszakerecseny H 145 G5
Tiszakeszi H 151 B6
Tiszakürt H 150 D5
Tiszalök H 145 G3
Tiszalúc H 145 G3
Tiszanagyfalu H 145 G3
Tiszanána H 150 B6
Tiszaörs H 150 B6
Tiszapalkonya H 145 H3
Tiszapüspöki H 150 C5
Tiszaroff H 150 C5
Tiszasas H 150 D5
Tiszasüly H 150 C5
Tiszaszalka H 145 G5
Tiszaszentimre H 150 C6
Tiszasziget H 150 E5
Tiszatarján H 147 F12
Tiszatelek H 145 G4
Tiszatenyő H 150 C5
Tiszaug H 150 D5
Tiszaújváros H 145 H3
Tiszavárkony H 150 C5
Tiszavasvári H 145 H3
Titaguas E 47 E10
Titel SRB 158 C5
Ţiţeşti RO 160 C6
Tithorea GR 175 B6
Tito I 60 B5
Titova Korenica HR 156 C4
Titov Drvar BIH 156 D5
Titran N 104 D4
Tittelsnes N 94 C3
Titting D 75 E9
Tittmoning D 76 F3
Titu RO 161 D7
Titulcia E 46 D5
Tiukuvaara FIN 117 C13
Tiurajärvi FIN 117 C12
Tivat MNE 163 E6
Tivenys E 42 F5
Tiverton GB 13 D8
Tivissa E 42 E5
Tivoli I 62 D3
Tizzano F 37 H9
Tjæreborg DK 86 E3
Tjäkkjokk S 109 E15
Tjällmo S 92 B6
Tjåmotis S 109 C16
Tjappsåive S 109 E17
Tjärmyrberget S 106 C9
Tjärn S 107 D13
Tjärnäs S 98 A6
Tjärnberg S 107 A15
Tjärstad S 92 C7
Tjärutråsk S 118 B8
Tjautas S 116 D5
Tjeldnes N 111 D11
Tjeldstø N 100 E1
Tjelle N 100 A7
Tjentište BIH 157 F10
Tjöck FIN 122 F6
Tjøme N 90 A7
Tjønnefoss N 90 B4
Tjorhom N 94 E5
Tjörnarp S 87 D13
Tjøtta N 108 E3
Tjuda FIN 126 E8
Tjuvskjær N 111 C13
Tkon HR 156 E3
Tleń PL 138 C5
Tlmače SK 147 E7
Tłuchowo PL 139 E7
Tlumačov CZ 146 C5
Tłuszcz PL 139 F11
Toab GB 3 F14
Toaca RO 152 D5
Tóalmás H 150 C4
Toano I 66 D2
Tobar an Choire IRL 6 D5
Tobarra E 55 B9
Tobercurry IRL 6 D5
Tobermore GB 4 F3
Tobermory GB 4 B4
Tobo S 99 B9
Tobyn S 97 C8
Tocane-St-Apre F 29 E6
Tocco da Casauria I 62 C5
Tocha P 44 D3
Töcksfors S 96 C6
Tocón E 53 B9
Todal N 104 E5
Toddington GB 13 B11
Todi I 62 B2
Todireni RO 153 B10
Todireşti RO 153 B8
Todireşti RO 153 C9
Todireşti RO 153 D10
Todmorden GB 11 D7
Todolella E 42 F3
Todorići BIH 157 D7
Todor-Ikonomovo BG 161 F10
Todorovo BG 161 F9
Todtmoos D 27 E8
Todtnau D 27 E8
Toén E 38 D4
Toft GB 3 E14
Toft N 108 F3
Tofta S 87 A10
Tofta S 93 D12
Tofte N 95 C13
Töftedal S 91 B10
Tofterup DK 86 D3
Toftir FO 2 A3
Toftlund DK 86 E4
Tofyeli BY 133 E5
Togher IRL 7 E10
Togher IRL 7 F7
Togher IRL 8 E4
Togston GB 5 E13
Tohmajärvi FIN 125 F14
Tohmo FIN 115 E2
Toholampi FIN 123 C12
Toija FIN 127 E9
Toijala FIN 127 C10
Toila EST 132 C2
Toirano I 37 C8
Toivakka FIN 119 B17
Toivakka FIN 123 F16
Toivala FIN 124 E9
Toivola FIN 128 C6
Tojaci MK 169 B6
Töjby FIN 122 E6
Tök H 149 A11
Tokachka BG 171 B9
Tokaj H 145 G3
Tokarnia PL 143 E9
Tokarnia PL 147 B9
Tokod H 149 A11
Tököl H 149 B11
Tokrajärvi FIN 125 E15
Toksovo RUS 129 E14
Tolastadh Úr GB 2 J4
Tolbaños E 46 C3
Tolbert NL 16 B6
Tolcsva H 145 G3
Toledo E 46 E4
Tolentino I 67 F7
Tolfa I 62 C1
Tolga N 101 B14
Toliejai LT 135 F10
Tolja FIN 119 B17
Tolk D 82 A7
Tolkmicko PL 139 B8
Tollarp S 88 D5
Tollered S 91 D11
Tollesbury GB 15 D10
Tollo I 63 C6
Tølløse DK 87 D9
Töllsjö S 91 D12
Tolmachevo RUS 132 D6
Tolmezzo I 73 D7
Tolmin SLO 73 D8
Tolna H 149 D11
Tolnanémedi H 149 C10
Tolne DK 90 E7
Tolo GR 175 D6
Tolocăneşti MD 153 A11
Tolonen FIN 117 E14
Tolosa E 32 D1
Tolosa P 44 F5
Tolosenmäki FIN 125 F14
Tolox E 53 C7
Tolšići BIH 157 D10
Tolva E 42 C5
Tolva FIN 121 B12
Tolvayarvi RUS 125 F16
Tolve I 60 B6
Tomai MD 154 D2
Tomai MD 154 E3
Tomar P 44 E4
Tomares E 51 E7
Tomaševac SRB 158 C6
Tomaševo MNE 163 C8
Tomašica BIH 157 C6
Tomášikovo SK 146 E5
Tomášovce SK 147 E9
Tomaszów Lubelski PL 144 C7
Tomaszów Mazowiecki PL 141 G2
Tomatin GB 3 L9
Tombebœf F 33 A6
Tomelilla S 88 D5
Tomelloso E 47 F6
Tomeşti RO 151 E10
Tomeşti RO 151 F9
Tomeşti RO 153 C11
Tomice PL 147 B8
Tomiño E 38 E2
Tomintoul GB 3 L10
Tomislavgrad BIH 157 E7
Tømmerneset N 111 E10
Tommerup DK 86 E6
Tomnavoulin GB 3 L10
Tömörkény H 150 D5
Tompa H 150 E4
Tomra N 100 A5
Tomşani RO 161 D8
Tona E 43 D8
Tonara I 64 C3
Tonbridge GB 15 E9
Tondela P 44 C4
Tønder DK 86 F3
Tonezza del Cimone I 69 B11
Tongeren B 19 C11
Tongland GB 5 F8
Tongue GB 2 J8
Tönisvorst D 183 C8
Tonkopuro FIN 115 E4
Tonna GB 13 B7
Tonnay-Boutonne F 28 D4
Tonnay-Charente F 28 D4
Tonneins F 33 B6
Tonnerre F 25 E10
Tonnes N 108 C5
Tönning D 82 B5
Tønsberg N 95 D12
Tönsen S 103 D12
Tonstad N 94 E5
Tonsvik N 111 A17
Toombeola IRL 6 F3
Toomebridge GB 4 F4
Tootsi EST 131 D9
Topalu RO 155 D2
Topana RO 160 D5
Topares E 55 D8
Toparlar TR 181 C9
Topchii BG 161 F9
Topchin D 80 B5
Topčić-Polje BIH 157 D8
Topcliffe GB 11 C9
Töpen D 75 B10
Topeno FIN 127 D11
Tophisar TR 173 D9
Topleţ RO 159 D9
Topliceni RO 161 C10
Topli Do SRB 165 C6
Topliţa RO 152 D6
Topliţa RO 159 B10
Töplitz D 79 B12
Topojë AL 168 C1
Topola SRB 158 E6
Topolčani MK 168 B5
Topoľčany SK 146 D6
Topoľčianky SK 146 E6
Topolia GR 178 E6
Topólka PL 138 E6
Topolnica SRB 159 E9
Topoľníky SK 146 F5
Topolog RO 155 D2
Topolovac HR 149 F6
Topolovăţu Mare RO 151 F8
Topoloveni RO 160 D6
Topolovgrad BG 166 E6
Topolovnik SRB 159 D7
Topolovo BG 166 F4
Topolšica SLO 73 D11
Toponica SRB 158 F6
Toporec SK 145 E1
Toporivtsi UA 153 A8
Toporów PL 81 B8
Toporu RO 161 E7
Toporzyk PL 85 C10
Toppenstedt D 83 D8
Topraisar RO 155 E2
Topsham GB 13 D8
Topusko HR 156 B4
Torá E 43 D6
Toral de los Guzmanes E 39 D8
Toral de los Vados E 39 C6
Torano Castello I 60 E6
Torasalo FIN 125 F10
Toras-Sieppi FIN 117 C11
Torbali TR 177 C9
Torbjörntorp S 91 C14
Torbygget S 102 A4
Torchiara I 60 C4
Torchiarolo I 61 C10
Torcy F 30 B5
Torda SRB 158 B5
Tordas H 149 B11
Tordehumos E 39 E9
Tordera E 43 D9
Tordesillas E 39 E10
Tordesilos E 47 C9
Töre S 118 C9
Töreboda S 91 B15
Toreby DK 83 A11
Torekov S 87 C11
Torella del Sannio I 63 D7
Torellano E 56 E3
Torelló E 43 C8
Toreno E 39 C6
Torestorp S 91 E12
Torgau D 80 C3
Torgelow D 84 C6
Torgiano I 62 A2
Torhamn S 89 C9
Torhout B 19 B7
Tori EST 131 E9
Torigni-sur-Vire F 23 B10
Torija E 47 C6
Torino I 68 C4
Toritto I 61 B7
Torkanivka UA 154 A4
Torkovichi RUS 132 D7
Torla E 32 E5
Torma EST 131 D13
Tormac RO 159 B7
Törmänen FIN 113 E19
Törmänen FIN 115 A2
Törmänki FIN 117 E13
Törmänmäki FIN 121 E10
Törmäsenvaara FIN 121 C13
Törmäsjärvi FIN 119 B12
Tormestorp S 87 C13
Tormón E 47 D10
Tormore GB 4 D6
Tornadizos de Ávila E 46 C3
Tornaľa SK 145 G1
Tornavacas E 45 D9
Tornby DK 90 D6
Tornemark DK 87 E9
Tornes N 100 A6
Tørnes N 111 D11
Tornesch D 82 C7
Torneträsk S 111 D18
Tornimäe EST 130 D6
Tornio FIN 119 C12
Tornjoš SRB 150 F4
Torno I 69 B7
Tornos E 47 C10
Tornow D 84 D4
Toro E 39 E9
Torö S 93 B11
Törökbálint H 149 B11
Törökszentmiklós H 150 C5
Torony H 149 B7
Toros BG 165 C9
Toroshino RUS 132 F4
Torp FIN 99 B13
Torpa S 92 D6
Torphins GB 3 L11
Torpo N 101 E9
Torpoint GB 12 E6
Torpsbruk S 88 A7
Torpshammar S 103 B11
Torquay GB 13 E7
Torquemada E 40 D3
Torralba de Calatrava E 54 A5
Torralba E 47 D8
Torralba I 64 B2
Torralba de Aragón E 41 E10
Torralba de El Burgo E 40 E6
Torralba de los Sisones E 47 C10
Torralba de Oropesa E 45 E10
Torrão P 50 C3
Torrböle S 107 D17
Torre-Alháquime E 51 F9
Torre Annunziata I 60 B2
Torrebaja E 47 D10
Torreblanca E 48 D5
Torreblascopedro E 53 A9
Torrebruna I 63 D7
Torrecaballeros E 46 C4
Torrecampo E 54 C3
Torre Canne I 61 B8
Torre-Cardela E 55 D6
Torrecilla de Alcañiz E 42 F3
Torrecilla de la Jara E 46 E3
Torrecilla de la Orden E 45 B10
Torrecilla del Rebollar E 42 F1
Torrecillas de la Tiesa E 45 E9
Torrecuso I 60 A3
Torre da Gadanha P 50 B3
Torre das Vargens P 44 F5
Torre de Coelheiros P 50 C4
Torre de Dona Chama P 38 E5
Torre de Embesora E 48 D4
Torredeita P 44 C4
Torre de Juan Abad E 55 B6
Torre del Bierzo E 39 C7
Torre del Burgo E 47 C6
Torre del Campo E 53 A9
Torre del Greco I 60 B2
Torre del Mar E 53 C8
Torredembarra E 43 E6
Torre de Miguel Sesmero
E 51 B6
Torre de Moncorvo P 45 B6
Torre de'Passeri I 62 C5
Torre de Santa María E 45 F8
Torredonjimeno E 53 A9
Torre do Terrenho P 44 C6
Torrefarrera E 42 D5
Torregamones E 39 F7
Torregrossa E 42 D5
Torreiglesias E 46 B4
Torreira P 44 C3
Torrejoncillo E 45 E8
Torrejoncillo del Rey E 47 D7
Torrejón de Ardoz E 46 D6
Torrejón del Rey E 46 C6
Torrejón el Rubio E 45 E9
Torrelacarcel E 47 C10
Torrelaguna E 46 C5
Torrelapaja E 41 E8
Torrelavega E 40 B3
Torrellas E 41 E8
Torrelles de Foix E 43 E7
Torrelobatón E 39 E9
Torrelodones E 46 C5
Torremaggiore I 63 D8
Torremanzanas-La Torre de les
Macanes E 56 D4
Torremayor E 51 B6
Torremegía E 51 B7
Torre Mileto I 63 D9
Torremocha E 45 F8
Torremocha de Jiloca E 47 C10
Torremolinos E 53 C7
Torrenostra E 48 D5
Torrent E 48 F4
Torrente del Cinca E 42 E4
Torrenueva E 55 B6
Torreorgaz E 45 F8
Torre Orsaia I 60 C4
Torre-Pacheco E 56 F3
Torre Pellice I 31 F11
Torreperogil E 55 C6
Torres E 53 A9
Torresandino E 40 E4
Torre San Giovanni I 61 D10
Torre Santa Susanna I 61 C9
Torres de Albánchez E 55 C7
Torres de Berrellén E 41 E9
Torres de la Alameda E 46 D6
Torres del Carrizal E 39 E8
Torresmenudas E 45 B9
Torres Novas P 44 F3
Torres Vedras P 44 F2
Torrevelilla E 42 F3
Torrevieja E 56 F3
Torrice I 62 D4
Torricella I 61 C9
Torricella in Sabina I 62 C3
Torricella Peligna I 63 C6
Torricella Sicura I 62 B5
Torricella Taverne CH 69 A6
Torrico E 45 E10
Torri del Benaco I 69 B10
Torridon GB 2 K5
Torriglia I 37 B10
Torrijas E 48 D3
Torrijo E 41 F8
Torrijo del Campo E 47 C10
Torrijos E 46 E4
Torrin GB 2 L4
Tørring DK 86 D4
Tørring N 105 C10
Torrita di Siena I 66 F4
Torroal P 50 C2
Torroella de Montgrí E 43 C10
Torrox E 53 C9
Torrubia del Campo E 47 E7
Torrubia de Soria E 41 E7
Tørrvika N 104 C7
Torsåker S 98 A6
Torsång S 97 B14
Torsås S 89 C10
Tørsbøl DK 86 F4
Törsbole S 107 E15
Torsborg S 102 A5
Torsby S 97 B9
Torsby S 97 C9
Torsebro S 88 C6
Torshälla S 98 D6
Tórshavn FO 2 A3
Torsholma FIN 126 E5
Torsken N 111 B13
Torslanda S 91 D10
Torsminde DK 86 C2
Torsö S 91 B14
Torsvåg N 112 C4
Törtel H 150 C4
Tortellà E 43 C9
Torteval GBG 22 B6
Torthorwald GB 5 E9
Tortinmäki FIN 126 D7
Tórtola de Henares E 47 C6
Tórtoles de Esgueva E 40 E3
Tortolì I 64 D4
Tortomanu RO 155 E2
Tortona I 37 B9
Tortora I 60 D5
Tortoreto I 62 B5
Tortorici I 59 C6
Tortosa E 42 F5
Tortozendo P 44 D5
Tortuera E 47 C9
Tortuna S 98 C7
Toruń PL 138 D6
Torun' UA 145 F8
Torup S 87 B13
Tõrva EST 131 E11
Tor Vaianica I 62 D2
Tõrvandi EST 131 E13
Torvenkylä FIN 119 F11
Torvik N 100 B3
Torvik N 104 F4
Torvikbukt N 104 F3
Tørvikbygd N 94 B4
Torvinen FIN 117 D17
Torvizcón E 55 F6
Torvsjö S 107 C12
Torysa SK 145 E2
Torzym PL 81 B8
Tosbotn N 108 F4
Toscolano-Maderno I 69 B10
Tossa E 43 D9
Tossåsen S 102 A5
Tossåsen S 102 A7
Tossavanlahti FIN 123 D16
Tosse F 32 C3
Tösse S 91 B12
Tossicia I 62 B5
Tosside GB 11 C7
Tõstamaa EST 131 E7
Tostedt D 82 D7
Tószeg H 150 C5
Toszek PL 142 F6
Totana E 55 D10
Totebo S 93 D8
Tôtes F 18 E3
Toteşti RO 159 B10
Tótkomlós H 150 E6
Totland GB 13 D11
Totnes GB 13 E7
Totra S 103 E13
Tótszerdahely H 149 D7
Tøttdal N 105 C10
Tottijärvi FIN 127 C9
Totton GB 13 D12
Tótvázsony H 149 B9
Touça P 45 B6
Toucy F 25 E9
Touffailles F 33 B8
Touget F 33 C7
Toul F 26 C4
Toulon F 35 D10
Toulon-sur-Allier F 30 B3
Toulon-sur-Arroux F 30 B5
Toulouges F 34 E4
Toulouse F 33 C8
Tounj HR 156 B3
Touques F 23 B12
Tourch F 22 D4
Tourcoing F 19 C7
Tourlaville F 23 A8
Tournai B 19 C7
Tournan-en-Brie F 25 C8
Tournay F 33 D6
Tournecoupe F 33 C7
Tournefeuille F 33 C8
Tournon-d'Agenais F 33 B7
Tournon-St-Martin F 29 B7
Tournon-sur-Rhône F 30 E6
Tournus F 30 B6
Tourny F 24 B6
Tourouvre F 24 C4
Tours F 24 F4
Tourteron F 19 E10
Tourtoirac F 29 E8
Toury F 24 D6
Tous E 48 F3
Tõusi EST 131 D7
Touvois F 28 B2
Toužim CZ 76 B3
Tovačov CZ 146 C4
Tovariševo SRB 158 C3
Tovarné SK 145 F4
Tovarnik HR 157 B11
Toven N 108 D5
Tovrljane SRB 164 C3
Towcester GB 14 C7
Tower IRL 8 E5
Toymskardlia N 106 A5
Töysä FIN 123 E11
Traar D 183 C9
Trabada E 38 B5
Trabanca E 45 B8
Trabazos E 39 E7
Traben D 21 E8
Trąbki PL 144 D1
Trąbki Wielkie PL 138 B6
Traboch A 73 B10
Trabotivište MK 165 F6
Traby BY 137 E12
Trachili GR 175 B9
Tradate I 69 B6
Trädet S 91 D14
Trædal N 111 D14
Trafrask IRL 8 E3
Tragacete E 47 D9
Tragana GR 175 B7
Tragano GR 174 D3
Tragjas AL 168 D2
Tragwein A 77 F7
Traian RO 153 D10
Traian RO 155 C1
Traian RO 155 C2
Traian RO 160 E4
Traian RO 160 F6
Traian Vuia RO 151 F9
Traid E 47 C9
Traiguera E 42 F4
Train D 75 E10
Traînel F 25 D9
Traînou F 24 E7
Traisen A 77 F9
Traiskirchen A 77 F10
Traismauer A 77 F9
Traitsching D 75 D12
Trakai LT 137 D10
Trakovice SK 146 E5
Traksėdžiai LT 134 F2
Tralee IRL 8 D3
Trá Li IRL 8 D3
Tramacastilla E 47 D9
Tramagal P 44 F4
Tramariglio I 64 B1
Tramatza I 64 C2
Tramayes F 30 C6
Tramelan CH 27 F7
Trá Mhór IRL 9 D8
Tramonti di Sopra I 73 D6
Tramonti di Sotto I 73 D6
Tramore IRL 9 D8
Tramutola I 60 C5
Tranås S 92 C5
Tranbjerg DK 86 C6
Trancoso P 44 C6
Tranebjerg DK 86 D7
Tranemo S 91 E13
Trången S 105 D15
Trånghalla S 92 D4
Trängslet S 102 D6
Trångsviken S 105 E16
Trani I 61 A6
Trannes F 25 D12
Tranovalto GR 169 D6
Tranøy N 111 D10
Trans F 23 D8
Trans-en-Provence F 36 D4
Transtrand S 102 D5
Transtrand S 102 E5
Tranum DK 86 A4
Tranvik S 99 D11
Trapani I 58 C2
Trapene LV 135 B13
Traplice CZ 146 C4
Trappes F 24 C7
Trarbach D 185 E7
Traryd S 87 B13
Trasacco I 62 D5
Träskvik FIN 122 F7
Trasmiras E 38 D4
Trasobares E 41 E8
Tratalias I 64 E2
Traun A 76 F6
Traunreut D 73 A6
Traunstein D 73 A7
Traunstein D 73 A6
Traupis LT 135 E9
Trava SLO 73 E10
Trävad S 91 C13
Travagliato I 66 A1
Travanca do Mondego P 44 D4
Travassô P 44 C4
Travemünde D 83 C9
Travenbrück D 83 C8
Travers CH 31 B10
Traversetolo I 66 C1
Trávnica SK 146 E6
Travnik BIH 157 D8
Travo I 37 B11

Trawniki PL 141 H8
Trawsfynydd GB 10 F4
Trbovlje SLO 73 D11
Trbuk BIH 157 C9
Trebaseleghe I 72 E5
Trebatice SK 146 D5
Trebatsch D 80 B6
Trebbin D 80 B4
Třebechovice pod Orebem CZ 77 B9
Trebel D 83 E10
Treben D 79 D11
Třebenice CZ 76 B5
Trebenow D 84 D5
Trèbes F 33 D10
Trébeurden F 22 C4
Třebíč CZ 77 D9
Trebinje BIH 162 D5
Trebisacce I 61 D7
Trebišov SK 145 F4
Trebnje SLO 73 E11
Trebolle E 38 C4
Třeboň CZ 77 D7
Trebsen D 79 D12
Trebujena E 51 F7
Trebur D 21 E10
Trecastagni I 59 D7
Trecate I 68 C6
Trecchina I 60 C5
Trecenta I 66 B3
Tredegar GB 13 B8
Tredington GB 13 A11
Tredozio I 66 D4
Treehoo IRL 7 D8
Trefaldwyn GB 10 F5
Trefeglwys GB 10 F4
Treffen A 73 C8
Treffort-Cuisiat F 31 C7
Treffurt D 79 D7
Trefriw GB 10 E4
Trefynwy GB 13 B9
Tregaron GB 13 A7
Trégastel F 22 C4
Tregde N 90 C2
Tregnago I 66 A3
Tregony GB 12 E5
Trégueux F 22 D6
Tréguier F 22 C5
Trégunc F 22 E4
Tregynon GB 10 F5
Trehörna S 92 C5
Trehörningsjö S 107 D15
Treia D 82 A6
Treia I 67 F7
Treignac F 29 D9
Treigny F 25 E9
Treimani EST 131 F8
Treis D 185 D7
Trekanten S 89 B10
Treklyano BG 165 D6
Trélazé F 23 F11
Trelech GB 12 B6
Trélissac F 29 E7
Trelleborg S 87 E12
Trelleck GB 13 B9
Trélon F 19 D9
Tremadog GB 10 F3
Tremblay-les-Villages F 24 C5
Tremedal de Tormes E 45 B8
Tremelo B 19 C10
Trémentines F 23 F10
Tremês P 44 F3
Tréméven F 22 E4
Tremezzo I 69 B7
Trémolat F 29 F7
Třemošná CZ 76 C4
Trémouilles F 34 B4
Tremp E 42 C5
Trenance GB 12 E4
Trenčianska Turná SK 146 D6
Trenčianske Jastrabie SK 146 D6
Trenčianske Stankovce SK 146 D5
Trenčianske Teplice SK 146 D6
Trenčín SK 146 D6
Trendelburg D 21 A12
Trengereid N 94 B3
Trensacq F 32 B4
Trent D 84 A4
Trenta SLO 73 D8
Trentels F 33 B7
Trento I 69 A11
Tréon F 24 C5
Treorchy GB 13 B7
Trepča HR 148 F5
Treppeln D 81 B7
Trept F 31 D7
Trepuzzi I 61 C10
Trequanda I 66 F4
Tres Cantos E 46 C5
Trescléoux F 35 B10
Trescore Balneario I 69 B8
Tresenda I 69 A9
Tresfjord N 100 A6
Tresigallo I 66 C4
Tresjuncos E 47 E7
Treski EST 132 F2
Treskog S 97 C8
Trešnjevica SRB 158 F5
Tresnuraghes I 64 C2
Trespaderne E 40 C5
Tressait GB 5 B9
Třešť CZ 77 D8
Tretower GB 13 B8
Trets F 35 D10
Tretten N 101 D12
Treuchtlingen D 75 E8
Treuenbrietzen D 79 B12
Treungen N 90 A4
Trévé F 22 D6
Trevélez E 55 F6
Tréveray F 26 C3
Trèves F 34 B5
Trevi I 62 B3
Treviana E 40 C5
Trévières F 23 B10
Treviglio I 69 B8
Trevignano Romano I 62 C2
Trévillers F 27 F6
Treviño E 40 C6
Treviso I 72 E5
Trevllazër AL 168 C2
Trevões P 44 B6
Trévoux F 30 D6
Trézelles F 30 C4
Trezzo sull'Adda I 69 B8
Trgovište SRB 164 E5
Trhová Hradská SK 146 F5
Trhové Sviny CZ 77 E7
Trhovište SK 145 F4
Trhový Štěpánov CZ 77 C8
Triacastela E 38 C5
Triaize F 28 C3
Trianta GR 181 D8
Triantaros GR 176 D5
Tribalj HR 67 B10
Tribanj-Krušćica HR 156 D3
Tribehou F 23 B9
Tribsees D 83 B13
Tribunj HR 156 E4
Tricarico I 60 B6
Tricase I 61 D10
Tricesimo I 73 D7
Trichiana I 72 D5
Tricot F 18 E6
Trieben A 73 A9
Triebes D 79 E11
Trie-Château F 18 F4
Trier D 21 E7
Trierweiler D 186 B2
Trieste I 73 E8
Trie-sur-Baïse F 33 D6
Trieux F 20 F5
Trifeşti RO 153 C11
Trifeşti RO 153 D9
Triftern D 76 F4
Trigaches P 50 C4
Trigance F 36 D4
Triggiano I 61 A7
Triglitz D 83 D12
Trignac F 23 F7
Trigrad BG 165 F9
Triguères F 25 E8
Triqueros E 51 E6
Trigueros del Valle E 39 E10
Triigi EST 130 D5
Trikala GR 169 E6
Trikāta LV 131 F11
Trikeri GR 175 A7
Trilj HR 157 E6
Trillevallen S 105 E14
Trillick GB 7 D8
Trillo E 47 C7
Trilofo GR 174 E5
Trilofos GR 169 D8
Trilport F 25 C8
Trim IRL 7 E9
Trimdon GB 5 F14
Trimley St Mary GB 15 D11
Trimmis CH 71 D9
Trimsaran GB 12 B6
Trindade P 38 F5
Trindade P 50 D4
Třinec CZ 147 B7
Tring GB 15 D7
Trinità d'Agultu I 64 B2
Trinitapoli I 60 A6
Trino I 68 C5
Trins A 72 B3
Trinta P 45 C6
Trinwillershagen D 83 B13
Triollo E 39 C10
Triora I 37 D7
Tripkau D 83 D10
Tripoli GR 174 D5
Tripotama GR 174 D4
Tripotamos GR 169 C7
Trippstadt D 21 F9
Triptis D 79 E10
Tritenii de Jos RO 152 D4
Trittau D 83 C8
Trittenheim D 21 E7
Trivalea-Moşteni RO 160 E6
Trivento I 63 D7
Trivero I 68 B5
Trivigno I 60 B5
Trizac F 29 E11
Trnakovac HR 157 B7
Trnava CZ 146 C5
Trnava SK 146 E5
Trnava SRB 158 F5
Trnavá Hora SK 147 D7
Trnjani BIH 157 C6
Trnovci MK 168 B5
Trnovec Bartolovečki HR 149 D6
Trnovec nad Váhom SK 146 E5
Trnovica BIH 157 F9
Trnovo BIH 157 E9
Tro N 108 E4
Troarn F 23 B11
Tröbitz D 80 C4
Trochtelfingen D 27 D11
Trödje S 103 E13
Troense DK 86 E7
Trofa P 38 F2
Trofaiach A 73 B11
Trofors N 108 E5
Trogir HR 156 E5
Trøgstad N 95 C14
Troia I 60 A4
Tróia P 50 C2
Troianul RO 160 F6
Troina I 59 D6
Troisdorf D 21 C8
Troisfontaines F 186 D3
Trois-Ponts B 19 D12
Troissereux F 18 F5
Trois-Vèvres F 30 B3
Troisvierges L 20 D6
Troiţsoe MD 154 D4
Trojane SLO 73 D10
Trojanów PL 141 G5
Troldhede DK 86 D3
Trollbukta N 113 C19
Trollhättan S 91 C11
Trollvik N 112 D6
Tromello I 69 C6
Tromsdalen N 111 A16
Tromsø N 111 A16
Tromvik N 111 A15
Tronco P 38 E5
Trondenes N 111 C12
Trondheim N 104 E8
Trones N 105 B13
Trongisvágur FO 2 B3
Tronnes N 108 C8
Trönninge S 87 B11
Trönningeby S 87 A10
Trönö S 103 D12
Trontano I 68 A5
Tronvik N 105 D9
Tronville-en-Barrois F 26 C3
Tronzano Vercellese I 68 C5
Troo F 24 E4
Troon GB 4 D7
Trooz B 183 D7
Tropaia GR 174 D4
Tropea I 59 B8
Trory GB 7 D7
Trosa S 93 B11
Troshan AL 163 F8
Trösken S 98 B7
Troškūnai LT 135 E9
Trošmarija HR 148 F4
Trossin D 79 C12
Trossingen D 27 D10
Tröstau D 75 B10
Trostberg D 75 F12
Trostyanets' UA 145 E9
Trostyanets' UA 153 A12
Troszyn PL 139 D12
Troubky CZ 146 C4
Troubsko CZ 77 D10
Troutbeck GB 10 C6
Trouville-sur-Mer F 23 B12
Trouy F 29 A10
Troviscal P 44 E4
Trowbridge GB 13 C10
Troyan BG 165 D10
Troyanovo BG 167 D8
Troyes F 25 D11
Troyits'ke UA 154 B6
Troyits'ke UA 154 D6
Troyon F 26 B3
Trpanj HR 157 F7
Trpejca MK 168 C4
Trpezi MNE 163 D9
Trpinja HR 157 B10
Trsa MNE 157 F10
Trstená SK 147 C9
Trstené pri Hornáde SK 145 F3
Trstenik HR 162 D3
Trstenik SRB 163 B11
Trstice SK 146 E5
Trstín SK 146 D4
Trubar BIH 156 D5
Trubia E 39 B8
Truchas E 39 D7
Truchtersheim F 27 C8
Trud BG 165 E10
Trudovets BG 165 D8
Trudy BY 133 E6
Trujillanos E 51 B7
Trujillo E 45 F9
Trulben D 27 B8
Trŭn BG 165 D6
Trun CH 71 D7
Trun F 23 C12
Trŭnchovitsa BG 165 C11
Truro GB 12 E4
Truşeşti RO 153 B10
Trusetal D 79 E7
Trush AL 163 F7
Truskava LT 135 F8
Truskavets' UA 145 E8
Trŭstenik BG 161 F7
Trŭstenik BG 165 C9
Trustrup DK 87 C7
Trutnov CZ 81 E9
Try N 90 C2
Tryavna BG 166 D4
Trybusivka UA 154 A3
Tryfos GR 174 B3
Tryggelev DK 83 A9
Trygona GR 168 E5
Tryńcza PL 144 C6
Tryserum S 93 C9
Trysil N 102 D3
Tryškiai LT 134 D5
Trysunda S 107 E15
Tržac BIH 156 C4
Trzcianka PL 85 D10
Trzcianka PL 139 E12
Trzcianne PL 140 D7
Trzciel PL 81 B9
Trzebiatów PL 85 B8
Trzebiechów PL 81 B9
Trzebiel PL 81 C7
Trzebielino PL 85 B12
Trzebień PL 81 D9
Trzebieszów PL 141 G7
Trzebieszowice PL 77 B11
Trzebież PL 84 C7
Trzebinia PL 143 F7
Trzebiszewo PL 81 A8
Trzebnica PL 81 D12
Trzebnice PL 81 D10
Trzebownisko PL 144 C5
Trzeciewiec PL 138 D5
Trzemeszno PL 138 E4
Trzemeszno Lubuskie PL 81 B8
Trześcianka PL 140 E8
Trześniów PL 145 D4
Trzeszczany Pierwsze PL 144 B8
Tržič SLO 73 D9
Trzrcińsko-Zdrój PL 84 E7
Trzyciąż PL 143 F8
Trzydnik Duży PL 144 B5
Tsagkarada GR 169 F9
Tsakarisianos GR 174 C2
Tsalapitsa BG 165 E10
Tsamantas GR 168 E3
Tsaparevo BG 169 A9
Tsareva Livada BG 166 D4
Tsarev Brod BG 167 C8
Tsarevo BG 167 E9
Tsarimir BG 165 E10
Tsaritsani GR 169 E7
Tsar Kaloyan BG 161 F8
Tsar-Petrovo BG 159 F10
Tschagguns A 71 C9
Tschernitz D 81 C7
Tsebrykove UA 154 C6
Tselina BG 166 E4
Tsenovo BG 166 B5
Tserovo BG 165 C7
Tserovo BG 165 E9
Tsiistre EST 131 F14
Tsirguliina EST 131 F12
Tsivaras GR 178 E7
Tsooru EST 131 F13
Tsotili GR 168 D5
Tsoukalades GR 174 B2
Tsŭrvaritsa BG 165 E6
Tsvetino BG 165 F8
Tsyatsyerki BY 133 E2
Tua N 105 D9
Tuaim IRL 6 E5
Tuaim Beola IRL 6 F3
Tuam IRL 6 E5
Tuamgraney IRL 8 C5
Tubbercurry IRL 6 D5
Tubbergen NL 17 D7
Tubilla del Agua E 40 C4
Tübingen D 27 C11
Tubize B 19 C9
Tubre I 71 D10
Tučepi HR 157 F7
Tuchan F 34 E4
Tüchen D 83 D12
Tuchheim D 79 B11
Tuchola PL 138 C4
Tuchomie PL 85 B12
Tuchów PL 144 D3
Tuchowicz PL 141 G6
Tuckur FIN 122 D8
Tuczna PL 141 G8
Tuczno PL 85 D10
Tudela E 41 D8
Tudela de Duero E 40 E2
Tudora RO 153 B9
Tudor Vladimirescu RO 155 B1
Tudu EST 131 C13
Tudulinna EST 131 C14
Tudweiliog GB 10 F2
Tuejar E 47 E10
Tuenno I 72 D3
Tufeni RO 160 E5
Tufeşti RO 155 D1
Tuffé F 24 D4
Tufjord N 113 A12
Tuhkakylä FIN 125 B10
Tui E 38 D2
Tuili I 64 D2
Tuin MK 168 A5
Tuiskula FIN 122 E8
Tūja LV 135 B8
Tukhkala RUS 121 C16
Tukhol'ka UA 145 F7
Tukums LV 134 C6
Tula I 64 B2
Tulach Mhór IRL 7 F8
Tulare SRB 164 D3
Tuławki PL 136 F2
Tulbing A 77 F10
Tulca RO 151 D8
Tulce PL 81 B12
Tulcea RO 155 C3
Tulčík SK 145 E3
Tulette F 35 B8
Tulgheş RO 153 D7
Tuli BIH 162 D5
Tuliszków PL 142 B5
Tulje BIH 162 D5
Tulka S 99 B11
Tulla IRL 8 C5
Tullaghan IRL 6 D6
Tullamore IRL 7 F8
Tulle F 29 E9
Tullebølle DK 87 F7
Tulleng N 111 A15
Tulleråsen S 105 E16
Tullingsås S 106 D9
Tullins F 31 E7
Tulln A 77 F10
Tullow IRL 9 C9
Tully GB 7 D7
Tully GB 7 D8
Tullyallen IRL 7 E10
Tullyvin IRL 7 D8
Tulnici RO 153 F9
Tulos RUS 125 C14
Tulovo BG 166 D5
Tułowice PL 139 F9
Tułowice PL 142 E4
Tulppio FIN 115 C6
Tulsk IRL 6 E6
Tulstrup DK 87 D10
Tulucești RO 155 B2
Tumba S 93 A11
Tumbo S 98 D6
Tume LV 134 C6
Tummel Bridge GB 5 B8
Tumšupe LV 135 B9
Tun S 91 C12
Tunadal S 103 B13
Tuna-Hästberg S 97 B13
Tunari RO 161 D8
Tunbridge Wells, Royal GB 15 E9
Tunga GB 2 J4
Tungozero RUS 121 C17
Tunnerstad S 92 C4
Tunnhovd N 95 B9
Tunnsjø-Røyrvika N 105 B14
Tunsjön S 107 E12
Tunstall GB 15 C11
Tuntenhausen D 72 A5
Tunvågen S 102 A8
Tuohikotti FIN 128 C7
Tuohikylä FIN 115 E5
Tuolluvaara S 116 C4
Tuomikylä FIN 122 E9
Tuomioja FIN 119 E14
Tuorila FIN 126 B6
Tuoro sul Trasimeno I 66 F5
Tuovilanlahti FIN 124 D8
Tupilaţi RO 153 C9
Tuplice PL 81 C7
Tuppurinmäki FIN 125 E10
Tura H 150 B4
Turanlar TR 177 D10
Turany SK 147 C8
Turawa PL 142 E5
Turba EST 131 C8
Turbe BIH 157 D8
Turbenthal CH 27 F10
Turburea RO 160 D3
Turceni RO 160 D2
Turcia E 39 C8
Turčianske Teplice SK 147 D7
Turcifal P 44 F2
Turcinești RO 160 C2
Turcoaia RO 155 C2
Turda RO 152 D3
Turdaş RO 151 F11
Turégano E 46 B4
Turek PL 142 B6
Tureni RO 152 D3
Turenki FIN 127 D12
Turew PL 81 B11
Turgeliai LT 137 E12
Türgovishte BG 167 C7
Turgut TR 181 B8
Turgutalp TR 177 A10
Turgutbey TR 173 B7
Turgutlu TR 177 C10
Turgutreis TR 177 F9
Türi EST 131 D10
Turi I 61 B8
Turia RO 153 E8
Turić BIH 157 C10
Turie SK 147 C7
Turija BIH 157 C9
Turija SRB 158 B4
Turija SRB 159 D8
Turís E 48 F3
Turiya BG 166 D4
Türje H 149 C8
Turka UA 145 E7
Türkeve H 150 C6
Türkgücü TR 173 B8
Türkheim D 71 A11
Turki LV 135 D12
Türkmenli TR 171 E10
Turkova BY 133 E4
Turkoviči BIH 162 D4
Turku FIN 126 E7
Turlava LV 134 C3
Turleque E 46 E5
Turmantas LT 135 E12
Turmenti BIH 162 D5
Turna LV 131 F11
Tŭrnak BG 165 C9
Turňa nad Bodvou SK 145 F2
Turnau A 148 A4
Tŭrnava BG 165 B8
Turnberry GB 4 E7
Turners Hill GB 15 E8
Turnhout B 16 F3
Turnišče SLO 149 C6
Türnitz A 77 G9
Turnov CZ 81 E8
Turnu Măgurele RO 160 F5
Turnu Roşu RO 160 B4
Turnu Ruieni RO 159 C9
Turobin PL 144 B6
Turośl PL 139 C12
Turośl PL 139 D12
Turów PL 141 G7
Turowo PL 85 C11
Turquel P 44 F3
Turrach A 73 C8
Turre E 55 E9
Turri I 64 D2
Turriff GB 3 K12
Tursi I 61 C6
Turţ RO 145 H7
Turtel MK 164 F5
Turtola FIN 117 E11
Turulung RO 145 H7
Turup DK 86 E5
Tur"ya-Bystra UA 145 F6
Tur"ya-Polyana UA 145 F6
Turyatka UA 153 A8
Tur"ye UA 145 E7
Tur"yi Remety UA 145 F6
Turynka UA 144 C9
Turza Wielka PL 139 D9
Turzovka SK 147 C7
Tusa I 58 D5
Tuscania I 62 C1
Tuse DK 87 D9
Tuset N 105 E10
Tušilović HR 148 F5
Tuşnad RO 153 E7
Tussenhausen D 71 A11
Tüßling D 75 F12
Tuszów Narodowy PL 143 F11
Tuszyma PL 143 F12
Tuszyn PL 143 C8
Tutbury GB 11 F8
Tutjunniemi FIN 125 F13
Tutora RO 153 C11
Tutova RO 153 E11
Tutow D 84 C4
Tutrakan BG 161 E9
Tuttlingen D 27 E10
Tütüncü TR 173 D8
Tutzing D 72 A3
Tützpatz D 84 C4
Tuudi EST 130 D7
Tuukkala FIN 127 B16
Tuuliharju FIN 117 D13
Tuulimäki FIN 121 F11
Tuulos FIN 127 C12
Tuupovaara FIN 125 F15
Tuuri FIN 123 E11
Tuusjärvi FIN 125 E10
Tuusniemi FIN 125 E10
Tuusula FIN 127 E12
Tuv N 101 E8
Tuv N 108 B8
Tuvattnett S 106 D7
Tuve S 91 D10
Tuvnes N 104 D5
Tuvträsk S 107 B15
Tuxford GB 11 E10
Tuzburgazi TR 177 D9
Tuzculu TR 177 B8
Tŭzha BG 166 D4
Tuzi MNE 163 E7
Tužina SK 147 D7
Tuzla BIH 157 C10
Tuzla RO 155 E3
Tuzla TR 171 E10
Tužno HR 148 D6
Tuzora MD 154 C2
Tuzsér H 145 G5
Tvååker S 87 A10
Tvärålund S 107 C17
Tvärån S 118 C6
Tvärträsk S 107 A13
Tvardița MD 154 E3
Tvärsele S 106 B8
Tvärskog S 89 B10
Tvede DK 86 B6
Tvedestrand N 90 B4
Tveit N 90 C3
Tveit N 94 D4
Tverai LT 134 E4
Tverečius LT 135 F13
Tverrå N 108 D7
Tverråmo N 109 B10
Tverrelmo N 111 C18
Tversted DK 90 D7
Tving S 89 C8
Tvis DK 86 C3
Tvøroyri FO 2 B3
Tvorozhkovo RUS 132 E4
Tvrdošín SK 147 C9
Tvrdošovce SK 146 E6
Tvŭrditsa BG 166 D5
Twardogóra PL 142 D3
Twatt GB 3 G10
Tweedmouth GB 5 D12
Tweedsmuir GB 5 D10
Twello NL 16 D6
Twist D 17 C8
Twiste (Twistetal) D 17 F11
Twistringen D 17 C11
Two Mile Borris IRL 9 C7
Twomileborris IRL 9 C7
Two Mile Bridge IRL 7 F8
Tworóg PL 142 E6
Twyford GB 13 C12
Twyford GB 15 E7
Twyning GB 13 A10
Tyachiv UA 145 G8
Tychero GR 171 B10
Tychówko PL 85 C10
Tychowo PL 85 C10
Tychy PL 143 F6
Tyczyn PL 144 D5
Tydal N 105 E11
Tydavnet IRL 7 D8
Tyfors S 97 B11
Tygelsjö S 87 D11
Tyinkrysset N 101 D8
Tykocin PL 140 D7
Tylawa PL 145 E4
Tylissos GR 178 E9
Tyllinge S 93 C8
Tylmanowa PL 145 D1
Tylösand S 87 B11
Tylstrup DK 86 A5
Tymbark PL 144 D1
Tymień PL 85 B9
Tymowa PL 81 D10
Tympaki GR 178 E8
Tyndérö S 103 B14
Tyndrum GB 4 C7
Týnec nad Labem CZ 77 B8
Týnec nad Sázavou CZ 77 C7
Tynemouth GB 5 E14
Tyngsjö S 97 B10
Tyniewicze Małe PL 141 E8
Týniště nad Orlicí CZ 77 B10
Tynkä FIN 119 F12
Týn nad Vltavou CZ 77 D6
Tynset N 101 B13
Typpö FIN 119 F12
Typpyrä FIN 117 E14
Tyrämäki FIN 121 D12
Tyrävaara FIN 121 D12
Tyrawa Wołoska PL 145 D5
Tyresö S 99 D10
Tyringe S 87 C13
Tyristrand N 95 B12
Tyrjänsaari FIN 125 E15
Tyrnävä FIN 119 E15
Tyrnavos GR 169 E7
Tyrrellspass IRL 7 F8
Tyrväntö FIN 127 C11
Tysnes N 111 D10
Tysse N 94 B3
Tysse N 100 D2
Tyssebotnen N 100 E3
Tyssedal N 94 B5
Tystberga S 93 B10
Tyszowce PL 144 B8
Tytuvėnai LT 134 E6
Tyukod H 145 H6
Tyulenovo BG 167 B11
Tywyn GB 10 F3
Tzermiado GR 178 E9
Tykiluoto FIN 119 D14
Tzummarum NL 16 B5

U

Uachdar GB 2 L2
Uachtar Ard IRL 6 F4
Ub SRB 158 E5
Übach-Palenberg D 183 D8
Ubby DK 87 D8
Úbeda E 53 A10
Überherrn D 21 F7
Überlingen D 27 E11
Übersee D 72 A5
Ubli HR 162 D2
Ubli MNE 163 D6
Ubli MNE 163 D7
Ubrique E 53 C6
Ubstadt-Weiher D 21 F11
Ucciani F 37 G9
Uccle B 19 C9
Ucea RO 152 F5
Uceda E 46 C6
Ucel F 35 A7
Ucero E 40 E5
Ucha P 38 E2
Uchanie PL 144 B8
Uchaux F 35 B8
Uchizy F 30 B6
Uchte D 17 D11
Üchtelhausen D 75 B7
Uchtspringe D 79 A10
Uckange F 186 C1
Uckfield GB 15 F9
Uckro D 80 C5
Uclés E 47 E7
Üçpinar TR 177 B9
Uda RO 160 D5
Udanin PL 81 D10
Udavské SK 145 F4
Udbina HR 156 C4
Udby DK 87 D9
Uddebo S 91 E13
Uddeholm S 97 B10
Uddel NL 183 A7
Uddevalla S 91 C10
Uddheden S 97 C8
Uddington GB 5 D9
Uden NL 16 E5
Udenhout NL 16 E4
Udenisht AL 168 C4
Uderns A 72 B4
Üdersdorf D 21 D7
Udeşti RO 153 B8
Udiča SK 146 C6
Udine I 73 D7
Udorpie PL 85 B13
Üdruma EST 131 D8
Udrycze PL 144 B7
Uebigau D 80 C4
Ueckermünde D 84 C6
Uehlfeld D 75 C8
Uelsen D 17 D7
Uelzen D 83 E9
Uetendorf CH 31 B12
Uetersen D 82 C7
Uettingen D 74 C6
Uetze D 79 B7
Uffculme GB 13 D8
Uffenheim D 75 C7
Uffing am Staffelsee D 72 A3
Uftrungen D 79 C8
Ugāle LV 134 B4
Ugao SRB 163 C9
Ugarana E 40 B6
Uge DK 86 F4
Ugelbølle DK 86 C6
Ugento I 61 D10
Ugerløse DK 87 D9
Uggdal N 94 B2
Uggelheden S 102 E3
Uggelhuse DK 86 C6
Uggerby DK 90 D7
Uggerslev DK 86 D6
Uggiano la Chiesa I 61 C10
Ugíjar E 55 F6
Ugine F 31 D9
Üglen BG 165 C9
Uglev DK 86 B3
Ugljan HR 67 D11
Ugljane HR 157 E6
Ugljevik BIH 157 C11
Ugod H 149 B9
Ugŭrchin BG 165 C9
Uğurlu TR 171 D9
Uharte-Arakil E 32 E2
Uherské Hradiště CZ 146 C4
Uherský Brod CZ 146 C5
Uhingen D 74 E6
Uhldingen D 27 E11
Uhlířské Janovice CZ 77 C8
Uhlstädt D 79 E9
Uhniv UA 144 C8
Uhtna EST 131 C13
Uhyst D 81 D7
Uig GB 2 K4
Uimaharju FIN 125 E14
Uimila FIN 127 C15
Uitgeest NL 16 C3
Uithoorn NL 16 D3
Uithuizen NL 17 B7
Uivar RO 159 B6
Ujazd PL 141 G1
Ujazd PL 142 F5
Újezd CZ 77 C12
Újezd CZ 146 C5
Újfehértó H 151 B8
Újhartyán H 150 C3
Újkér H 149 B7
Újkígyós H 151 D7
Újléta H 151 C8
Újpetre H 149 E10
Ujście PL 85 D11
Ujsoły PL 147 C8
Újszalonta H 151 D7
Újszász H 150 C5
Újszentiván H 150 E5
Újszentmargita H 151 B7
Újszilvás H 150 C4
Újtikos H 145 H3
Újudvar H 149 C7
Ukhozhany UA 154 A5
Ukkola FIN 125 E14
Ukmergė LT 135 F9
Ukri LV 134 D6
Ula BY 133 F6
Ula TR 181 B8
Ulamiş TR 177 C8
Uland S 103 A14
Ulan-Majorat PL 141 G6
Ulanów PL 144 C5
Ulaş TR 173 B8
Ulassai I 64 D4
Ula Tirso I 64 C2
Ulbjerg DK 86 B4
Ulbroka LV 135 C8
Ulbster GB 3 J10
Ulcinj MNE 163 F7
Uldum DK 86 D5
Ulefoss N 95 D10
Uleila del Campo E 55 E8
Ülenurme EST 131 E13
Ulëz AL 163 F8
Ulfborg DK 86 C2
Ulft NL 16 E6
Ulhówek PL 144 C8
Ulič SK 145 F5
Ulicoten NL 182 C5
Ulieş RO 152 E6
Ulieşti RO 161 D6
Ulila EST 131 E12
Uljanik HR 149 E8
Uljma SRB 159 C7
Ullånger S 107 E14
Ullapool GB 2 K6
Ullared S 87 A11
Ullatti S 116 D7
Ullava FIN 123 C11
Ullbergsträsk S 107 A17
Ulldecona E 42 F4
Ulldemolins E 42 E5
Ullerslev DK 86 E7
Ullervad S 91 B14
Üllés H 150 E4
Ulleskelf GB 11 D9
Ullisjaur S 107 A10
Ullits DK 86 B4
Üllő H 150 C3
Ullsfjord N 111 A18
Ulm D 74 F6
Ulma RO 152 B6
Ulmbach D 74 B5
Ulme P 44 F4
Ulmen D 21 D7
Ulmeni RO 151 C11
Ulmeni RO 161 C9
Ulmeni RO 161 E9
Ulmi RO 161 D6
Ulmu RO 161 D10
Ulmu RO 161 E8
Ulog BIH 157 F9
Uløybukta N 112 D6
Ulricehamn S 91 D13
Ulrichsberg A 76 E5
Ulrichstein D 21 C12
Ulrika S 92 C6
Ulriksberg S 97 B12
Ulriksfors S 106 D9
Ulrum NL 16 B6
Ulsberg N 101 A11
Ulsta GB 3 D14
Ulsted DK 86 A6
Ulsteinvik N 100 B3
Ulstrup DK 86 C5
Ulstrup DK 87 D7
Ulsvåg N 111 D10
Ultrå S 107 E16
Uluabat TR 173 D9
Ulucak TR 177 B9
Ulucak TR 177 C9
Ulukonak TR 181 A7
Ulvåker S 91 C14
Ulvenhout NL 16 E3
Ulverston GB 10 C5
Ulvik N 100 E5
Ulvila FIN 126 C6
Ulvöhamn S 107 E15
Ulvsjön S 102 C7
Ulvsjön S 103 B11
Ulvvik S 103 A14
Ul'yanovka UA 154 A6
Ul'yanovo RUS 136 D5
Umag HR 67 B8
Umberleigh GB 12 D7
Umbertide I 66 F5
Umbrăreşti RO 153 F10
Umbriatico I 61 E7
Umbukta N 108 D8
Umčari SRB 158 D6
Umeå S 122 C4
Umfors S 108 E9
Umgransele S 107 B14
Umhausen A 71 C11
Umin Dol MK 164 E4
Umka SRB 158 D5
Umkirch D 27 D8
Umljanović HR 156 E5
Ummeljoki FIN 128 D6
Ummern D 79 A7
Umnäs S 109 F11
Ümraniye TR 173 B11
Umurbey TR 172 D6
Umurga LV 135 A9
Uña E 47 D9
Uña de Quintana E 39 D7

Unaja FIN 126 C6
Únanov CZ 77 E10
Unapool GB 2 J6
Unari FIN 117 D15
Unbyn S 118 C7
Uncastillo E 32 F3
Undenäs S 92 B4
Undereidet N 112 D9
Underfossen N 113 C18
Undersåker S 105 E14
Undingen D 27 D11
Undløse DK 87 D9
Undva EST 130 D3
Undy GB 13 B9
Unelanperä FIN 120 F9
Ungerhausen D 71 A10
Ungheni MD 153 C11
Ungheni RO 152 E4
Ungheni RO 160 E5
Ungra RO 152 F6
Ungurașl RO 152 C4
Ungureni RO 153 B9
Ungureni RO 153 D10
Ungurpils LV 131 F9
Unhais da Serra P 44 D5
Unhais-o-Velho P 44 D5
Unhošť CZ 76 B6
Uničov CZ 77 C12
Uniejów PL 142 C6
Unieux F 30 E5
Unín SK 146 D4
Unirea RO 152 E3
Unirea RO 155 C1
Unirea RO 155 F3
Unirea RO 159 B10
Unirea RO 159 E11
Unirea RO 161 E11
Unisław PL 138 D5
Unkel D 21 C8
Unken A 73 A6
Unlingen D 71 A9
Unna D 17 E9
Unnaryd S 87 B13
Unnau D 185 C8
Unntorp S 102 D7
Unset N 101 C14
Unsholtet N 101 A14
Unstad N 110 D6
Untamala FIN 122 D9
Untamala FIN 126 D6
Unteni RO 153 B9
Unterägeri CH 27 F10
Unterammergau D 71 B12
Unterdießen D 71 B11
Untergriesbach D 76 E5
Unterhaching D 75 F10
Unterkulm CH 27 F9
Unterlüß D 83 E8
Untermaßfeld D 75 A7
Untermerzbach D 75 B8
Untermünkheim D 74 D6
Unterneukirchen D 75 F12
Unterpleichfeld D 75 C7
Unterreit D 75 F11
Unterschächen CH 71 D7
Unterschleißheim D 75 F10
Untersiemau D 75 B8
Untersteinach D 75 B10
Unterweißenbach A 77 F7
Unterwössen D 72 A5
Unverre F 24 D5
Upavon GB 13 C11
Upenieki LV 134 C5
Upenieki LV 135 D12
Upesgrīva LV 134 B6
Upgant-Schott D 17 A8
Úpice CZ 77 A10
Upinniemi FIN 127 E11
Uplyme GB 13 D9
Upninkai LT 137 C10
Upper Knockando GB 3 L10
Upperlands GB 4 F3
Upphärad S 91 C11
Uppingham GB 11 F10
Upplanda S 99 B9
Upplands-Väsby S 99 C9
Uppsala S 99 C9
Uppsälje S 97 A11
Uppsete N 100 E5
Uppsjö S 103 C12
Upton upon Severn GB 13 A10
Upyna LT 134 E5
Upyna LT 134 F4
Upytė LT 135 E8
Urafirth GB 3 E14
Urago d'Oglio I 69 B8
Uraiújfalu H 149 B7
Uras I 64 D2
Ura Vajgurore AL 168 C2
Uraz PL 81 D11
Urbach D 21 C9
Urbania I 66 E6
Urbar D 185 D8
Urbe I 37 C9
Urberach D 187 B6
Urbino I 66 E6
Urbisaglia I 67 F7
Urbise F 30 C4
Určice CZ 77 D12
Urda E 46 F5
Urdari RO 160 D2
Urdax-Urdazuli E 32 D2
Urdorf CH 27 F9
Urdos F 32 E4
Urduña E 40 C6
Ure N 110 D6
Urecheni RO 153 C9
Urechești RO 153 E10
Urechești RO 161 B10
Urë e Shtrenjtë AL 163 E8
Urepel F 32 D3
Ureterp NL 16 B6
Urga LV 131 F9
Úrhida H 149 B10
Úri H 150 C4
Uri I 64 B2
Uricani RO 159 C11
Uriménil F 26 D5
Uringe S 93 A11
Uriu RO 152 C4
Urjala FIN 127 C10
Urk NL 16 C5
Ürkmez TR 177 C8
Úrkút H 149 B9
Urla TR 177 C8
Urlați RO 161 D8
Urlingford IRL 9 C7
Urmeniș RO 152 D4
Urmince SK 146 D6
Urnäsch CH 27 F11
Urnieta E 32 D2
Üröm H 150 B3
Urovica SRB 159 E9
Urrea de Gaén E 42 E3
Urrea de Jalón E 41 E9
Urretxu E 32 D1
Urriés E 32 E3
Urros P 45 B6
Urroz E 32 E3
Urrugne F 32 D2
Ursberg D 71 A10
Ursensollen D 75 D10
Urshult S 89 B7
Ursviken S 118 E6
Urszulin PL 141 H8
Urt F 32 D3
Urtenen CH 31 A11
Urtimjaur S 116 E5
Urueña E 39 E9
Ururi I 63 D8
Urville Nacqueville F 23 A8
Urzjdów PL 144 B5
Urzica RO 160 F4
Urziceni RO 151 B9
Urziceni RO 161 D9
Urzicuța RO 160 E3
Urzulei I 64 C4
Urzy F 30 A3
Usagre E 51 C7
Ušari BIH 157 C7
Ušće SRB 163 C10
Uschlag (Staufenberg) D 78 D6
Uście Gorlickie PL 145 D3
Uście Solne PL 143 F10
Uscio I 37 C10
Usedom D 84 C5
Usellus I 64 D2
Useras E 48 D4
Ushachy BY 133 F5
Ušī LV 130 F5
Usingen D 21 D11
Usini I 64 B2
Usk GB 13 B9
Uskali FIN 125 F14
Uskedal N 94 C3
Üsküdar TR 173 B11
Üsküp TR 167 F8
Uslar D 78 C6
Usma LV 134 B4
Úsov CZ 77 C12
Uspenivka UA 154 E5
Usquert NL 17 B7
Ussana I 64 E3
Ussassai I 64 D3
Usseglio I 31 E11
Ussel F 29 D10
Ussel F 30 E2
Usson-du-Poitou F 29 C7
Usson-en-Forez F 30 E4
Ustaoset N 95 B8
Ustaritz F 32 D3
Ust'-Chorna UA 145 G8
Ust'-Dolyssy RUS 133 D7
Úštěk CZ 80 E6
Uster CH 27 F10
Ustibar BIH 163 B7
Ustica I 58 B3
Ustikotlina BIH 157 E10
Ústí nad Labem CZ 80 E6
Ústí nad Orlicí CZ 77 C10
Ustiprača BIH 157 E11
Ustirama BIH 157 E8
Ustka PL 85 A11
Ust'-Luga RUS 132 B3
Ustou F 33 E8
Ustovo BG 171 A7
Ustrem BG 167 E6
Ustroń PL 147 B7
Ustronie Morskie PL 85 B9
Ustrzyki Dolne PL 145 E6
Ustya UA 154 A5
Ustyluh UA 144 B9
Usurbil E 32 D1
Uszew PL 144 D2
Uszód H 149 C11
Utajärvi FIN 119 E16
Utåker N 94 C3
Utakleiv N 110 D6
Utanede S 103 A12
Utanen FIN 119 E16
Utansjö S 103 A14
Utanskog S 107 E14
Utarp D 17 A8
Utbjoa N 94 C3
Utebo E 41 E10
Utelle F 37 D6
Utena LT 135 F11
Utersum D 82 A4
Uthaug N 104 D7
Uthleben D 79 D8
Uthlede D 17 B11
Utiel E 47 E10
Utne N 94 B5
Utö S 93 B12
Utoropy UA 152 A6
Utrecht NL 16 D4
Utrera E 51 E8
Utrillas E 42 F2
Utrine SRB 150 F4
Utro N 104 C8
Utsjoki FIN 113 D18
Utskor N 110 C8
Uttendorf A 72 B6
Uttendorf A 76 F4
Uttenweiler D 71 A9
Utterbyn S 97 B9
Utterliden S 109 F17
Uttersberg S 97 C14
Uttersjö S 107 D14
Utterslev DK 87 F8
Utti FIN 128 D6
Utting am Ammersee D 71 A12
Uttoxeter GB 11 F8
Utula FIN 129 C9
Utvalnäs S 103 E13
Utvik N 100 C5
Utvorda N 105 B9
Utzedel D 84 C4
Uuemõisa EST 130 D7
Uukuniemi FIN 129 B13
Uulu EST 131 E9
Uura FIN 121 F10
Uurainen FIN 123 E14
Uuro FIN 122 F8
Uusikaarlepyy FIN 122 C9
Uusikartano FIN 126 D7
Uusikaupunki FIN 126 D5
Uusikylä FIN 123 D12
Uusikylä FIN 127 D15
Uusi-Värtsilä FIN 125 F14
Uva FIN 121 E11
Uvac BIH 158 F4
Uvåg N 110 C8
Úvaly CZ 77 B7
Uvanå S 97 B10
Uvdal N 95 B9
Üvecik TR 171 E10
Uvernet-Fours F 36 C5
Uv'jaršto N 113 D12
Uxbridge GB 15 D8
Uxeau F 30 B5
Üxheim D 21 D7
Uyeasound GB 3 D15
Uza F 32 B3
Užava LV 134 B2
Uzdin SRB 158 C6
Uzel F 22 D6
Uzer F 35 A7
Uzerche F 29 E9
Uzès F 35 B7
Uzhhorod UA 145 F5
Uzhok UA 145 F6
Užice SRB 158 F4
Uzlovoye RUS 136 D5
Uznovë AL 168 C2
Užpaliai LT 135 E11
Uzrechcha BY 133 F3
Uzundzhovo BG 166 F5
Uzunköprü TR 172 B6
Uzunkuyu TR 177 C8
Užventis LT 134 E5

V

Vaadinselkä FIN 115 E5
Vaajakoski FIN 123 F15
Vaajasalmi FIN 124 E7
Vääkiö FIN 121 D12
Vaala FIN 119 E17
Vaalajärvi FIN 117 D16
Vaale D 82 C6
Vaalimaa FIN 128 D8
Vaals NL 20 C6
Vaarakylä FIN 121 C11
Vaarankylä FIN 121 F10
Vaaranniva FIN 121 D11
Vaaraperä FIN 121 C13
Vaaraslahti FIN 123 D17
Väärinmaja FIN 124 G2
Vaas F 24 E3
Vaasa FIN 122 D7
Vaassen NL 16 D5
Väätäiskylä FIN 123 E13
Väätsa EST 131 D10
Vaattojärvi FIN 117 D12
Vabalninkas LT 135 E9
Vabole LV 135 D12
Vabre F 33 C10
Vabres-l'Abbaye F 34 C4
Vác H 150 B3
Văcărești RO 161 D6
Vaccarizzo Albanese I 61 D6
Váchartyán H 150 B3
Vacheresse F 31 C10
Vachlia GR 174 D4
Väckelsång S 89 B7
Vacov CZ 76 D5
Vacqueyras F 35 B8
Vácrátót H 150 B3
Văculești RO 153 B8
Vad RO 152 C3
Vad S 97 B14
Vadakste LV 134 D5
Vadaktai LT 135 E7
Vădastra RO 160 F4
Vădăstrița RO 160 F4
Vaddas gruver N 112 D8
Vădeni RO 155 C1
Väderstad S 92 C5
Vad Foss N 90 B5
Vadheim N 100 D3
Vadla N 94 D4
Vadocondes E 40 E4
Vadokliai LT 135 F8
Vado Ligure I 37 C8
Vadskinn N 111 C11
Vadsø N 114 C7
Vadstena S 92 C5
Vadu Crișului RO 151 D10
Vadu lui Isac MD 155 B2
Vadu Izei RO 145 H8
Vadul lui Vodă MD 154 C4
Vadul Turcului MD 154 B3
Vadum DK 86 A5
Vadu Moldovei RO 153 C8
Vadu Motilor RO 151 E10
Vadu Pașii RO 161 C9
Vaduz FL 71 C9
Vadžgirys LT 134 F5
Væggerløse DK 83 A11
Vafaiika GR 171 B7
Vafiochori GR 169 B8
Våg N 94 D2
Vågaholmen N 108 C5
Vågåmo N 101 C10
Vagan BIH 157 D6
Vågan N 111 B14
Vågdalen S 106 D9
Våge N 94 B3
Våge N 94 G6
Vaggatem N 114 E6
Vaggeryd S 92 E4
Våghølmane N 100 A4
Vagia GR 175 C7
Văgiulești RO 159 D11
Vaglia I 66 E3
Vaglio Basilicata I 60 B5
Vagli Sotto I 66 D1
Vagney F 26 D6
Vagnhärad S 93 B11
Vagnsunda S 99 C11
Vagos P 44 C3
Vågseidet N 100 E2
Vågsele S 107 B14
Vågsodden N 108 E3
Vágur FO 2 C3
Vähäjoki FIN 119 B14
Vähäkangas FIN 123 B13
Vähäkyrö FIN 122 D8
Vähäniva FIN 116 B9
Vahanka FIN 123 E13
Vahastu EST 131 D10
Vahenurme EST 131 D8
Vähikkälä FIN 127 D12
Vahojärvi FIN 127 B9
Váhovce SK 146 E5
Vahterpää FIN 127 E15
Vahto FIN 126 D7
Vaiamonte P 44 F6
Vaiano I 66 E3
Vaickūniškės LT 137 D10
Vaida EST 131 C9
Vaidava LV 135 B10
Vaideeni RO 160 C3
Vaidotai LT 137 D11
Vaiges F 23 D11
Vaiguva LT 134 E5
Väike-Maarja EST 131 C12
Väike-Pungerja EST 131 C14
Vaikijaur S 116 E3
Vaikko FIN 125 D11
Vailly-sur-Aisne F 19 F8
Vailly-sur-Sauldre F 25 F8
Vaimastvere EST 131 D12
Väimela EST 131 F14
Vaimõisa EST 131 D8
Vainikkala FIN 129 D9
Vainode LV 134 D3
Vainotiškiai LT 134 F7
Vainupea EST 131 B12
Vairano Patenora I 60 A2
Vairano Scalo I 60 A2
Väisälä FIN 121 E11
Vaison-la-Romaine F 35 B9
Vaïssac F 33 B9
Vaišvydava LT 137 D9
Vaivio FIN 125 E12
Vaivre-et-Montoille F 26 E5
Vaja H 145 H5
Vajangu EST 131 C12
Vajdácska H 145 G4
Våje N 90 B4
Våje N 110 D5
Vajkal AL 168 A3
Vajmat S 109 C18
Vajska SRB 157 B11
Vajszló H 149 E9
Vajta H 149 C11
Vakarel BG 165 D8
Vakern S 97 B11
Vakıflar TR 173 B8
Vaklino BG 155 F2
Vaksdal N 94 B3
Vaksevo BG 165 E6
Vaksince MK 164 E4
Vál H 149 B11
Valada P 44 F3
Vålådalen S 105 E13
Valadares P 38 D3
Valajanaapa FIN 119 C15
Valajaskoski FIN 119 B14
Valaliky SK 145 F3
Valand N 90 C2
Valandovo MK 169 B8
Vålånger S 103 A14
Valanida GR 169 E7
Valanjou F 23 F10
Valareña E 41 D9
Vålåsjø N 101 B10
Valaská SK 147 D9
Valaská Belá SK 146 D6
Valašská Bystřice CZ 146 C6
Valašská Polanka CZ 146 C5
Valašské Klobouky CZ 146 C6
Valašské Meziříčí CZ 146 C5
Välax FIN 127 E14
Valberg F 36 C5
Valberg N 110 D6
Vålberg S 97 D9
Valbiska HR 67 B9
Valbo S 103 E13
Valbom P 44 B3
Valbona E 48 D3
Valbondione I 69 A9
Valbonë AL 163 E8
Valbonnais F 31 F8
Valbonne F 36 D6
Valbuena de Duero E 40 E3
Valča SK 147 C7
Valcabrère F 33 D7
Valcău de Jos RO 151 C10
Vâlcele RO 153 F7
Vâlcele RO 160 E5
Vâlcelele RO 161 C10
Vâlcelele RO 161 E10
Valdagno I 69 B11
Valdahon F 26 F5
Valdaora I 72 C5
Valddak N 113 C14
Valdealgorfa E 42 E3
Valdeblore F 37 C6
Valdecaballeros E 45 F10
Valdecañas de Tajo E 45 E9
Valdecarros E 45 C10
Valdecilla E 40 B4
Valdecuenca E 47 D10
Valdefuentes E 45 F8
Valdeganga E 47 F9
Valdekļ LV 134 C5
Valdelacasa E 45 C9
Valdelacasa de Tajo E 45 E10
Valdelamusa E 51 D6
Valdelinares E 48 D3
Valdemanco del Esteras E 54 B3
Valdemärpils LV 134 B5
Valdemarsvik S 93 C9
Valdemeca E 47 D9
Valdemorillo E 46 C4
Valdemoro E 46 D5
Valdemoro-Sierra E 47 D9
Valdenoches E 47 C6
Valdeobispo E 45 D8
Valdeolivas E 47 C8
Valdepeñas E 55 B6
Valdepeñas de Jaén E 53 A9
Valderas E 39 D9
Val-de-Reuil F 18 F3
Valderice I 58 C2
Valderiès F 33 B10
Valderøy N 100 A4
Valderrobres E 42 F4
Val de San Domingo E 46 D4
Valdestillas E 39 F10
Valdetormo E 42 F4
Valdetorres E 51 B7
Valdeverdeja E 45 E10
Valdevimbre E 39 D8
Valdgale LV 134 B5
Valdice CZ 77 B8
Valdidentro I 71 E10
Valdilecha E 47 D6
Val-d'Isère F 31 E10
Valdisotto I 71 E10
Valdivienne F 29 B7
Val-d'Izé F 23 D9
Valdobbiadene I 72 E4
Valdoie F 27 E6
Valdunquillo E 39 D9
Vale GBG 22 B6
Våle N 95 D12
Våle S 103 A8
Valea Adîncă MD 154 A3
Valea Argovei RO 161 E9
Valea Călugărească RO 161 D8
Valea Chioarului RO 151 C11
Valea Ciorii RO 161 D11
Valea Crișului RO 153 F7
Valea Danului RO 160 C5
Valea Doftanei RO 161 C7
Valea Dragului RO 161 E8
Valea Ierii RO 151 D11
Valea Largă RO 152 D4
Valea lui Mihai RO 151 B9
Valea Lungă RO 152 E4
Valea Lungă RO 161 C7
Valea Măcrișului RO 161 D9
Valea Mare MD 153 C11
Valea Mare RO 160 D3
Valea Mare RO 160 D6
Valea Mare RO 160 E4
Valea Mare-Pravăț RO 160 C6
Valea Mărului RO 153 F11
Valea Moldovei RO 153 C8
Valea Nucarilor RO 155 C3
Valea Râmnicului RO 161 C10
Valea Salciei RO 161 C9
Valea Sării RO 153 F9
Valea Seacă RO 153 C9
Valea Seacă RO 153 E10
Valea Stanciului RO 160 F3
Valea Teilor RO 155 C3
Valea Ursului RO 153 D10
Valea Viilor RO 152 E4
Valea Vinului RO 151 B11
Vale da Rosa P 50 E4
Vale das Mós P 44 F4
Vale de Açor P 44 F5
Vale de Açor P 50 D4
Vale de Cambra P 44 C4
Vale de Cavalos P 44 F3
Vale de Espinho P 45 D7
Vale de Estrela P 45 C6
Vale de Figueira P 44 F3
Vale de Lobo P 50 E3
Vale de Prazeres P 44 D6
Vale de Reis P 50 C3
Vale de Salgueiro P 38 E5
Vale de Santarém P 44 F3
Vale do Peso P 44 F5
Válega P 44 C3
Valeggio sul Mincio I 66 B2
Valen N 94 C3
Valença P 38 D2
Valença do Douro P 44 B5
Valençay F 24 F6
Valence F 30 F6
Valence F 33 B7
Valence-d'Albigeois F 33 B10
Valence-sur-Baïse F 33 C6
Valencia E 48 F4
Valencia de Alcántara E 45 F6
Valencia de Don Juan E 39 D8
Valencia de las Torres E 51 C7
Valencia del Mombuey E 51 C5
Valencia del Ventoso E 51 C7
Valenciennes F 19 D8
Văleni RO 153 D11
Văleni RO 160 E5
Vălenii de Munte RO 161 C8
Valensole F 35 C10
Valentano I 62 B1
Valentigney F 27 F6
Valenza I 37 A9
Valenzano I 61 A7
Valenzuela E 53 A8
Valenzuela de Calatrava E 54 B5
Våler N 95 D13
Våler N 101 E15
Valera de Arriba E 47 E8
Valernes F 35 B10
Vales Mortos P 50 D5
Valestrand N 94 A2
Valevåg N 94 C2
Valfabbrica I 66 F6
Valfarta E 42 D3
Valfroicourt F 26 D5
Valfurva I 71 E10
Valga EST 131 F12
Valgalciems LV 134 B5
Valgale LV 134 B4
Valgrisenche I 31 D11
Valgu EST 131 D9
Valguarnera Caropepe I 58 E5
Valgunde LV 134 C7
Valhelhas P 44 D6
Valhermoso E 47 C9
Vålhovd N 101 E12
Välijoki FIN 119 B15
Välikangas FIN 119 B16
Väli-Kannus FIN 123 C11
Valikardhë AL 168 A3
Välikylä FIN 123 C11
Valimi GR 174 C5
Välitalo FIN 117 C16
Väliug RO 159 C9
Väli-Viirre FIN 123 C11
Valjala EST 130 E5
Valjevo SRB 158 E4
Valjok N 113 D16
Valjunquera E 42 F4
Valka LV 131 F12
Valkeajärvi FIN 123 F12
Valkeakoski FIN 127 C11
Valkeakoski S 117 E11
Valkeala FIN 128 D6
Valkeiskylä FIN 124 C8
Valkeiskylä FIN 125 D10
Valkenburg NL 19 C12
Valkenswaard NL 16 F4
Valkininkai LT 137 E10
Valkla EST 131 C10
Valko FIN 127 E15
Valkó H 150 B4
Valla S 93 A8
Valla S 107 E10
Valladolid E 39 E10
Valladolises E 56 F2
Vållaj H 151 B9
Vallåkra S 87 D11
Vallargärdet S 97 D10
Vallata I 60 A4
Vallauris F 36 D6
Vallberga S 87 C12
Vallbo S 105 E14
Vallbona d'Anoia E 43 D7
Vallda S 91 E10
Valldal N 100 B6
Vall d'Alba E 48 D4
Valldemossa E 49 E10
Valle E 40 B3
Valle LV 135 C9
Valle N 90 A2
Valle N 90 B6
Valle N 108 B6
Valle Castellana I 62 B5
Vallecorsa I 62 E4
Valle de Abdalajís E 53 C7
Valle de la Serena E 51 B8
Valle de Matamoros E 51 C6
Valle de Santa Ana E 51 C6
Valle di Cadore I 72 D5
Valledolmo I 58 D4
Valledoria I 64 B2
Valleiry F 31 C8
Vallelunga Pratameno I 58 D4
Valle Mosso I 68 B5
Vallen S 107 D11
Vallen S 118 F6
Vallenca E 47 D10
Vallendar D 185 D8
Vallentuna S 99 C10
Vallerås S 102 E6
Valleraugue F 35 B6
Vallermosa I 64 E2
Vallerotonda I 62 D5
Vallersund N 104 D7
Vallervatnet N 105 B15
Vallet F 23 F9
Valley D 72 A4
Valley GB 10 E2
Vallfogona de Riucorb E 42 D6
Vallières F 29 D10
Vallioniemi FIN 121 B12
Vallmoll E 42 E6
Valløby DK 87 E10
Vallo della Lucania I 60 C4
Vallo di Nera I 62 B3
Valloire F 31 E9
Vallombrosa I 66 E4
Vallon-en-Sully F 29 B11
Vallon-Pont-d'Arc F 35 B7
Vallorbe CH 31 B9
Vallorcine F 31 C10
Vallouise F 31 F9
Vallrun S 105 D16
Valls E 42 E6
Vallsbo S 103 E12
Vallsjön S 103 A11
Vallsta S 103 C11
Vallstena S 93 D13
Vallvik S 103 D13
Valmadrera I 69 B7
Valmadrid E 41 F10
Valmen N 101 D15
Valmiera LV 131 F10
Valmiermuiža LV 131 F10
Valmojado E 46 D4
Valmont F 18 E2
Valmontone I 62 D3
Valmorel F 31 E9
Valmy F 25 B12
Valnes N 108 B7
Valognes F 23 A9
Valongo P 44 B4
Valongo P 44 F5
Valor E 55 F6
Valoria la Buena E 40 E2
Valøy N 105 B9
Valøy N 105 C11
Valpaços P 38 E5
Valpalmas E 41 D10
Valpelline I 31 D11
Valperga I 68 C4
Valpovo HR 149 E10
Valpperi FIN 126 D7
Valras-Plage F 34 D5
Valréas F 35 B8
Valros F 34 D5
Vals CH 71 D8
Valsavarenche I 31 D11
Valse DK 87 F9
Valseca E 46 B4
Valsequillo E 51 C9
Valsgård DK 86 B5
Valsgarth GB 3 D15
Valshed S 103 E9
Valsinni I 61 C6
Valsjöbyn S 105 C16
Valsjön S 103 B11
Valška SRB 158 E6
Valskog S 97 D14
Vals-les-Bains F 35 A7
Valsøybotn N 104 E5
Välsta S 103 C13
Valstagna I 72 E4
Val-Suzon F 26 F2
Valtablado del Río E 47 C8
Valtero GR 169 B9
Valtesiniko GR 174 D5
Valtice CZ 77 E11
Valtiendas E 40 F4
Valtierra E 41 D8
Valtimo FIN 125 C11
Valtola FIN 128 C7
Valtopina I 62 A3
Valtos GR 171 A10
Valtotopi GR 169 C10
Valtournenche I 68 B4
Valtura HR 67 C8
Valu lui Traian RO 155 E2
Valun HR 67 C9
Väluste EST 131 E11
Valverde de Burguillos E 51 C6
Valverde de Júcar E 47 E8
Valverde de la Virgen E 39 C8
Valverde del Camino E 51 D6
Valverde de Leganés E 51 B6
Valverde del Fresno E 45 D7
Valverde de Llerena E 51 C8
Valverde del Majano E 46 C4
Valverde de Mérida E 51 B7
Valvika N 108 B8
Valvträsk S 118 B7
Valyra GR 174 E4
Vama RO 145 H7
Vama RO 153 B7
Vama Buzăului RO 161 B7
Vamberk CZ 77 B10
Vamdrup DK 86 E4
Vămhus S 102 D7
Vamlingbo S 93 F12
Vammala FIN 127 C8
Vammen DK 86 B5
Vamos GR 178 E7
Vámosmikola H 147 F7
Vámospércs H 151 B8
Vámosújfalu H 145 G3
Vampula FIN 126 C8
Vamvakofyto GR 169 B9
Vamvakou GR 169 F7
Vanaja FIN 127 D12
Vana-Koiola EST 131 F14
Vânători RO 152 E5
Vânători RO 153 C9
Vânători RO 153 F10
Vânători RO 155 B2
Vânători RO 159 E10
Vânătorii Mici RO 161 E7
Vânători-Neamț RO 153 C8
Vanault-les-Dames F 25 C12
Vana-Vigala EST 131 D8
Vana-Võidu EST 131 E11
Váncsod H 151 C8
Vanda FIN 127 E12
Vandel DK 86 D4
Vandellós E 42 E5
Vandenesse F 30 B4
Vandenesse-en-Auxois F 25 F12
Vandœvre-lès-Nancy F 186 D1
Vandoies I 72 C4
Vändra EST 131 D10
Vändträsk S 118 C6
Vandzene LV 134 B5
Vandžiogala LT 135 F7
Vāne LV 134 C5
Väne-Åsaka S 91 C11
Vänersborg S 91 C11
Vañes E 40 C3
Vang N 101 D9
Vånga S 92 B7
Vangaži LV 135 B9
Vänge S 93 E13
Vängel S 107 D10
Vangshamn N 111 B15
Vangshylla N 105 D10
Vangsnes N 100 D5
Vangsvik N 111 B14
Vanha-Kihlanki FIN 117 C10
Vanhakylä FIN 122 F7
Vänjaurbäck S 107 C15
Vänjaurträsk S 107 C15
Vânjuleț RO 159 E10
Vânju Mare RO 159 E10
Vannareid N 112 C4
Vännäs S 122 C3
Vännäsberget S 118 B9
Vännäsby S 122 C3
Vannavalen N 112 C4
Vånne N 90 B2
Vannes F 22 E6
Vannvåg N 112 C4
Vannvikan N 104 D8
Vänö FIN 126 F7
Vansbro S 97 A11
Vanse N 94 F5
Vänsjö S 103 C9
Vantaa FIN 127 E12
Vanttausjärvi FIN 119 B17
Vanttauskoski FIN 119 B17
Vanvey F 25 E12
Vanyarc H 147 F8
Vanzone I 68 B5
Vaour F 33 B9
Vápenná CZ 77 B12
Vaplan S 105 E16
Vaqueiros P 50 E4
Vara EST 131 D13
Vara S 91 C12
Vara del Rey E 47 F8
Varades F 23 F9
Vărădia RO 159 C8
Vărădia de Mureș RO 151 E9
Varages F 35 C10
Varaire F 33 B9
Varajärvi FIN 119 B13
Varajoki FIN 121 F14
Varakļāni LV 135 C13
Varallo I 68 B5
Varangerbotn N 114 C5
Varano de'Melegari I 69 D8
Varapayeva BY 133 F2
Varapodio I 59 C8
Vărăști RO 161 E8
Văratec RO 153 C8
Varaždin HR 149 D6
Varaždinske Toplice HR 149 D6
Varazze I 37 C9
Varberg S 87 A10
Vărbilău RO 161 C7
Varbla EST 130 E7
Varbó H 145 G2
Varbola EST 131 C8
Varces-Allières-et-Risset F 31 E8
Vărciorog RO 151 D9
Varda GR 174 C3
Vardali GR 174 A5
Varde DK 86 D2
Vardim BG 161 F6
Vardište BIH 158 F3
Vårdö FIN 99 B14
Vardø N 114 C10
Vårdomb H 149 D11
Varejoki FIN 119 B13
Varekil S 91 C10
Varel D 17 B10
Varėna LT 137 E10
Varengeville-sur-Mer F 18 E2
Varenna I 69 A7
Varennes-en-Argonne F 19 F11
Varennes-St-Sauveur F 31 C7
Varennes-sur-Allier F 30 C3
Varennes-Vauzelles F 30 A3
Vareš BIH 157 D9
Varese I 69 B6
Varese Ligure I 37 C11
Varetz F 29 E8
Vârfu Câmpului RO 153 B8
Vârfuri RO 161 C7
Vârfurile RO 151 E10
Vårgårda S 91 C12
Vărgata RO 152 D5
Vărghiș RO 153 E7
Vargön S 91 C11
Vargträsk S 107 C15
Varhaug N 94 E3
Vari GR 175 D8
Vari GR 176 E4
Variaș RO 151 E6
Varik NL 183 B6
Variku EST 130 C7
Varilhes F 33 D9
Varimbombi GR 175 C8
Varín SK 147 C7
Våring S 91 B14
Variņi LV 135 B12
Variskylä FIN 121 F9
Varislahti FIN 125 E11
Varistaipale FIN 125 E11
Varjakka FIN 119 E14
Varjisträsk S 109 D18
Varkaliai LT 134 E3
Varkaus FIN 125 F9
Värkava LV 135 D13
Varkhi BY 133 E7
Várlezi RO 153 F11
Varlosen (Niemetal) D 78 D6
Vārme LV 134 C4
Värmlandsbro S 91 A13
Varna BG 167 C9
Varna I 72 C4
Varna SRB 158 D4
Värnamo S 88 A6
Värnäs S 97 B9
Varnavas GR 175 C8
Varnhem S 91 C14
Varniai LT 134 E4
Varnja EST 131 E14
Varnsdorf CZ 81 E7
Varntresken N 108 E7
Varnyany BY 137 D13
Väröbacka S 87 A10

Viişoara RO 153 A9
Viişoara RO 153 D8
Viisoara RO 153 E11
Viişoara RO 160 F6
Viitaila FIN 127 C13
Viitala FIN 123 E10
Viitamäki FIN 123 C16
Viitaniemi FIN 125 D10
Viitapohja FIN 127 B11
Viitaranta FIN 115 D3
Viitaranta FIN 121 B12
Viitasaari FIN 123 D15
Viitavaara FIN 121 E13
Viitavaara FIN 121 F12
Viitka EST 132 F1
Viitna EST 131 C12
Viivikonna EST 132 C2
Vijciems LV 131 F11
Vik N 90 C4
Vik N 94 B2
Vik N 108 B9
Vik N 108 F3
Vik N 110 D7
Vik S 88 D6
Vika FIN 117 E16
Vika N 101 A15
Vika S 97 A14
Vikajärvi FIN 117 E16
Vikan N 104 E5
Vikan N 105 B10
Vikarbyn S 97 B15
Vikarbyn S 103 E9
Vikartovce SK 145 F1
Vikbyn S 97 B15
Vike N 100 E3
Vike S 103 A12
Vikebukt N 100 A6
Vikedal N 94 D3
Viken S 87 C11
Viken S 103 B9
Viken S 103 B11
Vikersund N 95 C11
Vikesâ N 94 E4
Vikevåg N 94 D3
Vikholmen N 108 D4
Viķi LV 131 F9
Vikingstad S 92 C6
Vikmanshyttan S 97 B14
Vikna N 105 B9
Vikoč BIH 157 F10
Vikøyri N 100 D5
Vikran N 111 A16
Vikran N 111 C12
Vikran N 113 A12
Viksberg S 97 B14
Viksjö S 103 A13
Viksjöfors S 103 D10
Viksmon S 107 E12
Vīksna LV 133 B2
Viktarinas LT 137 E8
Vikten N 110 D5
Viktorivka UA 154 C6
Vikýřovice CZ 77 C11
Vila E 38 E3
Vila Boa P 45 D7
Vila Boa do Bispo P 44 B4
Vila Caiz P 38 F3
Vila Chã de Sá P 44 C5
Vila Cova da Lixa P 38 F3
Vilada E 43 C7
Viladamat E 43 C10
Vila da Ponte P 38 E4
Viladecans E 43 E8
Vila de Cruces E 38 C3
Vila de Frades P 50 C4
Vila de Rei P 44 E4
Vila do Bispo P 50 E2
Vila do Conde P 38 F2
Viladrau E 43 D8
Vilafamés E 48 D4
Vilafant E 43 C9
Vila Fernando P 51 B5
Vila Flor P 38 F5
Vila Franca das Naves P 45 C6
Vilafranca de Bonany E 57 B11
Vilafranca del Penedès E 43 E7
Vila Franca de Xira P 50 B2
Vilagarcía de Arousa E 38 C2
Vilajuïga E 34 F5
Viļaka LV 133 B3
Vilalba E 38 B4
Vilallonga E 33 F10
Vilamartín E 38 D5
Vilamarxant E 48 E3
Vilamoura P 50 E3
Viļāni LV 133 C1
Vila Nogueira de Azeitão P 50 B1
Vilanova E 38 B5
Vila Nova da Baronia P 50 C3
Vila Nova da Barquinha P 44 F4
Vilanova d'Alcolea E 48 D5
Vilanova de Arousa E 38 C2
Vila Nova de Cacela P 50 E4
Vila Nova de Famalicão P 38 F2
Vila Nova de Foz Coa P 45 B6
Vila Nova de Gaia P 44 B3
Vilanova de la Barca E 42 D5
Vilanova de L'Aguda E 42 D6
Vilanova de Meià E 42 D6
Vila Nova de Paiva P 44 C5
Vila Nova de Poiares P 44 D4
Vilanova de Prades E 42 E5
Vila Nova de São Bento P 50 D5
Vilanova de Sau E 43 D8
Vilanova i la Geltrú E 43 E7
Vila Pouca da Beira P 44 D5
Vila Pouca de Aguiar P 38 E4
Vila Praia de Âncora P 38 E2
Vilar P 38 E3
Vilar P 44 F2
Vilarandelo P 38 E5
Vilarchao E 38 D4
Vilar da Veiga P 38 E3
Vilar de Andorinho P 44 B3
Vilar de Barrio E 38 D4
Vilar de Santos E 38 D4
Vilardevós E 38 E5
Vila Real P 38 F4
Vila Real de Santo António P 50 E5
Vilarelho da Raia P 38 E5
Vilar Formoso P 45 C7
Vilarinho da Castanheira P 45 B6
Vilarinho do Bairro P 44 D3
Vilariño de Conso E 38 D5
Vila-rodona E 43 E6
Vila Ruiva P 50 C4
Vila Seca P 38 E2
Vilaseca de Solcina E 42 E6
Vilassar de Mar E 43 D8
Vilasund S 108 D8
Vila Velha de Ródão P 44 E5
Vila Verde P 38 E3
Vila Verde P 38 F4
Vila Verde P 44 D3
Vila Verde da Raia P 38 E5
Vila Verde de Ficalho P 51 D5
Vila Viçosa P 50 B5
Vilce LV 134 D7
Vilches E 55 C6
Vildbjerg DK 86 C3
Vilémov CZ 77 C9
Vilgāle LV 134 C3
Vilhelmina S 107 B11
Vilia GR 175 C7
Viljakkala FIN 127 B9
Viljandi EST 131 E11
Viljevo HR 149 E10
Viljolahti FIN 125 F10
Vilkaviškis LT 136 D7
Vilkene LV 131 F9
Vilkija LT 137 C8
Vilkjärvi FIN 128 D8
Vilkyškiai LT 134 F4
Villa Bartolomea I 66 B3
Villabate I 58 C3
Villablanca E 51 E5
Villablino E 39 C7
Villabona E 32 D1
Villabrágima E 39 E9
Villabuena del Puente E 39 F9
Villac F 29 E8
Villacañas E 46 E6
Villa Carcina I 69 B9
Villacarriedo E 40 B4
Villacarrillo E 55 C6
Villa Castelli I 61 B8
Villacastín E 46 C4
Villach A 73 C8
Villacidro I 64 E2
Villaciervos E 41 E6
Villaconejos E 46 D6
Villaconejos de Trabaque E 47 D8
Villada E 39 D10
Villa d'Almè I 69 B8
Villa del Prado E 46 D4
Villa del Río E 53 A8
Villadepera E 39 E7
Villa de Ves E 47 F10
Villadiego E 40 C3
Villadose I 66 B4
Villadossola I 68 A5
Villaeles de Valdavia E 39 C10
Villaescusa de Haro E 47 E7
Villaescusa la Sombría E 40 D5
Villafáfila E 39 E8
Villafeliche E 47 B10
Villaflores E 45 B10
Villafranca d'Asti I 37 B8
Villafranca de Córdoba E 53 A7
Villafranca de Ebro E 41 E10
Villafranca del Bierzo E 39 C6
Villafranca del Campo E 47 C10
Villafranca del Cid E 48 D4
Villafranca de los Barros E 51 B7
Villafranca de los Caballeros E 46 F6
Villafranca di Verona I 66 B2
Villafranca in Lunigiana I 69 E8
Villafranca-Montes de Oca E 40 D5
Villafranca Tirrena I 59 C7
Villafranco del Guadalquivir E 51 E7
Villafrati I 58 D3
Villafrechos E 39 E9
Villafruela E 40 E4
Villafuerte E 40 E3
Villagarcía de Campos E 39 E9
Villagarcía de la Torre E 51 C7
Villagarcía del Llano E 47 F9
Villagio Mancuso I 59 A10
Villagonzalo E 51 B7
Villagrande Strisaili I 64 D4
Villaharta E 54 C3
Villähde FIN 127 D14
Villahermosa E 55 B7
Villahermosa del Campo E 47 B10
Villahermosa del Río E 48 D4
Villaherreros E 40 D3
Villahizán E 40 D4
Villahoz E 40 D4
Villaines-en-Duesmois F 25 E12
Villaines-la-Juhel F 23 D11
Villajoyosa E 56 D4
Villala FIN 125 F13
Villala FIN 129 D9
Villa Lagarina I 69 B11
Villalago I 62 D5
Villalar de los Comuneros E 39 E9
Villa Latina I 62 D5
Villalba I 58 D4
Villalba de Duero E 40 E4
Villalba de Guardo E 39 C10
Villalba del Alcor E 51 E7
Villalba de la Sierra E 47 D8
Villalba de los Alcores E 39 E10
Villalba de los Barros E 51 B6
Villalba del Rey E 47 D7
Villalba dels Arcs E 42 E4
Villalba de Rioja E 40 C6
Villalcampo E 39 E7
Villalcázar de Sirga E 40 D2
Villalengua E 41 F8
Villalgordo del Júcar E 47 F8
Villa Literno I 60 A2
Villalobos E 39 E9
Villalón de Campos E 39 D9
Villalonga E 56 D4
Villalpando E 39 E9
Villalpardo E 47 F9
Villaluenga de la Sagra E 46 D5
Villalumbroso E 39 D10
Villamalea E 47 F9
Villamañán E 39 D8
Villamandos E 39 D8
Villamanrique E 55 B7
Villamanrique de la Condesa E 51 E7
Villamanta E 46 D4
Villamar I 64 D2
Villamartín E 51 F8
Villamartín de Campos E 39 D10
Villamassargia I 64 E2
Villamayor E 45 C9
Villamayor de Calatrava E 54 B4
Villamayor de Campos E 39 E9
Villamayor de Santiago E 47 E7
Villamayor de Treviño E 40 D3
Villamblard F 29 E7
Villamediana E 40 D3
Villamediana de Iregua E 32 F1
Villamejil E 39 C7
Villamesías E 45 F9
Villamiel E 45 D7
Villa Minozzo I 66 D1
Villamo FIN 122 F7
Villamor de los Escuderos E 39 F8
Villamuelas E 46 E5
Villamuriel de Cerrato E 40 E3
Villandraut F 32 B5
Villanova I 61 B9
Villanova d'Albenga I 37 C8
Villanova d'Asti I 37 B7
Villanova del Battista I 60 A4
Villanovafranca I 64 D3
Villanova Monferrato I 68 C5
Villanova Monteleone I 64 B1
Villanova Truschedu I 64 D2
Villanova Tulo I 64 D3
Villanterio I 69 C7
Villanúa E 32 E4
Villanubla E 39 E10
Villanueva de Alcardete E 47 E6
Villanueva de Alcorón E 47 C8
Villanueva de Algaidas E 53 B8
Villanueva de Argaño E 40 D4
Villanueva de Bogas E 46 E5
Villanueva de Cameros E 41 D6
Villanueva de Castellón E 56 C4
Villanueva de Córdoba E 54 C3
Villanueva de Gállego E 41 E10
Villanueva de Gómez E 46 C3
Villanueva de la Cañada E 46 D5
Villanueva de la Concepción E 53 C7
Villanueva de la Fuente E 55 B7
Villanueva de la Jara E 47 F9
Villanueva de la Reina E 53 A9
Villanueva del Arzobispo E 55 C6
Villanueva de las Cruces E 51 D5
Villanueva de la Serena E 51 B8
Villanueva de la Sierra E 45 D8
Villanueva de las Torres E 55 D6
Villanueva de la Vera E 45 D10
Villanueva del Campo E 39 E9
Villanueva del Duque E 54 C3
Villanueva del Fresno E 51 C5
Villanueva de los Castillejos E 51 D5
Villanueva de los Infantes E 55 B7
Villanueva del Rey E 51 C9
Villanueva del Río Segura E 55 C10
Villanueva del Río y Minas E 51 D8
Villanueva del Rosario E 53 C8
Villanueva del Trabuco E 53 B8
Villanueva de Mesía E 53 B8
Villanueva de San Carlos E 54 B5
Villanueva de San Juan E 51 E9
Villanueva de Tapia E 53 B8
Villanueva de Valdegovia E 40 C5
Villanuño de Valdavia E 40 C2
Villány H 149 E10
Villa Opicina I 73 E8
Villapalacios E 55 B7
Villaperuccio I 64 E2
Villapiana I 61 D6
Villapiana Lido I 61 D6
Villa Poma I 66 C3
Villapourçon F 30 B4
Villaputzu I 64 E4
Villaquejida E 39 D8
Villaquilambre E 39 C8
Villaralbo E 39 F8
Villaralto E 54 C3
Villarcayo E 40 C4
Villard-Bonnot F 31 E8
Villard-de-Lans F 31 E8
Villar de Cañas E 47 E7
Villar de Chinchilla E 55 B9
Villar de Ciervo E 45 C7
Villardeciervos E 39 E7
Villardefrades E 39 E9
Villar del Arzobispo E 48 E3
Villar de la Yegua E 45 C7
Villar del Buey E 39 F7
Villar del Cobo E 47 D9
Villar del Humo E 47 E9
Villar de los Barrios E 39 C6
Villar de los Navarros E 42 E1
Villar del Pedroso E 45 E10
Villar del Rey E 45 F7
Villar del Salz E 47 C10
Villar de Olalla E 47 D8
Villar de Peralonso E 45 B8
Villar de Rena E 45 F9
Villar de Torre E 40 D6
Villardompardo E 53 A8
Villareal E 48 E4
Villarejo de Fuentes E 47 E7
Villarejo de Montalbán E 46 E3
Villarejo de Orbigo E 39 D8
Villarejo de Salvanés E 47 D6
Villa Rendena I 69 A10
Villarente E 39 C9
Villares de la Reina E 45 B9
Villargordo E 53 A9
Villargordo del Cabriel E 47 E10
Villarino de los Aires E 39 F7
Villarluengo E 42 F2
Villarosa I 58 D5
Villarquemado E 47 C10
Villarramiel E 39 D10
Villarrasa E 51 E6
Villarreal de Huerva E 47 B10
Villarrín de Campos E 39 E8
Villarrobledo E 47 F7
Villarrodrigo E 55 C7
Villarroya de la Sierra E 41 F8
Villarroya de los Pinares E 42 F2
Villarrubia de los Ojos E 46 F5
Villarrubia de Santiago E 46 E6
Villarrubio E 47 E7
Villars F 29 E7
Villars F 30 E5
Villars-Colmars F 36 C5
Villars del Saz E 47 E8
Villars-les-Dombes F 31 D7
Villars-sur-Var F 36 D6
Villar-St-Pancrace F 31 F10
Villarta E 47 F9
Villarta de los Montes E 46 F3
Villarta de San Juan E 46 F6
Villasalto I 64 E3
Villasana de Mena E 40 B5
Villasandino E 40 D3
Villa San Giovanni I 59 C8
Villa San Pietro I 64 E3
Villa Santa Maria I 63 D6
Villasante de Montija E 40 B5
Villa Santina I 73 D6
Villasarracino E 40 D3
Villasavary F 33 D10
Villasayas E 41 F6
Villasbuenas E 45 B7
Villasdardo E 45 B8
Villaseca de Laciana E 39 C7
Villaseca de la Sagra E 46 E5
Villaseco de los Gamitos E 45 B8
Villaseco de los Reyes E 45 B8
Villaseco del Pan E 39 F8
Villasequilla de Yepes E 46 E5
Villasimius I 64 E4
Villasmundo I 59 E7
Villasor I 64 E2
Villaspeciosa I 64 E2
Villasrubias E 45 D7
Villastar E 47 D10
Villasur de Herreros E 40 D5
Villatobas E 46 E6
Villatoro E 45 C10
Villatoya E 47 F10
Villatuerta E 32 E2
Villaturiel E 39 C9
Villaumbrales E 39 D10
Villaurbana I 64 D2
Villava E 32 E2
Villavallelonga I 62 D5
Villavelayo E 40 D6
Villaverde de Guadalimar E 55 C7
Villaverde del Río E 51 D8
Villaverde y Pasaconsol E 47 E8
Villavernia I 37 B9
Villaviciosa E 39 B9
Villaviciosa de Córdoba E 54 C2
Villaviciosa de Odón E 46 D5
Villavieja E 48 E4
Villavieja de Yeltes E 45 C8
Villaviudas E 40 E3
Villayón E 39 B6
Villazanzo de Valderaduey E 39 C10
Villé F 27 D7
Villebois-Lavalette F 29 E6
Villebrumier F 33 C8
Villecomtal-sur-Arros F 33 D6
Villecomte F 26 E3
Villecroze F 36 D4
Villedaigne F 34 D4
Villedieu-la-Blouère F 23 F9
Villedieu-les-Poêles F 23 C9
Villedieu-sur-Indre F 29 B9
Ville-en-Tardenois F 20 F1
Villefagnan F 28 C6
Villefontaine F 31 D7
Villefort F 35 B6
Villefranche-d'Albigeois F 33 C10
Villefranche-d'Allier F 30 C2
Villefranche-de-Lauragais F 33 D9
Villefranche-de-Lonchat F 28 F6
Villefranche-de-Panat F 34 B4
Villefranche-de-Rouergue F 33 B10
Villefranche-du-Périgord F 33 A8
Villefranche-sur-Cher F 24 F6
Villefranche-sur-Mer F 37 D6
Villefranche-sur-Saône F 30 D6
Villefranque F 32 D3
Villegas E 40 D3
Villel E 47 D10
Villelaure F 35 C9
Villemandeur F 25 E8
Villemorien F 25 D11
Villemoustaussou F 33 D10
Villemur-sur-Tarn F 33 C9
Villena E 56 D3
Villenauxe-la-Grande F 25 C10
Villeneuve CH 31 C10
Villeneuve F 33 B10
Villeneuve F 35 C10
Villeneuve-au-Chemin F 25 D10
Villeneuve-d'Allier F 30 E3
Villeneuve-d'Ascq F 19 C7
Villeneuve-de-Berg F 35 A8
Villeneuve-de-Marsan F 32 C5
Villeneuve-de-Rivière F 33 D7
Villeneuve-la-Guyard F 25 D9
Villeneuve-l'Archevêque F 25 D10
Villeneuve-lès-Avignon F 35 C8
Villeneuve-lès-Béziers F 34 D5
Villeneuve-Loubet F 36 D6
Villeneuve-sur-Allier F 30 B3
Villeneuve-sur-Lot F 33 B7
Villeneuve-sur-Yonne F 25 D9
Villeneuve-Tolosane F 33 C8
Villepinte F 33 D10
Villercomtal F 33 A11
Villeréal F 33 A7
Villerest F 30 D5
Villerías E 39 E10
Villerouge-Termenès F 34 D4
Villers-Bocage F 18 E5
Villers-Bocage F 23 B10
Villers-Bretonneux F 18 E6
Villers-Carbonnel F 18 E6
Villers-Cotterêts F 19 F7
Villers-Écalles F 18 E2
Villers-en-Argonne F 25 B12
Villersexel F 26 E5
Villers-Farlay F 31 A8
Villers-le-Bouillet B 183 D6
Villers-le-lac F 31 A10
Villers-lès-Nancy F 26 C5
Villers-Outréaux F 19 D7
Villers-Semeuse F 19 E10
Villers-sur-Glâne CH 31 B11
Villers-sur-Mer F 23 B11
Villerville F 23 B12
Villery F 25 D11
Villeseneux F 25 C11
Ville-sur-Tourbe F 20 F3
Villetta Barrea I 62 D5
Villeurbanne F 30 D6
Villeveyrac F 35 C6
Villevocance F 30 E6
Villié-Morgon F 30 C6
Villiers-Charlemagne F 23 E10
Villiers-en-Lieu F 25 C12
Villiers-en-Plaine F 28 C4
Villiers-le-Sec F 26 D3
Villiers-St-Benoît F 25 E9
Villiers-St-Georges F 25 C9
Villieu-Loyes-Mollon F 31 D7
Villikkala FIN 128 D6
Villingen D 27 D9
Villingsberg S 97 D12
Villmar D 185 D9
Villoldo E 39 D10
Villora E 47 E9
Villorba I 72 E5
Villoria E 45 C10
Villoruela E 45 B10
Villotte-sur-Aire F 26 C3
Villshärad S 87 B11
Villvattnet S 118 E4
Vilnius LT 137 D11
Vilovi d'Onyar E 43 D9
Vilppula FIN 123 F12
Vilpulka LV 131 F10
Vils A 71 B11
Vils DK 86 B3
Vilsbiburg D 75 F11
Vilseck D 75 C10
Vil'shanka UA 154 A3
Vilshofen D 76 E4
Vilshult S 88 C7
Vilslev DK 86 E3
Vilsted DK 86 B4
Vilsund Vest DK 86 B3
Vilusi BIH 157 C7
Vilusi MNE 162 D6
Viluste EST 132 F1
Vilvestre E 45 B7
Vilvoorde B 19 C9
Vilzēni LV 131 F10
Vima Mică RO 152 C3
Vimbodí E 42 E6
Vimeiro P 44 F2
Vimercate I 69 B7
Vimianzo E 38 B1
Vimieiro P 50 B4
Vimioso P 39 E6
Vimmarvattnet S 107 D9
Vimmerby S 92 D7
Vimory F 25 E8
Vimoutiers F 23 C12
Vimpeli FIN 123 D11
Vimperk CZ 76 D5
Vimy F 18 D6
Vinac BIH 157 D7
Vinadio I 37 C6
Vinaixa E 42 E5
Vinařice CZ 76 B6
Vinaròs E 42 G4
Vinarsko BG 167 D8
Vinäs S 102 E8
Vinassan F 34 D5
Vinay F 31 E7
Vinberg S 87 B11
Vinça F 34 E4
Vinča SRB 158 D6
Vincey F 26 D5
Vinchiaturo I 63 E7
Vinci I 66 E2
Vind DK 86 C3
Vindblæs DK 86 B4
Vindeballe DK 86 F6
Vindeby DK 86 E7
Vindel-Ånäset S 118 F3
Vindelgransele S 107 A14
Vindeln S 107 C17
Vinderei RO 153 E11
Vinderslev DK 86 C4
Vinderup DK 86 C3
Vindhella N 100 D7
Vindinge DK 87 D10
Vindinge DK 87 E7
Vindsvik N 94 D4
Vinebre E 42 E5
Vineuil F 24 E5
Vineuil F 29 B9
Vinga RO 151 E7
Vingåker S 92 A7
Vingäng S 102 E4
Vingrau F 34 E4
Vingrom N 101 D12
Vingsand N 104 C8
Vinhais P 39 E6
Vinhas P 39 E6
Vinica HR 148 D6
Vinica MK 164 F5
Vinica SK 147 E8
Vinica SLO 67 B11
Viničné SK 146 E4
Viniegra de Arriba E 40 D6
Vinine BIH 157 G8
Viniśće HR 156 F5
Vinje N 94 C7
Vinje N 100 E4
Vinjeøra N 104 E5
Vinkovci HR 149 F11
Vinkt B 182 C2
Vinliden S 107 B13
Vinné SK 145 F4
Vinnes N 94 B3
Vinnesvåg N 94 B2
Vinni EST 131 C12
Vinninga S 91 C13
Vinningen D 27 B8
Vinodol SK 146 E6
Vinograd BG 166 C5
Vinogradets BG 165 E9
Vinon-sur-Verdon F 35 C10
Vinsa S 116 E9
Vinslöv S 87 C13
Vinsobres F 35 B9
Vinsternes N 104 E4
Vinstra N 101 C11
Vintervollen N 114 D8
Vintilă Vodă RO 161 C9
Vintjärn S 103 E11
Vintrosa S 97 D12
Vintturi FIN 123 C11
Vinţu de Jos RO 152 E2
Viñuelas E 46 C6
Vinuesa E 40 E6
Vinzelberg D 79 A10
Viöl D 82 A6
Violay F 30 D5
Violès F 35 B8
Vipava SLO 73 E8
Vipe LV 135 D12
Viperești RO 161 C8
Vipiteno I 72 C3
Vipperød DK 87 D9
Vipperow D 83 D13
Vir BIH 157 E7
Vir HR 67 D11
Vir SLO 73 D10
Vira S 93 B8
Virawlya BY 133 E7
Virazeil F 33 A6
Virbalis LT 136 D6
Virbi LV 134 B5
Virče MK 165 F6
Vire F 23 C10
Virešl LV 135 B12
Vireux-Molhain F 184 D2
Vireux-Wallerand F 19 D10
Virey-sous-Bar F 25 D11
Virgen A 72 B5
Virginia IRL 7 E8
Viriat F 31 C7
Virieu-le-Grand F 31 D8
Virigneux F 30 D5
Virignin F 31 D8
Viriville F 31 E7
Virķēni LV 131 F10
Virkkala FIN 127 E11
Virkkula FIN 121 B13
Virkkunen FIN 121 C10
Virklund DK 86 C5
Virmaanpää FIN 124 E8
Virmaila FIN 127 C13
Virmutjoki FIN 129 C10
Virolahden kk FIN 128 D8
Virolahti FIN 128 D8
Virovitica HR 149 E8
Virpazar MNE 163 E7
Virpe LV 134 B4
Virrat FIN 123 F11
Virsbo S 97 C15
Virserum S 89 A9
Virtaniemi FIN 114 F4
Virtasalmi FIN 124 F8
Virton B 19 E12
Virtsu EST 130 D7
Virttaa FIN 126 D8
Viru-Jaagupi EST 131 C12
Viru-Nigula EST 131 C13
Viry F 31 C9
Vis HR 63 A10
Visaginas LT 135 E12
Višakio Rūda LT 137 D7
Visan F 35 B8
Vişani RO 161 C10
Visåsen S 103 A13
Visbek D 17 C10
Visborg DK 86 B6
Visby DK 86 E3
Visby S 93 D12
Visé B 19 C12
Višegrad BIH 158 F3
Visegrád H 149 A11
Viserba I 66 D6
Viseu P 44 C5
Vişeu de Jos RO 152 B4
Vişeu de Sus RO 152 B4
Vishnyeva BY 137 E13
Vishovgrad BG 166 C4
Visiedo E 42 F1
Visikums LV 133 B2
Vişina RO 160 E5
Vişina RO 160 F4
Vişineşti MD 154 E2
Vişineşti RO 161 C7
Visingsö S 92 C5
Visjövalen S 105 E12
Viskafors S 91 D12
Viskan S 103 B11
Viškļ LV 135 D13
Vislanda S 88 B6
Visnes N 94 D2
Višnja Gora SLO 73 E10
Višnjićevo SRB 158 D3
Višňová CZ 81 E8
Višňové CZ 77 E10
Višňové SK 147 C7
Visoca MD 153 A11
Viso del Marqués E 55 B5
Visokë AL 168 C2
Visoko BIH 157 E9
Visone I 37 B9
Visonta H 150 B5
Visp CH 68 A4
Vissac-Auteyrac F 30 E4
Vissani GR 168 E4
Visselfjärda S 89 B9
Visselhövede D 82 E7
Vissenbjerg DK 86 E6
Visso I 62 B4
Vissoie CH 68 A4
Vist N 105 D10
Vistabella del Maestrazgo E 48 D4
Vistbäcken S 118 C5
Viştea RO 152 F5
Vistheden S 118 C5
Visthus N 108 E4
Vištytis LT 136 E6
Visuvesi FIN 123 F11
Visznek H 150 B5
Vita I 58 D2
Vitå S 118 C8
Vitaby S 88 D6
Vitåfors S 118 C8
Vitanová SK 147 C9
Vitanovac SRB 159 F6
Vitanovac SRB 164 C5
Vitaz SK 145 F2
Vitberget S 118 C4
Viterbo I 62 C2
Viterne F 26 C5
Vitez BIH 157 D8
Vítězná CZ 77 B9
Viti RKS 164 E3
Vitigudino E 45 B8
Vitina BIH 157 F8
Vītiņi LV 134 D5
Vitis A 77 E8
Vítkov CZ 146 B5
Vitkovići BIH 157 E10
Vītoliņi LV 134 C7
Vitolište MK 169 B6
Vitomireşti RO 160 D4
Vitomiricë RKS 163 D9
Vitorchiano I 62 C2
Vitoria-Gasteiz E 41 C6
Vitoševac SRB 159 F8
Vitovlje BIH 157 D8
Vitré F 23 D9
Vitrey-sur-Mance F 26 E4
Vitrolles F 35 D9
Vitry-en-Artois F 18 D6
Vitry-en-Perthois F 25 C12
Vitry-le-François F 25 C12
Vitry-sur-Loire F 30 B4
Vittangi S 116 C7
Vittaryd S 87 B13
Vitteaux F 25 F12
Vittel F 26 D4
Vittikko FIN 115 E4
Vittikko FIN 119 B13
Vittikkovuoma FIN 117 E12
Vittinge S 98 C8
Vittjärv S 118 C7
Vittoria I 59 F6
Vittorio Veneto I 72 E5
Vittsjö S 87 C13
Vitulano I 60 A3
Vitulazio I 60 A2
Vitvattnet S 102 B8
Vitvattnet S 107 D16
Vitvattnet S 119 B10
Vitzenburg D 79 D10
Viuruniemi FIN 125 E11
Vivario F 37 G10
Vivastbo S 98 B7
Viveiro E 38 A4
Vivel del Río Martín E 42 F2
Viver E 48 E3
Viverols F 30 E4
Viveros E 55 B7
Vivier-au-Court F 19 E10
Viviers F 35 B8
Viviez F 33 A10
Vivild DK 86 C6
Viv-le-Fesq F 35 C7
Vivonne F 29 C6
Vix F 25 E12
Vix F 28 C4
Vizantea-Livezi RO 153 F9
Vize TR 173 A8
Vizille F 31 E8
Vižinada HR 67 B8
Viziru RO 155 C1
Vizitsa BG 167 E9
Vizovice CZ 146 C5
Vizslás H 147 E9
Vizsoly H 145 G3
Vizzini I 59 E6
Vlaardingen NL 16 E2
Vlachata GR 174 C2
Vlacherna GR 174 D5
Vlachia GR 175 B8
Vlachiotis GR 175 F6
Vlachokerasia GR 174 E5
Vlachovice CZ 146 C5
Vlădaia RO 159 E11
Vladaya BG 165 D7
Vlădeni RO 153 B9
Vlădeni RO 153 C10
Vlădeni RO 155 D1
Vlădeşti RO 154 F2
Vlădeşti RO 160 C4
Vlădeşti RO 160 C5
Vladičin Han SRB 164 D5
Vlădila RO 160 E4
Vladimir MNE 163 E7
Vladimir RO 160 D3
Vladimirci SRB 158 D4
Vladimirescu RO 151 E7
Vladimirovac SRB 159 C6
Vladimirovo BG 161 F11
Vladimirovo BG 165 B7
Vladinya BG 165 C10
Vladislav CZ 77 D9
Vlad Ţepeş RO 161 E10
Vladychen' UA 155 B3
Vlăhiţa RO 153 E7
Vlahovići BIH 157 F9
Vlanduk BIH 157 D8
Vlaole SRB 159 E8
Vlase SRB 164 D4
Vlasenica BIH 157 D10
Vlašići HR 156 D3
Vlašim CZ 77 C7
Vlasina Okruglica SRB 164 D5
Vlăsineşti RO 153 B9
Vlasotince SRB 164 D5
Vlatkovići BIH 157 D7
Vlčany SK 146 E5
Vlčnov CZ 146 D5
Vledder NL 16 C6
Vleuten NL 16 D4
Vlijmen NL 16 E4
Vlissingen NL 16 F1
Vlochos GR 169 E7
Vlorë AL 168 D1
Vlotho D 17 D11
Vlycho GR 174 B2
Vnanje Gorice SLO 73 D9
Vnorovy CZ 146 D4
Vočin HR 149 E9
Vöcklabruck A 76 F5
Vöcklamarkt A 76 F4
Voden BG 161 F9
Voden BG 167 E7
Voderady SK 146 E5
Vodica BIH 157 F6
Vodice HR 67 B9
Vodice HR 156 E4
Vodinci HR 157 B10
Voditsa BG 166 C6
Vodjenica BIH 156 C5
Vodňany CZ 76 D6
Vodnjan HR 67 C8
Vodskov DK 86 A6
Vodstrup DK 86 B3
Voe GB 3 E14
Voel DK 86 C5
Voerde (Niederrhein) D 17 E7
Voerendaal NL 183 D7
Voerladegård DK 86 C5
Voerså DK 86 A6
Vogatsiko GR 168 D5
Vogelenzang NL 182 A5
Vogelgrun F 27 D8
Vogelsang D 84 D4
Vogelsdorf D 80 B5
Vogelweh D 21 F9
Voghera I 37 B10
Voghiera I 66 C4
Vognill N 101 A11
Vognsild DK 86 B4
Vogošća BIH 157 E9
Vogt D 71 B9
Vogtareuth D 72 A5
Vogüé F 35 A7
Vohburg an der Donau D 75 E10
Vohenstrauß D 75 C11
Vöhl D 21 B11
Võhma EST 130 D4
Võhma EST 131 D11
Vohonjoki FIN 120 B9
Vöhringen D 27 D10
Vöhringen D 75 F7
Voiceşti RO 160 D4
Void-Vacon F 26 C4
Voikkaa FIN 128 D6
Voikoski FIN 128 C6
Voila RO 152 F5
Voillecomte F 25 C12
Voineasa RO 160 C3
Voineşti RO 153 C10
Voineşti RO 160 C6
Voiron F 31 E8
Võiste EST 131 E8
Voiteg RO 159 C7
Voiteur F 31 B8
Voitsberg A 73 B11
Voivodeni RO 152 D5

Závažná Poruba SK 147 C9
Zaventem B 19 C9
Zavet BG 161 F9
Zavidovići BIH 157 D9
Zavlaka SRB 158 E3
Zăvoaia RO 161 D10
Závod SK 77 E12
Zăvoi RO 159 B9
Zavoj SRB 165 C6
Zavutstsye BY 133 F4
Zavyachellye BY 133 F5
Zavydovychi UA 144 D8
Zawada PL 81 C9
Zawada PL 141 G1
Zawada PL 142 E4
Zawada PL 143 E7
Zawada PL 144 B7
Zawady PL 140 D7
Zawadzkie PL 142 E5
Zawichost PL 144 B4
Zawidów PL 81 D8
Zawidz Kościelny PL 139 E8
Zawiercie PL 143 F7
Zawoja PL 147 B9
Zawonia PL 81 D12
Zaytsevo RUS 132 F4
Žažina HR 148 E6
Zázrivá SK 147 C8
Žažvic HR 156 E4
Zbąszyn PL 81 B9
Zbąszynek PL 81 B9
Zbehy SK 146 E6
Zberoaia MD 153 D12
Zbiczno PL 139 D7
Zbiersk PL 142 C5
Zbiroh CZ 76 C5
Zblewo PL 138 C5
Zbludowice PL 143 F10
Zbójna PL 139 D12
Zbójno PL 139 D7
Zborov SK 145 E3
Zborovice CZ 146 C4
Zborov nad Bystricou SK 147 C7
Zbraslav CZ 77 D10
Zbraslavice CZ 77 C8
Zbrzeźnica PL 140 D6
Zbuczyn Poduchowny PL 141 F6
Ždala HR 149 D8
Ždánice CZ 77 D12
Žďár CZ 77 A8
Žďár nad Sázavou CZ 77 C9
Zdenci HR 149 E9
Ždiar SK 145 E1
Zdice CZ 76 C5
Zdihovo HR 67 B11
Zdíkov CZ 76 D5
Ždírec nad Doubravou CZ 77 C9
Zdounky CZ 146 C4
Ždralovac BIH 157 E6
Zdravets BG 167 C9
Zdravinje SRB 164 C3
Ždrelac HR 156 D3
Ždrelo SRB 159 E8
Zdunje MK 164 F3
Zduńska Wola PL 143 C6
Zduny PL 81 C12
Zduny PL 141 F1
Zdynia PL 145 E3
Zdziarzec PL 143 F11
Zdziechowa PL 85 E13
Zdzieszowice PL 142 F5
Zdziłowice PL 144 B6
Zjbowice PL 142 E5
Žebrák CZ 76 C5
Zebreira P 45 E6
Zebrene LV 134 C5
Zebrzydowa PL 81 D8
Zechlinerhütte D 84 D3
Zeddam NL 183 B8
Zeddiani I 64 D2
Zedelgem B 19 B7
Zederhaus A 73 B8
Žednik SRB 150 F4
Žjdowice PL 142 E6
Zeebrugge B 19 B7
Zeeland NL 16 E5
Zeewolde NL 183 A7
Zegama E 32 E1
Żegiestów PL 145 E2
Žegljane MK 164 E4
Żegocina PL 144 D1
Zehdenick D 84 E4
Zehna D 83 C12
Žehra SK 145 F2
Zehren D 80 D4
Zeilarn D 76 F3
Žeimelis LT 135 D8
Žeimiai LT 135 F8
Zeiselmauer A 77 F10
Zeiskam D 187 C5
Zeist NL 16 D4
Zeithain D 80 D4
Zeitlofs D 74 B6
Zeitz D 79 D11
Zejmen AL 163 F8
Želazków PL 142 C5
Zele B 19 B9
Želechlinek PL 141 G2
Želechów PL 141 G5
Zelena UA 152 A5
Zelena UA 152 B5
Zelena UA 153 A9
Zeleneč SK 146 E5
Zeleni Jadar BIH 158 E3
Zelenikovo BG 166 E4
Zelenikovo MK 164 F4
Zelenogorsk RUS 129 E12
Zelenogradsk RUS 136 D1
Zelenohirs'ke UA 154 B6
Želetava CZ 77 D9
Železná Ruda CZ 76 D4
Železné SK 147 D8
Železnice CZ 77 B8
Železniki SLO 73 D9
Železný Brod CZ 81 E8
Zelhem NL 16 D6
Želiezovce SK 147 E7
Zelina HR 148 E6
Zelinja BIH 157 C9
Želino MK 164 F3
Želiv CZ 77 C8
Željuša BIH 157 F8
Żelków-Kolonia PL 141 F6
Zell D 75 B10
Zell (Mosel) D 21 D8
Zella-Mehlis D 79 E8
Zell am Harmersbach D 27 D9
Zell am Main D 187 B8
Zell am See A 73 B6
Zell am Ziller A 72 B4
Zell im Wiesental D 27 E8
Zellingen D 74 C6
Zell-Pfarre A 73 D9
Zelmeņi LV 134 D6
Želovce SK 147 E8
Zelów PL 143 D7
Zeltingen-Rachtig D 21 E8
Zeltiņi LV 135 B13
Zeltweg A 73 B10
Želva LT 135 F10
Zelzate B 19 B8
Žemaičių Naumiestis LT 134 F3
Žemberovce SK 147 E7
Zemblak AL 168 C4
Zembrów PL 141 E6
Zembrzyce PL 147 B9
Zemen BG 165 E6
Zemeno GR 175 C6
Zemeş RO 153 D8
Zemianska Oľča SK 146 F5
Zemīte LV 134 C5
Zemitz D 84 C5
Zemmer D 21 E7
Zemné SK 146 F6
Zempléanagárd H 145 G5
Zemplínske Hámre SK 145 F5
Zemst B 19 C9
Zemun SRB 158 D5
Zenica BIH 157 D8
Zennor GB 12 E3
Zentene LV 134 B5
Žepa BIH 157 E11
Žepče BIH 157 D9
Žeravice CZ 146 C4
Zerbst D 79 C11
Zerf D 21 E7
Zerind RO 151 D8
Żerków PL 142 B4
Zernez CH 71 D10
Zernien D 83 D9
Zernitz D 83 E12
Zero Branco I 72 E5
Zerpenschleuse D 84 E5
Zerrenthin D 84 D6
Zestoa E 32 D1
Žetale SLO 148 D5
Zetea RO 152 E6
Zetel D 17 B9
Zet'ovo BG 166 E4
Zeulenroda D 79 E10
Zeven D 17 B12
Zevenaar NL 16 E6
Zevenbergen NL 16 E3
Zevgolatio GR 175 D6
Zevio I 66 B3
Zeytinalani TR 181 C9
Zeytinbağı TR 173 D10
Zeytindağ TR 177 B9
Zeytineli TR 177 C8
Zeytinli TR 173 E6
Zeytinliova TR 177 B10
Zgierz PL 143 C7
Zgłobice PL 143 G10
Zgornje Bitnje SLO 73 D9
Zgornje Jezersko SLO 73 D9
Zgornji Duplek SLO 148 C5
Zgorzelec PL 81 D8
Zgropolci MK 169 A6
Zguriţa MD 153 A11
Zhabinka BY 141 F10
Zhabokrychka UA 154 A3
Zhdeniyevo UA 145 F7
Zhegër RKS 164 E3
Zheleznodorozhnyy RUS 136 E3
Zhelyazkovo BG 167 E8
Zhelyu Voyvoda BG 167 D6
Zheravna BG 167 D6
Zhilino RUS 136 D4
Zhitkovo RUS 129 D11
Zhitnitsa BG 167 C9
Zhitom AL 168 C2
Zhodzishki BY 137 D13
Zhorany UA 141 H9
Zhovkva UA 144 C8
Zhovtantsi UA 144 D9
Zhovtneve UA 144 B9
Zhovtneve UA 155 B3
Zhovty Yar UA 154 F5
Zhuprany BY 137 E13
Zhur RKS 164 E2
Zhvyrka UA 144 C9
Zhydachiv UA 145 E9
Zhyrmuny BY 137 E11
Žiar nad Hronom SK 147 D7
Zibalai LT 137 C10
Zibello I 66 B1
Zibreira P 44 F3
Zicavo F 37 H10
Žichovice CZ 76 D5
Zickhusen D 83 C10
Zidani Most SLO 73 D11
Zidarovo BG 167 E8
Židikai LT 134 D4
Židlochovice CZ 77 D11
Ziduri RO 161 C10
Zijbice PL 81 E12
Ziedkalne LV 134 D6
Ziegelroda D 79 D9
Ziegendorf D 83 D11
Ziegenrück D 79 E10
Ziegra D 80 D4
Zieleniewo PL 85 B9
Zieleniewo PL 85 D9
Zielitz D 79 B10
Zielkowice PL 141 F2
Zielona PL 139 D8
Zielona Chocina PL 85 C12
Zielona Góra PL 81 C9
Zielona Góra PL 85 E11
Zielonka PL 139 F11
Zielonki PL 143 F8
Zieluń PL 139 D8
Ziemeri LV 131 F14
Ziemnice Wielkie PL 142 E4
Ziemupe LV 134 C2
Zierenberg D 17 F12
Zierikzee NL 16 E1
Ziersdorf A 77 E9
Zierzow D 83 D11
Ziesar D 79 B11
Žiežmariai LT 137 D9
Žigljen HR 67 C10
Žīguri LV 133 B3
Žihárec SK 146 E5
Žihle CZ 76 B4
Žilaiskalns LV 131 F10
Žilina SK 147 C7
Žilinai LT 137 E10
Zillis CH 71 D8
Ziltendorf D 81 B7
Zilupe LV 133 D4
Zimandu Nou RO 151 E7
Zimbor RO 151 C11
Zimmersrode (Neuental) D 21 B12
Zimnicea RO 160 F6
Zimnitsa BG 167 D7
Žindaičiai LT 134 F5
Zingst D 83 B13
Zinkgruvan S 92 B6
Zinnowitz D 84 B5
Ziras LV 134 B3
Zirc H 149 B9
Zirchow D 84 C6
Žiri SLO 73 D9
Zirndorf D 75 D8
Zîrneşti MD 154 E2
Zirņi LV 134 C4
Ziros GR 179 E11
Žirovnice CZ 77 D8
Zistersdorf A 77 E11
Žitište SRB 158 C6
Žitkovac SRB 164 B4
Žitni Potok SRB 164 C4
Žitomislići BIH 157 F8
Žitorsđa SRB 164 C4
Žitoše MK 168 B5
Zitsa GR 168 E4
Zittau D 81 E7
Zitz D 79 B11
Živaja HR 157 B6
Živinice BIH 157 D10
Živogošće HR 157 F7
Žiželice CZ 77 B8
Zizers CH 71 D9
Zizurkil E 32 D1
Zlarin HR 156 E4
Zlata SRB 164 C4
Zlatar BG 167 C7
Zlatar HR 148 D6
Zlatar-Bistrica HR 148 D6
Zlataritsa BG 166 C5
Zlaté Hory CZ 142 F3
Zlaté Klasy SK 146 E4
Zlaté Moravce SK 146 E6
Zlaten Rog BG 159 E10
Zlatitsa BG 165 D9
Zlatna RO 151 E11
Zlatna Panega BG 165 C9
Zlatograd BG 171 B8
Zlatokop SRB 164 D4
Zławieś Wielka PL 138 D5
Žlebič SLO 73 E10
Žleby CZ 77 C8
Zlēkas LV 134 B3
Zletovo MK 164 F5
Žlibinai LT 134 E4
Zlín CZ 146 C5
Zliv CZ 76 D6
Žljebovi BIH 157 D10
Zllakuqan RKS 164 D2
Złocieniec PL 85 C10
Złoczew PL 142 D6
Zlokuchene BG 165 E8
Zlonice CZ 76 B6
Złota PL 141 G2
Złota PL 143 F10
Złotniki Kujawskie PL 138 E5
Złotoryja PL 81 D9
Złotów PL 85 D12
Złoty Stak PL 77 B11
Zlozela BIH 157 D7
Žlutice CZ 76 B4
Zmajevac BIH 156 C5
Zmajevac HR 149 E11
Zmajevo SRB 158 C4
Zmeyovo BG 166 E5
Żmigród PL 81 D11
Zmijavci HR 157 F7
Žminj HR 67 B8
Żmudź PL 144 A8
Znamensk RUS 136 D3
Žnin PL 138 E4
Znojmo CZ 77 E10
Zoagli I 37 C10
Zöblitz D 80 E4
Zoelen NL 183 B6
Zoersel B 16 F3
Zoetermeer NL 16 D2
Zofingen CH 27 F8
Zogno I 69 B8
Zografou GR 175 D8
Zola Predosa I 66 C3
Zolder B 19 B11
Zoldo Alto I 72 D5
Żółkiewka-Osada PL 144 B6
Zölkow D 83 C11
Zollikofen CH 31 A11
Zollikon CH 27 F10
Zolotkovychi UA 144 D6
Żółtnica PL 85 C11
Zołynia PL 144 C5
Zomba H 149 D11
Zomergem B 19 B8
Zonhoven B 19 C11
Zoni GR 171 A10
Zoniana GR 178 E8
Zonnebeke B 18 C6
Zonza F 37 H10
Zórawina PL 81 E12
Zörbig D 79 C11
Zorita E 45 F9
Zorita del Maestrazgo E 42 F3
Zorleni RO 153 E11
Zorlenţu Mare RO 159 C8
Zorneding D 75 F10
Zornheim D 21 E10
Zörnigal D 79 C12
Zornitsa BG 167 C9
Zornitsa BG 167 E7
Zory PL 142 F6
Zossen D 80 B4
Zottegem B 19 C8
Zoutkamp NL 16 B6
Zoutleeuw B 183 D6
Zovi Do BIH 157 F9
Zovka RUS 132 E4
Zreče SLO 148 D4
Zrenjanin SRB 158 C5
Zrin HR 156 B5
Zrinski Topolovac HR 149 D7
Zrmanja Vrelo HR 156 D5
Zrnovci MK 164 F5
Zruč CZ 76 C4
Zruč nad Sázavou CZ 77 C8
Zsadány H 151 D7
Zsáka H 151 C7
Zsámbék H 149 A11
Zsámbok H 150 B4
Zsana H 150 E4
Zschaitz D 80 D4
Zscherben D 79 D10
Zschopau D 80 E4
Zschortau D 79 D11
Zsombó H 150 E4
Zuberec SK 147 C9
Zubia E 53 B9
Zubiaur E 40 B6
Zubići BIH 157 D8
Zubiena I 68 C5
Zubieta E 32 D1
Zubieta E 32 D2
Zubin Potok RKS 164 D2
Zubiri E 32 E2
Zubří CZ 146 C6
Zubrohlava SK 147 C9
Zubrów PL 81 B8
Žuć SRB 164 C3
Zucaina E 48 D4
Zuchwil CH 27 F8
Zudaire E 32 E1
Zudar D 84 B4
Zuera E 41 E10
Zufre E 51 D7
Zug CH 27 F10
Zuhatzu-Kuartango E 40 C6
Zuheros E 53 A8
Zuid-Beijerland NL 182 B4
Zuidhorn NL 16 B6
Zuidland NL 182 B4
Zuidlaren NL 17 B7
Zuidwolde NL 17 C6
Zuienkerke B 182 C2
Zújar E 55 D7
Żuków PL 141 F2
Żuków PL 141 G8
Żukowice PL 81 C9
Żukowo PL 138 B5
Žuljana HR 162 D3
Žulová CZ 77 B12
Zülpich D 21 C7
Zulte B 19 C7
Zumaia E 32 D1
Zumarraga E 32 D1
Zundert NL 16 F3
Zungri I 59 B8
Zunzarren E 32 E3
Zuoz CH 71 D9
Županja HR 157 B10
Zūras LV 134 B3
Zūrgena E 55 E8
Zürich CH 27 F10
Zurndorf A 77 G12
Zūrnevo BG 161 F10
Żuromin PL 139 D8
Zurow D 83 C11
Zusmarshausen D 75 F8
Züsow D 83 C11
Züssow D 84 C5
Žuta Lokva HR 67 C11
Žutautai LT 134 E2
Zutendaal B 19 C12
Zutphen NL 16 D6
Žuženberk SLO 73 E10
Zveçan RKS 164 D2
Zvejniekciems LV 135 B8
Zverino BG 165 C8
Zvezdë AL 168 C4
Zvezdel BG 171 B8
Zvezdets BG 167 E8
Zvolen SK 147 D8
Zvolenská Slatina SK 147 D8
Zvonce SRB 164 D6
Zvoriştea RO 153 B8
Zvornik BIH 157 D11
Zwartemeer NL 17 C8
Zwartsluis NL 16 C6
Zweeloo NL 17 C7
Zweibrücken D 21 F8
Zweisimmen CH 31 B11
Zwenkau D 79 D11
Zwethau D 80 C4
Zwettl A 77 E8
Zwevegem B 19 C7
Zwevezele B 182 C2
Zwickau D 79 E12
Zwiefalten D 27 D11
Zwierzyn PL 85 E9
Zwierzyniec PL 144 B6
Zwiesel D 76 D4
Zwijndrecht B 19 B9
Zwijndrecht NL 16 E3
Zwinge D 79 C7
Zwingen CH 27 F8
Zwingenberg D 21 E11
Zwochau D 79 D11
Zwoleń PL 141 H5
Zwolle NL 16 C6
Zwönitz D 79 E12
Zwota D 75 B11
Zyabki BY 133 F4
Zyal'ki BY 133 E4
Zyalyonka BY 133 E5
Zychlin PL 143 B8
Żydowo PL 85 B11
Żydowo PL 85 F13
Žygaičiai LT 134 F4
Zygos GR 171 B6
Zygry PL 143 C6
Žyniai LT 134 F2
Żyraków PL 143 F11
Żyrardów PL 141 F2
Żyrzyn PL 141 H6
Żytkiejmy PL 136 E6
Żytniów PL 142 D6
Żytno PL 143 E8
Żywiec PL 147 B8
Żywocice PL 142 F4

Æ

Ærøskøbing DK 86 F6

Ø

Ødis DK 86 E4
Ødsted DK 86 D4
Øie N 105 B12
Økdal N 101 A12
Øksfjord N 112 C9
Øksnes N 110 C8
Øksneshamn N 110 D9
Ølen N 94 C3
Ølgod DK 86 D3
Ølholm DK 86 D5
Ølsted DK 86 D5
Ølsted DK 87 D10
Ølstykke DK 87 D10
Ønslev DK 83 A11
Øra N 112 C8
Ørbæk DK 86 E7
Ørgenvika N 95 B11
Ørjavik N 104 F2
Ørje N 96 D6
Ørnes N 108 C6
Ørnhøj DK 86 C3
Ørslev DK 87 E9
Ørsnes N 100 A5
Ørsta N 100 B4
Ørsted DK 86 C6
Ørting DK 86 D6
Ørum DK 86 C5
Ørum DK 86 C7
Øsby DK 86 E5
Østbirk DK 86 D5
Østby N 91 A9
Østby N 102 D4
Østengård DK 86 D4
Øster Assels DK 86 B3
Øster Bjerregrav DK 86 C5
Øster Brønderslev DK 86 A5
Østerby DK 86 A5
Øster Hornum DK 86 B5
Øster Hurup DK 86 B6
Øster Højst DK 86 E4
Østerild DK 86 A3
Øster Jølby DK 86 B3
Østerlars DK 89 E7
Øster Lindet DK 86 E4
Østermarie DK 89 E8
Øster Tørslev DK 86 B6
Øster Ulslev DK 83 A11
Øster Vedsted DK 86 E3
Østervrå DK 90 E7
Øster Vrøgum DK 86 D2
Østese N 94 B4
Østrup DK 86 B4
Øverbygd N 111 C17
Øvergard N 111 B18
Øvre Alta N 113 D11
Øvre Kildal N 112 D7
Øvrella N 95 C10
Øvre Rendal N 101 C14
Øvre Årdal N 100 D7
Øvre Åstbru N 101 D13
Øyangen N 104 E7
Øydegarden N 104 E4
Øyenkilen N 91 A8
Øyer N 101 D12
Øyeren N 96 B7
Øyjord N 108 B9
Øynes N 108 B9
Øynes N 111 C11
Øyslebø N 90 C2
Øyvatnet N 111 C12

Å

Å N 104 F7
Å N 110 E4
Å N 111 B12
Å N 111 C13
Åberget S 109 E18
Åbo S 103 C10
Åbodarna S 107 E14
Åbogen N 96 B7
Åbosjö S 107 D13
Åby S 89 A7
Åby S 93 B8
Åbyen DK 90 D7
Åbyggeby S 103 E13
Åbyn S 118 D6
Åbytorp S 92 A6
Ådalsliden S 107 E11
Ådum DK 86 D3
Åfarnes N 100 A7
Åfjord N 104 D8
Åfoss N 90 A6
Ågerup DK 87 D10
Ågotnes N 94 B2
Ågskaret N 108 C5
Åheim N 100 B3
Åhus S 88 D6
Åkarp S 87 D12
Åkerbränna S 107 D11
Åkerby S 99 B9
Åkerholmen S 118 C6
Åkersberga S 99 D10
Åkers styckebruk S 98 D8
Åkerstrømmen N 101 C14
Åknes N 110 C9
Åkran N 105 D12
Åkrehamn N 94 D2
Åkullsjön S 118 F5
Åkvisslan S 107 E13
Ål N 101 E9
Ålberga S 93 B9
Ålbo S 98 B7
Ålbæk DK 90 D7
Åle DK 86 D5
Åled S 87 B11
Ålem S 89 B10
Ålen N 101 A14
Ålesund N 100 B4
Ålgnäs S 103 D12
Ålgård N 94 E3
Ålhult S 92 D7
Ålloluokta S 109 B17
Ålmo N 104 E4
Ålsrode DK 87 C7
Ålstad N 110 E9
Ålund S 118 D6
Ålvik N 94 B4
Ålvund N 101 A9
Ålvundeid N 101 A9
Ålåsen S 106 D7
Åmdals Verk N 95 D8
Åminne FIN 122 E7
Åminne S 87 A14
Åmland N 94 F5
Åmli N 90 A3
Åmli N 90 B3
Åmmeberg S 92 B6
Åmot N 94 C7
Åmot N 95 B11
Åmot N 95 C8
Åmot N 95 C11
Åmot S 103 E11
Åmotfors S 96 C7
Åmsele S 107 B16
Åmsosen N 94 D3
Åmynnet S 107 E15
Åmål S 91 A12
Åmål S 91 B12
Åmøyhamn N 108 C5
Åna-Sira N 94 F4
Åndalsnes N 100 A7
Åneby N 95 B13
Ånes N 104 E4
Ånge S 103 A10
Ånge S 109 E14
Ångelsberg S 97 C15
Ångersjö S 102 C8
Ånn S 105 E13
Ånstad N 110 C8
Ånsvik N 109 B9
Ånäset S 118 F6
Årbostad N 111 C13
Årby DK 87 D8
Årbyn S 118 C8
Årdal N 100 C4
Årdalstangen N 100 D7
Åre S 105 E14
Årfor N 105 B11
Årgård N 105 C10
Århult S 89 A10
Årjäng S 96 D7
Årnes N 95 B14
Årnes N 104 F5
Årnes N 111 B15
Årnäs S 91 B14
Åros N 95 C12
Årosjåkk S 111 E17
Årre DK 86 D3
Årrenjarka S 109 C15
Årsandøy N 105 A12
Årsdale DK 89 E8
Årset N 105 A11
Årslev DK 86 E6
Årstein N 111 C14
Årsunda S 98 A7
Årvik N 100 B3
Årviksand N 112 C6
Årvågen N 104 E5
Åryd S 89 B7
Åryd S 89 C8
Årøybukta N 111 A19
Årøysund N 90 A7
Ås N 95 C13
Ås N 105 E11
Ås S 96 C7
Ås S 97 C12
Ås S 106 E7
Ås S 107 E11
Åsa N 95 B12
Åsa S 91 E11
Åsan N 105 B12
Åsarna S 102 A7
Åsby S 87 A10
Åse N 111 B10
Åsebyn S 96 D7
Åseda S 89 A8
Åsegg N 105 C9
Åsele S 107 C12
Åselet S 118 D4
Åsen N 105 D10
Åsen S 102 C7
Åsen S 102 D6
Åsen S 106 E7
Åsen S 109 E16
Åsenbruk S 91 B11
Åseral N 90 B1
Åshammar S 103 E12
Åskilje S 107 B13
Åskogen S 118 C7
Åsli N 101 E11
Åsljunga S 87 C12
Åsmansbo S 97 B13
Åsmarka N 101 D13
Åsskard N 104 E5
Åsta N 101 D14
Åstan N 104 E7
Åsteby S 97 B9
Åstorp S 87 C11
Åstrand S 97 B9
Återvänningen S 103 A13
Åtorp S 92 A4
Åträsk S 118 B7
Åträsk S 118 D5
Åttonträsk S 107 C14
Åtvidaberg S 92 C7
Åva FIN 126 E5
Åvestbo S 97 C14
Åvist FIN 122 D9

Ä

Äetsä FIN 126 C8
Ähtäri FIN 123 E12
Ähtärinranta FIN 123 E12
Äijäjoki FIN 116 B10
Äijälä FIN 123 E16
Äkäsjokisuu FIN 117 D11
Äkäslompolo FIN 117 C12
Ålandsbro S 103 A14
Älgarås S 92 B4
Älgered S 103 B12
Älghult S 89 A9
Älmestad S 91 D13
Älmhult S 88 B6
Älmsta S 99 C11
Älta S 99 D10
Älvdalen S 102 D7
Älvho S 102 D8
Älvkarleby S 103 E13
Älvkarleö S 99 A8
Älvros S 102 B8
Älvsbyn S 118 C6
Älvsered S 87 A11
Älvängen S 91 D11
Ämmälänkylä FIN 123 E9
Ämmänsaari FIN 121 E12
Åmådalen S 102 D8
Äng S 92 D5
Änge S 105 E16
Ängebo S 103 C11
Ängelholm S 87 C11
Ängersjö S 122 C3
Ängeslevä FIN 119 E15
Ängesträsk S 118 B8
Ängesån S 116 E8
Ängom S 103 B13
Äppelbo S 97 B11
Ärla S 98 D7
Ärnäs S 102 D5
Ärnäs S 102 E5
Ärtled S 103 E9
Ärtrik S 107 E11
Äsarp S 91 C14
Äsbacka S 103 D11
Äsköping S 92 A8
Ässjö S 103 B12
Ätran S 87 A11
Äyskoski FIN 123 D17
Äystö FIN 122 F7
Äänekoski FIN 123 E15

Ö

Öckerö S 91 D10
Ödeborg S 91 B10
Ödeshog S 92 C5
Ödkarby FIN 99 B13
Ödsmål S 91 C10
Ödåkra S 87 C11
Öja FIN 123 C9
Öja S 93 E12
Öjarn S 106 D8
Öje S 102 E6
Öjebyn S 118 D6
Öjeforsen S 103 B9
Öjingsvallen S 103 C8
Öjung S 103 C10
Öksajärvi S 116 C8
Öllölä FIN 125 F15
Ölmbrotorp S 97 D13
Ölme S 97 D11
Ölsboda S 92 A4
Ömossa FIN 122 F7
Önnestad S 88 C6
Önningby FIN 99 B14
Öratjärn S 103 C10
Öravan S 107 B14
Öravattnet S 106 E9
Örbyhus S 99 B9
Örbäck S 97 C15
Örebro S 97 D13
Örebäcken S 102 C4
Öregrund S 99 B10
Öreström S 107 C16
Öretjändalen S 103 A10
Örkelljunga S 87 C12
Örnsköldsvik S 107 E15
Örnäsudden S 109 E13
Örsbäck S 107 D17
Örserum S 92 C5
Örsjö S 89 B9
Örsundsbro S 99 C8
Örträsk S 107 C15
Örviken S 118 E6
Ösmo S 93 B11
Östa S 98 B7
Östanfjärden S 119 C10
Östansjö S 92 A5
Östansjö S 109 E16
Östanskär S 103 A13
Östanvik S 103 D9
Östanå S 88 C6
Östavall S 103 B9
Östbjörka S 103 E9
Östby S 107 D13
Österbybruk S 99 B9
Österbymo S 92 D6
Österede S 107 E11
Österforse S 107 E12
Österfärnebo S 98 B7
Östergarn S 93 E13
Östergraninge S 107 F12
Österhankmo FIN 122 D7
Österjörn S 118 D4
Österlisa S 99 C11
Östermark FIN 126 E8
Österoret S 107 C12
Östero FIN 122 D8
Österskucku S 102 A8
Östersund S 106 E7
Östersundom FIN 127 E13
Östervåla S 98 B8
Österås S 107 E12
Östhammar S 99 B10
Östloning S 103 A13
Östmark S 97 B8
Östmarkum S 107 E14
Östnor S 102 D7
Östra Ed S 93 C9
Östra Frölunda S 91 E13
Östra Granberg S 118 C4
Östra Grevie S 87 E12
Östra Husby S 93 B9
Östra Ljungby S 87 C12
Östra Lovsjön S 106 D7
Östra Löa S 97 C13
Östra Ormsjö S 107 C10
Östra Ryd S 93 C8
Östra Skråmträsk S 118 E5
Östra Stugusjö S 103 A9
Östra Sönnarslöv S 88 D6
Östra Vemmerlöv S 88 D6
Östra Yttermark FIN 122 E6
Östra Åliden S 118 D4
Överammer S 107 E9
Överberg S 102 B7
Överbyn S 103 C12
Överhogdal S 102 B8
Överhörnäs S 107 E15
Överissjö S 107 C13
Överkalix S 119 B9
Överlida S 91 E12
Överlännäs S 107 E13
Övermalax FIN 122 E7
Övermark FIN 122 E6
Övermorjärv S 118 B9
Övernäs S 109 D14
Överstbyn S 118 B7
Övertorneå S 119 B11
Överturingen S 102 B8
Övertänger S 103 E10
Överum S 93 D8
Överäng S 105 D14
Överö FIN 99 B15
Öv Långträsk S 109 E16
Övra S 107 D11
Övre Bredåker S 118 C6
Övre Fläsjön S 118 B7
Övre-Konäs S 105 D14
Övre Soppero S 116 B7
Övre Tväråsel S 118 C5
Övsjöbyn S 107 E9
Öxabäck S 91 E12

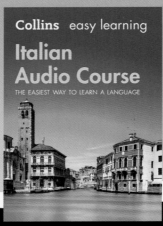
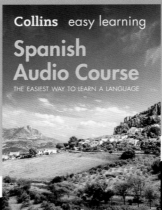

i-SPY

Collins

Look around you and discover the world with i-SPY

i-SPY In the countryside

What can you spot?

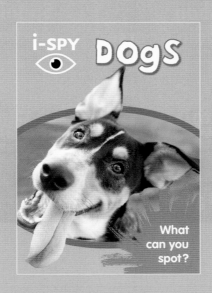

i-SPY Dogs

What can you spot?

i-SPY Creepy crawlies

What can you spot?

Spy it
up to 200 fun things to spot around you

Spot it
tick off what you see as you go

Score it
score points for each spot and receive your super-spotter certificate and badge!

i-SPY Birds

What can you spot?

collins.co.uk/i-SPY

@Collins4Parents f facebook.com/collins4parents

What can you spot?

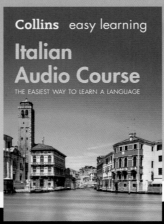
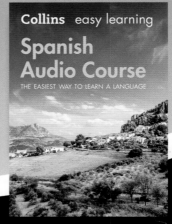

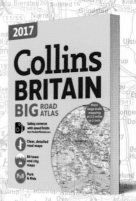

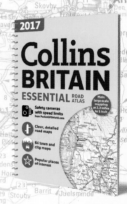
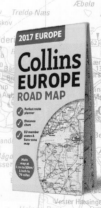
 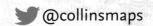